Early childhood intervention is a young and rapidly growing field. In little more than a decade it has been transformed from an emerging service with a primitive empirical base, scant funding, and virtually no public mandate to a robust area of theory, research, and practice. Moreover, since the passage of the Education of the Handicapped Act Amendments of 1986 (Public Law 99-457), early intervention has acquired a growing national audience, increased funding, a promise of more comprehensive programs and services, and unprecedented attention from major state and federal policymaking groups.

The *Handbook of Early Childhood Intervention* has been designed to serve as a core textbook for those who are interested in young children with disabilities or developmental vulnerabilities, and their families. Its intent is to integrate the theory, research, and practical knowledge that guide current practice in this field and to frame the agenda for its continued growth and maturation.

The editors of this volume have brought together an outstanding collection of contributions from many of the most creative thinkers and influential leaders in the field. The overall goal of the *Handbook* is to present sophisticated, state-of-the-art material in a format that is accessible to a broad audience that cuts across such diverse disciplines as education, psychology, social service, pediatrics, nursing, speech and language pathology, occupational and physical therapy, public health, and child care. Within and across each of these professional domains, the *Handbook of Early Childhood Intervention* can serve as a definitive source for those involved in academic training programs, research and scholarly endeavors, policy development, and service provision.

Handbook of early childhood intervention

Handbook of
early childhood intervention

Edited by SAMUEL J. MEISELS
and
JACK P. SHONKOFF

 CAMBRIDGE
UNIVERSITY PRESS

3795

To our families

?

Published by the Press Syndicate of the University of Cambridge
The Pitt Building, Trumpington Street, Cambridge CB2 1RP
40 West 20th Street, New York, NY 10011-4211, USA
10 Stamford Road, Oakleigh, Melbourne 3166, Australia

© Cambridge University Press 1990

First published 1990
Reprinted 1990, 1992, 1993

Printed in the United States of America

Library of Congress Cataloging-in-Publication Data
Handbook of early childhood intervention / edited by Samuel J.
Meisels, Jack P. Shonkoff.
p. cm.
ISBN0-521-34371-2 – ISBN 0-521-38777-9 (pbk.)
1. Developmental disabilities – Prevention.   2. Child health
services.   I. Meisels, Samuel J.   II. Shonkoff, Jack P.
RJ135.H48   1989
362.1'968–dc20   89-25312
                                                                    CIP

A catalogue record for this book is available from the British Library.

ISBN 0-521-34371-2 hardback
ISBN 0-521-38777-9 paperback

Contents

v

Foreword

EDWARD F. ZIGLER

The preparation of this *Handbook* represents a coming of age of the field of early childhood intervention. Although programs like the Richmond-Caldwell Infant program in Syracuse and Susan Gray's Preschool program in Nashville predated Head Start, it was the implementation of the Head Start program in 1965 that provided the major impetus for programs designed for young children. This *Handbook* thus represents a summing-up of our knowledge after approximately one-quarter century of effort.

It has been a time characterized by controversy, theoretical excesses, and instances of denigrating those whom we were trying to help. The major controversy, of course, was whether early intervention did indeed have any long-term benefits for children (see Zigler & Berman, 1983, for more details). Not until the publication of the Cornell Consortium data (Darlington, Royce, Snipper, Murray, & Lazar, 1980) and the more recent findings reported by the High/Scope group (Berrueta-Clement, Schweinhart, Barnett, Epstein, & Weikart, 1984) and the Department of Health and Human Services (Copple, Cline, & Smith, 1987) was this controversy finally put to rest. In regard to economically disadvantaged children, a consensus now exists among behavioral scientists, policymakers, and even taxpayers that early intervention is a cost-effective method for combating the effects of poverty experienced early in life.

On the political scene, early intervention was first championed primarily by liberal policymakers. Today, programs for poor children are endorsed by more conservative elements such as the economic community (Committee for Economic Development, 1987). During the recent political campaign the moderate-conservative candidate George Bush voiced his enthusiasm for the Head Start program. His more conservative predecessor, Ronald Reagan, included Head Start in his safety net of programs that were kept in place during his term of office. Thus, early intervention is now embraced by all elements of the political spectrum. Further, it is now viewed as being of value not only for poor children but for other high-risk groups, including developmentally disabled and abused children. Evidence for the efficacy of early intervention for a variety of at-risk populations was recently presented by the American Psychological Association under the title of *Fourteen Ounces of Prevention* (Price, Cowen, Lorion, & Ramos-McKay, 1988). It is more than a coincidence that this *Handbook* appears at the same time that our nation is embarking on a major early intervention effort on behalf of developmentally disabled children under Public Law 99-457.

The wide acceptance of the value of early childhood intervention should not lead to hubris on the part of workers in the field. This *Handbook* represents a tangible

ix

benchmark of progress, but many questions remain, questions that will only be answered by future empirical efforts. Although a complete consensus exists that early intervention for economically disadvantaged children has long-term effects, there is no agreement among workers as to exactly what processes mediate these benefits. The great empirical task of the future will be to identify these mediating processes. The future must also see a much more fine-grained approach to the efficacy issue. No early intervention program results in equal benefits to all those enrolled. We must strive to illuminate what factors determine which participants are aided by our interventions and which are not.

Our humility should be further anchored by noting the errors of the past quarter of a century. We must be careful to trod a middle ground in which we avoid both the overoptimism of the early 1960s and the pessimism that was a reaction to it – exemplified in the premature statement by Jensen (1969) that "compensatory education has been tried and it apparently has failed." We have certainly learned by now that permanently changing the developmental trajectory of a human life is an immense task that will never be accomplished with minimal or token efforts. Our early overoptimism can clearly be seen in our nation's original Head Start program, which amounted to a 6- to 8-week intervention during the summer preceding the child's entry into school. With the wisdom of hindsight it is difficult to imagine how so many people believed that such a brief program for children from America's urban and rural slums would ameliorate all the bad effects of poverty they had experienced all their young lives, and would actually inoculate them from any further damage.

Whereas most workers agree that human development is characterized by a considerable degree of plasticity (i.e., influenced by environmental events), this plasticity is not limitless. At this juncture in our history we can only be amused by the extreme ideas of major workers in the early 1960s who lead parents to believe that cognitive development was so plastic that even so simple and minimal an intervention as hanging a mobile over a baby's crib would enhance intellectual growth. The problem, of course, is that applied efforts flow from and cannot outdistance the theoretical corpus that gives rise to them. The theoretical underpinnings of early intervention can be traced primarily to McVicker Hunt's *Intelligence and Experience* (1961), and to a lesser extent to Benjamin Bloom's *Stability and Change in Human Characteristics* (1964). These formulations gave us the extremely plastic child and started us on our search for those critical periods during which relatively minor environmental interventions would result in major long-term benefits.

Infancy and preschool years were not the only acclaimed magic period; other theorists emphasized other ages, such as the prenatal period, the early school years, and even adolescence. I take point with each of these claims individually; however, I support them all when taken in unison. That is, there is no one magic period in the life of a child. Each and every period is a magical and important one. My view is that we must commit ourselves to the principle of the continuity of human development. Each period of development naturally grows out of each preceding period. Given this fact, we should realize the dangers of trying to provide societal supports at only one stage, as if intervention at that time would absolve us from the need to be concerned with other ages as well. Our task, therefore, is not to find the right age at which to intervene, but to find the right intervention for each age.

Optimal development is enhanced by providing appropriate developmental nutrients at each age, with the particular nutrients required dependent on the child's stage of development. Thus, an optimal intervention would not take place at one age alone, but would consist of a series of interfacing interventions over the life of the child, from conception through adolescence. As Victoria Seitz and I noted earlier (Zigler & Seitz, 1982), this form of maximal intervention may be understood best from the obvious example of an intervention program in nature: a good secure family. Families do not care for their children only when they are very young, when they enter school, or when they become adolescents. The form of care that a family provides certainly changes at each age, but there is continual care nonetheless. With such an approach we shall never again hear those scholars who criticized the Head Start program because the intervention (at age 4) was too late in the life cycle to be of value. In point of fact, the continuity principle influenced decision makers responsible for Head Start, and can clearly be seen in the implementation of Parent and Child Centers for children younger than Head Start age and the Follow-Through program for school-age children.

The clearest programmatic exemplar of the continuity principle may be seen in the short-lived Child and Family Resource Program. This program provided a collection of interventions for children and their families starting at birth and extending to 8 years of age. This effort also recognized the heterogeneity that characterizes economically disadvantaged families, and attempted to avoid the error of forcing each family to fit themselves to a single type of program. Instead, a number of services were made available and each family had an opportunity to select those they thought would be of benefit. We see in this program the early seeds of our nation's current family support (or family resource) movement (Kagan, Powell, Weissbourd, & Zigler, 1987).

This empowerment of parents and respect for the choices they might make was consistent with the Head Start philosophy; and it represented a further attempt to undermine the deficit model of early intervention that did little more than blame the victims of poverty. Again, one can only be amused at the early period of the intervention movement when scholars so cavalierly advanced the thesis that poor families suffered from "cultural deprivation." Thus, poor minority children were viewed as suffering a double handicap: a biologically based innate inferiority, and a culture whose bad features attenuated the child's developmental course. Since literally no child can be deprived of a culture, the cultural deprivation concept was little more than an assertion that a variety of cultures were inferior to the mainstream middle socioeconomic status (SES) culture. This denigration of culture and heritage is now avoided in early intervention efforts, and the family's cultural embeddedness is respected and viewed as a factor that can be utilized in optimizing human functioning.

In the 1960s the views of Hunt and his stress on intellectual development, and Bloom's questionable assertion that "half of learning of the child is over by the age of 4," gave early childhood intervention an overly cognitive emphasis. Since the beginning of intervention efforts, both taxpayers and decision makers have been legitimately concerned with whether these programs succeed or fail. They have rightfully held the programs accountable for the public funds invested in them. By far the most commonly used outcome measure in the early years was the IQ score or, more specifically, the magnitude of the change in IQ as a result of intervention. The reason that the IQ score became the most popular measure for outcome evaluations is easily understood: The standard IQ tests are well-developed instruments with psychometric properties that are so well documented that they allow the user to avoid difficult measurement problems; they are relatively easy to administer; they are related to a number of other behaviors that are of theoretical and practical significance; and, finally, because of the lure of being able to demonstrate almost immediate results of a program in the form of increased IQ scores.

I take issue with the use of IQ as the ultimate outcome measure of intervention programs for a number of reasons. First, there is now considerable evidence that the reported increases in IQ reflect motivational changes that influence the children's test performance rather than changes in the actual quality of cognitive functioning. Consider for a moment the child who refuses to answer any questions on the IQ test. This surely does not mean an absolute lack of cognitive ability or knowledge. Rather, what is reflected here is an apprehensive, perhaps skeptical child who is minimizing all contact with the object of his or her apprehension, the tester. However, a child who has participated in an intervention effort, even a short 6-week program, is likely to feel more self-confident and comfortable with an adult tester and therefore to score higher on the standardized test. This explains why Eisenberg and Conners (1966) were able to find 10-point increases in IQ after only a short summer of intervention.

The difficulty of effecting true increases in IQ was recently noted by Herman Spitz (1986; see Zigler, 1988, for a more complete discussion of this issue). Interestingly, the long-term effects of intervention that have been found do not include permanently elevated IQ scores but rather everyday competence indicators such as being in the right grade for age and avoiding delinquency behaviors (Berrueta-Clement et al., 1984; Darlington et al., 1980). This brings me to my second objection to the use of the IQ score as *the* standard for evaluating intervention programs. I do not believe IQ tests measure what intervention efforts are trying to achieve. The goal of intervention programs is to affect increased social competence, an aim that includes but is not limited to measured intelligence. We must consider the child as more than a walking cognitive system, for cognitive ability alone will not dictate how well that child will function in our world. Again, this is related to our discussion of appreciating continuity within the child's life. Even the most gifted child will not do well in school if he or she does not know how to interact with teachers or peers. Furthermore, we cannot even hope that children will achieve academically if they have not received the proper nutrition needed to function in their daily lives. A sick child will never be a competent child. The aim, therefore, of intervention efforts must be to affect positively all aspects of the child's development: social, emotional, and physical, as well as intellectual. This is critical because all of these aspects are interrelated – one does not function independently of the other.

Readers familiar with the field will recognize that what I have just described is the "whole child approach" to development, an approach I have championed for the last 25 years. It should be obvious from the discussion thus far that the adoption of a whole child approach demands a commitment to interdisciplinary work. It is therefore extremely heartening to witness the production of this *Handbook*. The multidisciplinary approach taken in this book is obvious from the list of people who have contributed – pediatricians, advocates, psychologists, educators, economists, and psychiatrists. Shonkoff and Meisels have indeed produced a handbook that takes into account the development of the "whole child."

Concern for the child as a complete and multifaceted entity means that we must also go beyond the child. Fortunately, historical happenings guided us along this path. Since the theoretical foundations we had for early intervention in the 1960s clearly led us into many errors, the field could not have advanced had not a new theoretical paradigm been forthcoming. Thankfully, a new paradigm took firm root in the 1970s. Arnold Sameroff provided us with his transactional model, and perhaps of greatest importance, Urie Bronfenbrenner provided us with his ecological model. As a result of these theoretical developments the entire approach to early intervention changed. Prior to this time early interventionists often viewed themselves as "child savers." We would take the child from the negative environment provided in the home, place the child in our intervention program, and thanks to our ministrations, the child would become a more adequate person. This approach reached its zenith (or perhaps nadir) when Bruno Bettelheim proposed that economically disadvantaged children be taken from their parents and placed in centers like those he saw in the Israeli kibbutzim. Today successful programs see the unit of intervention not as the individual child, but the family unit including the child. This of course demands a more complicated systems approach in which family members are seen as being in constant reciprocal interaction. The early seeds of this type of thinking may be seen in Head Start's commitment to family involvement and participation. This may well have been due to the important role that Urie Bronfenbrenner played in the conceptualization and implementation of the Head Start program.

The family systems approach provides us with a viable hypothesis to explain the long-term effects of early intervention. Victoria Seitz, Ron Lally, and I have all advanced the view that the long-term effects are not due to the half-day program experienced by the child for 1 year during preschool, but are rather due to the parents. As a result of their involvement with the intervention, parents become more optimal socializers of the child throughout the rest of the day and, indeed, throughout the child's formative years.

Thanks to the ecological model, we are now aware that the child's development is not only influenced by the family system, but by other systems far removed from the family's control. The child is thus influenced by the family, which in turn is influenced by the nature and effectiveness of our major social systems, such as the world of work, the school, the media, and available health services. Thus, any complete evaluation of an early intervention program would assess whether the entire ecology of the child has become more conducive for human development. Again, early seeds of such evaluation may be found in the history of Head Start. Whereas many scholars are aware of the negative findings of the Westinghouse report, few appear conversant with the findings of the Kirschner report that indicated that the presence of Head Start in a community acted as a catalyst for improvements in two major systems impacting the child, the school and the health system.

The ecological model has clear implications that we not oversell what we can realistically accomplish with current early intervention programs. In many instances these programs simply cannot change enough of the ecology or the larger environment to make a real difference in the lives of families. The problems of many families will not be solved by early intervention efforts, but only by changes in the basic features of the infrastructure of our society. No amount of counseling, early childhood curricula, or home visits will take the place of jobs that provide decent incomes, affordable housing, appropriate health care, optimal family configurations, or integrated neighborhoods where children encounter positive role models.

This concern and others will be found in the pages of this *Handbook*. The book is quite amazing in that it attempts and succeeds in summarizing and synthesizing the vast knowledge base of the early intervention field. It struggles with complicated issues such as toward whom services should be directed and how these services should be evaluated, and it covers these many different topics from a variety of perspectives. The list of those who have contributed to this volume comprises a "Who's Who" roster of the early intervention field, and their efforts have been bound together to create a book that includes no less than the state-of-the-art knowledge of this field.

Meisels and Shonkoff should be congratulated for producing a book that is an absolute necessity for anyone interested in early childhood intervention. The *Handbook* is so thoughtful and comprehensive that it is sure to serve as a guide for workers in this field well into the twenty-first century.

REFERENCES

Berrueta-Clement, J. R., Schweinhart, L. J., Barnett, W. S., Epstein, A. S., & Weikart, D. P. (1984). *Changed lives: The effects of the Perry Preschool Program on youths through age 19* (Monographs of the High/Scope Educational Research Foundation, No. 8). Ypsilanti, MI: High/Scope.

Bloom, B. (1964). *Stability and change in human characteristics.* New York: Wiley.

Committee for Economic Development. (1987). *Children in need: Investment strategies for the educationally disadvantaged.* Washington, DC: Author.

Copple, C. E., Cline, M. G., & Smith, A. N. (1987). *Path to the future: Long-term effects of Head Start in the Philadelphia school district.* Washington, DC: U.S. Department of Health and Human Services.

Darlington, R. B., Royce, J. M., Snipper, A. S., Murray, H. W., & Lazar, I. (1980). Preschool programs and later competence of children from low-income families. *Science, 208,* 202–204.

Eisenberg, L., & Conners, C. K. (1966, April 11). The effect of Head Start on the developmental process. Paper presented at the 1966 Joseph P. Kennedy, Jr., Foundation Scientific Symposium on Mental Retardation, Boston.

Hunt, J. McV. (1961). *Intelligence and experience.* New York: Ronald Press.

Jensen, A. R. (1969). How much can we boost IQ and scholastic achievement? *Harvard Educational Review, 31,* 1–123.

Kagan, S. L., Powell, D., Weissbourd, B., & Zigler, E. (Eds.). (1987). *America's family support programs.* New Haven: Yale University Press.

Price, R. H., Cowen, E. L., Lorion, R. P., & Ramos-McKay, J. (Eds.). (1988). *Fourteen ounces of prevention: A casebook for practitioners.* Washington, DC: American Psychological Association.

Spitz, H. (1986). *The raising of intelligence: A selected history of attempts to raise retarded intelligence.* Hillsdale, NJ: L. Erlbaum.

Zigler, E. (1988). The IQ pendulum. [Review of H. Spitz, *The raising of intelligence*]. *Readings, 3*(2), 4–9.

Zigler, E., & Berman, W. (1983). Discerning the future of early childhood intervention. *American Psychologist, 38,* 894–906.

Zigler, E., & Seitz, V. (1982). Social policy and intelligence. In R. Sternberg (Ed.), *Handbook of human intelligence* (pp. 586–641). New York: Cambridge University Press.

Preface

Early childhood intervention is a young and rapidly growing field. In little more than a decade it has been transformed from an emerging service with a primitive empirical base, scant funding, and virtually no public mandate to a robust area of theory, research, and practice. Moreover, since the passage of the Education for All Handicapped Children Act Amendments of 1986 (Public Law 99-457), early intervention has acquired a growing national audience, increased funding, a promise of more comprehensive programs and services, and unprecedented attention from major state and federal policymaking groups.

This book has been designed to serve as a vehicle for communication across the many disciplines that contribute to early intervention services. The intent of the *Handbook* is to integrate the theory, research, and practical experiences that lie at the foundation of current practice, and to facilitate the further growth and maturation of the field.

In its current form, early childhood intervention is based on two fundamental assumptions. The first concerns interdisciplinary activity. Since the problems confronting young children with disabilities or specific vulnerabilities are potentially so diverse, the range of services required to meet their needs must reflect this breadth. Thus, early intervention incorporates a host of service providers that cut across many disciplines and theoretical orientations including medicine, education, social service, child care, speech and language pathology, occupational and physical therapy, nursing, respite care, public health, and psychology. Indeed, a thorough understanding of early intervention requires a comfort with professional pluralism, a recognition that no single formula or prescription can be applied universally to early intervention's heterogeneous population, and a realization that no unidimensional research focus or design can capture adequately all of its dynamics.

The second key assumption emerges from the view that the needs of infants who are enrolled in intervention programs can only be fully appreciated and understood within a family context. In turn, families must be seen as dynamic units embedded within a larger social system. This focus on the child within the family and the family within the larger social context represents one of the most far-reaching provisions of the new federal law, and affects all aspects of early intervention – from prevention, to identification, to assessment, to service delivery. In short, providing early intervention services implies providing services that are sensitive to family concerns, that build on family strengths, that seek to enhance family adaptation, and that create within families new capabilities to support and facilitate infant and toddler development and prevent developmental problems.

xv

These two assumptions can be combined into a general definition:

> Early childhood intervention consists of multidisciplinary services provided for develop-
> mentally vulnerable or disabled children from birth to age 3 years and their families.
> These programs are designed to enhance child development, minimize potential delays,
> remediate existing problems, prevent further deterioration, limit the acquisition of
> additional handicapping conditions, and/or promote adaptive family functioning. The
> goals of early intervention are accomplished by providing developmental and therapeutic
> services for children, and support and instruction for their families.

The comprehensive nature of this definition reflects the underlying rationale for early
childhood intervention services – that behavior and developmental potential are neither
fixed in early life by genetic factors, nor limited by a critical period beyond which
change is impossible.

The essays in this *Handbook* reflect these assumptions and definitions. Conceived as a
core textbook for all those interested in young disabled and developmentally vulnerable
children and their families, this volume is addressed to a diverse range of individuals,
including those identified with academic training programs, research and scholarly
endeavors, policy development, and service provision.

The book is divided into seven sections. The first consists of an introductory chapter
that places the concept of early intervention into historical context and identifies new
challenges to be addressed by the field in the coming years. The second section
examines sources of developmental vulnerability (biological, familial, and social) that
can have deleterious impacts on development, in conjunction with a discussion of
protective factors that can buffer individuals from such hazards. The next section
explores four theoretical bases of early intervention, including approaches that can be
described as transactional, psychodynamic, behavioral-ecological, and neurobiological.
All of these chapters present a strong rationale for early childhood intervention, each
from a different perspective.

The fourth section of the book explores the area of assessment. Reflecting the
comprehensive nature of early intervention services, the six chapters in this section
review existing knowledge regarding current evaluation strategies and assessment instruments from several vantage points: a traditional interdisciplinary model of infant
assessment, alternative strategies for evaluating young children, and approaches to
evaluating parent–child interaction, families, and social support. Included as well is a
discussion of the potential therapeutic aspects of the assessment process.

Next, five models of service delivery are explored in separate chapters. These essays
reflect the multiple approaches to service delivery that mark early intervention efforts.
Three of the chapters focus on models that target specific primary service recipients:
the child, the caregiver, and the family. The last two chapters explore models that are
directed toward specific caregiving environments: hospital-based services and community-based programs for children from low-income families.

Although every chapter in the *Handbook* carefully reviews the available research base
that is pertinent to its specific focus, the sixth section of the book identifies four
discrete areas of efficacy research for intense scrutiny. The first reviews comprehensively our knowledge about the effects of intervention on children. The second chapter in
this section explores research about the family as the focus for intervention, and the
next provides an overview of early intervention's economic costs and benefits. The final
chapter in this section critically analyzes a range of research approaches to the evaluation of service effectiveness.

The book's final section is devoted to explorations of a broad range of policy issues and programmatic directions. Included are chapters on the identification of service recipients, issues related to primary prevention, paraprofessionals, parent advocacy, personnel preparation, and interagency coordination. These chapters are intended to highlight some of the current policy and programmatic agendas of early intervention, and to examine some of the decisions that must be made in the future if early childhood intervention is to continue to expand in scope and in impact.

The contributors to this *Handbook* include many of the leaders of this pioneering field. The breadth of scholarship contained in this volume reflects the overall depth of the special world of early childhood intervention. Our hope for this book is that it will cast the past and the present in sharp relief so that the future for vulnerable young children and their families will be more hopeful and personally more fulfilling.

One of the special pleasures of working in the field of early childhood intervention is the opportunity it affords to develop an abundance of personal and professional relationships – reflected in no small-measure by the shared editorial responsibility we took for this volume. To the many mentors, colleagues, trainees, students, parents, and children who have taught us so much over the years (and whose names, if listed, would fill many pages) we would like to express our deepest gratitude. To Irving Harris and Ruth Belzer of the Harris Foundation, we offer special thanks for providing financial support for the preparation of this book. Of course, we are indebted to the valued contributors of this book, without whom this project could not have come to fruition. And finally, to our families, Alice, Seth, and Reba Meisels and Fredi, Michael, and Adam Shonkoff, we express our fondest appreciation for their love, their emotional support, and their generous tolerance of our passion for our work.

SAMUEL J. MEISELS
JACK P. SHONKOFF

Contributors

Nicholas J. Anastasiow, Ph.D.
Thomas Hunter Professor
*Hunter College and Graduate Center
City University of New York*

Donald B. Bailey, Ph.D.
Director, *Early Childhood Research
Frank Porter Graham Child Development
Center*
Clinical Associate Professor, *School of
Education
University of North Carolina at Chapel
Hill*

Kathryn E. Barnard, R.N., Ph.D.
Professor of Nursing and Associate
Dean for Academic Programs
*Department of Parent and Child Nursing
University of Washington
Seattle, Washington*

W. Steven Barnett, Ph.D.
Assistant Professor and Research
Associate, *Center for Research on
Human Development and Education
Temple University
Philadelphia, Pennsylvania*

Leila Beckwith, Ph.D.
Professor, *Department of Pediatrics
University of California at Los Angeles*

Diane Bricker, Ph.D.
Professor of Special Education
Director, *Early Intervention Program
Center on Human Development
University of Oregon
Eugene, Oregon*

Philippa Campbell, Ph.D.
Director, *Family Child Learning Center
Tallmadge, Ohio*

Dante Cicchetti, Ph.D.
Professor of Psychology and Psychiatry
Director, *Mt. Hope Family Center
University of Rochester
Rochester, New York*

Carl J. Dunst, Ph.D.
Director, *Family, Infant and Preschool
Program
Western Carolina Center
Morganton, North Carolina*

Colette M. Escobar, M.S.
Research Associate, *Early Intervention
Research Institute
Utah State University
Logan, Utah*

Dale C. Farran, Ph.D.
Professor and Chair, *Child Development-
Family Relations
University of North Carolina at
Greensboro*

Barbara H. Fiese, Ph.D.
Assistant Professor of Psychology
*Syracuse University
Syracuse, New York*

Mary B. Fleck, M.Ed.
Graduate Student, *Doctoral Program in
Educational Psychology*

Rutgers University, Graduate School of
  Education
New Brunswick, New Jersey

James J. Gallagher, Ph.D.
Kenan Professor of Education
Director, *Carolina Policy Studies*
  Program
University of North Carolina at Chapel
  Hill

James Garbarino, Ph.D.
President, *Erikson Institute for Advanced*
  Study in Child Development
Chicago, Illinois

Linda Gilkerson, Ph.D.
Director, *Infant Care Program*
Evanston Hospital
Evanston, Illinois
Co-Director, *Infant Studies Program*
Erikson Institute
Chicago, Illinois

Barbara Glazewski, Ed.D.
Assistant Professor of Speech,
  Language, and Hearing Sciences
Rutgers University
New Brunswick, New Jersey

Peter A. Gorski, M.D.
Division Head, *Behavioral &*
  Developmental Pediatrics
The Evanston Hospital and Northwestern
  University Medical School
Evanston, Illinois

Stanley Greenspan, M.D.
Clinical Professor of Child Health and
  Development
George Washington University Medical
  School
Washington, DC
Supervising Child Psychoanalyst,
  Psychoanalytic Institute
Bethesda, Maryland

Robert Halpern, Ph.D.
Professor, *Erikson Institute*
Chicago, Illinois

Gloria L. Harbin, Ph.D.
Associate Director, *Carolina Policy*
  Studies Program

Frank Porter Graham Child Development
  Center
The University of North Carolina at
  Chapel Hill

Penny Hauser-Cram, Ed.D.
Research Associate, *Department of*
  Pediatrics
University of Massachusetts Medical
  School
Worcester, Massachusetts

Francine Jacobs, Ed.D.
Assistant Professor of Child Study
Tufts University
Medford, Massachusetts

Barbara Kalmanson, Ph.D.
Psychologist, *Infant-Parent Program*
Department of Psychiatry
University of California at San Francisco

Jean F. Kelly, Ph.D.
Research Associate, *Department of*
  Parent and Child Nursing
University of Washington
Seattle, Washington

Nancy K. Klein, Ph.D.
Professor and Associate Dean, *College of*
  Education
Cleveland State University
Cleveland, Ohio

Marty Wyngaarden Krauss, Ph.D.
Assistant Professor, *Heller Graduate*
  School
Brandeis University
Waltham, Massachusetts

Paul C. Marshall, M.D.
Associate Professor of Pediatrics and
  Neurology
University of Massachusetts Medical
  School
Worcester, Massachusetts

Cecilia McCormick, Ph.D.
Early Childhood Coordinator, *Olympia*
  School District
Olympia, Washington

Lorraine McCune, Ed.D.
Associate Professor

Rutgers University, Graduate School of
*   Education*
New Brunswick, New Jersey

Brian A. McNulty, Ph.D.
Executive Director, *Special Education*
Colorado Department of Education
Denver, Colorado

Samuel J. Meisels, Ed.D.
Professor, *School of Education*
Research Scientist, *Center for Human*
*   Growth and Development*
The University of Michigan
Ann Arbor, Michigan

Judith S. Musick, Ph.D.
Visiting Scholar, *Northwestern University*
Evanston, Illinois

Polly Panitz, M.D.
Fellow, *Division of Behavioral &*
*   Developmental Pediatrics*
The Evanston Hospital and Northwestern
*   University Medical School*
Evanston, Illinois

Steven J. Parker, M.D.
Assistant Professor of Pediatrics
Boston University School of Medicine
Director, *Developmental Assessment*
*   Clinic*
Boston City Hospital

Peggy Pizzo, M.Ed.
Senior Program Associate, *National*
*   Center for Clinical Infant Programs*
Washington, D.C.

Sally Provence, M.D.
Professor Emeritus of Pediatrics and
*   Child Development*
Senior Research Scientist, *Yale*
*   University Child Study Center*
New Haven, Connecticut

Christine L. Salisbury, Ph.D.
Associate Professor of Special Education
Division of Education, School of
*   Education & Human Development*
State University of New York at
*   Binghamton*

Arnold J. Sameroff, Ph.D.
Professor of Psychiatry and Human
*   Behavior, Brown University*
Director of Research, *E.P. Bradley*
*   Hospital*
East Providence, Rhode Island

Victoria Seitz, Ph.D.
Research Scientist, *Yale University Child*
*   Study Center and Department of*
*   Psychology*
New Haven, Connecticut

Jack P. Shonkoff, M.D.
Professor of Pediatrics
Chief, *Division of Developmental and*
*   Behavioral Pediatrics*
University of Massachusetts Medical
*   School*
Worcester, Massachusetts

Joan Sillari, B.S.
Director, *Early Intervention Program*
The Children's Center
Edison, New Jersey

Rune J. Simeonsson, Ph.D.
Professor and Investigator
School of Education and Frank Porter
*   Graham Child Development Center*
University of North Carolina at Chapel
*   Hill*

Frances Stott, Ph.D.
Professor, *Erikson Institute*
Chicago, Illinois

Philip Strain, Ph.D.
Associate Professor of Psychiatry and
*   Special Education*
Western Psychiatric Institute and Clinic
University of Pittsburgh

Annette Tessier, Ed.D.
Professor, *Division of Special Education*
California State University at Los Angeles

Carol M. Trivette, M. A.
Associate Director, *Center for Family*
*   Studies*
Western Carolina Center
Morganton, North Carolina

Contributors

Carole Christofk Upshur, Ed.D.
Associate Professor, *College of Public and Community Service*
University of Massachusetts at Boston

Margaret Veltman, M.A.
Coordinator, Model Demonstration Program, *Early Intervention Program*
Center on Human Development
University of Oregon
Eugene, Oregon

Lisbeth J. Vincent, Ph.D.
Professor, *Department of Rehabilitation Psychology and Special Education*
University of Wisconsin
Madison, Wisconsin

Sheldon Wagner, Ph.D.
Department of Psychology
University of Rochester
Rochester, New York

Barbara A. Wasik, Ph.D.
Associate Research Scientist, *Center for Social Organization of Schools*
Johns Hopkins University
Baltimore, Maryland

Emmy E. Werner, Ph.D.
Professor of Human Development and Research Child Psychologist
University of California at Davis

Edward F. Zigler, Ph.D.
Sterling Professor of Psychology
Yale University
New Haven, Connecticut

Barry S. Zuckerman, M.D.
Professor of Pediatrics, *Boston University School of Medicine*
Director, *Division of Behavioral and Developmental Pediatrics*
Boston City Hospital

PART I

Introduction

1 Early childhood intervention: The evolution of a concept

JACK P. SHONKOFF AND SAMUEL J. MEISELS

The field of early childhood intervention is a model of remarkable accomplishment and unfulfilled opportunity. Its agenda ranges from scholarly reflection to service delivery. Its successes include specialization as well as enhanced cross-disciplinary collaboration. Its unmet challenges are both theoretical and pragmatic. And it draws upon a wide range of intellectual resources in child and family development, education, health, economics, social policy, and philosophy.

In recent testimony before the Senate Committee on Labor and Human Resources and the House Committee on Education and Labor, David Hamburg, president of the Carnegie Corporation of New York, closed with the following remarks:

> What we do early in life lays the foundation for all the rest. The early years can provide the basis for a long, healthy life-span. Early preventive intervention can be exceptionally valuable. Health and education are closely linked in the development of vigorous, skillful, adaptable young people. Investments in health and education can be guided by research in biomedical and behavioral sciences in ways likely to prevent much of the damage now being done to children. We have learned a lot in recent years about ways of preventing damage to children – prenatal and perinatal care, early education, immunization, nutrition, and much more. The great challenge now is to be sufficiently resourceful and persistent to find ways of putting that knowledge to use for healthy child development in a rapidly changing socio-technical context. If there is a more fundamental task for human beings, I wonder what it could be (Hamburg, 1987, pp. 49–50).

That task – to merge the knowledge and insights of scholars and practitioners with the creative talents of those who design and implement social policy initiatives, and to invest the products of such an alliance in the future of our children – reflects the fundamental purpose of early childhood intervention.

The concept of support for infants and young children would seem, at first glance, to generate little controversy. One would think that a child with a disability, or one whose early life experiences are dominated by the material deprivations of poverty, or by the caregiving of a disorganized, isolated, or abusive parent, would be the uncontested beneficiary of adequately funded public services. Indeed, many have proposed that the allocation of resources for this most vulnerable and most disenfranchised group within our population should be based on its moral imperative alone (e.g., Caldwell, 1986; Edelman, 1987; Schorr, 1988; Turnbull & Turnbull, 1985). Nevertheless, evidence is emerging that an "investment" in young children will also return monetary dividends in the form of decreased subsequent need for such costly services as special education,

3

custodial care, welfare support, and incarceration for delinquent behavior (Barnett, 1985; Barnett & Escobar, this volume).

Despite its intrinsic appeal, however, the field of early childhood intervention has not been embraced uniformly or supported consistently. It has endured battles over the delineation of its goals and objectives (Clarke & Clarke, 1976; Ferry, 1981), the specification of program models and methods (Anastasiow & Mansergh, 1975), and the selection of service providers and recipients (Bricker & Slentz, 1988). It has tried to respond to the challenge to document its effectiveness while struggling with the methodological and logistical constraints of inadequate outcome measures, unavoidable sample attrition, limited funds to sustain long-term longitudinal studies, and ethical barriers to the maintenance of untreated control groups of children with documented problems (Meisels, 1985; Shonkoff, Hauser-Cram, Krauss, & Upshur, 1988).

This chapter is divided into three sections. The first explores the diverse origins of the field of early childhood intervention prior to the 1960s. The second section provides an overview of the dramatic advances of the past three decades. Finally, the chapter closes with an examination of the conceptual and programmatic challenges of the future.

The history of early childhood intervention in the United States illustrates the power of an idea that has evolved over time. Whereas its early roots were established in a variety of fields that have converged in recent years, its theoretical foundation continues to mature as it gains from both the successes and the disappointments of its pioneers. Standing on the threshold of the final decade of the twentieth century, the concept of early childhood intervention faces a formidable array of political, bureaucratic, and theoretical challenges and opportunities. Its antecedent pathways and their links to the tasks of the present and the future are the focus of this chapter.

HISTORICAL ROOTS AND EARLY FOUNDATIONS

The overall framework of contemporary early childhood intervention has evolved from multiple perspectives. The first part of this chapter will focus on the historical contributions of four discrete fields: early childhood education, maternal and child health services, special education, and child development research.

Early childhood education

The intellectual roots of early childhood education are often traced to the relatively recent historical recognition of childhood as a unique period in life and to the writings of the European philosophers of the seventeenth and eighteenth centuries (Aries, 1962). Comenius (1592–1670) characterized the "School of the Mother" as the most appropriate vehicle for education in the first six years of life and advocated that the child learn "spontaneously...in play whatever may be learned at home" (Eller, 1956, p. 116, cited by Clarke-Stewart & Fein, 1983). Locke (1632–1704) popularized the notion of the tabula rasa, suggesting that children from birth are a blank slate, thereby challenging the commonly held concept of genetically predetermined behavior and competence. Rousseau (1712–1778), an even stronger advocate of the unspoiled nature of the child, urged a laissez-faire approach to the early childhood years in order to allow for the natural unfolding of individual talents. These views were largely echoed by the nineteenth century educational experiments of Tolstoy (1967) and by those of A. S. Neill (1960) in more recent years. In contrast to the humanistic attitudes toward child development that emerged in Europe, however, child-rearing practices in the American colonies during the seventeenth and eighteenth centuries were dominated by a harsh puritan influence that focused on the central goal of spiritual salvation and advocated rigid discipline in early education to counteract the inborn "sinful" tendencies of young children (Greven, 1973; Wishy, 1968).

KINDERGARTEN. The first formal kindergarten classes, which were based on a philosophy grounded in traditional religious values and in a belief in the importance of learning through supervised play, were established in Germany by Friedrich Froebel in the early 1800s. During the latter half of the nineteenth century, these ideas were transported across the Atlantic and stimulated the proliferation of experimental programs throughout the United States. Shortly after the first public school kindergarten was established in St. Louis in 1872, the National Educational Association made an official recommendation that kindergarten become a regular part of the public school system (Peterson, 1987).

The social context in which the kindergarten movement began in the United States was molded by the interactive influences of industrialization, urbanization, and secularization. With much early support coming from private agencies and philanthropic groups, advocates of formal kindergarten programs emphasized the potential benefits for poor children and focused particularly on those who had recently immigrated to the United States and were living in urban slums (Braun & Edwards, 1972).

Within a few decades of its early popularization in the United States, however, the kindergarten movement was beset with a series of battles over goals and curricula. Traditionalists remained loyal to the philosophy of Froebel and defended their value-driven educational practices. In contrast, reformists worked to liberalize the kindergarten experience and looked beyond its moralistic foundation to the emerging discipline of child psychology for more empirically derived principles based on the systematic observations, data collection, and analyses of early child development researchers (Hill, cited in Braun & Edwards, 1972). During the early 1900s, the developmental approach to early childhood curriculum advocated by G. Stanley Hall and the pragmatic emphasis on the functional purposes of education promoted by John Dewey were particularly influential.

As research about the developmental process progressed, and as social and political forces shifted, sharp disagreements over the goals of kindergarten have persisted throughout the twentieth century. Its primary objectives continue to alternate between an emphasis on early academic achievement and the nurturing of noncompetitive social and emotional development. Although publicly supported programs are not yet available in all parts of the country, kindergarten is considered a standard component of the American educational system, and it has become an important vehicle for introducing ideas about childhood development into the educational mainstream.

NURSERY SCHOOLS. Nursery schools, like kindergarten, originated in Europe. The first nursery school in London was established by Rachel and Margaret MacMillan, who began in 1910 with a health clinic that was later expanded into an open-air school. The mission of this experimental program was to provide comprehensive, prevention-oriented services to meet the social, physical, emotional, and intellectual needs of young children. Unlike the religious orientation of Froebel's kindergarten, the MacMillans' curriculum was based on secular social values and focused on the development of self-care, individual responsibility, and educational readiness skills (Peterson, 1987).

While the MacMillans were developing their model of early medical–educational intervention in England, Maria Montessori was opening the first nursery school in the slums of Rome. A physician and former director of an institution for mentally retarded children, Montessori applied the methods she had developed for training children with retardation to the preschool education of nondisabled, urban, poor children. The Montessori method departed significantly from traditional early childhood curricula in its emphasis on individualized self-teaching by children within a carefully prepared classroom environment.

The initial introduction of the Montessori approach to preschool education in the United States had minimal impact, as it was lost amidst the battles then being waged among the Froebelian conservatives, the liberal-progressive adherents of the philosophy of Dewey, and the newly emerging "American" positivism championed by such prominent psychologists as Thorndike and Kilpatrick (Braun & Edwards, 1972). Consequently, interest in the Montessori method remained essentially dormant in the United States until the 1960s. The relatively recent rise in its popularity has, however, been greatest among the middle classes, rather than among those who work with poor or disabled children – the populations for whom the method was originally designed (Peterson, 1987).

The nursery school movement first began to gain popularity in the United States in the 1920s based upon an adaptation of the MacMillans' model, an adaptation that attached a great deal of importance to parent involvement within the school program. In contrast to the kindergarten focus on school readiness, early nursery school programs were designed to nurture exploration and to facilitate the social-emotional development of children. By the early 1930s, approximately 200 nursery schools existed in the United States, half of which were associated with colleges and universities, including some of the most productive child development laboratories in the country. The remainder of the programs were operated as private schools or were sponsored by child welfare agencies (Peterson, 1987).

During the depression (1930s), the number of nursery schools increased dramatically as federal relief programs were developed to subsidize unemployed teachers. With the onset of World War II, the need for women to work in defense plants led to further expansion of the schools and to the establishment of federally supported day-care centers under the Lanham Act of 1940 (Morgan, 1972). Prior to this period, day-care services were utilized primarily by the working poor. The employment of large numbers of middle-class women to support the war effort blurred the distinctions between day-care programs and nursery schools. After the war ended, however, federal support for child care terminated, large numbers of women left the work force to raise families, and many programs closed. Without public resources, nursery schools drifted from their early mission of serving poor children and became increasingly available only to those who could afford private tuition.

In recent years, as women have chosen or been compelled by circumstances to combine both child rearing and employment outside the home, the distinctions between child-care programs and nursery schools have become blurred once again. In this social context, the debate about the balance between "care" and "education" in the early preschool years has resumed (see Kahn & Kamerman, 1987; Provence, Naylor, & Patterson, 1977).

SUMMARY. An examination of the historical roots of early childhood education in the United States tells us much about our enduring traditions and changing values. First, it reveals a willingness to explore ideas that were developed in other societies and a determination to adapt them to our own perceived needs. Second, it emphasizes the extent to which the interests of young children and their families are always addressed within the constraints of concurrent political and social demands. Third, it highlights the degree to which early childhood programs have alternatively been developed to meet the particular needs of poor children or middle-class children and their families. Finally, it underlines the extent of inevitable overlap that exists among the generic health, educational, and social needs of all young children regardless of socioeconomic status.

Early childhood intervention services have been influenced significantly by our history of education for young children prior to traditional school entry. The central features of these early programs that have become firmly embedded in current intervention efforts include a child-centered curriculum focus; an emphasis on early socialization of the child outside of the family; an enhanced understanding of child development and the practical applications of developmental theory; and a belief in the importance of the early years as a foundation for later social, emotional, and intellectual competence. This conceptual legacy, in conjunction with the wealth of materials, resources, and techniques that have been refined over the years, is woven throughout the day-to-day activities of contemporary early intervention programs.

Maternal and child health services

In much the same way that the industrialization and secularization of the nineteenth century provided fertile ground for the development of new concepts in early childhood education, persistently high mortality rates among young children promoted greater concern for their physical health. In fact, many pediatric authorities in the late 1800s urged a deemphasis on educational stimulation before 5 years of age to prevent the diversion of "vital forces" from activities that promoted physical well-being (Griffith, 1895; Holmes, 1857). In a classic textbook, one of the most prominent pediatricians at the turn of the century wrote,

> Great injury is done to the nervous system of children by the influences with which they are surrounded during infancy, especially during the first year....Playing with young children, stimulating to laughter and exciting them by sights, sounds, or movements until they shriek with apparent delight may be a source of amusement to fond parents and admiring spectators, but it is almost invariably an injury to the child....It is the plain duty of the physician to enlighten parents upon this point, and insist that the infant shall be kept quiet, and that all such playing and romping as has been referred to shall, during the first year at least, be absolutely prohibited (Holt, 1897, p. 5).

THE CHILDREN'S BUREAU. In 1912, in an attempt to address the widespread problems of high infant mortality, poor physical health, and exploitation of working children, Congress established a Children's Bureau in the Department of Labor "to investigate and report...upon all matters pertaining to the welfare of children and child life among all classes of our people" (quoted in Lesser, 1985, p. 591). In its first annual report, the Bureau acknowledged its responsibility to serve all children, but noted that particular attention would be focused on "those who were abnormal or subnormal or suffering from physical or mental ills" (Bradbury, 1962, cited in Lesser, 1985, p. 591). Based on a decision to emphasize the concept of prevention, and having addressed the issue of infant mortality as the object of its first investigation, the

Children's Bureau proceeded to conduct early studies in such subject areas as day care, institutional care, mental retardation, the health of preschool children in selected cities, and the care of "crippled children" (Lesser, 1985).

As the first official acknowledgment of a federal responsibility for children's welfare, the establishment of the Children's Bureau provided a foundation for governmental data collection and federal grants to promote the health and development of the nation's most vulnerable children. In its earliest studies, the bureau highlighted striking correlations between socioeconomic factors and infant and maternal deaths. These data established a firm justification for programs supported by the Sheppard-Towner Act during the 1920s that increased public health nursing services and stimulated the creation of state child hygiene divisions and permanent maternal and child health centers throughout the country (Steiner, 1976).

Although the development of programs for children with disabilities progressed more slowly than services for those who were poor, data collected by the Children's Bureau through its state surveys served to highlight marked unmet needs in this area as well. Consequently, the 1930 White House Conference on Child Health and Protection recommended that federal funds be made available to each of the states to establish programs for "crippled children" that reflected cooperation among medical, educational, social welfare, and vocational rehabilitation agencies to provide a comprehensive array of diagnostic and treatment services (Lesser, 1985).

TITLE V. When the Social Security Act was enacted in 1935, the importance of a federal responsibility for the well-being of children and their mothers was reinforced explicitly. Title V of that landmark legislation contained three major components that established the framework for resource allocation and program development that has influenced national health policy for children over the succeeding half century (see Magee & Pratt, 1985).

Part I (Maternal and Child Health Services) authorized financial assistance to states to develop services designed to promote the general health of mothers and children, with special emphasis on program initiatives for rural and economically depressed areas. The most common activities supported by such funds included prenatal care, well baby clinics, school health services, immunization programs, public health nursing and nutrition services, and health education.

Part II (Services for Crippled Children) created the first federal program to provide matching funds for states to deliver medical services to a targeted patient group. The law was clear in its intent to develop a comprehensive service system, including case finding, diagnosis, treatment, and follow-up care. The prevention of "crippling" diseases and the amelioration of secondary handicaps were highlighted as central goals, and each state was required to promote cooperative efforts between health and welfare groups in order to achieve such ends. The definition of crippled children was left to the states, and although more than three-quarters of those who received services in the 1930s and 1940s had orthopedic problems, by the mid 1950s that proportion had dropped to less than 50% as increasing numbers of children with other chronic disabilities (e.g., heart disease, seizure disorders, etc.) were identified.

Part III (Child Welfare Services) of the Title V program authorized funding to state welfare agencies to develop programs (especially in rural areas) for the care and protection of homeless, dependent, and neglected children, and children considered to be in danger of becoming delinquents (Lesser, 1985).

In 1939, nonmatching Title V funds were appropriated for "special projects of regional and national significance" (SPRANS grants) to enable states to develop innovative programs beyond the core of mandated services. Subsequently, these grants provided support for such wide-ranging initiatives as improved care of premature infants, training of professionals, and applied research on children with a wide variety of chronic illnesses and disabling conditions, including sensory impairments, seizure disorders, and congenital heart disease.

EPSDT. In 1965, the Medicaid provisions of the Social Security Act were signed into law in order to improve the quality and accessibility of medical services for all those living in poverty. Although designed primarily as a medical reimbursement program to be administered by the states and jointly financed by state and federal funds, Medicaid does include mandated programs that reflect specific federal interest in early childhood intervention for poor children. One of the best known of these efforts is the Early and Periodic Screening Diagnosis and Treatment Program (EPSDT).

EPSDT was initiated in the late 1960s as part of a national effort to improve the health and welfare of poor children. It mandated the early and periodic medical, dental, vision, and developmental screening, diagnosis, and treatment of all children and youth under 21 years of age whose families qualified for Medicaid eligibility. One of the incentives for formulating and enacting this new program was a recognition of the prevalence of a range of apparently preventable problems among the nation's youth (Foltz, 1982). Thus, EPSDT was designed to assure early identification of such problems and to provide funds for subsequent intervention. Indeed, this program was conceived as an attempt to break the cycle of poverty, to remedy the health consequences of uneven economic circumstances, and to improve poor children's health by providing services designed to have a high payoff in later health and welfare (Meisels, 1984). Unfortunately, however, EPSDT's record of success has been very uneven, and recent analyses of its effectiveness suggest that major changes should take place in its formulation and organization (Foltz, 1982; Margolis & Meisels, 1987; Meisels & Margolis, 1988).

SUMMARY. Unlike education, which is accepted as a traditional responsibility of state and federal government, health care services in the United States are provided by a complex amalgamation of public and private resources and delivery systems. Thus, any attempts on the part of the federal government to regulate or otherwise influence the organization or delivery of medical services are always met with some degree of organized opposition and/or noncompliance in the private sector. In this context, the early history and subsequent growth of publicly supported maternal and child health and crippled children's services is striking. Indeed, it reflects a powerful and persistent underlying consensus within the American political system that the care and protection of the health of children is too important to be left to the "wisdom" of the free market, particularly for those who are poor or those who have a chronic disabling condition.

Special education

The history of special education services for children with disabilities provides a third lens through which we can examine the evolution of early childhood intervention services. In ancient times, young children with physical anomalies or obvious disabilities were often the victims of active or passive euthanasia. During the Middle Ages and succeeding centuries, retarded individuals were either tolerated as court jesters or street beggars (see Aries, 1962), or were imprisoned or otherwise institutionalized (see Chase, 1980).

Most historical overviews of the field of special education begin with the attempts by Itard, in the late eighteenth century, to teach the "wild boy of Aveyron," using a set of sensory training techniques and what is currently characterized as behavior modification. However, Itard's student, Edouard Seguin, is generally acknowledged as the most important pioneer in this field. As director of the Hospice des Incurables in Paris, Seguin developed a "physiological method of education" for disabled children. This method was based on a detailed assessment of individual strengths and weaknesses and a specific plan of sensorimotor activities designed to correct specific difficulties. Through painstaking observations Seguin described the early signs of developmental delay and emphasized the importance of early education (Crissey, 1975). As noted earlier, his methods were later adapted by Montessori for the education of poor preschool children in Rome.

Seguin's pessimism about the benefits of special education initiated later in life was complemented by his belief in the critical importance of early intervention. He stated, "If the idiot cannot be reached by the first lessons of infancy, by what mysterious process will years open for him the golden doors of intelligence" (quoted in Talbot, 1964, p. 62). Seguin was, indeed, one of the first "early interventionists."

RESIDENTIAL PLACEMENTS. Inspired by Seguin's work in Paris, educational programs for persons with mental retardation proliferated throughout the world during the early 1800s. In the latter half of the nineteenth century residential institutions were built in the United States and, stimulated by Seguin's immigration to this country, his teaching techniques were incorporated into many of these newly opened facilities. In 1876, the Association of Medical Officers of American Institutions for Idiotic and Feeble-Minded Persons was formed, with Seguin as its first president, to provide a mechanism for communication among those interested in the education of mentally retarded persons. (In 1906, the name of the organization was changed to the American Association for the Study of the Feeble-Minded; in 1933, it was changed again to the American Association on Mental Deficiency; and in 1987, the name was changed for the third time – reflecting contemporary changes in attitude – to the American Association on Mental Retardation.) By the end of the nineteenth century, residential institutions in the United States were well established, highly invested in the development of teaching strategies, and firmly committed to the integration, albeit in limited form, of disabled persons into community life (Crissey, 1975).

In the early decades of the twentieth century, however, residential institutions changed their mission from training and planned social integration to custodial supervision and isolation. Among the forces that influenced this dramatic shift were the activities of such prominent psychologists as Henry Goddard and Louis Terman, who embraced the prejudices of the eugenics movement and employed the newly developed technology of individual intelligence testing to identify target groups for discrimination, if not systematic exclusion, from American society (Chase, 1980). Data providing "scientific validation" of the link between mental retardation and criminal behavior were disseminated, and intelligence test scores were used to justify the legislation of racist immigration restrictions and compulsory sterilization procedures for the "mentally defective" (Kamin, 1974). Harsh rhetoric from the psychology community challenged the early optimism of special education, and residential institutions were transformed into dreary warehouses for neglected and forgotten individuals.

PUBLIC SCHOOL PROGRAMS. In the public schools, the development of special education programs began slowly and served relatively small numbers of children. Youngsters with moderate to severe disabilities were either sent to institutions or were kept at home, while most children with mild disabilities were simply enrolled in regular classes from which they ultimately dropped out at very high rates. During the depression and the world war that followed, special education resources for the public schools were curtailed, and greater reliance was placed on already overcrowded and educationally limited residential institutions.

During the postwar period, children with disabilities began to receive more benevolent attention. This renewed interest in the needs of developmentally vulnerable youngsters was stimulated in part by the results of massive testing of military personnel during World War II, which revealed the striking prevalence of young men and women with physical, mental, or behavioral disabilities. It was also stimulated by changes in societal attitudes toward disabled persons, in general, brought about by the large numbers of war veterans who returned with physical disabilities. In 1946, a Section for Exceptional Children was established within the United States Office of Education, which later (in 1966) became the Bureau of Education for the Handicapped and then (in 1980) the Office of Special Education and Rehabilitation Services. By the late 1950s, legislation at both the state and federal levels was beginning to promote greater access to special education for wider segments of the population.

SUMMARY. Shifts in attitudes and practices regarding the education of children with disabilities have been described in evolutionary terms by Caldwell (1973), who identified three major historical periods. The first, labeled "Forget and Hide," refers to the practice in the first half of this century through which handicapped children were kept out of public view presumably to avoid embarrassing their families. The second period corresponds to the prevailing attitudes of the 1950s and 1960s, and is called "Screen and Segregate." In this period, children with disabilities were tested, labeled, and then isolated once again in special facilities, based on the assumption that they needed protection and could not function independently in the mainstream. Caldwell named the third period "Identify and Help." Beginning in the mid-1970s, with the passage of landmark special education legislation and continuing to the present day, this stage has been marked by efforts to screen for special needs in the early years of life in the hopes of providing appropriate intervention services at as young an age as possible. The goals of this era are to contain the consequences of disabling conditions, prevent the occurrence of more severe disorders, assist the families of children with disabilities, and increase the opportunities for all children to grow to their full potential.

Child development research

Although fundamental decisions regarding program design and resource allocation are typically motivated by sociopolitical considerations, the evolving conceptual context of early childhood services has been influenced substantially by the scholarly study of the development of young children. Thus, a fourth lens through which the history of early childhood intervention can be examined focuses on the contributions of the academic child development community. Despite the fact that a comprehensive overview of the history of child development research is beyond the scope of this chapter, a brief mention of several influential theoretical and empirical contributions is essential. In this regard, two critical research themes will be addressed: the nature–nurture controversy and the importance of the caregiver–child relationship.

THE NATURE–NURTURE DEBATE. Interest in the determinants of competence in young children is a relatively recent phenomenon. Although systematic evaluations of the emerging abilities of infants were conducted by a New Orleans physician in the late nineteenth century (Chaille, 1887), the cataloguing of early achievements and the methods of childhood assessment were not well developed until the early decades of the twentieth century.

The dominant figure in the emerging field of child developmental evaluation was Arnold Gesell, a pediatrician and psychologist. As the director of one of several child study centers supported by the Laura Spelman Rockefeller Memorial Fund, Gesell conducted extensive studies of the skills of normally developing children, the abilities of youngsters with Down syndrome, and the developmental accomplishments of those who were born prematurely or who sustained perinatal injuries (Gesell, 1925, 1929). His observational methods produced a wealth of data that continue to influence the construction of developmental assessment instruments to this day.

Gesell's theoretical orientation was clear, and his impact on the clinical study of children was enormous. He was a strong believer in the primacy of biologically determined maturation. His disdain for the relative impact of experience on the developmental process was striking, and the possibility of altering that process through early intervention was viewed as futile. The conceptual legacy of Gesell's maturational perspective was a linear model of human development that was used by clinicians to predict long-term outcomes based on the rate of acquisition of specific developmental milestones in early infancy. During the 1950s, this model was linked to the growing recognition of a correlation between adverse perinatal events and later neurodevelopmental disorders, which resulted in the popularization of an influential paradigm of biological determinism known as the "continuum of reproductive casualty" (Lilienfeld & Parkhurst, 1951; Lilienfeld & Pasamanick, 1954).

As the maturationist view of development attracted support during the first half of the twentieth century, its influence was countered by the comparably powerful concepts of behaviorism. The behaviorists believed that in the absence of significant brain damage, developmental outcomes in children are controlled largely by environmental forces. One of the most eloquent early spokespersons for this interventionist approach to human development was John B. Watson, a prominent psychologist, who wrote, "Since the behaviorists find little that corresponds to instincts in children, since children are made not born, failure to bring up a happy child, a well adjusted child – assuming bodily health – falls upon the parents' shoulders. The acceptance of this view makes child rearing the most important of all social obligations" (Watson, 1928, p. 8).

The controversy over the relative impact of nature and nurture on the developmental process in early childhood has been an enduring one. While the maturationists championed the belief in biological determination, the behaviorists advocated the tenets of operant conditioning and environmental manipulation. Each position has had strong support. Yet, when examined in isolation, both perspectives have been found to be quite limited.

With the advent of Piaget's "cognitive revolution" in the fifties and sixties (Cairns, 1983), the stage was set for a rapprochement between the polarities of nature and nurture. This was facilitated by a recognition that biological and social factors in development mutually influence one another, thereby creating a need to go beyond the traditional nature–nurture debate. In fact, research findings even led some scholars to adopt the paradoxical position that all behavior is completely inherited as well as completely determined by experience. As Goldberg (1982) noted, "Unless capacities for behavior are inherited, a behavior can never occur (e.g., chimpanzees will never talk regardless of what experiences are provided). But...the actual occurrence of behavior depends on appropriate experience (e.g., a human infant will not learn to speak without hearing the speech of others)" (pp. 35–36). In other words, many researchers began to acknowledge that the distinctions between biological and social explanations for developmental outcomes are, if not arbitrary and incomplete, at least ambiguous.

One of the most influential conceptualizations of the reciprocal relationship that exists between nature and nurture was articulated by Sameroff and Chandler (1975). In a challenge to the previously popular paradigm of a "continuum of reproductive casualty," they formulated the notion of a "continuum of caretaking casualty" to describe the transactional effects of familial, social, and environmental factors on human development. In Sameroff's (1975) terms, "Although reproductive casualties may play an initiating role in the production of later problems, it is the caretaking environment that will determine the ultimate outcome" (p. 274). For the field of early childhood intervention, acceptance of the transactional model of development meant that biological insults could be modified by environmental factors, and that developmental vulnerabilities could have social and environmental etiologies. This focus on the bidirectionality of social and biological factors proved to have a major impact on both research and service delivery.

THE IMPORTANCE OF EARLY RELATIONSHIPS. As the child development community first began to explore the process through which developmental outcomes could be affected by the child-rearing environment, a number of investigations were launched to study the adverse consequences of deprivation in early human relationships. Guided by a psychoanalytic framework, these ground-breaking "natural experiments" first focused attention on the effects of institutionalization on the cognitive and socioemotional development of infants (Provence & Lipton, 1962; Spitz, 1945). Such studies documented the developmentally destructive impact of the sustained isolation and understimulation typical of life in many orphanages, poorly staffed hospital wards, and other institutional settings. The features of this syndrome, which Spitz (1945) characterized as "hospitalism," included growth retardation, maladaptive social relationships, and health-related problems in young, otherwise normal children.

A complementary set of seminal studies in this area focused on the degree to which the developmental sequelae of early deprivation are modifiable. Beginning with a classic experiment on children who were institutionalized for mental retardation (Skeels & Dye, 1939), investigators manipulated living arrangements and levels of stimulation for a range of institutionalized populations and demonstrated that a responsive and stimulating environment could reverse the effects of negative, isolated, and otherwise deleterious experiences in early infancy (Dennis, 1960, 1973; Skeels, 1966). The growing empirical literature generated by such studies highlighted the malleability of early human development, thereby establishing a rationale for intervention within the early years of life (also see Kirk, 1958).

On a conceptual level, the work of John Bowlby provided a theoretical framework for the empirical findings of the early deprivation studies. With support in the 1950s from the World Health Organization, Bowlby investigated the problems of homelessness and maternal deprivation, and examined their consequences for mental health in children.

In his classic monograph on maternal and child health, Bowlby (1951) called attention to the critical importance of the mother–child relationship for healthy child development. His subsequent formulation of the construct of attachment provided a theoretical foundation for the development over the ensuing decades of critically important studies of the socioemotional adaptation of young children (Ainsworth, 1969; Ainsworth, Blehar, Waters, & Wall, 1978; Bowlby, 1969; Bretherton & Waters, 1985; Sroufe, 1983).

Much of the empirical research that demonstrated the marked influence of the caretaking environment and thereby supported the validity of the transactional model of development emerged from a number of landmark longitudinal studies that were initiated in the 1950s and 1960s. Two of these investigations focused on the growth and development of large birth cohorts; the others delineated the emerging abilities of young children with specifically defined risk factors.

The most extensive longitudinal data on the developmental impact of biological and social risk factors in a birth cohort were generated by the Collaborative Perinatal Project of the National Institute of Neurological Diseases and Blindness, which enrolled a national sample of more than 53,000 pregnant women and followed their children through the early school years (Broman, Nichols, & Kennedy, 1975). A second, remarkably rich investigation, known as the Kauai Studies, collected longitudinal data from the neonatal period through adulthood on more than 1,000 children born on the Hawaiian island of Kauai (Werner, Bierman, & French, 1971; Werner & Smith, 1977, 1982). The major findings of both studies documented the significant influence on developmental outcomes of maternal education and the quality of the caregiving environment, except in cases of severe brain damage.

A number of pioneering prospective studies of the development of infants with documented risk factors or diagnosed disabilities were similarly enlightening. Investigations of young children with histories of perinatal anoxia, for example, revealed the extent to which adverse neurological sequelae were often found to be transient, as many at-risk children displayed normal development over the ensuing preschool years (Graham, Ernhart, Thurston, & Craft, 1962; Graham, Pennoyer, Caldwell, Greenman, & Hartmann, 1957). Similarly, detailed longitudinal assessments of young children with such diagnosed developmental disorders as Down syndrome and phenylketonuria (PKU) provided reliable databases for assessing individual outcomes, highlighted the extent to which levels of disability varied within diagnostic categories, and demonstrated the limitations of early developmental predictions (Fishler, Graliker, & Koch, 1964; Share, Webb, & Koch, 1961).

The data generated by these diverse studies contributed important insights to the growing interest in early intervention services for vulnerable children. The process of development was found to be complex and transactional, and it was becoming increasingly clear that outcomes are mediated by the mutual effects of both nature and nurture (see Beckwith, this volume; Garbarino, this volume; Shonkoff & Marshall, this volume; Werner, this volume).

SUMMARY. During the early decades of the twentieth century, questions regarding child development were framed within relatively simple paradigms that reflected the competing influences of organic endowment and individual experience. Subsequent research on the development of young children extended our knowledge of the essential transactional nature of the developmental process and of the potential benefits of early intervention services. The degree to which the quality of the caregiving environment was demonstrated to influence the effects of biological risk factors provided substantial support for the development of intervention strategies to modify that environment. The design of such interventions has reflected a range of conceptual perspectives and has been based on a wide variety of empirically and theoretically based practices (see Anastasiow, this volume; Greenspan, this volume; Sameroff & Fiese, this volume; Vincent, Salisbury, Strain, McCormick, & Tessier, this volume).

THREE DECADES OF GROWTH AND DEVELOPMENT

The philosophical and pragmatic roots of early childhood intervention prior to the 1960s emerged from a variety of sources. In each domain – early childhood education, maternal and child health, special education, and child development research – interactions between professional expertise and sociopolitical exigencies helped to lay a foundation for the educational, psychological, public health, and public policy developments of the last thirty years. Among the themes that persisted through the early years, despite the occasional opposition they encountered, are a belief in the responsibility of society to provide care and protection for young children; a commitment to the special needs of children who are particularly vulnerable as a result of a chronic disabling condition or as a consequence of growing up under conditions of poverty; and a sense that prevention is better than treatment and that earlier intervention is better than later remediation. These three themes reflect the spiritual origins of early childhood intervention. They provide an organizing framework for examining the major initiatives that have unfolded during the last three decades and that are likely to influence the field in years to come.

The sixties: a broad agenda with an ambitious promise

The decade of the 1960s marks the beginning of the modern era in early childhood intervention. It was a time of optimism and creative program development. Public support for investing in human services was broad based, and resources flowed from the federal government to promote the achievement of ambitious social goals. Within this context the convergence of several critical social issues served to frame the agenda for early childhood services. These included President Kennedy's interest in mental retardation, the political impact of the civil rights movement, and President Johnson's commitment to wage war on the sources and consequences of poverty.

Due in part to his family's personal experience with mental retardation, John F. Kennedy in 1961 appointed a presidential commission to explore current knowledge in this area and to develop a national strategy of prevention. In 1963, the enactment of Public Law 88-156 provided new federal funding under Title V of the Social Security Act for special projects for children with mental retardation. Screening programs for inborn errors of metabolism, such as PKU, and Maternity and Infant Care Projects to help reduce the incidence of mental retardation caused by complications of childbearing, are examples of such projects.

As the decade opened with President Kennedy's interest in the prevention of mental retardation, it closed with President Johnson's commitment to the educational needs of young children with disabilities. In 1968, the enactment of Public Law 90-538, the Handicapped Children's Early Education Assistance Act, authorized funds to stimulate the development, evaluation, refinement, and dissemination of model demonstration programs for the education of disabled infants, preschoolers, and their parents.

Through grants to demonstration programs, and with the initiation of federal support to specialized university teacher-training programs, a new field of study was born.

Closely related to this new discipline of early childhood special education in many of its underlying principles, but distinct and separate in its political beginnings, the concept of early childhood intervention also received considerable support in the 1960s as a potential weapon in the war on poverty. As a result of the efforts of civil rights activists, progressive politicians, and social scientists, Americans became painfully aware of the extent of poverty in the United States and the degree to which the consequences of marked socioeconomic inequalities threatened the well-being of the nation (deLone, 1979). In its own analysis of the "poverty cycle" the President's Panel on Mental Retardation echoed the prevailing stereotype of "cultural deprivation" as a major cause of recurrent, multigenerational retardation (Albee, 1968). Based on its belief that education was the key to breaking this cycle, the panel recommended the widespread establishment in economically disadvantaged communities of preschool programs designed to foster "the specific development of the attitudes and aptitudes which middle-class culture characteristically develops in children, and which contributes in large measure to the academic and vocational success of such children" (The President's Panel on Mental Retardation, 1963, quoted in Zigler & Valentine, 1979, p. 12).

The theoretical rationale for proposals to intervene in the lives of disadvantaged children emerged from a growing body of evidence that questioned previous, widely accepted assumptions regarding the immutable, genetic determination of intelligence. Supported by the recently published scholarly work of J. McVicker Hunt (1961) and Benjamin Bloom (1964), social activists emphasized the powerful influence of experience on the development of competence in young children, and focused on the particular vulnerability and malleability of the first years of life. In the decade of social experimentation that followed, interactions between academic researchers and program developers flourished. "Experimental preschool programs were created in the laboratories of child development researchers and tested in communities across the country . . . . Developmental psychologists were ready to change the world; their proposals to structure children's experiences in ways different from those traditionally accomplished by untutored parents at home were made with enthusiasm and optimism" (Clarke-Stewart & Fein, 1983, p. 918).

In 1965, the most far-reaching experiment of the decade, Head Start, began as an 8-week pilot program for children in more than 2,500 communities around the country. Originally developed under the auspices of the Office of Economic Opportunity, it was elaborated under the leadership of Edward F. Zigler, a prominent academic psychologist who was appointed as the first director of the Office of Child Development. Head Start was based on a belief in the crucial impact of early childhood experiences on later development. Its founders assumed that socioeconomically impoverished environments contain biological (e.g., poor health and nutritional status) and experiential (e.g., understimulation and reduced motivation) risk factors that can affect early childhood adversely. They were convinced that compensatory programs in the preschool period could facilitate better school adjustment and performance for children who were disadvantaged by the consequences of poverty and social disorganization (Zigler & Valentine, 1979).

Head Start was conceived as a multidimensional, comprehensive service system designed to strike at the roots of disadvantage for poor families with young children (Zigler & Valentine, 1979). It harnessed the expertise of a broad array of professionals to provide educational, medical, dental, nutritional, psychological, and social services. It invested a great deal of energy in parent involvement at both the volunteer and decision-making levels and included training programs for low-income adults from the community to facilitate employment mobility. Head Start provided a bold and dramatic model for the field of early childhood intervention that continues to the present day (Peters & Kontos, 1987; Reese, 1985). Its insistence on combining health, education, and social services was critical. Its provisions for parent participation in both the classroom and on administrative policy committees was unprecedented in American education policy. Its approach to the client–professional relationship as a vehicle for shared decision making was revolutionary.

The achievements and political resilience of Head Start have been well documented (Hubbell, 1983; Zigler & Valentine, 1979). In its triumphs and in its disappointments it provides a microcosm of the sixties. The beneficial effects on children, families, and their communities have been extolled frequently (Lazar & Darlington, 1982). The program has not, however, resulted in the complete elimination of school failure, welfare dependency, delinquent behavior, or any of the other social consequences of poverty. Perhaps one of the greatest lessons that Head Start has to teach the field of early childhood intervention is that programs should establish explicit and realistic goals and objectives. The legacy of the sixties teaches us to be cautious about the promises we make, and it reminds us that there are no magic solutions to complex social problems.

The seventies: The political ascendence of developmental disabilities

While much of the creative intervention energies of the sixties were channeled into the War on Poverty, the seventies witnessed a greater investment in the needs of children with disabilities. As the social and political upheavals of the previous decade subsided and the nation worried more about the effects of inflation on the middle class than about the effects of poverty on the development of young children, increased attention was focused on the social status and legal rights of persons with handicapping conditions (Gliedman & Roth, 1980).

Federally supported demonstration and outreach projects proliferated at a rapid rate (DeWeerd, 1981). Funds from both the Bureau of Education for the Handicapped and the Division of Maternal and Child Health supported multidisciplinary training programs at university-affiliated facilities across the country and produced new cadres of professionals to work with handicapped children. Early childhood special education became a higher priority as the demand increased for teachers of preschool children with special needs and as state departments of education began to develop guidelines for certification in this new area of specialization (Stile, Abernathy, Pettibone, & Wachtel, 1984).

⟶ In 1972, Public Law 92-424 (the Economic Opportunity amendments) mandated that all Head Start centers reserve at least 10% of their enrollment for children with identified disabilities. In 1973, the Division for Early Childhood (DEC) was established as a new entity within the Council for Exceptional Children (CEC), thereby reflecting the sense of a distinct professional identity felt by early childhood special educators. In 1974, the federal government earmarked separate funding for state implementation grants to assist states in the planning and development of services for infants and preschoolers with disabilities.

⟵ In 1975, with the passage of Public Law 94-142 (the Education for All Handicapped

Children Act), the right to a free and appropriate public education was established for all children of school age, regardless of the presence of a disability. This landmark legislation mandated the development of individualized education plans (IEPs) based on the results of a nondiscriminatory assessment, specified requirements for parent involvement in the construction of such plans, spelled out principles of due process for both children and parents in the planning and implementation of educational services, and articulated requirements that IEPs be carried out in the least restrictive environment (Singer & Butler, 1987). Although the provisions of P.L. 94-142 did not require states to offer services for infants, toddlers, or preschoolers with disabilities, the new federal law endorsed the importance of such services and provided financial incentives for states to serve children as young as 3 years of age. During this period of cautious interest in infant intervention, the National Center for Clinical Infant Programs (NCCIP) was founded in 1977 in an effort to focus the nation's attention on the needs of the very youngest children and their families.

Complementing their achievements in the area of public education, advocates for disabled persons borrowed some of the strategies used so successfully by civil rights groups during the sixties and brought their message to both the Congress and the court system in a battle to end discrimination on the basis of disability in all aspects of society (Gliedman & Roth, 1980). The first federal civil rights law specifically directed toward the rights of persons with disabilities (Public Law 93-112, the Vocational Rehabilitation Act, Sec. 504), which focused primarily on employment, was passed in 1973. The following year it was amended under Public Law 93-516 to establish rights for nondiscrimination in employment, admission into institutions of higher learning, and access to public facilities. Supportive legislation, multiple successful class-action suits, and a rising public consciousness about the injustice of discrimination against people with disabilities characterized much of the legacy of the 1970s.

The eighties: Governmental retrenchment and the formation of new alliances

The decade of the eighties began with a new national mandate based on a different set of values about the role of government. In 1981, the Omnibus Budget Reconciliation Act was passed by a coalition of politically conservative forces bent on reducing the investment of federal resources in social programs and shifting the responsibility for such efforts (and the concomitant financial burden) to the states. Thus, while Congress endorsed substantial reductions in federal taxes (in conjunction with the sharpest increases in military expenditures ever recorded during peacetime) many domestic programs began to be dismantled and others suffered significant decreases in funding (Edelman, 1987; Schorr, 1988). Formula grants to the states were consolidated into block grants, and overall appropriations for social programs were reduced. The newly conceived Maternal and Child Health Block Grant, for example, incorporated funding for eight categorical programs that previously received separate grants, with an overall budget reduction of 18% in the first 2 years (Lesser, 1985). The eight programs whose previous support was combined into a single block grant included crippled children's, maternal and child health, and genetic disease testing and counseling services; prevention programs for lead paint poisoning, sudden infant death syndrome, and adolescent pregnancy; hemophilia diagnostic and treatment centers; and Supplemental Security Income for disabled children. The immediate result of their consolidation in a block grant was the pitting of categorical programs against each other in a fight for a fair share of the smaller amount of government social spending.

The fact that early childhood intervention programs survived the federal polices of the eighties attests to the depth of their political and social strength and to the breadth of their constituency groups. At a time when the war on poverty was all but eliminated from federal policy making, Head Start was included in the Reagan administration's so-called safety net and continued to receive federal funds. In an era when presidential advisers talked about the advisability of abolishing the United States Department of Education, federal expenditures for the education of young children with disabilities continued to grow, and the most sweeping piece of legislation for disabled children since P.L. 94-142 was enacted, despite the opposition of the Secretary of Education and the threat of a presidential veto. The explanation for the survival of Head Start and for the continued progress of early intervention services for young children with disabilities is clear. Each developed and nurtured a powerful array of advocates and constituency groups both within and outside government. Moreover, the basic principles of early intervention for vulnerable children and their families had gained wide national support (Schorr, 1988).

As the 1980s come to a close and we enter the last decade of the twentieth century, our evolving conceptualization of early childhood intervention is best represented in both the spirit and the provisions of the Education for the Handicapped Act Amendments of 1986 (P.L. 99-457). The philosophy of service delivery that the new law prescribes, and the political energy that secured its enactment, reflect both a culmination of the work of the past and a blueprint for the tasks of the future.

Public Law 99-457

The Education for All Handicapped Children Act Amendments of 1986 is the most important legislation ever enacted for developmentally vulnerable young children. Proposed, passed, and signed into law within a 6-month period in 1986, the statute calls for "a statewide, comprehensive, coordinated, multidisciplinary, interagency program of early intervention services for all handicapped infants and their families" (P.L. 99-457, Sec. 671). Although the bill does not mandate universal services for all children younger than 6 years old, it strengthens incentives for states to serve 3–6-year-olds, and it establishes a discretionary program (Part H of the statute) that provides services for children from birth to 3 years.

Specifically, the bill contains three main provisions. The first part (Part H of the existing Education of the Handicapped Act) establishes the new discretionary program for states to facilitate the development of comprehensive systems of early intervention services for infants and toddlers with developmental delays or disabilities. Although such services are not required by the law, all states elected to begin planning activities, as prescribed in Part H (Campbell, Bellamy, & Bishop, 1988). The second part requires states, by the early 1990s, to provide free and appropriate public education and related services for all eligible children with disabilities from the age of 3 to the age of 5 in order to receive any federal preschool funds. The last part of the law reauthorizes a number of discretionary programs under the Education of the Handicapped Act, such as services for deaf-blind children, early childhood research institutes, and grants for personnel training.

Early intervention is defined narrowly under the new law as "developmental services which...are designed to meet a handicapped infant's or toddler's developmental needs in any one or more of the following areas: physical development; cognitive development; language and speech development; psychosocial development; or self-help skills"

(Sec. 672). Although the language in Part H (which refers to the "development" rather than the "education" of the infant or toddler with disabilities) reinforces a spirit of comprehensiveness, health services are included only to the extent that they are "necessary to enable the infant or toddler to benefit from the other early intervention services" (Sec. 672). Nevertheless, the statute clearly recognizes that effective early intervention services will require the contributions of professionals from many different disciplines and orientations. Thus, multiple perspectives are woven throughout the planning and implementation of the law, and the activities prescribed under Part H must be guided by an Interagency Coordinating Council.

An Analysis of P.L. 99-457

As a federal initiative, P.L. 99-457 provides for states to exercise considerable discretion regarding organizational and programmatic decision making. In fact, the range of implementation options is sufficiently broad that there could eventually be as many different service systems in place as there are states. Nevertheless, the law prescribes a number of critical components that each state must plan for and make operational (see Hauser-Cram, Upshur, Krauss, & Shonkoff, 1988).

LEAD AGENCIES. In order to receive Part H funds, each state is required to select a lead agency to administer its service system and must appoint an Interagency Coordinating Council to assist in its planning, development, and implementation. The intent of this requirement is to overcome the typically fragmented systems of services currently found within most states (Meisels, 1985; Meisels, Harbin, Modigliani, & Olson, 1988). At the time of the passage of P.L. 99-457, services for infants and toddlers with disabilities were delivered through a wide variety of programs supported by local and state taxes, Medicaid, and by the U.S. Department of Health and Human Services, (e.g., Developmental Disabilities programs, or the Maternal and Child Health Block Grant) and through a similar diversity of programs supported by the U.S. Department of Education (e.g., demonstration projects funded through the Handicapped Children's Early Education Program) (Meisels, Harbin, Modigliani, & Olson, 1988). Although Part H is administered by the federal Department of Education, each state is given full authority to designate its own lead agency. In the first year, about one-third of the states chose departments of education as their lead agency, slightly fewer selected departments of health, and the remainder designated other agencies, such as departments of mental health or human services (Garwood, Fewell, & Neisworth, 1988).

HEALTH AND EDUCATION COLLABORATION. Traditional relationships between the health care (public and private) and education communities concerning the care of infants and toddlers with disabilities have been uneven and complex. Thus, coordination between health care and education agencies at both the state and federal levels is viewed as particularly critical to the successful implementation of Part H (Smith & Strain, 1988). Although physicians are usually the professionals best situated to identify very young children with disabling conditions (as well as those who are at risk for developmental problems), attitudes toward early intervention services within the pediatric community are variable (Green, Ferry, Russman, Shonkoff, & Taft, 1987; Guralnick, Heiser, Eaton, Bennett, Richardson, & Groom, 1988). Furthermore, despite the fact that many infants with disabilities have associated health problems (e.g., seizures, sensory impairments, growth disorders) that require sophisticated medical management to assure optimal early intervention efficacy, successful medical–educational collaboration has evolved slowly and inconsistently across the country (Gartner & Lipsky, 1987).

To counteract jurisdictional boundaries and disputes over funding responsibilities between health and education agencies, P.L. 99-457 urges collaborative efforts, and formal interagency agreements have been negotiated at the federal level between the Bureau of Maternal and Child Health and Resources Development, Department of Health and Human Services, and the Office of Special Education Programs, Department of Education. The need to develop local service systems based on functional medical–educational cooperation in the context of the bureaucratic division of medical and educational resources, however, remains a perplexing policy challenge for the 1990s (Butler, Starfield, & Stenmark, 1984).

PROGRAMMATIC DECISIONS. Beyond their influence on bureaucratic organization, the provisions of Part H create a framework within which a number of crucial programmatic decisions must be made about the evolving nature of early childhood intervention services. Each state, for example, is required to develop its own definition of developmental delay, which must be based on appropriate diagnostic procedures that cover five areas of performance (cognitive, physical, language and speech, self-help, and psychosocial development). However, although all states indicated an interest in developing an early intervention service system, only half had reached agreement on a definition of developmental delay to determine their target population within one year of the passage of the law (Gallagher, Harbin, Thomas, Wenger, & Clifford, 1988).

A second issue related to service eligibility involves the problem of developmental "risk." The law requires that early intervention services be made available for two major target groups: those experiencing developmental delay at the time of referral and assessment and those who have a diagnosed condition that has a high probability of resulting in subsequent delay. Each state has the additional option of including children who are "at risk of having substantial developmental delays if early intervention services are not provided" (Sec. 672). Children in this discretionary third category have traditionally been characterized as "biologically at risk" and/or "environmentally at risk" (Tjossem, 1976). Difficulties in identifying such children, however, have been monumental, and will present a significant challenge to states (Meisels & Wasik, this volume). The financial implications related to definitions that increase the potential size of the service population are likely to be a particular focus of contention (see Upshur, this volume).

A third major task presented by the new law is the requirement that an individualized family service plan (IFSP) be developed by a multidisciplinary team (which must include a parent or guardian) for each child and family enrolled in an early intervention program (Sec. 677). Based on an assessment of the needs of the entire family, the IFSP must articulate specific child and family goals, describe the criteria, methods, and timing to be used to evaluate goal attainment, specify the services needed to meet each goal, and identify a case manager who is responsible for insuring the implementation of the plain.

THE ROLE OF THE FAMILY. In explicitly acknowledging the family (rather than the child in isolation) as the central focus of the service, the concept of an IFSP reflects contemporary theoretical perspectives about child development (Beckwith, this volume; Sameroff & Fiese, this volume), current practices in many early intervention programs

(Simeonsson & Bailey, this volume), and empirically based findings regarding enhanced outcomes for children whose parents are involved actively in their early intervention program experiences (Gallagher, this volume; Shonkoff & Hauser-Cram, 1987). The IFSP provision of Part H, however, has generated considerable controversy as a matter of public policy. On the one hand, it is both a logical extension of the mandated parental involvement for school-age children embedded within P.L. 94-142 and a formal endorsement of the family oriented approach that characterizes the current state of the art for services in the early years of life (Healy, Keesee, & Smith, 1985). On the other hand, the IFSP can also be viewed as a catalyst for radical change in early childhood programs that imposes a significant intrusion into family life (Krauss, 1988). The selection of sensitive evaluation strategies to identify family needs (see Krauss & Jacobs, this volume), and the development of appropriate new training experiences to enable existing and future service providers to conduct, interpret, and utilize such assessment protocols constructively (see Klein & Campbell, this volume), will determine the extent to which the concept of an IFSP will be a major step forward or an unworkable federal requirement.

TRANSITIONS. The transition across service systems at 3 years of age presents another potential dilemma in the implementation of P.L. 99-457. The proposed regulations require that the IFSP include a plan to support the transfer of service responsibility from the early intervention system to a preschool program (*Federal Register*, 1987, Sec. 303.68) and that a case manager must be responsible for the development of such a plan (*Federal Register*, 1987, Sec. 303.6). Disputes over the determination of appropriate educational plans, delays in starting services, and disagreements about whether all children enrolled in early intervention programs necessarily qualify for special education classes at age 3 years have all been reported (Association for Retarded Citizens, 1986; Kerns, 1988), therefore development of effective transition procedures will require considerable thought and effort (Hanline & Knowlton, 1988).

SUMMARY. From the perspective of public policy, P.L. 99-457 represents a bold initiative that raises a number of critical challenges for the field of early childhood intervention (Hauser-Cram et al., 1988; Meisels, in press). It combines an enduring national commitment to the needs of vulnerable young children with the "new federalism" of the 1980s that has transferred responsibility for many social programs into the hands of state policymakers. Under the new law, each state must make independent decisions about the definition of developmental delay, the service eligibility of children at risk for developmental disabilities, the criteria and methods to be used for family assessment, and the strategies needed to identify a lead service agency, constitute an Interagency Coordinating Council, and facilitate a smooth transition of children and families from early intervention programs to preschool special education services. How these decisions are reached, whose views are solicited by state policymakers, how research is used to inform and defend specific decisions, and how the impacts of existing state practices are assessed, will require the participation of diverse constituencies from the academic, policy, and service delivery arenas. The task is formidable, but the rewards are potentially very great.

EARLY CHILDHOOD INTERVENTION: THE NEXT CHALLENGES

As each state seeks its own path in meeting the challenges of P.L. 99-457, conceptual battles and political struggles will shape the agenda for early childhood intervention in the nineties. The final section of this chapter examines four broad issues whose consideration offers considerable promise for launching an exciting new era of services for young, vulnerable children and their families.

Rethinking traditional disciplinary boundaries

Although the contributions of multiple professional orientations continue to influence the delivery of early intervention services, current conceptualizations of the process of early childhood development underline the futility of attempting to divide the needs of young children into discrete components defined by traditional disciplinary boundaries. Debates about the demarcation between health concerns and educational interests, for example, generally become exercises in semantic frustration. If a 2-year-old has recurrent otitis media with a fluctuating hearing loss and associated deficits in communication, is this a medical problem, an educational problem, or perhaps a combination of the two? What about the 800-gram neonate who was born after a 29-week pregnancy to a 15-year-old mother who is living alone supported only by public assistance? Are the needs of this infant primarily medical, educational, or developmental, or are they more appropriately classified within the realm of social service? And what about the 3-year-old with a poor attention span and aggressive, disorganized behavior who poses significant management problems in a Head Start program? Are these problems essentially educational? If the child is found to be malnourished and anemic, do the problems become medical? If the child has been physically abused or severely neglected, are we now more likely to consider the problems as a mental health or social service concern?

The list of examples that illustrate the difficulties inherent in a strict categorical approach to the needs of young children is virtually endless. Furthermore, it is not a list of hypothetical situations; rather, it is a catalogue of the kinds of problems that make up an average caseload in a typical early intervention program. The boundaries among the domains of social welfare, physical and mental health, and early childhood education have become less clear, and the more sophisticated we become in our understanding of the complexities of early human development, the more difficult it becomes to sharpen them.

The progressive and inevitable ambiguity of disciplinary boundaries represents one of the central challenges facing the field of early childhood intervention, and the role of the case manager in P.L. 99-457 may be one of the primary vehicles for successfully communicating among the disciplines. The need to rethink traditional disciplinary boundaries demands an intellectually flexible orientation toward the definition of adaptive functioning and individual needs in young children – an orientation that strikes at the very core of the professional identities of a wide variety of disciplines that have played key roles in shaping our concepts of development and intervention. The stresses that accompany such critical reexamination of the boundaries of disciplinary expertise must not be underestimated, and the implications of this phenomenon for the content of professional training programs are enormous (see Klein & Campbell, this volume). However, despite the formidable nature of the task, such change must occur if we are to move toward the design and implementation of truly integrated services for young children and their families.

Redesigning service delivery systems

At the level of individual service delivery, appropriately trained and experienced professionals are able to deal effectively with the kind of disciplinary overlap and ambiguity just described. At the level of service system organization, however, and particularly at the point where decisions are made about the allocation of public resources, vague boundaries are a bureaucratic nightmare. In simple terms, this generally comes down to the basic question of, Who will pay?

Departments of health, education, mental health, social service, and public welfare were all established at certain points in history in order to accomplish specific purposes. Each reflects the expertise of a distinct professional discipline and each focuses on an explicitly defined human service domain. As a consequence of this organizational structure, most public programs tend to adopt narrow goals, and well-integrated comprehensive approaches to social problems are rare. In contrast, early childhood intervention efforts demand a coordinated array of inputs from a range of disciplinary perspectives in order to devise a unified approach that views young children as multidimensional, yet essentially indivisible.

Thus, our evolving theoretical sophistication about the process of human development suggests that the traditional bureaucratic organization of services is becoming increasingly dysfunctional for the delivery of early childhood intervention services. Models of interagency collaboration and the designation of lead agencies and coordinating councils represent the first stage in a process designed to reduce the fragmentation and inefficiency that characterizes current agency structures. Such arrangements are likely to proliferate in the nineties, as states seek to fulfill the mandates of P.L. 99-457 for collaborative planning and implementation of comprehensive service systems (see Harbin & McNulty, this volume).

The ultimate challenge for the field of early childhood intervention would be a reconceptualization and reorganization of human service agencies at the community, state, and ultimately the federal level. Such reorganization would require bold, creative political leadership and strong support from constituency groups willing to invest considerable energy and resources in a long-term process of change. Although the bureaucratic inertia and interest group activity that would oppose fundamental restructuring is great, one cannot help but wonder about the long-term viability of a system that continues to ask questions about which aspects of early childhood intervention should be paid for with health dollars, which with education dollars, and which from other agency appropriations. Mandates for the sharing of administrative responsibilities and costs represent an important step in the development of new infrastructures that will facilitate more integrated services delivery.

Matching service goals and recipients

The anticipated growth of a wide variety of child-care services, generic family support programs, and specifically focused early intervention services highlights the need for a clearer definition of target populations and service goals and objectives. Thus, the broad diversity of families and children who could benefit from early childhood programs demands a comparable diversity in the availability of service options (see Bricker & Veltman, this volume; Gilkerson, Gorski, & Panitz, this volume; Halpern, this volume; Musick & Stott, this volume; Seitz, & Provence, this volume; Simeonsson, & Bailey, this volume). As this diversity grows, it becomes increasingly important that we develop criteria for matching specific service models to individual child and family needs.

Some program models concentrate on the basic needs of all parents with young children (Kagan, Powell, Weisbourd, & Zigler, 1987). Rather than focusing on the unique needs of youngsters with specific disabilities and their families, such generic family support programs are fueled by the recognition that all young children and their parents need support. Recent demographic trends, such as increased isolation of small nuclear families from extended kinships, larger percentages of working parents, higher numbers of single parents, and greater economic stresses in general serve to create significant burdens for all those who rear young children.

Some programs target their activities to the specific vulnerabilities exhibited by particular subgroups of children or their parents. The identification of appropriate service recipients for such programs will require a more refined understanding of developmental risk as an extremely complex and multidimensional construct extending far beyond the simple presence of univariate "organic" and "experiential" factors. The result of such expanded thinking inevitably will complicate what was once considered to be a deceptively straightforward process of selecting children for services (Meisels & Wasik, this volume).

Closely linked to the task of identifying the target population and specifying individual program objectives more precisely is the responsibility for ongoing evaluation of service efficacy (see Hauser-Cram, this volume). In some cases, intervention or support programs can have substantial impact. Under other circumstances, their effects may be relatively small compared to those of other influences. The investigations of the nineties will require a full recognition of the rich range of individual differences found among children, families, and the social contexts in which they live (see Farran, this volume). Evaluations must focus both on the broad range of children's abilities that programs seek to enhance (see Cicchetti & Wagner, this volume; McCune, Kalmanson, Fleck, Glazewski, & Sillari, this volume) and on the equally important effects that services may have on parents, siblings, and on the family system as a whole (see Barnard & Kelly, this volume; Dunst & Trivette, this volume; Krauss & Jacobs, this volume; Parker & Zuckerman, this volume). Finally, future investigators must acknowledge the diverse audiences for whom efficacy data are needed, including scholars of human development, makers of public policy, providers of direct services, and the children and families for whom programs are and will be designed (Shonkoff et al., 1988).

Reconsidering parent–professional relationships

One of the most important legacies of the human service programs of the past decade, whose spirit is reflected in the provisions of P.L. 99-457, is the growing recognition of the need for a more collaborative, less hierarchical relationship between service providers and service recipients. The degree to which our reexamination of these relationships moves beyond the facade of simple slogans, and the extent to which we are able to examine the substance and complexity of these extremely sensitive interactions, will be an important gauge of how our service system matures.

The 1990s are likely to be a decade in which relationships between parents of young developmentally vulnerable children and providers of early childhood intervention services undergo critical examination and redefinition. However, in order for this process to be successful, its complexity and the importance of individual differences must be appreciated. Some parents of young children with developmental disabilities, for example, have the personal resources and motivation to assume responsibility quickly for all aspects of decision making regarding their child's care and education. Others may require a longer period of dependence on professional guidance, and still others may resist greater autonomy for indefinite periods of time.

Advocates of "parent empowerment" correctly emphasize the critical role that parents play in the development of their children, as well as the enduring responsibility they maintain long after program resources are gone. Some suggest, however, that the concept of empowerment itself can be paternalistic if it is viewed as the giving of power to parents by professionals, rather than the assumption of power by parents themselves (see Pizzo, this volume). Notwithstanding the critical need for the parenting role to be strengthened, all families who seek the resources of an early childhood intervention program begin inevitably from a position of dependence. Differences among parents are reflected in the time frame within which a transfer of power can take place, and the nature of the transition process itself.

The needs of professionals cannot be ignored in this process, and an endorsement of the ultimate value of parental autonomy must not be tantamount to a dismissal of the value of professional expertise. Service providers are also people with needs for respect, appreciation, and reinforcement of self-worth. Early childhood intervention programs require professional staff with highly refined skills and sensitivities. In many circumstances, years of formal education and practical experience culminate in jobs whose rewards come more from the satisfaction of "making a difference" in a family's life than from significant financial remuneration. Thus, the process in which parental competence is affirmed cannot succeed if it depends upon a devaluation of professional expertise. It is only when the roles of both partners in the relationship are respected that the potential contributions of each can be realized optimally. Under such circumstances, the professional service provider may be viewed best as the generalist regarding early childhood development, while the parent is considered the ultimate specialist who knows her or his individual child best.

Finally, the extent to which decision-making powers can be shared optimally between parents and professionals depends upon the often-complex dilemma of determining who represents "the best interests of the child" when there is disagreement. In all matters related to a child's well-being, the parent's claim must be (and usually is) presumed to be paramount. There are, however, circumstances under which such presumptions are unwarranted and potentially dangerous. Some parents, for example, inflict physical abuse upon their children. Others may neglect their children's needs and may demonstrate consistently poor judgment in their child-rearing decisions. Circumstances of abuse or neglect involve the most delicate and difficult challenges for the parent–professional relationship, and highlight the dangers of an unequivocal endorsement of parental supremacy in all circumstances. On the other hand, too many professionals have, without any justification, usurped decision-making powers from parents who are capable of making appropriate decisions on behalf of their own children.

The social and political pressures for a reexamination of the balance between parental and professional control over decision making in early childhood intervention programs are clear. The traditional asymmetry of the parent–professional relationship has been challenged, and the demands for greater equality in that relationship that have been advanced by a variety of advocacy groups have been strengthened by the due process provisions of P.L. 99-457. Much work remains to be done in this highly sensitive area.

A FINAL RECAPITULATION

The concept of early childhood intervention has roots that extend back to the earliest years of our country's history. Its foundations are humanistic, scholarly, and, above all, sociopolitical. The development of service models in the next decade must balance a responsiveness to children's and families' needs with a respect for the privacy of family life and a commitment to parental autonomy in child rearing. Consequently, the best early childhood programs will aim for maximal support and minimal intrusion in the lives of those who can benefit from their assistance. Ultimately, early childhood intervention must reflect our best attempts to translate ever-growing knowledge about the process of human development into the formation of the best kind of environment in which a child can grow.

In an analysis of the recent history of early intervention efforts, Zigler and Berman (1983) observed: "With the wealth of early childhood intervention experience behind us and a commitment to become and remain an experimenting society, in the next decades we can successfully build and improve on the achievements of the past" (p. 904). The history of early childhood intervention in the United States has been one of continuous experimentation. It reflects our interest in pragmatic solutions to human problems and our loyalty to enduring social values within the context of an ever-changing, pluralistic society. Early childhood intervention is a concept that continues to evolve. It reflects our willingness to invest in young children and our determination to help them and their families take charge of their lives and have a greater influence on their future.

REFERENCES

Ainsworth, M. D. S. (1969). Object relations dependency and attachment: A theoretical review of the mother–infant relationship. *Child Development, 40*, 969–1025.
Ainsworth, M. D. S., Blehar, M. D., Waters, E., & Wall, S. (1978). *Patterns of attachment: A psychological study of the Strange Situation.* Hillsdale, NJ: L. Erlbaum.
Albee, G. W. (1968). Needed – a revolution in caring for the retarded. *Transaction, 3*, 37–42.
Anastasiow, N. J., & Mansergh, G. P. (1975). Teaching skills in early childhood programs. *Exceptional Children, 41*, 309–317.
Aries, P. (1962). *Centuries of childhood: A social history of family life.* New York: Knopf.
Association for Retarded Citizens. (1986). *Transition practices for handicapped youngsters in early childhood settings.* Boston: Author.
Barnett, W. S. (1985). Benefit-cost analysis of the Perry Preschool Program and its policy implications. *Educational Evaluation and Policy Analysis, 7*, 333–342.
Bloom, B. S. (1964). *Stability and change in human characteristics.* New York: Wiley.
Bowlby, J. (1951). *Maternal care and mental health.* Geneva: World Health Organization.
Bowlby, J. (1969). *Attachment and loss* (Vol. 1). New York: Basis Books.
Braun, S. J., & Edwards, E. P. (1972). *History and theory of early childhood education.* Worthington, OH: Charles A. Jones.
Bretherton, I., & Waters, E. (1985). Growing points of attachment: Theory and research. *Monographs of the Society for Research in Child Development, 50* (1–2, Serial No. 209).
Bricker, D., & Slentz, K. (1988). Personnel preparation: Handicapped infants. In M. C. Wang, M. C. Reynolds, & H. J. Walberg (Eds.), *Handbook of special education: Research and practice* (Vol. 3, pp. 319–345). Elmsford, NY: Pergamon Press.
Broman, S. H., Nichols, P. L., & Kennedy, W. A. (1975). *Preschool IQ: Prenatal and early developmental correlates.* Hillsdale, NJ: L. Erlbaum.
Butler, J. A., Starfield, B., & Stenmark, S. (1984). Child health policy. In H. W. Stevenson & A. E. Siegel (Eds.), *Child development research and social policy* (pp. 110–188). Chicago: University of Chicago Press.
Cairns, R. B. (1983). The emergence of developmental psychology. In W. Kessen (Ed.), *History, theory, and methods: Vol. 1. Handbook of child psychology* (pp. 41–102). New York: Wiley.
Caldwell, B. M. (1973). The importance of beginning early. In M. B. Karnes (Ed.), *Not all little wagons are red: The exceptional child's early years* (pp. 2–10). Arlington, VA: Council for Exceptional Children.
Caldwell, B. M. (1986). Education of families for parenting. In M. W. Yogman & T. B. Brazelton (Eds.), *In support of families* (pp. 229–241). Cambridge: Harvard University Press.

Campbell, P. H., Bellamy, G. T., & Bishop, K. K. (1988). State-wide intervention systems: An overview of the new federal program for infants and toddlers with handicaps. *Journal of Special Education, 22*, 25–40.

Chaille, S. (1887). Infants. Their chronological process. *New Orleans Medical and Surgical Journal, 14*, 893–902.

Chase, A. (1980). *The legacy of Malthus: The social costs of the new scientific realism.* New York: Knopf.

Clarke, A. M., & Clarke, A. D. B. (1976). *Early experience: Myth and evidence.* New York: The Free Press.

Clarke-Stewart, A., & Fein, G. (1983). Early childhood programs. In P. Mussen (Ed.), *Handbook of child psychology* (Vol. 2, pp. 917–999). New York: Wiley.

Crissey, M. S. (1975). Mental retardation – past, present, and future. *American Psychologist, 30*, 800–808.

deLone, R. H. (1979). *Small futures: Children, inequality, and the limits of liberal reform.* New York: Harcourt, Brace, Jovanovich.

Dennis, W. (1960). Causes of retardation among institutionalized children: Iran. *The Journal of Genetic Psychology, 96*, 47–59.

Dennis, W. (1973). *Children of the crèche.* New York: Appleton-Century-Croft.

DeWeerd, J. (1981). Early education services for children with handicaps: Where have we been, where are we now, and where are we going? *Journal of the Division for Early Childhood, 2*, 15–23.

Edelman, M. W. (1987). *Families in peril: An agenda for social change.* Cambridge: Harvard University Press.

Eller, E. (Ed.) (1956). *The school of infancy by John Amos Comenius.* Chapel Hill: University of North Carolina Press.

Federal Register (1987, November 18) U.S. Department of Education. (34 CFR Part 303) Early Intervention Program for Infants and Toddlers with Handicaps: Notice of Proposed Rule-making. Washington, DC: U.S. Government Printing Office.

Ferry, P. C. (1981). On growing new neurons: Are early intervention programs effective. *Pediatrics, 67*, 38–41.

Fishler, K., Graliker, B. V., & Koch, R. (1964). The predictability of intelligence with Gesell developmental scales in mentally retarded infants and young children. *American Journal of Mental Deficiency, 69*, 515–525.

Foltz, A. M. (1982). *An ounce of prevention: Child health politics under Medicaid.* Cambridge: MIT Press.

Gallagher, J. Harbin, G., Thomas, D., Wenger, M., & Clifford, R. (1988). *A survey of current status on implementation of infants and toddlers legislation* (P.L. 99-457, Part H). Chapel Hill, NC: Frank Porter Graham Child Development Center.

Gartner, A., & Lipsky, D. K. (1987). Beyond special education: Toward a quality system for all students. *Harvard Educational Review, 57*, 367–595.

Garwood, S. G., Fewell, R. R., & Neisworth, J. T. (1988). Public Law 94-142: You can get there from here! *Topics in Early Childhood Special Education, 8*, 1–11.

Gesell, A. (1925). *The mental growth of the preschool child.* New York: Macmillan.

Gesell, A. (1929). *Infancy and human growth.* New York: Macmillan.

Gliedman, J., & Roth, W. (1980). *The unexpected minority: Handicapped children in America.* New York: Harcourt, Brace, Jovanovich.

Goldberg, S. (1982). Some biological aspects of early parent–infant interaction. In S. G. Moore & C. R. Cooper (Eds.), *The young child – Review of research* (Vol. 3, pp. 35–56). Washington, DC: National Association for the Education of Young Children.

Graham, F. K., Ernhart, C. B., Thurston, D. L., & Craft, M. (1962). Development three years after perinatal anoxia and other potentially damaging newborn experiences. *Psychological Monographs, 76* (3, Whole No. 522).

Graham, F. K., Pennoyer, M. M., Caldwell, B. M., Greenman, M., & Hartmann, A. T. (1957). Relationships between clinical status and behavior test performance in a newborn group with histories suggesting anoxia. *Journal of Pediatrics, 50*, 177–189.

Green, M., Ferry, P., Russman, B., Shonkoff, J., & Taft, (1987). Early intervention programs: When do pediatricians fit in? *Contemporary Pediatrics, 4*, 92–118.

Greven, P. (Ed.) (1973). *Child rearing concepts, 1628–1861.* Itasca, IL: F. E. Peacock.

Griffith, J. P. C. (1895). *The care of the baby – A manual for mothers and nurses.* Philadelphia: Saunders.

Guralnick, M. J., Heiser, K. E., Eaton, A. P., Bennett, F. C., Richardson, H. B. & Groom, J. M. (1988). Pediatricians' perceptions of the effectiveness of early intervention for at-risk and handicapped children. *Journal of Developmental and Behavioral Pediatrics, 9,* 12–18.

Hamburg, D. (1987, September 9). *Early intervention to prevent lifelong damage: Lessons from current research.* Testimony for the Senate Committee on Labor and Human Resources and the House Committee on Education and Labor.

Hanline, M. F., & Knowlton, A. (1988). A collaborative model for providing support to parents during their child's transition from infant intervention to preschool special education public school programs. *Journal of the Division for Early Childhood, 12,* 116–125.

Hauser-Cram, P., Upshur, C., Krauss, M., Shonkoff, J. (1988). Implications of Public Law 99–457 for early intervention services for infants and toddlers with disabilities. *Social Policy Report of the Society for Research in Child Development, 3* (3), 1–16.

Healy, A., Keesee, P., & Smith, B. (1985). *Early services for children with special needs: Transactions for family support.* Iowa City: The University of Iowa.

Holmes, D. (1857). *The child's physician: A popular treatise on the management of diseases of infancy and childhood.* Providence, RI.

Holt, L. E. (1897). *The diseases of infancy and childhood.* New York: D. Appleton and Company.

Hubbell R. (1983). *A review of Head Start research since 1970.* Washington, DC: U.S. Department of Health and Human Services.

Hunt, J. M. (1961). *Intelligence and experience.* New York: Ronald Press.

Kagan, S. L., Powell, D. R., Weissbourd, B., & Zigler, E. F. (1987). *America's family support programs.* New Haven/London: Yale University Press.

Kahn, A. J., & Kamerman, S. B. (1987). *Child care: Facing the hard choices.* Dover, MA: Auburn House.

Kamin, L. (1974). *The science and politics of I.Q.* Potomac, MD: L. Erlbaum.

Kerns, G. M. (1988). *Transition for young children with special needs in New Hampshire: Perceptions of parents and early intervention program directors.* Paper presented at the 112th Annual Meeting of the American Association on Mental Retardation, Washington, DC.

Kirk, S. A. (1958). *Early education of the mentally retarded.* Urbana, IL: The University of Illinois Press.

Krauss, M. (in press). A new precedent in family policy: The individualized family service plan. *Exceptional Children.*

Lazar, I., & Darlington, R. (1982). Lasting effects of early education: A report from the Consortium for Longitudinal Studies. *Monographs of the Society for Research in Child Development, 47,* (2–3, Serial No. 195).

Lesser, A. J. (1985). The origin and development of maternal and child health programs in the United States. *American Journal of Public Health, 75,* 590–598.

Lilienfeld, A. M., & Parkhurst, E. (1951). A study of the association of factors of pregnancy and parturition with the development of cerebral palsy: A preliminary report. *American Journal of Hygiene, 53,* 262–282.

Lilienfeld, A. M., & Pasamanick, B. (1954). Association of maternal and fetal factors with the development of epilepsy, I: Abnormalities in the prenatal and paranatal periods. *Journal of the American Medical Association, 155,* 719–724.

Magee, E. M., & Pratt, M. W. (1985). *1935–1985: 50 years of U.S. federal support to promote the health of mothers, children, and handicapped children in America.* Vienna, VA: Information Sciences Research Institute.

Margolis, L. H., & Meisels, S. J. (1987). Barriers to the effectiveness of EPSDT for children with moderate and severe developmental disabilities. *American Journal of Orthopsychiatry, 57,* 424–430.

Meisels, S. J. (1984). Prediction, prevention, and developmental screening in the EPSDT program. In H. W. Stevenson & A. E. Siegel (Eds.), *Child development research and social policy* (pp. 267–317). Chicago: University of Chicago Press.

Meisels, S. J. (1985). The efficacy of early intervention: Why are we still asking this question? *Topics in Early Childhood Special Education, 5,* 1–8.

Meisels, S. J. (1985). A functional analysis of the evolution of public policy for handicapped young children. *Educational Evaluation and Policy Analysis, 7,* 115–126.

Meisels, S. J. (in press). Meeting the mandate of Public Law 99-457: Early childhood intervention in the nineties. *American Journal of Orthopsychiatry.*

Meisels, S., Harbin, G., Modigliani, K., & Olson, K. (1988). Formulating optimal state early childhood intervention policies. *Exceptional Children, 55,* 159–165.

Meisels, S. J., & Margolis, L. H. (1988). Is EPSDT effective with developmentally disabled children? *Pediatrics, 81*, 262–271.

Morgan, G. (1972). The Kaiser child service centers. In S. J. Braun & E. P. Edwards (Eds.), *History and theory of early childhood education* (pp. 368–372). Worthington, OH: Charles A. Jones.

Neill, A. S. (1960). *Summerhill: A radical approach to child rearing.* New York: Hart Publishing.

Peters D. L., & Kontos, S. (1987). Continuity and discontinuity of experience: An intervention perspective. In D. L. Peters and S. Kontos (Eds.), *Continuity and discontinuity of experience in child care* (pp. 1–16). Norwood, NJ: Ablex Publishing.

Peterson, N. (1987). *Early intervention for handicapped and at-risk children – An introduction to early childhood – special education.* Denver: Love Publishing.

Provence, S., & Lipton, R. C. (1962). *Infants in institutions.* New York: International Universities Press.

Provence, S., Naylor, A., & Patterson, J. (1977). *The challenge of day care.* New Haven: Yale University Press.

Reese, C. (1985). Head Start at 20. *Children Today, 14*, 6–9.

Sameroff, A. J. (1975). Early influences on development: Fact or fancy? *Merrill-Palmer Quarterly of Behavior and Development, 21*, 267–294.

Sameroff, A. J., & Chandler, M. J. (1975). Reproductive risk and the continuum of caretaking casualty. In F. D. Horowitz, M. Hetherington, S. Scarr-Salapatek, & G. Siegel (Eds.), *Review of child development research* (Vol. 4, pp. 187–244). Chicago: University of Chicago Press.

Schorr, L. B. (1988). *Within our reach: Breaking the cycle of disadvantage.* New York: Anchor Press.

Share, J., Webb, A., & Koch, R. (1961). A preliminary investigation of the early developmental status of mongoloid infants. *American Journal of Mental Deficiency, 66*, 238–241.

Shonkoff, J. P., & Hauser-Cram, P. (1987). Early intervention for disabled infants and their families – A quantitative analysis. *Pediatrics, 80*, 650–658.

Shonkoff, J. P., Hauser-Cram, P., Krauss, M. W., & Upshur, C. C. (1988). Early intervention efficacy research: What have we learned and where do we go from here? *Topics in Early Childhood Special Education, 8*, 81–93.

Singer, J., & Butler, J. A. (1987). The Education for All Handicapped Children Act: Schools as agents of social reform. *Harvard Educational Review, 57*, 125–152.

Skeels, H. M. (1966). Adult status of children with contrasting early life experiences. *Monographs of the Society for Research in Child Development, 31*, 1–65.

Skeels, H. M., Dye, H. B. (1939). A study of the effects of differential stimulation on mentally retarded children. *Proceedings of the American Association of Mental Deficiency, 44*, 114.

Smith, B. J., & Strain, P. S. (1988). Early childhood special education in the next decade: Implementing and expanding P.L. 99-457. *Topics in Early Childhood Special Education, 8*, 37–47.

Spitz, R. A. (1945). Hospitalism: An inquiry into the genesis of psychiatric conditions in early childhood. In R. S. Eissler (Ed.), *Psychoanalytic study of the child.* New Haven: Yale University Press.

Sroufe, L. A. (1983). Infant–caregiver attachment and patterns of adaptation in preschool: The roots of maladaptation and competence. In M. Perlmutter (Ed.), *The Minnesota symposia on child psychology* (Vol. 16, pp. 41–84). Hillsdale, NJ: L. Erlbaum.

Steiner, G. Y. (1976). *The Children's Cause.* Washington, DC: The Brookings Institution.

Stile, S., Abernathy, S., Pettibone, T., & Wachtel, W. (1984). Training and certification for early childhood special education personnel: A six-year follow-up study. *Journal of the Division for Early Childhood, 11*, 66–73.

Talbot, M. E. (1964). *Edward Seguin – A study for an educational approach to the treatment of mentally defective children.* New York: Columbia University Teachers College.

Tjossem, T. (1976). Early intervention: Issues and approaches. In T. Tjossem (Ed.), *Intervention strategies for high risk infants and young children* (pp. 3–33). Baltimore: University Park Press.

Tolstoy, L. (1967). *Tolstoy on education.* Chicago: University of Chicago Press.

Turnbull, A. P., & Turnbull, H. R. (1985). Stepping back from early intervention: An ethical perspective. *Journal of the Division for Early Childhood, 10*, 106–117.

Watson, J. (1928). *Psychological care of infant and child.* New York: Norton.

Werner, E. E., Bierman, J. M., & French, F. E. (1971). *The children of Kauai: A longitudinal study from the prenatal period to age ten.* Honolulu: University of Hawaii Press.

Werner, E. E., & Smith, R. S. (1977). *Kauai's children come of age.* Honolulu: University of Hawaii Press.

Werner, E. E., & Smith, R. S. (1982). *Vulnerable but invincible: A longitudinal study of resilient children and youth.* New York: McGraw-Hill.

Wishy, B. (1968). *The child and the republic – The dawn of modern American child nurture.* Philadelphia: University of Pennsylvania Press.

Zigler, E., & Berman, W. (1983). Discerning the future of early childhood intervention. *American Psychologist, 38,* 894–906.

Zigler, E., & Valentine, J. (Eds.) (1979) *Project Head Start: A legacy of the War on Poverty.* New York: The Free Press.

PART II

Concepts of developmental vulnerability

2 *Biological bases of developmental dysfunction*

JACK P. SHONKOFF AND PAUL C. MARSHALL

Human development and behavior unfold through a complex and highly interactive process in which both biological regulation and experiential influences are substantial. Although most attention in the field of early childhood intervention has been focused on the role of experience in that process, the contribution of the biological substrate requires equal scrutiny. Thus, in order to achieve a balanced understanding of the transaction between nature and nurture, it is essential that we examine the normal development of the central nervous system (CNS) and explore the effects of specific abnormalities and injuries on its functioning.

Extensive research conducted over the past few decades has resulted in a dramatic increase in our knowledge about the normal development of the brain (Moore, 1985; Volpe, 1987). The biology of neuromaturation has been shown to be controlled by genetic mechanisms whose timing is regulated precisely and whose unfolding is sensitive to a variety of environmental influences. Despite the growing sophistication of our understanding of the evolution of brain structure and neurochemistry, our knowledge of the operation of the central nervous system is rudimentary. Thus, the neurological bases of such complex behaviors as attention, problem solving, communication, and creative thinking are largely a mystery.

The immediate and long-term consequences of specific biological insults or malformations that impinge on the developing brain have also been the subject of intense investigation and review (Gabriel & McComb, 1985; Lemire, Leoser, Leech, Alvord 1975). Growing bodies of data have increased our understanding of the developmental effects of such variables as the specific nature of the injurious agent, the dosage of the insult, and its timing in the sequence of brain development (Moore, 1985). Furthermore, as the variability in the functional impact of brain injury has become clear, differences in the degree to which individuals may be susceptible to specific insults have become better appreciated.

Although knowledge in this area continues to evolve, our current understanding of the impact of brain insult rests more on a concept of greater developmental vulnerability rather than inevitable disability. Within such a model, the ultimate outcome of any specific injury to the central nervous system is potentially mediated by a broad range of protective factors, both within each child and in the environment in which he or she is reared. Some children, for example, may be highly resistant on a genetic basis to the adverse effects of a high level of maternal alcohol ingestion during pregnancy. Others may be born with some of the features of the fetal alcohol syndrome after only a

35

moderate exposure to this potential teratogen (Clarren & Smith, 1978). Some newborns may be quite resilient and survive an asphyxiating delivery without sequelae, while others who appear to sustain a comparable degree of oxygen deprivation may manifest the signs of cerebral palsy later in the first year (Nelson & Ellenberg, 1979, 1981). A premature infant who struggles through multiple medical complications and is discharged from a neonatal intensive care unit to a nurturing home with excellent social supports is likely to do well developmentally; another baby with an identical medical history who is reared in an unstable environment by an isolated, disorganized, and highly stressed single parent is likely to have a host of developmental difficulties (see Beckwith, this volume). Thus, biological insults to the central nervous system have variable effects on the development of the young child. This diversity in outcomes reflects the impact of individual differences in constitutional resilience of children and the critical influence of the caregiving environment on early childhood development. In essence, it refutes earlier views of the immutability of brain injury and highlights the mutual impact of nature and nurture.

This chapter will focus on the neurological basis of development in early childhood. It begins with an overview of the normal process of development and maturation of the central nervous system from conception through infancy. Next, a selection of neurological determinants of disability and dysfunction will be examined, with particular consideration given to the nature of the specific pathologic influence, the timing of the insult, and the range and variety of subsequent consequences it may have for later developmental and behavioral competence. The chapter concludes with an exploration of the process through which neurological vulnerabilities interact with environmental factors to produce variable functional outcomes in the early years of life.

DEVELOPMENT OF THE CENTRAL NERVOUS SYSTEM

The orderly progression of human development from a fertilized egg to a highly differentiated yet immature infant is determined by an exquisitely tuned sequence of events that is controlled by genetic regulation and influenced by intrauterine environmental factors. This section provides a broad overview of the embryogenesis and early maturation of the central nervous system. Interested readers can find more detailed accounts elsewhere (Moore, 1985; Volpe, 1987).

The human nervous system begins its differentiation as a simple plate of neuroectodermal cells that is present as early as 16 days after fertilization. Over the following 2 weeks, this neural plate folds into a tube or cylinder whose head (rostral) end will develop into the upper spinal cord and brain. By day 28 of gestation, the neural tube is completely closed and major subdivisions of the nervous system are identifiable. Although most biological insults during this early stage of brain development result in spontaneous miscarriage, a localized failure of closure of the neural tube can have nonfatal, but significant, consequences. If, for example, the rostral end fails to close, the child may be born with anencephaly, an invariably fatal condition in which there is an absence of cerebral cortex. Failure of closure of the tail (caudal) end of the neural tube can result in myelodysplasia or spina bifida, a nonfatal disorder with variable prognosis.

By 5 weeks gestational age, the neural tube will have divided lengthwise to form two cerebral hemispheres with bilateral ventricles. Further cleavage and folding in other planes result in the structural differentiation of the major parts of the central nervous system. At this point in embryogenesis, specific insults or interruptions of development are likely to result in severe anomalies. An example of such a malformation is holo-prosencephaly, or single-sphered brain, which is found in children with a chromosomal abnormality (trisomy 13) in which there is a failure of cleavage of the developing brain into hemispheres.

With the closure and differentiation of the neural tube completed by the end of the first 6 weeks of pregnancy, the brain is a primitive but recognizable organ. At this point in time, the nervous system proceeds rapidly through a contemporaneous and time-limited process of cellular proliferation and migration. Any significant interference with this process may result in a marked reduction in the number of viable neurons available for later brain function. Radiation exposure or a congenital infection (such as rub lla) represent the types of insults known to interfere with this process of extensive cell division. The result of such an insult is a marked decrease or destruction of cerebral tissue, leading to a condition termed microcephaly, which literally means *small brain*.

As primitive neural and supporting cells (glia) multiply, they migrate to adjacent or distant parts of the brain where further differentiation takes place. This migration process is highly regulated. For example, in the cortex the neurons are guided to their final destination by specialized glial cells that provide the ladder on which the neurons climb into position. The first neurons to reach the evolving cerebral cortex reside in the lower cell layer, followed by further waves of neurons that migrate to layers that are closer to the brain surface, thereby resulting in an inside out topography of cortical development. Although the biologic triggers that regulate the initiation and termination of this precisely controlled migration of cells have not yet been fully elucidated, it is known that interference with this process can result in severe disruption of the further development of appropriate neuronal interconnections or networks.

A dramatic example of a disorder of neuronal migration is the failure of formation (agenesis) of the corpus callosum. The corpus callosum is a broad band of white matter that serves as the major connecting link between the two hemispheres. Formation of the corpus callosum generally begins at about 11 to 12 weeks of gestation and is complete by 20 weeks. If a significant insult affects callosal development in its early stages, complete agenesis results. If the disruption occurs somewhat later, a lesser degree of the interhemispheric connection is lost, resulting in partial agenesis. Another example of migrational dysfunction occurs early in the embryonic development of children who have certain neurocutaneous syndromes, such as neurofibromatosis and tuberous sclerosis. In such cases, genetic mechanisms that are not yet understood appear to result in glial overgrowth and disorganization that interfere with neuronal migration. It is assumed that the resulting structural abnormalities of the brain explain the mental retardation and seizures that often accompany these syndromes.

By 6 months of gestation, under normal circumstances, the adult complement of neurons is achieved. Beyond this period, however, and extending into adult life, the process of neuronal differentiation continues, with considerable variability from one part of the nervous system to another. Although the genetic programming of this process is presumed to be substantial, environmental influences mediated by chemical interactions among cells have a significant impact as well.

Maturing neurons differentiate primarily by the growth of appendages – axons and dendrites – that are the connecting links through which nerve cells communicate with each other. This elaboration of axons and dendrites, which has been characterized as a process of arborization or treelike branching, is accompanied by a parallel process called synaptogenesis, which involves the development of spines or the sites of connec-tion between the appendages of adjacent neurons. These resultant synapses represent the final step in the establishment of the basic circuitry of the central nervous system. As the point of functional interaction between two neurons, each synapse is highly specialized in its morphology and chemical specificity. The primary sensory and motor systems demonstrate the greatest degree of early connection specificity. Although many aspects of this intricate process are not yet understood, it is presumed that the highly individualized and specific nature of each synapse, and its capacity to be modified, play a large role in the plasticity and capacity for adaptation that is characteristic of a young brain (see Anastasiow, this volume).

The development of synaptic connections (synaptogenesis) continues at a brisk pace well into the first year of postnatal life to the point where there appears to be an overabundance of synapses. At that stage, there begins a process of selective elimination of synapses and neuronal branches that results in a more highly organized and efficient brain. Thus, an immature brain has an abundance of neuronal connections. In fact, half of the neurons in any given network may eventually be eliminated during the stage of selective neuronal death that appears to characterize brain maturation in infancy. Although this process has been noted to begin in prenatal life, it continues through infancy and childhood and requires environmental stimulation for its proper elaboration.

Parallel to the process of neuronal differentiation and the establishment of synapses, the supporting tissue network (which is composed of glial cells) also undergoes dramatic proliferation and differentiation. In addition to their important role in neuronal migration, glial cells appear to provide neurons with the appropriate metabolic milieu for normal function. In producing the myelin sheath that surrounds axons and facilitates their efficient function in neural transmission, these cells make a critical contribution to the process of neuromaturation.

Myelination involves the encasement of axons similar to the placement of insulation around electric wires. It facilitates the capacity of the central nervous system to transmit messages further and faster. Although myelination begins in the prenatal period, it becomes most significant in the first year of postnatal life and continues into the third decade. Certain inborn errors of metabolism, such as metachromatic leukodystrophy, can disturb the myelination process, leading to significant cerebral dysfunction.

In summary, the process of brain development and overall neuromaturation is highly complex and precisely programmed. It unfolds through a series of interactive steps that are genetically regulated according to a highly predictable timetable and that are influenced by factors in the intrauterine environment. The early stages of this process are characterized by the rapid proliferation and highly controlled migration of neurons. Subsequent stages are characterized by cell differentiation, synapse formation, and selective cell death and elimination of neuronal connections. Disruptions in brain development can be caused by intrinsic factors (such as genetic disorders) or by a wide variety of extrinsic influences (such as infection, toxins, asphyxia, etc.), whose ultimate impact is determined by the nature, dose, and timing of the insult, by individual differences in susceptibility, and by the subsequent interplay between the resulting biological vulnerability and early life experiences.

ORIGINS OF CENTRAL NERVOUS SYSTEM DYSFUNCTION AND DISABILITY

Although the manifestations of neurological dysfunction can be identified on the basis of a comprehensive clinical examination, an understanding of the specific etiology or underlying pathophysiological mechanism is often limited. In some cases, a structural abnormality in the brain can be identified through sophisticated diagnostic procedures, such as computerized tomography (CT scan) or magnetic resonance imaging (MRI). In many conditions, however, the brain itself appears normal to conventional imaging and neurophysiological evaluation techniques despite its impaired functioning. Some disabilities, such as Down syndrome, are known to be associated with a well-defined chromosomal abnormality, yet we do not understand how additional or incomplete chromosomal material produces the atypical physical features and mental retardation that characterize such children. Under other circumstances, such as after a congenital infection from cytomegalovirus (CMV), the causal mechanisms of the neurological sequelae may be more clear, but we are still left with unanswered questions about wide variations in individual susceptibility and different outcomes in children who sustained apparently comparable infection in utero. More commonly, the precise etiology of a neurologically based disability is completely unknown. The following sections provide a selected overview of some of the malformations and insults that have been demonstrated to affect the central nervous system adversely.

Genetic disorders

Developmental disabilities can result from abnormalities of chromosomes or single genes, or through the mechanisms of multifactorial inheritance.

CHROMOSOMAL ABNORMALITIES. Although the diagnosis of a chromosomal anomaly is specific and unambiguous, its developmental manifestations can be quite variable. Individuals with *Down syndrome*, for example, which is associated with extra genetic material from chromosome 21, may function anywhere between a level of severe mental retardation to borderline normal intelligence (Pueschel, 1978). In contrast, most persons with disorders secondary to an abnormal number of sex (X or Y) chromosomes (e.g., Turner or Klinefelter syndrome) have normal intelligence, although some are mildly retarded and many women with Turner syndrome have relatively stronger verbal skills and less well developed spatial abilities (Garron, 1977; Silbert, Wolff, & Lilienthal, 1977).

X-LINKED MENTAL RETARDATION AND FRAGILE-X SYNDROME. Descriptions of *X-linked mental retardation* and the *fragile-X syndrome* (each of which involves abnormalities of the X chromosome) represent some of the most important recent advances in the study of the causes of mental retardation (Chudley & Hagerman, 1987; Hagerman, 1987; Opitz, 1984). Emerging data suggest that the fragile-X syndrome is second only to Down syndrome in frequency among the known chromosomal disorders. The range of IQ scores among individuals with this syndrome extends from 20 to 80, although boys with learning disabilities and attentional problems with normal intelligence have been reported (Hagerman, Kemper, & Hudson, 1985). As many as one-third of female carriers of the fragile-X chromosome may have intellectual deficits (Jacobs, 1982), and it has been proposed that as much as 10% of mild retardation in females may be related to X-linked inheritance (Herbst & Miller, 1980). Overall, it is believed that the fragile-X syndrome accounts for approximately one-third of all X-linked mental retardation, with the remainder reflecting a wide variety of other syndromes that are markedly heterogeneous in their physical features and levels of impairment (Lubs, 1983).

SINGLE-GENE ABNORMALITIES. Single-gene abnormalities may be inherited through a variety of genetic patterns, including autosomal dominant (transmitted by either parent alone), autosomal recessive (transmitted by both parents together), X-linked dominant (transmitted by either parent alone), or X-linked recessive (asymptomatic in females and symptomatic in males) mechanisms. A number of inborn errors of metabolism, for example, are inherited as autosomal recessive disorders. Many of these conditions are accompanied by moderate to severe retardation, and the known disorders in this category are responsible for approximately 4% to 6% of all severe mental retardation (Moser, 1985). Some metabolic disorders, such as Tay-Sachs disease, result in progressive neurological impairment and death with no treatment options available at the present time. Others, such as phenylketonuria (PKU), whose toxic effects are also produced by a specific enzyme deficiency, can be treated through specific dietary therapy that prevents the potential complications, including seizures and mental retardation. Many inborn errors of metabolism are detectable through prenatal diagnosis.

MULTIFACTORIAL INHERITANCE. The least well understood genetic pattern, multifactorial inheritance, refers to the process whereby the presence of a disorder is determined by the interactive effects of one or more minor genes and specific environmental facilitators. Neural tube defects (Carter, 1974) and schizophrenia (Kety, 1978) are important examples of disorders that appear to have a multifactorial genetic basis. Spina bifida, for example, has been reported both to occur with greater frequency in some families and to have a two to four times higher incidence among lower socioeconomic groups (Nevin, Johnston, & Merritt, 1981). These data have led to one hypothesis that suboptimal maternal nutrition may be a contributing factor in the pathogenesis of myelodysplasia among those women who have a genetic predisposition toward bearing children with this disorder. Recent therapeutic trials of multivitamin supplementation in the early weeks of pregnancy for women who had previously given birth to a child with a neural tube defect suggest potential benefits regarding a reduced risk of recurrence (Smithells et al., 1983). More research in this area is needed, however, before definitive conclusions and recommendations for routine treatment can be made.

   In summary, many disorders with associated mental retardation have a genetic basis. However, the variability of expression among specific inherited conditions reflects marked differences in their effects on ultimate brain function and renders meaningless generalizations about the genetic basis of developmental disabilities.

Early brain malformations

Detectable malformations of the CNS may be associated with known genetic disorders that are predetermined from the moment of conception, or with random yet identifiable prenatal insults. They may also be of completely obscure etiology. Although they reflect a *structural* departure from normal brain development, the *functional* consequences of central nervous system malformations can be extremely variable, ranging from profound disability to essentially normal development.

MYELODYSPLASIA. Myelodysplasia (myelomeningocele or spina bifida) is the most commonly encountered anatomical malformation of the central nervous system. As described earlier in the chapter, this condition probably results from the incomplete closure of the caudal portion of the neural tube during the first month of pregnancy. As a consequence of the defective closure, the skeletal and soft tissue coverings of the spinal cord do not develop, and the spinal cord itself and the nerves that exit the spinal canal at that location are abnormal (dysplastic), covered only by a thin membrane. This membrane can easily rupture, leading to meningitis, if surgical repair is not instituted promptly after birth. When meningitis does occur, the risk for additional complications, such as hearing impairment and mental retardation, is increased significantly.

The nature of the neurological handicap associated with myelomeningocele is determined by the location of the spinal defect. Over 80% of affected children have their lesion in the lumbar or lumbosacral region, which results in varying degrees of lower extremity motor impairment (paraparesis), sensory loss, and bowel and bladder dysfunction, depending on the location of the defect and the integrity of the underlying dysplastic neural elements. If the lesion is located in the thoracic region, a severe curvature of the spine (kyphoscoliosis) develops as a frequent result of the malfunction of the adjacent (paraspinal) muscle groups. Almost 90% of children with lumbosacral myelomeningocele have the associated Chiari malformation (a variable malformation of the brain stem and cerebellum) and hydrocephalus.

Despite the multiplicity of clinical problems that are associated with myelodysplasia, developmental outcomes are extremely variable and are, in part, determined by the availability of aggressive medical and surgical treatment. One review of 200 consecutive unselected patients with myelomeningocele and hydrocephalus (all of whom received aggressive treatment) found a mortality rate by 3 to 7 years of 14%, with nearly three-quarters of the survivors having IQ scores greater than 80 and a comparable number reported to be ambulatory (McClone et al., 1985). When associated cerebral anomalies of greater severity are present, the mortality and morbidity rates are higher. Thus, the simple diagnosis of meningomyelocele does not necessarily imply a poor developmental prognosis. Rather, associated anomalies (over which we have little control) and the quality of medical and surgical care (over which we have substantial control) contribute additional sources of risk and protection, which interact with factors in the child's caregiving environment to determine ultimate outcome.

HYDROCEPHALUS. A common clinical problem among children with myelodysplasia, hydrocephalus can also be caused by a variety of other lesions that interrupt the circulation and/or reabsorption of cerebrospinal fluid. Such interruptions can arise from other malformations, such as aqueductal stenosis, or from scarring secondary to infection or hemorrhage within the ventricular system.

Under normal circumstances, spinal fluid is produced continuously within the cerebral ventricles. This fluid circulates through the ventricular system and then out of the brain into the subarachnoid space, where it bathes the spinal cord and the brain surface before it is eventually reabsorbed. Any interruption in the continuous circulation of cerebrospinal fluid results in fluid backup, increased intracranial pressure, and eventual expansion of the ventricles. If the ventricles expand slowly, the brain can compensate. Under such circumstances, through either spontaneous resolution or surgical placement of a shunt (which drains fluid from the cerebral ventricles to the abdominal cavity), there is little, if any, functional impairment. Prolonged hydrocephalus, on the other hand, which results in marked compression of the cerebral cortex, can produce significant developmental effects. This problem is particularly striking among children surviving with intrauterine hydrocephalus who demonstrate a 54% rate of intellectual impairment (McCullough & Balzer-Martin, 1982). The extent of disability, however, is not simply determined by the degree to which the cerebral cortex is decreased in size as a result of prolonged elevation of intracranial pressure. Thus, on an individual basis, brain adaptation is variable and accurate prediction of ultimate cognitive outcomes is extremely difficult, even when cerebral imaging techniques, such as computerized tomography, offer the option of measuring the thickness of the cerebral cortex.

Children with hydrocephalus who are identified early and treated appropriately can have a reasonably optimistic prognosis for future development. In a study of children with myelomeningocele and hydrocephalus, that compared youngsters with and without shunt infection, those who had not had infected shunts demonstrated a mean IQ on follow-up of 95, while those with shunt infections had a mean IQ of 73. A control population of children with myelomeningocele without hydrocephalus had a mean IQ of 102 (McClone et al., 1982). Thus, it appears that hydrocephalus that is treated promptly and is not complicated by infection does not necessarily lead to significant cognitive limitations.

MICROCEPHALY. Microcephaly, a less common malformation that may be suspected clinically among children with microcrania, is defined by a head circumference greater than three standard deviations below the mean. This problem can be caused by any of a number of intrauterine insults, including congenital infection, intracranial infarction, or excessive exposure to radiation. Familial microcephaly, a genetic disorder presumably related to deficient neuronal proliferation, initially may appear indistinguishable in its clinical manifestations and be diagnosed only on the basis of a positive family history.

Like other cerebral anomalies or malformations, the functional consequences of a small head can be quite variable. Although significant reductions in head size often reflect abnormal brain development, a head circumference below the 2nd percentile is not a guarantee of neurological disability or intellectual impairment. In fact, most individuals with a head circumference just below the normal range are intellectually quite normal (Sells, 1977).

MEGALENCEPHALY. Magalencephaly is defined operationally as a head circumference greater than the 98th percentile for age. Once again, this physical finding by itself does not necessarily imply neurological dysfunction (Lorber & Priestly, 1981). A large head can be associated with a genetically large brain or it can be secondary to hydrocephalus or a space-occupying lesion, such as a tumor or subdural fluid collection. Neuroimaging techniques, a thorough family history, and a careful clinical examination for associated anomalies usually help with this differential diagnosis. Once again, no developmental prognosis can necessarily be attached to this clinical finding without further investigation.

AGENESIS OF THE CORPUS CALLOSUM. In its partial or complete form, agenesis of the corpus callosum is among the more common major structural defects of the brain itself. This malformation is usually part of a syndrome of associated findings and is frequently seen in conjunction with other anomalies of midline structures, such as cleft lip and cleft palate. Despite the severity of the anatomical disruption, at least 15% of individuals with this diagnosis have normal intelligence. Of those with identified disabilities, impairments range from mild to severe (Lemire et al., 1975).

In summary, although a number of specific anatomical malformations of the brain have been described, their developmental consequences are variable and often difficult to predict during early infancy. Although a great deal more needs to be learned about these abnormalities, it is clear that differences in both biological adaptability and early childhood experiences contribute to the diversity of outcomes.

Infections of the central nervous system

Acute or chronic infections of brain tissue (encephalitis) or of the meninges (the covering membrane for the central nervous system) and contiguous brain structures (meningitis) are an important cause of chronic neurological impairment. During the prenatal period, a number of organisms have been demonstrated to produce recognizable congenital syndromes with a range of adverse neurological sequelae. Postnatally, bacterial meningitis remains a potentially devastating illness whose consequences can range from negligible to severe.

CYTOMEGALOVIRUS (CMV). CMV is the most common of the congenital infections that can lead to neurological impairment. The frequency of infection among newborns ranges from 0.2% to 8.0% of all live births worldwide, with an average in the United States of 1% (Hanshaw, 1981). Of those infants who are born with active infection, between 5% and 10% show evidence of clinically overt disease. Such youngsters demonstrate multiple organ system involvement characaterized by intrauterine growth retardation, microcephaly, chorioretinitis (damage to the eyes), hepatosplenomegaly (enlargement of the liver and spleen), and often signs of significant meningoencephalitis. The neurological outcome for this overtly symptomatic group is generally considered to be overwhelmingly poor (Pass, Stangno, Myers, & Alford, 1980), although a recent study raises the possibility of a subgroup with mild developmental sequelae (Conboy et al. 1987).

More than 90% of children with congenital CMV are relatively asymptomatic at birth. Although the majority of these youngsters are presumed to have a good prognosis developmentally, as many as 10% to 20% have been reported to develop intellectual or perceptual deficits, as well as significant hearing impairment (Hanshaw et al. 1976; Kumar, Nankervis, & Gold, 1973; Melish & Hanshaw, 1973). A recent study, however, suggests that for those with normal hearing, the risks for impairment of intelligence or learning are negligible (Conboy et al. 1986).

RUBELLA. Although encountered less frequently because of successful immunization programs, rubella was once the prototypic example of the consequences of congenital infection (Cooper & Krugman, 1966). In its symptomatic form, congenital rubella in young children is manifested by growth retardation, cataracts and retinitis (eye problems), microcephaly, hepatosplenomegaly, petechiae (a rash related to a blood dysfunction), and congenital heart disease. In the most severe cases, active signs of central nervous system infection with seizures may be seen. Only 25% of children with congenital rubella, however, demonstrate neurological symptoms at birth. Such neonates present with marked irritability, diminished head size, and hypotonia as the predominant features of the syndrome. By the end of the first year of life, over one-third of children with congenital infection demonstrate signs of psychomotor retardation. Behavioral disorders are also common, and a small percentage of children show features of childhood autism (Chess, 1974). Although the number of children with demonstrated hearing loss at birth is relatively small, over 20% have progressive hearing impairment, which can only be diagnosed in later childhood. Progressive visual deficits, secondary to retinitis or cataracts, are also common and are usually obvious. In rare cases, a progressive and fatal brain infection (panencephalitis) has been reported. Some children with congenital rubella show significant sequelae in early infancy. Others are relatively asymptomatic at birth, only to demonstrate progressive impairments over the first few years of life. A large percentage of children exposed to the rubella virus in utero, however, appear to remain unaffected. Although the timing of the insult is critical, differences in susceptibility among individual fetuses are presumed also to play a major role in the observed variability of sequelae.

TOXOPLASMOSIS. Congenital *toxoplasmosis* is caused by the protozoan parasite, *Toxoplasma gondii*. Women who contract this infection during their pregnancy are generally asymptomatic and transfer the parasite to their fetus through the placenta. Approximately 10% of children with congenital toxoplasmosis are symptomatic with severe disease in the newborn period characterized by prematurity, microcephaly, hydrocephalus, seizures, and chorioretinitis (Desmonts & Couvreur, 1979). Such youngsters develop severe disabilities and their mortality rate is high (Stray-Pederson, 1980). Most infants who acquire congenital infection with toxoplasmosis, however, are initially asymptomatic. The most common problem found in those children with subclinical cases at birth is chorioretinitis, which often results in unilateral or bilateral blindness. Hearing loss and intellectual deficits are also common, although their appearance may be delayed. Antimicrobial treatment appears to be promising for children with relatively mild symptoms at birth, although further studies are needed to determine its effect on long-term sequelae (Wilson, Remington, Stagno, & Reynolds, 1980).

SUMMARY. Infections of the central nervous system can be associated with a variety of outcomes ranging from normal function to severe disability. In some cases, devastating sequelae are immediate and dramatic. Under other circumstances, the impact of an infectious assault on the brain can be more insidious and may be characterized by the gradual appearance of a subtle or increasingly significant impairment. Although the actual injury from a congenital infection may be nonprogressive, symptoms may not emerge until later, as in the case of cerebral palsy. In other circumstances the infectious insult may be ongoing and cumulative, as in the case of a progressive impairment of vision or hearing. As with other injuries to the central nervous system, the timing of the infection and differences in fetal susceptibility account for marked variability in developmental outcomes.

Toxic insults to the central nervous system

Although the number of exposures to potentially toxic substances during an average pregnancy is undoubtedly high, specific birth defects (teratogenic effects) attributed to particular chemicals or drugs have been well documented in only a small number of instances. Attempts to understand the relation between individual toxic exposures and their possible link to subsequent developmental disability are plagued by methodological challenges. To illustrate some of these problems, the influences of alcohol on fetal and childhood development are examined in this section.

Within the past two decades investigators have explored a distinctive syndrome characterized by craniofacial anomalies, pre- and postnatal growth deficiency, and psychomotor retardation with microcephaly, that is estimated to occur (in its partial or complete form) in three to five infants per thousand live births (Clarren & Smith, 1978; Jones, Smith, Wheland, & Streissguth, 1973). However despite the relatively high incidence of the disorder and the presence of fairly characateristic clinical features, the precise nature of the so-called fetal alcohol syndrome remains elusive. Although pathological studies have revealed disturbances in the expected migration of neurons, in conjunction with marked decrease in brain size, abnormalities of brain development that can be ascribed to almost every period of intrauterine life have been reported (Clarren, Alvord, Sumi, Streissguth, & Smith, 1978), including suggestions of a link between maternal alcohol ingestion and neural tube defects (Friedman, 1982). Questions also have been raised about whether the teratogenic effects of alcohol are toxic in nature or whether they are secondary to associated nutritional deficiencies. Despite the growing interest of researchers, however, the underlying cause of the disorder remains unclear.

A number of serious methodological deficiencies in the existing literature raise questions about the reliability and validity of available data and highlight the problem of attributing a potentially toxic exposure to a specific neurological impairment. Difficulty in collecting reliable data regarding the amount of alcohol consumed during a pregnancy presents one of the most basic limitations. Unsuccessful attempts to demonstrate correlations between the extent of the atypical physical features and the degree of intellectual impairment have thwarted the search for parameters to measure dose-related alcohol effects. And once again, the issue of variation in the manifestations of the syndrome creates major diagnostic problems regarding developmental sequelae.

Children with physical features suggesting a fetal alcohol effect have been reported to demonstrate abilities ranging from moderate retardation to borderline normal intelligence. Alternatively, some youngsters demonstrate normal intelligence yet have greater problems with attention and learning (Shaywitz, Cohen, & Shaywitz, 1980); others show mild to severe speech dysfunction with or without behavior problems (Iosub, Fuchs, Bingol, & Gromisch, 1981). For the present, prenatal exposure to alcohol remains a potential risk factor for subsequent developmental disability. Its variable biological expression, however, and its frequent association with caregiving dysfunction contribute to the complexity of its pathogenesis.

Malnutrition

An association between malnutrition in infancy and subsequent intellectual abilities has been well documented, particularly in developing countries. When severe calorie and protein deprivation exists during the prenatal period and into early childhood, mental retardation and behavioral disorders generally have been frequent and irreversible. The effects of moderate or chronic low-grade malnutrition, however, are less well understood (Scrimshaw & Gordon, 1968).

Extensive research on laboratory animals suggests that the timing of a nutritional insult relative to the maturational status of the brain will have an important influence on ultimate developmental outcome. Studies in rats, for example, have shown that comparatively mild nutritional restrictions during periods of rapid cell proliferation result in permanent changes in the adult brain that cannot be reversed subsequently by a better diet, but significant undernutrition before or after the growth-spurt period produces no detectable effect that has not been demonstrated to be reversible by later dietary supplementation (Dobbing & Sands, 1971).

In human development, the sensitive period of rapid brain growth appears to include two important phases. The first extends from mid-pregnancy until the end of the second year of life and is characterized by early neuronal proliferation and a later increase in glial cell numbers. The second phase extends well into the third and fourth years and is characterized by rapid myelination in association with the continuous elaboration of increasingly complex dendritic branching and synaptic connections (Dobbing, 1974). Thus, current evidence suggests that periods of human brain growth that are vulnerable to the effects of malnutrition exist both before and after birth. In a review of seven studies, Chase (1973) reported significant intellectual impairment among malnourished children ages 2 to 14 years in all but one report. Other investigators have noted greater deficits in behavioral characteristics, such as attentiveness, curiosity, activity, and social responsiveness, than in measured intelligence per se.

Several epidemiologic studies have documented significant nutritional vulnerabilities among poor children in the United States that suggest increased risk for developmental sequelae. In a review of data on pregnant women, infants, and children under age 4 years from the Ten-State Nutrition Survey, Livingston, Calloway, MacGregor, Fisher, and Hastings (1975) found that nearly 60% of all pregnant women living below the poverty level in the United States were consuming calories at a rate low enough to affect fetal brain development adversely. Of children ages 1 to 4 years living in poverty, 18% were categorized as vulnerable to defective brain development according to data from that same survey (U.S. Department of Health, Education, and Welfare, 1972). The Preschool Nutrition Survey reported a still higher frequency of 24% at risk (Owen, Kram, Garry, Lowe, & Lubin, 1974). The Select Panel for the Promotion of Child Health (1981) estimated that approximately one-third of all black children in the United States were at risk for some kind of nutritional defect, as compared to less than 15% of white children.

The most obvious methodological problem in human studies on the effects of malnutrition has been the almost universal association of poor nutrition with poverty, whose correlates typically have an independent negative influence on intellectual development (McKay, Sinisterra, McKay, Gomez, & Lloreda, 1978). A few reports, however, have been published of studies involving malnutrition in the absence of significant socioeconomic deprivation. Lloyd-Still, Hurwitz, Wolff, and Shwachman (1974) studied 41 middle-class subjects, ages 2–21 years, who were substantially malnourished in infancy secondary to cystic fibrosis or congenital defects of the gastrointestinal tract. Significant differences in scores on the Merrill-Palmer Scales were found up to age 5 years, but no differences were observed on the Wechsler Scales administered to the older subjects. Klein, Forbes, and Nader (1975) reported a followup study of 50 children, ages 5–14 years, who had brief periods of starvation in early infancy as a result of pyloric stenosis. When compared to siblings and matched controls, these children showed no significant difference in measures of global intelligence but did demonstrate significantly lower scores on subtests related to short-term memory and attention.

The risks for later developmental disabilities among children subjected to malnutrition in early life present a clear example of the synergistic effects of both biological and environmental vulnerability. Differential sensitivity to the biological impact of inadequate nutrition based on the maturational status of the brain is particularly noteworthy.

Perinatal insult

Beginning with W. J. Little's first description in 1862 of the association between intrapartum birth trauma and cerebral palsy, much has been learned over the past 100 years about the effects of perinatal brain "injury" on later function. However, with the development of improved fetal monitoring and obstetrical techniques, physical trauma is now rare (Rosen, 1985). Thus, the major clinical problems currently encountered in the perinatal period are associated with intraventricular hemorrhage and hypoxic-ischemic encephalopathy. The neuropathological substrate for each of these insults has been studied but many questions remain.

Intraventricular hemorrhage (IVH) is seen most typically in premature infants and is located at the center of the hemisphere adjacent to the ventricles. Bleeding in this area also may be termed subependymal germinal matrix hemorrhage. It is the most common type of bleeding found in the brains of preterm infants. This category of hemorrhage in and of itself, unless extensive, does not appear to result necessarily in irreversible brain injury. However, with secondary hydrocephalus or extension of the hemorrhage into the adjacent cerebral white matter, presumably as a result of infarction, significant disabilities may result.

Hypoxic-ischemic injury to the brain produces a variety of neuropathological consequences (Volpe, 1987). These include selective necrosis (destruction) of neurons, white matter injury, and cystic changes. Selective neuronal necrosis is the most common neuropathological sequelae. It can be widespread, involving not only the cerebral cortex but the brain stem, basal ganglia, and cerebellum as well. White matter injury often is concentrated near the ventricles (periventricular leukomalacia), but it too can be widespread, and may be related to prenatal factors, including maternal infection (Gilles, 1985). Widespread cystic changes in the brain generally are the result of severe ischemia in the perinatal period but the origins of less extensive lesions often are not known. The clinical outcomes for children with any of these major perinatal insults are variable and not correlated consistently with the specific pathological lesions.

Intraventricular hemorrhage currently represents the most common neurologic disorder of premature infants. Bleeding typically occurs between 30 and 36 hours after birth, and affects between 40 and 50% of infants who weigh less than 1,500 grams at birth or who were less than 35 weeks gestation (Brann, 1985). Intraventricular hemorrhages are graded on a scale of I to IV, based upon their severity. Grades I and II are characterized by bleeding that is confined to the subependymal region or less than half the ventricular area. Grades III and IV, on the other hand, are characterized by more extensive hemorrhage with rupture into the substance of the cerebral cortex. Although mortality rates are higher among infants who sustain any degree of hemorrhage, figures vary substantially from one study to another. Despite considerable variation in morbidity data as well, there is general agreement that infants with grade I or II hemorrhage do not have significantly increased risk for major neurological sequelae when compared to a control group (Papille, Munsick-Bruno, & Schaefer, 1983). However, infants with grade III or IV hemorrhage have a substantially increased risk of neurological abnormalities, most commonly in the form of spastic diparesis or quadriparesis, and often with some degree of mental retardation (Schub, Ahmann, Lazzara, Dykes, 1980). The ability to differentially predict precise outcomes for individual infants is imperfect, but better imaging techniques, such as nuclear magnetic resonance, are making great improvements in this area.

Neonatal hypoxic-ischemic encephalopathy refers to the consequences of both hypoxia (inadequate oxygen) and ischemia (inadequate blood supply), the two most common pathological events occurring in a neonate who is asphyxiated. The early clinical signs of hypoxic-ischemic encephalopathy in the newborn period are variable. They range from relatively minor differences in state control to a number of serious signs and symptoms, including seizures and abnormalities in muscle tone, posture, reflexes, respiratory patterns, and autonomic function. Although the full-term neonate who is at greatest risk for developing long-term neurological complications as a consequence of perinatal hypoxia-ischemia will demonstrate signs of neurologic dysfunction in the first weeks of life, 85% of infants in the National Collaborative Perinatal Project who had definite neurologic abnormalities at the time of hospital discharge did not have cerebral palsy at follow-up (Nelson & Ellenberg, 1979).

For many years it was believed that oxygen deprivation during delivery led to cerebral palsy, often with associated mental retardation. Recent data, however, indicate that the pathogenesis of cerebral palsy is far more complicated, and that simple cause–effect relations associated with perinatal difficulties are generally not substantiated (Freeman, 1985; Freeman & Nelson, 1988). The Apgar score, for example, which reflects the cardiorespiratory status of a newborn and is low for babies who are asphyxiated, has not been shown to reliably predict neurological outcomes in a large percentage of clinical cases. Thomson, Searle, and Russell (1977), for example, followed 31 full-term infants with 1-minute Apgar scores of 0 and found that 93% had no serious neurologic sequelae. Nelson and Ellenberg (1981) analyzed data from the National Collaborative Perinatal Project and found no major handicaps at school age in 80% of the survivors who had Apgar scores below 3 (out of a possible score of 10) at 10 minutes, including some surviving neonates with scores of less than 3 at 20 minutes who were also normal. Paneth and Stark (1983) summarized available data regarding etiologic factors contributing to cerebral palsy and concluded that the impact of perinatal events might be overestimated, since 50% of neonates who later developed cerebral palsy were not found to be clinically asphyxiated at birth.

Despite the fact that there is still a great deal more to be learned about the effects of perinatal hypoxia-ischemia and intracranial hemorrhage in the newborn period, three conclusions can be drawn from currently available data. First, more severe degrees of hypoxia-ischemia and hemorrhage are associated with greater risks for neurological sequelae. Second, most infants who have survived an hypoxic-ischemic episode in the newborn period, as well as those who have sustained milder degrees of intraventricular hemorrhage, will not have major developmental disabilities on follow-up, particularly if they are reared by competent caregivers. And, finally, evidence suggests that underlying vulnerabilities in the neonate or the mother (presumably of prenatal origin) appear to play an important role in determining the incidence and severity of cerebral palsy or other neurological problems and may also potentiate the effects of additional brain insults.

SUMMARY: THE DEVELOPMENTAL IMPACT OF BRAIN INJURY

The process of neurological adaptation that follows a specific insult to the brain is exceedingly complex. On the one hand, many severe disabilities demonstrate the limitations of the central nervous system for recovery. On the other hand, the ability of the brain to adapt to a wide variety of insults, with relatively minor residual sequelae, has been well documented. In many circumstances of neurological dysfunction, however, we have a limited ability to determine the precise nature, severity, and timing of the presumed insult with any reasonable degree of accuracy and therefore are constrained by significant limitations in our capacity to predict its ultimate impact on development.

Clearly the immature brain of a young child is capable of adaptive recovery to a far greater degree than the more differentiated and mature brain of an adult (see Anastasiow, this volume). Although the central nervous system may not be able to replace damaged neurons after the early stage of cell proliferation is completed, changes in the communication network among functioning cells can take place. That is to say, the axons and dendrites that transmit and receive impulses from one cell to another are capable of undergoing a process of "rewiring," although how this process is initiated and controlled is largely unknown. The degree to which sensory inputs and individual experiences may influence such repair processes continues to be explored (Anastasiow, this volume).

Neurological insult can take many forms. Specific injury to the brain may result from infection, exposure to a toxic substance, malnutrition, or an hypoxic-ischemic event. The sequelae of adverse influences on the central nervous system are variable and often unpredictable for individuals. In some cases, alterations of brain structure or functional relationships result in substantial disability within a rather narrow range of variability. In other circumstances, specific cortical insults can produce an extraordinarily wide variety of outcomes.

Young children vary in their apparent vulnerability to noxious biological experiences. The burden of an insult to the central nervous system may be insurmountable or may be a simple risk factor that can be neutralized by individual resilience or a nurturant, caregiving environment. The process of development is transactional and complex. All humans are endowed with a reservoir of biological adaptability, as well as sources of vulnerability. Such characteristics may be genetically determined or simple constitutional traits.

The development of competence is not determined by biology alone. Rather, it unfolds under the mutual influences of nurture and nature. Indeed, the maturation of the central nervous system itself is affected by the experiences that characterize each individual's personal environment. For the very young child, interactions and evolving relationships with his or her caregivers are the most crucial elements in that environment. When such relationships are dysfunctional, the most biologically resilient youngster will be at risk for later problems. When such relationships are supportive of adaptive development, the young child with extensive neurological vulnerabilities may still have a substantial opportunity to thrive (see Beckwith, this volume; Gabarino, this volume; Werner, this volume).

The field of early childhood intervention faces a number of critical challenges. Among these is the need to increase our ability to identify biological risk factors and to reduce their deleterious effects. Major advances in this area will require significant breakthroughs in the basic sciences of neurobiology, including a greater understanding of the molecular basis of neurological function and the prevention of neurological damage. In those circumstances in which biological insult cannot be avoided, the task before us is to enhance our understanding of human adaptation. This will require more extensive investigation of how protective factors in the child and in his or her environment can mitigate the adverse developmental impact of brain injury. Identifying and facilitating such protective factors is the central mission of early childhood intervention.

REFERENCES

Brann, A. (1985). Factors during neonatal life that influence brain disorders. In J. Freeman (Ed.), *Prenatal and perinatal factors associated with brain disorders* (NIH Publication No. 85–1149, pp. 263–358). Washington, DC: U.S. Department of Health and Human Services.

Carter, C. (1974). Clues to the aetiology of neural tube malformations. *Developmental Medicine and Child Neurology 32* (Suppl.), 3–15.

Chase, H. (1973). The effects of intrauterine and postnatal undernutrition on normal brain development. *Annals of the New York Academy of Science, 205*, 231–244.

Chess, S. (1974). The influence of defect on development in children with congenital rubella. *Merrill-Palmer Quarterly, 20*, 255–274.

Chudley, A. E., & Hagerman, R. J. (1987). Fragile X syndrome. *Journal of Pediatrics, 110*, 821–831.

Clarren, S. K., Alvord, E. C., Jr., Sumi, S. M., Streissguth, A. P., & Smith, D. W. (1978). Brain malformations related to prenatal exposure to ethanol. *Journal of Pediatrics, 92*, 64–67.

Clarren, S., & Smith, D. (1978). The fetal alcohol syndrome. *New England Journal of Medicine, 288*, 1063–1067.

Conboy, T. J., Pass, R. F., Stagno, S., Alford, C., Myers, G., Britt, W., McCollister, F., Summers, M., McFarland, C., & Boll, T. (1987). Early clinical manifestations and intellectual outcome in children with symptomatic congenital cytomegalovirus infection. *Journal of Pediatrics, 111*, 343–348.

Conboy, T. J., Pass, R. F., Stagno, S., Britt, W., Alford, C., McFarland, C., & Boll, T. (1986). Intellectual development in school-aged children with asymptomatic congenital cytomegalovirus infection. *Pediatrics, 77*, 801–806.

Cooper, L. Z., & Krugman, S. (1966). Diagnosis and management: Congenital rubella. *Pediatrics, 37*, 335–338.

Desmonts, G., & Couvreur, J. (1979). Congenital toxoplasmosis: A prospective study of the offspring of 542 women who acquired toxoplasmosis during pregnancy – pathophysiology of congenital disease. In O. Thalhammer, K. Baumgarten, & A. Pollak (Eds.), *Perinatal medicine, Sixth European Congress, Vienna, 1978* (pp. 51–60). Stuttgart: Georg Thieme Publishers.

Dobbing, J. (1974). The later growth of the brain and its vulnerability. *Pediatrics, 53*, 2–6.

Dobbing, J., & Sands, J. (1971). Vulnerability of the developing brain: IX. The effect of nutritional growth retardation on the timing of the brain growth-spurt. *Biological Neonatorum, 19*, 363.

Freeman, J. (1985). *Prenatal and perinatal factors associated with brain disorders.* (NIH Publication No. 85–1149). Washington, DC: U.S. Department of Health and Human Services.

Freeman, J., & Nelson, K. (1988). Intrapartum asphyxia and cerebral palsy. *Pediatrics, 82*, 240–249.

Friedman, J. M. (1982). Can maternal alcohol ingestion cause neural tube defects? *Journal of Pediatrics, 101*, 232–234.

Gabriel, R. S., & McComb, J. G. (1985). Malformations of the central nervous system. In J. H. Menkes (Ed.), *Textbook of child neurology* (pp. 189–270). Philadelphia: Lea & Febiger.

Garron, D. C. (1977). Intelligence among persons with Turner's syndrome. *Behavioral Genetics, 7*, 105–127.

Gilles, F. H. (1985). Neuropathologic indicators of abnormal development. In J. Freeman (Ed.), *Prenatal and perinatal factors associated with brain disorders* (NIH Publication No. 85–1149, pp. 53–108). Washington, DC: U.S. Department of Health and Human Services.

Hagerman, R. J. (1987). Fragile X syndrome. *Current Problems in Pediatrics, 17*, 621–674.

Hagerman, R., Kemper, M., & Hudson, M. (1985). Learning disabilities and attentional problems in boys with the Fragile X syndrome. *American Journal of Diseases of Children, 139*, 674–678.

Hanshaw, J. (1981). Cytomegalovirus infections. *Pediatrics in Review, 2*, 245–251.

Hanshaw, J., Scheiner, A., Moxley, A., Gaev, L., Abel, V., & Scheiner, B. (1976). School failure and deafness after "silent" congenital cytomegalovirus infection. *New England Journal of Medicine, 295*, 468–470.

Herbst, D. S., & Miller, J. R. (1980). Nonspecific X-linked mental retardation II: The frequency in British Columbia. *American Journal of Medical Genetics, 7*, 461–469.

Iosub, S., Fuchs, M., Bingol, N., & Gromisch, D. S. (1981). Fetal alcohol syndrome revisited. *Pediatrics, 68*, 475–479.

Jacobs, P. A. (1982). The William Allan Memorial Award Address: Human population cytogenetics. The first twenty-five years. *American Journal of Human Genetics, 34*, 689–698.

Jones, K. L., Smith, D. W., Wheland, C. N., & Streissguth, P. P. (1973). Pattern of malformations in offspring of chronic alcoholic mothers. *Lancet, 1*, 1267.

Kety, S. (1978). Genetic and biochemical aspects of schizophrenia. In A. Nicholi (Ed.), *Harvard guide to modern psychiatry.* Cambridge, MA: Belknap Press.

Klein, P., Forbes, G., & Nader, P. (1975). Effects of starvation in infancy (pyloric stenosis) on subsequent learning abilities. *Journal of Pediatrics, 87*, 8–15.

Kumar, M., Nankervis, G., & Gold, E. (1973). Inapparent congenital cytomegalovirus infection, a follow-up study. *New England Journal of Medicine, 288*, 1370–1372.

Lemire, P. J., Leoser, J. D., Leech, R. W., & Alvord, E. C. (1975). *Normal and abnormal development of the human nervous system.* New York: Harper & Row.

Little, W. (1862). On the influence of abnormal parturition, difficult labor, premature birth, and asphyxia neonatorum on the mental and physical condition of the child, especially in relation to deformities. *Transactions of the Obstetrical Society of London, 3,* 293–344.

Livingston, R., Calloway, D., MacGregor, J., Fisher, G., & Hastings, A. (1975). U.S. poverty impact on brain development. In M. Brazier (Ed.), *Growth and development of the brain* (pp. 377–394). New York: Raven Press.

Lloyd-Still, J., Hurwitz, I., Wolff, P., & Shwachman, H. (1974). Intellectual development after severe malnutrition in infancy. *Pediatrics, 54,* 306–312.

Lorber, J., & Priestly, B. L. (1981). Children with large heads: A practical approach to diagnosis in 557 children, with special reference to 109 children with megalencephaly. *Developmental Medicine and Child Neurology, 23,* 494–504.

Lubs, H. A. (1983). X-Linked mental retardation and the marker X. In A. E. H. Emery & D. L. Rimoin (Eds.), *Principles and practice of medical genetics* (pp. 216–223). Edinburgh: Churchill Livingstone.

McClone, D. G., Czyzurski, D., Raimondi, A. J., & Sommers, R. C. (1982). Central nervous system infections as a limiting factor in the intelligence of children with myelomeningocoele. *Pediatrics, 70,* 338.

McClone, D. G., Dias, L., Kaplan, W. E., & Sommers, M. W. (1985). Concepts in the management of spina bifida. *Concepts in Pediatric Neurosurgery, 5,* 97.

McCullough, P. & Balzer-Martin, L. (1982). Current prognosis in overt neonatal hydrocephalus. *Journal of Neurosurgery, 57,* 378–383.

McKay, H., Sinisterra, L., McKay, A., Gomez, H., & Lloreda, P. (1978). Improving cognitive ability in chronically deprived children. *Science, 200,* 270–278.

Melish, M., & Hanshaw, J. (1973). Congenital cytomegalovirus infection: Developmental progress of infants detected by routine screening. *American Journal of Diseases of Children, 126,* 190.

Moore, R. (1985). Normal development of the nervous system. In J. Freemen (Ed.), *Prenatal and perinatal factors associated with brain disorders* (NIH Publication No. 85-1149, pp. 33–52). Washington, DC: U.S. Department of Health and Human Services.

Moser, H. (1985). Biologic factors of development. In J. Freeman (Ed.), *Prenatal and perinatal factors associated with brain disorders* (NIH Publication No. 85-1149, pp. 121–161). Washington, DC: U.S. Department of Health and Human Services.

Nelson, K. B., & Ellenberg, J. H. (1979). Neonatal signs and predictors of cerebral palsy. *Pediatrics, 74,* 225–232.

Nelson, K. B., & Ellenberg, J. H. (1981). Apgar scores as predictors of chronic neurologic disability. *Pediatrics, 68,* 36–44.

Nevin, N. C., Johnston, W. P., & Merritt, J. D. (1981). Influence of social class on the risk of recurrence of anencephalus and spina bifida. *Developmental Medicine and Child Neurology, 23,* 155–159.

Opitz, J. M. (1984). *X-Linked mental retardation.* New York: Alan R. Liss.

Owen, G., Kram, K., Garry, P., Lowe, J., & Lubin, A. (1974). A study of nutritional status of preschool children in the United States, 1968–1970. *Pediatrics, 53,* 597–646.

Paneth, N., & Stark, R. I. (1983). Cerebral palsy and mental retardation in relation to indicators of perinatal asphyxia. *American Journal of Obstetrics and Gynecology, 147,* 960–966.

Papille, L., Munsick-Bruno, G., & Schaefer, A. (1983). Relationship of cerebral intraventricular hemorrhage and early childhood neurologic handicaps. *Journal of Pediatrics, 103,* 273–277.

Pass, R., Stagno, S., Myers, G., & Alford, C. (1980). Outcome of symptomatic congenital cytomegalovirus infection: Results of long-term longitudinal follow-up. *Pediatrics, 66,* 758–762.

Pueschel, J. (Ed.). (1978). *Down syndrome: Growing and learning.* Kansas City, KS: Andrews & McMeel.

Rosen, M. G. (1985). Factors during labor and delivery that influence brain disorders. In J. Freeman (Ed.), *Prenatal and perinatal factors associated with brain disorders* (NIH Publication No. 85-1149, pp. 237–262). Washington, DC: U.S. Department of Health and Human Services.

Schub, H. S., Ahmann, P., Lazzara, A., & Dyres F. D. (1980). Long-term developmental follow-up of premature infants with subependymal intraventricular hemorrhage: Reason for optimism. *Clinical Research, 28,* 874A.

Scrimshaw, N., & Gordon, J. (Eds.). (1968). *Malnutrition, learning, and behavior.* Boston: MIT Press.

Select Panel for the Promotion of Child Health. (1981). *Report to the U.S. Congress and the Secretary of Health and Human Services on better health for our children.* Washington, DC: U.S. Department of Health and Human Services.

Sells, C. J. (1977). Microcephaly in a normal school population. *Pediatrics, 59,* 262–265.

Shaywitz, S., Cohen, D., & Shaywitz, B. (1980). Behavior and learning difficulties in children of normal intelligence born to alcoholic mothers. *Journal of Pediatrics, 96,* 978–982.

Silbert, A., Wolff, P. H., & Lilienthal, J. (1977). Spatial and temporal processing in patients with Turner's syndrome. *Behavioral Genetics, 7,* 11.

Smithells, R. W., Seller, M. J., Harris, R., Fielding, D. W. Schorah, C. J., Nervin, N. C., Sheppard, S., Read, A. P., Walker, S., Wild, J. (1983). Further experience of vitamin supplementation for prevention of neural tube defect recurrences. *Lancet, 1,* 1027–1030.

Stray-Pedersen, B. (1980). Infants potentially at risk for congenital toxoplasmosis. *American Journal of Diseases of Children, 134,* 638–642.

Thomson, A. J., Searle, M., & Russell, G. (1977). Quality of survival after severe birth asphyxia. *Archives of Diseases of Childhood, 52,* 620–626.

U.S. Department of Health, Education, and Welfare. (1972). *Ten-state nutrition survey* (Publication No. 72–81334). Washington, DC: Author. U.S. Department of Health, Education, and Welfare.

Volpe, J. J. (1987). Human brain development. In J. Volpe (Ed.), *Neurology of the newborn* (pp. 1–65). Philadelphia: Saunders.

Wilson, C. B., Remington, J. S., Stagno, S., & Reynolds, D. W. (1980). Development of adverse sequelae in children born with subclinical congenital toxoplasma infection. *Pediatarics, 66,* 767–774.

3 Adaptive and maladaptive parenting – Implications for intervention

LEILA BECKWITH

The human infant develops in a social environment. From the moment of birth the infant must be protected and cared for by others. In the process of fulfilling those biologic needs to secure survival, parents, by the emotions they express to the infant and to others and by the content and timing of their behavior, influence their infant's emerging cognitive, linguistic, social, and emotional competencies.

A full decade ago, a review of the then-emerging field of caregiver–infant interaction as it related to early intervention stressed the formative influence of infancy (Beckwith, 1976). The review examined what was known about the dimensions of caregiver–infant interaction in normal parent–infant pairs, the contribution of the infant to those interactions, and the consequences of those interactions for later development. It suggested that similar analyses of atypical pairs would be a worthwhile strategy.

This chapter will review the changes that have occurred in the field in the decade that has elapsed since that publication. During that period, there has been a growing cross-fertilization between studies of parenting in normal families and the application of comparable methods and theories to clinical populations. The study of the dimensions of parenting as they influence developmental processes now includes biologically at-risk infants and infants at both biologic and social risk (e.g., those with mentally ill parents, parents who are substance abusers). These studies examine the processes that underlie emerging competence or dysfunction, in relation to both the nature of the disordered parental interactions and the deviance of the child's adaptation to developmental tasks. They also seek to determine the origins or etiology of distortions in the parental history, personality, or current spousal relationship, and external stresses.

The growing interest in observable specific behaviors during interaction has now broadened to include affect as it is expressed directly to the infant, as the infant seeks it out in regulating his or her own affective experience, and as its organization is regulated in the infant through experience with the parent (Dunn & Munn, 1985). The study of parent–infant interaction has been enriched further by examining that relationship in the context of competing and supporting relationships among multiple members of the family: that of the infant to the father, of the father to the mother, of the mother–father–infant, of the mother–infant–sibling, and of each parent to his or her own

Preparation of this chapter was supported by the Center for Prevention Research, Division of Prevention and Special Mental Health, National Institute of Mental Health, Grant No. MH 36902.

parents (Minuchin, 1985). Infants are now perceived as full participants in the social system that is the family, which is more than an aggregation of individuals.

It is becoming more evident that marital relationships are affected by parents' own childhood histories (Belsky & Isabella, 1985; Minuchin, 1985; Ricks, 1985; Rutter, 1987). These early experiences influence martial harmony, which in turn influences parental behavior and the emerging parent–infant relationship (Belsky, Gilstrap, & Rovine, 1984; Goldberg & Easterbrooks, 1984; Rutter & Quinton, 1984). The infant, in turn, influences the parents' marital relationship as well as the emotional bonds between them and their own parents. Further, the parents' influence on the infant's development is only in part coherent with their own goals and needs. The parents are responsive as well to the external environment over which they have limited control (Furstenberg, 1985).

The study of parenting has three essential aspects: characteristics or processes (How is parenting done?), the etiology of individual differences (Why is it done in that way?), and consequences (How does it influence the developing child?) (Belsky, 1984). These three questions are clearly critical to our understanding of early intervention. In the realm of primary prevention, before dysfunctional parenting becomes evident, it is essential to identify the stresses affecting the parent from within and outside the family as well as the vulnerabilities within the parent and infant that can be addressed by intervention. If there are presumed deficits in parenting ability, it is important to be able to specify the dimensions that will be both the focus of that intervention and will be measured in order to assess its effectiveness.

This chapter will begin with a consideration of the family as a social unit, as it influences parenting. Then will follow an examination of normative processes of parenting, as they facilitate competent development. Next, we will focus on individual differences, risk groups, and dysfunction. Finally, implications for intervention will be explored. The review will be selective rather than exhaustive, and will focus on recent research on infancy and the preschool years. (Many excellent relevant writings exist. The interested reader should review Campos, Barrett, Lamb, Goldsmith, & Stenberg, 1983; Lewis, 1987; Maccoby & Martin, 1983; Parke and Tinsley, 1987; Wachs & Gruen, 1982.)

THE FAMILY AS A SOCIAL UNIT

The family is embedded in a broad variety of social systems including extended family, friends and neighbors, work, schools, medical and religious institutions, and cultural group (Bronfenbrenner, Moen, & Garbarino, 1984). That larger environment acts as a source of both stress and support in its influence on the parent's relationship to the child (Cochran & Brassard, 1979; Crnic, Greenberg, Robinson, & Ragozin, 1984; Parke & Tinsley, 1987).

The nuclear family itself is made up of multiple, competing relationships that have both direct and indirect effects on the infant (Belsky, 1981; Lewis, 1987). It is not only the mother, but the father (Clarke-Stewart, 1980; Lamb, 1981; Lewis & Weintraub, 1976) and siblings (Dunn & Kendrick, 1982), as well as perhaps grandparents (Cohler & Grunebaum, 1981) and others, who influence the infant through their reciprocal interactions. Infants do not relate only to their mothers. The infant's relationship to either parent is more a function of the nature of their interactions than of an innate biological disposition (Kotelchuck, 1976).

Family members also influence each other and thereby alter the relationship of each parent to each child. The birth of a sibling alters the relationship of the parent to the older children (Dunn & Kendrick, 1982). Each parent behaves somewhat differently toward a child in the presence of the other parent than when alone with that child (Clarke-Stewart, 1978). Further, there is growing evidence that the quality of the marriage influences the attitudes and interactions of each parent and child (Maccoby & Martin, 1983). The father may be a source of marital satisfaction and maternal self-esteem, a focus of competition with the child for the mother's attention, or a source of discord, either enhancing or interfering with the maternal role. Even more, the marital relationship strongly predicts paternal involvement, with the level of mother-father harmony correlating positively with the level of father-infant interaction (Belsky, Gilstrap, & Rovine, 1984; Parke & Tinsley, 1987). Whereas the quality of a marriage is associated with mothers' and fathers' adaptation to the challenges of pregnancy, childbirth, and parenthood (Osofsky & Osofsky, 1984), it is not clear to what extent high marital quality acts as an emotional support that enhances parenting and to what extent personality characteristics are reflected simultaneously in both marital and parenting interactions.

One study examining the quality of marriage and its effects on parenting behavior found that parents' attitudes of warmth, encouragement of independence, and decreased aggravation with their toddlers were related significantly to their scores on a scale of marital adjustment. Furthermore, there were more secure infant–parent attachments in the high marital adjustment group, and more insecure infant–parent attachments in the low marital adjustment group (Goldberg & Easterbrooks, 1984).

In a longitudinal study of infant and family development from the last trimester of pregnancy through the first year of the infant's life, Belsky and his colleagues found that marital adjustment declined significantly within the group across the transition to parenthood (Belsky & Isabella, 1985; Belsky, Spanier, & Rovine, 1983). Individual differences in both kind and degree of change in marital satisfaction were found, however, and could be correlated with individual differences in the relationship histories of the parents in their own families of origin.

The notion that a person's childhood relationships with his or her parents would affect later parental behavior has begun to be studied empirically (Main, Kaplan, & Cassidy, 1985). Whereas no prospective study has been reported, there are two lines of evidence to support this hypothesis. One indicates that serious disruptions in the parent's own family of origin, due to death, separation, or discord, are related to later difficulties in parenting as well as to later marital disharmony. These phenomena increase parenting problems (Rutter, 1987). The second suggests that maternal memories of childhood relationships are related both to the quality of current parental behavior and to the child's security of attachment (Main et al., 1985; Ricks, 1985).

The determinants of individual differences in parenting can be examined within three domains: (1) the parents' own history and personal psychological resources; (2) contextual sources of stress and support; and (3) the child's characteristics (Belsky, 1984). Belsky argues that parental history and personality are the most influential determinants because they not only affect parenting directly but they indirectly determine the quality of support the parent receives through, for example, the selection of a spouse, the maintenance of stable friends, work and its satisfactions, and the quality of the relationships with others.

ADAPTIVE PARENTING

Functions

How should the functions of parenting an infant and young toddler be characterized? There is no single answer. Despite the variations in emphasis, most theorists and researchers now agree that successful parenting provides protection (Ainsworth, 1973; Bowlby, 1969), facilitates emotional organization (Emde, 1987), and encourages environmental exploration and learning (Bruner, 1975).

Although there are important individual differences in parenting, derived from the parent's own childhood history and psychological resources, extensive research supports the notion of a core foundation of genetically prewired behaviors that facilitate the basic processes of parenting (Ainsworth, 1973; Bowlby, 1969; Klaus & Kennell, 1976; Papousek & Papousek, 1987). Bowlby (1969) and Ainsworth (1973) emphasize the adult's natural tendency to hold, talk, smile, and respond to the infant cry as complementary to the infant's own biologically determined behaviors that together build attachment. Papousek and Papousek (1987) stress a special form of speaking – "motherese" – that is created universally by parents for their infants and is particularly informative to the infant who is in the process of acquiring language. Klaus and Kennell (1976) emphasize a priming mechanism for parenting behaviors labeled *bonding*, defined as the consequence of close physical contact between infant and mother in the first few hours or days following birth. Although conceptualized as a sensitive period, perhaps based on biochemical changes within the mother, the developmental effects of early and extended contact have been questioned, and the empirical literature in the area is controversial (Lamb & Hwang, 1982).

Processes

Whereas investigators during the 1960s and 1970s focused on specific parent–infant interactions, it is now clear that the parent–infant relationship is more complex than previously demonstrated (Campos et al., 1983). This chapter will discuss three processes within the parent–infant relationship that reflect current lines of research: content and timing of behavior, affect, and attachment.

CONTENT AND TIMING OF BEHAVIOR. The parent's ability to perceive and interpret the child's signals and intentions and to respond quickly and appropriately has been called sensitivity (Ainsworth, 1973). It is believed that through interactions with sensitive and predictably responsive adults, infants develop a concept of their own competence (Watson, 1972; Watson & Ramey, 1972). The infant recognizes that he or she is an effective agent who can at least partially determine his or her own experiences. Thus, not only do parents satisfy basic needs, but they facilitate contingencies between the infant's actions and effects in the environment through the manipulation of both inanimate objects and a wide range of social interactions involving parental talking, smiling, laughing, eye-to-eye contact, holding, touching, and postural adjustments that are gratifying to the infant (Emde, 1980).

Parents vary considerably in the extent to which they provide contingent and appropriate responses to their infant's signals. It has been shown that mothers who respond quickly and consistently to cries and nondistress vocalizations have infants who later show more advanced information processing, as demonstrated by faster rates of response decrement to repeated stimulation (Lewis & Goldberg, 1969). Mot. respond quickly and consistently to their infant's cries and nondistress vocah. foster mastery motivation that is manifested by greater interest in exploring the vironment (Yarrow, Rubenstein, & Pederson, 1975). Mothers who respond prompt. to their infants' cries in the early months of life have infants who later cry less and are more communicative in other ways (Bell & Ainsworth, 1972; Crockenberg & McClusky, 1986). The influence of sensitive, responsive caregiving during infancy has been demonstrated to promote cognitive competence, as shown in IQ scores taken concurrently and later (Beckwith, Cohen, Kopp, Parmelee & Marcy, 1976; Belsky, 1981; Bradley & Caldwell, 1984; Clarke-Stewart, Vanderstoep, & Killian, 1979).

Although parental sensitivity cannot be defined independently of the child, because infants differ in the clarity and degree to which they initiate signals, it is important to measure sensitivity and to understand the reasons for individual differences when planning intervention. Brody and Axelrod (1978) have suggested that ignorance, lack of interest, carelessness, intolerance, and excessive indulgence may explain parental insensitivity. Lamb and Easterbrooks (1981) have suggested that parental attitudes of perceived skill, perceived efficacy as a parent, and the value attributed to the parental role may influence their sensitivity to their young child. Sameroff and Feil (1985) consider that it is the parent's cognitive-developmental level that determines his or her ability to understand the child's perspective and to respond appropriately. Much intervention work has aimed to increase parents' ability to assess, elicit, and respond contingently to their infants, and a great deal of further investigation in this area is needed.

Closely related to the concept of parental sensitivity has been the emergence of the concept of synchrony between parent and infant. Synchrony focuses more heavily on the precise timing of interactions. It tends to depend on microanalytic techniques of measurement in the laboratory rather than naturalistic home observations and it specifically addresses the first few months of life. The most widely used behavior sample in this area of study is structured face-to-face interaction. There is a burgeoning research literature that details the variations in synchrony and mutual regulation that characterize mother–infant interaction in the first few months (Bakeman & Brown, 1977; Brazelton & Yogman, 1986; Stern, 1985; Tronick, Als, Adamson, Wise, & Brazelton, 1978). It examines how parents foster their infant's contribution to the interaction by organizing their own behavior in response to the infant's interactive capabilities. Most data support the notion that competent parents make it easy for their infants to take turns in interaction (Tronick, Ricks, & Cohn, 1982).

AFFECT. Emotions are regarded as active, ongoing, and adaptive. They are also considered to be highly patterned and organized. Emotions play a critical role in appraising the meaning of events as satisfying or dangerous and in guiding subsequent behavior. Moreover, they allow for self-monitoring (goals, well-being, intentions) and monitoring of others (intentions, needs, states of well-being and engagement) (Emde, 1987).

Emotions also regulate interpersonal processes. Both parental caregiving and infant behavior are guided by highly organized emotional signaling systems. Recent research has explored the communication of affect from infant to parent and from parent to infant in the process by which they regulate their interaction (Bretherton, Fritz, Zahn-Waxler, Ridgeway, 1986; Campos et al., 1983). In the course of the process, each reads facial, postural, and vocal cues in order to achieve access to the other's inner states.

By the end of the first year, infants begin to look to their parents' face to read the affective content of their expressions, in order to appraise an ambiguous or novel environmental situation. Thus, infants' reactions to other persons or to events are influenced by the indirect effect of observing their parents' response to that person or event. The ability of infants to learn vicariously is based, in part, on their ability to use the affective reaction of another, particularly the parent, as a means of appraising and understanding the environment (Feiring, Lewis, & Starr, 1984). Infants' social knowledge, therefore, arises from vicarious learning as well as from direct interaction.

This phenomenon has been demonstrated through several studies. Campos and Stenberg (1981) showed that a 10-month-old is much more likely to approach a remote-controlled robot if the mother smiles when the infant looks at her than if the mother frowns. In another study, infants whose mothers displayed disgust (as instructed by the experimenter) played less with a stimulus toy than infants whose mothers displayed positive affect or remained silently neutral (Hornik, Risenhoover, & Gunnar, 1987). In yet another study, infants responded differently to strangers as a second-order effect of their mother's affect expressions toward the strangers (Feinman & Lewis, 1983). Extending the knowledge that infants' behavior can be influenced by others' affect is the beginning research evidence that indicates that during the second year, if not sooner, toddlers become responsive to the distress and to the anger of other family members (Cummings, Zahn-Waxler, & Radke-Yarrow, 1981). It has further been found that toddlers respond with distress to background anger in a laboratory situation and show the aftereffects by increased aggressiveness in play with a familiar peer (Cummings, Iannotti, & Zahn-Waxler, 1985).

Since the now classic study by Schaffer and Emerson (1964) that demonstrated that the amount of time that the parent was present in the home with the infant was unrelated to the infant's preference for that parent, it has been accepted that mere physical availability is not enough for the infant to establish an affectional tie. Another critical feature, in addition to responsive behavior, is the parent's willingness to respond on an emotional level (Bowlby, 1973; Matas, Arend, & Sroufe, 1978). Such emotional availability is a state of readiness that communicates to the infant that the parent is aware of the infant's presence, is monitoring his or her behavior, and is available to respond appropriately (Emde, 1980).

The significance of emotional availability to the young child has been examined in experimental studies in the laboratory. In one investigation in which mothers were instructed to alternate between being emotionally unavailable (by reading) and then emotionally available to their infants, it was found that the infants showed less pleasure, were less active, vocalized and smiled less, and made fewer attempts to initiate interactions with their mothers under the unavailable condition. They also restricted their exploration of the unfamiliar environment, both with regard to a stranger and a novel toy. Thus, emotional availability is one parenting characteristic that determines the degree to which infants will explore and the pleasure with which they do so (Sorce & Emde, 1981). Emotional availability has also been shown, under more naturalistic conditions in the home, to affect levels of symbolic play. When the mother was available to play (while the experimenter was not engaging her in conversation), the child's level of pretend play increased (Slade, 1987). The level of play was highest and the duration of play episodes lengthened when the mother interacted actively with the child (O'Connell & Bretherton, 1984; Slade, 1987). These research data not only endorse the importance of emotional availability but also support Bruner's (1975) hypothesis that parents facilitate higher cognitive achievements in their children through scaffolding their actions by providing concrete support for emerging cognitive structures.

A related notion to that of emotional availability is the idea that there is a pr\
affect attunement between parents and infants in which they both can share ιɩ
states (Stern, 1985). Through this process the parents reflect back nonverbally ↙
infant's own experiences and, thereby, enable the child to perceive how he or she iʑ
perceived by others. Sometimes referred to as "affect matching" (Malatesta & Izard,
1984), or "intersubjectivity" (Trevarthan, 1979), this concept implies that the parent
"reads" the infant's internal state and that the infant "reads" the parent's response as a
reflection of the infant's original experience. The characteristic features of attunement
are (1) imitation that is not a simple duplicate of the infant's overt behavior;
(2) parental use of a different modality of expression from that used by the infant;
(3) reference for the match that is not an external behavioral act but an internal state;
(4) manifestation of the match in the parental expression of the infant's inner state; and
(5) a process that occurs almost automatically and largely out of awareness. Since attunement behaviors reference the internal state and do not reproduce external behavior,
attunement shifts the focus of attention to the feeling that is being shared rather than to
an observed activity. Attunement implies participating or sharing in another's experience without altering the other's behavior. It is distinguished from communication that
usually refers to an exchange of information (Stern, 1985).

In an experimental study designed to demonstrate infants' sense of their parents'
attunement, the parents were asked to misjudge purposely their infants' level of pleasurable affect (Stern et al., 1985). When they judged it to be at a higher or lower level
and responded accordingly, the infants stopped their ongoing behavior. When the
parents reacted appropriately, the infants did not respond and continued in their own
self-directed behavior. These findings support the idea that infants sense the extent of
matching and that a violation of the match is meaningful.

Attunement is considered to be an essential aspect of one's acquisition of a sense of
self and may be one of the bases of infants' emerging discovery by the last quarter of
the first year that they have a mind that is separate from the minds of other people.
Further, the infant comes to expect that his or her mind and the mind of another can
be related. It has been hypothesized that this discovery primes pointing gestures and
intentions to communicate as well as language acquisition (Bruner, 1975; Collis &
Schaffer, 1975).

ATTACHMENT. The most extensively developed and empirically supported theory of
parent–infant relationships is the concept of attachment (Ainsworth, 1973; Ainsworth,
Blehar, Waters, & Wall, 1978; Bowlby, 1969; Bretherton & Waters, 1985; Sroufe,
1985). As first proposed by Bowlby, attachment theory posits that the affectional tie
between infant and parent develops out of species-specific response patterns that are
preprogrammed to ensure that infants will be protected from predators and will be
nurtured so that the species will survive. The infant's primary behaviors of crying,
smiling, sucking, clinging, and, within a few months, following, are used to initiate
or maintain proximity between the infant and the parent. From the beginning, both
are active partners in initiating and maintaining contact, and both participate in the
development of a reciprocal system of interaction. Differences in the adult's tendency
to respond promptly and appropriately to the infant's signals influence the nature of the
affectional bond that develops between them, as well as the sense of security or basic
trust the infant feels in that relationship.

The attachment system is only one of several major behavioral systems within the
infants' repertoire (Ainsworth et al., 1978; Bowlby, 1969). The fear/wariness system
coordinates the monitoring and avoidance of events or people that are felt to be

dangerous. The affiliation system regulates playful social interaction. The exploration system controls the investigation of the animate and inanimate environment. During the second 6 months of life, behaviors begin to be organized into coherent systems governed by plans or goals. The goal of attachment is a certain degree of proximity to the attachment figure. Each system integrates subsystems that organize affective and cognitive appraisals of the self and the environment into multiple feedback loops with effector behaviors. Each system, dependent upon internal and external events, may be activated to a greater or lesser intensity at any particular time. Individual behavioral components vary according to circumstances as does the goal. Activation of any one of these systems affects the functioning of the others. An infant whose attachment figure has been inaccessible or available unreliably feels less secure and, therefore, may require greater proximity to the attachment figure, and do less exploration than an infant who has learned to count on the adult being available promptly.

Several studies now support, as Bowlby (1969) proposed, that early attachment relationships are critical influences on later personality development. Bowlby suggested that the infant gradually builds working models of others and of self, through which later events are perceived. These working models include representation of the attachment figure as either accessible, responsive, and emotionally available, or the opposite, and of the self as either worthy and lovable or unworthy and unlovable.

Ainsworth and her colleagues (Ainsworth et al., 1978) have emphasized that the parent's degree of sensitivity in responding to infant signals and communications, in the context of close bodily contact, is the basis of secure attachment. This sensitivity in response to infant signals relevant to feeding (Ainsworth & Bell, 1969), crying (Bell & Ainsworth, 1972), and face-to-face interaction (Blehar, Lieberman, & Ainsworth, 1977), as well as parental sensitivity and responsiveness in other diverse situations (Bates, Maslin, & Frankel, 1985; Egeland & Farber, 1984; Grossman, Grossman, Spangler, Suess, & Unzer, 1985; Sroufe & Fleeson, 1986), has been found to predict the quality of the infant–caregiver attachment.

In general, security of attachment does not correlate with differences in IQ scores (Sroufe & Fleeson, 1986). There are, however, differences in task persistence and enthusiasm, quality of play, and problem-solving behaviors that have been shown to be associated with level of security of attachment. Secure infants have been found to become 2-year-olds who are more enthusiastic, persistent, and likely to elicit and accept their mother's help in problem-solving tasks, and to show less distress and more positive affect in those tasks than infants who were rated as insecure (Matas et al., 1978). Secure infants also show more advanced inanimate and animate tool use than do insecure infants (Bretherton, Bates, Benigni, Camaioni, & Volterra, 1979). Secure infants tend to be more compliant and cooperative and to show more positive affect (Erickson & Crichton, 1981; Londerville & Main, 1981; Main, 1973; Sroufe & Rosenberg, 1982). At age 3 years, secure infants have been found to be more sociable with peers (Pastor, 1981; Waters, Wippman, & Sroufe, 1979) and at age 5 to show more ego resilience and ego strength, including greater self-esteem, positive affect, assertiveness, empathy, peer competence, and popularity, than children who had shown insecure attachments as infants (Sroufe & Fleeson, 1986).

Sometime during a child's second year, if not sooner, parents begin to impose rules and restrictions. At the same time, children begin to intend to control others (Lewis, 1987). Children's readiness to comply with the mild demands made on them by their parents and their parents' responsiveness to the mild bids that come from their children, become important in maintaining harmony and decreasing coercion (Parpal &

Maccoby, 1985). There is much evidence that securely attached infants are more compliant and cooperative with their attachment figure than are insecurely attached infants (e.g., Schaffer & Crook, 1980).

One of the perplexing questions in attachment theory is how infants integrate contrasting relationships, because security of attachment is specific to each individual attachment figure. It has been shown that children can and do form one kind of attachment to one parent and another kind to the other parent (Main & Weston, 1981). It has also been shown that the nature of the attachment to one parent, although it tends to remain stable, can change over time in response to factors that reflect instability within the family (Vaughn, Egeland, Waters, & Sroufe, 1979). Whereas it is undoubtedly true that stable, secure attachments to both parents facilitate a more secure model of self and others, it is not yet clear how conflicting models of attachment influence development. This question may be particularly significant for intervention services that have as one of their goals the improvement of a child's relationships and sense of self through the promotion of a more secure parent–child attachment.

RISK GROUPS AND PARENTING DYSFUNCTION

The contribution of the infant

It is posited that the influences between parent and infant are bidirectional and transactional; that is, both are active partners, and each contributes to and is changed in the process of their relationship (Sameroff & Chandler, 1975). Whereas the parent can be flexible in the face of a wide range of infant characteristics and can respond positively and appropriately, there are some babies who, by their own biologically rooted characteristics, are more difficult to care for and who contribute to the development of more complex relationships. Temperamentally "difficult" infants are one such group and preterm babies are another.

TEMPERAMENT. Temperamental "difficultness" was identified by Thomas and Chess (1977) as a syndrome of characteristics that includes high activity level, intense emotional reactions, difficulty in adapting to change, arhythmic biological patterns, and generally negative mood. Although it is reasonable to assume that such an infant would affect the parent–child relationship adversely, a direct causal association between differences in infant temperament and parental behavior has not been found (Bates, 1987).

Most measures of temperament rely on maternal report and are confounded by influences stemming from the mother's own individuality (Crockenberg, 1986). For example, there is evidence that a mother's perception of her infant is related to characteristics in her that existed prior to the infant's birth (Heinicke, 1984; Heinicke, Diskin, Ramsey-Klee, & Given, 1983; Sameroff, Seifer, & Elias, 1982; Vaughn, Deinard, & Egeland, 1980). Moreover, any relation between temperament and later parental behavior may be an effect of prior maternal behavior rather than a cause of maternal behavior (Washington, Minde, & Goldberg, 1986). A child's noncompliance, anger, or lack of confidence, for example, may result more from the mother's behavior and attribution than the child's intrinsic temperament.

Studies that seek to describe infant characteristics independent of parent perception and prior to any influence of their relationship show only a weak link between neonatal characteristics (rated by an objective observer) and the evolving parent–child relationship. That is, biologically rooted characteristics do not lead to an altered relationship or to altered developmental patterns unless other risk factors impinge on the parent (Crockenberg, 1986; Crockenberg & McClusky, 1986; Sroufe, 1985). One series of investigations (Crockenberg, 1981) found that an increased likelihood of maternal insensitivity at 12 months was jointly determined by both negative prenatal attitudes and increased newborn irritability, as assessed by the Neonatal Behavorial Assessment Scale. (Brazelton, 1979). Infant irritability only resulted in later insecure attachment if mothers reported little social support. When adolescent mothers experienced both rejection during their own childhood and limited support from their partners after the birth of their babies, they were likely to show punitive parenting regardless of the irritability of the infant, and their children were more likely to be angry and non-compliant. If, in addition, the children were irritable at 3 months, then they were particularly vulnerable to adverse parenting, and were more likely to be angry and noncompliant and to show less confidence than less irritable infants exposed to the same kind of parenting (Crockenberg, 1987). Although the development of the parent–child relationship is complex, these studies suggest that it is likely that temperamental characteristics contribute to differential vulnerability to adverse circumstances among infants.

PRETERM BIRTH. Preterm infants and their parents are a widely studied risk group for whom a variety of intervention efforts have been developed (Korner, 1987). Preterm infants often differ from full-term babies in ways that make early interactions with their parents more difficult and less satisfying. In the early months, preterm infants tend to be less alert and responsive, show poorer motor coordination, are often more irritable or drowsy, and may have a different cry (Field, 1977; Frodi et al., 1978; Goldberg, 1978). A few months later, many preterm infants are more likely than full-term infants to fuss or gaze avert, and are less likely to smile during face-to-face interactions (Crnic, Ragozin, Greenberg, Robinson, & Basham, 1983; Field, 1977, 1982). In studies of face-to-face interactions at 3 and 5 months, term dyads have shown higher coherence of affective involvement and more adaptive periodicities of the rhythms of social interaction than have preterm dyads. Term infants are also more likely to lead the interaction than are preterm infants (Lester, Hoffman, & Brazelton, 1985).

Given the differences among infants and the effects on parents of a preterm birth, with its resultant disruption and anxiety about the neonate's immediate survival and long-term development, it is not unexpected that early interactions of preterm infants with their parents differ significantly from those of full-term dyads. The parents of preterm babies often tend to compensate for their infants' deficits and behave more actively with them, even though their response may be less contingent to their infant's cues (Bakeman & Brown, 1980; Crnic et al., 1983; Goldberg, 1978). Further, both infant and mother have been observed to show less enjoyment and decreased positive affect in their interactions (Crnic et al., 1983).

Despite those alterations in the early parent–child relationship, many studies find no significant differences by the end of the first year between preterm and full-term infants in distribution of the major attachment classifications (Frodi & Thompson, 1985; Goldberg, Perrotta, Minde & Corter, 1986) or in patterns of affect expressions, at least in the attachment measure (Frodi & Thompson, 1985). There is conflicting evidence as well, however, that indicates that more preterm than full-term infants are only "marginally secure" (Goldberg et al., 1986) or that more insecure infants of the anxiously resistant type have been found among those infants who had been severely ill in the perinatal period (Plunkett, Meisels, Stiefel, Pasick, & Roloff, 1986; but not in Goldberg et al., 1986). Severely ill preterm infants also showed a greater sensitivity to distress arousal at low levels of stress and were less able to modulate distress once aroused than were infants who had been less ill in the perinatal period (Stiefel, Plunkett, & Meisels, 1987).

There is not yet enough information to be able to reconcile the conflicting findings. But it is evident that preterms are not a homogenous group, and that there are subgroups at high risk, such as infants with severe respiratory illness, who may be more vulnerable to developmental disturbances. Security of attachment may be more fragile in such infants. Early problems, however, may be transitory if the parent adapts to the characteristics of the preterm baby and is able to establish a sensitive, reciprocal caregiving style (Frodi & Thompson, 1985; Brachfeld, Goldberg, & Sloman, 1980). Consequently, persistent differences between preterm and full-term children are less likely to be apparent when preterm children are reared in families that have the emotional resources to compensate for their infants' early interactional deficits (Goldberg, 1977; Plunkett, Klein, & Meisels, 1988). On the other hand, significant differences in affect organization and quality of attachment may persist if preterm infants, particularly those of higher biological risk, are reared in more depleted or stressed homes.

The contribution of the parent

A continuum of parental risk conditions exists that ranges from lack of knowledge to alterations in affect and deficits in judgment. The conditions may be either transitory or persistent, and mild or severe. Risk conditions are usually not unitary, particularly if they persist, but typically include multiple adverse factors. Teenage mothers, for example, are likely not only to lack knowledge, but to be poor and less well educated, to have lower self-esteem, to have more conflicted relationships in their own family of origin, to lack the stable support of a husband, and to place other competing needs above those of the child (Klerman, 1986). Associated risk factors may be as significant in their effects on the developing child as the primary identified risk condition.

This section considers two categories of severe parenting risk: parents who are depressed and parents who maltreat their children. The variety of factors implicated in these conditions, the processes of associated infant–parent relationships, and their consequences for the developmental course of infants and toddlers are examined. These two groups of parents have not been commonly selected as specific targets of early intervention programs. Such programs have traditionally emphasized the facilitation of cognitive performance in infants of economically disadvantaged families, or those considered vulnerable because of preterm birth or biologically based disability. These vulnerable parenting conditions have been selected because of recent interest in the influence of normal and deviant affects on the parent–child relationship, in conjunction with the renewed impetus for preventive intervention strategies to break the cycle of familial transmission in psychopathology.

DEPRESSION. There is increasing evidence that an affective disorder in the parent puts the young child at increased risk for developmental problems. Although genetic vulnerability may be prominent in some families, especially if there is a parent with bipolar illness (Scarr & Kidd, 1983), it is also apparent that a dysfunctional parent–child relationship can result in other constitutional vulnerabilities.

One approach to investigating the parent–child relationships of depressed women has focused on the analysis of structured face-to-face interaction in both spontaneous interchanges and situations in which the mother is asked to simulate a depressive affect. Field (1984, 1987) studied women with symptoms of postpartum depression from a nonclinical sample and found that their infants behaved less positively during spontaneous face-to-face interactions than did infants of nondepressed mothers, and they showed little change during the simulated "depressed" interaction. In contrast, when exposed to the "depressed" sequence, infants of nondepressed mothers either attempted to reinstate a more positive interaction or seemed to be distressed, looked away, and protested. These latter findings were consistent with those of a previous study of normal mothers and infants (Cohn & Tronick, 1983).

In general, the behavior and affect of the infants of depressed mothers appeared to mirror the behavior and affect of their mothers. In spontaneous interactions, depressed mothers showed flat affect and lower activity levels as well as less contingent responses to their infants. They imitated their infants less, engaged in less game playing, and had more neutral facial expressions, yet they looked at and talked to their infants as much as the comparison group (Field, 1987). In their spontaneous interactions, infants of depressed mothers were less active, showed fewer contented expressions, and demonstrated more fussiness (Field, 1987). At birth, the neonates of depressed mothers have been shown to have reduced activity levels and reduced responsiveness to social stimulation, as assessed by the Brazelton Neonatal Behavioral Assessment Scale (Field et al., 1985). Such alterations in newborn responses may represent a genetic transmission of depression or may be a result of elevated stress during pregnancy. It has been suggested that maternal emotional factors may affect the fetus adversely such that it is less competent at birth, thereby intensifying subsequent interaction problems (Sameroff & Chandler, 1975).

Another study used the same research paradigm with women of low social class who had multiple problems, including high levels of chronic depression (Cohn, Matias, Tronick, Connell, & Lyons-Ruth, 1986). During the face-to-face interactions observed in this group, there was more variability in the behavior of the depressed mothers than had been expected. Although they were not uniformly withdrawn and muted in their range of affects, their expressions of positive affect were lower than in normal mothers and there was a general lack of contingent responsiveness. Some depressed mothers actually showed high levels of engagement, but primarily in the form of intrusive or angry behavior not seen in normal mothers. These angry and depressed mothers, when observed under spontaneous and more naturalistic conditions, tended to avoid their infants and initiated few interactions with them. The infants, too, were withdrawn and seldom showed positive affect. This same sample of women, when seen during naturalistic home observations when their infants were 12 months of age, showed significantly more covert hostility and interference with their infants' goal-directed behavior than normal controls (Lyons-Ruth, Zoll, Connell, & Grunebaum, 1986).

These studies indicate that there are several patterns of parent–child interaction among depressed mothers, perhaps dependent upon differences in chronicity, severity, or other risk factors. One pattern is characterized by flattened affect, reduced energy level, and social withdrawal. Another pattern is more overtly negative, and accompanied by hostility and interference. There may be yet another subgroup whose behavior is labile, alternating between disengagement and intrusive overstimulation (Lyons-Ruth et al., 1986). Thus, the depressed parent may provide too few or insufficiently contingent interactions, may be withdrawn emotionally, may be hostile, or may be available inconsistently. All of these behaviors can impede an infant's sense of control, pleasure, and felt security in the relationship (Tronick & Gianino, 1986).

Additionally, a child may be affected by the parent's own feelings of depression and anger through contagion of negative affects.

In an important study of infants of chronically ill women with schizophrenia, it was found that mothers with neurotic-depressive disorders, who were included as one of the comparison groups, actually fostered worse development in their children than mothers with schizophrenia or with personality disorders (Sameroff, Seifer, & Zax, 1982). Whereas there were few differences between the schizophrenic group and the normative control group, the neurotic-depressive group showed significant differences from the controls. Their infants had the worst obstetric histories and poorest newborn functioning. These mothers with neurotic-depressive disorders showed the least involvement with their infants at 4 months, and their infants were the least sociable with others. No differences were found among groups at 12 months, but at 30 months the mothers with neurotic depression reported their children to be less cooperative, more depressed, and emotionally more bizarre. The authors suggest that the affective quality of the parent–child relationship, particularly the withdrawal and depression, may have the most salient influence on the mothers' interactions with their infants. In general, however, the severity and chronicity of maternal psychopathology had more impact on the child's development than the specific diagnosis.

Research suggests that infants and toddlers are at risk for developmental problems of affect disturbance, insecure attachment, and lowered cognitive performance when at least one parent has a psychiatric history of depression (Tronick & Field, 1986). Children from families with bipolar affective disorders evidence even more problems. They have been shown to demonstrate more frequent and more intense aggression toward their peers despite their engagement in less peer interaction than was recorded for control children. They showed heightened upset during conflicts involving others but little pleasure after the conflict was resolved (Zahn-Waxler, Cummings, McKnew, & Radke-Yarrow, 1984). These same children showed more fear in free play situations, as well as greater anger in free play, in testing, and in response to the approach of a stranger (Gaensbauer, Harmon, Cytryn, & McKnew, 1984).

Insecure patterns of attachment have been documented to be more common among children of mothers with a major depression (bipolar or unipolar) than among children of mothers with minor or no depression. Moreover, atypical insecure attachments, in which the infant shifts from anxious-avoidant to anxious-resistant behavior, were found when mothers had histories of severe depression. Nevertheless, there are children of depressed mothers who do not show insecure attachments and children of normal mothers who do (Gaensbauer et al., 1984; Radke-Yarrow, Cummings, Kuczynski, & Chapman, 1985).

Although there is strong evidence for a genetic component in the depressive disorders, particularly for bipolar manic-depressive illness, most investigators have described multiple causal elements. The causal factors include, but are not restricted to, vulnerability in the infant, which is potentiated by the altered behavior and affect of the parent–child relationship. Intervention for mothers with mental illness buffers their infants' development (Musick, Stott, Spencer, Goldman, & Cohler, 1986) and facilitates significant increases in DQ/IQ. Those children who show the greatest gains generally have mothers who show more positive affect and emotional availability, are less self-involved and have friends, are more "likeable," and are actively willing to share the care of their child with other nurturing adults.

MALTREATMENT. Maltreatment represents a breakdown in the basic function of parenting, which is protection of the child. Abuse of children is defined within each culture and can include many forms, including physical battering, neglect (not providing adequate food, medical care, or adult supervision) and (in some parts of the United States) maternal use of illegal drugs during pregnancy. Although it is reasonable to propose that various types of maltreatment may affect a child's development differentially, it has been difficult to delineate types of maltreatment because physical injury, emotional mistreatment, and physical neglect often occur simultaneously (Schneider-Rosen, Braunwald, Carlson, & Cicchetti, 1985). Abused children also have poorer medical care; they lack immunizations, receive erratic treatment for illness (Martin, 1980), and may be in poorer health from inadequate nutrition, anemia, and from neglect of physical care by their parents. Moreover, although the actual perpetrator of the abuse is probably significant with respect to the child's attachment relationships, most studies focus on the mother–child relationship, regardless of the perpetrator.

It is clear that such adverse life situations as poverty, other sources of chronic stress, and lack of social supports may so deplete parental psychological resources that assault or neglect of children is possible (Garbarino & Gilliam, 1980; Parke & Tinsley, 1987). However, most parents who experience a high degree of stress do not abuse their children. A comparison of parents under high stress who did and did not abuse their children found that maltreatment was more likely if the parents had a history of violence in their own childhood or experienced concurrent interspousal violence, and if they had few satisfying social supports (e.g., an unrewarding marriage, no organizational affliations, and rare or no attendence at religious services) (Straus, 1980).

In a study of the social networks of mothers reported to have abused, neglected, and/or marginally maltreated their children, Crittenden (1985) found that adequate mothers had far more support and longer-lasting and more satisfying social relationships than mothers in the group characterized by either neglect or maltreatment. It was not true, however, that all maltreating families were isolated; rather, some had extensive contact with network members but did not form long-term reciprocal relationships. Women who neglected their children had mainly short-term friendships, infrequent contact with friends, very frequent contact with relatives, and dissatisfaction with the dependability of their supports.

Many parents who abuse their children report that they themselves were maltreated during their own childhood. Rutter and Quinton (1984) conclude that serious aberrations in parenting rarely arise without previous childhood adversities. They suggest that parents who maltreat their children are following predictable patterns of parent–child interaction that were basically determined by the way they themselves were cared for in early childhood. Yet it still must be explained why some families show intergenerational recurrence of abuse while others do not, and why some children who have grown up in a family with an abusing parent become abusive themselves while their siblings do not.

In an extensive analysis of the literature on personality characteristics of parents who maltreat their children, Parke and Collmer (1975) pointed out that it has been difficult to isolate a consistent set of specific and unique traits. Moreover, there is only a limited correlation between personality traits and actual parental behavior. One important study examined parent characteristics before the birth of a child who was later abused or neglected. Prenatally and at 3 months after birth, women who were later to maltreat their children scored lower on an intelligence test and showed higher aggression, defensiveness, and anxiety, lower social desirability, and lower encouragement of reciprocity in comparison to mothers who provided nurturant care despite poverty and stress. Mothers who eventually abused their children also responded negatively to the experience of pregnancy, and were more likely to describe themselves in disparaging terms (Brunquell, Crichton, Egeland, 1981; Egeland, Breitenbucher, & Rosenberg, 1980).

A review of the research literature on fathers who abuse their children highlights similarities in personality profiles to those of mothers who commit comparable acts. Social isolation, poor marital adjustment, unmanageable stress, low self-esteem, and a history of having been abused are important determinants of paternal as well as maternal child abuse (Tyler, 1986).

Attempts at early identification have been built on the previously discussed research, and have been successful statistically in identifying potential abusive parents. However, there is considerable risk of false positives (e.g., Gray, Cutler, Dean, & Kempe, 1977). In fact, child abuse is a relatively rare occurrence that is multiply determined, and parents who abuse their children overlap in personality characteristics and childhood histories with parents who do not.

There is growing evidence that parents who maltreat their children show deviant parental behavior and affect in many circumstances. Such mothers express more anger and annoyance and less sympathy in response to videotapes of crying infants than do those mothers who refrain from abuse (Frodi & Lamb, 1980). They are more likely to identify affect expressions incorrectly when shown slides of infants reflecting different emotional states (Kropp & Haynes, 1987).

Mothers who abuse their children tend to be extremely insensitive to them during infancy. Such mothers interfere insensitively with their infants' goal-directed behavior more frequently, and display more instances of covert hostility (Crittenden & Bonvillian, 1984; Lyons-Ruth, Connell, Zoll, & Stahl, 1987). Mothers who neglect their children more often show decreased interaction, including greater physical distance from the child, absence of affect expression, long pauses between conversational initiatives, and decreased eye contact. Normative mothers, on the other hand, are more responsive contingently to their infants, show more affectionate behavior, and demonstrate enjoyment of and responsiveness to their infants' goals (Crittenden & Bonvillian, 1984). Mothers who abuse their children also differ in the control techniques they use with their preschoolers. Compared to a normative group, abusive mothers use more commands, and more power-assertive and less positively oriented control strategies. They have been shown to be more intrusive and inconsistent in their use of techniques, to display more flattened affect throughout their interactions, and to be less flexible in their attempts to gain compliance from the child (Oldershaw, Walters, & Hall, 1986).

Some investigators suggest that the infant may contribute to his or her own abuse through those physical and/or behavioral characteristics, such as prematurity and difficult temperament (e.g., irritability and lack of clarity of cues), that make parenting more difficult (Parke & Collmer, 1975). Klaus and Kennell (1976) hypothesized that a premature child, with all of his or her attendant problems, may overtax the limited resources of some mothers. Furthermore, they suggested that underlying problems may result from early, prolonged separation, which can further impair the affectional tie of overstressed parents to their infant. Although the data on the effects of separation on later parenting of preterms are not persuasive (Lamb & Hwang, 1982), there is some evidence that a short period between birth and the initial contact between a mother and her full-term infant may buffer later parenting stresses (Vietze, Falsey, Sandler, O'Connor, & Altemeier, 1980).

In a study based on the work of Klaus and Kennell, parents at high risk for maltreating their infants were identified, and their newborns were randomly assigned to either a rooming-in group or a control group that was separated from their mothers until at least 12 hours after delivery (Vietze et al., 1980). Later maltreatment was reported for 1 of 143 rooming-in mothers and 9 of 158 control mothers, which represents a significant difference. The findings suggest that early contact does affect parents who are already predisposed to maltreatment. In contrast, those with greater resources may adapt to early separation from their infants with little difficulty.

Parents who abuse their children describe them as more irritable and more difficult to manage (Maccoby & Martin, 1983). It may also be that children who are abused send unclear social cues and are low in responsiveness (Bee, Disbrow, Johnson, Crowley, & Barnard, 1981). Further, maltreated children have been described as significantly more aggressive, frustrated, and noncompliant, and as demonstrating less positive affect than control children (Egeland & Sroufe, 1981). It may be that children who are maltreated are temperamentally more difficult; however, their noxious characteristics could be outcomes rather than causes of the abusive patterns found within their families (Belsky, 1981; Maccoby & Martin, 1983).

In 1975, Sameroff and Chandler reported that there were very few studies of the subsequent development of infants who had been abused. At that time, most of the data came from clinical descriptions. Recently, however, there have been a growing number of systematic studies with appropriate control groups. Most have examined quality of attachment (Egeland & Sroufe, 1981), parent–child interaction either in the laboratory (Egeland & Sroufe, 1981) or in the home (Burgess & Conger, 1978), or behavior at day-care centers (George & Main, 1979; Herrenkohl, Herrenkohl, & Toedter, 1983; Lewis & Schaeffer, 1981).

The preponderance of research clearly indicates that maltreatment is associated with insecure attachment to the mother (Egeland & Sroufe, 1981; Lamb, Gaensbauer, Malkin, & Schultz, 1985; Lyons-Ruth et al., 1987; Schneider-Rosen et al., 1985) or to the foster mother, but not if the source of maltreatment was someone other than the biological mother (Lamb et al., 1985). Most investigators have reported an increase in insecure avoidance (Lyons-Ruth et al., 1987; Schneider-Rosen et al., 1985); others have found more anxious resistance (Egeland & Sroufe, 1981; Schneider-Rosen et al., 1985); and still others have indicated the need for a new, atypical classification of both avoidance and resistance to describe infants who have been abused (Crittenden, 1985; Lyons-Ruth et al., 1987). Thus, the attachment behaviors of infants who have been maltreated may be organized so differently from those found in less disturbed relationships that the usual classifications do not fit.

Some infants who have been maltreated are able to form secure attachment relationships with their parents, although these tend to be unstable over time (Schneider-Rosen et al., 1985). It is not clear what it means to have a secure attachment under such conditions, nor is it known how much the abusing conditions modify the felt security.

Young children who have been abused have also been found to be more likely to respond to frustration with aggression (Herrenkohl et al., 1983), or to be more physically aggressive with their peers. They were found also to assault or threaten to assault caregivers, a behavior that was not observed in any control children. Children who have been abused avoid other children and avoid adult caregivers many times more often than controls (George & Main, 1979). In a follow-up study of preschool playmates, five pairs were identified in which one child victimized or exploited the other (e.g., hitting when the partner indicated an area of soreness; demonstrating sarcasm, derogation, and hostility; lying on top of the partner and not letting up). In each case, the victimizing child has been identified previously as having experienced abuse from a parent (Sroufe & Fleeson, 1986).

When observed in day-care settings, non-abused toddlers from disadvantaged, stressed families responded to the distress of their peers with interest or with concern, empathy, or sadness, consistent with studies of middle-class non-abused children. However, not one toddler who had been abused showed concern in response to the distress of another child. Instead, abused toddlers were likely to react to another's distress with physical attacks, fear, or anger, all behaviors not seen in a comparison group. A significant minority of the abused toddlers alternately attacked and attempted to comfort their peers in distress (Main & George, 1985).

There is growing evidence that toddlers who have been maltreated develop altered self-systems. Whereas most children react positively when they see themselves with rouge on their noses in a mirror, the majority of youngsters with histories of maltreatment show neutral or negative affect (Cicchetti & Schneider-Rosen, 1984). Further investigation of the development of the self-system, as it begins to be represented symbolically, shows that toddlers who have been maltreated talk less about their feelings or about the feelings of others than does a comparison group (Cicchetti & Beeghly, 1987). In both studies, youngsters who have been abused experience themselves in muted ways.

Available research has begun to detail the process by which an intergenerational cycle of abuse develops. It describes the abusive parent's behavior and the developing behavior of the child who is abused. The latter is often characterized by avoidance of persons who make friendly overtures; threatening and abusive behavior exhibited by the child; frequent response to others' distress with anger, fear, hostility, and nonconcern; and a tendency to experience oneself in negative or muted ways. (For a more extensive discussion of maltreatment, see Cicchetti & Carlson, 1987.)

IMPLICATIONS FOR INTERVENTION AND CONCLUSIONS

Two intriguing questions for the field of early intervention are Which parents and infants can be helped? and Which deficits in the parent–child relationship can be altered? Although it would be exceedingly useful to be able to answer these questions, existing data are too sparse. Mechanisms for change, who changes, and how that change takes place are not yet clear. A large and rapidly growing body of literature, however, suggests the following observations.

   1. Some families are so disordered that basic survival goals, – securing adequate nutrition and medical care, providing a safe environment with opportunities for exploration, providing appropriate child care, and reducing family violence – must be set before goals of sensitivity, reciprocity, or even security of attachment can be pursued.

   2. Cognitive training may be quite insufficient as a means of intervention for many families, given the primacy of affect in the parent–child relationship and the multiple factors that contribute to that relationship.

   3. Since the parent–infant relationship is affected by contextual sources of stress and support, intervention may be needed to help with broader ecological issues such as social services, job training, and child care for other siblings. A recent report of an intervention that provided such services, in addition to its focus on the parent–infant relationship, indicated long-lasting influences (Seitz, Rosenbaum, & Apfel, 1985).

   4. For some families, intervention may have to be provided directly to the child in order to supplement work with the parents.

   5. The fact that a parent's relationships with other significant persons affect the parent–child relationship implies that some intervention services may have to focus

on marital relationships, an area in which child development interventionists are often not skilled. For example, Minde and his colleagues (1983) relied on parent support groups in their intervention with parents of preterm infants, but found that the intervention group fostered more optimum development in the children at the cost of more marital divorce and separation. In this case, Minde suggests that the intervention helped disentangle nonsupportive spousal relationships that were interfering with the mother–infant relationship.

6. Intervention may affect parental attentiveness, and the level of animate and inanimate stimulation offered to the child, before it affects sensitivity. The child effects may then be seen in increases in intellectual performances, but not in security of attachment or affect regulation.

7. Rather than a singular focus on the development of the child as the primary measurement of intervention efficacy, it may be useful to measure changes in the family, both in parental competence and in improved relationships within the family (Heinicke, Beckwith, & Thompson, 1988). A recent intervention study, for example, did just that (Seitz et al., 1985). It was found that mothers who had received interventions completed more years of education, waited longer to have a second child, were more likely to become self-supporting and to maintain a nuclear family, and made greater use of remedial and supportive community services. Intervention did not produce lasting cognitive change in the children. But intervention children needed fewer special services, were better adjusted socially, were more cooperative, were happier, and got along better with other children. It is likely that the link between the intervention and the children's better school and social adjustment was mediated by the improved family functioning.

8. There is recent evidence that indicates that variation in parental intervention experience affects the efficacy of the intervention (Belsky, 1986; Worobey & Brazelton, 1986). Interventions differ in how they are delivered and how they are received. Qualities of the parent–child relationship that foster more optimum development in children (e.g., positive affect, sensitivity, and emotional availability) facilitate better rapport and involvement between parent and intervenor and thereby enhance the parental intervention experience.

9. Parenting is not a matter of hard-and-fast rules. To be a good enough parent is to project oneself into the child's world and at the same time try to understand one's own feelings and goals (Bettelheim, 1987). In order to understand the meaning of events to a child, it is helpful for parents to remember what similar events meant to them when they were children. Therefore, it is helpful for intervention to emphasize parents' feelings during their own childhood and parenthood as much as the infant's feelings. This dual emphasis fosters the spontaneity and authenticity of the parent–intervenor and parent–child relationship.

Parent–infant relationships are complex. The parent assumes multiple roles as protector, biological regulator, love object, teacher, and mediator of exploration in the environment. At the same time the parent must also deal with multiple competing and supporting relationships both within and outside the family. The task is demanding, and the responsibility is heavy; yet there are intuitive competencies within the parent and the infant that can be translated into success. The chances of success for risk groups are fostered when the community can provide adequate medical and child care as well as early intervention.

REFERENCES

Ainsworth, M. D. S. (1973). The development of infant–mother attachment. In B. M. Caldwell & H. N. Ricciuti (Eds.), *Review of child development research* (Vol. 3, pp. 1–94). Chicago: University of Chicago Press.

Ainsworth, M. D. S., & Bell, S. M. (1969). Some contemporary patterns of mother–infant interaction in the feeding situation. In A. Ambrose (Ed.), *Stimulation in early infancy* (pp. 133–170). New York: Academic Press.

Ainsworth, M. D. S., Blehar, M., Waters, S. E., & Wall, S. (1978). *Patterns of attachment.* Hillsdale, NJ: L. Erlbaum.

Bakeman, R., & Brown, J. V. (1977). Behavioral dialogues: An approach to the assessment of mother–infant interaction. *Child Development, 48,* 195–203.

Bakeman, R., & Brown, J. V. (1980). Early interaction: Consequences for social and mental development at three years. *Child Development, 51,* 437–447.

Bates, J. E. (1987). Temperament in infancy. In J. D. Osofsky (Ed.), *Handbook of infant development* (2nd ed., pp. 1101–1149). New York: Wiley.

Bates, J. E., Maslin, C. A., & Frankel, K. A. (1985). Attachment security, mother–child interaction, and temperament as predictors of behavior-problem ratings at age three years. In I. Bretherton & E. Waters (Eds.), Growing points of attachment theory and research. *Monographs of the Society for Research in Child Development, 50* (1–2, Serial No. 209).

Beckwith, L. (1976). Caregiver–infant interaction and the development of the high risk infant. In T. D. Tjossem (Ed.), *Intervention strategies for high risk infants and young children* (pp. 119–140). Baltimore: University Park Press.

Beckwith, L., Cohen, S. E., Kopp, C. B., Parmelee, A. H., & Marcy, T. G. (1976). Caregiver–infant interaction and early cognitive development in preterm infants. *Child Development, 47,* 579–587.

Bee, H. L., Disbrow, M. A., Johnson-Crowley, N., & Barnard, K. (1981). *Parent–child interactions during teaching in abusing and non-abusing families.* Paper presented at the meeting of the Society for Research in Child Development, Boston.

Bell, S. M., & Ainsworth, M. D. S. (1972). Infant crying and maternal responsivenss. *Child Development, 43,* 1171–1190.

Belsky, J. (1981). Early human experience: A family perspective. *Developmental Psychology, 17,* 3–23.

Belsky, J. (1984). The determinants of parenting: A process model. *Child Development, 55,* 83–96.

Belsky, J. (1986). A tale of two variances: Between and within. *Child Development, 57,* 1301–1305.

Belsky, J., Gilstrap, B, & Rovine, M. (1984). The Pennsylvania infant and family development project, I: Stability and change in mother–infant and father–infant interaction in a family setting at one, three, and nine months. *Child Development, 55,* 692–705.

Belsky, J., & Isabella, R. A. (1985). Marital and parental–child relationships in family of origin and marital change following the birth of a baby: A retrospective analysis. *Child Development, 56,* 342–349.

Belsky, J., Spanier, G. B., & Rovine, M. (1983). Stability and change in marriage across the transition to parenthood. *Journal of Marriage and the Family, 45,* 567–577.

Bettelheim, B. (1987). *A good enough parent. A book on child rearing.* Near York: Knopf.

Blehar, M., Lieberman, A. F., & Ainsworth, M. (1977). Early face-to-face interaction and its relation to later infant–mother attachment. *Child Development, 48,* 182–194.

Bowlby, J. (1969). *Attachment and loss: Vol. 1. Attachment.* New York: Basic Books.

Bowlby, J. (1973). *Attachment and loss: Vol. 2. Separation, anxiety and anger.* New York: Basic Books.

Brachfeld, S., Goldberg, S., & Sloman, J. (1980). Parent–infant interaction in free play at 8 and 12 months: Effects of prematurity and immaturity. *Infant Behavior and Development, 3,* 289–305.

Bradley, R. H., & Caldwell, B. M. (1984). The relation of infants' home environment to achievement test performance in first grade: A follow-up study. *Child Development, 55,* 803–809.

Brazelton, T. B. (1973). Neonatal behavioral assessment scale. *National Spastics Society Monograph.* Philadelphia: Lippincott.

Brazelton, T. B., & Yogman, M. W. (Eds.). (1986). *Affective development in infancy.* Norwood, NJ: Ablex Publishing.

Bretherton, I., Bates, E., Benigni, L., Camaioni, L., & Volterra, V. (1979). Relationships between cognition, communication, and quality of attachment. In E. Bates, L. Benigni, I. Bretherton, L. Camaion, & V. Volterra (Eds.), *The emergence of symbols: Cognition and communication in infancy* (pp. 223–269). New York: Academic Press.

Bretherton, I., Fritz, J., Zahn-Waxler, C., Ridgeway, D. (1986). Learning to talk about emotions: A functionalist perspective. *Child Development, 57*, 529–548.

Bretherton, I., & Waters, E. (Eds.). (1985). Growing points of attachment theory and research. *Monographs of the Society for Research in Child Development, 50*, (1–2, Serial No. 209).

Brody, S., & Axelrod, S. (1978). *Mothers, fathers, and children: Explorations in the formation of character in the first seven years.* New York: International Universities Press.

Bronfenbrenner, V., Moen, P., & Garbarino, J. (1984). Child, family, and community. In R. D. Parke (Ed.), *Review of child development research* (Vol. 7, pp. 283–328). Chicago: University of Chicago Press.

Bruner, J. S. (1975). The ontogenesis of speech acts. *Journal of Child Language, 2*, 1–19.

Brunquell, E., Crichton, L., & Egeland, B. (1981). Maternal personality and attitude in disturbances of child rearing. *American Journal of Orthopsychiatry, 51*, 680–691.

Burgess, R. L., & Conger, R. D. (1978). Family interaction in abusive, neglectful, and normal families. *Child Development, 49*, 1163–1173.

Campos, J. J., Barrett, K. C., Lamb, M. E., Goldsmith, H. H., & Stenberg, C. (1983). Socioemotional development, In M. Haith & J. J. Campos (Eds.), *Handbook of child psychology: Vol. 2. Infancy and developmental psychobiology* (pp. 783–916). New York: Wiley.

Campos, J. J., & Stenberg, C. (1981). Perception, appraisal and emotion: The onset of social referencing. In M. E. Lamb & L. R. Sherrod (Eds.), *Infant social cognition: Empirical and theoretical considerations* (pp. 273–314). Hillsdale, NJ: L. Erlbaum.

Cicchetti, D., & Beeghly, M. (1987). *Symbolic development in atypical children. New directions for child development.* (Series No. 36). San Francisco: Jossey-Bass.

Cicchetti, D., & Carlson, V. (Eds.). (1987). *The handbook of child maltreatment: Theory, research and intervention.* Cambridge: Cambridge University Press.

Cicchetti, D., & Schneider-Rosen, K. (1984). Toward a transactional model of childhood depression. *New directions for child development* (pp. 5–27). San Francisco: Jossey-Bass.

Clarke-Stewart, A. (1978). And daddy makes three: The father's impact on mother and young child. *Child Development, 49*, 466–478.

Clarke-Stewart, K. A. (1980). The father's contribution to children's cognitive and social development in early childhood. In F. A. Pedersen (Ed.), *The father–infant relationship* (pp. 111–146). New York: Praeger.

Clarke-Stewart, K. A., Vanderstoep, L. P., & Killian, G. A. (1979). Analysis and replication of mother–child relations at two years of age. *Child Development, 50*, 777–793.

Cochran, M. M., & Brassard, J. A. (1979). Child development and personal social networks. *Child Development, 50*, 601–616.

Cohler, B., & Grunebaum, H. (1981). *Mothers, grandmothers, and daughters. Personality and child care in three-generation families.* New York: Wiley.

Cohn, J. F., Matias, R., Tronick, E. Z., Connell, D., & Lyons-Ruth, K. (1986). Face-to-face interactions of depressed mothers and their infants. In E. Z. Tronick & T. Field (Eds.), *Maternal depression and infant disturbance. New directions for child development* (pp. 31–46). San Francisco: Jossey-Bass.

Cohn, J. F., & Tronick, E. Z. (1983). Three-month-old infants' reaction to simulated maternal depression. *Child Development, 54*, 185–193.

Collis, G. M., & Schaffer, H. R. (1975). Synchronization of visual attention in mother–infant pairs *Journal of Child Psychology and Psychiatry, 16*, 315–320.

Crittenden, P. M. (1985). Maltreated infants: Vulnerability and resilience. *Journal of Child Psychology and Psychiatry, 26*, 85–96.

Crittenden, P. M., & Bonvillian, J. D. (1984). The relationship between maternal risk status and maternal sensitivity. *American Journal of Orthopsychiatry, 54*, 250–262.

Crnic, K. A., Greenberg, M. T., Robinson, N. M., & Ragozin, A. S. (1984). Maternal stress and social support: Effects on the mother–infant relationship from birth to eighteen months. *American Journal of Orthopsychiatry, 54*, 224–235.

Crnic, K. A., Ragozin, A. S., Greenberg, M. T., Robinson, N. M., & Basham, R. B. (1983). Social interaction and developmental competence of preterm and full-term infants during the first year of life. *Child Development, 54*, 1199–1210.

Crockenberg, S. B. (1981). Infant irritability, mother responsiveness, and social support influences on the security of infant–mother attachment. *Child Development, 52*, 857–865.

Crockenberg, S. (1986). Are temperamental differences in babies associated with predictable differences in caregiving? In J. V. Lerner & R. M. Lerner (Eds.), *Temperament and psychosocial interaction in infancy and childhood: New directions for Child development* (pp. 53–72). San Francisco: Jossey-Bass.

Crockenberg, S. (1987). Predictors and correlates of anger toward and punitive control of toddlers by adolescent mothers. *Child Development, 58*, 964–975.

Crockenberg, S., & McClusky, K. (1986). Changes in maternal behavior during the baby's first year of life. *Child Development, 57*, 746–753.

Cummings, E. M., Ianotti, R. J., & Zahn-Waxler, C. (1985). Influence of conflict between adults on the emotions and aggression of young children. *Developmental Psychology, 21*, 495–507.

Cummings, E. M., Zahn-Waxler, C., & Radke-Yarrow, M. (1981). Young children's responses to expressions of anger and affection by others in the family. *Child Development, 52*, 1274–1282.

Dunn, J., & Kendrick, C. (1982). *Siblings: Love, envy and understanding.* Cambridge: Harvard University Press.

Dunn, J. F., & Munn, P. (1985). Becoming a family member: Family conflict and the development of social understanding in the second year. *Child Development, 56*, 480–492.

Egeland, B., Breitenbucher, M., & Rosenberg, D. (1980). Prospective study of the significance of life stress in the etiology of child abuse. *Journal of Consulting and Clinical Psychology, 48*, 195–205.

Egeland, B., & Farber, E. A. (1984). Infant–mother attachment: Factors related to its development and changes over time. *Child Development, 55*, 753–771.

Egeland, B., & Stroufe, L. A. (1981). Attachment and early maltreatment. *Child Development, 52*, 44–52.

Emde, R. N. (1980). Emotion availability: A reciprocal reward system for infants and parents with implications for prevention of psychosocial disorders. In P. M. Taylor (Ed.), *Parent–infant relationships* (pp. 87–115). New York: Grune & Stratton.

Emde, R. N. (1987). Infant mental health: Clinical dilemmas, the expansion of meaning, and opportunities. In J. D. Osofsky (Ed.), *Handbook of infant development* (pp. 1297–1320). New York: Wiley.

Erickson, M. F., & Crichton, L. (1981). *Antecedents of compliance in two-year-olds from a high risk sample.* Paper presented at the Biennial meeting of the Society for Research in Child Development, Boston.

Feinman, S., & Lewis, M. (1983). Social references at 10 months: A second-order effect on infants' responses to strangers. *Child Development, 54*, 878–887.

Feiring, C., Lewis, M., & Starr, M. D. (1984). Indirect effects and infants' reaction to strangers. *Developmental Psychology, 20*, 485–491.

Field, T. M. (1977). Effects of early separation, interactive deficits, and experimental manipulations on infant–mother face-to-face interaction. *Child Development, 48*, 763–771.

Field, T. M. (1982). Individual differences in the expressivity of neonates and young infants. In R. Feldman (Ed.), *Development of nonverbal behavior in children* (pp. 279–298). New York: Springer-Verlag.

Field, T. (1984). Early interactions between infants and their postpartum depressed mothers. *Infant Behavior & Development, 7*, 527–532.

Field, T. (1987). Affective and interactive disturbances in infants. In J. D. Osofsky (Ed.), *Handbook of infant development* (pp. 972–1005). New York: Wiley.

Field, T., Sandberg, D., Garcia, R., Vega-Lahr, N., Goldstein, S., Guy, L. (1985). Pregnancy problems, postpartum depression and early mother–infant interactions. *Developmental Psychology, 21*, 1152–1156.

Frodi, A. M., Lamb, M. E., Leavitt, L. A., Donovan, W. L., Neff, C., & Sherry, D. (1978). Fathers' and mothers' responses to the faces and cries of normal and premature infants. *Developmental Psychology, 14*, 490–498.

Frodi, A. M., & Lamb, M. E. (1980). Child abusers' responses to infant smiles and cries. *Child Development, 51*, 238–241.

Frodi, A., & Thompson, R. (1985). Infants' affective responses in the strange situation: Effects of prematurity and of quality of attachment. *Child Development, 56*, 1280–1291.

Furstenberg, F. F., Jr. (1985). Sociological ventures in child development. *Child Development, 56*, 281–288.

Gaensbauer, T. J., Harmon, R. J., Cytryn, L., & McKnew, D. H. (1984). Social and affective development in infants with a manic-depressive parent. *American Journal of Psychiatry, 141,* 223–229.

Garbarino, J., & Gilliam, G. (1980). *Understanding abusive families.* Lexington, MA: Lexington Press.

George, C., & Main, M. (1979). Social interactions of young abused children: Approach, avoidance, and aggression. *Child Development, 50,* 306–318.

Goldberg, S. (1977). Social competence in infancy: A model of parent–infant interaction. *Merril-Palmer Quarterly, 23,* 163–177.

Goldberg, S. (1978). Prematurity: Effects on parent–infant interaction. *Journal of Pediatric Psychology, 3,* 137–144.

Goldberg, S., Perrotta, M., Minde, K., & Corter, C. (1986). Maternal behaviors and attachment in low-birth-weight twins and singletons. *Child Development, 57,* 34–46.

Goldberg, W. A., & Easterbrooks, M. A. (1984). Role of marital quality in toddler development. *Developmental Psychology, 20,* 504–514.

Gray, J. D., Cutler, C., Dean, J., & Kempe, C. H. (1977). Prediction and prevention of child abuse and neglect. *Child Abuse and Neglect, 1,* 45–58.

Grossman, K., Grossman, K. E., Spangler, G., Suess, G., & Unzner, L. (1985). Maternal sensitivity and newborns' orientation responses as related to quality of attachment in northern Germany. In I. Bretherton & E. Waters (Eds.), Growing points of attachment theory and research. *Monographs of the Society for Research in Child Development, 50* (1–2, Serial No. 209).

Heinicke, C. M. (1984). Impact of prebirth parent personality and marital functioning on family development: A framework and suggestions for further study. *Developmental Psychology, 20,* 1044–1053.

Heinicke, C. M., Beckwith, L., & Thompson, A. (1988). Early intervention in the family systems: A framework and review. *Infant Mental Health Journal, 9,* 111–141.

Heinicke, C., Diskin, S., Ramsey-Klee, D., & Given, K. (1983). Prebirth characteristics and family development in the first year of life. *Child Development, 54,* 194–208.

Herrenkohl, E., Herrenkohl, R., & Toedter, L. (1983). Perspectives on the intergenerational transmission of abuse. In D. Finkelor, R. Gelles, G. Hotaling, & M. Straus (Eds.), *The dark side of families: Current family violence research* (pp. 305–316). Beverly Hills: Sage.

Hornik, R., Risenhoover, N., & Gunnar, M. (1987). The effects of maternal positive, neutral, and negative affective communications on infant responses to new toys. *Child Development, 58,* 937–945.

Klaus, M. H., & Kennell, J. H. (1976). *Maternal–infant bonding.* St. Louis: Mosby.

Klerman, L. V. (1986). Teenage pregnancy. In M. W. Yogman & T. B. Brazelton (Eds.), *In support of families* (pp. 211–223). Cambridge: Harvard University Press.

Korner, A. F. (1987). Prevention intervention with high-risk newborns: Theoretical, conceptual and methodological perspectives. In J. D. Osofsky (Ed.), *Handbook of infant development* (pp. 1006–1036). New York: Wiley.

Kotelchuck, M. (1976). The infant's relationships to the father: Experimental evidence. In M. E. Lamb (Ed.), *The role of the father in child development* (pp. 329–344). New York: Wiley.

Kropp, J. P., & Haynes, O. M. (1987). Abusive and nonabusive mothers' ability to identify general and specific emotion signals of infants. *Child Development, 58,* 187–190.

Lamb, M. E. (Ed.). (1981). *The role of the father in child development* (2nd ed.). New York: Wiley.

Lamb, M. E., & Easterbrooks, M. A. (1981). Individual differences in parental sensitivity: Some thoughts about origins, components and consequences. In M. E. Lamb & L. R. Sherrod (Eds.), *Infant social cognition: Empirical and theoretical considerations* (pp. 127–153). Hillsdale, NJ: L. Erlbaum.

Lamb, M. E., Gaensbauer, T. J., Malkin, C. M., & Schultz, L. A. (1985). The effects of child maltreatment on security of infant-adult attachment. *Infant Behavior and Development, 8,* 35–45.

Lamb, M. E., & Hwang, C. (1982). Maternal attachment and mother–infant bonding: critical review. In M. E. Lamb & A. L. Brown (Eds.), *Advances in developmental psychology* (Vol. 2, pp. 1–39). Hillsdale, NJ: L. Erlbaum.

Lester, B. M., Hoffman, J., & Brazelton, T. B. (1985). The rhythmic structure of mother–infant interaction in term and preterm infants. *Child Development, 56,* 15–27.

Lewis, M. (1987). Social development in infancy and early childhood. In J. D. Osofsky (Ed.), *Handbook of infant development* (pp. 419–493). New York: Wiley.

Lewis, M., & Goldberg, S. (1969). Perceptual-cognitive development in infancy: A generalized expectancy model as a function of the mother–infant interaction. *Merrill-Palmer Quarterly, 15,* 81–100.

Lewis, M., Schaeffer, S. (1981). Peer behavior and mother–infant interaction in maltreated children. In M. Lewis & L. Rosenblum (Eds.), *The uncommon child* (pp. 193–223). New York: Plenum.

Lewis, M., & Weintraub, M. (1976). The father's role in the infant's social network. In M. Lamb (Ed.), *The role of the father in child development* (pp. 157–184). New York: Wiley.

Londerville, S., & Main, M. (1981). Security of attachment, compliance and maternal training methods in the second year of life. *Developmental Psychology, 17,* 289–299.

Lyons-Ruth, K., Connell, D. B., Zoll, D., & Stahl, J. (1987). Infants at social risk: Relations among infant maltreatment, maternal behavior, and infant attachment behavior. *Developmental Psychology, 23,* 223–232.

Lyons-Ruth, K., Zoll, D., Connell, D., & Grunebaum, H. (1986). The depressed mother and her one-year-old infant: Environmental context, mother–infant interaction and attachment, and infant development. In E. Tronick & T. Field (Eds.), *Maternal depression and infant disturbances. New directions for child development* (pp. 61–82). San Francisco: Jossey-Bass.

Maccoby, E. E., & Martin, J. A. (1983). Socialization in the context of the family: Parent–child interaction. In E. M. Hetherington (Ed.), *Handbook of child psychology: Vol. 4. Socialization, personality, and social development* (pp. 1–101). New York: Wiley.

Main, M. (1973). *Exploration, play, and cognitive functioning as related to mother–child attachment.* Unpublished doctoral dissertation, Johns Hopkins University, Baltimore.

Main, M., & George, C. (1985). Responses of abused and disadvantaged toddlers to distress in age mates: A study in the day-care setting. *Developmental Psychology, 21,* 407–412.

Main, M., Kaplan, N., & Cassidy, J. (1985). Security in infancy, childhood, and adulthood: A move to the level of representation. In I. Bretherton & E. Waters (Eds.), *Growing points of attachment theory and research. Monographs of the Society for Research in Child Development, 50* (1–2, Serial No. 209).

Main, M., & Weston, D. (1981). The quality of the toddler's relationship to mother and father: Related to conflict behaviors and the readiness to establish new relationships. *Child Development, 52,* 932–940.

Malatesta, C. Z., & Izard, C. E. (1984). The ontogenesis of human social signals: From biological imperative to symbols utilization. In N. A. Fox & R. J. Davidson (Eds.), *The psychobiology of affective development.* Hillsdale, NJ: L. Erlbaum.

Martin, H. P. (1980). The consequences of being abused and neglected: How the child fares. In C. H. Kempe & R. E. Helfer (Eds.), *The battered child* (pp. 347–365). Chicago: University of Chicago Press.

Matas, L., Arend, R., & Sroufe, L. A. (1978). Continuity of adaptation in the second year: The relationship between quality of attachment and later competence. *Child Development, 49,* 547–556.

Minde, K., Shosenberg, N., & Thompson, J. (1983). Self-help groups in a premature nursery-infant behavior and parental competence one year later. In E. Galenson & J. Call (Eds.), *Frontiers of infant psychiatry* (pp. 264–271) New York: Basic Books.

Minuchin, P. (1985). Families and individual development: Provocations from the field of family therapy. *Child Development, 56,* 289–302.

Musick, J. S., Stott, F. M., Spencer, K. K., Goldman, J., & Cohler, B. J. (1986). Maternal factors related to vulnerability and resilience in young children at risk. In E. J. Anthony & B. Cohler (Eds.), *The invulnerable child.* New York: Guilford Press.

O'Connell, B., & Bretherton, I. (1984). Toddler's play, alone and with mother: The role of maternal guidance. In I. Bretherton (Ed.), *Symbolic play* (pp. 337–366). Orlando: Academic Press.

Oldershaw, L., Walters, G. D., & Hall, D. K. (1986). Control strategies and noncompliance in abusive mother–child dyads: An observational study. *Child Development, 57,* 722–732.

Osofsky, J. D., & Osofsky, H. J. (1984). Psychological and developmental perspectives on expectant and new parenthood. In R. D. Parke, R. N. Emde, H. P. McAdoo, & G. P. Sackett (Eds.), *Review of child development research* (Vol. 7, pp. 372–397). Chicago: University of Chicago Press.

Papousek, H., & Papousek, M. (1987). Intuitive parenting: A dialectic counterpart to the infant's integrative competence. In J. D. Osofsky (Ed.), *Handbook of infant development* (pp. 669–720). New York: Wiley.

Parke, R. D., & Collmer, C. W. (1975). Child abuse: An interdisciplinary analysis. In E. M. Hetherington (Ed.), *Review of child development research* (Vol. 5, pp. 509–590). Chicago: University of Chicago Press.

Parke, R. D., & Tinsley, B. J. (1987). Family interaction in infancy. In J. D. Osofsky (Ed.), *Handbook of infant development* (pp. 579–641). New York: Wiley.

Parpal, M., & Maccoby, E. E. (1985). Maternal responsiveness and subsequent child compliance. *Child Development, 56*, 1326–1334.

Pastor, D.L. (1981). The quality of mother–infant attachment and its relationships to toddlers' initial sociability with peers. *Developmental Psychology, 17*, 326–335.

Plunkett, J. W., Klein, T., Meisels, S. J. (1988). The relationship of preterm infant–mother attachment to stranger sociability at three years. *Infant Behavior and Development, 11*, 83–96.

Plunkett, J. M., Meisels, S. J., Stiefel, G. S., Pasick, P. L., & Roloff, D. W. (1986). Patterns of attachment among preterm infants of varying biological risk. *Journal of the American Academy of Child Psychiatry, 25*, 794–800.

Radke-Yarrow, M., Cummings, E. M., Kuczynski, L., & Chapman, M. (1985). Patterns of attachment in two- and three-year-olds in normal families and families with parental depression. *Child Development, 56*, 884–893.

Ricks, M. H. (1985). The social transmission of parental behaviors: Attachment across generations. In E. Bretherton & E. Waters (Eds.), Growing points of attachment theory and research. *Monographs of the Society for Research in Child Development, 50* (1–2, Serial No. 209).

Rutter, M. (1987). Continuities and discontinuities from infancy. In J. D. Osofsky (Ed.), *Handbook of infant development* (pp. 1256–1296). New York: Wiley.

Rutter, M., & Quinton, D. (1984). Parental psychiatric disorder: Effects on children. *Psychological Medicine, 14*, 853–880.

Sameroff, A. J., & Chandler, M. (1975). Reproductive risk and the continuum of caretaking casualty. In F. D. Horowitz, M. Hetherington, S. Scarr-Salapatek, & G. Siegel (Eds.), *Review of child development research* (Vol. 4, pp. 187–244). Chicago: University of Chicago Press.

Sameroff, A. J., & Feil, L. A. (1985). Parental concepts of development. In I. E. Sigal (Ed.), *Parental belief systems. The psychological consequences for children* (pp. 83–105). Hillsdale, NJ: L. Erlbaum.

Sameroff, A. S., Seifer, R., & Elias, P. K. (1982). Sociocultural variability in infant temperament ratings. *Child Development, 53*, 164–173.

Sameroff, A. J., Siefer, R., & Zax, M. (1982). Early development of children at risk for emotional disorder. *Monographs of the Society for Research in Child Development, 47* (7, Serial No. 199).

Scarr, S., & Kidd, K. K. (1983). Developmental behavior genetics. In P. H. Mussen (Series Ed.), M. Haith & J. J. Campos (Vol. Eds.), *Handbook of child psychology: Vol. 2. Infancy and developmental psychobiology* (pp. 345–434). New York: Wiley.

Schaffer, H. R., & Crook, C. K. (1980). Child compliance and maternal control techniques. *Developmental Psychology, 16*, 54–61.

Schaffer, H. R., & Emerson, P. E. (1964). The development of social attachment in infancy. *Monographs of the Society for Research in Child development, 29*, (3, Serial No. 94).

Schneider-Rosen, K., Braunwald, K. G., Carlson, V., & Cicchetti, D. (1985). Current perspectives in attachment theory: Illustration from the study of maltreated infants. In I. Bretherton & E. Waters (Eds.), Growing points of attachment theory and research. *Monographs of the Society for Research in Child Development, 50*, (1–2, Serial No. 209).

Seitz, V., Rosenbaum, L. K., Apfel, N. H. (1985). Effects of family support intervention: A ten-year follow-up. *Child Development, 56*, 376–391.

Slade, A. (1987). A longitudinal study of maternal involvement and symbolic play during the toddler period. *Child Development, 58*, 367–375.

Sorce, J. F., & Emde, R. N. (1981). Mother's presence is not enough. *Developmental Psychology, 17*, 737–745.

Sroufe, L. A. (1985). Attachment classification from the perspective of infant–caregiver relationships and infant temperament. *Child Development, 56*, 1–14.

Sroufe, L. A., & Fleeson, J. (1986). Attachment and the construction of relationships. In W. Hartup & Z. Rubin (Eds.), *The nature and development of relationships* (pp. 51–71). Hillsdale NJ: L. Erlbaum.

Sroufe, L. A., & Rosenberg, D. (1982). *Coherence of individual adaptation in lower class infants and toddlers*. Paper presented at the meeting of the International Conference on Infant Studies, Austin, TX.

Stern, D. M. (1985). *The Interpersonal world of the infant*. New York: Basic Books.

Stern, D. M., Hofer, L., Haft, W., & Dore, J. (1985). Affect attunement: A descriptive account of the intermodal communication of affective status between mothers and infants. In T. Fields & N. Fox (Eds.), *Social perception in infants*. Norwood, NJ: Ablex Publishing.

Straus, M. A. (1980). Stress and child abuse. In C. H. Kempe & R. E. Helfer (Eds.), *The battered child* (pp. 86–103). Chicago: University of Chicago Press.

Stiefel, G. S., Plunkett, J. W., & Meisels, S. J. (1987). Affective expression among preterm infants of varying levels of biological risk. *Infant Behavior and Development, 10*, 151–164.

Thomas, A., & Chess, S. (1977). *Temperament and development*. New York: Brunner/Mazel.

Trevarthan, C. (1979). Communication and cooperation in early infancy: A description of primary intersubjectivity. In M. Bullowa (Ed.), *Before speech: The beginning of interpersonal communication* (pp. 321–347). New York: Cambridge University Press.

Tronick, E. Z., Als, H., Adamson, L., Wise, S., & Brazelton, T. B. (1978). The infant's response to entrapment between contradictory messages in face-to-face interaction. *Journal of the American Academy of Child Psychiatry, 17*, 1–13.

Tronick, E., & Field, T. (Eds.). (1986). *Maternal depression and infant disturbance. New directions for child development*. San Francisco: Jossey-Bass.

Tronick, E. Z., & Gianino, A. (1986). Interactive mismatch and repair: Challenges to the coping infant. *Zero to Three, 6*, 1–6.

Tronick, E. Z., Ricks, M., & Cohn, J. F. (1982). Maternal and infant affective exchange: Patterns of adaption. In T. M. Field (Ed.), *Emotion and early interaction* (pp. 83–100). Hillsdale. NJ: L. Erlbaum.

Tyler, A. H. (1986). The abusing father. In M. E. Lamb (Ed.), *The father's role: Applied perspectives*. New York: Wiley.

Vaughn, B., Deinard, A., & Egeland, B. (1980). Measuring temperament in pediatric practice. *Journal of Pediatrics, 96*, 510–514.

Vaughn, B., Egeland, B., Sroufe, L. A., & Waters, E. (1979). Individual differences in infant–mother attachment at twelve and eighteen months: Stability and change in families under stress. *Child Development, 50*, 971–975.

Vietze, P., Falsey, S., Sandler, H., O'Connor, S., & Altemeier, W. A. (1980). Transactional approach to prediction of child maltreatment. *Infant Mental Health Journal, 1*, 248–261.

Wachs, T. D., & Gruen, G. E. (1982). *Early experience and human development*. New York: Plenum.

Washington, J., Minde, K., & Goldberg, S. (1986). Temperament in preterm infants: Style and stability. *Journal of the American Academy of Child Psychiatry, 25*, 493–502.

Waters, E., Wippman, J., & Sroufe, L. A. (1979). Attachment, positive affect, and competence in the peer groups: Two studies in construct validation. *Child Development, 50*, 821–829.

Watson, J. S. (1972). Smiling, cooing, and "the game." *Merrill-Palmer Quarterly, 18*, 341–347.

Watson, J. S., & Ramsey, C. T. (1972). Reactions to response-contingent stimulation in early infancy. *Merrill-Palmer Quarterly, 18*, 219–228.

Worobey, J., & Brazelton, T. B. (1986). Experimenting with the family in the newborn period: A commentary. *Child Development, 57*, 1298–1300.

Yarrow, L. J., Rubenstein, J. L. & Pederson, F. A. (1975). *Infant and environment: Early cognitive and motivational development*. New York: Wiley.

Zahn-Waxler, C., Cummings, M., McKnew, D., & Radke-Yarrow, M. (1984). Altruism, aggression and social interactions in young children with a manic-depressive parent. *Child Development, 55*, 112–122.

4   *The human ecology of early risk*

INTRODUCTION AND OVERVIEW

An ecological perspective on developmental risk directs our attention simultaneously to two kinds of interactions. The first is the interaction of the child as a biological organism with the immediate social environment as a set of processes, events, and relationships. The second is the interplay of social systems in the child's social environment. This dual mandate to look both *outward* to the forces that shape social contexts and *inward* to the day-to-day interaction of the child in the family is both the beauty and the challenge of human ecology. It demands much of us intellectually and ideologically, if it is to be more than an academic exercise.

Ecology is the study of relationships between organisms and environments. Ecologists explore and document how the individual and the habitat shape the development of each other. Like the biologist who learns about an animal by studying its habitat, sources of food, predators, and social practices, the student of human development must address how people live and grow in their social environment. Whereas all students of animal ecology must accommodate to the purposeful actions of the organism, the human ecologist must go further and seek to incorporate the phenomenological complexity of the organism–environment interaction – the social and psychological maps that define human meaning.

Put this way, we must recognize that the habitat of the child at risk includes family, friends, neighborhood, church, and school, as well as less immediate forces that constitute the social geography and climate (e.g., laws, institutions, and values), and the physical environment. The interplay of these social forces and physical settings with the individual child defines the range of issues in the forefront of an ecological perspective. The most important characteristic of this ecological perspective is that it both reinforces our inclination to look inside the individual and encourages us to look beyond the individual to the environment for questions and explanations about individual behavior and development. It emphasizes development in context.

An ecological perspective constantly reminds us that child development results from the interplay of biology *and* society, from the characteristics children bring with them into the world and the way the world treats them, from nature *and* nurture. In this it reflects what Pasamanick (1987) calls social biology. In contrast to sociobiology, which emphasizes a genetic origin for social behavior (Wilson, 1978), social biology concentrates on the social origins of biological phenomena (e.g., the impact of poverty on

78

infant morbidity). Nevertheless, the two perspectives are not mutually exclusive. Indeed, sociobiologists see the *historical* (i.e., evolutionary) origins of biological phenomena (i.e., gene pool characteristics) in social phenomena (i.e., the differential life success of individuals) because of the *social* implications of their *genetically based* individual behavior (Wilson, 1978). They seek to explain how the social impact of biologically rooted traits affects the survival of organisms and thus the likelihood that those particular genetic patterns will be passed along to surviving offspring.

Children face different opportunities and risks for development because of their mental and physical makeup and because of the social environment they inhabit. Moreover, social environment affects the very physical makeup of the child. These effects may be negative (e.g., the impact of poverty on birth weight or the mutagenic influence of industrial carcinogens) or positive (e.g., intrauterine surgery or nutritional therapy for a fetus with a genetic disorder). When these social influences operate in psychological or sociological terms, we refer to them as sociocultural opportunities and risks.

When we refer to opportunities for development we mean relationships in which children find material, emotional, and social encouragement compatible with their needs and capacities as they exist at a specific point in their developing lives. For each child, the best fit must be worked out through experience, within some very broad guidelines of basic human needs, and then renegotiated as development proceeds and situations change. Windows of opportunity for intervention appear repeatedly across the life course, and what may be a critical threat at one point may be benign or even developmentally enhancing at another. For example, Elder's analyses (1974) of the impact of the economic crisis of the 1930s reveal that its effects were felt most negatively by young children. In fact, some adolescents even benefited from the fact that paternal unemployment often meant special "opportunities" for enhanced responsibility for teenage sons and daughters. Bronfenbrenner (1986) confirmed that the stress of urban life associated with family adversity is most negative and potent for young children, yet it may stimulate some adolescents.

Risks to development can come both from direct threats and from the absence of normal, expectable opportunities. Besides such obvious biological risks as malnutrition or injury, there are sociocultural risks that impoverish the developing individual's world of essential experiences and relationships and thereby threaten development. For example, abandoned children may suffer from their lack of the family ties and diverse role models that enrich those who live in large close-knit families. Similarly, children who are born at the low point of an economic depression may receive fewer benefits from preventive services than those who are born during more economically auspicious times. When sociocultural risks threaten, appropriate early intervention can help the child find new routes for adaptive development. Understanding the consequences of both sociocultural risks and opportunities and the role of social support networks is a central concern of human ecology.

Our goal here is to make use of a systems approach to clarify the complexity we face in attempting to understand the interplay of biological, psychological, social, and cultural forces in early developmental risks and their amelioration. A systems approach helps us discover the connections among what might at first seem to be unrelated events. It also can help us see that what often seems like an obvious solution may actually only make the problem worse. Forrester (1969) concludes that because systems are linked, and therefore influence each other (feedback), many of the most effective solutions to social problems are not readily apparent, and may even be "counter intuitive." According to Hardin (1966) the First Law of Ecology is, You can never do just one thing. Intersystem feedback ensures that any single action may reverberate and produce unintended consequences. This will become apparent as we proceed.

As individuals develop they play an ever more active role in an ever widening world. Newborns shape the feeding behavior of their mothers, but are confined largely to cribs or laps and have limited means of communicating their needs and wants. Ten-year-olds, on the other hand, influence many adults and other children in many different settings, and have many ways of communicating. The adolescents' world is still larger and more diverse, as is their ability to influence that world. Individuals and environments negotiate their relationships over time through a process of reciprocity. Neither is constant; *each* depends on the other. When asked, Does *X* cause *Y*? the answer is always, It depends. We cannot reliably predict the future of one system without knowing something about the other systems with which it is linked. And even then it may be very difficult. We see this when we ask, Does early day care enhance or harm development? It depends on the child's age, quality of parent–child attachment, the day-care provider's relationship to the child's parents, and the day-care provider's motivations and training, as well as the more obvious question of what *exactly* constitutes the experience of day care. In short, it depends (cf. Belsky, 1986).

We see this contextualism in all aspects of development. Thus, for example, the link between early developmental delay and later IQ deficit appears to differ across social-class groupings in the kind of social system present in most United States communities. In one classic study, 13% of the lower-class children who were developmentally delayed at 8 months showed an IQ of 79 or less at 4 years of age. In contrast, only 7% of the middle-class children who were delayed at 8 months of age were retarded at 4 years of age. For the upper-class children the figure was only 2% (Willerman, Broman, & Fiedler, 1970). Does developmental delay predict IQ deficit? It would seem that it depends upon the family and community environment in which the child is growing up. We might hypothesize that the social-class effect linked to family status would be exaggerated in some communities while it might also be diminished in others.

Is IQ influenced more by genetics or by environment, by nature or by nurture? It depends. For example, a reanalysis of twin study data reveals that when identical twins were separated at birth and reared in *similar* communities the correlation between their adult IQs was strong (.86). When identical twins were reared in *dissimilar* communities the correlation between their adult IQs was weak (.26) (Bronfenbrenner, 1975). Which is more important, nature or nurture? It depends.

We see the individual's experiences as subsystems within systems within larger systems, "as a set of nested structures, each inside the next, like a set of Russian dolls" (Bronfenbrenner, 1979, p. 22). In asking and answering questions about development, we can and should always be ready to look at the next level of systems "beyond" and "within" to find the questions and the answers (Garbarino et al., 1982). If we see parents and visiting nurses in conflict over the use of physical punishment in early childhood (the family system), we need to look to the community that establishes laws and policies about child abuse. We also should look to the culture that defines physical force as an appropriate form of discipline in early childhood. We also must look within the individual, as a psychological system that is affected by conscious and changing roles, unconscious needs, and motives, to know why and how each adjusts in ways that generate conflict. In addition, we must look "across" to see how the several systems involved (family, social services, social network, and economy) adjust to new conditions. Interaction among these social forces is the key to an ecological analysis of early developmental risk. They exist as linked social systems, implying that intervention can take place at each system level *and* that intervention at one level may well spill over to others.

This system approach examines the environment at four levels beyond the individual organism – from the micro to the macro. These systems have been catalogued in detail elsewhere (Bronfenbrenner, 1979, 1986; Garbarino et al., 1982). The goal here is to introduce them briefly in order to provide a context for discussing the ecology of early developmental risk.

Microsystems

Microsystems are the immediate settings in which individuals develop. The shared experiences that occur in each setting provide a record of the microsystem and offer some clues to its future. Microsystems evolve and develop much as do individuals themselves from forces generated both within and without. The quality of a micro-system depends upon its ability to sustain and enhance development, and to provide a context that is emotionally validating and developmentally challenging. This ability to enhance development in turn depends upon the capacity to operate in what Vygotsky (1934) called "the zone of proximal development," that is, the distance between what the child can accomplish alone (the level of actual development) and what the child can do when helped (the level of potential development).

Children can handle (and need) more than infants. Adolescents can handle (and need) more than children. We measure the social richness of an individual's life by the availability of enduring, reciprocal, multifaceted relationships that emphasize playing, working, and loving. And we do that measuring over time, because microsystems, like individuals, change over time. Risk, on the other hand, lies in patterns of abuse, neglect, resource deficiency, and stress that insult the child and thwart development (Garbarino, Guttmann, & Seeley, 1986).

The "same" day-care center is very different in June from what it was in September for the "same" infants who, of course, are themselves not the same as they were at the beginning of the year. The setting of the family, as the first-born child experiences it, is different from that experienced by subsequent offspring. Naturally, children themselves change and develop, as do others in the setting. It is also important to remember that our definition speaks of the microsystem as a pattern *experienced* by the developing person. Individuals influence their microsystems and those microsystems influence them in turn. Each participant acts on the basis of an emergent social map – a phenomenological record and projection.

Mesosystems

Mesosystems are relationships *between* microsystems in which the individual experiences reality. These links themselves form a system. We measure the richness of a meso-system in the number and quality of its connections. One example is the case of an infant's day-care group and his or her home. We ask, Do staff visit the child at home? Do the child's parents know his or her friends at day care? Do parents of children at the center know each other? A second example concerns a hospital and the home for a chronically ill child. What role do the parents play in the hospital regime? Do the same health care professionals who see the child in the hospital visit the home? Is the child the only one to participate in both? If he or she is the only "linkage," the mesosystem is weak and that weakness may place the child at risk. Research suggests that the strength of the mesosystem linking the setting in which an intervention is implemented with the settings in which the individual spends most significant time, is crucial to the long-term effectiveness of the intervention and to the maintenance of its effects (Whittaker, 1983).

Exosystems

Exosystems are settings that have a bearing on the development of children, but in which those children do not play a direct role. For most children, the key exosystems include the workplace of their parents (in general, most children are not participants there) and those centers of power such as school boards, church councils, and planning commissions that make decisions affecting their day-to-day life. Note that the concept of an exosystem illustrates the projective nature of the ecological perspective, for the same setting that is an exosystem for a child may be a microsystem for the parent, and vice versa. Thus, one form of intervention may aim at transforming exosystems into microsystems by initiating greater participation in important institutions for isolated, disenfranchised, and powerless clients, for example, by getting parents to visit the family day-care home or by creating on-site day care at the workplace.

In exosystem terms, both risk and opportunity come about in two ways. The first is when the parents or other significant adults in a child's life are treated in a way that impoverishes (risk) or enhances (opportunity) their behavior in the microsystems they share with children. Examples include elements of the parents' working experience that impoverish or enhance family life – unemployment, low pay, long or inflexible hours, traveling, or stress, on the one hand, in contrast to an adequate income, flexible scheduling, an understanding employer, or subsidies for child care, on the other (Bronfenbrenner & Crouter, 1982).

The second way risk and opportunity flow from the exosystem lies in the orientation and content of decisions made in those settings that affect the day-to-day experience of children and their families. For example, when the state legislature suspends funding for early intervention programs, it jeopardizes development. When public officials expand prenatal health services or initiate specialized day care in high-risk communities, they increase developmental opportunities (and may reduce infant mortality or morbidity).

Albee (1980) has gone so far as to identify powerlessness as the primary factor leading to impaired development and mental disability. It certainly plays a large role in determining the fate of groups of individuals via public policy and may even be very important when considering individual cases, such as whether or not parents have the "pull" to get a medically vulnerable child enrolled in a special treatment program. In many cases, risk and opportunity at the exosystem level are essentially political matters.

One of the most useful aspects of the ecological approach is its ability to highlight situations in which the actions of people with whom the individual has no direct contact significantly affect development. The following example illustrates the relationship between social policy and individual child development. Because of a leveraged corporate takeover, a board of directors decides to shift operations from one plant to another. Hundreds of families with young children are forced to move to new locations. Local services are underfunded in a period of escalating demand. Parents lose their jobs and thus their health insurance. The quality of prenatal and well-baby care declines; infant mortality increases. This is a classic illustration of an exosystem effect. It highlights the fact that exosystem events may establish much of the agenda for day-to-day early intervention on behalf of children at risk.

At this point it is worth emphasizing that the ecological perspective forces us to consider the concept of risk beyond the narrow confines of individual personality and family dynamics. In the ecological approach, both are causes of the child's developmental patterns and reflections of broader sociocultural forces. Mark Twain wrote, "If the only tool you have is a hammer you tend to treat every problem as if it were a nail." Inflexible loyalty to a specific focus (e.g., the parents) is often a stumbling block to effective intervention. However, the obverse must also be considered: If you define every problem as a nail, the only tool you will seek is a hammer. Viewing children at risk only in terms of organismic and interpersonal dynamics precludes an understanding of the many other avenues of influence that might be open to us as helpers, or that might be topics of study for us as scientists. This message provides a crucial guide to our discussion of early intervention.

Macrosystems

Meso- and exosystems are set within the broad ideological, demographic, and institutional patterns of a particular culture or subculture. These patterns are the *macrosystems* that serve as the master blueprints for the ecology of human development. These blueprints reflect a people's shared assumptions about how things should be done, as well as the institutions that represent those assumptions. Macrosystems are ideology incarnate. Thus, we contrast societal blueprints that rest upon fundamental institutional expressions, such as a collective versus individual orientation. Religion provides a classic example of the macrosystem concept because it involves both a definition of the world and a set of institutions reflecting that definition – both a theology and a set of roles, rules, buildings, and programs.

Macrosystem refers to the general organization of the world as it is and as it might be. Historical change demonstrates that "might be" is quite real, and occurs through either evolution (many individual actions guided by a common reality) or through revolution (dramatic change introduced by a small cadre of decision makers). The Iranian revolution of 1978–79, for example, overturned a modernizing society and embodied a changed institutional and ideological landscape that shaped the most basic experiences of childhood. Current efforts to modernize in China include a massive shift from collective reward to private initiative as the dominating economic force. More directly relevant still is China's one-child policy that has altered the demography of the family, and appears to be altering the social fabric at each level of the human ecology (Schell, 1982).

In the United States, the increasing concentration of high-risk families in a geographically concentrated underclass (Lemann, 1986; Wilson, 1987) is exerting dramatic influences on the need and the prognosis for early interventions. Pockets of marked vulnerability show poverty and infant mortality rates many times the average found in unafflicted communities. For early intervention services to be plausible in such high-risk ecological niches, they must target ecological transformation as the program goal. For example, Chicago's Center for Successful Child Development (The Beethoven Project) is an effort to prevent developmental delays among an entire birth cohort in a public housing project (i.e., all the children born in one year who live in the same kindergarten catchment area). The program employs home health visitors, early developmental screening, prenatal health care and parent education, job training for parents, infant day care, child abuse prevention programming, Head Start participation, and other transforming and supportive services (Barclay-McLaughlin, 1987; Musick & Stott, this volume). When such efforts are conducted in the context of thoughtful evaluation research they can serve as the kind of "transforming experiments" that advance an ecologically valid science of early intervention (Bronfenbrenner, 1979).

When all is said and done, an ecological perspective has much to contribute to the process of formulating, evaluating, and understanding early intervention. It gives us a kind of social map for navigating a path through the complexities of programming. It helps us see the relationships (potential and actual) among programs – how, for example, some programs are complementary while others may be competitive. It aids us in seeing the full range of alternative conceptualizations of problems affecting children and points us in the direction of multiple strategies for intervention. An ecological perspective provides a kind of checklist to use in thinking about what is happening, and what to do about it when faced with developmental problems and social pathologies that afflict children. It does this by asking us always to consider the micro, meso-, exo-, and macrosystem dimensions of developmental phenomena and interventions. It constantly suggests the possibility that context is shaping causal relationships. It always tells us "it depends" and stimulates an attempt to find out "on what."

THE ECONOMIC AND DEMOGRAPHIC CONTEXT OF EARLY CHILDHOOD IN THE UNITED STATES

Having laid out a set of terms to use in assessing the social system in which child development occurs, we can turn next to identifying current sources of risk in the human ecology of the young child. To accomplish this we must turn to a brief social history of early risk that must consider recent economic trends in the United States, particularly as they affect the experience and developmental prognosis of young children.

In reviewing the state of the nation during the 1970s, several blue-ribbon panels charged with the task of assessing risk to families deriving from the social environment, identified economic deprivation as the principal villain (e.g., the National Academy of Sciences, 1976, Keniston, 1977, which was suggested by the Carnegie Corporation). In the space of a decade, these reports have come to seem tame as the relative economic position of young children has deteriorated. Reversing the traditional pattern for the United States, in which poverty has been concentrated among the elderly, economic deprivation is now most common among families with young children. In 1985, for example, about 25% of America's children under age three were living in poverty, as compared with 13% of the general population, including the elderly (U.S. Census, 1980). For blacks and Hispanics, the rates are higher. Looking over the 10-year period from 1969 to 1979 (basically good times for the nation as a whole), roughly 25% of families slipped below the poverty line at least once, while about 3% (mainly black, one-parent households headed by women) remained below that level continuously (Duncan, Coe, & Hill, 1981). The social concern of the 1980s focused attention on this latter (and growing) group, now often called the underclass; but the larger group remains at risk, particularly if a period of temporary impoverishment coincides with the birth of a child.

Although chronic impoverishment poses a serious threat to child welfare, so does acute, episodic impoverishment – the much more common variety in our system. Many projections lead to the expectation that poverty will persist for one in four young children, particularly in single-parent households, unless there is some dramatic change in demography, policy, and/or the structure of the economy (Garbarino, 1988). This projection reflects the fact that the experience of single parenthood – a major correlate of poverty – is expected to continue as a feature of life for one in two children at some point in their first 18 years of life. It also reflects the expectation that outbreaks of unemployment will continue above and beyond the chronic unemployment and under-employment characterizing the inner-city underclass.

There is considerable debate about the exact processes that translate unemployment into developmental risk for children, but there is consensus that acute economic deprivation represents a challenge to the coping resources of individuals, families, and communities (Fisher & Cunningham, 1983). The connection between unemployment and developmental crisis is mainly indirect, but it is real nonetheless. Unemployment tends to diminish resources and precipitate problems in mental health and welfare. Male identity and parental status have traditionally been tied to occupational position. Unemployment diminishes that identity and gives rise to ambiguity or even outright conflict in the family. This psychic threat is compounded by the very practical fact that employment is the principal source of basic health and welfare services. Unemployment thus precipitates crises in both the psychic and the fiscal economy of the family. Both increase the likelihood of risky conditions for children and decrease the likelihood that such risky conditions will be observed and attended to effectively. This dynamic is particularly important for workers in financially marginal employment, where reserves are minimal or nonexistent – one paycheck away from disaster, as they are often described. This financial vulnerability heightens the importance of social resources of the kind discussed later in this chapter. One source of concern is the growing recognition that there has been a steady increase in the politically tolerable level of "normal" unemployment, from 4% in 1950 to 7% in 1986. It may go higher, and already is in fact higher, due to methods of public accounting that do not include those too discouraged to seek work, and others who are not fully employed. As recessions occur, they produce double-digit levels of unemployment (i.e., 10% or more), with localized hot spots in excess of 20%. These deteriorating economic conditions, characterized by increases in the number of people falling below the poverty level, are a major force driving the human ecology of early risk (Bronfenbrenner, Moen, & Garbarino, 1984).

In addition to the well-established connection between poverty and infant mortality, researchers have identified a link between economic deprivation and child maltreat-ment, certainly the bottom line when it comes to indicators of child welfare and family functioning (see Garbarino & Crouter, 1978a; Garbarino & Sherman, 1980; NCCAN, 1981; Pelton, 1978; Steinberg, Catalano, & Dooley, 1981). Briefly, these studies report a correlation between low income and the risk for child maltreatment on both the individual and community level. Thus, the rate of maltreatment (all forms of abuse and neglect combined) computed as part of the federally financed National Incidence Study (which dealt with many of the issues of class-biased reporting) ranges from 27.3 per 1,000 children among families with 1979 incomes of under $7,000, to 14.6 per 1,000 for families in the $15,000 to $24,999 range, and 2.7 per 1,000 for families with annual incomes in excess of $25,000 (NCCAN, 1981). Studies of rates at the community level tell the same story (Garbarino & Crouter, 1978b), as shall be discussed in greater detail later.

The kind of economic crisis that may occur in the 1990s – a crisis described as probable by some economic forecasters – could mean an epidemic of threats to child welfare (Garbarino et al., 1982; Garbarino, 1988). This happened during the 1980s in unemployment hot spots around the country as child maltreatment rates followed climbing unemployment rates. In Oregon, for example, where a depressed lumber industry prompted double-digit unemployment rates, officials reported a 46% increase in child maltreatment for 1981 (Birch, 1982). The resulting upsurge in the need for child welfare and other human services typically coincides with a diminished capacity of formal services to respond during troubled economic times. As an economic crisis unfolds, for example, it simultaneously increases demand for state-supported services across the spectrum from health care to food stamps, and typically decreases the tax revenues available to finance such services. A further disturbing trend is the finding that the economic recovery of the mid-1980s, with unemployment dipping below 7% in 1987, did not (and in all likelihood will not) reach the growing underclass, where unemployment, poverty, and demographic adversity are becoming ever more entrenched and chronic (Wilson, 1987).

While most industrialized societies entitle all families to maternal and infant health care and basic child-support subsidies, ours does not (Kahn & Kamerman, 1975; Kamerman & Kahn, 1976; Miller, 1987). Although the federal budget includes a substantial commitment to "entitlement" programs (some $362 billion in 1983), five-sixths goes to programs that disproportionately assist affluent adults, while relatively little goes to families in the service of child-welfare-related objectives (Fallows, 1982). As noted by Bronfenbrenner (1986), this may explain why correlations between measures of income or socioeconomic status and basic child outcomes are often higher in the United States than in other modern societies. That is, low income is a better predictor of deficits in the United States than in other countries because our social policies tend to exaggerate rather than minimize the impact of family income on access to preventive and rehabilitative services.

The current crisis in the United States comes in the wake of the economic track record of the post–World War II era that led most Americans, except perhaps the chronically impoverished underclass, to *expect* material affluence on a mass scale that is unprecedented in human history. Many now take for granted as necessities what were considered previously to be luxuries. The economic "miracle" of the last four decades has raised expectations, and it has led to more and more of daily life becoming part of the monetarized economy – that is, having a dollar price (Giarini, 1980). Many Americans have become accustomed to an affluent material standard of living that probably cannot be sustained over the next decade for many of the people much of the time. Data from the economic depression of the 1930s, when expectations were considerably lower, predict a pattern of increasing frustration, anger, depression, and hostility under such circumstances (Bronfenbrenner et al., 1984). Such negativity increases developmental risk for children.

It is the phenomenology of deprivation that concerns us here. Having become socialized into a highly monetarized life-style (that is, one in which a high proportion of the activities of day-to-day life involve cash transactions), it is difficult to retreat into a less monetarized way of living. Similarly, a drop in income is experienced relative to the prior standard, not some absolute conception of need. What does it take to meet the minimal standards for child care? Any statement of the budget for child care by a family reflects assumptions about the kinds of materials that are necessary. For example, prior generations used cloth diapers and made large investments of time and personal energy to maintain them. Currently, even families with small incomes and very limited prospects for earning have come to depend upon expensive disposable diapers as a basic necessity. These substitutes cost a great deal and their environmental impact is insidious.

The phenomenology of poverty is dominated by the experience of deprivation, and exacerbated by widespread promulgation of highly monetarized affluence as the standard. Low-paying jobs can come to be interpreted as an affront in such a context, the accoutrements of affluence a right. This inflation of expectations does not contribute to the well-being of young children. All of it sustains rage and despair. Add to this the geographic concentration of economically marginal families as communities become more homogeneous (e.g., through clustering public housing), and the developmental effects on children are profoundly disturbing. Children become the incidental and deliberate targets of concentrated and often unmitigated rage and despair, in the form of neglect and abuse. Children cost too much when their "caregivers" cannot generate enough income to meet popular expectations for participating in the monetarized economy of day-to-day life.

In a nation where everything costs money and continues to cost more, most families need two incomes to keep up, although because of divorce and single parenthood, more and more families have only one potential wage earner. This was *not* the case at the outset of the economic depression of the 1930s. Most families with children contained two adults, and wives represented a largely untapped resource that could be and was mobilized to generate cash income in response to the unemployment and income loss experienced by male workers (Elder, 1974). Now this resource has already been tapped to meet basic family expenses, and therefore does not represent a reserve in the sense that it did in the 1930s. Currently, employed wives earn on average about 60% of what their husbands do per hour, and in all contribute 26% of total family income (U.S. Department of Labor, 1981). Furthermore, children are increasingly an economic burden, directly because of what it costs to raise them and indirectly because of what they cost in lost parental income (i.e., time away from the job that over a childhood comes to tens of thousands if not hundreds of thousands of dollars).

Conventional economics

The relationship between developmental risk and economic crisis flows from both the current political climate and the conventional economic thinking that undergirds our political economy (Garbarino, 1988). The problem is thus both our political ideology and the conventional economic thinking that guides our institutions. Conventional economics was built and continues to rest on a foundation of ecologically flawed assumptions about prices, costs, and values.

Human activity – *particularly* economic activity – cannot *produce* anything material, only the social constructions that create or convey meaning. For example, humans produce cars, not the metal, petroleum, and other materials that go into that car. All that we do and can do is transform and (inevitably) degrade material resources into waste. Eventually the metal, plastics, and other components of the car become junk. Our economically productive activity transforms one state of matter into another by capturing and focusing energy. This transformed matter is, *for a period of time*, useful to us (it becomes a "utility" in economic terms), and then becomes waste. What we call "production" is thus really only "transformation," and the only real measure of value is the duration and nature of something's usefulness (Garbarino, 1988).

In the real social environment, human work (i.e., a job) is a vital psychological and sociological factor with many important ramifications for child welfare (Bronfenbrenner & Crouter, 1982). Conventional economics does not recognize the real material and social basis of production: Capital and labor are fully interchangeable only in the abstract calculations of conventional economics. Farmers farm not only to earn an income but because of their attachment to a particular kind of life. One person farming 10,000 acres using robots is not the same as 100 people each farming 100 acres using minimal mechanization.

Standard economics proceeds on the assumption that acts that do not have an immediate cash price (such as dumping pollutants into rivers or closing enterprises that are the lifeblood of a community because they do not return a high enough dividend) are free. Economists call these factors that are outside an enterprise's direct costs "externalities." Social and material costs are pushed onto the public in general, and specific communities and families in particular. Conventional economists tell us to assume that these costs are accounted for automatically in the marketplace and result in the general good.

The invalidity of this assumption is ever more apparent as the scale of human economic enterprise grows to the point at which it is sufficiently powerful to degrade the earth on global proportions. In the social domain it is evident in the increasingly unrealistic character of conventional economic analyses of the threats posed to children by the monetarily inadequate resource base for child care. Current policy initiatives aimed at welfare reform and improving child care do not consider fully the true costs. There are limits to the number of children that one caregiver can serve, without compromising development. Family day-care providers who serve less than affluent families are usually in a very difficult position. They cannot generate sufficient income per child served to set a proper limit on the number of children in their care. A recent analysis conducted in Illinois illustrates this problem (Gilkerson, 1987). Workers at the factory studied can afford to pay no more than $25 per week per child for care. A family day-care provider who accepts four children, the approved number, can thus earn only $5,000 per year. Most day-care providers respond by increasing the number of children cared for to eight and stay outside the licensing system. The cost of this pattern of care is borne in decreased developmental prospects for the children. The same analysis concludes that it costs at least $50 per week per child to provide adequate care. Who pays the missing $25? Questions like this must be at the top of our agenda when we speak of the economics of child development. We also need to ask such questions as, How can we afford to pay $2,000 a day for neonatal intensive care for one child, but not $2,000 per family in intensive prenatal care to prevent low birth weight and neonatal risk?

Some knowledge of these issues of economic motivation and analysis will be essential for an adequate understanding of the human ecology of early risk and the prospects for intervention. The implications of this analysis run counter to the laissez-faire themes put forward during the 1980s by political forces that have demanded less rather than more governmental responsibility for families and early childhood, thereby exacerbating the dynamics of family vulnerability and economic hardship (Garbarino, 1988).

The politics of early childhood risk and opportunity in the 1980s portend a long series of battles pitting the basic well-being of some children and their families against the affluence of others. The politics of choosing between those two thrusts will intensify as they become more clearly mutually competitive. The internal situation in the United States will thus mirror the global choices to be made between more luxuries for the haves versus more necessities for the have-nots. According to the Bureau of Labor Statistics, for a family of four in 1982 to live at a "high" level required about $38,000, while to live at a "lower" (struggling) level required about $15,000. Should the goal of policy be to bring as much of the population up to $15,000 as possible, or to enhance the prospects of those who have reached the $38,000 level? The former goal is much more germane to early intervention and the prevention of developmental risks; the latter may be more in keeping with the spirit of the time.

Economic issues play a very large role in the dynamics of early risk. At the micro-system level, family structure and activities interact with the parents' participation in the workforce. Macrosystem issues provide a context for this. To the degree to which the community's day-to-day life is monetarized, families as microsystems will be drawn or driven into the cash economy. If the exosystems of the community (local government, philanthropic institutions, etc.) remain aloof from this process, those who cannot generate sufficient cash income to participate in basic activities will become ever poorer. Impoverished microsystems will begin to form systematic patterns of deprivation – family, school, and social network will reinforce developmental delay and deviant socialization. We see this played out in the human ecology of infant mortality and child maltreatment, particularly in socially impoverished urban areas where the entire human ecology seems to operate in a concerted attack upon the foundations for successful child development. In this sense, the underclass represents a kind of ecological conspiracy against children.

THE CLINICAL SOCIOLOGY OF EARLY RISK: AN EMPIRICAL MODEL OF CHILD MALTREATMENT, INFANT MORTALITY, AND EARLY INTERVENTION IN HIGH-RISK COMMUNITIES

In contrast to the socially rich family environment stands the socially impoverished one, in which the parent–child relationship is denuded of enduring supportive relationships and protective behaviors. It is thus deprived of the essential elements of social support – nurturance and feedback systems (Caplan, 1974; Whittaker et al., 1983). The socially rich environment includes people who are "free from drain" (Collins & Pancoast, 1976). Such individuals can afford to give to and share with others, because the balance of needs and resources in their own lives markedly favors the latter. They offer "services" that do not involve cash transactions. Thus, they stand outside the monetarized human service sector (i.e., the services that involve salaries and wages, prices and financial contracts). They find nonmonetarized payoff in helping others.

What do these people who are free from drain do? One thing they do is provide "protective behaviors" to children. Emlen (1977) uses this concept to refer to the range of things neighbors and friends may do to keep children safe – everything from keeping an eye on them while they play outside, to offering assistance to parents with day-to-day or emergency care, to intervening on the child's behalf when threatened (even to reporting child maltreatment to protective service agencies). These individuals become one aspect of the socially rich neighborhood. Kromkowski (1976) puts it this way:

A neighborhood's character is determined by a host of factors, but most significantly by the kinds of relationships that neighbors have with each other. . . . A healthy neighborhood has some sort of cultural and institutional network which manifests itself in pride in the neighborhood, care of homes, security for children, and respect for each other (p. 228).

Socially impoverished neighborhoods, in contrast, lack people who are free from drain and therefore tend to operate on a "scarcity" economy when it comes to social relations. Mutuality is suppressed by fears of exploitation and of being a burden and excessively beholding. For example, residents may fear acts of neighboring such as generalized offers of shared child care because such open-ended acts can open a Pandora's box of requests and may lead to the expectation of reciprocity – a negative prospect if one distrusts the caregiving practices of one's neighbors.

This social impoverishment can occur independently of economic impoverishment. When it does, however, its consequences for young children are likely to be blunted because affluent families can gain access to monetarized services to compensate. Nonetheless, the affluent but socially impoverished environment may catch up with children and families as they face the transition to adolescence, when the need for social stability increases to compensate for the intrinsic psychological and physiological challenges of puberty (Garbarino et al., 1985). Thus, even a financially affluent social environment may lack the kind of enduring support systems that adolescents need to provide positive role models, caring adult supervision, and a sense of personal validation. The same may be true for the parents of those adolescents who may feel acutely embarrassed to admit difficulty with their adolescents in a community in which there is a presumption of competence and high expectations for achievement.

The greatest risks come when families lack the financial resources to purchase support services in the marketplace and are cut off from the informal helping relationships. It is when monetarized and nonmonetarized economy are both impoverished, however, that child maltreatment and infant mortality flourish, and the challenges to early intervention are greatest (Garbarino et al., 1980). This condition is seen most clearly in the urban underclass that has become the focal point for emergency intervention. Marginal or submarginal economic resources interact with diminished psychosocial resources born of violence, academic failure, exploitation, despair, fear, and deteriorated community infrastructure. For example, in a recent study of life for preschoolers in an inner-city public housing project, all the mothers cited "shooting" as their greatest fear for their children (Dubrow & Garbarino, 1987).

In this inner-city area every child has had a first-hand encounter with gunfire – including being in the arms of someone when that person was shot and having bullets come through apartment windows nearby while playing. In such environments most women experience their first pregnancy while still an unmarried teenager, living with very little prospect of economic self-sufficiency or two-parent family status. Many of these pregnancies result from sexual exploitations by much older men (Barclay-McLaughlin, 1987). These are the environments in which prenatal care is inadequate, intervals between births are often too short, beliefs about child care too often dysfunctional, access to and utilization of well-baby care inadequate, early intervention for child disabilities inadequate, and thus in which child mortality and morbidity are rampant.

We know from research that some individuals and families create and sustain patterns of interaction that generate infant mortality and child maltreatment (Belsky, 1980; Garbarino, 1977; Gaudin & Polansky, 1985; Polansky et al., 1981). However high-risk *families* are not the whole story. To understand the forces that create and sustain early developmental risk we must go further to identify and investigate high-risk *environments* in which such families live. Understanding infant mortality and child maltreatment is thus an issue for clinical *sociology* (see Pavenstedt, 1967; Roman & Trice, 1974) as much as for clinical psychology. Families both shape their social surroundings and are shaped by them. This interactive process can enhance or undermine family functioning (Garbarino, 1977; Martin, 1976). More systematic efforts to study and serve families in context can enrich research and intervention, both preventive and rehabilitative. For many practical purposes, this means examining high-risk neighborhoods as well as high-risk families (see Sattin & Miller, 1971).

Previous research has sought to explore and validate the concept of social impoverishment as a characteristic of high-risk family environments. The links between child maltreatment and social impoverishment are well known (Garbarino, 1977; Garbarino & Gilliam, 1980). Similarly, it has long been well known, and recently affirmed, that infant mortality rates serve as social indicators of impoverishment. Identifying the environmental correlates of child maltreatment (Garbarino, 1976; Garbarino, Crouter, & Sherman, 1977) has provided an empirical basis for screening neighborhoods to identify high- and low-risk areas. This work has been extended to incorporate infant mortality as well. In Chicago, for example, public health data document infant mortality rates in the poorest third of the city's neighborhoods five to ten times the rate observed in the most affluent third (Kostelny & Garbarino, 1987).

Multiple regression analyses employing measures of socioeconomic and demographic resources have been used to illuminate two meanings of high risk (Garbarino & Crouter, 1978b). The first, of course, refers to areas with a high absolute rate of child maltreatment and infant mortality (based on cases per unit of population). In this sense, concentrations of socioeconomically distressed families are most likely to be at high risk. In one city (Omaha, Nebraska), socioeconomic status accounts for about 40% of the variation across neighborhoods in child maltreatment ($r = .64$). Similar results obtain when infant mortality is the dependent variable of interest. In Chicago, for example, these same conditions account for some 60–75% of the variation among 77 community areas in child maltreatment and infant mortality (Kostelny & Garbarino, 1987).

We should note that the magnitude of these correlations may reflect a social policy effect. It seems reasonable to assume that in a society in which low income is *not* correlated with access to basic human services (e.g., where there is universal availability of maternal–infant health care) these correlations would be smaller; in a society totally devoid of policies to ameliorate the impact of family-level differences in social class the correlations might be even larger. The key is how social class (a "status" variable) is translated into the experiences of children and parents (i.e., the "process" variables).

Tulkin's (1972) classic analysis of the concept of "cultural deprivation" made this clear. On the one hand, it is not the culture of those living in poverty in some general sense that matters most. Rather it is those aspects of that culture that translate into an inability to meet the basic developmental needs of children that matter, for example, whether or not caregivers "accept" infant attachment, whether or not they "give up" too quickly on sick children, and whether or not it is normative to reject children with disabilities (Scheper-Hughes, 1987).

It is often easy to attribute blame generally incorrectly to beliefs and values of the poor, but it is much harder to recognize that in fact these beliefs bear no one-to-one correspondence with socioeconomic outcomes for an ethnic group. Tulkin, for example, cites the contrast between two culturally distinct groups of Jews in New York City. One is very successful academically; the other evidences a cultural deficit in this domain. The latter group does not inhabit the underclass, however, because of its strong economic resources and traditional commercial culture. The point is that there are multiple ways to escape poverty. Having said that, we can go still further to note that there are multiple possible consequences of being poor.

The community plays a vital role in deciding this issue. By establishing a strong and aggressive system of prenatal and maternal and child health care, and by making it easy to gain access and difficult to avoid it, a community can do much to dissociate poverty and infant mortality (Miller, 1987). By adapting a passive stance and allowing the free market to rule, a community can strengthen the links between poverty and early child death (Garbarino, 1988).

This hypothesis merits empirical exploration, but is consistent with the observation that socioeconomic status is a more potent predictor of child development outcomes in the United States than in some European societies. Furthermore, a replication of the Omaha study conducted in Montreal revealed a weaker association of socioeconomic status and child maltreatment rates, presumably because of that city's welfare policies that diminish the link between income and basic services (Bouchard, 1987). The direct correlational links between social class and social pathology constitute the first meaning of high risk – that is, the finding that poverty is a risk factor because it is associated with rates of infant mortality, child abuse, and so on.

However, it is the second meaning of high risk that may be of greatest relevance here. High risk can also be taken to mean that a social environment has a higher rate of child maltreatment or infant mortality than would be predicted knowing its socioeconomic character. Thus, two areas with similar socioeconomic and demographic profiles may have very different rates of child maltreatment and infant mortality. In this sense, one is high risk while the other is low risk, although both may have higher rates than other, more affluent areas. Figure 1 illustrates this.

Areas A and B have high actual observed rates of child maltreatment (36 per 1,000 and 34 per 1,000, respectively). Areas C and D have lower rates (16 per 1,000 and 14 per 1,000). However, areas A and C have higher actual observed rates than would be predicted (10 per 1,000 predicted for A, 7 per 1,000 for C), while areas B and D have lower actual observed than predicted rates (55 per 1,000 for B and 54 per 1,000 for D). In this sense, A and C are both high-risk while B and D are both low-risk. Areas E and F evidence a close approximation between predicted and actual rates. As we shall see, this classification system can provide the basis for identifying contrasting social environments.

What do low- and high-risk social environments look like? One way to answer this question is to examine a pair of neighborhoods with the same predicted but different observed rates of child maltreatment (i.e., one high-risk and the other low-risk for child maltreatment). This approach provides a test of the hypothesis that the two neighborhoods present contrasting environments for child rearing (Garbarino & Sherman, 1980). Relative to a low-risk area, and even though it is socioeconomically equivalent (i.e., has the same level of poverty), a high-risk neighborhood represents a socially improverished human ecology in the sense discussed earlier – that is, it has few people who are free from drain, a generalized fear of being exploited in neighborly interactions, and a lot of highly stressed and emotionally needy families.

To complement demographic and socioeconomic data from census records and individual perceptions from face-to-face interviews with parents, investigators can interview a wide range of "informants" – people who are familiar with a neighborhood in their professional roles as police, visiting nurses, principals, clergy, mail carriers, and the like. These observers are asked to provide information about the following domains: neighborhood public image, neighborhood appearance, social characteristics, neighborhood change, neighborhood "quality of life," child abuse and neglect, neighborhood involvement, and informal supports. The results obtained through blind open-ended questions are subjected to a content analysis and validate the identification

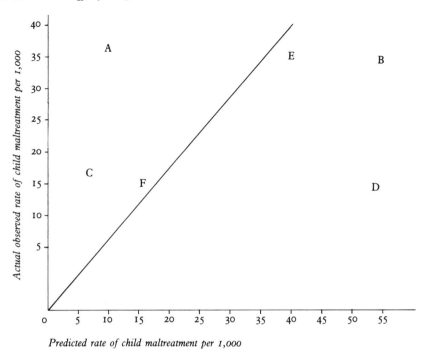

Figure 1. Two Meanings of *risk* in Assessing Community Areas

of one area as being relatively more socially impoverished than the other (Garbarino & Sherman, 1980). The observers may describe the high-risk neighborhood as deteriorated interpersonally and physically, as a dangerous place, as disorganized, and distrustful. In one study there was less positive neighboring and more stressful day-to-day interactions for families in the high-risk area (Garbarino & Sherman, 1980). In short, even though it has equal economic status with the low-risk area, the high-risk neighborhood violates all of Kromkowski's (1976) requisites for a good neighborhood: pride in the neighborhood, care of homes, security for children, and respect for each other.

Current research in metropolitan Chicago seeks to place evaluation of community-based prevention programs within an ecological perspective (Garbarino, Schellenbach, & Kostelny, 1986). It does so by focusing on the operation and impact of child abuse prevention, infant mortality reduction, and family support programs in four high-risk community areas. This provides a case study for applying the concepts of human ecology to the practice of evaluating the impact of early intervention.

The net result of these analyses will document the degree to which program operation is conditioned by community factors. This is an important issue for the field of early intervention, where family support programs seek to be community-based (cf. Kagan, Powell, Weissbourd, & Zigler, 1987). Such analyses can shed light on the degree to which program effectiveness is conditioned by community characteristics, and thus provide guidance for early interventionists, program managers, and community development specialists. Such analyses can serve as a model for the kind of program evaluation needed to make sense of the issues we face in making a community commitment to deal with developmental risk. It provides the operational basis for understanding the human ecology of early developmental risk.

The clinical sociology of early risk is one of the important underdeveloped resources for improving the life prospects of children. It requires further efforts to operationalize the concepts of social richness and social impoverishment. It requires further efforts to use these concepts in understanding the impact of social class on development. It requires further efforts to operationalize a community-based program evaluation model for assessing early intervention efforts. It is a crucial feature of our efforts to bring out into the field the ecological insight that when asked, Does X cause Y? the answer is always, It depends. Finding out the precise who, what, where, and when of that assertion of the importance of context is one of the major challenges we face in making further progress in a science of early intervention on behalf of children at risk.

CONCLUSION

In the Middle Ages half the children died by age five. Now, child death is relatively rare. As standards and expectations for the care and life prospects of children have improved in the last century, developmental risk has become a focal point for research and policy. Thus, our focus has shifted from sheer quantitative concern with child survival to a qualitative concern with development. This is a major accomplishment.

This chapter has explored the sources of developmental risk in the social environment. Its ecological perspective provides a challenge to researchers, policymakers, and clinicians. The challenge is both intellectual and spiritual. The intellectual challenge is to insist upon analytic models that are ecologically valid – that incorporate (or at least address) the full range of influences upon children, from the organismic to the macrosocial. This strains our intellectual resources to their limits, and sometimes beyond. The spiritual challenge is to refuse to despair when faced with the ecological "conspiracies" that envelope children in high-risk social environments. We must refuse to despair and refuse to capitulate to narrow intervention approaches, single-variable models, and other efforts to deny the importance of ecological validity. This is the agenda before us.

REFERENCES

Albee, G. (1980). Primary prevention and social problems. In G. Gerbner, C. J. Ross, & E. Zigler (Eds.), *Child abuse: An agenda for action* (pp. 106–117). New York: Oxford University Press.

Barclay-McLaughlin, G. (1987). *The Center for Successful Child Development.* Chicago, IL: The Ounce of Prevention Fund.

Belsky, J. (1986). Infant day care: A cause for concern? *Zero to Three, 6,* 1ff.

Belsky, J. (1980). Child maltreatment: An ecological interaction. *American Psychologist, 35,* 320–335.

Birch, T. (1982, May 25). *Memo on child abuse and neglect.* National Child Abuse Coalition.

Bouchard, C. (1987). *Child maltreatment in Montreal.* Montreal: University of Quebec.

Bronfenbrenner, U. (1975). Reality and research in the ecology of human development. *Proceedings of the American Philosophical Society, 119,* 439–469.

Bronfenbrenner, U. (1979). *The ecology of human development: Experiments by nature and design.* Cambridge: Harvard University Press.

Bronfenbrenner, U. (1986). Ecology of the family as a context for human development research perspectives. *Developmental Psychology, 22,* 723–742.

Bronfenbrenner, U., & Crouter, A. (1982). Work and family through time and space. In S. N. Kammerman & C. D. Hayes (Eds.), *Families that work: Children in a changing environment of work, family and community* (pp. 138–156). Washington, DC: National Academy of Sciences.

Bronfenbrenner, U., Moen, P., & Garbarino, J. (1984) Families and communities. In H. R. Parke (Ed.), *Review of child development research* (pp. 251–278). Chicago: University of Chicago Press.

Caplan, G. (1974). *Support systems and community mental health.* New York: Behavioral Publications.

Collins, A., & Pancoast, D. (1976). *Natural helping networks.* Washington, DC: National Association of Social Workers.

Dubrow, N., & Garbarino, J. (1987). *Living in the war zone: Mothers and children in public housing developments.* Chicago: Erikson Institute.

Duncan, G., Coe, R., & Hill, M. (1981). *The dynamics of poverty.* Ann Arbor: University of Michigan.

Elder, G. H. (1974). Children of the Great Depression. Chicago: University of Chicago Press.

Emlen, A. (1977, November). *If you care about children, then care about parents.* Address to the Tennessee Association for Young Children, Nashville.

Fallows, J. (1982). Entitlements. *The Atlantic Monthly, 250,* 51, 5ff.

Fisher, K., & Cunningham, S. (1983). The dilemma: Problem grows, support shrinks. *APA Monitor, 14,* 2, 1ff.

Forrester, J. (1969). *Urban dynamics.* Cambridge: MIT Press.

Garbarino, J. (1976). A preliminary study of some ecological correlates of child abuse: The impact of socioeconomic stress on mothers. *Child Development, 47,* 178–185.

Garbarino, J. (1977). The human ecology of child maltreatment: A conceptual model for research. *Journal of Marriage and the Family, 39,* 721–736.

Garbarino, J. (1988). *The future as if it really mattered.* Longmont, CO: Bookmakers Guild.

Garbarino, J., & Associates. (1982). *Children and families in the social environment.* Hawthorne, NY: Aldine Publishing.

Garbarino, J., & Associates (1985). *Adolescent development: An ecological perspective.* Columbus, OH: Merrill.

Garbarino, J., & Crouter, A. (1978a). Defining the community context of parent–child relations. *Child Development, 49,* 604–616.

Garbarino, J., & Crouter, A. (1978b). A note on assessing the construct validity of child maltreatment report data. *American Journal of Public Health, 68,* 598–599.

Garbarino, J., Crouter, A., & Sherman, D. (1977). Screening neighborhoods for intervention: A research model for child protective services. *Journal of Social Service Research, 1,* 135–145.

Garbarino, J., & Gilliam, G. (1980). *Understanding abusive families.* Lexington, MA: Lexington Books.

Garbarino, J., Guttmann, E., & Seeley, J. (1986). *The psychologically battered child.* San Francisco: Jossey-Bass.

Garbarino, J., Schellenbach, C., & Kostelny, K. (1986). *A model for evaluating the impact of family support and child abuse prevention programs in high-risk communities.* Chicago: Erikson Institute.

Garbarino, J., & Sherman, D. (1980). High-risk neighborhoods and high-risk families: The human ecology of child maltreatment. *Child Development, 51,* 188–198.

Garbarino, J., Stocking, S. H., & Associates (Eds.). (1980). *Protecting children from abuse and neglect.* San Francisco: Jossey-Bass.

Gaudin, J., & Polansky, N. (1985). Social distancing of the neglectful family. *Social Service Review, 58,* 245–253.

Giarini, O. (1980). *Dialogue on wealth and welfare.* New York: Pergamon.

Gilkerson, L. (1987). *Report of the Aurora Child Care Project.* Chicago, IL: Erikson Institute.

Hardin, G. (1966). *Biology: Its principles and implications.* San Francisco: W. H. Freeman.

Kagan, S., Powell, D., Weissbourd, B., & Zigler, E. (Eds.). (1987). *Family support programs.* New Haven: Yale University Press.

Kahn, A., & Kamerman, S. (1975). *Not for the poor alone: European social services.* Philadelphia: Temple University Press.

Kamerman, S., & Kahn, A. (1976). *Social services in the United States: Policies and programs.* Philadelphia: Temple University Press.

Keniston, K. (1977). *All our children.* New York: Harcourt Brace Jovanovich.

Kostelny, K., & Garbarino, J. (1987). *The human ecology of infant mortality: An analysis of risk in 76 urban communities.* Chicago: Erikson Institute.

Kromkowski, J. (1976, August). *Neighborhood deterioration and juvenile crime* (U.S. Department of Commerce). South Bend, IN: The South Bend Urban Observatory. (NTIS No. PB-260 473).

Lemann, N. (1986). The origins of the underclass. *Atlantic, 257*, 31–61.

Martin, H. (Ed.). (1976). *The abused child: A multidisciplinary approach to developmental issues and treatment.* Cambridge, MA: Ballinger.

Miller, A. (1987). *Maternal health and infant survival.* Washington, DC: National Center for Clinical Infant Programs.

Moen, P., Kain, E., & Elder, G. (1981, December 15). *Economic conditions and family life: Contemporary and historical perspectives.* Paper presented at the National Academy of Sciences, Assembly of Behavioral and Social Sciences, Committee on Child Development Research and Public Policy, New York.

National Academy of Sciences. (1976). *Towards a national policy for children and families.* Washington, DC: U.S. Government Printing Office.

National Center on Child Abuse and Neglect. (1981). *The national incidence study of child abuse and neglect: Report of findings.* Washington, DC: National Center on Child Abuse and Neglect.

Pasamanick, B. (1987, Winter). Social biology and aids. *Division 37 Newsletter.* Washington, DC: American Psychological Association.

Pavenstedt, E. (1967). *The drifters: Children of disorganized lower-class families.* Boston: Little, Brown.

Pelton, L. (1978). The myth of classlessness in child abuse cases. *American Journal of Orthopsychiatry, 48*, 569–579.

Polansky, N., Chalmers, M., Buttenwieser, E., & Williams, D. (1981). *Damaged parents.* Chicago: University of Chicago Press.

Roman, R., & Trice, H. (Eds.). (1974). *Exploration in psychiatric sociology.* Philadelphia: Davis.

Sattin, D., & Miller, J. (1971). The ecology of child abuse. *American Journal of Orthopsychiatry, 41*, 413–425.

Schell, J. (1982). *The fate of the earth.* New York: Knopf.

Scheper-Hughes, N. (1987). Culture, scarcity, and maternal thinking: Mother love and child death in northeast Brazil. In N. Scheper-Hughes (Ed.), *Child survival* (pp. 187–210). Boston: Reidel.

Steinberg, L., Catalano, R., & Dooley, D. (1981). Economic antecedents of child abuse and neglect. *Child Development, 52*, 975–985.

Tulkin, S. (1972). An analysis of the concept of cultural deprivation. *Developmental Psychology, 6*, 326–339.

United States Bureau of the Census. (1980). *Money, income and poverty studies of families and persons in the United States.* (Current population reports, Series P-60, No. 127).

United States Department of Labor. (1981, March 25). New income levels defining poverty. *New*, 81–156.

Vygotsky, L. S. (1934). *Thought and language.* London: MIT Press.

Whittaker, J., Garbarino, J., & Associates. (1983). *Social support networks.* Hawthorne, NY: Aldine Publishing.

Whittaker, J. (1983). Social support networks in child welfare. In J. Whittaker, J. Garbarino, & Associates, *Social Support Networks* (pp. 167–187). Hawthorne, NY: Aldine Publishing.

Willerman, L., Broman, S. H., & Fiedler, M. (1970). Infant development, preschool IQ, and social class. *Child Development, 41*, 69–77.

Wilson, E. (1978). *On human nature.* Cambridge: Harvard University Press.

Wilson, W. (1987). *The truly disadvantaged: The inner city, the underclass, and public policy.* Chicago: University of Chicago Press.

5   *Protective factors and individual resilience*

EMMY E. WERNER

> It is man's role
> in this evolving universe...
> to teach the terrors of his nature
> and his world to sing...
>   Lillian Smith, *The Journey*

Even in the most disorganized and emotionally impoverished homes, and beset with serious physical handicaps, some children appear to develop stable, healthy personalities and to display a remarkable degree of resilience. Such children have recently become the focus of attention of researchers who have asked, What is right with these children? and, by implication, How can we help others to becomes less vulnerable in the face of life's adversities?

A number of investigators from different disciplines – psychologists, psychiatrists, pediatricians, educators, and sociologists – are engaged in this venture, both in the United States and in Europe. But in contrast to the well-established track record of those who study high-risk children who go on to develop problems, research on protective factors and individual resilience is still in its infancy – "a new scientific region to explore" (Anthony, 1978).

The first objective of this chapter is a clarification of concepts, the second is an overview of the different methodological approaches that have been used to study protective factors and resilience, and a third is to summarize what is presently known about the role of protective factors in the development of children, families, and the community at large. The chapter concludes with a discussion of implications for early intervention that arise from our yet fragmentary knowledge of the roots of resilience in children.

CONCEPTS OF RESILIENCE AND PROTECTIVE FACTORS

The concepts of *resilience* and *protective factors* are the positive counterparts to the constructs of *vulnerability* (which denotes an individual's susceptibility to a negative outcome) and *risk factors* (which denote biological or psychosocial hazards that increase the likelihood of a negative developmental outcome).

Researchers who study children exposed to biological risk factors and stressful life events have gone through several stages in their approach to understanding vulnerability and resilience. First, emphasis was given to the negative developmental outcomes associated with single risk factors, such as low birth weight, or stressful life events, such as the loss of a parent. This was followed by a shift from a "main effect" model of risk research to one that considered interactional effects among multiple stressors, such

97

as the co-occurrence of perinatal complications and poverty. The most recent phase has been marked by a lessened emphasis on vulnerability and a greater focus on resilience. This approach stems from observations of many investigators, especially those engaged in longitudinal studies, that even among children exposed to potent risk factors, it is unusual for more than half to develop serious disabilities or persistent disorders (Rutter, 1978, 1985).

During the mid-1970s, Anthony (1974) introduced the analogy of three dolls – one made of glass, the second made of plastic, and the third made of steel – to contrast children who vary in their vulnerability to adversity. Under the blow of a hammer, the first doll shatters and the second is permanently scarred, but the third doll only emits a fine metallic sound – appearing to be invulnerable, like some of the children of psychotic parents observed in clinical settings. Thus, the concept of the *invulnerable child* has become a part of the literature of psychopathology (Anthony & Cohler, 1987).

As Rutter (1985) has pointed out, however, resistance to stress in children is relative, not absolute. Moreover, the bases of resistance are *both* environmental and constitutional, and the degree of resistance varies over time and according to life's circumstances. Consequently, most researchers today prefer the relative concepts of *resilience* or *stress resistance* rather than invulnerability (Garmezy & Tellegen, 1984; Rutter, 1987; Werner & Smith, 1982). This usage implies a track record of successful adaptation following exposure to biological and psychosocial risk factors and/or stressful life events, and an expectation of continued lower susceptibility to future stressors. Whereas resilience is a characteristic of the individual, *protective factors* include both individual and environmental characteristics that ameliorate or buffer a person's response to constitutional risk factors or stressful life events (Masten & Garmezy, 1985).

Garmezy, Masten, and Tellegen (1984) hypothesize that protective factors may operate through three different mechanisms: compensation, challenge, and immunization. In the *compensatory model*, stress factors and individual attributes are seen as combining *additively* in the prediction of outcome, and severe stress can be counteracted by personal qualities or sources of support. In the *challenge model*, stress is treated as a potential enhancer of competence (provided the degree of stress is not excessive), and the relation between stress and competence may, therefore, be *curvilinear*. In the *immunity model*, there is a *conditional* relation between stressors and protective factors. Such factors modulate the impact of stress on the quality of adaptation, but may have no detectable effects *in the absence* of a stressor.

The compensatory, challenge, and immunity models of stress resistance are not mutually exclusive. They may operate simultaneously or successively in the adaptive repertoire of a resilient individual, depending on his or her coping style and stage of development.

METHODOLOGICAL ISSUES IN THE STUDY OF RESILIENCE AND PROTECTIVE FACTORS

Our current understanding of the roots of resilience comes from a diverse body of literature that is markedly heterogeneous with regard to study design, selection of subjects, definitions of risk and stressors, measures of quality of adaptation, and timing of assessment.

In recent years, research on protective factors has demonstrated a significant shift from individual case studies, and retrospective and cross-sectional designs, to prospective longitudinal studies. The former type of research design suggests potential protective factors, and the latter serves to document and analyze their short-term versus long-term effects.

Some major studies in this area (whose findings will be reviewed in the next section) have been epidemiological in nature. Here, correlates of competence and pathology were observed in large, unselected populations of children in urban, suburban, and rural communities in different regions of the United States and Europe. Protective factors were inferred from correlates of positive outcomes, especially in the presence of adverse circumstances (Earls, Beardslee, & Garrison, 1987; Garmezy, 1987; Rutter, 1979; Werner & Smith, 1982).

In other investigations (a review of the findings follows) high-risk samples were selected for study. The common research paradigm in these studies has been an examination of at-risk infants and children in terms of whether they had good or poor outcomes at a later point in time. Variables associated with subsequent positive outcomes suggest possible protective factors. Definitions of risk in these investigations vary, however, by level of organization, that is, whether researchers conceive of the risk factors residing in the individual organism, in the immediate family, or in the broader sociocultural context that the child inhabits (Seifer & Sameroff, 1987).

So far, only a relatively small number of studies have focused on protective factors in infants and young children who were exposed to *biological insults* that affect the *individual organism*. These include studies of resilient children with perinatal complications, congenital heart defects, cerebral palsy, Down syndrome, and sensory deficits (Berry, 1987; Colona, 1981; Garmezy, 1987; Hrncir, 1987; Moriarty, 1987; O'Dougherty, Wright, Garmezy, Loewenson, & Torres, 1983; Werner & Smith, 1982; Williams, Williams, Landa, & Decena, 1987).

More exclusive and systematic research has been done with resilient children who were exposed to serious *caregiving deficits* in the *immediate family*. A number of investigators have conducted prospective studies of the resilient offspring of psychotic parents (Anthony & Cohler, 1987; Bleuler, 1978; Garmezy, 1974, 1984, 1985, 1987; Kauffman, Grunebaum, Cohler, & Gamer, 1979; Watt, Anthony, Wynne, & Rolf, 1984). Others have focused on protective factors in children of parents with alcoholism (Werner, 1986) and in the offspring of mothers prone to child abuse (Egeland & Sroufe, 1986; Farber & Egeland, 1987). There are also short-term longitudinal studies of resilient children of divorced parents (Hetherington, Cox, & Cox, 1982; Wallerstein & Kelley, 1980) and of competent offspring of teenage parents (Crockenberg, 1981; Furstenberg, 1976; Furstenberg, 1980; Furstenberg & Crawford, 1978).

Most numerous in the current research literature are studies of individual resilience under conditions of *poverty* among contemporary American children and among children who endured the Great Depression in the 1930s (Clark, 1983; Coles, 1967; Coles, 1972; Coles, 1973; Coles, 1978; Elder, 1974; Elder, Caspi, & Van Nguyen, 1985; Elder, Van Nguyen, & Caspi, 1984; Garmezy, 1981; Kellam, Ensminger, & Turner, 1977; Lewis & Looney, 1983; Long & Vaillant, 1984; Werner & Smith, 1982).

There has also been a growing body of literature on protective factors in the lives of young children who have experienced dramatic *upheavals of their social context*. Included are field studies of abandoned, orphaned, and refugee children, and of children who have experienced the horrors of the Nazi holocaust and of wars in Europe, Central America, the Middle East, and Southeast Asia (Ayala-Canales, 1984; Boothby, 1983; Felsman, 1984; Heskin, 1980; Moskovitz, 1983; Rosenblatt, 1983; Sheehy, 1987). Such studies provide an opportunity to test the cross-cultural universality of protective factors under more extreme conditions than prevail in the United States.

So far, most studies of vulnerable children have defined risk at only one level of organization. Data analyses that explore the interplay among multiple risks and protective factors at all three levels – the individual organism, the immediate family, and the larger social context – are still rare (Seifer & Sameroff, 1987; Werner & Smith, 1982). The availability of data for such complex analyses should be on the increase in the next decade as several prospective longitudinal studies with large numbers of children are "coming of age" (Anthony & Cohler, 1987; Magnusson, 1988; Silva & McGee, 1984; Werner, 1987).

Other methodological issues that confront researchers who study individual resilience and protective factors in children include: (1) the selection of age-appropriate measures of competence; (2) the need to use multiple criteria to discriminate high from low competence groups; (3) the timing of child assessment, that is, the need to observe children at risk at multiple measurement points rather than only at one point; and (4) the generalizability of findings from highly selected samples that are particularly vulnerable to samples or populations of infants and children that are at lesser risk (Fisher, Kokes, Cole, Perkins & Wynne, 1987).

Despite such methodological problems and the fragmentation of research efforts, one can discern in the growing body of literature on resilient children a common core of dispositions and sources of support that enable children to maintain a sense of competence and control in their lives, even when confronted with physical handicaps, a pathological family environment, or the adverse effects of poverty, war, and dislocation. The task for future research is to examine systematically the developmental processes that underlie the manifestations of such resilient behavior in children.

INDIVIDUAL RESILIENCE: PROTECTIVE FACTORS WITHIN THE CHILD

Infancy

So far, only a few prospective studies have focused on the roots of resilience in infants, but they are consistent in their findings that babies with good coping abilities under adverse conditions tend to have predictable temperamental characteristics that elicit positive responses from other people.

Beginning in the prenatal period, the Kauai Longitudinal Study has monitored the impact of a variety of biological and psychosocial risk factors, stressful life events, and protective factors on the development of 698 Asian and Polynesian children born in 1955 on a rural Hawaiian island. Half of the cohort lived in chronic poverty, the other half in relative affluence. Data on the children and their families were collected at birth, in the postpartum period, and at ages 1, 2, 10, 18, and 30 years (Werner, 1987, 1989; Werner, Bierman, & French, 1971; Werner & Smith, 1977; Werner & Smith, 1982).

One out of three children in this birth cohort developed learning or behavior problems in the first two decades. Most of the children with such problems had been exposed to multiple risk factors that included perinatal complications, parental psychopathology, family instability, and chronic poverty. But a group of 72 children (some 10% of the cohort), who had experienced four or more such risk factors *before the age of 2*, developed instead into competent and caring young adults. We called them "vulnerable, but invincible" (Werner & Smith, 1982).

The majority of these resilient boys and girls were characterized by their caregivers as very active, affectionate, cuddly, good-natured, and easy to deal with, when they were infants. Few had distressing feeding or sleeping habits. All tended to elicit a great deal of attention and warmth from their caregivers (Werner, 1985).

Positive temperamental characteristics that generated a great deal of attention from caregivers also characterized another high-risk sample of infants from the Kauai Longitudinal Study, the resilient offspring of parents with alcoholism (Werner, 1986).

Very few of the resilient infants in the Kauai Study had to share their parents' attention with a younger sibling during the first 20 months of their lives. Most of the resilient boys were first-born. Being a first-born son was also found to be a protective factor in a study of Philipino infants with congenital heart disease who had normal scores on the Metro-Manila Development Screening Test (MMDST) (Williams et al., 1987).

Spanning an age range similar to the Kauai Longitudinal Study, the Coping Project of the Menninger Foundation in Topeka, Kansas, reported strikingly similar findings based on clinical assessments of 32 middle-class Caucasian infants at 4–32 weeks. Observers noted a consistent positive relation between good energy resources, easy vegetative functioning, and resilience. An intense drive and vigor, and a notable responsiveness to people and objects characterized the successful copers in that study (Murphy, 1987; Murphy & Moriarty, 1976).

Moriarty (1987) illustrated the characteristics of such a resilient infant in her case study of a boy with sensory deficits (hearing loss and divergent strabismus). Even as early as 4 weeks, this child showed a high energy level and was able to express clear-cut preferences, such as being held upright rather than laid supine. He expressed protest forcefully by crying, but recovered quickly from discomfort. He utilized support well, cuddled comfortably, and responded positively to physical contact. Throughout his first year of life, in repeated home observations, he gave reliable evidence that he was an active and assertive baby, with high autonomic reactivity, social responsiveness, and a distinct capacity for self-expression through motor and preverbal channels.

Farber and Egeland (1987) report from the Minnesota Mother–Child Interaction Project that securely attached infants of abusing mothers were especially robust and able to elicit support from other caregivers. They appeared alert, easy to soothe, and socially responsive. Secure attachments in these infants were found to be associated with the presence of a supportive family member – if not the mother, then a grandmother or an older sibling.

Musick, Stott, Spencer, Goldman, and Cohler (1987) found similar interaction styles in babies of mentally ill mothers who profited from the availability of a therapeutic nursery when their mothers underwent treatment or were hospitalized. In spite of separations and family discord during their earliest months, these infants had a relationship with their mothers that was, at least some of the time, characterized by responsiveness and warmth. They also actively reached out for others – the well parent or grandparents.

Resilient infants appear to successfully elicit positive attention. They tend to be active, alert, responsive, and sociable babies, who have experienced nurturance and learned to trust in its availability.

Preschool years

Several investigators, in both short- and long-term longitudinal studies, have noted a pronounced sense of autonomy and social orientation in resilient preschool children.

The high-risk yet resilient toddlers in the Kauai Study met familiar adults and strangers (examining pediatricians and psychologists) on their own terms. During a potentially stressful situation, such as a series of developmental tests, they were described by the examiners as more alert, cheerful, responsive, self-confident, and independent than children of the same age and sex who later developed serious learning or behavior problems. They were also more advanced in communication, locomotion, and self-help skills, and engaged in more social play than the toddlers who later developed problems (Werner & Smith, 1982).

Here is an example of a resilient toddler from our case records: Jenny, a preterm infant, whose mother had a difficult pregnancy and delivery, was at 20 months a small frail-looking child. She appeared to be active and very alert to examiners. Her score on the Cattell Infant Intelligence Scale was in the average range (97), but she demonstrated superior self-help skills on the Vineland Social Maturity Scale (SQ 132). She was inclined "to throw things if not pleased or interested," but was generally cooperative. Jenny was perceived by her mother as an assertive, determined, and domineering little girl who could occasionally be disagreeable if she did not get her way. Her independence and autonomy was quite apparent, in spite of her physical frailty (Werner & Smith, 1982).

Murphy and Moriarty (1976) observed in the Menninger Coping Project that resilient preschoolers tended to play vigorously and to seek out novel experiences. Although notably fearless and self-reliant, they were able to use adults and peers as resources and to ask for help when they needed it.

In the Berkeley study of ego-resiliency and ego-control, Block (1981) looked at the relation between scores on an experimentally derived ego-resiliency index (based on performance under stress) and the independent behavioral ratings of nursery school teachers. Three-year-old children who scored high on the index were described by their teachers as more competent, novelty seeking, and self-reliant, and as less anxious, imitative, and in need of reassurance than their low-scoring peers.

In an epidemiological study of 3-year-olds in the northeastern United States, Earls et al. (1987) found that children classified as ego-resilient on the basis of play observations, were described by their parents as having easy temperaments. They demonstrated four outstanding characteristics: adaptability, positive response to environmental stress, self-initiation, and high involvement in play activities.

Farber and Egeland (1987) noted that abused children who were securely attached and competent at 24 months tended to be less vulnerable to the detrimental effects of abuse from their mothers when they were 42 months old. They were also more competent in their dealing with problem-solving tasks in a frustrating situation, such as the Barrier Box, than children who were insecurely attached. These competent children had been rated as more alert and attentive as newborns by independent observers.

Halverson and Waldrup (1974) monitored the behavior of 74 preschoolers (median age, 30 months) in a barrier situation in nursery school, and at age $7\frac{1}{2}$ years in test situations and free-play in grade school. Preschoolers who coped successfully with the barrier situation were characterized by their teachers as fearless and socially at ease, as showing initiative, and as engaging in vigorous play. These characteristics correlated positively with school-age measures of coping, imagination, and verbal development. Halverson and Waldrup noted that behavior in barrier situations reflects assumptions that young children make about their control of the environment. A child who can demonstrate at an early age that he or she is an agent capable of producing change in a frustrating situation tends to be active and competent in grade school as well.

Wallerstein and Kelley (1980) found similar characteristics among preschool children who weathered successfully the stresses of parental divorce. Such children related to both peers and teachers without excessive anxiety or need for attention. They appeared more socially mature than preschoolers who had difficulty coping with the marital breakup, and were able to distance themselves from their parents' conflict by establishing routines and order in their own lives.

By the time they reach preschool age, resilient children have evolved a coping pattern that combines autonomy (i.e., an ability to provide their own structure) with an ability to ask for support when needed. These characteristics, observed in a variety of high-risk situations and sociocultural contexts, also appear to be predictive of resilience in later years.

Middle childhood

At present we have more data on characteristics of resilience in middle childhood than for any other developmental period. Community-based cross-sectional and longitudinal studies of competent children who experienced stressful life events, and follow-up studies of resilient children who were exposed to poverty, parental psychopathology, or divorce, have yielded similar results in a variety of cultural and geographical contexts (Anthony, 1987; Boothby, 1983; Cohler, 1987; Felsman, 1984; Garmezy, 1983; Werner, 1985). A sense of competence and self-efficacy appears to be the general hallmark of these children.

The vulnerable, but invincible 10-year-olds in the Kauai Longitudinal Study were neither unusually talented nor intellectually gifted. They did, however, possess well-developed problem-solving and communication skills that they put to good use. Their teachers noted that they were not only sociable, but also remarkably independent. They were able to control their impulses and to concentrate on their schoolwork, even if they grew up in homes marred by chronic discord, parental alcoholism, or psychosis. Parental and self-reports indicated that these resilient children displayed a healthy androgyny in their interests and activities, and engaged in hobbies that were not narrowly sex-typed. Such activities gave them solace in adversity, and provided them with a sense of mastery and a reason to feel proud (Werner & Smith, 1982).

Other investigators have found similar characteristics among resilient children who grew up under conditions of chronic poverty in city slums in the United States and abroad (Cohler, 1987; Felsman, 1981; Felsman & Vaillant, 1987; Garmezy, 1981; Long & Vaillant, 1984; Masten, Garmezy, Larkin, & Tellegen, 1985). Children who were more stress-resistant in terms of achievement and behavior at school and adjustment at home share a number of common traits: (1) They were well liked by peers and adults; (2) their dominant cognitive style was reflective rather than impulsive; (3) they demonstrated an internal locus of control, a belief that they were capable of influencing their environment positively; and (4) they were able to use flexible coping strategies in overcoming adversity, including a sense of humor (Masten, 1986).

Sociability and a strong sense of independence are also personal qualities found among the resilient school-age children of psychotic parents (Anthony, 1987; Cohler, 1987; Kauffman et al., 1979; Worland, Weeks, & Janes, 1987). Anthony (1987) has noted that the children he studied in the St. Louis Risk Project resisted becoming engulfed in the parental psychopathology, showed curiosity in understanding what it was that troubled the psychotic parent, maintained a compassionate but detached approach to the mentally ill parent, and often discovered a refuge and source of self-esteem in the pursuit of hobbies and creative interests with schoolmates or friends.

The elementary age children who coped well with the stresses of parental divorce in the Wallerstein and Kelly (1980) study displayed similar characteristics. They enjoyed their classmates and teachers, they tended to be good students, they had a positive self-concept, and they were interested in many aspects of the world around them.

Resilient youngsters during the middle childhood years share a combination of attributes that traditionally have been stereotyped by gender. They provide us with a more androgynous model of competence that includes caring as well as risk taking for *both* boys and girls. Resilient girls tend to be autonomous and independent; resilient boys tend to be emotionally expressive, socially perceptive, and nurturant. Both sexes display flexible coping strategies that allow them to master adversity rather than to react in a rigid, narrowly sex-typed manner.

Adolescence

Studies of resilient adolescents are less numerous than those of younger children. They include studies of youth who have grown up in chronic poverty, in families with parental mental illness or drug abuse, and in families who experienced the stresses of divorce or teenage motherhood (Anthony, 1987; Blum, 1972; Furstenberg, 1980; Gonsalves, 1982; Lewis & Looney, 1983; Long & Vaillant, 1984; Wallerstein & Kelley, 1980; Werner & Smith, 1982; Worland et al., 1987).

Among the personality characteristics that differentiated the high-risk youth on Kauai from their peers with serious delinquencies and mental health problems were a more internal locus of control, a more positive self-concept, and higher scores on the California Psychological Inventory (CPI) scales for Responsibility, Socialization, Achievement via Conformance, and Femininity for *both* sexes (Werner & Smith, 1982).

Resilient youth have been shown to be more responsible and achievement-oriented than their age-mates. They attain a greater degree of social maturity by the time they graduate from high school. They prefer structure in their lives and have internalized a positive set of values. They also share a great interest in matters labeled feminine by conventional wisdom. They are more appreciative, gentle, nurturant, and socially perceptive than their peers who have difficulty coping with adversity (Werner, 1985).

This pattern of individual characteristics found among the Asian youth on Kauai shows a striking similarity to the CPI scores of competent black adolescents from working-class families (Lewis & Looney, 1983) and of academically successful Hispanic male high school students who grew up in poverty (Mason, 1967).

Investigations of two other resilient high-risk groups revealed similar personality dispositions. These groups included adolescents who coped well with the trauma of parental divorce (Wallerstein & Kelly, 1980), and teenage mothers who established stable relationships with a man, and improved their educational and financial status after the birth of their baby (Gonsalves, 1982). Youth in both groups were more responsible, independent, and socially mature than their peers who coped unsuccessfully under similar circumstances. The resilient teenage mothers also had a more outgoing, sociable temperament and a more internal locus of control (Werner, 1987).

Resilient youth are generally characterized by a pronounced social maturity and strong sense of responsibility. They retain a belief, even in the face of great adversity, that they can exert considerable control over their fate.

Intelligence and resilience

Even though there is little evidence that high intelligence *alone* promotes more effective coping, most studies of resilient children suggest that intelligence and central nervous system integrity, as measured by a variety of formal tests (such as the Wechsler Intelligence Scales for Children, the Primary Mental Abilities Test, and the Bender-Gestalt Test for Children), are positively associated with individual resilience. This relationship has been demonstrated in all the prospective longitudinal studies discussed (on Kauai, in Berkeley, in St. Louis, and in Topeka), in the community sample of Project Competence in Minnesota, and in follow-up studies of inner-city youth in Boston and London (Block & Block, 1984; Block & Gjerde, 1986; Garmezy, 1987; Garmezy & Devine, 1984; Felsman & Vaillant, 1987; Murphy & Moriarty, 1976; Rutter, Maughan, Mortimore, & Ouston, 1979; Werner & Smith, 1982; Worland et al., 1987).

It stands to reason that children who are better able to understand events in their lives are better able to figure out strategies for coping with adversities, either through their own efforts, or by actively reaching out to others for help. This association holds for all ethnic groups that have been studied, including Asians and Polynesians (Werner & Smith, 1982), Caucasians (Block & Gjerde, 1986), and blacks (Lewis & Looney, 1983; Looney & Lewis, 1982). Intelligence correlates with resilience among middle-class children (Murphy & Moriarty, 1976) and among children who live in poverty (Long & Vaillant, 1984).

Correlations between measures of intelligence and effective adaptation tend to increase from preschool age to middle childhood and adolescence, and are generally stronger for males than for females. Block and Gjerde (1986) suggest, on the basis of longitudinal data from the Berkeley Study, that ego resiliency may have stronger constitutional roots in boys, while early socialization factors may play a greater role for girls. This hypothesis needs to be tested more systematically through further longitudinal studies.

Protective factors that have been observed repeatedly in resilient children include temperamental characteristics, such as activity level and sociability, and intelligence – dispositions that have a strong genetic base (Scarr & McCartney, 1983). As infants, these children are successful in eliciting positive attention from other people, can structure a situation selectively so it meets their needs, and are able to recover quickly from discomfort. By the time they are preschoolers, they have evolved a strong sense of autonomy coupled with the ability to ask for support when needed. From repeated experiences in successfully overcoming frustrating situations, either on their own initiative or with the help of others, they derive in childhood a sense of self-efficacy and confidence that leads to a strong belief that they are able to influence their environment positively. These children tend to employ a wide range of flexible coping strategies that are not narrowly sex-typed. They select what they need from their environment, make active use of it, or change or restructure a situation so it meets their needs. They are optimistic and hopeful.

PROTECTIVE FACTORS WITHIN THE FAMILY

Despite the burden of parental psychopathology, family discord, or chronic poverty, most children identified as resilient have had the opportunity to establish a close bond with at least one person who provided them with stable care and from whom they received adequate and appropriate attention during the first year of life. The resilient offspring of alcoholics on Kauai, the resilient infants of abusive mothers in Minnesota, and the resilient babies of psychotic parents in Chicago, Rochester, and St. Louis *all* had enough good nurturing to form secure attachments and develop a basic sense of trust (Anthony, 1987; Farber & Egeland, 1987; Fisher et al., 1987; Kauffman et al., 1979; Musick et al., 1987; Werner, 1986; Werner & Smith, 1982).

Affectional ties with alternative caregivers

In high-risk families some of the nurturing often comes from alternative caregivers – the "kith and kin" who have remained relatively invisible in the child development literature (Werner, 1984). Among family members who play important roles as providers of stable care and positive models of identification, grandparents and older siblings often emerge as important buffers of stress in the lives of vulnerable children. A few examples illustrate their potential positive effects.

GRANDPARENTS. Crockenberg (1981) demonstrated that the social support provided by grandparents to mothers and babies during the first year of life was an important predictor of secure attachment for infants at age 1 year. This protective effect was especially potent for mothers with irritable babies. Crockenberg's evidence suggests that such support may mitigate the effects of unresponsive mothering by providing the infant with a responsive substitute. Musick et al. (1987) found that infants and preschoolers who attended a therapeutic nursery for offspring of psychotic mothers were more likely to bounce back from the effects of multiple separations from the ill parent if grandparents joined with the well parent in providing loving care for the child, and cooperated with the efforts of the nursery school staff.

Farber and Egeland (1987) report that few of the young children of abusive mothers in their study were competent and securely attached when they saw them at ages 22, 24, and 42 months. The exceptions were infants and toddlers who had grandmothers who provided them with emotional support.

This phenomenon was also demonstrated by Furstenberg (1976) in a rare longitudinal study of low-income, predominantly black teenage mothers from the Baltimore area who kept their babies. When the cognitive development of their offspring was assessed at ages 3–4 years, the children of these unmarried teenage mothers tended to have higher scores if they were cared for by more than one adult – in most cases by the maternal grandmother. Furthermore, unmarried teenage mothers who remained with their own parents were more likely to return to school, to graduate from high school, and to be employed and off welfare than teenage mothers who did not have such (grand)parental support (Furstenberg & Crawford, 1978).

Working with poor black elementary school children in a Chicago suburb, Kellam et al. (1977) discovered that grandparents made a positive contribution to the adaptation of their grandchildren in grades 1–3. Mother/grandmother families were nearly as effective as two-parent families in assuring that their offspring had positive relationships with peers and teachers, that they paid attention in class, and that they achieved commensurate with their abilities. Children from mother/grandmother families also showed fewer psychiatric symptoms and reported less sadness and nervousness than children reared by single mothers or in mother/stepfather families.

Several studies have shown that grandparents can also be a significant source of support for children of divorce. Whether they are preschoolers or adolescents, young-sters who cope well during and after the parental breakup often have ongoing rela-tionships with grandparents who are attentive to their needs (Wallerstein & Kelley, 1980). When grandparents live nearby, they may provide financial support, child care, and emotional sustenance. Grandfathers can play a particularly important role in skills training and the provision of activities for young grandsons in divorced families (Hetherington et al., 1982).

SIBLINGS. Sib caregiving seems to be another protective buffer for children who grow up in high-risk families. In cases of permanent father absence as a result of death, desertion, or divorce, such caregiving contributed to the pronounced sense of responsi-bility and social maturity we observed among the resilient youth on Kauai. Most of these youngsters were either first- or second-born in families with four or fewer children, and had siblings who were born more than 2 years apart. Involvement in sib caregiving, either as a provider or recipient, proved to be one of the major protective factors in their stressful lives (Werner & Smith, 1982). Studies of the effects of sib caregiving on the brothers and sisters of handicapped children similarly report that such siblings are generally characterized by greater emotional maturity and social responsibility than is commonly found in American youth (Simeonsson & McHale, 1981).

Sib caregiving tends to be more effective as a protective factor when it is *sup-plementary* rather than *substitute* parenting. But under some traumatic circumstances (such as those found in abusive homes or during wars), children have also served as surrogate parents for each other. A classic example are the "six orphans of Terezin" whose parents died in a concentration camp. When brought to a therapeutic nursery in England at the end of World War II, these children did not trust any adult. They had, however, developed strong attachments to each other and looked out for each other with fierce loyalty. Extremely sensitive to each other's needs, they provided mutual emotional support. Remarkable in their resilience as children, they have remained so as adults (Moskovitz, 1983).

In the long run, the availability of supplemental adult resources seems to be a crucial determinant of whether an older sibling will help or hinder a younger brother or sister. Among the resilient children of Kauai, when a parent was absent, alcoholic, or mentally ill, other concerned adults, relatives, and neighbors acted as such protective buffers (Werner & Smith, 1982). Resilient children seem to be especially adept at actively recruiting surrogate parents, even if they are not kin. These can come from the ranks of babysitters, nannies, or house mothers in orphanages or refugee centers (Ayala-Canales, 1984; Moskovitz, 1983; Sheehy, 1987).

Socialization practices

Both the Berkeley and the Kauai studies have noted characteristic child-rearing orienta-tions that appear to promote resilience differentially in boys and girls (Block & Gjerde, 1986; Werner & Smith, 1982). Resilient girls appear to come from households that combine an absence of overprotection, an emphasis on risk taking and independence, and reliable emotional support from the primary caregiver, whether she be mother, grandmother, sister, or aunt. Resilient boys, on the other hand, appear to come from households where there is greater structure, rules, and parental supervision, a male who serves as a model of identification (father, grandfather, older brother, or uncle), and where there is encouragement of emotional expressiveness. Socialization factors that emphasize independence and an absence of overprotection appear to have a greater impact on the resilience of girls than of boys (Block & Gjerde, 1986). The example of a mother who is gainfully and steadily employed appears to be an especially powerful model of identification for resilient girls raised in poverty, whether they are black (Clark, 1983), Hispanic (Gandara, 1982), or Asian-American (Werner & Smith, 1982), especially in households where the father is permanently absent.

Required helpfulness

Assigned chores and the need to take on domestic responsibilities and part-time work to help support the family have proved to be sources of strength and competence for resilient children. On Kauai, many of the high-risk resilient youth had responsibility for the care of younger siblings. Some managed the household when a parent was ill or hospitalized; others worked part-time after school to support their family (Werner & Smith, 1982).

Such acts of "required helpfulness" (Rachman, 1978) have also been noted by Anthony (1974) and Bleuler (1978; 1984) in their clinical studies of the resilient offspring of psychotic parents, by Johnson (cited in Stark, 1987) among the competent offspring of parents with alcoholism, and by Ayala-Canales (1984) and Moskovitz (1983) among resilient orphans of war. Studies of children who had lived during the Great Depression (Elder, 1974; Elder et al., 1985) and of contemporary black youth from working-class families (Clark, 1983; Lewis & Looney, 1983) have shown that such productive roles of responsibility, when associated with close family ties, are important protective factors during times of adversity.

Faith: A sense of coherence

A number of studies of resilient children from a wide variety of socioeconomic and ethnic backgrounds have noted that their families have held religious beliefs that provided stability and meaning to their lives, especially in times of hardship and adversity (Anthony, 1987; Blum, 1972; Lewis & Looney, 1983; Moskovitz, 1983; Murphy & Moriarty, 1976; Werner & Smith, 1982). The content of their faith varied from Buddhism to Mormonism to Catholicism and fundamental and liberal versions of Protestantism and Judaism. What such faith appears to give resilient children and their caregivers is a sense of rootedness and coherence (Antonovsky, 1979, 1987) a conviction that their lives have meaning, and a belief that things will work out in the end, despite unfavorable odds. This sense of meaning persists, even among children uprooted by wars or scattered as orphans and refugees to the four corners of the earth (Antonovsky, 1987; Ayala-Canales, 1984). It enables children to love despite hate, and to behave compassionately toward other persons (Moskovitz, 1983).

Resilient infants have had the opportunity to establish a secure attachment with at least one stable caregiver, (if not a parent, then a close relative, such as a grandparent, older sibling, uncle, aunt, or nanny). As these children grow older, they are especially adept at actively recruiting substitute parents if their own parents are absent, unavailable, or incapacitated. Their caregivers, in turn, tend to reward them for their risk taking and independence, encourage their assumption of responsibility, and model examples of helpfulness and caring. They also foster the belief that adversities can be overcome by personal effort and with the emotional support of kith and kin.

PROTECTIVE FACTORS IN THE COMMUNITY

Abundant data from both longitudinal and cross-sectional studies suggest that resilient children obtain a great deal of emotional support from outside their own family. They tend to rely on friends, neighbors, and teachers for counsel and comfort in times of transition or crisis (Bryant, 1985; Werner & Smith, 1982).

Friends

Even though they may come from poor, chaotic, and discordant homes, resilient children tend to be well liked by their playmates and classmates, and have one or more close friends (Garmezy, 1981; Kauffman et al., 1979; Werner & Smith, 1982). They tend to keep their childhood friends for long periods of time and rely on them for ongoing emotional support. This finding holds for females more than males (Werner, 1987).

Association with friends and the parents of friends who come from stable families can help resilient children to gain a perspective and maintain a constructive distance between themselves and their own households, which may be marred by discord, parental psychopathology, or alcoholism (Anthony, 1987; Werner & Smith, 1982). Investigators who have studied the role of friends in the lives of children whose parents divorce, have noted that peers may enrich and expand the quality of a resilient child's life, but, like siblings, they are more effective as supplements rather than as substitutes for a close and stable relationship with at least one family member in the home (Wallerstein & Kelley, 1980).

School

Most studies have noted that resilient children enjoy school, whether nursery school, grade school, or high school (Kellam et al., 1977; Musick et al., 1987; Werner & Smith, 1982). Even if they are not unusually gifted, those who ultimately show the greatest resilience tend to put whatever abilities they have to good use. In many cases, such children make school into a home away from home, a refuge from a disordered household.

Musick et al. (1987) provided a special therapeutic nursery school program for the offspring of mothers with psychiatric illness. They noted that such programs allow young children to bounce back from the effects of multiple separations from their hospitalized mothers.

In their studies of schools in inner London, Rutter et al. (1979) found that positive experiences in the classroom could mitigate the effects of considerable stress at home. In this regard, the more successful schools were characterized by appropriately high academic standards, the availability of incentives and rewards, effective feedback with ample praise for students from their teachers, the setting of good models of behavior by teachers, and the availability of positions of trust and responsibility for students. Children who attended such schools developed few, if any, emotional or behavior problems, despite considerable deprivation and discord at home.

Hetherington et al. (1982) found a remarkable similarity in the characteristics of both home and school environments that were associated with greater resilience among children of divorced families. In both settings, a greater degree of adaptive behavior among children was associated with a more responsive and nurturant atmosphere as well as a more organized and predictable environment, with clearly defined and consistently enforced standards, rules, and responsibilities. In fact, such structure, organization, rule enforcement, and assignment of responsibilities were more important for children from divorced than from nondivorced families. Structure and control appeared more salient for fostering resilience in boys; nurturance and the assumption of responsibility was more important for girls.

Such structural support in schools may be an especially potent protective factor for bright children from discordant, divorce-prone homes (Wallerstein & Kelley, 1980) and for talented minority children from economically disadvantaged backgrounds. Studies of high-achieving Hispanic females in *both* public and parochial schools in California, for example, have shown that attendance at integrated schools that demanded discipline and high academic standards was an important contributor to their success (Gandara, 1982; Luzania, 1986).

Teachers

Among the most frequently encountered positive role models in the lives of the children of Kauai, outside of the family circle, was a favorite teacher. For the resilient youngster a special teacher was not just an instructor for academic skills, but also a confidant and positive model for personal identification (Werner & Smith, 1982). Only a few studies have explored the role of teachers as protective buffers in the lives of children who overcome great adversity. Though they differ in their methodological approaches, the studies tend to agree that teachers of preschool and primary school children can have a lasting effect on their young charges.

Two investigations deserve special note. One is a follow-up study into middle adulthood of 24 child survivors of the Nazi holocaust who were sent from concentration camps and orphanages to a therapeutic nursery school in England at the close of World War II (Moskovitz, 1983). Excerpts from follow-up interviews after 30–40 years reveal an extraordinary affirmation of life. Furthermore, all of the resilient survivors considered *one* woman to be among the most potent influences in their lives – the nursery school teacher who provided warmth and caring, and taught them "to behave compassionately."

A second study employed path analysis to trace the direct and indirect effects of a first-grade teacher on the subsequent adult status of 60 children from a disadvantaged neighborhood (Pederson & Faucher, 1978). Results show clearly that an effective first-grade teacher conveys to pupils "a profound impression of the importance of school" and can influence their social mobility. None of these children remained in the lower class, one-third moved into the middle class, and the other two-thirds attained upper middle-class status in adulthood. This is one of the rare investigations that describes the process by which a good teacher shapes academic attainment and the self-concept of pupils. In such a case, an initial good foundation (all the students read by the end of first grade) yielded benefits in later life. More such studies are needed to demonstrate the direct and indirect effects of protective factors in the lives of resilient children across several developmental stages.

Among potent protective factors in the lives of resilient children are friends, neighbors, and teachers who provide emotional support, reward competence, and promote self-esteem. Such external sources of support appear particularly effective if they provide an organized and predictable environment for the young child that combines warmth and caring with clearly defined structure and rules.

CONCLUSIONS

Three types of protective factors emerge as recurrent themes from the diverse studies cited in this chapter: (1) dispositional attributes of the child that elicit predominantly positive responses from the environment, such as physical robustness and vigor, an easy temperament, and intelligence; (2) affectional ties and socialization practices within the family that encourage trust, autonomy, and initiative; and (3) external support systems that reinforce competence and provide children with a positive set of values. The preliminary data reviewed here suggest that these protective factors may have a more generalized effect on children's adaptation than those of specific risk factors or stressful life events. The qualities that define individual resilience have been demonstrated in children of all races, in different socioeconomic groups, and in different cultural contexts: "Resilience...seems to involve several related elements. Firstly, a sense of self-esteem and self-confidence; secondly, a belief in one's own self-efficacy and ability to deal with change and adaptations; and thirdly, a repertoire of social problem solving approaches" (Rutter, 1985).

The shifting balance between vulnerability and resilience

Just as vulnerability is relative, depending on complex interactions among constitutional factors and life circumstances, resilience is governed by a similar dynamic interaction among protective factors within the child, his or her family environment, and the larger social context in which he or she lives (Cohler, 1987). Longitudinal studies that have followed infants from birth to maturity indicate that at each developmental stage, there is a shifting balance between stressful life events that heighten children's vulnerability and protective factors that enhance their resilience. This balance changes not only with the stages of the life cycle, but also varies with the sex of the individual and the cultural context in which he or she grows up (Werner & Smith, 1982).

Both the American and European studies reviewed here have shown repeatedly that boys are more vulnerable than girls to the effects of biological insults or caregiving deficits in infancy and childhood. This trend is reversed in the second decade, with girls becoming more vulnerable in adolescence, especially with the onset of early childbearing. In young adulthood, the balance appears to shift back again in favor of the women. (Werner, 1987).

As long as the balance between stressful life events and protective factors is favorable, successful adaptation is possible. However, when stressful life events outweigh the protective factors, even the most resilient child can develop problems. Intervention may thus be conceived as an attempt to shift the balance from vulnerability to resilience, either by decreasing exposure to risk factors and stressful life events, or by increasing the number of available protective factors (e.g., competencies and sources of support) in the lives of vulnerable children.

Implications for early intervention

What then are some of the implications that we can draw from the still tentative and fragmentary findings of studies of resilient children? Most of all, they provide us with a more hopeful perspective than can be gleaned from reading only the literature on children who succumb to the negative consequences of biological insults, caregiving deficits, and/or ecological stressors. Research on protective factors and individual resilience gives us an awareness of the self-righting tendencies that move children toward normal development under all but the most persistent adverse circumstances.

Risk factors are not black boxes into which one fits children to be neatly labeled and safely stored away. Like protective factors, they are probability statements, the odds of a gamble whose stakes change with time and place. The identification and assessment of risk factors in infants and young children makes sense *only* if it plugs into intervention programs, and there is a periodic follow-up to determine the efficacy of education, rehabilitation, and treatment. Such efforts are based ultimately on the faith that the odds *can* be changed, if not for every vulnerable child, at least for many; if not all the time, at least some of the time; if not everywhere, at least in some places.

It needs to be kept in mind that, with very few exceptions, research on individual resilience and protective factors has focused on children who muddled through on their own, with informal support from kith and kin, *not* children who were recipients of early intervention services. Yet, there are some lessons such children can teach us about effective early intervention.

1. There are large individual differences among high-risk children in their responses to *both* negative and positive circumstances in their environment. The very fact of individual variation among infants and young children who live in adverse conditions suggests the need for greater assistance to some than to others.

2. We need to set priorities, to make hard choices, if we cannot extend early intervention services to every child from birth to 3 years of age. Such programs need to focus especially on infants and young children who appear most vulnerable because they lack, temporarily or permanently, some of the essential social bonds that appear to buffer stress. Among these vulnerable children are the survivors of neonatal intensive care; hospitalized children who are separated from their families for extended periods of time; the young offspring of alcoholic or psychotic parents; infants and toddlers whose mothers work full-time in the labor market, without access to stable child care; the babies of single or teenage parents with no other adult in the household; and young migrant and refugee children with no roots in a permanent community.

3. Assessment and diagnosis, the initial part of early intervention, need to focus not only on risk factors in the lives of children and families they serve, but also on the protective factors. These include the competencies and sources of informal support that *already* exist, that can be utilized to enlarge a young child's repertoire of problem-solving skills, and that can enhance his or her self-esteem.

4. Research on resilient children has shown repeatedly that if a parent is incapacitated or unavailable, other significant people in a young child's life can play an enabling role, whether they are grandparents, older siblings, family day-care providers, or nursery school teachers. In many situations, it may make better sense to strengthen such available informal ties to kin and community than to introduce additional layers of bureaucracy into the delivery of services, and it might be less costly as well.

5. In order for any early intervention program to be effective, a young child needs enough consistent nurturance to trust in its availability. Research on resilient children has shown us that they had at least one person in their lives who accepted them unconditionally, regardless of temperamental idiosyncracies, physical attractiveness, or level of intelligence.

6. Research has also shown us that the promotion of resilience in young children by caring adults does not rely on removing stress and adversity completely from their lives, but rather in helping them encounter graduated challenges that enhance their competence and confidence.

7. Such challenges appear to be most effective for young children in the context of an organized and predictable environment that combines warmth and caring with a clearly defined structure and an established setting of explicit limits that are consistently enforced.

8. Although studies show that some youngsters are constitutionally more resistant to stress than others, all children can be helped to become more resilient if their caregivers encourage their independence, teach them flexible ways of problem solving (including appropriate communication and self-help skills), boost their self-confidence, and model as well as reward acts of helpfulness and cooperation.

The life stories of resilient individuals have taught us that competence, confidence, and caring can flourish, even under adverse circumstances, if young children encounter persons who provide them with a secure basis for the development of trust, autonomy, and initiative. Evaluations of effective early intervention programs can, in turn, illuminate the process by which the chain of direct and indirect links among protective factors is established, which fosters escape from adversity for vulnerable children.

REFERENCES

Anthony, E. J. (1974). The syndrome of the psychologically invulnerable child. In E. J. Anthony & C. Koupernik (Eds.), *The child and his family: Vol. 3. Children at psychiatric risk* (pp. 529–544). New York: Wiley.

Anthony, E. J. (1978). A new scientific region to explore. In E. J. Anthony, C. Koupernik, & C. Chiland (Eds.), *The child and his family: Vol. 4. Vulnerable children* (pp. 3–15). New York: Wiley.

Anthony, E. J. (1987). Children at risk for psychosis growing up successfully. In E. J. Anthony & B. Cohler (Eds.), *The invulnerable child* (pp. 147–184). New York: Guilford Press.

Anthony, E. J., & Cohler, B. (Eds.). (1987). *The invulnerable child.* New York: Guilford Press.

Antonovsky, A. (1979). *Health, stress and coping: New perspectives on mental and physical well-being.* San Francisco: Jossey-Bass.

Antonovsky, A. (1987). *Unraveling the mystery of health: How people manage stress and stay well.* San Francisco: Jossey-Bass.

Ayala-Canales, C. E. (1984). *The impact of El Salvador's civil war on orphan and refuge children.* Unpublished master's thesis in child development, University of California, Davis.

Berry, P. (1987, July 15). *Risk and protective factors in the development of Down's syndrome children and adolescents.* Paper presented at the Ninth Biennial Meeting of the International Society for the Study of Behavioral Development, Tokyo.

Bleuler, M. (1978). *The schizophrenic disorders: Long-term patient and family studies.* New Haven: Yale University Press.

Bleuler, M. (1984). Different forms of childhood stress and patterns of adult psychiatric outcome. In J. S. Watt, E. J. Anthony, L. C. Wynne, & J. E. Rolf (Eds.), *Children at risk for schizophrenia: A longitudinal perspective* (pp. 537–542). London and New York: Cambridge University Press.

Block, J. H. (1981). Growing up vulnerable and growing up resistant: Preschool personality, pre-adolescent personality and intervening family stresses. In C. D. Moore (Ed.), *Adolescence and stress* (pp. 123–129). Washington, DC: U.S. Government Printing Office.

Block, J. H., & Block, J. (1984). A longitudinal study of personality and cognitive development. In S. A. Mednick, M. Harway, & K. M. Finello (Eds.), *Handbook of longitudinal research* (pp. 328–352). New York: Praeger.

Block, J., & Gjerde, P. F. (1986, August). *Early antecedents of ego resiliency in late adolescence.* Paper presented at the American Psychological Association Meeting, Washington, DC.

Blum, R. (1972). *Horatio Alger's children: The role of the family in the origin and prevention of drug risk.* San Francisco: Jossey-Bass.

Boothby, (1983). The horror, the hope. *Natural History, 92,* 64–71.

Bryant, B. K. (1985). The neighborhood walk: Sources of support in middle childhood. *Monographs of the Society for Research in Child Development* (Serial No. 210).

Clark, R. M. (1983). *Family life and school achievement: Why poor black children succeed or fail.* Chicago: University of Chicago Press.

Cohler, B. J. (1987). Adversity, resilience and the study of lives. In E. J. Anthony & B. J. Cohler (Eds.), *The invulnerable child* (pp. 363–424). New York: Guilford Press.

Coles, R. (1967). *Children of crisis: Vol. 1. A study of courage and fear.* Boston: Little, Brown.

Coles, R. (1972). *Children of crisis: Vol. 2. Migrants, sharecroppers, mountaineers.* Boston: Little, Brown.

Coles, R. (1973). *Children of crisis: Vol. 3. The south goes north.* Boston: Little, Brown.

Coles, R. (1978). *Children of crisis: Vol. 4. Eskimos, Chicanos, Indians.* Boston: Little, Brown.

Colona, A. (1981). Success through their own efforts. *Psychoanalytic Study of the Child, 36,* 133–144.

Crockenberg, S. B. (1981). Infant irritability, mother responsiveness, and social support influences on the security of infant–mother attachment. *Child Development, 52,* 857–865.

Earls, F., Beardslee, W., & Garrison, W. (1987). Correlates and predictors of competence in young children. In E. J. Anthony & B. Cohler (Eds.), *The invulnerable child* (pp. 70–83). New York: Guilford Press.

Egeland, B., & Sroufe, A. (1986, August). *Stressful life events and school outcome: A study of protective factors.* Paper presented at the American Psychological Association Meeting, Washington, DC.

Elder, G. H. (1974). *Children of the Great Depression.* Chicago: University of Chicago Press.

Elder, G. H., Caspi, A., & Van Nguyen, T. (1985). Resourceful and vulnerable children: Family influence in hard times. In R. Silbereisen & H. Eyferth (Eds.), *Development in context* (pp. 167–186). Berlin: Springer-Verlag.

Elder, G. H., Van Nguyen, T., & Caspi, A. (1984). Linking family hardships to children's lives. *Child Development, 56,* 361–375.

Farber, E. A., & Egeland, B. (1987). Invulnerability among abused and neglected children. In E. J. Anthony & B. Cohler (Eds.), *The invulnerable child* (pp. 253–288). New York: Guilford Press.

Felsman, J. K. (1981). *Street urchins of California: On risk, resiliency and adaptation in childhood.* Unpublished doctoral dissertation, Harvard University, Cambridge.

Felsman, J. K. (1984). Abandoned children: A reconsideration. *Children Today, 13*(3), 13–18.

Felsman, J. K., & Vaillant, G. E. (1987). Resilient children as adults: A 40-year study. In E. J. Anthony & B. Cohler (Eds.), *The invulnerable child* (pp. 289–314). New York: Guilford Press.

Fisher, L., Kokes, R. F., Cole, R. E., Perkins, P. M., & Wynee, L. C. (1987). Competent children at risk: A study of well-functioning offspring of disturbed parents. In E. J. Anthony & B. Cohler (Eds.), *The invulnerable child* (pp. 211–228). New York: Gulford Press.

Furstenberg, F. F. (1976). *Unplanned parenthood: The social consequences of teenage child-bearing.* New York: The Free Press.

Furstenberg, F. F. (1980). Burden and benefits: The impact of early childbearing on the family. *Journal of Social Issues, 36,* 64–87.

Furstenberg, F. F., & Crawford, A. G. (1978). Family support: Helping teenage mothers to cope. *Family Planning Perspectives, 10,* 322–333.

Gandara, P. (1982). Passing through the eye of the needle: High achieving Chicanas. *Hispanic Journal of Behavioral Sciences, 4,* 167–180.

Garmezy, N. (1974). The study of competence in children at risk for severe psychopathology. In E. J. Anthony & C. Koupernik (Eds.), *The child in his family: Vol. 3. Children at psychiatric risk* (pp. 77–98). New York: Wiley.

Garmezy, N. (1981). Children under stress: Perspectives on antecedents and correlates of vulnerability and resistance to psychopathology. In A. I. Rabin, J. Aronoff, A. M., Barclay, & R. A. Zucker (Eds.), *Further explorations in personality* (pp. 196–269). New York: Wiley.

Garmezy, N. (1983). Stressors of childhood. In N. Garmezy & M. Rutter (Eds.), *Stress, coping and development in children* (pp. 43–84). New York: McGraw-Hill.

Garmezy, N. (1984). Children vulnerable to major mental disorders: Risk and protective factors. In L. Grinspoon (Ed.), *Psychiatric update* (Vol. 3, pp. 91–104; 159–161). Washington, DC: American Psychiatric Press.

Garmezy, N. (1985). Stress-resistant children: The search for protective factors. In J. E. Stevenson (Ed.), Recent research in developmental psychopathology, *Journal of Child Psychology & Psychiatry, Book Supplement No. 4* (pp. 213–233). Oxford: Pergamon Press.

Garmezy, N. (1987). Stress, competence, and development: Continuities in the study of schizophrenic adults, children vulnerable to psychopathology, and the search for stress resistant children. *American Journal of Orthopsychiatry, 57*(2), 159–174.

Garmezy, N., & Devine, V. (1984). Project Competence: The Minnesota studies of children vulnerable to psychopathology. In N. F. Watt, E. J. Anthony, L. C. Wynne, & J. E. Rolf (Eds.), *Children at risk for schizophrenia: A longitudinal perspective* (pp. 289–303). London and New York: Cambridge University Press.

Garmezy, N., Masten, A. S., & Tellegen, A. (1984). The study of stress and competence in children: Building blocks for developmental psychopathology. *Child Development, 55*, 97–111.

Garmezy, N., & Tellegen, A. (1984). Studies of stress-resistant children: Methods, variables and preliminary findings. In F. Morrison, C. Lord, & D. Keating (Eds.), *Advances in applied developmental psychology* (pp. 231–287). New York: Academic Press.

Gonsalves, A. M. (1982). *Follow-up of teen-age mothers at age 25: A longitudinal study on the island of Kauai.* Unpublished masters thesis in child development, University of California, Davis.

Halverson, C. F., & Waldrup, M. P. (1974). Relations between preschool barrier behaviors and early school measures of coping, imagination and verbal development. *Developmental Psychology, 10*, 716–720.

Heskin, L. (1980). *Northern Ireland: A psychological analysis.* New York: Columbia University Press.

Hetherington, E. M., Cox, M., & Cox, R. (1982). Effects of divorce on parents and children. In M. Lamb (Ed.), *Non-traditional families* (pp. 223–285). Hillsdale, NJ: L. Erlbaum.

Hrncir, E. J. (1987, May 13). *Mother and infant affective contributors to resiliency in at-risk and non-risk infants.* Paper presented at the Fifth International Conference on Early Identification of Children at Risk, Durango, CO.

Kauffman,C., Grunebaum, L., Cohler, B., & Gamer, E. (1979). Superkids: Competent children of psychotic mothers. *American Journal of Psychiatry, 136*, 1398–1402.

Kellam, S. G., Ensminger, M. T., & Turner, R. J. (1977). Family structure and the mental health of children. *Archives of General Psychiatry, 34*, 1012–1022.

Lewis, J. M., & Looney, J. D. (1983). *The long struggle: Well functioning working class black families.* New York: Brunner/Mazel.

Long, J. V. F., & Vaillant, G. E. (1984). Natural history of male psychological health, XI: Escape from the underclass. *American Journal of Psychiatry, 141*, 341–346.

Looney, J. G., and Lewis, J. M. (1982, July). *Competent adolescents from different socio-economic and ethnic contexts.* Paper presented at the Tenth International Congress of Child and Adolescent Psychiatry, Dublin, Ireland.

Luzania, L. R. (1986). *Locus of control and academic achievement in U.S. born Mexican-American children.* Unpublished masters thesis in child development, University of California, Davis.

Magnusson, D. (1988). *Individual development from an interactional perspective: A longitudinal study.* Hillsdale, NJ: L. Erlbaum.

Mason, E. P. (1967). Comparison of personality characteristics of junior high school students from American Indian, Mexican and Caucasian ethnic backgrounds. *Journal of Social Psychology, 73*, 115–128.

Masten, A. S. (1986). Humor and competence in school-age children. *Child Development, 57*, 461–473.

Masten, A. S., & Garmezy, N. (1985). Risk, vulnerability and protective factors in developmental psychopathology. In B. B. Lahey & A. E. Kazdin (Eds.), *Advances in Clinical Child Psychology* (Vol, 8, pp. 1–52). New York: Plenum Press.

Masten, A., Garmezy, N., Larkin, K., & Tellegen, A. (1985, August). *Family factors related to stress and competence in children.* Paper presented at the American Psychological Association Meeting, Los Angeles.

Moriarty, A. E. (1987). John, a boy who acquired resilience. In E. J. Anthony & B. Cohler (Eds.), *The invulnerable child* (pp. 106–144). New York: Guilford Press.

Moskovitz, S. (1983). *Love despite hate: Child survivors of the holocaust and their adult lives.* New York: Schocken.

Murphy, L. B. (1987). Further reflections on resilience. In E. J. Anthony & B. Cohler (Eds.), *The invulnerable child* (pp. 84–105). New York: Guilford Press.

Murphy, L. R., & Moriarty, A. (1976). *Vulnerability, coping and growth from infancy to adolescence.* New Haven: Yale University Press.

Musick, J. S., Stott, F. M., Spencer, C. K., Goldman, J., & Cohler, B. J. (1987). Maternal factors related to vulnerability and resiliency in young children at risk. In E. J. Anthony & B. J. Cohler (Eds.), *The invulnerable child* (pp. 229–252). New York: Guilford Press.

O'Dougherty, M., Wright, F. S., Garmezy, N., Loewenson, R. B., & Torres, F. (1983). Later competence and adaptation in infants who survive severe heart defects. *Child Devleopment, 54,* 1129–1142.

Pederson, E., & Faucher, T. (1978). A new perspective on the effects of first grade teachers in children's subsequent adult status. *Harvard Educational Review, 18,* 1–31.

Rachman, S. F. (1978). *Fear and courage.* San Francisco: W. H. Freeman.

Rosenblatt, R. (1983). *Children of war.* Garden City, NY: Anchor Press.

Rutter, M. (1978). Early sources of security and competence. In J. Bruner & A. Garton (Eds.), *Human growth and development* (pp. 33–61). New York: Oxford University Press.

Rutter, M. (1979). Protective factors in children's responses to stress and disadvantage. In M. W. Kent & J. E. Rolf (Eds.), *Primary prevention of psychopathology* (Vol. 3, pp. 49–74). Hanover, NH: University Press of New England.

Rutter, M. (1985). Resilience in the face of adversity: Protective factors and resistance to psychiatric disorder. *British Journal of Psychiatry, 147,* 598–611.

Rutter, M. (1987). Psychosocial resilience and protective mechanisms. *American Journal of Orthopsychiatry, 57,* 316–331.

Rutter, M., Maughan, B., Mortimore, P., & Ouston, J. (1979). *Fifteen thousand hours: Secondary schools and their effects on children.* Cambridge: Harvard University Press.

Scarr, S., & McCartney, L. (1983). How people make their own environments: A theory of genotype-environment effects. *Child Development, 54,* 424–435.

Seifer, R., & Sameroff, A. J. (1987). Multiple determinants of risk and invulnerability. In E. J. Anthony & B. Cohler (Eds.), *The invulnerable child* (pp. 51–69). New York: Guilford Press.

Sheehy, G. (1987). *Spirit of survival.* New York: Bantam Books.

Silva, P. A., & McGee, R. (1984). *Growing up in Dunedin.* Dunedin Multidisciplinary Health and Development Research Unit, Department of Pediatrics and Child Health, University of Otago Medical School, Dunedin, New Zealand.

Simeonsson, R. J., & McHale, S. M. (1981). Review: Research on handicapped children: Sibling relationships. *Child Care, Health and Development, 7,* 153–171.

Wallerstein, J. S., & Kelley, J. B. (1980). *Surviving the breakup: How children and parents cope with divorce.* New York: Basic Books.

Watt, N. S., Anthony, E. J., Wynne, L. C., & Rolf, J. E. (Eds.). (1984). *Children at risk for schizophrenia: A longitudinal perspective.* London and New York: Cambridge University Press.

Werner, E. E. (1984). *Child care: Kith, kin and hired hands.* Baltimore: University Park Press.

Werner, E. E. (1985). Stress and protective factors in children's lives. In A. R. Nicol (Ed.), *Longitudinal studies in child psychology and psychiatry* (pp. 335–356). Chichester, England: Wiley.

Werner, E. E. (1986). Resilient offspring of alcoholics: A longitudinal study from birth to age 18. *Journal of Studies on Alcohol, 47,* 34–40.

Werner, E. E. (1987, July 15). *Vulnerability and resiliency: A longitudinal study of Asian-Americans from birth to age 30.* Address at the Ninth Biennial Meeting of the International Society for the Study of Behavioral Development, Tokyo.

Werner, E. E. (1989). High risk children in young adulthood: A longitudinal study from birth to 32 years. *American Journal of Orthopsychiatry 59*(1), 72–81.

Werner, E. E. Bierman, J. S., & French, F. E. (1971). *The children of Kauai: A longitudinal study from the prenatal period to age ten.* Honolulu: University of Hawaii Press.

Werner, E. E., & Smith, R. S. (1977). *Kauai's children come of age.* Honolulu: University of Hawaii Press.

Werner, E. E., & Smith, R. S. (1982). *Vulnerable but invincible: A longitudinal study of resilient children and youth.* New York: McGraw-Hill.

Williams, P. D., Williams, A. R., Landa, A., & Decena, A. (1987, May 13). *Risk and resilience: Another look at the excluded child.* Paper presented at the Fifth International Conference on Early Identification of Children at Risk, Durango, CO.

Worland, J., Weeks, D. G., & Janes, C. L. (1987). Predicting mental health in children at risk. In E. J. Anthony & B. Cohler (Eds.), *The invulnerable child* (pp. 185–210). New York: Guilford Press.

PART III

Theoretical Bases of Early Intervention

6 Transactional regulation and early intervention

ARNOLD J. SAMEROFF AND BARBARA H. FIESE

The prevention of children's psychosocial disorders has not been an easily accomplished task. In a critical appraisal of such efforts, Rutter (1982) was led to conclude that our knowledge of the topic is limited and that there are few interventions of proven value. What we hope to achieve here is to demonstrate that Rutter's assessment is accurate in what we have already been able to accomplish, but underestimates what we are capable of achieving with current knowledge. The two greatest myths identified by Rutter were the belief that there are single causes for disorders and the belief that these causes can be eliminated by treating the child as an individual. In his review of the literature he finds that the evidence contradicts these beliefs. Whatever substance can be found in this area of research points to multiple not single causation as the rule rather than the exception, and the need for intervening in the childrearing context as of equal or greater importance than treating the child.

This presentation will begin with an overview of traditional concepts of intervention and prevention. When these ideas are used to interpret causal factors in disease, a variety of paradoxes emerge that require a contextual systems analysis of developmental processes for their understanding. A transactional model will be described that explains behavioral outcomes as the mutual effects of context on child and child on context. The transactional model will be seen to be embedded in a regulatory system that is characteristic of all developmental processes. Based on the regulatory system, a number of intervention strategies will be described that are theoretically driven and that enhance the possibility of providing optimal outcomes for children.

DEFINING PREVENTION

For the last 30 years there has been a division of prevention efforts into primary and secondary categories. More recently, tertiary prevention has been added to the list (Leavell & Clark, 1965). *Primary prevention* is practiced prior to the origin of the disease. *Secondary prevention* is practiced after the disease has been identified but before it has caused disability. *Tertiary prevention* occurs after disability has been experienced, with the goal of reducing further deterioration.

Although secondary and tertiary prevention may be quite important, they do not have the connotation of priority associated with primary prevention (Lamb & Zusman, 1979). Especially for the nonprofessional community, the terms imply a *preferred*

119

priority, when only a qualitative distinction is intended. Cost-benefit analyses of many intervention efforts have found that the secondary treatment of a high-risk group may be far more efficient than a primary universal treatment (Gordon, 1983).

Distinctions among prevention categories may be even less clear when one turns from the primary prevention of biological diseases, where these definitions were formulated, to the primary prevention of psychological disease, where the complexity of the problem is further increased. Although clear linkages have been found between some germs and specific biological disorders (e.g., *diplococci* and pneumonia), this has not been true for behavioral disorders. Primary prevention of psychological disorders, in the sense of deterring a single biological factor, may have meaning in a very small percentage of cases, but these are usually the most severe and profound cases. In the vast majority of cases, behavioral or developmental disturbances are the result of a combination of factors that are more strongly associated with the psychological and social environment than any intrinsic characteristics of the affected individuals.

Traditionally, early intervention programs have been based on stable models of development in which children who were identified as doing poorly early in life were expected to continue to do poorly. The early childhood education movement as exemplified in the Head Start program was designed to improve the learning and social competence of children during the preschool years with the expectation that these improvements would be maintained into later life. Unfortunately, follow-up research of such children has found only moderate gains in measurable intellectual competence being maintained into adolescence (Zigler & Trickett, 1978), although there were reduced rates of school failure and need for special education (Lazar, Darlington, Murray, Royce, & Snipper, 1982; Schweinhart & Weikart, 1980).

From a different perspective, children who were identified early in life as being at risk because of such biological circumstances as birth complications were thought to have generally negative developmental outcomes. But longitudinal research in this area has demonstrated that the majority of children who experienced such biological conditions did not have intellectual or social problems later in life (Sameroff & Chandler, 1975; Sameroff, 1986).

In both domains early characteristics of the child have been overpowered by factors in the environmental context of development. The Kauai study of Werner and her associates (Werner, Bierman, & French, 1971; Werner & Smith, 1982) demonstrated that when family and cultural variables have fostered development, children with perinatal complications have been indistinguishable from children without complications. Where family cultural variables have hindered development, even infants without biological complications have developed severe social and cognitive deficits later in life.

Two conclusions emerge from this analysis that have major implications for intervention programs. The first is that the child's level of competency at any point in early development, whether reached through normal developmental processes or through some special intervention efforts, is not linearly related to the child's competence later in life. The second point is that in order to complete an equation predictive of later development, one needs to add the effects of the child's social and family environment that act to foster or impede the continuing positive developmental course of the child. In short, intervention programs cannot be successful if changes are made only in the individual child. Corollary changes in the environment must also occur that will act to enhance the existing competencies of the child and buffer the child from stressful life events in the future.

REPRESENTATIVE RISK FACTORS

Let us turn for a moment to research aimed at identifying representative risk factors in the development of cognitive and social-emotional competence. Such competencies of young children have been found to be strongly related to family mental health and especially social class (Broman, Nichols, & Kennedy, 1975; Golden & Birns, 1976; Werner & Smith, 1982). Efforts to prevent developmental dysfunctions must be based on an analysis of how families in different social classes differ on the characteristics that foster or impede psychological development in their children. These factors range from proximal variables like the mother's interaction with the child, to such intermediate variables as the mother's mental health, to distal variables such as the financial resources of the family.

Although casual models have been sought in which singular variables uniquely determine aspects of child behavior, a series of studies in a variety of domains have found that, except at the extremes of biological dysfunction, it is the number rather than the nature of risk factors that are the best determinants of outcome. Parmelee and Haber (1973) found this to be true for neurological factors in samples of infants with many perinatal problems, Rutter (1979) for family factors in samples of children with many psychosocial problems, and Greenspan (1981) for both biological and family factors in multirisk families.

In a study of 215 4-year-old children Sameroff, Seifer, Barocas, Zax, and Greenspan (1987) assessed a set of 10 environmental variables that are correlates of socioeconomic status (SES) but not equivalents of SES. They tested whether poor development was a function of low SES or the compounding of environmental risk factors found in low-SES groups. The 10 environmental risk variables were chronicity of maternal mental illness; maternal anxiety; a parental perspectives score derived from a combination of measures that reflected rigidity or flexibility in the attitudes, beliefs, and values that mothers had in regard to their child's development; spontaneous positive maternal interactions with the child during infancy; occupation of head of household; maternal education; disadvantaged minority status; family support; stressful life events; and family size.

When these risk factors were related to social-emotional and cognitive competence scores, major differences were found between those children with low multiple risk scores and those with high scores. In terms of intelligence, children with no environmental risks scored more than 30 points higher than children with eight or nine risk factors (see Figure 1). Similarly, the range in scores on an assessment of the social and emotional competencies of the children showed a similar spread over two standard deviations (Sameroff et al., 1987).

Several conclusions from this study are relevant to intervention efforts. One conclusion is that the *number* of risk factors was the prime determinant of outcome within each socioeconomic level, not the socioeconomic level itself. The second and more important conclusion for intervention strategies is that the same outcomes were the result of different combinations of risk factors. Data from the 79 families that had a moderate multiple risk score of 3, 4, or 5 were cluster analyzed. The families fell into five clusters with different sets of high-risk conditions. Different combinations of factors appear in each cluster (see Table 1). Cluster 2 has no overlapping variables with clusters 3, 4, or 5. Minority status is a risk variable in clusters 3, 4, and 5, but does not appear in clusters 1 or 2. Despite these differences the mean IQs were not different for

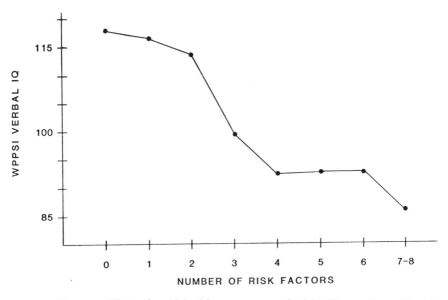

Figure 1. Effects of multiple risk scores on preschool intelligence (Sameroff et al., 1987)

children in the five clusters when compared in an analysis of variance. Thus, it seems that it was not any single variable but the combination of multiple variables that was associated with reduced intellectual performance. No single factor was regularly related to either poor or good outcomes. If this is the case, it is unlikely that universal interventions can be found for the problems of children. For every family situation a unique analysis of risk factors will require a unique set of intervention strategies embedded within a developmental model.

TRANSACTIONAL MODEL

One such developmental model that appears to apply in a number of scientific domains is the transactional model (Sameroff, 1983, 1987; Sameroff & Chandler, 1975). In this approach developmental outcomes are neither a function of the individual alone nor the experiential context alone. Outcomes are a product of the combination of an individual and his or her experience. To predict outcome, a singular focus on the characteristics of the individual, in this case the child, frequently will be misleading. An analysis and assessment of the experiences available to the child needs to be added.

Within this transactional model the development of the child is seen as a product of the continuous dynamic interactions of the child and the experience provided by his or her family and social context. What is innovative about the transactional model is the equal emphasis placed on the effects of the child and the environment, so that the experiences provided by the environment are not viewed as independent of the child. The child may have been a strong determinant of current experiences, but developmental outcomes cannot be systematically described without an analysis of the effects of the environment on the child. A concrete example of such a transactional outcome can be seen in Figure 2.

In this figure the child's outcome at any point in time is neither a function of the

Table 1. *Cluster analysis of families with moderate multiple-risk scores*

Cluster	Risk factor
1	Mental health
	Family support
	Mother education
	Anxiety
2	Mother–infant interaction
	Mental health
	Anxiety
3	Family support
	Minority status
4	Mother education
	Minority status
	Occupation
5	Parental perspectives
	Minority status
	Mother education

Source: Sameroff, Seifer, Barocas, Zax, and Greenspan (1987).

initial state of the child nor the initial state of the environment, but a complex function of the interplay of child and environment over time. For example, complicated childbirth may have made an otherwise calm mother somewhat anxious. The mother's anxiety during the first months of the child's life may have caused her to be uncertain and inappropriate in her interactions with the child. In response to such inconsistency, the infant may have developed some irregularities in feeding and sleeping patterns that give the appearance of a difficult temperament. This difficult temperament decreases the pleasure that the mother obtains from the child and so she tends to spend less time with her child. If adults are not actively interacting with the child, and especially speaking to the child, the child may not meet the norms for language development and may score poorly on preschool language tests.

What determined the poor outcome in this example? Was the poor linguistic performance caused by the complicated childbirth, the mother's anxiety, the child's difficult temperament, or the mother's avoidance of verbal and social interaction? If we were to design an intervention program for this family, where would it be directed? If we were to select the most proximal cause, it would be the mother's avoidance of the child, yet we can see that such a view would oversimplify a complex developmental sequence. Would primary prevention be directed at eliminating the child's difficult temperament or at changing the mother's reaction, or at providing alternative sources of verbal stimulation for the child? Each of these would eliminate a potential dysfunction at some contemporary point in the developmental system. But would any of these efforts insure the verbal competence of the child or, perhaps more important, insure the continued progress of the child after the intervention was completed?

The series of transactions described is an example of how developmental achievements are rarely sole consequences of immediate antecedents and even more rarely sole consequences of distal antecedents. Not only is the causal chain extended over time, but it is also embedded in an interpretive framework. The mother's anxiety is based on

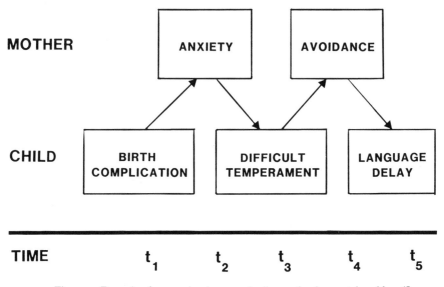

Figure 2. Example of transactional process leading to developmental problem (Samer-off, 1987)

an interpretation of the meaning of a complicated childbirth and her avoidance is based on an interpretation of the meaning of the child's irregular feeding and sleeping patterns. To understand the effects of interventions on the way parents behave toward their infants, there is a need to understand this interpretive framework. What follows is a description of the organization and operation of this interpretive scheme that offers the possibility of a richer understanding of why past intervention strategies were more or less successful. The ultimate goal of this description will be to provide a theoretical basis for the design of future intervention strategies that can be targeted at a level of developmental regulation appropriate to the desired change in a child's development.

THE ENVIRONTYPE

Just as there is a biological organization, the genotype, that regulates the physical outcome of each individual, there is a social organization that regulates the way human beings fit into their society. This organization operates through family and cultural socialization patterns and has been postulated to compose an *environtype* analogous to the biological genotype (Sameroff, 1985). The importance of identifying the sources of regulation of human development is obvious if one is interested in manipulating that development, as in the case of prevention or intervention programs. It is beyond the scope of even the most ambitious intervention program to manipulate all the parameters that influence child development. The alternative is to understand determinants of development in sufficient degree to choose a level of complexity appropriate to the problem to be solved, the developmental stages of the child and family, and available supports. The failures of intervention efforts can only be understood in terms of a failure to understand these regulatory systems. Each individual's environtype contains these regulatory patterns.

The environtype is composed of subsystems that not only transact with the child but also transact with each other. Bronfenbrenner (1977) has provided the most detailed descriptions of environmental organizations that influence developmental processes within categories of microsystems, mesosystems, exosystems, and macrosystems (also see Garbarino, this volume). The *microsystem* is the immediate setting of a child in an environment with particular features, activities, and roles (e.g., the home or the school). The *mesosystem* comprises the relationships between the major settings at a particular point in an individual's development (e.g., between home and school). The *exosystem* is an extension of the mesosystem that includes settings that the child may not be a part of but that affect the settings in which the child does participate (e.g., the world of work and neighborhoods). Finally, the *macrosystem* includes the overarching institutional patterns of the culture, including the economic, social, and political systems of which the microsystems, mesosystems, and exosystems are concrete expressions. Bronfenbrenner's ecological model has been fruitfully applied in the analysis of a number of clinical issues, including the effects of child abuse (Belsky, 1980) and divorce (Kurdek, 1981).

For our present purposes we will restrict the discussion to levels of environmental factors contained within the culture, the family, and the individual parent. Developmental regulations at each of these levels are carried within codes: the cultural code, the family code, and the individual code of the parent. These codes regulate cognitive and social-emotional development so that the child ultimately will be able to fill a role defined by society. They are hierarchically related in their evolution and in their current influence on the child. The experience of the developing child is partially determined by the beliefs, values, and personality of the parents; partially by the family's interaction patterns and transgenerational history; and partially by the socialization beliefs, controls, and supports of the culture. There is a distinction that must be recognized between codes and behaviors. The environtype is no more a description of the experiential environment than the genotype is a description of the biological phenotype. In each case the code must be actualized through behavior. The codes have an organizational and regulatory influence on parent behavior, but the behavior is not the same as the codes.

Although the environtype can be conceptualized independently of the child, changes in the abilities of the developing child are major triggers for regulatory changes and in most likelihood were major contributors to the evolution of a *developmental agenda* that is each environtype's timetable for developmental milestones. Although developmental milestones have always been thought to be a property of the child, their significance is much reduced unless there is a triggered regulation from the environtype. Different parents, different families, and different cultures may be sensitive to different behavior of the infant as a regulatory trigger (deVries & Sameroff, 1984). For example, in the United States it was not until the major changes in the educational system stimulated by Sputnik – that is, the evidence of advanced Soviet technology – that newborn intellectual competence, for example, the ability to perceive and learn, became an important milestone.

Most behavioral research on the effects of the environment has been limited to the study of mother–child interaction patterns, which is only one component of the environtype. Parke and Tinsley (1987), in an extensive review of family interaction research, have pointed to the important new trend of adding not only father–child interaction to the study of mother–child interaction, but the combination of these into studies of triadic interactions and behavioral patterns of the entire family. The be-

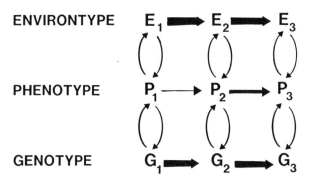

Figure 3. Regulation model of development with transactions among genotype, pheno-type, and environtype (Sameroff, 1985)

havioral research is slowly overcoming the technological difficulties embodied in anal-yses of multiple interacting individuals (Gottman, 1979; Sackett, 1978). Another growing empirical base comes from the direction of beliefs rather than behavior (Sigel, 1985). Parental belief systems include their understanding of child behavior, of the sources of developmental change (Sameroff & Feil, 1983), and their child-rearing values (Kohn, 1969). Investigators have become increasingly articulate at defining the dimensions of parental belief systems with the ultimate goal of describing the effects of these belief systems on parental behavior and, ultimately, on the behavior of the child. For the present, however, these research domains have provided primarily promis-sory notes of important future contributions to successful intervention efforts.

To summarize the overall model of developmental regulation, the child's behavior at any point in time is a product of the transactions between the phenotype, that is, the child, the environtype, that is, the source of external experience, and the genotype, that is, the source of biological organization (see Figure 3). Traditional research on child development has emphasized the child's utilization of biological capacities to gain experience and the role of experience in shaping child competencies, but there has been far less attention to how that experience is organized. Indeed, the organization of experience is explicit in the great amount of attention given to curriculum development and behavior modification plans, but far less attention is given to the implicit organiza-tion of experience found in the environtype we will describe.

Cultural code

The ingredients of the cultural code are the complex of characteristics that organize a society's child-rearing system and that incorporate elements of socialization and educa-tion. These processes are embedded in sets of social controls and social supports. They are based on beliefs that differ in the amount of community consensus ranging from mores and norms to fads and fashions. It is beyond the scope of this paper to elucidate the full range of cultural regulatory processes that are potentially relevant to interven-tion efforts. Only a few points will be highlighted to clarify the dimensions of the cultural code.

Many common biological characteristics of the human species have acted to produce similar developmental agendas in most cultures. For example, in most cultures formal education begins between the ages of 6 and 8 when most children have reached the cognitive ability to learn from such structured experiences (Rogoff, 1981). However, there are historical and cross-cultural differences where changes in child behavior are emphasized or ignored. For example, informal education can begin at many different ages, depending on the culture's attributions to the child. For example, some middle-class parents have been convinced that prenatal experiences will enhance the cognitive development of their children and consequently begin stimulation programs during pregnancy, but others believe it best to wait until the first grade before beginning formal learning experiences. Such examples demonstrate the variability of human developmental contexts, and the openness of the regulatory system to modification.

One of the major contemporary risk conditions toward which many intervention programs are directed in the United States is adolescent pregnancy. Although for certain young mothers pregnancy is the outcome of individual factors, for a large proportion it is the result of a cultural code that defines maturity, family relationships, and socialization patterns with adolescent motherhood as a normative ingredient. Teenage childbearing has never been uncommon in the United States (Wattenberg, 1976). In the 1950s close to one-half of all women wed in their teens and well over one-quarter had their first child before age 20 (Cherlin, 1981). The current concern results from two new trends. The first is that the number of families having children is declining in all age groups except adolescence; and the second is that the number of children born out-of-wedlock is increasing dramatically in this age-group (Furstenberg, Brooks-Gunn, & Morgan, 1987). The reduced rate of marriage overall adds further to the numbers of single adolescent mothers. During the 1950s there were estimates that 50% of women who married before the age of 20 were pregnant at the time (Cutright, 1972), but these premarital pregnancies were hidden by the consequent marriage. Furstenberg et al. (1987) point out that the current life-course perspective on families attributes the timing of marriage and childbearing to the interplay between personal, social, economic, and cultural beliefs about age-appropriate behavior. In such instances, to focus on the problem as one that resides wholly at the level of the pregnant individual would seriously undercut effective intervention efforts.

Family code

Just as cultural codes regulate the fit between individuals and the social system, family codes organize individuals within the family system. Family codes provide a source of regulation that allows a group of individuals to form a collective unit in relation to society as a whole. As the cultural code regulates development so that an individual may fill a role in society, family codes regulate development to produce members that fulfill a role within the family and ultimately are able to introduce new members into the shared system. Traditionally, new members are incorporated through birth and marriage, although more recently remarriage has taken on a more frequent role in providing new family members.

The family regulates the child's development through a variety of processes that vary in their degree of explicit representation and conduct. Families have *rituals* that prescribe roles and dictate conduct within family settings, *stories* that transmit orientations and accounts to each family member as well as to whomever will listen, shared *myths* that influence individual interactions and exaggerate aspects of family stories, and *paradigms* that change individual behavior when in the presence of other family members. Reiss (1989) has contrasted the degree to which these processes are articulated and readily recounted by individual members with the degree to which each family member's behavior is regulated by a common practice evident only when the family members are together. Whereas family rituals may be recounted by each family member, family paradigms are constructed through group processes. The most represented regulations are exemplified by family rituals and the least by family paradigms. Stories and myths provide regulatory functions intermediate to rituals and paradigms. Issues that will have importance for intervention efforts are the exact nature of how these forms are transmitted behaviorally among family members and how they are represented in cognition. Because of the paucity of empirical data in these areas, we shall put these issues aside at this point and restrict our discussion to the description of these family regulatory forms.

RITUALS. Rituals are the most clearly self-aware of the family regulatory forms (Bossard & Boll, 1950). Rituals are practiced by the whole family and are frequently documented. They may be times for taking photographs, exchanging gifts, or preserving mementos. Ritual activities are by definition set off from the normal routine and include family celebrations, traditions, and patterned interactions. The content of family rituals includes symbolic information as well as important preparatory phases, schedules, and plans. Rituals serve a regulatory function by assigning clear roles or tasks to each member of the family. For example, at Thanksgiving the family member who sits at the head of the table and carves the turkey is seen as the head of the household. In order to participate in the ritual, each family member must conform to the specific characteristics of the role.

The role of family rituals in regulating dysfunctional behavior has been most clearly demonstrated in families of alcoholics (Bennett, Wolin, Reiss, & Teitlebaum, 1987; Wolin, Bennett, Noonan, & Teitelbaum, 1980). In a study of married children of alcoholic parents certain aspects of family rituals were identified as protective factors that guarded against the children becoming alcoholics. Children who came from families that were able to preserve family rituals, such as distinctive dinner and holiday routines, were less likely to become alcoholics themselves. Wolin and his colleagues speculate that rituals provide stability for dysfunctional families (Wolin, Bennett, & Jacobs, 1988). Such research has not yet been applied to problems of early intervention, although there are beginning efforts at collecting normative data.

Rituals of early childhood can be extrapolated from research on children's stories. Hudson and Nelson (1983) have demonstrated that preschool and first-grade children recall stories about birthday parties prior to recalling stories about routine events such as baking cookies. There is a high degree of saliency to rituals that facilitate participation by children, and encoding of family structure. The child's participation in family rituals may be facilitated by the child's own creation of rituals that regulate other family members. Bedtime and mealtime rituals frequently occur during early childhood. Again, the lack of research in this area leaves many of these themes unconnected.

STORIES. Stories provide a second form for family regulations. Reiss (1989) notes that although stories have long been of interest to developmental and cognitive scientists as a tool for understanding cognitive development, there is little systematic work on the importance of stories that families tell about themselves.

In a study of family folklore, Zeitlin, Kotkin, and Baker (1982) collected large numbers of family stories. From their analysis they proposed three broad functions for such stories: (1) to highlight conspicuous heroes or rogues in the family's history, (2) to dramatize and conserve significant family transitions and stressful events, and (3) to enshrine and preserve certain family customs. Thus stories are seen as having a stabilizing effect by preserving important events and passing on a value system to the next generation (Reiss, 1989).

There is a strong developmental component to family stories. As a source of regulation, the practice of telling stories is a major feature of early relationships between young children and other family members. Ratner and Bruner (1977) proposed that this early storytelling provides a framework for the learning of conversational turn-taking and facilitates language development. During these early years the child engages in storytelling by being a story-listener and will often encourage others to tell or read a story.

Children are increasingly able to recall specific aspects of stories. Nelson and her colleagues found a developmental progression in the recall of stories (Nelson, 1981; Nelson & Gruendel, 1981). Preschool children readily talk about their experiential knowledge in scriptlike form and these scripts affect the way in which children interpret and remember stories and everyday events (Nelson, 1981; Nelson & Gruendel, 1981). Children are receptive to hearing stories and organizing experiences along story lines, which provides parents with the opportunity to pass down values through their storytelling.

MYTHS. A third source of regulation within the family code is family myths. Family myths are beliefs that go unchallenged in spite of reality. Myths may have a traumatic origin and frequently have a strong affective component (Kramer, 1985). Family myths are not open for discussion, nor are they readily recognized as distortions (Ferreira, 1963).

Some family myths help to regulate role definitions. For example, a traditional family may consider females as unable to handle professional responsibilities of the work world despite the fact that they are able to balance the family checkbook and organize a busy household. Subtle aspects of a particular role may become inflated and incorporated into the myth. For example, parents of a physically disabled child may believe that the child is also disabled cognitively despite examples of the child's intelligent behavior. A myth develops that casts the child in a "handicapped" role that encompasses behaviors outside of physical limitations. In the same context another family may create a myth that their mentally retarded child is unimpaired because of a bright-eyed look (Pollner & McDonald-Wikler, 1985; Roskies, 1972).

Developmental problems can arise when the child must accept a distorted family myth in order to be congruent with the family, or when the family imposes an inflated role on the child by creating a new myth. In the first instance, sexually abused children or witnesses to parental abuse may adapt their behavior to fit within the family structure (Belsky, 1980). In the second instance, a handicapped child may be treated as the youngest sibling despite birth order or chronological age (Sigel, 1985).

PARADIGMS. Family paradigms are a fourth form of family regulations. Reiss and his colleagues (Reiss, 1981; Reiss, Oliveri, & Curd, 1983) have described how families develop paradigms that include a set of core assumptions, convictions or beliefs that each family holds about its environment. The evidence that paradigms operate at the family level is that in the same problem-solving situations members will engage in different problem-solving strategies if they are with other members of their family than when they are alone. Reiss et al. (1983) argue that these paradigms generally persist for years, even generations, and are manifested "in the fleeting fantasies and expectations by all members of the family and, even more important, in the routine action patterns of daily life" (p. 20). Based on empirically derived dimensions of configuration, coordination, and closure, these investigators have identified a four-category typology of paradigms including environment-sensitive, consensus-sensitive, achievement-sensitive, and distance-sensitive families. Environment-sensitive and consensus-sensitive families both are highly cohesive and cooperative internally, but they differ in how they understand and respond to stress. Environment-sensitive families believe the world is understandable and problems are solvable, but the consensus-sensitive ones believe the world operates by unknowable random laws and they become self-protective in response to stress. In achievement-sensitive and distance-sensitive families, the members are in competition with each other. Where they differ is that the achievement-sensitive family members seek alliances outside the family to support their roles, but distance-sensitive family members cannot relate to anyone, in or out of the family group.

Paradigms appear to be the form of family regulation that is the least articulated in awareness although they can be expressed in family stories and myths. The importance of family paradigms for prevention efforts is that, although they have been identified only in the course of family problem-solving tasks, they are manifested in the relationships that family members, including children, form with other individuals and groups. Thus, the normal or disturbed behavior of children must to some degree be interpreted as an outgrowth of the family paradigm (Reiss et al., 1983).

Current research on the effects of family factors on child development have emphasized observed interactions among family members, that is, whether there are conflicted or harmonious relationships among family members. The family code is a domain of family functioning that organizes such behaviors and is only now being explored. A recognized risk condition for children is the effect of marital discord and divorce that produces behavioral problems in response to the family conflict or the absence of a parent (Wallerstein & Kelly, 1980). Studying the family code is important for understanding these problems because divorce involves a process of code disorganization and reorganization (Hetherington & Camara, 1984). As old members are less influential and new members are introduced through remarriage, existing family codes are altered. Hetherington and Camara (1984), for example, found major differences in roles given to and assumed by stepfathers as compared to fathers, and stepmothers as compared to mothers. To focus entirely on the individual child's reaction to the absence of a parent would ignore broader changes in the family context. To focus entirely on a parent's reaction to the child ignores the constraints that have been placed on the behavior of both by the family rituals, stories, myths, and paradigms.

Individual code of the parent

There is clear evidence that parental behavior is influenced by the family context. When operating as part of a family, the behavior of each member is altered (Parke & Tinsley, 1987), frequently without awareness of the behavioral change (Reiss, 1981). However, there is also no doubt that individuals bring their own contribution to family interactions. The contribution of parents is determined much more complexly than that of young children, given the multiple levels that contribute to their behavior. We have discussed the socializing regulations embodied in the cultural and family codes. We have not discussed the individualized interpretations that each parenting figure imposes on these codes. To a large extent these interpretations are conditioned by each parent's past participation in his or her own family's coded interactions, but they are captured uniquely by each member of the family. These individual influences further condition each parent's responses to his or her own child (see Beckwith, this volume). Main and Goldwyn (1984) have identified adult attachment categories that reflect parents' encoding of their interpretation of their attachment to their own parents. What is compelling about these adult attachment categories is that they operate across generations and are predictive of the attachment categories of the infant.

The richness of both health and pathology embodied in these parental responses is well described in the clinical literature. In terms of early development, Fraiberg (1980) and her colleagues have provided many descriptions of the attributions that parents bring to their parenting. These "ghosts" of unresolved childhood conflicts have been shown to "do their mischief according to a historical or topical agenda, depending upon the vulnerabilities of the parental past" (Fraiberg, Adelson, & Shapiro, 1980, p. 164).

The effect of parental deviance has long been recognized as a contributor to the poor developmental status of children (Sameroff, Seifer, & Zax, 1982). One of the major steps forward in current early intervention programs is the effort to facilitate the parent's caregiving behavior because of its importance for the development of the child. Although we acknowledge that influence, we must also be careful to add the importance of the contexts in which parental behavior is rooted, the family and cultural codes. To ignore these contexts that organize parental behavior would permit only limited additional success when parent involvement is added to intervention efforts that foundered when the child was the sole target of treatment. It is important to recognize the parent as a major regulating agency, but it is equally important to recognize that parental behavior is itself embedded in regulatory contexts that may require additional intervention strategies.

Regulations

The description of the contexts of development is a necessary prologue to the understanding of developmental problems and to the eventual design of intervention programs. Once an overview of the complexity of systems is obtained, we can turn to the search for nodal points at which intervention strategies can be directed. These points will be found in the interfaces among the child, the family, and the cultural systems, especially where regulations are occurring. To complete the picture we must elaborate on the complexity of regulatory processes reflected in their time span, purposiveness, level of representation, and the nature of the child's contribution. Developmental regulations have been divided into three categories based on these considerations: macroregulations, miniregulations, and microregulations (Sameroff, 1987). *Macroregulations* are predominantly purposive major changes in experience that continue for long periods of time, such as weaning or entry into school. *Miniregulations* are predominantly caregiving activities that occur on a daily basis, such as dressing, feeding, or disciplining. *Microregulations* are almost automatic patterns of momentary interactions such as attunement (Stern, 1977), on the positive side, or coercion (Patterson, 1986) on the negative.

MACROREGULATIONS. The most extensive types of regulations are macroregulations, which are part of the culture's developmental agenda. This agenda is a series of points in time when the environment is restructured to provide different experiences to the child. Weaning, toilet training, and schooling may be initiated at different times in the child's course of development based on different cultural codes. The Digo and Kikuyu are two distinct East African cultures that provide different experiences to infants according to cultural beliefs (deVires & Sameroff, 1984). The Digo view the infant as capable of learning within a few months after birth and begin socialization early on. The Kikuyu do not hold such beliefs and wait until the second year of life before educating their children. Cultural agendas are subject to change and are tolerant of variation found in contemporary Western culture.

Macroregulatory codes provide the basis for socialization in each culture. They are responses to behaviors from the child that are easily identifiable as distinct events and are expected of all members of a culture. Temporally, macroregulations are epochal in nature, reflecting changes that mark major milestones and a restructuring of the child's activities. Once the child's behavior triggers a restructuring of the environment, the culture is no longer active in providing additional regulations until the child's behavior triggers another restructuring. The validity of cultural developmental agendas is not in their particular details, but in the fact that the culture is successful in reproducing generation after generation of offspring. Macroregulations are the most highly articulated of the regulatory functions and are known to socialized members of each culture and may be openly discussed or written down in the form of laws (e.g., all children age 6 and above must be registered for school). In Western culture, the recording of developmental milestones is an institutionalized practice of health personnel and family members.

MINIREGULATIONS. The second level is characterized by miniregulations that operate within a shorter time span. They include the daily caretaking activities of a family. Temporally, they operate on a daily basis reflecting repeated demands within the family. Such activities include feeding children when they are hungry, changing their diapers when they are wet, and disciplining them when they misbehave. Miniregulations are susceptible to a wide range of individual variability while still conforming to cultural codes. The family provides the arena for most of the early developmental miniregulations and throughout much of the child's growth and development. Families may develop their own codes that are then transmitted to other members of the family (Sameroff & Fiese, 1989). Families may carry out caregiving practices such as disciplining in a variety of ways yet still conform to the cultural code. Deviances such as coercive parenting can have a detrimental effect on the child's behavior but may be maintained as a form of regulation within the family (Patterson, 1986). Most family members can agree upon miniregulations, although they may not be able to articulate them spontaneously (Reiss, 1989).

The child's contribution to miniregulations may be seen in instances where the caretaking behaviors of the family are restructured to meet the unique demands of the child. A child with cerebral palsy, for example, may present difficulties in established routine caretaking. However, adjustments are made to incorporate the child into daily routines through alterations in miniregulations.

MICROREGULATIONS. The third level of regulation consists of microregulations that operate on the shortest time base. Micro regulations are momentary interactions between child and caregiver that others have referred to as "behavioral synchrony" or "attunement" (Field, 1979; Stern, 1977). Microregulations are a blend of social and biological codes because, although they may be brought to awareness, many of these activities appear naturally and with seeming automaticity. Toward the biological end are the caregiver's smile in response to an infant's smile, and toward the socialized end are "micro social" patterns of interaction that increase or decrease antisocial behavior in the child (Patterson, 1986). The child's contribution to microregulations may be seen in the effects of infant activity level on maternal responsivity. Premature infants or infants who have experienced multiple prenatal complications may exhibit a lower activity level overall and require less active stimulation from their mother than that required by a healthy, full-term newborn (Field, 1977; Goldberg, Brachfeld, & DiVitto, 1980). Thus, adjustment in maternal microregulations can be stimulated in part by the child's behavior (Brazelton, Koslowski, & Main, 1974).

The three sources of regulations that have been outlined are organized at different levels of the environtype. Macroregulations are the modal form of regulation within the cultural code. Many cultural codes are written down or memorized and may be passed on to individual members of society through customs, beliefs, and mythologies, in addition to actual laws that are aimed at regulating child health and education. Miniregulations are modal within the family code where less formal interactions condition the caregiving behavior of family members. Microregulations come into play at the individual level where differences in personality and temperament balance with commonalities in human species-specific behavior in regulating reactions to the child.

During early childhood, the common pathway of these regulations is through the behavior of parental figures, and especially the primary caregiver, in their relationships with the infant. Thus, for present purposes early relationships become central to the development of normative and deviant infant adaptations.

Although these levels of regulation have been described independently, they are in constant interaction and even transaction. The family develops its caretaking routines influenced by the transactions between the cultural and family codes, that is, between social norms and family traditions. As children develop within the family, they participate increasingly in these transactions that serve as a foundation for social interaction. Families highlight the role defined for each child through rituals and develop myths that further regulate the child's development. The style of each family member contributes to the way in which the regulations will be carried out in relation to the individuality of each child.

The operation of the family code is characterized by a series of regulated transactions. The parents may hold particular concepts of development that influence their caretaking practices. As children are exposed to different role expectations and listen to the family stories, they make their own contribution by their particular styles. The child's acting out of roles within the family is incorporated into family stories, rituals, and myths. By becoming an active transactor in the family code, the child ultimately may affect the child-rearing practices of the parents and thereby influence the code to be passed down to the next generation.

TARGETING INTERVENTION EFFORTS

A sensitivity to the complexities of child development has encouraged the implementation of intervention strategies to include multiple members of the child's family (Dunst & Trivette, in press; Turnbull, Summers, & Brotherson, 1983) as well as multiple disciplines concerned with early childhood (Bagnato & Neisworth, 1985; Bricker, 1986; Bricker & Dow, 1980). Increasingly, early intervention programs designed today are based on a team approach that addresses the many facets of childhood problems. As it becomes less acceptable to focus on isolated aspects of developmental disorders, the total environmental context of the child is considered (Sameroff, 1982). Once multiple determinants have been recognized as being associated with childhood problems, a more targeted approach to implementing intervention is in order, based on the specific determinants identified in a specific situation.

A frequent problem in planning intervention strategies is deciding where to concentrate therapeutic efforts. As we have outlined, developmental regulatory systems may include individual, family, and cultural codes. Not only do economic and personnel limitations preclude global interventions across systems, but all these regulatory codes incorporate different aspects of the child's development and imply different intervention strategies. A careful analysis of the regulatory systems is necessary to define what may be the most effective avenue and form of intervention. The cultural, familial, and individual codes are embedded in temporal and behavioral contexts that vary in magnitude of time and scope of behavior. A basic point that emerges from this analysis is that there will never be a single intervention strategy that will solve all developmental problems. Cost-effectiveness will not be found in the universality of a treatment, but in the individuation of programs that are targeted at the relevant nodal points for a specific child in a specific family in a specific social context.

In consideration of the temporal dimensions of regulation, what are the implications for intervention? Frequently, models of intervention attempt to cover a wide range of contexts for a single identified problem. Some early intervention programs for disabled infants are designed to intervene on the level of the child, family, and occasionally the larger context of social support systems (Dunst & Trivette, this volume; Dunst, Trivette, & Cross, 1986). Although well-intentioned, a great deal of effort may be expended with minimal results. A more precise understanding of regulatory systems and diagnostic decision making may provide more effective forms of intervention. In line with the transactional model (Sameroff & Chandler, 1975), we would like to present a format for identifying targets of intervention as well as strategies of intervention.

TRANSACTIONAL MODEL OF INTERVENTION

The transactional model has implications for early intervention, particularly for identifying targets and strategies of intervention. The nonlinear premise that continuity in individual behavior is a systems property rather than a characteristic of individuals provides a rationale for an expanded focus of intervention efforts. According to the model, changes in behavior are the result of a series of interchanges between individuals within a shared system following specifiable regulatory principles. The multidirectionality of change is emphasized while pinpointing regulatory sources that mediate change. By examining the strengths and weaknesses of the regulatory system, targets can be identified that minimize the necessary scope of the intervention while maximizing cost efficiency. In some cases small alterations in child behavior may be all that is necessary to reestablish a well-regulated developmental system. In other cases changes in the parents' perception of the child may be the most strategic intervention. In a third category are cases that require improvements in the parents' ability to take care of the child. These categories of intervention strategies have been labeled remediation, redefinition, and reeducation, respectively (Sameroff, 1987).

Figure 4 is an abstraction of the regulatory model of development during early childhood that incorporates all biologically regulated changes into the child line of

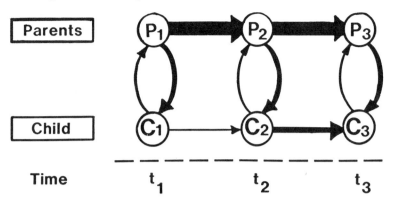

Figure 4. Developmental regulation through transactions between parent and child behavior

development and all environmentally regulated changes into the parent line of development (also see Figure 3). A set of arrows leads from the child's initial state (C_1) to the child's state at succeeding points in time. This dimension refers to the child's development of self-regulatory capacities. Early in infancy these are primarily biological regulations of autonomic and state variables, to which are added an increasingly rich behavioral repertoire (Brazelton, 1973). As children increase in age, the line gets thicker as they learn more skills for taking care of themselves and buffering themselves from stressful experiences. Another set of arrows leads from the parents' initial state (P_1) to the parents' state at succeeding points in time. This dimension refers to the continuity in the parents' understanding of the cultural code and their competence in regulating their child's development. Our discussion of intervention strategies will focus on the vertical arrows between parent and child and on the change in parents from time t_1 to time t_2. The arrows from child to parent represent changes in the child that transact with the parent and ultimately change the parents' behavior or attitudes. The downward arrow reflects changes in the parent that are directed toward eventual changes in the child. Horizontal arrows between P_1 and P_2 reflect changes initiated with the parent at t_1, which then influence the parents' behavior at t_2, which may then affect the child's behavior at t_2. Each direction of effect implies a different point and form of intervention.

A further abstraction of the regulatory model that focuses only on strategies of early intervention can be seen in Figure 5. Remediation changes the way the child behaves toward the parent. For example, in cases where children present with known organic disorders, intervention may be directed primarily toward remediating biological dysregulations. By improving the child's physical status, the child will be better able to elicit caregiving from the parents. Redefinition changes the way the parent interprets the child's behavior. Attributions to the child of difficulty or willfulness may deter a parent from positive interactions. By refocusing the parent on other, more acceptable attributes of the child, positive engagement may be facilitated. Reeducation changes the way the parent behaves toward the child. Providing training in positioning techniques for parents of handicapped children is an example of this form of intervention. Each category of intervention will be described further, with examples of early intervention techniques used for each regulatory code.

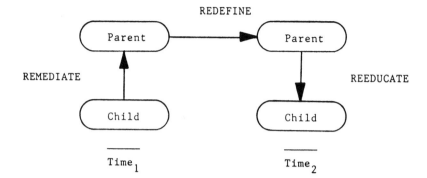

Figure 5. Depiction of intervention strategies in terms of child–parent transactions

Feeding disturbances are a common problem during infancy. The treatment of such problems will be used as the primary illustration of each aspect of this approach. During the first year of life, children's development is regulated in part by their nutritional status. Failure to maintain growth may result from a variety of conditions, each requiring different forms of intervention. Severe primary malnutrition is a problem not only in economically deprived countries, but also in the United States and other Western countries (Listernick, Christoffel, Pace, & Chicaramonte, 1985). The following discussion will serve to highlight how a basic condition such as nutritional status may be regulated by a variety of systems requiring different forms of intervention.

Remediation

As represented in Figure 5, the strategy of remediation is the class of intervention techniques designed to change the child, with eventual changes occurring in the parent (upward arrow). Remediation is not directed at changing the family or cultural codes. The intervention goal is to fit the child to preexisting caregiving competencies that could operate adequately given appropriate infant triggering responses. Remediation is typically implemented outside of the family system by a professional whose goal is to change an identifiable condition in the child. Once the child's condition has been altered, intervention is completed.

The most clearcut examples of remediation are those in which there are possibilities for structural repair of a biological condition, for example, the surgical correction of a mechanical blockage secondary to pyloric stenosis. The child is presented to the parents as cured and they proceed to engage in the normative child rearing appropriate to a healthy infant. Such direct solutions are excellent interventions for a number of early problems, but they occasionally involve controversial applications. The surgical alteration of the appearance of children with Down syndrome would be such a questionable procedure (Pueschel, 1984). In this example, the transactional hypothesis is the basis for the surgeon's belief that if the child looked more like a nonhandicapped child, he or she would be treated more like a nonhandicapped child, and consequently would have a developmental outcome more like a nonhandicapped child.

Less dramatic, but more behaviorally oriented remediations may be appropriate for preterm infants with feeding difficulties due to immaturity of sucking and poor coordination in swallowing. In such cases, feedings may be regulated initially through tubes inserted into the stomach while the infant is in the neonatal intensive care unit. Poor nutrition may complicate the care of such an infant, and delayed development of the sucking reflex may prolong hospitalization, leading to a parental perception of a sick child with the possibility of associated dysfunctions in child-rearing behavior. Bernbaum, Peneira, Watkins, and Peckham (1983) have demonstrated that through pairing nonnutritive sucking with gavage feedings premature infants have gained weight more rapidly than infants who did not receive oral stimulation. The increased weight gain in the infants provided with pacifiers is even more remarkable considering that the control infants received the same caloric intake. The orally stimulated infants were also discharged from the hospital sooner than the control infants. Thus, premature infants who receive an individualized remediation treatment in the special care nursery are able to normalize their feeding behavior earlier and be discharged from the hospital sooner. The consequence is fewer discrepant effects on the parents' behavior (Anderson, Burroughs, & Measel, 1983; Field et al., 1982).

Als and her colleagues (1986) have demonstrated that individualized treatment of the premature infant was associated with higher degrees of social turn taking, interactional synchrony, and overall quality of the interaction with their mothers during a free play session at 9 months of age. The remediation of the child as a neonate may have facilitated the parents' sensitivity in interacting with their child at a later age. The infants who did not receive the individualized intervention as neonates showed decreased levels of social interaction at 9 months of age.

The current emphasis on incorporating immediate members of the child's family and support group into intervention programs (Dunst & Trivette, in press) has been a result, in part, of the disappointing results obtained in using solely child-centered approaches to intervention. However, according to the principles of the transactional model and the regulatory system being presented here, there are circumstances where interventions directed toward the child alone may result in changes in the parent. In cases where the child's dysfunction is easily identified and successful intervention techniques are available, remediation of the child may lead to adaptive changes in the parent.

The case of treating malnutrition in infancy highlights how remediation with the child may influence the parents' behavior. Lower intelligence scores in infants who have been malnourished were originally believed to be the result of decreased cell growth in the brain (Stein & Susser, 1985). However, in cases where nutritional status could be improved, it has been demonstrated that poor intellectual performance in malnourished infants is the result of poor environments rather than poor biology (Cravioto & Arrieta, 1983; Read, 1982). Cravioto and DeLicardie (1979) found that the behavioral effects of malnutrition were most prevalent in families where mothers were more traditionally passive in their child care and provided little stimulation to their children. To examine how familial interactions may be influenced by nutritional status, Barrett, Radke-Yarrow, and Klein (1982) compared a group of children who had received caloric supplementation with a group that did not. The infants who received the nutritional supplements demonstrated greater social responsiveness, more expression of affect, greater interest in the environment, and higher activity at school age. Nutritional supplements obviously increased the infants' energy level. But it may not have been their increased energy level that increased their school-age social, emotional, and intellectual competence. Rather, by increasing their energy level, the nourished infants were better able to participate in the socialization process, whereas malnourished children are less able to elicit optimal caregiving behaviors (Rutter, 1987). Healthy, well-nourished children were better able to give cues about their condition and elicit a wide range of behaviors from their parents, including feeding. Their parents may have been prompted to provide more socially responsive stimulation, thereby further encouraging their children's interpersonal behavior.

Remedial interventions are regulations of child development in much the same way that the family and cultural code are regulators of development. The remediation strategies that we have described can be broken down into the level of regulation addressed. Microregulations were predominantly involved in the nutritional supplementation interventions. The child's ability to stimulate interactive sequences was enhanced, permitting parents to respond to the child's triggering cues. Alterations in miniregulations were more apparent in interventions that changed the child's overall behavioral repertoire, as in the sucking enhancement efforts. Here the change was not in the threshold or response to existing cues, but in the child's ability to produce a new organized behavioral episode. Finally, macroregulations change major domains of experience. Remediations that fit in this latter category are the one-time structural changes wrought by surgical interventions that alter the child's functioning for long periods of time. The agent of remediation is a part of an expanded concept of the cultural code that includes all social agencies responsible for fostering child development. Because of the vagaries of government support, a large proportion of early intervention programs are experimental or demonstration efforts that have not been incorporated into the cultural code. In contrast, there are times when legislative efforts convert such experimental programs into a component of the environtype, as was the case with acts supporting education of the handicapped.

These examples of remediation are directed toward changing the child, with the expectation that changes in child behavior will result in a more optimal caregiving environment. Remediation is indicated where there is a reasonable expectation that the child's condition can be altered and the family and cultural codes do not prevent implementation of the intervention effort. There are instances, however, in which the cultural or familial code cannot operate successfully and a second strategy needs to be implemented – the strategy of redefinition.

Redefinition

Redefinition as an intervention strategy is indicated when existing family codes do not fit with the child's behavior. Redefinition is represented by the horizontal arrow between the parents, P_1 and P_2, in Figure 5. Redefinition strategies are directed primarily toward the facilitation of more optimal parenting interactions and are warranted when the parents have defined the child as abnormal and are unable or unwilling to provide normal caregiving. Such difficulties in providing caretaking may arise from two sources: failure of parents to adapt to a disabling condition in the child, or failure of parents to distinguish between their emotional reactions to the child and the child's actual behavior. Examples of the first kind of problem are parents who disqualify themselves as adequate caregivers by automatically translating a child's physical or mental handicap into a condition that can only be treated by professionals (Roskies, 1972). Examples of the second kind are parents who become disenchanted with child rearing because they find a poor fit between their expectations of child behavior and the child's actual performance.

In the case of an atypical condition in the child, redefinition interventions are directed toward normalizing the parents' reactions to their child. An infant born with Down syndrome, for example, may be defined as abnormal because of differences in appearance or developmental pace or merely because of the label itself, leading the parents to believe that they are incapable of rearing such a child. Redefinition would be directed toward emphasizing to the parents the normal aspects of the child's behavior in order to facilitate caregiving behaviors that are in the parents' repertoire. Such normal child behaviors would include communication efforts like eye contact, emotional responsitivity like smiling and, eventually, laughing. Redefinition interventions directed toward parents when a deviant condition in the child is not identified focus on the parents' misperceptions of the child. Redefinition is directed toward changing interactions in the context of immediate experience rather than past events. The case of an infant with a diagnosis of nonorganic failure to thrive may serve to illustrate this process.

Failure to thrive (FTT) is a condition diagnosed in the first two years of life when a child's weight drops below the 3rd percentile of growth with no known organic etiology (Barbero & McKay, 1969). Nonorganic FTT, contrasted to organic FTT, is a diagnosis often made by the combined criteria of the exclusion of organicity and a weight gain in the hospital produced by nutritional supplements (Rosen, Loeb, & Jura, 1980). Children diagnosed with FTT are thought to be at risk for delays in cognitive development, behavior problems, and child abuse (Haynes, Cutler, Gray, & Kempe, 1984; Oates, Peacook, & Forrest, 1985; Singer, Drotar, Fagan, Devost, & Lake, 1983). A striking feature of nonorganic FTT infants is that upon hospitalization and removal from the home environment significant weight gain is recorded after implementing a standard nutritional program. In-hospital weight gain contrasted with in-home weight loss had led some to speculate that FTT is a failure in parenting (Haynes et al., 1984). However, there is increasing evidence that FTT may not represent a single syndrome but is a concommitant of a variety of disturbances in infancy (Gordon & Vazquez, 1985).

For redefinition to be the intervention of choice, a crucial aspect of the FTT case must be in the parental perception of the child. It has been reported that many parents of FTT infants describe their children as oppositional or "bad" (Ayoub & Milner, 1985), and have difficulty in accepting them (Casey, Bradley, & Wortham, 1984). Redefinition efforts in this case would be directed toward relabeling for the parent the child's emotional expressions. In the case of a mother who refuses to feed a crying infant because the infant is perceived as being stubborn, the infant's cry may be redefined as a signal for hunger rather than anger. Simple relabeling may be sufficient to alter the parent–child relationship so that effective feeding interactions can take place. However, some cases of FTT may not be responsive to altered labels of child behavior, and a more intensive effort directed toward the parents' past history may be indicated.

Fraiberg and her colleagues have described how past experiences of being parented influence current caretaking behaviors (Fraiberg et al., 1980). As parents engage in routine caretaking activities with their children, past experiences of their own childhoods are recalled. Individuals who experienced nurturant parenting recall these positive experiences as they parent their own children. However, individuals who have experienced inadequate parenting often repeat the same nonoptimal interactions. These "ghosts in the nursery" may influence how parents engage in routine caretaking activities. Returning to the case of FTT, mothers of FTT infants often recount their own upbringing as inadequate in nurturance (Haynes et al., 1985; Altemeir, O'Connor, Sherrod, & Vietze, 1985). In this case, redefinition interventions may be directed to the parents' memories of past experiences. Chatoor and her colleagues report that rede-fining the baby as the mother's own, rather than a symbol of past parenting experi-ences, has been effective in the treatment of infants failing to thrive (Chatoor, Dickson, Schaeffer, & Egan, 1985).

The mother, the father, or the entire family may be the source of inappropriate attributions concerning the infant. In fact, recognizing how a family may contribute to dysfunctions in the child is central to adapting the family code to fit the child's behavior. The family context may be particularly crucial in treating FTT infants (Drotar et al., 1985). Redefinition interventions may also be directed at how the family, as a whole, views the child, and what roles the family code permits the infant to play. Drotar and Malone (1982) report that minimizing the current influence of past parent-ing experiences can have a positive effect on caregiving in families with an FTT child.

The case of FTT has been presented to illustrate redefinition interventions. Redefini-tion may be directed toward parent–child interactions and a relabeling of the child's behavior. If a relabeling of behavioral interactions proves effective in facilitating weight gain, then no further intervention may be necessary. However, when relabeling is insufficient to facilitate change, redefinition efforts also may be directed toward examin-ing the parents' past experiences of being parented.

Most of the discussion of redefinition has been directed at the family code, but occasionally redefinition may be directed at the cultural code. For example, during the 1950s a healthy infant was typified by the Gerber Baby – full, round cheeks and a pudgy torso. This cultural image may have led to overfeeding and may possibly have accounted for weight problems later in childhood. As more emphasis has been placed on balanced nutrition, the image of the healthy baby in American culture has been redefined to emphasize a less rotund child. Cultural redefinitions are rarely in the purview of intervention programs. However, public education programs such as those directed toward defining the expectations of adequate parenting for teenage parents attempt to redefine behavior at the level of the cultural code.

Redefinitions at different levels of regulation move from a focus on specific child behaviors, to a focus on general attributions to a specific child, to a focus on attribu-tions to children in general. Interventions at the level of microregulation help parents to reinterpret their child's cues, for example, to redefine a cry as a cry of hunger instead of oppositionalism. Miniregulation interventions help parents redefine who their child is – "It is my baby and not myself as a baby, not my mother, not my father, and not my spouse" – so that the object of their caregiving becomes clarified. Interventions at the macroregulation level are directed at redefining cultural stereotypes in order to alter major segments of that culture's developmental agenda, for example, redefining the ideal baby as lean and mean instead of fat and happy.

Whereas redefinition interventions attempt to alter parenting patterns due to mal-adaptive perceptions or inadequate past parenting experiences, there are cases where the parents do not have the requisite skills for effective parenting. In this case reeduca-tion is indicated.

Reeducation

Reeducation refers to teaching parents how to raise their children. Reeducation is represented by the downward arrow from P_2 to C_2 in Figure 5. It is directed toward parents who do not have the knowledge base to use a cultural code to regulate their child's development.

Reeducation, like redefinition, has rarely involved intervention in the cultural code. However, public health initiatives have increasingly been utilized in such efforts. Teaching teenage fathers basic parenting skills is an example of reeducation at a cultural level that alters the expected roles for males. Providing information about the nutritional qualities of food types has been directed toward improving child-raising behaviors in impoverished societies (Messer, 1984). General cultural attitudes may also be altered to provide parents with enriched experiences as well. One such example is the recently adopted value that parents of healthy children should be educated about the newborn's interactive capabilities (Worobey & Belsky, 1982).

However, most reeducation efforts are directed at the family or individual parent level. Such efforts typically supply parents with information about specific caregiving skills.

The care and feeding of premature infants is an area that may serve to illustrate reeducation interventions. Premature infants present parents with particular challenges in routine caretaking since the infant's immaturity may be characterized by irregularities in maintaining homeostasis (Gorski, 1983), irregular sleep patterns (Parmelee & Sigman, 1984), and inconsistencies in social interaction (Field, 1980; Goldberg et al., 1980). An intervention program developed to address the caregiving concerns of parents of premature infants is reported by Minde and his colleagues (Minde et al., 1980). A series of discussion groups was offered to parents while the infants were still in the nursery. The discussion groups included a "veteran mother" who had had a similar premature infant. The later course of the intervention included discussions led by hospital personnel to review medical procedures and the developmental needs of premature babies. Three months following discharge from the hospital, the infants whose parents participated in the intervention groups fed significantly longer than did the control group. These changes were mediated by changes in the parents' behavior. Mothers who had participated in the intervention engaged their infants more through talking and looking than did the control group.

An even more highly structured and educational approach is reported by Nurcombe et al. (1984). Parents of 74 premature infants were assigned either to a control condition or were enrolled in an intervention program that consisted of 11 sessions with a trained pediatric nurse. The nurse trained the parents in developmental aspects of prematurity including state regulation, motor system development, and recognition of cues and patterns of temperament. Six months following discharge from the hospital and three months following the end of the intervention program, intervention and control families were assessed on measures of infant temperament, maternal role satisfaction, maternal attitude to child rearing, and maternal confidence. Mothers who participated in the intervention program were more confident in, more satisfied with, and more favorable toward child rearing than those in a low-birth weight control group. Intervention mothers perceived their infants as more adaptable, happy, and approachable, and less easily distressed. Reeducation efforts directed toward the parents influenced their caretaking abilities and confidence in parenting premature infants with special needs. This form of intervention may have led the parents to perceive their infants as less difficult to raise, and in turn made the parents more willing to interact with the babies in a social context.

In contrast with classroom programs for groups of parents are the individualized interactions in programs devoted to interactional coaching (Field, 1983). After videotaping dyadic interaction sessions, typically between infants and their mothers, the mothers are shown how changes in their interaction behavior produced changes in the infant's responsivity. Highlighting the relatively subtle cues produced by high-risk infants allows parents to participate in more optimal caregiving behaviors and facilitates the child's communication and interaction behaviors (Clark & Seifer, 1983).

The contrast between interventions at the level of macroregulations, miniregulations, and microregulations can be seen in these intervention programs. Macroregulations are involved when parents are taught in didactic programs about developmental milestones and about what changes should be made when the child is weaned, begins to walk, and begins to talk. Miniregulations are involved when parents are given more hands-on training and taught to change diapers or position the infant for feeding. Microregulations are involved when parents are given interaction coaching to improve their abilities to interpret subtle interactional cues. When intervention programs are targeted at one level of regulation, it is not clear whether there is spillover into other levels, or whether there needs to be. Important research questions concern whether teaching parents in a classroom will change the way they interact in face-to-face situations with their infants. The classroom situation is much less expensive, and will ensure that infants will at least get the right feeding formula. On the other hand, it may be in the face-to-face situation, or perhaps the lack of it, that many feeding difficulties arise. Alternatively, there may be spillover from programs that focus on microregulations to broader areas of parenting. For example, parents who feel better about their minute-to-minute interactions with their infant may alter their developmental goals for the child.

Reeducation interventions are directed toward families who are deficient in certain skills that are necessary for optimal parenting. Remediation and redefinition are not salient for such families because even if the parent makes appropriate attributions to a child who is making appropriate elicitations, the parent does not know how to respond appropriately. Recent advances in our knowledge about teaching parenting skills allows professionals to impart this knowledge to parents in need of information and skill training. Reeducation is the intervention of choice when parents are expected to make use of this information, thus producing beneficial changes in the child's developmental course.

TRANSACTIONAL DIAGNOSIS

We have argued that it may be helpful to focus intervention efforts according to problem identification and level of regulation involved. Such categorization would not only lead to better program design, but better evaluation models and research designs, as well. In the case of remediation, the child is identified as developmentally atypical and intervention would be necessary with any parent. The focus of remediation is to change the child. Redefinition interventions are prescribed when the child may be identified as having a problem, but the parent's relationship with the child inhibits the child's normal growth and development. Intervention is necessary because of the particular relationship between this child and this parent. The target of intervention is to change the parent's relationship with this child. Finally, in the case of reeducation, the parent has been identified as being deficient in certain skills or knowledge, whereas the child's condition is not in need of change. The purpose of intervention is then to change the parent's knowledge of all children or knowledge of their particular child's condition.

A decision tree can be described for choosing the appropriate form of intervention (see Figure 6). Because in almost every case the child is brought into a program because he or she is perceived as having a problem, the first decision to be made is whether

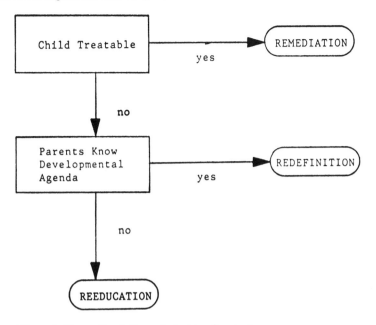

Figure 6. Transactional diagnosis decision flowchart

remediation is appropriate. For infants remediation usually takes medical, but sometimes behavioral, forms, for example, the introduction of nasogastric feedings or the behavioral stimulation of the sucking reflex to enhance feeding. Remediation cannot be achieved in two instances: a case where there is no procedure for changing the current condition of the child, for example, a preterm or handicapped infant; or a situation where nothing can be found that needs changing. In such cases, the parents' knowledge of the developmental agenda and their reactions to the child must be examined. When parents show evidence of knowing the cultural code but are not using it with their child, redefinition is necessary. When the child's problems are the result of the parent's lack of knowledge about the cultural code, reeduction is indicated.

Redefinition requires parents to identify areas of normal functioning in their child. For redefinition in the case of a disabled child, the parents need to rid themselves of attributions that may have arisen in their own histories that prevent them from interacting more productively with their child's actual characteristics, that is, getting rid of the ghosts in the nursery. In the case of a handicapped child, the parents need to be led to see the handicap as only one aspect of the child's behavior among many other characteristics that are responsive to normal caretaking, for example, appreciation of the child's social and emotional responsivity despite delays in cognitive functioning.

Reeducation would be evident in a program that instructed adolescent mothers how to rear their children. In the case of handicapped infants, reeducation takes the form of adapting the cultural code to the specific characteristics of the child. Training parents of motorically impaired infants in positioning techniques for feeding would be one example. Providing parents of preterm babies with interaction coaching or developmental information is another.

Once the form of intervention has been determined, the level of regulation should

Table 2. Examples of regulation-based intervention strategies for feeding disturbances in infancy

Levels of Regulation	Transactional categories		
	Remediate	Redefine	Reeducate
Microregulation	Increase child's ability to demonstrate hunger cues	Relabel child's crying as hunger not oppositionalism	Coach parents to be sensitive to infant's cues during interactions
Miniregulation	Provide supplemental oral stimulation to encourage sucking	Help parents to relate to real child instead of fantasized one	Provide educational program for parents of preterm babies
Macroregulation	Insert nasogastric feeding tube	Encourage balanced diet through public health advertising	Educate mothers to prolong liquid diet and delay feeding solid foods

be identified. Table 2 summarizes the interventions we have described that deal with feeding disturbances as examples of the three transactional categories and the three levels of regulation.

The transactional model of intervention is a working model at this point. It has been proposed to provide a framework for identifying more effective means of intervention while recognizing the complexities of human development. Several aspects of this model that may be salient for future research directives have not been addressed. Considering the systemic properties of change, for example, intervention focused in one area may lead to the need for intervention in another area. As a teenage mother becomes educated about child development, subsequent interventions may be directed toward redefining her relationship with her infant, given continued difficulties in the child's development. A better understanding of how the regulatory codes relate to each other and are involved in different processes of change may lead to more specific forms of intervention. An attempt to clarify the transactional model of intervention highlights again the complexities of human development. However, we are not discouraged by such complexities, but instead see complexities as the very reason for developing more adaptive and beneficial forms of intervention.

SUMMARY

The preceding discussion has been aimed at understanding the impact of contextual influences on development. Through an ecological analysis, some aspects of the environtype were highlighted as providing the regulatory framework for healthy child development. These factors included the cultural and family codes. A case was made that the environment is an active force in shaping outcomes. However, the shaping forces is constrained by the state and potentialities of the individual (Sameroff, 1983). In an attempt to incorporate both aspects in a coherent model of development, the utility of the transactional model for designing programs to prevent cognitive and social-emotional problems was explored. The development of these problems has been interpreted as deviations in a child-rearing regulatory system. The prevention of these problems has been defined as the adjustment of the child to better fit the regulatory system or the adjustment of the regulatory system to better fit the child.

Within this regulatory framework transactions are ubiquitous. Wherever parents change their way of thinking about or behaving toward the child as a result of something the child does, a transaction has occurred. Most of these transactions are normative within the existing cultural code and facilitate development. Intervention only becomes necessary where these transactions are nonnormative. In our progress toward effective intervention programs we have reached a key theoretical breakthrough. The problems of children are no longer seen as restricted to children. Social experience is now recognized as a critical component of all behavioral developments, both normal and abnormal. Unfortunately, we have not yet reached the level of sophistication in theory and research that would connect childhood problems with corollary regulatory problems. There are many possible regulations to solve the same problem and, therefore, many possible interventions. Future research should test the relative efficacies of interventions at the individual, family, and cultural level.

The complex model that characterizes our modern understanding of the regulation of development seems an appropriate one for analyzing the etiology of developmental disorders. It permits the understanding of intervention at a level necessary to identify targets of intervention. It helps us to understand why initial conditions do not determine outcomes, either positively or negatively. The model also helps us to understand why early intervention efforts may not determine later outcomes. There are many points in development where regulations can facilitate or retard the child's progress. The hopeful part of this model is that these many points in time represent opportunities for changing the course of development.

In sum, models that focus on singular causal factors are inadequate for either the study or manipulation of developmental outcomes. The evolution of living systems has provided a regulatory model that incorporates feedback mechanisms between the individual and regulatory codes. These cultural and genetic codes are the context of development. By appreciating the workings of the regulatory system, we can obtain a better grasp of the process of development and how to change it.

REFERENCES

Als, H., Lawhon, G., Brown, E., Gibes, R., Duffy, F. H., McAnulty, G., & Blickman, J. G. (1986). Individualized behavioral and environmental care for the very low birth weight preterm infant at high risk for bronchopulmonary dysplasia: Neonatal intensive care unit and developmental outcome. *Pediatrics, 78*, 1123–1132.
Altemeir, W. A., O'Connor, S. M., Sherrod, K. B., & Vietze, P. M. (1985). Prospective study of antecedents for nonorganic failure to thrive. *The Journal of Pediatrics, 106*, 360–365.
Anderson, G. E., Burroughs, A. K., & Measel, C. P. (1983). Nonnutritive sucking opportunities: A safe and effective treatment for preterm neonates. In T. Field & A. Sostek (Eds.), *Infants born at risk: Physiological, perceptual, and cognitive processes* (pp. 129–146). New York: Grune & Stratton.
Ayoub, C. C., & Milner, J. S. (1985). Failure to thrive: Parental indicators, types and outcomes. *Child Abuse and Neglect, 9*, 491–499.
Bagnato, S. J., & Neisworth, J. T. (1985). Efficacy of interdisciplinary assessment and treatment for infants and preschoolers with congenital and acquired brain injury. *Analysis and Intervention in Developmental Disabilities, 1*, 107–128.
Barbero, G., & McKay, N. (1969). Failure to thrive. In W. E. Nelson (Ed.), *Textbook of pediatrics* (pp. 1653–1654). Philadelphia: Saunders.
Barrett, D. E., Radke-Yarrow, M., & Klein, R. E. (1982). Chronic malnutrition and child behavior: Effects of early caloric supplementation on social and emotional functioning at school age. *Child Development, 18*, 541–556.
Belsky, J. (1980). Child maltreatment: An ecological integration. *American Psychologist, 35*, 430–435.

Bennett, L. A., Wolin, S., Reiss, D., & Teitelbaum, M. A. (1987). Couples at risk for the transmission of alcoholism: Protective influences. *Family Process, 26,* 111–129.

Bernbaum, J. C., Peneira, G. R., Watkins, J. B., & Peckham, G. J. (1983). Nonnutritive sucking during gavage feeding enhances growth and maturation in premature infants. *Pediatrics, 71,* 41–45.

Bossard, J. H. S., & Boll, E. S. (1950). *Ritual of Family Living.* Philadelphia: University of Pennsylvania Press.

Brazelton, T. B. (1973). Neonatal behavioral assessment scale. *Clinics in Developmental Medicine* (No. 50). Philadelphia: Lippincott.

Brazelton, T. B., Koslowski, B., & Main, M. (1974). The origins of reciprocity: The early mother–infant interaction. In M. Lewis & L. Rosenblum (Eds.), *The effect of the infant on its caregiver* (pp. 49–76). New York: Wiley.

Bricker, D. D. (1986). *Early education of at-risk and handicapped infants, toddlers, and preschool children.* Glenview, IL: Scott, Foresman.

Bricker, D. D., & Dow, M. (1980). Early intervention with the young severely handicapped child. *Journal of the Association for Severely Handicapped, 5,* 130–138.

Broman, S. H., Nichols, P. L., & Kennedy, W. A. (1975). *Preschool IQ: Prenatal and early developmental correlates.* Hillsdale, NJ: L. Erlbaum.

Bronfenbrenner, U. (1977). Toward an experimental ecology of human development. *American Psychologist, 32,* 513–531.

Casey, P. H., Bradley, R., & Wortham, B. (1984). Social and nonsocial home environments of infants with nonorganic failure to thrive. *Pediatrics, 73,* 348–353.

Chatoor, I., Dickson, S., Schaeffer, S., & Egan, J. (1985). A developmental classification of feeding disorders associated with failure to thrive: Diagnosis and treatment. In D. Drotar (Ed.), *New directions in failure to thrive: Implications for research and practice* (pp. 235–258). New York: Plenum Press.

Cherlin, A. J. (1981). *Marriage, divorce, remarriage.* Cambridge: Harvard University Press.

Clark, G. N., & Seifer, R. (1983). Facilitating mother–infant communication: A treatment model for high-risk and developmentally delayed infants. *Infant Mental Health Journal, 4,* 67–82.

Cravioto, J., & Arrieta, R. (1983). Malnutrition in childhood. In M. Rutter (Ed.), *Developmental Neuropsychiatry* (pp. 32–51). New York: Guilford Press.

Cravioto, J., & DeLicardie, E. R. (1979). Nutrition, mental development and learning. In F. Falkner & J. M. Turner (Eds.), *Human growth* (Vol. 3, pp. 481–508). New York: Plenum Press.

Cutright, P. (1972). Illegitimacy in the United States, 1920–1960. In C. W. Woestoff & R. Parke (Eds.), *Demographic and social aspects of population growth.* Washington, DC: U.S. Government Printing Office.

deVries, M. W., & Sameroff, A. J. (1984). Culture and temperament: Influences on temperament in three East African societies. *American Journal of Orthopsychiatry, 54,* 83–96.

Drotar, D., & Malone, C. A. (1982). Family-oriented intervention in failure to thrive. In M. Klaus & M. O. Robertson (Eds.), *Johnson and Johnson Pediatric Round Table: Vol. 6. Birth interaction and attachment* (pp. 104–112). Skillman, NJ: Johnson and Johnson.

Drotar, D., Woychik, J., Mantz-Clumpner, C., Brickell, C., Negray, J., Wallace, M., & Malone, C. (1985). The family context of failure to thrive. In D. Drotar (Ed.), *New directions in failure to thrive: Implications for research and practice* (pp. 295–310). New York: Plenum Press.

Dunst, C. J., & Trivette, C. M. (in press). A family systems model of early intervention. In D. P. Powell (Ed.), *Parent education and support programs: Consequences for children and families.* Norwood, NJ: Ablex Publishing.

Dunst, C. J., Trivette, C. M., & Cross, A. H. (1986). Mediating influences of social support: Personal, family and child outcomes. *American Journal of Mental Deficiency, 90,* 403–417.

Ferreira, A. (1963). Family myth and homeostasis. *Archives of General Psychiatry, 9,* 457–463.

Field, T. (1977). Effects of early separation, interactive deficits, and experimental manipulation in infant–mother face-to-face interaction. *Child Development, 48,* 763–771.

Field, T. M. (1979). Interaction patterns of preterm and term infants. In T. M. Field, A. M. Sostek, S. Goldberg, & H. H. Schuman (Eds.), *Infants born at risk: Behavior and development* (pp. 333–356). New York: Medical and Scientific Books.

Field, T. M. (1980). Interactions of preterm and term infants with their lower- and middle-class teenage and adult mothers. In T. Field, S. Goldberg, D. Stern, & A. M. Sostek (Eds.), *High-risk infants and children: Adult and peer interactions* (pp. 113–132). New York: Academic Press.

Field, T. M. (1983). Early interaction and intervention: Coaching of high-risk infants and parents. In M. Perlmutter (Ed.), *Development and policy concerns: Children with special needs. Symposium on Child Psychology.* Hillsdale, NJ: L. Erlbaum.

Field, T. M., Ignatoff, E., Stringer, S., Brennan, J., Greenberg, S., Widmayer, S., & Anderson, G. C. (1982). Nonnutritive sucking during tube feedings: Effects on preterm neonates in an intensive care unit. *Pediatrics, 70*(3), 381–384.

Fraiberg, S. (1980). *Clinical studies in infant mental health: The first year of life.* New York: Basic Books.

Fraiberg, S., Adelson, E., & Shapiro, V. (1980). Ghosts in the nursery: A psychoanalytic approach to the problems of impaired mother–infant relationships. In S. Fraiberg (Ed.), *Clinical studies in infant mental health: The first year of life* (pp. 164–196). New York: Basic Books.

Furstenberg, F. F., Brooks–Gunn, J., & Morgan, S. P. (1987). *Adolescent mothers.* Cambridge: Cambridge University Press.

Goldberg, S., Branchfeld, S., & DiVitto, B. (1980). Feeding, fussing and playing parent–infant interaction in the first year as a function of prematurity and perinatal problems. In T. Field, S. Goldberg, D. Stern, & A. Sostek (Eds.), *High-risk infants and children: Adult and peer interactions* (pp. 133–153). New York: Academic Press.

Golden, M., & Birns, B. (1976). Social class and infant intelligence. In M. Lewis (Ed.), *Origins of intelligence: Infancy and early childhood.* New York: Plenum Press.

Gordon, E. F., & Vazquez, D. M. (1985). Failure to thrive: An expanded conceptual model. In D. Drotar (Ed.), *New directions in failure to thrive: Implications for research and practice* (pp. 69–76). New York: Plenum Press.

Gordon, R. (1983). An operational definition of prevention. *Public Health Reports, 98,* 107–109.

Gorski, P. (1983). Premature infant behavioral and physiological responses to caregiving interventions in intensive care nursery. In J. D. Call, E. Galenson, & R. L. Tyson (Eds.), *Frontiers of infant psychiatry* (pp. 265–273). New York: Basic Books.

Gottman, J. M. (1979). Detecting cyclicity in social interaction. *Psychological Bulletin, 86,* 338–348.

Greenspan, S. I. (1981). *Psychopathology and adaptation in infancy and early childhood: Clinical infant reports no. 1.* Hanover, NH: University Press of New England.

Haynes, C. F., Cutler, C., Gray, J., & Kempe, R. S. (1984). Hospitalized cases of nonorganic failure to thrive: The scope of the problem and short-term lay health visitor intervention. *Child Abuse and Neglect, 8,* 229–242.

Hetherington, E. M., & Camara, K. A. (1984). Families in transition: The process of dissolution and reconstitution. In R. Parke (Ed.), *The family* (pp. 398–439). Chicago: University of Chicago Press.

Hudson, J., & Nelson, K. (1983). Effects of script structure on children's recall. *Developmental Psychology, 19,* 625–635.

Kohn, M. L. (1969). *Class and conformity: A study in values.* Homewood, IL: Dorsey Press.

Kramer, J. (1985). Family myth and homeostasis. *Archives of General Psychiatry, 9,* 457–463.

Kurdek, L. A. (1981). An integrative perspective on children's divorce adjustment. *American Psychologist, 36,* 856–866.

Lamb, H. R., & Zusman, J. (1979). Primary prevention in perspective. *American Journal of Psychiatry, 136*(1), 12–17.

Lazar, I., Darlington, R., Murray, H., Royce, J., & Snipper, A. (1982). Lasting effects of early education: A report from the consortium for longitudinal studies. *Monographs of the Society for Research in Child Development, 47* (2–3, Serial No. 195).

Leavell, H. R., & Clark, E. G. (1965) *Preventive medicine for a doctor in his community: An epidemiological approach* (3rd ed.). New York: McGraw-Hill.

Listernick, R., Christoffel, K., Pace, J., & Chicaramonte, J. (1985). Severe primary malnutrition in U.S. children. *American Journal of Diseases in Childhood, 139,* 1157–1160.

Main, M., & Goldwyn, R. (1984). Predicting rejection of her infant from mother's representation of her own experience: Implications for the abused and abusing intergenerational cycle. *Child Abuse and Neglect, 8,* 203–217.

Messer, E. (1984). Sociocultural aspects of nutrient intake and behavioral responses to nutrition. In J. Galler (Ed.), *Nutrition and behavior* (pp. 417–471). New York: Plenum Press.

Minde, K., Shosenberg, N., Marton, P., Thompson, J., Ripley, J., & Burns, S. (1980). Self-help groups in a premature nursery – a controlled evaluation. *The Journal of Pediatrics, 96,* 933–940.

Nelson, K. (1981). Social cognition in a script framework. In J. Flavell & R. Ross (Eds.), *Social cognitive development* (pp. 97–118). Cambridge: Cambridge University Press.

Nelson, K., & Gruendel, J. (1981). Generalized event representations: Basic building blocks of cognitive development. In A. Brown & M. Lamb (Eds.), *Advances in developmental psychology* (Vol. 1, pp. 131–158). Hillsdale, NJ: L. Erlbaum.

Nurcombe, B., Howell, D. C., Rauh, V. A., Teti, D. M., Ruoff, P., & Brennan, J. (1984). An intervention program for mothers of low-birthweight infants: Preliminary results. *The Journal of the American Academy of Child Psychiatry, 23,* 319–325.

Oates, R. K., Peacook, A., & Forrest, D. (1985). Long-term effects of nonorganic failure to thrive. *Pediatrics, 75,* 36–40.

Parke, R. D., & Tinsley, B. J., (1987). Family interaction in infancy. In J. Osofsky (Ed.), *Handbook of infancy* (2nd ed., pp. 579–641). New York: Wiley.

Parmelee, A. H., & Haber, A. (1973). Who is the at risk infant? *Clinical Obstetrics and Gynecology, 16,* 376–387.

Parmelee, A. H., & Sigman, M. (1984). Perinatal brain development and behavior. In J. J. Campos & M. M. Haith (Eds.), *Handbook of Child Psychology: Vol. 2. Infancy and developmental psychobiology* (pp. 95–155). New York: Wiley.

Patterson, G. R. (1986). Performance models for antisocial boys. *American Psychologist, 41,* 432–444.

Pollner, M., & McDonald-Wikler, L. (1985). The social construction of unreality: A case study of a family's attribution of competence to a severely retarded child. *Family Process, 24,* 241–254.

Pueschel, S. M. (1984). *The young child with Down syndrome.* New York: Human Sciences Press.

Ratner, N., & Bruner, J. (1977). Games, social exchange and the acquisition of language. *Journal of Child Language, 5,* 391–401.

Read, M. S. (1982). Malnutrition and behavior. *Applied Research in Mental Retardation, 3,* 279–291.

Reiss, D. (1981). *The family's construction of reality.* Cambridge: Harvard University Press.

Reiss, D. (1989). The represented and practicing family: Contrasting visions of family continuity. In A. J. Sameroff & R. N. Emde (Eds.), *Relationship disturbances in early childhood: A developmental approach.* New York: Basic Books.

Reiss, D., Oliveri, M. E., & Curd, K. (1983). Family paradigm and adolescent social behavior. In H. D. Grotevant & C. R. Cooper (Eds.), *Adolescent development in the family: New directions for child development, 22* (pp. 77–91). San Francisco: Jossey-Bass.

Rogoff, B. (1981). Schooling and the development of cognitive skills. In H. C. Triandis & A. Heron (Eds.), *Handbook of cross-cultural psychology: Developmental psychology* (Vol. 4, pp. 233–294). Boston: Allyn & Bacon.

Rosen, D., Loeb, J. S., & Jura, M. B. (1980). Differentiation of organic from nonorganic failure to thrive syndrome in infancy. *Pediatrics, 66,* 698–704.

Roskies, E. (1972). *Abnormality and normality: The mothering of thalidomide children.* Ithaca, NY: Cornell University Press.

Rutter, M. (1979). Protective factors in children's responses to stress and disadvantage. In M. W. Kent & J. E. Rolf (Eds.), *Primary prevention of psychopathology: Vol. 3. Social competence in children.* Hanover, NH: University Press of New England.

Rutter, M. (1982). Prevention of children's psychosocial disorders: Myths and substance. *Pediatrics, 70,* 883–894.

Rutter, M. (1987). Continuities and discontinuities from infancy. In J. Osofsky (Ed.), *Handbook of infant development* (2nd ed., pp. 1256–1296). New York: Wiley.

Sackett, G. P. (1978). *Observing behavior: Data collection and analysis method* (Vol. 2). Baltimore: University Park Press.

Sameroff, A. J. (1982). The environmental context of developmental disabilities. In D. Bricker (Ed.), *Intervention with at-risk and handicapped infants: From research to application* (pp. 141–152). Baltimore: University Park Press.

Sameroff, A. J. (1983). Developmental systems: Contexts and evolution. In W. Kessen (Ed.), *Handbook of child psychology: Vol. 1. History, theories, and methods* (pp. 238–294). New York: Wiley.

Sameroff, A. J. (1985). *Can development be continuous?* Paper presented at the Annual Meeting of the American Psychological Association, Los Angeles.

Sameroff, A. J. (1986). Environmental context of child development. *Journal of Pediatrics, 109,* 192–200.

Sameroff, A. J. (1987). The social context of development. In N. Eisenberg (Ed.), *Contemporary topics in developmental psychology* (pp. 273–291). New York: Wiley.

Sameroff, A. J., & Chandler, M. J. (1975). Reproductive risk and the continuum of caretaking casualty. In F. D. Horowitz, M. Hetherington, S. Scarr-Salapatek, & G. Siegel (Eds.), *Review of child development research* (Vol. 4, pp. 187–244). Chicago: University of Chicago Press.

Sameroff, A. J., & Feil, L. (1983). Parental concepts of development. In I. Sigel (Ed.), *Parent belief systems: The psychological consequences for children* (pp. 83–104). Hillsdale NJ: L. Erlbaum.

Sameroff, A. J., & Fiese, B. H. (1989). Conceptual issues in prevention. In D. Schaffer (Ed.), *Project Prevention: An intervention initiative* (OSAP Prevention Monograph No. 2). Washington, DC: U.S. Government Printing Office.

Sameroff, A. J., Seifer, R., Barocas, B., Zax, M., & Greenspan, S. (1987). IQ scores of 4-year-old children: Social-environmental risk factors. *Pediatarics, 79*(3), 343–350.

Sameroff, A. J., Seifer, R., & Zax, M. (1982). Early development of children at risk for emotional disorder. *Monographs of the Society for Research in Child Development, 47* (7, Serial No. 199).

Schweinhart, L., & Weikart, D. (1980). *Young children grow up: The effort of the Perry preschool program on youths through age 15* (Monographs of the High/Scope Educational Research Foundation No. 7). Ypsilanti, MI: High/Scope.

Sigel, E. (1985) *Parental belief systems: The psychological consequences for children.* Hillsdale, NJ: L. Erlbaum.

Singer, L. T., Drotar, D., Fagan, J. F., Devost, L., & Lake, R. (1983). The cognitive development of failure to thrive infants: Methodological issues and new approaches. In T. Field & A. Sostek (Eds.), *Infants born at risk* (pp. 211–242). New York: Grune & Stratton.

Stein, Z., & Susser, M., (1985). Effects of early nutrition on neurological and mental competence in human beings. *Psychological Medicine, 15*, 717–726.

Stern, D. (1977). *The first relationship: Infant and mother.* Cambridge: Harvard University Press.

Turnbull, A., Summers, J., & Brotherson, M. (1983). *Working with families with disabled members: A family systems approach.* Lawrence: University of Kansas Research and Training Center.

Wallerstein, J. S., & Kelly, J. B. (1980). *Surviving the break-up: How parents and children cope with divorce.* New York: Basic Books.

Wattenberg, B. J. (Ed.). (1976). *The statistical history of the United States: From colonial times to the present.* New York: Basic Books.

Werner, E. E., Bierman, J. M., & French, F. E. (1971). *The children of Kauai.* Honolulu: University of Hawaii Press.

Werner, E. E., & Smith, R. S. (1982). *Vulnerable but invincible: A longitudinal study of resilient children and youth.* New York: McGraw-Hill.

Wolin, S., Bennett, L., & Jacobs, S. (1988). Assessing family rituals. In E. Imber-Black, J. Roberts, & R. Whiting (Eds.), *Rituals and family therapy.* New York: Norton Press.

Wolin, S., Bennett, L., Noonan, D., & Teitelbaum, M. (1980). Disrupted family rituals: A factor in the intergenerational transmission of alcoholism. *Journal Studies of Alcoholism, 41*, 199–214.

Worobey, J., & Belsky, J. (1982). Employing the Brazelton scale to influence mothering: An experimental comparison of three strategies. *Developmental Psychology, 18*, 736–743.

Zeitlin, S. J., Kotkin, A. J., & Baker, H. C. (1982). *A Celebration of American family folklore.* New York: Pantheon Books.

Zigler, E., & Trickett, P. K. (1978). IQ, social competence, and evaluation of early childhood intervention programs. *American Psychologist, 33*, 789–799.

Comprehensive clinical approaches to infants and their families: Psychodynamic and developmental perspectives

STANLEY I. GREENSPAN

Psychodynamic perspectives emphasize that the infant and child in the family should be studied in the context of their cultural and social patterns. By definition, psychodynamic approaches consider underlying emotions and wishes as they relate to behavior. Specific capacities, such as sensory reactivity and processing, fine motor, gross motor, language, and cognition, are seen as aspects of human functioning that can be studied in their own right, but that can also be viewed in interaction with and as contribution to psychosocial adaptation. This chapter will elaborate on this perspective through a review of some important developments in the field of infant and early childhood intervention. It will also present a theoretical and clinical discussion of work with multirisk families and their infants, as well as with infants with unique developmental challenges in families that are coping relatively well. The developmental structuralist approach (Greenspan, 1979, 1981) will be presented as a model that integrates psychodynamic, developmental, and emerging empirical perspectives on infants, children, and families who are at risk for environmental and/or biological factors.

The past 30 years have been marked by enormous progress in understanding infancy and early childhood development. A wealth of observational and experimental studies have documented the infant's social and emotional growth in the first year of life (e.g., Ainsworth, Bell, & Stayton, 1974; Bowlby, 1951; Brazelton, Koslowski, & Main, 1974; Emde, Gaensbauer, & Harman, 1976; Sander, 1962; Sroufe, 1983; Stern, 1985). This information, coupled with knowledge of neuromotor and cognitive development, permits the development of a comprehensive perspective that includes physical, cognitive, emotional, and interactive patterns. Such comprehensive perspectives are the essence of a psychodynamic approach.

MULTIPLE LINES OF DEVELOPMENT

The view that the infant develops along multiple rather than unitary lines (i.e., physical, cognitive, social-emotional, and familial) is perhaps self-evident; however, this approach is not always put into practice. In order to approach problems in ways that will facilitate development in all areas of an infant's life, intervention strategies must take into account the existence of multiple lines of development. For example, clinical observations suggest that a baby born with an auditory and/or tactile hypersensitivity will tend to withdraw when talked to or held. A clinical approach would combine gentle exposure to the potentially noxious stimuli in low doses with such soothing experiences as rocking and soothing sounds. Recognizing the child's tendency to withdraw, the clinical staff might formulate special patterns of care that would help the parents "woo" the baby into greater emotional relatedness.

In contrast, an approach that focused, say, only on cognitive stimulation might attempt to enliven a withdrawn, seemingly "slow" baby through sensorimotor stimulation. Yet, if a child actually has an undiagnosed sensory hypersensitivity, the child could become even more irritable and less available for human relationships as a consequence of this type of intervention.

Failure to consider multiple lines of development in infancy may lead to impairment at a later age. In general, a youngster who responds to human stimulation with irritability, rigidity, and gaze aversion may very well be alert and show interest in the inanimate world with inanimate stimulation. From the point of view of physical and neurological development, such a child might develop adequate cognition during the first 12 to 18 months. However, the impairment of human relationships and capacity to organize and differentiate animate experience (coping and adapting skills) might not become clearly noticeable until the latter part of the second, or early in the third, year. It is during this period, when relationships with peers become important, that complaints related to unsocialized behavior or patterns of withdrawal (refusal to play with others) are heard from parents.

A COMPREHENSIVE CLINICAL APPROACH

A comprehensive clinical approach views infants in a context that includes not only multiple lines of development, but also the parents, other family members, and relevant social factors. A comprehensive approach, for example, would consider and work with the parents' predominant attitudes and feelings, family relationships, and other crucial contextual factors, such as the system of health and mental health services and relevant community structures.

A comprehensive clinical approach by definition considers the infant in the context of interactive, family, and social patterns. It must begin with an assessment consisting of a number of conceptually consistent categories, including the following six core areas.

1. *Prenatal and perinatal variables:* These variables all have some relative impact on the infant's constitutional status and developmental tendencies, although the extent of the impact is unknown. The prenatal variables include familial genetic patterns; mother's status during pregnancy, including nutrition, physical health and illness, personality functioning, mental health, and degree of stress; familial and social support systems; and characteristics of the pregnancy and the delivery process, including complications, time in various stages, and the infant's status after birth. The perinatal variables include maternal perceptions of her infant, maternal reports of the emerging daily routine, and observations of the infant and of maternal–infant interaction.

2. *Parental, familial, and environmental variables:* These variables include evaluations of parents, other family members, and individuals who relate closely to the family along a number of dimensions. These assessments include each member's personality organization and developmental needs, child-rearing capacity, and family interaction patterns. Evaluations of the support system used by or available to the family (e.g., extended family, friends, and community agencies) and of the total home environment (both animate and inanimate components) are also included.

3. *Primary caregiver and caregiver–infant/child relationship variables:* Evaluations in this area focus on the interaction between the infant and his or her important nurturing figure(s). Included are the quality of mutual rhythm, feedback, and capacity for joint pleasure, as well as the dyad's flexibility in tolerating tension and being able to return to a state of intimacy. Later in development, capacities to experience differentiation, form complex emotional and behavioral patterns, and construct representations are important.

4. *Infant variables – physical, neurological, physiological:* These variables include the infant's genetic background and status immediately after birth, including the infant's general physical integrity (size, weight, general health), neurological integrity, physiological tendencies, rhythmic patterns, and levels of alertness and activity. Special attention should be paid to the infant's physical integrity and how this factor could foster or hinder the child's capacities to experience internal and external stimulation; regulate internal and external experience and reach a state of homeostasis; develop human relationships; interact in cause-and-effect reciprocal patterns; form complex behavioral and emotional patterns; and construct representation to guide behavior and feelings.

5. *Infant variables – sensory, motor, and cognitive:* The variables in this category include the development, differentiation, and integration of the infant's motor and sensory systems, and the relationship of the infant's sensorimotor development to the infant's cognitive development.

6. *Infant variables – formation and internalization of human relationships:* These variables involve the interrelationships and capacities for relationships among the infant, parents, and other family members. Early relationships help the infant develop the capacity for manifesting a range of emotions in the context of a sequence of organizational stages. These stages include the capacity for purposeful interactions; complex, organized social and emotional patterns; constructing representations; and differentiating internal representations along self versus non-self and time-and-space dimensions.

There are also variables that focus on the mother and involve the mother's capacity to reach out and foster attachment; provide physical comfort and care; perceive basic states of pleasure and discomfort in her infant; respond with balanced empathy, that is, without either overidentification or isolation of feeling; and perceive and respond flexibly and differentially to the infant's cues, foster organized complex interactions, and support the infant's ability to symbolize his or her affective world.

DEVELOPMENTAL STRUCTURALIST APPROACH TO MILESTONES

Aspects of physical, sensorimotor, and cognitive development are already included in many approaches to working with infants and their families. Comprehensive clinical approaches require equal attention to emotional and social development. The focus on infants and their families from multiple aspects of development has encouraged the elaboration of new concepts of development that focus on an infant's social and emotional functioning. In this section, a model of emotional development will be presented that incorporates multiple perspectives.

Although there are no large-scale studies of infants and young children's affective patterns at different ages, there is extensive literature on the emotional development of infants who are presumed normal. Interestingly, during recent years there has been considerably greater documentation of normal emotional development in infants than probably any other age group (Barrett & Campos, 1987; Campos, Barrett, Lamb, Goldsmith, & Stenberg, 1983; Izard & Malatesta, 1987).

It is now well documented that infants are capable, even at birth or shortly thereafter, of organizing experience in an adaptive fashion. They can respond to pleasure and displeasure (Lipsitt, 1966; Stern, 1985); change behavior as a function of its consequences (Bower, 1982; Fagan, 1977; Gerwitz, 1965, 1969); form intimate bonds and make visual discriminations (Fernald, 1984; Klaus & Kennell, 1976; Meltzoff & Moore, 1977; Stern, 1977); organize cycles and rhythms, for example, sleep-awake alertness states (Condon & Sander, 1974; Kaye, 1982; Sander, 1962); evidence a variety of affects or affect proclivities (Ekman, 1972; Izard, 1978; Lewis & Michalson, 1983; Tomkins, 1963); and demonstrate organized social responses in conjunction with increasing neurophysiologic organization (Duffy, Mowrer, Jensen, & Als, 1984; Harmon, 1976). The infant from the early months demonstrates a unique capacity to enter into complex social and affective interactions (Brazelton & Als, 1979; Brazelton et al., 1974; Stern, 1974a, 1974b, 1977). It is interesting to note that this empirically documented view of the infant is, in a general sense, consistent with Freud's (1911/1958) early hypothesis and Hartmann's (1939) postulation of an early undifferentiated organizational matrix. That the organization of experience broadens during the early months of life to reflect increases in the capacity to experience and tolerate a range of stimuli, including responding in social interaction in stable and personal configurations, is also consistent with more recent empirical data (Brazelton et al., 1974; Bretherton & Waters, 1985; Campos et al., 1983; Emde et al., 1976; Escalona, 1968; Murphy & Moriarty, 1976; Sander, 1962; Sroufe, Waters, & Matas, 1974).

Increasingly complex patterns continue to emerge as the infant further develops, as indicated by such emotional responses as surprise (Charlesworth, 1969) and affiliation, wariness, and fear (Ainsworth et al., 1974; Ainsworth, Blehar, Waters, & Wall, 1978; Bowlby, 1969; Sroufe & Waters, 1977); exploration and "refueling" patterns (Mahler, Pine, & Bergman, 1975); behavior suggesting functional understanding of objects (Werner & Kaplan, 1963); and the eventual emergence of symbolic capacities (Bell, 1970; Bretherton & Waters, 1985; Gouin-Decarie, 1965; Piaget, 1962/1972).

In these studies there is a consensus that by 2–4 months of age at the latest, and often much earlier, healthy infants are capable of responding to their caregiver's faces, smiles, and voices with brightening or alerting and, often, with a smile and reciprocal vocalizations, as well as other reciprocal responses. Furthermore, as development proceeds the infant and caregiver's interaction patterns become progressively characterized by more complex social interaction.

In addition to the studies of normal infant emotional development, important observations concerning disturbed development complete the emerging picture of infant emotional functioning. Interestingly, the study of psychopathology in infancy is a new area, even though the historical foundation for identifying disturbances in the early years of life is very impressive.

Winnicott (1931) began describing the environment's role in early relationship problems in the 1930s. In the 1940s followed the well-known studies of the severe developmental disturbances of infants reared in institutions or in other situations of emotional deprivation (Bakwin, 1942; Bowlby, 1951; Hunt, 1941; Lowrey, 1940; Spitz, 1945).

The role of individual differences in the infant based on constitutional maturational and early interactional patterns became a focus of inquiry in the observations of

Burlingham and A. Freud (1942); Bergman and Escalona's (1949) descriptions of infants with "unusual sensitivities"; the work of Escalona and Heider (1959); Murphy and Moriarty's (1976) description of patterns of vulnerability; Thomas, Chess, and Birch's (1968) temperament studies; Cravioto and Delicardie's (1973) descriptions of the role of infant individual differences in malnutrition; and the impressive emerging empirical literature on infants (Als, Lester, Tronick, & Brazelton, 1982; Brazelton et al., 1974; Emde et al., 1976; Gerwitz, 1961; Haith & Campos, 1983; Kaye, 1982; Lipsitt, 1966; Osofsky, 1987; Rheingold, 1966, 1969; Sander, 1962; Stern, 1974a, 1974b; Wolff, 1987). More integrated approaches to understanding disturbances in infancy have been emphasized in descriptions of selected disorders and very insightful clinical case studies (Fraiberg, 1965, 1980; Greenspan et al., 1987; Provence, 1983).

DEVELOPMENTAL PATTERNS

In order to further understand both adaptive and disturbed infant functioning, we undertook an in-depth study of normal and disturbed developmental patterns in order to develop a systematic classification of adaptive and maladaptive infant and family patterns. Table 1 summarizes our observations (Greenspan, 1979; Greenspan & Lourie, 1981; Greenspan, Lourie, & Nover, 1979; Greenspan & Porges, 1981).

The capacities described by the stages are all present in some rudimentary form from early infancy. The sequence presented suggests not when these capacities begin, but when they become relatively prominent in organizing behavior and furthering development.

The first stage is the *achievement of homeostasis*, that is, self-regulation and emerging interest in the world through sight, sound, smell, touch, taste. Once the infant has achieved some capacity for regulation in the context of engaging the world, concurrent with central nervous system (CNS) maturation between 2 and 4 months of age, the infant becomes more attuned to interpersonal interaction. There is greater ability to respond to the external environment and to form a special relationship with significant primary caregivers.

A second, closely related stage is the *formation of human attachments*. If an affective and relatively pleasurable attachment (an investment in the human, animate world) is formed, then with growing maturational abilities the infant develops complex patterns of communication in the context of this primary relationship. Parallel to the development of the infant's relationship with the inanimate world, in which basic schemes of causality are developed (Piaget, 1962/1972), the infant's ability to engage in complicated human communications is enhanced (Charlesworth, 1969; Lewis & Michalson, 1983; Stern, 1974a, 1977, 1985; Tennes, Emde, Kisley, & Metcalf, 1972; Tronick, 1982; Yogman & Brazelton, 1986).

When there are distortions in the attachment process, as occurs when a mother responds in a mechanical, remote manner, or projects some of her own independent feelings onto her infant, the infant may not learn to appreciate causal relationships between people and to experience compassionate and intimate feelings. This situation can occur even though causality seems to be developing in terms of the infant's relationship to the inanimate world and the interpersonal human world.

The establishment of causal relationships between the infant and the primary caregiver is evidenced in the infant's growing ability to discriminate primary caregivers from others. The infant also becomes able to differentiate his or her own actions from their consequences – affectively, somatically, behaviorally, and interpersonally. Usually by 8 months of age or earlier the process of differentiation occurs along a number of developmental lines, including sensorimotor integration, affect, and relationships (see Barrett & Campos, 1987).

The third stage is *somatopsychologic differentiation* indicating processes that occur jointly at the somatic (sensorimotor) and emergent psychological levels. (In this context, psychologic refers to higher-level mental processes characterized by the capacity to form internal representations or symbols as a way to organize experience.) Although schemes of causality are being established in the infant's relationship to the interpersonal world, it is not at all clear whether these schemes exist at an organized representational or symbolic level. Rather, they appear to exist mainly at a somatic or behavioral level (Greenspan, 1979), even though the precursors of representational capacities are observed.

With appropriate reading of cues and systematic differential responses, the infant's or toddler's behavioral repertoire becomes complicated and communications take on more organized, meaningful configurations. By 12 months of age, the infant is connecting individual behaviors into larger organizations and exhibits such complex emotional responses as affiliation, wariness, and fear (Ainsworth et al., 1974; Bowlby, 1969; Sroufe & Waters, 1977). As the toddler approaches the third year of life, in the context of developing individuation (Mahler et al., 1975), an increased capacity exists for forming original behavioral schemes (Piaget, 1962/1972) and imitative activity and intentionality.

Learning through imitation, which is evidenced in earlier development, now seems to assume a more dominant role. As imitations take on a more integrated personal form, it appears the toddler is adopting or internalizing attributes of his or her caregivers.

To describe these new capacities, it is useful to consider a fourth stage, that of *behavioral organization, initiative, and internalization*. As the toddler approaches the end of the second year, internal sensations and unstable images become organized in a mental representational form that can be evoked with some stability (Bell, 1970; Gouin-Decarie, 1965; Piaget, 1962/1972). While this capacity is fragile between 16 and 24 months, it soon appears to become a dominant mode in organizing the child's behavior.

A fifth stage is the *formation of mental representations or ideas*. The capacity for "object permanence" is relative and goes through a series of stages (Gouin-Decarie, 1965; Uzgiris & Hunt, 1975, 1987); it refers to the toddler's ability to search for hidden inanimate objects. Representational capacity refers to the ability to organize and evoke internally organized multisensory experiences of the animate object. The capacities to represent animate and inanimate experiences are related and depend both on CNS myelination and appropriate experiences. The process of "internalization" may be thought of as an intermediary process. Internalized experiences eventually become sufficiently organized to be considered representations.

At a representational level the child again develops capacities for elaboration, integration, and differentiation. Just as causal schemes previously were developed at a somatic and behavioral level, now they are developed at a representational level (e.g., use of language and pretend play). The child begins to elaborate and eventually differentiate those feelings, thoughts, and events that emanate from within and those that emanate from others. The child begins to differentiate the actions of others from his or her own. This process gradually forms the basis for the differentiation of self-representations from the external world, animate and inanimate, and also provides the basis for such crucial personality functions as knowing what is real from unreal, impulse and mood

Table 1. Developmental basis for psychopathology and adaptation in infancy and early childhood

Stage-specific tasks and capacities	Capacities		Environment (caregiver)	
	Adaptive	Maladaptive (pathologic)	Adaptive	Maladaptive
Homeostasis (0–3 mo) (self-regulation and interest in the world)	Internal regulation (harmony) and balanced interest in world	Unregulated (e.g., hyperexcitable) or withdrawn (apathetic)	Invested, dedicated, protective, comforting, predictable, engaging and interesting	Unavailable, chaotic, dangerous, abusive; hypostimulating or hyperstimulating; dull
Attachment (2–7 mo)	Rich, deep, multisensory emotional investment in animate world (especially with primary caregivers)	Total lack of, or nonaffective, shallow, impersonal, involvement (e.g., autistic patterns) in animate world	In love and woos infant to "fall in love"; affective, multi-modality, pleasurable involvement	Emotionally distant, aloof, and/or impersonal (highly ambivalent)
Somatopsychologic differentiation (3–10 mo) (purposeful, cause-and-effect signaling or communication)	Flexible, wide-ranging, affective, multisystem, contingent (reciprocal) interactions (especially with primary caregivers)	Behavior and affects random and/or chaotic, or narrow, rigid, and stereotyped	Reads and responds contingently to infant's communications across multiple sensory and affective systems	Ignores infant's communications (e.g., overly intrusive, preoccupied, or depressed) or misreads infant's communication (e.g., projection)
Behavioral organization, initiative, and internalization (9–24 mo)	Complex, organized, assertive, innovative, integrated behavioral and emotional patterns	Fragmented, stereotyped, and polarized behavior and emotions (e.g., withdrawn, compliant, hyperaggressive, or disorganized toddler)	Admiring of toddler's initiative and autonomy, yet available, tolerant, and firm; follows toddler's lead and helps him or her organize diverse behavioral and affective elements	Overly intrusive, controlling; fragmented, fearful (especially of toddler's autonomy); abruptly and prematurely "separates"

| Representational capacity, differentiation, and consolidation ($1\frac{1}{2}$–4 yr) (the use of ideas to guide language, pretend play and behavior and eventually thinking and planning) | Formation and elaboration of internal representations (imagery) Organization and differentiation of imagery pertaining to self and nonself; emergence of cognitive insight Stabilization of mood and gradual emergence of basic personality functions | No representational (symbolic) elaboration; behavior and affect concrete, shallow, and polarized; sense of self and other fragmented and undifferentiated or narrow and rigid; reality testing, impulse regulation, mood stabilization compromised or vulnerable (e.g., borderline psychotic and severe character problems) | Emotionally available to phase-appropriate regressions and dependency needs; reads, responds to, and encourages symbolic elaboration across emotional behavioral domains (e.g., love, pleasure, assertion) while fostering gradual reality orientation and internalization of limits | Fearful of or denies phase-appropriate needs; engages child only in concrete (nonsymbolic) modes generally or in certain realms (e.g., around pleasure) and/or misreads or responds noncontingently or nonrealistically to emerging communications (i.e., undermines reality orientation); overly permissive or punitive |
| Capacity for limited extended representational systems and multiple extended representational systems (middle childhood through adolescence) | Enhanced and eventually optimal flexibility to conserve and transform complex and organized representations of experience in the context of expanded relationship patterns and phase-expected developmental tasks | Derivative representational capacities limited or defective, as are latency and adolescent relationships and coping capacities | Supports complex, phase- and age-appropriate experiential and interpersonal development (i.e., into triangular and posttriangular patterns) | Conflicted over child's age-appropriate propensities (e.g., competitiveness, pleasure orientation, growing competence, assertiveness, and self-sufficiency); becomes aloof or maintains symbiotic tie; withdraws from or over-engages in competitive or pleasurable strivings |

Source: Greenspan (1981), Greenspan and Greenspan (1985).

regulations, and the capacity to focus attention and concentrate in order to learn and interact.

The capacity for differentiating internal representations becomes consolidated as object constancy is established (Mahler et al., 1975). In middle childhood, representational capacity becomes reinforced by the child's abilities to develop derivative representational systems that are tied to the original representation and to transform them in accord with adaptive and defensive goals. This permits greater flexibility in dealing with perceptions, feelings, thoughts, and emerging ideals. Substages for these capacities include representational differentiation, the consolidation of representational capacity, and the capacity for forming limited derivative representational systems and multiple derivative representational systems, that is, structural learning (Greenspan, 1979).

PATHOLOGY AND ADAPTATION

At each of these stages, pathologic as well as adaptive formations are possible. These may be considered as relative compromises in the range, depth, stability, and personal uniqueness of the experiential organization that is consolidation at each stage. The infant can form adaptive patterns of regulation in the earliest stages of development. Internal states are harmoniously regulated and the infant is free to invest in the animate and inanimate world, thereby setting the basis for rich emotional attachments to primary caregivers. On the other hand, if regulatory processes are not functioning properly and the infant is either hypo- or hypersensitive to sensations, he or she may evidence homeostatic difficulties. From relatively minor compromises such as a tendency to withdraw and/or become hyperexcitable under stress, to a major deviation such as overwhelming avoidance of the animate world, the degrees to which the infant achieves a less-than-optimal adaptive structural organization can be observed even in the first months of life.

Thus, the early attachments can be warm and engaging or shallow, insecure, and limited in their affective tone. There are differences between an infant who reads the signals of the caregivers and responds in a rich, meaningful way to multiple aspects of the communications with multiple affects and behavioral communication, and one who can respond only within a narrow range of affect (for example, protest) or who cannot respond at all in a contingent or reciprocal manner (for example, the seemingly apathetic, withdrawn, and depressed child who responds only to internal cues). As the toddler becomes behaviorally more organized, and complex patterns appear that reflect originality and initiative in the context of the separation and individuation subphase of development, we can observe those toddlers who manifest this full adaptive capacity. They may be compared with others who are stereotyped in their behavioral patterns, reflecting no originality or intentionality; who remain fragmented, never connecting pieces of behavior into more complicated patterns; or who evidence polarities of affect, showing no capacity to integrate emotions, for example, the chronic negativistic, aggressive toddler who cannot show interest, curiosity, or love.

The child who can organize, integrate, and differentiate a rich range of affective and ideational life can be distinguished from one who remains without representational capacity; who is undifferentiated, that is, who has deficits in the areas of reality testing, impulse control, or focused concentration; or who may form and differentiate self and object representations only at the expense of extreme compromises in the range of tolerated experience, for example, the schizoid child who withdraws from relationships.

Similar adaptive or maladaptive structural organizations can be observed in later childhood latency and adolescence.

A more detailed discussion of this framework, including principles of prevention and intervention, is available (Greenspan, 1979, 1981; Greenspan et al., 1987). It should also be pointed out that through videotaped analyses of infant–caregiver interactions, these patterns have been found to evidence temporal stability and can be rated reliably (Greenspan & Lieberman, 1980; Hofheimer, Lieberman, Strauss, Greenspan, 1985; Hofheimer, Strauss, Poisson, & Greenspan, 1981; Poisson, Hofheimer, Strauss, & Greenspan, 1983).

The ability to monitor developmental progress using rather explicit guidelines facilitates the early identification of those infants, young children, and their families who are either not progressing in an appropriate manner or who are progressing less than optimally. For example, it is now possible to evaluate infants who continue to have difficulty regulating their state and developing the capacity for focused interest in their immediate environments, or who fail to develop a positive emotional interest in their caregivers. It is also possible to assess an infant's difficulty in learning "cause-and-effect" interactions and complex emotional and social patterns, or a child's inability, by age two or three, to create symbols to guide emotions and behavior.

In exploring the factors that may be contributing to less than optimal patterns of development, the focus on multiple aspects of development offers many advantages. Some infants, for example, may evidence a motor delay because of familial patterns where exploration and the practice of the motor system is discouraged. In other infants there may be a maturational variation that, together with family patterns, contributes to a motor lag. In still other cases, genetic maturational factors may explain the delay completely. Even with a symptom as common as a motor delay, unless aspects of all factors are explored, it is likely that important contributing factors will go unrecognized. The focus on multiple aspects of development, in the context of clearly delineated developmental and emotional landmarks, opens the door to comprehensive assessments, diagnosis, and preventive intervention strategies.

AT-RISK POPULATIONS

The clinical approach that attempts to study infants, children, and families from multiple perspective and to assess the degree to which developmental milestones are being met allows for rich clinical description of the characateristics of vulnerable infants and families. It has been known for some time that certain populations are clearly at greater risk than others for poor cognitive, social, or emotional development (e.g., teenage mothers, low-income families, infants with low birth weight, and chronic physical illness). However, the impact of cumulative risk factors, which include psychological as well as social characteristics, has not been clearly identified. Therefore, we identified the clinical criteria seen in multirisk families. Subsequently, data on a nonintervention high-risk population, originally studied by Sameroff and colleagues in their well-known Rochester studies (Sameroff, Seifer, & Zax, 1982) were reanalyzed using some of these clinical criteria.

In our study of multirisk families (Greenspan et al., 1987), we observed forty-seven families in-depth who were referred by various prenatal clinics or by other agencies because of the parents' limited child-rearing capacities (64% were referred by medical facilities, 11% by social services, and only 17% by mental health facilities). Multirisk families that are often thought of as "social" and "economic" challenges in fact have a high degree of psychiatric illness, including severe developmental interferences and disturbances in psychosocial functioning. In addition, early difficulties in their interactive abilities with their infants were observed. For example, 64% of the mothers came from families with a history of psychiatric disturbance, 34% had themselves experienced psychiatric hospitalization, and an additional 15% had some type of outpatient contact with a mental health provider.

Of the mothers in this program, 44% experienced physical abuse, 32% had been sexually abused prior to age 18, and 93% reported current physical abuse and a tendency to abuse or neglect their own children. (There were significant correlates between past and present abusive patterns.) Over two-thirds (69%) experienced significant disruptions of a parental relationship or parent-surrogate relationship prior to adolescence. More than 75% had impaired psychosocial functioning in either the family, school, peer, or work setting in childhood, adolescence, and early adulthood.

The study observed babies in the program who, during the first few days of life, were fairly healthy in terms of weight, size, and overall physical status but had difficulty in regulating social responsiveness, establishing habituation patterns, and organizing their motor responses. Some of them were withdrawn and unresponsive to animate stimuli, others irritable and overly responsive.

In general, babies in the program showed significantly less than optimal development as early as the first months of life. (Most of these babies were at risk prenatally but had normal patterns of development perinatally – prenatal intervention having assured adequate nutrition and other supports, including appropriate medical care.) Pediatric, neurologic, and Brazelton Neonatal Behavioral Assessment Scale examination at 1 month of age showed some developmental progression but not the increased capacity for orientation characteristic of a normative population. Interestingly, the group receiving comprehensive intervention was similar to normal comparison infants at birth but was slightly lower in their orientation capacity by 1 month. The study's high-risk group, which received only periodic evaluations, tended to show less optimal performance in a number of areas including orientation, habituation, and motor organization than both the normal and intervention groups at 1 month (Hofheimer et al., 1984).

By 3 months of age, instead of a capacity for self-regulation, organization, and an interest in the world, a number of babies showed increased tendencies toward lability, muscle rigidity, gaze aversion, and an absence of organized sleep–wake, alert, and feeding patterns. Their caregivers, instead of having an overall capacity for offering the babies comfort, protection, and an interest in the world, either tended to withdraw from them and avoid them, or overstimulate them in a chaotic and intermittent fashion.

Between 3 and 9 months of age, in the multiproblem families, the child's behavior and affect remained under the control of internal states in random and chaotic or narrow, rigid, and stereotyped patterns of interaction. The child's caregivers, instead of offering the expected optimal contingent responsiveness to the child's varied signals, tended to ignore or misread them. The child's caregivers were overly preoccupied, depressed, or chaotic.

Toward the end of the first year of life and the beginning of the second, children in multi-risk-factor families, instead of showing an increase in organized, complex, assertive, and innovative emotional and behavioral patterns (e.g., taking their mother's hand and leading her to the refrigerator to show her the kind of food they want), tended to exhibit fragmented, stereotyped, and polarized patterns. These toddlers were observed to be withdrawn and compliant, or highly aggressive, impulsive, and disorganized.

Their human environment tended to be intrusive, controlling, and fragmented. These toddlers may have been prematurely separated from their caregivers or the caregivers may have exhibited patterns 'of withdrawal instead of admiringly supporting the toddler's initiative and autonomy and helping to facilitate the organization of what would become more complex capacities for communicating, interacting, and behaving.

As the toddler's potential capacities continued to develop in the latter half of the second year and into the third (18–36 months), profound deficits could be observed more clearly. The child did not develop capacities for internal representations (imagery) that organize behavior and feelings, or that differentiate ideas, feelings, and thoughts pertaining to the self and the nonself. These children either developed no representational or symbolic capacity, or if the capacity did develop, it was not elaborated beyond the most elementary descriptive form. Thus, the child's behavior remained shallow and polarized. The sense of the emerging self, as distinguished from the sense of other people, remained fragmented and undifferentiated. The child's potentially emerging capacities for reality testing, impulse regulation, and mood stabilization seemed to be either compromised or to become extremely vulnerable to regression. In other words, patterns either consistent with later borderline and psychotic personality organization or severe asocial or antisocial impulse-ridden character disorders were observed.

At this stage, the underlying impairment manifested itself in the children's inability to use a representational or symbolic mode to organize their behavior. In essence, the distinctly human capacity of operating beyond the survival level, or using internal imagery to elaborate and organize complex feelings and wishes and to construct trial actions in the emotional sphere, and of anticipating and planning ahead, were compromised. In many of these families, the parents simply did not have these capacities. Even when they were not under emotional duress or in states of crisis or panic, they did not demonstrate a symbolic mode, as evidence in the paucity of verbal communication and in the absence of symbolic play. Such families tended to be fearful and to deny and fail to meet their children's needs. They engaged the child only in such nonsymbolic modes of communication as holding, feeding, and administering physical punishment, and at times they misread or responded unrealistically to the child's emergent communication, thus undermining the development in the child of a sense of self and a flexible orientation to reality.

Needless to say, the mastery of higher-level developmental tasks by the children in these families was severely curtailed. At each new level of development the infants and toddlers, who for a variety of reasons had survived earlier developmental phases intact, invariably would challenge the multi-risk-factor environment with their new capacities, for example, with the capacity for symbolic communication. The healthier the toddler, the more challenging and overwhelming the child was likely to be. In a pattern frequently observed, the child would move ahead of the parent (engaging, for example, in symbolic play around themes of dependency or sexuality), and the parent would become confused and either withdraw from or behave intrusively toward the child. Shortly, unless other more skillful caregivers became available, the child would begin to regress to presymbolic modes of behaving. These children may be able to consolidate higher-level capacities when they begin to receive support from other systems, such as the school, and when they become capable of understanding parental limitations. These capacities, however, can only develop when the child is older. The youngster who experiences developmental failures, including the failure to develop a full representational or symbolic capacity (the basis for formal school experience later on) will unquestionably be handicapped in subsequent opportunities for learning.

In order to further document the impact of multiple risk factors, we investigated a nonintervention sample. In a collaborative study with Sameroff and colleagues of a population of multirisk families, it was demonstrated that familial, psychological, and infant interactional patterns correlate with poor outcomes at age four when socioeconomic status is controlled. The study further showed that cumulative risk patterns during infancy can be used to predict as much as a 25-fold increase in the probability of poor outcomes at age four (Sameroff, Seifer, Barocas, Zax, & Greenspan, 1987). The results of this study suggest that cumulative risk factors place infants and families at greatest risk.

DESCRIPTION OF A MODEL COMPREHENSIVE APPROACH TO INFANTS, YOUNG CHILDREN, AND THEIR FAMILIES

In order to contend with cumulative risks, a model program should consider the multiple risks in the infant and family. From 1975 to 1983, we attempted to implement such a model program. The Clinical Infant Development Program (CIDP) implemented a pilot model program to develop the strategies for a larger scale demonstration of preventive interventions for various groups of infants and families. The program was able to study in depth for 2 or more years. The children in these families totaled more than 200. Details concerning the population, efforts made to recruit these families, and the clinical service approaches and assessments used are described elsewhere (Greenspan, 1981; Greenspan et al., 1987; Wieder, Jasnow, Greenspan, & Strauss, 1984).

The CIDP developed a regular pattern of services, including providing for such survival needs as food, housing, and medical care; ensuring a constant emotional relationship with the family; and, most important, offering special patterns of care including approaches to deal with the infant's and family's individual vulnerabilities and strengths. The program also had a special support structure to provide, at one site, partial or full therapeutic day care for the child, innovative outreach to the family, and ongoing training and supervision of the program staff.

To elaborate on these core services and to respond to the family's concrete needs, various community agencies were to be organized to build a foundation for the family's survival. However, this approach alone will not ensure success, since many of the families, for a variety of reasons, are adept at circumventing offers of traditional supports.

The second component of a comprehensive effort, and one that is absolutely necessary for these families, is a human relationship with one or more interventionists. However, such a relationship is not easy to establish because distrust may be ingrained in each parent as well as in the family as a unit. This human relationship must grow in ways that parallel the infant's development and should seek to help the parents facilitate that development. It must provide regularity, an emotional attachment, and a process that facilitates the description and examination of interpersonal patterns. To provide this human relationship, both a team and a single primary clinician were used. In order to give the critical ingredient – a relationship – its appropriate significance, the CIDP developed a therapeutic relationship scale that attempted to describe the steps in forming a relationship. This scale, which is shown in Table 2, could be rated reliably, could differentiate high- and low-risk groups, and correlated with other measures of caregiver functioning (Greenspan & Wieder, 1984).

However, organizing to respond to a family's concrete needs and offering the family a human relationship are not enough. The relationship must be designed to help the

Table 2. *Dimensions of the therapeutic relationship: steps in the therapeutic process*

Regularity and Stability	Attachment	Process
1. Willingness to meet with an interviewer or therapist to convey concrete concerns or hear about services	1. Interest in having concrete needs met that can be provided by anyone (e.g., food, transportation, etc.)	1. Preliminary communication, including verbal support and information gathering
2. Willingness to schedule meetings again	2. Emotional interest in the person of the therapist (e.g., conveys pleasure or anger when they meet)	2. Ability to observe and report single behaviors or action patterns
3. Meeting according to some predictable pattern	3. Communicates purposefully in attempts to deal with problems	3. Focuses on relationships involved in the behavior-action pattern
4. Meeting regularly with occasional disruptions	4. Tolerates discomfort or scary emotions	4. Self-observing function in relationship to feelings
5. Meeting regularly with no disruptions	5. Feels "known" or accepted in positive and negative aspects	5. Self-observing function in relationship to complex and interactive feeling states
		6. Self-observing function for thematic and affective elaboration
		7. Makes connections between the key relationships in life including the therapeutic relationship
		8. Identification of patterns in current, therapeutic, and historical relationships to work through problems and facilitate new growth
		9. Consolidation of new patterns and levels of satisfaction and preparing to separate from the therapeutic relationship
		10. Full consolidation of gains in the context of separating and experiencing a full sense of loss and mourning

Source: Greenspan & Wieder (1984).

parents understand some of their maladaptive coping strategies and to teach them how to deal with their own primary needs as well as those of their infant. In addition, special clinical techniques and patterns of care to reverse maladaptive developmental patterns in the areas of affect and social interaction, sensorimotor development, and cognition must be available at the appropriate time (Greenspan, 1981).

Consider, for example, a baby with a tactile hypersensitivity whose hyperactive, suspicious mother tends to deal with stress by hyperstimulating her baby. The correct approach would be to provide the baby with habituation and sensory integration approaches to overcome his or her special sensitivity. The mother is thus helped simultaneously to overcome her own tendency to undermine the baby's development.

Moreover, the intervention must occur over a sufficiently long period to allow the family's own strengths to take over and sustain it – in other words, not crisis intervention for only a few months, but an approach that can be available to families for several years at a minimum. After working with many of these families for as long as 2 years, the mothers' capacity to nurture and facilitate the development of a new baby was found to be significantly more advanced than when they entered the program pregnant with an earlier child (Wieder, 1987). In other words, when the helping relationship is offered over a sustained period of time, the frequently observed trend of multiproblem families to deteriorate further upon the birth of each subsequent baby begins to be reversed.

Another way to visualize the approach just discussed is from a developmental perspective. The tasks at each stage of development imply that certain components of the service system must be available to assure appropriate support for the functions of that stage (Greenspan, 1981). One might visualize preventive service approaches as a pyramid, as represented in Figure 1. The three levels of care in the service pyramid are further explicated in Figure 2. This figure emphasizes that specialized services – whether they be physical or occupational therapy, psychological counseling, or parent–infant interactional guidance – must be based on a foundation that deals with concrete survival issues and the formation of a regular, stable working relationship. The service pyramid, however, must contain ingredients that are sensitive to the changing developmental needs of infants and families. There are different service patterns within the pyramid for each stage of development (see Figure 2).

Maladaptive trends were observed in most of the families in the CIDP. By carefully pinpointing the area in which a child's development first began to go awry, and by using organized and comprehensive clinical techniques and service system approaches, the families often became capable of more adaptive patterns. For example, the CIDP found significant differences in a variety of measures of maternal functioning prior to and after 2 years in the program and in the functioning of children in such basic areas as the ability to experience pleasure, deal with impulses, and form relationships.

Many parents in the program began their child rearing as teenagers and experienced further deterioration in their own functioning and that of their infants with each subsequent birth. In most instances, however, even when a woman had four or more children, this pattern of deterioration reversed itself by means of appropriate clinical techniques and services. In a number of multi-risk-factor families, after they entered the program a gradual improvement took place in the mother and a modest but positive change in the first baby born thereafter. Then, if the family remained in the program and a second baby was born, the change in the family was more dramatic and was reflected in the new baby's more optimal development from the beginning.

Infants who received intensive intervention also showed a capacity to recover from early perinatal stress or developmental deviations (Hofheimer, Lieberman, Strauss, & Greenspan, 1984). Even when an infant's development had deteriorated during the first 3 months of life (as evidenced by lack of human attachment, chronic gaze aversion, muscle rigidity, and affect lability), appropriate interventions were often associated with adaptive homeostatic and attachment capacities within 1–4 months (Greenspan, 1981; Greenspan et al., 1987). The process of therapeutic work involved first figuring

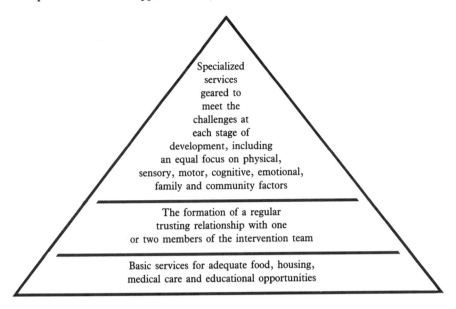

Figure 1. The service pyramid: preventive intervention services

out the types of experiences that were both aversive and satisfying for the infant, and the underlying feelings of the parents that might have interfered with their providing comforting and pleasurable interactions. Often it was then possible to help a family deal with their special individual differences when the infant had such unique problems as auditory or tactile sensitivities or extreme state or mood lability, or where there was severe psychopathology or patterns of rejection or overstimulation in the parents.

PRINCIPLES OF INTERVENTION FOR HANDICAPPED INFANTS AND THEIR FAMILIES

In the foregoing it was suggested that at each stage of emotional development specific sensory or motor challenges will create unique emotional challenges. The question is, How do we transform each challenge into a unique learning opportunity? For example, how do we help the infant with increased motor tone to correct the motor difficulty and, at the same time, learn to use his or her motor system for "falling in love," cause-and-effect emotional signaling, emotional thinking, and so forth? In considering the objective of integrating the child's physical and emotional needs, several guiding principles immediately suggest themselves.

> *Principle 1: Each activity aimed at improving sensory, motor, or cognitive capacities should also have, as its goal, facilitation of the relevant, age-expected, emotional pattern.*

For example, in working with an 8-month-old with motor delays and increased motor tone, the traditional approach would involve the use of positioning and handling techniques to normalize tone and to facilitate normal patterns of movement (i.e., mobilization of trunk, rotation patterns, and use of weight shifts and weight-bearing

Representation differentiation and consolidation

Age	Interagency collaboration	Basic requirements	Therapeutic relationship
24–40 months	Services to permit, as appropriate, more independent functioning and new relationships (e.g., nursery schools)	Facilitation of representational capacity and reality orientation	Work on capacity to shift between fantasy and reality and integrate wide range of affective and thematic issues
17–30 months	Services to permit direct psychotherapeutic work with toddler on as intensive basis as necessary	*Representational capacity* — Engagement of evolving representational (symbolic) capacities across a wide thematic and affective range	Work on capacity to use and elaborate fantasy
9–18 months	New services to permit direct exploratory work with the toddler now useful; remedial educational approach should also be available	*Behavioral organization, initiative, and internalization* — Secure availability while admiring and supporting greater behavioral organization, initiative, and originality	Further work on self-observing capacity permits integration of affective polarities around dependency and aggression and passivity and assertiveness
3–10 months	Services including educative and psychotherapeutic and, as necessary, auxiliary caretaker to facilitate reading of infant's communications	*Somatopsychological differentiation* — Reading and responding contingently to range of affective and behavioral cues	Includes work on capacity for self-observation to facilitate empathetic reading of the "other"
2–8 months	Special services to support consistent affective caretaker-infant relationship	*Attachment* — Rich investment in human world wooed and is wooed	Evolves in attachment that survives negative feelings
0–2 months	Health, mental health, social service, educational, legal	*Homeostasis* — Protection, care, engagement in world	Has a pattern that is predictable, regular, comforting

Figure 2. Schematic illustrations of levels of development and corresponding service system requirements and expected shifts in the therapeutic relationship

posture). Thus, one may position an 8-month-old infant with poor head control prone over a bolster so that the arms are in a forward position, while rotating the trunk and shoulder girdle to mobilize the spine. How does one at the same time create an opportunity for the emotional task of learning cause-and-effect emotional signaling? One might work toward teaching the infant to imitate simple movements of the hands (i.e., touching pictures, touching facial parts – "I do it; now, you do it"). One might also help the infant learn an emotional, relevant, intentional gesture indicating dependency, that is, reaching up to be held.

> *Principle 2: Each emotionally or socially relevant pattern, either in its incipient stages or in its complete form, should receive a timely, phase-specific, pleasurable, emotional response. This includes the caregiver's position (e.g., when possible, in front of the infant) and affective disposition (i.e., you can't fake pleasure).*

The fact that the caregiver's response should be developmentally phase-appropriate is illustrated by the motorically delayed 15-month-old who manages to crawl away from the caregiver and looks back with a smile of accomplishment. Clapping and admiring the infant's accomplishment from afar with distal communication support, that is, affective verbal and motor gestures, may at that moment be more phase-appropriate than a big hug and cuddle. The infant is learning to balance dependence and independence and to communicate across space with word and gesture. Distal communication modes, such as the use of words and gestures, support the infant's emergent ability to "be close" from across space. Because some motor exercises are carried out behind the infant or child, to facilitate purposeful communication innovative approaches should be developed to arrange for sufficiently flexible positioning for appropriate, face-to-face, emotional interactions.

> *Principle 3: Each emotionally relevant interaction should facilitate self-initiative in generating similar emotional patterns and the generalization and abstraction of these patterns to all areas and contexts of functioning.*

For example, in facilitating phase-specific emotional patterns, one should always ask, Am I doing it for the child, or am I creating a learning opportunity where the child is learning to take initiative? The 9-month-old who hears a "toot, toot" every time he presses his hand near his father's face, is learning to take initiative and make things happen. In contrast, the 9-month-old who is only read to is learning to receive information passively. The application of a new emotional skill in multiple contexts, for example, touching Daddy's face to make Daddy say "toot, toot," or pulling Mommy's finger to get her to stick out her tongue, facilitates the application of emotional-behavioral patterns and emotional-ideational patterns to multiple contexts through pretend play.

In addition to the challenge of learning to take initiative and to generalize new coping capacities, the infant or child with developmental disabilities, as well as the infant or child with cognitive lags or difficulties, faces another important challenge. This challenge relates to the critical psychological task of differentiating an emotional sense of self that is unique, encompasses the full range of human emotions, and is clearly separate from one's sense of others and nonself. Children with difficulties in sensory processing often have difficulty in discriminating subtle aspects of sensory-affective experience (e.g., Is she happy or sad? Does he intend to hold me or hurt me? Am I angry or scared? or Is my wish to bite a part of me?). Similarly, the child with tactile defensiveness and motor-planning problems who bumps into another child may yell,

"Stop hurting me! Watch where you are going!" Although such emotional interpretations relate to one's experiences, a basic difficulty in discriminating incoming information from information arising from one's own body (e.g., somatic affective cues) because of sensory processing problems would almost certainly make it particularly difficult to interpret confusing experiences. Cognitive lags may contribute to an inability to abstract the difficult emotional aspects of one's self into an organized pattern. Similarly, motor-planning or control difficulties would create an extra challenge in developing a secure sense of self in terms of body control, assertiveness, and handling aggression (e.g., If I can't make my body do what I want it to, then what can I control, and where does my self-initiative and control end and someone else's begin?).

To facilitate a differentiated sense of self across the full range of human emotions in a child who has sensory-affective discrimination, cognitive, motor-planning, or control difficulties requires that special experiences be made available. This leads to another principle.

> *Principle 4: To support and provide extra practice for self-differentiation. To accomplish this, provide extra opportunities for interpersonal interactions that have the elements of: (1) the infant or child elaborating the full range of human emotions and inclinations, including closeness or dependency, pleasure, assertiveness and curiosity, anger, protest, self-limit-setting, and, eventually, empathy and consistent love; and (2) caregiver responses that are clear and accurate in regard to the child's elaborations, including feedback that provides a sense of being understood and at the same time supports further self-initiated elaboration.*

For infants and children, special play times or "floor time" often provide the context for these types of interactions. Such play times, where dolls or soldiers may carry forth the emotional theme, may demand a great deal from the caregivers, including understanding their own emotional reactions to the child's dependency or aggression, as well as considerable patience and the realization that the child will need *extra* repetition at certain times and help with moving on at other times.

CONCLUSIONS

It is important to emphasize that recent understanding of infant and family emotional function now makes it possible to pinpoint emotional milestones much like neuromotor milestones. It is hoped that this road map will prove helpful in facilitating adaptive emotional growth in infants whose families have multiple emotional and social problems, as well as in infants whose sensory, motor, or physical differences set into motion unique family challenges.

The commitment to multiple approaches must always be remembered. Almost all infants and young children can learn, in different ways, to relate to others, interact intentionally, organize a sense of self, learn to use ideas to guide behavior and label feelings, test reality, modulate impulses and mood, experience positive self-esteem, and concentrate. The challenge is to provide infants, children, and their families – regardless of their special needs, their family difficulties, or the biological vulnerabilities in the infant – with the needed learning opportunities that are sensitive to their individual differences and unique potentials.

Enormous challenges lie ahead. Preventive interventions are generally efficacious despite the narrow focus of most programs. Yet, little is known about the degree to which preventive interventions hold up over time and the efficacy of specific types of interventions for specific types of problems. Furthermore, models that demonstrate how to work with multiple aspects of development, that is, physical, cognitive, emotional, and social and familial, are few and far between. The application of such models to a range of common challenges in primary care settings for infants, children, and their families, including motor and language delays, high-risk parenting situations, and emotional-social disorders, has not been implemented and evaluated with sufficient rigor.

In addition, although the normative developmental landmarks have been well delineated, studies documenting disturbed patterns in development have been relatively scarce. Such basic questions as the relative contributions of fine and gross motor delays to emotional problems or the contributions of difficulties in sensory processing to emotional, social, and intellectual difficulties have not been well studied. The demarcation of a developmental timetable involving cognitive, emotional, and social functioning now permits the study in greater detail of the factors that determine poor versus optimal developmental outcomes in both the short- and long-term. In addition, the ability to follow development from one phase to the next will permit short-term studies to have more meaning for longer-term investigations.

It is time to undertake new programs of research that can simultaneously look at the efficacy of comprehensive approaches to preventive intervention and offer the prospect of further understanding of the pathogenesis of psychomotor, cognitive, and emotional difficulties.

REFERENCES

Ainsworth, M., Bell, S. M., & Stayton, D. (1974). Infant–mother attachment and social development: Socialization as a product a reciprocal responsiveness to signals. In M. Richards (Ed.), *The integration of the child into a social world* (pp. 99–135). Cambridge, England: Cambridge University Press.

Ainsworth, M. D. S., Blehar, M. C., Waters, E., & Wall, S. (1978). *Patterns of attachment: A psychological study of the strange situation.* Hillsdale, NJ: L. Erlbaum.

Als, H., Lester, B. M., Tronick, E. C., & Brazelton, T. B. (1982). Towards a research instrument for the Assessment of Preterm Infants' Behavior (A.P.I.B.). In H. E. Fitzgerald, B. M. Lester, & M. W. Yogman (Eds.), *Theory and research in behavioral pediatrics* (Vol. 1, pp. 35–64). New York: Plenum Press.

Bakwin, H. (1942). Loneliness in infants. *American Journal of Diseases of Children, 63*, 30.

Barrett, K. C., & Campos, J. J. (1987). Perspectives on emotional development II: A functionalist approach to emotions. In J. D. Osofsky (Ed.), *Handbook of infant development* (2nd ed., pp. 555–578). New York: Wiley.

Bell, S. (1970). The development of the concept of object as related to infant–mother attachment. *Child Development, 41*, 219–311.

Bergman, P., & Escalora, S. (1949). Unusual sensitivities in very young children. *The psychoanalytic study of the child, 3–4*, 333.

Bower, T. G. R. (1982). *Development in infancy* (2nd ed.). San Francisco: W. H. Freeman.

Bowlby, J. (1951). *Maternal care and mental health* (WHO Monograph No. 2). Geneva: World Health Organization.

Bowlby, J. (1969). *Attachment and loss* (Vol. 1). London: Hogarth Press.

Brazelton, T. B., & Als, H. (1979). Four early stages in the development of mother–infant interaction. *The Psychoanalytic Study of the Child, 34*, 349–369.

Brazelton, T., Koslowski, B., & Main, N. (1974). The origins of reciprocity: The early mother–infant interaction. In M. Lewis & L. Rosenblum (Eds.), *The effect of the infant on its caregiver* (pp. 49–76). New York: Wiley.

Bretherton, I., & Waters, E. (Eds.). (1985). Growing points of attachment theory and research. *Monographs of the Society for Research in Child Development, 50* (1–2 Serial No. 209).

Burlingham, D., & Freud, A. (1942). *Young children in wartime.* London: Allen & Unwin.

Campos, J. J., Barrett, K. C., Lamb, M. E., Goldsmith, H. H., & Stenberg, C. (1983).

Socioemotional development. In M. M. Haith & J. J. Campos (Eds.), *Infancy and developmental psychobiology* (pp. 783–916). New York: Wiley.

Charlesworth, W. R. (1969). The role of surprise in cognitive development. In D. Elkind & J. H. Flavell (Eds.), *Studies in cognitive development: Essays* (pp. 257–314). London: Oxford University Press.

Condon, W. S., & Sander, L. W. (1974). Neonate movement is synchronized with adult speech: Interactional participation and language acquisition. *Science, 183*, 99–101.

Cravioto, J., & Delicardie, E. (1973). Environmental correlates of severe clinical malnutrition and language development survivors from kwashiorkor or marasmus. In *Nutrition, the nervous system and behavior* (PAHO Scientific Publication No. 251). Washington, DC.

Duffy, F. H., Mowrer, G., Jensen, F., & Als, H. (1984). Neural plasticity: A new frontier for infant development. In H.E. Fitzgerald, B. M. Lester, & M. W. Yogman (Eds.), *Theory and research in behavioral pediatrics* (Vol. 2, pp. 67–96). New York: Plenum Press.

Ekman, P. (1972). Universals and cultural differences in facial expressions of emotion. *Nebraska Symposium on Motivation*. Lincoln: University of Nebraska Press.

Emde, R. N., Gaensbauer, T. J., & Harmon, R. J. (1976). *Emotional expression in infancy: A biobehavioral study* (Psychological Issues Monograph No. 37). New York: International Universities Press.

Escalona, S. K. (1968). *The Roots of Individuality*. Chicago: Aldine.

Escalona, S. K., & Heider, G. (1959). *Prediction and outcome: A study in child development*. New York: Basic Books.

Fagan, J. F. (1977). Infant's recognition of invariant features of faces. *Child Development, 48*, 68–78.

Fernald, A. (1984). The perceptual and affective salience of mother's speech to infants. In L. Fagan, C. Garvey, & R. Golinkoff (Eds.), *The origin and growth of communication*. Norwood, NJ: Ablex Publishing.

Fraiberg, S. H. (1965). *The magic years: Understanding and handling the problems of early childhood*. New York: Scribner.

Fraiberg, S. (Ed.). (1980). *Clinical studies in infant mental health: The first year of life*. New York: Basic Books.

Freud, S. (1958). Formulations on the two principles of mental functioning. In J. Strachey (Ed. and Trans.), *The standard edition of the complete psychological works of Sigmund Freud* (Vol. 12, pp. 218–226).

Gerwitz, J. L. (1961). A learning analysis of the effects of normal stimulation, privation and deprivation on the acquisition of social motivation and attachment. In B. M. Foss (Ed.), *Determinants of infant behavior* (Vol. 1, pp. 213–299). London: Methuen.

Gerwitz, J. L. (1965). The course of infant smiling in four child rearing environments in Israel. In B. M. Foss (Ed.), *Determinants of infant behavior* (Vol. 3, pp. 205–260). London: Methuen.

Gerwitz, J. L. (1969). Levels of conceptual analysis in environment–infant interaction research. *Merrill-Palmer Quarterly, 15*, 9.

Gouin-Decarie, T. (1965). *Intelligence and affectivity in early childhood: An experimental study of Jean Piaget's object concept and object relations*. New York: International Universities Press.

Greenspan, S. I. (1979). *Intelligence and adaptation: An integration of psychoanalytic and Piagetian developmental psychology* (Psychological Issues Monograph No. 47/48). New York: International Universities Press.

Greenspan, S. I. (1981). *Psychopathology and adaptation in infancy and early childhood: Principles of clinical diagnosis and preventive intervention*. New York: International Universities Press.

Greenspan, S. I., & Greenspan, N. T. (1985). *First feelings: Milestones in the emotional development of your infant and child from birth to age 4*. New York: Viking Press.

Greenspan, S. I., & Lieberman, A. F. (1980). Infants, mothers, and their interaction: A quantitative clinical approach to developmental assessment. In S. I. Greenspan & G. H. Pollock (Eds.), *The course of life: Psychoanalytic contributions toward understanding personality development* (Vol. 1). (DHHS Publication No. [ADM] 80–786). Washington, DC: Government Printing Office.

Greenspan, S. I., & Lourie, R. S. (1981). Developmental structuralist approach to the classification of adaptive and pathologic personality organization: Application to infancy and early childhood. *American Journal of Psychiatry, 136*(6), 725–735.

Greenspan, S. I., Lourie, R. S., & Nover, R. A. (1979). A developmental approach to the classification of psychopathology in infancy and early childhood. In J. Noshpitz (Ed.), *The* basic handbook of child psychiatry (Vol. 2, pp. 157–164). New York: Basic Books.

Greenspan, S. I., & Porges, S. W. (1984). Psychopathology in infancy and early childhood: Clinical perspectives on the organization of sensory and affective-thematic experience. *Child Development, 55*, 49–70.

Greenspan, S. I., & Wieder, S. (1984). Dimensions and levels of the therapeutic process. *Psychotherapy, 21*(1), 5–23.

Greenspan, S. I., Wieder, S., Lieberman, A., Nover, R., Lourie, R., & Robinson, M. (Eds.). (1987). *Clinical infant reports: No. 3. Infants in multirisk families: Case studies in preventive intervention.* New York: International Universities Press.

Haith, M. M., & Campos, J. J. (Eds.). (1983). *Infancy and developmental psychobiology.* New York: Wiley.

Hartmann, H. (1939). *Ego psychology and the problem of adaptation.* New York: International Universities Press.

Hofheimer, J. A., Lieberman, A. F., Strauss, M. E., & Greenspan, S. I., (1984). *Short term temporal stability of mother–infant interactions in the first year of life.* Unpublished paper.

Hofheimer, J. A., Lieberman, A., Strauss, M., & Greenspan, S. I. (1985). *Short-term stability in observations of mother–infant interactions.* Paper presented at the Ninety-third Annual Meeting of American Psychological Association, Los Angeles.

Hofheimer, J. A., Strauss, M. E., Poisson, S. S., & Greenspan, S. I. (1981). *The reliability, validity and generalizability of assessments of transactions between infants and their caregivers: A multicenter design* (Working Paper, Clinical Infant Development Program). Bethesda, MD: National Institute of Mental Health.

Hunt, J. M. (1941). Infants in an orphanage. *Journal of Abnormal Social Psychology, 36*, 338.

Izard, C. E. (1978). On the development of emotions and emotion-cognition relationships in infancy. In M. Lewis & L. Rosenblum (Eds.), *The development of affect.* New York: Plenum Press.

Izard, C. E., & Malatesta, C. Z. (1987). Perspectives on emotional development I: Differential emotions theory of early emotional development. In J. D. Osofsky (Ed.), *Handbook of infant development* (2nd ed., pp. 494–554). New York: Wiley.

Kaye, K. (1982). *The mental and social life of babies: How parents create persons.* Chicago: University of Chicago Press.

Klaus, M., & Kennell, J. (1976). *Maternal–infant bonding: The impact of early separation or loss on family development.* St. Louis: Mosby.

Lewis, M., & Michalson, L. (1983). *Children's emotions and moods: Theory and measurement.* New York: Plenum Press.

Lipsitt, L. (1966). Learning processes of newborns. *Merrill-Palmer Quarterly, 12*, 45–71.

Lowrey, L. G. (1940). Personality distortion and early institutional care. *American Journal of Orthopsychiatry, 10*, 546.

Mahler, M. S., Pine, F., & Bergman, A. (1975). *The psychological birth of the human infant.* New York: Basic Books.

Meltzoff, A., & Moore, K. (1977). Imitation of facial and manual gestures by human neonates. *Science, 198*, 75–78.

Murphy, L. B., & Moriarty, A. (1976). *Vulnerability, coping and growth.* New Haven: Yale University Press.

Osofsky, J. D. (Ed.). (1987). *Handbook of infant development* (2nd ed.). New York: Wiley.

Piaget, J. (1972). The stages of the intellectual development of the child. In S. Harrison & J. McDermott (Eds.), *Childhood psychopathology* (pp. 157–166). New York: International Universities Press. (Original work published 1962)

Poisson, S. S., Hofheimer, J. A., Strauss, M. E., & Greenspan, S. I. (1983). *Interobserver agreement and reliability assessments of the GLOS measures of caregiver–infant interaction.* Unpublished manuscript, National Institute of Mental Health, Department of Health and Human Services.

Provence, S. (Ed.). (1983). *Clinical infant reports: No. 2. Infants and parents: Clinical case reports.* New York: International Universities Press.

Rheingold, H. (1966). The development of social behavior in the human infant. *Monographs of the Society for Research in Child Development, 31*, 1.

Rheingold, H. (1969). Infancy. In D. Sills (Ed.), *International encyclopedia of the social sciences.* New York: Macmillan.

Sameroff, A. J., Seifer, R., & Zax, M. (1982). Early development of children at risk for emotional disorder. *Monographs of the Society for Research in Child Development, 47* (No. 199).

Sameroff, A., Seifer, R., Barocas, R., Zax, M., & Greenspan, S. (1987). IQ scores of 4-year-old children: Social-environmental risk factors. *Pediatrics, 79*, 343–350.

Sander, L. (1962). Issues in early mother–child interaction. *Journal of the American Academy of Child Psychiatry, 1*, 141.

Spitz, R. (1945). Hospitalism. *Psychoanalytic Study of the Child, 1*, 53.

Sroufe, L. A. (1983). Infant–caregiver attachment and patterns of adaptation in preschool: The roots of maladaption and competence. In M. Perlmutter (Ed.), *The Minnesota Symposia on Child Psychology* (Vol. 16, pp. 41–84). Hillsdale, NJ: L. Erlbaum.

Sroufe, L., & Waters, E. (1977). Attachment as an organizational construct. *Child Development, 48*, 1184–1199.

Sroufe, L., Waters, E., & Matas, L. (1974). Contextual determinants of infant affective response. In M. Lewis & L. Rosenblum (Eds.), *The origins of fear* (pp. 49–72). New York: Wiley.

Stern, D. (1974a). Mother and infant at play: The dyadic interaction involving facial, vocal and gaze behaviors. In M. Lewis & L. Rosenblum (Eds.), *The effect of the infant on its caregiver*. New York: Wiley.

Stern, D. (1974b). The goal and structure of mother–infant play. *Journal of the American Academy of Child Psychiatry, 13*, 402–421.

Stern, D. (1977). *The first relationship: Infant and mother*. Cambridge: Harvard University Press.

Stern, D. N. (1985). *The interpersonal world of the infant: A view from psychoanalysis and developmental psychology*. New York: Basic Books.

Tennes, K., Emde, R., Kisley, A., & Metcalf, D. (1972). The stimulus barrier in early infancy: An exploration of some formulations of John Benjamin. In R. Holt & E. Peterfreund (Eds.), *Psychoanalysis and contemporary science* (Vol. 1, pp. 206–234). New York: Macmillan.

Thomas, A., Chess, S., & Birch, H. G. (1968). *Temperament and behavior disorders in children*. New York: New York University Press.

Tomkins, S. (1963). *Affect, imagery, consciousness* (Vol. 1). New York: Springer Publishing.

Tronick, E. Z. (Ed.). (1982). *Social interchange in infancy*. Baltimore: University Park Press.

Uzgiris, I., & Hunt, J. McV. (1975). *Assessment in infancy: Ordinal scales of psychological development*. Urbana: University of Illinois Press.

Uzgiris, I., & Hunt, J. McV. (1987). *Infant performance and experience: New findings with the ordinal scales*. Urbana: University of Illinois Press.

Werner, H., & Kaplan, B. (1963). *Symbol Formation*. New York: Wiley.

Wieder, S. (1987). Reaching the unreachable: Measuring change in relation to intervention. In S. I. Greenspan, S., Wieder, A. F. Lieberman, R. A. Nover, R. S. Lourie, & M. E. Robinson (Eds.), *Clinical Infant Reports: No. 3. Infants in multirisk families: Case studies in preventive intervention*. New York: International Universities Press.

Wieder, S., Jasnow, M., Greenspan, S. I., & Strauss, M. (1984). Identifying the multi-risk family prenatally: Antecedent psychosocial factors and infant developmental trends. *Infant Mental Health Journal, 4*, 165–201.

Winnicott, D. W. (1931). *Clinical notes on disorders of childhood*. London: Heineman.

Wolff, P. H. (1987). *The development of behavioral states and the expression of emotions in early infancy: New proposals for investigation*. Chicago: University of Chicago Press.

Yogman, M. W., & Brazelton, T. B. (Eds.). (1986). *In support of families*. Cambridge: Harvard University Press.

8 A behavioral-ecological approach to early intervention: Focus on cultural diversity

LISBETH J. VINCENT, CHRISTINE L. SALISBURY,
PHILLIP STRAIN, CECILIA MCCORMICK,
ANNETTE TESSIER

In this chapter we discuss the use of a behavioral-ecological approach to early intervention. The chapter is divided into three major sections. In the first section, we provide a brief review of the powerful impact that a behavioral (operant) approach to intervention can have on the development of services for young children and their families. In the second section we review available demographic data on the changing ecology of families in this country, paying particular attention to minority families and examining cultural diversities that can play a significant role in the design of early intervention services. In the final section we build upon the information and foundations of the first two sections and explore how the addition of an ecological perspective strengthens the behavioral approach, allowing for applications with culturally diverse families in diverse settings. We then examine how this behavioral-ecological approach can be applied to assessment, intervention, and program evaluation efforts.

OPERANT FOUNDATIONS AND CONTRIBUTIONS TO EARLY INTERVENTION

At first glance, the relationship between operant learning experiments with pigeons and rats and the delivery of quality services to young children with handicaps seems remote. Yet, the links are real, and the influence has been profound.

The operant experiments by B. F. Skinner and his students brought to light a radically new and different approach to the study of behavior and learning. This approach, and its subsequent influence on early intervention, had as its basic premise the belief that behavior is largely a function of environment.

Behavior is largely a function of environment

The operant paradigm was used to demonstrate that the most simple behavior, for example, key pecking by a pigeon, and the most extraordinarily complex behavior, for example, children playing together, could be understood and controlled to a large degree by a careful analysis of the temporal antecedents and consequences of behavior.

Appreciation is extended to Mary Fish, Julianna Quinn, Diane Hinckley, Maria Gutierrez, and Daria Kirby for assistance in preparation of this chapter.

In no way did early operant theory and practice deny biology. Rather, it showed the great range of behavior that was possible under various environmental manipulations.

The notion that behavior was largely attributable to the impact of the environment, and that purposeful experiments could document the point, had a profound influence on the pioneers of early intervention. Consider for example, Bijou's (1966) reconceptualization of mental retardation:

It is suggested that developmental retardation be treated as observable, objectively defined stimulus-response relationships without recourse to hypothetical mental constructs such as "defective intelligence" and hypothetical biological abnormalities such as "clinically inferred brain injury." From this point of view, a retarded individual is one who has a limited repertoire of behavior shaped by events that constitute his history (p. 2).

A careful analysis of Bijou's comment reveals many of the fundamental propositions that have been promoted by behaviorally oriented early interventionists. These include the following.

1. The child does not behave in a retarded fashion because he or she has the condition of retardation, but because he or she has yet to be taught to behave otherwise (Baer, 1981; Bijou, 1966; Bricker, 1970; Sailor & Guess, 1983).
2. The proper analysis of the child is here and now, not historical. That is, trauma may indeed have damaged the nervous system at some point in history, but only an analysis of the contemporary, *instructional* environment is relevant to intervention (Sidman, 1960).
3. The critical relationships between the child's behavior and the environment are directly observable. In other words, one need not assess mental states or internal capacities in order to apply an effective technology of instruction (Baer, 1981; Bijou, 1966; Sidman, 1960).

Basic principles of behavior change are highly replicable

Beginning with the early operant conditioning experiments, it became clear (at least to operant conditioners) that certain principles of behavior change, such as the operation of reinforcement and punishment schedules, stimulus control, and stimulus and response generalization, were to be found at all levels of the phylogenetic scale and at all levels of behavioral sophistication (see Sailor & Guess, 1983, for a complete description of these principles of behavior change as they are applied to the education and treatment of children). Thus, the "educability" of children with developmental disabilities was seen as being controlled not by their disability but by the selection of an appropriate response to teach in the appropriate settings. This "universality" of operant principles, as demonstrated in literally hundreds of experimental replications, led to an important and imposing view of early intervention. Specifically, if the principles of operant conditioning are universally applicable, then failure to achieve a certain outcome can likely be traced to an inadequate instructional environment, rather than to a universal defect in the learner. This fundamental shift from "blaming" the learner to "blaming" the instruction is clearly reflected in the words of another pioneer of early intervention, W. Bricker (1970):

Finally, I wish to affirm my belief in the importance of the nervous system and to indicate a conviction that a host of events could do damage to it and its functioning. However, only the failure of a perfectly valid, perfectly reliable, perfectly efficient program of training will convince me that the identification of the deficit is sufficient reason to stop trying to educate the child. Somehow, I cannot feel that we have reached perfection in the development of training programs (p. 13).

Over a decade later, Baer (1981) suggested that poor *procedures* may not be the only instructional explanation for poor intervention outcomes.

Failure to teach a behavior in the discipline of operant conditioning, can of course mean faulty technique..., but can also mean faulty response analysis. Specifically, it may mean that the behavior being taught unsuccessfully has essential behavioral prerequisites, and that until these are identified and taught, the teaching of their dependent behavior will remain unsuccessful. (By way of a homely example, consider the prospects of teaching a child long division before addition, subtraction, multiplication, and short division are mastered and fluent) (p. 96).

Thus, the wide-spread demonstration of *replicable* behavior change in the operant laboratory, and in early clinical work, brought with it a certain optimism, if you will, regarding failures to teach effectively. That optimism, in turn, has been supported methodologically by single-case designs and their idiosyncratic focus on child behavior (see Guess & Noonan, 1981, for a discussion of this methodology). Exactly how have these experimental designs, with their operant roots, contributed to early intervention?

Single-case designs and early intervention

In order to appreciate fully the contribution of single case research methodology to early intervention, a few words about group designs are necessary. Suppose that the following question is put: What is the effect of Intervention X on preschool children's social interaction with peers? In a group-design format, one group of youngsters, chosen randomly, might receive the prescribed intervention while a similarly selected group might receive no intervention or an alternative intervention. To answer the question at hand, the average performance of one group would be compared to that of the other using an assessment prior to and after intervention. For the sake of example, suppose that Intervention X is quite potent, and is clearly superior to no intervention. We might also suspect that if we looked at the individuals that comprise the Intervention X group, some might have stayed the same, some might have improved marginally, and some might have improved spectacularly. It is important to note, however, that such individually grounded information is often unavailable in group designs.

Single-subject methodology brings an entirely different logic to the question. Here, Intervention X might be applied to an individual subject's interactions with class peers after considerable data have been gathered on performance prior to intervention. At the same time, baseline or no-intervention data might be collected on the individual's interactions with unfamiliar age-peers and siblings. Presuming that Intervention X produced a clear change in interactions with class peers, the procedure would be applied sequentially to the other behaviors, namely interactions with unfamiliar peers and siblings. If behavioral improvement was noted only when intervention was applied to the three behavioral targets, one could argue that teaching via Intervention X was functionally related to (caused) improved performance. This same paradigm, a multiple baseline across behaviors, would then be applied to other subjects in order to test the range of conditions under which Intervention X is effective. At any point in time, if performance does not improve, then we might see that Intervention X is *altered* to accommodate the idiosyncratic needs of new subjects.

Note that several features of the single-subject methodology are particularly consistent with and compatible with early intervention. The first area of high compatibility is *repeated* and *intensive* assessment of children in order to document change, or, for that matter, baseline performance. Regardless of one's theoretical orientation to early intervention, it is widely accepted that the behavior of young children and particularly young handicapped children is highly variable, and stability of even the most stable of measures (e.g., IQ) has been highly suspect.

Thus, what is typical may be described as follows. Sometimes the child seems to possess a skill or concept, but sometimes not. Sometimes it appears that the display of the skill or concept is under the control of certain environmental events (having a favorite toy to play with) or constitutional events (having or not having a bout of otitis media), but sometimes not. Such uncertainty or variability in the primary subject matter of early intervention would seem to demand repeated and intensive assessments of child behavior and contemporaneous environments, the very assessment method that is the centerpiece of single-subject designs.

The second area of high compatibility between early intervention practices and single-case methods is the strong adherence to the idiosyncratic needs of participants (Strain, Kohler, & Smith, 1988). Here, too, there seems to be general professional consensus that best practice and a focus on the individual's strengths and weaknesses are synonymous. Most often we do not hear that a certain invariant intervention is best for all children or even for children of a narrow class, such as biologically at-risk infants. Just as the competent early interventionist tailors interventions to fit the need of individuals, so too does the single-subject researcher modify procedures to produce the best outcomes for individual subjects. It is here that we find the widest conceptual gulf between group and single-subject designs. For group-design users, a varied intervention brings error, lack of interpretability, and criticism to the study at hand. For the single-subject researcher who, as Sidman (1960) suggested, is conducting an "ever-changing" experiment, a varied intervention represents sensitivity to incoming data, potentially important analyses of how to make things work when they do not work the first time (a problem that any early interventionist can certainly relate to), and a reconfirmation of the wisdom of studying the behavior of individuals, not groups.

In summary, operant principles and methodology have made the following contributions to early intervention:

1. produced evidence to suggest that failures to teach a skill are most reasonably attributed (in terms of scientific and technological advancement) to faulty procedures (see Baer, 1981, for a discussion);
2. focused the attention of practitioners and researchers on those events in the child's contemporaneous environment that are readily changed and potentially relevant to behavioral improvement;
3. changed the focus of attention of child assessment from the infrequent sampling of traits and states to the daily observation of child behaviors in interaction with critical elements of the instructional universe (e.g., teacher guidance, caregiver intervention, curriculum materials, peers' behavior); and
4. provided an evaluation methodology in the form of single-case designs that are highly compatible with the everyday practice of quality service delivery.

Many of the early model projects in early childhood/special education were based on a behavioral approach to intervention, for example, The University of Washington Down Syndrome Project (Hayden & Haring, 1976), the Toddler Project (W. Bricker & D. Bricker, 1974), and the Portage Project (Shearer, 1972). These projects focused strongly on the content and method of instruction for children. The developers of these projects recognized, however, that a focus on the family was also necessary for intervention to be successful, for the family is a prime component of the child's environment. The behavioral approach fostered the inclusion of a family focus also from the perspective of generalization of behavior learned by children in the educational or therapeutic context to natural home and community environments. In fact, most early intervention programs included a "home" component where early intervention staff visited families in the natural environment for all or part of the instructional experience. Such a focus developed out of the early recognition (Stokes & Baer, 1977) that children need to display learned behavior in the environments where the behavior will ultimately be required in order to function successfully in the community.

Strategies to promote generalization of learned behavior have been identified by many researchers. These include using natural materials in the training context, training responses that will involve reinforcing responses from people in the natural context, and training in several contexts (see Sailor & Guess, 1983, for a complete discussion). One strategy that is identified with early intervention is to employ trainers who will be present in most of the settings in which the child needs to function, that is, the child's parents. Thus, early intervention has often looked to family members to assume the role of teacher or generalizer of skills. Such an approach requires that interventionists understand who these teachers are and what influences them as teachers. This requires a look at the American family.

THE CHANGING ECOLOGY OF THE FAMILY

Since 1980 increased academic attention has been devoted to the composition of the American family. The last two decades have seen a dramatic change in how we, in America, define the family. Our concept of family has been broadened beyond the traditional depiction of father as breadwinner and mother as housewife and child rearer. Rather, family has come to have a broader, less structured, and more flexible meaning. What does family in America look like today and what do we project it will look like in the future? What impact will and should this have on the delivery of early intervention services?

The American family in the late 1980s

Over 60% of America's children born today will spend part of their life in a single-parent home (Vincent & Salisbury, 1988). A majority of these children will spend 5 years being raised by a single parent. Whereas historically single parenthood was caused by death of a parent, in the 1970s and 80s the cause has changed to divorce and to the increase in childbirth by unmarried women. Over half of black children born in America today will be born to a single mother; over one-quarter of Hispanic children will start life with a single mother; overall, 20% of American births are to single mothers (Norton & Glick, 1986). Many of these births will be to teenage mothers who have not completed a high school degree and will not complete the degree following the birth of the child (Halpern, 1987). Approximately 40% of America's children will experience the divorce of their parents by the time the children reach adulthood. With the increasing frequency of second marriage and the high rate of divorce in these "blended" families, about one-quarter to one-third of America's children will experience a second divorce ("Statistics Tell," 1987).

The financial stability as well as the composition of the American family is changing. With the increase in single parenthood has come an increase in the need for financial assistance from outside family sources. For example, in Wisconsin in 1985, 75% of single mothers were receiving Aid to Families of Dependent Children (AFDC) (Vincent & Salisbury, 1988). Nationally in 1985, 90% of AFDC recipients were single mothers and their children (Haskins, Schwartz, Akin, & Dobelstein, 1986). Most of these families were living at or below the poverty level. Added to the working families who are living in poverty, this means that 30% of American children were growing up in poverty (Vincent & Salisbury, 1988). Many of these children are at risk for developmental problems due to environmental and/or maternal caregiving factors. These children's parents are also at risk for being abusive and/or neglectful to their children (Vincent & Salisbury, 1988). Bristol, Reichle, and Thomas (1987) pointed out that although the age and life demands of these parents make them excellent candidates for services, this factor decreases the probability that they will participate. An ecological approach that looks at their life demands, values, and supports is essential to the achievement of desired program outcomes.

Changes in family composition and financial security are accompanied by changes in the demographics of American children. For example, in 1970 the California population was 78% white (i.e., non-Hispanic white), 7% black, 12% Hispanic, and 3% Asian. In 1985, the figures were 63% white, 8% black, 21% hispanic, and 8% Asian. By the year 2000 the prediction is that the population will be 53% white, 8% black, 27% Hispanic, and 21% Asian (California Assembly Office of Research, 1986). Only in the age group of those over 65 years will whites who are non-Hispanic be a majority. During the preschool years, the majority of children will be members of ethnic minorities (California Assembly Office of Research, 1986).

This dramatic change will also take place outside California. Chan (1986) predicted that by the year 2080 the demographics of America overall will resemble California. America's rural areas will be predominantly white and urban areas will be predominantly ethnic minority. Throughout the country, minorities will be responsible for a majority of new births. If the experience in California is paralleled elsewhere, a growing number of these children will be classified as "limited English proficient," a classification rendered when children are reared in non–English-speaking homes (California Assembly Office of Research, 1986).

Not only is the language base of such families different from that of white America, the values, priorities, and child-rearing practices may also differ. The stresses and life experiences of such families may also be different (Chan, 1986; Korbin, 1980; McAdoo, 1978).

Minority families

All families assume the role of socializing children to become part of the larger community. An examination and understanding of the differences between "mainstream" culture and its values, and the values of individual ethnic minority groups and individual families are part of the foundation of a behavioral-ecological approach to intervention. In the space of this chapter, reviewing the wealth of information now available on ethnic minority families is not possible. However, highlighting findings for several groups should be helpful.

Caution must be exercised when trying to describe any group in a generalized sense. There are often as many and as wide variations within a group as between groups. In an attempt to better understand cultural difference and variability we must always be careful not to perpetuate stereotypes (McAdoo, 1978). As A. Ortiz (1987) indicated, culture exists on a continuum. Early intervention must discern where on the continuum of assimilation into the majority culture a family functions, and recognize that this may change.

NATIVE AMERICAN FAMILIES. McAdoo (1978) provided an excellent synthesis of the experience of Native American families. She pointed out that they were on this continent before all other groups and that diversity in their cultures is as great as that of all European cultures. Patterns of marriage and family relationships reflected a wide spectrum both in structure and composition. Geography and economics played a large role in the development of families. Some tribes were matriarchal, others patriarchal, others a combination. Some tribes were polygamous, others monogamous. In contrast, early white settlers practiced only one form of marriage, monogamy, and saw the variety in the Native American population as uncivilized.

Currently, approximately half of the Native American population lives in urban areas, while half lives on or near reservations (Tafoya, 1987). There are similarities in how different tribes view families and child rearing and hence, in the children's styles of learning (A. Ortiz, 1987). Pride in one's heritage and tribal identity are important values taught to children. The clan or family comes first, the individual second. Some Native American languages have no word for "I." Thus, the Pueblo custom of not signing artwork and pottery can be seen as an example of the individual's effort on behalf of the clan (Tafoya, 1987). Elders are highly respected. In fact, in many tribes parenting is actually carried out by the grandparents, as the biological parents are viewed as too young to take on such an important role. Extended kinship structures are very common. Children are taught by example rather than direction. In many Indian tribes, telling someone what to do directly is viewed as unacceptable behavior. Similarly, standing out or being individually recognized may be viewed as not in the best interest of the clan. Nevertheless, each person is viewed as unique, with abilities and disabilities. "Guardian spirits" are available to help each person discern his or her role, the role that will best help the clan or tribe (Ortiz, 1987).

Reactions to a child with an obvious disability are varied. In some clans this is a sign of the clan behaving in a way that was objectionable to the "guardian spirits;" in others it is a sign of good luck (Tafoya, 1987). Interactions with professionals concerning a child's disability and intervention needs can be strained. As professionals we focus typically on the individual child, while the family may focus on the needs of the clan. Directly teaching skills to a child may be viewed as inappropriate if the culture values modeling or less structured approaches. Attempts at involving biological mothers and fathers may not be effective and may, in fact, alienate family members in whom greater authority is vested.

For Native Americans who have moved from the reservation to urban areas, the extended network of the clan and its support may be missing. Where an individual, parent, or family is in the acculturation process will need to be carefully studied. In addition, an assessment will be needed of which tribal values are still held. An ecological approach provides the best opportunity for obtaining and integrating this information successfully, for it places the greatest value on the context within which the individual child with disabilities functions.

BLACK AMERICAN FAMILIES. Black Americans come from highly diverse backgrounds. Early black Americans were brought to the United States from Africa as slaves. Depending on whether they were placed on large plantations or small farms, different family structures evolved. Later, black immigrants came from the Caribbean and Central and South America, bringing with them new cultures, religions, and family structures. Thus as with other minority groups, generalizing about the black American experience must be done with caution. One aspect of that experience that can be addressed is their common experience of racism, prejudice, and economic oppression (Hale, 1981; McAdoo, 1978; Mullings-Franco, 1987).

More than any other ethnic minority group, single-parent homes have predominated in black America in recent years (Norton & Glick, 1986). Single parenthood may be perpetuated in black American families for economic reasons. In some cities, the unemployment rate for young black men is 40%. Single parenthood affords mothers and children the opportunity to obtain financial assistance in the form of AFDC. As Bristol et al. (1987) pointed out, this does not mean that fathers are not significantly involved in these children's lives. In fact, as early as 1978, McAdoo pointed to the involvement of black fathers as much higher than expected. Economic oppression has forced black mothers and fathers to evolve more equalized roles. Kinship bonds are established not only within, but also across, households. The black family is multigenerational, and strong loyalty to relatives exists (Simon & Booth, 1987). Mullings-Franco (1987) characterized the typical urban black family as cutting across five or more households, guided by a dominant figure who could be male or female, and taking on the care of its own. Church attendance and church-based support have often been seen as central to the black experience (Hale, 1981). When a family has a member with a disability, the strong religious base may provide support, but also feelings of guilt that a child's disability may be due to parent wrongdoing.

Some researchers point to a unique learning style of African-American children (Hale, 1981). They suggest that these children are more accustomed to emotions, body language, and social nuance. Early intervention strategies must establish a match between the child's and the family's ecology of learning and should be delivered in a way that respects cross-generational and cross-familial bonds.

HISPANIC FAMILIES. Hispanic people have come to the United States from a wide variety of places (e.g., South and Central America, Puerto Rico, Mexico) and with many different experiences. Many differences in these cultures exist, but there are similarities in family and child-rearing customs. Hispanic people comprise the second largest minority group in America. Because of language, religion, and economic practices they are often isolated from the mainstream (McAdoo, 1978), and are more likely than families from the dominant culture to exist in an extended family framework. Grandparents, aunts, uncles, cousins, and "padrinos" (godparents), as well as the immediate family, are involved in child rearing and decision making (J. Ortiz, 1981). In Hispanic families the child is looked at first as a member of the extended family unit and then secondly as an individual. The family uses its extended family network to solve problems and hesitates to reach out to professional "outsiders" for help (Eagan, 1981). Some literature indicates that when outside help is sought, the medical community is more trusted than the educational community, as Hispanic Americans often see the educational community as discriminating against their children (Marion, 1980).

Roles within the family have traditionally been well defined. The father typically is the head of the household and is the authority figure. The mother is expected to be devoted to him and to her children and to place her needs last. Today's Hispanic family is facing stress from the acculturation process as women are becoming more unwilling to accept traditional roles. Unemployment has taken its toll on the ability of the Hispanic male to support his family. At times Hispanic women have an easier time finding employment, thus, leaving the male at home in an unnatural caregiving role.

Child-rearing practices take advantage of the extended family network. All adults are expected to discipline children, and older children are seen as competent caregivers of younger children. The oldest daughter is often involved in feeding, dressing, and supervising her siblings, even though she may still be a young child herself. Extended family members who live close by will check in occasionally and children can usually ask for and receive help from neighbors (Vandevier & Rodriguez, 1987). Within the dominant culture this practice is often viewed as parental irresponsibility and is sometimes characterized as child neglect. However, individual responsibility is generally expected of Hispanic American children earlier than their Anglo counterparts, and sibling rivalry is not as accepted in the Hispanic culture (Eagan, 1981). The teaching of good manners and acceptable "public" behavior is also stressed. To say that a child is "well educated" in Hispanic culture refers not to academic achievement, but to his knowledge of social norms and mores (e.g., talking to elders with downcast eyes as a sign of respect).

Hispanic-American families generally believe that a child with a disability is "God's will." Adaptation usually is based on using the extended family to protect and teach the child those skills that will make him or her "well educated." Marion (1980) and Luderus (1977) pointed out that Hispanic parents do not necessarily show the full range of negative emotional reactions that are characateristic of Anglo America (e.g., shock, anger, sadness). Such reactions would be viewed as maladaptive, since it is "God's will" that they raise their child. This basic cultural religiosity can be seen as an asset for a child with a disability. As Turnbull and Turnbull (1986) have indicated, religiosity has been correlated with positive family adaptation outcomes.

This acceptance of "God's will" influences how Hispanic families view planning for the future and the extent to which they follow through on services. The notion that "all will turn out as it should in the long run" may mean that the family carries out early intervention activities with less urgency than professionals would like. Early interventionists will need to involve families in selecting intervention goals so as to increase the likelihood of follow-through.

ASIAN FAMILIES. The largest group of immigrants entering the United States are people of Asian descent (Chan, 1986; Dung, 1984). Between 1980 and the year 2000, the Asian population in this country will have doubled. This population represents approximately 30 distinct ethnic groups with very diverse national origins and histories (Chan, 1986). From the initial immigration, Asians have faced discrimination and have formed segregated communities as a way of protecting themselves. Although this isolation has lessened to some degree in the last decade, recent immigrants from Vietnam, Thailand, and Cambodia have tended to establish self-contained ethnic communities where mother country language and culture are maintained (Chan, 1986). Nevertheless, while the Asian community is diverse, there are some common cultural traditions and mores that influence how these families raise children and relate to intervention services.

Chan (1986) pointed out that traditional Asian values derive from cultures that have existed for over 5,000 years. These values contrast markedly with Western cultural values. In Asian culture, for example, hierarchical roles and status govern behavior, and subordination and interdependence are valued. For instance, in the Vietnamese culture status is more important than wealth (Dung, 1984). Children are viewed as status, thus, the abundance of large families.

In traditional Asian cultures cooperation, obligation, and reciprocity are valued over Western competition, autonomy, and self-reliance (Chan, 1986). Rules and roles are most important in determining the context and content of social interaction. A parent who adheres to traditional cultural mores will be deferential and noninterfering in interactions with professionals. "Teachers" are highly regarded in Asian culture and are not to be questioned or contradicted (Chan, 1986). However, if the teacher presents a point of view that is markedly opposed by traditional values, his or her credibility with the family will be limited. This can often happen in early intervention programs due to the differences in belief about appropriate child-rearing practices between Asian families and early intervention professionals.

In Asian culture children are seen as "gifts from the Gods" (Chan, 1986). During infancy, Asian parents tend to be permissive by Western standards and to expect their child's attainment of developmental milestones in the self-help area to be slower than that expected by Western parents. The focus of interaction is on physical contact, not on verbal interaction. In contrast, during the preschool years, Asian parents have a tendency to set higher expectations in the self-help area than do Western parents and to place greater emphasis on the child learning the rules related to social interaction within the Asian community, since the child's behavior is felt to reflect on the family.

In traditional Asian cultures, the child's relationship with his or her parents is characterized by respect and obedience. Asian parents tend to be more rigid about discipline than Western parents (Chinn & Plata, 1986), with communication tending to be one-directional (i.e., parent to child). Children are not expected to express feelings, wants, likes, and dislikes. Given the focus in early intervention curriculum on communication as a social event, a sharp disagreement may emerge between early intervention professionals and Asian parents who hold traditional child-rearing values.

Disagreements may also exist between families and professionals in the areas concerning the cause of a child's disability, future prognosis, and appropriate treatment. Traditional Asian child development beliefs may attribute the birth of a child with a disability to moral transgressions committed by the parents, demons or ghosts, or to physiological imbalances in the life force caused by improper nutrition or health practices during pregnancy (Chan, 1986). All of these reasons can result in shame and "loss of face" for the Asian family. Even when professionals provide objective information that removes the blame from the family, the family still experiences the burden of the child being unable to carry out traditional life responsibilities. Thus the family's "wealth" and status are diminished.

The Asian cultural belief in humankind's need to accept fate and proceed stoically may conflict with professional expectations of outward grief and grieving. Thus, the Asian family may be misperceived as not dealing with or accepting their child's disability. In actuality, such grief and grieving may be an artifact of Western culture and may be incongruent with Asian values (Blacher, 1984; Chan, 1986; Lim-Yee, 1983).

In terms of prognosis, the traditional Asian belief is that children are good and will develop as a result of their family's teachings. Thus, professional predictions that a child at birth will be delayed in development or will be mentally retarded may be met with little acceptance. Many Asian languages do not have terms for mental retardation, and in translation, confusion may develop related to the concept of mental illness. The credibility of professionals who provide early assessment and diagnostic information rests on an understanding of these cultural beliefs. While Asian parents are not likely to publicly disagree with "teachers," they may simply ignore suggestions or not return for scheduled visits. Cautions must be exercised when dealing with a child's parents who are very accepting of the information given. The grandparents and extended family members who may be responsible for carrying out intervention activities may not be in agreement (Chinn & Plata, 1986).

The development of an Individualized Family Service Plan (IFSP) or Individualized Education Plan (IEP) that is based on family goals and directions may pose particular difficulty for the Asian family. As Chinn and Plata (1986) pointed out, Asian parents who have immigrated to the United States have often been raised in educational systems where "the teacher knows best." They may be confused by attempts on professionals' part to involve them in decision making, and, as Chan (1986) indicated, they may be reluctant to do so for fear of being wrong or offending professionals with their choices. Staff who are knowledgeable about Asian culture, values, and language are essential to the success of a behavioral-ecologically based early intervention program. At the present time, such staff are not generally available and the successful implementation of P.L. 99-457 will rest, in large part, on the availability of appropriately trained personnel.

The goals and strategies chosen for intervention for Asian families will need to be matched to traditional Asian and emerging American values. Families may prefer to see "indigenous healers" from their own culture, or employ herbal remedies, healing ceremonies, or acupuncture (Chan, 1986). They may employ healing practices that seem to be unscientific by Western cultural standards (Dung, 1984). Immigrant families may select these practices over a professionally based system of early intervention services, not only because of their cultural beliefs, but also because they may fear that needing publicly supported services will result in deportation (Chan, 1986). They tend to make fewer assumptions about entitlements to services than white families, and may be less likely to take advantage of those services that are offered.

THE BEHAVIORAL-ECOLOGICAL PERSPECTIVE

American families differ widely in composition, values, resources, and needs. Such diversity requires that the behavioral approach that was used to develop instructional strategies for children be broadened to look at larger family variables. Such an approach has been termed ecological in the literature and incorporates the behavioral focus discussed earlier.

The ecological perspective

The ecological perspective provides an additional basis for designing early intervention services. Such a perspective derives its support from both human ecology (Bronfenbrenner, 1979; Cochran & Brassard, 1979) and family systems (Carter & McGoldrick, 1980; Minuchin, 1974) theories. Like behavioral approaches, human ecology theory emphasizes the interactions and accommodations between the developing child and his or her environment, and seeks to explain how events in different ecological settings affect human behavior directly and indirectly (Dunst & Trivette, in press). Bronfenbrenner's ecological model of human development provides perhaps the most comprehensive foundation for understanding how we apply the ecological perspective to early intervention. Specifically, Bronfenbrenner proposed that there are four sources of influence on an individual's development: interactions within immediate settings (e.g., home, school, job – microsystem); the interrelations among major settings containing the individual (mesosystem); formal and informal social structures that affect the individual (e.g., media, neighborhoods, agencies – exosystem); and the ideological patterns of the culture and subcultures of the settings in which the individual functions (macrosystems). Because context is presumed to influence the development of the individual, early intervention efforts must be designed to address multiple sources of influence on the child and his or her family members. Behaviorally based projects had focused predominantly on the first source. However, behavioral principles can be used at all levels.

We extend Bronfenbrenner's model of individual development to the family as a unit by incorporating family systems theory as an additional aspect of the ecological approach. Family systems theory stresses the interactional nature of the family unit and suggests that events affecting any one member have an impact upon all family members, a position that is highly consistent with the behavioral foundations discussed earlier. The family is viewed as consisting of subsystems (e.g., parental, sibling, spousal, extrafamilial) whose membership and roles change over the life cycle of the family (Carter & McGoldrick, 1980). Taken together, the behavioral approach and an ecological perspective provide a useful basis for examining the transactional and developmental relationships that emerge as the child and family interact with complex social contexts over time.

For purposes of this chapter, the focus on the child and family as they interact within and among complex social systems will be termed a behavioral-ecological approach. Dunst and Trivette (this volume) provide a cogent analysis of the constructs and underpinnings of the social systems perspective, with particular attention drawn to the types of social supports that affect family functioning. Knowledge of such supports and their relationship to family functioning plays a critical role in the design, development, and implementation of early intervention services.

Although grounded in a strong theoretical base (Bronfenbrenner, 1979; Carter & McGoldrick, 1980; Minuchin, 1974) remarkably little has been written about the ecological perspective in early intervention since the reports on the large-scale efforts undertaken in the 1970s (cf. the Milwaukee Project). In examining the ecology of the child and the family, Siders, Riall, Campbell, and Crow (1987) noted that whereas research has historically recognized the typical infant as an active, competent learner, there is equal justification for attributing the same capabilities to the infant with handicaps or the infant at risk for handicapping conditions. Specifically, they state that "practitioners must move beyond viewing development in terms of a simple taxonomy of skills and begin to focus on the host of variables resulting from mutual transactions between the child and the social environment" (Siders et al., 1987, p. 3). In order to address adequately the myriad factors that can affect the child and his or her family unit, early interventionists must adopt a multidimensional model of assessment, intervention, and program evaluation. Such a model should be grounded in behavioral principles of measurement.

A behavioral-ecological perspective enables professionals to formulate coherent assessment strategies for examining relationships among child, family, and social context variables. Such an assessment provides a sound basis for making outcome projections and specific intervention plans. Dunst (1985) suggested that changes in child behavior are not solely dependent upon intervention by professionals, by rather can occur directly and indirectly from a variety of sources. Numerous researchers have highlighted the roles that family and social support play in the successful adaptation of a family to a child with a disability (cf. Crnic, Friedrich, & Greenberg, 1983; Dunst, Trivette, & Cross, 1986; Turnbull & Turnbull, 1986). Yet, when supports and assistance do not match family need, the child and family become vulnerable and are at risk for potentially negative effects of intervention services (Dunst & Trivette, 1987).

Only recently has attention been drawn to nontraditional families with handicapped and at-risk children. Vincent and Salisbury (1988), Halpern (1987), and Bristol et al. (1987) have pointed out how increases in teenage pregnancy and single parenthood have eroded the support available to families, particularly families of children who can be considered at risk for developmental problems. Thus, intervention programs must adopt models that are ecological in nature and provide services, not only to children, but also to parents and other family members.

Many authors have spoken of the need for such a focus (Chan, 1986; Dunst et al., 1987; Foster, Berger, & McClean, 1981; Korbin, 1980; Turnbull & Turnbull, 1986; Vincent & Salisbury, 1988), however, early intervention programs have not been uniformly successful in actively involving parents. For example, Bricker (1986) reported that only 20 to 40% of parents were actively involved in their infant's or toddler's early intervention program. Meyers and Blacher (1987) reported that even for children with severe disabilities, home–school communication was rare in 31% and nonexistent in 5% of the families in their program. About 50% of the parents reported no, little, or only some involvement in assessment, program planning, or parent groups.

Dropout from parent programs has been reported to be as high as 70% of initial attendance (Stile, Cole, & Garner, 1979). Brinckerhoff and Vincent (1987) summarized research on parents' involvement in selecting educational goals for their children. They indicated that over 90% of goals are chosen by professionals. Overall, efforts at developing models of intervention have not been ecologically successful. Although children have received professional services, families have not been active decision makers. Thus, the context of intervention has fallen short of what we know to be ideal.

Dunst et al. (1987) pointed out that a new "ecological" approach to intervention is needed because previous approaches focused on adult control over the child and did not view the child as an active learner, transactor, or initiator. A similar argument can be made about parent and family participation. To date, approaches have tended to exert professional control over family involvement, rather than develop family control over the content and delivery of services. Such an approach must change if the vision of family-focused services is to become a reality.

Bailey (1987) reviewed research on parent and professional priorities related to service delivery goals. He indicated that often professionals and parents do not agree about what is most important. Salisbury, Vincent, and Gorrafa (1987) reported a 23% overlap between the goals selected by professionals and those selected by parents of children with dual sensory impairments. Cadman, Goldsmith, and Bashim (1984) reported that professionals were much more likely to choose helping parents with family interactions as a priority than were parents. Similar results were reported by Blackard and Barsh (1982), who found that professionals were more likely than parents to predict that a child with a disability would have a negative impact on the family. Such a prediction leads not only to differences in what services are included in an intervention program, but also to expectations of parents and families that may be unjustified. Bailey (1987) summarized the issues in the area of parent–professional collaborative goal setting by pointing out that disagreements can arise over what goals are established for service provision or the methods by which services will be delivered.

Disagreement usually emerges from differences in values. Values about child rearing and parental roles are two areas where parents and professionals have been shown to disagree (Winton & Turnbull, 1981) and where disagreements are likely due to differences in life experience between professionals and the parents with whom they work. Understanding the ecology of the family is essential for a successful model of early intervention. It is essential that the content of services and methods of service delivery be matched to the needs, priorities, and preferences of the family. Strain (1987), Dunst et al. (1987), and others have pointed out that a change in the child is dependent, not just on professional skills or the child's disability, but also upon complex interrelationships among family values, intra- and extrafamily supports, and the extent to which services offered match what families need and want. Assessing and assuring the match is not easy, but recognition of its importance is prompting the design and development of promising assessment models (cf. Bailey et al., 1986; Dunst & Trivette, this volume). America's "family" has changed in the 1980s and is predicted to keep changing into the twenty-first century. Whereas the nature of child disabilities will generally remain the same as targets for intervention, the ecological contexts of intervention will undergo dramatic change. The behavioral approach to intervention offers the basis for responding to these dramatic changes, for at its core is a focus on the child and family as an individual case.

Application of the behavioral-ecological model with families

Richardson (1981) summarized the salient assumptions behind an ecological approach with particular reference to minority families. However, these assumptions are applicable to all families. First and foremost, she pointed out that there are many ways to be human. Similarly, there are many ways to be a family, to be parents, to be a member of a community. The diverse values that underlie ethnic minorities' approaches to family, parenting, and community have equal claim to validity, and, in fact, have often existed many centuries longer than the majority Anglo culture. Since diversity exists within the Anglo culture as well, there is likely to be disagreement based on geography, social class, and education. Korbin (1980) pointed out that as long as a culture, family, or clan was not abusing a child there was no right way to raise children. The issue is how we as a society define abuse and the rights of children versus the rights of parents.

Some of the healing practices of the minority cultures and rural majority cultures have been mistaken for abuse, (e.g., coining, the practice of rubbing a hot coin on the throat of a child with a sore throat to allow the infection to escape). Such judgments often grow out of the assumption that these families are not concerned about or caring for their children. We often judge parents to be uncaring when they care differently than we as professionals do. Richardson (1981) reminded us that parents do not fail to follow the advice of professionals without reason. We as professionals may be unwilling to hear the reason or may fail to comprehend the subtleties of what parents say to us. Parents may appear to be lazy, uncooperative, or resistant when in reality they may not have the necessary familial, societal, or financial support and resources to become actively involved. Although at times parents do not act in the best interest of their children, the vast majority of parents want to do what is best, as defined by their values and culture. Intervention programs must develop ways to interface with the family's ecology, and early interventionists must learn to identify both the obstacles that exist for families and the strategies to remove these obstacles that are consistent with the family's ecology. When intervention efforts with families do not succeed, we must return to our behavioral base and recognize that if the family is not acting in the child's best interest or following through on activities and services, it is because we have not taught them to do so, not because they are incapable or uncooperative. We must then use our knowledge of family systems and the ecological perspective to design new approaches.

As Baca (1987) indicated, teachers and other professionals are receiving little systematic training in how to deal with the cultural diversity that exists within the American "educational intervention system." In the present authors' experience, teacher education programs focus on teaching prescribed curriculum to children. The problem rests in part with the focus of instruction. Although early childhood special education training programs place more importance on the family, student teaching and field placements usually take place in classrooms, not homes or communities. Student concerns usually focus on whether they have control over the classroom (Zeichner, 1980), not whether the skills they are teaching are valued in the child's home environment and community. Such concerns have been addressed in the area of instruction with students in special education and take the form of what is referred to as "community referenced instruction" (Snell & Grigg, 1987) based upon "ecological inventories of subsequent environments" (Vincent et al., 1980). Application of these principles to early childhood special education would require modifications in the content and manner in which many programs provide training. This approach requires that environments where children will function on a day-to-day basis, currently and in the near future, be evaluated to determine what skills are needed for them to be successful. By then assessing what the environment (i.e., parents' homes) will require of the teacher-in-training, personnel preparation programs would design instruction that is appropriate in its content and valid in its method. Such an approach would be based upon direct assessments of home settings with parents, and would offer students field experiences in the settings (parents' homes) in which those skills are valued and needed. How to conduct such assessments is the basis of a behavioral approach.

The direct observation of the diverse environments in which young children function (e.g., home, day care, and grocery store), would be done based on an analysis with the family of what settings are most important to them. The recording of expected child behavior in relation to a particular adult, materials, or peer cues is a unique contribution of a behavioral-ecological approach. The assumption is that if we know how a child needs to behave in a given environment to be perceived as successful in that environment, we can teach the child the necessary behavior, or modify the environment so that other behaviors that a child already displays will be acceptable.

A behavioral-ecological perspective on assessment

Johnson and Beauchamp (1987) reported that nearly half of the teachers in early childhood special education they surveyed were using a particular assessment instrument because it was the only one they knew of or was already in use when they were hired. Such a finding implies that teachers may not see selection of assessment instruments and procedures as important to their success as teachers or to children's success as learners. Yet, as Peterson and Meier (1987) indicated, in a quality intervention program, assessment serves "as a guide for everything that happens to a child" (p. 276). Bailey and Wolery (1984) stated:

> The teacher's first task in designing an appropriate intervention program is to determine the skills the child needs to master and the sequence in which those skills should be taught. Determining instructional targets requires a basic understanding of child development, a knowledge of child assessment techniques, and the ability to relate developmental skills to the everyday demands placed on children (p. 25).

Added to this latter statement should be "by different cultures and settings at different points in development." In outlining methods of assessments, both sets of authors point to the role of direct testing, naturalistic observation, and parent interviewing. Peterson and Meier (1987) pointed out the relative novelty of an adaptive-transactive perspective that emphasizes the interaction between the child and his or her world rather than simply between the child and the test items. Such an approach is highly consistent with the behavioral methodology discussed earlier and is advantageous for gathering a wide range of information on the child's functional competencies in the natural environment. Naturalistic observation affords a similar vantage point to assessment if it is conducted in the full range of environments with the full range of people with whom the child usually interacts. Since many intervention programs are not able to observe children in the multitude of settings in which they function, it is fortunate that parents are generally as accurate as professionals in assessing children's behavior (Schafer, Bell & Spalding, 1987; Seibert, Hogan, & Mundy, 1987; Vincent, 1986). The inclusion of parents as equal members of the assessment team has been shown to change how educational goals are generated for children (Brinckerhoff & Vincent, 1986).

Assessment should go beyond an examination of child behavior. From an ecological perspective, assessment must also include a look at family needs and resources (Bailey, 1987; Turnbull & Turnbull, 1986; Vincent, 1986). Unfortunately, widely accepted standardized instruments are not available to assess family needs, resources, priorities, and values. A combination of methods is necessary to gather this information, including family self-report, structured interviews, and direct observation. Turnbull and Turnbull (1986) outlined sample techniques that they have used. Bailey et al. (1986) presented a functional model of family-focused intervention. Dunst and Trivette (1985) provided a comprehensive look at tools for assessing a wide range of family functioning variables. Their techniques would need to be adapted for use in cultural settings where parents rely on professional judgments, or rely on cultural spirit advisers or faith healers. A behavioral-ecological perspective makes one more aware that not only will we need to change the information we gather, we also must change how we gather information. Although many measures exist that have been used in more clinical settings with families, their application and appropriateness to early intervention are still being examined (Dunst & Trivette, this volume; Krauss & Jacobs, this volume). New techniques for examining each family's unique resources and needs must be developed. Intervention at the family systems level will only be successful if we begin with an appropriate assessment of the child-and-family context. This assessment must start from the concept that all families have needs and resources, not from the notion that we will identify weaknesses and strengths in the family. The latter implies that we can judge families and that we have a standard to judge them against. Such is not the case.

A behavioral-ecological perspective on intervention

A behavioral-ecological approach to the child and family can also be translated into how the "interventionist" will approach the child. These interventionists may be teachers, parents, therapists, cousins, godparents, grandparents, siblings, or neighbors. The content and strategies of the intervention will be based on an interaction between the family's beliefs about child development and child-rearing practices, and what we know from professional literature about how children acquire the most generalizable skills. There must be a focus on generalizability since young children usually function in more than one environment and will experience increasing numbers of environments as they grow up. Dunst et al. (1987) pointed to the importance of interactive competencies for young children (e.g., ability to attract the caregiver's attention) as opposed to the respondent skills (e.g., waves bye-bye when instructed), that is often taught in early intervention programs. Of interest is that many of the minority cultures reviewed earlier also place an emphasis on the child as an interactive developer during the early years. Considerable flexibility is given children concerning when they develop self-help skills. The child in relation to others is a focus in most of these cultures. Whether it is called transactive-adaptive (Peterson & Meier, 1987), or interactive (Dunst et al., 1987), is not the issue. What is important is that the targets that are selected for child competence fit the environment in which the child lives. Bailey and Wolery (1984) and Vincent et al. (1980) term this a functional approach to selecting intervention targets and note that behaviorally designed intervention strategies are among the most effective for achieving child change. The behaviors that are valued in the child's world are selected for teaching. The mechanism for teaching must also be addressed and matched to the child's culture and family's beliefs about how children learn. Dunst et al. (1987) strongly advocated against traditional didactic approaches to teaching as reducing infant and child competence. A behavioral-ecological approach can take into account both infant competence and more traditional teaching strategies.

The behavioral-ecological approach to intervention for young children with disabilities has evolved as we have tried various models in our intervention efforts. The components of the various approaches to early intervention that have been used and the problems that have resulted will be described to provide a background for the behavioral-ecological model.

One common approach to early intervention has been to combine developmentally based skill sequences and behavioral components into classroom curricula. A primary goal of many intervention programs has been to provide experiences that will help a child with disabilities develop skills that approximate or reach those that normal children develop (Hayden, McGinnes, & Dimitriev, 1976). Because of this, many curricula are based on normal developmental sequences of skills ordered to facilitate their attainment. In other words, normal developmental milestones are assumed to be critical skills for children with disabilities (Bailey, Jens, & Johnson, 1983).

There are some potential problems in using developmentally based skill sequences to generate curriculum goals for children with handicaps. First, many children with disabilities must learn adaptive functioning skills that may not be included in the normal developmental sequence. Second, children with multiple handicaps may have various functioning levels across domains. Another problem arises when the child's disability in one domain affects his or her ability to perform a task in another domain. For example, a child with poor fine motor skills may have difficulty performing a cognitive task involving retrieving objects out of reach. Failure on the task could be due to physical or cognitive disabilities or both.

The behavioral component of many early intervention curricula comprises specific teaching strategies, which are often called direct instruction. Components of direct instruction include analyzing tasks, breaking down tasks into a series of teaching steps, identifying and instructing target behavior, and applying systematic reinforcement procedures (Bailey et al., 1983). Direct instructional practices assign the teacher an active role in the child's educational process, often by employing considerable control and structure over the environment (Conn-Powers, 1982). These strategies are designed to maximize the child's attention to the specific behavior to be learned (Hart & Rogers-Warren, 1978).

Although the use of direct instructional practices has resulted in successful acquisition of targeted skills, some researchers have been concerned about poor generalization of those skills to functional, less structural settings (Guess, Sailor, Keogh, & Baer, 1978; Warren, Rogers-Warren, Baer, & Guess, 1980). A related problem has been the tendency to oversimplify the interactions between the child and his or her environment. By breaking down behavior into small measurable steps, proponents of the behavioral model have often neglected the contextually bound, experientially based characteristics of young children's learning (Blank, Rose, & Berlin, 1978; Cook-Gumperz, 1977; Rees, 1978).

Because this model of early intervention has also incorporated a high frequency of questions and directives by teachers, children's learning has tended to be highly response-oriented. This style may provide multiple opportunities to use a targeted skill, but at the same time restricts opportunities for spontaneous initiation of behavior (Corsaro, 1979; Dembro, Yoshida, Reilly, & Reilly, 1978). Children have been found to initiate more often when their conversational partners are less controlling (Conn-Powers, 1982; Corsaro, 1979; Prutting, Bayshaw, Goldstein, Juskowitz, & Umen, 1978).

Problems with this model of early intervention have led to the evolution of a different model of instruction. The model, which has been variously termed an interactional, transactional, or ecological approach to instruction (Bricker & Carlson, 1980; Bromwich, 1978; Dunst, 1980; Hanson, 1982; Mahoney & Weller, 1980), incorporates aspects of developmental and behavioral approaches with an additional consideration of the complex interactions that normally take place between the child and significant others.

The interactional or behavioral-ecological approach to instruction emphasizes the intimate relations among developmental processes such as cognition, social skills, and communication, without separating the domains for training purposes. The child is viewed as engaging in constant interactions with caregivers and the environment, which continually affect the developmental process (Bricker & Carlson, 1980, 1981; Dunst, 1980; Mahoney & Weller, 1980). Basic principles of an ecological approach include selecting intervention targets from the child's natural environment, training within the context of meaningful, naturally occurring situations, and actively involving parents or caregivers in the process (Mahoney & Weller, 1980).

The behavioral component of a behavioral-ecological approach to intervention incorporates many of the same principles of the traditional behavioral models. Although intervention targets are selected from an ecological or interactional perspective, and trained in meaningful (natural) contexts, targets are still broken down and sequenced in a systematic manner. Such an approach to instruction may be more easily incorporated into diverse family perspectives. The family can be involved in selecting targets, the professional can help determine a teaching sequence, if necessary, and the family can help select teaching methods.

A behavioral-ecological approach to program evaluation

Fewell and Vadasy (1987) pointed out that the changes that have taken place in the purposes, scope, and strategies employed in early intervention during the past two decades should be reflected in how we measure the success of that intervention. Whereas the initial goals of early intervention programs in the 1970s were related to changes in individual child behavior, the goals in the 1990s need to be broader, reflecting an integration of our knowledge of family, culture, and community. The behavioral-ecological approach dictates that program evaluation include measures, not only of child change, but also of family satisfaction and change. The measures of child change must move beyond performance assessments on standardized developmental or intelligence tests. Although these tests have traditionally been the cornerstone for measuring program success, their cultural and racial biases render their use with children from culturally diverse communities highly inappropriate. Where the goals of intervention are family change, family-level assessment measures must be used.

Measures of family change and satisfaction are beginning to emerge in the early intervention literature. Krauss and Jacobs (this volume) and Dunst and Trivette (this volume) review several scales that seem particularly effective for identifying family needs and sources of support. Although these measures begin to address the assessment of family change, we lack efficient and effective measures to assess the impact on the child of intervention with families. Recent research has described initial efforts at assessing the impact of social support on child, individual, and family outcomes (cf. Dunst et al., 1986). The need remains for those involved in model program design and evaluation to translate research procedures into practical strategies that can be used efficiently and effectively in a wide variety of applied settings.

SUMMARY

Early intervention programs and services will be called upon to meet the needs of more and more children and families within the next decade. These children and families will need services that are comprehensive, flexible, and family focused. Service providers will need to see children in the context of their family and the family in the context of its community. Individualized planning is required for each child and family unit. The behavioral-ecological model is particularly suited to this task because it provides a framework within which to work with each child and family in ways that will uniquely meet their needs.

REFERENCES

Baca, L. (1987). Bilingual special education teacher training for American Indians. In M. J. Johnson & B. A. Ramirez (Eds.), *American Indian exceptional children and youth* (pp. 25–30). ERIC Clearinghouse on Handicapped and Gifted Children, Council for Exceptional Children, Reston, VA.

Baer, D. N. (1981). A hung jury and Scottish verdict: "Not proven." *Analysis & Intervention in Developmental Disabilities, 1,* 91–98.

Bailey, D. B. (1987). Differences in values and priorities for services. *Topics in Early Childhood Special Education, 7,* 59–71.

Bailey, D. B., Jens, K. G., & Johnson, N. (1983). Curricula for handicapped infants. In R. R. Fewell & S. G. Garwood (Eds.), *Educating handicapped infants* (pp. 387–415). Rockville, MD: Aspen Systems.

Bailey, D. B., Simeonsson, R., Winton, P. J., Huntington, G. S., Comfort, M., Isbell, P., O'Donnell, K. J., & Helm, J. M. (1986). Family focused intervention: A functional model for planning, implementing, and evaluating individualized family services in early intervention. *Journal of the Division for Early Childhood, 10,* 156–171.

Bailey, D. B., & Wolery, M. (1984). *Teaching infants and preschoolers with handicaps.* Columbus, OH: Merrill.

Bijou, S. W. (1966). Theory and research in mental (developmental) retardation. *Psychological Record, 13,* 95–110.

Blacher, J. (1984). Sequential stages of parental adjustment to the birth of a child with handicaps: Fact or artifact. *Mental Retardation, 22,* 55–68.

Blackard, M. K., & Barsh, E. T. (1982). Parents' and professionals' perceptions of the handicapped child's impact on the family. *Journal of the Association for the Severely Handicapped,
7*, 62–70.

Blank, M., Rose, S. A., & Berlin, L. J. (1978). *The language of learning: The preschool years.* New
York: Grune & Stration.

Bricker, D. (1986). *Early education of at-risk and handicapped infants, toddlers, and preschool
children.* Glenview, IL: Scott, Foresman.

Bricker, D., & Carlson, L. (1980). An intervention approach for communicatively handicapped
infants and young children. In D. D. Bricker (Ed.), *New directions for exceptional children:
Language intervention with children* (pp. 33–48). San Francisco: Jossey-Bass.

Bricker, D., & Carlson, L. (1981). Issues in early language intervention. In R. L. Schiefelbusch &
D. D. Bricker (Eds.), *Early language: Acquisition and intervention* (pp. 479–515). Baltimore:
University Park Press.

Bricker, W. A. (1970). *Identifying and modifying behavioral deficits.* Unpublished manuscript,
George Peabody College, Nashville.

Bricker, W. A., & Bricker, D. (1974). An early language training strategy. In R. Schiefelbusch &
L. Lloyd (Eds.), *Language perspectives: Acquisition, retardation, and intervention.* Baltimore:
University Park Press.

Brinckerhoff, J. L., & Vincent, L. J. (1986). Increasing parental decision-making at their child's
individualized educational program meeting. *Journal of the Division for Early Childhood, 11*,
46–58.

Bristol, M. M., Reichle, N. C., & Thomas, D. D. (1987). Changing demographics of the
American family: Implications for single parent families of young handicapped children.
Journal of the Division for Early Childhood, 12, 56–69.

Bromwich, R. (1978). *Working with parents and infants: An interactional approach.* Austin, TX:
PRO-ED.

Bronfenbrenner, U. (1979). *The ecology of human development: Experiments by nature and design.*
Cambridge: Harvard University Press.

Cadman, D., Goldsmith, C., & Bashim, P. (1984). Values, preferences, and decisions in the care
of children with developmental disabilities. *Developmental and Behavioral Pediatrics, 5*, 60–
64.

California Assembly Office of Research. (1986). *California 2000. A people in transition.* California
House of Representatives, Sacramento, CA.

Carter, E., & McGoldrick, M. (1980). *The family life cycle: A framework for family therapy.* New
York: Gardner Press.

Chan, S. (1986). Parents of exceptional Asian children. In M. K. Kitano & P. C. Chinn (Eds.),
Exceptional Asian Children and Youth (pp. 36–53). ERIC Clearinghouse on Handicapped and
Gifted Children, Council for Exceptional Children, Reston, VA.

Chinn, P., & Plata, M. (1986). Perspectives and educational implications of Southeast Asian
students. In M. K. Kitano & P. C. Chinn (Eds.), *Exceptional Asian Children and Youth* (pp.
12–28). ERIC Clearinghouse on Handicapped and Gifted Children, Council for Exceptional
Children, Reston, VA.

Cochran, N., & Brassard, J. (1979). Child development and personal social networks. *Child
Development, 50*, 601–616.

Conn-Powers, M. (1982). *The effect of developmental and interactive-based teaching strategies on the
acquisition and generalization of vocabulary in young developmentally delayed children.* Unpublished doctoral dissertation, University of Wisconsin, Madison.

Cook-Gumperz, J. (1977). Situated instructions language socialization of school age children. In
S. Ervin-Tripp and C. Mitchell-Kernan (Eds.), *Child Discourse* (pp. 103–121). New York:
Academic Press.

Corsaro, W. A. (1979). Sociolinguistic patterns in adult–child interaction. In E. Ochs & B.
Schieffelin (Eds.), *Developmental Pragmatics* (pp. 373–389). New York: Academic Press.

Crnic, K. A., Friedrich, W. A., & Greenberg, M. T. (1983). Adaptation of families with
mentally retarded children: A model of stress, coping, and family ecology. *American Journal
of Mental Deficiency, 88*, 125–138.

Dembro, M. H., Yoshida, R. K., Reilly, T., & Reilly, V. (1978). Teacher–student interaction in
special education classroom. *Exceptional Education, 45*, 212–213.

Dung, J. N. (1984). Understanding Asian families: A Vietnamese perspective. *Children Today, 13*,
10–12.

Dunst, C. J. (1980, March). *An ecological approach to infant cognitive linguistic development and intervention.* Paper presented at the Project Imprint Special Topics Conference, George Mason University, Fairfax, VA.

Dunst, C. J. (Ed.). (1985). Early intervention [Special issue]. *Analysis and Intervention in Developmental Disabilities, 5* (112).

Dunst, C. J., Lesko, J. J., Holbert, K. A., Wilson, L. L., Sharpe, K. L., & Lies, R. F. (1987). A systematic approach to infant intervention. *Topics in Early Childhood Special Education, 7,* 19–37.

Dunst, C. J., & Trivette, C. M. (1985). *A guide to measures of social support and family behaviors.* Chapel Hill, NC: Technical Assistance Development System.

Dunst, C. J., & Trivette, C. M. (1987). Enabling and empowering families: Conceptual and intervention issues. *School Psychology Review, 16,* 327–342.

Dunst, C. J., & Trivette, C. M. (in press). A family systems model of early intervention with handicapped and developmentally at-risk children. In D. Powell (Ed.), *Parent education and support programs: Consequences for children and families.* Norwood, NJ: Ablex Publishing.

Dunst, C. J., Trivette, C. M., & Cross, A. (1986). Mediating influences of social support: Personal, family and child outcomes. *American Journal of Mental Deficiency, 90,* 403–417.

Eagan, G. R. (1987). *Chicano and Hispanic families.* Paper presented at Reaching Out to Families in a Multicultural Society Conference, Santa Fe, NM. Sponsored by Technical Assistance for Parents Program and the University of Oregon.

Fewell, R. R., & Vadasy, P. F. (1987). Measurement issues in studies of efficacy. *Topics in Early Childhood Special Education, 7,* 85–96.

Foster, M., Berger, M., & McLean, M. (1981). Rethinking a good idea: A reassessment of parent involvement. *Topics in Early Childhood Special Education, 1,* 55–65.

Guess, D., & Noonan, M. J. (1981). Curricula and instructional procedures for severely handicapped students. *Focus on Exceptional Children, 14,* 1–12.

Guess, D., Sailor, W., Keogh, W. J., & Baer, D. M. (1976). Language development programs for severely handicapped children. In N. G. Haring & L. J. Brown (Eds.), *Teaching the severely handicapped* (Vol. 1, pp. 301–326). New York: Grune & Stratton.

Hale, J. (1981). Black Children: Their roots, culture and learning styles. *Young Children, 36,* 37–50.

Halpern, R. (1987). Major social and demographic trends affecting young families: Implications for early childhood care and education. *Young Children, 42,* 34–40.

Hanson, J. J. (1982). Issues in designing intervention approaches from developmental theory and research. In D. D. Bricker (Ed.), *Intervention with at-risk and handicapped infants* (pp. 249–267). Baltimore: University Park Press.

Hart, B., & Rogers–Warren, A. (1978). A milieu approach to teaching language. In R. L. Schiefelbusch (Ed.), *Language intervention strategies* (pp. 195–235). Baltimore: University Park Press.

Haskins, R., Schwartz, J. B., Akin, J. S., & Dobelstein, A. W. (1986). How much child support can absent fathers pay? *Policy Review, 14,* 201–222.

Hayden, A. H., & Haring, N. G. (1976). Programs for Down's syndrome children at the University of Washington. In T. Tjossem (Ed.), *Intervention strategies for high risk infants and young children* (pp. 573–608). Baltimore: University Park Press.

Hayden, A. H., McGinnes, G. D., & Dimitriev, V. (1976). Early and continuous intervention strategies for severely handicapped infants and very young children, In N. G. Haring & L. J. Brown (Eds.), *Teaching the severely handicapped* (pp. 239–276). New York: Grune and Stratton.

Johnson, L. L., & Beauchamp, K. D. F. (1987). Preschool assessment measures: What are teachers using? *Journal of the Division for Early Childhood, 12,* 70–76.

Korbin, J. E. (1980). The cross-cultural context of child abuse and neglect. In C. H. Kempe & R. E. Helter (Eds.), *The battered child* (pp. 21–35). Cambridge: Harvard University Press.

Lim-Yee, N. (1983). *Parental reactions to a special needs child: Cultural differences and Chinese families.* Paper presented at the Annual Convention of the Western Psychological Association, San Francisco.

Luderus, E. (1977). *Family environment characteristics of Mexican-American families of handicapped and non-handicapped preschool children.* Unpublished doctoral dissertation. University of Texas, Austin.

Mahoney, G., & Weller, E. (1980). An ecological approach to language intervention. In D. D.

194   VINCENT, SALISBURY, STRAIN, MCCORMICK, AND TESSIER

Bricker (Ed.). *New directions for exceptional children: Language intervention with children* (pp. 17–32). San Francisco: Jossey-Bass.

Marion, R. L. (1980). Communicating with parents of culturally diverse exceptional children. *Exceptional Children, 46*, 616–625.

McAdoo, H. (1978). Minority families. In J. H. Stevens & M. Matthews (Eds.), *Mother/child, father/child relationships* (pp. 177–195). Washington, DC: National Association for the Education of Young Children.

Meyers, C. B., & Blacher, J. (1987). Parent's perceptions of schooling for severely handicapped children: Home and family variables. *Exceptional Children, 53*(5), 441–449.

Minuchin, S. (1974). *Families and family therapy.* Cambridge: Harvard University Press.

Mullings-Franco, P. (1987). *The Urban Black Family.* Paper presented at Reaching Out to Families in a Multicultural Society Conference, Santa Fe, Sponsored by Technical Assistance for Parents Programs and the University of Oregon.

Norton, A. J., & Glick, P. C. (1986). One-parent families: A social and economic profile. *Family Relations, 35*, 9–17.

Ortiz, A. A. (1987). The influence of locus of control and culture on learning styles of language minority students. In J. J. Johnson & B. A. Ramierez (Eds.), *American Indian exceptional children and youth* (pp. 9–16). ERIC Clearinghouse on Handicapped and Gifted Children, Council for Exceptional Children, Reston, VA.

Ortiz, J. M. (1981). Cultural pluralism in the delivery of services to high risk minority children. In V. Weinstein (Ed.), *An ecological model of services to inner city minority handicapped infants* (pp. 17–22). Los Angeles: Charles R. Drew Postgraduate Medical School, Pediatrics Department.

Peterson, N. L., & Meier, J. L. (1987). Assessment and evaluation processes. In Peterson, N. L. (Ed.), *Early intervention for handicapped and at-risk children: An introduction to early childhood–special education* (pp. 275–326). Denver: Love Publishing.

Prutting, C. A., Bayshaw, N., Goldstein, H., Juskowitz, S., & Umen, I. (1978). Clinician–child discourse: Some preliminary questions. *Journal of Speech and Hearing Disorders, 43*, 123–129.

Rees, N. S. (1978). Pragmatics of language: Applications to normal and disordered language development. In R. L. Schiefelbusch (Ed.), *Bases of language intervention.* Baltimore: University Park Press.

Richardson, B. B. (1981). Human service delivery for high risk infants. In V. Weinstein (Ed.), *An ecological model of services to inner city minority handicapped infants* (pp. 12–16). Los Angeles: Charles R. Drew Postgraduate Medical School, Pediatrics Department.

Sailor, W., & Guess, D. (1983). *Severely handicapped students: An instructional design.* Boston: Houghton Mifflin.

Salisbury, C., Vincent, L., & Gorrafa, S. (1987). *Involvement in the educational process: Perceptions of parents and professionals of dual sensory impaired children.* Unpublished manuscript, State University of New York, Binghamton.

Schafer, D. S., Bell, A. P., & Spalding, J. B. (1987). Parental vs. professional assessment of developmentally delayed children after periods of parent training. *Journal of the Division for Early Childhood, 12*, 47–55.

Seibert, J. M., Hogan, A. E., & Mundy, P. C. (1987). Assessing social and communication skills in infancy. *Topics in Early Childhood Special Education, 7*, 38–42.

Shearer, D. (1972). *The Portage guide to early education.* Portage, VI: Cooperative Educational Service Agency No. 12.

Siders, J., Riall, A., Campbell, R., & Crow, R. E. (1987). Gulf coast early intervention conference: Overview. *Topics in Early Childhood Special Education, 7*, 1–5.

Sidman, M. (1960). *Tactics of scientific research.* New York: Basic Books.

Simon, R., & Booth, E. (1987). Paper presented at Reaching Out to Families in a Multicultural Society Conference, Santa Fe, NM. Sponsored by Technical Assistance for Parent Programs and the University of Oregon.

Snell, M. E., & Grigg, N. C. (1987). Instructional assessment and curriculum development. In M. E. Snell (Ed.), *Systematic instruction of persons with severe handicaps* (3rd ed., pp. 64–109). Columbus, OH: Merrill.

Statistics tell the story. (1987). *Isthmus.* Madison, Wi: Madison Newspapers, Inc.

Stile, S. W., Cole, J. T., & Garner, A. Y. (1979). Maximizing parent involvement in programs for exceptional children: Strategies for education and related service personnel. *Journal of the Division for Early Childhood, 1*, 68–82.

Stokes, T. R., & Baer, D. M. (1977). An implicit technology of generalization. *Journal of Applied Behavior Analysis, 10*, 341–367.

Strain, P. (1987). Comprehensive evaluation of intervention for young autistic children. *Topics in Early Childhood Special Education, 7,* 97–110.

Strain, P. S., Kohler, S., & Smith, B. J. (1988). Some questions and answers about single subject design. *Journal of the Division of Early Childhood, 12,* 279–283.

Tafoya, T. (1987). *Native American families.* Paper presented at Reaching Out to Families in a Multicultural Society Conference, Santa Fe, NM. Sponsored by Technical Assistance for Parents Programs and the University of Oregon.

Turnbull, A. P., & Turnbull, H. R. (1986). *Families, professionals and exceptionality: A special partnership.* Columbus, OH: Merrill.

Vandevier, M., & Rodriguez, J. (1987). *Perspectives on Hispanic Cultures.* Paper presented at Reaching Out to Families in a Multicultural Society Conference, Santa Fe, NM Sponsored by Technical Assistance for Parent Programs and the University of Oregon.

Vincent, L. J. (1986). Family relationships. In National Center for Clinical Infant Programs, *Equals in this partnership: Parents of disabled and at-risk infants and toddlers speak to professionals* (pp. 33–41). Washington, DC: Author.

Vincent, L. J., & Salisbury, C. L. (1988). Changing economic and social influences on family involvement. *Topics in Early Childhood Special Education, 8,* 48–59.

Vincent, L. J., Salisbury, C., Walter, C., Brown, P., Gruenewald, J. J., & Powers, M. (1980). Program evaluation and curriculum development in early childhood special education: Criteria of the next environment. In W. Sailor, R. Wilcox, & L. Brown (Eds.) *Methods of instruction for severely handicapped students* (pp. 303–328). Baltimore: P. H. Brookes.

Warren, S., Rogers-Warren, A., Baer, D., & Guess, D. (1980). Assessment and facilitation of language generalization. In W. Sailor, B. Wilcox, & L. Brown (Eds.), *Methods of instruction for severely handicapped students* (pp. 227–258). Baltimore: P. H. Brookes.

Winton, P., & Turnbull, A. P. (1981). Parent involvement as viewed by parents of preschool handicapped children. *Topics in Early Childhood Special Education, 1,* 11–19.

Zeichner, K. M. (1980). Myths and realities: Field-based experiences in preservice teacher education. *Journal of Teacher Education, 31,* 45–50.

9 *Implications of the neurobiological model for early intervention*

NICHOLAS J. ANASTASIOW

INTRODUCTION

Neuropsychology is a field that studies the manner in which psychological processes are based in or arise out of neurological functioning in the central nervous system (CNS), specifically the brain. It is generally assumed that the brain is the location of memory and thinking and that these two major skills of man are stored in the cells of the brain (Greenough, 1978, 1986; Rosensweig, 1984). The major cells of the brain are called nerve cells, or *neurons*; hence, the word *neurology*, the study of the functioning of neurons. Neurons rarely, if ever, act alone, but are joined with other neurons into complex structures called modules.

Neurons communicate with other neurons through taillike structures called *dendrites* and *axons*. At the intersection of each dendrite and axon is a junction called a *synapse*, which serves as the specific site of intercellular communication (see Figure 1). Each neuron can generate many synapses, and thereby establish communication networks with many other neurons. Neurobiologists are interested in how these structures are established, how they function, and if the organization and functioning of these structures is influenced by intrinsic (biological) and/or extrinsic (environmental) factors.

Another name for this field of study is psychobiology. Psychobiologists make the same basic assumption as neuropsychologists, that is, that all of psychological functioning originates in biology. It is currently a widely accepted premise that the CNS develops as a function of both extrinsic and intrinsic factors (Greenough & Juraska, 1986; Scarr, 1982). The transactional or reciprocal nature of genetic-environmental influences has been discussed fully by Sameroff and Fiese (this volume). This chapter will review what is known about the effect of these transactions on the formation of structures within the brain, how these transactions facilitate or negatively influence the course of CNS development, and the genetic-environmental influences on brain behavior (Lerner & Hood, 1986).

One of the major reasons psychologists and educators have become interested in the neurosciences is that information from neuroscience may be directly applicable to understanding child development (Crnic & Pennington, 1987). Further, general prin-

Special thanks to Shirley Cohen, Shaul Harel, and Art Lewis who read and commented on an earlier draft of this chapter.

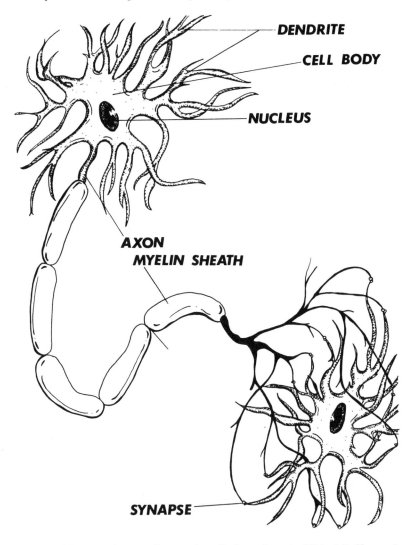

Figure 1. Neuron and neuronal connections (Redrawn by artist Michael P. Hegarty.)

ciples derived from neuroscience, particularly information illuminating the role of extrinsic experiences early in life, as compared to later in life, are important for understanding the development of learning and memory and for arranging environments to facilitate development and/or to provide remediation. More specifically for the reader of this volume, neuroscience can provide information that can assist in remediation and/or amelioration and intervention efforts with children who have disabilities. It can also provide insights concerning the appropriate timing for these interventions.

The basic assumption of the chapter is that the premise of development for healthy infants and children is the same as for children with disabilities. If we can understand this process of development, it can illuminate what may be interfered with by disabling conditions, and programs can be implemented to compensate for the lack of full healthy functioning. In addition, it is important to understand the limitations of the healthy organism during the course of development so as not to identify as impaired those immaturities that are normal. This chapter goes further to speculate about why we observe maturational stages of development and what neuroscience offers us as hypotheses to explain the operation of the CNS as it is correlated with the changes of behavior we note in the organism through the course of maturation.

This chapter will provide a summary of neurological research findings that can help us understand development. The evidence strongly supports the need for environmentally arranged experiences early in the child's life in order to facilitate development as well as to ameliorate risk conditions that are more difficult if not impossible to improve later.

BRAIN DEVELOPMENT

The following section presents an overview of how the brain develops, organizes itself into structures or modules, and how these structures are influenced by and depend upon extrinsic environmental experiences.

As the brain develops, areas within the brain reach their full maturation according to some predetermined biological timing. One major indication of brain area maturation is myelin. *Myelin* is a thin, fatty sheath that covers the long processes of axons, and thereby facilitates more rapid transmissions of impulses. As areas become myelinated, the areas mature and lose some of their plasticity and ability to change their fundamental functioning.

The brain gradually matures during myelinization over a long period of time, extending from before birth to around the age of 33 (Yakovlev & Lecours, 1967; Lecours, 1975). This gradual maturation of the brain is reflected in stages or levels of development. That is, as areas of the brain become myelinated, the individual is able to perform more complex tasks. Stages or levels of development have been documented by developmental psychologists (Piaget, 1971) and by neuropsychologists (Luria, 1973).

More recent evidence offers a link between brain maturation and the individual's increased behavioral competence (Fischer, 1983). Developmental psychologists have studied this link in terms of the question of when environmental learning should occur – before the brain maturation related to the skill in question, or after brain maturation. A tentative answer suggests that there are critical times for sensory development before maturation. The notion of critical periods suggests that experience should occur when the brain is most open (plastic) to the particular experiences, that is, before the area of the brain is myelinated (Goldman, 1976).

Through the course of evolution genes have been programmed to ready the CNS to record and store environmental experiences that are typical of man. Readiness for learning occurs throughout the brain and in all sensory modalities. Those typical experiences of the species (walking, talking, thinking) are called species-specific learnings. Genes also prepare the brain to be able to store unique experiences, that is, novel events that form everyone's personal history. Experiences once stored in neurons and communicated through synapses ensure the synapses' survival; unused synapses fade through a process known as cell death.

The brain goes through three major periods of development (Greenough & Green,

1981). The initial stage is one of relatively rapid change in which the brain is very receptive to extrinsic environmental experiences. This openness to storing experience coincides with the prenatal, perinatal, and early childhood stages of life. The changes that occur in the brain during this period are a normal and typical part of the organism's life (Lynch & Gall, 1979). By documenting the impact of extrinsic factors on brain structure during this first period of brain plasticity, strong research support can be marshaled for early intervention with handicapped children, a point that will be elaborated in later sections of this chapter.

The second period of brain development is the adult stage (Greenough & Green, 1981). The brain retains its ability to acquire and store new information, but with some limitations. The adult brain is relatively stable, and its ability to acquire new information appears in areas where expertise has already been established. For example, it is more likely that an adult who has acquired musical skills will persist and add to these skills throughout adulthood. However, it is unlikely that an adult who has not developed these skills in childhood will develop the same level of expertise as that of an early learner. The adult brain retains some plasticity, but not as much as during the first stage.

The third period of brain development concerns that of the aging brain (Greenough & Green, 1981). The aging brain retains limited plasticity; new information is likely to be gained only in areas where skills have been established previously. Although adults can demonstrate broad changes in response to environmental learning, these changes are more circumscribed in the aging brain (see also Cotman & Nieto-Sampedro, 1982). That is, the young brain is capable of massive learning in many areas, the adult brain less so, and the aging brain even less so.

It is important to understand that the sensory systems become established and fully mature during the young brain period. Experiences that enhance and are necessary for sensory development should occur during an early period of brain growth if the sensory systems are to function optimally as the gatherers of environmental information.

The anatomical and physiological changes in the brain that are reflected in behavior are the result of genetically programmed readiness in the brain to be receptive to self-generated extrinsic experience as well as to the training that the organism receives (Greenough & Juraska, 1986; Wittrock, 1986). As stated earlier, neuronal functioning is the basic level of operation of the brain, accounting for information storage and retrieval. During the embryonic formation of the brain, cellular multiplication of neurons, neural differentiation, and interneuronal connections are made. These are genetically programmed, species-specific structures that prepare the basic organization of the brain for the typical social culture, or niche, man occupies (Barnes, 1986; Gottlieb, 1983; Lerner, 1986).

The brain's basic organization is that of modules of neuronal connections, organized horizontally in complex systems (Fodor, 1983). Each of these modules, or areas of specialization, represents a perceptual system (visual, haptic, olfactory, gustatory) or an affective, cognitive, or linguistic system. The chemistry of these operations is being uncovered gradually, revealing a complex action of hormones and enzymes (see Panksepp, 1986, for a complete discussion).

Recall that neurons are connected to other neurons through cell structures called axons and dendrites (Greenough, 1975, 1986), and their junction is a structure called the synapse. It is across this synaptic space that neurons communicate with other neurons. A single neuron may have 100 to 1,000 synaptic connections to other neurons; in the adult brain there may be a quadrillion connections among neurons (Lerner,

1986). Early synaptic connection among neurons appears to be genetically programmed, with three-fourths of the total brain development occurring in the postnatal period (Prechtl, 1986). Shortly after birth, at 2–3 months of age, there is a rapid proliferation of synapses. These are called *experience-expectant* synapses (Greenough & Juraska, 1986). The proliferation of neural connections proceeds rapidly from 2 to 3 months to the second year of life in all areas of the brain (Rakic, Bourgeois, Echenhoff, Zecevic, & Goldman-Rakic, 1986). The synapses are programmed to be ready to receive experiences that are related to the species and that aid in adaptation (Greenough & Chang, 1985; Will, Schmitt, Dalympe, & Alford, 1986).

Experience-expectant synapses are developed in all sensory systems, for example, those in the visual area are ready to respond to light, and those in the motor area to motor events. Environmental experience causes the neurons to be activated, and neural activity tends to stabilize and make persistent synaptic connections (Fish, Mooney, & Rhoades, 1985). Following their stabilization, there is death of the unused, over-produced synapses (Chalupa & Williams, 1985; Hamburger & Oppenheim, 1982). This elimination process is called *pruning*.

Synapse stabilization is most vulnerable to environmental experiences during critical periods in development. (Critical periods will be discussed later in the chapter.) The retention of the genetically programmed experience-expectant synapses occurs during the first brain development period. These synapses store experience from the environment or become involved in neural structures that develop into functioning brain structures such as the visual system. The retention of synapses is directly related to the evolutionary adaptational function that the extrinsic experience adds to the organism's survival (Greenough & Juraska, 1986). As Greenough and Juraska (1986) point out, the information the organism receives must be correct. Incorrect information can be learned as well as correct information, which may irreversibly damage the expected or normal range of behavior of the organism (see the next section for a discussion of this point).

The second group of synapses are called *experience-dependent* synapses (Greenough & Juraska, 1986). These connections are not programmed by genes, but develop independently as a result of "unique" environmental experiences that occur to the individual in the environment. The experience-dependent synapses are hypothesized to be produced throughout life as long as the structures in which they develop retain some degree of plasticity. Experience-dependent synapses can also be generated as a result of insult to the brain (Hamburger & Oppenheim, 1982). Animals that have received surgically induced lesions tend to produce synaptic connections rapidly as a result of the lesion (this point is discussed more fully in the next section).

In summary, two systems that are of interest for intervention appear to operate in the construction of CNS structures. One is the rapid proliferation of synaptic connections readying the organism for species-specific, highly likely experiences. These are referred to as experience-expectant connections, or a readiness for experiences that have occurred in the history of the species. The second system of interest is the experience-dependent synaptic connections that can be generated as the individual receives novel experiences or training.

Humans have evolved to the point that genes roughly outline the pattern of neural connections, leaving the more specific details to be determined by the organism in interaction with the environment (Greenough, Black, & Wallace, 1987). Just how the environment fulfills this role will be discussed next.

Table 1. *Levels of development*

Brain maturation (Epstein, 1974; Lecours, 1975; Luria, 1973)	Piaget (1971)	Fischer (1980)
0–2 months	Sensorimotor Substage 1	First tier: single sensory
2–3 months	Substage 2 Substage 3	
7–9 months	Substage 4 Substage 5	Sensory
18–24 months	Substage 6 Preoperational	Sensory motor systems
4 years		Second tier: representational systems
5–7 years	Concrete operations	Representational mapping
9–11 years	Abstract reasoning	Systems of representations
14–15 years		Third tier: abstract mapping
22 years		Abstract systems
33 years		Systems of abstract systems

EXPERIENCE AND DEVELOPMENT

Research has shown that the human CNS develops in a series of stages, and that it is heavily influenced by the nature of the experience that is encountered, the manner in which the organism has experiences, and the time in the organism's development when the experience occurs. Evidence suggests that human learning is neither solely dependent on reinforcement nor on problem solving, but requires a combination of both, each complementing the other (Lerner, 1986).

Stages or levels of development have been documented by the course of myelinization and *arborization* (branch formation) of the brain from autopsy data (Epstein, 1974a, 1974b), differences in EEG brain patterns, sleep patterns, wake behavioral patterns (Emde, Gaensbauer, & Harmon, 1976), cultural observation and learning research (White, 1966), and more recently by positron emission tomography (PET) (Chugani & Phelps, 1986). Based on these data and others, Fischer (1980) has proposed a three-tier level of brain development. A summary of Fischer's model and the brain period data from other investigators are presented in Table 1.

Note that the brain maturation periods documented by Lecours (1975), Luria (1973), and Epstein (1974a, 1974b), closely match those of Piaget (1971) and Fischer (1980). There appears to be a gradual maturation of the brain, with each level of maturation displaying new competencies of the organism. The transitions signal higher levels of the organism's development and appear to be somewhat age dependent and biologically preprogrammed.

Fischer (1983), in a series of studies with his colleagues, has demonstrated stagelike progression of social development (Fischer, Pipp, & Bulloch, 1984), language development (Fischer & Corrigan, 1981), and cognitive development (Fischer & Bulloch, 1981). It is likely that the increasing abilities or skills of the individual over time, which we refer to as maturation, are essentially a transaction of genetically programmed responses to extrinsic events that display increasing hierarchical development as the areas of the brain become myelinated.

Timing of experience

The stages of brain development appear to be optimal times for certain types of learning (Gottlieb, 1983; Scott, 1978). That is, during a particular stage of development some experiences are of critical importance for the development of neural structures. An example of this is exposure to patterned light in the development of vision. If the appropriate experiences are not available, the structures may not be established, even after intense and dramatic intervention efforts (Rutter, 1981). For sensory systems the optimal time or critical period for development appears to be early in life (Greenough et al., 1987).

This may be clarified by research conducted with kittens (Grouse, Schrier, & Nelson, 1979; Hubel & Wiesel, 1970). In the first 8 weeks of life the visual system is very open (plastic) and is ready to respond to and develop visual structures in environments of patterned light. Kittens deprived of light during the first 8 weeks of life act as if they are blind, although their visual systems are normal. The presence of extrinsically provided light and shadows appears to be critical for the development of sight. Without this experience the neurons in the visual area apparently fail to transmit to other brain structures the visual information they receive (Blake & Hirsch, 1975).

Further, animals raised in low light conditions tend to develop structures that are viewed as abnormal, and if not corrected in the open, plastic period, may be irreversible (Greenough et al., 1987). Irreversibility arises due to the effect of the abnormal visual experience influencing the pattern of organization of synapses in the visual system. The principle at work apparently is that experience is recorded in species-specific expected ways (seeing) or in species-specific unexpected ways – squinting or acting as if one were blind. Following the plastic period of development, the synapses that could have been used to establish normal vision will have been lost.

Recent work with kittens deprived of light during the first 8 weeks shows that sight can be "restored" by the infusion of nonadrenalin (norepinephrine) into the visual cortex (Bateson, 1983). Thus, nonadrenalin serves a permissive role and may alter environmental deprivations by reestablishing plasticity. However, to maximize the probability of healthy functioning, experience should occur during the optimal developmental periods. For man, although the period of time for experience modification of brain structure is more extended, it is nevertheless circumscribed.

This phenomenon has been replicated with the human visual system. The first 4 years of life for humans appear to be the critical period for the development of the visual system, as documented with research on strabismis, a visual defect in which one eye cannot focus with the other due to an imbalance in the eye muscles. Humans with the disorder of strabismis typically have the disorder corrected before the age of five. Following that time it is very difficult to do so. Uncorrected strabismis has a negative effect on the organization of the visual system (Aslin, 1981). It appears that to maximize the probability of healthy sensory functioning, experience should occur during this early period. Intervention to facilitate sensory functioning for children with disabilities is most appropriate early in life when the CNS is being organized and when there are fewer constraints on its ability to change (Lerner, 1986). (Following Bornstein [1987], critical periods and sensitive periods are used synonymously in this discussion.)

As noted, the critical period for the development of vision in kittens appears to be the first 8 weeks of life, and in humans the first 4 years. Critical periods appear to be determined by the genetically programmed release of neurotransmitters (Greenough & Juraska, 1986). To Aslin (1981), critical periods are times in the organism's life when the phenotype is open to particular experiences. Some critical periods cover a broad time period and others a limited time period. One indication of a critical period is the appearance of a fixed-action pattern. Fixed-action patterns are coordinated sequences of responses that are cued by environmental stimulation (Gollin, 1981). Once the pattern is initiated and cued, the developed structure operates without further dependence on cueing. Fixed-action patterns of fowl following behavior (Lorenz, 1971) and of birds learning species-specific songs (Marler, 1961) have been well established. In humans, fixed-action patterns are referred to as fixed-behavior patterns and include reflexes, emotions, and emotional facial expressions (Ekman, 1980). For example, the sucking response usually appears at birth and will operate without prior learning when the infant is presented with the breast. The sucking response will continue to operate once initiated.

The social smile appears as a fixed-behavior pattern at around 2 to 3 months, and cued by a return smile, will remain. For the visually impaired infant, the smile may not persist unless cued by haptic stimulation (Fraiberg, 1977). Thus, some types of expected experiences may be largely dependent on the infant's ability to produce a stimulus (smile) that initiates a complementary stimulus in return (the adult smile) (Greenough et al., 1987).

In summary, the appearance of fixed-behavior patterns signal the organism's readiness for certain types of learning. In infancy, the fixed-action patterns we call reflexes are well known. Other fixed behavior patterns are being discovered, for example, the social smile at 2 to 3 months, the appearance of the first languagelike sound (cooing, comfort noises at 2–3 months), the facial expressions of anger, disgust, and joy in the first 7 months, the appearance of the social No at 18–20 months. These patterns are an indication of the organism's readiness for certain kinds of learning. The social smile clearly is involved in the formation of the attachment system, as is cooing with the development of language. These patterns offer a rich source of speculation concerning other periods documented by Fischer (see Table 1) and can be used to guide our intervention efforts. This point will be developed more fully in the final section.

BRAIN STRUCTURES AND THE NATURE OF EXPERIENCE

To this point we have seen that the CNS is prepared to receive species-specific expectant experiences, that there are critical times for experiences to occur, that these time periods are rather broad for humans, but that experiences early in life lay the foundation for normal sensory functioning. These assumptions have been documented by research with animals that clarifies how experience has direct impact on brain structures. These studies will be reviewed briefly.

In such animals as the cat, major advances have been made in understanding the exact nature of the impact of experience, lack of experience, and abnormal experience (Chalupa, & Williams, 1985). The impact of extrinsic experience has been demonstrated in other species, including the rhesus monkey, opossum, hamster, rat, ferret, chicken (Chalupa, & Williams, 1985), and even the fly, whose discriminations depend on experiences of light (Mimura, 1986).

The research strategy that typically has been employed to explore the impact of extrinsic experience on brain structure, particularly the formation or maintenance of synaptic connections, involves three environmental conditions: one that is deprived or isolated, one that is normal, and one that is enriched. For the rat, recent experiments have involved three groups of animals from the same litter. The first group consists of animals raised in isolation in single cages. The second group, the social group, contains animals raised with other animals. In the third group, the animals are raised in social groups and allowed to explore a room with reactive objects once a day. Reactive objects are ones that roll, swing, or in some manner respond when touched. The results have been summarized by several authors (Anastasiow, 1986a, 1986b; Greenough & Juraska, 1986; Rosensweig, 1984).

The typical outcome, demonstrated in replicated experiments, is that rats allowed to explore and discover properties of objects developed both brain structures and behavior skills that were absent in the other rats. The effects were significantly different when a rat from the enriched environment was compared with a socially raised rat, but were even stronger when the comparison was between an animal from the enriched environment and an isolated rat.

Those animals that were reared in an enriched environment, as opposed to isolation, had increased brain weight largely due to the development of an increased complexity of neuronal development including more dendritic treeing and synaptic connections. They possessed a higher number of neurological formations and branching to other neurons. In addition, the synapses were larger in size. Behaviorally, these animals learned to solve problems faster, and had better sleep patterns and healthier appetites. Further, chemical restoration of brain function after high levels of activity was quicker. That is, the CNS chemical balance in the environmentally enriched animals was more conducive to healthy functioning.

In addition, isolated animals demonstrated avoidance and low exploratory behavior, poor sleep patterns, and abnormal play and sexual behavior. Such deviant patterns appear to be difficult to reverse once established. When comparisons were made between animals reared in complex environments and animals housed in overcrowded conditions, it was found that the overcrowded animals demonstrated physiological and behavioral signs of stress, higher adrenal weight, higher pituitary weight, reduced stamina, reduced reproductive capacity, and bizarre behavior patterns. The conclusion is that species-specific normal behavior is obtained through optimal stimulation rather than through too little (isolation) or too much (overcrowding) stimulation.

Note, however, that an enriched environment does not imply training. In the enriched experience condition, the animal acted on the environment through its own species-determined exploratory activity. In humans this exploratory activity is called play. Training has an impact on brain structure, but less so than self-directed exploration (Greenough, 1978).

Two additional findings from animal research have direct implications for early intervention. First, the effects on the brain structures of environmental experiences are greater in young animals than in older ones (Greenough, 1978). Although some effects can be demonstrated in older animals, there is less plasticity, hence the effects are more limited. Second, animals that have received surgically induced lesions in the brain recover faster when placed in an enriched environment following surgery (Hamburger & Oppenheim, 1982). The animals in the enriched environment produced synaptic connections rapidly, and these connections in the areas immediately adjacent to the trauma serve in the recovery. The animals housed in enriched environments not only recovered faster then nonenriched ones. If their brains were examined later in life, it was found that the spread of the damage due to the surgery was less.

Evidently, the environment not only influences the formation of brain structure, but plays a role in recovery of function following insult, as has been shown recently in research on aging. Meaney, Aitken, Van Berkel, Bhatnager, and Salopsky (1988) demonstrated that handling neonatal rats daily from date of birth to weaning increased receptors in the hippocampus. These receptors, related to the positive management of stress, remained throughout life in the handled rats. Further, the handled rats experienced reduced effects of aging and had greater spatial memory ability than the non-handled rats. The authors suggests that "the relatively subtle early experience can alter profoundly the quality of aging years later" (p. 768).

Our knowledge of the formation of deviant structures is derived largely from studies of the cat's visual system, as reported earlier. However, the application of that knowledge to the potential for remediation of deviant sensory development as in strabismis is well known. One can speculate that deviant and maladaptive personality development, other than those syndromes that are genetically caused, arise out of abnormal environmental experiences. This premise has received support from studies of children's insecure and anxious attachment in the presence of severe environmental insults as seen in behavioral disorders at school age (Sroufe & Rutter, 1984). Much of childhood psychopathology arises from environmentally induced responses to nonfacilitating caregiver-child interactions, particularly the abusing, ignoring, or overindulgent parent (Axelrad & Brody, 1978). This point will be expanded in the last section.

In the next section, elements of what is known about CNS development and evidence from child development studies will be examined and interwoven to generate statements that can guide programs for children with known sensory impairments and children who are at risk for developmental delays.

EARLY EXPERIENCE AND THE HUMAN INFANT

As Trevarthen and his colleagues state, "contemporary knowledge of the state of the human brain at birth and how networks are formed remove doubts that infants could be born with elaborate foundations for mental activity of all kinds and that in the first three months of life the perceptual ability of infants is predominantly tuned to detect the action of persons and to interpret their experiences as having emotional value" (Trevarthen, 1983, p. 181). They note that there is currently strong neurological data to support this assumption. Other research shows that infants are competent learners and learn from pleasant and unpleasant events presented in the environment (Lipsitt, 1979). These early learnings of infants have an impact on the organization of the brain in the same manner as we have seen in animal research (Greenough & Juraska, 1986). The infant's activity in experiencing the environment in turn stabilizes the experience-expectant synapses and facilitates normal development. Infants are intrinsically motivated to explore and manipulate objects in their environment, and hence participate in their own development by such activities (Papousek & Papousek, 1983). Infant and child play is the natural mode of human learning and appears to be genetically initiated (Lerner, 1986). For humans, acquiring new knowledge is in itself reinforcing (Wittrock, 1986).

The caregiver who organizes the infant's life space by structuring feeding, sleeping, and waking patterns assists in the maturation of the infant as well as in establishing in the infant a preference and orientation to the caregiving figure (Lipsitt, 1979). Lack of such organizing features results in adaptive problems in an otherwise healthy infant (Hofer, 1981; Prechtl, 1981).

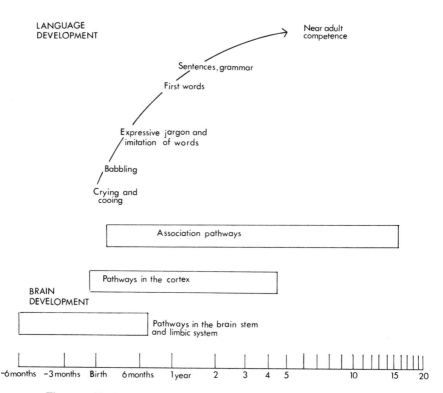

Figure 2. Myelogenetic cycles in the brain and the development of language (From *Human Development* by Kurt W. Fischer and Arlyne Lazenson. Copyright 1984. Reprinted with the permission of W. H. Freeman and Company. Redrawn by artist Michael P. Hegarty.)

A synthesis: Language development

In order to synthesize what has been presented, let us examine language learning. As Simon (1986) suggests, it is possible to build a macro theory without knowing all of the details of the underlying micro theory. What follows is a hypothesized macro theory of language development. Underlying or innate neurological function has been suggested by scientists from many different disciplines as a basis for language learning (Fischer & Pipp, 1984; Lecours, 1975; Lennenberg, 1967).

Fischer (1983) has displayed these transactions elegantly (see Figure 2). Note that as the myelination of the sensory tract matures and the connections in the brain are made, an individual's language development acquires more advanced and abstract forms. Recall that full myelin maturation for most areas of the brain is usually the last phase of development. Fischer's diagram presents the transactional course of language development. These biologically derived processes can be assumed to operate in impaired children as well as healthy children.

Gleitman (1986) concludes that language development is biologically programmed, although it can be modulated by experiences. That is, one can say that the capacity to learn language is genetically determined by synaptic connections and requires experiences during the early period of brain development for language learning to occur (Chall & Peterson, 1986). The rapidity with which humans learn language might well be accounted for by the preprogramming that occurs in synaptic expectant proliferation. As language is learned, these connections become stabilized. Once the language system is established, it remains open (plastic or flexible) throughout life with the ability to establish new synaptic connections to store new learning through language. These two methods of synaptic generation increase the brain's modifiability as cultures change. It allows the infant to learn any language of the world, provided that the infant experiences that language; and it allows the individual, once having learned a language system, to enlarge upon that knowledge and to enlarge the system. Gleitman (1986) perceives many of the features of language learning as a consequence of the innate biological structure of language. In essence, language development is a product of the transaction of cultural and genetic factors. One learns the language of one's culture in a genetically programmed universal sequence of stages, beginning with differentiated sound production at 2–3 months (Bloom & Lahey, 1978; Eimas & Tartles, 1979; Eimas, Siqueland, Juscyle, & Visorito, 1971) and culminating in the production of the first culturally relevant word at around 12 months of age. It is interesting to note that children initially learn language at relatively the same rate in homes where there have been very different amounts of language presented by the caregiver. This fact strongly suggests a biological base for the early stages of language development.

Children with sensory deficits such as visual or hearing impairments progress through the same genetically programmed production (Schiefelbusch, Sullivan, & Ganz, 1980). However, in the absence of hearing the production of culturally relevant sounds, hearing-impaired infants may not produce their first word unless their sound capacity is amplified. We know that the auditory tract begins to function around 7 months gestational age, and is myelinated in a series of stages at 7–9 months postnatally until 4 years of age (Lecours, 1975). According to Aslin (1981), the slow maturation of the auditory tract presents a wide critical period in which the neurological system is plastic and can profit from extended environmental experience. During this extended period of plasticity one finds that most of the basic sound-production elements of phonology and the structured elements of syntax are mastered (Anastasiow, 1986a, 1986b; Brainerd, 1983).

Gleitman (1986) points out that untrained deaf children will create their own unique signs for objects at the same time that normal hearing children speak their first word. Thus, in the absence of external input, the genetic program appears to propel the auditorally impaired child to create a symbol for an object. However, at the time that hearing children (around age two) are adding crucial closed classed words (e.g., in, on, the, and, etc.) to their production, the untrained hearing-impaired child does not create them. Closed class words seem to be environmentally provided, and the critical time for learning them appears to be about 2 years of age, the time Horton (1974) and Northcott (1981) suggest is the critical time at the latest for intervention with such children. Apparently genes require that oral language be provided to assist in the development of a language system. If language input is not provided by age five the child probably will not learn to speak (Lennenberg, 1967). If an alternative system such as American Sign Language is introduced, it can serve the same communicative function and should be introduced at the same age as oral language.

Across cultures children learn the names of things at about the same time (7–9 months) and will say the name for the object shortly thereafter. What is required is a person in the environment who provides the culturally appropriate sound patterns or word. In the absence of auditory capacity, the sound pattern equivalent can be provided by a sign. If the word or sign is not provided, children may make up a word for the object (Nelson, 1974). If words are not provided over an extended period of time, children will demonstrate anger or frustration and may eventually display withdrawn behavior.

It appears that humans are genetically programed to learn words and to produce them, and when frustrated in their attempts, they demonstrate behaviors that are considered inappropriate. The timing of learning is biologically determined. The conditions of learning are a caregiver responding to an infant's request for the culturally appropriate word. The child will learn about the object and its name through both behavioral (associated learning, stimulus–response connections) and cognitive (problem solving) techniques (Hirsh, 1974; Hull, 1920, Wittrock, 1986).

The rapid increase in communication output is genetically determined. What gets stored during the period of rapid learning is that which the culture, in this case the home environment, reinforces. The capacity of humans to hear the sounds of their culture begins before birth and continues with a very open system until approximately 5 years of age, when some of the plasticity of the system is lessened and children begin to filter out some culturally irrelevant sounds (Berlyne, 1965). However, if the system has been well developed, it retains great plasticity for culturally relevant language information and, with training, the child can learn new language sounds between the ages of from 5 to 7 and 15 years. More advanced language skills continue through life. For some disorders of language learning, the problem resides in the failure of the genetically laid out pattern to proceed according to plan. Other disorders may be acquired due to environmental inadequacies. In many cases, it is a combination of both. In the next section we will consider the importance of these findings for early interventionists.

EVIDENCE AND SPECULATIONS FOR EARLY INTERVENTION WITH
SPECIAL NEEDS CHILDREN

Data are available that demonstrate that child-rearing practices have an impact on the intellectual, social, and emotional development of healthy full-term and preterm infants, as well as on infants who sustained perinatal complications (Beckwith, this volume; Beckwith & Cohen, 1984; Broman, Nichols, & Kennedy, 1975; Sameroff & Fiese, this volume; Werner & Smith, 1982). The home environment is a strong predictor of outcome for many infants. The question asked here is: Are there data that directly relate these global findings to the neurological events previously described, most of which are based on data derived from animal research? The answer is that although there are few direct connections, there are some supportive data. The clearest support comes from Beckwith and Parmelee (1986), who studied the electro-encephalogram (EEG) patterns of 53 preterm infants in order to measure their level of maturity and integrity of neurophysiological function. They followed the preterm infants longitudinally, measuring caregiver–infant interactions in the home environment and various physiological and intellectual variables at standard periods of time until age eight. The major finding was that children with integrative and with nonintegrative EEG patterns did better in homes that consistently provided an attentive and responsive environment. Infants with nonintegrative (poor-state) EEG patterns who were raised in responsive homes, not only had significantly higher IQs than the poor-state infants raised in less responsive homes, their IQ as a group was as high as the well integrated preterms raised in responsive homes (IQs were 117 and 118, respectively). Beckwith and Parmelee report that their findings are "the first to show the buffering effect of family environment in ameliorating early risk factors expressed in brain activity in young infants" (p. 787).

Computer tomography and ultrasonography have made it possible to identify brain hemorrhages of various types, including intraventricular hemorrhage. Children with the most severe form of hemorrhage may not survive, and if they do they may have serious neurological problems. However, with milder hemorrhages, Beckwith and Parmelee (1986) report that many of these children appear to function well later in life if they have been raised in responsive and supportive environments.

Meisels and Plunkett (1988) present similar findings. That is, most early risk factors tend to be ameliorated by facilitative environments. They report, however, that a significant difference may be found in perceptual performance patterns at school age with preterms who are of low birth weight who have sustained risk factors such as intraventricular hemorrhage, chronic respiratory illness, and sepsis. These additional risk factors may account for long-term negative effects. They also report a significantly different pattern of attachment among the sick premature infants that they studied.

Meisels and Plunkett (1988) point out that very small and very sick preterm children who have been studied to ages five through eight have perceptual and intellectual problems usually associated with learning disabilities. They suggest that very low birth weight premature infants are at risk for several neurological impairments stemming from reduced diffusion of oxygen and blood flow leading to intracranial hemorrhage and/or to lesions associated with periventricular leukomalacia (PVL). PVL has been linked to cerebral palsy, and Meisels and Plunkett suggest that it may be related to some of the long-term cognitive effects that have been observed.

Low birth weight infants have been studied extensively, particularly infants whose survival depends on the facilities of a neonatal intensive care unit (NICU) (Gustaitis & Young, 1986). Field et al. (1986) found that tactile-kinesthetic (massage) stimulation of preterm infants in the NICU for 15 minutes, three times per day just before feeding over a 10-day period, resulted in higher survival rates, greater weight gain, and higher Brazelton scores than nonstimulated preterms. Note that the stimulation was a mild massage. Field (1983) and Als et al. (1986) have also shown that teaching parents to modify their stimulation by becoming less active with their preterms results in preterms who make positive gains in health and cognition. In addition, the parents became more alert to their infants' cues and were less stress-inducing in their interactions. Similarly, Turkewitz and Kenny (1985) cautioned that the timing of functional onset of perceptual systems in relation to other systems is critically important, and that a "little" stimulation may be "over" stimulation to the premature infant. In a review of animal research, they suggest that overstimulation of one sensory system prematurely (before typical onset of neural functioning) may cause it to act as if the animal is deprived or handicapped. Two functions occur during deprivation: (1) affected neural tissue that would serve an intact modality is reorganized and its functioning capacity increased, and (2) neural tissue normally used for processing is reallocated to a different modality.

Although little data from humans are available, the animal data are so strong that Turkewitz and Kenny suggest extreme caution be observed in providing stimulation to premature infants. In a commentary on the Turkewitz and Kenny article, Parmelee

(1985) agrees, noting that "The developmental changes in the brain between 26 and 40 weeks conceptual age are great. The immature brain may be more vulnerable to disorganization through exposure to excessive and inappropriate sensory stimulants in the NICU. The immature infant's general biological homeostatic mechanism is easily overwhelmed by almost any extra stimulation and the sicker the infant, the more likely this is" (p. 242).

Parmelee suggests that it be mandatory to attempt to protect the premature infant's sleep state and to provide a controlled interactive stimulation of face, voice, and touch when the infant is awake and interactive. These periods of awake interactive states in the premature infant are extremely limited, therefore, Parmelee's suggestions are for control of stimulation rather than provision of high levels of stimulation.

Thus, the current conclusion is that social stimulation should begin when the infant reaches 2 to 3 months of age for the full-term baby and at an age-equivalent stage for the premature infant (Huttenlocker, 1984). Medical intervention would of course begin at birth, as it would, for example, with hypothyroidism (abnormal thyroid functioning), which if untreated will result in the failure of myelinization in areas of the brain related to cognition (Trimeras, 1982), and retardation previously known as cretinism. Medical treatment for hypothyroidism beginning at birth and continued throughout life can prevent the retardation. In other cases we can only surmise about effects, since brain observational data are very limited.

It is well known that in children with Down syndrome, the course and timing of development, while slower, is very important. In addition, there is evidence that cell death of synaptic elimination may not occur as in the normally developing child (Huttenlocker, 1979). Thus, the child with Down syndrome may have too many synaptic connections rather than too few. Given the evidence that experience stimulates synaptic connection survival and elimination, the impact of early intervention programs for children with Down syndrome may have an impact on synaptic stabilization and elimination, because we know that early intervention leads to higher cognitive functioning in the child with Down syndrome (Guralnick & Bricker, 1987).

Given the rapid proliferation and overproduction of experience-expectant synapses in all areas of the brain, it can be hypothesized that this open plastic period is the underlying neurological reason for the beneficial impact of responsive environments and interventions in the early years of life. Few actual data are available to show the impact of experience on synaptic formulation. However, Purpura (1983) has demonstrated that very young infants who were in an NICU and died shortly after birth from health-related reasons had growth on at least 20 axons, whereas infants who did not experience the NICU and died from similar health problems of the lungs or heart had no such growth.

Another speculation can be derived from the knowledge of the course of myelination of the motor tract. The motor tract matures early in life and controls the behaviors related to many of the reflexes. This early maturation may be related to the belief held by physical therapists that atypical and abnormal motor patterns must be corrected as early in life as possible (Masi, 1979). The data concerning intervention effects on physically disabled children are not clear, because it is hard to find a large population of children with a single disability. However, Bricker (1985), Greenspan and White (1985), and Shonkoff and Hauser-Cram (1987) in their reviews of the intervention research conclude that programs for the physically disabled have helped to improve the functioning of these children in a wide variety of skill areas, particularly when the programs have been multidisciplinary and have been initiated early.

The data on myelinization of the visual tract indicate t̶
between 2–3 months and 7–9 months (Lecours, 1975). Fr̶
lack of visual stimulation during this period appeared to be̶
of abnormal behavior patterns and autistic-like behaviors. S̶
a rich program of haptic stimulation during this period ̶
appear. A hypothesis that seeks to explain these findings ̶
(myelinated) haptic system developed structures in lieu ̶
functioning structures may have prevented the developme̶

The success of programs for the hearing impaired beg̶
2 years of age might be explained by examining the course of myelinization in the auditory tract. The auditory system at 7–9 months is equivalently mature to the visual system at 2–3 months (Lecours, 1975). The auditory system at 4–5 years is as mature as the visual system was at 7–9 months. Thus, while the visual system and motor systems mature rapidly and provide major modes of learning (motor play and visual exploration), the auditory system has a longer period of plasticity that allows for the mastery of the language system. The recent success of treating stuttering at age three (when it usually begins) and particularly before the age of six (Curley & Perkins, 1984) may be related to the openness of the system at three and the closing off of its plastic nature by the full maturation of the auditory tract between 4 and 5 years of age.

The overwhelming documentation of the impact of the responsive and supportive social environment (home or intervention program) as not only facilitating normal development but also ameliorating a range of at-risk status, causes one to suspect that evolution expects a responsive supportive environment to fulfill its genetic role and to provide the environment in which the organism can experience health (Brazelton, 1986). When responsive supportive environments are not provided, abnormal patterns are established. Recall that experience will be recorded whether it is expected or deviant. The formation of the attachment system and its long-term correlates allows us to speculate on how this might be related in humans.

Attachment is the basic love system that is established between infants and their caregivers, usually the biological mother. Infants raised in responsive homes develop secure attachments that are predictive of social adjustment and positive personality variables at school age (Sroufe & Rutter, 1982). Children raised in less responsive, overindulgent, or punitive homes may develop attachment patterns that are related to a range of personality patterns that are viewed as maladaptive, and in some cases pathological (Sroufe & Rutter, 1982).

The self-system, which develops out of attachment transactions, does so in culturally perceived positive ways when the environment provides neither abusive nor indulgent settings (Anastasiow, 1986a, 1986b). One can surmise that the neurological structures that are built during this period become relatively stable and provide the continuity that we perceive in human personality development: Although a person changes, he or she remains the same (Emde, 1983).

CONCLUSION

Although any conclusions should be interpreted cautiously, the neurological data give strong support to the suggestion that the environment provides the input needed to complete the development of the sensory systems. In turn, these systems become the avenues for extracting information from the environment, which subsequently becomes the content stored in memory. Responsive environments facilitate these processes

...ive ones impede development, leading to traits considered culturally

...ods of rapid and open brain development for species-specific learning during ...period of brain growth suggest how the environment can fulfill its role in the ...opment of neural structures. As we have seen, structures will develop regardless of ...type of experience. Normality for humans appears to require an environment that is moderately interactive with the infant or child, providing psychological warmth, low physical punishment, and a push or encouragement to develop in culturally relevant ways (Werner & Smith, 1982). When sensory impairments exist, mild risk states can be remediated without much negative residue if intervention is begun early in life. More severe conditions will call for different efforts, but still require the supportive, responsive environment as a base on which therapies or treatments can be provided.

In some cases, severely handicapped children can be helped to function more normally at school age (McNulty, Soper, & Smith, 1984). Multihandicapped conditions may be extremely difficult to have an impact on, but evidence suggests that persistent efforts do lead to improvements. Sometimes changes are dramatic, although most often only a small increment of functioning is achieved (Bricker, 1985).

The genetic program is set at conception, but shows amazing flexibility in how it will respond to damage if treated. Consider the Sturge-Weber syndrome (Denis, 1982). In some cases of this syndrome one hemisphere of the brain is diseased and life threatening, and must be removed. When the diseased hemisphere is removed during the first 4 months of life, the remaining hemisphere will develop the skills normally developed in the two hemispheres. That is, traits that were typically developed in the hemisphere that was removed are not lost, but appear in the remaining hemisphere. This activity displays a remarkable capacity of neural cells both to fulfill and to adapt to circumstances, and to change their predetermined function.

The success of early intervention programs with sensory-impaired, disabled, and at-risk infants and young children is very likely related to the phenomena described in the Sturge-Weber syndrome, the Fraiberg studies, and the studies of hearing-impaired children. That is, neural tissue can respond to damage not only by creating new synapses to aid in recovery of function, but by changing the nature of their preprogrammed function to facilitate healthy functioning. Future neurological research will verify the accuracy of this hypothesis, or may suggest that something else is at the core of early intervention.

REFERENCES

Als, H., Lawhon, G., Brown, E., Gibes, R., Duffy, F. H., McAnulty, G., & Blickman, J. G. (1986). Individualized behavioral and environmental care for the very low preterm infant at high risk for bronchopulmonary dysplasia: Neonatal intensive care unit and developmental outcome. *Pediatrics, 78,* 1123–1132.

Anastasiow, N. J. (1986a). *Development and disability: A psychobiological analysis for special educators.* Baltimore: P. H. Brookes.

Anastasiow, N. J. (1986b) The case for early experience. In D. Tamir, A. Russell, & T. B. Brazelton (Eds.), *Intervention and stimulation in infant development* (pp. 1–16). Tel Aviv: Freund Publishers.

Aslin, R. N. (1981). Experimental influence and sensitive period in perceptual development: A unified model. In R. N. Aslin & F. Peterson (Eds.), *The development of perception* (Vol. 2, pp. 45–93). Orlando: Academic Press.

Axelrad, S., & Brody, S. (1978). *Mothers, fathers, children.* New York: International Universities Press.

Barnes, D. (1986). Brain architecture: Beyond genes. *Science, 233,* 155–156.

Bateson, P. (1983). The interpretation of sensitive periods. In A. Oliverio & M. Zappallin (Eds.), *The behavior of infants* (pp. 57–70). New York: Plenum Press.

Beckwith, L., & Cohen, S. E. (1984). Home environment and cognitive environment in preterm children during the first five years. In A. Gottfried (Ed.), *Home environments and early cognitive development* (pp. 235–272). New York: Academic Press.

Beckwith, L., & Parmelee, A. H., Jr. (1986). EEG patterns of preterm infants: Home environments and later IQ. *Child Development, 57.*

Berlyne, D. (1965). *Structure and direction in thinking.* New York: Wiley.

Blake, R., & Hirsch, H. V. B. (1975). Deficits in binocular depth perception in cats after alternating monocular deprivations. *Science, 190,* 1114–1116.

Bloom, L., & Lahey, M. (1978). *Language development and language disorders.* New York: Wiley.

Bornstein, M. H. (1987). *Sensitive periods in development.* Hillsdale, NJ: L. Erlbaum.

Brainerd, C. J. (Ed.). (1983). Recent advances in cognitive development. In Charles J. Lumsden (Ed.), *Gene culture linkage and the developing mind.* New York: Springer-Verlag.

Brazelton, T. B. (1986). Early Intervention: Does it pay? In D. Tamir, A. Russell, & T. B. Brazelton (Eds.), *Intervention and stimulation in infant development* (pp. 59–74). Tel Aviv: Freund Publishers.

Bricker, D. (1985). The effectiveness of early intervention with handicapped and medically at-risk infants. In M. Frank (Ed.), *Infant intervention programs* (pp. 51–65). New York: Haworth Press.

Broman, S. H., Nichols, P. L., & Kennedy, W. A. (1975). *Preschool IQ.* Hillsdale, NJ: L. Erlbaum.

Chall, J. S., & Peterson, R. W. (1986). The influence of neuroscience upon educational practice. In S. L. Friedman, K. A. Klivington, & R. W. Peterson (Eds.), *The brain, cognition and education* (pp. 287–318). Orlando: Academic Press.

Chalupa, L. M., & Williams, R. W. (1985). Formation of retina projection in the cat. In R. N. Aslin (Ed.), *Advances in neural and behavioral development* (Vol. 1, pp. 1–32). Norwood, NJ: Ablex Publishing.

Chugani, H. I., & Phelps, M. E. (1986). Maturation changes in cerebral function in infants determined by 18 RDG positron emission tomography. *Science, 23,* 840–845.

Cotman, C. W., & Nieto-Sampedro, M. (1982). Brain function, synapse renewal and plasticity. *Annual Review of Psychology, 33,* 371–401.

Crnic, L. S., & Pennington, B. F. (1987). Developmental psychology and the neurosciences: An introduction. *Child Development, 58,* 533–538.

Curley, R., & Perkins, W. (1984). *Nature and treatment of stuttering.* San Diego: College-Hill Press.

Denis, M. (1982). Language acquisition in a single hemisphere: Semantic organization. In D. Caplan (Ed.), *Biological studies of mental processes* (pp. 159–185). Cambridge: MIT Press.

Eimas, D. D., & Tartles, V. C. (1979). On the development of speech perception. In H. W. Reese & L. P. Lipsitt (Eds.), *Advances in child development and behavior* (Vol. 13, pp. 155–194). New York: Academic Press.

Eimas, P., Siqueland, E. R., Juscyle, P., & Visorito, J. (1971). Speech perception in infants. *Science, 171,* 303–306.

Ekman, P. (1980). *The face of man.* New York: Garland STPM Press.

Emde, R. N. (1983). The prerepresentational self and its affective care. *The Psychoanalytic Study of the Child, 38,* 165–192.

Emde, R. N., Gaensbauer, T. J., & Harmon, R. J. (1976). *Emotional expression in infancy.* New York: International Universities Press.

Epstein, H. T. (1974a). Phrenoblysis: Special brain and mind growth periods, part I: Human brain and skull development. *Developmental Psychology, 7,* 207–217.

Epstein, H. T. (1974b). Phrenoblysis: Special brain and mind growth periods, part II: Human mental development. *Developmental Psychology, 7,* 217–224.

Field, T. (1983). Early interactions and interaction coaching of high-risk infants and parents. In M. Perlmutter (Ed.), *The Minnesota Symposia in Child Psychology* (Vol. 16, pp. 1–34). Hillsdale, NJ: L. Erlbaum.

Field, T., Schanberg, S. M., Scafidi, F., Bauer, C. R., Vega-Lahr, N., Garcia, R., Nystrom, S., & Kuhn, C. N. (1986). Effects of tactile/kinesthetic stimulation on preterm neonates. *Pediatrics, 77,* 654–658.

Fischer, K. W. (1980). A theory of cognitive development. *Psychological Review*, 87, 477–531.

Fischer, K. W. (1983). Developmental level as periods of discontinuity. In K. W. Fischer (Ed.), *Levels and transitions in children's development* (pp. 1–7). San Francisco: Jossey-Bass.

Fischer, K. W., & Bulloch, D. (1981). Patterns of data: Sequence, synchrony, and constraint in cognitive development. In K. W. Fischer (Ed.), *Cognitive development* (pp. 1–20). San Francisco: Jossey-Bass.

Fischer, K. W., & Pipp, S. C. (1984). Process of cognitive development. In R. J. Sternberg (Ed.), *Mechanisms of cognitive development* (pp. 88–148). New York: W. H. Freeman.

Fischer, K. W., Pipp, S. L., & Bulloch, D. (1984). Detecting developmental discontinuities: Methods and measurements. In R. N. Emde & R. J. Harmon (Eds.), *Continuities and discontinuities in development* (pp. 95–121). New York: Plenum Publishing.

Fish, S. E., Mooney, R. D., & Rhoades, R. W. (1985). Development and plasticity of mammalean striate corticofugal pathway. In R. Aslin (Ed.), *Advances in neural and behavioral developments* (pp. 157–186). Orlando: Academic Press.

Fodor, J. A. (1983). *The modularity of mind*. Cambridge: MIT Press.

Fraiberg, S. (1971). *Insights from the blind*. New York: Basic Books.

Gleitman, L. R. (1986). Biological preprogramming for language learning. In S. L. Friedman, K. A. Klivington, & R. W. Peterson (Eds.), *The brain, cognition, and education* (pp. 120–151). Orlando: Academic Press.

Goldman, P. S. (1976). The role of experience in recovery of function following orbital prefrontal lesions in infant monkeys. *Neuropsychologia*, *14*, 401–411.

Gollin, E. S. (1981). *Development plasticity*. New York: Academic Press.

Gottlieb, G. (1983). The psychobiological approach to developmental issues. In P. H. Mussen (Ed.), *Handbook of child psychology* (Vol. 2, pp. 1–26). New York: Wiley.

Greenough, W. T. (1975). Experimental modifications of the developing brain. *American Scientist*, *63*, 37–46.

Greenough, W. T. (1978). Development and memory: The synaptic connection. In T. Teyler (Ed.), *Brain and learning* (pp. 127–145). Stamford, CT: Greylock Publishers.

Greenough, W. T. (1986). What's special about development? Thoughts on the bases of experience sensitive synaptic plasticity. In W. T. Greenough & J. M. Juraska (Eds.), *Developmental neuropsychobiology* (pp. 387–397). Orlando: Academic Press.

Greenough, W. T., Black, J. E., & Wallace, C. S. (1987). Experience and brain development. *Child Development*, *58*, 539–559.

Greenough, W. T., & Chang, F. L. F. (1985). Synaptic plasticity and remodeling. In I. C. Cutman (Ed.), *Brain plasticity* (pp. 335–372). New York: Guilford Press.

Greenough, W. T., & Green, E. J. (1981). Experience and the changing brain. In J. L. McGaugh, J. G. March, & S. B. Kiesler (Eds.), *Aging, biology, and behavior* (pp. 71–91). New York: Academic Press.

Greenough, W. T., & Juraska, J. M. (1986). *Developmental neuropsychobiology*. Orlando: Academic Press.

Greenspan, S. I., & White, K. R. (1985). The efficacy of preventive intervention: A glass half full? *Zero to Three*, *5*.

Grouse, L. D., Schrier, B. K., & Nelson, P. C. (1979). Effects of visual experience on gene expression during the development of stimuli specificity in cat brains. *Experimental Neurology*, *64*, 354–364.

Guralnick, M. J., & Bricker, D. D. (1987). The effectiveness of early intervention for children with cognitive and general developmental delays. In M. J. Guralnick & F. C. Bennett (Eds.), *The effectiveness of early intervention for at-risk and handicapped children* (pp. 115–174). New York: Academic Press.

Gustaitis, R., & Young, E. W. D. (1986). *A time to be born, a time to die*. Reading, MA: Addison-Wesley.

Hamburger, V., & Oppenheim, R. W. (1982). Naturally occurring normal deaths in vertebrates. *Neuroscience Commentary*, *1*, 39–55.

Hirsh, R. (1974). The hippocampus and contextual retrieval of information from memory: A theory. *Behavioral Biology*, 12–241.

Hofer, S. F. (1981). A new type of lesion-induced synaptogenesis. *Brain Research*, *222*, 15–27.

Horton, K. B. (1974). Infant intervention and language learning. In R. L. Schiefelbusch & L. L. Lloyd (Eds.), *Language perspectives: Acquisition, retardation, and intervention* (pp. 469–492). Baltimore: University Park Press.

Hubel, D. H., & Wiesel, T. N. (1970). The period of susceptibility to the physiological effects of unilateral eye closure in kittens. *Journal of Physiology, 206*, 419–436.

Hull, C. L. (1920). Quantitative aspects of the evolution of concepts. *Psychological Monographs, 123*.

Huttenlocker, P. R. (1979). Synaptic density in human frontal cortex–developmental changes and effects of aging. *Brain Research, 163*, 195–205.

Huttenlocker, P. R. (1984). Synapse elimination and plasticity in developing human cerebral cortex. *American Journal of Mental Deficiency, 88*, 488–496.

Lecours, A. R. (1975). Myelogenetic correlates of the development of speech and language. In E. H. Lennenberg & E. Lennenberg (Eds.), *Foundations of language development: A multi-disciplinary approach* (Vol. 1, pp. 121–135). New York: Academic Press.

Lennenberg, E. (1967). *Biological foundation of language*. New York: Wiley.

Lerner, R. M. (1986). *The nature of human plasticity*. New York: Cambridge Unviersity Press.

Lerner, R. M., & Hood, K. E. (1986). Plasticity in development: Concepts and issues for intervention. *Journal of Applied Developmental Psychology, 1*, 139–152.

Lipsitt, L. P. (1979). The newborn as informant. In R. B. Kearsley & I. E. Sigel (Eds.), *Infants at risk* (pp. 1–22). Hillsdale, NJ: L. Erlbaum.

Lorenz, K. (1971). *Studies in human and animal behavior, 29*. Cambridge: Harvard University Press.

Luria, A. R. (1973). *The working brain*. New York: Basic Books.

Lynch & Gall, C. (1979). Organization and reorganization in the central nervous system. In F. T. Falkner & J. M. Tanner (Eds.), *Neurobiology and nutrition*, (Vol. 3, pp. 57–71). New York: Plenum Press.

MacDonald, K. (1985). Early experience, relative plasticity and social development. *Developmental Research, 5*, 99–121.

Marler, P. (1961). The filtering of external stimuli during instinctive behavior. In M. W. Thorpe & O. L. Zangwill (Eds.), *Current problems in animal behavior* (pp. 389–449). London: Cambridge University Press.

Masi, W. (1979). Supplemental stimulation of the premature infant. In T. Field, A. Sostek, S. Goldberg, & H. Shuman (Eds.), *Infants born at risk* (pp. 367–388). New York: Spectrum.

McNulty, B., Smith, D., & Soper, E. (1984). *Effectiveness of early special education for handicapped children*. Denver: Colorado Department of Education.

Meaney, M. J., Aitken, D. H., Van Berkel, C., Bhatnager, S., & Sapolsky, R. M. (1988). Effect of neonatal handling on age-related impairments associated with the hippocampus. *Science, 239*, 766–768.

Meisels, S. J., & Plunkett, J. W. (1988). Developmental consequences of preterm birth: Are there long-term effects? In P. B. Baltes, D. L. Featherman, & R. M. Lerner (Eds.), *Life-span development and behavior* (Vol. 9, pp. 87–128). Hillsdale, NJ: L. Erlbaum.

Mimura, K. (1986). Development of visual pattern discrimination in the fly depends on high experience. *Science, 232*, 231–233.

Nelson, K. (1974). Concept, word, and sentence: Interrelations in acquisition and development. *Psychological Review, 81*, 267–285.

Northcott, W. H. (1981, April). Freedom through speech: Every child's right. *The Volta Review, 83*, 162–181.

Panksepp, J. (1986). The neurochemistry of behavior. *Annual Review of Psychology, 7*, 77–108.

Papousek, H., & Papousek M. (1983). The psychobiology of the first didactic program and toys in human infants. In A. Oliverio & M. Zappallin (Eds.), *The behavior of infants* (pp. 219–240). New York: Plenum Press.

Parmelee, A. (1985). Sensory stimulation in the nursery: How much and when? *Developmental and Behavioral Pediatrics, 6*, 242–243.

Piaget, J. (1971). *Biology and knowledge*. Cambridge: MIT Press.

Prechtl, H. F. R. (1986). New perspectives in early human development. *European Journal of Obstetrics, Gynecology and Reproductive Biology, 21*, 347–354.

Purpura, D. (1983). Cellular neurology of mental retardation. In F. Menolascino, R. Newman, & J. A. Stark (Eds.), *Curative aspects of mental retardation* (pp. 57–68). Baltimore: P. H. Brookes.

Rakic, P., Bourgeois, J. P., Echenoff, M. I., Zecevic, N., & Goldman-Rakic, P. S. (1986). Concurrent overproduction of synapses in diverse regions of the primate cerebral cortex. *Science, 252*, 232–237.

Rosenweig, M. S. (1984). Experience, memory and the brain. *American Psychologist, 39*, 365–376.
Rutter, M. (1981). Psychological sequelae of brain damage in children. *Journal of American Psychometric Association, 32*, 1553–1554.
Scarr, S. (1982). Development is internally guided, not determined. *Contemporary Psychology, 27*, 852–853.
Schiefelbusch, R. L., Sullivan, J. W., & Ganz, V. K. (1980). Assessing children who are at risk for speech disorder. In S. Harell & N. J. Anastasiow (Eds.), *The at risk infant* (pp. 277–284). Amsterdam: Excerpta Medica.
Scott, J. P. (Ed.), (1978). *Critical periods.* Stroudsburg, PA: Dowden, Hutchinson & Ross.
Shonkoff, J. P., & Hauser-Cram, P. (1987). Early intervention for disabled infants and their families: A quantitative analysis. *Pediatrics, 80,* 650–658.
Simon, H. A. (1986). The role of attention in cognition. In S. L. Friedman, K. A. Klivington, & R. W. Peterson (Eds.), *The brain, cognition, and education* (pp. 105–119). Orlando: Academic Press.
Sroufe, L. A., & Rutter, M. (1984). Salient developmental issues. *Child Development, 55,* 22.
Timeras, P. (1982). The timing of hormone signals in the orchestration of brain development. In R. N. Emde & R. J. Harmon (Eds.), *The development of attachment and affiliative systems* (pp. 47–64). New York: Plenum Press.
Trevarthen, C. (1983). Interpersonal ability of infants as generators for transmission of language and culture. In A. Oliverio & M. Zappallin (Eds.), *The behavior of infants* (pp. 145–176). New York: Plenum Press.
Turkewitz, G., & Kenny, P. A. (1985). The role of developmental limitation on sensory input in sensory/perceptual organization. *Developmental & Behavioral Pediatrics, 6,* 302–306.
Werner, E. E., & Smith, R. S. (1982). *Vulnerable, but invincible: A longitudinal study of resilient children and youth.* New York: McGraw-Hill.
Will, B. E., Schmitt, P., Dalympe, P., Alford, J. C. (1985). *Brain plasticity, learning, and memory.* New York: Plenum Press.
Wittrock, M. C. (1986). Education and recent research on attention and knowledge acquisition. In S. L. Freidman, K. A. Klivington, & R. W. Peterson (Eds.), *The brain, cognition, and education* (pp. 151–170). Orlando: Academic Press.
Yakovlev, P. I., & Lecours, A. (1967). The mylogenetic cycles of regional maturation of the brain. In A. Minkowski (Ed.), *Regional development of the brain in early life* (pp. 3–70). Oxford, England: Blackwell.

PART IV

Approaches to assessment

10 An interdisciplinary model of infant assessment

LORRAINE MCCUNE, BARBARA KALMANSON,
MARY B. FLECK, BARBARA GLAZEWSKI,
JOAN SILLARI

Infants, from birth, display complex patterns of interaction with the world. Their earliest behaviors and reactions form the basis of a broadening repertoire of skills and activities in the first 2 years of life. This continually unfolding sequence of skills was catalogued in detail during the 1920s and 1930s by Gesell (Gesell, 1928; Gesell, 1945; Gesell & Thompson, 1934) and by the Berkeley Growth Study (Bayley, 1933). In conjunction with the impetus provided by the intelligence testing movement of the late nineteenth and early twentieth centuries, these data served as the foundation for conventional modern techniques of infant evaluation (Brooks-Gunn & Weinraub, 1983). Rigorous psychometric tests for infants (e.g., Bayley, 1969) are an outgrowth of this earlier period.

Recently, attention has turned to the assessment of such specific abilities as sensorimotor skills (Corman & Escalona, 1969; Uzgiris & Hunt, 1975), language skills (Bzoch & League, 1971), and attentional processing (Brooks-Gunn & Lewis, 1981). In addition, federal legislation (i.e., P.L. 99-457, Education of the Handicapped Act Amendments of 1986) has increased the scope of assessment for the coming decade by shifting the attention of schools and other human service agencies to younger children. Moreover, emphasis in this legislation on the family highlights the importance of social and emotional assessment. This new emphasis requires careful deployment of established assessment procedures, supplemented by newly developed techniques to provide highly discriminating methodologies (Cicchetti & Wagner, this volume; Dunst & Trivette, this volume; Krauss & Jacobs, this volume).

The most striking feature of the evolution of infant assessment has been the shift from assessment of "intelligence" to assessment of a number of interrelated systems in very young children combined with a move toward discipline-oriented assessment. However, since babies view the world comprehensively, division of the infant's capacities along such lines as cognitive, motor, and social domains is not possible in the early weeks of life, and remains somewhat artificial throughout the first 3 years. Current developmental theory suggests that the capacities a baby exhibits in each domain draw upon a complex and dynamic underlying internal organization that provides both process and framework for specific development (Piaget, 1952; Piaget, 1962; Stern, 1985). Understanding of the baby's experience by others is facilitated, however, by considering infant behavior and capacity from a variety of topical perspectives, and integrating the information thus collected.

Assessment as considered in this chapter involves sampling behavior by presenting

219

specific tasks and observing the babies' responses in order to determine the nature of their underlying competencies and ways of organizing the world. Test items are therefore designed to elicit samples of behavior. When babies are asked to release a block into a cup, we hope to learn about their understanding of container and contained, about their motor control, and about how they relate to requests from an adult. From this perspective, the primary goals of assessment are to determine level of developmental accomplishment as well as the manner in which the child's organizing abilities appear to be operating at that time. Such an assessment should demonstrate a pattern of performance in a range of developmental domains and should suggest hypotheses about strengths that are enhancing development, and weaknesses that may be limiting ability to learn or perform. This information provides the basis for identifying children in need of early intervention services (Blackman, 1986).

PREDICTION VERSUS EARLY IDENTIFICATION

Measures of infant development are poor at predicting a child's ability at school age (Bayley, 1970; Escalona & Moriarty, 1961; McCall, Applebaum, & Hogarty, 1973; Shonkoff, 1983). Since behaviors measured in infancy differ substantially from behaviors assessed, for example, at 6 years of age, reliable and valid prediction of mental ability is questionable. In addition, it is difficult to obtain valid measures of infant competence. Infants have a limited behavioral repertoire and exhibit variability both in temperament (Brooks-Gunn & Weinraub, 1983) and in experience attributable to environmental factors (Cohen & Parmelee, 1983). Their performance is also dependent on motivation and attention, which may vary in the course of a day. These limitations on obtaining valid assessments further complicate the prediction issue.

Conventional test formats in infancy rely on performance of gross and fine motor tasks, imitation, speech, and the child's compliance with the examiner (Zelazo, 1982). If a child has difficulty or is handicapped in one or more of these areas, the assessment probably provides only a minimal estimate of the child's ability. However, for children with severe developmental disabilities and delays, long-term prediction is generally more accurate (Honzik, 1983). McCall, Hogarty, and Hurlburt (1972) suggested that prediction might be made more accurate if formal test scores were used in combination with other informal measures, including parent reports. They also suggested that analysis of performance on specific items from infant tests rather than total scores might enhance prediction.

In general, the best statistical predictor of childhood IQ from infancy remains parent education or parent IQ (Kopp & McCall, 1982; McCall, 1981). Additionally, Cohen and Parmelee (1983) demonstrated that parent–infant interaction and quality of parenting during the second year of life were strong predictors of 5-year outcomes for infants at risk. Bee et al. (1982) reported that standardized test scores become more predictive of later development after 24 months of age, whereas aspects of family environment and parent–infant interaction predict later IQ and language performance more effectively earlier in infancy. This suggests that family assessment and supportive intervention soon after birth may be a powerful tool for prevention of developmental disabilities.

One reason for the critical need to predict which at-risk infants will indeed have atypical development is the decision regarding which infants require early intervention. Theoretical models of early development suggest different approaches to the problem (Bornstein & Sigman, 1986). Kopp and McCall (1982), adopting a ''discontinuity'' model, suggested that the reason early infant tests do not predict later performance is that biologically based processes of development include highly similar organization and strong "self righting tendencies" during the first year of life, and later development (beyond 18 months) is characterized by varying levels of proficiency in human abilities and increased stability in individual differences. However, Siegel (1981) found continuity in her studies, showing that early scores on the Bayley (Bayley, 1969) and the Uzgiris-Hunt scales (Uzgiris & Hunt, 1975) were correlated significantly with cognitive and language scores at 2 years of age, and were reasonably accurate in identifying those children at risk for developmental delay.

Clinical experience suggests that babies who show very poor functioning or substantial gaps in development are unlikely to catch up on their own. For example, sensorimotor problems in infancy, such as delayed understanding of the permanence of objects and the means–end relationship for simple problem solving may wane, only to be followed by learning difficulties later (Siegel, 1979). In cases where a "low score" is observed in the presence of a number of risk conditions and with such other observations as ineffective ability to communicate, later normal development can neither be assumed nor ruled out. It may be that biologically compromised infants require intervention in support of the organization that develops so spontaneously in nondisabled infants. A simple example involves the baby who is apparently intact cognitively but has a sensory or motor impairment. Specific experiences provided in early intervention can support alternate sensorimotor routes to later cognitive organization at school age. Early intervention aims to exploit the plasticity of early infant development processes, making positive outcomes more likely (Anastasiow, this volume).

MULTIPLE MEASURES IN INTERDISCIPLINARY TEAM ASSESSMENT

Traditional measures of infant assessment comprise three major categories. The first, norm-referenced measures, provides a comparison of the child's performance with a relevant normative population (e.g., Bayley, 1969; Frankenburg, Dodds, Fandal, Kazuk, & Cohrs, 1975; Frankenburg, Fandal, Sciarillo, & Burgess, 1981). The work most frequently referenced in such tests is that of Gesell and his colleagues, who established an extensive data base for understanding the course of infant development (Shonkoff, 1983). The second category consists of ordinal scales (e.g., Dunst, 1980; Nicolich, 1977; Uzgiris & Hunt, 1975) that were designed to assess forms of behavior that are progressively more complex, sequential, and hierarchical in nature. Piaget's theory of sensorimotor intelligence and early symbolic development provides the basis for the development of ordinal scales. Finally, curriculum-based assessment provides a means to assess children and monitor their program based on a developmental sequence of tasks to be learned in each of several domains (Bagnato, Neisworth, & Capone, 1986). Such assessments were developed in response to the need for instruments that linked assessment findings with intervention planning.

All three types of traditional measures have the goal of quantifying a child's abilities. Such quantitative goals, however, often fail to address the need in current clinical practice to address the more qualitative aspects of a child's development, such as social competence, attentional abilities, and appropriateness of movement patterns (Hauser-Cram & Shonkoff, 1988). Anticipating this limitation of her normative measure, Bayley (1969) cautioned that "the examiner of exceptional children will probably wish to supplement the score, or age equivalent, with a careful qualitative study of the test protocol in order to observe the particular areas of strength and weakness" (p. 34). In contrasting ordinal scales with conventional psychometric tests, Dunst and Gallagher

(1983) noted that in attaining the same score on a psychometric measure, two children may have done so by passing very different items, and therefore may exhibit disparate cognitive competence. The use of ordinal scales permits the specification of such disparities by providing a description of how the child performed. Domain-specific measures also respond to the need to supplement global scores by delineating more clearly the level of functioning in each discrete area of development.

A critical challenge for the examiner is the integration of diverse test data into a comprehensive evaluation. When several measures are used in combination, a more thorough understanding of the child's developmental status is obtained, and changes in development can be monitored more adequately. The global score of the norm-referenced measure is complemented and enhanced by the clinical insight gained through the use of an ordinal scale and the specific skill level description in each domain afforded by the curriculum-based measures.

An integrated team approach to assessment facilitates an understanding of the infant's experience, behaviors, and capacities. The following professionals are most commonly involved in multidisciplinary assessment teams: psychologist (clinical, developmental, or educational); physician and/or nurse; physical therapist and/or occupational therapist; speech and language pathologist or therapist; social worker; and educator (early childhood and/or special education). In some settings, a pediatric neurologist is the primary assessor.

How can several individuals be involved in assessment without distressing, distracting, and tiring the baby and alarming the parents? These are problems that must be considered and solved individually in each setting (see Parker & Zuckerman, this volume). Because the parents and baby can be overwhelmed by a large number of people in a room, yet more than one individual may need to work with the baby, a "primary assessor" or team leader can sometimes be designated who performs most of the assessment in cooperation with the parents. One or two others might observe either from inside the room or through a one-way mirror. If a comprehensive core instrument is used by one examiner, this, with the addition of a free play observation, can be observed by several professionals, thus providing a large proportion of the assessment information. To facilitate understanding of the process involved in this approach, Figure 1 presents a procedure for an interdisciplinary team to follow when conducting an assessment.

Beginning with the administration of a core instrument by one examiner while the other professionals observe, the team can use the data obtained to analyze patterns of performance and, if appropriate, compute standardized scores. Since many items on domain-specific measures overlap with items on standardized general development measures, it is even possible to score several "domains" from a single administration (specific examples are described later in the chapter). From this analysis, it is then possible to both generate hypotheses for the performance patterns noted and determine whether any supplementary assessment techniques are needed to provide an accurate understanding of an infant's developmental level and functioning. For example, if results from the standardized instrument reveal uneven development with low scores in language and questionable social development, the team might decide to have the speech and language specialist conduct a home visit, including administration of a specific language measure and observation of the infant's communication style at home. Once all of the relevant data are collected and analyzed by the team, recommendations for early intervention or other follow-up services can be made. If early intervention is needed, the team can then use the data to determine the type, content, and frequency of the intervention to be provided.

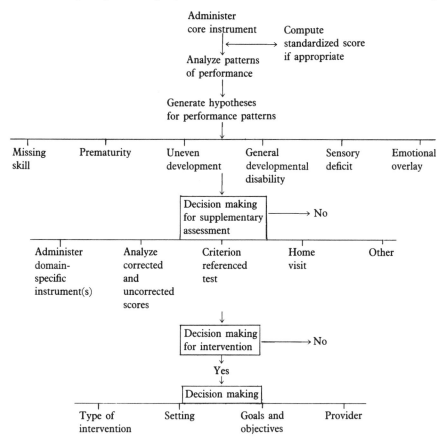

Figure 1. A procedure for interdisciplinary assessment using standardized and domain-specific instruments

USE OF A CORE ASSESSMENT INSTRUMENT

A core assessment instrument can provide a common framework within which a multidisciplinary team can use traditional measures in nontraditional ways. As a core instrument, the Bayley Scales of Infant Development (BSID) (Bayley, 1969) offer a broad range of items organized in developmental sequence with age ranges of typical performance based on a reasonably large number of subjects. Thus, the standard administration and scoring of the assessment instrument by designated team members provides quantitative information concerning the child's developmental level. Bayley (1969) stated that "the primary value of the developmental indexes is that they provide the basis for establishing a child's current status, and thus the extent of any deviation from normal expectancy" (p. 4). Furthermore, many other specific assessment instruments (Bzoch & League, 1971; Folio & Fewell, 1983; Nicolich, 1977) draw on the same pool of items as the BSID, so that a single administration can contribute to the scoring of several other assessment instruments. The interaction of team members while interpreting observations, analyzing items passed and failed, and providing input from any supplementary domain-specific tests, enhances the qualitative understanding of the child's strengths and weaknesses, which more readily translates into intervention plans and strategies.

The BSID contains important features consistent with the *Standards for Educational and Psychological Tests* (APA, AERA, & NCME, 1974) that make it an instrument of choice for a core measure. Intended to be used with children from 2 through 30 months of age, the BSID consists of three components–a mental scale, a motor scale, and a behavior record–each serving a specific purpose for assessment. The mental scale is a theoretically sound instrument that can be used to assess maturing cognition, specifically in the areas of sensorimotor and early symbolic functioning as described by Piaget (1952). The motor scale can be used to provide an index of physical maturation by measuring the degree of body control and gross and fine motor coordination. The behavior record provides a means for describing naturally occurring observed behaviors and the child's response to the environment. In addition to its clinical use in assessing the developmental status of young children, the BSID can be a valuable tool in infant research.

The technical aspects of the BSID are well documented (Collard, 1972; Damarin, 1978; Holden, 1972). The standardization process utilized a stratified sample design to collect data and establish norms, while controlling for sex and race within age groups, residence (urban, rural), and education of head of household. The original plan called for 1,400 children with 100 at each of the 14 ages (2, 3, 4, 5, 6, 8, 10, 12, 15, 18, 21, 24, 27, and 30 months) who were "normal" and living at home. The final sample totaled 1,262 children. Validity was determined by correlating the scores on the Mental Scale for 2-year-olds in the standardization sample with their scores on the Stanford-Binet Intelligence Test (Terman & Merrill, 1960) yielding a correlation of .57. Satisfactory split-half reliability coefficients were obtained for the Mental Scale (.81–.93) and the Motor Scale (.68–.92). Although the test manual does not specify the procedures used for item selection, reference is made to Bayley's 40 years of research and development of earlier versions of the scale in which the content of items was studied closely and revised.

Although the Mental Scale includes 163 items, many fewer items are actually used for any individual infant. Several items can be scored from a single task presentation (e.g., builds tower of two, three, six, or eight cubes), and the same materials are used for various items (e.g., puts nine cubes in a cup) or can be observed incidentally (e.g., bangs in play, transfers objects hand to hand), so that an experienced examiner can move through the administration rather smoothly. For example, the examiner testing a 12-month-old might begin by giving the baby several of the 1-inch cubes. Through the infant's use of and response to the cubes, the examiner is able to ascertain the infant's approximate range of abilities, and then use clinical judgment in presenting subsequent items beyond that range to establish a basal (a score of pass on 10 successive items) and ceiling level (failure on 10 successive items) in a manner that facilitates the infant's optimal performance, while minimizing undue frustration.

A presentation of the BSID can be considered a structured play session that should be enjoyable for parents, child, and examiner. Indeed, maintaining the child's comfort and rapport with the examiner is a primary requirement for this assessment. Testing takes place with the mother or caregiver present, and items may be presented by the parent when the examiner thinks this is indicated. Most items involve presenting the child with an object or social overture and observing the child's performance or reaction. Since no particular order of item presentation is required, and an item can be presented again later if a child shows no interest at first, the structure of the session can be varied to suit the child's apparent interests and skills.

When the testing is completed the examiner should be able to draw a number of conclusions from the resulting pattern of item performances. A raw score is generated from the number of items passed, including those below the basal level. Raw scores from the Mental and Motor scales are converted respectively into a Mental Development Index (MDI) and a Psychomotor Development Index (PDI), both based on the child's chronological age. These normalized standard scores are similar in numerical characteristics to the familiar deviation IQ, which is based on a mean of 100 and a standard deviation of 16. However, the concept of developmental index rather than intelligence is thought to better describe the nature of the construct being measured due to the uncertainty of what comprises intelligence in infancy. Occasionally a child may exhibit a score that is close to the standard score of 100, yet demonstrate consistent failures in one area, such as expressive language. Any child who is failing many age-appropriate items, or items in a specific domain, needs further evaluation (see Figure 1).

ADMINISTRATION, SCORING, AND INTERPRETATION FOR THE INFANT AT RISK

There are many well-documented problems in the administration, scoring, and interpretation of the performance of atypical infants on normative scales (Bayley, 1969; Brinker & Lewis, 1982; Brooks-Gunn & Lewis, 1983; Dunst, 1980; Dunst & Gallagher, 1983; Shonkoff, 1983). Because the Bayley Scales and other standardized instruments did not include disabled, premature, and other at-risk children in their norming samples, published norms are inappropriate for such atypical groups. Furthermore, in view of the heterogeneous nature of each such group, the determination of "appropriate norms" is extremely problematic (Pasick, 1985). One must consider with prematurity, for example, the range of risks (in addition to early birth) that may or may not characterize an individual premature baby (e.g., respiratory distress syndrome).

Most of the disadvantages of conventional measures for infants with disabilities can be overcome by sensitive administration and careful clinical interpretation. Although standardized scores are of limited usefulness in some cases, item information can be important. One must take special care that standardized scores are not used to characterize children's cognitive level when sensory and/or motor difficulties limit their ability to perform some tasks. It is also critical that the transition from assessment to intervention focus not on the test items themselves, but on underlying skills. The pattern of items that are passed and failed allows an analysis of skill development that can form the basis of an intervention plan. The following section will provide sample interpretations of atypical patterns of performance that may have to take into account the specific impacts of obvious motor disabilities; prematurity; suspected or confirmed sensory deficits; an emotional problem that impairs the child's ability to engage in the assessment; uneven development of cognitive, language, or other abilities; or an inadequate assessment session because of significant fussiness, hunger, fatigue, or illness. The examiner of infants at risk for or with disabilities should be aware of such special considerations and must take them into account during the assessment and later when scoring the test and examining patterns of performance.

Effects of a missing motor skill

Let us consider testing a 6-month-old boy. The examiner puts some cubes on the table and encourages him to play with them. The baby appears to be listening and is oriented toward the cubes, but does not reach to pick one up. The examiner asks the mother to encourage him, and after a few minutes she places a cube in her infant's hand. He handles it and shows interest in holding another that is placed in his hand, but does not reach. Other evidence in the testing situation might clarify why the infant does not reach, but for the moment let us focus solely on the effect of this missing skill on the child's test score. A child of 6 months who is not reaching will necessarily fail 10 items usually passed at this age (see Table 1).

Consider some hypothetical situation that might surround the baby's performance. First, suppose he passed all other items on the BSID up to item 75. His raw score would be 65 because of the 10 items missed, yielding an MDI of 85. This places his performance one standard deviation below the mean and would suggest the need for further assessment. No doubt the examiner would realize that reaching was absent, and a subsequent motor assessment could establish whether there were specific physical disabilities. A request for an informal description of the baby's daily activities, direct questioning, or observation during a home visit could clarify whether the child has had little previous experience with objects. If other aspects of the complete assessment (e.g., vision, sound production, etc.) indicate deficits or delays, a more comprehensive evaluation protocol may be indicated.

Not only test results, but development in general is hindered by the inability to reach. Unless someone places objects in the baby's hands, he will not be able to explore objects tactually in a manner that facilitates other developmental goals. Recent studies have indicated that for premature infants, effectiveness of manual exploratory strategies at 9 months is significantly related to Bayley Scale results at 24 months (McCune & Ruff, 1985; Ruff, McCarten, Kurtzburg, & Vaughn, 1984). Manual exploration is an example of a simple sensorimotor activity that promotes infant development in a variety of domains of function. The baby who cannot engage in this behavior will have difficulty learning about objects, experiencing his or her effect on the environment, and enjoying pleasure in the achievement and motivation to learn more. Parental enjoyment of the baby's accomplishments may also be lessened.

Suppose the 6-month-old boy has Down syndrome. In this case the child may already be enrolled in an early intervention program, and the score of 85 is no lower than the range of expected scores on developmental tests at school age for this population. Because of his lack of the spontaneous skill of reaching, this baby needs help in experiencing the world of objects. There may be additional problems, other than those expected for infants with Down syndrome, that are contributing to the baby's difficulties.

Suppose rather than Down syndrome, this is a case of premature birth by 2 months. In this case, the delayed accomplishment of directed reaching may be due to a slower maturational timetable, or there may be reason to suspect serious overall motor compromises. Although a developmental quotient can be computed correcting for prematurity (in this case yielding a score of 137, which is more than two standard deviations above the mean), this does not suggest exceptionally advanced development, but rather reflects the baby's solid performance on the nonreaching items. Follow-up assessment in a few months is still indicated to ensure that reaching has emerged. A pattern of additional deficits other than not reaching, such as asymmetrical movement

Table 1. *Bayley items that require reaching at 6 months and 9 months*

Item no.	Mean age, mo.	Item description
49	4.1	Reaches for cube (6 mo.)
51	4.4	Eye–hand coordination in reaching (6 mo.)
54	4.6	Picks up cube (6 mo.)
59	4.9	Recovers rattle in crib (6 mo.)
60	5.0	Reaches persistently (6 mo.)
63	5.2	Lifts inverted cup (6 mo.)
64	5.4	Reaches for second cube (6 mo.)
70	5.7	Picks up cube deftly and directly (6 mo.)
71	5.7	Pulls string, secures ring (6 mo.)
73	5.8	Lifts cup with handle (6 mo.)
80	7.1	Pulls string adaptively, secures ring (9 mo.)
82	7.6	Attempts to secure three cubes (9 mo.)
86	8.1	Uncovers toy (9 mo.)
88	9.0	Picks up cup, secures cube (9 mo.)

patterns and atypical muscle tone, might indicate the need for early intervention. These and other issues relevant to prematurity will be reviewed subsequently.

A baby seen at 9 months who is not reaching would continue to show a low developmental quotient (maximum raw score 74, with an MDI of 63 for a full-term baby). A 2 month correction for the prematurely born infant would yield an MDI of 86. In either case, such impoverished ability to interact with objects at this age would call for a more careful assessment to determine whether early intervention is appropriate.

An example of sensory impairment

Fraiberg (1977) explored the development of reaching in blind babies. She presented the profile of a baby who had experienced no prior intervention and who was evaluated for the first time at 5 months of age. His head was erect when he sat, his hands were open, and he grasped objects placed in them. However, his hands remained at shoulder height while making exploratory movements, even when a favorite musical toy had been taken from his grasp and placed in front of him. His hands met at midline only by accident and in passing. Without help it seemed unlikely that this baby would develop exploratory strategies that would contribute to his later development.

In attempting to determine why the baby without vision was impeded in reaching, Fraiberg noted the possibility of mistakenly assuming the baby was deaf, mentally retarded, or affected by a specific central nervous system deficit. These possibilities can be judged by careful assessment. Age-graded items from the Bayley Scales that are not dependent on vision can be helpful in this regard, but it may be necessary first to accustom the baby to interacting tactually with objects placed in his hands.

Fraiberg described three adaptive problems that prevent the otherwise nondisabled blind baby from achieving the milestones of reaching and grasping in a manner similar to the infant with normal vision: (1) midline organization of the hands is impeded by blindness; (2) the lure of the seen object is missing; and (3) the baby has no way of realizing there are things "out there" before sound becomes associated with the presence of substantial objects.

Fraiberg's delineation of these problems, through both direct observation of the babies and analyses of the tasks they face is a marvelous example of the type of problem solving that every infant specialist must undertake in the assessment of infants who have or who are at risk for disabilities. How can we determine which aspects of the cognitive and motor systems are operating well and enhance those, while helping the young child find alternative strategies to substitute for missing skills that simply cannot be reconstructed? Decarie (1969) proposed a similar approach for babies with limb anomalies secondary to fetal thalidomide exposure whose missing or stunted limbs precluded typical infant exploratory behavior.

Uneven development and other impediments to test interpretation

A number of circumstances may suggest that a baby should not be expected to perform in an easily interpretable fashion on a standardized test such as the BSID. In some of these cases, it is still useful to determine which items such children are capable of passing, based on what is known of their difficulties. For example, for a 2-year-old child with spastic cerebral palsy, the successful completion of items more sophisticated than his or her everyday activities can indicate unsuspected cognitive strengths. In such a case, the examiner may have to adapt items to the child's physical condition without altering their underlying cognitive character. Under such circumstances, standardized scores would not be computed, but a profile of items passed could be compiled.

Similarly, an 18-month-old with cleft palate or hearing impairment might be unable to perform some age-appropriate language tasks. In such cases, it is vitally important to ascertain the age placement of nonlanguage items for which the child is showing adequate performance. While a standard score cannot be computed for such children, the age-graded nature of the items allows identification of some areas of cognitive strength.

Occasionally, a few minutes of working with a child indicates that a complete assessment is unlikely because he or she is unwilling or unable to accept a broad range of items and engage in a calm give-and-take with the examiner. If this is atypical behavior for the child, the assessment can be rescheduled. Alternatively, the parent may be more successful than the examiner in presenting test items. However, even if it is not possible to complete a scorable testing session, the child's performance on a few items can give clues about developmental status and reasons for problems with performance.

A child who begins to look restless and tired, and who refuses items requiring movement, may be showing the effects of a chronic health impairment, such as congestive heart failure, or an emotional disturbance that interferes with his or her exercise of competence. A child who tries each task once and then throws items angrily at the examiner may be expressing extreme anxiety about potential failure. Sometimes a child will show a willingness to work hard at one task only, and demonstrate age-appropriate performance, while refusing or failing at other tasks. These small indicators of performance, given the age-graded nature of test items, may be very useful in discovering positive signs of adaptive ability in the midst of what may be a picture of global delays. Alternative forms of assessment may be helpful under such circumstances (see Cicchetti & Wagner, this volume).

Scoring and interpreting the BSID with premature infants

Premature infants comprise a heterogeneous population ranging from minimally premature, healthy babies to those born as much as 4 months early (24–28 weeks gestation), with very low birth weight and severe illnesses that require invasive medical treatment and prolonged hospitalization (Pasick, 1985). Whether, and for how long, one should use corrected scores when interpreting the test performance of preterm infants is an issue of professional debate linked to at least two points of view. Those who explain development in maturational terms support the use of corrected scores. Ungerer and Sigman (1983) argue for the use of corrected rather than postnatal age based on their findings that delays in development are related to biological maturation. However, their study population was composed of infants not very premature whose general developmental level was in the average range. Those who explain development in terms of environmental influences support the use of uncorrected scores. Siegel (1983); Field, Dempsey, and Shuman (1979); and Miller, Dubowitz, and Palmer (1984) suggest that uncorrected scores are better predictors of later outcomes. Nonetheless, whereas corrected scores may mask subtle, suboptimal developmental problems, uncorrected scores may lead to overidentification of pathology. The analysis of both types of scores provides a balanced approach (Pasick, 1985). Alternatively, Siegel (1983, 1985) suggests the use of corrected scores early in development because of the significance of biologically based maturational factors, and the use of uncorrected scores to account for environmental influences by 1 year of age. In view of the absence of empirically based data, the decision about when to correct scores for gestational age rests with the clinical judgment of the examiner and depends on the presenting situation for the individual infant. In general, the use of both scores is recommended, particularly if the uncorrected score continues to indicate delays. Regardless of the choice of summary score, the emerging pattern of item performance that provides clinical insight into a child's functioning is unaffected.

The decision to defer or omit standardized assessment

There are cases where the use of the Bayley Scales or other standardized instruments is inappropriate. For example, a 14-month-old girl who enters an early intervention program showing no ability to bring her hands under voluntary control either to midline, to the mouth, or for reaching out, and who demonstrates no language and little vocalization, would not benefit from the administration and scoring of a conventional psychometric measure. After several months of intervention, such a child might be able to reach and grasp clumsily, vocalize with familiar adults, and protest by crying and vocalization to certain parts of her therapy. The developmental timetable and sequence represented in the BSID would have no meaning for characterizing this child's growth and development. Her inability to interact intentionally with the environment is entirely obvious, the discouragingly low age levels associated with her emerging skills are generally not useful, and the presentation of age-graded scores to the parents of such a child can be disturbing and destructive. If the child is able to develop a broader repertoire of communication later, this will provide an avenue for assessment.

In the case of a young child with Down syndrome, or with another known cause of mental retardation, standardized cognitive testing often highlights the baby's deficits unnecessarily. Parents who become invested in their interactions with their child, despite the youngster's inevitable disability, can enjoy and take pride in the child's behaviors despite the fact that they are developmentally immature. Little is gained by confronting parents with dire predictions or discouraging them by continuing to calculate the extent of the child's deficit relative to age expectations. This is particularly true when the child's eventual level of performance may not be predicted very well by infant assessment results. In such circumstances, a Bayley score is generally less useful, and it may be appropriate to use criterion-referenced or curriculum-based assessment techniques to determine appropriate intervention strategies and to monitor progress (Bagnato et al., 1986). Formal assessment should be considered part of the clinical process of helping parents to be informed and to cope with their child's strengths and limitations (see Parker & Zuckerman, this volume).

THE USE OF SUPPLEMENTAL ASSESSMENT INSTRUMENTS

Because of the acknowledged limitations of standardized testing with infants at risk, the use of other assessment instruments is often indicated to provide supplemental information on the developmental status of the child. The following section will examine the appropriate measures for each developmental domain and their relationship to the administraton of the BSID as the core instrument.

Cognitive assessment

From a psychometric perspective, infant cognition is considered to be analogous to the concept of "intelligence" in school-aged children and adults and is measured through standardized tests such as the Bayley Scales. These measures use the total number of items passed in relation to the average score at the infant's age to assess the adequacy of development. Children who score significantly below this average are considered delayed. With the influence of Piagetian theory on infant assessment (e.g., Uzgiris & Hunt, 1975), infant cognition can be considered as a set of processes and active abilities that contribute to the growth of later knowledge. Assessment of cognition from this perspective is not based solely on the number of items passed, but takes into account the sensorimotor processes the child uses to approach and solve problems.

Piaget (1952, 1954, 1962) described two general principles of functioning that affect intelligence: organization (the tendency to integrate structures into higher order systems) and adaptation (the tendency to adapt to the environment). Adaptation consists of the two complementary processes of assimilation and accommodation. Assimilation is the process by which individuals adjust to an environmental event in terms of their current structures, and accommodation is the process by which individuals change in response to environmental demands. Based on naturalistic observations, Piaget described the theoretical framework for sensorimotor and symbolic development during the first 24 months of life, which details the changing approaches infants use to solve problems as development proceeds. This development is manifest in several domains of functioning: object permanence, means for bringing about environmental events (means–end), vocal and gestural imitation, causality, spatial relations, and play (Dunst, 1980; McCune-Nicolich, 1981; Uzgiris & Hunt, 1975). Progress within the various domains and ages of attainment of particular abilities vary greatly. Each sequence is assessed as an ordinal scale, that is, one in which the sequence of behavior attained at lower levels within a domain is essential for the mastery of subsequent levels. For example, a child will only be able to find a hidden object under one of two screens after developing the ability to find an object hidden under a single screen.

Understanding the child's sensorimotor and representational abilities helps an examiner understand the learning strategies and processes available to that child. The sequences of abilities measured by these ordinal scales of cognition form the basis for a variety of observable skills. For example, means–end development influences children's ability to use vocal and gestural means for communicative purposes (Bates, 1976; Bates, Benigni, Bretherton, Camaioni, & Volterra, 1979). Entrance into the final sensorimotor stage in object permanence occurs either prior to, or at the same time as, the use of conventional words for communication (Corrigan, 1979; McCune-Nicolich, 1981). The ability to apply specific appropriate actions to objects (schemes relating to objects) reflects the child's ability to learn specific information about the world and to use it appropriately. Sensorimotor actions suited to particular objects, like crinkling paper, wiggling string between the fingers, or banging a block, demonstrate meanings at the level of action. Treating a doll as a baby, using one object to stand for another, and other pretend acts demonstrate increasing levels of representational development. Children with specific disabilities who do not interact with their environment in age-appropriate ways may need help with activities that promote these developments.

Infants' level of development in these cognitive domains can be assessed using a variety of published techniques (e.g., Corman & Escalona, 1969; Corrigan, 1978; Dunst, 1980; Uzgiris & Hunt, 1975). However, because of the variability in ages at which specific stages are attained, the use of norms in this type of assessment is not particularly appropriate or helpful. Special caution is needed in assessing cognitive development based on the Piagetian perspective. Piaget's observations were conducted informally and involved many different eliciting situations presented to the infants to determine the maturity of the processes they used in problem solving. If ordinal scales are used repeatedly with little variation in procedure, the infant may learn how to solve a particular problem (e.g., that pulling a string brings an object) rather than learn the more general principle (that if two objects are connected in space, movement of one will influence movement of the other). If these tasks are used for intervention as well as assessment, it becomes even more important to use a variety of situations with varying materials to determine how well the baby has integrated the concept, rather than merely whether an item is passed or failed.

Certain items presented in the BSID are identical, or nearly so, to tasks administered as part of Piagetian cognitive measures. The Bayley items listed in Table 2, for example, provide useful information about the development of object permanence, means–ends relations, and pretend play that can be used as informal estimates of a child's skills in each of these cognitive areas. Because of the broad age range indicated as appropriate for passage of each item, performance on the Bayley Scales does not determine specific sensorimotor stage. One can, however, judge a child's relative strength in specific cognitive and social domains by examining items grouped in this manner. If further information is needed, additional items from a Piagetian assessment can be given.

For example, if a 15-month-old neither attempts to engage his or her caregiver socially, nor requests help when needed, various explanations are possible. By examining the Bayley performance of such a child in a domain-specific way, an examiner can begin to distinguish these cases. For example, the baby may not yet have established the means-end competence that provides the cognitive underpinning for intentional communication. Alternatively, the cognitive basis may be established, but the social use

Table 2. *Bayley items that sample ordinal aspects of cognitive development*

Item no.	Age, mo. Mean (Range)	Domain and item description
		Object permanence
86	8.1 (6–12)	Uncovers toy
88	9.0 (6–14)	Picks up cup, secures toy
91	9.5 (8–14)	Looks for contents of box
96	10.5 (8–17)	Unwraps cube
102	12.0 (9–17)	Uncovers blue box
131	19.7 (14–30+)	Finds two objects
		Means–end
71	5.7 (4–8)	Pulls string, secures ring
80	7.1 (5–10)	Pulls string adaptively, secures ring
83	7.8 (5–13)	Rings bell purposively
109	13.4 (10–19)	Removes pellet from bottle
122	17.0 (12–24)	Attains toy with stick
		Pretend play
92	9.7 (8–15)	Stirs with spoon in imitation
99	11.3 (8–15)	Pushes car along
126	17.8 (14–26)	Follows directions, doll
154	26.1 (19–30+)	Train of cubes

not yet demonstrated. A 17- or 18-month-old who does not yet make requests with words may be quite strong in other representational skills, such as play and object permanence, or might exhibit a representational deficit such that few of these items are passed.

A nonverbal child who fails age-appropriate language items, yet passes the items in Table 2, provides less cause for worry than one who fails in both. This pattern of performance signals the need to look at motor speech skills but also to feel somewhat secure that the child is developing the representational system appropriate for language. Item 131 (Finds two objects), for example, requires that a child find either a bunny or a ball, on command, thus combining language comprehension and object permanence. However, three trials that do not require language comprehension are presented where the child must find a ball located under one of two cups. Passage of these trials is similar to passing a Piagetian object permanence task. A higher level skill involves finding an object that is first hidden in the hand or a small box, then released under a cloth, out of the child's view. The child must infer that the object was released (i.e., represent its release) even though this occurred out of view. Where children are nonverbal, or low verbal, it is probably useful to present some additional items of this type (Dunst, 1980). It is also essential to ascertain whether a child has intact hearing and physical capability for speech.

Play assessment

Play assessment is particularly useful for determining representational capacity. A free-play session, in addition to more structured standardized testing, provides the opportunity to observe children's cognitive development at work, as they organize their interactions with toys and play partners. This session also provides a foundation for speech and language assessment, for obtaining ancillary information about movement capability in a more open atmosphere than a structured testing session, and for social assessment. McCune (1986) described a format for collecting a sample of play with mother or examiner using a standard set of toys. Play behavior observed using this technique is easily assigned to one of five developmental levels based on Piaget's (1962) research, which is now well documented in the child development literature (Belsky & Most, 1981; McCune, 1980; Nicolich, 1977) (see Table 3). The emergence of these play abilities is related to developmental level rather than chronological age (Hill & McCune-Nicolich, 1981), and the acquisition of language milestones has been associated with particular levels of play (McCune-Nicolich, 1981; McCune-Nicolich & Bruskin, 1981). Table 3 describes the play levels that have been identified.

In addition to assignment of a play level, measures of play complexity and variety are also useful. For example, a child might play only at feeding a doll with a bottle, repeating the same actions with minor variations, or the child's play might be much richer, including a variety of themes. It is possible to count the number of play acts in each play sequence, or the number of different acts in the sequence, and obtain an index of the breadth of the child's representational play skill. McCune (1980, 1986) describes this methodology in detail. See also Cicchetti and Wagner (this volume) for additional approaches.

The meanings in play provide clues to emotionally important issues for the baby. For example, the baby who repeatedly plays "bye-bye" with a purse may be commenting on the fact that mother has recently returned to work. A child with an eating disorder may mime both drinking and vomiting when playing with a cup.

Social and emotional assessment

The Bayley Infant Behavior Record (IBR) can be used as a psychosocial screening instrument to identify children at risk. Clinical observation made during a Bayley assessment can provide clues to socioemotional problems and to the impact of affective considerations on cognitive performance. The IBR provides a vehicle for organizing clinically relevant informal observations that arise in this situation. Wolf and Lozoff (1985) used data from the Bayley norming sample (Bayley, 1969; $N = 1,262$) and the Louisville Twin Study (Matheny, Dolan, & Wilson, 1974; $N = 132-213$) at each of six ages to obtain an empirical basis for defining "suspect" behavior patterns, that is, observations indicative of the need for further assessment. Behavior ratings were categorized as suspect if they were (a) clinically identified as poorly adaptive; (b) separated in the cumulative frequency distribution by a substantial margin from ratings reflecting more adaptive behavior; and (c) infrequent in the large normative samples. The authors suggest that babies receiving ratings in the suspect range on several items should receive more extensive socioemotional assessment. Table 4 lists the items Wolf and Lozoff (1985) found that differentiated suspect behavior patterns. These can serve as a guide for developing local procedures for clinical applications of the IBR.

During the administration of a standardized instrument, a focus on the baby's relationship with his or her parent and the examiner can yield valuable information about socioemotional development, some aspects of which can be quantified using the IBR. For example, an infant who does not take pleasure in interpersonal relationships may mechanically build a tower, but will not look to the parent or examiner as a social

Table 3. *Structure of pretend play, 10–24 months (1977)*

Levels and criteria	Examples

Sensorimotor period

Level 1. Presymbolic scheme: The child shows understanding of object use or meaning by brief recognitory gestures.
  No pretending.
  Properties of present object are the stimulus.
  Child appears serious rather than playful.

The child picks up a comb, touches it to his or her hair, drops it.
The child picks up the telephone receiver, puts it into ritual conversation position, sets it aside.
The child gives the mop a swish on the floor.

Level 2. Auto-symbolic scheme: The child pretends at self-related activities.
  Pretending.
  Symbolism is directly involved with the child's body.
  Child appears playful, seems aware of pretending.

The child simulates drinking from a toy baby bottle.
The child eats from an empty spoon.
The child closes his or her eyes, pretending to sleep.

Symbolic stage 1

Level 3. Single scheme symbolic games: Child extends symbolism beyond his or her own actions by:
Level 3.1. Including other actors or receivers of action, such as a doll.
Level 3.2. Pretending at activities of other people or objects such as dogs, trucks, and trains.

Child feeds mother or doll.
Child grooms mother or doll.
Child pretends to read a book.
Child pretends to mop floor.
Child moves a block or toy car with appropriate sounds of vehicle.

Level 4. Combinatorial symbolic games:
Level 4.1. Single scheme combinations: One pretend scheme is related to several actors or receivers of action.

Child combs own, then mother's hair.
Child drinks from the bottle, feeds doll from bottle.
Child puts an empty cup to mother's mouth, then experimenter, and self.

Level 4.2. Multi-scheme combinations: Several schemes are related to one another in sequence.

Child holds phone to ear, dials.
Child kisses doll, puts it to bed, puts spoon to its mouth.
Child stirs in the pot, feeds doll, pours food into dish.

Level 5. Planned symbolic games: Child indicates verbally or nonverbally that pretend acts are planned ahead.
Level 5.1. Planned single scheme symbolic acts – transitional type. Activities from levels 2 and 3 that are planned.
  Type A: Symbolic identification of one object with another.

Child finds the iron, sets it down, searches for the cloth, tossing aside several objects. When cloth is found, he or she irons it.
Child picks up play screwdriver, says "toothbrush" and makes the motions of toothbrushing.

Table 3. *(cont.)*

Levels and criteria	Examples
Type B: Symbolic identification of the child's body with some other person or object.	Child picks up the bottle, says "baby," then feeds the doll and covers it with a cloth.
Level 5.2. Combinations with planned elements: These are constructed of activities from levels 2 to 5.1, but always include some planned element. They tend toward realistic scenes.	Child puts play foods in a pot, stirs them. Then says "soup" or "Mommy" before feeding the mother. He or she waits, then says "more?" offering the spoon to the mother.

Source: Nicolich (1977), McCune (1986)

reference point. This baby may experience private pleasure in the tasks themselves, but will turn to neither parent nor examiner to share the pleasure. Such a baby may never warm up to the examiner. Alternatively, a baby may turn to parent and examiner after placing each block, apparently unable to initiate a subsequent act without verbal encouragement from those present. Such a baby may appear to be accepting the examiner, but actually may need these continued external overtures to cover a deeper sense of isolation or insecurity.

Difficulty in self-organization can accompany limitations in the ability to use adult mediation (Stern, 1985). This can be expressed in an unwillingness to relinquish toys as the testing proceeds from one item to another, or an unwillingness to engage sufficiently with a particular set of material to complete the required task. Reassurance from a parent, or an examiner's attempts to manage the transition, may not relieve the infant's anxiety.

Withdrawn fearfulness or extreme vigilance can be seen in infants who are not able to derive meaning from events in their environment. Such babies may seem unwilling to reach for or touch objects. At the other end of the continuum an infant may appear highly distracted and unable to focus on a single task. Some infants will be easily frustrated and unable to persevere with tasks that are not mastered immediately. Others seem to operate only on their own agenda and cannot become interested in any items that are presented.

The parent's relationship to infant and examiner during the testing session can alert the assessment team to difficulties in the parent–child relationship that may be impeding the infant's development. Signs to look for during the assessment session include a parent's attunement or responsiveness to the infant's bids for parental attention or involvement, as well as the parent's capacity to provide appropriate social cues, such as reassurance or encouragement. A parent who is extremely anxious about the child's performance may be intrusive or try to take over the assessment process. This may be manifested in insistent attempts to present items of no interest to the baby, or in actual physical manipulation of the child's hands to perform the task. Such a parent cannot tolerate waiting even a moment to find out what the baby will do with the material unaided. In contrast, some parents may be unwilling to allow the examiner to attend to the baby. Such parents may demand constant attention from the examiner and seem to

Table 4. *Suspect ratings for 6–30-month-old infants on IBR general behavioral scales*

Scale	Suspect ratings	Bayley Standardization Sample (BSS)		Louisville Twin Study (LTS)	
		Mean % of infants receiving suspect ratings	Mean % difference between suspect and nonsuspect categories	Mean % of infants receiving suspect ratings	Mean % difference between suspect and nonsuspect categories
1. Responsiveness to persons	1–4	10	25	3	17
2. Responsiveness to examiners	1–2	15	34	12	30
3. Responsiveness to mother	1–3	22	46	7	74
4. Cooperativeness	nu	nu	nu	nu	nu
5. Fearfulness	4–9	25	33	18	23
6. Tension	6–9	5	25	12	39
7. Happiness	1–4	14	22	19	33
8. Object orientation	1–4	4	26	11	38
11. Persistence	1–4	29	47	27	52
12. Attention span	1–4	16	38	17	47
13. Endurance	1–4	9	26	17	37
14. Activity	1–4	15	49	19	61
15. Reactivity	1–4	8	26	10	48
25. Energy level	1–2	na	na	11	79
26. Gross coordination	4–5	na	na	20	69
27. Fine coordination	4–5	na	na	18	74
Mean (n = 12 scales) ± SEM		14.3 ± 2.3	33.1 ± 2.8	14.3 ± 1.9	41.6 ± 4.6
Mean (n = 15 scales) ± SEM		na	na	14.7 ± 1.6	48.1 ± 5.1

Note: na = not available, nu = not uniform with age.
Source: Wolf and Lozoff (1985)

have a need to be the central focus of the examiner's interest throughout the assessment session. A parent who has withdrawn from the relationship with the baby may turn the infant over to the examiner and remain in the room as if not present. This parent may fail to resume normal parental functions even when called upon by the examiner.

The most appropriate approach to comprehensive socioemotional assessment is a longitudinal procedure including several unstructured observations in the home that can be used in conjunction with more formal assessment procedures (Fraiberg, 1980). This procedure provides the examiner a much more valid and reliable picture of the affective context of the baby's development than a clinic visit. In cases where more formal assessment leads to early intervention, longitudinal socioemotional assessment can occur during the beginning weeks of intervention. Unstructured home visits have several advantages over formalized procedures as a means for assessing the mental health of infant and parent. It is the examiner and not the baby who makes the adjustment to an unfamiliar setting. This eliminates the often negative effects of expecting an infant at risk to warm up and perform on command in a strange environment, and making parents feel ill at ease and scrutinized. With reduced stress, the examiner is in a position to observe the infant's abilities and relationships with all members of the household.

Home visits offer opportunities to investigate the potential multiplicity of influences contributing to a developmental problem. Are there ample opportunities to explore the environment? Does the baby spend the day in the crib and lack adequate motor control and social experience? Are the effects of hospitalization or disability affecting the frequency or depth of interactions offered the infant? Home visits offer opportunities to inquire about parental perception of the baby's spontaneous behavior as it occurs, taking advantage of the heightened feelings of the moment for exploration and interpretation. From observation one can learn if and how parental capacities and incapacities are affecting the baby. There is an opportunity to assess parental ego strengths as well as areas of conflict that may be creating obstructions to a mutually gratifying relationship. Recording the data collected during the home visit, whether through the use of a structured instrument such as the Home Observation for Measurement of the Environment Inventory (Bradley & Caldwell, 1980; Caldwell & Bradley, 1984) or the writing of clinical notes, requires that the examiner-visitor be sensitive so as not to detract from the spontaneity of the interaction. Actual writing and note taking are best deferred until after the visit.

Most important, observations made over time increase the likelihood of a more accurate assessment of the socioemotional domain, and continued focus on family assessment can occur even after the child begins the intervention sessions. In the course of four to six sessions, one can expect to have reduced the parents' anxieties about the assessor and have established sufficient trust to permit relatively ordinary family interactions to occur during the visits. An open-ended home visit in which one tries to learn about the parents' experience of the baby is quite different from a clinic observation of externally structured behavior in which the parent is asked to interact with the baby, while several professional onlookers observe, clipboards in hand.

The parents' previous experiences with other professionals prior to and during referral influence the emotional tone that they present at the assessment. Their feelings about treatment by other professionals (as well as historical authority figures in their lives) will influence their expectations about the assessment process and the team members. What have they been told about the infant's difficulties and about the actions they should take? Often they have already received conflicting advice. This history affects their manner of relating to the assessment team and their availability to meet the momentary needs of the baby (see Parker & Zuckerman, this volume). For these reasons a single observation, especially in a clinic setting, may provide only limited information concerning socioemotional issues. The initial interview should offer parents every opportunity to ask questions in order to increase their security and sense of control. The slow pace of an expanded assessment allows them the opportunity to tell their own story in their own time. Rather than attempt to take a developmental history that places a questionnaire between the parents and their feelings, the story can unfold in a sequence governed by the parents' affective experience.

Speech and language assessment

Comprehensive evaluation of infants at risk for developmental problems should include a variety of speech and language techniques. An oral-peripheral examination for both structure and function by an appropriately trained professional helps to determine the infant's neurological potential for efficient respiration and feeding, as well as for appropriate, volitional sound production (Morris, 1984). Hearing screening, for example, using the calibrated noisemakers in the *Hear Kit* (Downs, 1979), allows a gross behavioral estimate of hearing ability that identifies children who should be referred for a complete audiological evaluation. Collection of an informal language-communication sample and making an estimate of language ability in relation to a normed instrument form the final components of the evaluation.

Informal observation in a comfortable setting is more important for speech and language evaluation than the use of any specific standardized measure. Early language and communicative behavior is so dependent on the situation that children may be unwilling to display their skill to strangers in an unfamiliar environment. With advancing age, all forms of assessment come to depend more and more on the use of language both in understanding instructions and in producing responses. Therefore, children who may be hearing impaired, or whose native language is not that of the assessor or the evaluation instrument, pose particular assessment challenges.

In a clinic-based evaluation, a natural language sample can be obtained by setting aside time for a play session between parent and baby, and providing them with age-appropriate toys and picture books. Such sessions are often videotaped or audiotaped and supplemented with contextual notes. A home-based session allows more comfort and freedom on the part of the child and parent, leading to a richer language sample. The natural language sample becomes more important with age, and beyond 18 months becomes a critical feature of assessment.

Language development seems to be particularly vulnerable to various sources of risk. Although there is wide variation in the rate of language development between birth and 3 years, it is critical that children who show weak comprehension accompanied by the absence of verbal production be identified by 18 months of age. In the 18–36 months age range, a variety of published formats for evaluating a language sample are available (e.g., Bloom & Lahey, 1978; Chapman, 1981; Miller, 1981). Content, form, and use should be included in the analysis. Content, or the semantic component of language, is observable in the child's receptive and expressive vocabularies, and in the number of different word meanings the child is able to incorporate. Form is observable in the areas of phonology, morphology, and syntax. Phonological assessment considers the vocalizations or sounds a baby produces in babbling and later those sounds a child produces in syllables, words, and connected speech, in order to determine whether there are any error patterns, other than those expected at the early stages of acquisition, that need to be monitored across time. Morphological assessment examines the child's use of inflectional units of meaning within words in the form of free morphemes (e.g., "dog" or "mama", with each word representing one free-standing or unattached unit of meaning) and bound morphemes (e.g., "dogs," representing both a free morpheme, "dog," and a bound morpheme, "s," serving as a plural marker for more than one dog). Syntax analysis focuses on the ordered production of combined or connected words in multiword utterances. Finally, use of the pragmatic component of language is observable in terms of the child's intentions for communicative attempts (e.g., to request, to inform, to regulate) and can be analyzed in gestural, vocal, and verbal communication attempts or in any combination of these modalities. For instance, a child may point to the refrigerator while saying "juice" as a means for requesting a drink.

A number of formal instruments are available for speech and language assessment. They share a variety of problems: reliance on parent reporting, small numbers of items in the early age ranges, and weak or nonexistent norming procedures. The Bzoch-League Receptive-Expressive Emergent Language Scale (REEL) (Bzoch & League, 1971) is used very frequently because it has a relatively large number of items for the early ages and is easy to administer. However, it relies heavily on parental report and the basis for age placement of the items is unclear, given the absence of reports of a published norming study. Comparison of age placement for similar items on the BSID and the Sequenced Inventory of Communication Development-Revised (SICD) (Hendrick, Prather, & Tobin, 1984) indicates that the REEL expects behaviors at consistently earlier ages than the two other instruments. Since children produce more language that is related to behavior at home, parents would be expected to observe behaviors earlier. However, the SICD also frequently relies on parental reporting, and the discrepancies seem too large to be accounted for in this manner (Glazewski, 1987).

The Bayley Mental Scale can provide a preliminary estimate of language development, since it includes many items that appear on the REEL. It might be useful to combine the Bayley and REEL scales while relying on the Bayley age expectations, which are based on a well-normed sample, in contrast to the overly optimistic age placements of items on the REEL. Where the REEL and the SICD have overlapping items, the SICD age placements, which are based on a small norming sample, seem more appropriate than those of the REEL (Glazewski, 1987). Otherwise, the SICD adds little to the REEL below 24 months of age because of its extensive reliance on parental report and its limited number of items. When an informal language sample is obtained, the REEL might be used to score the sample. As an example of how these measures compare, Table 5 lists language items from the BSID in the 7–12-month average age range, with corresponding items and ages from the REEL. The REEL provides three expressive and three receptive items at each 2-month age span, so an additional 20 items can be observed in this age range. As shown in Table 5, age placements of items on the REEL tend to overlap, yet be lower than the means for the BSID.

Movement assessment

The assessment of movement is a critical aspect of the evaluation of any infant at risk. In the early months of life, preterm infants are more likely to show motor than cognitive delays (Gorga, Stern, & Ross, 1985). Siegel (1981), who reported no statistical differences in corrected mental development scores for a sample of moderately preterm and full-term infants at 2 years of age, did find a difference in motor scores.

Most motor scales (e.g., Bayley, 1969; Folio & Fewell, 1983) present a summary of

Table 5. *Language items from the Bayley Scales (7–12 months) and age placement (in months) on the REEL*

Item no.	Age, mo. Mean (Range)	Bayley item description	REEL no.	Age, mo.
79	7.0 (5–12)	Vocalizes four different syllables	E17	5–6
81	7.6 (5–12)	Cooperates in games	E23	7–8
84	7.9 (5–14)	Listens selectively to familiar words	R19	6–7
85	7.9 (5–14)	Says "da-da" or equivalent	E19	6–7
89	9.1 (6–14)	Responds to verbal request	R25	8–9
90	9.4 (6–13)	Puts cube in cup on command	R31	10–11
93	10. (7–16)	Looks at pictures in book	R27	8–9
94	10.1 (7–16)	Inhibits on command	R26	8–9
101	12. (9–18)	Jabbers expressively	E30	9–10
106	12.5 (9–18)	Imitates words	E33	10–11

milestones to be observed in the course of normal development, but provide no means for describing the quality of movement as the child changes position or accomplishes the milestone skills assessed. Several pediatric physical therapists and occupational therapists have developed descriptive instruments that quantify their clinical judgments and provide uniformity of procedure within a particular assessment setting (e.g., Gorga & Stern, 1979; Sillari, n.d.). Recently, quantitative scoring approaches for previously published neurologic exams have been developed (e.g., Ellison, Browning, Larson, & Denny, 1983), and a new instrument has been published, the Movement Assessment of Infants (MAI) developed specifically to meet the needs for early motor assessment (Chandler, Andrews, & Swanson, 1980). Ultimately, however, the assessment of movement is extremely dependent on the clinical skill of a trained examiner.

At the present time, few professionals who lack formal neurological training from either a medical or movement-specialized curriculum with a pediatric component are capable of screening a baby, even with the support of an appropriate instrument, to determine whether comprehensive motor assessment is called for. Professionals involved in infant assessment should ensure that their particular assessment procedure addresses this problem, either by including an individual competent in motor assessment in every evaluation, or by securing in-service training for other professionals so that they can make appropriate referrals.

In addition to the milestones assessed in the BSID, an evaluation of motor skills must address such areas as muscle tone, primitive reflexes, automatic reactions, and volitional movement. Any single milestone can be exhibited by a baby in a manner that will form the basis for later normal development, or in a manner characteristic of a specific motor dysfunction that will inhibit the development of later skills. Examples from the Bayley Motor Scale can illustrate the problem.

Bayley item 33 ("pre-walking progression"; mean age of achievement 7.1 month, range 5–11 months) is credited if the baby makes "9 inches or more" of forward progress by crawling, creeping, moving on feet and hands, or hitching along in a sitting position. Unimpaired babies show great variation in early locomotion, often to the amusement of their parents. For the disabled baby, however, some atypical forms of early locomotion may suggest the need for intervention so that later maladaptive patterns of movement can be minimized.

Consider the case of a baby with Down syndrome at 14 months who could belly crawl for 9 inches and reach a toy, but then would be too exhausted to pick it up and examine it. She attained the crawling position by widely separating her legs (straddle split) and falling forward. The positioning of her legs was either frightening to observe or a cause for wonder, like a skill we associate with a trained dancer. When placed in a standing position, she "fixed" her legs rigidly and locked them in place. Any destabilization led to immediate collapse and fearful crying because she had no ability to right herself.

Although she could pass Bayley Motor Scale item 36 ("pulls to standing position holding the examiner's thumbs"; mean age of achievement 8.1 months, range 5–12 months), she did this rigidly, with stiffening of her legs rather than moving through a sitting position. In fact, she avoided pulling to stand from a sitting position, crying and collapsing when this was attempted. She made no attempts to stand by furniture on her own (item 38, mean age of achievement 8.6 months, range 6–12 months).

This baby showed low muscle tone and little voluntary control. Because of the low muscle tone, she could achieve a prone position without volitional rotation of her legs, so her forward locomotion was not reflective of the level of organization normally needed for this skill. Her crawling strategy did little to improve her sense of balance or to contribute to upright stability. In this case, therapy was needed to help the child achieve volitional control of standing and lateral upright movements.

Preterm babies weighing less than 1,500 grams at birth or born 2 months early are known to be at risk for cerebral palsy. Concomitantly, they have a tendency to exhibit low or high muscle tone and slow waning of primitive reflexes, as well as other possible signs of neurological dysfunction related to complications of prematurity (Deitz, Crowe, & Harris, 1987; Palisano, 1986). Unlike babies with Down syndrome, not all preterms receive or require early intervention, thus, appropriate motor assessment of this group is crucial. Differences in the fine motor skills of preterm infants in the first year of life have been associated with lower Bayley Mental Scale Scores at 2 years of age (Ruff et al., 1984). It may be that fine motor limitations make it more difficult for the baby to explore the environment in ways that lead to cognitive growth (McCune & Ruff, 1985). Table 1 presents Bayley Mental Scale items that rely on reaching. Many other items also depend on fine motor skills, emphasizing the implicit relationship between early cognition and motor development. Yet the Bayley Scales do not provide for an assessment of the quality of movement. If a pediatric motor specialist is not part of the assessment team, a low score on the Mental Scale for babies in the 6–18-month age range may indicate the need for referral for further motor evaluation, even if Bayley motor milestones seem adequate, to determine whether poor movement quality is inhibiting exploration.

Babies experiencing psychosocial risk may show motor delays due to depression and low motivation. Their parents may be unaware of the need for free movement or unable to facilitate it. Infants who are failing to thrive may lack energy as well as motivation. Motor assessment cannot be neglected for this group either.

SUMMARY

Sensitive administration and interpretation of conventional assessment instruments with infants requires careful investigation of the multiple factors that contribute to developmental status. To accomplish this, we have proposed an interdisciplinary approach to assessment and resultant decision making concerning the needs of an infant and family, which is summarized in Figure 1. This procedure centers on the use of a strong core instrument, such as the Bayley Scales of Infant Development. The best use of such a core assessment is to determine not only a global measure of the child's current developmental level as compared with well established norms, but also, and more importantly, to identify patterns of performance through specific item analysis. Given a child's performance on the Bayley Scales, one can then formulate hypotheses and determine what additional information should be obtained through the administration of supplemental domain-specific instruments and/or observations of the child and family.

There has been considerably greater emphasis in the past on cognitive, language, motor, and medical assessment than on psychosocial assessment. However, there is increasing recognition of the prognostic value of socioemotional data (Bee et al., 1982; Cohen & Parmelee, 1983; Kopp & McCall, 1982). Furthermore, clinical evidence points to the efficacy of psychosocial intervention with families experiencing infant mental health problems (Fraiberg, 1980). With the legal mandate of P.L. 99-457 it becomes imperative for interdisciplinary teams to devote attention to evaluating the psychosocial needs of handicapped infants and their families, and to devising appropriate cost-effective strategies for incorporating psychosocial interventions. Ultimately, the challenge of the assessment process is for the team to analyze the multiple interrelated aspects of development, both to understand the nature and course of development for each child and to determine priorities for intervention.

REFERENCES

American Psychological Association, American Educational Research Association, and National Council on Measurement in Education. (1974). *Standards for educational and psychological tests*. Washington, DC: American Psychological Association.

Bagnato, S. J., Neisworth, J. T., & Capone, A. (1986). Curriculum-based assessment for the young exceptional child: Rationale and Review. *Topics in Early Childhood Special Education*, 6, 97–110.

Bates, E. (1976). *Language in context: The acquisition of pragmatics*. New York: Academic Press.

Bates, E., Benigni, L., Bretherton, I., Camaioni, L., & Volterra, V. (1979). *The emergence of symbols: Cognition and communication in infancy*. New York: Academic Press.

Bayley, N. (1933). Mental growth during the first three years. *Genetic Psychology Monographs, 14*, 1–92.

Bayley, N. (1969). Bayley Scales of Infant Development. New York: Psychological Corporation.

Bayley, N. (1970). Development of mental abilities. In P. H. Mussen (Ed.), *Carmichael's manual of child psychology* (vol. 1, pp. 1163–1210). New York: Wiley.

Belsky, J., & Most, R. (1981). From exploration to play: A cross-sectional study of infant free play behavior. *Developmental Psychology, 17*, 630–639.

Bee, H. L., Barnard, K. E., Eyres, S. J., Gray, C. A., Hammond, M. A., Spietz, A. L., Snyder, C., & Clark, B. (1982). Prediction of IQ and language skill from perinatal status, child performance, family characteristics, and mother–infant interaction. *Child Development, 57*, 1134–1156.

Blackman, J. (1986). *Warning signals: Basic criteria for tracking at-risk infants and toddlers*. Washington, DC: National Center for Clinical Infant Programs.

Bloom, L., & Lahey, M. (1978). *Language development and language disorders*. New York: Wiley.

Bornstein, M., & Sigman, M. (1986).Continuity in mental development from infancy. *Child Development, 57*, 251–274.

Bradley, R., & Caldwell, B. (1980). The relation of home environment, cognitive competence and IQ among males and females. *Child Development, 51*, 1140–1148.

Brinker, R., & Lewis, M. (1982). Discovering the competent handicapped infant: A process approach to assessment and intervention. *Topics in Early Childhood Special Educaton, 2*, 1–16.

Brooks-Gunn, J., & Lewis, M. (1981). Assessing young handicapped children: Issues and solutions. *Journal of the Division for Early Childhood, 2,* 84–95.

Brooks-Gunn, J., & Lewis, M. (1983). Screening and diagnosing handicapped infants. *Topics in Early Childhood Special Education, 3,* 14–28.

Brooks-Gunn, J., & Weinraub, M. (1983). Origins of infant intelligence tests. In M. Lewis (Ed.), *Origins of intelligence* (pp. 25–66). New York: Plenum Press.

Bzoch, K. R., & League, R. (1971). *The Bzoch-League Receptive-Expressive Emergent Language Scale: For the measurement of language skills in infancy.* Baltimore: University Park Press.

Caldwell, B., & Bradley, R. (1984). *Home observation for measurement of the environment.* Little Rock: University of Arkansas.

Chandler, L. S., Andrews, M. S., & Swanson, M. W. (1980). *Movement assessment of infants.* Rolling Bay, WA: Movement Assessment of Infants.

Chapman, R. (1981). Exploring children's communicative intents. In J. Miller (Ed.), *Assessing language production in children* (pp. 111–238). Baltimore: University Park Press.

Cohen, S. E., & Parmelee, A. H. (1983). Prediction of five-year Stanford-Binet scores in preterm infants. *Child Development, 54,* 1242–1253.

Collard, R. (1972). Review of the Bayley Scales of Infant Development. In O. K. Buros (Ed.), *The seventh mental measurement yearbook* (pp. 727–729). Highland Park, NJ: Gryphon Press.

Corman, H. H., & Escalona, S. K. (1969). Stages of sensorimotor development: A replication study. *Merrill-Palmer Quarterly, 15,* 351–361.

Corrigan, R. (1978). Language as related to stage six object permanence development. *Journal of Child Language, 5,* 173–189.

Damarin, F. (1978). Review of the Bayley Scales of Infant Development. In O. K. Buros (Ed.), *The eighth mental measurement yearbook* (pp. 291–293). Highland Park, NJ: Gryphon Press.

Decarie, T. G. (1969). A study of the mental and emotional development of the thalidomide child. In B. M. Foss (Ed.), *Determinants of infant behavior* (Vol. 4, pp. 167–187). London: Methuen.

Deitz, J. C., Crowe, T. K., & Harris, S. R. (1987). Relationship between infant neuromotor assessment and preschool motor measures. *Physical Therapy, 67,* 14–17.

Downs, M. (1979). *Hear Kit.* Denver: Bam World Markets.

Dunst, C. (1980). *A clinical and educational manual for use with assessment in infancy: Ordinal scales of psychological development.* Baltimore: University Park Press.

Dunst, C., & Gallagher, J. (1983). Piagetian approaches to infant assessment. *Topics in Early Childhood Special Education, 3,* 44–62.

Education of the Handicapped Act (1986). Part H–99–457–Title 34 of the United States Code, 20 U.S.C. Secs. 1401–1485, Supplement 181.

Ellison, P., Browning, C. A., Larson, B., & Denny, J. (1983). Development of a scoring system for the Milani-Comparetti and Gidoni method of assessing neurologic abnormality in infancy. *Physical Therapy, 9,* 1414–1423.

Escalona, S. K., & Moriarty, A. (1961). Prediction of schoolage intelligence from infant tests. *Child Development, 31,* 597–605.

Field, T., Dempsey, J., & Shuman, H. H. (1979). Bayley behavioral ratings of normal and high-risk infants: Their relationship to Bayley Mental Scores. *Journal of Pediatric Psychology, 4,* 277–283.

Folio, M. R., & Fewell, R. R. (1983). *Peabody developmental motor scale and activity cards.* Allen, TX: Teaching Resources.

Fraiberg, S. (1977). *Insights from the blind.* New York: Basic Books.

Fraiberg, S. (Ed.). (1980). *Clinical studies in infant mental health: The first year of life.* New York: Basic Books.

Frankenburg, W., Dodds, J., Fandal, A., Kazuk, E., & Cohrs, M. (1975). *Denver Developmental Screening Test.* Denver: LADOCA Publishing Foundation.

Frankenburg, W., Fandal, A., Sciarillo, W., & Burgess, D. (1981). The newly abbreviated and revised Denver Developmental Screening Test. *Journal of Pediatrics, 99,* 996–998.

Gesell, A. (1928). *Infancy and human growth.* New York: Macmillan.

Gesell, A. L. (1945). *The embryology of behavior: The beginnings of the human mind.* New York: Harper.

Gesell, A., & Thompson, H. (1934). *Infant behavior: Its genesis and growth.* New York: McGraw-Hill.

Glazewski, B. (1987). Assessment of communication in infancy: A review of the instruments.

Unpublished doctoral qualifying paper, Rutgers University, New Brunswick.

Gorga, D., & Stern, F. (1979). *The neuromotor behavioral inventory*. New York: New York Hospital-Cornell Medical Center.

Gorga, D., Stern, F., & Ross, G. (1985). Trends in neuromotor behavior of preterm and full-term infants in the first year of life: A preliminary report. *Developmental Medicine & Child Neurology, 27*, 756–766.

Hauser-Cram, P., & Shonkoff, J. (1988). Rethinking the assessment of child focused outcomes. In H. Weiss & F. Jacobs (Eds.), *Evaluating family programs* (pp. 73–94). Hawthorne, NY: Aldine Publishing.

Hendrick, D. L., Prather, E. M., & Tobin, A. R. (1984). Sequenced Inventory of Communicative Development–revised. Seattle: University of Washington Press.

Hill, P. M., & McCune-Nicolich, L. (1981). Pretend play and patterns of cognition in Down's syndrome children. *Child Development, 52*, 611–617.

Holden, R. (1972). Review of the Bayley Scales of Infant Development. In O. K. Buros (Ed.), *The seventh mental measurement yearbook* (p. 729). Highland Park, NJ: Gryphon Press.

Honzik, M. (1983). Measuring mental abilities in infancy: The value and limitations. In M. Lewis (Ed.), *Origins of Intelligence* (pp. 67–107). New York: Plenum Press.

Kopp, C. B., & McCall, R. B. (1982). Predicting later mental performance for normal, at-risk, and handicapped infants. In P. Baltes & O. Brim (Eds.), *Life span development and behavior* (Vol. 4, pp. 33–64). New York: Academic Press.

Matheny, A. P., Dolan, B., & Wilson, R. (1974). Bayley's Infant Behavior Record: Relations between behavior and early mental test scores. *Developmental Psychology, 10*, 696.

McCall, R., Hogarty, P. S., & Hurlburt, N. (1972). Transitions in infant sensorimotor development and the prediction of childhood IQ. *American Psychologist, 27*, 728–748.

McCall, R. B., Applebaum, M. I., & Hogarty, P. S. (1973). Developmental changes in mental performance. *Monographs of the Society for Research in Child Development 3* (Serial No. 150).

McCall, R. (1981). Early predictions of later IQ: The search continues. *Intelligence, 5*, 141–147.

McCune, L. (1980). A manual for analyzing free play: Experimental edition. New Brunswick: Rutgers University Press.

McCune, L. (1986). Symbolic development in normal and atypical infants. In G. Fein & M. Rivkin (Eds.), *The young child at play: Reviews of research*, (Vol., 45–61). Washington, DC: NAEYC.

McCune-Nicolich, L. (1981). Toward symbolic functioning: Structure of early pretend games and potential parallels with language. *Child Development, 52*, 785–797.

McCune-Nicolich, L., & Bruskin, C. (1981). Combinatorial competency in symbolic play and language. In K. Rubin (Ed.), *The play of children: Current theory and research* (pp. 1–14). Basel, Switzerland: Korger.

McCune, L., & Ruff, H. (1985). Infant special education: Interactions with objects. *Topics in Early Childhood Special Education*, 59–68.

Miller, J. (1981). *Assessing language production in children*. Baltimore: University Park Press.

Miller, G., Dubowitz, L., & Palmer, P. (1984). Follow-up of pre-term infants: Is correction of the developmental quotient for prematurity helpful? *Early Human Development, 9*, 137–144.

Morris, S. E. (1984). *Pre-speech assessment scale: A rating scale for the measurement of pre-speech behaviors from birth through two years*. Clifton, NJ: J. A. Preston.

Nicolich, L. McCune. (1977). Beyond sensorimotor intelligence: Assessment of symbolic maturity through analysis of pretend play. *Merrill-Palmer Quarterly, 23*, 89–101.

Palisano, R. J. (1986). Use of chronological and adjusted ages to compare motor development of healthy preterm and fullterm infants. *Developmental Medicine and Child Neurology, 28*, 180–187.

Pasick, P. (1985). *Specific developmental outcomes of premature infants with respiratory illness*. Doctoral dissertation, University of Michigan, Ann Arbor.

Piaget, J. (1952). *The origins of intelligence in children*. New York: International Universities Press.

Piaget, J. (1954). *The construction of reality in the child*. New York: Basic Books.

Piaget, J. (1962). *Play, dreams and imitation in childhood*. New York: Norton.

Ruff, H., McCarten, C., Kurtzburg, D., & Vaughn, H. (1984). Preterm infants' manipulative explorations with objects. *Child Development, 55*, 1166–1173.

Shonkoff, J. (1983). The limitations of normative assessment of high-risk infants. *Topics in Early Childhood Special Education, 3*, 29–43.

Siegel, L. S. (1979). Infant perceptual, cognitive and motor behaviors as predictors of subsequent cognitive and language development. *Canadian Journal of Psychology/Review of Canadian Psychology, 33,* 382–395.

Siegel, L. S. (1981). Infant tests as predictors of cognitive and language development at two years. *Child Development, 52,* 545–557.

Siegel, L. (1983). Correction for prematurity and its consequences for the assessment of the very low birth weight infant. *Child Development, 54,* 1176–1188.

Siegel, L. S. (1985). A risk index to predict learning problems in preterm and fullterm children. In W. K. Frankenburg, R. N. Emde, & J. W. Sullivan (Eds.), *Early identificaton of children at risk: An international perspective.* New York: Plenum Press.

Sillari, J. (n.d.). *Gross motor and fine motor evaluation.* Metuchen, NJ: Cerebral Palsy Association of Middlesex County.

Stern, D. (1985). The interpersonal world of the human infant: A view from psychoanalysis and developmental psychology, New York: Basic Books.

Terman, L. M., & Merrill, M. A. (1960). *Stanford-Binet Intelligence Scale.* Boston: Houghton-Mifflin.

Ungerer, J., & Sigman, M. (1983). Developmental lags in preterm infants from one to three years of age. *Child Development, 54,* 1217–1228.

Uzgiris, I. C., & Hunt, J. McV. (1975). *Assessment in infancy: Ordinal scales of psychological development.* Urbana: University of Illinois Press.

Wolf, A. W., & Lozoff, B. (1985). A clinically interpretable method for analyzing the Bayley Infant Behavior Record. *Journal of Pediatric Psychology, 10,* 199–214.

Zelazo, P. (1982). An information processing approach to infant cognitive assessment. In M. Lewis & L. Taft (Eds.), *Developmental disabilities: Theory, assessment and intervention* (pp. 229–255). New York: Spectrum Publications.

11 *Alternative assessment strategies for the evaluation of infants and toddlers: An organizational perspective*

DANTE CICCHETTI AND SHELDON WAGNER

INTRODUCTION

In recent years we have witnessed the emergence of an intensified national commitment to provide educational services for handicapped and high-risk children. As a direct consequence of these efforts, there has been a dramatic increase in the number of intervention programs available to children with disabilities and their families. However, despite the enthusiastic proliferation of services for this heterogeneous group of youngsters, the efficacy of these programs has not, in the main, been demonstrated empirically. In part, this state of affairs may be attributed to the paucity of assessment instruments that provide a rich enough picture of the developmental organization of children with atypical development. Because not all disabled children, even those with the same condition, develop similarly in all domains of functioning, it follows that intervention goals should be broader than mere cognitive stimulation and that different needs may profit from different types of programs (e.g., see Cicchetti, 1987; Cicchetti & Pogge-Hesse, 1982; Cicchetti, Toth, & Bush, 1988; Kopp, 1983).

Until recently the majority of studies conducted on disabled and high-risk children have used standardized normative tests as outcome measures. These conventional assessment instruments often lack the theoretical power and empirical specificity necessary to devise a successful intervention program to meet the specific needs of a particular child (Keogh & Kopp, 1978). Not only must we find some way to define and assess early maladaptation, we need to validate our diagnoses by illustrating their relation to later outcomes. Thus, a developmental scheme is necessary for tracing the etiology and nature of maladaptation so that interventions can be timed and guided appropriately.

Throughout history researchers have primarily conceptualized the development of disabled children as being qualitatively different from that of children without handi-

The writing of this chapter was supported by grants from the John D. and Catherine T. MacArthur Foundation Network on Early Childhood, the March of Dimes Foundation, the National Center on Child Abuse and Neglect (90-C-1929), the National Institute of Mental Health (RO1-MH37960-01), and the Spencer Foundation to author Cicchetti, and by a grant from the National Institute of Mental Health (1 RO3 MH 42189-01) to author Wagner. Special thanks are due to Jody Ganiban and to Sheree Toth for their valuable help, feedback, and suggestions, and to Victoria Gill for typing this manuscript.

246

caps. We propose that a more valuable perspective is to conceive of the development of children with a disability as an *organized system*, not unlike that of normally developing children (Cicchetti & Pogge-Hesse, 1982; Cicchetti & Sroufe, 1978; Hodapp & Zigler, in press; Zigler, 1969). Viewed within this framework, effective intervention strategies can be implemented more appropriately (Greenspan et al., 1987). Moreover, as we will illustrate, this organizational perspective on development is broad and integrative enough to deal effectively with individual differences within and between subgroups of handicapped and high-risk children (Cicchetti & Aber, 1986; Cicchetti & Beeghly, in press; Cicchetti & Olsen, in press; Cicchetti & Pogge-Hesse, 1982; Cicchetti & Schneider-Rosen, 1986; Cicchetti & Sroufe, 1978).

In recent years an increasing number of researchers have directed their attention toward elucidating the organization of development in high-risk children (e.g., children with a greater probability of developing maladaptively) and on uncovering the relation between the quality of early adaptation and later developmental outcomes (Kopp, 1987; Lewis, Feiring, McGuffog, & Jaskir, 1984; Main, Kaplan, & Cassidy, 1985; Sroufe, 1979a, 1983). By explaining abnormal ontogenetic processes in the social, emotional, cognitive, and linguistic domains, contributions can be made to theories of normal development. In addition, this developmental perspective broadens our understanding of the deviations and distortions that occur in high-risk and psychopathological conditions (Cicchetti, 1984, in press; Rutter & Garmezy, 1983). According to this perspective, disabilities can be viewed both in terms of how they do and do not exert an impact upon the developmental process. Moreover, this approach leads to a view of individual differences that is much more differentiated than a simple assessment of degree of cognitive retardation.

RATIONALE FOR ALTERNATIVE ASSESSMENT STRATEGIES

The uncritical application of traditional psychometric assessments to infants and toddlers with varying risk and handicapping conditions merely confirms what is already known about these youngsters from observations of their day-to-day functioning, and serves only to classify children at a particular level of intellectual functioning. Moreover, even if two children have the same IQ score, it does not necessarily follow that the underlying structural organization of their intellectual functioning is the same (cf. Fischer, 1980; Piaget, 1952). Furthermore, the assumption that youngsters with developmental difficulties can be assessed adequately using traditional assessment batteries is doubtful. The extension of conventional assessment techniques to populations whose life course may include such events as frequent illnesses, physical problems (including vision, speech, and hearing impairments), emotional difficulties, environmental risks, and poor quality caretaking is of questionable validity. Thus, any diagnostic evaluation of a child with a disability that is limited to cognitively based evaluations may seriously misjudge the child's competence as well as the source of the child's functional impairments. By focusing on a unitary area of deficit, the assessment may fail to uncover other problems or to elucidate areas of strength. Therefore, evaluations of children with disabilities, or those struggling with adverse environmental circumstances, need to assess a broad range of developmental domains (see McCune, Kalmanson, Fleck, Glazewski, & Sillari, this volume). The use of assessment paradigms that allow for the exploration of the full range of capabilities yields a much richer portrayal of functioning.

When evaluating children with handicapping or risk conditions, we believe that assessments should be targeted at multiple domains. We begin with a general discussion of assessment in infancy and toddlerhood, provide a theoretical discussion of the underlying assumptions and the purpose of traditional evaluations, and then explore nontraditional procedures. We believe that in conjunction with traditional forms of assessment instruments, utilization of alternate paradigms for assessing perceptual-cognitive, socioemotional, and representational capacities may be useful in providing a more comprehensive understanding of the developmental organization of special populations of children.

ASSESSMENT DURING INFANCY AND TODDLERHOOD

As the technology of medical management has become increasingly sophisticated and more successful, the number of surviving infants who are at risk for nonoptimal development is growing rapidly (Kopp, 1987). Likewise, as our knowledge base with regard to environmental risk factors has increased, evaluations that can identify incipient or nascent psychopathology have become even more necessary (Cicchetti, 1987). Because the identification of pathognomonic indicators of developmental deviations in infancy is difficult, the assessment of disturbances in infancy and toddlerhood requires sophisticated evaluative procedures that can identify the subtle developmental nuances associated with the early years of life. This requires the use of broad-band measures that assess the interrelations among biological, perceptual-cognitive, linguistic, and socioemotional domains. Multicontextual evaluations that incorporate input from a variety of settings and informants also can elucidate problem areas and lead to more well-informed decision making (Achenbach, McConaughy, & Howell, 1987). Before exploring pragmatic considerations, we wish to provide a theoretical overview of assessment in general. Next, we present a framework, the organizational perspective, that guides our philosophy about how alternative assessments should be designed and conducted.

THEORY OF ASSESSMENT

In the broadest sense, assessment is the measurement of the relative position of an individual in a larger defined population with respect to some psychological construct. It is the psychological counterpart to a medical examination, and both lead in some sense to a diagnosis and to the formulation of a treatment plan. However, there are important differences between the medical model, which generally starts from the individual's cluster of symptoms to deduce the individual's group membership (disease X), and psychological assessment. In psychological assessment it is generally the case that an individual's *relative* position in the group is ascertained, that is, how *much* of construct X she or he displays.

This difference in focus is a consequence of a fundamental distinction between the medical and psychological models. Psychology is primarily interested in *groups*, not individuals; psychology attempts to characterize groups of individuals based on the variations in performance of those individuals. Medicine starts from the individual and tries to determine the group in which he or she belongs. This basic difference in approach leads to problems in extending the research findings of psychological constructs to clinically useful diagnostic instruments.

PRINCIPLES OF ASSESSMENT

There are three fundamental assumptions of all assessment instruments: representativeness, continuity, and relatedness. The principle of *representativeness* requires that the instrument properly samples the psychological construct; that is, the microdevelopmental time of the testing session should be representative of the child's functioning in the macrodevelopmental time of the normal ontogenetic process. All traditional assessment instruments assume this principle. In the "strange situation," for example (Ainsworth & Wittig, 1969), the anxiety felt by the child at separation is assumed to be the same as felt in real-life situations – and the mother's reactions are considered to be a valid reflection of the dyad's day-to-day interaction patterns.

The principle of *continuity* requires that the construct assessed be fairly stable over time (Messick, 1983). If constructs were inherently evanescent, then there would be little utility in creating an assessment instrument to sample them. This does not mean that transient and/or infrequent psychological events (e.g., mental telepathy, moods) are inherently uninteresting – indeed they might be of great theoretical importance. This issue is of special concern to the development and utilization of nontraditional assessment instruments.

The principle of *relatedness* requires that the construct being assessed be of some real psychological importance. There is never any difficulty in finding a construct upon which people will differ. There are in fact an infinite number of such differences between any two individuals and any two groups. The key is to find a difference (i.e., measure a construct) that is related to something else of importance (either theoretical or practical). The principle of relatedness enjoins us to describe a difference as a difference *only* if it *makes* a difference.

WHY WE CONDUCT ASSESSMENTS

There are two major reasons to do assessment: prediction and anchoring. Any assessment is implicitly a prediction based on the principles of continuity and representativeness. If a child's relative position on an instrument is not maintained over time, then it is because some other force has acted upon the child. If no change occurs, then we assume that there was no force and the null hypothesis is maintained.

Anchoring refers to the establishment of a base from which one can monitor change. An assessment is done to establish the position of an individual, then an intervention occurs, followed by a subsequent assessment. In this way, the effect of the intervention can be determined experimentally. The purpose of the intervention is, in some sense, to "invalidate" the principle of continuity.

REASONS FOR NONTRADITIONAL ASSESSMENTS

There are three major reasons to conduct nontraditional assessments: population differences, domain or construct differences, and sensitivity concerns.

Population differences

If one is interested in an individual from a population that is not represented in the original standardization sample of a measure – such as infants and toddlers who are blind, deaf, or mentally retarded – then an assessment with the traditional instrument violates the principle of representativeness. Whereas the measurements may be useful for relative comparisons of individuals within the group of interest, they are fundamentally invalid. Population differences are one of the major reasons for nontraditional assessment. Nontraditional measurements should be used for those situations when the investigator is concerned with an individual who is not represented in the sample of traditional assessment instruments.

Domain or construct differences

A second reason for nontraditional assessments is that one is interested in a construct for which there are no useful standard assessment instruments. For example, one might be interested in tool-making ability, in the ability to transfer information acquired in one modality to another, in the appearance of anxiety in novel situations, or in the facility for making friends. Many nontraditional measures presume that the existence of a difference between two groups on the measure is *sufficient* evidence for the importance of the construct underlying the measure. Obviously there must be good reason to believe that such constructs are of some real psychological importance.

Sensitivity concerns

The third major reason for nontraditional assessments has to do with the sensitivity of traditional instruments. Let us imagine that one is convinced that a certain variable (e.g., prematurity or child neglect) should have an effect on the optimal development of the child. If traditional measures such as IQ or receptive language ability do not confirm this, then one could argue that the measures are insensitive to the actual differences that exist. Any and all tests have inherent error because the principle of representativeness can never be fulfilled perfectly. However, since it is always possible to accuse any instrument of being insensitive, one must be circumspect in employing such a criticism.

Nontraditional assessment tools often are used because of dissatisfaction with the sensitivity of a conventional instrument. It cannot be overemphasized, however, that sensitivity is a two-edged sword. The coarser the test, the more likely the principle of relatedness will obtain; the finer or more sensitive the test, the less likely the principle of relatedness will obtain. Take, for example, graphomotor abilities. If two groups differ on such a gross discrimination (one that requires the orchestration of several mental "subroutines"), then they are likely to differ consistently on other variables. If they differ on a more sensitive measure, say, a reaction-time variable, or a variable tapping only one mental system, then they are less likely to be *consistently* different on other variables (because one had to go all the way down to the supersensitive level of reaction time to find a *difference* to begin with).

At this point, it will be useful to establish some additional terminology. Let us assume that any assessment instrument can be scaled in such a way as to have a *pass score* and a *fail score*. For instance, a fail score might be a certain number of "wrong" answers on some screening test. The *criterion*, or *cut-point*, is the number of wrong answers on the screening test that is required before an individual "fails" the test. If one predicts outcome on another instrument (e.g., 6-year-old IQ, where a fail score is some arbitrary point on the IQ distribution, say, < 80) or on the same one later on, then there are four possible outcomes and two kinds of errors. We can predict that there will be a bad outcome when there is not and we can predict that there is no problem when there is. By convention, the first error is called a *false alarm*, or *false positive*, and the second error is called a *miss*, or *false negative*. The proportion of times we predict failure when in fact there is a failure is called the *hit rate* (hits/[hits + misses]). The proportion of times we predict a failure when there is no failure is called the *false alarm rate* (false alarms/[false alarms + correct rejection]). These two rates are independent of each other and need not have the same denominator. The hit rate is often called the *sensitivity of the instrument*. The complement of the false alarm rate is called the *specificity of the instrument*, the *true negative rate* (see Figure 1). The "ideal" or perfectly "accurate" instrument has a 100% hit rate and a 0% false alarm rate (obviously not a very common instrument).

Several points are worth noting. First, it is impossible to evaluate adequately any screening instrument when we do not know *both* the miss *and* the false alarm rate. Knowing one error rate does not allow one to predict the other. An instrument *could* have both a 100% hit rate and a 100% false alarm rate or even a 0% miss rate and a 100% false alarm rate (obviously not a very useful instrument). The *accuracy* of an instrument is basically how far apart the hit and false alarm rates are from one another. The greater the spread between the two, the more accurate the test. The statistic that measures this spread is called *d-prime* and originates in Signal Detection Theory (Green & Swets, 1966).

There are some nonintuitive consequences of this view of accuracy. First, a test with a sensitivity of 40% and a specificity of 90% is as "accurate" as a test with a 90% sensitivity and a 40% specificity, even though the first test is missing 60% of the time while the second is missing only 10% of the time. Although these are clearly not the same tests, they have equal relative error rates (i.e., the same *d-prime*). The selection of one test over the other reduces to an issue of which kind of error one prefers to make. In the first case (sensitivity, 75%; specificity, 25%), the high hit rate is accompanied by a high false positive rate (but a low miss or false negative rate). The second case (sensitivity, 25%; specificity, 75%) has a low hit rate. It misses fully 75% of the true positives. However, it has a much lower false alarm rate. The tests are from a statistical point of view, "equally accurate." However, depending on the nature of the instrument and how one defines a hit, they are psychologically different.

Second, if performances on the two tests are normally distributed, then changing the criterion-point of the screening test will simply reduce one error in favor of the other. It will have no effect on the test's accuracy (the *d-prime*). A screening test such as the Denver Pre-Screening Developmental Questionnaire (DPDQ) (Frankenburg, Fandal, Sciarillo, & Burgess, 1981) is designed to have a low false alarm rate. It rarely says a person fails who does not end up failing (that is, if we define hit as "predict fail, outcome fail"). This is because the criterion point is set very high (e.g., more than five "no's" on the DPDQ). However, its low false alarm rate is acquired at the cost of a high miss rate (it passes many who will end up experiencing a significant delay).

One might think that reducing the criterion to, say, four "no's," would lower the miss rate. Indeed it does, but it does so at the expense of increasing the false alarm rate (specifically, the test will start to label failures that end up as passes). Reducing one error rate *necessarily* increases the other. There is no solution to this dilemma if we confine ourselves to the criterion. We cannot limit ourselves to reducing only one of the error rates because the other will go up proportionately to the decline of the other. The choice of the criterion point is a matter of policy, not statistics, and depends on whether the professional is more worried about misses or false alarms.

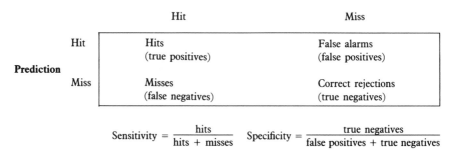

Figure 1. Possible outcomes of criterion "cut-points" on assessment instruments

Another crucial consideration in the evaluation of a test's effectiveness or usefulness is the base-rate of the particular condition that is being screened for. The prevalence of the condition being assessed (e.g., mental retardation) will dramatically affect the *meaning* of a positive or negative prediction. Consider the hypothetical example of some condition whose incidence is 1 in 10,000 and where the false alarm rate is conservatively estimated at 0.5% and the hit rate (specificity) is an incredible 99%. The probability that someone who has been screened as "positive" really has the condition is only 2%! Fully 98% of those who test positive will not have the condition. However, if the base-rate or incidence of the condition is 1 in 2, then the same false alarm rate results in a positive test being correct over 99% of the time! Even if a test is considered to have a 100% hit rate, the associated false alarm rate (even when assumed to be as low as 0.1%), can result in a positive test being wrong 91% of the time (if the incidence is as low as 1 in 10,0000).

These considerations amplify the caution we must employ in interpreting screening test results. As the incidence of the condition under study declines, the predictive power of the screening test plummets (all other things being equal). There is no test in the entire psychological literature that even approaches a hit rate as high as 90% and a miss rate of 5%.

In sum, in any consideration of a screening instrument, we need to know the hit rate, the false alarm rate, and the base-rate, and we need to realize that the accuracy of the instrument is unaffected by where we decide to set the criterion point that separates failures from passes. Reducing both errors simultaneously requires changing the instrument. Nevertheless, any assessment tool should compute the relevant *d*-prime statistic to allow it to be compared to other instruments.

THE PRACTICE OF ASSESSMENT AND DIAGNOSTIC CLASSIFICATION

Before we explore alternative evaluation strategies in the area of early intervention, it is necessary to review the purpose of assessment and traditional attitudes toward assessment. When a referral for evaluation occurs, a problem already has been identified. The source of a developmental lag may stem from constitutional limitations within the child or from factors in the home environment that may be limiting access to needed experiences. Despite differences among actual problem conditions, the fundamental goal of assessment is to identify accurately adaptive abilities and the nature of the difficulties so that appropriate intervention can be provided.

With the altered political climate of recent years, accurate assessment, supported by data documenting the developmental course of children with early disorders, has become increasingly important. One major area of assessment related to service provision involves the issue of special education labeling. During the 1960s and the early 1970s, the field of assessment reflected societal attitudes toward personal individuality, and there was a move toward discontinuing diagnostic classification. However, as dollars have become tighter, it has become ever more necessary to document *why* a child should receive services. Consequently, mental health professionals have had not only to reconsider their resistance to the stigma associated with diagnosis, but also to work toward the development of improved assessment strategies. Recent legislation (such as P.L. 99-457) places additional responsibility on professionals to develop assessment strategies that will result in the assignment of accurate categorization of developmental concerns in very young children, as well as facilitate the provision of appropriate services.

Current classification systems typically attempt to force childhood disorders into systems developed to identify adult psychopathology, for example, the *Diagnostic and Statistical Manual* (*DSM*-III-R) (American Psychiatric Association, 1987). Although similar patterns may be present in children, a major flaw of psychiatric classification systems to date is their failure to attend adequately to developmental considerations and vicissitudes.

Like most psychiatric nosologies (Blakemore, 1981), the *DSM*-III-R uses discrete symptomatology to diagnose disorders. However, because a given symptom can serve multiple systems or have multiple functions (Goldstein, 1939; Werner & Kaplan, 1963), sole reliance upon overt symptoms may result in an inordinate number of false positive and false negative diagnoses – a state of affairs that can have major ramifications for infants, toddlers, and their families. Furthermore, because most psychiatric research relies upon adult models of dysfunction for conceptualizing psychopathology, the assessment tools, diagnostic instruments, and classification systems of adult psychiatry often are applied to children without acknowledgment or awareness of the major developmental reorganizations that occur in the growing child's biological, socio-emotional, cognitive, and linguistic systems (Bemporad & Schwab, 1986; Cicchetti & Schneider-Rosen, 1986; Emde, Gaensbauer, & Harmon, 1976).

A number of early classification schemes have focused on such relational pathologies. For example, Spitz's (Spitz & Wolf, 1946; Spitz, 1951) classic research on hospitalism and anaclitic depression, Bowlby's (1951) work on the effects of maternal deprivation (see also Rutter, 1981), and Provence and Lipton's (1962) studies on the effects of institutionalization upon infant development provide exemplars of how dysfunctions within the caretaker–child–environment system may result in disturbances in infant functioning. The vast majority of the disorders of the early years of life can best be characterized as such transactional "relational pathologies" and not as disorders arising solely "within the child" (cf. Greenspan & Porges, 1984; Sroufe & Fleeson, 1986). Thus, the purpose of early assessment, as well as the types of difficulties that emerge in infancy and early toddlerhood, support the need for alternate intervention strategies. Specifically, assessment must attend to all domains of development and to the nature of the parent–child–environment system. Current instruments cannot identify these problems accurately.

THE ORGANIZATIONAL PERSPECTIVE ON DEVELOPMENTAL PSYCHOPATHOLOGY

Historically, a number of eminent scientists, theoreticians, and researchers have adopted the premise that knowledge about normal and abnormal development can inform each other. Developmental psychopathology has begun to emerge as a logical extension of the outgrowth of such thinking, which emphasizes that the developmental approach can be applied to any unit of behavior or discipline and to all cultures or populations, normal or atypical (Werner, 1948). From this developmental "world view" (Pepper, 1942), *any* handicapping condition or psychopathology can be conceived as a distortion in the normal ontogenetic process. Moreover, the study of disabled, high-risk, or psychopathological populations from a developmental perspective is believed to contribute to our understanding of both normal and abnormal ontogenesis (Cicchetti, in press; Rutter & Garmezy, 1983; Sroufe & Rutter, 1984).

By virtue of its emphasis on the interrelation among ontogenetic domains (e.g., perceptual-cognitive, linguistic, social, emotional, and biological development), the organizational perspective necessitates a multisystem approach to the assessment of children, parents, and environments (cf. Cicchetti & Sroufe, 1978; A. Freud, 1965; Goldstein, 1943). In contrast, investigators working with and writing about high-risk or disabled and normally developing children typically have focused primarily on their cognitive and linguistic development. This traditional orientation implies (a) that social and emotional development are not as important as intellectual development, and (b) that it is possible to understand cognitive development without also comprehending a child's development as a socioemotional being. Although those seeking to understand the psychological and biological organization of developmentally vulnerable children certainly have not intended such implications, they are the unfortunate by-product of a genuine concern about the cognitive and linguistic impairments that often characterize these conditions.

Historically, most organismic theories have focused primarily on cognition (Cicchetti & Pogge-Hesse, 1981; Kaplan, 1967). Since the 1970s, however, there has been a burgeoning interest in the nature of affect–cognition relations (Cicchetti & White, in press; Izard, 1977; Sroufe, 1979b). Our focus on stage-salient developmental issues, on tasks that require the child to coordinate cognition, affect, and behavior, and on multiple developmental systems, causes us to search for assessment strategies and interventions that include, yet are much broader than, single developmental domains such as cognition or language.

THE TRANSACTIONAL MODEL

Inherent in the organizational perspective on development is the recognition of the importance of transacting genetic, constitutional, neurobiological, biochemical, psychological, and social factors in the determination of behavior (Sameroff, 1983; Sameroff & Feiss, this volume). Throughout time, etiological models of handicap, "risk," or psychopathology have been "main effect" or "linear" in nature. According to the main-effect model, handicaps or psychopathology are the direct and inevitable results of some specific early pathogenic experience or inherent biological or biochemical dysfunction that exerts a profound impact on the individual throughout the life span. Although the past two decades have witnessed the emergence of more interactional models (e.g., the argument that *both* genetics and a poor environment are necessary and sufficient for the emergence of schizophrenia [Gottesman & Shields, 1972]), there still exists great dissatisfaction with these prevalent conceptualizations of handicap and psychopathology (cf. Engel, 1977). Proponents of the transactional model contend that the various factors that operate in normal or pathological conditions do not occur in isolation, but together influence the developmental process through a hierarchy of dispositions in a reciprocal, dynamic fashion (Cicchetti & Aber, 1986; Sameroff & Chandler, 1975).

When assessing the ability of a young child, a departure from the traditional focus on cognitive development is indicated. The transactional model of assessment, when applied to very young children, evaluates each component of the parent–child–environment system (cf. Cicchetti & Rizley, 1981). Regardless of the identified area of primary deficit, the importance of assessing multiple domains of functioning cannot be underestimated.

Unfortunately, all too frequently, areas of functioning are compartmentalized. For example, the effect of impaired speech on socioemotional functioning (or vice versa – see Cicchetti & Beeghly, 1987), or the impact of an emotional problem on cognitive development is often disregarded. This is especially problematic for very young children prior to initiation of formal schooling. Because many guidelines require that impaired *learning* be evidenced and the recognition of the potential impact of difficulties on learning has yet to be acknowledged widely, high-risk populations or children of average intelligence with emotional problems often fail to receive needed services. Such children often must experience increasing problems or failures before their needs are addressed. This presents an important challenge to the role of developmental assessment in the early years of life.

In order to explore the application of nontraditional methods of assessment to infancy and toddlerhood, approaches designed to assess development in perceptual-cognitive, socioemotional, and representational domains will be presented. These assessments should be used in conjunction with more traditional types of evaluations to provide a comprehensive portrayal of functioning. Although these domains are presented singly for purposes of clarity, we want to stress the importance of assessing multiple domains concurrently in order to maximize predictive efficiency of the test battery.

PERCEPTUAL-COGNITIVE DEVELOPMENT

It is true that perinatal trauma is not a *necessary* condition for later developmental delay; however, infants born prematurely or small for their gestational age, or those who have experienced severe perinatal complications, are represented disproportionately among children with learning disabilities, attention deficit disorders, or other academically related difficulties (Sameroff & Chandler, 1975). These effects, while mitigated by higher socioeconomic status, are preserved regardless of the social class of the infants and their families. There are a number of studies that show that despite near normal IQ, premature infants to take one example, may exhibit greater deficits in language (DeHirsch, Jansky, & Langford, 1966; Field, Dempsey, & Shuman, 1983; Hunt, Tooley, & Harmin, 1982); perceptual-motor skills (Caputo, Goldstein, & Tabu, 1979; Field et al., 1983; Hunt, 1981; Siegel, 1983; Tabu, Goldstein, & Caputo, 1977; Wallace, 1984); quantitative abilities (Caputo et al., 1979; Sell & Williams, 1983), and learning (Drillien, Thompson, & Burgoyne, 1980).

The issue of socioeconomic status is important because the amount of variance in childhood intellectual ability (as measured by IQ scores) that is attributable to social class generally outweighs that attributable to perinatal insult (Sameroff & Chandler, 1975). Yet the search for a performance measure in infancy that can – *independently* of social class – predict later outcome has been thwarted consistently by the failure of all standardized infancy measures to reliably predict later childhood IQ (see Fagan & Singer, 1983; Kopp, 1983; and Kopp & McCall, 1982, for representative reviews). McCall (1981a, 1981b) points out that the correlations of scores on such standard tests of infant development as the Bayley Scales of Infant Development (Bayley, 1969) with later IQ are so low as to be "conceptually uninteresting and clinically useless" (p. 141). This conclusion is borne out for normally developing infants as well as those at risk for developmental delay.

Although individual studies vary in specific outcomes, the average correlation of the Bayley Mental Developmental Index (MDI) assessed at 6–12 months with IQ at 5–7 years can only be characterized as minimal. Fagan and Singer (1983) reviewed 26 studies and reported an average correlation of 0.11 for normal populations. This correlation improves somewhat the later in infancy that the Bayley is administered and, more significantly, if high-risk or handicapped populations are included. Even in these extreme cases, however, the median correlations range between .20 and .30. Social class, on the other hand, predicts over 10 times the variance in childhood IQ that the Bayley does (Cohen, Sigman, Parmelee, & Beckwith, 1982; Kopp, 1983; McCall, 1981a).

The fact that standard infant tests cannot predict later outcome (as measured by IQ) does not mean that they are useless. They are perfectly valid indicators of *current* level of functioning. Although they cannot predict *which* 12-month-old infants will be retarded or who will be gifted, they can tell us how a particular infant is doing relative to his or her age peers.

For many investigators, the poor predictive ability of traditional developmental measures is an affront to the notion of intellectual continuity from the sensorimotor period to early childhood. Some (e.g., McCall, 1979) argue that this is due to the fact that intelligence itself is qualitatively different during the sensorimotor stage, when compared to the intelligence of later childhood. Others note that sensorimotor intelligence is highly genetically determined (Fishbein, 1976) and a vestige of our ancient evolutionary past. The symbolic thought of later intelligence is of a different species altogether. Just as we would not be surprised by low correlations between athletic ability and intelligence, we should not be surprised by low correlations between infant intelligence and later symbolic thought – or so the argument might go.

Alternatively, several investigators of infant perceptual and cognitive development (Caron & Caron, 1981; Caron, Caron, & Glass, 1983; Fagan, 1985; Fagan & McGrath, 1981; Fagan & Singer, 1983; Rose, 1981; Rose, Gottfried, & Bridger, 1978; and Rose & Wallace, 1985a,b) have suggested that failures in predicting later developmental outcome stem from fundamental flaws in the infant tests themselves. It has been postulated that the principal confound is their reliance on sensorimotor competence for the passing of items, in conjunction with the lack of tasks that tap the same kinds of perceptual discrimination and competence in memory required to do well on later intelligence tests. To be able to predict later intelligence, one must sample the same processes as behaviors known to be related to later intelligence (principle of relatedness).

The field of basic research into the cognitive and perceptual capacities of human infants represents one of the most fertile territories and greatest challenges for the use of nontraditional assessment. Infants are difficult to study both because of their relative motoric incompetence and the fact that they have limited formal language. We cannot ask them questions as we do older children, they do not readily follow instructions, and they are difficult to motivate and to keep on task for any length of time. In fact, they are so difficult to work with experimentally that it is only recently that techniques or paradigms have evolved whereby we can ask the questions psychologists have been wanting to ask of infants for centuries.

A revolution has occurred in the past 10 years in our understanding and appreciation of the abilities of human infants. The catalogue of infant skills is large and impressive. Young infants have been found to be able to form abstract concepts after only limited exposure to categorical exemplars (Cohen, 1979); they can recognize objects that they have felt but never seen (Gottfried, Rose, & Bridger, 1977, 1978); they can understand "metaphors" (Wagner, Winner, Cicchetti, & Gardner, 1980); and they can recognize emotional expressions in abstracted forms (Caron, Caron, & Myers, 1982).

Much of the revolution in the study of infant perceptual and cognitive abilities has come about through the application of four fundamental paradigms. These paradigms or procedures are generally simple and designed such that passive attention – either visual or auditory or tactual – is all that is required. Consequently, they are ideally suited for use with children who have difficulty in moving or speaking, or are otherwise disabled developmentally. They hold great promise for use in situations where traditional assessment batteries are either not applicable or not available.

Preferential-looking paradigm

Perhaps the simplest of techniques consists of presenting the infant with two visual targets that differ on some experimentally controlled feature. To the extent that attention is differentially directed to one of the targets, we can conclude that the infant has discriminated one of the features that distinguishes the two targets. Of course, obvious confounding variables such as right–left positioning of the targets must be controlled. Note that we are less interested in discovering the actual preferences of the infants than in establishing their discrimination thresholds.

In its simplest application, preferential looking has been used by Dobson and Teller (1978) to determine very precise estimates of the development of visual acuity in infants during the first year of life. The basis of the procedure consists in presenting gratings of differing stripe-width (spatial frequencies) corresponding to different Snellen acuity values (e.g., 20/100) paired with a homogeneous gray target. Infants prefer patterned stimuli to nonpatterned stimuli, therefore, when they no longer prefer the grating to the pure gray card, we can estimate their acuity. This technique would be appropriate for any population when verbal responses cannot be gathered and where visual evoked potential studies are not practical.

It should be stressed that preferential looking (PL) is not limited to establishing psychophysical thresholds. Differences between stimuli can be made arbitrarily complex. We have previously adapted PL to a situation in which we could show that infants of 6–12 months can associate dotted lines with pulsed tones and straight lines with pure tones and rising and falling sweep tones with arrows that are pointed up or down. These abilities could be called "metaphorical mappings" because the events are related only in abstract ways (i.e., dotted lines and pulsed tones have nothing "physical" in common) (Wagner et al., 1980). This paradigm demonstrates the presence of conceptual abilities that might go undetected by traditional methods of assessment.

Habituation paradigm

The habituation paradigm depends on the well-documented fact that infants (like all humans) lose interest when presented with a repetitive stimulus. Infants who are shown a visual target repeatedly will eventually reduce the average time they spend in looking at the stimulus. If a new target that differs on some experimentally important feature is introduced (usually when the infant's attention has declined to 50% of what it was initially), then the infant may increase his or her attention to the new target. If this occurs, then one can be confident that the infant has detected a change in the stimulus. If, on the other hand, attention does not increase, then we cannot conclude necessarily that the infant has not discriminated the experimentally manipulated change. In such circumstances the change may simply not be interesting enough to elicit an increase in attention. This is a very important point. Absence of evidence is not evidence of absence.

An increase in attention, however, is relatively unambiguous. The habituation procedure is extremely simple. But it is also extremely powerful, because differences between the habituation and test targets can be conceptual as well as perceptual.

It is important to note that habituation is subject-controlled (i.e., the subject controls the flow of information through the percentage of time spent in looking at a target). Habituation offers enormous promise to the assessment of not only infants, but also of children with motoric difficulties and those who are nonverbal and developmentally delayed. The only behavioral requirement of the paradigm is that the subject be able to fixate visually. Visual acuity per se is not really a limiting factor, as the sizes of the objects and the distances of the subject can be controlled experimentally. Indeed the procedure is so sensitive that it can even be used to assess visual acuity.

Whereas the great majority of studies employing the habituation paradigm have depended on the visual modality, there is an important variant of the technique called the high amplitude sucking procedure (HASP) that can be modified to establish discriminations in auditory and linguistic domains. In the HASP procedure, the infant is given a pacifier that contains a pressure transducer. A procedure is set up whereby the infant is presented an auditory (or visual) event as long as he or she sucks above a certain rate. If the rate declines below a prescribed level, the presentation is attenuated. At a prearranged point, the experimenter introduces some change in the stimulus. If the sucking rate increases after the change, the experimenter can conclude that the infant has discriminated the change.

This procedure, although somewhat technically complicated to set up, has been used with great profit in a variety of contexts. Eimas (1975) was able to discover that young infants have the same categorical boundaries for identification of phonemes as do adults. Entus (1975) was able to determine that 4-month-olds process musical tones in the right hemisphere and linguistic stimuli (phonemes) in the left hemisphere.

A variant of this technique was used by DeCasper and his students (DeCasper & Fifer, 1980; DeCasper & Spence, 1986) to reveal newborns' recognition of their mothers' voices at 3 days of age, as well as their recognition of stories and songs they had heard repeatedly during the third trimester of pregnancy. Siqueland (1981), using the HASP procedure, found negative correlations between recognition of novelty and frequency of maternal birth complications. Obviously, it is only the imagination of the experimenter that places limits on this assessment technique.

Familiarization-novelty paradigm

The habituation paradigm depends on the natural tendency of humans to attend to changes in their environment. The familiarization-novelty paradigm (FN) is designed around this fact. In this method, the infant is presented with a target for a certain preset number of "familiarization" trials, followed by a test trial in which the familiarization stimulus is paired with a novel stimulus. The important difference from the habituation paradigm is that the FN procedure does not wait for the infant to reach his or her own level of reduced attention (the total exposure is controlled by the experimenter, not the child) and there are two target stimuli to test (not just the one).

The FN procedure (sometimes called the paired-comparison technique) is generally more efficient than habituation in that it is quicker to administer and is more useful for making group comparisons. It is extremely general because the differences between the novel and familiar stimulus can be made arbitrarily complex by the experimenter. This procedure is probably the most frequently used of the infant perceptual discrimination paradigms.

The FN procedure has provided researchers with an opportunity to document enormously sophisticated information-processing capacities on the part of infants (Zelazo, 1979). One such capacity that potentially has great clinical importance is cross-modal object recognition. For example, if we are allowed to explore an object haptically without visual feedback, and then are subsequently shown the object paired with a novel object, we would generally have little trouble distinguishing the two. This seemingly trivial capacity is in reality quite complex because it requires that we have requisite cortical centers for the initial sensory processing, and sufficient capacity to translate and compare the visual and tactile information. Verbal language affords older children and adults this ability. In order for infants to be capable of solving such problems, however, they must possess a preverbal means of coding sensory events from one modality into the terms of another. Using the FN procedure, researchers have demonstrated such complex cross-modal discriminations in infants from birth to 1 year (Bushnell, 1986; Gottfried et al., 1977; Meltzoff & Borton, 1979; Rose, 1983; Wagner & Sakovits, 1986). Furthermore, Rose (1983) showed that cross-modal identification abilities were correlated with severity of prematurity and perinatal medical complications.

Another cognitive ability of young infants that was not suspected until recently has to do with abstract concept formation: categorization. Categorization is fundamental to thought and is defined as response equivalence to perceptually discriminable exemplars. It is our categorical ability that allows us to consider a whale as more similar to a mouse than to a shark. While infants have not demonstrated this particular ability, they have shown the capacity to form perceptual categories that are adultlike in nature based on limited exposure to selected exemplars (see Cohen, 1979, for a review).

Conditioning paradigm

Conditioning is one of the oldest assessment methods in the psychologist's arsenal. It is by far the most "demanding" of the infant paradigms in terms of cost, complexity, hardware requirements, and subject loss (i.e., due to time requirements, active compliance may decrease). It is, however, one of the most sensitive and powerful techniques available to the infancy researcher. The single greatest discriminating feature of the three other paradigms is that they are directed principally to the investigation of *group* differences. Their findings come from the comparison of preference scores to novel versus familiar objects, yet no *individual* infant's preference can be compared to some statistical standard (i.e., chance) because not enough trials are completed by any one subject. This point will be discussed when we present data concerning clinical samples.

Conditioning, on the other hand, offers an opportunity to examine the abilities of individual infants and toddlers. It offers substantial control and predictive validity possibilities. It is especially suited for intervention strategies, and it is used routinely in institutions around the world. At present, however, there are no standardized problems to which one could compare different populations. Although conditioning represents a powerful treatment tool, it is not an effective assessment technique.

Applications

Together these four paradigms have opened up new vistas of research into the perceptual and cognitive development of infants. They have facilitated the discovery of new abilities in infants and revisions in our theories of development. They also open up new possibilities for formalized assessment of infants, including those with developmental disabilities. Nonetheless, we still need to demonstrate that the abilities on which these methods depend (attention and preference for novel objects) have some clinical relevance. The question to be addressed is whether a young child who looks more quickly or for longer durations of time at a previously unseen or unexplored object will be more or less likely to develop greater competence later in life.

Fagan (1985) catalogued 15 studies that employed the novelty preference paradigm in the assessment of primarily premature infants who ranged in age from 3 to 12 months and were subsequently tested from 2 to 7.5 years of age. The 15 samples (total $N =$ 423, $M = 28.2$, $sd = 12.8$) yield an average predictive validity correlation of .44 (median = .42; range = .33 to .66; $sd = .09$), and the correlations are much higher if one limits them to at-risk populations or infants who are "failing-to-thrive." In these latter cases (three separate samples), the average correlation is .66 with a standard deviation of .06.

Rose and Wallace (1985a, b) extend the conclusions reached by Fagan and others. In their studies, premature infants were assessed on the Bayley Scales at 6, 12, and 24 months; on a novelty preference measure at 6, 12, and 24 months; and on a measure of IQ (Stanford-Binet and WISC-R) at 3, 4, and 6 years. Two findings are of note. First, the correlations of novelty preference with 6-year-old IQ average .54 and .64, compared with the Bayley MDI, which correlates with IQ -0.27 and $-.14$. Second, and more significantly, novelty preference measures predict IQ *independently* of socioeconomic status. Each variable alone contributes equally to the variance in IQ when the other is partialled out (the semipartial correlation of infant novelty to 6-year IQ is .5), but novelty preference level and socioeconomic status (i.e., mother's education) are not intercorrelated. This has been independently demonstrated by Fagan and Singer (1983).

If one assumes that the novelty preference paradigm (in significant contrast to the Bayley Scales and other conventional infancy instruments) is tapping the same *kinds* of cognitive processes that are assessed by conventional IQ tests (i.e., perceptual integration, visual recognition memory, similarity recognition, etc.), these are not surprising results. Clearly, many babies who are born prematurely or who sustain significant birth complications demonstrate cognitive difficulties later in childhood. It has been difficult, however, to identify *in infancy* those particular infants who are going to exhibit such deficits. It is reasonable to suggest that visual attention measures may achieve some success in this regard.

Many other studies have confirmed both the predictive and concurrent validity of attention and recognition memory scores (see Bornstein & Sigman, 1986, for a review). Fagan, Singer, Montie, and Shepherd (1986) administered a standardized FN test to infants suspected to be at risk for later mental retardation. The sample included children born prematurely (birth weight < 1,500 g) and those with intrauterine growth retardation, hypothyroidism, failure to thrive, or a history of maternal diabetes. The recognition memory test was administered four times between 3 and 7 months of age. Using a preestablished "risk-criterion," Fagan's test generated hits (sensitivity to delay), false alarms, misses, and correct rejections (specificity to normality) of .90, .19, .10 (complement of .90), and .81 (complement of .19), respectively. These compared to .45 sensitivity and .38 specificity for the Bayley Scales. In fact, a flip of a coin would have yielded higher sensitivity and specificity coefficients than did the Bayley Scales! Several other studies have reported differences between preterm infants and normal controls on both cross-modal recognition and visual recognition tests (Cohen, 1981; Rose, 1981; Rose et al., 1978; Rose & Wallace, 1985a,b).

All of these investigations have centered on recognition memory for objects that vary in shape. One could argue that these tests are screening devices for significant delay because the perceptual function of shape recognition is so fundamental to later conceptual abilities. That is, if a child has trouble differentiating a circle from a square, then she or he is very likely to experience later delays – or so one might argue. Some investigators have tried to extend these paradigms to tasks that go beyond the simple recognition of geometric shape. Caron and Caron (1981) explored whether more sophisticated cognitive processes such as the ability to process invariant information, in particular the ability to extract invariant relational information, might also differentiate high-risk from normal populations. Employing the FN paradigm (presenting problems that tested for recognition of face–nonface, above–below, same–different face, and smiling–neutral face), they found that preterms (27–36 weeks) performed less well than term infants on all four problems. McDonough and Cohen (1982) employed the habituation paradigm, using a problem requiring the infants to extract the concept of a "stuffed animal" from a series of six exemplars, to study a group of 16-month-old infants with cerebral palsy. These disabled infants were less able to extract the concept than age-matched normal controls, although the difference was not found for 22-month-olds.

In summary, the validity of the novelty preference paradigm to predict cognitive delay has been established. Recognition memory is more valid both concurrently and predictively than conventional assessment instruments (at least when one limits the analyses to the level of *group* differences). In addition, it has the rare virtue of being uncontaminated by social class.

The fact that recognition memory scores predict group differences based on some metric of developmental disability, however, does not mean that they have all the advantages of a *standardized* score, such as the Bayley MDI. A Bayley score tells us exactly where a particular infant lies relative to his or her age peers. This is not yet the case for the results of recognition memory type tests, although some steps are being made in that direction. Fagan et al. (1986), for example, have devised a standardized battery of objects for infant assessment, with norms computed for individual trial times and ages. This protocol is based on the FN paradigm and consists of a set of individual problems that are administered to the infants. An average novelty score is computed for each child based on his or her scores on three to four single problems. That score can be considered as a "novelty preference coefficient."

A slightly different approach has been taken by Wagner and Sakovits (1986). Their approach is based on a model of infant visual attention that is potentially well suited to predicting long-term developmental outcome.

The model stems from a dissatisfaction with the general attentional model underlying the standard novelty preference paradigm. Basically, the model posits that the novelty preference that is measured in the standard paradigm is the end point in a four-stage sequence whereby infants move from random (R) to familiarity (F) to random (R) to novelty (N) preference as the amount of exposure to the familiarizing stimulus is varied. Familiarity preference is not normally observed because, in general, the amount of time given for infants to explore the familiarization stimulus in the different experiments is sufficient to explore the object exhaustively and thus results in the infant preferring the novel object. The RFRN model, as it is called, assumes there is a direct relationship between duration of processing and preference. Prior research on the RFRN model has demonstrated its validity in both intramodal and cross-modal conditions, with object pairs of systematically varied complexity, with systematically varied exposure times to the familiarization stimuli, and with 6-, 9-, and 12-month-old infants (see Wagner & Sakovits, 1986, for a fuller elaboration).

If the RFRN model is a more complete characterization of infant attention and recognition memory, then it is natural to expect that it is better suited to predicting later developmental delay in at-risk infants. Other studies have centered on raw novelty preference averaged over a maximum of three trials per session, which results in low reliability between individual trials, and thus statistically limits the maximum predictive correlation. Familiarity preference (scores less than 50% novelty preference) would tend to depress correlations. Furthermore, infants with no preference (i.e., around 50% looking to the novel object) cannot be grouped with infants who show familiarity preference. What is needed is a way to compare an infant's individual profile with norms from all four phases of RFRN.

This raises a critical issue regarding the validity of attention measures. Virtually all studies have used group designs and, therefore, it is not possible to use the data to predict how well a *particular* infant will perform as a 6-year-old. Because of this unfortunate design feature of the traditional novelty preference paradigm, an individual's particular score on a novelty test *cannot* be separated from his or her preference for that object *independently* of its novelty. That is why the small number of trials per session in the previous studies is unfortunate. This can only inflate the miss rate of the instrument. The RFRN model suggests a design that allows us to chart the flow of attention over time for each infant. This individual profile can then be compared to the normalized one for that infant's age group, thus minimizing variations in looking related to the relative salience of individual objects and due to the temporal parameter.

In summary, the infant perceptual and cognitive paradigms hold significant promise both for the detection and the prediction of cognitive delay in groups of infants 9 months of age and older. Significant problems remain in extending these tasks to the prediction of outcome in individual clinical subjects, but there is reason to be optimistic about the long-term standardization potential of some of the visual recognition memory tasks (e.g., Fagan et al., 1986).

SOCIOEMOTIONAL DEVELOPMENT

Attempts to unravel the complexities and nuances of socioemotional development require an understanding of the growing child as an integrated, organized, and dynamic system (see Cicchetti & Pogge-Hesse, 1981; Hesse & Cicchetti, 1982; and Sroufe, 1979b, for an elaboration of this viewpoint). In studying the unfolding of joy, fear, and the other emotions, we encounter such processes as memory, expectation, relational abilities, intentionality, the ability to distinguish persons, and other major themes in cognitive development. In order to better understand socioemotional development, it is useful to look at the emergence of stage-salient tasks. Stage-salient tasks are thought to be those developmental issues that are most critical for the adaptive functioning of the child at a given point in time, and that require coordination of affect, cognition, and behavior (Cicchetti, Toth, Bush, & Gillespie, 1988; Erikson, 1950; Sroufe, 1979a).

Homeostatic regulation and the development of a reliable signaling system

One of the earliest stage-salient issues involves the development of homeostatic regulation. With the appearance of the social smile at around 2 to 3 months, a qualitatively new phase of development and behavioral organization emerges (Emde et al., 1976). During this stage, the infant first laughs in response to vigorous stimulation and exhibits frustration and/or rage in response to failed expectations. Mastery of homeostatic regulation and the development of reliable patterns of signaling contribute to an increased capacity for sustained attention to the environment. As a result, the infant begins to engage with both the animate and inanimate world in a more organized manner (Sroufe & Waters, 1976). Behaviors that were previously stimulated endogenously and were primarily reflexive in nature become replaced by contingent responses to exogenous stimulation. This stage is characterized by increased intensity and differentiation in the expression of affect (Sroufe, 1979b).

The assessment of positive affect

Sroufe and Wunsch (1972) developed a standard protocol of 30 items designed to assess the development of smiling and laughter in normal infants which was presented by mothers to their infants monthly in their homes from 4–12 months of age. Cicchetti and Sroufe (1976, 1978) conducted a parallel longitudinal study of the ontogenesis of smiling and laughter in babies with Down syndrome from 4–24 months of age and found that affective and cognitive development, though intimately related, were nonetheless independent developmental systems. Specifically, infants with Down syndrome manifested far less positive affect than was demonstrated by their mental age-matched counterparts. These findings suggest that other factors, including slower information processing, generalized hypotonicity, and physiological and biochemical anomalies, must also be taken into consideration in order to understand the organization of emotional development in infants with Down syndrome (cf. Cicchetti & White, in press).

In a subsequent investigation, Motti, Cicchetti, and Sroufe (1983) found that indices of both positive and negative affect obtained in early infancy in children with Down syndrome (cf. Cicchetti & Sroufe, 1978) predicted later cognitive and symbolic functioning between the ages of 3 and 5 years. These data reinforce the importance of considering the widespread influence that emotions may have on other developmental domains. Indeed, continued research and theorizing about the relation between emotional development and other ontogenetic domains may very well prove to be a rich prognostic index for later adaptation. Whereas it may be onerous to conduct monthly home-based assessments of the development of smiling and laughter in infants and young toddlers, the possible predictive power of affect assessments may make it especially worthwhile to incorporate several longitudinal assessments of positive affect using an abridged battery of items.

The assessment of a secure attachment

The development of a secure, adaptive attachment relationship with a primary caregiver is a stage-salient issue that has generated considerable research (Ainsworth, Blehar, Waters & Wall, 1978; Bowlby, 1982). As an evolving process, a secure attachment is marked by increased attention and attunement to interpersonal interaction (Stern, 1985). Although the basic capacity for attachment originates in earlier stages, overt manifestations of this issue reach ascendency in the latter half of the first year of life (Sroufe, 1979a). During this period the infant develops an increasing ability to coordinate a broad variety of behavioral responses into an adaptive and flexible "goal-corrected" response repertoire. Dyadic interactions that are marked by relatedness and synchrony, resiliency to stress, and appropriate affective interchange are associated with successful adaptation during this stage (Sroufe, 1979b). Inadequate response contingent stimulation, on the other hand, is likely to exert a negative impact on the infant's ability to master the tasks of this stage. In the absence of regular and reliable contingent responsivity, neither infant nor caregiver develop feelings of efficacy, and the development of a secure attachment relationship may be impeded (Ainsworth et al., 1978; Belsky, Rovine, & Taylor, 1984; Lamb, Thompson, Gardner, Charnov, & Estes, 1984).

The "strange situation" is a reliable and valid measure for assessing the quality of the caregiving–child attachment relationship between the ages of 12 and 48 months (Ainsworth & Wittig, 1969; Ainsworth et al., 1978; Cicchetti, Cummings, Greenberg, & Marvin, in press; Greenberg, Cicchetti, & Cummings, in press; Schneider-Rosen, Braunwald, Carlson, & Cicchetti, 1985). It is a procedure consisting of a series of seven 3-minute episodes, each entailing a change in the social environment of a novel laboratory playroom (see Ainsworth et al., 1978, for a description of the procedures and the scoring criteria). The episodes consist of: (1) mother and child alone in the playroom; (2) the entrance of a stranger who begins to interact with mother and child; (3) mother's departure, leaving the child alone with the stranger; (4) reunion of mother and child (stranger departs); (5) mother's second departure, leaving the child alone in the playroom; (6) the stranger's return; and (7) the second reunion of the mother and child (stranger departs). Thus, the episodes are arranged to create gradually escalating stress for the child so that consequent changes in his or her responses to the mother can be observed. Following the recommendation of Ainsworth and her colleagues (1978), separation episodes, 3, 5, and 6 are curtailed if the child is highly distressed.

The child's response to the caregiver in the reunion episodes is especially important for evaluating the quality of the attachment relationship. Based upon the organization of the child behaviors observed during the strange situation, children are classified into one of three categories. Those in Groups A and C are considered to be insecurely attached to their caregiver and will either avoid her (Group A) or manifest angry, resistant behavior alternating with proxmity-seeking or passive behavior (Group C) upon reunion. In contrast, securely attached children (Group B) use their caregiver as a secure base from which to explore the environment. If distressed, they will first approach the caregiver to seek comfort and will then return to play. If not distressed, they will greet the caregiver positively and will actively initiate contact. Approximately 70% of all nonclinical samples of youngsters, regardless of race or socioeconomic status, are securely attached, while 30% (20% A, 10% C) are insecurely attached to their primary caregiver (Ainsworth et al., 1978).

Recent refinements in the attachment coding system have led to the identification of a new attachment pattern, labeled "disorganized and disoriented" or Group D (Main & Solomon, 1986). Children classified as Group D display bizarre and unusual combinations of behavior in the strange situation. For example, they may be characterized by fear or wariness of their attachment figure, dazed and disoriented facial expressions, stereotypic and anomalous postures, or the manifestation of contradictory attachment behaviors belonging to mutually exclusive attachment categories. For example, many children in Group D behave simultaneously like a Group A and a Group C child.

The assessment of the quality of a child's attachment relationship with his or her primary caregiver has been shown to be an excellent predictor of later functioning on a variety of stage-salient issues, including self-development (Schneider-Rosen & Cicchetti, 1984), self-regulation (Matas, Arend, & Sroufe, 1978), communicative development (Gersten, Coster, Schneider-Rosen, Carlson, & Cicchetti, 1986), peer relations (Waters, Wippman, & Sroufe, 1979), ego resiliency and ego control (Arend, Gove, & Sroufe, 1979), and adaptation to school (Sroufe, 1983). Many high-risk children have been shown to manifest insecure attachment, especially those who have been maltreated or are the offspring of mothers with unipolar or bipolar depression (Crittenden, 1988; Radke-Yarrow, Cummings, Kuczynski, & Chapman, 1985; Schneider-Rosen et al., 1985). Those children who have been maltreated are prone to develop disorganized and disoriented attachments (Carlson, Cicchetti, Barnett, & Braunwald, 1989). In contrast, infants and toddlers with Down syndrome primarily form secure attachment relationships with their caregivers (Blacher & Myers, 1983; Thompson, Cicchetti, Lamb & Malkin, 1985). These results underscore the vicissitudes of parenting and highlight the importance of assessing parent–child relationships when conducting assessments of the emotional development of infants and toddlers. Observational measures should be a required part of assessment of infants and toddlers who have been maltreated or who are suspected of having emotional handicaps.

The assessment of autonomy and the capacity for self-regulation

The child's emergent acquisition of a sense of self, seen as encompassing both affective and cognitive dimensions, is a significant developmental task during toddlerhood (Lewis & Brooks-Gunn, 1979; Mahler, Pine, & Bergman, 1975; Stern, 1985). The evolution of this ability enables the toddler more fully to understand environmental occurrences that are external to the self and facilitates greater comprehension of personal functioning as a separate and independent entity. Issues of body management begin to emerge from the context of the mother–infant relationship into the realm of autonomous function. The infant becomes increasingly invested in self-managing due to new cognitive and motor achievements, as well as more sophisticated notions about self and other. Empathic acts also begin to emerge at this time, again as a manifestation of the realization that the self can have an impact on others (Zahn-Waxler & Radke-Yarrow, 1982). Between the ages of 24 and 36 months, toddlers develop the ability to construct even more differentiated mental representations of animate and inanimate objects (Greenspan & Porges, 1984). Additionally, the use of language and play to represent early conceptions of self and other is an age-appropriate manifestation of children's growing awareness of self and other. Caregiver sensitivity, or ability to tolerate the toddler's strivings for autonomy, and the capacity to set age-appropriate limits are crucial to the successful resolution of this issue. In contrast, an intolerance for infant initiative may impede the necessary development of autonomy. Caregivers who tend to feel rejected by their infants' increasing independence and/or become overwhelmed by their infants' actively initiated demands may inhibit the emergence of age-appropriate autonomy (Mahler et al., 1975).

The primary measurement technique used for assessing the development of visual self-recognition in infants and young toddlers is the mirror-and-rouge paradigm (Lewis & Brooks-Gunn, 1979). In this procedure, an infant observes his or her reflection in a mirror for a brief period of time in the presence of the mother and an experimenter. After this short inspection, the experimenter surreptitiously wipes a dot of rouge on the infant's nose. The presence of visual self-recognition is inferred from the infant touching his or her nose while simultaneously viewing his or her reflection. In addition, observations of infants' affective reactions to their rouge-marked mirror images can provide suggestive evidence of their feelings about themselves.

Whereas only 25% of babies evidence visual self-recognition at 18 months, by 24 months of age this figure rises to 75% (Lewis & Brooks-Gunn, 1979). During this period, most youngsters display positive affect in response to their rouge-altered mirror images. Yet, several studies suggest that many disabled and emotionally disturbed youngsters manifest problems in visual self-recognition, especially around the affective concomitants of this task. For example, both Spiker and Ricks (1984), in their studies of children with autism, and Schneider-Rosen and Cicchetti (1984), through investigations of children who were maltreated, found that these youngsters demonstrated primarily neutral or negative affect in response to recognizing themselves in a mirror. In contrast, toddlers with Down syndrome evinced normal positive affective reactions once they had attained visual self-recognition (Mans, Cicchetti, & Sroufe, 1978).

Matas et al. (1978) developed a *tool-use–problem-solving paradigm* to assess a toddler's emergent autonomy, independent exploration of the environment, and ability to cope with frustration at 24 months. In this procedure, young children are presented with a difficult problem that requires the use of a simple tool to solve (e.g., use of a block to hold down a lever in order to obtain a desirable lure). Mothers are instructed to let their children attempt to solve the problem and to give them whatever help they see fit. The situation is filmed for 6 minutes and subsequently coded for both maternal (e.g., sensitive prompting of child, supportive presence, etc.) and child (e.g., persistence, enthusiasm, temper tantrums, etc.) behaviors. Egeland and Sroufe (1981), employing this procedure, have demonstrated that children who have been maltreated have great difficulties with self-regulation. In contrast, Matas et al. (1978) have shown that securely attached toddlers manifest subsequent successful self-regulation on this paradigm.

These examples of strategies for assessing socioemotional development hold rich promise for providing a more comprehensive portrayal of functioning in populations of disabled children. Although additional work needs to be done in order to establish norms against which individual functioning can be compared, current paradigms can provide important information on patterns of adaptation and maladaptation.

REPRESENTATIONAL DEVELOPMENT

An additional means of assessing the growing sense of self and the representational abilities of toddlers is through the assessment of communicative and language development and of play. These can be studied in the context of structured and semistructured mother–child interactions that can be scored live or videotaped in a laboratory and coded subsequently. Two such interactional paradigms are presented.

SEMISTRUCTURED 30-MINUTE PLAY SESSION. Mother and child are brought into a playroom. They are provided with a standard set of age-appropriate toys. The mother is seated in a chair near one corner of the playroom, several feet away from the toys. During the first and last 10 minutes, the mother is asked to refrain from initiating any interaction with her child. During the middle 10-minute period she is invited to engage her child in playful interaction as she would at home. She is instructed to let her child initiate any interaction that the child wishes and to respond in a natural manner.

UNSTRUCTURED 20-MINUTE FREE PLAY. The mother is told that we are interested in seeing how she plays and communicates with her child. She and her child are seated on the floor of the playroom. A second set of assorted toys, different from those used in the semistructured play session, is placed in the middle of the room and the mother is instructed to play with her youngster as she normally would at home. The mother is free to initiate conversation and interaction whenever she desires.

Describing the child's language

After transcripts of videotaped mother–child interactions are made, coding of linguistic performance and communicative behavior can proceed. Speech and concomitant nonverbal behaviors of both members of the dyad can be recorded. The structural complexity of the child's utterances can be assessed by calculating the Mean Length of Utterance (MLU) according to the rules devised by Brown (1973). Productive vocabulary development can be assessed by calculating the total number of *words* as well as the total number of *different* words used by the child. For the latter determination, words may be divided into nouns, verbs, pronouns, modifiers (adjectives and adverbs) and social-expressive words (including personal names and stock phrases such as "bye-bye" and "all gone").

Overall communicative behavior can be assessed by a detailed analysis of the social and pragmatic function of a child's utterances. Based on previous work (Bates, 1976; Bloom & Lahey, 1978; Dore, 1979; Greenberg, 1980), we have developed a system sampling the major functions of communication. This system includes: imitating another, naming objects, seeking information, requesting others to act, repeating prior utterances, discussing the self, describing objects and events, and discussing other's thoughts and actions (see Gersten et al., 1986). Communications are coded to take into account the surface grammatical form, intonational contour, and other contextual cues needed to determine the functional intent of the message (cf. Dore, Gearhart, & Newman, 1978).

The mother's communicative behavior also can be assessed from the transcripts of the mother–child interactions. This investigation may include assessment of her total utterances, the complexity of her utterances, proportion of eliciting utterances, proportion of descriptive utterances, and proportion of utterances discussing others.

In normally developing children, the use of language to represent early conceptions of self and other is an age-appropriate achievement that unfolds during the second and third years of life (Bretherton, 1984), as they increasingly provide verbal accompaniments to their ongoing behavior (Kagan, 1981). In addition, children become more able to label emotional states, intentions, and cognitions (Bretherton & Beeghly, 1982), and begin to use their own name and personal pronouns appropriately. The use of self-related language becomes increasingly decontextualized, as children first speak primarily about themselves in the here-and-now, and then move on to discuss the actions and internal states of both themselves and of other hypothetical contexts.

In a series of recent studies, Gersten and her colleagues (1986) found that securely attached toddlers demonstrated a more elaborate vocabulary and conversed more about themselves and about others than did insecurely attached youngsters. In contrast, Cicchetti and Beeghly (1987) reported that youngsters who have been maltreated use less emotion-oriented language (i.e., talk less about their internal states) than do demographically matched comparison children who have not been maltreated.

Describing the child's play

Children demonstrate their growing social understanding in symbolic play. As in other forms of symbolization, the representation of self and other in play undergoes a process of decentration, decontextualization, and integration (Fenson, 1984). Toddlers first play at being themselves and then project their own behavior onto other recipients, such as dolls. By the end of the third year children are able to represent the behavior of several interacting replicas in an integrated fashion, and engage in sociodramatic play involving rudimentary role-playing (Watson & Fischer, 1977).

Three sets of measures that assess the cognitive, affective-motivational, and social dimensions of free-play behavior can be generated from codings of both structured and unstructured situations. The first involves coding the *maturity of a child's object and social play*. For example, the frequency of occurrence (in 15-second intervals) of mutually exclusive categories of object and social play can be tallied from videotaped records. These categories are based on dimensions that reflect developmental progressions in play maturity and that are related to cognitive development in normal children and in children with handicaps of varying etiology (e.g., Beeghly & Cicchetti, 1987; Belsky & Most, 1981; Hill & McCune-Nicolich, 1981). The most developmentally mature level of play is scored in each 15-second interval, with eight summary categories included in the final analyses. These categories are simple object manipulation, combinatorial object manipulation, presymbolic and functional play, self-related (auto-symbolic) symbolic play, decontextualized symbolic play, structured social (nonobject) play involving turntaking with mother, simple attending to mother, and no play. For all of these summary categories, frequencies are converted to percentages based on the proportion of time intervals spent in each category (relative to total number of time intervals in the play session). In addition, a ninth (double-coded) category is included that assesses the absolute frequency (in 15-second intervals) of simple communicative acts (giving, showing, social object labeling).

A second coding scheme assesses developmental progression in the complexity and maturity of children's *symbolic* play (Beeghly & Cicchetti, 1987). This 15-point developmental scale, which ranges from single pretend schemes to multischemed, hierarchically integrated episodes, is coded for complexity, and the final score is based on the highest level of symbolic play observed at least twice during the session.

A third set of measures produces global ratings of children's *affective motivational play style.* These scales include ratings of children's overall positive affect during the session (including affect expressed vocally and bodily, as well as with facial expression), the quality of object exploration, and affective engagement in play. Each dimension of play style is rated repeatedly in 10-minute intervals, and final scores for each dimension are based on averages of these ratings (see Beeghly & Cicchetti, 1987).

The study of play can be an important window on children's development. The sets of measures we've described provide but a sampling of the possible ways that free-play behavior may be coded and only a glimpse of how such observations may provide important information about the developmental organization of high-risk and disabled youngsters (see Bretherton, 1984; and Rubin, Fein, & Vandenburg, 1983, for reviews). For example, investigators of play development in atypical populations have replicated studies reported originally in the normal play literature that document a significant relationship between level of cognitive development and symbolic play maturity (see, for example, Hill & McCune-Nicolich, 1981; Motti et al., 1983). Wing, Gould, Yeates, and Brierly (1977), in a study of children with disabilities of varying etiology and degree of handicap, reported that no child with a mental age under 20 months engaged in symbolic play. Among subgroups of children with biologically based disabilities, youngsters with Down syndrome exhibited the most fluent and flexible symbolic play (Wing et al., 1977). Furthermore, Beeghly and Cicchetti (1987) found that, although emerging at a delayed pace, the symbolic play of children with Down syndrome progresses through the same developmental sequences of decentration, decontextualization, and integration in object and social play that characterize the play development of normally developing children (Bretherton, 1984). Moreover, close correspondence has been found between the affective and cognitive dimensions of symbolic play (see Motti et al., 1983), and affective motivational "play style" (persistence, enthusiasm, positive affect) has been shown to correlate significantly with level of cognitive development, symbolic play maturity, and social play (Beeghly & Cicchetti, 1987).

As children enter toddlerhood, traditional assessment instruments contain an increasing proportion of items requiring language skills. Therefore, the application of measures of representational development to children with handicaps is especially important because impaired language often precludes an accurate assessment of cognitive development in these children. Accordingly, it is essential to find a means of assessing cognition in children with impaired language. The close correspondence found between symbolic play and cognitive development identifies play as a potentially language-free method for assessing cognitive and symbolic capacity. Thus, assessments of play may provide a fuller understanding of youngsters who manifest expressive language delays or impairments, such as deaf children (Goldin-Meadow & Mylander, 1984) or children with Down syndrome (Beeghly & Cicchetti, 1987). Moreover, a careful assessment of both play and parent–child interaction may help uncover the nature of manifest linguistic deficits and may help to answer such questions as whether they are due to environmental factors such as parental input problems and insecure attachment relationships or whether they are a function of intrinsic speech or language handicaps per se.

APPLICATION OF ALTERNATIVE ASSESSMENT STRATEGIES

Although our discussion of alternative assessment strategies within the perceptual-cognitive, socioemotional, and representational arenas has provided a framework for conceptualizing early assessment, guidelines are necessary if these principles are to be applicable to actual clinical settings. Alternatives to traditional assessments are indicated not only for very young populations, but also for children who, due to some form of impairment, are not able to respond to more traditional measures. For example, in assessing a young child with limited verbal skills, a perceptual/cognitive task or an examination of symbolic play may provide information that a traditional evaluation would fail to generate.

The application of nontraditional assessment strategies to clinical settings can pose some obstacles. The paradigms presented in this chapter may appear unwieldy and too unconventional to gain ready acceptance. Rather than replacing traditional assessments with newer alternatives, we recommend the integration of alternate measures into standard assessment batteries. Although implementation of these procedures will require additional time, the gains with regard to predictive validity and a more well-rounded portrayal of strengths and weaknesses may very well be worth the effort. Obviously, not all alternatives will be necessary for all assessments, and evaluators will need to develop batteries based on referral questions, in conjunction with a step-wise decision process as an evaluation proceeds.

Because a primary goal of assessment is to provide information that can be applied to the development of intervention programs, it is important to review our suggestions for alternative assessment within this context. In thinking about the development of intervention strategies, a multidomain, multicontextual approach is indicated (Cicchetti & Toth, 1987). By gaining information related to transactions among parent-child-environment factors and to multiple domains of child functioning, areas requiring intervention can be identified and the most beneficial type of intervention can be provided (see Cicchetti et al., 1988).

Although we have focused on multidomain assessments in this chapter, it also is important to collect this information in multiple settings (e.g., home, laboratory, clinic, day-care center). This is especially critical because children do not necessarily respond similarly with all individuals or across all settings. Multicontextual assessments will better enable determinations of the respective contributions of constitutional (e.g., temperament) and socioemotional (e.g., parent–child relationships) factors to be made.

In addition to issues related to varied contexts, intervention decisions need to focus on within-child domains of deficit. Recognition of the interrelations among domains must again be emphasized. Even if a referral question identifies a circumscribed problem area (e.g., speech delays), the ramifications of this difficulty on other domains of functioning suggest broader assessment in order to inform intervention plans. For example, in the hypothetical case of a delay in the acquisition of language, implications for parent–child attachment and future socioemotional development must be considered (cf. Gersten et al., 1986).

CONCLUSION AND FUTURE PRESCRIPTIONS

The description of research-derived approaches to assessment in infancy and toddlerhood presented in this chapter highlights the unfortunate schism that exists between professionals involved in research and those engaged in service provision. If the field of clinical assessment is to benefit from increased knowledge in the area of child development, improved channels of communication between those who conduct research and those who apply these theories and research-derived principles will be necessary. As in many other areas, the realm of assessment emphasizes the clear need for an improved research–clinical interface.

One way of facilitating the development of this interface is through training. It is incumbent upon individuals and institutions involved in clinically relevant research to see that their findings reach professionals who can benefit from their application. Likewise, it is important that clinicians strive to apprise themselves of opportunities to incorporate new information and procedures. Increased reciprocity with respect to ideas and information could facilitate progress in both domains.

In addition to sharing information, it may be necessary for agencies within a given community to pool resources. For example, a medical center or a clinical research facility with the equipment and space necessary to conduct alternative assessments may consider opening its facilities to service agencies within the community. Conversely, channeling of specific clinical populations through a centralized system, or disbursement of results obtained from alternative evaluations, could expedite the acquisition of information, thereby benefiting both researcher and direct service provider.

Increased efforts to conduct longitudinal follow-up studies of the developmental progression of infants initially assessed with alternative intervention strategies also are necessary if the predictive validity of these techniques is to be established. Charting outcomes associated with varied types of disabling conditions (e.g., speech and language disorders, emotional problems, learning disabilities, etc.) and exploring the effects of specific interventions on these conditions also can have implications for treatment planning. In addition, a comparison between diagnostic status and the long-term outcomes associated with the findings of both traditional and alternative assessment batteries could be helpful in clarifying which situations result in greater predictive validity when alternative assessments are incorporated into traditional batteries.

Finally, the data obtained through the utilization of alternative assessment strategies may have implications for social policy decisions. Allocations of funds for special education could be influenced by the availability of information regarding the developmental outcome of children with various handicapping conditions. Moreover, the implementation of alternative assessment strategies may result in more accurate baseline and follow-up information about handicapped and high-risk youngsters. As a consequence, we should be better able to assess the effects of various interventions on the developmental process. At the very least, we are at a point in our knowledge where we can no longer afford to implement changes that affect children with handicapping conditions and their families without applying the best available procedures. Guided by the tenets of the organizational perspective, we stress the importance of assessing multiple domains of development concurrently. Through the application of this approach, we think that our understanding of handicapped and high-risk children will improve greatly, thereby facilitating our ability to provide developmentally appropriate interventions and to influence clinical decision making.

REFERENCES

Achenbach, T. M., McConaughy, S. H., & Howell, C. T. (1987). Child/adolescent behavioral and emotional problems: Implications of cross-informant correlations for situational specificity. *Psychological Bulletin, 101*, 213–232.

Ainsworth, M. D. S., Blehar, M. C., Waters, E., & Wall, S. (1978). *Patterns of attachment: A psychological study of the strange situation.* Hillsdale, NJ: L. Erlbaum.

Ainsworth, M., & Wittig, B. A. (1969). Attachment and exploratory behavior of 1-year-olds in a strange situation. In B. M. Foss (Ed.), *Determinants of infant behavior* (Vol. 4). New York: Wiley.

American Psychiatric Association Committee on Nomenclature. (1987). *Diagnostic and statistical manual of mental disorders, III* (rev. ed.). Washington, DC: American Psychiatric Association.

Arend, R., Gove, F. L., & Sroufe, L. A. (1979). Continuity of individual adaptation from infancy to kindergarten: A predictive study of ego-resiliency and curiosity in preschoolers. *Child Development, 50,* 950–959.

Bates, E. (1976). *Language and context: The acquisition of pragmatics.* New York: Academic Press.

Bayley, N. (1969). *The Bayley Scales of Infant Development.* New York: Psychological Corporation.

Beeghly, M., & Cicchetti, D. (1987). An organizational approach to symbolic development in children with Down syndrome. *New Directions for Child Development, 36,* 5–29.

Belsky, J., & Most, R. (1981). From exploration to play: A cross-sectional study of infant free play behavior. *Developmental Psychology, 17,* 630–639.

Belsky, J., Rovine, M., & Taylor, D. (1984). The Pennsylvania Infant and Family Development Project III. Origins of individual differences in infant–mother attachment: Maternal and infant contributions. *Child Development, 55,* 706–717.

Bemporad, J. R., & Schwab, M. E. (1986). The DSM-III and clinical child psychiatry. In T. Millon & G. L. Klerman (Eds.), *Contemporary directions in psychopathology: Toward the DSM-IV* (pp. 135–150). New York: Guilford Press.

Blacher, J., & Myers, C. (1983). A review of attachment formation and disorder of handicapped children. *American Journal of Mental Deficiency, 87,* 359–371.

Blakemore, C. (1981). The future of psychiatry in science and society. *Psychological Medicine, 11,* 27–37.

Bloom, L., & Lahey, M. (1978). *Language development and language disorders.* New York: Wiley.

Bornstein, M., & Sigman, M. (1986). Continuity in mental development from infancy. *Child Development, 57,* 251–274.

Bowlby, J. (1951). *Maternal care and mental health* (WHO Monograph No. 2). Geneva: World Health Organization.

Bowlby, J. (1982). *Attachment and loss* (2nd ed., Vol. 1). New York: Basic Books.

Bretherton, I. (Ed.). (1984). *Symbolic play.* Orlando: Academic Press.

Bretherton, I., & Beeghly, M. (1982). Talking about internal states: The acquisition of an explicit theory of mind. *Developmental Psychology, 18,* 906–921.

Brown, R. (1973). *A first language: The early stages.* Cambridge: Harvard University Press.

Bushnell, E. (1986). The basis of infant visual-tactual functioning amodal dimensions or multimodal compounds? In L. Lipsitt & C. Rovee-Collier (Eds.), *Advances in Infancy Research* (Vol. 4, pp. 182–194). Norwood, NJ: Ablex Publishing.

Caputo, D. V., Goldstein, K. M., & Taub, H. B. (1979). The development of prematurely born children through middle childhood. In T. M. Field, A. M. Sostek, S. Goldberg, & H. H. Shuman (Eds.), *Infants born at risk: Behavior and development* (pp. 219–247). Jamaica, NY: Spectrum Publications.

Carlson, V., Cicchetti, D., Barnett, D., & Braunwald, K. (1989). Finding order in disorganization: Lessons from research on maltreated infants' attachment relationships to their caregivers. In D. Cicchetti & V. Carlson (Eds.), *Child maltreatment: Theory and research on the causes and consequences of child abuse and neglect.* New York: Cambridge University Press.

Caron, A. J., & Caron, R. F. (1981). Processing of relational information as an index of infant risk. In S. L. Friedman & M. Sigman (Eds.), *Preterm birth and psychological development* (pp. 219–240). New York: Academic Press.

Caron, A. J., Caron, R. F., & Glass, P. (1983). Responsiveness to relational information as a measure of cognitive functioning in nonsuspect infants. In T. Field & S. Sostek (Eds.), *Infants born at risk: Psychological, perceptual, and cognitive processes* (pp. 181–209). New York: Grune & Stratton.

Caron, R., Caron, A., & Myers, R. (1982). Abstraction of invariant face expression in infancy. *Child Development, 53,* 1008–1015.

Cicchetti, D. (1984). The emergence of developmental psychopathology. *Child Development, 55,* 1–7.

Cicchetti, D. (1987). Developmental psychopathology in infancy: Illustration from the study of maltreated youngsters. *Journal of Consulting and Clinical Psychology, 6,* 837–845.

Cicchetti, D. (In press). An historical perspective on the discipline of developmental psychopathology. In J. Rolf, A. Masten, D. Cicchetti, K., Neuchterlein, & S. Weintraub (Eds.), *Risk and protective factors in the development of psychopathology.* New York: Cambridge University Press.

Cicchetti, D., & Aber, J. L. (1986). Early precursors to later depression: An organizational perspective. In L. Lipsitt & C. Rovee-Collier (Eds.), *Advances in infancy* (Vol. 4, pp. 87–137). Norwood, NJ: Ablex Publishing.

Cicchetti, D., & Beeghly, M. (1987). Symbolic development in maltreated youngsters: An organizational perspective. In D. Cicchetti & M. Beeghly (Eds.), *Atypical symbolic development* (pp. 47–68). San Francisco: Jossey-Bass.

Cicchetti, D., & Beeghly, M. (Eds.). (In press). *Children with Down syndrome: A developmental perspective.* New York: Cambridge University Press.

Cicchetti, D., Cummings, M., Greenberg, M., & Marvin, R. (In press). An organizational perspective on attachment beyond infancy: Implications for theory, measurement, and research. In M. Greenberg, D. Cicchetti, & M. Cummings (Eds.), *Attachment during the preschool years.* Chicago: University of Chicago Press.

Cicchetti, D., & Olsen, K. (In press). The developmental psychopathology of child maltreatment. In M. Lewis & S. Miller (Eds.), *Handbook of Developmental Psychopathology.* NY: Plenum Press.

Cicchetti, D., & Pogge-Hesse, P. (1981). The relation between emotion and cognition in infant development: Past, present, and future perspectives. In M. Lamb & L. Sherrod (Eds.), *Infant social cognition: Empirical and theoretical considerations.* (pp. 205–272). Hillsdale, NJ: L. Erlbaum.

Cicchetti, D., & Pogge-Hesse, P. (1982). Possible contributions of the study of organically retarded persons to developmental theory. In E. Zigler & D. Balla (Eds.), *Mental retardation: The developmental-difference controversy* (pp. 277–319). Hillsdale, NJ: L. Erlbaum.

Cicchetti, D., & Rizley, R. (1981). Developmental perspectives on the etiology, intergenerational transmission, and sequelae of child maltreatment. *New Directions for Child Development, 11*, 31–55.

Cicchetti, D., & Schneider-Rosen, K. (1986). An organizational approach to childhood depression. In M. Rutter, C. Izard, & P. Read (Eds.), *Depression in young people: Clinical and developmental perspectives* (pp. 71–134). New York: Guilford Press.

Cicchetti, D., & Sroufe, L. A. (1976). The relationship between affective and cognitive development in Down syndrome infants. *Child Development, 47*, 920–929.

Cicchetti, D., & Sroufe, L. A. (1978). An organizational view of affect: Illustration from the study of Down's syndrome infants. In M. Lewis & L. Rosenblum (Eds.), *The development of affect* (pp. 309–351). New York: Plenum Press.

Cicchetti, D., & Toth, S. (1987). The application of a transactional risk model to intervention with multi-risk maltreating families. *Zero to Three, I*, 1–8.

Cicchetti, D., Toth, S., & Bush, M. (1978). Developmental psychopathology and incompetence in childhood: Suggestions for intervention. In B. Lahey & A. Kazdin (Eds.), *Advances in clinical child psychology.* (pp. 1–73). New York: Plenum Press.

Cicchetti, D., Toth, S., Bush, M. A., & Gillespie, J. F. (1988). Stage-salient issues in infancy and toddlerhood: Implications for a transactional model of intervention. *New Directions for Child Development, 39*, 123–145.

Cicchetti, D., & White, J. (In press). Emotion and developmental psychopathology. In N. L. Stein, B. L. Leventhal, & T. Trabasso (Eds.), *Psychological and biological approaches to emotion.* Hillsdale, NJ: L. Erlbaum.

Cohen, L. B. (1979). Our developing knowledge of infant perception and cognition. *American Psychologist, 34*, 894–899.

Cohen, L. B. (1981). Examination of habituation as a measure of aberrant infant development. In S. L. Friedman & M. Sigman (Eds.), *Preterm birth and psychological development* (pp. 241–253). New York: Academic Press.

Cohen, L. B., Sigman, M., Parmelee, A. H., & Beckwith, L. (1982). Perinatal risk and developmental outcome in preterm infants. *Seminars in Perinatology, 6*, 334–339.

Crittenden, P. M. (1988). Relationships at risk. In J. Belsky & T. Nezworski (Eds.), *Clinical implications of attachment theory* (pp. 136–174). Hillsdale, NJ: L. Erlbaum.

DeCasper, A. J. & Fifer, A. P. (1980). Of human bonding: Newborns prefer their mothers' voices. *Science, 208*, 1174–1176.

DeCasper, A. J., & Spence, M. J. (1986). Prenatal maternal speech influences in newborns' perception of speech sound. *Infant Behavior and Development, 9*, 133–150.

DeHirsch, K., Jansky, J., & Langford, W. S. (1966). Comparisons between prematurely and maturely born children at three age levels. *American Journal of Orthopsychiatry, 36*, 616–628.

Dobson, V., & Teller, D. (1978). Visual acuity in human infants: A review and comparison of behavioral and electrophysiological studies. *Vision Research, 18*, 1469–1483.

Dore, J. (1979). Children's illocutionary acts. In R. Freedle (Ed.), *Discourse processes: Advances in research and theory.* Norwood, NJ: Ablex Publishing.

Dore, J. Gearhart, M., & Newman, D. (1978). The structure of nursery school conversation. In K. Nelson (Ed.), *Children's language* (Vol. 1). New York: Gardner Press.

Drillien, C. M., Thompson, A. J. M., & Burgoyne, K. (1980). Low-birth weight children at early school age: A longitudinal study. *Developmental Medicine and Child Neurology, 22,* 26–47.

Egeland, B., & Sroufe, L. A. (1981). Developmental sequelae of maltreatment in infancy. *New Directions for Child Development, 11,* 77–92.

Eimas, P. D. (1975). Speech perception in early infancy. In L. B. Cohen & P. Salapatek (Eds.), *Infant perception from sensation to cognition* (Vol. 2, pp. 193–231). New York: Academic Press.

Emde, R. N., Gaensbauer, T., & Harmon, R. (1976). *Emotional expression in infancy: A biobehavioral study.* New York: International Universities Press.

Engel, G. (1977). The need for a new medical model: A challenge for bio-medicine. *Science, 196,* 129–135.

Entus, A. K. (1975). *Hemispheric asymmetry in processing dichotically presented speech and nonspeech stimuli to infants.* Paper presented at the meeting of the Society for Research in Child Development, Denver.

Erikson, E. (1950). *Childhood and society.* New York: Norton.

Fagan, J. R. (1985). *Early novelty preferences and later intelligence.* Paper presented at the meeting of the Society for Research in Child Development, Toronto.

Fagan, J. F., & McGrath, S. K. (1981). Infant recognition memory and later intelligence. *Intelligence, 5,* 121–130.

Fagan, J. F., & Singer, L. T. (1983). Infant recognition memory as a measure of intelligence. In L. P. Lipsitt (Ed.), *Advances in infancy research* (Vol. 2, pp. 31–78). Norwalk, NJ: Ablex Publishing.

Fagan, J. F., Singer, L., Montie, J., & Shephard, P. (1986). Selective screening device for the early detection of normal or delayed cognitive development in infants at risk for later retardation. *Pediatrics, 78,* 1021–1026.

Fenson, L. (1984). Developmental trends for action and speech in pretend play. In I. Bretherton (Ed.), *Symbolic play* (pp. 249–270). Orlando: Academic Press.

Field, T., Dempsey, J., & Shuman, H. H. (1983). Five-year follow–up of preterm respiratory distress syndrome and post-term postmaturity syndrome. In T. Field & S. Sostek (Eds.), *Infants born at risk: Psychological, perceptual, and cognitive processes* (pp. 317–335). New York: Grune & Stratton.

Fischer, K. W. (1980). A theory of cognitive development: Control and construction of hierarchies of skills. *Psychological Review, 87,* 477–531.

Fishbein, H. D. (1976). *Evolution, development and children's learning.* Pacific Palisades, CA: Goodyear Publishing.

Frankenburg, W. K., Fandel, A. W., Sciarillo, W., & Burgess, D. (1981). The newly abbreviated and revised Denver Developmental Screening Test. *The Journal of Pediatrics, 99,* 995–999.

Freud, A. (1965). *Normality and pathology in childhood.* New York: International Universities Press.

Gersten, M., Coster, W., Schneider-Rosen, K., Carlson, V., & Cicchetti, D. (1986). The socio-emotional bases of communicative functioning: Quality of attachment, language development, and early maltreatment. In M. E. Lamb, A. L. Brown, & B. Rogoff (Eds.), *Advances in developmental psychology* (Vol. 4, pp. 105–151). Hillsdale, NJ: L. Erlbaum.

Goldin-Meadow, S., & Mylander, C. (1984). Gestural communication in deaf children: The effects and noneffects of parental involvement on early language development. *Monographs of the Society for Research in Child Development, 49* (3–4, Serial No. 207).

Goldstein, K. (1939). *Human nature in the light of psychopathology.* Cambridge: Harvard University Press.

Goldstein, K. (1943). The significance of psychological research in schizophrenia. *The Journal of Nervous and Mental Disease, 97,* 261–279.

Gottesman, I., & Shields, J. (1972). *Schizophrenia and genetics: A twin study vantage point.* New York: Academic Press.

Gottfried, A., Rose, S., & Bridger, W. (1977). Cross-modal transfer in human infants. *Child Development, 48,* 118–123.

Gottfried, A., Rose, S., & Bridger, W. (1978). Effects of visual, haptic, and manipulatory experiences on infants' visual recognition memory of objects. *Developmental Psychology, 14,* 305–312.

Green, D. M., & Swets, J. A. (1966). *Signal detection theory and psychophysics.* New York: Krieger.

Greenberg, M. (1980). Social interaction between deaf preschoolers and their mothers: The effect of communication method and communicative competence. *Developmental Psychology, 16,* 465–474.

Greenberg, M., Cicchetti, D., & Cummings, M. (Eds.). (In press). *Attachment during the preschool years.* Chicago: University of Chicago Press.

Greenspan, S. I., & Porges, S. W. (1984). Psychopathology in infancy and early childhood: Clinical perspectives on the organization of sensory and affective-thematic experience. *Child Development, 55,* 49–70.

Greenspan, S. I., Weider, S., Lieberman, A., Nover, R., Lourie, R., & Robinson, M. (Eds.). (1987). *Infants in multi-risk families: Case studies in preventive intervention.* New York: International Universities Press.

Hesse, P., & Cicchetti, D. (1982). Toward an integrative theory of emotional development. *New Directions for Child Development, 16,* 3–48.

Hill, P., & McCune-Nicolich, L. (1981). Pretend play and patterns of cognition in Down's syndrome infants. *Child Development, 23,* 43–60.

Hodapp, R., & Zigler, E. (In press). Applying the developmental perspective to individuals with Down syndrome. In D. Cicchetti & M. Beeghly (Eds.), *Children with Down syndrome: A developmental perspective.* New York: Cambridge University Press.

Hunt, J. V. (1981). Predicting intellectual disorders in childhood for preterm infants with birthweights below 1501 grams. In S. L. Friedman & M. Sigman (Eds.), *Preterm birth and psychological development* (pp. 329–351). New York: Academic Press.

Hunt, J. V., Tooley, W. H., & Harmin, D. (1982). Learning disabilities in children with birth weights ≤ 1,500 grams. *Seminars in Perinatology, 6,* 280–287.

Kagan, J. (1981). *The second year.* Cambridge: Harvard University Press.

Kaplan, B. (1967). Meditations on genesis. *Human Development, 10,* 65–87.

Keogh, B., & Kopp, C. (1978). From assessment to intervention. In F. Minifie & L. Lloyd (Eds.), *Communicative and cognitive abilities: Early behavior assessment.* Baltimore: University Park Press.

Kopp, C. B. (1983). Risk factors in development. In P. H. Mussen (Ed.), *Manual of child psychology.* (4th ed., Vol. I, pp. 1081–1188). New York: Wiley.

Kopp, C. B. (1987). Developmental risk: Historical reflections. In J. Osofsky (Ed.), *Handbook of infant development* (2nd ed., pp. 881–912). New York: Wiley.

Kopp, C. B., & McCall, R. B. (1982). Predicting later mental performance for normal, at-risk, and handicapped infants. in P. B. Baltes & O. G. Brim (Eds.), *Life-span development and behavior* (Vol. 4). New York: Academic Press.

Lamb, M., Thompson, R., Gardner, W., Charnov, E., & Estes, D. (1984). Security of infantile attachment as assessed in the strange situation: Its study and biological interpretation. *Behavioral and Brain Sciences, 7,* 124–147.

Lewis, M., & Brooks-Gunn, J. (1979). *Social cognition and the acquisition of self.* New York: Plenum Press.

Lewis, M., Feiring, C., McGuffog, C., & Jaskir, J. (1984). Predicting psychopathology in six-year-olds from early social relations. *Child Development, 55,* 123–136.

Lubchenco, L. O. (1981). Gestational age, birth weight, and the high-risk infant. In C. C. Brown (Ed.), *Infants at risk: Assessment and intervention* (pp. 12–17). New York: Johnson & Johnson.

Mahler, M., Pine, F., & Bergman, A. (1975). *The psychological birth of the human infant.* New York: Basic Books.

Main, M., Kaplan, N., & Cassidy, J. C. (1985). Security in infancy, childhood and adulthood: A move to the level of representation. In I. Bretherton & E. Waters (Eds.), Growing points of attachment theory and research. *Monographs of the Society for Research in Child Development, 50* (1–2, Serial No. 209), 66–104.

Main, M., & Solomon, J. (1986). Discovery of an insecure-disorganized/disoriented pattern. In T. B. Brazelton & M. Yogman (Eds.), *Affective development in infancy.* Norwood, NJ: Ablex Publishing.

Mans, L., Cicchetti, D., & Sroufe, L. A. (1978). Mirror reactions of Down's syndrome infants and toddlers: Cognitive underpinnings of self-recognition. *Child Development, 49,* 1247–1250.

Matas, L., Arend, R., & Sroufe, L. A. (1978). Continuity in adaptation in the second year: The relationship between quality of attachment and later competence. *Child Development, 49,* 547–556.

McCall, R. B. (1979). Qualitative transitions in behavioral development in the first three years of life. In M. H. Bornstein & W. Kessen (Eds.), *Psychological development from infancy* (pp. 183–224). Hillsdale, NJ: L. Erlbaum.

McCall, R. B. (1981a). Predicting developmental outcome: Resume and redirection. In C. C. Brown (Ed.), *Infants at risk: Assessment and intervention.* New York: Johnson & Johnson.

McCall, R. B. (1981b). Early predictors of later IQ: The search continues. *Intelligence, 5,* 141–147.

McDonough, S. C., & Cohen, L. B. (1982). *Use of habituation to investigate concept acquisition in cerebral palsied infants.* Paper presented at the meeting of the International Conference for Infant Studies, Austin, TX.

Meltzoff, A. N., & Borton, R. W. (1979). Intermodal matching by human neonates. *Nature, 282,* 403–404.

Messick, S. (1983). Assessment of children. In P. Mussen (Ed.), *Manual of child psychology* (Vol. 1, pp. 477–526). New York: Wiley.

Motti, F., Cicchetti, D., & Sroufe, L. A. (1983). From infant affect expression to symbolic play: The coherence of development in Down syndrome children. *Child Development, 54,* 1168–1175.

Pepper, S. (1942). *World hypotheses.* Berkeley: University of California Press.

Piaget, J. (1952). *The origins of intelligence in children.* New York: International Universities Press.

Provence, S., & Lipton, R. (1962). *Infants in institutions.* New York: International Universities Press.

Radke-Yarrow, M., Cummings, E. M., Kuczynski, L., & Chapman, M. (1985). Patterns of attachment in two- and three-year-olds in normal families and families with parental depression. *Child Development, 56,* 884–893.

Rose, S. A. (1981). Lags in the cognitive competence of prematurely born infants. In S. L. Friedman & M. Sigman (Eds.), *Preterm birth and psychology development* (pp. 255–269). New York: Academic Press.

Rose, S. A. (1983). Differential rates of visual information processing in full-term and preterm infants. *Child Development, 54,* 1189–1198.

Rose, S. A., Gottfried, A. W., & Bridger, W. H. (1978). Cross-modal transfer in infants: Relationship to prematurity and socioeconomic background. *Developmental Psychology, 14,* 643–652.

Rose, S. A., & Wallace, I. F. (1985a). Visual recognition memory: A predictor of later cognitive development in preterms. *Child Development, 56,* 843–852.

Rose, S. A., & Wallace, I. F. (1985b). Cross-modal and intramodal transfer as predictors of mental development in full-term and preterm infants. *Developmental Psychology, 21,* 949–962.

Rubin, K., Fein, G., & Vandenberg, B. (1983). Play. In P. Mussen (Ed.), *Handbook of child psychology* (Vol. 4, pp. 693–774), New York: Wiley.

Rubin, R. A., Rosenblatt, C., & Balow, B. (1973). Psychological and educational sequelae of prematurity. *Pediatrics, 52,* 352–363.

Rutter, M. (1981). *Maternal deprivation reassessed* (2nd ed.). Harmondsworth, Middlesex: Penguin Books.

Rutter, M., & Garmezy, N. (1983). Developmental psychopathology. In P. Mussen (Ed.), *Manual of child psychology.* (Vol. 4, pp. 775–911). New York: Wiley.

Sameroff, A. (1983). Developmental systems: Contexts and evolution. In P. Mussen (Ed.), *Handbook of child psychology* (Vol. 1, pp. 237–294). New York: Wiley.

Sameroff, A., & Chandler, M. (1975). Reproductive risk and the continuum of caretaking casualty. In F. Horowitz (Ed.), *Review of child development research* (Vol. 4, pp. 187–244). Chicago: University of Chicago Press.

Schneider-Rosen, K., Braunwald, K., Carlson, V., & Cicchetti, D. (1985). Current perspectives in attachment theory: Illustration from the study of maltreated infants. In I. Bretherton & E. Waters (Eds.), Growing points in attachment theory and research. *Monographs of the Society for Research in Child Development, 50* (Serial no. 209), 194–210.

Schneider-Rosen, K., & Cicchetti, D. (1984). The relationship between affect and cognition in maltreated infants: Quality of attachment and the development of visual self-recognition. *Child Development, 55,* 648–658.

Sell, E., & Williams, E. (1983). *Preschool prediction of later learning problems in children who received neonatal intensive care.* Paper presented at the meeting of the Society for Research in Child Development, Detroit.

Siegel, L. S. (1983). The prediction of possible learning abilities. In T. Field & S. Sostek (Eds.),

Infants born at risk: Physiological, perceptual, and cognitive process. New York: Grune & Stratton.

Siqueland, E. R. (1981). Studies of visual recognition memory in preterm infants: Differences in development as a function of perinatal morbidity. In S. L. Friedman & M. Sigman (Eds.), *Preterm birth and physiological development* (pp. 271–288). New York: Academic Press.

Spiker, D., and Ricks, M. (1984). Visual self-recognition in autistic children: Developmental relationships. *Child Development, 55,* 214–225.

Spitz, R. (1951). The psychogenic diseases of infancy: An attempt at their etiologic classification. *Psychoanalytic Study of the Child, 6,* 255–275.

Spitz, R., & Wolf, K. (1946). Anaclitic depression: An inquiry into the genesis of psychiatric conditions in early childhood, II. *Psychoanalytic Study of the Child, 2,* 313–342.

Sroufe, L. A. (1979a). The coherence of individual development. *American Psychologist, 34,* 834–841.

Sroufe, L. A. (1979b). Socioemotional development. In J. Osofsky (Ed.), *Handbook of infant development* (pp. 462–516). New York: Wiley.

Sroufe, L. A. (1983). Infant–caregiver attachment and patterns of adaptation in preschool: The roots of maladaptation and competence. In M. Perlmutter (Ed.), *The Minnesota Symposia on Child Psychology* (Vol. 16, pp. 41–81). Hillsdale, NJ: L. Erlbaum.

Sroufe, L. A., & Fleeson, J. (1986). Attachment and the construction of relationships. In W. Hartup & Z. Rubin (Eds.), *Relationships and development.* Hillsdale, NJ: L. Erlbaum.

Sroufe, L. A., & Rutter, M. (1984). The domain of developmental psychopathology. *Child Development, 55,* 1184–1199.

Sroufe, L. A., & Waters, E. (1976). The ontogenesis of smiling and laughter: A perspective on the organization of development in infancy. *Psychological Review, 83,* 173–189.

Sroufe, L. A., & Wunsch, J. (1972). The development of laughter in the first year of life. *Child Development, 43,* 1326–1344.

Stern, D. (1985). *The interpersonal world of the infant: A view from psychoanalysis and developmental psychology.* New York: Basic Books.

Taub, H. B., Goldstein, K. M., & Caputo, D. V. (1977). Indices of prematurity as discriminators of development in middle childhood. *Child Development, 48,* 797–805.

Thompson, R., Cicchetti, D., Lamb, M., and Malkin, C. (1985). The emotional responses of Down syndrome and normal infants in the strange situation: The organization of affective behavior in infants. *Developmental Psychology, 21,* 828–841.

Wagner, S., & Sakovits, L. (1986). A process analysis of infant visual and cross-modal recognition memory: Implication for an amodal code. In L. Lipsitt & C. Rovee-Collier (Eds.), *Advances in infancy research* (Vol. 4, pp. 196–217). Norwood, NJ: Ablex Publishing.

Wagner, S., Winner, E., Cicchetti, D., & Gardner, H. (1980). Metaphorical mapping in human infants. *Child Development, 52,* 728–731.

Wallace, I. F. (1984, April). Indicators of cognitive functioning in school-age low birth weight children. In L. S. Siegel (Chair), *The relationship between prematurity and functioning in the school age child: The role of biological and environmental factors.* Symposium held at the International Conference on Infant Studies, New York.

Waters, E., Wippman, J., & Sroufe, L. A. (1979). Attachment, positive affect, and competence in the peer group: Two studies in construct validation. *Child Development, 50,* 821–829.

Watson, M., & Fischer, K. (1977). A developmental sequence of agent use in late infancy. *Child Development, 48,* 828–836.

Werner, H. (1948). *Comparative psychology of mental development.* New York: International Universities Press.

Werner, H., & Kaplan, B. (1963). *Symbol formation: An organismic-developmental approach to language and the expression of thought.* New York: Wiley.

Wing, L., Gould, J., Yeates, S., & Brierly, L. (1977). Symbolic play in severely mentally retarded and in autistic children. *Journal of Child Psychology and Psychiatry, 18,* 167–178.

Zahn-Waxler, C., & Radke-Yarrow, M. (1982). The development of altruism: Alternative research strategies. In N. Eisenberg (Ed.), *Development of social behavior.* New York: Academic Press.

Zelazo, P. (1979). Reactivity to perceptual-cognitive events: Application for infant assessment. In R. Kearsley & I. Sigel (Eds.), *Infants at risk: Assessment of cognitive functioning* (pp. 49–83). Hillsdale, NJ: L. Erlbaum.

Zigler, E. (1969). Developmental versus difference theories of mental retardation and the problem of motivation. *American Journal of Mental Deficiency, 73,* 536–556.

12 Assessment of parent–child interaction

KATHRYN E. BARNARD AND JEAN F. KELLY

INTRODUCTION

Parent–child interaction is increasingly recognized as an important focus of early intervention programs, as research has shown that the interaction between a parent and child is important to optimal child development (e.g., Beckwith, 1976; Bee et al., 1982; Clarke-Stewart, 1973; Hammond, Bee, Barnard, & Eyres, 1983; Thoman, Becker, & Freeze, 1978). Brazelton (1988) explained the importance of viewing the interaction system as a reciprocal process in which each member of the dyad sensitively observes and adjusts personal behavior to the other member. He pointed out that interventions provide the opportunity to guide new parents toward mutually rewarding relations with their infants. Barnard, Booth, Mitchell, and Telzrow (1988) reported the results of an intervention program designed to facilitate parent–child adaptation and synchrony with at-risk infants and mothers. Their work demonstrated the importance of parent–child interaction and stimulation to cognitive development, and the effectiveness of intervention begun in the first few months of life. They maintained that for families where either parent or child has nonoptimal characteristics, a parent–child intervention program should be available as part of a standard preventive child health program.

Recent federal legislation for early intervention programs (Public Law 99-457) mandates a stronger emphasis on family involvement. These program regulations reflect a recognition of the important role parents and other family members have in the success of early intervention.

In order to understand more fully the interaction between an infant and parent and to develop appropriate methods for improving the infant's educational and social experiences, systematic assessment of the parent–infant interaction process is needed. Researchers, using a variety of measurement approaches, have identified discrete elements in that process and have examined their relation to the development of the child and the parent–child relationship (e.g., Beckwith & Cohen, 1984; Belsky, Rovine, & Taylor, 1984; Brazelton, 1988; Coates & Lewis, 1984; Stern, Caldwell, Hersher, Lipton, & Richmond, 1973). In addition, many research efforts have been devoted to identifying how parent–child interaction is affected when the infant is disabled or at risk for developmental delays (e.g., Barnard, Bee, & Hammond, 1984; Brooks-Gunn & Lewis, 1982; Eheart, 1982; Field, 1983; Mahoney, Finger, & Powell, 1985; Richard, 1986). With the identification of important elements in the interaction, it has become possible to develop assessment instruments to guide and evaluate intervention efforts.

278

During recent years a wide variety of measurement approaches and assessment scales have been used to measure parent–infant interaction, both for research and early intervention purposes (e.g., Bakeman & Brown, 1980; Bakeman & Gottman, 1986; Barnard, 1979; Booth & Mitchell, 1988; Bromwich, 1983; Farran, Kasari, Comfort, & Jay, 1986; Maccoby & Martin, 1983; Mahoney et al., 1985).

In this chapter we discuss four aspects of parent–infant interaction. First, we define its important elements and present examples of research studies that have employed a variety of measurement techniques to identify these elements. Second, we examine the differences reported in the literature between the interactions of parents with children who are disabled and those who are not disabled, and discuss the potential significance of these differences for assessment and intervention. Third, we introduce several approaches to the measurement of parent–infant interaction, and, fourth, we discuss a selection of specific scales designed to measure parent–infant interaction.

Although this chapter addresses the general concept of parent–child interaction, it is important to recognize that most studies have collected data only on maternal behaviors. This does not deny the importance of the father's role, but rather reflects the tendency to observe the most available partner, who is usually the mother.

IDENTIFICATION OF IMPORTANT ELEMENTS OF PARENT-INFANT INTERACTION

In recent years increasing effort has been devoted to understanding the nature of early parent–infant interaction. Several investigators have used a variety of measurement techniques to identify the important elements in that interaction. These elements include the behavioral repertoire of both the infant and parent, and the reciprocity that develops as both partners in an interaction respond and adapt to each other. This section discusses several studies that illustrate the importance of parent–infant interaction for child development, identifies the essential elements in that interaction, and examines their effect on the development of the parent–child relationship.

Importance of parent–infant interaction to child development

Researchers have discovered important links between certain aspects of parent–infant interaction and the child's skill development. Lewis and Goldberg (1969) found positive correlation between maternal responsiveness to infant behavior and the cognitive development of the infant at 3 months of age. They observed 20 mothers and infants in two situations, a controlled naturalistic setting and an experimental situation. Maternal responsiveness was measured by recording the occurrence of various behaviors, for example, mother looking at, smiling at, vocalizing to, holding, or touching the infant. Each time the infant exhibited specific behaviors, for example, eyes opened or closed, movement, crying, or vocalizing, the observer rated the nature and intensity of the maternal response. The data consistently indicated that there was a positive correlation between maternal response to infant behavior and the cognitive development of the infant as measured by response decrement in a habituation paradigm. This research suggested that the mother's increasing importance as a reinforcer of behaviors is one indication that the infant has learned to expect rewards from environmental interactions, and thus is the basis for future learning.

Stern et al. (1973) conducted a factor-analytic study concerned with learning more about mutually influential patterns of social behavior. Data were collected from clinic interviews and observations of 30 mothers and their infants. Seventy-nine items were designed to rate mother and infant characteristics. The factor analysis of the 79 variables yielded nine factors based on composites of the mother's and child's personality and behavior, and the child's mental and motor development. The authors state that the patterns of the loadings in each case suggest a causal sequence of relationships between the personality characteristics of the mother, the modes of maternal behavior she adopts, and the responses and development of the child. For example, one factor represented mothers who were loving, attentive, skillful, and emotionally involved; the infants shared only one thing in common, that is, accelerated development. In contrast, a different factor described mothers who were indifferent and disorganized in their interactions; their infants' behaviors were similarly lacking in purpose and plan.

Barnard (1979) discussed results of the Nursing Child Assessment Project (NCAP), a longitudinal study designed to assess infant and early childhood care systems that included assessments of infant characteristics, maternal characteristics, and mother–infant interaction. Among other things, the investigation examined the relation between maternal involvement and responsiveness and the child's mental and motor development. The researchers observed 193 mothers in the laboratory setting when their children were 2 years old, and the Bayley Scales of Infant Development were administered to each child. Mothers scoring high on maternal involvement and responsiveness, as measured by the first subscale of Caldwell's Home Observation for Measurement of the Environment (HOME) (Caldwell & Bradley, 1978) and on a number of behavioral items rated while the mother was teaching the child a new task, had babies who scored significantly higher on the Mental Development Index than did mixed or low-scoring mothers. In another study with a sample of socially high-risk mothers and their infants, maternal and infant behaviors during a teaching interaction were measured with the Nursing Child Assessment Satellite Training (NCAST) Teaching Scale. The Teaching Scale score at 3 months correlated positively with secure attachment at 12 months (Barnard et al., in press).

Beckwith (1971) showed that maternal verbal and physical responsiveness was related positively to Cattell scores in adopted middle-class infants, while maternal restriction of exploration was correlated negatively with developmental status. Ainsworth (1973) demonstrated that infants acquire a sense of security through the countless interactions they have with their mothers during the first year. When mothers demonstrate sensitive responsiveness to infants in the first months of life, the infants demonstrate secure attachment later and are able to use the parent as a secure base for exploration and as a source of comfort in time of stress. Ainsworth and Bell (1973) found that mothers who are sensitive in responding to their infants and who allow them freedom to explore have infants who are accelerated in development as measured on the Griffiths Scale. These and numerous other studies (Bateson, 1975; Beckwith & Cohen, 1984; Bee et al., 1982; Bell & Ainsworth, 1972; Belsky et al., 1984; Clarke-Stewart, 1973; Coates & Lewis, 1984; Elardo, Bradley, & Caldwell, 1975; Engel & Keane, 1975; Nelson, 1973; Olson, Bates, & Bayles, 1984; Ramey, Farran, & Campbell, 1979; Rubenstein, 1967; Snow et al., 1974; Tulken & Covitz, 1975; Wachs, Uzgiris, & Hunt, 1971) have demonstrated the strong relationship between parent–infant interaction and child competence.

Individual characteristics of parent and child

Many researchers have examined the individual characteristics of the caregiver and child and have explored how these characteristics relate to the formation of interactional patterns. Some have shown that infants contribute their own unique behaviors to the interaction (e.g., Bell, 1974; Brazelton, Koslowski, & Main, 1974; Cohen & Beckwith, 1979; Lewis & Rosenblum, 1974; Robson & Moss, 1970). As early as 1959, Chess, Thomas, and Birch (1959) hypothesized that various child-care practices were determined not only by what the mother feels and does, but also by the specific pattern of behavioral responses that characterize the individual child. Korner (1971) stated that individual infant differences at birth may affect later development, including the manner in which different infants will perceive the world around them. She suggested that for mutuality to develop between the mother and child, the individual infant behaviors must evoke differences in mothering. In summarizing her research and that of others, Korner reported that individual characteristics of the newborn, such as amount of crying behavior, soothability, and capacity to take in and synthesize sensory stimuli, will affect short- and long-range adaptation to the environment. She emphasized that parents must tune in to the infant and deal with his or her behavior differentially.

Stern (1977) concluded that "the infant arrives with an array of innately determined perceptual predelictions, motor patterns, cognitive and thinking tendencies, and abilities for emotional expressiveness and perhaps recognition" (p. 10). Beebe and Stern (1977) described the infant's coping behaviors that let the caregiver know when he or she is ready for interaction. Infant engagement and disengagement allow the infant to manage stimulation within a comfortable range or prompt the responsive mother to alter her behavior if it is uncomfortable. Booth (1985) found that both social status and neonatal state regulation (such behaviors as cuddliness, consolability, hand-to-mouth facility, and self-quieting activity) predicted the amount of synchrony in mother–infant interaction at 10–12 months. Hess (1970) and Bell (1974) proposed that the infant's physical appearance affects maternal responsiveness. Hess described features, called "babyishness," that heighten visual attention and serve as innate releasers for other parental behaviors.

In addition to the effect of individual infant characteristics, the influence of maternal characteristics on the interaction have also been examined. Booth, Barnard, Mitchell, and Spieker (1987) point out that, in general, mothers in difficult circumstances – for example, those with a low educational level, little support, multiple chronic problems, or high life stress – tend to have interactions with their infants that are less optimal than those of mothers who do not have such difficulties (see also Barnard et al., 1988; Bee et al., 1982; Crnic, Greenberg, Ragozin, Robinson, & Basham, 1983; Crnic, Greenberg, Robinson, & Ragozin, 1984; Egeland & Sroufe, 1981). Barnard and Eyres (1979) studied 200 families and found that mothers who were more involved and responsive with their children had higher educational levels, reported higher father involvement during pregnancy, and had low or moderate life change. A good relationship between parents correlated with the mother's involvement and responsiveness with the child, as did the mother's realistic expectations about the child's behavior. Barnard et al. (1985) found that variables such as maternal education, family income, and parent occupational status, and the total amount of social support for the mother were related positively to the child's scores on the Wechsler Intelligence Scale for Children (WISC-R), the Peabody Individual Achievement Test (PIAT), and the Myklebust Pupil Rating Scale (PRS).

The development of reciprocity between parent and child

The research literature substantiates the assertion that mother and child each come to the interaction with unique characteristics. It is the merging of the parent's and child's individual styles, however, that determines the success of the mother–child relationship. Several authors have described and labeled the development of this relationship. Spitz (1964) spoke of the interaction as a dialogue composed of action cycles. The dialogue can be impaired by meaningless exchange or inappropriate reactions. Spitz further emphasized that the breakdown of a dialogue in infancy had consequences for each subsequent developmental state. He pointed out that the newborn cannot empathize with the mother's inner processes; therefore, the mother's role is to empathize with what she understands from her baby's behaviors. Only with an empathic perspective will the interaction be meaningful; without empathy the parent is likely to initiate actions that might not apply to the child's needs or might interrupt responses before completion.

Stern (1984) discussed empathy as an important aspect of the parent–child relationship. He gave it the label of affect attunement, the ability to know what another is experiencing subjectively. The mental state of one partner must first become visible through his or her overt behaviors. Attunement occurs when the other partner perceives this state and produces a meaningful response. For example, a child tenses his or her body to make the final effort to grab a toy (overt behavior), and the mother at this precise time says "uuuuuh . . . uuuuuh!," with her vocal effort matching the child's physical effort. Although affect attunement is a matching process, it goes beyond simple matching and focuses on the internal state of the partner (See Beckwith, this volume).

Sander (1964) described the parent–infant relationship as a process of adaptation. He identified five stages during the first 2 years that are differentiated by the predominant behaviors of the child. It is the active tendencies of both parent and child that determine the development of a positive reciprocal relationship, marked by harmony and turn taking. At each stage, a type of refitting must be negotiated. The stages defined for the first year are primary modulation (birth–3 months); social-affective (3–6 months); initiative (6–9 months); and focalization (9–12 months). The final stage, which occurs after 1 year, is characterized as self-assertion, and is related directly to the development of autonomy and independent action. Sander's work reminds us that this independence is coordinated and achieved through an adaptive parent–child interaction.

Brazelton et al. (1974) studied the communication system that develops between infants and their caregivers within the first few months of life. They videotaped caregiver and infant behaviors simultaneously and reported that rhythmicity between the primary caregiver and the infant is an essential characteristic of the developing relationship; that is, there seems to be a positive interaction when each member of the dyad responds to the needs of the other. When one member is out of phase with the other, there appears to be a negative quality to the interaction. The strength of the interdependence of the dyad seems to be more powerful in shaping each member's behavior than does any other factor.

Thoman (1975) also reported on the mother–infant adaptation process, concluding that each baby has his or her own capabilities for providing cues to the mother, and each mother has unique ways of responding to her baby. Thoman described the process of adaptation as a behavior pattern developed in a three-part cue-response sequence: (1) cue giving by the baby, (2) cue-responsiveness by the mother, and (3) the response of the baby to the mother's action.

Kaye (1975, 1976) described the process of "turn taking," in which each partner learns the rules for beginning and ending his or her turn from the other partner's feedback. Over time both mother and infant behaviors are mutually shaped, and each becomes more competent at influencing the other partner's behavior. Stern (1974) observed gaze behavior of 3- and 4-month-old infants and their mothers, and Strain and Vietze (1975) studied vocal behaviors of 3-month-old infants and their mothers. Both research groups found evidence of this mutual regulation of mother and child behaviors during interaction.

Barnard et al. (in press) described four necessary features of the mutually adaptive "dance" between partners. First, each of the partners in this conversation must possess a sufficient repertoire of behaviors. If either partner lacks important qualities, the dance may be less satisfying. Among the crucial skills the child brings are the abilities to see, hear, and visually attend to the mother; smiling; body adaptation to holding or movement; soothability; and regularity with predictability of response. The parent brings the ability and willingness to read and respond appropriately to infant cues, and a repertoire of behaviors to stimulate and engage the infant. Second, the responses of the partners need to be contingent on one another. The contingent quality of parental responsiveness appears to be significant in the development of a secure attachment to the parent (Ainsworth, Blehar, Waters, & Wall, 1978; Belsky et al., 1984; Blehar, Lieberman, & Ainsworth, 1977; Crockenberg, 1981) and affects the subsequent development of competency in the child (Beckwith & Cohen, 1984; Coates & Lewis, 1984; Goldberg, 1977; Lewis & Coates, 1980). Third, there needs to be a richness of the interactive content. The amount of time the mother spends with the child, and the range of toys and activities presented are examples of measures of the level of richness. Fourth, the specific adaptive patterns between parent and child must change over time. Recent reports have noted that the ways that mothers and children interact with each other change with the development of the child (Belsky et al., 1984; Olson et al., 1984). This mutual adaptation process, as a developmental phenomenon, needs further investigation.

The studies described in this review illustrate the process that has contributed to an understanding of the importance of parent–child interaction to optimal child development and of the specific elements in the parent–child interaction. These elements include the individual behavioral repertoire of both the infant and parent, and the reciprocity that develops as both partners in an interaction respond and adapt to each other. Research has shown that infants come to the interaction with a unique set of characteristics. For a synchronous relationship to develop, these individual characteristics must evoke differences in mothering. For example, work with premature infants and their mothers has demonstrated the necessity for mothers to adjust the amount of their stimulation to the infant's capacity to handle sensory input (Field, 1982). In addition to infant characteristics, the individual characteristics of the parent affect the interaction. Barnard et al. (1988) pointed out that parents' awareness of their child's development and abilities and the parents' level of energy in using this awareness are major factors in the development of a growth-fostering interaction. Finally, the reciprocity that develops as both partners in an interaction respond and adapt to each other is the basis for a mutually satisfying relationship between the mother and child. The research discussed in this review described this process of developing reciprocity in many different ways. Spitz (1964) spoke of "action cycles"; Stern (1984) discussed "affective attunement"; Sander (1964) developed five stages of adaptation; Brazelton (1988) explained the reciprocity model as a feedback process that allows for flexibility, disruption, and organization. Thoman (1975) had previously described a similar process as a cue-response sequence, and Kaye (1975, 1976) described the process of "turn taking." Barnard et al. (in press) suggested the term "mutually adaptive dance" and described four necessary features of the dance.

In all these studies, researchers are defining the process of mutual regulation and adaptation that occurs in optimal interactions. For assessment purposes, the description of these elements in specific terms facilitates the construction of measurement procedures that make it possible to identify the important strengths and needs of the individual parent–child relationship. This resulting assessment information can be used to further research efforts and to plan appropriate intervention techniques.

PARENT–CHILD INTERACTION WHEN THE INFANT IS DISABLED OR AT RISK FOR DISABILITY

As the importance of early childhood intervention gained momentum in the 1970s, researchers started examining the interaction of parents and infants when the infants were disabled or at risk for developmental problems. Several studies have attempted to characterize differences in the interaction by comparing groups of infants who are delayed with groups of nondelayed infants.

Brooks-Gunn and Lewis (1982) studied play behavior in disabled and normal infants. Among many findings, they concluded that mothers tailor play interaction to their child's ability and behavior. However, mothers of infants with disabilities may not encourage independent or infant-initiated toy play because of their perceptions of their children's deficits. Maternal initiation of toy play, for example, was observed to occur much more often with the disabled children, reinforcing the belief that these mothers were controlling the interaction much longer than were mothers of normal children.

Jones (1977) compared the interactional exchanges between mothers and their nondelayed infants with those between mothers and infants with Down syndrome. He found that the children in the two groups showed no difference in their frequency of participation in interactive exchanges; there was a trend, however, toward more mother-directed interactions in the group with Down syndrome, as contrasted to more child-directed interactions in the nondelayed group. Although the babies with Down syndrome produced just as many vocalizations, they and their mothers did not engage in as much turn taking and displayed more vocal clash than in the control group. Buckhalt, Rutherford, and Goldberg (1978) concurred with these findings.

Eheart (1982) compared mother–child dyads with both mentally retarded and cognitively normal infants on interaction patterns demonstrated during free-play sessions. She found that mothers of children with mental retardation dominated the play sessions and perceived themselves as trying to change their children's behavior more often than did comparison mothers. The children with retardation responded less frequently to their mothers' initiations and initiated less than half as many interactions as control children. Mothers of disabled children were noted to be more dominating, and their infants correspondingly seemed less involved than observed for the nondelayed child–parent dyads.

Barnard et al. (in press) discussed the importance of a good repertoire of mother and infant behaviors in order for a comfortable interaction to develop. Perhaps this repertoire seems less reciprocal and more mother-dominated when an infant is delayed because of the differences in infant characteristics. There are some data to support the assumption that delayed infants' cues are less frequent and more subtle, and that this may result in less contingent behavior on the part of the mother. Fraiberg (1974) found that in a sample of 10 mothers and their blind infants, only 2 mothers were able to establish good communication systems through tactile means without some professional guidance. She explained that the infants seemed to be less responsive, to vocalize less, and to be slower than sighted children in learning to localize objects by sound. It is important to recognize that Fraiberg's intervention efforts sensitized parents to the subtle cues that blind infants display in communication attempts. These intervention strategies were possible to use only after carefully observing the infants' specific behavioral cues (e.g., signs of pleasure, interest, discomfort, or need).

Richard (1986) maintained that the differences in social interaction between mothers of nondisabled infants and those of infants with disabilities appear to be most related to infant characteristics. She reviewed the literature comparing infants without disabilities and those with Down syndrome on several infant characteristics and found evidence of significant differences in temperament (Rothbart & Hanson, 1983), gaze behavior (Gunn, Berry, & Andrews, 1979; Krakow & Kopp, 1983; Rothbart, 1984), gestures (Bricker & Carlson, 1980; Cicchetti & Sroufe, 1978; Dunst, 1980; Emde, Katz, & Thorpe, cited in Fogel, 1982; Jens & Johnson, 1982), vocalization (Buckhalt et al., 1968; Gisel, Lange, & Niman, 1984; Harris, 1983; Smith & Oller, 1981; Stevenson, Leavitt, & Silverberg, 1985), and proximity to caregivers (Smith & Hagen, 1984).

Mahoney et al. (1985) attempted to identify patterns of maternal behavior that are related to different levels of children's development for youngsters with mental retardation. They studied the play behavior of 60 organically impaired infants with retardation and their mothers, and rated 18 global maternal behaviors and 4 child behaviors. One of their major findings was that many of the maternal behaviors that were associated with the child's positive or negative cognitive functioning have also been associated with positive or negative cognitive functioning of children without retardation. For example, a group of facilitating behaviors, including sensitivity to the child's state, enjoyment, responsiveness, and appropriate teaching were related positively to the children's scores on the Bayley Scales, while other behaviors, including maternal directiveness and control, and insensitivity to the child's interests, were related negatively to their developmental scores. The authors pointed out that most intervention programs emphasize teaching strategies that are highly didactic and/or carefully structured to obtain preplanned objectives (e.g., Bailey & Wolery, 1984). Yet in this study, mothers whose infants had the highest Bayley Scores allowed their children to lead the activity, and were more concerned about supporting activities that their children initiated than they were about directing them. This finding has important implications for what interventionists see as their major goals and for which assessment instruments they use to plan their intervention. Measurement scales and intervention techniques that recognize the importance of maternal responsiveness are probably among the most potentially useful guides in planning intervention efforts.

Many researchers have studied parent–infant interaction when the infant is premature. Studies of differences between term infants and preterm infants report that the premature infant has a decreased level of behavioral responsiveness and less organization of sleep–wake activity (Kang & Barnard, 1979; Telzrow, Kang, Mitchell, Ashworth, & Barnard, 1982). Initially parents of preterm infants try harder to stimulate their infant, yet preterm infants are less responsive (Beckwith & Cohen, 1980; Brown & Bakeman, 1979; Divitto & Goldberg, 1979; Field, 1977, 1979; Goldberg, Brachfeld, & Divitto, 1980).

Field (1983) conducted research to determine whether high-risk infants are less attentive and show less positive affect and game playing during interaction. Her data showed that preterm and postterm infants were less attentive to their mothers and appeared to have less fun in early interactions than full-term infants. Field (1982) summed up the literature and concluded that the problem relates to finding an optimal level of stimulation, since low levels do not elicit responses from these infants and high levels may result in gaze aversion and fussiness. In general, a mother's stimulating behavior can best be defined as overstimulating, overcontrolling, or overdominating if it results in subtle or potent disengagement cues from the infant. The result of such behaviors can only be determined by assessing the individual dyad's interactions.

Barnard et al. (1984) found that interactions between preterm infants and their mothers at 4 months were characterized by intense maternal involvement and limited infant responsiveness. In contrast, 8-month interactions were characterized by a less attentive and involved mother and a more alert and responsive infant. By 2 years of age, mothers of preterm infants provided less stimulation than did mothers of term infants. Beckwith and Cohen (1983) presented confirming data to support this phenomenon of apparent "parent burnout" during the first year.

A related adjustment problem might sometimes be evident in the interaction between mothers and infants with disabilities. In normal interactions, turn taking increases with the developmental age of the child, while the relative frequency of simultaneous vocalizations decreases, indicating that turn taking is the more appropriate form for the development of mature communication (Schaffer, Collis, & Parson, 1977; Stern, Jaffe, Beebe, & Bennett, 1975). Berger and Cunningham (1983) recorded the vocal inter-actions of six infants with Down syndrome and seven nondisabled infants with their mothers during the first 6 months of life. They found a qualitative difference in the turn-taking behaviors of the two groups of mother–infant dyads, which reflected more than the different rates of the infants' vocal development. Their data suggest that there is an increasing age-related trend toward vocal "clashing" versus turn taking in the interaction between infants with Down syndrome and their mothers when compared to dyads without disabled infants.

The analysis of the turn-taking aspects of interaction suggests that with increasing age, the dyads that included a child with a disability became less successful at adapting mutually and regulating their vocal behaviors than did their nondisabled counterparts. These results extend the findings of Jones (1977) and Buckhalt et al. (1978), which indicate a high incidence of interactive clashing and asynchrony for mother–infant pairs involving children with Down syndrome during the second year of life. They suggest that the distortion of the interactive process begins during the first 6 months of life.

Vietze, Abernathy, Ashe, and Stich (1978) studied infants with and without delays. Results for the delayed and nondelayed groups at 1 year of age were strikingly similar, in that both showed a great deal of reciprocal vocal interaction. However, when the infants with delays were divided into two groups, one having scored higher on the Bayley Scales than the other, the failure of the lower scoring group to differentiate between the presence and absence of maternal vocalizations eventually affected the interactive style of the mothers. The authors maintained that this failure may lead to less contingent maternal responses.

Goldberg (1977) suggested that as parents become more sensitive to infant cues and better at predicting the outcomes of an act, they become more self-confident as parents. She stressed, however, that there are broad individual differences among infants in the clarity of their cues, so that even the most sensitive parent can have interactions that are noncontingent and chaotic if the infant is less readable or predictable. An important goal of intervention, therefore, could be to help parents become good observers of their own babies. Bromwich (1981), in describing her intervention program, pointed out:

The kinds of comments that accompanied our observations of the child's play, language, affective cues, social responses, and motor behavior called the parent's attention to the details of behavior that revealed important developmental changes in the child, no matter how small.... The discussions that ensued from the observations were motivating to the parent to continue to observe, and they gave her additional ideas about what was important to look for in order to help her interact more pleasurably and effectively with her child (pp. 176–177).

Summary

This review demonstrates that there are differences in mother–child interaction when the infant is disabled or at risk for disabilities. There is still great need for more conclusive research to determine why these differences occur and to elucidate their positive or negative effects. It is possible, however, to draw some initial conclusions based on this research, and to apply this knowledge cautiously when interpreting assessment information and designing intervention strategies.

First, *individual parent and infant characteristics must be considered in assessment.* The literature indicates that when the infant is at risk or disabled, the parent often tends to dominate the interaction for a longer period of time than do parents of infants without disabilities. This behavior may be due to the lack of readable infant cues and responses; that is, because the infant contributes less, the mother contributes more. In some interactions, parents become overcontrolling and overstimulating, leading the infant to become even less responsive and more avoiding. Therefore, assessment must include measurement of the type and frequency of infant cues and responses, as well as measurement of the type and frequency of the parent's initiations and responses. The variability in infant cues and responses is often greatest among children with disabilities. Thus, it is difficult to generalize about the interaction between parents and their disabled infants.

Second, *the contingent nature of the interaction must be assessed.* The literature demonstrates that individual infant and parent cues affect the interaction and that the ability of the infant and parent to merge their unique styles into a contingent and reciprocal relationship determines the success of the interaction. If the goal of intervention is the enhancement of this mutually enjoyable interaction, then mutuality or reciprocity must be measured. For example, one-third of the items on the Nursing Child Assessment Satellite Training Teaching and Feeding Scales (described later in this chapter) are contingency items. That is, they measure the degrees to which the parent's and infant's responses are contingent on the other's behavior.

Third, *the assessment must measure adaptations and changes over time.* Several studies indicate that when an infant is at risk or is disabled, parent–infant interaction changes over the first year (Barnard et al., 1984; Beckwith & Cohen, 1983; Berger & Cunningham, 1983; Vietze et al., 1978). These studies suggest that the behaviors of the dyad are affected by individual infant and parent characteristics and that the interaction can be adversely affected over time if mutuality is not established. Individual assessment must therefore be repeated at regular intervals so that intervention strategies that encourage and sustain the relationship can be devised and implemented.

METHODS USED TO MEASURE PARENT–INFANT INTERACTION

A variety of approaches are used to study the nature and importance of the parent–infant relationship. This section briefly discusses parent report methods and then provides a more lengthy discussion of observational methods, including systematic observation and global rating scales.

Parent report measures

Maccoby and Martin (1983) reported that most of the early studies of the relationship between parental practices and child outcomes used parents' introspective and descriptive reports as a primary source of data (e.g., Newson & Newson, 1968; Schaefer & Bell, 1958; Sears, Maccoby, & Levin, 1957). They point out that using carefully designed interview and questionnaire methods that rely on parents as informants have both advantages and disadvantages. These measures can assess behavior that extends over time, occurs in a variety of situations, and is usually not displayed in public. Several researchers, however, have criticized the accuracy of these types of measures (e.g., Bakeman & Gottman, 1986; Brekstad, 1966; Chess, Thomas, & Birch, 1966; Mednick & Schaffer, 1963; Yarrow, Campbell, & Burton, 1968). Ramey, Farran, Campbell, and Finkelstein (1978) pointed out that although interviews are less time-consuming and less expensive to perform than naturalistic observations, they are subject to bias due to selective memory for past events or the tendency to answer questions in a socially desirable way.

Zahn-Waxler, Radke-Yarrow, and King (1979) developed a parent report measure that was aimed at eliminating inaccurate recall of events. They trained mothers to observe and report all episodes of certain types of incidents occurring in the home over a period of weeks or months. A brief but specific written maternal report describes the mother and child behaviors preceding and following each incident. These reports can then be coded for the frequency of mother and child behaviors, and limited sequential analysis can be employed.

Observational methods

The development of observational methods has been a response to the limitations of parent report measures in studying the complex nature of parent–infant interaction. Several decisions must be made when employing such techniques. Observational measures can be conducted in the home or in the clinic or laboratory; they can be used to conduct research or to design intervention programs; and, finally, they can serve as systematic techniques designed to quantify specific behaviors, or as more global ratings of parent–infant interactions.

THE SETTING. One of the first decisions an investigator makes is where to collect information about parent–infant interaction – the home or the laboratory. Booth and Mitchell (1988) discuss the advantages and disadvantages of each setting for research purposes. An advantage to recording observations in the participants' homes is that their behavior will be more "natural." Carrying out observations in the home, however, can be more time-consuming and expensive. Alternatively, observations in a contrived setting may be less realistic, and therefore not as valid a representation of actual life experience. On the other hand, laboratory observations are more likely to be comparable from one participant to the next and are more likely to contain the kinds of interactive behaviors that are of interest to the investigator. Finally, most laboratory studies are less time-consuming and less expensive than comparable work in natural settings.

The decision to observe in the home or in the laboratory will be influenced by whether the purpose for gathering data is to develop appropriate intervention activities or to conduct research. Bromwich (1983) points out that it is important to build rapport with the family, to observe spontaneous parent–infant interaction, and to talk informally with the parent in order to gather information to be used in an ongoing intervention program. She suggests that the assessment period include two home visits to observe and interact with the family in a natural setting, and a third (clinic) session to collect additional information. Ultimately, the choice of setting depends on the purposes for gathering observational data, the type of information to be collected, and the available resources.

SYSTEMATIC OBSERVATIONAL TECHNIQUES VERSUS BEHAVIORAL RATING SCALES. Bakeman and Gottman (1986) define systematic observation as a particular approach in which predefined catalogs of behavioral codes are utilized by reliable observers. Although rating scales also make use of reliable observers, they focus not so much on how the behavior is manifested and for how long and how often, but whether the defined behavior is present in the individual's behavioral repertoire. The example offered by Bakeman and Gottman to distinguish the two observational approaches is instructive. Imagine that investigators are interested in the responsivity of two individuals to each other. They can define discrete behavior codes, code the stream of observed behavior, and then note how and how often each individual is responsive to the other (systematic, continuous observation). Alternatively, they can train observers to rate the level of responsivity that characterizes the observed interaction (rating scale). If a researcher wants to describe exactly how mothers are responsive and how their behavior changes over time, then systematic observation is indicated. If, on the other hand, an investigator is conducting an intervention program to change maternal responsivity to infant cues, then the far less stringent and time-demanding option of a time-sample rating scale would be preferable.

SYSTEMATIC OBSERVATION. If an investigator chooses a systematic observational scheme to collect data, several decisions must be made regarding the design of the coding protocol. The first consideration is whether the observer will code specific events as they occur (continuous event coding) or will record behavior at certain predetermined times (interval coding). A second consideration is whether the investigator is interested in coding the general stream of behaviors as they occur, or in identifying the sequential nature of the behaviors.

Booth and Mitchell (1988) define time (interval) and event coding and discuss when to employ each method. In time-triggered coding, the observer records behaviors at certain predetermined times. For example, the observer might record the occurrence or nonoccurrence of aggressive behaviors every 10 seconds on a continuous basis, or the observer might watch for 30 seconds but record for only 20 seconds (discontinuous time sampling).

In event-triggered coding, the observer begins recording behaviors when an event of interest occurs or when an event changes. For example, the observer of mother–infant interaction might begin to collect data only when the mother introduces a new toy, or the observer might continuously collect data about the interaction and simply change codes when the new toy is introduced. Three different schemes for event-triggered coding are available. A frequency scheme can be used if the interest is in whether and how frequently a behavior occurs. If the length of a behavior is important, then a frequency-plus-duration coding system can be employed. If the researcher is interested in recording a specific sequence of events, then a cross-classification of events is required. For example, the observer of a mother–infant interaction might choose to code (1) what happened right before the mother introduced a new toy, (2) how the mother introduced the toy, and (3) how the infant responded to the introduction.

Booth and Mitchell (1988) suggest using time-triggered coding if the behavior studied takes place over a long period of time, many coding categories exist, and the investigator is not interested in the sequence of behaviors. If sequences of behavior are important and the number of behaviors coded is limited, then an event-triggered system is most appropriate.

Nonsequential observation can be used to answer questions about how individuals distribute their time among various activities. Such data can be used to ask questions regarding how different groups or individuals vary or change with age. Sequential techniques, on the other hand, can be used to answer questions as to how behavior is sequenced in time, which in turn help us to understand how behavior functions within an ongoing interaction (Bakeman & Gottman, 1986).

Several researchers have developed systematic observational systems to examine sequential behavior (e.g., Gottman & Bakeman, 1979; Martin, Maccoby, Baran, & Jacklin, 1981; Stern, 1974, 1984). Booth, Lyons, and Barnard (1984) developed a systematic observational scheme to examine sequential behaviors of mothers and babies during an interaction. They coded all current behaviors of the mother and baby, and developed categories of behaviors described as Mother Signal, Baby Signal, and Interact. *Mother Signal* referred to the mother's attempt to engage the infant when the infant did not respond; *Baby Signal* was the converse; and *Interact* referred to mutual signaling, such as "mother and baby signal together," or "baby is held, plays game with mother." From these categories, a measure of dyadic synchrony was calculated. A high synchrony score resulted if there was a large amount of interaction occurring relative to the efforts of both the mother and baby to interact. Only a sequential analysis can yield information about the amount of synchrony in the mother–child relationship. It should be noted that it is primarily the availability of high-speed computers and videotaping equipment that makes the analysis of behavioral sequences possible. Maccoby and Martin (1983) provide a brief discussion of the microanalytic techniques that are used to analyze these moment-to-moment contingencies.

GLOBAL RATING SCALES. If the purpose of measurement is an overall rating of parent–infant interaction for research or clinical purposes, a global rating scale incorporates the knowledge base provided by studies using systematic observation, yet does not require as complicated coding and analysis procedures. Cairns and Green (1979) noted that frequency counts and ratings, both based on behavioral observation, have different strengths and weaknesses. Although behavior-count observations (systematic observations) give maximal information on situational variability, raters tend to report the central tendency of an individual's behavior, averaging out the moment-to-moment changes in situations.

Bakeman and Brown (1980) discuss the usefulness of ratings versus microanalytic scores (i.e., scores used to describe the sequential recording of behaviors). They coded videotapes using time-interval coding, while observers rated mothers and infants on more global characteristics. Whereas significant correlations were found between certain ratings made during the infant's first 3 months and the child's social competence at age 3 years, the microanalytic scores did not predict the child's subsequent social behaviors. These investigators concluded:

We think it may be more fruitful to think of characteristics of early interaction, like responsiveness, not as frequencies or sequences of particular acts, but rather as a disposition which permeates all of the mother's and/or all of the baby's interactive behavior. And in that case, global rating scales, and not sequential recording of minute particular behaviors followed by various microanalyses, might be the method of choice. Or perhaps most fruitful, would be an approach which combines features of molar (rating scale) and micro methods (p. 445).

In conclusion, no single observational method can be advocated as appropriate for all purposes (Maccoby & Martin, 1983). If resources permit, it is preferable for the investigator or clinician to use more than one approach to assess the nature of the parent–child interaction. If it is necessary to choose a preferred method, then the investigator must make a decision based on the purpose(s) for collecting the data and the type of information needed.

SPECIFIC MEASURES USED TO ASSESS PARENT–CHILD INTERACTION

Most of the examples of measurement strategies previously described in this chapter have been designed to answer specific research questions. This section describes examples of four measurement scales designed to rate the overall quality of the parent–child interaction. These scales have been used in multiple studies and are appropriate for use in both research and clinical settings. The global nature of the scales makes it possible to design intervention strategies based on the measurement and/or to evaluate overall program effectiveness. All four examples have published reliability and validity data. The four scales are the Nursing Child Assessment Satellite Training (NCAST) Teaching and Feeding Scales (Barnard, 1979); the Parent Behavior Progression (PBP) (Bromwich, 1983); the Maternal Behavior Rating Scale (MBRS) (Mahoney et al., 1985); and the Parent/Caregiver Involvement Scale (PCIS) (Farran et al., 1986).

NCAST Teaching and Feeding Scales

The Teaching and Feeding Scales (Barnard, 1979) are global observational scales that can be used in research to continue to advance important theoretical notions about parent–child interactions, and in clinical settings to plan individual intervention strategies and measure their outcome.

The paradigm is based on the assumption that parent–child interaction is reciprocal and, therefore, there are distinct parent and child contributions to the interaction. Several items on the scales measure the amount of responsive behavior exhibited by parent and child, that is, the behavior that occurs in response to an action of the other member of the dyad. Observational schemes are based on two quite different situations, one familiar and one novel. The familiar situation focuses on feeding, an event that occurs at least five or six times each day, which represents the longest interaction opportunities in the early months of life, and which parents often view as a central issue in their developing relationship with their infants. The second context involves a novel situation in which the parent is asked to "teach" the child two tasks, one at the child's age level and one at about $1\frac{1}{2}$ months beyond the expected ability of the child. Although parents instruct their child continuously, they often are not consciously aware of doing so. Therefore, asking them to teach specific tasks creates an unusual demand on both parents and children.

In the process of selecting scale items, it was necessary to establish a taxonomy of engagement and disengagement cues because the majority of infant communication is nonverbal (Beebe & Stern, 1977; Eriks, 1979; Givens, 1978). Engagement cues indicate the infant's or child's receptivity to interaction. The more potent cues are smiling, facing gaze, mutual gazes, and reaching toward the caregiver. The more subtle engagement cues include eye widening, facial brightening, and head raising. Disengagement cues are more numerous and serve to help the infant and young child control the timing and amount of interaction. When an interaction is too stimulating, one might see any number and sequencing of facial and body or extremity movements, such as eye clinch, gaze aversion, yawn, hiccoughs, leg kicking, and moving hand to back of neck or behind head. These engagement and disengagement cues are built into the feeding and teaching scale items. For example: "The parent slows the pace of feeding when the child averts gaze, places hand to ear, hand to mouth, hand behind head, hand to back of neck, hands over stomach, yawns, rubs eye, or displays feet movement."

The Teaching and Feeding Scales are each composed of four parent categories and two child categories. The parent areas include sensitivity to the child's cues, response to distress, social-emotional growth fostering, and cognitive growth fostering. The child categories include clarity of cues and responsiveness to parents. The Teaching Scale is composed of 76 yes or no items, and the Feeding Scale is composed of 73 items.

There are several scores generated that can be used to describe the parent–infant interaction: (1) a total score, calculated from the number of yes items received out of the potential total of 76 or 73 items; (2) a separate score of yes items for the parent; (3) a separate score of yes items for the child; and (4) a score on each subscale. In addition to the total or subscale scores, the Teaching Scale generates a Contingent Responsiveness Score. This score includes all parent and child items where one member's behavior is contingent on the other's act; for example, Item 3: "Parent gets the child's attention before beginning the task at the outset of the teaching interaction." Psychometric and normative data on the scales are reported by Barnard et al. (in press).

Particular strengths of the NCAST Teaching and Feeding Scales are that the contingent and reciprocal nature of the interaction is assessed, and the infant as well as maternal characteristics are examined. Some research and clinical programs might find it difficult to use the scales because direct training by an NCAST certified instructor is required.

Parent Behavior Progression

The PBP (Bromwich, 1983) was empirically derived from 5 years of home intervention experience by staff of the UCLA Infant Studies Project. The PBP training manual explains the purposes of the scale, the procedures for use, and the scoring system. The primary functions of the PBP are to help infant specialists focus on parent–infant interactions as well as to increase their awareness and sensitivity to parenting behaviors. This awareness allows the specialist to support positive behaviors already in the parent's repertoire and to help the parent acquire new behavior patterns that enhance infant–parent interaction and the infant's development. The PBP consists of a checklist of defined behaviors at each of six levels of parent involvement.

> *Level I*   The parent enjoys her infant.
> *Level II*   The parent is a sensitive observer of her infant, reads his or her behavioral cues accurately, and is responsive to them.
> *Level III*   The parent engages in a quality and quantity of interaction with her infant that is mutually satisfying and that provides opportunity for the development of attachment.
> *Level IV*   The parent demonstrates an awareness of materials, activities, and experiences suitable for her infant's current stage of development.

    Level V The parent initiates new play activities and experiences based on principles that she has internalized from her own experience, or on the same principles as activities suggested to or modeled for her.

    Level VI The parent independently generates a wide range of developmentally appropriate activities and experiences, interesting to the infant, in familiar and in new situations and at new levels of the infant's development.

Bromwich (1983) explains that progression on the PBP from one level to another suggests the behavioral sequence that many parents follow as they grow with their infants. Enjoyment of the infant leads to recognizing and responding to cues, and the combination of enjoyment of baby and sensitivity and responsiveness to cues leads to mutuality of interaction. When Levels I, II and III have been established, the parent progresses toward increasing competence in providing the infant with a growth-fostering environment (Levels IV, V, and VI). However, this sequence should not be thought of as a rigid structure to follow in setting goals for intervention. Behaviors at Level I do not have to be established before behaviors at subsequent levels can be expected. For example, it might be easier to begin intervention efforts by involving an unresponsive mother in activities at Level IV. When the parent sees the positive effect she is having, her feelings of competence will increase. A more positive feeling toward herself is often an important first step toward a parent's enjoyment of and sensitive responsiveness to her infant. For reports on the reliability and validity of the PBP, see Bromwich and Parmelee, 1979; Silcock and Rogers, 1981; Lewis and Latzko, 1979; and Allen, Affleck, McQueeny, and McGrade, 1982.

The PBP is particularly useful if researchers or service providers are working with an infant population with disabilities or at risk for disabilities. The assessment profile, having been developed for use with these populations, is structured for intervention purposes. The progression outlines developmental levels that sensitize and guide infant specialists in their intervention efforts. The PBP is limited, however, in that the focus is on the parent, and, consequently, individual infant characteristics are not assessed.

The Maternal Behavior Rating Scale

The MBRS (Mahoney et al., 1985) was originally developed for use in a research project designed to investigate the relationship between maternal behavioral style and the cognitive developmental status of 1-, 2-, and 3-year-old children with disabilities. The results of this study are discussed earlier in this chapter. The MBRS was developed to assess the quality of mother and child behavior during a 10-minute videotaped play session. The scale consists of 18 global maternal behaviors that are rated using a five-point Likert Scale. For the most part the MBRS includes only items that other investigators have found to be related to variability in children's rates of intellectual, language, or social development. Efforts were made to exclude items that assessed dimensions of maternal behavior that had been reported to be unrelated to the development of normal children. Examples of behaviors included in the scale are enjoyment, sensitivity to child state, responsivity, appropriate stimulation, and directiveness. The specific behavior for each of the possible one through five ratings is described for each of the 18 global behaviors. For example, for "expressiveness," the description of rating two is: "Low overt expressiveness. Mother emits strong expression only in one circumstance. She may occasionally smile or frown." For reliability and validity data on the MBRS see Mahoney et al. (1985) and Mahoney, Powell, and Finger (1986).

Mahoney et al. (1986) reported a shortened version of the scale that compared favorably with the original version, both in terms of the components of maternal behavior assessed and of the concurrent correlation between these factors and children's level of mental development. The authors state that the main advantage to the short form is that it provides a convenient vehicle to assess maternal interactive behavior on the basis of a small set of items. They recommend training to a 90% interrater reliability agreement, and caution that observations of mother–child interaction must occur under the same set of conditions (e.g., home observation of toy play versus clinic observation of teaching task) if scores are to be compared. A particular strength of the MBRS, especially the shortened version, is its effectiveness in assessing maternal interactive behavior on the basis of a small set of items. Mahoney and Powell (in press) described their use of the shortened form in evaluating the effects of an intervention program for birth to 3-year-old handicapped children. If the objectives of an intervention program correspond to the dimensions measured by the scale, then it could be a convenient and appropriate means for evaluating program effectiveness over them. However, the Scale does not measure infant behaviors, and therefore it is difficult to assess the contingent nature of the interaction with this instrument.

The Parent/Caregiver Involvement Scale

The PCIS (Farran et al., 1986) is designed to describe caregiver behaviors during interactive play with an infant or toddler. The scale can be used in research or as a clinical tool for assessing caregiver behavior, particularly in families with young high-risk or disabled children. The profiles that result from scoring the scale can be used to tailor intervention services to individual family needs, to evaluate the impacts of family services, and to compare family outcomes across intervention programs (Comfort & Farran, 1986).

The PCIS is focused on the caregiver's behavior with the child (Farran et al., 1987). Eleven types of caregiver behavior are defined. Examples of these behaviors are physical involvement, verbal involvement, teaching behavior, and positive and negative emotions. Each type of behavior is divided into three distinct aspects: amount, quality, and appropriateness. Amount is a neutral concept, relating strictly to the level of involvement of the caregiver without regard to quality. It asks how much the caregiver demonstrates each of these behaviors. The more the caregiver shows each of the behaviors, the more positively or negatively involved the caregiver is with the child. Quality assesses how well the caregiver carries out the behavior and with what degree of intensity, for example, how much warmth and acceptance the caregiver shows by each of these behaviors. The third area, appropriateness, refers to how closely matched the caregiver's behaviors are to the child's development, interest level, and motor capabilities. A final section of the PCIS provides an opportunity for the rater to make a global assessment of the parent–child interaction.

All behaviors are rated on a Likert Scale from one to five. The ratings are based on behaviors, not on general impressions. When the PCIS is used to rate interactions from videotapes, the observer actually has a checklist to tally behaviors during the interaction sequence. The observer uses the checklist to make judgments after viewing the videotape. When the scale is used in the home, a mental tally of behaviors must be used during the visit to enable accurate completion of the interaction sheet after the home observation.

The PCIS has been used with three different populations of children and their mothers: (1) the Carolina Abecedarian Project which is a longitudinal study of children whose socioeconomic situation places them at risk for developmental delay and school failure, (2) the Parent–Child Reciprocity Project, which focuses on infants who are biologically impaired, and (3) the Families Project which, unlike the other two projects, observed infants and families in their homes. Reliability and validity data on the scale are available (Farran et al., 1987).

Particular strengths of the PCIS are that it has been used in research and applied settings with several different populations of infants and their mothers. The scale yields a description of the child environment that is provided by the mother and can be used to tailor intervention services to individual family needs and to evaluate the effectiveness of services. A videotape and workbook are available for training in the use of the PCIS. The tape provides an introduction to the scale and practice sessions with feedback regarding scoring procedures. The PCIS does not focus on child behaviors nor the child's contribution to parent–child interaction. The developing reciprocity and contingent nature of the interaction would be difficult to assess with this scale.

The descriptions of these four assessment scales illustrate the similarities, differences, strengths, and drawbacks of various measurement systems. It is important that researchers continue their efforts to identify the elements of the parent–child interaction that are most important to the successful functioning of the child and the family, and to develop scales based on these elements that are effective for intervention and evaluation purposes.

SUMMARY

Studies described in this chapter demonstrate that there are important links between parent–infant interaction and the child's later social and cognitive development. Specific elements that affect that interaction are derived from the individual behavioral repertoires of both the infant and the parent, and the reciprocity that develops as both partners respond and adapt to each other. These identified elements are important because they affect both the emergence of a mutually satisfying relationship between the parent and child and the development of competence in the child. Research that has identified and described these elements in specific terms has facilitated the development of assessment procedures that reflect intervention and program evaluation needs.

Several studies have shown that there are differences in parent–child interaction when the infant is disabled or at risk for disability. There is some evidence that mothers of children with disabilities dominate the interchanges and their infants seem to be correspondingly less involved in the interaction than is the case with mothers and their nondisabled infants. Furthermore, there are data to suggest that over time mothers and infants who are disabled or premature are less successful at mutually adapting their behaviors to each other than are dyads with nondisabled infants.

Although there is still a great need for more conclusive research to determine why such differences occur and to assess the positive or negative effects of those differences on interactions, it is possible to draw some tentative conclusions based on available data and to apply this knowledge when selecting and interpreting assessment strategies. Specifically, individual parent and infant characteristics must be considered in assessment because of the variability in infant cues among infants who are disabled or premature. Second, the development of a good relationship depends on the mutuality that develops between parent and child; therefore, the contingent nature of the interaction must be assessed. Third, interactions change over time; therefore, assessment procedures must measure adaptations and changes at regular intervals.

A variety of approaches can be used to assess the nature and importance of the parent–infant relationship. Parent report measures such as questionnaires and interviews are used to measure behavior that extends over time and occurs in a variety of settings. In order to assess parent–child interaction more precisely, investigators have developed observational methods, both systematic observational schemes and more global rating scales. These assessment strategies have been developed for use in research and in clinical settings to plan individual intervention strategies and to measure their outcomes.

Present knowledge confirms the salience of parent–infant interaction and the importance of enhancing that interaction when the infant is at risk or disabled. As Cunningham (1986) points out, "We may have some of the emphases in our intervention wrong. The data we have suggest it is the interactions and the adaptation and the attachment processes and some of these social, within-family effects that are important." Thus, several reviews of early intervention efforts have called for a shift in evaluating program effectiveness. Instead of concentrating on child change measured in terms of IQ or developmental level, it has been suggested that we look at broader and perhaps more modifiable aspects of the child's early social (interactive) environment (Bricker, Bailey, & Bruder, 1984; Dunst, 1986; Fewell & Vadasy, 1987; Shonkoff & Hauser-Cram, 1987; White & Casto, 1985).

With the general acceptance of the importance of parent–infant interaction and the availability of empirically based assessment scales, it is now important for investigators to move forward in several ways. First, there is a need to include the facilitation of parent–infant interaction in intervention goals and to select the best available assessment strategies to measure the effects of interventions. Second, it is important to design longitudinal studies that include assessment profiles in order to identify the short- and long-term results of assessment and intervention on both the child and family. This type of research will facilitate the further development and refinement of appropriate assessment strategies and effective intervention goals and plans.

Finally, research and intervention studies should investigate further how assessment techniques can be adapted most effectively to the needs of such specific populations as parents and infants socially at risk, premature infants, and infants with diagnosed disabilities or delays. As discussed in this chapter, the individual characteristics of infants and parents greatly affect the development of reciprocal and mutually rewarding relationships. Therefore, assessment scales and intervention goals and plans should reflect individual characteristics as well as the contingent nature of the interaction. With a better understanding of how to assess areas of individual strengths and concerns in the parent–infant relationship, we will be able to provide families with more appropriate and helpful services.

REFERENCES

Ainsworth, M. D. (1973). The development of the infant–mother attachment. In B. Caldwell & H. Ricciuti (Eds.), *Review of child development research* (Vol. 3). Chicago: University of Chicago Press.

Ainsworth, M. D., & Bell, S. M. (1974). Mother–infant interaction and the development of competence. In K. Connolly & J. Bruner (Eds.), *The growth of competence.* New York: Academic Press.

Ainsworth, M., Blehar, M., Waters, E., & Walls, S. (1978). *Patterns of attachment: A psychological study of the strange situation.* Hillsdale, NJ: L. Erlbaum.

Allen, D. A., Affleck, G., McQueeny, M., & McGrade, B. J. (1982). Validation of the parent behavior progression in an early intervention program. *Mental Retardation, 20,* 159–163.

Bailey, D. B., & Wolery, M. (1984). *Teaching infants and preschoolers with handicaps.* Columbus, OH: Merrill.

Bakeman, R., & Brown, J. V. (1980). Early interaction: Consequences for social and mental development at three years. *Child Development, 51,* 437–447.

Bakeman, R., & Gottman, J. M. (1986). *Observing interaction, an introduction to sequential analysis.* New York: Cambridge University Press.

Barnard, K. E. (1979). *Instructor's learning resource manual.* Seattle: NCAST Publications, University of Washington.

Barnard, K. E., Bee, H. L., & Hammond, M. A. (1984). Developmental changes in maternal interactions with term and preterm infants. *Infant Behavior and Development, 7,* 101–113.

Barnard, K. E., Booth, C. L., Mitchell, S. K., & Telzrow, R. (1988). Newborn nursing models: A test of early intervention to high-risk infants and families. In E. Hibbs (Ed.), *Children and families: Studies in prevention and intervention* (pp. 63–81). Madison, CT: International Universities Press.

Barnard, K. E., & Eyres, S. J. (Eds.). (1979). *Child health assessment, part 2: The first year of life* (DHEW Publication No. HRA 79–25). Washington, DC: U. S. Government Printing Office.

Barnard, K. E., Hammond, M. A., Booth, C. L., Bee, H. L., Mitchell, S. K., & Spieker, S. J. (in press). Measurement and meaning of parent–child interaction. In F. Morrison, C. Lord, & D. Keating (Eds.), *Applied developmental psychology* (Vol. 3). New York: Academic Press.

Barnard, K. E., Hammond, M., Mitchell, S. K., Booth, C. L., Spietz, A., Snyder, C., & Elsas, T. (1985). Caring for high-risk infants and their families. In M. Green (Ed.), *The psychosocial aspects of the family* (pp. 245–266). Lexington, MA: Lexington Books.

Bateson, M. C. (1975). Mother–infant exchanges: The epigenesis of conversational interaction. In D. Aaronson & R. W. Rieber (Eds.), *Developmental psycholinguistics and communication disorders.* New York: New York Academy of Sciences.

Beckwith, L. (1971). Relationships between attributes of mothers and their infants' IQ scores. *Child Development, 42,* 1083–1098.

Beckwith, L. (1976). Caregiver–infant interaction and the development of the high risk infant. In T. D. Tjossem (Ed.), *Intervention strategies for high risk infants and young children.* Baltimore: University Park Press.

Beckwith, L., & Cohen, S. E. (1980). Interactions of preterm infants with their caregivers and test performance at age 2. In T. M. Field, S. Goldberg, D. Stern, & M. Sostek (Eds.), *High-risk infants and children: Adult and peer interactions.* New York: Academic Press.

Beckwith, L., & Cohen, S. E. (1983, April). *Continuity of caregiving with preterm infants.* Report presented at the meeting of the Society for Research in Child Development, Detroit.

Beckwith, L., & Cohen, S. E. (1984). Home environment and cognitive competence in preterm children during the first 5 years. In A. W. Gottfried (Ed.), *Home environment and early cognitive development.* New York: Academic Press.

Bee, H., Barnard, K., Eyres, S., Gray, C., Hammond, M., Spietz, A., Snyder, C., & Clark, B. (1982). Prediction of IQ and language skill from perinatal status, child performance, family characteristics, and mother–infant interaction. *Child Development, 53,* 1134–1156.

Beebe, B., & Stern, D. (1977). Engagement-disengagement early object experiences. In N. Freeman & S. Grand (Eds.), *Communicative structures and psychic structures* (pp. 35–55). New York: Plenum Press.

Bell, R. Q. (1974). Contributions of human infants to caregiving and social interaction. In M. Lewis & L. A. Rosenblum (Eds.), *The effect of the infant on its caregiver* (pp. 1–19). New York: Wiley-Interscience.

Bell, S. M., & Ainsworth, M. D. S. (1972). Infant crying and maternal responsiveness. *Child Development, 43,* 1171–1190.

Belsky, J., Rovine, M., & Taylor, D. G. (1984). The Pennsylvania Infant and Family Development Project, III: The origins of individual differences in infant–mother attachment: Maternal and infant contributions. *Child Development, 55,* 718–728.

Berger, J., & Cunningham, C. C. (1983). Development of early vocal behaviors and interactions in Down's syndrome and non-handicapped infant–mother pairs. *Developmental Psychology, 19,* 322–331.

Blehar, M. C., Lieberman, A. F., & Ainsworth, M. D. S. (1977). Early face-to-face interaction and its relation to later infant–mother attachment. *Child Development, 48,* 182–194.

Booth, C. L. (1985, April). *New and old predictors of cognitive and social outcomes in high social-risk toddlers.* Paper presented at the meeting of the Society for Research in Child Development, Toronto.

Booth, C. L., Barnard, K. E., Mitchell, S. K., & Spieker, S. J. (1987). Successful intervention with multiproblem mothers: Effects on the mother–infant relationship. *Infant Mental Health Journal, 8,* 288–306.

Booth, C. L., Lyons, N. B., & Barnard, K. E. (1984). Synchrony in mother–infant interaction: A comparison of measurement methods. *Child Study Journal, 14,* 95–114.

Booth, C. L., & Mitchell, S. K. (1988). Observing human behavior. In N. F. Woods & M. Catanzaro (Eds.), *Nursing research – theory and practice.* St. Louis: Mosby.

Brazelton, T. B. (1988). Importance of early intervention. In E. Hibbs (Ed.), *Children and families: Studies in prevention and intervention* (pp. 107–120). Madison, CT: International Universities Press.

Brazelton, T. B., Koslowski, B., & Main, M. (1974). The origins of reciprocity: The early mother–infant interaction. In M. Lewis & L. R. Rosenblum (Eds.), *The effect of the infant on its caregiver* (pp. 49–76). New York: Wiley-Interscience.

Brekstad, A. (1966). Factors influencing the reliability of anamnestic recall. *Child Development, 37,* 603–612.

Bricker, D., Bailey, E., & Bruder, M. B. (1984). Efficacy of early intervention and the handicapped infant: A wise or wasted resource. *Advances in Developmental and Behavioral Pediatrics, 5,* 373–423.

Bricker, D., & Carlson, L. (1980). *The relationship of object and prelinguistic social-communicative schemes to the acquisition of early linguistic skills in developmentally delayed infants.* Paper presented at the Conference on Handicapped and At-Risk Infants: Research and Applications, Asilomar, Monterey, CA.

Bromwich, R. (1981). *Working with parents and infants: An interactional approach.* Baltimore: University Park Press.

Bromwich, R. (1983). *Parent Behavior Progression – manual and 1983 supplement.* Northridge, CA: The Center for Research Development and Services, Department of Educational Psychology, California State University.

Bromwich, R. M., & Parmelee, A. H. (1979). An intervention program for preterm infants. In T. M. Field, A. Sostek, S. Goldberg, & H. H. Shuman (Eds.), *Infants born at risk.* New York: Spectrum Publications.

Brooks-Gunn, J., & Lewis, M. (1982). Development of play behavior in handicapped and normal infants. *Topics in Early Childhood Special Education, 2,* 14–27.

Brown, J. M., & Bakeman, R. (1979). Relationships of human mothers with their infants during the first year of life: Effect of prematurity. In R. W. Bell & R. Bakeman (Eds.), *Maternal influences and early behavior.* New York: Spectrum Publications.

Buckhalt, J. A., Rutherford, R. B., & Goldberg, K. E. (1978). Verbal and nonverbal interaction of mothers with their Down's syndrome and nonretarded infants. *American Journal of Mental Deficiency, 82,* 337–343.

Cairns, R. B., & Green, J. A. (1979). How to assess personality and social patterns. Observations or ratings? In R. B. Cairns (Ed.), *The analysis of social interactions.* Hillsdale, NJ: L. Erlbaum.

Caldwell, B. M., & Bradley, R. H. (1978). *Manual for the Home Observation for Measurement of the Environment.* Little Rock: University of Arkansas.

Chess, S., Thomas, A., & Birch, H. (1959). Characteristics of the individual child's behavior responses to the environment. *American Journal of Orthopsychiatry, 29,* 791–802.

Chess, S., Thomas, A., & Birch, H. G. (1966). Distortions in developmental reporting made by parents of behaviorally disturbed children. *Journal of the American Academy of Child Psychiatry, 5,* 226–234.

Cicchetti, D., & Sroufe, A. (1978). An organizational view of affect: Illustration from the study of Down's syndrome infants. In M. Lewis & L. A. Rosenblum (Eds.), *The development of affect* (pp. 309–349). New York: Plenum Press.

Clarke-Stewart, K. A. (1973). Interactions between mothers and their young children: Characteristics and consequences. *Monographs of the Society for Research in Child Development, 38*(6–7, Serial No. 153).

Coates, D. L., & Lewis, M. (1984). Early mother–infant interaction and infant cognitive status as predictors of school performance and cognitive behavior in six-year-olds. *Child Development, 55,* 1219–1230.

Cohen, S. E., & Beckwith, L. (1979). Preterm infant interaction with the caregiver in the first year of life and competence at age two. *Child Development, 50,* 767–776.

Comfort, M., & Farran, C. (1986, April). *Systematic assessment of maternal behavior during interactions with handicapped infants.* Paper presented at the Conference on Human Development, Nashville.

Crnic, K. A., Greenberg, M. T., Ragozin, A. S., Robinson, N. M., & Basham, R. B. (1983). Effects of stress and social support on mothers and premature and full-term infants. *Child Development, 54*, 209–217.

Crnic, K. A., Greenberg, M. T., Robinson, N. M., & Ragozin, A. S. (1984). Maternal stress and social support: Effects on the mother–infant relationship from birth to eighteen months. *American Journal of Orthopsychiatry, 54*, 224–235.

Crockenberg, S. B. (1981). Infant irritability, mother responsiveness, and social support influences on the security of infant–mother attachment. *Child Development, 52*, 857–865.

Cunningham, C. (1986, April). *Patterns of development in Down's syndrome.* Paper presented at the Third International Down's Syndrome Congress, Brighton, England. As cited in Fewell, R. R., and Vadasy, P. F. (1987). Measurement issues in studies of efficacy. *Topics in Early Childhood Special Education, 7*, 85–96.

Divitto, B., & Goldberg, S. (1979). The effects of newborn medical status on early parent–infant interaction. In T. M. Field, A. Sostek, S. Goldberg, & H. H. Shuman (Eds.), *Infants born at risk.* New York: Spectrum Publications.

Dunst, C. (1980, April). *Developmental characteristics of communicative acts among Down's syndrome infants and nonretarded infants.* Paper presented at the biennial meeting of the Southeastern Conference on Human Development, Alexandria, VA.

Dunst, C. J. (1986). Overview of the efficacy of early intervention programs: Methodological and conceptual considerations. In L. Bickman & D. Weatherford (Eds.), *Evaluating early intervention programs for severely handicapped children and their families* (pp. 79–147). Austin, TX: PRO-ED.

Egeland, B., & Sroufe, L. A. (1981). Developmental sequelae of maltreatment in infancy. In R. Rirley & D. Cicchetti (Eds.), *Developmental perspectives on child maltreatment: New directions for child development.* San Francisco: Jossey-Bass.

Eheart, B. K. (1982). Mother–child interactions with nonretarded and mentally retarded preschoolers. *American Journal of Mental Deficiency, 87*, 20–25.

Elardo, R., Bradley, R., & Caldwell, B. (1975). The relation of infants' home environments to mental test performance from six to thirty-six months: A longitudinal analysis. *Child Development, 46*, 71–76.

Emde, R., Katz, E., & Thorpe, J. (1978). Emotional expression in infancy: Early deviations in Down's syndrome. In M. Lewis & L. Rosenblum (Eds.), *The development of affect.* New York: Plenum Press. As cited in Fogel, A. (1982). Social play, positive affect and coping skills in the first six months. *Topics in Early Childhood Special Education, 2*, 53–65.

Engel, M., & Keane, W. M. (1975, April). *Black mothers and their infant sons: Antecedents, correlates, and predictors of cognitive development in the second and sixth year of life.* Paper presented at the biennial meeting of the Society for Research in Child Development, Denver.

Eriks, J. (1979). Infant "talk." In *Instructor's learning resource manual.* Seattle: NCAST Publications, University of Washington.

Farran, D., Kasari, C., Comfort, M., & Jay, S. (1986). *Parent/Caregiver Involvement Scale.* For further information contact Dale Farran, Child Development-Family Relations, University of North Carolina at Greensboro.

Farran, D. C., Kasari, C., Yoder, P., Harber, L., Huntington, G., & Comfort-Smith, M. (1987). Rating mother–child interactions in handicapped and at-risk infants. In D. Tamir (Ed.), *Stimulation and intervention in infant development.* London: Freund Publishing.

Fewell, R. R., & Vadasy, P. F. (1987). Measurement issues in studies of efficacy. *Topics in Early Childhood Special Education, 7*, 85–96.

Field, T. (1977). Effects of early separation, interactive deficits and experimental manipulations on infant–mother face-to-face interaction. *Child Development, 48*, 763–771.

Field, T. (1979). Interaction patterns of high-risk and normal infants. In T. M. Field, A. Sostek, S. Goldberg, & H. H. Shuman (Eds.), *Infants born at risk.* New York: Spectrum Publications.

Field, T. (1982). Interaction coaching for high-risk infants and their parents. *Prevention in Human Services, 1*, 5–54.

Field, T. (1983). High-risk infants "have less fun" during early interactions. *Topics in Early Childhood Special Education, 3*, 77–87.

Fraiberg, S. (1974). Blind infants and their mothers: An examination of the sign system. In M. Lewis & L. A. Rosenblum (Eds.), *The effect of the infant on its caregiver.* New York: Wiley-Interscience.

Gisel, E., Lange, L., & Niman, C. (1984). Tongue movement in 4- and 5-year-old Down syndrome children during eating: A comparison with normal children. *American Journal of Occupational Therapy, 38*, 660–665.

Givens, D. G. (1978). Social expressivity during the first year of life. *Sign Language Studies, 20*, 251–274.

Goldberg, S. (1977). Social competence in infancy: A model of parent–infant interaction. *Merrill-Palmer Quarterly, 23*, 163–177.

Goldberg, S., Brachfeld, S., & Divitto, B. (1980). Feeding, fussing, and play: Parent–infant interaction in the first year as a function of prematurity and perinatal medical problems. In T. M. Field, S. Goldberg, D. Stern, & M. Sostek (Eds.), *High-risk infants and children: Adult and peer interactions.* New York: Academic Press.

Gottman, J. M., & Bakeman, R. (1979). The sequential analysis of observational data. In M. E. Lamb, S. J. Suomi, & G. R. Stephenson (Eds.), *Social interaction analysis: Methodological issues* (pp. 185–206). Madison: University of Wisconsin Press.

Gunn, P., Berry, P., & Andrews, R. (1979). Vocalizations and looking behavior of Down syndrome infants. *British Journal of Psychology, 70*, 259–263.

Hammond, M., Bee, H. L., Barnard, K. E., & Eyres, S. J. (1983). *Child health assessment. Part 4: Follow-up at second grade* (Final report of project). Supported by grant No. RO1-NU-00816, Division of Nursing, Bureau of Health Professions, Health Resources and Services Administration, U.S. Public Health Service. Seattle: NCAST Publications, University of Washington.

Harris, S. (1983). *Improving oral-motor control in young children with motor handicaps: A neurodevelopmental treatment approach.* Unpublished paper.

Hess, E. H. (1970). Ethology and developmental psychology. In P. H. Mussen (Ed.), *Carmichael's manual of child psychology* (Vol. 1). New York: Wiley.

Jens, K., & Johnson, N. (1982). Affective development: A window to cognition in young handicapped children. *Topics in Early Childhood Special Education, 2*, 17–24.

Jones, O. H. M. (1977). Mother–child communication with pre-linguistic Down's syndrome and normal infants. In H. R. Schaffer (Ed.), *Studies in mother–infant interaction* (pp. 379–401). San Francisco: Academic Press.

Kang, R., & Barnard, K. (1979). Using the Neonatal Behavioral Assessment Scale to evaluate premature infants. In *Birth defects: Original article series* (Vol. 15, no. 7) (pp. 119–144). The National Foundation. New York: Alan R. Liss.

Kaye, K. (1975, September). *Toward the origin of dialogue.* Paper presented at the Loch Lomond Symposium, University of Strathclyde.

Kaye, K. (1976). Infants' effects on their mothers' teaching strategies. In J. Glidwell (Ed.), *The social context of learning and development.* New York: Gardner Press.

Korner, A. F. (1971). Individual differences at birth: Implications for early experience and later development. *American Journal of Orthopsychiatry, 41*, 608–619.

Krakow, J., & Kopp, C. (1983). The effects of developmental delay on sustained attention in young children. *Child Development, 54*, 1143–1155.

Lewis, J., & Latzko, T. (1979). *Progress report and evaluation of infant intervention program.* San Francisco: Family Development Center.

Lewis, M., & Coates, D. L. (1980). Mother–infant interaction and cognitive development in twelve-week-old infants. *Infant Behavior and Development, 3*, 95–105.

Lewis, M., & Goldberg, S. (1969). Perceptual-cognitive development in infancy: A generalized expectancy model as a function of the mother–infant interaction. *Merrill-Palmer Quarterly, 15*, 81–100.

Lewis, M., & Rosenblum, L. A. (1974). *The effect of the infant on its caregiver.* (Introduction). New York: Wiley-Interscience.

Maccoby, E. E., & Martin, J. A. (1983). Socialization in the context of the family: Parent–child interaction. In E. M. Hetherington (Ed.), *Handbook of child psychology* (Vol. 4). New York: Wiley.

Mahoney, G., Finger, I., & Powell, A. (1985). Relationship of maternal behavioral style to the development of organically impaired mentally retarded infants. *American Journal of Mental Deficiency, 90*, 296–302.

Mahoney, G., & Powell, A. (1988). Modifying parent–child interaction: Enhancing the development of handicapped children. *Journal of Special Education, 22*, 82–96.

Mahoney, G., Powell, A., & Finger, I. (1986). The Maternal Behavior Rating Scale. *Topics in Early Childhood Special Education, 6*, 44–56.

Martin, J. A., Maccoby, E. E., Baran, K. W., & Jacklin, C. N. (1981). The sequential analysis of mother–child interaction at 18 months: A comparison of microanalytic methods. *Developmental Psychology, 17*, 146–157.

Mednick, S. A., & Schaffer, B. P. (1963). Mothers' retrospective reports in child-rearing research. *American Journal of Orthopsychiatry, 33*, 457–461.

Nelson, K. (1973). Structure and strategy in learning to talk. *Monographs of the Society for Research in Child Development, 38*(1–2, Serial No. 149).

Newson, J., & Newson, E. (1968). *Four years old in an urban community.* London: Allen & Unwin.

Olson, S. L., Bates, J. E., & Bayles, K. (1984). Mother–infant interaction and the development of individual differences in children's cognitive competence. *Developmental Psychology, 20*, 166–179.

Ramey, C. T., Farran, D. C., & Campbell, F. A. (1979). Predicting IQ from mother–infant interactions. *Child Development, 50*, 804–814.

Ramey, C. T., Farran, D. C., Campbell, F. A., & Finkelstein, N. W. (1978). Observations of mother–infant interactions: Implications for development. In F. D. Minifie & L. L. Lloyd (Eds.), *Communication and cognitive abilities – early behavior assessment* (pp. 397–441). Baltimore: University Park Press.

Richard, N. B. (1986). Interaction between mothers and infants with Down syndrome: Infant characteristics. *Topics in Early Childhood Special Education, 6*, 54–71.

Robson, K. S., & Moss, H. A. (1970). Patterns and determinants of maternal attachment. *Journal of Pediatrics, 77*, 967–985.

Rothbart, M. K. (1984). Social development. In M. Hanson (Ed.), *Atypical infant development* (pp. 207–236). Austin, TX: PRO-ED.

Rothbart, M. K., & Hanson, M. (1983). A caregiver report comparison of temperamental characteristics of Down syndrome and normal infants. *Developmental Psychology, 19*, 766–769.

Rubenstein, J. (1967). Maternal attentiveness and subsequent exploratory behavior in the infant. *Child Development, 38*, 1089–1100.

Sander, L. W. (1964). Adaptive relationships in early mother–child interaction. *American Academy of Child Psychiatry, 3*, 231–263.

Schaefer, E., & Bell, R. (1958). Development of a parental attitude research instrument. *Child Development, 29*, 339–361.

Schaffer, H. R., Collis, G. M., & Parson, G. (1977). Vocal interchange and visual regard in verbal and pre-verbal children. In H. R. Schaffer (Ed.), *Studies in mother–infant interaction* (pp. 291–324). London: Academic Press.

Sears, R. R., Maccoby, E. E., & Levin, H. (1957). *Patterns of child rearing.* Evanston, IL: Row Peterson.

Shonkoff, J. P., & Hauser-Cram, P. (1987). Early intervention for disabled infants and their families: A quantitative analysis. *Pediatrics, 80*, 650–658.

Silcock, A., & Rogers, Y. (1981). *Parenting behavior in mothers of infants with birthweights below 1500 grams.* Paper presented at the Conference of Behavioral Psychology, Toronto.

Smith, L., & Hagen, V. (1984). Relationship between the home environment and sensorimotor development of Down syndrome and non-retarded infants. *American Journal of Mental Deficiency, 89*, 124–132.

Smith, B. L., & Oller, D. K. (1981). A comparative study of pre-meaningful vocalizations produced by normally developing and Down syndrome infants. *Journal of Speech and Hearing Disorders, 46*, 46–51.

Snow, C. E., Arlman-Rupp, A., Hassing, Y., Jobse, J., Joosten, J., & Vorster, J. (1974). *Mothers' speech in three social classes.* Unpublished paper, Institute for General Linguistics, University of Amsterdam.

Spitz, R. A. (1964). The derailment of dialogue. *Journal of American Psychoanalytic Associaton, 12*, 752–775.

Stern, D. N. (1974). Mother and infant at play: The dyadic interaction involving facial, vocal and gaze behaviors. In M. Lewis & L. A. Rosenblum (Eds.), *The effect of the infant on its caregiver* (pp. 187–214). New York: Wiley-Interscience.

Stern, D. (1977). The first relationship: Infant and mother. From *The Developing Child Series.* Cambridge: Harvard University Press.

Stern, D. N. (1984). Affect attunement. In J. D. Call, E. Galenson, & R. L. Tyson (Eds.), *Frontiers of infant psychiatry.* New York: Basic Books.

Stern, D. N., Jaffe, J., Beebe, B., & Bennett, S. L. (1975). Vocalizing in unison and in alternation: Two modes of communication within the mother–infant dyad. In D. Aaronson & R. W. Rieber (Eds.), *Developmental psycholinguistics and communication disorders.* New York: New York Academy of Sciences.

Stern, G. G., Caldwell, B. M., Hersher, L., Lipton, E. L., & Richmond, J. B. (1973). Early social contacts and social relations: Effects of quality of early relationship. In L. J. Stone, T. Smith, & L. B. Murphy (Eds), *The competent infant* (pp. 1097–1111). New York: Basic Books.

Stevenson, M. B., Leavitt, L. A., & Silverberg, S. B. (1985). Mother–infant interaction: Down syndrome case studies. In S. Harel & N. J. Anastasiow (Eds.), *The at-risk infant: Psychosocial aspects* (pp. 389–395). Baltimore: P. H. Brookes.

Strain, B. A., & Vietze, P. M. (1975, April). *Early dialogues: The structure of reciprocal infant-mother vocalization.* Paper presented at the meeting of the Society for Research in Child Development, Denver.

Telzrow, R. W., Kang, R. R., Mitchell, S. K., Ashworth, C. D., & Barnard, K. E. (1982). An assessment of the behavior of the preterm infant at forty weeks conceptional age. In L. P. Lipsitt & T. M. Field (Eds.), *Perinatal risk and newborn behavior.* Norwood, NJ: Ablex Publishing.

Thoman, E. B. (1975, May). *Mother–infant adaptation: The first five weeks.* Paper presented at the Perinatal Nursing Conference, Battelle Seattle Research Center, Seattle.

Thoman, E. B., Becker, P. T., & Freese, M. P. (1978). Individual patterns of mother–infant interaction. In G. P. Sackett (Ed.), *Observing behavior: Vol. 1. Theory and application in mental retardation.* Baltimore: University Park Press.

Tulkin, S. R., & Covitz, F. E. (1975, April). *Mother–infant interaction and intellectual functioning at age six.* Paper presented at the meeting of the Society for Research in Child Development, Denver.

Vietze, P. M., Abernathy, S. R., Ashe, M. L., & Stich, F. (1978). Contingent interaction between mothers and their developmentally delayed infants. In G. P. Sackett (Ed.), *Observing behavior* (Vol. 1). Baltimore: University Park Press.

Wachs, T. D., Uzgiris, I. C., & Hunt, J. McV. (1971). Cognitive development in infants of different age levels and from different environmental backgrounds: An exploratory investigation. *Merrill-Palmer Quarterly, 17,* 283–317.

White, K., & Casto, G. (1985). An integrative review of early intervention efficacy studies with at-risk children: Implications for the handicapped. *Analysis and Intervention in Developmental Disabilities, 5,* 7–31.

Yarrow, M. R., Campbell, J. D., & Burton, R. (1968). *Child rearing, an inquiry into research and methods.* San Francisco: Jossey-Bass.

Zahn-Waxler, C., Radke-Yarrow, M., & King, R. A. (1979). Child rearing and children's prosocial initiations toward victims of distress. *Child Development, 50,* 319–330.

13 *Family assessment: Purposes and techniques*

MARTY WYNGAARDEN KRAUSS
AND FRANCINE JACOBS

INTRODUCTION

The current intense interest in early intervention obscures its more humble and uncertain beginnings. The field has survived lean years, when limited public funding and questions of legitimacy, efficacy, and necessity plagued parents, advocates, and committed program personnel. With the passage of the 1986 Amendments to the Education for All Handicapped Children Act (P.L. 99-457), public policy now acknowledges the value of early intervention both for children with disabilities and for those who are developmentally vulnerable because of environmental factors. Moreover, in the past decade, professionals have come to realize that infants and toddlers are inextricably embedded within families – at least within the mother–child dyad. Thus, most early intervention programs today are expected to have an impact not only on children, but also on the families in which their development occurs. This emerging support for family-oriented services represents a significant shift in public policy, which previously had reserved such services for families who were poor, disadvantaged, or "pathological" (Moroney, 1987; Whittaker, 1983).

Many factors have contributed to this shift, including advances in family-oriented practice at the individual program level (Peterson, 1987), promising research establishing the transactional nature of early development (Sameroff & Chandler, 1975), refinements in ecological theory (Belsky, 1981; Lamb, 1984), and the application of family and social systems concepts to early childhood programming (Cataldo, 1987; Long, 1983). The increasing focus on families, as represented in state and federal early intervention policies, provides additional impetus. In light of these developments, the need for well-considered family assessment strategies has gained widespread attention. The purposes of family assessment within early intervention programs parallel those typically articulated for child assessment: to evaluate family needs and strengths, to establish appropriate short- and long-term goals, to determine relevant program services, and to establish a basis upon which program effects may be evaluated (Bailey et al., 1986; Healy, Keesee, & Smith, 1985).

After a brief discussion of these catalyzing factors, this chapter will present the theoretical underpinnings of family assessment and review traditional approaches to the evaluation of families within early intervention programs. It will then offer recommendations for the integration of core components of family assessment within these service programs and discuss issues in achieving an appropriate match between programs and assessment strategies.

303

FAMILY ASSESSMENT AND EARLY INTERVENTION POLICY

Whereas early child development was once viewed as a relatively stable, predictable unfolding of natural endowments, it is now considered to be a complex negotiation between innate capacities and external influences (Sameroff & Chandler, 1975; Werner & Smith, 1982). In recent years, attempts to identify the parameters of and facilitative influences on healthy early development have been framed in contextual terms, examining patterns of attachment, interaction, socialization, and cognitive stimulation involving the child and his or her environment (Bronfenbrenner, 1979; Crnic, Greenberg, Ragozin, Robinson, & Basham, 1983; Lamb & Easterbrooks, 1981).

The evolving interest among developmental psychologists in the context of growth has reinforced the ecologically oriented approach of early interventionists, though in many respects research has lagged behind, rather than informed, practice. In fact, the relative paucity of well-articulated theories of family development and behavior within the child development tradition has prompted several observers to conclude that early intervention programs often operate atheoretically (Dunst, 1986; Jacobs & Weiss, 1988). Programs often exhibit a diffuse commitment to family involvement without a clear understanding of why certain services should yield particular results.

Historically, program developers have relied on discipline-specific training rather than on general theories of human development and behavior, such as family and general systems theory, social network theory, and family sociology (Walker & Crocker, 1988). Each of these fields has a rich history and literature of its own, yet until quite recently, none has been examined seriously by early intervention proponents or researchers (Bailey et al., 1986; Bristol & Gallagher, 1982; Kazak, 1987). However, contemporary perspectives on early intervention include evidence of the cross-fertilization that ideally should have occurred in an earlier generation. For example, family development and life cycle issues (from family sociology) and descriptions of clinical interventions with families (from family systems theory) appear frequently in current early intervention materials (Bailey & Simeonsson, 1986; Healy et al., 1985).

Public policy has also moved in the direction of supporting intervention not only for disabled and at-risk children, but for their families as well. The Education for All Handicapped Children Act of 1975 (P.L. 94-142) mandated parental involvement in the education of children with disabilities. Additionally, this federal law and its companion state special education codes opened the door to serving parents and families directly through their "related services" provisions. For example, family counseling related to the child's disability and/or educational placement was listed as a reimbursable service. This augured well for future early intervention services. P.L. 94-142 also broke ground in its support of states' statutory involvement with the education of preschool handicapped children, a group historically excluded from the public schools' jurisdiction. This provision aided early intervention advocates indirectly by sensitizing the public to the need for supporting educational programs for young children with disabilities.

Until recently, early intervention policy was established at the state level. The wide variation across states in program philosophy and eligibility, funding levels, services provided, and state agency auspices has been well documented (Meisels, 1985; Meisels, Harbin, Modigliani, & Olson, 1988). With P.L. 99-457, Congress moved early intervention into the national policy arena, because it now sets eligibility and service guidelines to be used in state-level interagency planning for future early intervention programming. Among its provisions is the requirement for Individualized Family Service Plans (IFSP), the most explicit statement to date of the family-as-client approach to promoting the development of young children. As states embark on implementing the provisions of the law, their need for sound family assessment procedures will add renewed incentive for closing the gaps among research, policy, and service delivery interests.

Advances in the study of families from a clinical as well as theoretical perspective have been rapid during the past decades. Developing sound family assessment strategies for early intervention will require that programs be as conversant with family development issues as they are with child development issues. Although family assessment practices in early intervention programs are rarely driven theoretically, a brief review of some of the current theories about family development and functioning provides a more generalized context in which to place existing and recommended assessment practices.

THEORETICAL ISSUES IN FAMILY ASSESSMENT

Family assessment techniques are derived from theoretical assumptions about the nature of family life, particularly with regard to the ways families cope with both predictable and unpredictable crises. There are a variety of theoretical lenses through which the development and functioning of a family may be assessed; each provides a different focus by accentuating specific dimensions hypothesized to be relevant in explaining family behavior or accounting for family or child outcomes.

Perspectives from family sociology

Family sociologists conceptualize family functioning in terms of enduring dimensions of family life that can be observed and compared to hypothesized or empirically based norms. This body of work is notable for its emphasis on describing "normal" family functioning and identifying the boundaries that signal "atypical" or pathological functioning (Epstein, Bishop, & Baldwin, 1982; Forman & Hagan, 1983; Holman & Burr, 1980; Moos & Moos, 1976; Olson, Russell, & Sprenkle, 1983).

Moos and Moos (1976) identified three broad areas in which families differ: *relationship dimensions* (covering aspects of the family's cohesion, expressiveness, and degree of conflict), *personal growth dimensions* (including the value placed on independence, achievement, intellectual and cultural, active and recreational, and moral and religious aspects of family life), and *system maintenance dimensions* (including the family's organizational and control structures). Their conceptualization of family environments is operationalized in the Family Environment Scale (FES), which has been found to be predictive of marital satisfaction (Abbott & Brody, 1985), children's academic performance (Tabackman, 1977), and the adjustment of children with mental retardation (Nihira, Meyers, & Mink, 1980).

Another sociological perspective on family functioning is presented in the Circumplex Model of Marital and Family Systems (Olson et al., 1983; Olson, Sprenkle, & Russell, 1979). The Circumplex Model focuses on three central concepts: *adaptability* (the ability of a family to change its power structure, role relationships, and relationship rules in response to situational and developmental stress), *cohesion* (the emotional bonding that members have with one another and the degree of individual autonomy a person experiences in the family system), and *communication* (a facilitating dimension that enables families to move or change their patterns of adaptability and cohesion). These family processes have been operationalized in several versions of the Family

Adaptability and Cohesion Evaluation Scales (FACES) (Olson, Portner, & Bell, 1982), which place a family into one of 16 family types. Effective family functioning, as defined in the Circumplex Model, is characterized by nonextreme behavioral patterns in the adaptability and cohesion domains. Thus, balanced families are conceptualized as those that are neither overly rigid nor chaotic (in terms of adaptability) and those that are neither totally disengaged nor enmeshed (in terms of cohesion).

Perspectives from family systems theory

Another lens for conceptualizing family functioning comes from family systems theory, based in large part on general systems theory as proposed by von Bertalanffy (1969), Bateson (1972), and others. Within the family systems perspective, the family is viewed as an open, interactive system that operates according to a generalized set of principles (Walsh, 1980). Although there are multiple theoretical and clinical strains within family systems theory (see, e.g., Ackerman, 1958; Jackson, 1965; Minuchin, 1974), its core principles, as described by Walsh (1980) and others (Epstein, Bishop, & Levin, 1978; Hoffman, 1980) are:

1. circular casuality, whereby changes in any one member affect other individuals and the group as a whole;
2. nonsummativity, in which the family as a whole is greater than the sum of its parts, and family behavior therefore represents an interlocking system;
3. equifinity, whereby similar stimuli may lead to different outcomes and similar outcomes may result from different stimuli;
4. communication, in which all behavior is viewed as interpersonal messages that contain both factual and relationship information;
5. family rules, which operate as norms within a family and serve to organize family interactions;
6. homeostasis, whereby a steady, stable state is maintained in the ongoing interaction system through the use of family norms and a mutually reinforcing feedback loop; and
7. morphogenesis, whereby families also require flexibility to adapt to internal and external change.

Family systems theory underlies major clinical approaches to families and represents a significant departure from traditional methods of clinical assessment and therapy that focus on the symptoms of individuals rather than on the family context in which the individual lives. Within a systems perspective, individual dysfunction is seen as symptomatic of family dysfunction. Family assessment must take into account the perspectives of each family member as well as the behavior of the family as a unit, and must acknowledge the multiple causes and transactional nature of individual behavior that accrues from family membership.

Most standardized family assessment techniques that incorporate a systems perspective rely on detailed observational ratings of a family interaction. For example, both the Beavers-Timberlawn Family Evaluation Scale (Beavers, Hampson, & Hulgus, 1985) and the McMaster Model of Family Functioning (Epstein et al., 1978) are multidimensional assessment systems that require trained observers to evaluate family characteristics such as structure, flexibility, and competence. Whereas these assessment strategies have been found to differentiate the quality of adaptation within families with retarded children (Beavers, Hampson, Hulgus, & Beavers, 1986), the use of assessment strategies grounded in family systems theory within early intervention programs has not been reported.

Perspectives from family stress theory

A third related approach to the conceptualization of family functioning has emerged from the study of families under chronic and acute stress. McCubbin and his colleagues, building on the seminal work of Hill (1949), have proposed a model for understanding differential coping capacities of families experiencing a major stressful event (McCubbin et al., 1980; McCubbin & Patterson, 1982). Their Double ABCX Model postulates that family adaptation to a crisis is explained by several factors: the nature of the crisis event, the internally and externally based resources available, and the definition or meaning ascribed to the event. Over time, as the crisis either continues or subsides, the quality of the adaptation may vary as new stressors, resources, and/or meanings are integrated into the family and reshape its coping mechanisms. The theoretical formulation of the Double ABCX Model has been accompanied by the development of a host of instruments to measure the key components of stress identified in the model (McCubbin & Patterson, 1981). Although the utility of the instruments for family assessment and/or program planning has not been established, some evidence exists that the Coping Health Inventory for Parents (an instrument measuring coping patterns in families caring for a chronically ill member) is predictive of child health status and family adaptation (McCubbin et al., 1983).

Perspectives from family life cycle theory

A fourth lens, one that links the preceding three, is the theory that, like individuals, families have a fairly predictable life cycle governing their growth, development, and functioning. The identification of stages in family development, proposed initially by Duvall (1962), has generated a rich literature describing the developmental careers of families (Carter & McGoldrick, 1980) and the consequences of being thwarted in passing through the normal sequence (Farber, 1960; Haley, 1973). Although family development theorists differ in the suggested number of stages that constitute the family life cycle, all include the salient events of marriage, the birth and rearing of children, the departure of family members from the household, and changes in the status of the primary wage earner. Of particular interest to family life cycle theorists are the processes by which families negotiate transitions between stages, and the adaptive reformulations of such core family processes as role allocations, communication patterns, and goal attainment strategies.

CURRENT PRACTICES IN FAMILY ASSESSMENT

Whereas it is commonly noted that assessment should precede service delivery (Bailey & Simeonsson, 1984; Bailey et al., 1986; Dunst & Trivette, 1988), there is no consensus within early intervention programs about "best practice" procedures for their assessment. There are, however, critical opportunities during the course of a family's involvement with early intervention services that constitute key points for the family's assessment. On the basis of a sound evaluation, better decisions can be made about a family's needs for services (independent of demonstrated delays in the child's development), and more individualized service plans can be prepared (including the designation of which conditions or factors would signal the appropriate termination of family-focused services). In addition, systematic assessment contributes to the value of studies of the effectiveness of specific services for a particular family or type of family. Each of these critical assessment points will be discussed more fully.

The intake process

In general, eligibility decisions for early intervention are made primarily on the basis of delays in a child's development, rather than on an assessment of the family's strengths and weaknesses in providing a nurturing, stimulating environment to facilitate that development. If children are judged to be disabled or delayed, they and consequently their families are eligible for services, and are expected to participate.

Extensive family assessment is not often conducted during the program intake process, because most service providers rely on program-developed interviews and questionnaires designed to serve a variety of informational needs other than family evaluation. Such protocols usually restrict family-related information to basic sociodemographic data, including parents' education and employment status, the membership and characteristics of the nuclear and extended family, and the availability of other resources for help with the index child.

Information may also be collected to identify the presence of high-risk family environmental characteristics. Trohanis, Meyer, and Prestridge (1982) report that a variety of factors are commonly used to identify at-risk infants by screening their mothers or parents. Notably, these factors target individual (rather than family-level) status or characteristics and include

> maternal age (adolescent or advanced),
> maternal substance abuse,
> maternal illness or trauma,
> genetic factors,
> low parental education status,
> parental mental retardation,
> parental exposure to environmental hazards,
> parental history of abuse or neglect, and
> low family income.

The need to establish rational criteria for identifying families with known or assumed high-risk factors presents a formidable challenge. However, single marker variables or characteristics – which would simplify the intake process by focusing on discrete, objective status conditions – are poor predictors of child development (Broman, Nichols, & Kennedy, 1975; Rutter, Tizard, Yule, Graham, & Whitmore, 1976; Sameroff & Chandler, 1975). Multiple variables, on the other hand, can serve as useful predictors, as documented by Sameroff, Seifer, Barocas, Zax, and Greenspan (1987), who studied the verbal IQ scores of a socially heterogeneous sample of 215 four-year-olds. They found that children from high-risk environments (defined by a combination of 10 variables that focused on the social and familial environment) were more than 25 times as likely to have an IQ score below 85 than were low-risk children, and concluded that "the multiple pressures of environmental context in terms of amount of stress from the environment, the family's resources for coping with that stress, the number of children that must share those resources, and the parents' flexibility in understanding and dealing with their children all play a role in fostering or hindering of child intellectual and social competencies" (p. 349).

The finding that environmental risk is defined by *multiple* (rather than single) factors in the child and family is becoming more widely appreciated. However, it poses a considerable challenge to early intervention programs in designing efficient and feasible screening and intake batteries to identify children whose family circumstances place them at risk for developmental delay (see Meisels & Wasik, this volume).

Developing individualized family service plans

A persistent theme in many analyses of parental involvement in service systems is that greater individualization of services for parents be incorporated into program structures (Bailey et al., 1986; Bricker & Casuso, 1979; Turnbull & Turnbull, 1982; Winton & Turnbull, 1981). As Bristol and Gallagher (1982) commented, "It is not unusual to visit programs for high-risk or handicapped infants that have highly individualized programs for each infant, but only a single 'package' for involving parents" (p. 149).

In reality, most early intervention programs use maternal report as the primary source of information about the family, or rely on providers' clinical impressions of family functioning and needs (Bailey et al., 1986). Rarely is a formal (i.e., standardized) evaluation of the family conducted. Rather, family assessment proceeds, if at all, based on the collection and analysis of information gleaned from family history questionnaires, locally developed measures of such family domains as social support and family functioning, impressionistic data collected through observations or interviews during service provision (e.g., home visits, parent–child groups), and information shared at mothers' support groups. Such informal assessment procedures have serious drawbacks, including the questionable validity of locally developed measures (Bailey & Simeonsson, 1984) and the potential for cultural and class bias in observation (Howrigan, 1988).

In theory, programmatic decisions about appropriate services for families should be based on a systematic, multidimensional assessment of the family's strengths, needs, resources, current functioning, coping strategies, and parent–child interaction styles (Fewell, 1986; Harris, 1984). Assessments should tap the perspectives and behaviors of all family members, including fathers and siblings, and those of the family as a unit. Information about other current and past stresses in the family also needs to be incorporated. The methods of assessment should rely on both self-report activities and on objective ratings by the assessor. Finally, the assessment should tap the family's goals for the "target" child, for other individual family members, and for the total family. The results of such a comprehensive assessment can then be translated into an individualized family service plan that reflects both the family's goals and the judgments of the early intervention staff on needed services.

Most families of children in early intervention programs receive services, but it is not clear that specific information on individual families, collected either during or subsequent to the intake process, affects the particular services prescribed. As already noted, most programs typically offer a standard set of services. Although some differentiation in family-oriented programming occurs, it seems to be based on a more general categorization of family type rather than on individual family needs. For example, families of environmentally at-risk children may receive a different constellation of services than do families of children with established risks.

Finally, family assessments are rarely considered in developing the child's individual developmental plans, so that the potential to enhance child progress through the parents' involvement with the program is reduced substantially. Treatment plans requiring home-based activities should take into account the family's values and priorities, the family's sense of boundaries or its comfort with outsiders inside the home (Kantor & Lehr, 1975), the cultural meaning for the family of having a child with a disability, and the family's capacity to act in collaboration with service providers. For example, some parents may subscribe to the "parent as educator" role, whereas others place greater emphasis on the family's role as provider of affection and recreation

(Turnbull, Summers, & Brotherson, 1986). These factors will necessarily affect the success of child-directed programming.

Measuring overall program impact

The high visibility and popularity of early intervention services has increased demands for evaluations to determine program effectiveness (Bickman & Weatherford, 1986; Jacobs, 1988). Most studies evaluating these programs have relied on standardized measures of a narrow range of child outcomes and have substantially neglected the impacts on families (Gallagher, this volume; Hauser-Cram, this volume; Shonkoff & Hauser-Cram, 1987). Whereas researchers continue to develop child-focused assessments that are more applicable to children served in early intervention programs (Cicchetti & Wagner, this volume; McCune, Kalmanson, Fleck, Glazewski, & Sillari, this volume), the inclusion of a variety of family level outcomes in evaluation studies is requested increasingly by program funders and supporters.

There is considerable discussion in the literature and among practitioners of the potential impact on parents and families accruing from their participation in early intervention programs (Krauss, 1988; Mott et al., 1986; Zigler & Balla, 1982). Some areas of impact frequently described are

> reduction of parenting stress,
> development of positive parent–child interactions and child-rearing practices,
> strengthening of parental and familial social support networks,
> promotion of healthy family functioning,
> enhancement of education,
> increase in income and employment opportunities, and
> promotion of positive development among siblings.

The consensus with which these outcomes have been articulated is especially striking in light of the atheoretical and unstandardized approach most programs take toward assessing families upon entry, during service delivery, or at the termination of services.

The evaluation of family changes attributable to early intervention services is rarely incorporated as a programmatic activity. Most programs do not conduct routine or even episodic internal evaluations to determine service efficacy for particular families in a systematic manner. This omission jeopardizes a program's ability to refine its understanding of which services are most effective for which families; it also limits the effects on public policy that well-designed studies of this nature can have.

Practical constraints on family assessment

What accounts for the limited use of family assessment within early intervention programs? The major barriers appear to be the inadequate integration of family development issues in theories of early child development, the historical focus on the child in many early intervention programs, the absence of clear legislative or policy mandates (until recently) regarding families as an appropriate target for intervention, and the unavailability of well-designed assessment techniques.

Historically, families were viewed primarily as promoters of their children's development, rather than as legitimate service recipients themselves. Although early intervention increasingly has been defined as a family service, many staff remain ambivalent about a host of activities related to families: conducting family assessments, developing family-centered goals for service plans, and providing direct, sometimes necessarily therapeutic, services to families.

One influence mitigating against the transition to a greater family focus is the philosophical stance many programs maintain about their preferred relationship with families. Because early intervention professionals rarely describe themselves as family therapists, and few have undertaken clinical family training, the relationship between service providers and parents is typically viewed as a partnership rather than a clinical, "helper–client" arrangement (Dunst & Trivette, 1988; Weiss & Jacobs, 1988; Zeitlin, Williamson, & Rosenblatt, 1987). The partnership model assumes that families are capable of articulating their own needs and that, in concert with professionals, a mutually determined set of services will be prescribed. It does not assume, however, that professionals should probe more deeply into family styles and behaviors than parents initially are willing to allow, or that clinical appraisal of the family's functioning through techniques other than direct responses to questions is necessary.

This situation creates a conflict. The ability to probe and to appraise are essential conditions for most family assessment protocols, yet these conditions may be avoided by staff who are uncomfortable with the professional posture they require. Having been trained in child-centered disciplines, many service providers feel that doing "family work" overextends their expertise. As one staff person stated, "Parents are here because their kid has a handicap, not because they need services" (early intervention program director, confidential communicaton, June 12, 1987).

This resistance to family work affects the choice and use of family techniques. Unwilling to explore sensitive topics, untrained in conducting systematic family interviews, and unpracticed in discussing in-depth family needs and resources, many early interventionists often forego both formal and informal individual family assessments (early intervention program director, confidential communication, June 18, 1987). As a result, their assessments are quite informal and "underground." One program director suggested that parents who discover that someone thinks *their family* needs help will be angry and withdraw from the program. As a result, family assessments and family services are often a "hidden agenda . . . the thought behind dealing with families doesn't get into the case documentation," noted one early intervention director. Thus, the assumed generic needs of the group, "families with handicapped children," often dictate the services offered (early intervention program director, confidential communication, June 20, 1987).

An additional influence, however, is the significant gap between research and practice in the development of clinically relevant assessment batteries that focus on family life and development (Bailey & Simeonsson, 1984, 1986; Walsh & Wood, 1983) or on a core set of "predictors" or characteristics of families associated with programmatically relevant outcomes. The lack of rigor or sophistication in current practices for family assessment contrasts sharply with the more detailed and structured assessments commonly used to evaluate children. Many of the standardized assessment tools used in programs that have made a conscious effort to incorporate family assessment protocols were initially developed for research rather than clinical use and may, therefore, require special staff training for their proper administration and interpretation. Further, although some studies are honing in on specific family-based factors that place children at risk for poor development (Broman et al., 1975; Kochanek, Kabacoff, & Lipsitt, 1987; Sameroff et al., 1987), the chance of a false positive identification for any particular family is unacceptably high for most service providers to readily adopt any existing screening or assessment protocol.

Thus, limitations inherent in current family assessment procedures conspire with the proclivities and training of many staff within early intervention programs to prevent adequate family assessment from taking place. However, given the incentives and

pressures to refine family assessment strategies, programs will have to confront these
practical and ideological issues.

CORE DIMENSIONS AND SPECIFIC MEASURES IN FAMILY ASSESSMENT

Many early intervention providers are keenly interested in establishing more rigorous
and comprehensive assessment protocols for families, yet few have identified a core set
of instruments or procedures that works well for all families served, or that is useful
given staff capabilities and training. In this section, we present some recommended
areas for inclusion within family assessment procedures.

The literature on adaptation and coping in families with a disabled child (Bristol,
1984; Byrne & Cunningham, 1985; Crnic, Friedrich, & Greenberg, 1983) suggests that
there are, at a minimum, three core dimensions that should be included in an assessment battery for families receiving early intervention services. These dimensions are
parental and familial stress (defined as the perception of internally or externally based
demands exceeding the resources available to meet the demands), coping strategies
and resources (defined as psychological and social support resources used to manage
stress), and characteristics of the family environment (defined as the structures and
processes by which the family operates as a unit).

Each of these dimensions can be examined through a variety of methods, for
example, direct observations, structured interviews, self-administered instruments. The
choice of method typically is determined by the capabilities and training of the program's staff, its access to consultants to supplement core staff, and the appropriateness of the specific methods given the characteristics of the families served. Because
early intervention programs have little experience with the use of standardized instruments for the assessment of key family issues, the following discussion identifies potentially useful instruments that could supplement and expand existing clinical or intake
interview procedures.

Parental and family stress

The first core area in the assessment of families with young children with developmental disabilities is the amount and type of stress currently being experienced at the family
or individual level. The study of stress is thought to consist of three components: the
sources of stress (both acute and chronic events), the mediators of stress (coping styles
and social support), and the manifestations of stress (including physiological and overt
emotional and behavioral expressions) (Pearlin, Lieberman, Menaghan, & Mullan,
1981).

There is a voluminous literature describing the emotionally charged reactions of
parents to learning of their child's disability, and of the stress that accompanies the
initial period of determining the nature and extent of the handicap (Crnic, Friedrich,
& Greenberg, 1983; Gallagher, Beckman, & Cross, 1983; Wikler, 1986). There is
also considerable interest in how families marshal their resources to cope with the
heightened stress of this period (Byrne & Cunningham, 1985; Foster & Berger,
1985; McCubbin et al., 1980; Reiss & Oliveri, 1980; Turnbull et al., 1986) and with
the recurrent and cumulative stress that accompanies the required adaptations and
adjustments.

Identifying parents or families experiencing extreme levels of stress should be an integral component of family assessment procedures, since empirical studies have confirmed clinical findings on the relation between high levels of stress and adverse child and family outcomes (Crnic, Greenberg et al., 1983; Gallagher et al., 1983; Roghmann & Haggerty, 1972; Sherman & Cocozza, 1984). One of the basic services available in most early intervention programs – parent support groups – is specifically designed to provide parents with an outlet for their concerns and with an environment in which stress and its manifestations can be discussed comfortably (McKinney & Peterson, 1987). Given the priority most programs place on supporting families in their adaptation to the task of parenting a disabled or at-risk child, the integration of additional techniques for evaluating degrees of parental or family stress is critical.

Assessment protocols that focus on either an individual's level of stress or on stress at the family level have been reviewed elsewhere (Fewell, 1986; Krauss, 1988). Among the most commonly used instruments for measuring individual stress are the Parenting Stress Index (PSI) (Abidin, 1983; Loyd & Abidin, 1985), the Questionnaire on Resources and Stress (Friedrich, Greenberg, & Crnic, 1983; Holroyd, 1974; Salisbury, 1985), and the Life Experience Survey (Sarason, Johnson, & Siegal, 1978). Among those designed to measure family-level stress are instruments developed by McCubbin and his colleagues, such as the Family Inventory of Life Events and Changes (FILE) and a companion version for use with adolescents (A-FILE) (McCubbin & Patterson, 1981). The Impact-on-Family Scale (Stein & Reissman, 1978, 1980) has also been recommended as a potentially valuable instrument in the assessment of families receiving early intervention services (Mott et al., 1986).

Most of these measures have reference group norms against which scores may be compared. The manual for the PSI (Abidin, 1983), in particular, contains an unusually detailed description of clinical interpretations for particular scores. All are self-administered questionnaires, and although they vary in length and administration time, none is generally considered burdensome to complete, score, or interpret. However, the sensitivity of the scales to change over short periods of time is not well established.

Coping strategies and resources

Coping strategies are defined as an individual's or a family's active efforts to manage stressful situations through the use of psychological and social resources (Pearlin & Schooler, 1978; Schilling, Gilchrist, & Schinke, 1984). Pearlin and Schooler (1978) identified three categories of coping behaviors: responses that modify or alter the stressful situation, responses that function to control the meaning of the situation, and responses that function to control stress itself.

Variability in the recovery from or adaptation to intensely stressful situations is often attributed to the presence and activation of specific coping behaviors (Goldfarb, Brotherson, Summers, & Turnbull, 1986). For example, McKinney and Peterson (1987) report that spouse support, internal locus of control (a coping resource), and child characteristics were significantly related to the amount of stress reported by mothers of children in early intervention programs. Others have demonstrated that for families of children with a chronic illness, specific coping patterns – maintaining an optimistic definition of the situation, preserving self-esteem and social support, and receiving accurate factual information about the situation – are related to improved child health status and family adaptation (McCubbin et al., 1983). Clearly, the most consistently enumerated components of coping strategies, as defined by theoretical and empirical studies, are the activation of social support networks (an externally based coping mechanism) and the use of psychological resources (an internally based coping mechanism).

Programs designed to enhance the coping skills of families focus primarily on the provision of referral information to relevant agencies, the sponsorship of parent support groups in which common experiences and feelings can be shared, and the promotion of parental advocacy techniques through which parents develop a feeling of control and competence in securing services for their child and family. These strategies instill a more positive perspective on the experience of parenting a child with a disability and are critical forms of social support. Within early intervention programs, the entire complement of services to the family is often described as a means for enhancing the family's coping skills through the provision of social support (Dunst & Trivette, this volume; Healy et al., 1985).

The theoretical and empirical basis for examining social support networks among families with young handicapped or at-risk children is described by Dunst and Trivette (this volume) and elsewhere (Crnic, Greenberg et al., 1983; Kazak, 1987; McKinney & Peterson, 1987; Shonkoff, 1984). There is considerable evidence that social support, measured in terms of the breadth and degree of satisfaction with available supports, serves as a powerful buffer from stress for families (Dean & Lin, 1977; Whittaker & Garbarino, 1983) and may have a direct effect on parental well-being, family integrity, and child functioning (Cochran & Brassard, 1979; Dunst, Trivette, & Cross, 1986).

Given the centrality of social support to current conceptualizations of coping resources, the integration of formal assessment measures is clearly indicated. A number of instruments have been developed to assess the size, sources, and perceived helpfulness of an individual's social support network (Antonucci & Akiyama, 1987; Cleary, 1988; Dunst & Trivette, this volume). For example, the Family Support Scale (FSS) (Dunst, Jenkins, & Trivette, 1984), is an 18-item, self-report measure that assesses the extent to which different sources of support have been helpful to the family in rearing a young child. The Carolina Support Scale (CSS) (Bristol, 1984) is similar in structure but focuses on an individual's social support network. Antonucci and Akiyama's (1987) approach requires the enumeration of specific individuals in a person's social network based on the emotional proximity of the network members to the individual.

The merits of these instruments include their brevity, ease of administration, and straightforward interpretation. None contains intrusive or emotionally threatening items, and any could be incorporated readily in program screening or intake procedures. Antonucci and Akiyama's (1987) social network instrument yields more detailed information about the giving and receiving of support between the individual and his or her network members than is obtained through the FSS and CSS. These latter two instruments, although appealingly succinct, may be viewed by program staff as too cursory for service decision making. They may be well used, however, in conjunction with other measures.

There also are instruments that measure psychological resources as coping mechanisms, although their psychometric properties and utility for program planning are not well established (Krauss, 1988). For example, the Ways of Coping Checklist is a 68-item self-report instrument designed to measure coping behaviors used for managing day-to-day stress (Folkman & Lazarus, 1980). It incorporates multiple psychological strategies to manage stress, such as defensive coping (e.g., avoidance, intellectualization, isolation, suppression), information seeking, problem solving, direct action and magical thinking. In a study of coping strategies used by students taking college examinations, the Checklist revealed that different strategies are used in the anticipatory stages of a stressful event than are used in the management of the actual event

(Folkman & Lazarus, 1985). Early intervention programs may find the Checklist useful in documenting the range of psychological resources available to parents to cope with stress. Although the Checklist is easy to administer, its scoring and interpretation are not well described in the instrument's documentation. A revised and shortened version of the Checklist is available that demonstrates adequate reliability and construct validity properties (Vitaliano, Russo, Carr, Maiuro, & Becker, 1985).

The measures developed by McCubbin and Patterson (1981) to operationalize the Double ABCX Model (described earlier) contain several instruments that focus on the coping strategies utilized by families, such as the Family Inventory of Resources for Management (FIRM), the Coping Health Inventory for Parents (CHIP), and the Family Coping Inventory (FCI). Each is self-administered and contains multiple subscales that distinguish among different types of coping strategies. For example, the FCI has five subscales labeled maintaining family integrity, developing interpersonal relationships and social support, managing psychological tension and strain, believing in the value of the spouse's profession and maintaining an optimistic definition of the situation, and developing self-reliance and self-esteem. Whereas the psychometric properties of these coping scales appear satisfactory, none of the scales has been used widely in either research or clinical settings.

Family environment

A third component to systematic family assessment procedures is an evaluation of the home environment. Early life experiences and the social climate of the family – its values, attitudes, and behavioral style – have been identified as important contributors to a child's development (Bronfenbrenner, 1974; Hunt, 1961; Rutter, 1985). Mother–child interaction patterns have often been used as indicators of the quality of the child's home experiences (see Barnard & Kelly, this volume), but these dyadic interactions are embedded in the family and the larger social context (Auerswald, 1971; Bronfenbrenner, 1979; Garbarino, this volume, Garber & Heber, 1977). In accounting for different child and family outcomes, the relative salience of different aspects of the family environment – for example, maternal verbal behavior, availability of stimulating play materials and opportunities, the priorities placed on different dimensions of family life, strategies for intrafamily conflict resolution – has been the focus of research for decades (Erlardo, Bradley, & Caldwell, 1975; Mink & Nihira, 1987; Mink, Nihira, & Meyers, 1983; Ramey, Mills, Campbell, & O'Brien, 1975; Stevens & Bakeman, 1985; Wachs, Uzgiris, & Hunt, 1971). However, identifying specific features of the home environment that warrant direct assessment for a given family or for a group of families categorized by ethnicity, socioeconomic status, and type or severity of the child's disability is a complex process.

Most early intervention programs collect some relevant information on which a general description of a family's circumstances can be based. For example, the family's living conditions, financial resources, and membership structure are typically included in intake and assessment procedures. Home visit observations offer a clinical impression of such variables as the level of parental attachment, the degree of structure present in the home, the presence of appropriate toy and play materials for the child, and the degree of family cohesion. Interviews with parents also may yield insights into the family's values and its capacity to integrate therapeutic programs into its normal routines. Although explicit descriptions of the "quality of the family environment" frequently go unrecorded, informal assessments of this nature often occur.

More systematic evaluations of both specific and general features of the family environment are possible through the use of standardized measures (Bagarozzi, 1985; Forman & Hagan, 1983; Moos & Moos 1981; Straus & Brown, 1977; Walker & Crocker, 1988). Among the most widely used for evaluating the adequacy of a child's early developmental environment is the Home Observation for Measurement of the Environment (HOME) (Bradley & Caldwell, 1984), which covers the following family characteristics: frequency and stability of adult contact; amount of developmental and vocal stimulation; need gratification; emotional climate; avoidance of restriction on motor and exploratory behavior; available play materials; and home characteristics indicative of parental concern with achievement.

Because its administration is based on a home observation and discussion with the parent, the HOME can be easily integrated with home visiting procedures in early intervention programs. Its use enables professionals to assess the characteristics of the child's environment against standardized norms in order to identify those family settings in which the social and emotional context is less than optimal. The HOME has been criticized because of its high correlation with family socioeconomic status and its reliance on maternal report rather than observed child behavior for a substantial number of items (Halpern, 1984; Howrigan, 1988). However, its focus on environmental features that are particularly important in early childhood has made it a popular tool in this field.

Instruments also are available that tap other significant dimensions of the family's environment. For example, the Family Adaptability and Cohesion Evaluation Scales (FACES) (Olson et al., 1982) is a self-administered questionnaire that measures adaptability and cohesion within a family, an area of particular interest for clinicians serving families coping with unusual and extreme stress. The Beavers-Timberlawn Family Evaluation Scale (Lewis, Beavers, Gossett, & Phillips, 1976) is an observational assessment strategy that examines the overall functioning of the family system on key process (e.g., task efficiency, negotiation, clarity of expression) and structural (e.g., power, coalitions, closeness) characteristics.

Obviously, the ultimate selection of instruments is affected by the programmatic orientation of the service setting, the time, energy, and costs associated with different assessment protocols, and the skills and training of the program's staff. An additional selection factor is the acceptability of the protocols to the families being assessed. As noted earlier, many families and program staff perceive early intervention services as primarily oriented toward the child's development rather than as a service for the family as a unit. Thus, the addition of a staff member who is trained in and comfortable with the process of family assessment may be required.

APPLICATIONS OF FAMILY ASSESSMENT TECHNIQUES

The selection of appropriate family assessment strategies is affected by the organizational, philosophical, and programmatic characteristics of individual programs. For example, organizational features such as the age, numbers, and profiles of children and families served, staffing patterns, and agency auspices and funding levels can either enhance or constrain a program's flexibility in incorporating increasingly sophisticated family assessment goals. The philosophical orientation of staff and parents, staff training and interest in the clinical and research components of assessment, and the types of services provided also should be considered in the selection of assessment strategies.

The type of assessment appropriate for any particular program may vary; however, all programs must critically examine their existing strategies and make modifications based on a graduated model. For example, it is likely to be counterproductive to pressure small new programs, or those uncomfortable for some reason with the process, into adherence to sophisticated family assessment protocols. However, even these programs can be expected to collect basic sociodemographic information on families, with the possibility that, after gaining some experience in utilizing such data to shape their family services, such programs may be interested in more rigorous family assessment stategies. This approach, described in detail elsewhere (Jacobs, 1988), is based on the premise that every family support and education program, be it a "grassroots" low-budget operation or a well-funded demonstration project, should engage in evaluation activities at a level of effort appropriate for that particular program. A similar model could be applied to early intervention programs regarding the realm of family assessment.

The evaluation of families presents relatively new challenges that require a program-level assessment of structure and content. For example, who on the staff is committed to performing these assessments; how much time will they take and what budgetary alterations need to be made; how will families and staff respond to this additional component and how can proponents make these individuals more comfortable with the concept of family assessment; how willing are staff members to give up some of their control in assessing families' needs to the families themselves (and to more objective paper-and-pencil measures); and, finally, to what extent are programs prepared to change their services, their expectations for families, and their views of their own roles in the assessment process? Each program will have different responses to these questions, and therefore each should attempt somewhat individualized family assessment procedures.

Multimodal, multimeasure assessments provide programs with the depth and breadth of information necessary to make optimal decisions about family and child service plans, and to evaluate individual family progress and overall program effectiveness over time. The following three distinct approaches to family assessment within early intervention programs are illustrative of the integral relationship between assessment and service (Simeonsson, Bailey, Huntington, & Comfort, 1986) and demonstrate how standardized protocols can be incorporated into the service structure.

Family, Infant, and Preschool Program

The Family, Infant and Preschool Program (FIPP) in North Carolina defines its purpose as being a social support service to families of disabled or delayed infants and toddlers. In order to evaluate the families' current level of support, program staff have developed a comprehensive assessment battery that requires less than two hours to complete (Dunst & Trivette, 1988, this volume). In addition to a videotaped assessment of parent–child interaction during a free-play situation, information is collected that incorporates five major areas: parental characteristics (education, age, etc.); family characteristics (socioeconomic status, etc.); child characteristics (age, sex, etc.); child diagnosis; and social support.

The multifaceted assessment of social support conducted by FIPP is especially noteworthy since it utilizes five separate instruments. These cover family social support (The Family Support Scale by Dunst, Jenkins, & Trivette, 1984), maternal social support (The Maternal Social Support Index by Pascoe, Loda, Jeffries, & Earp, 1981), family resources (The Family Resources Scale by Dunst & Leet, 1987), parental roles (The Parental Role Scale by Gallagher, Cross, & Scharfman, 1981), and a psychosocial kinship inventory (by Pattison, Defancisco, Wood, Frazier, & Crowder, 1975). These measures of social support have been refined over several years, ensuring that they tap relevant dimensions for families with disabled children. Their approach also includes periodic reassessment of families using their standardized protocol.

Family-Focused Intervention Model

The assessment procedures used in the Family-Focused Intervention Model (Bailey et al., 1986) combine paper-and-pencil measures, direct observational procedures, and a focused face-to-face interview with parents. The cornerstone of the process is the interview, which covers specific issues derived from theoretical models of family coping (the family's current resources, its definition and perception of the stressful event, and its current coping strategies) and from models of family functioning (the family's priorities or values placed on basic functions that it performs). The goal of the interview, therefore, is to help the family articulate its strengths and needs in order to develop a list of family-focused goals and strategies for their implementation.

Whereas the model assumes that parents will be able to select appropriate family-focused areas for intervention, the interviewer may target additional goals (and inform the parents of these goals) if the parents neglect or resist awareness of problematic issues that surface in the assessment process. A goal attainment scale is then developed that specifies a weighted or ranked set of goals for the family and describes the range of possible outcomes (from worst possible to best possible) for each goal. Periodic reassessments of the family are made during the intervention period to establish their progress in meeting each goal.

COPING Project

Assessment in the COPING Project (Zeitlin et al., 1987), is based on a transactional model of coping with stress that acknowledges the reciprocal relationships among four hypothesized steps in the adaptation process: cognitive appraisal, decision making, action and reappraisal, and evaluation of the coping effort. The 1-hour family assessment process occurs over a 3-week period, after a family and child are enrolled in the program, and includes a battery of self-rated instruments completed by both parents at home or during the provision of services.

The instruments, initially developed elsewhere for research purposes, were selected by early intervention staff based on their applicability to the population served (families facing a chronic stress), the skills of the staff members (social workers and psychologists), and the efficiency of the instruments in tapping multiple dimensions of stress and coping behaviors. The results are summarized in terms of the family's and each parent's strengths and vulnerabilities. Through review of the written summary with the parents, a family service plan is prepared. Goals incorporated into the plan cover three areas: acquiring information, receiving support and guidance, and participating in counseling or therapy.

These three models of family assessment just described creatively integrate interviews, pencil-and-paper measures, and observational information. They also illustrate the importance of matching the assessment protocol to the specific structure and content of the intervention program.

The COPING Project focuses on developing effective familial and parental coping strategies for families with young disabled children. Its emphasis on reshaping the cognitive processes that define stress at the individual level accounts for its use of a wide array of instruments that focus on ways in which events are perceived and interpreted by the individual. Although the COPING and FIPP programs share a commitment to adaptive individual and family functioning, their approaches, and thus their assessment protocols, differ substantially.

The FIPP is designed to enhance and extend the social support networks of the families and children served, interpreting behavioral deficiencies in parents as a result of poor social supports rather than as personal weaknesses. Both FIPP and the Family-Focused Intervention Model use the assessment process as a vehicle for empowering parents in the decision-making process.

CONCLUSIONS

The field of early intervention is in the midst of a developmental transition. It has grown from a small collection of local entities to a national network of publicly supported programs. It has moved beyond the boundaries of state policy, with federal legislation exerting new influences on its development, capacities, and directions. It has embraced a broader constituency, focusing on children with environmental vulnerabilities in addition to those with established risks, and including parents as well as children.

Kahn and Kamerman (1982) distinguish between *family-oriented* programs that acknowledge the central role assumed by the families in their children's development but primarily serve children, and *family-focused* programs that design services to meet the needs of all family members and that assess the impacts of services on the family unit in addition to the target child. Early intervention services may accurately be described as a system moving from the former program type to the latter. This shift brings family assessment into bold relief.

The selection of family assessment procedures is only one of several critical family-related tasks to be undertaken by early intervention programs. Before such procedures can be selected, programs must articulate criteria for determining positive family functioning and for measuring how desired change in families occurs. Subsequently, family assessment can be structured not primarily on intuitive beliefs among program staff, but on the deliberate evaluation of the applicability of theoretically and empirically defensible models of family development.

A stronger commitment to family assessment without a concurrent commitment to examining family services in early intervention is like getting all dressed up with nowhere to go. The results of more finely grained family assessments likely will raise questions about the appropriateness of a standard range of services offered by many early intervention programs. A healthy, evolving early intervention system will respond to these questions flexibly, by entertaining new programming ideas and modifying present offerings.

Programs must also acknowledge that "family work" requires specialized training and skills. The traditional staffing structure of early intervention programs may need modification in order to incorporate professionals with a commitment to and competence in the assessment of families. It is unlikely that family assessment can be conducted with the sophistication and credibility it merits without substantial in-service training efforts or the addition of specialized staff.

Clinicians outside the traditional child development fields with perhaps the most to offer early intervention services at this juncture are family systems therapists or, as

Wynne, McDaniel, and Weber (1987) have defined the role, family systems consultants. A trained family systems consultant can offer support, education, and assessment in addition to, or exclusive of, therapy. The addition of staff members with a systemic orientation to service delivery could help many programs at each of the critical points in their interactions with families.

Early intervention has moved through a period of consolidation and achievement, and now must respond to and incorporate new demands – in this case, the integration of family assessment. These demands, which arise both from inside and outside the field, should not be seen as intrusions into an already highly satisfactory service system. Rather, they should be viewed as opportunities to enable early intervention to remain a vibrant and useful endeavor, growing to reflect new understandings of how better to serve vulnerable children and their families.

REFERENCES

Abbott, D. A., & Brody, G. H. (1985). The relation of child age, gender, and number of children to the marital adjustment of wives. *Journal of Marriage and the Family, 47*, 77–84.

Abidin, R. R. (1983). *Parenting Stress Index*. Charlottesville, MD: Pediatric Psychology Press.

Ackerman, N. W. (1958). *The psychodynamics of family life*. New York: Basic Books.

Antonucci, T. C., & Akiyama, H. (1987). Social networks in adult life and a preliminary examination of the convoy model. *Journal of Gerontology, 42*, 519–527.

Auerswald, E. H. (1971). Families, change and the ecological perspective. *Family Process, 10*, 263–282.

Bagarozzi, D. A. (1985). Dimensions of family evaluation. In L. L'Abate (Ed.), *The handbook of family psychology and therapy* (Vol. 2, pp. 989–1005). Homewood, IL: Dorsey Press.

Bailey, D. B., & Simeonsson, R. J. (1984). Critical issues underlying research and intervention with families of young handicapped children. *Journal of the Division for Early Childhood, 9*, 38–48.

Bailey, D. B., & Simeonsson, R. J. (1986). Design issues in family impact evaluation. In L. Bickman & D. L. Weatherford (Eds.), *Evaluating early intervention programs for severely handicapped children and their families* (pp. 209–230). Austin, TX: PRO-ED.

Bailey, D. B., Simeonsson, R. J., Winton, P. J., Huntington, G. S., Comfort, M., Isbell, P., O'Donnell, K. J., & Helm, J. M. (1986). Family-focused intervention: A functional model for planning, implementing, and evaluating individualized family services in early intervention. *Journal of the Division for Early Childhood, 10*, 156–171.

Bateson, G. (1972). *Steps to an ecology of mind*. New York: Ballantine Books.

Beavers, W. R., Hampson, R. B., & Hulgus, Y. F. (1985). Commentary: The Beavers Systems approach to family assessment. *Family Processes, 24*, 398–405.

Beavers, J., Hampson, R. B., Hulgus, Y. F., & Beavers, W. R. (1986). Coping in families with a retarded child. *Family Process, 25*, 365–378.

Belsky, J. (1981). Early human experience: A family perspective. *Developmental Psychology, 17*, 3–23.

Bickman, L., & Weatherford, D. L. (Eds.). (1986). *Evaluating early intervention programs for severely handicapped children and their families*. Austin, TX: PRO-ED.

Bradley, R. H., & Caldwell, B. M. (1984). 174 children: A study of the relationship between home environment and cognitive development during the first 5 years. In A. W. Gottfried, (Ed.), *Home environment and early cognitive development* (pp. 5–56). Orlando: Academic Press.

Bricker, D., & Casuso, V. (1979). Family involvement: A critical component of early intervention. *Exceptional Children, 46*, 108–116.

Bristol, M. M. (1984). Family resources and successful adaptation to autistic children. In P. Schopler & G. Mesibov (Eds.), *The effects of autism on the family* (pp. 289–311). New York: Plenum Press.

Bristol, M. M., & Gallagher, J. J. (1982). A family focus for intervention. In C. T. Ramey & P. L. Trohanis (Eds.), *Finding and educating high-risk and handicapped infants* (pp. 137–161). Baltimore: University Park Press.

Broman, S. H., Nichols, P. L., & Kennedy, W. A. (1975). *Preschool IQ: Prenatal and early developmental correlates*. Hillsdale, NJ: L. Erlbaum.

Bronfenbrenner, U. (1974). *Is early intervention effective? A report on longitudinal evaluations of preschool programs* (Vol. 2). Washington, DC: Department of Health, Education, and Welfare, Office of Child Development.

Bronfenbrenner, U. (1979). *The ecology of human development: Experiments by nature and design.* Cambridge: Harvard University Press.

Byrne, E. A., & Cunningham, C. C. (1985). The effects of mentally handicapped children on families: A conceptual review. *Journal of Child Psychology, 26,* 847–864.

Carter, E., & McGoldrick, M. (1980). *The family life cycle: A framework for family therapy.* New York: Gardner Press.

Cataldo, C. (1987). *Parent education for early childhood.* New York: Teachers College Press.

Cleary, P. D. (1988). Social support: Conceptualization and measurement. In H. Weiss & F. Jacobs (Eds.), *Evaluating family programs* (pp. 195–216). Hawthorne, NY: Aldine Press.

Cochran, M., & Brassard, J. (1979). Child development and personal social networks. *Child Development, 50,* 601–616.

Crnic, K. A., Friedrich, W. N., & Greenberg, M. T. (1983). Adaptation of families with mentally retarded children: A model of stress, coping, and family ecology. *American Journal of Mental Deficiency, 88,* 125–138.

Crnic, K. A., Greenberg, M. T., Ragozin, N. M., Robinson, N. M., & Basham, R. B. (1983). Effects of stress and social support on mothers of premature and full-term infants. *Child Development, 54,* 209–217.

Dean, A., & Lin, N. (1977). Stress-buffering role of social support. *Journal of Nervous and Mental Disease, 165,* 403–417.

Dunst, C. J. (1986). Overview of the efficacy of early intervention programs: Methodological and conceptual consideration. In L. Bickman & D. Weatherford (Eds.), *Evaluating early intervention programs for severely handicapped children and their families* (pp. 79–147). Austin, TX: PRO-ED.

Dunst, C. J., Jenkins, V., & Trivette, C. M. (1984). Family Support Scale: Reliability and validity. *Journal of Individual, Family and Community Wellness, 1,* 45–52.

Dunst, C. J., & Leet, H. E. (1987). Measuring the adequacy of resources in households with young children. *Child: Care, Health and Development, 13,* 111–125.

Dunst, C. J., & Trivette, C. M. (1988). Toward experimental evaluation of the Family, Infant and Preschool Program. In H. Weiss & F. Jacobs (Eds.), *Evaluating family programs* (pp. 315–346). Hawthorne, N.Y.: Aldine Press.

Dunst, C. J., Trivette, C. M., & Cross, A. H. (1986). Mediating influences of social support: Personal, family and child outcomes. *American Journal of Mental Deficiency, 90,* 403–417.

Duvall, E. M. (1962). *Family development.* Philadelphia: Lippincott.

Epstein, N. B., Bishop, D. S., & Baldwin, L. M. (1982). McMaster model of family functioning: A view of the normal family. In F. Walsh (Ed.), *Normal family processes* (pp. 115–141). New York: Guilford Press.

Epstein, N. B., Bishop, D. S., & Levin, S. (1978). The McMaster model of family functioning. *Journal of Marriage and Family Counseling, 4,* 19–31.

Erlardo, R., Bradley, R., & Caldwell, B. M. (1975). The relation of infants' home environments to mental test performance from six to thirty-six months: A longitudinal analysis. *Child Development, 46,* 71–76.

Farber, B. (1960). Family organization and crisis: Maintenance of integration in families with a severely mentally retarded child. *Monographs of the Society for Research in Child Development, 25,* (1, Serial No. 75).

Fewell, R. R. (1986). The measurement of family functioning. In L. Bickman & D. L. Weatherford (Eds.), *Evaluating early intervention programs for severely handicapped children and their families* (pp. 263–307). Austin, TX: PRO-ED.

Folkman, S., & Lazarus, R. S. (1980). An analysis of coping in a middle-aged community sample. *Journal of Health and Social Behavior, 21,* 219–239.

Folkman, S., & Lazarus, R. S. (1985). If it changes it must be a process: Study of emotion and coping during three stages of a college examination. *Journal of Personality and Social Psychology, 48,* 150–170.

Forman, B. D., & Hagan, B. J. (1983). A comparative review of total family functioning measures. *American Journal of Family Therapy, 11,* 25–40.

Foster, M., & Berger, M. (1985). Research with families with handicaped children: A multilevel systemic perspective. In L. L'Abate (Ed.), *The handbook of family psychology and therapy* (pp. 741–780). Homewood, IL: Dorsey Press.

Friedrich, W. N., Greenberg, M. T., & Crnic, K. (1983). A short-form of the Questionnaire on Resources and Stress. *American Journal of Mental Deficiency, 88,* 41–48.

Gallagher, J. J., Beckman, P., & Cross, A. H. (1983). Families of handicapped children: Sources of stress and its amelioration. *Exceptional Children, 50,* 10–19.

Gallagher, J. J., Cross, A. H., & Scharfman, W. (1981). Parental adaptation to a young handicapped child: The father's role. *Journal of the Division for Early Childhood, 3,* 3–14.

Garber, H., & Heber, F. R. (1977). The Milwaukee project: Indications of the effectiveness of early intervention in preventing mental retardation. In P. Mittler (Ed.), *Research to practice in mental retardation: I. Care and intervention* (pp. 119–127). Baltimore: University Park Press.

Goldfarb, L. A., Brotherson, M. J., Summers, J. A., & Turnbull, A. P. (1986). *Meeting the challenge of disability or chronic illness: A family guide.* Baltimore: P. H. Brookes.

Haley, J. (1973). *Uncommon therapy.* New York: Norton.

Halpern, R. (1984, July). *Some comments on the Caldwell HOME.* (Available from Harvard Family Research Project, Harvard University, Appian Way, Cambridge, MA 02138)

Harris, S. (1984). Intervention planning for the family of the autistic child. A multi-level assessment of the family system. *Journal of Marital and Family Therapy, 10,* 157–166.

Healy, A., Keesee, P., & Smith, B. (1985). *Early services for children with special needs: Transactions for family support.* Iowa City: University of Iowa.

Hill, R. (1949). *Families under stress.* New York: Harper & Row.

Hoffman, L. (1980). The family life cycle and discontinuous change. In E. A. Carter & M. McGoldrick (Eds.), *The family life cycle: A framework for family therapy* (pp. 53–68). New York: Gardner Press.

Holman, T. B., & Burr, W. R. (1980). Beyond the beyond: The growth of family theories in the 1970s. *Journal of Marriage and the Family, 42,* 729–741.

Holroyd, J. (1974). The Questionnaire on Resources and Stress: An instrument to measure family response to a handicapped member. *Journal of Community Psychology, 2,* 92–94.

Howrigan, G. (1988). Evaluating parent–child interaction outcomes of family support and education programs. In H. Weiss & F. Jacobs (Eds.), *Evaluating family programs* (pp. 95–130). Hawthorne, NY: Aldine Press.

Hunt, J. McV. (1961). *Intelligence and experience.* New York: Roland Press.

Jackson, D. D. (1965). The study of the family. *Family Process, 4,* 1–20.

Jacobs, F. (1988). The five-tiered approach to evaluation: Context and implementation. In H. Weiss & F. Jacobs (Eds.), *Evaluating family programs* (pp. 37–68). Hawthorne, NY: Aldine Press.

Jacobs, F., & Weiss, H. (1988). Lessons in context. In H. Weiss & F. Jacobs (Eds.), *Evaluating family programs* (pp. 497–505). Hawthorne, NY: Aldine Press.

Kahn, A., & Kamerman, S. (1982). *Helping America's families.* Philadelphia: Temple University Press.

Kantor, D., & Lehr, W. (1975). *Inside the family: Toward a theory of family process.* New York: Harper & Row.

Kazak, A. E. (1987). Families with disabled children: Stress and social support networks in three samples. *Journal of Abnormal Child Psychology, 15,* 137–146.

Kochanek, T. T., Kabacoff, R. I., & Lipsitt, L. P. (1987). Early detection of handicapping conditions in infancy and early childhood: Toward a multivariate model. *Journal of Applied Developmental Psychology, 8,* 411–420.

Krauss, M. W. (1988). Measures of stress and coping in families. In H. Weiss & F. Jacobs (Eds.), *Evaluating family programs* (pp. 177–194). Hawthorne, NY: Aldine Press.

Lamb, M. E. (1984). Social and emotional development in infancy. In M. H. Bornstein & M. E. Lamb (Eds.), *Developmental psychology: An advanced textbook* (pp. 241–276). Hillsdale, NJ: L. Erlbaum.

Lamb, M. E., & Easterbrooks, M. A. (1981). Individual differences in parental sensitivity: Origins, components, and consequences. In M. Lamb & L. Sherrod (Eds.), *Infant social cognition: Empirical and theoretical considerations* (pp. 127–153). Hillsdale, NJ: L. Erlbaum.

Lewis, J. M., Beavers, W. R., Gossett, J. T., & Phillips, V. (1976). *No simple thread: Psychological health in family systems.* New York: Brunner/Mazel.

Long, F. (1983). Social support networks in day care and early child development. In J. Whittaker & J. Garbarino (Eds.), *Social support networks: Informal helping in the human services* (pp. 189–217). Hawthorne, NY: Aldine Press.

Loyd, B. H., & Abidin, R. R. (1985). Revision of the Parenting Stress Index. *Journal of Pediatric Psychology, 10,* 169–177.

McCubbin, H. I., Joy, C. B., Cauble, A. E., Comeau, J. K., Patterson, J. M., & Needle, R. H.

(1980). Family stress and coping: A decade review. *Journal of Marriage and the Family, 42,* 855–871.

McCubbin, H. I., McCubbin, M. A., Patterson, J. M., Cauble, A. E., Wilson, L. R., & Warwick, W. (1983). CHIP: Coping Health Inventory for Parents: An assessment of parental coping patterns in the care of the chronically ill child. *Journal of Marriage and the Family, 45,* 359–370.

McCubbin, H. I., & Patterson, J. M. (1981). *Systematic assessment of family stress, resources and coping: Tools for research, education and clinical intervention.* St. Paul: Family Social Science.

McCubbin, H. I., & Patterson, J. M. (1982). The family stress process: The Double ABCX Model of adjustment and adaptation. In H. I. McCubbin, M. B. Sussman, & J. M. Patterson (Eds.), *Social stress and the family: Advances and developments in family stress theory and research* (pp. 7–38). New York: Haworth Press.

McKinney, B., & Peterson, R. A. (1987). Predictors of stress in parents of developmentally disabled children. *Journal of Pediatric Psychology, 12,* 133–150.

Meisels, S. J. (1985). A functional analysis of the evolution of public policy for handicapped young children. *Educational Evaluation and Policy Analysis, 7,* 115–126.

Meisels, S. J., Harbin, G., Modigliani, K., & Olson, K. (1988). Formulating optimal state early childhood intervention policies. *Exceptional Children, 55,* 159–165.

Mink, I. T., & Nihira, K. (1987). Direction of effects: Family life styles and behavior of TMR children. *American Journal of Mental Deficiency, 92,* 57–64.

Mink, I. T., Nihira, K., & Meyers, C. E. (1983). Taxonomy of family life styles: I. Homes with TMR children. *American Journal of Mental Deficiency, 87,* 484–497.

Minuchin, S. (1974). *Families and family therapy.* Cambridge: Harvard University Press.

Moos, R. H., & Moos, B. S. (1976). A typology of family social environments. *Family Process, 15,* 357–370.

Moos, R. H., & Moos, B. S. (1981). *Family Environment Scale manual.* Palo Alto: Consulting Psychologists Press.

Moroney, R. M. (1987). Social support systems: Families and social policy. In S. Kagan, D. Powell, B. Weissbourd, & E. Zigler (Eds.), *America's family support programs* (pp. 21–37). New Haven: Yale University Press.

Mott, S. E., Fewell, R. R., Lewis, M., Meisels, S. J., Shonkoff, J. P., & Simeonsson, R. J. (1986). Methods for assessing child and family outcomes in early childhood special education programs: Some views from the field. *Topics in Early Childhood Special Education, 6,* 1–15.

Nihira, K., Meyers, C. E., & Mink, I. (1980). Home environment, family adjustment, and the development of mentally retarded children. *Applied Research in Mental Retardation, 1,* 5–24.

Olson, D. H., Portner, J., & Bell, R. (1982). *FACES II: Family Adaptability and Cohesion Evaluation Scales.* St. Paul: Family Social Science, University of Minnesota.

Olson, D. H., Russell, C. S., & Sprenkle, D. H. (1983). Circumplex model of marital and family systems: VI. Theoretical update. *Family Process, 22,* 69–83.

Olson, D. H., Sprenkle, D. H., & Russell, C. S. (1979). Circumplex model of marital and family systems: I. Cohesion and adaptability dimensions, family types and clinical applications. *Family Process, 18,* 3–28.

Pascoe, J., Loda, F., Jeffries, V., & Earp, J. (1981). The association between mothers' social support and provisions of stimulation to their children. *Developmental and Behavioral Pediatrics, 2,* 15–19.

Pattison, E. M., Defancisco, D., Wood, P., Frazier, H., & Crowder, J. A. (1975). A psychosocial kinship model for family therapy. *American Journal of Psychiatry, 132,* 1246–1251.

Pearlin, L. I., Lieberman, M. A., Menaghan, E. G., & Mullan, J. T. (1981). The stress process. *Journal of Health and Social Behavior, 22,* 337–356.

Pearlin, L. I., & Schooler, C. (1978). The structure of coping. *Journal of Health and Social Behavior, 19,* 2–21.

Peterson, N. L. (1987). *Early intervention for handicapped and at-risk children: An introduction to early childhood-special education.* Denver: Love Publishing.

Ramey, C. T., Mills, P., Campbell, F. A., & O'Brien, C. (1975). Infants' home environment: A comparison of high risk families and families from the general population. *American Journal of Mental Deficiency, 80,* 40–42.

Reiss, D., & Oliveri, M. (1980). Family paradigm and family coping: A proposal for linking the family's intrinsic adaptive capacities to its responses to stress. *Family Relations, 29,* 431–444.

Roghmann, K. J., & Haggerty, R. J. (1972). Family stress and the use of health services. *International Journal of Epidemiology, 1,* 279–286.

Rutter, M. (1985). Family and school influences: Meanings, mechanisms, and implications. In A.

R. Nichol (Ed.), *Longitudinal studies in child psychology and psychiatry* (pp. 357–401). New York: Wiley.

Rutter, M., Tizard, J., Yule, W., Graham, P., & Whitmore, K. (1976). Research report: Isle of Wight studies, 1964–1974. *Psychological Medicine, 6,* 313–332.

Salisbury, C. L. (1985). Internal consistency of the short-form of the Questionnaire on Resources and Stress. *American Journal of Mental Deficiency, 89,* 610–616.

Sameroff, A., & Chandler, M. (1975). Reproductive risk and the continuum of caretaking casualty. In F. Horowitz (Ed.), *Review of child development research* (Vol. 4, pp. 187–244). Chicago: University of Chicago Press.

Sameroff, A. J., Seifer, R., Barocas, R., Zax, M., & Greenspan, S. (1987). Intelligence quotient scores of 4-year-old children: Social-environmental risk factors. *Pediatrics, 79,* 343–350.

Sarason, I. G., Johnson, J. H., & Siegal, J. M. (1978). Assessing the impact of life changes: Development of the Life Experiences Survey. *Journal of Consulting and Clinical Psychology, 46,* 932–946.

Schilling, R. F., Gilchrist, L. D., & Schinke, S. P. (1984). Coping and social support in families of developmentally disabled children. *Family Relations, 33,* 47–54.

Sherman, B. R., & Cocozza, J. J. (1984). Stress in families of the developmentally disabled: A literature review of factors affecting the decision to seek out-of-home placements. *Family Relations, 33,* 95–103.

Shonkoff, J. P. (1984). Social support and the development of vulnerable children. *American Journal of Public Health, 74,* 310–312.

Shonkoff, J. P., & Hauser-Cram, P. (1987). Early intervention for disabled infants and their families: A quantitative analysis. *Pediatrics, 80,* 650–658.

Simeonsson, R. J., Bailey, D. B., Huntington, G. S., & Comfort, M. (1986). Testing the concept of goodness of fit in early intervention. *Infant Mental Health Journal, 7,* 81–94.

Stein, R., & Reissman, C. K. (1978). *Impact on Family Scale.* New York: Albert Einstein College of Medicine.

Stein, R., & Reissman, C. K. (1980). The development of an Impact on Family Scale: Preliminary findings. *Medical Care, 18,* 465–472.

Stevens, J. H., & Bakeman, R. (1985). A factor analytic study of the HOME scale for infants. *Developmental Psychology, 21,* 1196–1203.

Straus, M. A., & Brown, B. W. (1977). *Family measurement techniques.* Minneapolis: University of Minnesota Press.

Tabackman, M. (1977). A study of family psycho-social environment and its relationship to academic achievement in gifted adolescents (Doctoral dissertation, University of Illinois, Urbana-Champaign) *Dissertation Abstracts International, 37,* 638A.

Trohanis, P. L., Meyer, R. A., & Prestridge, S. (1982). A report on selected screening programs for high-risk and handicapped infants. In C. T. Ramey & P. L. Trohanis (Eds.), *Finding and educating high-risk and handicapped infants* (pp. 83–100). Baltimore: University Park Press.

Turnbull, A. P., Summers, J. A., & Brotherson, M. J. (1986). Family life cycle: Theoretical and empirical implications and future directions for families with mentally retarded members. In J. J. Gallagher & P. M. Vietze (Eds.), *Families of handicapped persons: Research, programs, and policy issues* (pp. 45–66). Baltimore: P. H. Brookes.

Turnbull, A. P., & Turnbull, H. R. (1982). Parent involvement in the education of handicapped children: A critique. *Mental Retardation, 20,* 115–122.

Vitaliano, P. P., Russo, J., Carr, J. E., Maiuro, R. D., & Becker, J. (1985). The Ways of Coping Checklist: Revision and psychometric properties. *Multivariate Behavioral Research, 20,* 3–26.

von Bertalanffy, L. (1969). General systems theory and psychiatry: An overview. In W. Gray, F. J. Duhl, & N. D. Rizzo (Eds.), *General systems theory and psychiatry* (pp. 33–46). Boston: Little, Brown.

Wachs, T., Uzgiris, I., & Hunt, J. McV. (1971). Cognitive development in infants of different age levels and from different environmental backgrounds: An exploratory investigation. *Merrill-Palmer Quarterly, 17,* 283–317.

Walker, D. K., & Crocker, R. W. (1988). Measuring family systems outcomes. In H. B. Weiss & F. H. Jacobs (Eds.), *Evaluating family programs* (pp. 153–176). Hawthorne, NY: Aldine Press.

Walsh, F. (Ed.). (1980). *Normal family processes.* New York: Guilford Press.

Walsh, W. M., & Wood, J. I. (1983). Family assessment: Bridging the gap between theory, research and practice. *American Mental Health Counselors Association Journal, 5,* 111–120.

Weiss, H. B., & Jacobs, F. H. (1988). Family support and education programs: Challenges and opportunities. In H. B. Weiss & F. H. Jacobs (Eds.), *Evaluating family programs* (pp. xix–xxix). Hawthorne, NY: Aldine Press.

Werner, E., & Smith, R. (1982). *Vulnerable but invincible: A study of resilient children.* New York: McGraw-Hill.

Whittaker, J. (1983). Social support networks in child welfare. In J. Whittaker & J. Garbarino (Eds.), *Social support networks: Informal helping in the human services* (pp. 167–187). Hawthorne, NY: Aldine Press.

Whittaker, J. K., & Garbarino, J. (Eds.). (1983). *Social support networks: Informal helping in the human services.* Hawthorne, NY: Aldine Press.

Wikler, L. M. (1986). Family stress theory and research on families of children with mental retardation. In J. J. Gallagher & P. M. Vietze (Eds.), *Families of handicapped persons: Research, programs, and policy issues* (pp. 167–196). Baltimore: P. H. Brookes.

Winton, P., & Turnbull, A. P. (1981). Parent involvement as viewed by parents of preschool handicapped children. *Topics in Early Childhood Special Education, 1,* 11–19.

Wynne, L. C., McDaniel, S. H., & Weber, T. T. (1987). Professional politics and the concepts of family therapy, family consultation and systems consultation. *Family Process, 26,* 153–166.

Zeitlin, S., Williamson, G. G., & Rosenblatt, W. P. (1987). The coping with stress model: A counseling approach for families with a handicapped child. *Journal of Counseling and Development, 65,* 44–65.

Zigler, E., & Balla, D. (1982). Selecting outcome variables in evaluations of early childhood special education programs. *Topics in Early Childhood Special Education, 1,* 11–22.

14 Assessment of social support in early intervention programs

CARL J. DUNST AND CAROL M. TRIVETTE

The ways in which we conceptualize and think about social concerns certainly influence how we in turn view solutions to social problems. Early intervention has historically been seen as a way of preventing or ameliorating developmental disabilities associated with organismic or environmental deterrents. Early intervention practices traditionally have been based upon the assumption that treatments provided young at-risk children are a necessary condition for optimizing developmental outcomes, and that other experiences cannot be adequately substituted for educational and therapeutic interventions. Such a viewpoint generally fails to recognize or chooses to ignore the broader-based ecological influences affecting human development (Bronfenbrenner, 1979) and specifically disregards the influences a family's personal social network has on directly and indirectly promoting child development (Cochran & Brassard, 1979). The social network influences that parents experience as part of their child-rearing efforts and daily lives are referred to as *social support*. Strategies for conceptualizing, assessing, and enhancing social support constitute the foci of this chapter.

Social support refers to the resources – potentially useful information and things – provided to individuals or social units (e.g., a family) in response to the need for aid and assistance (Cohen & Syme, 1985; Dunst, Trivette, & Deal, 1988b). The persons and institutions with which a family and its members come in contact – either directly or indirectly – are referred to as the family's *personal social network*, and it is this network that is the primary source of support to families and individual family members.

Operationally, one can differentiate between *informal* and *formal* sources of social support. Informal support networks include both individuals (kin, friends, neighbors, minister, etc.) and social groups (church, social clubs, etc.) that are accessible to provide support as part of daily living, usually in response to both normative and nonnormative life events. Formal support networks include both professionals (physicians, infant specialists, social workers, therapists, etc.) and social agencies (hospitals, early intervention programs, health departments, etc.) that are, on an a priori basis,

Appreciation is extended to Pat Condrey, Norma Hunter, Wilson Hamer, and Wendy Jodry for assistance in preparation of this chapter. The work described herein was supported in part by grants from the National Institute of Mental Health, Prevention Research Branch (#MH38862), and the National Institute of Child Health and Human Development, Mental Retardation/ Developmental Disabilities Branch (#HD23038).

326

formally organized to provide aid and assistance to persons seeking needed resources (Mitchell & Trickett, 1980).

The importance of social support derives from both its empirical relationship with individual and family functioning, and the potential that it holds as a major form of intervention. The stress-buffering and health-promoting influences of social support have been so well documented (see e.g., Cohen & Syme, 1985; Sarason & Sarason, 1985) that it is now almost axiomatic to state that social support both enhances well-being and lessens the likelihood of emotional and physical distress. There is a growing body of evidence that social support directly and indirectly influences other aspects of individual and family functioning, including family well-being (Patterson & McCubbin, 1983), adaptations to life crises (Moos, 1986), satisfaction with parenting (Crnic, Greenberg, Ragozin, Robinson, & Basham, 1983), attitudes toward one's child (Colletta, 1981), parental styles of interaction (Trivette & Dunst, in preparation), aspirations for self and child (Lazar, Darlington, Murray, Royce, & Snipper, 1982), and child behavior and development (Affleck, Tennen, Allen, & Gersham, 1986; Crnic, Greenberg, & Slough, 1986).

The extent to which different aspects of social support and resources influence parent, family, and child functioning has been a major focus of our own research efforts (Dunst, 1985; Dunst, Cooper, & Bolick, 1987; Dunst & Leet, 1987; Dunst, Leet, & Trivette, 1988a; Dunst & Trivette, 1986, 1987a, 1988b, 1988c, 1988e; Dunst, Trivette, & Cross, 1986a, 1986b; Dunst, Vance, & Cooper, 1986; Trivette & Dunst, 1987, in press). Our data have shown that adequacy of different types and forms of support, *especially aid and assistance that match family identified needs*, enhances parent and family well-bring, decreases time demands placed upon a family by a disabled or at-risk child, promotes positive caregiver interactive styles, decreases the display of interfering caregiver interactive styles, enhances positive parental perception of child functioning, and indirectly influences a number of child behavior characteristics, including affect, temperament, and motivation.

At least one consistent finding from our research should be mentioned at this point, since it influences the ways in which we believe social support must be both assessed and operationalized within the context of early intervention programs. We have repeatedly found that an *indicated need* for support is a necessary condition for support to have positive influences on family functioning. That is, provision of support has its greatest impact when it is offered in response to a family-identified need. In contrast, support has minimal and in some cases negative effects when it is offered to a family that has not indicated a need for that particular type of aid or assistance. This finding has led us to argue for a needs-based approach to working with families (Dunst et al., 1988b; Trivette, Deal, & Dunst, 1986) in which support is provided and offered to families specifically and *only* in response to what is considered needed from the family's and not a professional's perspective. Thus, a maxim and fundamental condition of successful social support interventions is an *adequate determination of a family's needs as a basis for identifying resources and mobilizing support from personal social network members.*

The fact that social support has positive influences on parent, family, and child functioning is of special interest to professionals working in early intervention programs. On the one hand, the effects that social support have on behavior and development suggest an expanded conceptualization of early intervention. On the other hand, the effects suggest that we mobilize resources from different sources of support as a way of meeting family needs. Based upon available evidence concerning the causal and mediating influences of social support, Dunst (1985) proposed a broad-based definition of early intervention as "the provision of support to families of infants and young children from members of informal and formal social support networks that impact both *directly* and *indirectly* upon parent, family, and child functioning" (p. 179). Stated differently, early intervention can be conceptualized as the aggregation of the many different types of aid, assistance, and resources that individuals and groups provide to families of young children. Involvement in a preschool special education program is one type of early intervention, but so is compassion from a friend, advice from a physician, respite and child care, counseling by a minister, role sharing between a husband and wife, and so on. Thus, to the extent that personal social networks can be mobilized in a way that matches resources with family identified needs, social support should have positive influences on family functioning.

A social systems framework is utilized in this chapter for defining the meaning of support, specifying its components and dimensions, and illustrating how support can be operationalized as an "intervention" for influencing parent, family, and child functioning. The chapter is divided into three major sections. The first describes the major components of support, examines the relationships among the components, and briefly reviews available data regarding the manner in which support influences behavior and development in families of disabled and developmentally at-risk preschoolers. The second section examines a number of approaches for assessing social support, with particular attention to the characteristics of support that are known to influence family functioning. The third section discusses the manner in which social support can be mobilized as part of early intervention practices, particularly in terms of identifying and meeting the individualized needs of families.

THE SOCIAL SUPPORT DOMAIN

The term social support tends to be operationalized differently depending upon the perspective of the researcher or practitioner interested in the construct. There is, however, general consensus that the social support domain is multidimensional in nature, and that differing aspects of support have differential influences on individual and family functioning. Conceptually and operationally, the social support domain is made up of distinct *components* and specific *dimensions* within components (Cohen, Meimelstein, Kamarck, & Hoberman, 1985; House & Kahn, 1985). Figure 1 shows how the different dimensions of a social support component may be depicted graphically.

A number of conceptual frameworks have been proposed for specifying the components of support, their dimensional features, and the relationships among components (Barrera, 1986; Cohen et al., 1985; Dunst & Trivette, 1987a, 1988b, 1988e; Hall & Wellman, 1985; House & Kahn, 1985; Kahn, Wethington, & Ingersoll-Dayton, 1987; Tardy, 1985; Turner, 1983). An integration of available evidence regarding the social support domain suggests that it comprises five major components (relational support, structural support, constitutional support, functional support, and support satisfaction) and various dimensions within components.

Relational support refers to the existence and quantity of social relationships, including marital and work status, number of persons in one's personal social network, and membership in such social organizations as a church. The existence of social relationships, as well as the breadth of these relationships, sets the occasion for supportive exchanges. Relational support is oftentimes described in terms of the persons, groups, and organizations that are important to individuals (Wills, 1985).

Structural support refers to any number of quantitative aspects of personal social

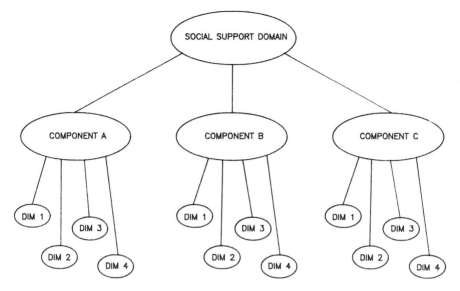

Figure 1. A model for representing the social support domain as made up of separate components and different dimensions (DIM)

networks, including physical proximity to social network members, duration and stability of relationships, frequency of contacts with network members, and reciprocity (give and take) in social relationships (see especially Hall & Wellman, 1985). The various dimensions of structural support are designed as ways of capturing the specific features of social relationships that are thought to be crucial for interactions to be supportive in nature (Gottlieb, 1981). Social network analysis is generally described as structural support.

Constitutional support refers to the indicated need for help and the congruence or match between needed support and the type of support offered. The term constitutional is used to refer to resources that a person believes are basic and essential for maintaining or improving his or her health and well-being; hence, it reflects a highly personalized view of what is important and needed. The notion of constitutional support has evolved from our own work on explicating the nature of supportive exchanges, and has emerged as one of the most important determinants of positive influences on family functioning (Dunst & Leet, 1987; Dunst et al., 1988a; Dunst & Trivette, 1988b). That is, the influences of social support are greatest when resources are offered in response to a family-indicated need for support, and when the resources offered match what is specifically requested.

Functional support refers to the type, quantity, and quality of aid and assistance. Types of support include, but are not limited to, informational, emotional, material, and instrumental (e.g., child care) aid and assistance that are offered by personal social network members. Quantity of support refers to how much support is provided by network members. Quality of support refers to the manner in which support is requested from and provided by network members (e.g., willingness of relatives to provide child care in an emergency).

Support satisfaction refers to the extent to which aid and assistance are viewed as helpful and useful. During and at the completion of a social exchange, people generally evaluate subjectively the nature of the support provided by others. Unless a person is subjectively satisfied with the support he or she is provided, the influences of support are diminished considerably.

Because the term *social support* has been used to refer to the various dimensions of social exchanges that make up the content of each of the five support components, each must be measured as part of assessing the personal social support networks of families participating in early intervention programs. Operationally, relational support is assessed in terms of the existence and quantity of social relationships; structural support is assessed in terms of the structural features that exist among and between sets of social relationships; constitutional support is assessed in terms of the need for certain types of aid and assistance and the congruence between what is needed and offered; functional support is assessed in terms of the particular types of aid and assistance that are offered by personal social network members and the manner in which support is offered; and satisfaction with support is assessed in terms of the subjective evaluation of the degree to which one feels "supported." The major goal of the assessment of social support is not to know the minute details of every extant and potential social relationship that exists or might exist for a family; rather, the goal is to gain insight about the ways in which resources and support flow between the family and personal network members. This in turn provides a basis for making suggestions and recommendations about mobilization of resources for meeting needs.

Relationships among the support components

Although it is possible to distinguish operationally among the five different support components, they are, as one might suspect, conceptually, logically, and empirically interrelated. Figure 2 shows graphically the ways in which we believe the five components of support are interconnected. The existence and quantity of relational support is viewed as a necessary condition for and hence a partial determinant of (a) defining needs (constitutional support), (b) the structural characteristics of one's social network, and (c) the types of help and assistance available from network members. Similarly, both constitutional needs and network structure may partially determine the particular types of support that are sought and offered. Finally, the types of support provided, especially the relationship between constitutional and functional support, will in part determine the degree to which one finds the aid and assistance helpful, and thus the extent to which one is satisfied with the support. Taken together, these five components and the potential connections among them provide a basis for understanding the nature of social relationships that set the occasion for supportive or nonsupportive exchanges. For example, a supportive exchange is likely to transpire when the members of an individual's personal social network have resources that can be provided to that individual in response to an indicated need, the recipient of support and his or her network members like one another, and the exchange of resources is deemed worthwhile with respect to the mutual benefits that are likely to accrue from the supportive act. In contrast, social relationships are likely to be nonsupportive when the relationships among personal network members are already strained or conflicted, network members are unwilling to reach out in response to a request for help, and relationships are inconsistent or unstable.

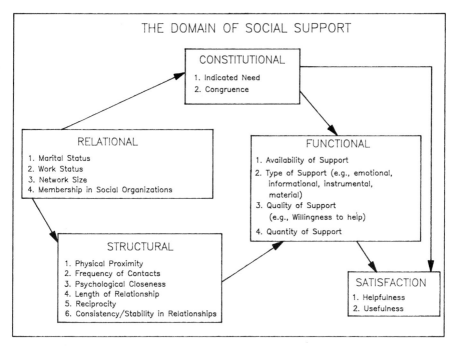

Figure 2. A conceptual framework for defining the major components of social support and their separate dimensions

Major dimensions of social support

Based upon extensive research examining the particular dimensions of social support that are related to different aspects of family functioning, certain dimensions within the social support domain consistently emerge as being the most important with respect to having stress-buffering and health-promoting influences on individual and family behavior and development (e.g., Affleck et al., 1986; Brown & Bifulco, 1985; Cauce, 1986; Cobb, 1976; Cohen & Syme, 1985; Cutrona & Troutman, 1986; Dean & Lin, 1977; Dimatteo & Hays, 1981; Dunst, 1985; Dunst, Jenkins, & Trivette, 1984; Dunst et al., 1987, 1988a, 1988b; Fiore, Coppel, Becker, & Cox, 1986; Hirsch, 1980; Lin, Dean, & Ensel, 1981; McCubbin et al., 1980; Mitchell & Trickett, 1980; Phillips, 1981; Procidano & Heller, 1983; Sarason, Levine, Basham, & Sarason, 1983; Wills, 1985). The following are some particular dimensions of support that have been found to be related consistently to well-being and other behavioral outcomes.

1. *Network size:* the number of persons who are members of an individual's or family's personal social network
2. *Existence of social relationships:* particular social relationships (e.g., marriage) and membership in social organizations or clubs
3. *Frequency by contacts:* how often an individual or family has contact with personal social network members, either face-to-face or in a group
4. *Need for support:* extent to which an individual or family indicates a need for support

5. *Type and amount of support:* type and amount of support offered or provided by personal social network members
6. *Congruence:* extent to which the types of support offered or provided by personal social network members match the indicated need for specific types of support
7. *Utilization:* extent to which an individual or family employs personal network members as sources of aid and assistance in times of need
8. *Dependability:* extent to which an individual or family can depend or rely upon personal network members for aid and assistance in times of need
9. *Reciprocity:* extent to which there is give-and-take (balance) in the exchange of support and resources between an individual or family and personal social network members
10. *Closeness:* extent to which an individual or family has positive or negative feelings toward personal social network members, and/or the extent to which personal network members are considered trusted confidants
11. *Satisfaction:* extent to which an individual or family indicates whether support provided by personal social network members is helpful or useful

Both our research and clinical experience tell us that any combination of these factors interact and influence the extent to which the provision of support will have positive influences on parent, family, and child functioning (Dunst, 1985; Dunst & Leet, 1987; Dunst & Trivette, 1987a, 1988b, 1988c, 1988e; Dunst et al., 1988a, 1988b; Trivette et al., 1986; Trivette & Dunst, 1987).

Evidence regarding the social support domain

There have been a host of studies in which the individual dimensions of support that make up the different support components have been found to be significantly related to one another (Barrera, Sandler, & Ramsay, 1981; Birkel & Repucci, 1983; Cauce, 1986; Cohen, McGowan, Fooskas, & Rose, 1984; Fiore et al., 1986; Hirsch, 1980; Lin et al., 1981; Oritt, Paul, & Behrman, 1985; Potasznik & Nelson, 1984; Procidano & Heller, 1983; Vaux & Harrison, 1985; Vaux et al., 1986). In one of the only studies examining the relationships among the different support components, Kahn et al. (1987) found modest but significant correlations among relational (situational in their terminology), structural, and functional support.

The extent to which different components of support are interrelated as well as influence parent, family, and child functioning has been the focus of investigation in three studies with families of disabled and at-risk preschoolers enrolled in the Family, Infant and Preschool Program (Dunst, 1985; Dunst & Trivette, 1988a, 1988e). Information about the social support networks of the families was obtained from both interview and self-report measures (Dunst et al., 1984; Dunst & Trivette, 1988a; Gallagher, Cross, & Scharfman, 1981; Pascoe, Loda, Jeffries, & Earp, 1981; Pattison, DeFrancisco, Wood, Frazier, & Crowder, 1975; Trivette & Dunst, 1988). The information obtained from the administration of these scales was used to derive measures of the five support components, and scores for each component intercorrelated. The findings from the three studies showed that although conceptually distinct, the different components of the support domain were, with few exceptions, significantly related to one another as predicted. The manner in which the different components influenced the behavior of the support recipients is presented next.

Social support and parent well-being

Figure 3 shows a simplified version of how we believe social support directly and indirectly affects parent, family, and child functioning. According to this model, social

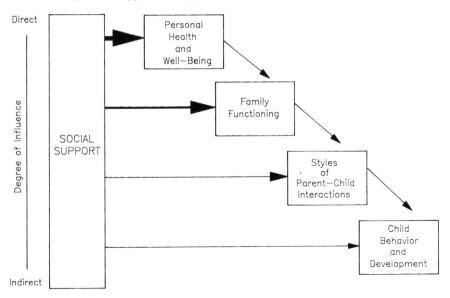

Figure 3. A conceptual model for depicting the direct and indirect influences of social support on parent, family, parent–child, and child functioning

support influences parent well-being and health; support and well-being influence family functioning; support, well-being, and family functioning influence styles of parent–child interactions; and support, well-being, family functioning, and interactive styles influence child behavior and development. Within this framework of direct and indirect relationships, well-being, family functioning, and interactive styles function as both independent and dependent variables depending upon the juncture at which one is assessing the influences of social support. We have presented elsewhere the bulk of evidence that provides support for these hypothesized relationships (see Dunst & Trivette, 1987a, 1988a, 1988b, 1988c). The extent to which the different support components are related to parent well-being is briefly examined here to illustrate the relationships between support and health outcomes.

In the three studies just described, the parents also completed measures of health and well-being. The well-being measures included the Emotional and Physical Health subscale of the Questionnaire on Resources and Stress (QRS) (Holroyd, 1974, 1985), the Psychological Well-Being Index (PWI) (Bradburn & Caplovitz, 1965), and the Personal Well-Being Index (WBI) (Trivette & Dunst, 1985). Global indices of well-being or specific components of well-being (child-related, general life) were used as measures of physical and emotional health. Two or more well-being measures were used in each study.

Canonical correlation analysis was used to determine both the overall relationship between social support and well-being and the unique contributions of the separate support subcomponents to well-being (Levine, 1977; Thompson, 1984). Each produced a significant multiple R (canonical correlation) ranging from $R = .58$ to $R = .78$, indicating that there was a substantial amount of shared variance between the support and well-being measures. Most notable, however, is the fact that in both the second and third studies, each support measure (with one exception) was significantly related to the composite canonical score, indicating that the separate support components made *independent contributions* to the relationship between support and well-being. Thus, whereas the different support components were generally interrelated, the separate components uniquely influenced the well-being outcomes.

These results are consistent with the findings from other studies that have demonstrated that social support influences well-being and other health outcomes (e.g., Cobb, 1976; Cohen & Syme, 1985; Dean & Lin, 1977; Dimatteo & Hays, 1981; McCubbin et al., 1980; Mitchell & Trickett, 1980). These data, together with evidence documenting the direct and indirect influences of social support on other aspects of family functioning (Dunst & Trivette, 1987a, 1988e), build a strong case for conceptualizing social support as a form of early intervention that can be used as a means to influence parent, family, and child behavior and development. A first step in mobilizing resources and support to meet family identified needs is an adequate assessment of a family's personal social support network.

ASSESSING SOCIAL SUPPORT

This section of the chapter is designed to accomplish two aims. First, it provides a brief description of a general system for assessing social support that has been developed specifically from an intervention rather than research perspective. Second, it briefly describes a number of social support scales with particular attention to those instruments that have greatest utility for early intervention practices.

At the outset it should be reemphasized that the assessment and mobilization of social support as part of early intervention practices must be done within the context of the family system and the family's indicated need for support. This stance toward working with families was stated in the following way by Pilisuk and Parks (1986) in terms of the relationship between a family and help giver (interventionist) as part of social support interventions:

The [family] defines the need for service. *(A) need for assistance is not assumed until the [family] has set forth such a need* [italics added]. This request for assistance might originate with one individual or with the...[family] system....(T)he social support facilitator helps the [family] crystallize the [concern] (pp. 162–163).

Thus, a determination of an indicated need for aid and assistance (constitutional support) is the first and fundamentally most important part of social support interventions, and *all* intervention efforts must be based on these family identified needs if they are to be successful in affecting parent, family, and child functioning.

A second consideration should also be mentioned before proceeding with a description of the methods used to assess social support. To the extent possible, major emphasis should be placed upon identification of informal personal network members as sources of support and resources for meeting family needs. So often, we professionalize all types of services in early intervention programs, which only interferes with and precludes opportunities to build and strengthen more natural family and community support networks (Hobbs et al., 1984). An example may help illustrate how we can go astray despite well-intentioned efforts. Child care is often identified as a need by families of handicapped youngsters. Quite often the needs of the children require some kind of special training for those who care for special needs children. A typical response to this set of circumstances is to create some type of respite care program where professional or paraprofessional respite providers are trained to provide specialized types of child care. This response to family needs fails to recognize the fact that if persons the family does not know can be trained to provide child care, so can friends, neighbors, and other family members to the extent that they desire and are willing to care for children with handicaps or other special needs. A rule of thumb that should be followed in assessing and mobilizing social support is to strengthen natural support systems rather than create new ones. The latter only serves to weaken personal social ties, which in turn may have detrimental influences on other aspects of social relationships.

A general system for assessing social support

In our own work on measuring and promoting mobilization of support to families of children participating in early intervention programs, a general system for assessing social support has evolved that is useful for both intervention and research purposes. The system is based upon House's (1981; House & Kahn, 1985) model for assessing the multiple dimensions of social support. It is designed to be economical in the sense that it requires minimal time and energy, yet yields a wealth of information (direct and derived) about the multidimensionality of social support.

The system, known as SASSI (Systematic Assessment of Social Support Inventory), employs both interview and self-report methods for obtaining five classes of social support information. The information obtained from administering SASSI permits one to derive a multitude of social support indices depending upon the purposes of the assessment. Table 1 shows the particular support dimensions that are measured by each of the five SASSI categories.

The following types of information are obtained using SASSI.

1. *The indicated need for particular types of support*, including the congruence or match between what is required and offered: An assessment of the need for support is done either by interview (see Dunst et al., 1988b) or self-report measures (e.g., Dunst & Leet, 1987), or a combination of both. Congruence is generally measured by rating scales used by the respondent to indicate the extent to which needed resources are adequate, and the degree to which people generally provide aid and assistance that match indicated needs.

2. *The members of an individual's or family's personal social network*, including the respondent's relationship with these persons (spouse or partner, relative, friend, neighbor, co-worker, church affiliate, etc.): First the respondent is asked to list all persons with whom she or he (a) has contact on a regular basis (regardless of his or her feelings toward the people) and (b) feels close to and can trust (regardless of how often she or he has contact with the people). The respondent is also asked to list all the social groups that she or he interacts with on a regular basis in order to establish the existence of social ties that potentially set the occasion for supportive exchanges. The process of identifying individuals and groups that constitute the person's personal social network is referred to as "network mapping," and this process provides a picture of existing and potential sources of support.

3. *The types of support generally offered by personal social network members*, including how often resources are both requested and provided by specific network members: The types of support that are assessed include (but are not limited to) emotional (e.g., someone to talk to about a difficulty or concern), companionship (e.g., someone with whom to enjoy social activities), instrumental (e.g., babysitting or child care), informational (e.g., child-rearing advice), and material (e.g., borrowing a car or

Table 1. *SASSI support categories and corresponding support components and dimensions*

SASSI categories	Support components	Dimensions
Need for support	Constitutional	Indicated need Congruence
Social network members	Relational	Network size Existence of social relationships (e.g., marital and work status) Social group membership
Types of support	Functional	Source of support Type and amount of support Quality of support exchanges
Social relationship ties	Structural	Frequency of contacts Closeness Utilization and dependability Reciprocity Relationship stability
Support satisfaction	Satisfaction	Helpfulness Usefulness

money). The manner in which different types of support are offered is generally assessed in terms of the degree to which different types and amounts of aid and assistance are sought or volunteered (e.g., Barrera et al., 1981).

4. *The nature of social ties with personal social network members*, including frequency of contacts, dependability, utilization, reciprocity, and closeness: These dimensions of support are generally assessed by rating scales in order to obtain both quantitative and qualitative information about social ties (e.g., Oritt et al., 1985). This information is useful for asking the respondent about his or her social support network, and is especially helpful in determining the extent to which certain support sources are more or less likely to represent potential resources for meeting needs.

5. *Satisfaction with aid and assistance obtained from personal social network members*, especially in terms of how helpful and useful one finds currently available support: Both helpfulness and usefulness are assessed by rating scales for the different types of support provided by specific network members (e.g., Dunst et al., 1984).

SASSI is designed to yield information that can be used both for gleaning as complete an understanding as possible about an individual's personal network and for making suggestions and recommendations about potential sources of support and ways to mobilize resources for meeting needs. The assessment system provides a mechanism for systematizing the collection and organization of social support information. The specific assessment and measurement scales that can be used for these purposes are described below. We preface the description of these tools and measurement instruments with a brief discussion of several procedural considerations that guide the administration of social support scales.

Procedural considerations

The process of employing social support scales for assessment and intervention purposes is designed to answer four questions: (1) What are the family's needs? (2) What resources are required to meet these needs? (3) Who and what are the major existing sources of support for accessing resources for meeting needs? and (4) Who and what are potential but currently untapped sources of support that can be accessed for meeting needs? The process for answering these questions can be divided into two steps: identification of family needs, and identification of sources of support and resources for meeting needs. The information gleaned from both parts of the assessment process can then be used for making recommendations and implementing interventions for mobilizing sources of support and resources. A number of considerations related to each of these steps are discussed next in order to place the use of social support scales for intervention purposes in proper perspective.

IDENTIFYING FAMILY NEEDS. The use of social support scales as part of family-level assessment procedures provides a basis for gaining insight about what a family perceives as important and needed. However, our experience tells us that the information obtained from these scales should not be used directly for intervention purposes. Rather, the information should be used as a basis for helping the family to *clarify* and *define* what they consider important enough to deserve their time and energy (see especially Dunst et al., 1988b; McKillip, 1987). For example, an item on an assessment tool might assess the adequacy of food and shelter. A family that completes the scale indicates that food and shelter is a need. The assessor should not base an intervention on this response, but would rather use the response to further identify the conditions that make this a need and base the intervention on these factors and not the needs itself (e.g., "You indicated that you feel you do not have adequate food to feed your family. Can you tell me more about this so I get a better idea about this concern?").

We have found that the following steps and considerations should be taken into account when social support scales are used as a basis for assessing individual and family needs. First, it is important to state explicitly why the family is being asked to complete the scale (e.g., "Could you please take the time to fill out this scale about what you might need so that I can be of assistance to you and your family"). Second, it is important to be very clear about how the results will be used (e.g., "After you complete the scale, I'd like us to go over your responses to get a better idea about your concerns and needs"). Third, responses can be used as a way of helping the family clarify and define what they perceive to be a concern or need (e.g., "You indicated that child care is a need. Can you tell me more about what types of child care you feel would be most beneficial"). Fourth, it is useful to restate the needs as they are clarified in order to be sure the family agrees with the interviewer's perceptions (e.g., "If I understand you correctly, you are saying that because you will be going back to work, you must find day care that is available during hours that fit with your work schedule"). Attention to these four considerations helps specify needs and the types of resources required to meet needs. With practice, early intervention practitioners can become proficient in using self-report scales for needs-identification purposes.

IDENTIFYING SOURCES OF SUPPORT FOR MEETING NEEDS. The use of social support scales to identify sources of support for meeting family-identified needs provides a basis for exploring existing and potential options within the family's social network. In addition, it can provide a basis for exploring the characteristics of family and professional helpgiver exchanges that promote or impede mobilization of those resources (see especially Dunst et al., 1988b).

The use of self-report or clinically administered social support scales yields information that forms the basis for further discussion with families, and should be guided by the same explanatory statements described before when using assessment tools for identifying family needs. Discussions during these interactions can explore which sources of support are most and least helpful, which sources are options for meeting needs, how the family feels about asking for help, how the family thinks persons will respond to being asked for help, and so on.

The process of identifying potential resources for meeting needs begins by "mapping" a family's personal social network (relational support) to identify social ties that might form the basis for requesting and seeking help and assistance. Network mapping involves nothing more than identification of the persons and groups with whom a family comes in contact, and the nature of the relationships with personal network members. Once existing and potential sources of aid and assistance are identified, a quantitative and qualitative (structural and functional support) assessment of support can be made. The network mapping process, together with queries about the family's quantitative and qualitative descriptions of their personal social network, is a simple yet highly efficient process of matching resources with needs.

The process of identifying and evaluating the usefulness of different sources of support for meeting needs, although simple and efficient, requires that one be sensitive to the verbal and nonverbal behavior of the family when matching resources to needs. This is especially true in terms of the willingness of the family to seek and ask for help and the willingness of different network members to provide aid and assistance. Therefore, one should be sensitive to how the family responds to different options for meeting needs, and use their responses as a basis for prompting clarifications (e.g., "You indicated that your aunt might be able to provide transportation to take your child to therapy, but I sense that you are hesitant about asking her. Is there some reason why you feel this way?"). This type of follow-up question provides a way of helping family members clarify their reasons for not wanting to ask for assistance, and provides a basis for exploring ways of making a particular source of support a viable option or for exploring alternative options. One should not assume that because a network member has a resource a family could use to meet a need that it automatically means this is an appropriate source of support to the family. One must be careful to take into consideration qualitative aspects of social exchanges as a basis for making suggestions about viable sources of support.

The processes for identifying needs and resources and mobilizing sources of support for meeting needs does require some shift and expansion in the roles early interventionists employ in interactions with families and their personal social network members (see especially Dunst et al., 1988b; Trivette et al., 1986). With practice, early interventionists can become proficient in assessing and mobilizing support. Both self-report and interviewer administered social support scales are particularly useful for accomplishing this goal.

Social support scales

The increased interest in the role that social support plays in affecting health and well-being (Cohen & Syme, 1985) has been accompanied by a proliferation of social support scales (see Bruhn & Philips, 1984; Dunst & Trivette, 1988b; Fewell, 1986; House & Kahn, 1985; Tardy, 1985, for extensive lists and critical reviews of these scales). There are literally hundreds of scales that measure one or more dimensions of support, and any attempt to review all the scales that are useful for intervention purposes can quickly become overwhelming. With few exceptions, the majority of available scales was developed for research and not intervention purposes. Many, however, have practical utility, and when used properly (see especially Dunst et al., 1988b), can aid in the assessment and enhancement of support to families participating in early intervention programs.

Based both on a review of existing instruments and our clinical and research experience using social support scales for assessment and intervention purposes, we have selected a number of instruments we believe have the greatest potential for yielding information that can be used by early intervention practitioners for meeting family-identified needs. The scales we chose yield information that provides the intervention practitioner with a "picture" of an individual's personal network. These scales also prompt questions that allow a practitioner to link a family with existing or potential sources of support required to meet needs (Hobbs et al., 1984). Table 2 lists instruments that can be useful for intervention purposes. Each of the entries includes the dimensions of support that the scale measures and summarizes data regarding both the reliability and validity of the instrument.

PSYCHOSOCIAL KINSHIP INVENTORY (PATTISON ET AL., 1975). This scale can be particularly helpful for assessing various aspects of an individual's personal social network. It includes procedures for both identifying the members of an individual's or family's personal network and for assessing 11 separate dimensions of support for each network member. The 11 dimensions include *kind* of feelings and thoughts toward the respondent's network members, *strength* of these feelings and thoughts, *help* provided by the network members, degree of *emotional support* they provide, frequency of *contact* with them, degree of *stability* of the relationships, physical *proximity* to the network members, *kinds* of feelings and thoughts believed held toward the respondent by the network members, *strength* of feelings believed held toward the respondent, *help* provided to network members, and *emotional support* provided to these kinship members. Each of these dimensions are rated on a 5-point scale for each person listed by the respondent. The results generate a detailed picture of an individual's social network and provide a basis for exploring which network members are used for meeting needs and which network members represent potential but untapped sources of aid and assistance.

SUPPORT NETWORK INVENTORY (ORITT ET AL., 1985). This is a particularly useful instrument because of its multidimensional format. It provides an objective method for determining the members of an individual's or a family's personal network, the respondent's relationships with these people, the types of support they provide, the manner in which support is provided, and the extent to which the respondent is satisfied with that support. The respondent is first asked to list all the people she or he would ordinarily go to if help or assistance were needed, then indicate what types of support she or he would generally seek from these people, and finally rate a number of qualitative aspects of support exchanges (e.g., reciprocity, conflict, initiation). Although the scale was developed for research purposes, it does have clinical utility because it measures those aspects of personal social networks that have been found to influence decisions about seeking and accepting help (Dunst & Trivette, 1988d).

MATERNAL SOCIAL SUPPORT INDEX (PASCOE ET AL., 1981). This is an eight-item scale that assesses several dimensions of social support, including role demands and role sharing, frequency of contact with personal network members, dependability,

Table 2. Selected list of social support scales that have utility for intervention purposes

Scale (Source)	Relational: Network size	Relational: Membership	Relational: Social relationships	Structural: Contacts	Structural: Dependability	Structural: Utilization	Structural: Reciprocity	Structural: Closeness	Constitutional: Indicated need	Constitutional: Congruence	Functional: Type of support	Functional: Support source	Functional: Quantity	Satisfaction: Helpfulness	Satisfaction: Usefulness	Reliability: Internal consistency	Reliability: Short-term stability	Reliability: Long-term stability	Factor structure (# of dimensions)	Validity: Criterion (Health outcomes)
Psychosocial Kinship Inventory (Pattison, DeFrancisco, Wood, Frazier, & Crowder, 1975)	x	x	x	x			x	x				x							2–3	.27 (Well-being: Dunst, Cooper, Bolick, 1987)
Support Network Inventory (Oritt, Paul, & Behrman, 1985)	x		x		x	x	x				x	x			x	.60	.79			
Maternal Social Support Index (Pascoe, Loda, Jeffries, & Earp, 1981)		x			x									x						.46 (Well-being: Dunst, 1985)
Arizona Social Support Inventory (Barrera, 1980; Barrera, Sandler, & Ramsay, 1981; Sandler & Barrera, 1984)	x								x	x	x	x	x	x			.88			.41 (Well-being)
Social Support Resources Scale (Vaux & Harrison, 1985)	x		x	x			x	x			x	x		x			.86			−.39 (Depression)
Social Support Questionnaire (Sarason, Levine, Basham, & Sarason, 1983)	x										x			x		.95	.87		1	−.24 (Anxiety & depression)
Personal Projects Matrix (Little, 1983)									x	x										
Family Resource Scale (Dunst & Leet, 1987)									x							.92	.52		8	.57 (Well-being)
Support Functions Scale (Dunst & Trivette, 1988a)									x							.87	.62		5	.33 (Well-being)
Inventory of Supportive Behaviors (Barrera et al., 1981; Barrera & Ainsley, 1983)											x		x			.93	.88		4	.35 (Family functioning)
Family Support Scale (Dunst, Jenkins, & Trivette, 1984)												x		x		.77	.91	.47	6	.30 (Well-being: Dunst, 1985)

[a] In cases where two or more reliability and validity coefficients were reported, the separate coefficients were averaged to obtain an overall reliability or validity estimate. All criterion validity (correlation) coefficients are significant beyond the .05 level. Criterion validity coefficients were obtained from the source reference(s) included in the table or from the cited reference.

membership in social organizations, and satisfaction with help and assistance provided by personal social network members. The scale is useful for obtaining information about a number of dimensions of a respondent's personal social network, which in turn permits queries about the ways in which existing network members are helpful, who might represent viable options for resources to meet needs, and so on.

ARIZONA SOCIAL SUPPORT INVENTORY (BARRERA, 1980). This interview-administered scale assesses both personal social network size and satisfaction with support from network members. A respondent is first asked to list all the people who provided up to six different types of support (e.g., talk about private feelings) during the preceding month. Second, the respondent is asked to indicate, on a 3-point rating scale, the extent to which he or she was satisfied with the support that was requested or offered. The findings from this scale are especially useful for identifying the types of aid and assistance that are procured from and offered to the respondent. When used in conjunction with a needs-based support scale, it can provide a basis for determining the types of support that are used and from whom support is obtained. The latter information is useful for "matching" resources with needs.

SOCIAL SUPPORT RESOURCES SCALE (VAUX & HARRISON, 1985). This scale yields a wealth of information about nearly all components and dimensions of the social support domain. It first asks the respondent to indicate which members of his or her social network are important in terms of five different categories of support. Second, the respondent is asked to assess his or her relationship with each network member in terms of a number of specific dimensions of support, including frequency of contacts, closeness (intimacy), balance (reciprocity), and complexity of relationships. Finally, the respondent is asked to rate how satisfied he or she is in terms of the types of support that are provided by network members. This scale can be especially useful as a tool for obtaining a complete picture of a family's support system, which in turn provides a basis for making suggestions and recommendations about ways in which to mobilize resources to meet needs.

SOCIAL SUPPORT QUESTIONNAIRE (SARASON ET AL., 1983). This scale includes 27 questions that ask the respondent to indicate who he or she can depend upon for different types of support. The scale also permits an assessment of the degree to which the respondent is satisfied with each type of support that is available for network members. It provides a way of determining who is important and close to the respondent, and thus which network members might represent viable options for meeting needs.

PERSONAL PROJECTS MATRIX (LITTLE, 1983). This scale provides a unique way of determining a person's needs and aspirations. A respondent is first asked to list up to 10 personal projects that occupy his or her time and energy. Second, the individual rates each of the projects in terms of its importance, enjoyment, difficulty, stress, impact (both positive and negative), and "progress" toward meeting the goals (needs, achieving an aspiration), and so forth. On the one hand, this assessment system provides a direct way of determining the activities a person considers important enough to warrant time and energy (i.e., his or her needs). On the other hand, it provides a way of assessing a number of qualitative aspects of the projects with respect to the respondent's perceptions of how the activities impinge upon his or her life. The latter can be especially useful for determining the extent to which efforts to complete projects will occur.

FAMILY RESOURCE SCALE (DUNST & LEET, 1987). This scale measures the extent to which different types of resources are adequate in households with young children. The scale includes 30 items that tap the adequacy of both physical and human resources, including food, shelter, transportation, time to be with family and friends, health care, money to pay bills, child care, and the like. Each item is rated on a 5-point scale ranging from "Not At All Adequate" to "Almost Always Adequate." The scale can be completed by a parent or another family member. It can help identify family needs and provide a basis for deciding upon the appropriate targets for intervention. Those items rated "Not At All Adequate" or "Seldom Adequate" may be taken as evidence that these needs are not being met, and provide a basis for exploring with the family more precisely what resources are lacking and why they are needed.

SUPPORT FUNCTIONS SCALE (DUNST & TRIVETTE, 1988A). This scale measures parents' need for different types of help and assistance. An extended and short-form version of the scale includes 20 and 12 items, respectively. (The items on the short-form version were based on the factor analysis results of the extended version of the scale.) The items measure the need for emotional, material, instrumental, social participation, and informational assistance on a 5-point scale ranging from "Never" need this type of support to "Quite often" need this type of support. The scale can help identify family needs and is useful for prompting questions concerning the needs and wants of a family.

INVENTORY OF SOCIALLY SUPPORTIVE BEHAVIORS (BARRERA ET AL., 1981). This scale consists of 40 items that describe different types of supportive acts that might have been experienced during the preceding month (e.g., looked after a family member when the respondent had to be away, listened to the respondent talk about private feelings). Each item is rated on a 5-point scale ranging from "Has Not Occurred At All" to "Occurs Almost Every Day." The findings from this scale can provide a clear picture of the types of support that are provided by network members as well as how often these types of aid and assistance are needed. It can be useful as a tool for prompting questions that permit one to make suggestions and recommendations about ways to mobilize resources for meeting needs.

FAMILY SUPPORT SCALE (DUNST ET AL., 1984). This is an 18-item self-report measure that assesses the degree to which different support sources are helpful to families rearing a young child. The sources of support include the respondent's own parents, spouse or partner, friends, neighbors, co-workers, the church, professionals, and social groups and organizations. Each item is rated on a 5-point scale ranging from "Not At All Helpful" to "Extremely Helpful." The results from the scale can be used to query persons about members of their social network, including who is helpful and why, who is not helpful and why, and which sources of support are used and not used and why.

Any of these scales could be used for obtaining information necessary to conduct social support interventions. The final section of the chapter describes a family systems intervention model that helps structure the manner in which one can assist a family to mobilize resources to meet needs.

CONDUCTING SOCIAL SUPPORT INTERVENTIONS

The approach to developing and implementing social support interventions described in this section is based on principles and guidelines for practice (Dunst et al., 1988b) that operationalize a needs-based approach to intervention proposed originally by Hobbs et al. (1984). This model takes very complex material regarding social and family systems theory and reduces it to a set of principles that can be used to meet the needs of families in a way that increases the likelihood that interventions will have positive effects on child, parent, and family functioning (Dunst & Trivette, 1987a, 1988b, 1988e).

Philosophical bases of the model

The implementation of the assessment and intervention model is guided by a number of beliefs that emphasize a proactive, highly responsive approach to working with families. First, major emphasis is placed on both enabling and empowering families (Dunst, 1986, 1987, 1988; Dunst & Trivette, 1987b, 1988d). Enabling families means creating opportunities for family members to become more competent, independent, and self-sustaining with respect to their abilities to mobilize their social networks to get needs met and attain desired goals (Hobbs et al., 1984). Empowering families means carrying out interventions in a manner in which family members acquire a sense of control over their own developmental course as a result of their efforts to meet needs (Rappaport, 1981, 1987).

Second, major emphasis is placed on strengthening families and their natural support networks without usurping decision-making or supplanting their support networks with professional services (Hobbs et al., 1984). Strengthening families means supporting and building upon the things the family already does well as a basis for promoting and encouraging the mobilization of resources among the family's network members (Stinnett & DeFrain, 1985).

Third, major emphasis is placed on enhancing families' acquisitions of a wide variety of competencies that permit them to become capable of meeting needs through mobilization of their support networks. Enhancing the acquisition of competencies means providing families with the information and skills necessary for them to become more self-sustaining and thus better able to promote personal well-being as well as have positive influences in other areas of family functioning (Dunst, 1985, 1986; Dunst & Trivette, 1987a, 1987b, 1988b, 1988d). Enabling, empowering, and strengthening families constitute the major goals of the assessment and intervention process.

A Family Systems Assessment and Intervention Model

The family-level assessment and intervention model is divided into four components: identification of family needs, identification of intrafamily resources (strengths and capabilities), identification of extrafamily source of support and resources, and proactive interventionist roles in helping families mobilize both intrafamily and extrafamily resources to meet needs. The operationalization of each of these components is described next.

1. *Identification of family concerns, issues, and priorities using needs-based assessment procedures and strategies.* The purpose of this component of the model is to identify the needs and projects that a family considers important enough to warrant their time and energy. The ability to identify family needs and projects adequately requires that

one employ a broad-based needs hierarchy perspective, where needs may be thought of as varying along a continuum from basic needs (food, shelter, etc.) to enrichment (community, job, adult education, child-level intervention, etc.) to generativity (sharing experiences with others, security, etc.). It cannot be emphasized enough that identification of family needs should be the focus of the needs-based assessment process. People who leave their own agenda outside the assessment process, and simply listen to what family members have and want to say, will be able to identify what the family views as important, and consequently will be able to adequately identify family needs. Stoneman (1985) stated this in the following way: "To be effective [in work with families], service providers must want to hear what parents have to say and must be truly interested in understanding the family's concerns and needs" (p. 463). The procedures for identifying needs were described in the preceeding section, Assessing Social Support.

2. *Identification of family strengths and capabilities as a basis for emphasizing the things the family already does well, and for identifying the intrafamily resources that increase the likelihood of the successful mobilization of extrafamily resources to meet needs.* The purpose of this component of the model is to identify a family's unique functioning style both in terms of existing intrafamily resources as well as strengths and capabilities that can be used to secure additional resources. Family strengths include the skills employed in response to demands placed upon the family, the competencies used to mobilize resources, and any other abilities that "make the family work well." Family functioning style includes both the strengths and capabilities that constitute intrafamily resources for meeting needs and the ways in which a family employs strengths and capabilities as a basis for securing or creating additional resources. The importance of this step in the assessment and intervention model cannot be stressed enough. Identification and knowledge of family strengths and capabilities provides the basis for building upon the things a family already does well, and is more likely to result in the investment of time and energy required to mobilize resources. Dunst et al. (1988b) describe methods that can be used for assessing family strengths.

3. *"Mapping" of the family's personal social network in terms of existing sources of support and resources and of untapped but potential sources of aid and assistance.* The purpose of this component of the model is to identify existing sources of intrafamily and extrafamily support, and untapped but potential sources of aid and assistance that match family identified needs. The procedures to accomplish this goal were described in the preceding section on assessing social support. Our experience tells us that many existing and potential sources of support are oftentimes overlooked by early intervention practitioners because they fail to consider the full range of social support options available to families. Social support network mapping provides a mechanism for ensuring that no possible options are overlooked and that we do not "overprofessionalize" families when less formal sources of support can be used to meet needs.

4. *Use of a number of different help-giving roles to enable and empower families so they may become better able to mobilize resources to get their needs met and achieve desired goals.* The purpose of this component of the model is to employ helping behaviors that enable families to maximize the use of their existing competencies and empower families with new competencies that make them more self-sustaining in terms of mobilizing resources to meet needs. The ability to attain this goal is guided by a proactive approach to working with families, a shift and expansion in the professional roles, and a set of guidelines that are both enabling and empowering (see Dunst et al., 1988b; Dunst, Trivette, Davis, & Cornwell, 1988; Trivette et al., 1986). In contrast to

the previous three components, which emphasize assessment of different aspects of the family, this component focuses on the ways in which professionals work with families in a manner that the families are likely to become more competent and self-sustaining (empowered) with respect to their ability to mobilize resources for meeting their needs.

One consistent theme has surfaced repeatedly as part of both our research and clinical experiences with assessing and mobilizing social support to meet family needs: *It is not just a matter of whether needs are met but rather the manner in which mobilization of resources and support occurs that is a major determinant of enabling and empowering families* (Dunst, 1986; Dunst & Trivette, 1987b, 1988d). To be both enabling and empowering in a way that promotes a family's capabilities and competencies, the family must be actively involved in the process of identifying and mobilizing resources, and the interventionist must derive personal and intrinsic gratification and enjoyment from seeing others become more capable and competent. Maple (1977), in his book *Shared Decision Making*, noted that when helpgivers see themselves as singularly responsible for rescuing families from their troubles, "the rescuer becomes a star. It is [my] view that your goal as helpers is not to learn how to become a star, but rather to help [others] become the 'star' in some aspects of their lives" (p. 7). To do so cannot but have a significant positive influence on family functioning, especially with respect to supporting and strengthening families (Dunst et al., 1988b; Hobbs et al., 1984).

SUMMARY AND IMPLICATIONS

This chapter focused on three aspects of social support: definition, assessment considerations and strategies, and procedures for mobilizing support to meet family-identified needs. All three aspects were discussed from a family and social systems framework specifically designed for intervention purposes (see especially Dunst et al., 1988b; Hobbs et al., 1984). This framework has evolved from efforts to understand the meaning of social support and how it functions as an intervention that promotes positive change in parent, family, and child behavior and development (Dunst & Trivette, 1988b, 1988c, 1988e).

The major conclusion to be drawn from the material presented in this chapter, as well as from the research and clinical evidence upon which the material is derived, is that the assessment and mobilization of support to meet family-identified needs must be guided by a framework that promotes an understanding of the major components and dimensions of support, and how support potentially influences family functioning. SASSI, which systematizes the collection and interpretation of social support information, provides a framework for assessing social support within the context of early intervention programs. Early intervention practitioners should find this assessment system useful for measuring the need for support and identifying sources of resources to meet these needs.

The material presented in this chapter also has several other major practical implications beyond providing a framework for conceptualizing, assessing, and mobilizing social support. First, it broadens both the meaning of early intervention (Dunst, 1985) and the roles that early intervention practitioners can use in order to enable families to identify needs and mobilize resources to meet needs (Dunst et al., 1988b). As previously noted, early intervention may be conceptualized as the aggregation of the different types of support that are provided by professional and nonprofessional helpgivers, and what interventionists do to mediate support extends beyond simply direct provision of services to children and families. Second, it suggests the optimal conditions under which support is most likely to have the greatest impact on family functioning; that is, when it is provided in response to family-identified needs by people in whom the family has confidence and trust. On the one hand, this model indicates that persons identified as sources of support should, to the extent possible, be individuals with whom the family has positive attributions, and on the other hand, indicates the necessity for early intervention practitioners to establish positive and proactive partnerships with families if the assistance and advice that they provide is to have broad-based positive influences.

The greatest positive impacts of early intervention will most likely be realized if a social support perspective is employed for identifying and meeting family needs. The material presented in this chapter provides the necessary framework for ensuring that early interventionists and early intervention practices support and strength family functioning.

REFERENCES

Affleck, G., Tennen, H., Allen, D. A., & Gershman, K. (1986). Perceived social support and maternal adaptation during the transition from hospital to home care of high-risk infants. *Infant Mental Health Journal, 7*, 6–18.

Barrera, M., Jr. (1980). A method for the assessment of social support networks in community survey research. *Connections, 3*, 8–13.

Barrera, M., Jr. (1986). Distinctions between social support concepts, measures, and models. *American Journal of Community Psychology, 14*, 413–445.

Barrera, M., Jr., & Ainslay, S. L. (1983). The structure of social support: A conceptual and empirical analysis. *American Journal of Community Psychology, 11*, 133–143.

Barrera, M., Jr., Sandler, I. N., & Ramsay, T. B. (1981). Preliminary development of a scale of social support: Studies on college students. *American Journal of Community Psychology, 9*, 435–447.

Birkel, R. C., & Repucci, N. D. (1983). Social networks, information-seeking, and the utilization of services. *American Journal of Community Psychology, 11*, 185–205.

Bradburn, N. M., & Caplovitz, D. (1965). *Reports on happiness*. Chicago: Aldine.

Bronfenbrenner, U. (1979). *The ecology of human development: Experiments by nature and design*. Cambridge: Harvard University Press.

Brown, G., & Bifulco, A. (1985). Social support, life events and depression. In I. G. Sarason & B. R. Sarason (Eds.), *Social support: Theory, research and applications* (pp. 349–370). Dordrecht, The Netherlands: Martinus Nijhoff Publishers.

Bruhn, J. G., & Philips, B. U. (1984). Measuring social support: A synthesis of current approaches. *Journal of Behavioral Medicine, 7*, 151–169.

Cauce, A. M. (1986). Social networks and social competence: Exploring the effects of early adolescent friendships. *American Journal of Community Psychology, 14*, 607–628.

Cobb, S. (1976). Social support as a moderator of life stress. *Psychosomatic Medicine, 38*, 300–314.

Cochran, M., & Brassard, J. (1979). Child development and personal social networks. *Child Development, 50*, 601–616.

Cohen, L. H., McGowan, J., Fooskas, S., & Rose, S. (1984). Positive life events and social support and the relationship between life stress and psychological disorder. *American Journal of Community Psychology, 12*, 567–587.

Cohen, S., Meimelstein, R., Kamarck, T., & Hoberman, H. (1985). Measuring the functional components of social support. In I. G. Sarason & B. R. Sarason (Eds.), *Social support: Theory, research and applications* (pp. 73–94). Dordrecht, The Netherlands: Martinus Nijhoff Publishers.

Cohen, S., & Syme, S. L. (1985). *Social support and health*. Orlando: Academic Press.

Colletta, N. (1981). Social support and the risk of maternal rejection by adolescent mothers. *Journal of Psychology, 109*, 191–197.

Crnic, A., Greenberg, M., Ragozin, A., Robinson, N., & Basham, R. (1983). Effects of stress and social support on mothers of premature and full-term infants. *Child Development, 54*, 209–217.

Crnic, K. A., Greenberg, M. T., & Slough, N. M. (1986). Early stress and social support influences on mothers' and high-risk infants' functioning in late infancy. *Infant Mental Health Journal, 7*, 19–48.

Cutrona, C. E., & Troutman, B. R. (1986). Social support, infant temperament and parenting self-efficacy: A mediational model of postpartum depression. *Child Development, 57*, 1507–1518.

Dean, A., & Lin, N. (1977). The stress-buffering role of social support. *The Journal of Nervous and Mental Disease, 165*, 403–417.

DiMatteo, M. R., & Hays, R. (1981). Social support and serious illness. In B. H. Gottlieb (Ed.), *Social networks and social support* (pp. 117–148). Beverly Hills: Sage Publications.

Dunst, C. J. (1985). Rethinking early intervention. *Analysis and Intervention in Developmental Disabilities, 5*, 165–201.

Dunst, C. J. (1986, October). *Helping relationships and enabling and empowering families.* Paper presented at the 11th Annual Regional Intervention Program Expansion Conference, Cleveland, OH.

Dunst, C. J. (1987, December). *What is effective helping?* Paper presented at the Fifth Biennial National Training Institute of the National Center for Clinical Infant Programs, Washington, DC.

Dunst, C. J. (1988, March). *Enabling and empowering families: Caveats, considerations and consequences.* Paper presented at the Early Intervention: Innovations in Service Delivery Conference, Danbury, CT.

Dunst, C. J., Cooper, C., & Bolick, F. (1987). Supporting families of handicapped children. In J. Garbarino, P. Brookhouser, & K. Authier (Eds.), *Special children, special risks: The maltreatment of children with disabilities* (pp. 17–46). New York: Aldine de Gruyter.

Dunst, C. J., Jenkins, V., & Trivette, C. M. (1984). Family Support Scale: Reliability and validity. *Journal of Individual, Family, and Community Wellness, 1*, 45–52.

Dunst, C. J., & Leet, H. (1987). Measuring the adequacy of resources in households with young children. *Child: Care, Health and Development, 13*, 111–125.

Dunst, C. J., Leet, H., & Trivette, C. M. (1988a). Family resources, personal well-being, and early intervention. *Journal of Special Education, 22*, 108–116.

Dunst, C. J., & Trivette, C. M. (1986). Looking beyond the parent–child dyad for the determinants of maternal styles of interaction. *Infant Mental Health Journal, 7*, 69–80.

Dunst, C. J., & Trivette, C. M. (1987a, April). Social support and positive functioning in families of developmentally, at-risk preschoolers. Presentation at biennial meeting of the Society for Research in Child Development, Baltimore.

Dunst, C. J., & Trivette, C. M. (1987b). Enabling and empowering families: Conceptual and intervention issues. *School Psychology Review, 16*, 443–456.

Dunst, C. J., & Trivette, C. M. (1988a). Support Functions Scale. In C. J. Dunst, C. M. Trivette, & A. G. Deal, *Enabling and empowering families: Principles and guidelines for practice* (pp. 143–145). Cambridge, MA: Brookline Books.

Dunst, C. J., & Trivette, C. M. (1988b). Toward experimental evaluation of the Family, Infant and Preschool Program. In H. Weiss & F. Jacobs (Eds.), *Evaluating family programs.* New York: Aldine de Gruyter.

Dunst, C. J., & Trivette, C. M. (1988c). Determinants of caregiver styles of interaction used with developmentally at-risk children. In K. Marfo (Ed.), *Parent–child interaction and developmental disabilities: Theory, researach, and intervention.* New York: Praeger.

Dunst, C. J., & Trivette, C. M. (1988d). Helping, helplessness, and harm. In J. Witt, S. Elliott, & F. Gresham (Eds.), *Handbook of behavior therapy in education.* New York: Plenum Press.

Dunst, C. J., & Trivette, C. M. (1988e). A family systems model of early intervention with handicapped and developmentally at-risk children. In D. Powell (Ed.), *Parent education as early childhood intervention: Emerging directions in theory, research, and practice* (pp. 131–180). New York: Ablex.

Dunst, C. J., Trivette, C. M., & Cross, A. (1986a). Mediating influences of social support: Personal, family, and child outcomes. *American Journal of Mental Deficiency, 90*, 403–417.

Dunst, C. J., Trivette, C. M., & Cross, A. (1986b). Roles and support networks of mothers of handicapped children. In R. Fewell & P. Vadasy (Eds.), *Families of handicapped children: Needs and supports across the life span* (pp. 167–192). Austin, TX: PRO-ED.

Dunst, C. J., Trivette, C. M., Davis, M., Cornwell, J. C. (1988). Enabling and empowering families of children with health impairments. *Children's Health Care, 17*(2), 71–81.

Dunst, C. J., Trivette, C. M., & Deal, A. G. (1988b). *Enabling and empowering families: Principles and guidelines for practice.* Cambridge, MA: Brookline Books.

Dunst, C. J., Vance, S. D., & Cooper, C. S. (1986). A social systems perspective of adolescent pregnancy: Determinants of parent and parent–child behavior. *Infant Mental Health Journal,* 7, 34–48.

Fewell, R. R. (1986). The measurement of family functioning. In L. Bickman & D. L. Weatherford (Eds.), *Evaluating early intervention programs for severely handicapped children and their families* (pp. 263–310). Austin, TX: PRO-ED.

Fiore, J., Coppel, D., Becker, J., & Cox, G. B. (1986). Social support as a multifaceted concept: Examination of important dimensions of adjustments. *American Journal of Community Psychology,* 14, 93–112.

Gallagher, J. J., Cross, A. H., & Scharfman, W. (1981). *Parent Role Scale.* Unpublished scale, University of North Carolina, Frank Porter Graham Child Development Center, Chapel Hill, NC.

Gottlieb, B. H. (1981). Social networks and social support in community mental health. In B. H. Gottlieb (Ed.), *Social networks and social support* (pp. 11–42). Beverly Hills: Sage Publications.

Hall, A., & Wellman, B. (1985). Social networks and social support. In S. Cohen & S. L. Syme (Eds.), *Social support and health* (pp. 23–42). New York: Academic Press.

Hirsch, J. B. (1980). Natural support and coping with major life changes. *American Journal of Community Psychology,* 8, 159–172.

Hobbs, N., Dokecki, P. R., Hoover-Dempsey, K. V., Moroney, R. M., Shayne, M. W., & Weeks, K. H. (1984). *Strengthening families.* San Francisco: Jossey-Bass.

Holroyd, J. (1974). The Questionnaire on Resources and Stress: An instrument to measure family responses to a handicapped family member. *Journal of Community Psychology,* 2, 92–94.

Holroyd, J. (1985). *Questionnaire on Resources and Stress Manual.* Unpublished scale, University of California, Neuropsychiatric Institute, Department of Psychiatric and Behavioral Sciences, Los Angeles.

House, J. S. (1981). *Work stress and social support.* Reading, MA: Addison-Wesley.

House, J. S., & Kahn, R. L. (1985). Measures and concepts of social support. In S. Cohen & S. L. Syme (Eds.), *Social support and health* (pp. 83–108). New York: Academic Press.

Kahn, R. H., Wethington, E., & Ingersoll-Dayton, B. (1987). Social support and social networks: Determinants, effects, and interactions. In R. P. Abeles (Ed.), *Life-span perspectives and social psychology* (pp. 139–165). Hillsdale, NJ: L. Erlbaum.

Lazar, I., Darlington, R., Murray, H., Royce, J., & Snipper, A. (1982). Lasting effects of early education: A report from the consortium for longitudinal studies. *Monographs of the Society for Research in Child Development,* 47(2–3, Serial No. 195).

Levine, M. S. (1977). *Canonical analysis and factor comparison.* Sage University Paper series on Quantitative Applications in the Social Sciences, 07-006. Beverly Hills: Sage Publications.

Lin, N., Dean, A., & Ensel, W. M. (1981). Social support scales: A methodological note. *Schizophrenia Bulletin,* 7, 73–88.

Little, B. R. (1983). Personal projects: A rationale and method for investigation. *Environment and Behavior,* 19, 273–309.

Maple, F. F. (1977). *Shared decision making.* Beverly Hills: Sage Publications.

McCubbin, H. I., Joy, C. B., Cauble, A. E., Comeau, J. K., Patterson, J. M., & Needle, R. H. (1980). Family stress and coping: A decade review. *Journal of Marriage and the Family,* 42, 855–871.

McKillip, J. (1987). *Needs analysis: Tools for the human services and education.* Beverly Hills: Sage Publications.

Mitchell, R. E., & Trickett, E. J. (1980). Task Force Report: Social networks as mediators of social support: An analysis of the effects and determinants of social networks. *Community Mental Health Journal,* 16, 27–44.

Moos, R. H. (Ed.). (1986). *Coping with life crisis: An integrated approach.* New York: Plenum Press.

Oritt, E. C., Paul, S. C., & Behrman, J. A. (1985). Perceived Support Network Inventory. *American Journal of Community Psychology,* 13, 565–582.

Pascoe, J. M., Loda, F. A., Jeffries, V., & Earp, J. (1981). The association between mothers' social support and provision of stimulation to their children. *Journal of Developmental and Behavioral Pediatrics,* 2, 15–19.

Patterson, J. M., & McCubbin, H. I. (1983). Chronic illness: Family stress and coping. In C. R.

Figley & H. I. McCubbin (Eds.), *Stress and the family: Vol. II. Coping with catastrophe* (pp. 21–36). New York: Brunner/Mazel.

Pattison, E. M., DeFrancisco, D., Wood, P., Frazier, H., & Crowder, J. (1975). A psychosocial kinship model for family therapy. *American Journal of Psychiatry, 132,* 1246–1251.

Phillips, S. L. (1981). Network characteristics related to the well-being of normals: A comparative base. *Schizophrenia Bulletin 7,* 117–123.

Pilisuk, M., & Parks, S. H. (1986). *The healing web: Social networks and human survival.* Hanover, NH: University Press of New England.

Potasznik, H., & Nelson, G. (1984). Stress and social support: The burden experienced by the family of a mentally ill person. *American Journal of Community Psychology, 12,* 589–607.

Procidano, M. E., & Heller, K. (1983). Measures of perceived social support from friends and from family: Three validation studies. *American Journal of Community Psychology, 11,* 1–24.

Rappaport, J. (1981). In praise of paradox: A social policy of empowerment over prevention. *American Journal of Community Psychology, 9,* 1–25.

Rappaport, J. (1987). Terms of empowerment/exemplars of prevention: Toward a theory for community psychology. *American Journal of Community Psychology, 15,* 121–128.

Sandler, I. N., & Barrera, M., Jr. (1984). Toward a multimethod approach to assessing the effects of social support. *American Journal of Community Psychology, 12,* 37–52.

Sarason, I. G., Levine, H. M., Basham, R. B., & Sarason, B. R. (1983). Assessing social support: The Social Support Questionnaire. *Journal of Personality and Social Psychology, 44,* 127–139.

Sarason, I. G., & Sarason, B. R. (Eds.). (1985). *Social support: Theory, research and applications.* Dordrecht, The Netherlands: Martinus Nijhoff Publishers.

Stinnett, N., & DeFrain, J. (Eds.). (1985). *Secrets of strong families.* New York: Berkley Books.

Stoneman, Z. (1985). Family involvement in early childhood special education programs. In N. H. Fallen & W. Umansky (Eds.), *Young children with special needs* (2nd ed., pp. 442–469). Columbus, OH: Merrill.

Tardy, C. H. (1985). Social support measurement. *American Journal of Community Psychology, 13,* 187–202.

Thompson, B. (1984). *Canonical correlation analysis: Uses and interpretation.* Sage University Paper series on Quantitative Applications in the Social Sciences, 07-047. Beverly Hills: Sage Publications.

Trivette, C. M., Deal, A., & Dunst, C. J. (1986). Family needs, sources of support, and professional roles: Critical elements of family systems assessment and intervention. *Diagnostique, 11,* 246–267.

Trivette, C. M., & Dunst, C. J. (1985). *Personal Well-Being Index.* Unpublished scale, Family, Infant and Preschool Program, Western Carolina Center, Morganton, NC.

Trivette, C. M., & Dunst, C. J. (1987). Proactive influences of social support in families of handicapped children. In H. G. Lingren et al. (Eds.), *Family strengths: Vol. 8–9. Pathways to well-being.* Lincoln: University of Nebraska Press.

Trivette, C. M., & Dunst, C. J. (1988). Inventory of Social Support. In C. J. Dunst, C. M. Trivette, & A. G. Deal, *Enabling and empowering families: Principles and guidelines for practice* (pp. 159–163). Cambridge, MA: Brookline Books.

Trivette, C. M., & Dunst, C. J. (in press). Characteristics and influences of role division and social support among mothers of handicapped preschoolers. *Parenting Studies.*

Trivette, C. M. & Dunst, C. J. (in preparation). Caregiver styles of interaction: Child, parent, family, and extrafamily influences.

Turner, R. J. (1983). Direct, indirect, and moderating effects of social support on psychological distress and associated conditions. In H. B. Kaplan (Ed.), *Psychosocial stress: Trends in theory and research* (pp. 105–135). New York: Academic Press.

Vaux, A., & Harrison, D. (1985). Support network characteristics associated with support satisfaction and perceived support. *American Journal of Community Psychology, 13,* 245–268.

Vaux, A., Phillips, J., Holly, L., Thomson, B., Williams, D., & Stewart, D. (1986). The Social Support Appraisals (SS-A) Scale: Studies of reliability and validity. *American Journal of Community Psychology, 14,* 195–219.

Wills, T. A. (1985). Supportive functions of interpersonal relationships. In S. Cohen & S. L. Syme (Eds.), *Social support and health* (pp. 61–82). Orlando: Academic Press.

15 *Therapeutic aspects of the assessment process*

STEVEN J. PARKER AND BARRY S. ZUCKERMAN

INTRODUCTION

The process of intervention begins with an assessment. The goal of this assessment has traditionally been to quantify specific areas of a child's developmental or behavioral functioning and use this information to both guide the therapeutic interventions and gauge their efficacy. Used in this way, the assessment is viewed as subordinate to, rather than a part of, the therapeutic process. Its goals are narrow, confined to circumscribed areas of functioning, and the results are not easily integrated into a coherent view of the whole child.

This chapter examines the therapeutic potential of the assessment process and proposes an expansion of its traditional goals. The term *developmental assessment* will refer to the process of a structured or semistructured evaluation of a child's neurobehavioral functioning. Whatever the explicit reason for the assessment – for example, an evaluation of educational potential, motor function, language competence, or parent–child interactions – the therapeutic potential of this process is considerable. As professionals become more aware of the special opportunities provided by the assessment process, greater benefits for the child and family can occur. By expanding its theoretical and practical goals, the arbitrary distinction between assessment and intervention can be erased.

The theoretical basis for expanding the goals of assessment to include therapeutic outcomes emanates from the transactional theory of child development. According to this viewpoint, each aspect of a child's developmental and behavioral functioning interacts with, modulates, and is transformed by the caretaking environment. As an example, a child's speech may be sparse due to a combination of an intrinsic language disorder and inadequate environmental stimulation. The lack of environmental reinforcement for verbal output may also cause the child to be depressed. The depression further diminishes communicative efforts and, at the same time, the child's increasing silence elicits even less reinforcement from the caretakers. By focusing purely on the intrinsic language deficit and ignoring the reasons for inadequate environmental stim-

This chapter was written with support from grants from the Boston Foundation, the Jessie B. Cox Charitable Trust, and the Bureau of Health Care Delivery and Assistance, Maternal and Child Health Branch (MCJ-009094). The authors thank Margaret Stanhope for her help in preparing the manuscript.

ulation, the assessment process is limited in a way that neither promotes an understanding of that child nor provides a foundation for effective interventions.

In this chapter we will discuss the reasons for the heightened sensitivity and vulnerability of parents to the assessment process, discuss the available literature on using a developmental assessment as an intervention, and highlight the therapeutic opportunities inherent in the assessment process.

THE CONTEXT OF THE ASSESSMENT PROCESS

Parental responses to a child with a disability

There is a large body of literature that discusses parents' reactions to having a child with a developmental disability. Because these reactions and ongoing adaptations contribute to the emotional state brought by parents to the assessment process, an understanding of these feelings, expectations, hopes, and fears is a key to maximizing the therapeutic benefits of any developmental assessment.

The study of parents' responses to a child with disabilities evolved from Lindemann's (1944) classic descriptions of the symptomatology and evolution of grieving. He documented the reactions of families, friends, and survivors to the deaths of 491 people in a nightclub fire. The initial responses to this tragedy were universal and included somatic distress, preoccupation with the image of the loved one, feelings of guilt, hostile reactions, and disorganization of the normal patterns of behavior. Some were able to resolve these feelings and constructively continue with their lives, but others remained emotionally distraught and unable to cope with the demands of everyday life. According to Lindemann, those who successfully adapted had engaged in active "grief work." Poor psychological adjustment, on the other hand, was ascribed to "morbid grief reactions." These occurred when persistent denial prevented the grief work from even beginning or when, once underway, the grieving process became distorted, intensified, and inadequately resolved.

This description of grief reactions became the reference point for the literature from the 1950s and early 1960s that presented clinical examples of parents' responses to having a child with a disability. Kanner (1953) described parents of children with mental retardation as needing to express

their emotional involvements in the form of questions, utterances of guilt, open and sometimes impatient rebellion against destiny, stories of frantic search for causes, pathetic accounts of matrimonial dissensions about the child's condition, regret about the course that has been taken so far, anxious appraisals of the child's future, and tearful pleas for reassurance (p. 375).

Olshansky (1962) rejected the notion that parental responses followed an inevitable progression of stages. He believed that "parents who have a mentally defective child suffer chronic sorrow throughout their lives." He chastised professionals who viewed "having a mentally defective child less as a tragedy than as a psychiatric problem" (p. 192) and who criticized parents for resolving their grief too slowly. He recommended that professionals allow parents "the opportunity to ventilate and clarify their feelings, and to receive support for the legitimacy of the feelings they were expressing" (p. 192), rather than demanding that the parents unambivalently accept and cheerfully adapt to the new realities of their lives.

Solnit and Stark (1961) examined the birth of a "defective child" from a psychoanalytic perspective. In their view, such an event represented a severe injury to the ego of the parents:

The simultaneous loss of one child – the expected and narcissistically invested one – and adaptation to the deviant or defective child makes a demand that is very likely to be overwhelming. . . . Thus, at a time the mother is prepared to be nurtured by the satisfaction of her creative experience and to begin nurturing her child, her adaptive capacities are sapped because she failed to create what she intended (p. 526).

In the authors' view, the role of professionals is to facilitate the resolution of the mourning process by synchronizing the interventions with the parents' stage of grieving.

Beyond these clinical descriptions, several empirical studies were conducted during the 1950s and early 1960s. These studies, however, suffered from numerous methodologic limitations, including sampling biases, inadequate control groups, and incomplete outcome measures (Jordan, 1962). One early study attempted to overcome some of these limitations by comparing the responses of mothers of children with mental retardation to mothers of children with chronic illnesses or neurotic symptoms (Cummings, Bayley, & Rie, 1966). This study found mothers of children with retardation to experience less pleasure in parenting, increased tendencies to reject their child, and lower self-esteem in their maternal role, compared to the control group. Similar negative outcomes and an additional pattern of long-term social withdrawal were also demonstrated in a later study of fathers of children with retardation (Cummings, 1976).

More recent studies of parental reactions to a child with a disability have employed interviews or questionnaires (Drotar, Baskiewicz, Irvin, Kennell, & Klaus, 1975; Emde & Brown, 1978; Kennedy, 1970; Wikler, 1981) or have synthesized available clinical and published observations (Howell, 1973; Huber, 1979; MacKeith, 1973; Menolascino, 1968; Miller, 1968; Sieffert, 1978; Wright, 1976). Although each author conceptualized the stages of adjustment somewhat differently, common themes are evident. Following initial awareness of their child's disability, parental responses usually include shock, denial, and bewilderment. During this stage parents may be unable to comprehend the nature of their child's disability, no matter how sensitively or repeatedly it is explained. Most observers view this as an essential coping mechanism – "nature's anesthetic" according to Wright (1976) – that allows parents to assimilate bad news gradually and continue to fulfill their day-to-day responsibilities (Geleerd, 1965).

As these initial responses subside, the grieving process begins. Following the initial shock and denial, characteristic parental responses include guilt, anger, hostility, depression, bitterness, envy, lowered self-esteem, sorrow, and shame (Blacher, 1984). Positive feelings may also emerge at this time as parents become able to focus on normal aspects of their child's behavioral and developmental functioning (Drotar et al., 1975). The ambivalent nature of this stage is striking, with the dualities of despair–hope, denial–acceptance, rejection–attachment, guilt–blamelessness, and anger–equanimity in a constant dynamic interplay.

The final stage of adaptation is usually described as one of adjustment and/or acceptance. Through successful grief work, parents are enabled to accept emotionally and intellectually their child's condition. This allows them to realistically modify their expectations for the child, accept support and intervention services, resume a constructive life, and remain free of chronic emotional disorganization.

These descriptions of the reactions and feelings experienced by parents are extremely useful in the clinical setting. However, there is considerable controversy over whether they represent discrete and/or sequential stages (Blacher, 1984). It is stated frequently, for example, that sorrow is a recurrent phenomenon in parents' lives (Wilker, Wasow, & Hatfield, 1981), that parents fluctuate freely between these stages at different stages of their child's development (Featherstone, 1980), and that life with a handicapped child mandates ongoing readjustments to cope with ever-changing challenges (Bray, Coleman, & Bracken, 1981; Dunlap, 1979; Wikler, 1981).

Most of these studies examined parental adaptation to children with *established* disabilities (e.g., Down syndrome or cerebral palsy). There are only a few reports, however, describing parental responses to children with a *marginal* or *ambiguous* handicap. In such cases it is not clear that a problem actually exists or what its potential impact on long-term functioning may be. The parents' denial of their child's problem may reflect this clinical uncertainty, rather than represent a stage of acute grieving (Matheny & Vernick, 1969). Parental anger may be due to the ambiguity of the diagnosis and prognosis, and not a defense mechanism (Stacey, 1980). Willner and Crane (1979) suggest that parents of mildly handicapped children suffer from *chronic disappointment*, rather than chronic sorrow. The parents' emotional turmoil may be initially less intense but more prolonged, as the uncertainty of the child's limitations leads to unfulfilled developmental and behavioral expectations throughout life.

A time of heightened parental sensitivity

The emotional context in which parents experience a developmental assessment is dependent on the nature of their adaptation to the child's real or potential problems. Mandelbaum and Wheeler (1960) asserted that the goals of an initial evaluation should be to "assist the parents toward arriving at some resolution of their painful, conflicted feelings, of the anger and guilt that torment them, of the self-doubts that assail them, and of the distortions of reality that lead to irrational planning" (p. 366).

Featherstone (1980) emphasized that the assessment process occurs during a time of emotional fragility for the family: "Parents looking for a diagnosis are frightened and immensely vulnerable. They may have already suffered days, months, even years of agonizing doubt. They stand exposed and powerless before the 'experts.' Indifference, condescension, or equivocation wound them deeply" (p. 38).

Evaluators must be aware that under such circumstances parents are likely to have intense emotions regarding any assessment of their child's development. Even years later, discussions with parents frequently return to the initial assessment as a time of heightened feelings (Featherstone, 1980; Turnbull & Turnbull, 1978). In fact, parents of children with mental retardation or learning disabilities have ranked the experience of the first professional diagnosis of their child's condition as second in emotional impact only to the search for appropriate educational services (Bray et al., 1981). This time of emotional vulnerability makes it especially important to use the assessment process to assist parents in their adaptation. Intervention should begin with an assessment that informs and initiates the therapeutic process through its sensitivity to the parents' emotional state.

ASSESSMENT AS INTERVENTION: RESEARCH FINDINGS

Although clinical experience supports the therapeutic potential of the assessment process, there are few controlled studies to confirm or refute this view. Only the utilization of the Neonatal Behavioral Assessment Scale (NBAS) (Brazelton, 1984) as a therapeutic intervention has been well documented. The NBAS evaluates infant neurobehavioral functioning in such areas as interactive behaviors, self-regulatory abilities, physiologic vigor, and neurologic integrity. Studies have examined whether administering the NBAS in the presence of the parents can enhance the understanding of their baby's behavior and thereby improve parent–child outcomes.

Widmayer and Field (1981), for example, assessed the impact of using the NBAS as an intervention for 30 black teenage, low socioeconomic status mothers of healthy preterm infants. The mothers were assigned either to an experimental group who observed the administration of the NBAS with their babies, or to a control group who received routine care. The experimental group continued to formally assess their child's subsequent behavior and development at 1-week intervals for the first month of life, utilizing a version of the NBAS adapted for parents. The infants were then evaluated at 1, 4, and 12 months of age.

At 1 month, the experimental group manifested more optimal interactive skills, compared to the routine care group. At 4 months, the experimental group of infants showed better fine motor and adaptive abilities and more synchronous interactive behaviors with their mothers. At 1 year, the infants in the experimental group scored significantly higher on the Mental Scale of the Bayley Scales of Infant Development. The authors concluded that this use of the NBAS as an intervention may have helped the mother to "become more sensitized to the unique abilities of her infant, more interested in observing his or her development, and more active in promoting and providing stimulation to facilitate this development" (p. 713).

Worobey and Belsky (1982) demonstrated the necessity for parents to participate *actively* in the administration of the NBAS if enhanced mother-infant interactions were to be found 1 month later. Passively watching the exam, on the other hand, led to few discernible changes in maternal behaviors.

A study with a middle-class sample taught a group of parents to perform the NBAS on their own infants (Myers, 1982). Four weeks later, these parents scored higher in their knowledge of infant behavior, compared to a control group. Fathers who observed this NBAS were also more involved in the caretaking responsibilities of their infants. However, no improvements in parent–child interactions were noted. Liptak, Keller, Feldman, and Chamberlin (1983) were likewise unable to demonstrate significant benefits for parent–child interactions in a middle-class sample of parents who observed the NBAS. One interpretation of these negative results is that a "ceiling effect" had been achieved in families who were already primed for positive interactions with their infants.

Belsky (1985) used the NBAS as an intervention with middle-class families and failed to find any differences in outcomes at 1, 3, and 9 months between the experimental and control groups. He suggested that the determinants of family outcomes are complex and that any single intervention, such as the NBAS, can have only a small effect. This conclusion resulted in a published exchange of commentaries that addressed methodologic issues in the involved studies and questioned if those parents who participated actively in the NBAS administration might have demonstrated positive outcomes (Belsky, 1986; Worobey & Brazelton, 1986). To address these issues, Belsky reanalyzed the data and found that the parents who appeared most involved in the initial administration of the NBAS appeared to show modest long-term improvements in measures of their interactions with their infant, compared to the control group (Belsky, 1986).

Whereas conclusions regarding the efficacy of the NBAS as the intervention are still somewhat controversial, certain clinical implications are persuasive:

1. Assessments must be performed sensitively and expertly if they are to be therapeutic.
2. Assessments are most beneficial for parents who are less knowledgeable regarding

their child's behavior and development, and more at-risk for suboptimal interactions.
3. Active parental involvement in the assessment process is necessary to achieve therapeutic results.
4. Ongoing assessments can have a greater positive impact than any single evaluation.
5. Assessments are best utilized as part of a comprehensive therapeutic program to enhance family functioning.

Apart from studies examining the NBAS, there are few empirical data to support or refute the effectiveness of assessments as interventions. Important unresolved questions include: What is the impact of routine assessments on parents? What kind of developmental assessments are best able to enhance parent and child functioning? What are the deleterious effects on a family of an insensitively conducted assessment? Until these questions are addressed in controlled studies, we will have to rely on clinical impressions to gauge the benefits and pitfalls of utilizing assessments as interventions.

THERAPEUTIC GOALS OF THE ASSESSMENT PROCESS

Professionals help families in four ways. They identify and explain the child's problems. They can show respect for the child, the parent, and the relationship between them. They offer concrete assistance – services such as therapy, education, or corrective surgery. And they support the parents emotionally. (Featherstone, 1980, p. 178)

The available literature suggests that the assessment process itself can engender therapeutic outcomes. In this section we will examine four of the mechanisms through which such benefits may be achieved: (1) by enhancing the parents' understanding of the child, (2) by promoting the "goodness-of-fit" between parent and child, (3) by empowering and supporting the parents, and (4) by modeling constructive interactions with the child.

Enhancing the parents' understanding of the child

A successful assessment increases the parents' understanding of their child's behavior and level of developmental functioning. As parents observe their child's performance during formal testing, they are often surprised by what their child can (or cannot) do. One study evaluated 25 mothers from low socioeconomic circumstances who observed the administration of the Bayley Scales of Infant Development on their infants. Of these women, 96% reported that they learned something new about their baby's behavior or development during the assessment, 40% saw the baby perform a task that they did not know he or she could do, 28% were surprised at the length of their baby's attention span and ability to cooperate with a stranger, and 16% felt that they had to readjust their thinking because their developmental expectations had been too high (Stein, 1988).

Many parents anticipate only a numerical test score to be the outcome of an assessment. Although quantification of the child's abilities is important, the *quality* of his or her functioning throughout the examination provides equally useful information. The child's learning style, coping mechanisms, approach to problem solving, sense of mastery, and self-esteem are some of the more subtle aspects of performance that can be identified and discussed with the parents. This information enriches the parents' understanding of their child and enables them to fashion a more appropriate environment to facilitate the acquisition of developmental and behavioral skills.

An assessment further presents the opportunity to help parents have appropriate developmental expectations for their child. Parents may have unrealistically high or low expectations for their child's performance that become apparent during the assessment (Strom, Rees, Slaughter, & Wurster, 1981). A study by Crouchman (1985), for example, demonstrated that, independent of socioeconomic status, 47% of the mothers of newborn babies believed their infants to be blind at birth. These mothers may not provide appropriate visual stimulation for their infants early in life because they underestimate their babies' abilities. Conversely, if parental expectations are too high, they may frustrate their child by demanding the completion of tasks beyond his or her capacities.

Alternatively, parents may accurately grasp their child's abilities but be unaware of normative developmental milestones. Consequently, they may not interact in a way that facilitates the achievement of the next goal. During an assessment, the evaluator can discuss a reasonable timetable for the emergence of new skills based on the child's current level of functioning and previous rate of developmental progress. With the aid of this information, parents can adjust their expectations and interactions with their child more appropriately (Matheny & Vernick, 1969).

Promoting the goodness-of-fit between parent and child

A developmental assessment provides the opportunity to observe the interactions between parent and child. The fit between the child's temperament and the parents' caretaking characteristics is especially important to note. Thomas and Chess (1984) originally described nine domains of temperament in the 133 children they followed from childhood to adulthood.

1. Activity level
2. Rhythmicity: the predictability of any biologic function (e.g., sleep pattern, hunger)
3. Approach–withdrawal: the nature of response to a new or novel stimulus
4. Adaptability: the ease of modifying behavior to meet the needs of a new situation
5. Threshold of responsiveness: the intensity level of a stimulus needed to evoke a response
6. Intensity of reaction: the energy level of response
7. Quality of mood: pleasant–unpleasant, friendly–unfriendly, happy–sad
8. Distractibility: the ability of extraneous stimuli to interfere with ongoing purposeful behavior
9. Attention span and persistence with task completion

They defined temperament as the "how" of behavior, in contrast to the child's abilities (the "what" of behavior) and motivations (the "why" of behavior). Thomas and Chess noted that infants with a constellation of difficult temperamental traits were prone to behavioral problems in early and middle childhood. The most powerful predictor of behavioral pathology in late childhood and early adulthood, however, was not the child's inherent behavioral style but what they termed the "goodness-of-fit" between parent and child, that is, how sensitively and appropriately the caregivers responded to the child's behaviors.

An implicit goal of the assessment process can be to identify and enhance the goodness-of-fit between parent and child. When areas of parent–child conflict are identified during an assessment, the temperamental and behavioral characteristics of the child that triggered the incident can be noted, and inappropriate parental responses and expectations addressed.

Empowering and supporting the parents

The assessment process can enable parents to feel more confident in their ability to promote their child's development. Conversely, an insensitively performed assessment can engender parental feelings of doubt and ineptitude. These feelings may adversely affect their overall relationship with their child and diminish parental participation in the intervention process. This may be an especially detrimental outcome for early intervention programs in which parental participation is an important component (Bromwich, 1981; Bronfenbrenner, 1974; Comptroller General, 1979; Goodson & Hess, 1975; Welsh & Odum, 1981), particularly in programs for children with disabilities (Bricker & Casuso, 1979; Enzer, 1975; Menolascino & Coleman, 1980).

Bricker and Casuso (1979) summarized the advantages of parental involvement in early intervention programs as increasing intervention time for the child, improving parental self-confidence, reducing the risk of alienation from the child, and providing a broader base of information for the parent. Bronfenbrenner (1974) went so far as to state that "without family involvement, intervention is likely to be unsuccessful, and what few effects are achieved are likely to disappear once the intervention is discontinued" (p. 470).

To date, however, there is little empirical evidence to support or refute this clinical truism. White and Casto (1985) performed a "meta-analysis" of the existing studies concerning the efficacy of early intervention programs for children through 5 years of age who were at biologic, environmental, and/or established risk. Their analyses showed little to no demonstrable benefit for child outcomes in those programs with high parental involvement, compared to those with low parental participation. On the other hand, a similar meta-analysis performed by Shonkoff and Hauser-Cram (1987) demonstrated that active parental participation was associated with significantly better outcomes in programs specifically for children less than 3 years with established disabilities. The authors suggested that parental involvement may be more critical for younger children with biologically based disabilities than for older, more heterogeneous groups.

The available studies have methodologic flaws that prohibit drawing firm conclusions about whether parental involvement in early intervention programs is either necessary or sufficient to achieve long-term gains (Gray & Wandersman, 1980). For example, the usual measures of outcome (e.g., IQ tests) may not identify the most beneficial outcomes of parental involvement, such as improved family functioning. Additionally, the *degree* of parental involvement in a program is critical for achieving benefits, but rarely described in the literature. Finally, it is likewise unresolved which *type* of parental participation may be most beneficial. Some programs are curriculum-focused, with the goal of strengthening the parents' role as educators of their child, whereas others are interaction-focused, with the goal of improving the parent–child relationship (Affleck, McGrade, McQueeny, & Allen, 1982).

Some authors have cautioned that parental participation in early intervention programs can also have negative consequences. Bromwich (1979), for example, warned that programs may actually lower parental self-esteem by fostering a dependence on specialists. Winton and Turnbull (1981) found that 21 of 31 mothers preferred *informal* rather than *formal* involvement with their child's intervention program. These women viewed respite from their caretaking responsibilities as a major benefit of intervention programs. Finally, Tyler, Kogan, and Turner (1974) found more negative affect expressed by mothers and children when the mother adopted the role of therapist with her child.

Despite these caveats and the absence of definitive empirical support, most clinicians agree that active parental participation should be fostered during the initial assessment and that it is an important element for the success of any ongoing intervention, including physical therapy (Gross, Eudy, & Drabman, 1982), occupational therapy (Anderson & Hinojosa, 1984), and educational programs (Welsh & Odum, 1981). A goal of the assessment process should be to identify those parents for whom intervention duties would prove constructive and those for whom a limited role would be more beneficial.

Whatever the goal for parental participation in their child's intervention program, an assessment affords the opportunity to empower and support them in their role as the child's most important caregivers. This can be achieved by explicitly acknowledging during the assessment that it is the parents, not the assessor or intervention program, who are really the crucial figures in the child's life. The examiner can also explore and validate the parents' perceptions of their child. Although parents tend to rate their child's intelligence or abilities slightly higher than do teachers (Gradel, Thompson, & Sheehan, 1981), there is still a high concordance in their assessments of young children (Blacher-Dixon & Simeonsson, 1981). A therapeutically oriented assessment supports the parents, whenever possible, as trusted and accurate observers of their child's abilities.

Finally, parents can be encouraged to facilitate their child's performance during the formal testing session. They may even administer selected items of the test to best elicit certain skills. This helps the parents to see themselves as a valuable resource for professionals and increases their confidence in their ability to play a significant role in the ongoing assessment and therapeutic processes.

Modeling constructive interactions with the child

Because most parents are vigilant observers of all aspects of the assessment process, there is great potential for the evaluator's behaviors to serve as a model for them. A growing body of literature supports modeling as one of the most effective means of teaching parents how to deal with their children. For example, modeling has proven superior to the use of written manuals or verbal instructions in teaching parents ways to provide positive reinforcement for their child (O'Dell et al., 1982) and in utilizing the "time-out" technique for disciplining their child (Flanagan, Adams, & Forehand, 1979).

Hudson (1982) compared different programs designed to train parents how to modify target behaviors of their handicapped children and found that modeling enabled parents to be more successful than did verbal instructions. Minor, Minor, and Williams (1983) compared an experimental program for parents using participatory modeling in the techniques of early intervention with a standard program utilizing only verbal instructions. After 5 months of training, the children in the experimental group showed significantly higher developmental gains than did the control group. The authors suggested that modeling taught the parents new methods of working with their children, increased their self-confidence as teachers, and allowed for greater generalization to other areas of the parent–child interaction.

The behavior of professionals can be of significant value as a model for parents of constructive ways to interact with their child. When parents observe the evaluator eliciting the child's best performance during the formal testing or demonstrating consistent and effective limit-setting techniques, they may consciously or unconsciously incorporate these approaches in their own interactions with their child. Evaluators must remain aware that *how* they interact with the child may be of more significance for parents than *what* is actually done.

THE STAGES OF THE ASSESSMENT PROCESS

The assessment process is composed of the following six stages:

1. Formation of a therapeutic alliance
2. History taking
3. Informal observations
4. Formal test administration
5. Formulation of the child's strengths and weaknesses
6. Feedback and discussion

During each of these stages, special opportunities exist to support therapeutic goals and enhance long-term outcomes.

Formation of a therapeutic alliance

A therapeutic alliance between parents and service providers is a prerequisite for any successful intervention. All subsequent steps in the assessment and intervention process may be facilitated or hindered by the nature of the relationship established during the initial assessment. For example, parental dissatisfaction with a professional encounter diminishes compliance with subsequent professional recommendations (Cadman, Shurvell, Davies, & Bradfield, 1984; Francis, Korsch, & Morris, 1969) and increases parental "shopping" behaviors for alternative diagnoses and treatments (Anderson, 1974).

There are many ways to form a therapeutic alliance. It is useful to begin an assessment with a comment recognizing the parents as individuals with needs and interests of their own (Korsch, 1987). Parental satisfaction with a medical visit and subsequent compliance with recommendations has been demonstrated to be related to the amount of time spent by professionals being friendly and discussing nonclinical topics (Pantell, Stewart, Dias, Wells, & Ross, 1982). By acknowledging them as more than merely the child's parents, a professional can set a respectful and empathic tone for the rest of the evaluation.

Following a description of the goals and structure of the session, parents should be encouraged to voice their hopes and expectations for the session. Redman-Bentley (1982) interviewed 66 parents who had preschool children with a variety of developmental disabilities and elicited their expectations for professional encounters. She found that parents wanted (in order of importance): to have a say in the decision-making process, to have diagnostic results explained, to be provided with instructions on how to care for their child, to be kept informed of their child's progress, to be informed of the purpose of treatment measures, and to have their role in the treatment process explained.

Although parents may have clear expectations for the assessment, Korsch, Gozzi, and Francis (1968) found that patients explicitly verbalized these expectations to a physician in only 35% of visits. At the same time, patient satisfaction with the visit depend, in large part, on whether these expectations had been addressed by the professional. It is critical to actively elicit and address the parents' expectations for the assessment process in order to avoid unrealistic hopes and fears, and to establish mutually agreeable goals.

The therapeutic alliance is furthered by the maintenance of a non-judgmental demeanor toward the parents throughout the assessment (Green, 1984). Parents should not be given reason to believe that the evaluator views them as incompetent, inaccurate, mean-spirited, or unobservant. All parental questions and comments must receive a respectful and thoughtful response. If parents sense disapproval, they will find it difficult to form a bond with the evaluator and are less likely to participate in the assessment process.

Finally, evaluators must avoid clinical jargon and the use of words or concepts that parents do not understand. Korsch et al. (1968) found technical language to be a barrier to communication in more than half of the studied encounters. The use of jargon serves to distance parents from evaluators (Mathews, 1983). For example, such commonly used terms as "work-up," "expressive and receptive language," "muscle tone," "information processing," "central nervous system," "range of motion," and "etiology" may be confusing to parents who are often too embarrassed or intimidated to ask their meanings. In a study of 234 parents of children with learning disabilities, the most frequent recommendation offered by parents to the psychologists who tested their children was, "Use terminology we can understand!" (Dembinski & Mauser, 1977).

History taking

The process of forming a relationship continues during the history taking. Parents initially may believe that they should limit their remarks to specific areas of their child's developmental or behavioral functioning, and that it is inappropriate to bring up their feelings, worries, or hopes during an assessment. It is during the history taking that the professional can broaden the range of acceptable topics for discussion by addressing the parents' concerns regarding their child, themselves, and their family.

Issues that may be especially relevant to parents of children with disabilities can be found in the Questionnaire on Resources and Stress (QRS) (Holroyd, 1974). This questionaire explores the impact of a disabled or chronically ill child on his or her parents and other family members. A list of the content areas of the questionnaire follows.

Parent problems
1. Poor health or mood
2. Excess time demands
3. Negative attitudes toward child
4. Overprotectiveness or dependency
5. Lack of social support
6. Overcommitment or martyrdom
7. Pessimism

Family problems
8. Lack of family integration
9. Limits on family opportunity
10. Financial problems

Child problems
11. Physical incapacitation
12. Lack of activities
13. Occupational limitations
14. Social obtrusiveness
15. Difficult personality characteristics

Each of these areas has been validated as important to many families of children with a disability (Friedrich & Friedrich, 1981).

Increased stress, for example, is commonly seen in families of children with a disability. Beckman (1983) related the degree of parental stress to specific behavioral characteristics of the child. She found that parents experienced the most stress if their child was relatively unresponsive to the environment, possessed a difficult temperament, manifested repetitive behavior patterns, and/or engendered burdensome or unusual caregiving demands. The behaviors of the child that exacerbate family stress should be explored in the history taking.

Likewise, other factors that affect family adaptation may be discussed. These include socioeconomic status (Nihira, Mink, & Meyers, 1981), social support (Friedrich & Friedrich, 1981), religious beliefs (Zuk, Miller, Bartram, & Kling, 1961), the parents' preexisting personality characteristics (Gath, 1977), and the stability of the marriage (Friedrich, 1979). As an example, the impact of the child's problems on marital functioning may be touched upon during the history taking. Farber (1968) found marital disintegration to be a frequent feature of families with handicapped children. Friedrich and Friedrich (1981) also showed lower marital satisfaction for parents with handicapped children, compared to a control group. A study by Waisbren (1980), on the other hand, could not demonstrate a deleterious effect of a child with special needs on the quality of the marriage. Such variability suggests that the effects on the marital relationship associated with the birth of a child with a disability are influenced by many factors. These have been shown to include the severity of the disability, the age of the child, the preexisting nature of the marriage, the individual coping styles of the parents, and their support systems (Crnic, Friedrich, & Greenberg, 1983). In some cases the marital relationship may actually be strengthened by such a shared experience. Sultz, Schlesinger, and Mosher (1961) found such a positive effect in 26% of the 390 families they studied. Knowledge of the quality of the parents' marriage may prove to be a key factor in understanding the child's needs and devising an effective treatment plan.

Parental feelings regarding the assessment process itself may also be important to elicit, especially when the child has had previous evaluations. Most parents of children with mental retardation regard the initial diagnostic evaluation of their child as unsatisfactory (Abramson, Gravink, Abramson, & Sommers, 1977; Wolfensberger & Kurtz, 1974). Subsequent assessments may be approached by these parents with feelings of anger or fear that derive from their negative past experiences. By explicitly addressing these feelings, parents are given the license to ventilate their past grievances toward professionals and lessen their tendency to project these feelings onto the current evaluation.

Any, all, or none of these issues may be pursued in depth during the history-taking process. Clinical judgment is always needed to distinguish when it is appropriate to expand and when to narrow the content of the discussions. The professional must be aware that some parents find it helpful to discuss their feelings, whereas others experience personal questions as intrusive and unnecessary. Bloch (1978) cautioned that aggressive, insensitive history taking can lead to heightened parental anxiety and uncertainty:

We do not confront parents with their denial or anger or seek to elicit their feelings about their child's handicap, although we do not avoid opportunities to enable both mother and father to make contact with and express their painful inner feelings. The intent of our contacts during this first stage is to support parents, to begin the process of problem-solving, and to reduce unproductive parental preoccupations with guilt and etiology (p. 6).

The key to helping families during the history taking is an awareness of what, how, and when to probe, and, equally important, when to inhibit discussion and wait for cues from the parents to explore a potentially sensitive area.

Informal observations

The traditional goal of a developmental assessment is to quantify a child's performance by administering and scoring a standardized test. However, equally valuable information can be gathered during informal observations made before, during, and after the testing. The parent–child interactions and behaviors may be more spontaneous and less self-conscious when relatively unstructured. Critical aspects of their relationship, such as warmth, controlling or rejecting behaviors (Ricci, 1970), and attachment behaviors (Blacher & Meyers, 1983; Kogan, Tyler, & Turner, 1974) may be best revealed during informal observations.

Careful observation of a child's behavior before beginning the formal testing can make the difference between a successful and unsuccessful evaluation. For example, a child who is observed to be hypersensitive to environmental stimulation may require a low-key style for successful test administration. The child's coping strategies and self-esteem, for example, may become apparent during early observations as the child interacts with the parents, evaluator, and the novel setting into which he or she is thrust. The following list outlines some of the parent and child behaviors that can be noted throughout the assessment. These observations may affect not only the way in which the assessment is conducted, but how the test results are integrated into an understanding of the whole child.

Attachment behaviors (child)
1. Does the child use the parents as a secure base from which to explore the environment?
2. Does the child look to the parents for positive or negative responses to his or her behavior?
3. Does the child appear to expect to be praised or punished by the parents for his or her behaviors?
4. Is the child distressed if the parents leave the room?
5. Does the child respond more positively to the parents than the evaluator?

Attachment behaviors (parent)
1. Are the parents warm to the child during the exam?
2. Do the parents avidly watch the child's performance or are they indifferent?
3. Do the parents take pleasure in the child's successes or appear worried at the child's failures?
4. Do the parents appear angry with the child?
5. Are the parents attuned to the child's needs?

Coping style
1. How does the child deal with the stress of the assessment?
2. Does the child withdraw, regress, act out, tantrum, or the like when stressed?
3. Do the child's coping mechanisms enhance or detract from his or her performance?
4. What seems most stressful to the child?

Self-esteem
1. Is the child pleased with himself or herself completing a task?
2. Does the child behave as if he or she anticipates praise from the environment?
3. Does the child persist in attempting to perform tasks beyond his or her level, or does the child immediately give up?

Formal test administration

Most assessments employ formal tests to evaluate a child's functioning. However, focusing solely on the quantitative scores of these tests overlooks a great deal of valuable information. For example, a child may be labeled as "untestable" because he or she refuses to participate in the examination. Although this refusal indicates an inability to respond well to the structure of the test itself, important areas can nonetheless be observed and evaluated, such as the child's attentional ability, learning style, sense of mastery, emotional development, self-help, and socialization skills.

For the experienced evaluator, a standarized test establishes only the structure and content by which a child's specific task-oriented abilities and behaviors can be observed. It is the clinical acumen of the evaluator that allows an equally detailed assessment of the *quality* of these abilities. For example, one child who fails to perform a task may persist in attempts to succeed, whereas another passively accepts the failure and ceases all efforts. Conversely, two children may succeed in a task although one has performed it with confidence, the other quite tentatively. These children may generate identical test scores, but their qualitative differences may imply different prognoses and individualized intervention plans.

Formulation of the child's strengths and weaknesses

A child's development and behavior must be understood in the context of the ecology of his or her world. This requires integrating all of the phases of the assessment process and formulating a comprehensive list of the child's strengths and weaknesses. By highlighting the child's strengths, the assessment can allow parents room for cautious optimism, if appropriate, and promote their adaptation by pointing out positive features of their child's functioning. Identification of the child's strengths can also enhance the treatment plan by building on those strengths to circumvent the weaknesses.

The assessment process should also be used to evaluate the parents' ability to fulfill any therapeutic responsibilities. For example, if maternal depression adversely affects the mother's ability to care for her child, then ameliorating the depression must be high on the intervention agenda before participation in her child's intervention program will prove productive (Zuckerman & Beardslee, 1987). To be effective, a therapeutic plan must be informed by an assessment of the family's ability to provide help for the child.

An integrated approach to assessment mandates a more comprehensive approach to intervention. If a child is malnourished and hungry, for example, most therapies will be ineffective. If the environment is understimulating, 2 hours of specialized therapy per week are unlikely to ameliorate the deficits. A complete assessment evaluates all salient aspects of the child's functioning and places them in the context of his or her caretaking environment. Only after such an assessment can the intervention plan be comprehensive enough to provide the necessary supports to promote optimal development.

Feedback and discussion

The feedback and discussion between the parents and the professional mark the culmination of the assessment process. This dialogue is the time when diagnostic, prognostic, and therapeutic issues are addressed explicitly. As such, it is also the most stressful of all the stages of the assessment for parents (Bernheimer, Young, & Winton, 1983) and may even have a long-term impact on the way they adjust to their child (Springer & Steele, 1980). Despite its importance, studies have consistently shown that approximately one-half of parents are dissatisfied with the feedback they received from their disabled child's initial assessment (Abramson et al., 1977; Bernheimer et al., 1983; Koch, Graliker, Sands, & Parmelee, 1959; Quine & Pahl, 1987).

Frequent parental dissatisfaction with the way in which they were first informed of their child having Down syndrome has been especially well documented (Gayton &

Walker, 1974; Pueschel & Murphy, 1976; Quine & Pahl, 1987). In response to this finding, Cunningham, Morgan, and McGucken (1984) devised a model program to communicate this diagnosis to parents. The key elements of their program were that the diagnosis was transmitted to the family as soon as possible, both parents were told at the same time, a private place was utilized for the discussion, the infant was present during the discussion, there was unlimited time for questions, various support services were offered, and a follow-up interview was scheduled. Parental satisfaction with this method of learning the diagnosis was reported at 100%, compared to 20% for the group of parents who received the diagnosis via the usual practice. This study confirmed that parental satisfaction with the manner in which negative diagnostic and prognostic information is given can be markedly increased by an approach that is sensitive to their needs.

Down syndrome represents a diagnosis of established risk with a predictable range of long-term outcomes. However, even experienced clinicians have difficulty communicating information to parents when the etiology and prognosis of the child's condition are uncertain (Lipton & Svarstad, 1977). Under such circumstances, one study found 69% of the parents sampled were dissatisfied with the feedback they received (Quine & Pahl, 1987). The authors found that professionals withheld more information, made more insensitive comments, and provided more inaccurate information to parents when either the diagnosis or prognosis was uncertain.

The success of the feedback stage is built upon the previous stages of the assessment process (Stacey, 1980). Parents are more accepting of ambiguous professional feedback when it is presented in an empathic and encouraging way (Wasserman, Invi, Barriatua, Carter, & Lippincott, 1984). If a therapeutic alliance has been established prior to feedback, it is easier for both evaluator and parents to discuss and accept clinical uncertainty.

A goal of the feedback stage may be to help parents cope with the ambiguity of the diagnosis or prognosis, rather than convey a sense of certainty in order to allay their anxiety. The clinician must also achieve a balance between offering overly optimistic predictions, thereby creating unrealistic parental expectations, and underestimating the child's potential outcome, thereby generating self-fulfilling negative prophecies. The therapeutic alliance is better served by acknowledging the inherent ambiguities of any developmental assessment (Calnan, 1984) than by feigning certainty or providing empty reassurance. Parents can better tolerate clinical ambiguity if they know that they will not be abandoned by professionals and that there is an ongoing process that will ultimately provide more definitive answers.

Other important influences on parents' satisfaction with feedback from assessments have been identified. These include the adequacy of the provider's rationale for therapy, how well the parent was listened to during the assessment, and the amount of time set aside for discussion of the findings (Cadman et al., 1984). Some parents, however, continue to deny the intended messages, regardless of how sensitively and repetitively they are presented. Waller, Todres, Cassem, & Anderten (1979) suggest sharing prognostic information with parents according to the following guidelines:

1. Information concerning prognosis is best given to parents when they request it;
2. Information should be presented with tact and sensitivity, and with regard to how the parents will react;
3. Clinicians must acknowledge their uncertainty about the future;
4. Parents should be asked to describe the nature of their current understanding about the prognosis before new information is given;
5. Parents should be offered emotional support to help complete their grief work.

In helping parents to come to terms with their child's disabilities, diagnostic terms and future outcomes must be addressed. At the same time, the evaluator must remain aware of the benefits and dangers of affixing labels to the child. In cases where the diagnosis is clear, parents may need to hear the words "mental retardation" or "cerebral palsy" in order to understand and accept their child's condition. When such emotionally charged terms are used, however, the evaluator is obligated to explain exactly what they mean. Many parents have inaccurate and distorted perceptions of the meaning of diagnostic terms (Sherman, Austrian, & Shapiro, 1981; Svarstad & Lipton, 1977; Wolfensberger & Kurtz, 1974). The term "cerebral palsy", for example, may conjure up images only of the most severely handicapped child, even though the child in question actually may have a mild disability. In such a case, the evaluator must explain the wide range of outcomes encompassed by the term cerebral palsy and ensure that parental misconceptions have been dispelled.

An assessment should always end with the evaluator asking the parents to recapitulate what they have learned from the assessment process. Professionals should never assume that the parents have grasped all that was observed or understood all that was discussed. By asking the parents what they have learned from the process, the key points can be reiterated. As it began, the assessment can then close with a statement that acknowledges the importance and worth of the parents, and supports them in their future efforts. The assessment process thus comes full circle as it initiates and promotes the therapeutic interventions to follow.

SUMMARY AND IMPLICATIONS

In the past, many developmental assessments focused on singular areas of functioning. The rigid administration of standardized tests and a lack of breadth and depth in content areas were the hallmarks of such assessments. This led to fragmented views of a child's functioning and to a neglect of the larger environmental context in which he or she operated. It was difficult to devise an integrated and comprehensive intervention program based on such incomplete information about the child. Furthermore, by compartmentalizing the child in this way, a valuable opportunity was lost to benefit families by way of the assessment process itself.

Assessments must expand their goals in order for the intervention process to afford families maximum therapeutic outcomes. An assessment should address a wide range of child and parent behaviors, and these content areas must then be placed in the broader context of the child's entire experiential world. To neglect the emotional state of the family during an assessment, for example, is to ignore an aspect of the child's life that may ultimately have a larger impact on his or her developmental outcomes than will any test performance. An opportunity is also lost to connect empathically with a family who might derive immediate and long-term benefits from such a therapeutic relationship. Finally, an insensitively conducted assessment may prove destructive to both child and family by promoting a distrust of professionals, a purely pathological view of the child's problems, a misunderstanding of the diagnosis and prognosis, increased family stress, a dismantling of necessary defense mechanisms, and poor compliance with the treatment plan.

The distinction between assessment and intervention is an arbitrary one. The assessment process itself should seek to enhance parents' understanding of their child, improve the fit between the parents' caretaking style and the child's behaviors, empower and support the parents in their crucial role as the child's most significant caregivers, and model constructive ways to interact with the child. By addressing those aspects of the child's world that traditionally have been the province of separate disciplines, this model challenges all professionals to transcend the narrow focus of their particular specialty. The outcome of such an approach can provide immediate therapeutic benefits for families and more comprehensive information to assist the intervention team in planning integrated, coherent, and effective treatment plans.

REFERENCES

Abramson, P., Gravink, M., Abramson, L., & Sommers, D. (1977). Early diagnosis and intervention of retardation: A survey of parental reactions concerning the quality of services rendered. *Mental Retardation, 15,* 28–31.

Affleck, G., McGrade, B., McQueeny, B., & Allen, D. (1982). Promise of relationship-focused early intervention in developmental disabilities. *Journal of Special Education, 16,* 413–430.

Anderson, J., & Hinojosa, J. (1984). Parents and therapists in a professional partnership. *American Journal of Occupational Therapy, 38,* 452–462.

Anderson, K. (1974). Mothers of retarded children who shop for professional help. *Clinical Pediatrics, 13,* 159–161.

Beckman, P. (1983). Influence of selected child characteristics on stress in families of handicapped infants. *American Journal of Mental Deficiency, 88,* 150–156.

Belsky, J. (1985). Experimenting with the family in the newborn period. *Child Development, 56,* 407–414.

Belsky, J. (1986). A tale of two variances: Between and within. *Child Development, 7,* 1301–1305.

Bernheimer, L., Young, M., & Winton, P. (1983). Stress over time: Parents with young handicapped children. *Journal of Developmental and Behavioral Pediatrics, 4,* 177–181.

Blacher, J. (1984). Sequential stages of parental adjustment to the birth of a child with handicaps: Fact or artifact?. *Mental Retardation, 22,* 55–68.

Blacher, J., & Meyers, C. (1983). A review of attachment formation and disorder of handicapped children. *American Journal of Mental Deficiency, 87,* 359–371.

Blacher-Dixon, J., & Simeonsson, R. (1981). Consistency and correspondence of mothers' and teachers' assessment of young handicapped children. *Journal of the Division for Early Childhood, 3,* 64–71.

Bloch, J. (1978). Impaired children: Helping families through the critical period of first identification. *Children Today, 7,* 2–6.

Bray, N., Coleman, J., Bracken, M. (1981). Critical events in parenting handicapped children. *Journal of the Division for Early Childhood, 3,* 26–33.

Brazelton, T. (1984). *Neonatal Behavioral Assessment Scale.* Philadelphia: Lippincott.

Bricker, D., & Casuso, V. (1979). Family involvement: A critical component of early intervention. *Exceptional Children, 46,* 108–115.

Bromwich, R. (1981). *Working with parents and infants: An interactional approach.* Baltimore: University Park Press.

Bronfenbrenner, U. (1974). *Is early intervention effective?* (Publication No. (CHD) 74–25). Washington, DC: Department of Health, Education, and Welfare, Office of Child Development.

Cadman, D., Shurvell, B., Davies, P., & Bradfield, S. (1984). Compliance in the community with consultants' recommendations for developmentally handicapped children. *Developmental Medicine and Child Neurology, 26,* 40–46.

Calnan, M. (1984). Clinical uncertainity: Is it a problem in the doctor–patient relationship? *Sociology of Health and Illness, 6,* 74–85.

Comptroller General's report to the Congress (1979). *Early childhood and family development programs improve the quality of life for low income families* (Report No. HRD-79-40). Washington, DC: U.S. Government Printing Office.

Crnic, K., Friedrich, W., & Greenberg, M. (1983). Adaptation of families with mentally retarded children: A model of stress, coping and family ecology. *American Journal of Mental Deficiency, 88,* 125–138.

Crouchman, M. (1985). What mothers know about their newborns' visual skills. *Developmental Medicine and Child Neurology, 27,* 455–460.

Cummings, S. (1976). The impact of the child's deficiency on the father: A study of fathers of mentally retarded and of chronically ill children. *American Journal of Orthopsychiatry, 46,* 246–255.

Cummings, S., Bayley, H., & Rie, H. (1966). Effects of the child's deficiency on the mother: A study of mentally retarded, chronically ill, and neurotic children. *American Journal of Orthopsychiatry, 36,* 595–608.

Cunningham, C., Morgan, P., & McGucken, R. (1984). Down's syndrome: Is dissatisfaction with disclosure of diagnosis inevitable?. *Developmental Medicine and Child Neurology, 26,* 33–39.

Dembinski, R., & Mauser, A. (1977). What parents of the learning disabled really want from professionals. *Journal of Learning Disabilities, 10,* 49–55.

Drotar, P., Baskiewicz, A., Irvin, N., Kennell, J., & Klaus, M. (1975). The adaptation of parents to the birth of and infant with a congenital malformation: A hypothetical model. *Pediatrics, 56,* 710–717.

Dunlap, W. (1979). How do parents of handicapped children view their needs? *Journal of the Division for Early Childhood, 1,* 1–10.

Emde, R., & Brown, C. (1978). Adaptation to the birth of a Down's syndrome infant. *Journal of the American Academy of Child and Adolescent Psychiatry, 17,* 299–323.

Enzer, N. (1975). Parents as partners in behavior modification. *Journal of Research and Development in Education, 8,* 24–33.

Farber, B. (1968). *Mental retardation: Its social context and social consequences.* Boston: Houghton-Mifflin.

Featherstone, H. (1980). *A difference in the family: Life with a disabled child.* New York: Basic Books.

Flanagan, S., Adams, H., & Forehand, R. (1979). A comparison of four instructional techniques for teaching parents to use time-out. *Behavioral Therapy, 10,* 94–102.

Francis, V., Korsch, B., & Morris, M. (1969). Gaps in doctor–patient communication: Patients' response to medical advice. *New England Journal of Medicine, 280,* 535–540.

Friedrich, W. (1979). Predictors of coping behavior of mothers of handicapped children. *Journal of Consulting and Clinical Psychology, 47,* 1140–1141.

Friedrich, W., & Friedrich, W. (1981). Psychosocial aspects of parents of handicapped and nonhandicapped children. *American Journal of Mental Deficiency, 85,* 551–553.

Gath, A. (1977). The impact of an abnormal child upon the parents. *British Journal of Psychiatry, 130,* 405–410.

Gayton, W., & Walker, L. (1974). Down syndrome: Informing the parents. *American Journal of Diseases of Children, 127,* 510–512.

Geleerd, E. (1965). Two kinds of denial: Neurotic denial and denial in the service of the need to survive. In M. Schur (Ed), *Drives, affects and behavior* (p. 118). New York: International Universities Press.

Goodson, B., & Hess, R. (1975). *Parents as teachers of young children* (DHEW/OE No. ED 136967). Washington, DC: Bureau of Educational Personnel Development.

Gradel, K., Thompson, M., & Sheehan, R. (1981). Parental and professional agreement in early childhood assessment. *Topics in Early Childhood Special Education, 1,* 31–39.

Gray, S., & Wandersman, L. (1980). The methodology of home-based intervention studies: Problems and promising strategies. *Child Development, 51,* 99–109.

Green, M. (1984, October). Interview techniques that get results. *Contemporary Pediatrics,* 52–60.

Gross, A., Eudy, C., & Drabman, R. (1982). Training parents to be physical therapists with their physically handicapped child. *Journal of Behavioral Medicine, 5,* 321–327.

Holroyd, J. (1974). The questionnaire on resources and stress: An instrument to measure family response to a handicapped family member. *Journal of Community Psychology, 2,* 92–94.

Howell, S. (1973). Psychiatric aspects of habilitation. *Pediatric Clinics of North America, 20,* 203–219.

Huber, C. (1979). Parents of the handicapped child: Facilitating acceptance through group counseling. *Personnel and Guidance Journal, 57,* 267–269.

Hudson, A. (1982). Training parents of developmentally handicapped children: A component analysis. *Behavioral Therapy, 13,* 325–333.

Jordan, T. (1962). Research on the handicapped child and the family. *Merrill-Palmer Quarterly, 8,* 243–260.

Kanner, L. (1953). Parents' feelings about retarded children. *American Journal of Mental Deficiency, 57,* 375–383.

Kennedy, J. (1970). Maternal reactions to the birth of a defective baby. *Social Casework, 51,* 410–417.

Koch, R., Graliker, B., Sands, R., & Parmelee, A. (1959). Attitude study of parents with mentally retarded children. *Pediatrics, 23,* 582–584.

Kogan, K., Tyler, N., & Turner, P. (1974). The process of interpersonal adaptation between mothers and their cerebral palsied children. *Developmental Medicine and Child Neurology, 16,* 518–527.

Korsch, B. (1987, January). Strengthening the therapeutic alliance. *Contemporary Pediatrics,* 93–105.

Korsch, B., Gozzi, E., & Francis, V. (1968). Gaps in doctor–patient communication. *Pediatrics, 42,* 855–870.

Lindemann, E. (1944). Symptomatology and management of acute grief. *American Journal of Psychiatry, 101,* 141–148.

Liptak, G., Keller, B., Feldman, A., & Chamberlin, R. (1983). Enhancing infant development and parent–practitioner interaction with the Brazelton Neonatal Assessment Scale. *Pediatrics, 72,* 71–78.

Lipton, H., & Svarstad, B. (1977). Sources of variation in clinicians' communication to parents about mental retardation. *American Journal of Mental Deficiency, 82,* 155–161.

MacKeith, R. (1973). The feelings and behavior of parents of handicapped children. *Developmental Medicine and Child Neurology, 15,* 524–527.

Mandelbaum, A., & Wheeler, M. (1960). The meaning of a defective child to parents. *Social Casework, 41,* 360–367.

Matheny, A., & Vernick, J. (1969). Parents of the mentally retarded child: Emotionally overwhelmed or informationally deprived?. *Journal of Pediatrics, 74,* 953–959.

Mathews, J. (1983). The communication process in clinical settings. *Social Science in Medicine, 17,* 1371–1378.

Menolascino, F. (1968). Parents of the mentally retarded: An operational approach to diagnosis and management. *Journal of the American Academy of Child Psychiatry, 7,* 589–602.

Menolascino, F., & Coleman, R. (1980). The pilot parent program: Helping handicapped children through their parents. *Child Psychiatry and Human Development, 11,* 41–48.

Miller, L. (1968). Toward a greater understanding of the parents of the mentally retarded child. *Journal of Pediatrics, 73,* 699–705.

Minor, S., Minor, J., & Williams, P. (1983). A participant modeling procedure to train parents of developmentally disabled infants. *Journal of Psychology, 115,* 107–111.

Myers, B. (1982). Early intervention using Brazelton training with middle-class mothers and fathers. *Child Development, 52,* 462–471.

Nihira, K., Mink, I., & Meyers, E. (1981). Relationship between home environment and school adjustment of TMR children. *American Journal of Mental Deficiency, 86,* 8–15.

O'Dell, S., O'Quin, J., Alford, B., O'Briant, A., Bradlyn, A., & Giebenhain, J. (1982). Predicting the acquisition of parenting skills via four training methods. *Behavioral Therapy, 13,* 194–208.

Olshansky, S. (1962). Chronic sorrow: A response to having a mentally defective child. *Social Casework, 43,* 190–193.

Pantell, R., Stewart, T., Dias, J., Wells, P., & Ross, A. (1982). Physician communication with children and parents. *Pediatrics, 70,* 396–402.

Pueschel, S., & Murphy, A. (1976). Assessment of counseling practices at the birth of a child with Down's syndrome. *American Journal of Mental Deficiency, 81,* 325–330.

Quine, L., & Pahl, J. (1987). First diagnosis of severe handicap. A study of parental reactions. *Developmental Medicine and Child Neurology, 29,* 232–242.

Redman-Bentley, D. (1982). Parent expectations for professionals providing services to their handicapped children. *Physical and Occupational Therapy in Pediatrics, 2,* 13–27.

Ricci, C. (1970). Analysis of child-rearing attitudes of mothers of retarded, emotionally disturbed, and normal children. *American Journal of Mental Deficiency, 74,* 756–761.

Sherman, M., Austrian, R., & Shapiro, T. (1981). Labeling and unlabeling: Perceptions of diagnostic terms among mothers and professionals. *Developmental and Behavioral Pediatrics, 2,* 93–96.

Shonkoff, J., & Hauser-Cram, P. (1987). Early intervention for disabled infants and their families: A quantitative analysis. *Pediatrics, 80,* 650–658.

Sieffert, A. (1978). Parents' initial reactions to having a mentally retarded child: A concept and model for social workers. *Clinical Social Work Journal, 6,* 33–43.

Solnit, A., & Stark, M. (1961). Mourning and the birth of a defective child. *Psychoanalytic Study of the Child, 16,* 523–537.

Springer, A., & Steele, M. (1980). Effects of physicians' early parental counseling on rearing Down's Syndrome children. *American Journal of Mental Deficiency, 85*, 4–15.

Stacey, M. (1980). Charisma, power, and altruism: A discussion of research in a child development center. *Sociology of Health and Illness, 2*, 64–85.

Stein, H. (1988). *The effects of infant developmental assessment on the mother's understanding of infant behavior and development*. Unpublished dissertation.

Strom, R., Rees, R., Slaughter, H., & Wurster, S. (1981). Child rearing expectations of families with atypical children. *American Journal of Orthopsychiatry, 51*, 285–295.

Sultz, H., Schlesinger, E., & Mosher, W. (1961). *Long-term Childhood Illness*. Pittsburgh: University of Pittsburgh Press.

Svarstad, B., & Lipton, H. (1977). Informing parents about mental retardation: A study of professional communication and parent acceptance. *Social Science in Medicine, 11*, 645–651.

Thomas, A., & Chess, S. (1984). Genesis and evolution of behavioral disorders: From infancy to early adult life. *American Journal of Psychiatry, 141*, 1–9.

Turnbull, A., & Turnbull, H. (Eds.). (1978). *Parents speak out*. Columbus, OH: Merrill.

Tyler, N., Kogan, K., & Turner, P. (1974). Interpersonal components of therapy with young cerebral palsied children. *American Journal of Occupational Therapy, 28*, 395–400.

Waisbren, S. (1980). Parents' reaction to the birth of a developmentally disabled child. *American Journal of Mental Deficiency, 84*, 345–351.

Waller, D., Todres, D., Cassem, N., & Anderten, A. (1979). Coping with poor prognosis in the pediatric intensive care unit. *American Journal of Diseases of Children, 133*, 1121–1125.

Wasserman, R., Invi, T., Barriatua, R., Carter, W., & Lippincott, P. (1984). Pediatric clinicians' support for parents makes a difference: An outcome-based analysis of clinician–parent interaction. *Pediatrics, 74*, 1047–1053.

Welsh, M., & Odum, C. (1981). Parent involvement in the education of the handicapped child: A review of the literature. *Journal of the Division for Early Childhood, 3*, 15–25.

White, K., & Casto, G. (1985). An integrative review of early intervention efficacy studies with at-risk children: Implications for the handicapped. *Analysis and Intervention in Developmental Disabilities, 5*, 7–31.

Widmayer, S., & Field, T. (1981). Effects of Brazelton demonstrations for mothers on the development of preterm infants. *Pediatrics, 67*, 711–714.

Wikler, L. (1981). Chronic stresses of families of mentally retarded children. *Family Relations, 30*, 281–288.

Wikler, L., Wasow, M., & Hatfield, E. (1981). Chronic sorrow revisited: Parent vs. professional depiction of the adjustment of parents of mentally retarded children. *American Journal of Orthopsychiatry, 51*, 63–70.

Willner, S., & Crane, R. (1979). A parental dilemma: The child with a marginal handicap. *Social Casework, 60*, 30–35.

Winton, P., & Turnbull, A. (1981). Parent involvement as viewed by parents of preschool handicapped children. *Topics in Early Childhood Special Education, 1*, 11–19.

Wolfensberger, W., & Kurtz, R. (1974). Use of retardation-related diagnostic and descriptive labels by parents of retarded children. *Journal of Specdial Education, 8*, 131–142.

Worobey, J., & Belsky, J. (1982). Employing the Brazelton to influence mothering: An experimental comparison of three strategies. *Developmental Psychology, 18*, 736–743.

Worobey, J., & Brazelton, T. (1986). Experimenting with the family in the newborn period: A commentary. *Child Development, 57*, 1298–1300.

Wright, L. (1976). Chronic grief: The anguish of being an exceptional parent. *Exceptional Child, 23*, 160–169.

Zuckerman, B., & Beardslee, W. (1987). Maternal depression: An issue for pediatricians. *Pediatrics, 79*, 110–117.

Zuk, G., Miller, R., Bartram, J., & Kling, F. (1961). Maternal acceptance of retarded children: A questionnaire of attitudes and religious background. *Child Development, 32*, 525–540.

PART V

Models of service delivery

16 *Early intervention programs: Child-focused approaches*

DIANE BRICKER AND MARGARET VELTMAN

INTRODUCTION

Comparing contemporary early intervention programs with the status of service delivery 20 years ago is exhilarating. In the early 1960s, intervention programs were unavailable for infants and young children with disabilities. Parents whose children were identified as being disabled during these early years were generally advised to institutionalize their youngsters. Today, progressive state and federal legislation, most recently the passage of Public Law 99-457, has left few communities without early intervention programs – programs that permit children to remain with their families and to work toward the development of independent functioning. In a period of just two decades, the field of early intervention has made significant progress toward becoming an important component in the public education and health care service systems.

The authors of this chapter have been asked to review and analyze child-focused early intervention programs, including only those early intervention programs that provide "a systematic and planned effort to promote development through a series of manipulations of environmental or experiential factors initiated during the first 5 years of life" (Guaralnick & Bennett, 1987, p. 19). In addition, the review is limited to programs that primarily serve children with developmental disabilities. Programs for children determined to be "at risk" for developmental delay because of biological and/or environmental factors are not included. Finally, this review is directed to describing early intervention programs or aspects of programs that are focused on the child. Other chapters in this volume describe caregiver-focused and family-system–focused programs (see Seitz & Provence, this volume; Simeonsson & Bailey, this volume).

Given the indicated orientation, this chapter has five purposes: (1) to discuss the theoretical underpinnings of child-focused early intervention programs; (2) to identify an associated set of assumptions related to program development; (3) to identify common elements in child-focused early intervention programs; (4) to provide a general analysis of selected program practices; and (5) to briefly discuss programmatic

Preparation of this chapter was provided, in part, by a grant (G008400748) from the Office of Special Education Programs to the Center on Human Development, University of Oregon.
The authors would like to thank Angela Notari for her helpful editing of the manuscript and Karen Lawrence for preparation of the manuscript.

changes that may enhance the quality of services provided to infants and children with handicaps.

An examination of the early intervention literature, observations of programs, and conversations with interventionists as well as researchers indicate that child-focused programs have evolved from a set of widely held sociopolitical positions and theoretical assumptions. Two theoretical assumptions appear to have provided the basic rationale for the development of child-focused early intervention programs: (1) genetic and biological problems can be overcome or attenuated, and (2) early experience is important to children's development. Without believing that it is possible to overcome and/or reduce the impact of a handicapping condition, little justification exists for intervention. Further, one must acknowledge the potential importance of development during the first years of life if intervention efforts during a child's early years are to be encouraged and supported.

During the late 1800s and early 1900s, many authorities responsible for the management of handicapped people held positions of predeterminism or genetic determinism (Sarason & Doris, 1969). Major tenets of these views are that development is dictated by an individual's inherent genetic constitution, and that environmental conditions are of little consequence in the development of intelligence and personality (see Matarazzo, 1972, for discussions of heredity and IQ). Acceptance of genetic determinism negates the importance of a child's formative years and the importance of experience in shaping developmental outcomes, and leads logically to the establishment of facilities that offer custodial rather than rehabilitative treatment (Wolfensberger, 1969). Compensatory and rehabilitative programs for poverty and disabled groups were not initiated in earnest until alternative philosophical and theoretical positions stressing the importance of the environment gained acceptance.

In particular, early intervention programs began to develop when genetic determinism was replaced by a more optimistic theoretical perspective that emphasized the importance of environmental influences on young children. Data suggesting the plasticity of the nervous system (Issacson, 1976; St. James-Roberts, 1979) and the influence of the environment on the human organism (Dennis, 1963; Erdman & Olson, 1966; Hunt, 1961; Skeels, 1966; Young, 1969) supported theoretical positions that were consonant with the initiation of intervention efforts during children's early years.

The two theoretical assumptions that provide the rationale for early intervention programs serve to generate other theoretical positions specific to program development:

1. Children with developmental problems require more and/or different early experience from nondisabled age-mates.
2. Formal programs with trained personnel are necessary to provide the required early experience to compensate for developmental problems.
3. Developmental progress is enhanced in children with handicaps who participate in early intervention programs.

Figure 1 is a schematic of the two theoretical assumptions that provide the basic rationale for early intervention programs and the three associated theoretical assumptions that underlie program development. The schematic illustrates how the notions of children needing and benefiting from formally structured programs evolve from the general premises that early experience is important and that environmental arrange-

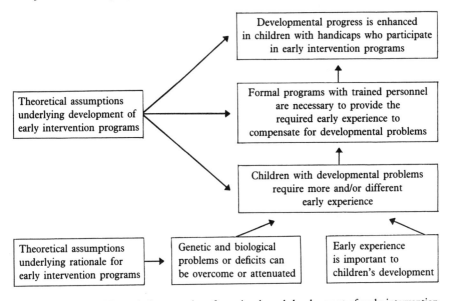

Figure 1. Theoretical assumptions for rationale and development of early intervention programs

ments can compensate for or attenuate biological deficits. The requirement of a formal structure then provides the basis for further program development. A formal structure implies that instructional strategies derived from developmental theory are applied systematically by trained interventionists to facilitate behavior change.

THEORETICAL GUIDELINES FOR CHILD LEARNING

In addition to theoretical assumptions that provide the basis for program rationale and program development, theory has provided a number of useful guidelines for infant and child learning within intervention programs, for example:

> The central nervous system must be aroused,
> Attention must be focused,
> Active participation must occur,
> Learning is facilitated through environmental manipulation that produces disequilibrium in children.

The arousal of the nervous system is implicated in learning because children's attention and responsivity to visual, auditory, vestibular, and other stimuli is related to the child's physiological state (Bell, 1974; Gardner & Karmel, 1983; Wilson, 1980). Young children have the capacity to respond to stimuli by changing state, and to control a stimulus (e.g., caregiver attention) by prolonging it. There also appear to be states of arousal that are optimal for certain activities. Alert inactivity, for instance, has been suggested as the optimal state for learning in infants (Clarke-Stewart & Koch, 1983; Korner, 1979). In visually alert states, infants will usually fixate and pursue objects visually (Korner, 1974). An infant who is quiet and alert will smile at the sound of an inanimate object, human voice, or game of pat-a-cake. A child who is irritable may cry when subjected to the same stimuli (Sherrod, Vietze, & Friedman, 1978). Als, Lester, and Brazelton (1979) have suggested that preterm infants can be easily over-aroused, whereas handicapped children such as those with Down syndrome appear to have arousal deficits that interfere with efficient interactions (Richard, 1986). The role of arousal in learning and its effect on responsiveness has also been mentioned as a worthwhile line of inquiry for educators working with students experiencing profound handicaps (Rainforth, 1982).

Another theory-derived guideline that is related to physiological state of arousal is the notion that the child's attention must be focused. The significance of attentional behavior to a child's development is common to many theoretical positions. Theorists who suggest that the mother–infant relationship forms the basis for the child's subsequent psychological growth claim attentive behavior as a component of early mother–child interaction (Brazelton, Koslowski, & Main, 1974).

There is wide variability in the attentional capabilities of young children, but the reason for this is not yet clear (Rothbart, 1984). Sigman (1983) notes that "those infants who cannot maintain their attention to salient stimuli for even brief periods must be handicapped if this behavior is maintained" (p. 290). In contrast, attentive full-term infants cry less and are talked to more by their mothers, whereas preterm children tend to be either overly attentive to moderately salient stimuli (Sigman, 1983) or less actively engaged (Goldberg & DiVitto, 1983).

In a study of the attention and exploratory behavior of infants with Down syndrome, Vietze, McCarthy, McQuiston, MacTurk, and Yarrow (1983) reported that a disproportionately high amount of visual attention was displayed by children with Down syndrome as compared to normal infants who participated in a previous study. Krakow and Kopp (1982) found that the quantity of attention in children with Down syndrome was comparable to that of normal controls, but the play patterns of the subjects with Down syndrome were repetitive and stereotypic. Vietze et al. (1983) also reported that decreases in visual attention in their subjects were accompanied by increases in manual exploration. Attention deficits have also been implicated in the cognitive difficulties experienced by persons with mental retardation (Thurman & Widerstrom, 1985).

Another theory-based guideline suggests that active participation is a prerequisite for infant or child learning. Most interventionists appear to operate under the assumption that active participation of the child is necessary for the acquisition of new responses or the modification of existing behavior. Whether inspired by the Piagetian contention of constructivism (Flavell, 1977), the behavior analyst's position of active responding (Brinker, 1985), or Dewey's thoughts on learning by doing (Dewey, 1916), most programs are designed to elicit the active involvement of children. Considerable documentation is available on the early capabilities of infants to participate actively in environmental events. Newborns can actively discriminate stimuli (Fantz, 1973; Flavell, 1985; Sherrod et al., 1978; Warren & Rogers-Warren, 1982) and participate as partners in interactions with primary caregivers (Bell, 1974; Tronick, 1980). Where children have been deprived of active roles in controlling environmental events, deleterious effects on development are noted or suspected (Jennings, Connors, Stegman, Sankaranarayan & Mendelsohn, 1985; Kempe, Cutler & Dean, 1980).

A corollary theory-based guideline is the premise that learning is facilitated through environmental manipulation that produces disequilibrium in children. The notion of disequilibrium is based on the Piagetian notions of assimilation and accommodation. Flavell (1985) provides the following definitions:

Assimilation essentially means interpreting or construing external objects or events in terms of one's own presently available and favored ways of thinking about things.... Accommodation roughly means noticing and taking cognitive account of the various real properties and relationships among properties that external objects and events possess; it means the mental apprehension of the structural attributes of environmental data (p. 5).

Disequilibrium is apparently created when the child is unable to assimilate a property or event to existing schemes and must resolve the integration by first accommodating to its novel characteristics. There are research findings that tend to confirm children's increased attention and interest in objects and events moderately discrepant from previous experiences (Clarke-Stewart & Koch, 1983; Flavell, 1985). Such findings indicate that children appear to be most intrigued by and motivated to engage in activities that are partially but not entirely assimilated to existing cognitive structures (Flavell, 1985).

Summary

A number of theoretical assumptions underly the rationale for early intervention programs, program development, and child learning. Although theoretical positions supporting early intervention may not be explicit, these theoretical perspectives serve as a foundation for most child-focused programs.

Kopp (1982) made an appeal for the use of theory to guide research efforts focusing on children with handicaps. She argued that without a theoretical framework, research findings are difficult to categorize and integrate into useful outcomes. Kopp's appeal for theory to guide research efforts should be extended to the use of theory to directly guide program development and operation. Without an explicit theoretical structure it is difficult to understand the relationship between a program's purpose and its outcomes.

Bricker (1986) has also argued that adoption of a sound theoretical position lends cohesiveness and consistency to early intervention programs by directing decision-making processes in at least five critical areas: (1) the identification of program goals and objectives, (2) the selection of assessment and curricular tools, (3) the development of individual program plans, (4) the selection of instructional strategies, and (5) the determination of appropriate evaluation methods to assess the outcome of the intervention.

In addition, it stands to reason that better prepared educators would be more efficient in the interpretation of theory and research findings, and more competent in translating this information into practice. Educators with knowledge of developmental theory and training in instructional strategies should be much better equipped to act as models and resources for parents. This is of particular importance in child-focused programs where teachers are frequently involved in training parents to teach their child skills (Bagnato, Munson, & MacTurk, 1987; Bruder & Bricker 1985). Cole and Gilkerson (1982) claim that considerable experience in the field of child development is necessary for educators to work "effectively and flexibly" as developmental consultants.

We believe that theory should guide the important aspects of program development and provide the continuity necessary to ensure that the early intervention practices selected match the purposes for which the program was established.

FROM THEORY TO PRACTICE: CHILD-FOCUSED PROGRAMS

We have chosen to examine selected practices common to child-focused early intervention programs rather than reproduce descriptions of exemplary efforts. Thus the analysis is conducted at a general level, and involves reviewing program practices and synthesizing them into a general model of child-focused early intervention programs.

Most child-focused programs operate within a three-phase context. Phase One, Entry, encompasses finding, identifying, and referring children to programs for services. Phase Two, Program Implementation, includes activities relevant to service delivery; and Phase Three, Exit, is focused on systems for the transition of children from the early intervention program to the next appropriate intervention setting, often a public school classroom. Figure 2 illustrates a general program model.

A perfunctory examination of professional early childhood special education journals, dating from 1980 to the present, will allow interested readers to gauge the relative levels of attention given to each phase. It should be readily apparent from this exercise that much more time and effort has been spent on Phases One and Two than on Phase Three. Phase Three activities have also been largely excluded from program descriptions supplied in the 1985–86 Directory of the Handicapped Children's Early Education Program (Decker, 1986) – a federally funded program of grants to individual sites to develop model early childhood demonstration programs. Regardless of the conspicuous absence of Phase Three activities in the literature, transitions from program to program are handled in some way by all early intervention programs. Therefore, the activities of each phase will be described in terms of prevalent activities.

Phase One: Entry

Substantial time and energy has been expended on screening and diagnostic efforts, often conducted by multidisciplinary teams, largely because of the consensus concerning the importance of identifying groups of children who are handicapped or may be at risk for developmental delay (Frankenburg, Emde, & Sullivan, 1985; Lichtenstein & Ireton, 1984). Several states, such as Washington and Iowa, have instituted early screening programs for populations of at-risk infants (National Center for Clinical Infant Programs, 1985). Most states provide screening for children entering kindergarten, and the national Early and Periodic Screening, Diagnosis and Treatment (EPSDT) program provides medical, dental, and developmental screening, diagnosis, and treatment of children under 21 whose parents are receiving Medicaid (Keogh, Wilcoxen, & Bernheimer, 1986; Meisels, 1987).

Interestingly, a recent report from the National Center for Clinical Infant Programs (1986) indicates that only 10% of eligible children participate in EPSDT. However, the success of the program may vary widely from state to state. Meisels and Margolis (1988) report that in 1984, 39% of Medicaid-eligible recipients in Michigan received screening services from EPSDT.

Children identified through screening are referred to an appropriate agency for more comprehensive and in-depth diagnostic testing. Before children can be placed in special education programs, they are entitled by law to receive a comprehensive, diagnostic individual evaluation of their educational needs (Fallen, 1985). The general goal of this process is to determine whether a child is handicapped and, if so, the extent and nature of educational and related services required for intervention. Federal mandates require that assessment procedures be multifactorial and be derived from multiple sources, and

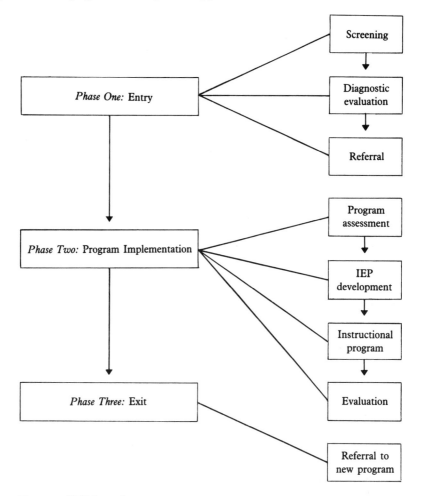

Figure 2. Child-focused program components

that they be conducted by multidisciplinary professional teams. The composition of the teams may be static or may vary according to each child's unique characteristics; state regulations, however, generally provide guidelines for minimum representation. Similarly, each state interprets the intent of the law to set standards for the content of the evaluation (Superintendent of Public Instruction, 1984). The information obtained from the comprehensive diagnostic assessment is used to determine the child's eligibility for special, state-subsidized services.

Historically, there has been a mismatch between the information provided by diagnostic assessments and the information sought by early interventionists functioning in direct service capacities (Bagnato & Neisworth, 1981; Bricker & Campbell, 1980). Initially, educators operated under the assumption that information gathered in diagnostic assessments would be useful in the development of instructional programs.

Such information is rarely provided, however, except on a very general level. Diagnostic tools yield information more relevant to current medical, social, and developmental status than to developing specific intervention content and procedures. Though steps in the same process (i.e., securing and providing educational services), diagnostic assessment and instructional program development serve quite different functions. If this disparity is clearly comprehended, there is no reason to believe that information generated in one activity can be used for the other. The disillusionment over the usefulness of diagnostic assessment is often due to the failure to comprehend its function.

Phase Two: Program Implementation

Children found eligible for early intervention services based on a diagnostic assessment are referred to Phase Two (see Figure 2). Although there are exceptions, most early intervention programs have intake procedures that require children to receive additional assessments upon program entry. Program personnel employ a variety of assessment tools and procedures to develop individualized educational plans (IEPs) for participating children. These initial assessments yield a level of behavioral functioning against which future behavioral change will be compared. In early intervention programs, this is sometimes referred to as a "baseline."

The major differences in programs with respect to intake or initial assessment activities are in the types of tools or procedures used, and how directly the outcomes can be used to develop IEPs and detailed instructional programs. For example, a cohesive Piagetian-based program may use the Infant Scales of Psychological Development (Uzgiris & Hunt, 1975) to assess specific domains of sensorimotor development, and Dunst's Infant Learning Curriculum to design instructional programs (Dunst, 1981). Unfortunately, assessment outcomes do not always reflect the developmental orientation of the program, nor are they always relevant or adequate for constructing individual program plans and instructional strategies.

IEP development follows program assessment on the service delivery continuum for child-focused programs. In most early intervention programs, formal procedures have been implemented to meet the standards stipulated by the Education for All Handicapped Children's Act (P.L. 94-142). As with most other practices, the way in which the law is interpreted by individual agencies largely determines the way in which IEP activities are conducted (e.g., the extent of parent involvement, who attends, what issues take precedence).

In child-focused programs, goals directly related to children or their behavior are priorities. In other respects, the IEP process is probably similar to that practiced in all early intervention programs.

Once the IEP is written and approved, program personnel typically operationalize children's goals into a set of instructional objectives with accompanying programs designed to move children toward established developmental targets. Again, variability exists in child-focused programs as to the curricular content and instructional strategies adopted by program personnel. Many prepared curricula are presently available that include recommended instructional sequences (e.g., long-range goals with associated short-term objectives), such as those found in the Evaluation and Programming System: For Infants and Young Children (Bricker, Gentry, & Bailey, 1985), and/or suggested activities (e.g., use diapering to encourage vocalization) to assist teachers and parents in eliciting the desired behavior, such as those compiled in the Carolina Curriculum for Handicapped Infants and Infants At Risk (Johnson-Martin, Jens, & Attermeier, 1986).

Program descriptions suggest that the most frequent child-focused approaches are developmental and task analytical. It is not surprising that many programs use a combination of these strategies, as certain child and parent learning styles and certain skills lend themselves more easily to certain teaching and learning paradigms. For instance, when intervening with children learning to use a bilateral reaching response, teachers may use a detailed teaching sequence with children presenting severe handicaps as opposed to encouraging bilateral reaching and manipulation by offering a variety of objects to children with mild to moderate developmental delay.

A related area in which major differences exist across programs is the focus on child-initiated versus teacher-initiated activity. Some child-focused programs are teacher-initiated and driven totally by the interventionist's choice of activity and schedule. Other programs permit children to select activities and the general sequence of instruction. Many programs combine approaches allowing child-initiated activity to be interwoven with teacher-initiated instruction.

Another practice included in Phase Two is evaluation. Published descriptions of child-focused programs often claim extensive evaluation efforts. These efforts fall into two main categories: evaluation to ascertain individual child progress for instructional purposes, and evaluation of global outcome data to determine program impact (most commonly, changes in I.Q. or developmental level). Descriptions of procedures and outcomes on child progress are usually brief and rarely supported by socially valid empirical evidence such as number of children placed in regular education classes, or financial savings. A number of analyses have been conducted and published on global evaluation data (see, e.g., Guralnick & Bennett, 1987), but few analyses published indicate more general societal outcomes (Strain, 1984).

Phase Three: Exit

As previously mentioned, Phase Three, the transition of children to the next appropriate setting, has received relatively little scholarly attention. However, transitions are an integral component of early intervention programs. Moreover, the care with which transitions are executed may make the difference in whether children will experience success or failure in their next placement (Vincent et al., 1980). Most early intervention programs conduct transition procedures informally, but there are strategies worth noting. Vincent et al. (1980) suggest incorporating "survival skills" needed for children's successful assimilation into the next environment within the curricula of early intervention programs. Another strategy involves systematic information sharing between exit and entry agencies regarding individual children's needs. Such systems can be helpful in planning and implementing transitions for children and parents between programs.

Summary

Child-focused early intervention programs generally provide a continuum of services that in some cases begin with screening, and then progress through diagnostic assessment, referral, initial (program) assessment, IEP development, development of instructional programs, evaluation, and transition to the next setting. Where laws provide guidelines for services (e.g., IEP development, diagnostic assessment), early intervention practices across programs can be similar. However, there is great variety among program assessment tools, procedures used in the development of instructional programs, evaluation techniques, the quality of the linkage among various program components, and their consistency with the framework guiding program development.

The overview of prevalent practices in child-focused early intervention programs provides a context within which selected issues of particular relevance to child-focused programs can be examined.

PROGRAM ANALYSIS

The theoretical assumptions underlying the development of early intervention programs for young children with handicaps appear to have changed little since the 1960s; however, program goals, assessment, intervention content, and instructional and evaluation strategies have undergone significant transformations. Early attempts to assist young handicapped children lacked the scope and sophistication of today's approaches. These early efforts can best be characterized as exploratory ventures that evolved into defensible and comprehensive programs directed by trained personnel.

The present analysis examines several important features of contemporary intervention programs for young children with handicaps. Specifically, we explore aspects of: population, assessment, IEP development, instructional content, teaching strategies, and evaluation.

Population

There is no central source or agency charged with the task of gathering, synthesizing, and disseminating information on populations served in child-focused early intervention programs. The federal government and most states attempt to collect and report some information on populations served in early intervention programs; however, these data are incomplete and difficult to integrate because they tend to include only programs that receive state or federal support. Historically, many programs for young children with handicaps have been operated by private agencies. Further, these data are lacking in specificity because prior to the passage of P.L. 99-457, programs were not mandated for preschool children at the federal level. Finally, the wide variation in definitions or classifications makes the combination of information across programs suspect. Thus, no central authority has efficiently cataloged information on the demographics of preschool populations served.

Many of the initial programs were categorical, serving specific populations of children with obvious impairments such as Down syndrome (Hayden & Haring, 1978; Rynders & Horrobin, 1975). Although categorical programs still exist today, additional groups of children with special needs have been identified and are receiving attention. These groups include youngsters who are developmentally delayed but have no overt motoric or sensory impairment, and infants and older children considered to be at risk developmentally because of medical or environmental factors. Concern for these groups of children has resulted in the broadening of eligibility criteria in many intervention programs.

The 1978–9 edition (TADS/WESTAR, 1978–9) and the 1985–6 edition (Decker, 1986) of the *Handicapped Children's Early Education Program Directory* were reviewed to examine changes in program populations. These annual directories provide a brief summary of the Handicapped Children's Early Education Program (HCEEP) demonstration and outreach projects funded by the U.S. Office of Special Education Programs.

Table 1. *Comparison of percentages of child population served by age in HCEEP in 1978–1979 and 1985–1986*

Year	0–3	3–5	0–6[a]	Other[b]	Not specified[c]
1978–9 N = 127	24	13	37	20	6
1985–6 N = 102	42	10	34	8	6

[a] Includes programs that exceeded 0–3 or 3–5 ages. For example, 2–6, 0–6, 0–4, and 2–4 years.
[b] Includes programs that exceeded 0–6 years. For example, 0–12, 2–7, 5–8, and 3–10 years.
[c] Includes programs that did not specify age of population served.

Of particular interest are changes in age and type of populations served in the HCEEPs during 1978 and 1986, an 8-year interval. In the 1978 directory, 127 demonstration programs were described, and in the 1986 directory, 102. Table 1 compares the age of the children served in HCEEPs in 1978 and 1986. A review of Table 1 indicates two major shifts in the age of children served. First, almost twice as many programs in 1986 than in 1978 (42% as compared to 24%, respectively) reported serving infants exclusively. Second, only 8% of the programs in 1986 reported serving youngsters older than age 6 years, as compared to 20% of the programs in 1978. These two changes indicate a clear trend toward serving younger children.

Another 1978–86 HCEEP comparison examined the categories of children served. We examined the percentage of programs that served children who were handicapped and at risk and noted the number of programs that had categorical versus noncategorical groupings. Programs in both 1978 and 1986 served children with handicaps in predominantly noncategorical programs (as shown in Table 2). The major change was in the increased percentage of programs serving at-risk populations in 1986. In 1978, 9% of the population served were at risk, whereas in 1986, the percentage of at-risk children served had almost doubled (16%).

A final comparison involved determining differences in the level of child impairment. Table 3 presents this comparison. The marked shift in the number of programs serving children at risk is consonant with the data presented in Table 2. Also, in 1986 HCEEPs appeared to be operating more programs serving children with a range of impairments; however, because a large number of programs (57% in 1978 and 49% in 1986) did not specify levels of impairment, caution must be exercised in drawing firm conclusions about the level of impairment typified by children served in the HCEEP network.

If HCEEPs are representative of early intervention programs as a whole, and the descriptions listed in the directories are accurate, the results demonstrate two trends worth mentioning. First, increasing numbers of programs are serving infants and, second, increasing numbers of programs are serving at-risk populations.

It is important to note that the shift to infants and at-risk populations does not appear to interfere with or detract from serving children with identified handicapping conditions. Programs are expanding to accommodate younger and less impaired children rather than choosing which different groups of children to serve.

Several factors are likely responsible for the noted changes in children being served. Among them are advances in medical technology, research efforts focused on newborn

Table 2. *Comparison of percentage of child population served by category in HCEEP in 1978–1979 and 1985–1986*

| Year | Handicapped | | At risk[c] | Not specified[d] |
	Cross-categorical[a]	Categorical[b]		
1978–9 N = 127	75	16	9	8
1985–6 N = 102	69	15	16	1

[a] Includes programs that serve children with different handicapping conditions and multiply handicapped.
[b] Includes programs that exclusively serve children with a particular impairment, for example, hearing-impaired, visually impaired, autistic.
[c] Includes programs that serve children at risk for medical or environmental reasons, for example, teenage mothers, prematurity, low birth weight.
[d] Includes programs that did not specify type of children served.

Table 3. *Comparison of percentages of child population served by level of impairment in HCEEP in 1978–1979 and 1985–1986*

Year	At risk	Mild	Moderate	Severe	Mixed[a]	Not specified[b]
1978–9 N = 127	9	0	8	13	20	50
1985–6 N = 102	15	0	0	6	30	49

[a] Includes programs that served children with different levels of impairments, for example, moderate and severe; mild, moderate, and severe; at risk and mild.
[b] Includes programs that did not specify levels of impairment of children served.

follow-up, and broader legislative mandates. Certainly advances in medical technology have contributed significantly to the survival as well as morbidity rate among young children. Harrison (1983) reported that before the days of modern intensive care, 40,000 babies died annually of respiratory distress syndrome (RDS). As of 1983, 85% of the 30,000–60,000 infants diagnosed annually with RDS survive.

In recent years, neurological and behavioral testing of newborns has supplemented information supplied by the Apgar score and other perinatal variables, and undoubtedly improved the identification of babies with impairments. Tracking systems designed to monitor the developmental progress of infants beyond the neonatal period have emerged to solve both the identification problem and questions relevant to the developmental sequelae of children born at risk for developmental delay (Bricker, Squires, Kaminski, & Mounts, 1988).

Individual states and the federal government are continuing to enact more comprehensive legislation for serving young children with special needs (Weiner & Koppelman, 1987). As a result, intervention services are being expanded and improved through the constant influx of recommendations from relevant research and efficacy studies. Although significant financial hurdles exist, programs for young children are now considered a legitimate component of the human services delivery system.

Assessment

From the inception of early intervention programs, there has been a need for instruments and procedures for accurately measuring the capabilities of young children, and the effects of intervention programs on their behavior. Moreover, the increased concern with early identification and the inclusion of children experiencing a wider range of handicapping conditions in early intervention programs has forced a reexamination of existing assessment procedures. Concomitant redefinition of appropriate assessment procedures has increased awareness and spurred the development of alternative tools and procedures (Cicchetti & Wagner, this volume; Fewell & Sandall, 1986; Vietze & Coates, 1986).

Simeonsson, Huntington, and Parse (1980) identified several issues pertinent to the assessment of young children with severe handicaps that will provide the context for the following discussion. They contend that the limitations imposed upon the valid assessment of young children with severe handicaps emanate from four sources: definitional issues, child limitations, instrument limitations, and examiner limitations.

The concern over definitional issues centers around the stigmatizing and often demeaning consequences associated with the description of the development of persons with significant handicaps in terms of a relative position to normative standards. A solution to this problem is the use of measures that include sequential levels on which all individuals can be placed, irrespective of age or severity of handicap. The levels describe an absolute level of functioning rather than one that is relative to the performance of a nonhandicapped age-mate from the standardization sample (most likely a decrement or deviation). The belief supporting this practice is that the more positive description will result in more optimistic expectations for the handicapped child, and influence the caregiver's and interventionist's behavior accordingly.

Increased considerations for the limitations of young children with handicaps has spawned many changes in the area of assessment. Several assessment instruments, designed specifically for educational purposes (Phase Two) now include suggestions for modifying testing procedures for motorically and/or sensory impaired children, for example, the Battelle Developmental Inventory (Newborg, Stock, Wnek, Guidubaldi, & Svinicki, 1984). There are also assessment tools designed specifically for children with certain handicapping conditions such as the Callier-Azusa Scale for deaf-blind children (Stillman, 1975). Finally, alternative response modes have been examined (e.g., heart rate, visual fixation) for children unable to manage more conventional means of demonstrating their abilities (Vietze & Coates, 1986; Zelazo, 1982).

Consideration for the idiosyncratic behavior of infants and young children with handicaps has also influenced testing procedures. Very young children, as well as children experiencing physical, sensory, and neurological impairments, may exhibit highly variable performance levels from one observation to another due to physiological fluctuations (Lester, 1983; Prechtl, 1983). Attention to children's physiological state of arousal has prompted test developers to suggest repeated administrations of test items to ensure measurement of the child's best response (Brazelton, 1973).

Environmentally induced phenomena, either in combination with physiological instability or alone, may also account for variable performance levels. Newborns, for instance, appear less alert if their mothers are given sedatives prior to delivery. Anticonvulsant drug therapy for controlling children's seizures may also produce undesirable behavior. Likewise, lighting conditions, examiner characteristics, and amount of extraneous stimuli are some environmental factors that may interfere with children's optimal performance (Gaylord-Ross, 1980).

Instrument limitations have been acknowledged and, as previously mentioned, adaptations have been instituted. Unfortunately, psychometric data are unavailable on many of these tools, and therefore their validity is questionable (Sheehan, 1982).

Examiner bias may also contribute to invalid assessment of children's capabilities. Major obstacles may be orientation or expectation bias, invalid assumptions, and procedural errors (Simeonsson et al., 1980). Concerns may be at least partially allayed by the growing number of specialized training programs in early childhood special education. Many states now require early childhood special education certification of personnel deploying intervention services in state subsidized programs for young children with handicaps (Bricker & Slentz, 1988). The requirements for training of early childhood educators vary from state to state, and even from institution to institution where guidelines do not yet exist for certification (Bricker & Slentz, 1988; Stile, Abernathy, Pettibone, & Wachtel, 1984). Certainly, standards for certification are needed to circumvent erroneous judgments associated with assessment practices.

The concerns and suggestions of Simeonsson et al. (1980) with respect to young children with severe handicaps are applicable to young children experiencing a wide range of disabilities. There are at present notable trends based on these and similar arguments (Bricker, 1986).

Many assessment tools now are composed of sequences of hierarchically arranged items used to assess children's developmental levels and to design interventions. Criterion-referenced tools are now used extensively, replacing norm-referenced tools for individualized program planning and evaluation. Finally, multivariate assessment procedures are allowing more comprehensive testing of children's capabilities by tapping many areas of functioning. The latter trend includes such innovations as the use of comprehensive tools (i.e., those testing across several developmental areas such as gross and fine motor, cognitive, communicative, and social skills), the incorporation of the parent's assessment of children's developmental skills, and curriculum-based assessment that provides information directly relevant to the development of children's instructional programs and IEPs.

IEP Development

A frequent activity of early intervention personnel, particularly in programs sponsored by educational agencies, is the development of individualized education plans. The IEP process is closely tied to the enrollment of children, their initial assessment, and subsequent end-of-the-year completion activities. The purpose of the IEP is to develop a comprehensive individual instructional plan that can serve as a blueprint for intervention.

Although IEPs have been required for school-age children since the passage of P.L. 94-142 in 1975, serious problems continue to exist in their development and use (Goldstein & Turnbull, 1982). Two interrelated difficulties relevant to child-focused approaches appear to be the development of quality plans and their systematic implementation. Many early interventionists are poorly equipped to develop quality IEPs for the infants and young children in their programs (Notari, 1988). Speculation about the cause of this problem necessitates a closer examination of possible influences. First, a substantial percentage of the personnel in early intervention programs may have had little formal training in early childhood special education (ECSE). For example, a statewide survey conducted in Nebraska to gather information about personnel providing services to their handicapped preschool population revealed that of the 139 teachers responding, only 48% had some type of ECSE endorsement or certification (Nebraska Department of Education, 1986). When teachers were asked to rate the adequacy of the training they received prior to employment, they rated preparation in medical considerations, planning intervention, assessment, family systems resources, and teaching adult learners as only "adequate." Although limited, these data, if representative, indicate that many early interventionists may have a minimum of formal training in the area of ECSE, and that they perceive their own expertise as merely adequate.

Another consideration concerning the quality of IEPs focuses on the possibility that the assessment and evaluation tools used by many programs do not lend themselves to the development of appropriate IEPs. In other words, they do not yield outcomes that are programmatically relevant. Thus, interventionists often have little useful or appropriate information from which to develop sound instructional programs.

Instructional content

Instructional or curricular content is the substance or matter that constitutes what interventionists are attempting to teach children. Determining the nature of curricular content from reviews of early intervention programs can be difficult because program descriptions often lack adequate specificity. Despite the lack of detailed descriptions of program content, it is clear that a range of curricular foci and content are represented in early intervention programs. Programs that serve infants and toddlers tend to be more developmentally oriented (i.e., focusing on global milestones), whereas programs that serve older children tend to have an increased preacademic focus (i.e., skills prerequisite to success in reading, writing, and mathematics) (Cohen & Gross, 1979). Specific skills (e.g., sorting and sequencing) are targeted for instruction in preacademic classrooms, as opposed to general processes (e.g., walking and talking) in programs for younger children (Bailey, Jens, & Johnson, 1983). Another difference in curricula is apparent in the organization of content. In developmental curricula, content is sequenced and presented according to normal developmental age levels (Alberto, Briggs, & Goldstein, 1983). Adherence to this sequence is not necessarily a characteristic of programs employing preacademic curricula for older children. It is important to note that this is a generality, and one can find exceptions in programs for infants that target specific skills (Shearer & Shearer, 1976) and programs for older children that are focused on general processes (Haywood, Brooks, & Burns, 1986).

Despite obvious variations in application, some generally accepted curricular practices are found in early intervention programs (Mori & Neisworth, 1983). Young children rarely present isolated developmental deficits that can be addressed directly by a professional representing a single discipline. Much more commonly the disability is pervasive, affecting many areas of functioning and requiring a multifaceted approach to instructional content. Children with genetic disorders (e.g., Down syndrome), serious motor impairments (e.g., spastic quadriplegia), and significant sensory impairments (e.g., visual and hearing impairments), have problems that result in a generalized inability to acquire important skills and information at an age-appropriate rate.

For example, children with Down syndrome often have motor, cognitive, communication, and socialization delays or deficits (Pueschel, Tingey, Rynders, Crocker, & Crutcher, 1987). Narrowly focused intervention such as articulation therapy is not usually seen as appropriate for this population of children or other populations with serious impairments. Rather, since cognitive, social, communicative, and motoric development are so interrelated in the behavioral repertoires of young children, quality intervention programs are designed to assist them in all development areas. It is of questionable value to enhance a child's intelligibility if the child has nothing to say.

Moving from discussing specific practices to a global level of content analysis, Bailey et al. (1983) reported some findings of interest. They reviewed 15 curricula for children with handicaps and found that most of them grouped skills into developmental domains (e.g., gross motor, fine motor, problem solving, communication, socialization, and self-help); however, the number of specific items per test and per domain varied considerably. Most of these curricula had procedures for determining children's entry levels and for monitoring change over time. However, Bailey et al. (1983) reported little indication that any of the curricula evolved from sound theoretical bases, or had empirical evidence attesting to their effectiveness.

Our analysis agrees with the conclusions of Bailey et al. (1983). First, there are a number of comprehensive curricula available (e.g., ABACUS [McCarthy, Lund, & Bos, 1987]). Second, for the most part the authors of these curricula have not specified their theoretical bases adequately. Finally, objective data on the reliability, validity, and utility of these curricular materials are lacking.

Instructional strategies

Instructional strategies refer to the methods or procedures for teaching children to acquire selected instructional goals and objectives. As with instructional content, there is variability in the instructional approaches used by early interventionists; however, there are also consistencies. The consistencies reflect important trends in instructional approaches used with young children. In particular, there are three trends that appear to have gained acceptance by leaders in the field of early childhood special education: the need for child-initiated activity, for increased attention to generalization of learned responses, and for training within daily activities and familiar contexts. These changes are embodied in approaches that are referred to as ecologically based (Bagnato & Neisworth, 1987).

Ecologically based approaches perceive the child as an organism developing in interaction with the environment (Thurman & Widerstrom, 1985). Children's development is assumed to occur within the context of their ecological systems, from which it derives meaning. Therefore strategies designed to ameliorate developmental disabilities must be conducted within the constraints of the ecological context. Traditional programs for preschool-age children with handicaps have their evolutionary roots in programs created in institutions for individuals with mental retardation (Bricker & Carlson, 1981). These programs employed operant procedures to teach narrowly defined and specific responses. The teaching strategy complemented the rather restrictive curricular goals, which were often geared toward making individuals more manageable and instilling in them the most rudimentary of skills (Baer, Peterson, & Sherman, 1967). It was believed that such structure was necessary to change behavior and generate behavioral options for institutionalized populations. When community-based programs for young handicapped children emerged, many procedures that had been found effective with institutional populations were transferred from those settings to the newly established programs (Bricker & Bricker, 1971; Wolf, Risley, & Mees, 1964). Feedback from professionals (Meisels, 1979), parents (MacMillan & Turnbull, 1983), and child outcome data (specifically the lack of generalization of training to other situations) suggested change was necessary. Although the instructional principles were sound, the manner in which they were applied to young children in community settings was objectionable (e.g., giving young children food rewards for correct responses). This recognition led to the adoption of instructional approaches more in tune with the child's ecological context.

Ecologically based approaches to instruction are designed to maximize the development of functional skills, in particular social-communication skills (Mahoney, 1975; Warren & Rogers-Warren, 1985). These approaches have several important features. First, there is an emphasis on child initiation. This aspect of the approach has been deemed necessary because a number of investigations indicate that infants and other children with handicaps initiate interactions significantly less often than nonhandicapped peers (Jones, 1977; Mahoney & Robenalt, 1986).

A second important facet of ecologically based approaches is that instruction is conducted under conditions in which the desired responses are embedded in a frequently occurring transaction. For instance, if the desired outcome is an increase in the number of objects a child names, the names of objects are provided to children who then are encouraged to choose among those objects or activities according to their interests. Using such strategies is thought to enhance the generalization of responses and remove the need for artificial consequences such as those that occur when children are rewarded for labeling pictures in tutorial sessions.

Ecological approaches include caregivers and other family members in the child's instructional program (MacDonald, 1985). Parents are thought to be pivotal to child change since they often interact more frequently with and are naturally salient to their children. In addition, consistency in the handling and the expectations for young children should produce greater progress. Parents and family members should be included as part of the intervention team if consistency is to occur.

The instructional strategies incorporated in ecological approaches (e.g., child-initiated interactions, the embedding of desired responses in naturally occurring events, and the increased attention to the caregiving context) have significantly changed the way in which intervention is conducted with infants and young children. By approximating the conditions that are thought to promote learning in typical children, interventionists avoid the problems of more restrictive strategies, such as the child's reliance on others to provide interactions, the use of artificial cues and reinforcing experiences, and the alienation of caregivers as well as peers from the children's instructional programs (Warren & Kaiser, 1988). The ecological approach is practical and may have far-reaching benefits, not the least of which is the reduction of teacher burnout, a by-product of client-focused strategies characterized by a unilateral flow of the teacher's energy and emotional support to the student (Weiskopf, 1980).

Different child-focused approaches advocate different roles for the interventionist. Those programs reflecting the more teacher-directed approaches are the programs that tend to begin training focused on specific targets using highly controlled presentation formats. The ecologically based approaches are characterized by the use of distributed rather than massed presentations of instructional cues and attempts to follow the child's attentional lead, and teaching within the form and context of naturally occurring events (Warren & Kaiser, 1988). The approach is child- rather than teacher-oriented, implying that the teacher's role is to facilitate, enhance, and expand interactions selected by the child.

Evaluation

In spite of national philosophical leanings toward the importance of early experience for children, some critics still question the investment of resources in an enterprise they see as nonproductive (see, e.g., Ferry, 1981; Gibson & Field, 1984; Piper & Pless, 1980). Even after publication of an extensive array of studies on program efficacy, the controversy continues (Dunst & Snyder, 1986; Mastropieri, White, & Fecteau, 1986; Shonkoff & Hauser-Cram, 1987; Strain & Smith, 1986; Tingey, 1987).

Although one cannot deny the existence of controversy over the efficacy of early intervention, other factors attenuate the relevance of the dispute. Foremost is the belief that efficacy studies are focusing on the wrong questions (Anastasiow, 1986; Bricker, 1987). Both Anastasiow (1986) and Bricker (1987) point out that the question of whether early intervention programs should be continued is not a research question but a socioethical issue. Relevant research questions concern how best to deliver intervention services. Wolery and Bailey insist that "individual programs generally should not spend time and resources in efforts to justify early intervention" (1984, p. 28). The more important challenge is rather to measure progress toward established instructional objectives in order to make sound educational decisions about the effectiveness of children's instructional programs.

In most early intervention programs, the evaluation of child progress and of program impact (i.e., grouped child progress data) is accomplished through test administration, observation under specific conditions, completion of a protocol, or some combination of these techniques. Single-subject analysis, whereby an individual's behavior is compared to his or her own performance over repeated observations, is the most common form of evaluating child change (see Hersen & Barlow, 1976). Standardized tests, published curricula, and "homemade" tests and protocols are frequently used to measure group effects. An application of the latter might be measuring the increase in interactions between children with and without handicaps in an integrated program. Typically, the number and type of interactions are recorded, rather than the responses and initiations of particular individuals.

The example described may be used as an illustration of one of the difficulties in evaluating child-focused programs: assessing the relationship between program elements (in this case, instructional strategies), and desired outcomes (in our example, increased interactions). When descriptions of program elements (i.e., instructional strategies, curricula, parent training strategies) and outcomes are general, they provide little assistance in determining exactly what was done to produce change in children's behavior. Most program analyses to date provide few insights into the functional relationship between independent (e.g., instructional strategy) and dependent (e.g., child change) variables (Dunst & Snyder, 1986).

The inability to tie program elements to program outcomes represents a serious barrier to determining the integrity of specific program content in promoting the development of young children with handicaps. White and his colleagues have attempted to solve this and related measurement dilemmas through the use of metaanalysis (White, Mastropieri, & Casto, 1984). Conducting a metaanalysis involves (1) obtaining a complete sample of studies on a specific topic; (2) transforming the outcomes of each study into a standard numerical value; (3) coding program characteristics (e.g., child characteristics, program elements, outcome measures) that may affect results; and (4) using correlational and descriptive statistical methods to summarize findings so that relationships between and among child and program variables are evident (Casto &

Table 4. *Diversity of studies and measures used in six early intervention efficacy reviews*

Area of development or deficit	Total number of studies	Total number of measures across studies	Total number of different measures cited
Cognition[a]	24	54	27
Motor[b]	13	24	18
Language[c]	30	43	29
Vision[d]	7	18	18
Hearing[e]	8	27	23
Autism[f]	3	7	6

Note: Information taken from chapters by [a] Guralnick & Bricker, [b] Harris, [c] Snyder-McLean & McLean, [d] Olson, [e] Meadow-Orlans, [f] and Simeonsson, Olley, & Rosenthal in M. Guralnick and F. Bennett (Eds.), (1987). *The effectiveness of early intervention for at-risk and handicapped children.* New York: Academic Press.

Mastropieri, 1986). A number of flaws in this approach have been noted. Strain and Smith (1986) insist that outcomes from the White et al. (1984) metaanalysis should be interpreted with caution because of serious omissions in the data base used for the analysis (for example, the exclusion of single-subject studies). Another concern is the practice of combining all studies to produce an overall effect size despite important differences in populations, procedures, and outcomes measures. Shonkoff and Hauser-Cram (1987) demonstrate that adherence to selected criteria can significantly influence the outcomes when using metaanalytic approaches.

There is also considerable diversity in measures used by child-focused programs to assess and evaluate child change. To illustrate this diversity, an analysis was conducted on a group of six chapters that reviewed efficacy studies for children with cognitive, motor, language, hearing, and vision impairments, and autism (Guralnick & Bennett, 1987). Using data gleaned from tables presented in the six chapters, we constructed a composite table that indicates the numbers and types of measures found in investigations critiqued by authors of the six chapters. As shown in Table 4, the efficacy studies included in each chapter reported the use of many different measures.

In addition to the diversity of procedures and tools employed, the field has used a variety of experimental designs to examine program impact. Dunst and Rheingrover (1981) examined 49 efficacy studies and reported that none of these studies was completely free from threats of internal validity. This finding suggests that the field has important barriers to overcome in documenting child progress and program impact.

Another approach to program evaluation has been to review investigations selectively that meet specific criteria. For example, Odom and Fewell (1983) and White et al. (1984) analyzed results from projects approved by the Joint Dissemination Review Panel (JDRP). (The JDRP is a committee of experts appointed to judge the adequacy of program evaluation for projects receiving federal support and interested in disseminating their model.) This procedure has the advantage of allowing confidence in the outcomes, yet the generalizability of these outcomes is of concern. The representativeness of such selected reviews has been questioned as well as the selection criteria for including and excluding studies from the review (White, Bush, & Casto, 1986).

A final approach has been to review a large number of studies using a full range of classification schemes (i.e., grouped by experimental design, focus of intervention, service delivery model, or nature of outcome measure(s)). Such reviews have been conducted by Bricker, Bailey, and Bruder (1984); Dunst and Rheingrover (1981); Gibson and Field (1984); Haskins, Finkelstein, and Stedman (1978); and Simeonsson, Cooper, and Scheiner (1982). Recently, an entire book was dedicated to reviewing the efficacy of early intervention for motorically, sensory, cognitively, communicatively, biologically, and psychologically impaired, and environmentally at-risk children (Guralnick & Bennett, 1987).

As the field has matured, early intervention personnel have become more knowledgeable about tests, measurement, and methodological controls. This awareness is evidenced in the adoption of more sophisticated and comprehensive evaluation plans and strategies by early intervention programs (Bailey et al. 1986; Odom & Shuster, 1986). For instance, Beckman, Robinson, Jackson, and Rosenberg (1986) suggest a four-step procedure for incorporating and evaluating theoretical information and research findings into practice: identify findings, identify applications, systematize applications, and document applications. Following such systematic procedures should enhance the evaluation procedures used by early interventionists.

HOW TO MAKE A GOOD THING BETTER

At the beginning of this chapter, we indicated that the field of early intervention has made significant progress toward delivering quality services to young children with handicaps. In closing, we would like to emphasize the growing expertise in assessment, curricular approaches, instructional strategies, personnel perparation, and program evaluation. However, important problems still need resolution.

First, more complete descriptions of program operation are necessary in order to determine the content, strategies, and circumstances that make a difference in producing change in children. A global experiential approach to instruction is contraindicated, since this strategy blurs the strength and direction of relationships among variables. Approaches directed to meet children's specific needs should be employed and carefully described, including details of program operation and procedures. More detailed accounts of how programs function will assist researchers in making useful comparisons across programs and discriminating among variables that enhance child change. Clarity at the content and strategy level will undoubtedly have a facilitative effect on IEP development.

Although most early intervention program personnel develop IEPs, the quality and thus the usefulness of these IEPs are questionable. In a recently completed study Notari (1988) found that early interventionists often write long-range goals that are so vague that the measurement of children's progress is impossible. It seems imperative that long-range goals and short-term objectives be written to provide a functional intervention plan for professional personnel and parents.

Developing useful and relevant IEPs for children will require increased training efforts of two kinds. First, systematic in-service training focused on early childhood development needs to be provided to early intervention personnel who are operating programs for young handicapped children and their families. Often special education teachers and other interventionists have had little or no explicit training in working with infants and young children. These interventionists may have a poor grasp of early development and thus develop IEPs with content and intervention strategies that are inconsistent with the cognitive and behavioral repertoires of infants and young children. Systematic, on-the-job training is needed to assist interventionists in gaining the knowledge and skills to become more effective in their IEP development and subsequent intervention strategies.

Although interventionists completing early childhood special education training programs may be able to develop quality IEPs, preservice training also needs expansion. The curricular content of many early childhood–special education personnel preparation programs is focused primarily on working with young children only (Bricker & Slentz, 1988). At best, students are offered one class on parent involvement and very little on the principles of adult education. Much of the intervention effort, particularly for infants and young children, is focused on assisting adult caregivers in working more effectively with their children. Personnel preparation programs need to broaden their curricular focus to include adult education. Interventionists need to learn techniques that will enable them to involve parents more effectively in the development of IEPs and in the subsequent intervention process.

Assessment and evaluation instruments that yield useful and relevant instructional content are necessary to support the efforts of well-trained personnel in developing useful educational plans. The advent of curriculum-based assessment should make a significant contribution to improving the quality of IEPs (Bagnato, Neisworth, & Capone, 1986; Notari, Slentz, & Bricker, in press). These tools provide assessment information that can be used to formulate IEPs and thus make the links direct and functional between assessment, IEP development, and intervention. Curriculum-based assessments yield information on what skills or behaviors children can successfully complete and those behaviors they have not yet acquired. Assessment outcomes can be used to select specific educational targets for children and also may be tied directly to curricular activities. For example, if the assessment indicates a child can pull to stand, sidestep while holding on, but not walk without support, independent walking becomes an IEP goal. The curriculum associated with the assessment will then provide the interventionist with suggestions and curricular activities for encouraging independent walking. Tools that yield information related directly to the development of long-range goals, short-term objectives, and specific instructional steps make intervention efforts efficient and effective.

Not only do assessment and evaluation instruments need to provide information for the development of instructional programs, there still exists the need for assessment and evaluation systems that provide a direct link between the three phases of program entry, implementation, and exit as illustrated in Figure 2. Systems that relate assessment, intervention, and evaluation activities are essential if program personnel are to deliver quality services efficiently. Further, these systems will permit more appropriate evaluation of child progress and program impact. Fortunately, systems that link assessment, intervention, and evaluation are under development and are becoming available, for example, the Arizona Basic Assessment and Curriculum Utilization System (McCarthy et al., 1987), Coordinating Assessment and Programming for Preschoolers (Karnes & Johnson, 1987) and the Evaluation and Programming System: For Infants and Young Children (Bricker et al., 1985).

Another area of concern is transition, or the process of moving infants and other children from one program to another. More time and energy are needed to develop sound procedures for transferring children to other settings without confusion, loss of valuable information, or waste of time in the duplication of data and information. In addition, objective information about the effectiveness of transition strategies is necessary to improve the transfer of children across programs.

A final barrier to improvement of early childhood–special education services is our proclivity to take complicated factors and interactions and treat them as if they were simple and linear. Treating complex variables such as early versus later entry into early intervention programs as dichotomous clouds rather than illuminates the issue. To take the position for all children that early is more profitable than later entry, or the reverse, is simplistic and probably inaccurate. As with most activities human beings encounter, there are numerous variables that will affect when it is more beneficial to begin intervention for individual children. The sensible approach is to have programs available that can be accessed by children when entry is deemed appropriate by parents and professionals.

The reality is that children, parents, and interventionists are complex organisms who must function in dynamic and interactive sociopolitical settings. Recognizing this complexity must undergird our theory and practice if we are to develop a better understanding of the requirements for making the future more profitable and satisfying for young children with handicaps.

REFERENCES

Alberto, P. A., Briggs, T., & Goldstein, D. (1983). Managing learning in handicapped infants. In S. G. Garwood & R. R. Fewell (Eds.), *Educating handicapped infants* (pp. 417–454). Rockville, MD: Aspen Systems.

Als, H., Lester, B., & Brazelton, B. (1979). Dynamics of the behavioral organization of the premature infant: A theoretical perspective. In T. M. Field, A. M. Sostek, S. Goldberg, & H. H. Shuman (Eds.), *Infants born at risk* (pp. 173–192). Jamaica, NY: Spectrum Publications.

Anastasiow, N. M. (1986). The research base for early intervention. *Journal of the Division for Early Childhood*, 10, 99–105.

Baer, D. M., Peterson, R. F., & Sherman, J. A. (1967). The development of imitation by reinforcing behavioral similarity to a model. *Journal of Experimental Analysis of Behavior, 10*, 405–416.

Bagnato, S. J., Munson, S. M., & MacTurk, R. H. (1987). Exceptional infants and toddlers. In J. T. Neisworth & S. J. Bagnato (Eds.), *The young exceptional child: Early development and education* (pp. 180–205). New York: Macmillan.

Bagnato, S. J., & Neisworth, J. T. (1981). *Linking developmental assessment and curricula: Prescriptions for early intervention.* Rockville, MD: Aspen Systems.

Bagnato, S. J., & Neisworth, J. T. (1987). Normal and exceptional early development. In J. T. Neisworth & S. J. Bagnato (Eds.), *The young exceptional child: Early development and education* (pp. 64–100). New York: Macmillan.

Bagnato, S. J., Neisworth, J. T., & Capone, A. (1986). Curriculum-based assessment for the young exceptional child: Rationale and review. *Topics in Early Childhood Special Education, 6*, 97–110.

Bailey, D. B., Jens, K. G., & Johnson, N. (1983). Curricula for handicapped infants. In S. G. Garwood & R. R. Fewell (Eds.), *Educating handicapped infants* (pp. 387–415). Rockville, MD: Aspen Systems.

Bailey, D. B., Simeonsson, R. J., Winton, P. J., Huntington, G. S. Comfort, M., Isbell, P., O'Donnell, K. J., & Helm, J. M. (1986). Family-focused intervention: A functional model for planning, implementing, and evaluating individualized family services in early intervention. *Journal of the Division for Early Childhood, 10*, 156–171.

Beckman, P. J., Robinson, C. C., Jackson, B., & Rosenberg, S. A. (1986). Translating developmental findings into teaching strategies for young handicapped children. *Journal of the Division for Early Childhood, 10*, 45–52.

Bell, R. Q. (1974). Contributions of human infants to caregiving and social interaction. In M. Lewis & L. A. Rosenblum (Eds.), *The effect of the infant on its caregiver* (pp. 1–19). New York: Wiley.

Brazelton, T. B. (1973). *Neonatal behavior assessment scale.* Philadelphia: Lippencott.

Brazelton, T. B., Koslowski, B., & Main, M. (1974). The origins of reciprocity: The early mother–infant interaction. In M. Lewis & L. A. Rosenblum (Eds.), *The effect of the infant on its caregiver* (pp. 49–76). New York: Wiley.

Bricker, D. D. (1986). *Early education of at-risk and handicapped infants, toddlers, and preschool children.* Glenview, IL: Scott, Foresman.

Bricker, D. (1987). Impact of research on social policy for handicapped infants and children. *Journal of the Division for Early Childhood, 11,* 98–105.

Bricker, D. D., Bailey, E. J., & Bruder, M. B. (1984). The efficacy of early intervention and the handicapped infant: A wise or wasted resource? M. Wolraich & D. Routh (Eds.), *Advances in Developmental and Behavioral Pediatrics* (Vol. 5, pp. 373–423). Greenwich, CT: JAI Press.

Bricker, D. D., & Bricker, W. A. (1971). *Toddler research and intervention project report: Year 1.* (IMRID Behavioral Science Monograph No. 20). Nashville: Institute on Mental Retardation and Intellectual Development, George Peabody College.

Bricker, D. D., & Carlson, L. (1981). Issues in early language intervention. In R. Schiefelbusch & D. Bricker (Eds.), *Early language: Acquisition and intervention* (pp. 477–515). Baltimore: University Park Press.

Bricker, D. D., Gentry, D., & Bailey, E. J. (1985). *Evaluation and Programming System: For Infants and Young Children: Assessment level I: Developmentally 1 month to 3 years.* Eugene: University of Oregon.

Bricker, D. D., & Slentz, K. L. (1988). Personnel preparation: Handicapped infants. In M. Wang, H. Walberg, & M. Reynolds (Eds.), *The handbook of special education: Research and practice* (Vol. 3, pp. 319–345). Oxford: Pergamon Press.

Bricker, D. D., Squires, J., Kaminski, R., & Mounts, L. (1988). The reliability, validity and cost of a parent-completed questionnaire system to evaluate at-risk infants. *Journal of Pediatric Psychology, 13,* 56–68.

Bricker, W. A., & Campbell, P. H. (1980). Interdisciplinary assessment and programming for multihandicapped students. In W. Sailor, B. Wilcox, & L. Brown (Eds.), *Methods of instruction for severely handicapped students* (pp. 3–45). Baltimore: P. H. Brookes.

Brinker, R. (1985). Curricula without recipes: A challenge to teachers and a promise to severely mentally retarded students. In D. Bricker & J. Filler (Eds.), *The severely mentally retarded: From research to practice* (pp. 208–229). Reston, VA: Council for Exceptional Children.

Bruder, M. B., & Bricker D. D. (1985). Parents as teachers of their children and other parents. *Journal of the Division for Early Childhood, 9,* 136–150.

Casto, G., & Mastropieri, M. A. (1986). The efficacy of early intervention programs: A meta-analysis. *Exceptional Children, 52,* 417–424.

Clarke-Stewart, A., & Koch, J. B. (1983). *Children: Development through adolescence.* New York: Wiley.

Cohen, M. A., & Gross, P. J. (1979). *The developmental resource: Behavioral sequence for assessment and program planning* (Vol. 2). New York: Grune & Stratton.

Cole, J. G., & Gilkerson, L. (1982). Developmental consultation: The role of the parent/infant educator in a hospital/community coordinated program for high-risk premature infants. In A. Waldstein, D. Gilderman, D. Taylor-Hershel, S. Prestridge, & J. Anderson (Eds.), *Issues in neonatal care* (pp. 107–122). Monmouth/Chapel Hill, NC: WESTAR/TADS.

Decker, M. (Ed.). (1986). *The 1985–86 handicapped children's early education program directory.* Chapel Hill, NC: TADS.

Dennis, W. (1963). Environmental influences upon motor development. In W. Dennis (Ed.), *Readings in child psychology* (2nd ed., pp. 83–94). Englewood Cliffs, NJ: Prentice-Hall.

Dewey, J. (1916). *Democracy and education.* New York: MacMillan.

Dunst, C. J. (1981). *Infant learning: A cognitive-linguistic intervention strategy.* Hingham, MA: Teaching Resources Corporation.

Dunst, C. J., & Rheingrover, R. (1981). An analysis of the efficacy of infant intervention programs with organically handicapped children. *Evaluation and Program Planning, 4,* 287–323.

Dunst, C. J., & Snyder, S. W. (1986). A critique of the Utah State University early intervention meta-analysis research. *Exceptional Children, 53,* 269–276.

Erdman, R. L., & Olson, J. L. (1966). Relationships between educational programs for the mentally retarded and the culturally deprived. *Mental Retardation Abstracts, 3,* 311–318.

Fallen, N. H. (1985). Assessment: Techniques, processes and issues. In N. H. Fallen & W. Umansky (Eds.), *Young children with special needs* (2nd ed., pp. 61–131). Columbus, OH: Merrill.

Fantz, R. L. (1973). Visual perception from birth as shown by pattern selectivity. In L. J. Stone, H. T. Smith, & L. B. Murphy (Eds.), *The competent infant: Research and commentary* (pp. 622–630). New York: Basic Books.

Ferry, P. C. (1981). On growing new neurons: Are early intervention programs effective? *Pediatrics, 67,* 38–41.

Fewell, R. R., & Sandall, S. R. (1986). Developmental testing of handicapped infants: A measurement dilemma. *Topics in Early Childhood Special Education, 6,* 86–99.

Flavell, J. H. (1977). *Cognitive development* Englewood Cliffs, NJ: Prentice-Hall.

Flavell, J. H. (1985). *Cognitive development* (2nd ed.). Englewood Cliffs, NJ: Prentice-Hall.

Frankenburg, W. K., Emde, R. N., & Sullivan, J. W. (1985). *Early identification of children at risk: An international perspective.* New York: Plenum Press.

Gardner, J. M., & Karmel, B. Z. (1983). Attention and arousal in preterm and full-term neonates. In T. Field & A. Sostek (Eds.), *Infants born at risk: Physiological, perceptual and cognitive processes* (pp. 69–98). New York: Grune & Stratton.

Gaylord-Ross, R. (1980). A decision model for the treatment of aberrant behavior in applied settings. In W. Sailor, B. Wilcox, & L. Brown (Eds.), *Instruction for severely handicapped students* (pp. 135–158). Baltimore: P. H. Brookes.

Gibson, D., & Field, D. (1984). Early stimulation programs for Down's syndrome: An effectiveness inventory. In W. Wolraich & D. Routh (Eds.), *Advances in developmental and behavioral pediatrics* (Vol. 5, pp. 331–372). Greenwich, CT: JAI Press.

Goldberg, S., & DiVitto, B. A. (1983). *Born too soon: Preterm birth and early development.* New York: W. H. Freeman.

Goldstein, S., & Turnbull, A. P. (1982). Strategies to increase parent participation in IEP conferences. *Exceptional Children, 48,* 360–361.

Guralnick, M. J., & Bennett, F. C. (1987). A framework for early intervention. In M. J. Guralnick & F. C. Bennett (Eds.), *The effectiveness of early intervention for at-risk and handicapped children* (pp. 3–29). Orlando: Academic Press.

Harrision, H. (1983). *The premature baby book: A parent's guide to coping and caring in the first years.* New York: St. Martin's Press.

Haskins, R., Finkelstein, N., & Stedman, D. (1978). Infant-stimulation programs and their effects. *Pediatrics Annual, 7,* 123–144.

Hayden, A., & Haring, N. (1978). The acceleration and maintenance of developmental gains in Down's syndrome school-age children. In P. Mittler (Ed.), *Research to practice in mental retardation. Vol. I: Care and intervention* (pp. 129–141). Baltimore: University Park Press.

Haywood, H. C., Brooks, P., & Burns, S. (1986). Stimulating cognitive development at developmental level: A tested, non-remedial preschool curriculum for preschoolers and older retarded children. In M. Schwebel & C. Mahr (Eds.), *Facilitating cognitive development: International perspectives, programs and practices* (pp. 127–147). New York: Haworth Press.

Hersen, M., & Barlow, D. (1976). *Single case experimental designs.* New York: Pergamon Press.

Hunt, J. McV. (1961). *Intelligence and experience.* New York: Ronald Press.

Issacson, R. L. (1976). Recovery "?" from early brain damage. In T. D. Tjossem (Ed.), *Intervention strategies for high risk infants and young children* (pp. 37–62). Baltimore: University Park Press.

Jennings, K. D., Connors, R. E., Stegman, C. E., Sankaranarayan, P., & Mendelsohn, S. (1985). Mastery motivation in young preschoolers: Effect of a physical handicap and implications for educational programming. *Journal of the Division for Early Childhood, 9,* 162–169.

Johnson-Martin, N., Jens, K., & Attermeier, S. (1986). *The Carolina curriculum for handicapped infants and infants at risk.* Baltimore: P. H. Brookes.

Jones, O. (1977). Mother–child communication with prelinguistic Down's syndrome and normal infants. In H. Schaffer (Ed.), *Studies in mother–infant interaction* (pp. 379–401). New York: Academic Press.

Karnes, M., & Johnson, L. (1987). *Coordinating Assessment and Programming for Preschoolers (CAPP). Field Test Edition.* Champaign, IL: Developmental Service Center.

Kempe, R. S., Cutler, C., & Dean, J. (1980). The infant with failure-to-thrive. In C. H. Kempe & R. E. Helfer (Eds.), *The battered child* (3rd ed., pp. 163–182). Chicago: University of Chicago Press.

Keogh, B. K., Wilcoxen, A. G., & Bernheimer, L. (1986). Prevention services for risk children: Evidence for policy and practice. In D. C. Farran & J. D. McKinney (Eds.), *Risk in intellectual and psychosocial development* (pp. 287–316). New York: Academic Press.

Kopp, C. B. (1982). The role of theoretical frameworks in the study of at-risk and handicapped young children. In D. D. Bricker (Ed.), *Intervention with at-risk and handicapped infants: From research to application* (pp. 13–30). Baltimore: University Park Press.

Korner, A. F. (1974). The effect of the infant's state, level of arousal, sex, and ontogenetic stage on the caregiver. In M. Lewis & L. A. Rosenblum (Eds.), *The effect of the infant on its caregiver* (pp. 105–121). New York: Wiley.

Korner, A. F. (1979). Maternal rhythms and waterbeds: A form of intervention with premature infants. In E. B. Thoman (Ed.), *Origins of the infant's social responsiveness* (pp. 95–124). Hilldale, NJ: L. Erlbaum.

Krakow, J. B., & Kopp, C. B. (1982). Sustained attention in young Down syndrome children. *Topics in Early Childhood Special Education*, *2*, 32–42.

Lester, B. M. (1983). Change and stability in neonatal behavior. In T. B. Brazelton & B. M. Lester (Eds.), *New approaches to developmental screening of infants* (pp. 51–75). New York: Elsevier Science Publishing Co., Inc.

Lichtenstein, R., & Ireton, H. (1984). *Preschool screening: Identifying young children with developmental and educational problems.* Orlando: Grune & Stratton.

MacDonald, J. D. (1985). Language through conversation: A model for intervention with language-delayed persons. In S. F. Warren & A. K. Rogers-Warren (Eds.), *Teaching functional language* (pp. 89–122). Baltimore: University Park Press.

MacMillan, D. L., & Turnbull, A. P. (1983). Parent involvement with special education: Respecting individual preferences. *Education and Training of the Mentally Retarded, 18*, 5–9.

Mahoney, G. (1975). Ethological approaches to delayed language acquisition. *American Journal of Mental Deficiency, 80*, 139–148.

Mahoney, G., & Robenalt, K. (1986). A comparison of conversational patterns between mothers and their Down syndrome and normal infants. *Journal of the Division for Early Childhood, 10*, 172–180.

Mastropieri, M. A., White, K. R., & Fecteau, F. (1986). Introductions of special education textbooks: What they say about the efficacy of early intervention. *Journal of the Division for Early Childhood, 11*, 59–66.

Matarazzo, J. D. (1972). *Wechsler's measurement and appraisal of adult intelligence* (5th ed.). New York: Oxford University Press.

McCarthy, J. M., Lund, K. A., & Bos, C. S. (1987). *The Arizona Basic Assessment and Curriculum Utilization System.* Denver: Love Publishing.

Meisels, S. J. (1979). Special education and development. In S. J. Meisels (Ed.), *Special education and development: Perspectives on young children with special needs* (pp. 3–10). Baltimore: University Park Press.

Meisels, S. J. (1987). Using criterion-referenced assessment data to measure the progress of handicapped children in early intervention programs. In G. Casto, F. Ascione, & M. Salehi (Eds.), *Perspectives in infancy and early childhood research* (pp. 59–64). Logan, UT: DCHP Press.

Meisels, S. J., & Margolis, L. H. (1988). Is EPSDT effective with developmentally disabled children? *Pediatrics 81*, 262–271.

Mori, A. A., & Neisworth, J. T. (1983). Curricula for early childhood education: Some generic and situational considerations. *Topics in Early Childhood Special Education*, *2*, 1–8.

National Center for Clinical Infant Programs (1985). *Keeping track: Tracking systems for high risk infants and young children.* Washington, DC: Author.

National Center for Clinical Infant Programs (1986). *Infants can't wait.* Washington, DC: Author.

Nebraska Department of Education (1986). *Survey of early childhood special education service providers* (Final Report, Special Education Office). Lincoln: Author.

Newborg, J., Stock, J., Wnek, L., Guidubaldi, J., & Svinicki, J. (1984). *Battelle Developmental Inventory.* Allen, TX: DLM Teaching Resources.

Notari, A. (1988). *The utility of a criterion-referenced instrument in the development of individualized education plans for infants and young children.* Unpublished doctoral dissertation, University of Oregon, Eugene.

Notari, A., Slentz, K. L., & Bricker, D. D. (in press). Assessment-curriculum packages for early childhood special education. In R. Brown & D. Mitchell (Eds.), *Early intervention for disabled and at-risk infants* (Vol. 4). London: Croom Helm.

Odom, S., & Fewell, R. (1983). Program evaluation in early childhood special education: A meta-evaluation. *Educational Evaluation and Policy Analysis, 5*, 445–460.

Odom, S., & Shuster, S. (1986). Naturalistic inquiry and the assessment of young handicapped children and their families. *Topics in Early Childhood Special Education, 6*, 68–82.

Piper, M., & Pless, I. (1980). Early intervention for infants with Down syndrome: A controlled trial. *Pediatrics, 65*, 463–468.

Prechtl, H. F. (1983). Risk factors and the significance of early neurological assessment. In T. B. Brazelton & B. M. Lester (Eds.), *New approaches to developmental screening of infants* (pp. 125–135). New York: Elsevier Science Publishing Co., Inc.

Pueschel, S. M., Tingey, C., Rynders, J. E., Crocker, A. C., & Crutcher, D. M. (1987). *New perspectives on Down syndrome.* Baltimore: P. H. Brookes.

Rainforth, B. (1982). Biobehavioral state and orienting: Implications for educating profoundly retarded students. *The Journal of the Association for the Severely Handicapped, 6*, 33–37.

Richard, N. B. (1986). Interaction between mothers and infants with Down syndrome: Infant characteristics. *Topics in Early Childhood Special Education, 6*, 53–71.

Rothbart, M. K. (1984). Social development. In M. Hanson (Ed.), *Atypical infant development* (pp. 207–236). Austin, TX: Pro-Ed.

Rynders, J. E., & Horrobin, J. M. (1975). Project Edge: The University of Minnesota's communication stimulation program for Down's syndrome infants. In B. Friedlander, G. Sterritt, & G. Kirk (Eds.), *Exceptional infant* (Vol. 3, pp. 173–192). New York: Brunner/Mazel.

St. James-Roberts, I. (1979). Neurological plasticity, recovery from brain insult, and child development. In H. W. Reese & L. P. Lipsitt (Eds.), *Advances in child development and behavior* (Vol. 14, pp. 253–319). New York: Academic Press.

Sarason, S., & Doris, J. (1969). *Psychological problems in mental deficiency.* New York: Harper & Row.

Shearer, D., & Shearer, M. (1976). The Portage project: A model for early childhood intervention. In T. Tjossem (Ed.), *Intervention strategies for high-risk infants and young children* (pp. 335–350). Baltimore: University Park Press.

Sheehan, R. (1982). Infant assessment: A review and identification of emergent trends. In D. Bricker (Ed.), *Intervention with at-risk and handicapped infants: From research to application* (pp. 47–61). Baltimore: University Park Press.

Sherrod, K., Vietze, P., & Friedman, S. (1978). *Infancy.* Monterey: Brooks/Cole.

Shonkoff, J. P., & Hauser-Cram, P. (1987). Early intervention for disabled infants and their families – a quantitative analysis. *Pediatrics, 80*, 650–658.

Sigman, M. D. (1983). Individual differences in infant attention: Relations to birth status and intelligence at five years. In T. Field & A. Sostek (Eds.), *Infants born at risk: Physiological, perceptual and cognitive processes* (pp. 271–293). New York: Grune & Stratton.

Simeonsson, R. J., Cooper, D., & Scheiner, A. (1982). A review and analysis of the effectiveness of early intervention programs. *Pediatrics, 69*, 635–641.

Simeonsson, R. J., Huntington, G. S., & Parse, S. A. (1980). Assessment of children with severe handicaps: Multiple problems – multivariate goals. *Journal of the Association for the Severely Handicapped, 5*, 55–72.

Skeels, H. M. (1966). Adult status of children with contrasting early life experiences. *Monographs of the Society for Research in Child Development, 31* (3, Serial No. 105).

Stile, S. W., Abernathy, S. M., Pettibone, T. J., & Wachtel, W. J. (1984). Training and certification for early childhood special education personnel: A six-year follow-up study. *Journal of the Division for Early Childhood, 8*, 69–73.

Stillman, R. D. (1975). *Assessment of deaf-blind children: The Callier-Azusa scale.* Reston: The Council for Exceptional Children.

Strain, P. S. (1984). Efficacy research with young handicapped children: A critique of the status quo. *Journal of the Division for Early Childhood, 9*, 4–10.

Strain, P. S., & Smith, B. J. (1986). A counter-interpretation of early intervention effects: A response to Casto and Mastropieri. *Exceptional Children, 53*, 260–265.

Superintendent of Public Instruction, Olympia Washington. (1984). *Implementation guide for early childhood special education programs.* Olympia: Author.

TADS/WESTAR. (1979). *Handicapped children's early education program 1978–79: Overview and directory.* Washington, DC: U.S. Office of Education.

Thurman, S. K., & Widerstrom, A. H. (1985). *Young children with special needs: A developmental and ecological approach.* Newton, MA: Allyn & Bacon.

Tingey, C. (1986). Early intervention: Learning what works. *The Exceptional Parent, 16*, 32–33.

Tronick, E. (1980). Infant communicative intent. In A. P. Reilly (Ed.), *The communication game* (pp. 4–10). Skillman, NJ: Johnson & Johnson.

Uzgiris, I., & Hunt, J. McV. (1975). *Assessment in infancy: Ordinal scales of psychological development*. Urbana: University of Illinois Press.

Vietze, P. M., & Coates, D. (1986). Using information processing strategies for early identification of mental retardation. *Topics in Early Childhood Special Education, 6,* 72–85.

Vietze, P. M., McCarthy, M., McQuiston, S., MacTurk, R., & Yarrow, L. J. (1983). Attention and exploratory behavior in infants with Down's syndrome. In T. Field & A. Sostek (Eds.), *Infants born at risk: Physiological, perceptual and cognitive processes* (pp. 251–268). New York: Grune & Stratton.

Vincent, L. J., Salisbury, C., Walter, G., Brown, P., Grunewald, L. J., & Powers, M. (1980). Program evaluation and curriculum development in early childhood special education: Criteria of the next environment. In W. Sailor, B. Wilcox, & L. Brown (Eds.), *Methods of instruction for severely handicapped students* (pp. 303–328). Baltimore: P. H. Brookes.

Warren, S. F., & Kaiser, A. P. (1988). Research in early language intervention. In S. L. Odom & M. B. Karnes (Eds.), *Research in early childhood special education* (pp. 89–108). Baltimore: P. H. Brookes.

Warren, S. F., & Rogers-Warren, A. K. (1982). Language acquisition patterns in normal and handicapped children. *Topics in Early Childhood Special Education, 2,* 70–79.

Warren, S. F., & Rogers-Warren, A. K. (1985). Teaching functional language: An introduction. In S. F. Warren & A. K. Rogers-Warren (Eds.), *Teaching functional language* (pp. 3–23). Baltimore: University Park Press.

Weiner, R., & Koppelman, J. (1987). *From birth to 5: Serving the youngest handicapped children.* Alexandria, VA: Capitol Publications.

Weiskopf, P. E. (1980). Burnout among teachers of exceptional children. *Exceptional Children, 47,* 18–23.

White, K. R., Bush, D., & Casto, G. (1985–1986). Learning from reviews of early intervention. *The Journal of Special Education, 19,* 417–428.

White, K. R., Mastropieri, M., & Casto, G. (1984). The efficacy of early intervention for handicapped children: An analysis of special education early childhood projects approved by the joint dissemination review panel. *Journal of the Division for Early Childhood, 9,* 11–26.

Wilson, A. L. (1980). Promoting a positive parent–baby relationship. In C. H. Kempe & R. E. Helfer (Eds.), *The battered child* (3rd ed., pp. 401–419). Chicago: University of Chicago Press.

Wolery, M., & Bailey, D. B. (1984). Alternatives to impact evaluations: Suggestions for program evaluation in early intervention. *Journal of the Division for Early Childhood, 9,* 27–37.

Wolf, M., Risley, T., & Mees, H. (1964). Application of operant conditioning procedures to the behavior problems of an autistic child. *Behavior Research and Therapy, 1,* 305–312.

Wolfensberger, W. (1969). The origin and nature of our institutional models. In R. Kugel & W. Wolfensberger (Eds.), *Changing patterns in residential services for the mentally retarded* (pp. 59–171). Washington, DC: President's Committee on Mental Retardation.

Young, W. M., Jr. (1969). Poverty, intelligence, and life in the inner city. *Mental Retardation, 7,* 24–29.

Zelazo, P. R. (1982). Alternative assessment procedures for handicapped infants and toddlers: Theoretical and practical issues. In D. Bricker (Ed.), *Intervention with at-risk and handicapped infants: From research to application* (pp. 107–128). Baltimore: University Park Press.

17 *Caregiver-focused models of early intervention*

VICTORIA SEITZ AND SALLY PROVENCE

Early intervention efforts that focus on the child's caregivers recognize the central importance of parents for the health, well-being, and development of the infant and young child. Parents protect the child's health, transmit social and cultural tradition, are the principal guides for the young child's development as a thinking, acting, and feeling person, and are the unique persons who enable the child to experience intimacy, security, and love. One of the most important roles of the professional is to support parents and other caregivers through the skilled use of knowledge about health and development and through a sensitive regard for the importance of a child's family for his or her physical, emotional, and intellectual well-being.

This chapter focuses on what is currently known about how professionals can enable parents and other caregivers to support and facilitate the child's development. It describes the types of intervention efforts that have been made, whether translated into programs or individual practice, and it analyzes the characteristics of those services that are effective. Finally, it presents research evidence to support the expectation that children benefit when services are directed toward their caregivers. As these topics indicate, there are both theoretical and empirical issues to be considered in determining the potential impact of directing services for children primarily toward their caregivers. In this chapter we will first address issues concerning how services might best be delivered, then we will examine evidence concerning what is known about the effects of caregiver-focused programs.

THE DELIVERY OF CAREGIVER-FOCUSED SERVICES

Essentials for clinically effective programs

The principle that children benefit when services are directed toward caregivers has so much face validity that we wish to advance it as a reasonable working hypothesis that should routinely be adopted by those who design intervention programs. For a number of reasons we describe later, this hypothesis has rarely been adequately tested empirically, although the existing evidence supports it. A critical modification of the principle

Preparation of this chapter was supported by grant HD03008 from the National Institute of Child Health and Human Development.

400

is that the services should be clinically sound and well delivered. Even well-meaning efforts can be badly designed and may be rejected or viewed as irrelevant by the intended recipients.

Some guidance about how to design clinically sound programs can be derived from examining whether common principles appear to be true across programs that serve parents and children who differ considerably in the kinds of problems that they present. In a volume devoted to infant mental health issues (Provence, 1983a), evidence of this kind was provided by practitioners who described six different programs. The case reports described how clinicians work with parents and infants and described the changes or lack of changes in the lives of the children and parents during the work. Whereas settings, treatment approaches, and infants' presenting problems varied considerably from case to case, certain shared beliefs and attitudes could be recognized:

It is assumed that diagnosis and treatment can best be carried out when parents have an opportunity to become involved in a therapeutic alliance with those who offer help. Such an alliance usually forms gradually, based on professionals' ability to engender feelings of trust in the parent regarding their competence, interest, and availability. When care is episodic, discontinuous, or fragmented because of personnel changes – even in settings staffed by competent professionals – work with individual clients and parents is impeded, and many a good beginning lost (Provence, 1983b, p. 2).

Parents seek help for their children and know most about them. Part of the practitioner's task is to recognize the parents' knowledge and enable them to share what they know about their child, as well as their concerns and questions. This requires time, the ability to listen and inquire sensitively, and to provide information or advice in a clear and considerate manner.

There is no substitute for careful individualization of treatment for each child and parent in clinical work. Among the more encouraging results of work with disadvantaged families, and with parents whose infants are temperamentally difficult or disabled, are the continuing benefits to the child and parent of having the right kind of help at the time when it is needed. It is also assumed that parents and their children must be enabled to work actively in their own behalf and that helping them to do so is part of the function of the clinician. Some individuals and families are able to do so more promptly, and more fully, than others.

Families who have children whose needs for special care extend over months and years are subject to chronic stress with periods of acutely stressful events. To serve those families well, practitioners must be endowed with a capacity for sustained attention and service. Case studies and reports seldom convey how difficult and often discouraging the work may be. Little is said from the practitioners' side about the periods, sometimes long ones, when nothing very good seems to be happening in the life of the child, or when things are not going well between them and their clients or patients, or when the outcome for a particular child is especially grim. At such times colleagues, mentors, or consultants may be of great service, not only in reevaluating a particular case, but also in sharing the frustration, anxiety, and perplexity practitioners feel when the therapeutic goals they have set seem unattainable and when they feel less than adequate as healers or teachers.

Based upon these observations and on clinical experience, we suggest that there are at least three basic principles or concepts that favor successful early intervention with caregivers: *competence, continuity,* and *partnership.*

COMPETENCE OF SERVICE PROVIDERS. Basic knowledge and practical skills are vitally important for successful intervention with vulnerable and disabled children. When the skills of the providers match the needs of child and family, the maximum benefit of the services is likely to ensue. In other words, service providers ought to know what they are doing.

The need for competence implies the advantage of having a team of persons with different areas of expertise to provide services. The competence principle also implies that professional training in many areas would be enhanced if more careful attention were given to how to work with parents. For example, professionals who choose careers as early childhood specialists may be poorly trained in how to work with caregivers, and thus be less effective than their skill with the child would suggest. The competence principle is applicable to other professionals in the health, mental health, education, social service, and legal systems as well as to those who act as parent surrogates in day-care, foster care, and residential settings.

This principle does not imply that only highly trained professionals can be effective in intervening with caregivers. Paraprofessionals and lay home visitors can play a central role in service delivery (see Musick & Stott, this volume; Halpern, this volume). What is needed, however, is a backup system so that persons with special expertise are available when the need arises.

CONTINUITY OF CARE FROM SERVICE PROVIDERS. It is well known that utilization of services and the satisfaction of clients and patients are enhanced by parents' ability to see and count on being seen by the same service providers over time. It is also known that physicians, nurses, teachers, and others are more effective in their healing and supportive functions when they know the parent and child well. Thus, the utilization of a common clinic model, in which needed services are made available from whomever is on call at a particular time, is not recommended in delivering early intervention services to caregivers.

WORKING PARTNERSHIP BETWEEN PROVIDER AND CAREGIVER ON BEHALF OF THE CHILD. The ideal outcome of a caregiver-focused delivery model occurs when the service providers are successful in creating a working partnership with the caregivers on behalf of the child. It is extremely rare that a parent would not be needed as a partner in intervention efforts for the child. In those situations in which a parent is unavailable or unable to function as the child's nurturer, an adult substitute must become a part of the therapeutic team, because the caregiver's ability to sustain the child and contribute to the therapeutic program is vitally important to its success. The days when professionals expected themselves to be the source of all expertise and wisdom and to bestow it on the child are no more. Rather, it is clear that establishing a partnership and a therapeutic alliance with the caregiver on behalf of the child is a goal to be sought with persistence and all the skills we have available. Thomas (1988) has recently emphasized the problems that may arise for children with complex health care needs when parents and professionals become competitive over who is to control the child's treatment. Such problems include competition in regard to decision making with professionals seeing families as troublesome and interfering and families coming to regard professionals as excessively controlling and often prone to error.

There are unquestionably other principles that could guide the development of effective service delivery models, but we view these three as being particularly critical.

We believe these principles are essential fundamentals necessary if caregivers are going to be supported effectively in their ability to promote their childen's physical, emotional, and intellectual well-being.

Some models of intervention

Working with child and parent simultaneously, or conjointly, is often the intervention model of choice. Here the aim is to influence the way in which parent and child interact in order to improve the child's development or behavior. Four of the most commonly used strategies are (1) parent as recipient of developmental guidance, (2) parent and child models, (3) parent as therapist, and (4) parent as teacher. Their descriptions follow.

PARENT AS RECIPIENT OF DEVELOPMENTAL GUIDANCE (GENERAL PEDIATRICS MODEL). Giving advice to parents about how to keep their children healthy and how to care for them when they are ill, hurt, or disabled has been at the center of the work of many early childhood specialists. Developmental guidance as a method focused on the caregiver is generally educative. But it is usually conceived as a process in which facts and information, although important, are provided as part of a working relationship between a parent and a clinician who is able to provide them sensitively and with regard to what a parent is ready to hear and able to use.

Developmental guidance is recognized as an important part of the practitioner's role in child care and is an expectable occurrence in the practice of pediatricians, nurses, and family practitioners. The tradition of well-baby care, for example, includes advice about preventive measures, not only regarding immunization and nutrition, but also about the safety of the environment. It also includes a tradition of anticipatory guidance – looking forward to the next expected events in the baby's development – or guidance regarding current issues or problems in behavior or development. When the infant has a handicapping condition or is medically fragile, these same factors operate but become more complex. The assumption in each case is that such guidance, which includes but is not limited to providing information to the parents, will have a beneficial influence on the adult's ability to function comfortably and competently in the parental role. The child is the primary focus of attention, but the work goes on between the caregiver and practitioner. Such advice is likely to be most helpful and effective when a working alliance has been developed between the parent and physician or nurse, when the professional is seen as trustworthy and interested, and when sufficient time is allowed for the parents' questions and concerns to be discussed.

PARENT AND CHILD MODELS. Three models of working with child and parent in the presence of a professional are given as examples of therapy in which both child and parent are participants in the process, but the effectiveness is due primarily to changes brought about in the parent. The presence and participation of the child is primarily a catalyst in that his or her development, actions, and reactions to parent and therapist facilitate and shape the direction of the work. One of the great advantages of working both with parent and child is that the therapist can more promptly appreciate changes that influence the dynamic relationship between them.

Parent and child in dyadic treatment. Dyadic treatment refers to approaches in which psychodynamic change is brought about through working with child and parent together. The interactions between child and parent, parent and therapist, and child and therapist provide the material for the dialogue. The elements of emotional support, of interpretation of behavior, and of guidance and counseling are integral to the process.

The method of parent–infant psychotherapy developed by Fraiberg and her colleagues (Fraiberg, Adelson, & Shapiro, 1980) is one in which the treatment of the parent is foremost. Indeed, the problem in the infant is seen to be a result of conflict between parent and infant arising from the mother's unresolved problems with figures in her own past – the old "ghosts" that have invaded the nursery. Meaningful links between past and present are made through interpretation that will lead to insight. In the course of parental treatment, however, there is always a return to the baby. The choice of this treatment modality is dependent on the parent's ability to make use of such a focus and, as Fraiberg notes, may be contraindicated when there is ego impairment that cannot sustain inquiry into causes and motives. However, experience with this method demonstrates that it can be used successfully in a broad range of cases, including parents who are depressed, borderline, adolescent, or "acting out," and whose problems have adversely affected their infants.

Tripartite Therapeutic Design. The Tripartite Therapeutic Design developed by Mahler (1968) is one in which parent and therapist join in the rehabilitation of the psychotic child in sessions 2–3 hours long. The mutual exchanges of information and understanding between parent and therapist during these sessions have great advantages in Mahler's view. In these very difficult, long-term interventions the parent is also helped to engage in an emotional-intellectual learning experience that permits her or him to assume and maintain the corrective experiences for the child developed through the therapy. Improvement in some very impaired children through this treatment modality has led to its use with other kinds of cases, for example, with young infants with severe hearing impairments to alleviate problems in social and emotional communication between child and parent (Fields, Blum, & Scharfman, in press).

Parent and child interaction model. Still another model in which the nature of the parent–child interaction is the focus of intervention is exemplified in the work of Bromwich (1981). Designated as the Parent–Infant Interaction Model, it focuses on the process of bonding and attachment and the reciprocal reading and responding to cues that form the core of a complex interactional system between parent and infant. It is the role of the intervention, Bromwich, says, to "assess the nature of the interactive process...and to intervene to make their behavior with each other more reciprocal and their interaction more mutually pleasurable" (1981, p. 9). That the infant exerts a powerful influence on parental behavior is a concept that has been demonstrated repeatedly by clinicians and investigators during the past 15 years (Bell, 1968; Bell & Harper, 1977). The infant who is unpredictable, unresponsive, or difficult to read for whatever reason is at risk of missing environmental stimuli that are important for optimum development. Intervention that focuses on parent–infant interaction can improve the interaction by modifying the way in which the parent perceives and behaves toward the baby. But, as Bromwich emphasizes, "the fact that the reciprocity of effect within the parent–infant dyad has become more generally accepted does not detract from recognition of the powerful influences that the parent's feelings, attitudes and behavior exercise on the behavior of her infant" (1981, p. 11). Such feelings may be particularly powerful when the baby is mentally retarded or otherwise disabled (Hodapp, 1988; Solnit & Stark, 1961). Thus a goal of such intervention is to enable the caregiver to behave toward the baby in ways that favor development. The consequences of a positive outcome in the short-term for such an intervention can have long-range favorable results because parents will have gained skill in observing their infants, in understanding the importance of play, and in learning to anticipate changes in behavior and needs as a part of development. A greater sense of adequacy in their parenting role and confidence in their ability to favorably influence their child's development characterize the successful intervention.

PARENT AS THERAPIST. Efforts in which parents are enabled to function as therapists doing what professionals would do for their children have been made for a variety of disabling conditions. Parents have been enabled by generations of nurses; speech, occupational, and physical therapists; and teachers to carry out part of the educational and therapeutic program for children with special needs. In recent years parents have assumed major responsibility for the home care of technologically dependent infants with complex health care needs, such as those with respiratory, gastrointestinal, neurological, and urological problems. It has become important that parents learn, for example, to master techniques for the use of nebulizers, humidifiers, tracheostomy or nasogastric tubes, catheters, and a host of other methods formerly associated only with professional care. There is increased activity in the training of professionals who can provide parents with the necessary education and psychological support to care for such infants effectively (Desguin, 1988; Harvey & Johns, 1988). Psychotherapy of young children in selected cases has been accomplished successfully through working not with the child but with the parent, who has become the child's therapist providing interpretations in much the same way as a professional psychotherapist might do (Bonnard, 1950; Furman, 1957). Freud's treatment of the phobia of Little Hans via the father is perhaps the best-known example (1909/1955).

In deciding to use the approach of parent as therapist, it is essential to assess the child carefully to understand how the child's condition contributes to the problem. One may then decide that the child does not need direct work and that therapy may be carried out through guiding the parent. It is important to keep in mind, however, that the child's well-being remains at the center of the work between clinican and parent. It is the adult as parent that is the focus in the model, not the adult as adult patient.

In adopting a parent-as-therapist approach, practitioners need to be aware that something beyond the ordinary parent–child relationship is involved. The parent is being asked to assume a role that is task-oriented and targeted to a particular problem in the child. The child is asked to cooperate in much the same way the professional therapist requires. But not every parent can be an effective therapist or cotherapist for his or her child. Anxiety, tension, and anger with the child can operate to prevent the process from working well for either parent or child. One problem is that the child may develop the fear that if unable to do what is asked, for example, learning new words or other skills, he or she will lose the parent's love. The stress on child and parent may engender emotional complications beyond those that already exist because of the child's disability. It is also possible that periods of successful involvement of parent as therapist may be followed by periods when the effectiveness of therapy would be enhanced and stress diminished if the parent is not a therapist or cotherapist. This places an important responsibility on professionals for careful, continuing evaluation of the therapeutic plan. They must be sensitive enough to realize when too much stress is being placed on the parent–child relationship and when to relieve parent and child, temporarily at least, of the responsibility of working together as therapist and patient.

PARENT AS TEACHER. When a child's primary problem has been perceived as intellectual slowness arising from a presumed lack of adequate cognitive stimulation, parents have sometimes been enlisted to provide intellectual stimulation to their children at home. Levenstein's Verbal Interaction Project (1970) provides one example of this approach. In this model a trained home visitor, called a "toy demonstrator," makes home visits, bringing carefully chosen toys or games. (Parents also can be shown how to create toys from common household objects.) The toy demonstrator shows how the child can be engaged actively in playing with cognitively challenging toys and asks the parent to regularly spend time every day playing in the same manner with the child. In other projects, parents have been encouraged to talk with their preschoolers more and to read to them on a regular basis (Gordon, Guinagh, & Jester, 1977).

Conceptually, the parent-as-teacher model is similar to the parent-as-therapist approach described earlier. In practice, however, the intensity of necessary effort tends to be less in the parent-as-teacher approach. Also, the model is more likely to be imposed on parents by others who are concerned about the child's development rather than to be adopted because the parents perceive a problem and seek help. In general, the parent-as-teacher model has been more associated with research efforts than with clinical practice, and it tends to have been employed principally with economically impoverished populations (Gordon et al., 1977; Karnes, Teska, & Hodgins, 1970; Levenstein, 1970).

EFFECTS OF CAREGIVER-FOCUSED PROGRAMS

Research information on effects of caregiver-focused programs arises primarily from three sources. Programs have been designed for families whose children are believed to be at risk of poor outcomes (1) because of environmental circumstances (especially poverty), (2) because the child may pose unusual difficulties for the caregiver (e.g., premature or disabled infants), or (3) because the parents have special vulnerabilities (e.g., depressed mothers, adolescent mothers). We will examine each of these areas in turn.

Poverty or low socioeconomic status

COGNITIVE-FOCUSED PROGRAMS. Most intervention programs for economically impoverished children have focused directly on the children and have been designed for the purpose of influencing their cognitive development. Even in such programs, the importance of recognizing the caregiver's role became apparent very early. In a review of early childhood intervention programs over a decade ago, Bronfenbrenner (1975) concluded that the effects of such programs were greatly enhanced when parents were given a meaningful role in the intervention. In Bronfenbrenner's analysis, "The involvement of the child's family as an active participant is critical to the success of any intervention program. Without such family involvement, any effects of intervention, at least in the cognitive sphere, appear to erode fairly rapidly once the program ends" (p. 595).

The nature of parental involvement in the programs upon which this conclusion was based can be characterized as parents serving as teachers to their preschool children. Specifically, in some of the more successful early programs, parents were encouraged to view themselves as being competent to help their children learn and were given materials in the home with which to engage them in learning experiences (e.g., Gordon et al., 1977; Karnes et al., 1970; Levenstein, 1970). Parents were also encouraged to read aloud to their children. The emphasis in such programs was upon having parents learn to use toys and play as vehicles of instruction.

HEALTH AND SOCIAL OUTCOME PROGRAMS. Within the past decade, a number of researchers have attempted to influence health and social outcomes for poor children in addition to, or instead of, cognitive outcomes. The interventions implemented by these researchers have been much more explicitly caregiver-focused than were the majority of earlier programs.

THE UNIVERSITY OF ROCHESTER NURSE HOME VISITATION PROGRAM. One of the most ambitious studies in terms of size, scope, and quality of evaluation design has been an experimental study by Olds and his colleaquges (Olds, Henderson, Tatelbaum, & Chamberlain, 1986, 1988; Olds, Henderson, Chamberlain, & Tatelbaum, 1986) of the effects of intervention on 400 pregnant and parenting low-income women in a small, semirural county in the Appalachian region of New York State. The intervention in this study was provided by nurses who made home visits to women who were pregnant with their firstborn child. For some women, visits were made only during their pregnancy; for others, visiting continued postnatally until the children were 2 years old. In addition to nurse home visits, the project staff provided free transportation so that the women could visit their doctors for prenatal care and take their babies for well-child checkups.

The home visits offered considerable opportunity for contact between the nurse and the mother. During pregnancy, there were an average of 9 visits, each lasting approximately 1 hour and 15 minutes. Mothers in the postnatal visit group received about 30 such visits over 2 years. During the home visits nurses carried out three major activities: parent education, enhancement of the mothers' informal support system, and linkage of the family with other community health and human services. In terms of parent education, for example, the nurses provided mothers with information about fetal development, prenatal health care, and the significance of nutrition, smoking, and alcohol for the baby's health. Postnatally, nurses provided information about infant temperament, especially crying and its meanings, the infant's socioemotional and cognitive development, and physical health care needs. Both during pregnancy and postnatally, nurses attempted to enhance the support available to the mother from family and friends, and they connected families with community health and human service agencies. For example, they urged the mothers to make and keep medical appointments for prenatal care and for regular well-baby checkups, and they clarified and reinforced the recommendations of the families' physicians. When appropriate, nurses also referred mothers to a variety of other social services.

The results of this extensive intervention were impressive. The most striking results of nurse home visitation during pregnancy were found in health outcomes for the babies born to young adolescents and to mothers who were smokers. Teenagers who were less than 17 years of age and who were visited by a nurse during pregnancy gave birth to newborns who had significantly higher birth weights than those born to their nonvisited counterparts. Women who smoked and were visited by nurses significantly reduced the number of cigarettes they smoked and exhibited a 75% reduction in the incidence of preterm delivery compared to nonvisited smokers (Olds et al., 1986a).

The effects of the program were also examined for the outcomes of preventing child abuse and neglect (Olds, Henderson, Chamberlain, Tatelbaum, 1986). During the babies' second year of life, infants of nurse-visited women were seen in the emergency room fewer times, and were seen by physicians less frequently for injuries and poisonings than were babies of women who did not receive postnatal visits. For mothers considered to be at especially high risk – poor unmarried teenagers – there was lower incidence of verified child abuse and neglect during the children's first 2 years of life (4% for postnatally nurse-visited versus 19% for other poor unmarried teenagers). These high-risk mothers were also observed in their homes to restrict and punish their children less frequently and to provide more appropriate play materials.

Olds and his colleagues have recently examined the effects of the intervention for the mothers' own life course development (Olds et al., 1988). Nurse home visitation, regardless of timing, was found to lead to a higher likelihood that the mothers would return to school. Two other positive outcomes – employment and delay of subsequent pregnancy – occurred for specific subgroups of postnatally visited women. For older mothers (those over 19 years), those visited postnatally were nearly three times as likely to be employed in the first year after their babies' birth than were unvisited mothers or those who were visited during their pregnancy alone. Poor unmarried teenaged mothers who were visited postnatally had a very low rate of repeat pregnancy by the follow-up time of 22 months postpartum, a rate approximately one-fourth that for teen mothers who were not visited or who received only prenatal visits.

Because of the large sample size and random group assignment, considerable confidence can be placed in the results of this study. It provides one of the clearest indications to date that directing intervention efforts toward caregivers can result in significant benefits for their children. The results are also important in revealing that effects of programs will sometimes be found only for certain subgroups of at-risk parents. This finding has the methodological implication that evaluators of intervention programs should not accept an overall finding of no results without performing a diligent search for possible subgroups for which the treatment does have effects. It is reasonable to believe that subject-by-treatment interactions will be common in intervention programs and that eventually programs can be targeted to reach the most appropriate recipients. As long as meaningful subgroups can be defined based on objective criteria (e.g., young age or smokers), this is a defensible and highly recommended strategy.

MONTREAL HOME VISITATION STUDY. A second caregiver-focused study of both substantive and methodological importance was conducted by Larson (1980). As in the Olds et al. study, Larson examined the effects of prenatal and postpartum home visits, but the home visitors were not nurses. Rather, they had undergraduate degrees in child psychology and were extensively trained by the study's director, a pediatrician, to deliver the project's services. The recipients of this program were 115 working-class Canadian women who were between 18 and 35 years old, had no more than a high school education, experienced no serious illnesses during pregnancy, had no prior history of psychiatric hospitalization, and delivered healthy full-term babies.

Three different service formats were examined, varying in amount and timing of home visitation. Group A mothers received one prenatal visit in the seventh month of pregnancy, one postpartum hospital visit, and 9 postnatal home visits until the baby was 15 months old (half of these visits occurred during the initial 6 weeks at home). Group B received 10 home visits, from the age of 6 weeks to 15 months postpartum. Group C mothers received no visits or other forms of intervention. Mothers who received postpartum visits thus received a total of 10, but these differed in the time they were received. Assignment to groups B and C was random and ended when 80 subjects had been entered. Group A mothers were then entered into the study until a predetermined date. This time-lag approach was used to prevent contamination across conditions, since a pilot study had revealed that women who received a hospital visit shared their experience with other women in the same room.

The home visitors provided counseling and advice in four areas: general caretaking, mother–infant interaction, social status, and child development. General caretaking covered topics such as feeding, sleep and scheduling, bathing and clothing, injury prevention, and encouragement to seek out appropriate well-child care. The visitors encouraged mothers to interact frequently with their babies, as in talking to them during feeding and responding to their vocalizations. "Social status" referred to the visitor's reviewing the mother's support systems, her relationship with the baby's father, and any area of exceptional stress or concern. Child development counseling included reviewing with the mother the child's developmental competence and suggesting types of activities she could engage in to promote her child's capabilities.

Results of this study showed that the children in Group A had significantly fewer injuries than did those in Group B, who in turn had fewer injuries than did the Group C children. (The injury rate for Group C was quadruple that for Group A at 6 months and double at 12 months of age.) The quality of the home environment was assessed using the HOME scale (Caldwell & Bradley, 1979), a widely used measure that has been shown to be predictive of infants' cognitive development. Group A mothers consistently scored higher on the HOME scale than did Group B and C mothers, who did not differ from each other. Effects were particularly evident for the HOME subscale measuring the provision of appropriate play materials for the babies. Observers' ratings of the quality of maternal behavior with the child (e.g., "positive involvement with baby," "skill in caregiving," "responsiveness of behavior") consistently favored Group A over Group B and C mothers, with the differences being particularly pronounced in the earliest assessments (at 6 weeks and 6 months). Finally, Group A and B mothers were compared in the number of problems observed by the home visitors. Group B mothers were observed to have significantly more feeding problems and mother–child interaction problems than did Group A mothers. There were also significantly more nonparticipant fathers in Group B than in Group A (22% versus 4%, respectively).

Larson concluded that the timing of visitation with caregivers was a highly important factor influencing the effectiveness of such visitation. His results indicate that *early* home visits, beginning prenatally and resuming early in the postpartum period, can lead to a reduction in injuries, increased sensitivity and responsiveness toward the child, and the establishment of a more stimulating home environment. The provision of visits during the postnatal period alone had a beneficial effect on injury rates but no other significant consequences.

Larson's findings are very similar to those obtained by Olds and his colleagues for effects of postnatal home visitation. Because Larson's most intensive intervention condition provided such comparable results to the other study, one implication is that the home visitor need not be a nurse. Because visitation that did not begin until 6 weeks into the postnatal period had relatively few effects, it is clear that timing deserves careful consideration in planning caregiver-focused interventions. Larson suggests that beginning home visitation postnatally may be a poor strategy; however, it is unclear whether postnatal programs alone might not be effective if they were begun sooner than 6 weeks after the baby is born. After 6 weeks, parents may come to feel that they are adjusting adequately and may view advice from home visitors as unnecessary and intrusive. Supportive services begun in the first week might be welcomed much more enthusiastically. Or it may be, as Larson hypothesizes, that beginning contact with a parent before the baby is born brings special benefits because the nature of the contact is inherently less threatening. As Larson has pointed out, "Contact with a mother during her pregnancy permits the initiation of services at a time when prevention rather than problem detection can be emphasized" (1980, p. 197).

THE YALE CHILD WELFARE PROGRAM. The projects described thus far have been evaluated when the children whose parents received services were still very young. There is reason to believe that the most important consequences of caregiver-focused intervention will be seen much later in the families' lives. In the authors' own research, effects of an early, intensive caregiver-focused program were found to be considerably greater 10 years after the program had ended than they were soon after services were terminated (Provence & Naylor, 1983; Provence, Naylor, & Patterson, 1977; Rescorla, Provence, & Naylor, 1982; Seitz, Rosenbaum, & Apfel, 1985; Trickett, Apfel, Rosenbaum, & Zigler, 1982).

The intervention sample consisted of 17 impoverished women who were expecting a first born child, who had no serious complications of pregnancy, who were not obviously retarded or psychotic, and who delivered healthy babies at the Women's Clinic of the Yale–New Haven Hospital. The initial contact was made during the mother's pregnancy, when the nature of the project's services was described. Services were provided until 30 months postpartum and included pediatric care, a regular home visitor, day care, and regular developmental examinations for the children.

Each pediatrician saw the newborn and mother at least daily during the postdelivery hospital stay and scheduled a home visit within the first week. Each made house calls if needed and responded to telephoned concerns promptly and sympathetically. The children received from 13 to 17 regular well-baby exams over the 30-month period, each scheduled to permit a full hour's interchange between mother and physician.

Home visits were made by a clinical social worker, a psychologist, or a nurse; families received an average of 28 visits over the 30-month period. Home visitors listened sympathetically to the parents' concerns, helped to solve such immediate problems as reducing physical dangers or obtaining more adequate food or housing, and assisted in solving larger life problems, such as helping parents come to satisfying educational, marital, and career decisions. They also provided a liaison with other service providers in the immediate project and in the community.

Day care and/or a toddler program were provided for all but one of the children for periods ranging from 2 to 28 months. On the average, the children received 13 months of day care. Each child had a primary caregiver; thus, the principle of individualized personalized care was extended to children in the day-care setting as well as to their parents in the other services that were provided. The staff actively tried to achieve continuity between their child-care practices and those of the parents, discussing any problems with parents in an effort to work out mutually agreeable methods of handling them. The primary focus was on the children's emotional and social development (e.g., helping the children learn to handle aggression, dealing with problem of separation from the parents, and fostering good peer interactions).

The children also received from seven to nine regularly scheduled developmental examinations, using the Yale Developmental Schedules (Provence & Leonard, 1986), a measure that is similar to the Bayley Scales of Infant Development. Without making any direct effort to teach facts about development, the examiner could nevertheless capitalize on the parent's interest and curiosity about the significance of the child's performance. Parents also had the opportunity to witness the examiner's techniques for handling difficult behavior and to discuss their concerns about it.

During the program, each family interacted with a team of four persons: a home visitor, pediatrician, primary day-care worker, and developmental examiner. This "family team" provided long-term continuity for each family, because at least one member could be dependably available at any time. In short, the intervention employed a teamwork approach providing continuity of care by familiar and skilled professionals; it focused on the social and emotional adjustment of the parents and children, and its aim was to strengthen parents in their caregiving ability and their ability to solve their own life problems.

One of the 17 families had a second child during the intervention period, and this child was added to the intervention sample. As a control group, the project staff recruited a sample of eighteen 30-month old children after the project had ended. The clinic records were searched in the same manner as had occurred in identifying the experimental subjects. From the group of mothers who met the original criteria, and who would have been invited to participate in the project had it continued, potential control children were matched with the experimental children on sex, income level of the family, number of parents in the home, and ethnicity of the mother. The investigators thus employed a time-lag strategy, as did Larson (1980), in order to obtain a control group.

Significant results of the project at the close of the intervention, when the children were 30 months old, were limited to language development: Intervention children showed better language development than did control children. A 10-year follow-up study revealed a number of additional differences between intervention and control families. Intervention mothers had obtained significantly more education than had control mothers, and they were significantly more likely to be employed and self-supporting. Intervention mothers had also chosen to bear fewer children than had control mothers, and to space the births of their children more widely. The two groups of children did not differ in IQ or in performance on a standardized academic achievement test. However, intervention children had better school attendance, and striking differences in school adjustment were found among the boys. Control boys were much more likely to require costly special school services than were intervention boys (on the average, control boys cost more than $1,000 more per child in this one year alone for services than did intervention boys), and teachers rated control boys much more negatively in describing their behavior in the classroom. Intervention mothers were significantly more likely than control mothers to seek out information from their children's teachers about their school performance. Intervention mothers were also more likely than control mothers to report that they enjoyed their children and that their children showed open affection toward them.

Perhaps the most noteworthy aspect of these results is the discovery that the long-term effects of an intervention program can be much greater than its short-term effects. Had the evaluation of this program been limited to the time period immediately following its completion, the most important consequences would have been missed. Intervention and control mothers did not differ in education or in being self-supporting when their firstborns were $2\frac{1}{2}$ years old. In the subsequent 10 years, however, control families remained essentially static on these dimensions, whereas intervention families showed a slow, steady improvement, and the two groups eventually diverged radically from each other. Almost all intervention families had become self-supporting by the time their firstborns were $12\frac{1}{2}$ years old. Since Olds et al. (1986) also reported higher maternal return to school for intervention mothers, an implication is that programs directed toward impoverished new parents have considerable potential to lead such parents to make beneficial changes in their lives. The very low rate of subsequent childbearing for intervention mothers (who waited a median of 9 years before having a second child) is an outcome that could not have been assessed in the earliest years following the program. Other consequences, such as a better parent–child relationship, are simply easier to measure when children are older. The impaired socialization of a child who has experienced many years of poor parenting can eventually become so readily apparent that subtle measurement techniques are not necessary. Ratings by teachers who dealt with these children daily made it clear that control boys were likely to show aggressive, acting-out, predelinquent behavior serious enough to require such actions as placement in classrooms for emotionally disturbed children or suspension from school following excessively aggressive behavior. Mothers of control boys also reported such problems as the son staying out all night without the mother's knowledge of where he was, stealing, and behaving aggressively toward parents and siblings. When parents can be led early in the child's life to be more confident and competent caregivers, the benefits are likely to become increasingly evident over time. Since improving the long-term parent–child relationship is a major goal of all caregiver-focused programs, it follows that the actual effectiveness of such programs cannot be adequately assessed without long-term follow-up.

Without more longitudinal research it is not possible to determine whether caregiver-focused or child-focused approaches are relatively more effective ways to design interventions. The limited information currently available suggests that, at least for poverty populations, caregiver-focused approaches may lead to more comprehensive changes for families and therefore to a broader range of beneficial outcomes for children than will child-focused approaches. As the very least, the existing data provide considerable encouragement to investigators to examine this hypothesis more fully.

Children posing unusual caregiving problems

Children who are born prematurely, who have a handicapping condition, or whose development is otherwise atypical are likely to present such difficult caregiving challenges that their parents are clearly in need of intervention services. It is very difficult to evaluate the effects of such services because ethical problems presented by creating control groups of unserved parents with disabled infants are particularly formidable. However, an informative line of research is emerging in the area of programs for parents of premature infants.

PREMATURE INFANTS. Whereas most attention has been focused on the medical needs of premature infants, many researchers have begun to address the unusual difficulties that low birth weight infants pose for their caregivers. In a widely noted study, Minde and his associates examined the efficacy of self-help groups for parents of premature infants (Minde et al., 1980). The babies whose parents were studied were very low birth weight (less than 1,501 grams), singleton birth infants who had no physical abnormalities or serious complications affecting the likelihood of their survival or eventual normal cerebral functioning. Parents of babies meeting the study criteria were alternately assigned, in blocks of four, to experimental and control conditions with a total of almost 30 subjects in each group. Control parents experienced the standard procedures of the hospital's premature nursery. Experimental parents were invited to meet the project's nurse coordinator during their first hospital visit and were informed about the parent support groups. Each group consisted of up to 10 parents, a nurse coordinator, and a "veteran parent" who had given birth to a similar small baby about a year earlier and who served as the group's "official animator." Groups met weekly for $1\frac{1}{2}$–2 hours. In the first few meetings, much of the group activity was directed at permitting parents to share their feelings about having given birth to a premature infant. Gradually, instructional content was added to the sessions, with information being given about the treatment procedures of the neonatal intensive care unit (NICU) and about appropriate infant stimulation and developmental needs.

Assessments of program effects were made during parental visits to their infants in the NICU and in home visits, up to 3 months after discharge. Experimental mothers visited their babies in the NICU significantly more often than control mothers did and, during their babies' hospitalization, were observed to interact with them increasingly more often over time, touching, looking in the en face position, and talking to their babies more than control mothers did. After discharge, experimental mothers were observed to spend more time than control mothers feeding their babies. In an interview at discharge, experimental mothers were more satisfied than control mothers with the medical and nursing care their child had received; they also had a better understanding of their infant's condition, more interaction with other parents, more knowledge of community resources, and more confidence in their ability to care for their infant at home. The intervention thus appeared both to reduce the emotional stresses associated with having given birth to a premature baby and to improve the quantity and quality of parent–infant interaction.

A second study of a hospital-based supportive program for parents of premature infants has been reported by Zeskind and Iacino (1984). The intent of the program was specifically to promote maternal visitation to infants in the NICU. The premature babies whose parents were studied were similar to those in the Minde et al. study – except that they were not limited to very low birth weight infants – in that they showed no gross signs of brain damage, severe central nervous system insult, respiratory distress, genetic anomalies, cardiac problems, or other significant medical problems likely to affect their survival. Twenty-six parents of such babies were assigned to experimental or control groups, approximately half by random assignment and half by matching on a number of variables to parents already assigned.

The control condition consisted of routine NICU treatment: A staff person visited the mother in her hospital room, accompanied her during her first visit to the NICU, explained her baby's condition, was available for explanations whenever requested (although opportunities for such interchanges were not routinely scheduled), and provided well-baby information at discharge. Mothers in the experimental condition were visited in their hospital room by a project staff member who offered advocacy and support. The interventionist explained the NICU procedures, clarified information about the baby, and encouraged the mother to visit her baby and to interact as much as was medically permissible. The interventionist made a weekly appointment for the mother to visit her baby and provided transportation for such visits if necessary. Finally, the interventionist made weekly home visits (30–90 minutes in length) for 6 weeks postdischarge to answer questions about the infant's development and provide well-baby information.

As was true in the Minde et al. study, experimental mothers chose to visit their babies more often than did control mothers. Experimental mothers made more than twice as many self-initiated visits to their babies than did control mothers. Perhaps this greater contact explains a second finding: Experimental mothers had more realistic, although negative, perceptions of their infants' behaviors at discharge than did control mothers. Nevertheless, experimental mothers were more positive than control mothers about their children's long-term prognosis. Finally, Zeskind and Iacino reported that the intervention group babies were hospitalized for a significantly shorter time than were control infants (by an average of about 8 days). After ruling out possible arti-factual causes for this finding, these investigators speculated that the greater maternal visitation to the baby "may have facilitated the recovery of the infant" (p. 1887).

A third predominantly hospital-based program was provided by Nurcombe and his associates (Nurcombe et al., 1984). Parents of premature babies were offered a total of 11 sessions with a pediatric nurse, focusing on helping them to resolve the emotional crisis associated with premature delivery and on teaching the mothers to be sensitive and responsive to their babies' physiological and social cues. Parents in this study had delivered premature, low birth weight infants (less than 37 weeks gestational age and less than 2,200 grams) who were hospitalized for 10 days or longer in the NICU. Single mothers, multiple births, and babies with congenital anomalies were excluded from the study sample. Seventy-eight parents of babies meeting the sample criteria were ran-domly assigned to experimental and control conditions. Parents in the experimental group met daily with the pediatric nurse intervenor in the hospital during the week prior to their baby's discharge and received four home visits from the nurse during the 3 months following discharge. The visits followed a preset plan, beginning with a demonstration of the baby's capabilities with the Brazelton Neonatal Behavioral Assessment Scale (BNBAS) (Brazelton, 1973), and progressing through such topics as posture, tone and movement, state regulation, attention, alertness and responsivity, feeding, diapering, bathing, play, and temperament.

Results were assessed when the babies were 6 months old (corrected for prematur-ity). The two groups of babies were comparable in mental and motor development on the Bayley Scales of Infant Development. They differed in temperament, however, as rated by their mothers. Experimental mothers rated their babies as more adaptable, happy, and approachable, and as less easily distressed compared with ratings of control group babies by their mothers. Intervention group mothers also were more confident in and more satisfied with child rearing than were control mothers.

In all three projects described thus far, there were indications of greater parental involvement in or satisfaction with the parental role following intervention. But the consequences for the babies have been more mixed. Both Minde et al. and Zeskind and Iacino limited their study of child outcomes to the length of hospitalization, with one study finding a positive effect of intervention and the other study no effects. Nurcombe et al. found no effects of their caregiver-focused intervention for the babies' cognitive and motor development, but they did report beneficial effects in parental perceptions of their babies' temperament. Clearly, the range of possible outcomes for children needs much more extensive study. At this point it remains an underexamined area for studies of hospital-based programs.

In studies that have relied extensively upon home visits as a vehicle for delivering programs, child outcomes have been examined much more extensively. Differences following intervention have been reported frequently and they uniformly favor babies in the intervention group over controls. A study by Scarr-Salapatek and Williams (1973) provides a conceptual bridge between the predominantly hospital-based pro-grams described thus far and other programs to be described that have relied extensively on home visitation to parents of premature babies. The Scarr-Salapatek and Williams study was not exclusively caregiver-focused, because the earliest phase of the intervention consisted of giving sensory enrichment directly to infants in the NICU. The infants in the study were 30 consecutively born neonates who weighed between 1,300 and 1,800 grams. The mothers of all these infants were low-income, black women, mostly unmarried and young (average age 21 years, range 16–32). Subjects were alternately assigned to experimental and control conditions.

Intervention infants were given a colorful mobile to look at within their isolette, whereas control infants were not provided with any special visual stimulation. When they were sufficiently well to permit the procedure, the intervention infants were picked up and talked to during feeding; control infants did not receive this special social and kinesthetic stimulation. Following discharge from the hospital, a social worker made weekly home visits to the intervention group mothers until the babies were 12 months of age. She gave instruction and provided demonstrations on how to play with the baby, how to provide stimulating care, and how to observe the infant sensitively. She gave the mothers suitable toys, a mobile, and an infant seat. The social worker also provided counsel and direct aid concerning the mothers' personal and practical problems, such as finding an apartment or job, obtaining AFDC, and dealing with depression, boyfriends, and relatives.

Because of the frequency of visits and the breadth of issues addressed by the home visitor, it is unfortunate that no data were reported in this study regarding changes in the caregivers. However, significant effects were found for the babies. In the NICU the intervention babies gained significantly more weight than did control babies. At 1 year of age, intervention babies scored significantly higher on the Cattell Infant Intelligence Test (Cattel, 1970) than did control babies (mean of 95 versus 86, respectively). The long-term effects are somewhat difficult to interpret because of attrition, because almost half of the control group was lost to follow-up by age 12 months. The finding of better cognitive development for the intervention infants, however, is consistent with results of a number of other caregiver-focused programs for low-income parents of premature infants, as will be described.

To better understand the effects of caregiver-focused programs, it would be a productive research strategy to compare different models of intervention within a single study. In a study conducted with a mixed socioeconomic status (SES)-Canadian sample, Barrera, Rosenbaum, and Cunningham (1986) employed such a strategy. One experimental condition, "developmental programming intervention," was designed to be similar to the program employed by Scarr-Salapatek and Williams (1973) in providing specific curriculum activites to stimulate the infants' cognitive development. A second experimental condition, "parent–infant interaction," was modeled after a program described by Bromwich and Parmelee (1979) that was designed to enhance the parent–infant interaction through sensitive observation, discussion, modeling, therapeutic suggestion, and encouragement (Bromwich, 1981).

Families who had delivered preterm infants (birth weight less than 2,000 grams and gestational age less than 37 weeks) were assigned by a stratified random assignment procedure to one of the two experimental interventions or to a control group. In addition, Barrera et al. studied a comparison group of full-term infants of comparable family backgrounds. Intervention began after the infant's discharge from the NICU (therefore, only the home-visiting portion of the Scarr-Salapatek and Williams procedure was replicated). Families in the two treatment groups received an average of 23 home visits during the first year following the baby's birth. These visits, 1–2 hours in duration, were made by therapists who "had academic and practical training in early child development and intervention working with parents" (Barrera et al., 1986, p. 22). Babies and their mothers were assessed at 4, 8, 12, and 16 months.

A number of effects of intervention were found, but few differences were found between the two intervention models. In terms of the babies' cognitive development, both intervention groups made significant gains on the Bayley Mental Development Index; neither the preterm nor the full-term control group changed significantly over time. The practical result of this finding is that whereas the intervention babies had lower mental development scores at 4 months compared with full-term babies, at 16 months they were comparable. No treatment effects were found for the babies' motor development or for measures of their temperament. On the HOME scale, both intervention groups became comparable to the full-term control group over time, with the parent–infant interaction group doing so more quickly. Particular improvement over time for intervention mothers was seen in the areas of "provision of materials" and "variety of stimulation." In the premature control group, HOME scores did not change appreciably and were lower than all other groups' scores by the age of 16 months. The investigators argued that, without intervention, premature infants tended to be raised in a relatively unstimulating manner and that "the effect of intervention was to 'normalize' the home environment of the preterm infant" (Barrera et al., 1986, p. 31). Finally, results of intervention were found on measures of both infant and maternal interaction: By 16 months of age, intervention infants displayed significantly more verbal independent play than did preterm controls. Also by 16 months, mothers of preterm controls were found to have become less responsive to their infants than were intervention or full-term control mothers.

This study is interesting for its demonstration that two models of intervention differing in focus (cognitive stimulation versus parent–infant interaction) nevertheless had similar beneficial effects. The study is also important for its indication that, without intervention, premature infants in low-income homes appear to be vulnerable to being raised in unstimulating environments, and that this effect persists into the children's toddlerhood. This finding specifically documents how adverse environmental factors may significantly compound the initial biological vulnerabilities that can compromise the prematurely born child's chances for optimal development (see Sameroff & Chandler, 1975).

Two studies focusing on parent–infant interactions but using fewer home visits than those in the study just described provide results that replicate those of Barrera et al. Field and her colleagues (Field, Widmayer, Stringer, & Ignatoff, 1980) randomly assigned low-SES, black teenage mothers of preterm infants either to an intervention that provided home visits or to a control condition with no visits. Ross (1984) employed a time-lag design to study a very similar intervention procedure but with a more general low-SES population of parents of premature infants. Field provided a total of only 12 home visits, ending at 8 months; Ross provided a total of 15 visits, ending at 12 months. In both studies the intervention team taught the mothers specifics about infant development and caretaking and provided instruction about games and exercises to facilitate infant performance. Instruction was provided about appropriate expectations for premature babies and how to handle specific difficulties in feeding, sleeping, respiration, irritability, and motor development.

Intervention group babies in both studies showed significantly better cognitive development (e.g., mean Bayley mental scores of 99.2 versus 89.4 for intervention and control babies, respectively [Ross, 1984]), but did not differ in motor development.

Intervention mothers rated their babies' temperaments more favorably than did control mothers, describing them as being more likely to approach than to withdraw, more adaptable, and as having a more positive mood. Intervention mothers also scored higher than control mothers on the HOME scale, showing better emotional and verbal responsiveness, better organization of the environment, more provision of appropriate play materials, and greater involvement with the child. Both studies provide a very clear demonstration of positive effects for infants and caregivers following a caregiver-focused intervention.

In several of the studies just reviewed, intervention consisted of a lengthy period of home visitation. Widmayer and Field (1981) have conducted a study that is provocative because of the large effects reported following relatively less intense intervention efforts. The mothers in this study were low-SES black teenagers who had delivered healthy preterm infants (less than 37 weeks gestation, but with average birth weight less than 2,500 grams). Thirty such mothers were randomly assigned to one of two intervention groups or to a control group. Mothers in one intervention group (Group 1) witnessed their newborn receiving the BNBAS and were asked to complete a Mother's Assessment of the Behavior of her Infant (MABI) Scale (see Field, Dempsey, Hallock, & Shuman, 1978), which is an adaptation of the Brazelton scale based on maternal report. Mothers completed the MABI at birth and weekly thereafter for 4 weeks. Mothers in the second intervention group (Group 2) did not witness the BNBAS, but they were asked to complete the MABI Scale on the same schedule as the mothers in the first group. The control group mothers were asked to complete a weekly assessment of developmental milestones and a questionnaire on child-rearing attitudes. Assessments were made by testers unaware of the families' intervention group status, when the babies were 1, 4, and 12 months of age (corrected for prematurity).

Results indicated benefits of the intervention for babies and mothers at all assessment times. At 1 month, mothers in both intervention groups were more attentive and appropriate with their babies during feeding and face-to-face interactions, and their babies were more attentive to them than was true for control group mother–infant pairs. The Group 1 mothers, who had witnessed the BNBAS, had somewhat better interactions than the Group 2 mothers, who had not: Their babies scored higher on the Brazelton interaction score and spent less time with averted gaze, and the mothers vocalized more to their infants than did control group subjects. By 4 months, there were no differences between the two intervention groups. Both groups of mothers had babies who were more responsive during face-to-face interactions and who had higher adaptability scores on the Denver Developmental Screening Test (Frankenburg & Dodds, 1967) than did control group babies. At 12 months, intervention group babies scored significantly higher on the Mental Development Index of the Bayley Scales than did control infants (means were 127, 122, and 97 for Group 1, Group 2, and control infants, respectively). There were no group differences in motor development.

SUMMARY. Taken together, the studies of caregiver-focused programs for parents of premature infants yield several consistent findings. In all but one of the studies reviewed, the investigators examined some aspect of the quality of the mother–child interaction. Whenever measures of such an outcome have been included in a study, investigators have consistently found evidence that the caregiver-focused interventions resulted in better mother–child interactions and in better infant temperament and responsiveness during interactions. Thus there is good reason to believe that caregiver-focused programs, ranging widely in intensity and specific approach, have considerable likelihood of affecting the quality of the relationship that develops between the parent and the preterm child.

There is also good evidence that focusing on caregivers has benefits for the babies. Measures of the babies' health, such as weight gain and length of hospitalization, showed significant positive changes following intervention in three of the four studies that were reviewed. Most studies measured the babies' cognitive and motor development, with the consistent finding that motor development was unaffected by all the intervention programs. In contrast, for mental development, all four intervention programs for low-SES families resulted in significant increases in the babies' scores on standardized tests of cognitive growth. Programs with mixed or unspecified SES populations demonstrated either no effects on the babies' mental development (two cases) or did not include a measure of this outcome (two cases).

In their influential analysis a decade ago, Sameroff and Chandler (1975) observed that the long-term effects of prematurity appear to be much more negative for children raised in impoverished, as opposed to socioeconomically more advantaged, environments. As the present review suggests, where experimental interventions have been employed, low-SES parents of low birth weight infants have been very receptive to such services and they and their infants appear to benefit markedly from them.

Although Ross (1984) has noted that "middle-class families are frequently able to provide interventions that minimize disabilities caused by prematurity" (p. 263), the extent to which middle-class parents of low birth weight infants may benefit from intervention efforts has not yet been well tested. With one exception, the programs given to mixed-SES samples have been of shorter duration than those employed with low-SES samples, and the investigators have measured very few outcomes. Both the Minde et al. and the Zeskind and Iacino studies, for example, limited their measures of child effects to a single outcome of length of hospitalization. It may be the case that higher-SES parents of premature babies are less in need of intervention than their lower-SES counterparts, but this hypothesis needs more rigorous testing before it can be accepted. Certainly the available research shows that middle-class parents have become more responsive to their low birth weight babies following intervention, and the likelihood that such parental changes can affect the babies merits fuller examination.

Given the relative recency of the proliferation of intervention programs for parents of premature infants, it is not surprising that information about their efficacy is limited to short-term outcomes. As described earlier, research with poverty populations has indicated that long-term effects of programs can be substantially greater than short-term effects. This generates the expectation that greater parental sensitivity and provision of increased stimulation in the home environment – consistently found as outcomes for interventions with caregivers of premature infants – may initiate patterns of more optimal caregiving that will lead to a considerable magnification of beneficial outcomes in middle childhood and adolescence. The need for long-term longitudinal studies in this area is obvious.

HANDICAPPED OR DISABLED INFANTS. Children who are mentally or physically disabled represent another group for whom caregiver-focused interventions may be particularly well suited. In a recent review of family-focused interventions, Bailey et al. (1986) pointed out that most interventions for handicapped children have been child-focused. They conclude, however, that programs that have targeted specific aspects of family involvement have led to improved parental teaching skills (Rosenberg, Robinson, & Beckman, 1984), changes in children's behavior as a result of improved parental teaching abilities (Filler & Kasari, 1981), better social interactions between handicapped infants and their caregivers (Kelly, 1982; McCollum & Stayton, 1985), and reduced parental stress (Vadasy, Fewell, Mayer, Schell, & Greenberg, 1984). Shonkoff and Hauser-Cram (1987) have also reported better child outcomes for programs that work with parent and child together.

A central problem in evaluating programs for handicapped infants, whether they are child- or family-focused, is that it is extremely difficult to obtain control groups. As Bricker and Sheehan very cogently phrased the problem, "Programs cannot ethically withhold educational or medical services from a child in need of assistance if resources are available for such intervention" (1981, p. 23). Without control groups, however, it is almost impossible to determine whether improvements that children show are the result of treatment or might have occurred without it.

A clear example of this dilemma is provided by an exemplary program at the University of Oregon where the Preschool Program at the Center on Human Development provided services for children with Down syndrome, cerebral palsy, sensory impairments, and general developmental delays (Bricker & Sheehan, 1981). In addition to offering educational services for the children, the program had extensive parental involvement. Parent education was offered by individual instruction and group meetings. In weekly home visits, parents were taught to deliver such services as physical therapy to their children. A social worker offered services for specific problems, such as marital counseling, and helped with such practical issues as arranging for transportation. Finally, parents were supported and encouraged in their advocacy efforts "to become articulate spokespersons for their children" (p. 13). The great majority of children (60%–90%) showed statistically significant increases in their cognitive abilities and social skills while enrolled in the program. Without a control group, however, it cannot be determined whether children might have improved even without treatment, since children's cognitive and social skills typically improve as they grow older. Because the absence of control groups necessarily will continue to be usual in the area of services for children with disabilities, it seems most reasonable to view such strikingly positive results as those reported for this program as at least supportive of the hypothesis that caregiver-focused interventions can be highly effective for families with handicapped children. Although rigorous scientific proof is unlikely to be forthcoming, the existing data are encouraging of further efforts.

There is considerable agreement that parental involvement is an important component of early intervention efforts on behalf of handicapped children. Simeonsson, Cooper, and Scheiner (1982), for example, reported that home and combined home and center programs make up approximately two-thirds of reported studies of intervention with handicapped children, and that most programs have specified roles for parents and report some aspect of parent support or training by staff. Whereas many of the studies they reviewed had no control or contrast group, the overwhelming majority (93%) reported effectiveness on the basis of clinical conclusions.

A particularly elegant example of a model of working conjointly with parent and child is provided by the work of Fraiberg and her associates with blind infants (Fraiberg, 1971, 1977; Fraiberg, Smith, & Adelson, 1969). Fraiberg and her colleagues provided home visits twice a month to 10 families whose infants were blind from birth but had no other known handicapping condition. The intervention was individually tailored to meet each family's specific needs. The staff extensively shared knowledge and insights with parents, demonstrated the babies' capabilities, and enlisted parental help in providing an environment designed to stimulate the infants' optimal development.

Evidence of the effectiveness of their approach was provided by comparing babies who were enrolled in the project from their earliest months with those who were not identified and enrolled in the project until they were several months old. Also, Fraiberg and her colleagues compared the children in their project with older blind children who were born before their project was initiated, thus making use of a time-lag strategy to obtain control subjects.

In examining older blind children, the staff noted that blind babies are at risk of failing to develop an investment in persons and solid human attachments. While investigating why this occurs and attempting to design strategies to correct the situation, Fraiberg and her colleagues discovered that blind babies generally smile less than do sighted babies and that they do not initiate a social interaction with a smile. Caregivers are likely to misinterpret this lessened smiling as a rejection. The staff was able to demonstrate to parents that although their babies did not respond reliably to the sound of their voices by smiling, they were much less likely to smile at an unfamiliar examiner's voice. The babies' smiling, although irregular, was clearly selective to the sound of the parents' voices, and parents found demonstrations of this fact reassuring. Similarly, blind infants' tactile exploration of their familiar caregivers' faces was much more extensive and obviously satisfying to them than was their fleeting exploration of unfamiliar faces. Demonstration of this fact also helped strengthen the parents' feelings of attachment and satisfaction with their babies.

Noting that the blind baby "has an impoverished repertoire of facial signs" (Fraiberg, 1977, p. 101), Fraiberg and her associates learned to become sensitive observers of infants' hands and shared their discovery and observational techniques with the parents. The staff was able to develop an educational approach that encouraged blind infants to explore for objects with their hands at the midline of the body, just as sighted infants learn to do spontaneously. A baby who had not received intervention and was introduced to the program at 5 months was observed to maintain his hands "at shoulder height in the neonatal posture. The hands are open, and...the empty hands are seen to execute occasional grasping-ungrasping motions or to engage in inutile fingering in mid-air....If a favorite toy is in his hand and he drops it, his face registers no emotion, and he will not make a gesture of search for it" (Fraiberg, 1977, p. 153).

To promote midline organization of the hands, the staff and parents developed strategies to bring the hands together. During feeding, for example, mothers were encouraged to place the baby's hands on the bottle. Staff members encouraged patty-cake games and other hand-clapping games with rhythmic chants, all designed to create an "interesting space" at midline. In the crib, for example, parents and staff suspended dangling toys, for which a midline reach led to interesting tactual and auditory results. They placed interesting objects on a tray top when the baby could sit with support. The babies responded to such procedures by using their hands to explore more and more actively. "By furnishing the blind baby's near space we saw that we could create incentives for mobility in sit, in prone, and later in cruising and free walking" (p. 162). Without such intervention, blind babies were often found to develop such behaviors as stereotyped rocking – getting into an all-fours crawl position, but rocking rather than attempting to explore actively. Helping the baby make the discovery that mobility leads to obtaining interesting objects eliminated this stereotyped rocking.

The value of providing the right kind of stimulation to allow the blind child to develop incentives to motion is illustrated by the dismal results of failing to do so:

Clearly, if the baby has not yet demonstrated "reach on sound," all efforts to entice him to creep with a distant voice or sound will fail....Many parents and educators may attempt to "teach" a blind baby to creep by putting him through the exercise of creeping, manipulating his legs and arms. It is a method doomed to failure and typically results in a resistant and outraged baby who flips over on his back and has a monumental temper tantrum (Fraiberg, 1977, p. 179).

It is now evident that many of the stereotyped postures and behaviors once thought to be inevitable consequences of blindness (e.g., holding the hands inactive at shoulder height, rocking) can be prevented by sensitive early intervention, and that caregivers play a very significant role in providing this effective service.

Parents with special vulnerabilities

Certain groups of caregivers, because of their age or past experiences, may be likely to have special difficulty nurturing children, and should be viewed as particularly good candidates for caregiver-focused intervention. Parents who are depressed or psychiatrically ill or who were abused as children fall into this category, as do parents who are adolescents. As the literature on programs for adolescent parents is relatively more extensive and methodologically sound, we will use this area to consider the potential effects of caregiver-focused intervention for unusually vulnerable parents.

ADOLESCENT PARENTS. The common negative consequences of adolescent parent-hood are well documented both for the adolescent parents and for their children. For example, very young mothers are at elevated risk of delivering babies who are not full-term and healthy (Sarrel & Klerman, 1969; Zachler, Andelman, & Bauer, 1969). Whereas it was initially believed that the increased risk reflected some kind of biological problem associated with pregnancy at a very young age, more recently researchers have documented that the risks are largely a function of such adolescent behaviors as failing to obtain early and regular prenatal care and of failing to maintain good nutritional habits (Sarrel & Klerman, 1969; Zachler et al., 1969). Thus, as discussed earlier, the nurse home visitation provided by Olds and his colleagues led to increased birth weight for babies of young adolescents. Similarly, positive health outcomes have been reported for pregnant teenagers attending a special school whose staff arranged and supervised their visits for prenatal care (Osofsky & Osofsky, 1970). From these studies, it is now well established that intervention programs that lead teenagers to receive adequate prenatal health care and nutrition during pregnancy are highly effective in reducing the health risks associated with early parenthood (Sarrell & Klerman, 1969; Zachler et al., 1969).

For the adolescent caregiver, educational curtailment, frequent and rapid subsequent pregnancies, and eventual poverty as the uneducated and welfare-supported head of a single-parent family are documented life risks (Hardy, Welcher, Stanley, & Dallas, 1978; Moore, Hofferth, Caldwell, & Waiter, 1979; Osofsky & Osofsky, 1978). In a review of programs for pregnant and parenting teenagers, Jekel and Klerman (1982) therefore stressed the importance of the *comprehensiveness* of such programs. That is, service interventions must simultaneously address the three kinds of problems associated with early childbearing: medical, educational, and social.

The Olds study discussed earlier showed the effectiveness of intervention with impoverished teenage parents in leading mothers to return to school after delivering their babies. This program also led to a significant reduction in the rate of subsequent pregnancy for teenage mothers. In addition to this specific project, evidence on this topic has been generated from several comprehensive programs for school-aged parents that have been in existence for a considerable time. The Young Mothers Educational Development Program (YMED), in Syracuse, New York, for example, provided an alternative high school for pregnant and parenting students (Osofsky & Osofsky, 1970). Classes were taught so that students could continue to earn academic credit, help was provided with day care for the babies, and medical services were arranged. Compared with other student mothers, those in the YMED Program were reported to have much higher rates of educational success (Osofsky & Osofsky, 1970).

Hardy and her associates (Hardy, King, Shipp, & Welcher, 1981) described a comprehensive program provided through a hospital rather than a school. Teenage mothers in this study received high-quality prenatal care; approximately half then received a postnatal program until the baby was 3 years old. Services included health supervision and counseling as well as family planning and small-group parent-training sessions for the teenagers. Infant health screening and supervision were provided, as was active outreach with regular home visits, educational counseling, referrals to appropriate agencies as needed, and group activities with other young mothers. The results of this comprehensive program were very positive. Eighty-five percent of the teenagers who received it were still in school or had graduated by the 2-year follow-up, compared with only about 20% of teens who received no services. The program also reduced the likelihood that teenagers would become pregnant again within 1 year (7.5% of experimental vs. 21% of controls) or within 2 years (21% of experimental versus 39% of controls).

The results from programs for adolescent parents have been very encouraging. A wide variety of service delivery models, including nurse home visitation, child health supervision, alternative high schools, and hospital-based programs, have led to similar positive results for the babies and for the adolescents. Relatively little is known as yet about whether adolescent parents will be as responsive to efforts to improve the quality of their caregiving. As described earlier, Field and her colleagues (Field et al., 1980; Widmayer & Field, 1981) have found evidence to suggest that intervention with teenage mothers of prematurely born infants can lead to more responsive caregiving, better parent–child interaction, the provision of a more stimulating home environment, and higher developmental quotients for the babies. Such research on the effects of intervention for adolescent parents is relatively new but very promising. Again, long-term follow-up studies of such interventions are very much needed.

CONCLUDING COMMENTS

Lack of clarity in defining the intervention is one of the most serious impediments to determining effects of caregiver-focused programs. Earlier we suggested that therapeutic competence, continuity, and the establishment of a working alliance with parents should be critical to the success of any caregiver-focused program. Both the clinical and research literature are incomplete in permitting the assessment of the validity of our argument. In the clinical literature detailed aspects of therapeutic attempts are provided, but little or no information is given about the adequacy of formal evaluation efforts. In the research literature ample details of subject selection and measurement of outcomes are usually given, but descriptions of how programs were administered are sketchy. If we are to fully determine the potential of caregiver-focused programs, researchers will need to devote more care both to designing services that are clinically sound and to describing these services completely so that any effects – or lack of effects – can better be understood.

The ideal study of effects of caregiver-focused intervention would have a clearly defined intervention given to a large number of persons who were randomly selected to receive it. A breadth of outcomes would be examined. For the caregivers, these would include such areas as education, employment, and subsequent childbearing, as well as relatively more subtle psychological outcomes such as nurturance, attachment, and parental competence. For the children, social and emotional development would be assessed in addition to the more ubiquitously measured changes in cognition and motor performance. Effects of the programs would be assessed longitudinally, preferably until the children of the caregivers had attained their own adulthood.

The ideal study does not yet exist, and reviewers must attempt to sketch from the existing approximations a picture of what such studies might be expected to reveal. Some of the present research has yielded such promising results that this is a task worth attempting. The kinds of outcomes that appear open to influence through caregiver-focused early intervention include:

> the prevention of premature birth;
> raising children's DQs and IQs;
> improving children's school adjustment;
> increasing maternal education;
> increasing maternal spacing of subsequent childbearing;
> improving the quality of parent–child interaction;
> improving parental responsiveness to children; and
> improving children's socialization.

The particular populations and procedures involved may vary, but, at least in principle, this breadth of outcome has been shown to exist following interventions focused on caregivers. Perhaps of greatest importance, the data also indicate that the long-term effects of early intervention can be much greater than the short-term effects.

It is important to recognize that there is not a clear line either conceptually or in practice between child-focused and caregiver-focused approaches to intervention. In principle, it might seem possible to design interventions addressed exclusively toward parents or toward children. In practice, however, programs typically involve a mixed focus. In establishing programs intended for caregivers, for example, as a general principle such programs will operate most effectively if a child is made the basis for the interactions between program providers and recipients. The child provides the catalyst and reason for the dialogue between service providers and caregivers. The reality of a child and a child's problem provides the motivation for a dialogue. In practice, caregiver-focused programs are unlikely to operate effectively without the existence of and inclusion of the child.

Intervention programs presumably designed for children alone also must involve their parents in some way, at least to the minimal level needed for informed consent. This fact is well illustrated in considering the 11 studies that have been combined together and reported as the Consortium for Longitudinal Studies (Lazar & Darlington, 1982). These studies are usually viewed as representing the effects of preschool cognitive stimulation programs for low-income children. Over half of the studies, however, also employed frequent home visits to involve parents (Beller, 1974; Deutsch, Deutsch, Jordan, & Grallo, 1983; Gordon et al., 1977; Gray & Klaus, 1970; Levenstein, 1970;

Weikart, Deloria, Lawser, & Wiegerink, 1970). Even for the Consortium programs without home visits, the program descriptions reveal that parents were involved in such ways as parent–teacher conferences at school (Karnes et al., 1970), having parents choose the curriculum model to be employed (Seitz, Apfel, Rosenbaum, & Zigler, 1983), encouraging parents to observe their children during cognitive stimulation sessions (Palmer, 1983), or having parents serve as aides in the classroom one day per month (Woolman, 1983). Although it might conceivably be possible to direct services toward children alone, in practice intervenors seem not to have done so.

Because interventions will typically involve both caregivers and children to some degree, it is not practical to ask whether caregiver-focused or child-focused programs are more effective. The more productive questions are: How should the needs of both caregivers and children be addressed productively in a program? How should their needs be balanced? How can one create a working partnership with parents on behalf of the child? These are the questions to be addressed in future research on early intervention programs.

REFERENCES

Bailey, D. B., Jr., Simeonsson, R. J., Winton, P. J., Huntington, G. S., Comfort, M., Isbell, P., O'Donnell, K. J., & Helm, J. M. (1986). Family-focused intervention: A functional model for planning, implementing, and evaluating individualized family services in early intervention. *Journal of the Division for Early Childhood, 10*, 156–171.
Barrera, M. E., Rosenbaum, P. L., & Cunningham, C. E. (1986). Early home intervention with low-birth-weight infants and their parents. *Child Development, 57*, 20–33.
Bell, R. Q. (1968). A reinterpretation of the direction of effects in studies of socialization. *Psychological Review, 75*, 81–95.
Bell, R. Q., & Harper, L. V. (1977). *Child effects on adults*. Hillsdale, NJ: L. Erlbaum.
Beller, E. K. (1974). Impact of early education on disadvantaged children. In S. Ryan (Ed.), *A report on longitudinal evaluations of preschool programs* (Vol. 1, pp. 15–48) (DHEW Publication No. (OHD) 74–24). Washington, DC: U.S. Government Printing Office.
Bonnard, A. (1950). The mother as therapist in a case of obsessional neurosis. *Psychoanalytic Study of the Child, 5*, 391–408.
Brazelton, T. (1973). *Neonatal Behavioral Assessment Scale*. London: Spastics International Medical Publications.
Bricker, D., & Sheehan, R. (1981). Effectiveness of an early intervention program indexed by measures of child change. *Journal of the Division for Early Childhood, 4*, 11–27.
Bromwich, R. M. (1981). *Working with parents and infants: An interactional approach*. Baltimore: University Park Press.
Bromwich, R. M., & Parmelee, A. H. (1979). An intervention program for pre-term infants. In T. M. Field, A. M. Sostek, S. Goldberg, & H. H. Shuman (Eds.), *Infants born at risk: Behavior and development* (pp. 389–411). New York: Spectrum Medical & Science Books.
Bronfenbrenner, U. (1975). Is early intervention effective? In M. Guttentag & E. L. Struening (Eds.), *Handbook of evaluation research* (Vol. 2, pp. 519–603). Beverly Hills: Sage.
Caldwell, B., & Bradley, R. (1979). *Home observation for measurement of the environment*. Little Rock: University of Arkansas Press.
Cattell, P. (1970). *The measurement of intelligence of infants and young children* (rev. ed.). New York: Johnson Reprint Corp.
Desguin, B. W. (1988). Preparing pediatric residents for the primary care of children with chronic illness and their families: The Chronic Illness Teaching Program. *Zero to Three, 8*, 7–10.
Deutsch, M., Deutsch, C. P., Jordan, T. J., & Grallo, R. (1983). The IDS program: An experiment in early and sustained enrichment. In Consortium for Longitudinal Studies (Ed.), *As the twig is bent* (pp. 377–410). Hillsdale, NJ: L. Erlbaum.
Field, T. M., Dempsey, J., Hallock, N., & Shuman, D. (1978). Mothers' assessments of the behavior of their infants. *Infant Behavior and Development, 1*, 156–165.
Field, T. M., Widmayer, S. M., Stringer, S., & Ignatoff, E. (1980). Teenage, lower-class, black

mothers and their preterm infants: An intervention and developmental follow-up. *Child Development*, *51*, 426–436.

Fields, B., Blum, E., & Scharfman, H. (in press). Mental health intervention with very young children and their parents: A model based on the infant death. In S. Provence (Ed.), *A stitch in time: Clinical responses to infants and families*. New York: International Universities Press.

Filler, J., & Kasari, C. (1981). Acquisition, maintenance, and generalization of parent-taught skills with two severely handicapped infants. *Journal of the Association for the Severely Handicapped*, *6*, 30–38.

Fraiberg, S. (1971). Intervention in infancy: A program for blind infants. *Journal of the American Academy of Child Psychiatry*, *10*, 381–405.

Fraiberg, S. (1977). *Insights from the blind: Comparative studies of blind and sighted infants*. New York: Basic Books.

Fraiberg, S., Adelson, E., & Shapiro, V. (1980). Ghosts in the nursery: A psychoanalytic approach to the problems of impaired infant–mother relationships. In S. Fraiberg (Ed.), *Clinical studies in infant mental health* (pp. 146–196). New York: Basic Books.

Fraiberg, S., Smith, M., & Adelson, E. (1969). An educational program for blind infants. *Journal of Special Education*, *3*, 121–139.

Frankenburg, W. K., & Dodds, J. B. (1967). The Denver Developmental Screening Test. *The Journal of Pediatrics*, *71*, 181–191.

Freud, S. (1955). Analysis of a phobia in a five year old boy. In J. Strachey (Ed. and Trans.), *The standard edition of the complete psychological works of Sigmund Freud* (Vol. 10, pp. 5–149). London: Hogarth Press. (Original work published 1909)

Furman, E. (1957). Treatment of under-fives by way of parents. *Psychoanalytic Study of the Child*, *12*, 250–262.

Gordon, I. J., Guinagh, B. J., & Jester, R. E. (1977). The Florida parent education infant and toddler programs. In M. C. Day & R. K. Parker (Eds.), *The preschool in action* (2nd ed., p. 281–305). Boston: Allyn & Bacon.

Gray, S. W., & Klaus, R. G. (1970). The early training project: A seventh year report. *Child Development*, *41*, 909–924.

Hardy, J. B., King, T. M., Shipp, D. A., & Welcher, D. W. (1981). A comprehensive approach to adolescent pregnancy. In K. G. Scott, T. Field, & E. Robertson (Eds.), *Teenage parents and their offspring* (pp. 265–282). New York: Grune & Stratton.

Hardy, J. B., Welcher, D. W., Stanley, J., & Dallas, J. R. (1978). Long-range outcome of adolescent pregnancy. *Clinical Obstetrics and Gynecology*, *21*, 1215–1232.

Harvey, C., & Johns, N. F. (1988). Training parents for home care of babies who have bronchopulmonary dysplasia: The role of the parenting specialist. *Zero to Three*, *8*, 19–22.

Hodapp, R. M. (1988). The role of maternal emotions and perceptions in interactions with young handicapped children. In K. Marfo (Ed.), *Parent–child interaction and developmental disabilities: Theory, research, and intervention* (pp. 32–46). New York: Praeger.

Jekel, J. R., & Klerman, L. V. (1982). Comprehensive service programs for pregnant and parenting adolescents. In E. R. McAnarney (Ed.), *Premature adolescent pregnancy and parenthood* (pp. 295–310). New York: Grune & Stratton.

Karnes, M. S., Teska, J. A., & Hodgins, A. S. (1970). The effects of four programs of classroom intervention on the intellectual and language development of four-year-old disadvantaged children. *American Journal of Orthopsychiatry*, *40*, 58–76.

Kelly, J. F. (1982). Effects of intervention on caregiver–infant interaction when the infant is handicapped. *Journal of the Division for Early Childhood*, *5*, 53–63.

Larson, C. (1980). Efficacy of prenatal and postpartum home visits on child health and development. *Pediatrics*, *66*, 191–197.

Lazar, I., & Darlington, R. (1982). Lasting effects of early education: A report from the Consortium for Longitudinal Studies. *Monographs of the Society for Research in Child Development*, *47*, (2–3, Serial No. 195).

Levenstein, P. (1970). Cognitive growth in preschoolers through verbal interaction with mothers. *American Journal of Orthopsychiatry*, *40*, 436–442.

Mahler, M. S. (1968). *On human symbiosis and the vicissitudes of individuation*: Vol. 1. *Infantile psychosis*. New York: International Universities Press.

McCollum, J. A., & Stayton, V. D. (1985). Infant/parent interaction: Studies and intervention guidelines based on the SIAI Model. *Journal of the Division for Early Childhood*, *9*, 125–135.

Minde, K., Shosenberg, N., Marton, P., Thompson, J., Ripley, J., & Burno, S. (1980). Self-help groups in a premature nursery – a controlled evaluation. *The Journal of Pediatrics, 96,* 933–940.

Moore, K., Hofferth, S. L., Caldwell, S. B., & Waite, L. J. (1979). *Teenage motherhood: Social and economic consequences.* Washington, DC: The Urban Institute.

Nurcombe, B., Howell, D. C., Rauh, V., Teti, D. M., Ruoff, P., & Brennen, J. (1984). An intervention program for mothers of low-birthweight infants: Preliminary results. *Journal of the American Academy of Child Psychiatry, 23,* 319–325.

Olds, D. L., Henderson, C. R., Jr., Chamberlain, R., & Tatelbaum, R. (1986). Preventing child abuse and neglect: A randomzied trial of nurse home visitation. *Pediatrics, 78,* 65–78.

Olds, D. L., Henderson, C. R., Jr., Tatelbaum, R., & Chamberlain, R. (1986). Improving the delivery of prenatal care and outcomes of pregnancy: A randomized trial of nurse home visitation. *Pediatrics, 77,* 16–28.

Olds, D. L., Henderson, C. R., Jr., Tatelbaum, R., & Chamberlain, R. (1988). Improving the life-course development of socially disadvantaged mothers: A randomized trial of nurse home visitation. *American Journal of Public Health, 78,* 1436–1445.

Osofsky, H. J., & Osofsky, J. D. (1970). Adolescents as mothers: Results of a program for low-income pregnant teenagers with some emphasis upon infants' development. *American Journal of Orthopsychiatry, 40,* 825–834.

Osofsky, J. D., & Osofsky, H. J. (1978). Teenage pregnancy: Psychosocial considerations. *Clinical Obstetrics and Gynecology, 21,* 1161–1173.

Palmer, F. H. (1983). The Harlem Study: Effects of type of training, age of training, and social class. In The Consortium for Longitudinal Studies (Ed.), *As the twig is bent* (pp. 201–236). Hillsdale, NJ: L. Erlbaum.

Provence, S. (Ed.). (1983a). *Infants and parents: Clinical case reports.* New York: International Universities Press.

Provence, S. (1983b). Introduction. In S. Provence (Ed.), *Infants and parents: Clinical case reports* (pp. 1–8). New York: International Universities Press.

Provence, S., & Leonard, M. (1986). *Manual for the Yale Developmental Schedules* (rev. ed.). Unpublished manuscript, Yale University Child Study Center, New Haven.

Provence, S., & Naylor, A. (1983). *Working with disadvantaged parents and their children: Scientific and practice issues.* New Haven: Yale University Press.

Provence, S., Naylor, A., & Patterson, J. (1977). *The challenge of daycare.* New Haven: Yale University Press.

Rescorla, L. A., Provence, S., & Naylor, A. (1982). The Yale Child Welfare Research Program: Description and results. In E. F. Zigler & E. W. Gordon (Eds.), *Day care: Scientific and social policy issues* (pp. 183–199). Boston: Auburn.

Rosenberg, S., Robinson, C., & Beckman, P. (1984). Teaching Skills Inventory: A measure of parent performance. *Journal of the Division for Early Childhood, 8,* 107–113.

Ross, G. S. (1984). Home intervention for premature infants of low-income families. *American Journal of Orthopsychiatry, 54,* 263–270.

Sameroff, A. J., & Chandler, M. J. (1975). Reproductive risk and the continuum of caretaking casualty. In F. D. Horowitz, E. M. Hetherington, S. Scarr-Salapatek, & G. M. Siegel (Eds.), *Review of child development research* (Vol. 4, pp. 187–244). Chicago: University of Chicago Press.

Sarrell, P., & Klerman, L. (1969). The young unwed mother. *American Journal of Obstetrics and Gynecology, 105,* 575–578.

Scarr-Salapatek, S., & Williams, M. L. (1973). The effects of early stimulation of low-birth-weight infants. *Child Development, 44,* 94–101.

Seitz, V., Apfel, N. H., Rosenbaum, L. K., & Zigler, E. (1983). Long-term effects of Projects Head Start and Follow Through: The New Haven project. In The Consortium for Longitudinal Studies (Ed.), *As the twig is bent* (pp. 299–332). Hillsdale, NJ: L. Erlbaum.

Seitz, V., Rosenbaum, L. K., & Apfel, N. H. (1985). Effects of family support intervention: A ten-year follow-up. *Child Development, 56,* 376–391.

Shonkoff, J. P., & Hauser-Cram, P. (1987). Early intervention for disabled children and their families – a quantitative analysis. *Pediatrics, 80,* 650–658.

Simeonsson, R. J., Cooper, D. H., & Scheiner, A. D. (1982). A review and analysis of the effectiveness of early intervention programs. *Pediatrics, 69,* 635–641.

Solnit, A., & Stark, M. (1961). Mourning and the birth of a defective child. *The Psychoanalytic Study of the Child, 16,* 523–537.

Thomas, R. B. (1988). The struggle for control between families and health care providers when a child has complex health care needs. *Zero to Three, 8,* 15–18.

Trickett, P. K., Apfel, N. H., Rosenbaum, L. K., & Zigler, E. F. (1982). A five-year follow-up of participants in the Yale Child Welfare Research Project. In E. F. Zigler & E. W. Gordon (Eds.), *Day care: Scientific and social policy issues* (pp. 200–222). Boston: Auburn.

Vadasy, P. F., Fewell, R. R., Meyer, D. J., Schell, G., & Greenberg, M. T. (1984). Involved parents: Characteristics and resources of fathers and mothers of young handicapped children. *Journal of the Division for Early Childhood, 8,* 13–25.

Weikart, D., Deloria, D., Lawser, S., & Wiegerink, R. (1970). *Longitudinal results of the Ypsilanti Perry Preschool Project* (Monographs of the High/Scope Educational Research Foundation, No. 1). Ypsilanti, MI: High/Scope.

Widmayer, S. M., & Field, T. M. (1981). Effects of Brazelton demonstrations of mothers on the development of preterm infants. *Pediatrics, 67,* 711–714.

Woolman, M. (1983). The micro-social learning environment. A strategy for accelerating learning. In The Consortium for Longitudinal Studies (Ed.), *As the twig is bent* (pp. 265–298). Hillsdale, NJ: L. Erlbaum.

Zachler, J., Andelman, S., & Bauer, F. (1969). The young adolescent as an obstetric risk. *American Journal of Obstetrics and Gynecology, 103,* 305–312.

Zeskind, P., & Iacino, R. (1984). Effects of maternal visitation to preterm infants in the neonatal intensive care unit. *Child Development, 55,* 1887–1893.

18 *Family dimensions in early intervention*

RUNE J. SIMEONSSON AND DONALD B. BAILEY, JR.

The field of early intervention has undergone major shifts in emphasis since the first programs were launched on behalf of handicapped infants. The earliest efforts focused on the amelioration of developmental deficits through general programs of sensory stimulation (Stedman & Eichorn, 1964). Based on the assumption that early stimulation could offset subsequent developmental delays, the infant was the primary target of intervention. In the decades that followed there have been variations in both the targets and nature of intervention (Simeonsson, Cooper, & Scheiner, 1982). Viewed from a qualitative perspective, these variations can be grouped into four different forms of intervention for handicapped infants and their families, each of which has been characterized by distinct roles for the handicapped infants, their families, and interventionists.

FORMS OF FAMILY INVOLVEMENT

One of the earliest and perhaps most widely implemented forms of intervention consisted of prescribed programs of stimulation or therapy administered to the infant by an interventionist who assumed the role of teacher or therapist. Although parents accompanied their child to therapy sessions or may have hosted interventionists in their homes, their role was often that of a passive bystander. Parent involvement was thus likely to be very limited.

A second form of intervention began in the early seventies with the recognition of the importance of family involvement in programs on behalf of handicapped children (Winton & Turnbull, 1981). This recognition was formalized for school-aged children in the provisions of P.L. 94-142, which specified the rights of parents to participate in the educational planning process on behalf of their handicapped child. This concept of the parent as a member of the intervention team was also recognized as important in

The preparation of this manuscript was supported in part by Special Education Programs, Special Education and Rehabilitation Services, U.S. Department of Education, Grant #G008401614. The opinions expressed do not necessarily reflect the position or policy of the U.S. Department of Education, and no official endorsement by the U.S. Department of Education should be inferred.

Appreciation is expressed to Deedee Dransfield of Southeastern Ohio Special Education Regional Resource Center, Athens, Ohio, for contributing to the conceptualization of the dimensions of family involvement.

428

early intervention, although the process of involving parents was less formalized. This form of early intervention can thus be seen as one in which parents were encouraged to become involved in their child's program, although the nature of that involvement was usually not well defined and varied widely from program to program (Simeonsson et al., 1982).

In a third form of early intervention, parent involvement was formalized by training family members to extend the teaching and therapist roles of the interventionists (Hanson, 1985). Parents were encouraged to carry out instructional or therapeutic activities with their handicapped child, either as cotherapists with interventionists or as the primary intervention agents themselves. In some cases this teaching role was extended to members of the family other than the parents, with siblings assuming training and teaching roles with the handicapped child (Simeonsson & Bailey, 1986).

In the early eighties, families began to be viewed as important recipients of services in their own right. This fourth form of family involvement is currently gaining increased attention through the formal requirements for family assessment, family goals, and family services spelled out by the provisions of P.L. 99-457. Whereas the distinctness of these forms can be debated, the importance of increased family involvement and the recognition of the family as a legitimate client in early intervention seems clear. The family empowerment model is a very specific example of this form of family involvement (Dunst, Trivette, & Deal, 1988). The nature and form of family involvement in early intervention is thus likely to be further examined in the coming years in order to identify effective strategies as well as to explore the feasibility, appropriateness, and general efficacy of a more family-focused approach to early intervention.

RATIONALE FOR A FAMILY FOCUS

The increased emphasis on families may be attributable to a number of findings. One factor that may account for increased family involvement in early intervention is the general growth in parent involvement on behalf of their children (Turnbull & Turnbull, 1982). Parents generally are becoming more sophisticated consumers of services for their children and more knowledgeable about the dimensions of services that they and their children require. Parental recognition of their own need for early intervention services has been paralleled by interventionist recognition of the need to extend the focus of intervention beyond the infant. Thus, a second factor is the equivocal evidence for the effectiveness of early intervention when focused on children alone, leading to an intensified interest in family outcomes (Simeonsson et al., 1982). Findings from the behavior modification literature revealing the success of parents in modifying child behavior can be seen as a third factor supporting a family emphasis in early intervention (Kaiser & Fox, 1986). Repeated evidence that parents were successful behavioral change agents resulted in a variety of strategies to involve them in the provision of services for their handicapped children. A final factor has been both formal and informal evidence that families often have specific needs related to the presence of a handicapped infant or young child. For example, Bailey and Simeonsson (1988a) report that mothers and fathers of young handicapped children showed similar patterns of concerns about their children, with information and resource needs emerging as the highest priorities.

Converging on these practical factors were a number of conceptual contributions that reinforced the importance of family involvement in early intervention. The transactional model of child development formulated by Sameroff (1975) has played a significant role in promoting the involvement of the family in early intervention (see also Sameroff and Fiese, this volume). As defined by the model, the family is the essential component of the caregiving environment that influences and is influenced by the child over time, resulting in differential outcomes for child and family. A conceptual contribution that complements and extends the emphasis in the transactional model on the caregiving environment is Bronfenbrenner's (1979) view of the family as one system embedded in a larger ecological framework of systems. Viewing the family from a systems perspective has been a major trend in family theory (Massey, 1986) and family therapy (Campbell & Draper, 1985), and there is a growing emphasis on consideration of families with handicapped children (Harris, 1981; Skrtic, Summers, Brotherson, & Turnbull, 1984). The implications of the transactional model and the family systems approach for early intervention have been twofold. First, because the influence of family members is reciprocal, intervention should adopt a systems orientation. Second, because the family system is embedded in a larger ecology, assessment and intervention should consider different levels of reciprocal effects involving the immediate family, the community, and the society in which the family is situated.

As a result of these converging practical and conceptual contributions, approaches to family involvement in early intervention have become more diverse. One indication of this diversity can be seen in a program's adherence to a particular theoretical framework with its attendant clinical implications. In programs based on behavior modification principles, for example, family members assume the role of contingency managers of the handicapped child's behavior. A major assumption underlying early intervention in such programs is that the development and behavior of the handicapped infant can be influenced by the management of contingencies by family members. Other programs may be built on the premise that family needs are as important to address as a child's needs because child and family are seen as an integrated system. The diversity of approaches may, on the other hand, simply reflect the responses of programs to the growing expectation for involving parents in services without a clear conceptual framework for that involvement.

Although a review of the current literature documents an increasingly diverse emphasis on family involvement in early intervention, it also reveals that interventions are still likely to be primarily child-oriented, as evidenced by a monograph devoted to early intervention efficacy studies (Garwood & Fewell, 1985). In that monograph only one of four studies reported outcomes in terms of family change. A similar predominance of child-oriented outcomes was evident in reviews of early intervention research by Bailey and Bricker (1984) and by Marfo and Kysela (1985), in which only 25% or fewer of the studies reported family change as outcomes. It should be pointed out that parent involvement may, in fact, have been a component in a larger proportion of these programs, but if this were the case it was not represented in the outcome measures. In general, however, the reviews are consistent with the conclusion that although family involvement has been promoted as an important component of early intervention for some time, its implementation has not been systematic.

DIMENSIONS OF FAMILY INVOLVEMENT

As the need for early intervention services continues to grow, it would be useful to examine how families have been involved in early intervention and what associations there may be between such involvement and child and family outcomes. Recently there have been several reviews of the early intervention literature addressing program and evaluation variables (Marfo & Kysela, 1985); home-based intervention (Bailey & Simeonsson, 1988b); a journal issue devoted to the topic of efficacy (Dunst, 1985a); and evaluative efforts using meta-analytic procedures (Casto & Mastropieri, 1986; Shonkoff & Hauser-Cram, 1987). In light of the availability of these comprehensive reviews, this chapter will have an analytic rather than an evaluative focus. To this end, representative studies on early intervention will be examined to identify dimensions and correlates of family involvement. Drawing on the conceptualization of forms of family involvement developed earlier in this paper, family involvement will be reviewed in two ways: families as participants in the provision of services to their children, and families as clients and recipients of services.

Families as participants in service provision

Families have assumed a number of roles as service providers in early intervention. These roles involve the family in planning intervention for their handicapped infant as well as in delivering services through training, teaching, or the provision of therapy. Each of these roles can be seen as specific instances in which the family, typically represented by the mother, becomes a member of the early intervention team to implement or extend its service. This perspective is exemplified in Hanson's (1985) description of parent involvement in the transdisciplinary approach as one in which "parents were considered crucial members of the team" (p. 40).

A recent study by Barrera, Watson, and Adelstein (1987) illustrates several of these parental roles in early intervention. In a home-based program for Down syndrome infants with and without heart defects, parents were assisted in becoming more adept at assessing their child's needs and in planning and implementing developmental stimulation. Parents were also provided information and emotional support by the home interventionist. Results of the study indicated that intervention effects reflected a complex interaction between intervention and the condition of the child. The environment provided by mothers was significantly better at follow-up for infants without heart defects than for those with heart defects. In this case the heart condition may have constituted an individual difference that mediated intervention effects. These findings emphasize the importance of individualizing interventions to take into account characteristics of handicapped infants that may influence the nature and effectiveness of interventions.

A variety of roles for parent participation have also been described by Hanson (1985) in an early intervention program for youngsters with moderate or severe disabilities. In a combination home- and center-based program, families carried out educational and therapeutic procedures as members of a transdisciplinary team. Interestingly, in keeping with individualized education plans for the infant, parent involvement plans were also developed for each family. Evaluation of the program revealed developmental progress of children as well as changes in parenting behavior.

Several studies examined specific features of the nature of the teaching or training roles of families. The intensity of training provided by a parent was a feature of family involvement studied by Sloper, Glenn, and Cunningham (1986) in a program involving parents of infants with Down syndrome. Parents in the intense training group were taught to administer a daily structured program, whereas a matched group of parents was given general advice. A comparison of results revealed small short-term effects associated with intense training, but no long-term effects.

Another feature of the parental teaching role pertains to the domain in which training is done. Lombardino and Mangan (1983) described an intervention program in which parents were trained to plan and carry out language teaching strategies with their developmentally delayed youngsters. Parents implemented the teaching strategies in structured and free-play contexts and kept daily records of the sessions. Evaluation of the 10-week intervention indicated consistent but statistically nonsignificant gains in parental use of language teaching strategies as measured by a structured rating scale. Significant differences, however, were obtained for five language stimulation strategies used by parents in free-play situations (i.e., parallel talking, referencing, questioning, replying, demanding). A mastery of 64% was also found for the language items presented to the children in the home training program. The authors concluded that systematic instruction can help parents become successful language teachers of their children. A significant role for mothers in planning and implementing language training for their handicapped infants has also been described in a study by Mahoney and Snow (1983). Results indicated substantial changes in language acquisition on pre- and posttest measures.

A number of studies have focused on training parents in a particular methodology, behavior modification being the most common method (Cash & Evans, 1975; Kaiser & Fox, 1986). These programs are based on the premise that parents trained in behavior modification principles can be more effective in stimulating development and in managing the behavior of their children. Bidder, Bryant, and Gray (1975) provide a good example of this approach to family involvement in early intervention. A comparison was made of mothers of 2-year-old children with Down syndrome provided either usual services or specific training in behavior modification techniques for a period of 6 months. Significant differences were found in measures of language and performance for children of mothers receiving training in behavior modification skills. It was concluded that the behavioral training given to mothers contributed not only to the developmental progress of their children but also helped mothers to better understand the management of their children's behavior.

The extent to which families are seen as participants on the early intervention team is evident in the designation of parents as primary therapists (Goodman, Cecil, & Barker, 1984). In a program focusing on individualization of treatments, parent involvement took the form of working with their children and the staff in a preschool setting and at home in order to promote developmental processes such as imitation and increased attention. The effects of the intervention were evaluated by assessing child changes in intellectual functioning on standardized measures. A comparison of the treatment group with a contrast group receiving more typical community services revealed a significantly greater gain for children in the experimental program. Another specific example of the designation of the parent as therapist was described by Gross, Eudy, and Drabman (1982). Using modeling and fading techniques, parents were trained to be physical therapists for their physically handicapped children. The finding of positive results was interpreted as supportive evidence for parent training as an effective way to extend the provision of needed physical therapy services.

The studies illustrate the diverse ways in which the concept of family involvement has been implemented to promote the role of the parent as teacher or therapist. Despite differences in the specific nature of parental roles, an assumption common to all of these approaches appears to be that family involvement can contribute directly or indirectly to the developmental progress of the child. This assumption is exemplified in a study that examined the effectiveness of parent education focused on developmental issues, as compared to education that focused on more general child management principles (Moxley-Haegert & Serbin, 1983). Parents of developmentally delayed infants receiving developmental education were more involved in home treatment programs, and their infants made more progress than those whose parents had child management education or no educational program at all. It was concluded that developmental education sensitized parents to the assessment and promotion of more subtle developmental skills, thereby enhancing engagement with their children. Such sensitivity may be essential to the effectiveness of any family involvement that calls upon the parent to fill a teacher or therapist role.

It should be noted that the research on parents as teachers also reports certain findings that suggest caution in implementing such programs. Reviews of research on parents as teachers (Breiner & Beck, 1984; O'Dell, 1985) conclude that although initial training may be effective, generalization and maintenance of effects are less well documented. This finding prompted Reese and Serna (1986) to suggest that in any intervention effort activities that promote generalization and maintenance of parent training should be formalized. However, Allen and Hudd (1987) caution that we may be going too far in "professionalizing parents," since many factors may determine the interest of parents in serving as teachers.

Families as clients of intervention services

Whereas studies examining family involvement in the form of various teaching and training roles have been quite extensive, the number of studies focusing on the family as the client or beneficiary of intervention has been limited. There may be several reasons for this situation, one being the relative recency of the family emphasis in early intervention and the associated lack of information about addressing needs of families. A second and related reason may be the fact that the resources of programs as well as expertise available to provide comprehensive support for families are limited. A third reason that may account for the situation is that the boundaries for family involvement in early intervention have not been clearly defined. There may thus be ambiguity surrounding the nature and extent of services that early intervention should provide. A broad interpretation of the family emphasis in early intervention would be to address all family needs in an inclusive, systems-oriented manner. A conservative interpretation, on the other hand, would take a more limited approach, in which intervention with families would focus on concerns directly linked with the needs of the handicapped infant. There are at least two issues that need to be considered in defining the boundaries for family involvement in early intervention. One of these pertains to the efficient deployment of human service programs. An important goal here should be to reduce overlap between early intervention services and those of other agencies (e.g., mental health, social service, etc.). A second issue pertains to accountability for the provision of services. The question in this regard is in what ways and to what extent are early intervention programs responsible in meeting the needs of families of handicapped infants?

A review of available studies suggest three approaches to defining the involvement of the family in client roles. One of these approaches builds on the parent training model but recognizes that, in addition to child effects measured in terms of motor or language achievements, there may also be family effects observed in terms of parental competence and attitude change. Illustrative of this approach is a study by Sandler, Coren, and Thurman (1983) that examined parent training effects on mother, father, and child. The training program focused on helping parents instruct their children in the areas of fine and gross motor skills, receptive and expressive communication, self-help skills, and cognitive development. It was assumed, however, that increased maternal involvement and enhanced child competence would in turn positively affect the knowledge and attitude of both parents. The study yielded differential results in that the knowledge and interactive skills of mothers improved, whereas no significant effects were found for fathers.

A second approach to family involvement is represented by a program for fathers of handicapped children described by Vadasy, Fewell, Greenberg, Dermond, and Meyer (1986). The purpose of the fathers' program was to provide an information and support system uniquely suited to paternal needs. The actual program involved father–child activities, informational sessions, and group discussions providing peer and professional support. Although fathers were the targets of intervention services, assessments were also made of mothers in order to determine if there were any second-order effects of father involvement. Measurements of social support, stress, grief, depression, information needs, and the family environment were obtained on a pre–post basis. A number of significant changes were observed with reduced stress and decreased depression found for both mothers and fathers, whereas other changes were specific to either mothers or fathers. Although the authors acknowledged the limitations of a causal interpretation of the positive effects of this intervention, they stressed the importance of involving the family as a unit and the potential benefits of second-order effects of interventions. An intervention program with similar intent has been described by Kirkham, Schilling, Norelius, and Schinke (1986) for reducing stress in mothers of handicapped children. Results indicated that the intervention was associated with improvements in family coping skills and enhancement of social support.

The previous two approaches to intervening with families rely on the application of general intervention techniques across families. The individualization of interventions based on a systematic assessment of family needs represents a third approach to family involvement in early intervention. Drawing on family systems theory, Dunst (1985b) has proposed that early intervention should focus on helping parents acquire the services and skills needed to facilitate the adaptation and development of the family and the handicapped child. Central to the family empowerment model described by Dunst and his colleagues (1988) is the identification and alignment of social support to strengthen the family unit (see Dunst & Trivette, this volume). Implementation of the intervention model has been associated with developmental achievements in handicapped infants and an increase in the effective use of resources and supports by families.

A second example of the individualization of intervention at the level of the family system is the Family Focused Intervention model (Bailey et al., 1986). This model takes a functional approach and consists of six steps: (1) comprehensive child and family assessment, (2) generation of initial hypotheses regarding intervention goals, (3) a focused interview to discuss family needs and negotiate intervention goals, (4) operationalization and scaling of goals, (5) implementation of intervention services, and (6) evaluation of goal attainment and documentation of child and family outcomes. The model builds on the goodness-of-fit concept (Chess, 1986) in which intervention is seen as a means for optimizing the fit between the capabilities of the family and the demands the family faces. Findings that support family involvement have emerged from implementation of the model in a statewide network of home-based early intervention programs. The emphasis placed upon the family system in the model was reflected by the fact that the interventionists wrote approximately an equal number of intervention goals for the family and for the target handicapped child. The importance of involving the family in the negotiation of intervention goals was also evident in the fact that the focused interview resulted in the deletion or modification of 20% of the original goals and the addition of 10% new goals. An analysis of the extent to which intervention goals were attained revealed that about two-thirds of the goals reached the level of expected outcome (Simeonsson, Bailey, Huntington, & Brandon, 1988). In addition to these attainments, changes were also obtained in parental perceptions of needs and family impact. In sum, the study supports the use of a functional model for assessing family needs and for planning, implementing, and evaluating the attainment of specified child and family goals.

A CONTINUUM OF FAMILY INVOLVEMENT

The studies reviewed in this chapter clearly demonstrate that family-focused early intervention, just as child-focused early intervention, is not a unitary construct. Rather, it can be seen as a continuum varying in form, focus, and complexity depending upon the interaction of child, family, and program variables. At one end of the continuum, family involvement is nonexistent, that is, families elect not to be involved in early intervention. A minimal level of involvement may take the form of accessing only child-focused services, for example, securing physiotherapy or speech therapy for the child. At a more complex level, family involvement may take the form of increasingly active and invested participation. As early intervention services expand and become more formalized, it may be useful to explore frameworks in which the range and diversity of family and professional roles can be fully represented. Such frameworks can serve to define and help establish priorities among early intervention efforts. They may also help to define boundary issues in early intervention in a systematic manner. Doherty and Baird (1987) have described a model of family-centered medical care that defines services by levels of practitioner involvement. Drawing on this model, an expanded framework applicable to early intervention is proposed in Table 1. In recognition of the fact that levels of intervention are mutually determined, the dimensions of involvement in the table are defined in terms of the family as well as the interventionist.

The levels defined in Table 1 are hierarchical in nature, reflecting qualitative differences in the focus and degree of involvement of the family and the interventionist. Each successive level reflects an increase in the comprehensiveness of services provided by the interventionist and the family's desire for, and investment in, these services. A similar ordinal conceptualization has also been proposed by Dunst and Leet (1987) in their hierarchical approach to the assessment of family resources. Viewed from an ordinal perspective, dimensions of family involvement can be defined as qualitatively different levels of investment made jointly by family and interventionist. It should be emphasized that higher levels include and extend all the services and provisions of lower levels. The actual level of family and interventionist involvement may be a function of characteristics of the family as well as the early intervention program. Turnbull and Turnbull (1982) argued for a similar graduated approach to family involvement in the education of handicapped children in which levels of involvement reflected evolving family preferences and needs. The needs, values, and life-style of the family are factors that are likely to influence its level of involvement. Correspondingly, the nature and comprehensiveness of services and the degree of investment of the interventionist are program factors likely to influence family involvement. As Doherty and Baird (1987) have pointed out in the sphere of medical care, "the appropriate level

Table 1. *Hierarchical dimensions of family involvement in early intervention: family and interventionist roles*

Level	Dimensions of involvement	Family role	Interventionist role	Example
O	Elective noninvolvement	Rejects available services	Informs and offers available services	Family elects not to be involved
I	Passive involvement	Acknowledges but does not use services	Tracks and advises families	Family allows tracking
II	Consumer involvement	Consumer of child-related services	Provider or broker of child-related services	Provision of developmental stimulation and allied therapies
III	Involvement focusing on informational and skills needs	Information seeking; acquiring teaching and management skills	Consultant and teacher role in information sharing	Provision of anticipatory guidance for families
IV	Personal involvement to secure or extend personal or social support	Seeking support to build or strengthen formal or informal resources	Advocacy and relationship building	Identification of informal or formal support network
V	Behavioral involvement to define and deal with reality burdens	Partnership to identify, prioritize, and implement interventions	Goal setting to develop interventions	Coordination of services to facilitate family coping
VI	Psychological involvement to define and deal with value conflicts	Client role in seeking psychological change at family or personal level	Therapist or counselor role to help with psychological or existential issues	Provision and coordination of comprehensive therapeutic services

of physician involvement with a family in a particular case must be determined not only by the needs and desires of the patient and the family, but also by the skill, motivation, time and other resources of the physician" (p. 4). It is reasonable to assume that the same premise holds true in early intervention. Some families prefer, and are content with, a limited consumer role in which they obtain services with a minimal degree of involvement with the program. Other families seek services that require greater involvement on their part and greater investment on the part of interventionists. As Dunst and Leet (1987) have suggested, the adequacy of resources available to a given family is likely to be a determining factor in their commitment to and involvement in early intervention activities. It is important to recognize, however, that the level of family involvement is not a static phenomenan but may shift from one level to another as a function of developmental and/or situational factors in the family.

The family's involvement in terms of informational needs (level III) requires a mutual level of investment in which the family and the interventionist can communicate openly and effectively, albeit primarily in a factual domain. The need for information is a high priority among families in early intervention (Bailey & Simeonsson, 1988a). The degree of mutual investment is successively increased in levels IV, V, and VI, reflecting increased complexity and intensity of interventions. The interaction between family and interventionist at level IV reflects a supportive relationship – one that focuses on personal as well as practical concerns. At level V the interaction between family and interventionist represents a mutual investment in effecting changes pertaining to the ways in which the family manages current practical demands. Level VI represents a mutual engagement to address significant issues of a personal and psychological nature. The distinction between levels V and VI in terms of the involvement of the family and the investment of the interventionist may be clarified by drawing on Menolascino and Egger's (1978) differentiation of reality burdens and value conflicts. Interventions with families to relieve reality burdens (level V) are concerned with the identification of practical strategies and resources to help the family cope with ongoing needs and demands. Level VI addresses value conflicts or concerns of the family that are of a psychological or existential nature and that will often require a significant therapeutic engagement of family and interventionist. Defining the criteria for distinguishing levels of involvement is not a problem that is unique to early intervention. Kraemer (1987) has discussed the ambiguity that surrounds the issue of distinguishing between casework and psychotherapy in working with parents. Although casework and psychotherapy can be defined as distinct interventions with different emphases that require different competencies, Kraemer points out that the line between the two may be quite blurred. In most cases an early interventionist may feel neither qualified nor responsible to provide level VI services directly. The involvement of the interventionist, however, can take the form of referring families for appropriate services, and supporting them in a service coordination or case management role. Furthermore, as Kraemer (1987) suggests, in practice the level of involvement depends on the competencies of the interventionist. The engagement of family and interventionists may thus reflect "a delicate balance, the worker taking a casework attitude, but using therapeutic skills" (p. 210).

IMPLICATIONS

The trend toward greater family involvement in early intervention has important implications for practice, research, policy, and training. The review and synthesis of research has suggested two primary forms of parent involvement – that of participant and that of client. There has already been a significant emphasis on parent involvement in cotherapist or coteacher roles in early intervention. With the implementation of P.L. 99-457, and the requirement of an Individualized Family Service Plan, it is clear that the client role of the family will increase. Furthermore, it is also likely that the variability of family involvement in early intervention programs will continue to reflect an overlap between family characteristics and program variables. Given such potential variability, what are the specific implications of family involvement in early intervention?

Practice

The central implication of family involvement for early intervention practice focuses on the individualization of services. Carney (1983) has emphasized that the unique needs of families cannot be met by providing the same prescribed set of services for each family. The nature of family involvement may vary from family to family as a function of the needs and level of development of the handicapped child and the family. However, individualizing interventions is not an easy task due to the fact that there are no well-established models for the parent–interventionist relationship. As Halpern (1986) has pointed out, the lack of defined rules for the family–interventionist relationship in home-based intervention necessarily results in the evolution of this relationship through successive interactions. The lack of defined models is further complicated by ambiguities in the timing of intervention, the diagnosis of child and family needs, and the purpose of the intervention. To address these problems, Halpern (1986) emphasized the importance of an incremental diagnostic approach in which the intervention can be modified to fit changing needs and family configurations. In this regard it may be helpful to consider family assessment and intervention as complementary components of a continuing diagnostic process in which changes are made in the implementation of the intervention based on new information.

Specific models have emerged that reflect the importance of individualizing early intervention services. Barrera and Rosenbaum (1986) described a transactional model of home intervention that focused on the ongoing transactions within the family as the basis for intervening with the child and family. Dunst et al. (1988) proposed a family systems approach as a framework for the model of Proactive Empowerment through Partnership for Families with Handicapped Children. The key elements of the model focus on building on the parent–professional partnership in order to strengthen the family's skill in gaining access to and control of resources. The Family-Focused Intervention Model stresses individualization of early intervention through comprehensive assessment of both the family and the child, and the active involvement of the family in the negotiation and planning of intervention priorities (Bailey et al., 1986). Each of the models discussed shares a common emphasis in conceptualizing early intervention services in frameworks that are comprehensive in scope and foster an active role for the family in the intervention process. Implementation of individualized interventions should proceed on the recognition that early intervention, like family-centered medical care (Doherty & Baird, 1987), can reflect qualitatively different levels of involvement as a function of family and program characteristics.

Research

The examination of family involvement as a research issue has progressed from early concerns regarding limited considerations of its role in early intervention (Simeonsson et al., 1982) to more precise questions about relevant family dimensions (Bailey & Simeonsson, 1988b). Concerns about the lack of substantive support for the claim of efficacy of early intervention for developmentally disabled infants led Dunst (1985a) to argue for broader conceptualizations of family intervention and greater precision in the measurement and evaluation of outcomes. A key issue in investigations of efficacy is documentation of the relationship between intervention and outcomes. In this context, Halpern (1984) stressed the need for research to test causal models of intervention. In order to test for causal relationships between intervention variables and outcome variables, it is necessary to define and operationalize the complex elements that account for child and family functioning. The extent to which evidence can support a causal role for intervention can be strengthened by comprehensive measurement that documents treatment and outcome (Simeonsson, 1985). The recognition that differences in family functioning may be greater among families with handicapped children than in comparison families without such children (Kazak, 1987), further underscores the fact that interventions should be individualized. In order to maximize the efficiency of intervention, it is necessary to identify more precisely the populations and conditions under which interventions are effective. It may be particularly important to investigate factors that constitute specific limitations on intervention effectiveness. In this regard Halpern (1984) has suggested that there may be limitations inherent in some situations or with some families that preclude intervention effects. If, in fact, some minimum conditions are necessary for a family to benefit from early intervention efforts, identification of such factors would facilitate treatment planning.

Policy

The issue of family involvement also has clear implications for early intervention policy. One issue that can be identified as important to consider from a policy standpoint pertains to defining boundaries for family involvement in intervention services. Implicit in family-focused early intervention are widely held assumptions that not only is parent and family involvement desirable, but that more involvement is preferable to less intervention. These assumptions are open to question, at least with regard to some forms of involvement. Winton and Turnbull (1981) have shown that some parents neither value nor want a teaching role with their preschool handicapped children. In other words, careful attention should be paid to the expectation for family involvement to ensure that families do not experience it as intrusive or obligatory. The boundary issue is also of importance for the interventionist to consider as the scope of early intervention continues to evolve. Since the purposes and activities of early intervention encompass a very comprehensive effort (Halpern, 1984), translation into actual services may vary from family to family as a function of the investment of the family and the competence of the interventionist. Realistic and efficient boundaries governing program investment and family involvement in early intervention are thus critical to define. Writing about the unique problems of dealing with long-term needs of clients in the community, Lamb (1980) has argued for the role of a "therapist–case manager," a professional who provides case management in the context of a therapeutic relationship. As the role of the case manager or service coordinator becomes more formalized in early intervention, it may be useful to examine that role in terms of qualitatively different levels of professional competencies, responsibility, and investment, as proposed earlier in this chapter.

The conceptualization of family involvement in a hierarchical model (see Table 1) leads to several considerations in the provision of early intervention services. The hierarchical nature of the model implies that the roles and activities of family and interventionist at lower levels are incorporated into higher levels. Thus, it is clear that a handicapped or at-risk infant may be receiving physical therapy while the parents are engaged in a therapeutic program to resolve value conflicts (level VI). The distinguishing feature of each level lies in the intensity of involvement and personal investment rather than in the nature of the intervention services themselves. A second consideration is that the level of involvement is a prerogative of the families. Their needs, priorities, and personal styles dictate the level of investment they are willing to make and the expectations they hold. A final consideration pertains to the assumptions that professionals hold about family involvement. Since the degree of family investment is a significant determinant of the success of any intervention effort, it is important to approach families on the basis of expressed family preference rather than prior assumptions by the interventionist about a desired degree of family involvement. To consider the issues in this regard it may be helpful to draw an analogy to the principle of the *least restrictive placement* concept in educational services for school-aged disabled children. To ensure appropriate provision of early intervention services for families, a comparable approach would be to design and implement family interventions on the principle of *least intrusive involvement*. Such a principle would hold that intervention as well as assessment activities with families should be guided by considerations that seek to ensure practices and procedures that respect the family's values, privacy, and self-determination. Translation of this principle into practice will require ongoing clinical sensitivity and appraisal of family needs and may well constitute one of the more demanding tasks of the interventionist.

Ethical issues constitute a second set of implications for family involvement with regard to early intervention policy. With the growing focus on family involvement it is possible to consider at least two clients for early intervention services: the infant and the family. If subsets of the family are considered separately, there may be three or more distinct clients. Ethical dilemmas may arise when the needs and best interests of these clients conflict or are incompatible (Reader, 1984). The key issue in these dilemmas is to determine for whom the best interest principle should be advanced to guide intervention policy. It is not difficult to envision situations in which intervention activities deemed to be in the best interest of the infant may not be perceived as in the best interests of the parents by virtue of intrusion of privacy or excessive time demands. Alternatively, the best interests of siblings may be at risk when parental involvement focuses primarily on the nurturance or stimulation of the disabled infant at the expense of sibling needs. In extreme cases, the best interest of the disabled or at-risk child may, for reasons of neglect or abuse, only be assured in environments other than the primary family. The resolution of ethical dilemmas such as these is clearly not an easy matter. In some instances it may be possible to resolve "best interest" dilemmas through various combinations of training, counseling, and support. In most cases, however, the incompatibility of competing needs is such that no solution is likely to be completely satisfactory or free from compromise of someone's best interest. The primary criterion that may need to be considered in this regard is that of *doing no harm*. It is important for interventionists to recognize that the concept of best interest needs to be considered within a subjective, personal perspective that is idiosyncratic to each participant in early intervention. A careful analysis of each of the competing points of view through perspective taking may be a positive way in which interventionists can seek to appreciate the complex needs of families in early intervention (Simeonsson & Simeonsson, 1980).

A related ethical dilemma exists when the needs of the family and the interventionist are incompatible. Such incompatibility may involve role expectations, priorities, or values. In regard to role expectations, interventionists and families may differ in terms of independence and assumption of responsibility. Some families may want to assume a passive role while the interventionist is advocating the family to take an active role in the intervention. The needs and role expectations may be reversed in other family–interventionist considerations in which families assume active roles while the interventionist would prefer a more traditional service provider role. Rodgers (1986) has explored this dilemma in terms of the common professional expectation that parents ought to assume roles as teachers or therapists. Rodgers cautions interventionists to be realistic and to recognize the primacy of the caregiving and parental role of families. A fundamental premise that applies to many of the ethical concerns is that family-focused intervention should first and foremost be supportive of the family.

Training

The need for professionals to respond to a range of potential family dimensions in early intervention programs undoubtedly will have significant implications for training. Although professionals from disciplines such as social work or psychology usually have extensive training in working with families, others such as early childhood special educators, physical therapists, occupational therapists, and speech-language pathologists have typically had more child-focused training.

It is thus likely that many professionals will need new skills. Among these are the ability to assess family needs and strengths, communicate effectively with family members, establish positive and collaborative relationships with families, jointly identify family goals, provide selected services for families, act as case managers, and refer to other sources for support when appropriate. For some professionals, however, the expanded dimensions of family involvement in early intervention many represent a significant challenge to expected roles and responsibilities. They may have concerns about their ability to work effectively with families and about their desire to take on roles for which they feel inadequate. Thus skill-based training will need to be combined with significant discussions about the role of various professionals in early intervention programs. Ultimately it is likely that traditional child-focused conceptualizations will need to be augmented by a broader view of professional responsibility in which *each* professional recognizes the need for sensitivity to family needs, values, and priorities for services.

SUMMARY

The involvement of families in early intervention has generally taken two forms, one as teacher-therapist participants in service provision and another as clients of interventions. Although these are not mutually exclusive forms of involvement, they do build on different assumptions about the purpose and nature of early intervention efforts. As such, they have important and distinct implications for early intervention practice and policy. Involvement of the family is an important objective in early intervention. The degree of that involvement, however, varies from family to family and may be best approached in terms of qualitatively different levels determined by the needs and preferences of the family, the resources of the program, and the investment of the interventionist.

Under ideal circumstances, the full range of services should be available to accommodate a particular family's needs and desire for involvement. In reality, the level of family involvement a program can accommodate may vary substantially from a few services to a full array, depending upon fiscal resources as well as the quality of personnel and services. Problems may arise when families want or need services that are not available or for which expertise is limited. In other situations the intervention program may engage the family at a level more complex or intense than the family desires. Successful intervention reflects mutual involvement of parent and intervention-ist based on sensitive, clinical judgment of the clinician and a negotiation of priorities with the family.

REFERENCES

Allen, D. A., & Hudd, S. S. (1987). Are we professionalizing parents? Weighing the benefits and pitfalls. *Mental Retardation, 25,* 133–139.

Bailey, D. B., & Simeonsson, R. J. (1984). Critical issues underlying research and intervention with families of young handicapped children. *Journal of the Division for Early Childhood, 9,* 38–48.

Bailey, D. B., & Simeonsson, R. J. (1988a). Assessing the needs of families with handicapped infants. *Journal of Special Education, 22,* 117–127.

Bailey, D. B., & Simeonsson, R. J. (1988b). Home-based early intervention. In S. L. Odom & M. B. Karnes (Eds.), *Research in early childhood special education* (pp. 199–215). Baltimore: P. H. Brookes.

Bailey, D. B., Simeonsson, R. J., Winton, P. J., Huntington, G. S., Comfort, M., Isbell, P., O'Donnell, K. J., & Helm, J. (1986). Family-focused intervention: A functional model for planning, implementing, and evaluating individualized family services in early intervention. *Journal of the Division for Early Childhood, 10,* 156–171.

Bailey, E. J., & Bricker, D. (1984). The efficacy of early intervention for severely handicapped infants and young children. *Topics in Early Childhood Special Education, 4,* 30–51.

Barrera, M. E., & Rosenbaum, P. (1986). The transactional model of early home intervention. *Infant Mental Health Journal, 7,* 121–131.

Barrera, M. E., Watson, L. J., & Adelstein, A. (1987). Development of Down's syndrome infants with and without heart defects and changes in their caretaking environment. *Child: Care, Health and Development, 13,* 87–100.

Bidder, R. T., Bryant, G., & Gray, O. P. (1975). Benefits to Down's syndrome children through training their mothers. *Archives of Disease in Childhood, 50,* 383–386.

Breiner, J., & Beck, S. (1984). Parents as change agents in the management of their developmen-tally delayed children's noncompliant behaviors: A critical review. *Applied Research in Mental Retardation, 5,* 259–278.

Bronfenbrenner, U. (1979). *The ecology of human development: Experiments by nature and design.* Cambridge: Harvard University Press.

Campbell, D., & Draper, R. (1985). *Applications of systemic family therapy.* London: Grune & Stratton.

Carney, I. H. (1983). Services for families of severely handicapped preschool students: Assump-tions and implications. *Journal of the Division for Early Childhood, 7,* 78–81.

Cash, W. M., & Evans, I. M. (1975). Training preschool children to modify their retarded sibling's behavior. *Journal of Behavioral Therapy and Experimental Psychiatry, 6,* 13–16.

Casto, G., & Mastropieri, M. A. (1986). The efficacy of early intervention programs: A meta-analysis. *Exceptional Children, 52,* 417–424.

Chess, S. (1986). Early childhood development and its utilization for analytic theory and practice. *American Journal of Psychoanalysis, 46,* 122–148.

Doherty, W. J., & Baird, M. A. (1987) *Family centered medical care: A clinical casebook.* New York: Guilford Press.

Dunst, C. J. (1985a). Editor's introduction. *Analysis and Intervention in Developmental Disabilities, 5,* 1–5.

Dunst, C. J. (1985b). Rethinking early intervention. *Analysis and Intervention in Developmental Disabilities, 5,* 165–201.

Dunst, S. J., & Leet, H. E. (1987). Measuring the adequacy of resources in households with young children. *Child: Care, Health and Development, 24,* 111–125.

Dunst, C., Trivette, C., & Deal, A. (1988). *Enabling and empowering families.* Cambridge, MA: Brookline Brooks.

Garwood, G., & Fewell, R. (1985). From the editors. *Topics in Early Childhood Special Education, 5,* ix–xi.

Goodman, J. F., Cecil, H. S., & Barker, W. F. (1984). Early intervention with retarded children: Some encouraging results. *Developmental Medicine and Child Neurology, 26,* 47–55.

Gross, A. M., Eudy, C. & Drabman, R. S. (1982) Training parents to be physical therapists with their physically handicapped child. *Journal of Behavioral Medicine, 5,* 321–327.

Halpern, R. (1984). Lack of effects for home-based early intervention? Some possible explanations. *American Journal of Orthopsychiatry, 54,* 33–42.

Halpern, R. (1986). Home-based early intervention: Dimensions of current practice. *Child Welfare, 65,* 387–398.

Hanson, M. J. (1985). An analysis of the effects of early intervention services for infants and toddlers with moderate and severe handicaps. *Topics in Early Childhood Special Education, 5,* 36–51.

Harris, S. H. (1981). Effects of neurodevelopmental therapy on motor performance of infants with Down syndrome. *Developmental Medicine and Child Neurology, 23,* 477–483.

Kaiser, A. P., & Fox, J. J. (1986). Behavioral parent training research. In J. J. Gallagher & P. Vietze (Eds.), *Families of handicapped persons* (pp. 219–235). Baltimore: P. H. Brookes.

Kazak, A. E. (1987). Families with disabled children: Stress and social networks in three samples. *Journal of Abnormal Psychology, 15,* 137–146.

Kirkham, M. A., Schilling, R. F., Norelius, K., & Schinke, P. (1986). Developing coping styles and social support networks: An intervention outcome study with mothers of handicapped children. *Child: Care, Health and Development, 12,* 313–323.

Kraemer, S. (1987). Working with parents: Casework or psychotherapy? *Journal of Child Psychology and Psychiatry, 28,* 207–213.

Lamb, R. H. (1980). Therapist–case managers: More than brokers of service. *Hospital and Community Psychiatry, 31,* 762–764.

Lombardino, L., & Mangan, N. (1983). Parents as language trainers: Language programming with developmentally delayed children. *Exceptional Children, 49,* 358–361.

Mahoney, G., & Snow, K. (1983). The relationship of sensorimotor functioning to children's response to early language training. *Mental Retardation, 21,* 248–254.

Marfo, K., & Kysela, G. M. (1985). Early intervention with mentally handicapped children: A critical appraisal of applied research. *Journal of Pediatric Psychology, 10,* 305–324.

Massey, R. F. (1986). What/who is the family system? *American Journal of Family Therapy, 14,* 23–39.

Menolcascino, F. J., & Egger, M. L. (1978). *Medical dimensions of mental retardation.* Lincoln: University of Nebraska Press.

Moxley-Haegert, L., & Serbin, L. A. (1983). Developmental education for parents of delayed infants: Effects on parental motivation and children's development. *Child Development, 54,* 1324–1331.

O'Dell, S. L. (1985). Progress in parent training. *Progress in Behavior Modification, 19,* 57–108.

Reader, L. (1984). Pre-school intervention programmes. *Child: Care, Health and Development, 10,* 237–251.

Reese, R. M., & Serna, G. (1986). Planning for generalization and maintenance in parent training: Parents need I.E.P.s too. *Mental Retardation, 24,* 87–92.

Rodgers, S. (1986). Parents as therapists: A responsible alternative or abrogation of responsibility. *Exceptional Child, 33,* 17–27.

Sameroff, A. (1975). Early influences on development: Fact or fancy. *Merrill-Palmer Quarterly, 21,* 267–294.

Sandler, A., Coren, A., & Thurman, S. K. (1983). A training program for parents of handicapped preschool children: Effects upon mother, father, and child. *Exceptional Children, 49,* 355–358.

Shonkoff, J. P., & Hauser-Cram, P. (1987). Early intervention for disabled infants and their families. *Pediatrics, 80,* 650–658.

Simeonsson, R. J. (1985). Efficacy of early intervention: Issues and evidence. *Analysis and Intervention in Developmental Disabilities, 5,* 203–209.

Simeonsson, R. J., & Bailey, D. B. (1986). Siblings of handicapped children. In J. J. Gallagher & P. Vietze (Eds.), *Families of handicapped persons* (pp. 67–77). Baltimore: P. H. Brookes.

Simeonsson, R. J., Bailey, D. B., Huntington, G. S., & Brandon, L. (1988). *Scaling and attainment of goals in family-focused intervention.* Unpublished manuscript, University of North Carolina, Chapel Hill.

Simeonsson, R. J., Cooper, D. H., & Scheiner, A. P. (1982). A review and analysis of the effectiveness of early intervention programs. *Pediatrics, 69,* 635–641.

Simeonsson, R. J., & Simeonsson, N. E. (1980). Parenting handicapped children: Psychological perspectives. In J. Paul (Ed.), *Parents of handicapped children* (pp. 51–58). New York: Holt, Rinehart & Winston.

Skrtic, T. M., Summers, J. A., Brotherson, M. J., & Turnbull, A. P. (1984). Severely handicapped children and their brothers and sisters. In J. Blacher (Ed.), *Young severely handicapped
children and their families: Research in review* (pp. 215–246). New York: Academic Press.

Sloper, P., Glenn, S. M., & Cunningham, C. C. (1986). The effect of intensity of training on
sensorimotor development in infants with Down's syndrome. *Journal of Mental Deficiency
Research, 30*, 149–162.

Stedman, D. J., & Eichorn, D. H. (1964). A comparison of the growth and development of
institutionalized and home-reared mongoloids during infancy and early childhood. *American
Journal of Mental Deficiency, 69*, 391–401.

Turnbull, A. P., & Turnbull, H. R. (1982). Parent involvement in the education of handicapped
children: A critique. *Mental Retardation, 20*, 115–122.

Vadasy, P. F., Fewell, R. R., Greenberg, M. T., Dermond, N. L., & Meyer, D. J. (1986).
Follow-up evaluation of the effects of involvement in the father's program. *Topics in Early
Childhood Special Education, 6*, 16–31.

Winton, P., & Turnbull, A. (1981). Parent involvement as viewed by parents of preschool
handicapped children. *Topics in Early Childhood Special Education, 1*, 11–19.

19 Hospital-based intervention for preterm infants and their families

LINDA GILKERSON, PETER A. GORSKI, POLLY PANITZ

Early intervention refers generally to community-based programs that provide educational, therapeutic, and family support services for infants and toddlers and their families. In contrast, hospitals provide medical treatment, diagnostic services, and in certain cases, limited individual developmental therapies that all too often are not coordinated with other community-based services. In this chapter we will examine the delivery of early intervention services to hospitalized preterm infants within the confines of a hospital setting, as well as the opportunities that exist for linking hospitals more effectively with community programs.

We begin by defining the context of the hospital caregiving environment and by contrasting the institutional characteristics of this setting with community-based early intervention programs. Then we focus on one aspect of hospital-based intervention: developmental intervention in the neonatal intensive care unit (NICU). Finally, we discuss approaches that have been successful in linking hospitals and community-based intervention programs.

THE HOSPITAL AS A SOCIAL SYSTEM

Hospitals have a particular social organization that has been studied by medical sociologists for the past 30 years (Parsons, 1951). Whereas considerable sociological attention has been focused on the nature of the doctor–patient relationship (Parsons, 1951, 1975; Parsons & Fox, 1952) and on the social roles and hierarchies of power and authority within the medical profession (Starr, 1982), sociologists have not attempted to analyze the characteristics of the health care system as they relate to community-based human service programs such as early intervention. The analysis that follows focuses on six variables that differentiate hospital and community early intervention programs: (1) acute versus chronic care, (2) individual versus systems approach, (3) medical science versus social science base, (4) horizontal versus vertical organization, (5) unilateral versus shared authority, and (6) reactive versus proactive management. It is our assumption that by articulating and understanding the underlying dynamics of these two systems, professionals in both settings will be able to work with each other more effectively, thereby developing more successful linkages.

The authors wish to thank David Beer of the Erikson Institute in Chicago for valuable discussions on the sociology of hospitals.

445

Acute versus chronic care

Although the provision of medical care during the acute phases of illness is the hallmark of the modern hospital, in their earliest forms hospitals were religious and charitable institutions that cared for poor homeless persons and the mentally ill. The transformation to the more familiar model of hospitals as centers for short-term medical treatment, rather than long-term social welfare, was well under way by the early 1900s. Starr (1982) cites several factors that were responsible for this shift: increasing urbanization, an accompanying weakening of the traditional value of self-sufficiency and care for the ill within the family, and a growing respect for technical competence and specialization. Further, the growth of medical education required that hospitals not fill their beds entirely with the chronically ill, but maintain a steady flow of patients with a variety of conditions. Thus, "the sick began to enter hospitals, not for an entire siege of illness, but only during the acute phase to have some work performed upon them. The hospital took on a more activist posture; it was no longer a well of sorrow and charity but a work place for the production of health" (Starr, 1982, p. 146).

This pattern of high-volume, short-term acute care, focused on medical needs rather than social concerns, characterizes the modern hospital. The NICU represents the apex of the acute care model. Infants are delivered in or are transported to specially designated hospitals with highly trained staff and with the most advanced technological equipment. Neonatologists and neonatal nurses approved to care for the critically ill and ventilator-dependent infant provide treatment for premature and sick full-term newborns during the most critical phase of their care. Neonatology and neonatal nursing are emergency medicine specialities; physicians and nurses are attracted to this field because of the critical nature of the care they dispense.

The most critical function of the hospital is to preserve life. Accordingly, a hierarchy of activities clearly exists in which life-threatening situations take precedence over other activities. For example, NICU nurses may cancel meetings at the last minute or simply not show up for appointments when there is a crisis on their unit. Residents may sleep through a pediatric conference or a Grand Rounds presentation when they have been awake all night helping to admit triplets or care for a severely ill newborn.

As soon as the infants are medically stable, they are moved to a Level II or intermediate unit (i.e., a section of the hospital that is approved to care for moderately ill infants) either within the same institution or in an affiliated community hospital. Here again the focus is on caring for the baby through the initial stages of recovery and discharging the infant to the home for care by the family as soon as the baby's condition permits. In this postcritical phase, more attention can be given to parent participation in providing care, parent teaching, identification of the infant's and family's needs in preparation for discharge, and mobilization of community resources to facilitate the transition home.

The organization of early intervention programs provides a dramatic contrast with the high-volume, acute care, medically oriented focus of the hospital. First, with regard to volume, the number of infants cared for annually in an NICU is typically greater than the number served in an early intervention program. To illustrate, an average NICU, with 20 beds, admits approximately 300 infants per year. Larger units with 50 beds may care for as many as 500 babies. Staff size can vary from 30 nurses with 4 attending physicians in 20-bed units to 200 nurses with 15 physicians in large units. In Illinois, the average early intervention program serves 50 families (J. Deppe, personal communication, 1988); in Massachusetts, 80 families (A. Schuman-Weiss, personal communication, 1988); and in Texas, 120 families (D. Samuelson, personal communication, 1988). Caseloads range from 10 to 30 families per worker, with an average of approximately 15 families. Staff size can vary from 3 to 40.

To maintain its high volume, a hospital often draws patients from a wide geographical area, especially hospitals that are regional centers for high-risk deliveries. Thus, staff must relate not only to a high volume of patients, but also to a large number of community support programs. Because the immediate demands of direct patient care have priority, and because hospitals tend to function in isolation from the community, hospital personnel typically do not have first-hand knowledge of community resources. Referrals may tend to go to a few agencies with which the hospital staff is familiar. Programs are evaluated through reports from parents, or from other colleagues who may have obtained their information second- or third-hand, rather than by direct contact. Because staff generally does not have a context in which to interpret negative feedback, and because hospitals are cautious about referring patients to outside services, one or two negative reports on a program may prevent future referrals. Since it is very hard for hospital staff to update or correct misinformation, referrals may not resume even after the problem has changed or the problem has been resolved.

Early intervention programs vary greatly in the geographical areas they cover. A regional program can serve a rural county with a radius of 50 miles; an inner-city center can be responsible for a much smaller area with many more services and many more clients; a coastal community program may fly early intervention staff to neighboring islands. While early intervention programs face a challenge similar to hospitals in knowing about services, the likelihood of their succeeding in this task is enhanced by two factors: (1) early intervention catchment areas are usually narrower than those of high-risk deliverly centers (e.g., Evanston Hospital in Illinois serves 30 surrounding communities but local early intervention programs serve no more than 2 or 3 communities), and (2) early intervention programs are more likely than NICUs to define outreach into the community as one of their major responsibilities, particularly outreach across institutional boundaries (e.g., hospital to early intervention program). Later we will return to this distinction in our discussion of horizontal versus vertical institutions.

Whereas the length of stay in an NICU ranges from 1 to 2 days for observation to more than a year for comprehensive care for a small number of the smallest and sickest neonates, early intervention programs are available to families for the first 3 years of their child's life. NICUs may have greater breadth of exposure to different families; early intervention specialists may have greater depth of contact. The relationship between an early intervention staff and a family can begin soon after discharge and continue through the child's third year of life. This relationship may include home as well as center contacts, and may focus on the full functioning of the family in addition to the child's developmental progress. This long-term relationship provides early intervention staff with the knowledge of how families adapt over time and how they function when they are not in a state of crisis. Turnbull (1988) urges early intervention specialists to adopt an even longer-term view – a life span perspective – and to teach families "marathon skills" that reach beyond the "sprint race" of the early childhood years.

This long-term perspective tends to be more future-oriented and more process-oriented than the fast-paced, present-oriented, emotionally labile atmosphere of the NICU. Community infant programs respond to the immediate needs of families; however, it is more likely that an early intervention staff knows in advance about major events such as a child's transition to preschool or the enrollment of new children. (Contrast the regularly scheduled weekly intake staffings of early intervention programs with the open admissions policy of the NICU in which babies can be admitted virtually any time – day or night – with little or no advance notice.) Typically, early intervention programs have time to develop plans and to follow up on them. Value is placed on a consensus style of decision making in inter- and transdisciplinary early intervention teams.

Community personnel may use a group process to make decisions, but medical personnel tend to defer to authority figures and to scholarly literature as sources of problem solving, and may resent the time needed to process decisions (Swanson, 1981). In acute care, such as on a cardiopulmonary resuscitation team, it may be a requirement that one person take charge. When seconds can make a difference between life and death, the communication style tends to be direct and, if needed, confrontational. Terse commands and direct challenges are not uncommon during a crisis on the unit. Given the central value of hospitals – to save lives – there is an informal understanding among professional staffs, especially in acute care, that there are times when one just has to get the job done and pick up the pieces later. These "pieces" may be administrative and tied to policies that were not followed; managerial and tied to meetings or tasks not completed; or interpersonal and tied to situations where feelings could not be considered at the time (Konner, 1987).

Individual versus systems approach

Hospitals and early intervention programs differ in their conceptual models of disease and disability and therefore in their targets for intervention. The biomedical model conceives of disease as a biochemical abnormality within the individual. Symptoms are seen as manifestations of an underlying biological reality. "The primary tasks of the clinician, then, are to 'decode' the patient's complaints – 'a process of converting observed evidence into names of diseases' (Feinstein, 1973) – and to carry out 'rational treatment' (Kety, 1974), based on knowledge of a causal chain at the biological level" (Good & Delvecchio-Good, 1980, p. 166). Medical interventions tend to be directed at one individual and one disease. An ideal scenario is the isolation and treatment of a single or small cluster of physiological variables. Hospitals, as powerful as they might be, do not reach out to address the broad environmental, social, and cultural factors that may influence an individual's symptoms, treatment, or recovery. Although sociologists and medical anthropologists have criticized the biomedical model for its reductionist view (Kleinman, 1980) and have proposed alternative clinical models that incorporate an ecological perspective as well as attribution of meaning to the illness by the individual (Good & Delvecchio-Good, 1980), hospitals continue to organize their care around an individual rather than around a systems model, thus denying rather than utilizing the patient's relatedness to the social environment.

Theoretical models underlying the development of early intervention services embrace a systems approach. Turnbull & Turnbull (1986) describe a family systems model that challenges providers to develop early intervention approaches that take into account the impact of the interventions recommended for the target child on all the subsystems of the family: spouses as partners, spouses as parents, siblings, and extended family and friends. Dunst and Trivette (this volume) present a social systems model for early intervention that places priority on helping families identify and use their social support networks. In this model, the staff is trained to use goals identified by families for themselves and for their children, rather than staff-determined goals that may or may not address the issues as families see them.

Medical science versus social science base

Hospitals, once on the periphery of medical practice, now are the focal point of the medical profession. Starr (1982) traces the evolution of the medical profession from a relatively low-status occupation to a highly powerful role of cultural authority, economic power, and political influence. The medical profession, because of its close ties to modern science, has enjoyed a dominance not characteristic of other professions (e.g., law, clergy, education).

Unlike law and the clergy, it enjoys close bonds with modern science, and at least for most of the last century, scientific knowledge has held a privileged status in the hierarchy of belief. Even among the sciences, medicine occupies a special position. Its practitioners come into direct and intimate contact with people in their daily lives; they are present at the critical transitional moments of existence. They serve as intermediaries between science and private experience, interpreting personal troubles in the abstract language of scientific knowledge. For many people, they are the only contact with a world that otherwise stands at a forbidding distance. . . . The therapeutic definition of the profession's role also encourages its acceptance: its power is avowedly enlisted in the interests of health – a value of usually unambiguous importance to its clients and society. On this basis, physicians exercise authority over patients, their fellow workers in health care, and even the public-at-large in matters within, and sometimes outside their jurisdiction (pp. 4–5).

Allied health disciplines – one step removed from the aura of medical science and the privilege to diagnose, define treatment regimes, and control access to such resources as medications, therapy, and payment for supportive services – have had to struggle for their share of power, authority, and recognition in relation to the professional domination of medicine. Nursing has sought to define itself as a separate and equally essential partner in the health care field. Physical therapists have lobbied to gain "occupational control" from physicians who, by law, serve as gatekeepers to the physical therapist's practice. Social science disciplines even further removed from medical science, such as social work, psychology, education, and child life may occupy the bottom rungs of the ladder in this hierarchical system. This stratification of disciplines originating in the social dynamics of the hospital is reenacted on early intervention teams when therapists dominate team decisions in their particular areas and teachers are hard-pressed to identify a nonredundant role for themselves. Teacher self-confidence and self-esteem is emerging as a national issue in elementary and secondary school systems. Educators on early intervention teams may grapple with a double dose of professional doubt – from society at large and from the carryover of oppression among subgroups in the health system.

Physicians themselves experience differential social rankings based on the degree of perceived technological competence required in their specialty, its reliance on medical research, the resulting amount of social distancing between patient and physicians, and the ability of the patient to return benefits to the hospital. Primary care pediatricians are given lower status and lower salaries than their counterpart colleagues who treat adults. Developmental services typically have a lower status, lower priority, and lower revenue-generating capacity than medical or certainly surgical services. Developmentalists work diligently within the medical establishment to secure their roles in relation to the "hard scientists" whose use of highly technical diagnostic and treatment procedures permits independent judgment of the nature of the problem and the response to treatment. This ability to diagnose and treat with limited input from the patient creates greater social distancing and higher prestige (Starr, 1982).

Ironically, the most sophisticated developmental services may appear invisible to the untrained eye, whereas the most basic medical treatments may be patently obvious to the layperson. The anticipatory guidance of the developmental pediatrician; the developmentally appropriate interventions using common objects and infant toys recommended by the early intervention specialist; the playful, peek-a-boo games encouraged by the parent-infant psychotherapist; or the clinical interviewing of the social worker at intake can leave the impression that "nothing much happened," in contrast to drawing blood, taking a CAT scan, or performing surgery to release tightened heel cords.

Physicians in developmental roles where curing the patient is not the goal tend to operate from both a medical and a social science base. They generally have a longer-term perspective and are experienced and comfortable with both methods of decision-making – consensus and authoritarian. This merger of medicine and the social sciences is also present in the roles and functioning of other health professionals who are involved in the long-term care of developmentally disabled or at-risk children, for example, public health and visiting nurses, infant follow-up team staff, and personnel on chronic care units.

Vertical versus horizontal organization

Hospitals are self-contained, highly stratified social systems with their own rules that govern behavior. They are designed to be a complete community – for the staff and for the patients. Since their goal is self-sufficiency (Starr, 1982), hospitals duplicate most of the basic services of the communities in which they exist. They have a library, power plant, police department, plumbers, electricians, town government (administration), restaurants (hospital staff rarely goes into the community to eat on work days), shops, different neighborhoods with different personalities (newborn nursery versus adult oncology); they even have a local newspaper!

Hospitals prefer to care for a patient totally, providing all required treatment within their own walls and by their own professionals. The extent to which hospitals succeed in creating a horizontal organization, or total institution, is the extent to which they become isolated from the community and from other hospitals with parallel, competing facilities. Because of the uniformity of services and the traditional lack of coordination among hospitals (Starr, 1982), there is a natural tendency for hospitals to be suspicious of other medical institutions because they also provide the same services. This caution spills over to early intervention programs when hospital personnel perceive that medical services are provided as part of early intervention. Since the whole inertia of the hospital is toward self-sufficiency, it is not surprising that hospitals have difficulty in reaching out to community programs.

Further constricting its perspective, the hospital tends to function as a closed institution that highly regulates the professionals who can enter and can have the privilege of practicing there. Legitimacy of authority must be granted to outsiders before hospital personnel will refer "their" patients. The inherent suspicion and resulting need for validation can be met by such formal means as licensing, publications, or membership in professional societies. Informal validation can be bestowed through recommendation of a trusted colleague or through personal contact. Legitimacy for in-house referrals may also have to be established through similar means. These referrals might include referrals to Infant Follow-up from the NICU or to a developmental clinic from a gastrointestinal specialist for a behavioral workup on a failure-to-thrive infant.

Paradoxically, whereas the medical profession closely monitors who can participate in the system, the organizational structure is highly decentralized and characterized by a great deal of professional (medical) autonomy and self-regulation (Konner, 1987). Starr (1982) describes the hospital as an incompletely integrated institution lacking a single clear line of authority, an anomaly from the standard model of bureaucratic organizations. Hospitals, in fact, have three separate centers of authority – the trustees, the physicians, and the administration – that are held together in a fluid alliance. Although intrainstitutional coordination of a loose confederation of independent departments and programs poses an enormous challenge to a hospital, one only needs to speculate on the difficulty this lack of coordination causes community programs.

Because of the sovereignty of professional autonomy, hospital practices are frequently tied to the beliefs and priorities of the individuals currently in charge. Interchangeability of staffs – a vital component of self-sufficiency – further adds to this dynamic, as the beliefs of this month's attending physician may encourage early intervention referrals but next month's physician may prohibit it. Referrals may drop off when a head nurse who has had a special needs child takes another position, or when the unit is understaffed and direct care is the only priority.

Coordination between hospitals has traditionally been highly decentralized (Starr, 1982), with very little communication and virtually no central interinstitutional administration. Therefore, although there may be a great deal of duplication of services, each hospital may organize the same basic services very differently. NICUs can have highly organized systems of primary care where families are served by a consistent team of a primary nurse and a primary physician, or there can be little coordination of care with different nurses having responsibility each day and no single physician identified to communicate regularly with the family. Depending on the unit, discharge planning can be delegated to nursing, social work, or continuing care. Infant follow-up programs can vary greatly in primary focus (research or clinical service), eligibility criteria, staffing, length of follow-up and frequency of visits, and practices regarding referral to community services.

Early intervention programs are, by definition, organized vertically, seeking to provide developmental and family support services for high-risk and delayed infants and toddlers through the provision of direct services and through the coordination of community resources. Typically, early intervention programs do not have either the resources or the need to be a total institution providing every type of service under one roof. In fact, early intervention programs may assume a community consultation role in order to develop the capacity of day-care homes, recreation programs, or nursery schools to provide additional or alternative services to their population.

Although the organization of early intervention programs generally varies with that of their sponsorship, experience suggests that the lines of authority in early intervention are generally simpler than the tripartite model of the hospital, and often show a democratic organization of team functioning with the program director assuming, when required, an authoritative but not authoritarian role. Policies and procedures may be flexible, but basic program structures – types of services offered, amount of service, team composition, and so on – are relatively stable. Variability in program services is encouraged to meet the different needs of families; thus, variations in practice are more likely to be tied to the individual characteristics of families than to the professionals in charge of serving them. In short, early intervention programs may vary greatly from one another in states where no standards are in force, or they may possess a common core of characteristics where staffing patterns, service options, and reimbursement strategies are regulated by such standards.

Unilateral versus shared authority

Parsons (1951) described the necessary relationship between patient and physician as asymmetrical.

The patient has a need for technical services because he doesn't – nor do his lay associates, family members, etc. – "know" what is the matter or what to do about it, nor does he control the necessary facilities. The physician is the technical expert who by special training and experience, and by an institutionally validated status, is qualified to "help" the patient in a situation institutionally defined as legitimate in a relataive sense but needing help (p. 439).

In Western cultures, society institutionalizes this relationship by holding the physician legally responsible for restoring the patient to normality (West, 1984). Thus, according to Wolinsky (1980), "The practitioner must have control over the interaction with the patient, ensuring that the patient will comply with the prescribed regimen. If patient compliance is not ensured, then the ability of the practitioner to return the patient to a normal functioning state is undermined" (p. 163). Parsons (1951) equates this interactional control over patients with the ability to treat them; thus, asymmetry in the relationship is a required therapeutic agent.

West (1984) identifies three sources that give physicians power over their patients. These same sources are present to varying degrees in early intervention services: situational dependency because the patient or client needs health or early intervention services and cannot provide them himself or herself; situational authority because the physician or early intervention specialist has technical knowledge; and professional prestige of the physician or early intervention specialist over the layperson. The degree to which an early intervention program resembles or diverges from the authoritarian approach of the medical model depends on the program's philosophy about its clients and their needs and about its staff members and their roles.

In general, several contrasts can be made between the traditional model of medical services and what could be considered an interactive model of early intervention such as that developed by Bailey et al. (1986), Bromwich (1978), or Dunst and Trivette (1987).

First, the early interventionist does not have legal authority in relationship to the client; the interventionist has professional responsibility and ethical accountability, but no legal authority. Thus, control over the client's behavior is not a requirement to fulfill the early intervention specialist's professional role. In fact, having control over the client's behavior or the client's family's behavior is counterproductive to the ultimate goals of early intervention: self-sufficiency for the child and self-determination for the family.

Rather, early intervention seeks to develop symmetrical relationships defined by Alexander (1980, p. 313) as those "in which the relating parties express or exchange the same kind of behavior." The early intervention specialist seeks to form a relationship where parents are equal partners and the authority for decision making and goal setting is shared. Although the power of professionals lies in dependence on their knowledge and competence and a suspension of "private judgment" in deference to the professional's judgment (Starr, 1982), Dunst and Trivette (1987) advocate that early intervention programs adopt a model of helping in which clients are expected to play a major role in deciding what is important to them, what options they will choose to achieve intentions, and what actions they will take in carrying out plans. The client is the essential agent of change; the help giver supports, encourages, creates opportunities for the client to become competent....This is all done in a co-operative, partnership approach that emphasizes joint responsibility between the help seeker and help giver (p. 18).

Bailey et al. (1986) have institutionalized parent input into program planning in early intervention by the addition of a family-focused interview between the assessment and intervention phases in the Family-Focused Intervention Model. During the family-focused interview, the family reviews the recommendations of the professionals, plans are revised based on the family's input, and then the services begin. Vincent et al. (1986) have developed a form that families complete to provide detailed information about the child in the home setting so that a family is prepared with their report during an educational planning meeting just as the professionals are – a vivid example of a symmetrical relationship where professionals and parents exchange the same kind of information. The arena assessment model used as part of a transdisciplinary team is another example of the systematic inclusion of parents in a parallel role to the professional. The roles are differentiated in that the professionals' training prepares them to assess and recommend needed interventions; the roles merge as parents help set priorities, make their own observations, and carry out interventions. Clearly, in health care parents are needed to carry out procedures (e.g., catheterization of children with spina bifida, antibiotic treatment and dressing changes for infected wounds, range-of-motion activities for children with cerebral palsy). In early intervention parents are also involved in helping to determine the priorities and the procedures that are to be followed and in the delivery of services (see Seitz & Provence, this volume).

Reactive versus proactive management

Because of the acute nature of health care (high volume of patients for short stays during the most critical phases of their illnesses), staff members are continuously faced with a diverse set of often unanticipated demands. Responding to the immediate needs of the clinical staff requires a reactive rather than a proactive approach to management. Proactive management is characterized by preplanned, focused blocks of time to address specific concerns. Managers depend upon datebooks, timetables, advance notice, and an orderly sequence of activities that can be broken down into manageable components.

Management of a clinical setting in a hospital requires a more flexibly organized process to meet the demands as they arise. Being present and available is the key to the success of this style. Being out of the hospital at meetings or in the community is in conflict with the high visibility and accessibility expected of the reactive manager. Here lies another example of the hospital as a horizontal institution or complete community, limiting contact of staff members with the outside world.

The reactive manager has ample unscheduled time when he or she is in the office with the door open or walking through the units on what functions as administrative rounds. Any topic is fair game, and the manager is willing to make a recommendation or an on-the-spot decision. The reactive manager usually knows what he or she thinks and is quick to respond.

Hospitals rely upon a social network of many brief contacts that go on intermittently throughout the day. Gilkerson (1981) referred to this communication style as a "stop and go" pattern. What appear as unplanned interactions are actually an accepted and effective way of doing business in a setting where time is at a premium, needs are immediate, and staff schedules can change daily. Whereas hospital administrators rely on written memos, clinical staffs tend to keep paper communication (with the exception of clinical notes and charts) to a minimum. This lack of reliance on written communication probably results from the pressures of time and the immediacy of need.

Proactive management is more characteristic of early intervention programs where the time frame is longer and the population is more stable. The entire goal-setting process and Individualized Family Service Plan (IFSP) development model relies on a proactive strategy of thoughtful preplanning, consensus discussions, long-range goals, periodic review, and follow-up. The administrative style reflects this systematic approach to the management of resources and time. Program directors and coordinators are able to set predictable schedules for program activities. Staff meetings and case conferences provide an important forum where issues can be discussed and decisions made. The moment-by-moment availability and responsiveness of the reactive manager is also a part of the role of the early intervention director, but typically does not predominate in the way it does in the health care setting.

In short, hospitals and early intervention programs reflect very different social contexts. Their characteristic organizational frameworks and professional values shape both the day-to-day interactions among professionals in each setting and the interactions across settings. Further, these contextual differences affect how infants and their families are viewed and how care is provided. Pressures for cost containment within the health care system are shifting the organizational framework and moving hospitals more toward increased coordination and decreased professional autonomy. Further, the nature of primary presenting problems for the practicing pediatrician is changing from that of illness and disease to that of behavior and development. Thus, the traditional medical model described here is in a state of flux, potentially moving more toward a framework of shared values, including the importance of a social science base in behavioral-developmental change and a focus on a systems orientation that pediatric practice has begun to embrace.

EARLY INTERVENTION SERVICES DURING NEONATAL HOSPITALIZATION

Thus far, this chapter has portrayed the NICU as a social environment that differs sharply from early intervention programs whose vertical professional organization, longitudinal temporal orientation, and developmental priorities accept and foster slow, progressive growth within a child and family. However, such distinctions are likely to change somewhat because they no longer reflect accurately the nature and needs of many infants at high risk for developmental disabilities who are now being born into NICUs. Today, the smallest and highest risk NICU patients are likely to spend a long period of time in the hospital in order to gain weight and pass through several stages of neurobehavioral development. The NICU, then, becomes an important site for early intervention on behalf of optimizing an infant's development and a family's adaptation.

To better appreciate the present need for developmental care during neonatal hospitalization, one should understand the enormous progress in the medical treatment of high-risk neonates that has been accomplished within a relatively brief period of time. The modern era of neonatal medicine was launched just 20 years ago with the first successful application of mechanical ventilatory support (in the form of continuous positive airway pressure [CPAP]) for premature infants with hyaline membrane disease

(Gregory, Kitterman, Phibbs, Tooley, & Hamilton, 1971). At that time and until the early 1980s, medical challenges in NICUs involved resuscitation and stabilization of acutely ill but relatively mature neonates. Without the aid of contemporary science and technology, small, very prematurely born infants rarely survived the neonatal period. Indeed, whereas prior to 1975 infants born weighing less than 750 grams had little chance for survival, by the late 1970s there was a 40% survival rate with 67% of these survivors having normal developmental outcomes and 22% surviving with functional abnormalities (Hirata, Epcar, & Walsh, 1983). As of the mid-1980s, outcome data have again improved. Limited studies of 24–29 week gestational age neonates document a drop in mortality during this decade from 52% to 16% as well as a significantly decreased medical morbidity (Kwong, Egan, & Notter, 1985; Merritt, Hallman, & Bloom, 1986). Accompanying and largely accounting for these dramatic changes have been such newly available treatments as high-frequency jet ventilators (Boros et al., 1985) and exogenous administration of natural or synthetic surfactant (Enhorning et al., 1985; Hallman, Schneider, Merritt, & Gluck, 1981).

Accordingly, NICUs are increasingly populated by tiny newborns (less than 1,000 grams) who breathe spontaneously, oxygenate effectively, and are likely to survive well beyond the noenatal period. Yet, these same infants require the specialized medical services of an NICU. Moreover, the physiological immaturity of all their organ systems other than their pulmonary alveoli demand prolonged hospitalization in high-risk neonatal medical centers. These are medically stable yet extremely fragile infants whose central nervous systems, despite pulmonary surfactant, are appropriately immature and vulnerable, given their gestational age at birth. Resting in their isolettes for weeks and months, these infants are exposed to an abundance of sensory stimuli from the caregivers and the caregivers' facilities. Therefore, for these infants, developmental care deserves parity with acute and chronic medical attention.

Indeed, studies (Gorski et al., 1984; Gorski & Huntington, 1988; Lawson, Daum, & Turkewitz, 1977; Linn, Horowitz, & Fox, 1985; Long, Lucey, & Philip, 1980) suggest that attention to environmental conditions and caregiver interventions, both medical and social, may influence acute physiological events as well as physical and developmental outcome following premature birth. Over the past decade studies have been conducted that systematically examine the sensory characteristics of an NICU, the caregiver protocols and patterns of medical as well as social intervention, and infant behavioral and physiological responses in interaction with this level of care (Gorski, Davison, & Brazelton, 1979; Gorski, Hole, Leonard, & Martin, 1983; Gorski et al., 1984; Gorski & Huntington, 1988). Since these studies did not impose any changes in caregiver behavior, they provide an excellent view of the sensory conditions normally experienced by premature infants in an NICU.

Continuous computerized observations of infant sleep–wake state, activity level, skin color, and discrete behaviors were recorded together with reports of caregiver presence and action. These recordings, lasting 4 to 6 hours, were coupled to simultaneous, automatically digitized, and time-synchronized files of infant heart rate and oxygenation. From the thousands of data points collected on caregivers and premature infants between 28 and 36 weeks gestational age, it has been possible to investigate caregiver routines (High & Gorski, 1985), infant sleep patterns (High & Gorski, 1985), and the effects of caregiving interventions and conditions on the physiological stability of infants (Gorski, 1982; Gorski et al., 1983; Gorski et al., 1984; Gorski & Huntington, 1988). These studies have illustrated the extraordinary nature of caregiver–infant interactions during hospitalization in an NICU. The results have, for example, exposed the caregiving environment as one that alternatively provides a bombardment of stimuli from sheer numbers of different caregivers and procedures, as well as one that deprives infants of frequent patterns of contact and direct observation from the human (as compared with mechanical) caregivers (High & Gorski, 1985). Also discovered was an absence of consistent temporal association between the sleep or awake state of infants and the onset of either medical or, surprisingly, social interventions by caregivers (High & Gorski, 1985). Moreover, the synchronized behavioral and physiological recordings documented statistically significant connections between such potentially life-threatening events as bradycardia (heart rate decelerations) and antecedent medical or social interventions (Gorski et al., 1984; Gorski & Huntington, 1988).

Als and her colleagues (Als, Lawhon, & Brown, 1986), discussed later in this chapter, have tested the validity of these interactive phenomena as a guiding framework for integrating individualized behavioral care into the professional handling of premature infants in an NICU. Their preliminary results hold great promise for demonstrating the physiological benefit of integrating such behavioral considerations into current medical treatment protocols.

Such research findings underscore the point that, in order to survive, premature infants must succeed in physiological and behavioral adaptation to the extrauterine environment. How well, then, does the NICU serve as a caregiving environment in support of adaptive growth and development? What form, intensity and pattern of sensory input, caregiver interaction, and parent support lead to optimal neurodevelopmental outcome following premature birth? To answer these critical questions, we will examine the research that begins to inform the field about the efficacy of early intervention efforts on behalf of high-risk infants and parents during neonatal hospitalization.

Understandably, studies of developmental intervention in NICUs test hypotheses that in turn derive from personal philosophies about the nature of stimulation already provided by the NICU environment. Three perspectives have dominated the field and are evidenced in the research and practices performed on developmental interventions during neonatal hospitalization. The ongoing debate centers on whether (1) the NICU environment deprives infants of necessary stimulation, (2) the NICU bombards infants with continuous overstimulation, or (3) the NICU lacks a contingent pattern of stimulation organized around maturationally determined physiological and/or behavioral cues from the infants.

Those who believe that the NICU deprives infants of sensory input test the effects of providing supplemental forms of stimulation. Researchers who incline toward seeing the NICU as already overstimulating study methods of protecting infants from potentially costly responses to sensory inputs from the environment. Investigators who perceive inadequate consideration for timing of interventions in the NICU design studies that do not regard the amount of stimulation so much as test the effects of offering interventions at systematically different times.

Supplemental stimulation

During the 1960s and early 1970s very few technical procedures were available to treat medically fragile infants. No wonder then that in this setting developmental specialists regarded the caregiving environment to be isolating and sensorily impoverished. Parents themselves were only beginning to be allowed to visit their infants for extended periods of time (Barnett, Leiderman, Grobstein, & Klaus, 1970).

The intervention studies that arose from these circumstances generally tested the utility of introducing supplemental amounts of stimulation to hospitalized premature infants. All interventions were directed at the infants, neglecting to support the needs or integrate the importance of parents during hospitalization. These infant-focused stimulation programs usually offered some combination of visual (Leib, Benfield, & Guidubaldi, 1980; Resnick, Eyler, & Nelson, 1987), auditory (Katz, 1971), tactile (Bernbaum, Pereira, & Watkins, 1983; Field, Ignatoff, & Stringer, 1982; Field, Schanberg, & Scafidi, 1986; White & Labarba, 1976), or vestibular-kinesthetic stimuli (Korner, Guilleminault, & Van den Hoed, 1978; Korner, Kraemer, & Haffner, 1975; Korner & Schneider, 1983), often applying more than one at a time (Kraemer & Pierpoint, 1976; Powell, 1974; Resnick et al., 1987; Scarr-Salapatek & Williams, 1973; Thoman & Graham, 1986).

Although almost all of these intervention studies reported positive effects, methodological weaknesses present challenges to their clinical utility and generalizability. To begin with, stimulation programs sometimes report similar results despite employing disparate forms and combinations of interventions. Even those that concentrated their efforts on providing one form of sensory input, such as auditory stimulation, varied with respect to the type of auditory stimulus used. One study, for example, periodically offered the infant a tape recording of a mother's voice (Katz, 1971). Other studies used a source of nonhuman sound in the form of music or human heartbeat (Barnard & Bee, 1983), or the staff provided unregulated singing or talking during intervention procedures (Leib et al., 1980; Scarr-Salapatek & Williams, 1973) to alternately soothe or arouse infants.

The intervention programs differed widely as to the onset, frequency, and duration of the experimental intervention tested (Bennett, 1987). Some started at an arbitrary time, such as 2 weeks of age, whereas others began at birth, and still others after the infants became physiologically stable by some clinical criteria. Although all the investigations provided some form of stimulation each day, they varied as to how often or regularly this stimulation took place. Some offered the stimuli at several hour intervals, others before or after feedings, and still others intervened in response to an infant's behavior, for example, during motorically quiet periods. Duration ranged as widely as did time of onset and frequency of intervention. Some programs lasted 1 week, others continued until discharged from the hospital, and a few persisted through home follow-up after hospitalization. Without temporal standards across studies, we are unable to determine the optimal starting time, frequency, or duration of intervention needed to achieve best results.

More problematic still, these same studies often failed to report baseline sensory conditions and practices prior to onset of intervention. Without this information, we are unable to confidently attribute change to the intervention program alone. Furthermore, infants studied were sometimes all within one small gestational age range, limiting the generalizability of effects to many other infant populations of different neuromaturation.

The opposite problem existed in other studies (Korner & Schneider, 1983). When the same stimuli were used on a small number of infants of scattered gestational age, potentially positive effects may have been reversed or reduced by results from infants who may have been at a developmental stage potentially unresponsive to that type of intervention. Indeed, the nursery intervention literature is confused with reports based on very diverse study populations (Meisels, Jones, & Stiefel, 1983).

Another issue to which the reader must remain critically sensitive concerns the wide variety of dependent outcome measures used across studies to assess the efficacy of intervention. There is, of course, the overall concern that when researchers choose to regard or report one or several areas of possible intervention effect, they may miss other positive or untoward effects. Interpreting the existent literature similarly suffers from a cloud created by the inconsistent use of outcome measures across studies. Some report developmental changes in infants before and after intervention. These range from assessments of muscle tone to activity to sensory-perceptual skills (Barnard & Bee, 1983; Katz, 1971; Kramer, Chamorro, Green, & Kundtson, 1975; Powell, 1974). Other studies document medical progress in subjects with or without extra stimulation (Als et al., 1986; Korner et al., 1978; Kraemer & Pierpoint, 1976). These measures often track head circumference, weight gain, formula intake, incidence of apnea, and length of hospitalization. Still other projects monitor patterns of parent visitation or parent–infant interaction (Minde et al., 1978; Powell, 1974).

All of the research thus far reported on neonatal developmental intervention suffers from a relatively brief follow-up assessment of the long-term efficacy of the interventions tested. Should we care that an infant can be provoked to sustain alerting responses during the neonatal period or gain weight faster in the hospital? Such questions are difficult to decide and can be convincingly argued from both sides. Research (Beckwith, Cohen, Kopp, Parmelee, & Marcy, 1976) has led to a modern theoretical perspective (Sameroff & Chandler, 1975) that views long-term development as a process that depends on multiple influences interacting over time to produce an outcome that could not be fully predicted from any one time period, no matter how seemingly critical the experience appears at the moment. Logically, however, the infant's condition at each point in time directly influences the immediately succeeding challenges and opportunities for growth and development. Therefore, it seems, we must interest ourselves in supporting optimal conditions regardless of their ultimate significance, as long as long-term costs do not prove to outweigh short-term benefits. Early successes, especially concerning caregiving, have at least the advantage of building confidence for meeting future challenges.

Finally, a limitation shared by almost all neonatal intervention programs relates to the paucity of knowledge yet acquired about the functional organization of the premature infant's central nervous system (CNS). Because of little understanding about CNS regulation of preterm autonomic control of heart rate and respiration or of regulation and use of alerting responses, stimulation practices often lack a theoretical or empirical rationale specific to premature infant neuromaturation. We must therefore remain extremely careful when studying the effects of these early interventions to search seriously for untoward and unexpected side effects that could render the desired main effect of the intervention too costly to achieve. For example, if in the interest of stimulating more awake, alert time in 32-week gestation infants, the tactile stimulus also results in depressed levels of oxygen within the infant's bloodstream for several minutes following the intervention (Gorski, Huntington, & Lewkowicz, 1987; Long et al., 1980), the potential physiologic compromise to the cerebral circulation in the brain may negate the value of the behavior produced. Most of the earlier studies of hospital-based stimulation programs were conducted on populations of infants who would be medically low-risk by today's standards. We must be particularly observant when applying such techniques to the much more fragile, gestationally immature infants now surviving into neonatal care.

Protection at all costs

No formal research has been attempted to discover the effects of withholding all forms of medical or social stimulation from infants treated in an NICU. This would be impossible to achieve given the large staff and numbers of procedures essential for providing life support for high-risk newborns. Several clinical programs and a handful of research studies have operated from a premise that infants should, for the most part, be spared any unnecessary exposure to stimuli from the caregiving environment in the NICU (Als et al., 1986). In order to protect infants from depleting low energy reserves through wasted involuntary responses to animate and inanimate stimuli, many NICUs impose standing policies of no or minimal handling of infants at all times or at least at regular times, such as the end of nursing shifts, when no medical tests or treatments can be conducted unless urgently needed and when the staff members refrain from speaking to each other.

While awaiting results from formal investigations, such approaches tread a very delicate line between guarding the limited strength of premature infants against over-stress from the environment and understimulation of emerging CNS structures. The classic studies of Spitz and Cobeliner (1965) and Skeels (1966) informed us about the fatal risks of neglecting to engage the interactive capacities of institutionalized infants, granted in markedly different circumstances. An environment rich in social and percep-tual experience appears to foster infant brain growth and organization when compared with environments relatively deprived of stimulation (Diamond, Ingham, Johnson, Bennett, & Rosenzweig, 1976; Greenough, 1975). These studies, however, were con-ducted on populations of initially healthy, full-term subjects. Their results, therefore, which suggest that more stimulation leads to more optimal development, did not consider the special needs of high-risk infants whose nervous systems might be more vulnerable to the physiologically destabilizing effects of caregiving stimuli to which healthy full-term infants are routinely exposed. Clearly, then, optimal developmental care must derive from additional considerations that go beyond the absolute amount of stimulation required.

Contingency-based and developmentally based interventions

Beginning with the pioneering efforts of Brazelton (1973, 1980, 1984) that demon-strated the competence of full-term neonates in using behavior to signal their needs to caregivers, researchers and clinicians have been trying to identify reliable meanings of the behaviors of less organized premature infants. Neuroanatomical (Parmelee & Sig-man, 1983) as well as behavioral research with fetuses (Birnholz, 1981; Birnholz & Benacearraf, 1983; Birnholz, Stephens, & Faria, 1978; Hooker, 1952) and premature infants (Aylward, 1982) teaches us the limits of comparability between full-term and preterm infant behavioral responses. Despite the relative dearth of social signals avail-able to the more fragile and physiologically stressed preterm infants, researchers and clinicians have attempted to assign quantitative or qualitative value to commonly observed facial movements, activity, irritability, sleep and awake states, postures, as well as patterns of heart rate, respiration, and oxygenation (Als et al., 1986).

Several intervention programs designed caregiver efforts to occur only when trig-gered by some specific infant behaviors. Two such studies will be cited as examples of this current trend in intervention design. Both studies share a regard for individualized, temporally patterned interventions directed by some behavior emitted by the infant subject. Barnard and Bee (1983) tested the hypothesis that stimulation offered following a period of infant inactivity might foster the infant's emerging organization of quiet sleep. This proved to be partially fulfilled because a group of infants who experienced quasi-self-activated stimulation scored higher on subsequent measures of behavioral organization than did either the fully self-activated experimental group or the control group.

Als et al. (1986) studied an approach to nursing care that was individually planned and periodically updated and modified the infant's environment based on observations of behavioral responses to stress. Infant behaviors were labeled either "stress behaviors" or "self-regulatory behaviors." Infants who received the individualized nursing care plan compared favorably with their chronological peer control group on selected measures of medical progress in hospital as well as on developmental strides during the first year after discharge. Unfortunately, the strength of the findings was limited by differences that already distinguished the groups prior to any intervention. Several of the experimental group infants were extubated and were breathing room air before the intervention period started and, therefore, may have progressed initially for reasons other than the intervention program. A second study, as yet unpublished (H. Als, personal communication, 1988), confirms the positive benefits attributable to the contingency-based developmental intervention program.

At this time, we can derive cautious optimism from such pioneering studies. Cautious, indeed, since complex programs that combine multiple forms of intervention must determine which aspects of the intervention support optimal processes of growth and development and which strategies actually neutralize some of the overall benefit found when the entire intervention program is evaluated as if it were a single intervention. Additional basic research needs to parallel and support the current line of intervention studies.

Our own naturalistic observations of infant–caregiver interactions during NICU hospitalization begin to confirm temporal associations between certain infant "distress" behaviors and physiological crises such as bradycardia (Gorski et al., 1983; Huntington & Gorski, 1988). However, intervention efforts often attempt to change or shape some behavioral pattern whose teleological function remains poorly understood. Is it healthy to alter the percentage of time spent in various awake states at the expense of other states at a given period of neuromaturation? We tend to believe, for example, that whatever produces longer visual interaction between infant and caregiver benefits neurodevelopment. Further studies should address the possible repercussions of losing states or breathing patterns that might serve some less obvious but equally vital purpose during a particular stage of maturation.

Summary

Very early intervention programs during NICU hospitalization represent perhaps the boldest new effort to actively consider and support infant and family development at the beginning of extrauterine life. Certainly, methodological problems weaken the generalizability of the first generation of research in this burgeoning field of scientific and clinical interest. We have detailed common inadequacies related to small sample sizes, insufficient demographic data to ensure subject comparability prior to intervention, limited descriptions of both routine and experimental caregiving protocols, simultaneous use of multiple intervention modalities, limited involvement of parents, and short-term follow-up periods.

Much useful and positive experience has also been acquired as a result of these same investigations. We can safely conclude that the NICU environment does not, by itself, ensure optimal developmental outcome following premature birth, since premature infants rarely function as well as full-term neonates when both are tested at 40 weeks postconception (Aylward, 1982). Indeed, many common medical complications, such as bronchopulmonary dysplasia, necrotizing enterocolitis, and severe apnea and hypoxemia, encountered by premature infants result from the stress of having to adapt physiologically to the extrauterine caregiving environment.

Recent investigations, such as those discussed, raise the hope that attention to emerging neuroregulatory mechanisms in premature infants may augment current high standards of neonatal medical care that are now focused on treating the heart, lungs, and digestive systems. Such studies of early developmental processes instruct us to recognize and treat premature infants as individuals, as was long ago acknowledged about full-term infants and parents. Through understanding the critical role for parents in guiding the continued health and development of infants following hospital discharge (Beckwith et al., 1976; Sameroff & Chandler, 1975), hospital staffs are beginning to explore methods for helping parents feel involved, respected, and supported as primary caregivers. Similarly, medical staffs are beginning to act on the growing realization that optimal developmental outcome requires close coordination between the hospital and community services for infants and families.

LINKING HOSPITALS AND COMMUNITY PROGRAMS

In addition to advances in the care of preterm infants during hospitalization, increased focus has been placed on the postdischarge needs of these infants and their families. Following hospitalization, providers' and parents' priorities shift from the infant's survival and health status to the infant's future and the infant's developmental progress at home. Close coordination between infant follow-up programs, primary health care providers, community health nursing and visiting nursing associations, and early intervention programs is essential to the successful transition of infants from tertiary centers to community hospitals to home.

Given the focus of this volume, we shall discuss approaches to linking hospitals with community early intervention programs. However, efforts to integrate the services of infant follow-up, home health nursing, and primary care pediatrics with tertiary care units are equally important and must be considered when developing comprehensive discharge practices. (For a description of the best practices and the problems in providing access to infant follow-up and community health nursing services for NICU graduates, see Project ACCESS, 1985.)

A clear need for the linkage of hospitals and early intervention programs was demonstrated in a survey of 17 community-based intervention programs in the New England area (Project ACCESS, 1985). In these sites, from 6% to 57% of the children in early intervention had previously been cared for in an NICU, with eight programs reporting that from one-third to one-half of their clients were NICU graduates. In Massachusetts, statewide data collected from 43 early intervention programs revealed that 37% of the client population received some type of neonatal intensive care (Massachusetts Department of Public Health, 1985).

Whereas a substantial number of children who eventually receive early intervention are NICU graduates, only a small percentage of infants are referred to programs directly from the NICU. The four tertiary centers providing data in the New England survey estimated that from 5% to 14% of their population were referred to early intervention directly from the NICU. These tended to be infants with identifiable disabilities or infants from extremely high-risk environments. Although practice varies from hospital to hospital, typically the NICU has relied upon other follow-up services to determine the need for early intervention and to make appropriate referrals. Thus, the same four centers noted refer from 15% to 70% of the infants to community nursing and from 15% to 48% to hospital-based infant follow-up programs – two excellent sources of referral to early intervention.

For many infants and families, referral at a later point is highly appropriate. Infants leaving the unit with good primary care, with regular follow-up appointments, and/or with competent community health nursing involvement can be monitored effectively in the community and referred as the need arises. Families may want time away from the intensity of professional involvement that they have experienced in the NICU; some families see referral to early intervention as an extension of the control of outsiders at a time when parents most need to be in charge (Hartz, 1983). Families of infants at biological risk may be resistant to an early referral to a program that also serves disabled children. They may fear that their child will be labeled handicapped or will lack contact with children who have similar developmental abilities. Yet, whereas an early referral may be inappropriate for some families, for others it provides much needed developmental and family support during the very difficult early months at home.

Ideally, hospitals and community programs should jointly develop coordinated referral systems that are sensitive to the needs of individual families and that capitalize fully on the resources and expertise of each institution. As these systems are put into place, communities can avoid the more common pattern of referral that is characacterized by an arbitrary quality concerning who gets to early intervention and when and how the referral is made: "For every child in the [early intervention] program, there probably are other children in the community who are similar, who are not in the program and whether a child is actually receiving services or not is to some extent dependent on luck – who the parent came into contact with" (Project ACCESS, 1985, p. 63).

Institutional contrasts and strategies of collaboration

We propose that cooperative efforts between hospitals and early intervention programs are likely to succeed if the underlying dynamics of each organizational system are considered: both the strengths and resources and the limitations and constraints. Rather than act as barriers to collaboration, institutional differences – once articulated and understood – can inform interactions and can guide interinstitutional work.

Let us return to the contrasting organizational styles of tertiary centers and community early intervention programs and examine the opportunities for collaboration between the two systems on behalf of preterm infants and their families. Because hospitals tend to function as self-contained, horizontal institutions that are somewhat isolated from the community, and because their focus is primarily on the acute immediate needs of patients, early intervention programs may be best positioned to take the lead and initiate an ongoing relationship. The vertical organization of early intervention services supports outreach beyond institutional boundaries as an expected, accepted program component. The proactive administrative model more characteristic of early intervention staff members also enhances their ability to initiate contact, set up a meeting, go to the hospital site, and systematically follow through on resulting plans.

In designing effective referral systems, it is imperative that the receiving institution take primary responsibility for informing referral sources about the service and for providing feedback after the referral is made. Again, because of the self-contained nature of the hospital and its focus on medical rather than developmental concerns, it is particularly important that early intervention programs take the initiative in informing health care professionals about birth-to-three programs. Physicians and nurses surveyed by Project ACCESS reported that one of the major obstacles to referrals was lack of information about available services. Even in areas that reported a basic knowledge of early intervention programs, difficulty in keeping the information up-to-date interfered with the effectiveness of hospital-generated referrals. Further, when referrals were made, health care providers reported that they often had an inadequate understanding of what actually happened in the programs. P.L. 99-457 requires that each participating state prepare and distribute a centralized directory of early intervention programs. Such a directory not only will provide invaluable information on available services, but will also serve as a source of formal sanction of the state's early intervention network.

To maintain an ongoing relationship, other strategies that legitimize the authority of outside agencies and capitalize on their proactive approach can be designed. For example, an early intervention program might designate a single consistent contact person for each hospital. This individual can assume a number of roles that vary in function and frequency of contact. For example, the contact could make regularly scheduled rounds to the unit, discussing cases with the nursing staff or with a multidisciplinary team. Appropriate families could be referred prior to discharge, meeting the early intervention representative at the hospital. Other families might be offered the opportunity to meet the early intervention staff member, learn about the program, and, depending upon their needs, make a self-referral at a later point.

As the relationship between the contact and the hospital staff grows, other opportunities for consultation and collaboration may evolve. In one unit with a hospital-affiliated early intervention program, the early intervention contact, an occupational therapist, was asked to assume a consultation role. During her regular visits, she made rounds with the primary nurses, reviewed the developmental progress of each infant, suggested positioning and handling techniques, and assessed the need for future intervention. In another setting, the role of the contact, this time an educator, was extended to include participation in infant follow-up clinic visits for children from the early intervention program. In a third setting, an early intervention nurse developed a new home-visiting and parent support component for families of NICU graduates that was based on her experience as an NICU contact. Referrals to the specially designed program were easily facilitated through contact with the families prior to discharge and through the encouragement of the staff nurses who were knowledgeable about the new service and confident in its leadership.

Another helpful strategy that promotes consistent communication and systematic referral is shared staffing. For example, a nurse might work part-time for the infant follow-up program and part-time for the early intervention program, or a therapist might work part-time at a children's hospital while also consulting to an early intervention program. When functioning effectively in both roles, professionals can interpret the goals and practices of the two settings and serve as intermediaries in the referral and feedback process.

Because of the decentralized administration across hospitals and the high degree of professional autonomy, hospital settings are likely to vary in how they are organized. Health care professionals can take the lead in explaining the complexities and uniqueness of their settings. Health care professionals can inform early intervention programs about their unit's procedures for discharge planning, for example, whose job it is – nursing (primary nurse? clinical specialist? senior staff nurse who serves as a peer consultant?), social work, continuing care, or multidisciplinary team. Further, the physician's role in this setting should be clarified. The physician may have a strong role in discharge planning, as is traditional in community hospitals, and may be the only professional who can refer a family to early intervention. Alternatively, particularly in tertiary centers, physicians may have a more limited role in the psychosocial and developmental recommendations at discharge, leaving these decisions to nursing and/or social work. Some NICUs have a policy of not making referrals directly to early intervention; rather, they expect the infant follow-up program or the primary care physician in the community to make these decisions. All of these patterns can be understood and managed once they are articulated and cooperative plans have been made.

Still, because of the decentralized organization and professional autonomy within hospitals, intervention programs may need to have multiple contact points to cover all of the potential referral sources. These may include but not be limited to the NICU, infant follow-up, other developmental clinics, and specialty clinics such as neurology, orthopedics, failure-to-thrive, child abuse, feeding, and Down syndrome and other disabilities. Health care professionals within the system can be an invaluable source of information about the different services and about the approaches different persons take toward referral to early intervention. Further, these professionals can pave the way by informally validating – providing legitimacy for – contact with others in the setting through a phone call, a brief discussion in the hall, or, less likely, a written note.

Initial contacts with hospital staff designed to establish an ongoing relationship for referral and feedback may be facilitated more easily by professionals who already share a similar orientation; that is, who have a combined medical and social science base, rather than a solely medical base. Developmental pediatricians, infant follow-up program staff, or developmentally oriented nurses may be excellent first contacts. Relationships with neonatologists, neurologists, orthopedic surgeons, pediatric ophthalmologists, and others may develop more easily over time and through case-by-case contacts concerning individual families.

Knowing that medical professionals are likely to accord more status to interventions that maintain social distance from the client and that rely on sophisticated diagnostic procedures and treatment modalities that do not depend on patient interpretation, the early intervention professional can be better prepared to explain the rationale and the complexities of working interdependently with families. For example, articulating the underlying developmental processes exhibited in block play, or the subtle adjustments in positioning needed to develop muscle tone that a mother may use in a game of peek-a-boo with her infant with Down syndrome may help bridge the gap between the two perspectives. In addition, the IFSP offers early intervention specialists a new opportunity to present a family-focused philosophy of early intervention to physicians and nurses working in acute and primary care settings.

Finally, knowing that cultural values outside of personal relationships and individual characteristics influence how people understand the world and how they behave can help us depersonalize some of the issues in health care and early intervention collaboration, thus opening up new possibilities based on a deeper understanding of the underlying influences on behavior.

SUMMARY

As the nearly universal birthplace, hospitals have the natural opportunity to initiate support services on behalf of optimal recovery, growth, and development of infants born at risk. Although these opportunities exist, so too do some inherent obstacles within the structure and function of these large, acute care medical centers. This chapter has described the nature of these institutional challenges to providing early developmental intervention for infants and their families.

Despite such fundamental differences, hospitals and early intervention staffs have begun to communicate, to learn about each other's expertise and limitations, and to forge a new partnership dedicated to the common goal of supporting optimal developmental outcome. Such efforts are bound to create healthy self-inspection as well as critical evaluation by hospitals and community organizations. We welcome this process because of its potential to elevate hospital and community programs to positions of mutual regard and respect, thus helping to ensure a future based on reciprocal interaction and shared commitment to brightening the hopes of vulnerable children.

REFERENCES

Alexander, L. (1980). The double-bind between dialysis patients and their health practitioners. In L. Eisenberg & A. Kleinman (Eds.), *The relevance of social science for medicine* (pp. 307–329). Boston: Riedel.

Als, H., Lawhon, G., & Brown, E. (1986). Individualized behavioral and environmental care for the very low birth weight preterm infant at high risk for bronchopulmonary dysplasia: Neonatal intensive care unit and developmental outcome. *Pediatrics, 78*, 1123–1132.

Aylward, G. P. (1982). Forty-week full-term and preterm neurologic differences. In L. P. Lipsitt, & T. M. Field (Eds.), *Infant behavior and development: Perinatal risk and newborn behavior* (pp. 67–83). Norwood, NJ: Ablex Publishing.

Bailey, D. B., Jr., Simeonsson, R. J., Winton, P. J., Huntington, G. S., Comfort, M., Isbell, P., O'Donnell, K. J., & Helm, J. M. (1986). Family–focused intervention: A functional model for planning, implementing, and evaluating individualized family services in early intervention. *Journal of the Division for Early Childhood, 10*, 156–171.

Barnard, K., & Bee, H. (1983). The impact of temporally patterned stimulation on the development of preterm infants. *Child Development, 54*, 1156–1167.

Barnett, C. R., Leiderman, P. H., Grobstein, R., & Klaus, M. H. (1970). Neonatal separation: The maternal side of interactional deprivation. *Pediatrics, 45*, 197–205.

Beckwith, L., Cohen, S. E., Kopp, C. B., Parmelee, A. H., & Marcy, T. (1976). Caregiver–infant interaction and early cognitive development in preterm infants. *Child Development, 47*, 579–587.

Bennett, F. C. (1987). The effectiveness of early intervention for infants at increased biologic risk. In M. J. Guralnick & F. C. Bennett (Eds.), *The effectiveness of early intervention for at-risk and handicapped children* (pp. 79–112). Orlando: Academic Press.

Bernbaum, J., Pereira, G., & Watkins, J. (1983). Nonnutritive sucking during gavage feeding enhances growth and maturation in premature infants. *Pediatrics, 71*, 41–45.

Birnholz, J. (1981). The development of human fetal eye movement patterns. *Science, 213*, 679–681.

Birnholz, J., & Benacearraf, B. (1983). The development of human fetal hearing. *Science, 222*, 516–518.

Birnholz, J., Stephens, J., & Faria, M. (1978). Fetal movement patterns: A possible means of defining neurologic developmental milestones in utero. *American Journal of Roentgenology, 130*, 537–540.

Boros, S. J., Mammel, M. C., Coleman, J. M., Lewallen, P. K., Gordon, M. J., Bing, D. R., & Ophoven, J. P. (1985). Neonatal high-frequency jet ventilation: Four years' experience. *Pediatrics, 75*, 657–663.

Brazelton, T. B. (1973). *Neonatal behavioral assessment scale*. Philadelphia: Lippincott.

Brazelton, T. B. (1980). The behavioral competence of the newborn. In P. M. Taylor (Ed.), *Parent–infant relationships* (pp. 69–85). New York: Grune & Stratton.

Brazelton, T. B. (1984). *Neonatal behavioral assessment scale.* London: Blackwell Scientific Publications.

Bromwich, R. (1978). *Working with parents and infants: An interactional approach.* Baltimore: University Park Press.

Diamond, M. C., Ingham, C. A., Johnson, R. E., Bennett, E. L., & Rosenzweig, M. R. (1976). Effects of environment on morphology of rat cerebral cortex and hippocampus. *Journal of Neurobiology, 7,* 75–86.

Dunst, C., & Trivette, C. M. (1987). Enabling and empowering families: Conceptual and intervention issues. *School Psychology Review, 16,* 443–456.

Enhorning, G., Shennan, A., Pessinager, F., Dunn, M., Chen, C. P., & Milligan, J. (1985). Prevention of neonatal respiratory distress syndrome by tracheal instillation of surfactant: A randomized clinical trial. *Pediatrics, 76,* 145–153.

Feinstein, A. R. (1973). An analysis of diagnostic reasoning, parts 1 and 2. *Yale Journal of Biology and Medicine, 46,* 212–232, 264–283.

Field, T., Ignatoff, E., & Stringer, S. (1982). Nonnutritive sucking during tube feelings: Effects on preterm neonates in an intensive care unit. *Pediatrics, 70,* 381–384.

Field T., Schanberg, S., & Scafidi, F. (1986). Tactile/kinesthetic stimulation effects on preterm neonates. *Pediatrics, 77,* 654–658.

Gilkerson, L. (1981). Building relationships: Year 1 – The dignity of risk. In P. Gilderman, D. Taylor-Hershel, S. Prestridge, & J. Anderson (Eds.), *The healthcare/education relationship* (pp. 11–19). Chapel Hill: WESTAR/TADS.

Good, B. J., & Delvecchio-Good, J. J., (1980). The meaning of symptoms: A cultural hermeneutic model for clinical practice. In Eisenberg & A. Kleinman (Eds.), *The relevance of social science for medicine* (pp. 165–196). Boston: Reidel.

Gorski, P. A. (1982). Premature infant behavioral and physiological responses to caregiving interventions in an intensive care nursery. In J. D. Call, E. Galenson, & R. L. Tyson (Eds.), *Frontiers of infant psychiatry* (pp. 256–263). New York: Basic Books.

Gorski, P. A., Davison, M. F., & Brazelton, T. B. (1979). Stages of behavioral organization in the high-risk neonate: Theoretical and clinical considerations. *Seminars in Perinatology, 3,* 61–72.

Gorski, P. A., Hole, W. T., Leonard, C. H., & Martin, J. A. (1983). Direct computer recording of premature infants and nursery care. *Pediatrics, 72,* 198–202.

Gorski, P. A., & Huntington, L. (1988). Physiological measures relative to tactile stimulation in hospitalized preterm infants. *Pediatric Research, 23,* 210a.

Gorski, P. A., Huntington, L., & Lewkowicz, D. J. (1987). Handling preterm infants in hospitals: Stimulating controversy about timing stimulation. In N. Gunzenhauser (Ed.), *Infant stimulation* (Johnson & Johnson Pediatric Round Table No. 13, pp. 43–51). Skillman, NJ: Johnson & Johnson.

Gorski, P. A., Leonard, C., Sweet, D., Martin, J., Sehring, S., O'Hara, K., High, P., Lang, M., Piecuch, R., & Green, J. (1984). Caring for immature infants – a touchy subject. In C. C. Brown (Ed.), *The many facets of touch* (Johnson & Johnson Pediatric Round Table No. 10, pp. 84–91). Skillman, NJ: Johnson & Johnson.

Greenough, W. T. (1975). Experiential modification of the developing brain. *American Scientist, 63,* 37–46.

Gregory, G. A., Kitterman, J. A., Phibbs, R. H., Tooley, W. H., & Hamilton, W. K. (1971). Treatment of the idiopathic respiratory distress syndrome with continuous positive airway pressure. *New England Journal of Medicine, 284,* 1333–1340.

Hallman, M., Schneider, H., Merritt, T. A., & Gluck, L. (1981). Human surfactant substitution. *Pediatric Research, 16,* 290a.

Hartz, S. E., (1983). *Integrating pre-term infants and their families into early intervention programs.* Boston: Project Welcome, Wheelock College.

High, P. C., & Gorski, P. A. (1985). Womb for improvement – A study of preterm development in an intensive care nursery. In A. W. Gottfried & J. L. Gaiter (Eds.), *Infant stress under intensive care* (pp. 131–155). Baltimore: University Park Press.

Hirata, T., Epcar, J., & Walsh, A. (1983). Survival and outcome of infants 501 to 750 grams: A six-year experience. *Journal of Pediatrics, 102,* 741–748.

Hooker, D. (1952). *The prenatal origins of behavior.* Lawrence: The University of Kansas Press.

Huntington, L., & Gorski, P. A. (1988). Temporal relations between preterm infant behaviors and physiological distress. *Pediatric Research, 23,* 210a.

Katz V. (1971). Auditory stimulation and developmental behavior of the premature infant. *Nursing Research, 20,* 196–201.

Kety, S. (1974). From rationalization to reason. *American Journal of Psychiatry, 131*, 957–963.

Kleinman, A. (1980). *Patients and healers in the context of culture.* Berkeley: University of California Press.

Konner, M. (1987). *Becoming a doctor: A journey of initiation into medical school.* New York: Viking Press.

Korner, A., Guilleminault, C., & Van den Hoed, J. (1978). Reduction of sleep apnea and bradycardia in preterm infants on oscillating water beds: A controlled polygraphic study. *Pediatrics, 61*, 528–533.

Korner, A., Kraemer, H., & Haffner, E. (1975). Effects of waterbed flotation on premature infants: A pilot study. *Pediatrics, 5*, 361–365.

Korner, A., & Schneider, P. (1983). Effects of vestibular-proprioceptive stimulation on the neurobehavioral development of preterm infants: A pilot study. *Neuropediatrics, 14*, 170–175.

Kraemer, L., & Pierpoint, M. (1976). Rocking waterbeds and auditory stimuli to enhance growth of preterm infants. *Journal of Pediatrics, 88*, 297–299.

Kramer, M., Chamorro, I., Green, D., & Knudtson, F. (1975). Extra tactile stimulation on the preterm infant. *Nursing Research, 24*, 324–334.

Kwong, M., Egan, E., & Notter, R. (1985). Double-blind clinical trial of calf lung surfactant extract for the prevention of hyaline membrane disease in extremely premature infants. *Pediatrics, 76*, 585–599.

Lawson, K. R., Daum, C., & Turkewitz, G. (1977). Environmental characteristics of a neonatal intensive-care unit. *Child Development, 48*, 1633–1639.

Leib, S., Benfield, G., & Guidubaldi, J. (1980). Effects of early intervention and stimulation on the preterm infant. *Pediatrics, 66*, 83–89.

Linn, P., Horowitz, F., & Fox, H. (1985). Stimulation in the NICU: Is more necessarily better? *Clinics in Perinatology, 12*, 407–422.

Long, J., Lucey, J., & Philip, A. (1980). Noise and hypoxemia in the intensive care nursery. *Pediatrics, 65*, 143–145.

Massachusetts Department of Public Health, Division of Family Health (1985). Clinical Data System.

Meisels, S. J., Jones, S. N., & Stiefel, G. S. (1983). Neonatal intervention: Problem, purpose and prospects. *Topics in Early Childhood Special Education, 3*, 1–13.

Merritt, T., Hallman, M., & Bloom, B. (1986). Prophylactic treatment of very premature infants with human surfactant. *New England Journal of Medicine, 315*, 785–790.

Minde, K., Trehub, S., Corter, C., Boukydis, C., Celhoffer, L., & Marton, P. (1978). Mother–child relationships in the premature nursery: An observational study. *Pediatrics, 61*, 373–379.

Parmelee, H. P., & Sigman, M. D. (1983). Perinatal brain development and behavior. In P. H. Mussen (Ed.), *The handbook of child psychology* (pp. 95–139). New York: Wiley.

Parsons, T. (1951). *The social system.* Glencoe, IL: Free Press.

Parsons, T. (1975). The sick role and the role of the physician reconsidered. *Millbank Memorial Fund Quarterly, 53*, 257–277.

Parsons, T., & Fox, R. L. (1952). Illness, therapy, and the modern urban American family. *Journal of Social Issues, 8*, 31–44.

Powell, L. (1974). The effect of extra stimulation and maternal involvement on the development of low-birth-weight infants and on maternal behavior. *Child Development, 45*, 106–113.

Project ACCESS. (1985). *Access to Developmental Services for NICU Graduates.* Boston: Wheelock College.

Resnick, M., Eyler, F., & Nelson, R. (1987). Developmental intervention for low birth weight infants: Improved early developmental outcome. *Pediatrics, 80*, 68–74.

Sameroff, A. J., & Chandler, M. J. (1975). Reproductive risk and the continuum of caretaking casualty. In F. D. Horowitz, M. Hetherington, S. Scarr-Salapatek, & G. Siegel (Eds.), *Review of child development research* (Vol. 4, pp. 187–244). Chicago: University of Chicago Press.

Scarr-Salapatek, S., & Williams, M. (1973). The effects of early stimulation on low-birth weight infants. *Child Development, 44*, 94–101.

Skeels, H. M. (1966). Adults status of children with contrasting life experiences. *Monographs of the Society for Research in Child Development, 31* (105, 33).

Spitz, R. A., & Cobeliner, W. G. (1965). *The first year of life.* New York: International Universities Press.

Starr, P. (1982). *The social transformation of American medicine.* New York: Basic Books.

Swanson, J. (1981). Building relationships between the medical and educational communities:

What is, what was, and what might be. In D. Gilderman, D. Taylor-Hershel, S. Prestridge, & J. Anderson (Eds.), *The healthcare/education relationship* (pp. 21–29). Chapel Hill, NC: WESTAR/TADS.

Thoman, E., & Graham, S. (1986). Self-regulation of stimulation by premature infants. *Pediatrics, 78*, 855–860.

Turnbull, A. P. (1988). A lifespan perspective. *Family Resource Coalition Report, 2*, 13.

Turnbull, A. P., & Turnbull, H. R. (1986). *Families, professionals, and exceptionality: A special partnership.* Columbus, OH: Merrill.

Vincent, E., Davis, D., Brown, P., Broome, K., Funkhauser, K., Miller, J., & Gruenewald, L. (1986). *Parent inventory of child development in non-school environments.* Madison Metropolitan School District and Department of Rehabilitative Psychology and Special Education, University of Wisconsin, Madison.

West, C. (1984). *Routine complications.* Bloomington: Indiana University Press.

White, J., & Labarba, R. (1976). The effects of tactile and kinesthetic stimulation on neonatal development in the premature infant. *Developmental Psychobiology 9*, 569–577.

Wolinsky, F. (1980). *The Sociology of health: Principles, professions, and issues.* Boston: Little, Brown.

20   *Community-based early intervention*

ROBERT HALPERN

This chapter examines the state-of-the-art of community-based early intervention programs that serve low-income families with children from birth to 3 years of age. The chapter begins with a discussion of the characteristics that define community-based early intervention programs and then examines the recent historical roots of the current generation of programs, the social forces that are stimulating interest in these programs at the present time, and contemporary programmatic approaches. Finally, the chapter explores the conceptual, organizational, and political issues that must be addressed as community-based early intervention programs take a more significant place in social problem solving.

DEFINING CHARACTERISTICS OF COMMUNITY-BASED EARLY INTERVENTION

In recent years two main streams of practice have been developed to address parenting and related support needs in low-income families with young children. The first is a clinical stream, in which specially trained professional teams work in a therapeutic mode with families in which there is evidence of problems in parent–infant interaction. Although families served by clinical infant programs are disproportionately likely to be economically disadvantaged, these programs view poverty as a compounding stress, rather than a primary targeting criterion for intervention (see Garbarino, this volume).

The second stream, and the focus of this chapter, is community-based. Community-based early intervention programs typically target any family with children under three in a specific population of low-income families. This approach is based on the premise that the stressful familial and extrafamilial environment in which low-income families live poses inherent threats to both infants' and parents' well-being and development. Alternatively, some programs focus on specific families who are identified as being at risk for inattentive or inappropriate parenting due to such factors as lack of access to resources, social isolation, lack of knowledge of children's developmental needs, infant health problems, and other stressors associated with poverty. Adolescent parents constitute a special population within this group, due to the unique cluster of obstacles to nurturant parenting posed by their particular developmental needs.

469

A working definition

For purposes of this chapter, community-based early intervention programs will be defined as those in which neighborhood-based agencies employ lay family workers, sometimes in concert with professionals, to provide sustained goal-oriented support to low-income families during pregnancy and/or infancy. The components of that support typically include outreach to alert families to the program, information, guidance and feedback, joint problem solving, help with securing entitlements and services, encouragement, and psychological support.

Support is provided with the objective of promoting family conditions, parental competencies, and behaviors that contribute to maternal and infant health, maternal personal development, and healthy child development (Weiss & Halpern, 1988). A secondary but equally important goal is to identify and activate latent helping resources in low-income communities. This has the potential for fostering enduring helping relationships among community members, and may occasionally even stimulate collective action to address the unavailability or poor quality of services and other community problems.

Support is provided to families in community-based early intervention programs through individual formats such as home visiting, and/or group formats such as peer support groups and parent education classes. Programs can include none, few, or many of such additional services as developmental child care and respite care, health and/or developmental screening, toy lending, information and referral, adult education, and so forth. Community-based early intervention programs are sponsored by many kinds of community agencies, ranging from mental health and child welfare agencies to health agencies, churches, and federally funded community action agencies. In many cases programs are based in agencies that provide other more established helping services. But there are also a growing number of "family support centers," created for the purposes of providing the services just described.

The great majority of community-based early intervention programs are initiated locally, in response to perceived neighborhood needs, with relatively short-term funding. These are generally undertaken as service programs, although they may document numbers and characteristics of families served, and measure participant satisfaction. There has also been a small group of demonstration programs with significant research components. Evidence from these programs, which provide the empirical foundation for this program movement, will be examined in a later section of this chapter. In the past few years, a small number of states (notably Illinois, Maryland, and Connecticut) have initiated programs that explicitly or implicitly target low-income families (Weiss, 1989). These states typically provide a common funding base, some kind of mandate with regard to priority target population, program purpose, and components, and some level of technical assistance. Level and types of evaluation activity associated with these state initiatives vary, although none has yet completed a summative evaluation.

RECENT HISTORICAL ROOTS OF THE CURRENT GENERATION OF COMMUNITY-BASED EARLY INTERVENTION PROGRAMS

Several of the defining features of community-based early intervention in the late 1980s have their roots in the War on Poverty programs of the 1960s, especially those programs sponsored by the Office of Economic Opportunity. This history actually begins in the 1950s. Implicit in the growing civil rights movement of the 1950s, and in emerging sociological theory on the causes of deviance, was the notion that our closed opportunity system blocked families from lifting themselves out of poverty (Chilman, 1973). Concurrently, a number of strands of emerging social science research were focusing on the lifestyle and culture of poor families, particularly poor black families, positing an identifiable set of behaviors that were adaptive in the short-term, but ultimately served to perpetuate poverty from one generation to the next (Valentine, 1968).

The two causal frameworks – one focusing on the social system, the other on the poor themselves – were combined in the 1960s to yield the specific programs of the War on Poverty. The hallmark of these programs was a dual emphasis on opening up the opportunity system and preparing poor children, youth, and, to a lesser extent, adults to take advantage of new opportunities. Complementing these two emphases was a commitment to use social science knowledge to design interventions and social science methods to measure their effectiveness.

The strategic emphases were made operational in the human service programs sponsored by the Office of Economic Opportunity, in such generic elements as the targeting of a whole community of poor families, not selected "cases"; the use of indigenous paraprofessionals to provide direct services, creating new careers, and at the same time influencing the culture of the human service system; outreach to isolated or distrustful families in order to bring them into community life; advocacy and service brokerage on behalf of families; provision of an array of services in the same program; and attempts to embed programs physically and socially in neighborhood life.

These generic elements were applied to a specific set of priority problems, identified by a cadre of social scientists, consulted and in some cases recruited into government service by the Kennedy and Johnson administrations (Zigler & Valentine, 1979). Among these was a group of pediatricians and developmental psychologists concerned that "on their own, the poor are incapable of helping their children escape from poverty" (Skerry, 1983, p. 27). Their concerns and the social action principles of the early War of Poverty were synthesized in the Office of Economic Opportunity's Head Start program, which become the paradigmatic social program of the era.

The argument underlying Head Start was that even if poor children were given equal access to decent quality schooling, they would start out disadvantaged by patterns of parental care and nurturance that failed to prepare them to compete with economically more advantaged peers, by poor health and nutritional status due to lack of family resources and community services, and by lack of parent involvement in their children's educational careers. The model that emerged to address these problems was a neighborhood-based program for 3- and 4-year-old children, providing preschool education, health screening, meals, service brokerage for families, and varied opportunities for parent participation (although not parent education).

Head Start proved to be an effective vehicle for combining the strategic principles of the War on Poverty into a coherent program (Zigler & Valentine, 1979). It embodied the renewed, though deeply rooted, American faith in education as a path out of poverty. It provided human service employment and training opportunities for adults. And it provided a vehicle for mobilizing parents to become agents of wider community change.

Not least, Head Start rekindled interest in parent education as a strategy for fighting poverty. Parent education never became a significant element of the core program, in spite of a rationale that implied inadequate parenting among poor children. But by the late 1960s, stimulated by a variety of forces, the founders were arguing that "the only way to help poor children was to educate their parents as well" (Skerry, 1983, p. 22). One such force was the renewed attention to an old theme in the child development literature – that parents are the most important influence on and mediators of children's development, and the earliest years are a critical period for child development (Clarke-Stewart, 1981). Another was the equivocal findings of a major early Head Start evaluation (Cicirelli, 1969) that led the evaluators and others to conclude (prematurely) that Head Start was beginning too late, and that parents' distinct role as early educators needed to be addressed directly in early childhood intervention programs.

These criticisms had been anticipated to some extent by a small group of developmental and educational psychologists who had been experimenting since the early 1960s with home visiting programs designed to "teach" low-income mothers how to be better "teachers" of their young children, and in some cases directly provided stimulation to infants and toddlers (Deutsch, 1967; Klaus & Gray, 1968; Levenstein, 1971). Home visitors in these programs not only strived to teach mothers how to play with their infants and talk with them, but frequently brought learning materials into the home to be used during the home visit, or to be left there until the next visit.

These programs were premised on a group of overlapping theories positing dysfunctional maternal socialization and early teaching strategies as the principal cause of what appeared to be retarded cognitive and linguistic development in low-income, particularly low-income black, children. (For an overview and critique see Baratz & Baratz, 1970.) Reports and articles emanating from this group of applied researchers reclothed the historically rooted notion of inadequate family care among low-income families (Grubb & Lazerson, 1982) in state-of-the-art psychological terms. Perhaps more significantly, the dissemination efforts of this group of researchers put the rearing of low-income infants on the public agenda in a historically unprecedented way, complementing the early evaluation findings from Head Start itself.

The Office of Economic Opportunity responded to the basic and applied research findings on the importance and apparent inadequacy of early parenting in low-income families by launching the Parent–Child Center (PCC) program. The PCCs were envisioned initially to become a nationwide network of multipurpose family centers, providing parent education, health, and social services to low-income parents with infants birth to 3 years of age. Some 33 centers were established in the first few years, but shifting political forces and bureaucratic reorganization overtook the program, preventing its expansion. Nonetheless, the PCCs signaled a return to the historic focus on family functioning, rather than inadequacies in social structure, in public efforts to address the causes and consequences of poverty (Schlossman, 1978).

Another signal of this transition was the transfer of Head Start and the PCCs from the Office of Economic Opportunity to a new Office of Child Development (OCD). The early leaders of OCD were strongly committed to promoting parent education. But they were also aware that the emphasis on wide-scale social and institutional change of the preceding years was giving way to questions about accountability and effectiveness (Weissman, 1978). The approach thus adopted was to mount demonstration projects, carefully conceived, implemented, and evaluated, and then replicate them if they proved effective. Federal, and eventually foundation, sponsorship led to a decade of public and private sector demonstration activity that yielded some of the best evidence we have to this day about the parameters and conditions of effectiveness of parent support and education. (For reviews see Hewett, 1982; Zigler & Weiss, 1985; Weiss & Jacobs, 1988.)

Two notable public sector demonstrations of the era, the Parent–Child Development

Centers (PCDs) and the later Child and Family Resource Programs (CFRPs), will be described. These two initiatives reflect particularly well the evolution in premises and strategies of community-based early intervention during the 1970s, as well as the persistent contradictions and dilemmas that frame the genre to this day. Both demonstrations focused on improving low-income parents' ability to promote in their young children the skills and habits they would need to compete in the larger (middle-class) world, beginning with success in school. But the demonstrations combined in somewhat different measures the principles of the Office of Economic Opportunity's community action programs: emerging ecologically oriented child develoment theory arguing for attention to a range of extrafamilial obstacles to attentive parenting in programs serving low-income families (Weiss, 1987), and more traditional child development theory arguing that poor minority parents had to be taught middle-class parents' child-rearing practices in bringing up their children (Ogbu, 1985).

Parent–Child Development Centers

The PCDC experiment involved the development of parent education models suited to the needs of different groups of low-income families with children from birth to 3 years of age. Three PCDCs were selected for the experiment: Birmingham, serving both black and white families; Houston, serving Hispanic families; and New Orleans, serving black families. Program development, implementation, and evaluation were managed in each community by university-based researchers in consultation with community members. The three programs were developed and implemented within a common framework that focused on the crucial mediating role of maternal behavior on child development and also acknowledged the importance of addressing the range of situational difficulties facing poor families. All three included health, social services, meals, and transportation (Andrews et al., 1982).

Evaluation design in the PCDC experiment was site-specific, with a commitment to measuring a common core of variables. Outcome measurement had three main foci: maternal behavior measured along various dimensions, mother–infant interaction patterns, and infant development. Program features, evaluation design, methods, and findings are summarized in Table 1.

As Table 1 indicates, the PCDC experiment demonstrated significant program-favoring effects on maternal behaviors and maternal–infant interaction (Andrews et al., 1982). Program mothers' behavior was more positive than controls' in such areas as emotional responsiveness, demonstration of affection, praise, appropriate control, and encouragement of child verbalization. Infant development effects were more modest, which is not surprising since the interventions focused largely on maternal competencies. The Houston researchers managed to follow target children remaining in their sample at the end of the intervention up to ages 8–11 years, finding no differences in teacher-reported learning problems, but significantly more behavioral problems (i.e., aggressive, acting-out behavior) among control children, particularly among boys (Johnson & Walker, 1987).

One cautionary note in the findings, however, was a generally high attrition rate, an average of 50% across the three programs, with especially high attrition among women who were returning to work or school. Evidently, the lengthy and intense PCDC parenting interventions, although contributing to improved parenting, were not fully consonant with women's efforts to advance their education or focus their energies on economic self-sufficiency. This problem is addressed more fully in a later section of the

Table 1. *Parent–Child Development Centers: Program and evaluation features by site*

Program features	Birmingham	Houston	New Orleans
Program characteristics	Duration: infant age 3–36 mo. 1st yr: mothers spend three half-days weekly in parenting/child development classes, and participating with infants in nursery, where more experienced peers serve as models. 2nd yr: mothers "understudy." 3rd yr: they become peer models themselves.	Duration: infant age 12–36 mo. 1st yr: 30 weekly home visits by trained lay visitors. 2nd yr: mothers attend 3-hr sessions at center, 4 days a week; daily developmental program for children; weekend family workshops, evening meetings for family.	Duration: infant age 2–36 mo. For full 3 yr, two 3-hr classes per week, one on child development, the other on community resources; also strong health education component.
Sampling strategy	Random assignment to treatment (T) and control (C); recruitment door-to-door and agency referrals; controls received stipend.	Random assignment in two cohorts; Ts and Cs paid for taking tests; recruitment door-to-door.	Random assignment in two cohorts; recruitment from birth records of public hospital.
Sample characteristics	$N = 162$ Ts, 89 Cs; 100% black; average maternal age 22 yr; average education 11 yr.	$N = 97$ Ts, 119 Cs; 100% Mexican-American; average maternal age 28 yr; average education 7.5 yr.	$N = 67$ Ts, 59 Cs; 100% black; average maternal age 24 yr; average education 11 yr.
Sample attrition	57% Ts, 27% Cs; not random: Ts lost women returning to work; also lowest IQ females from T group.	50% Ts, 51% Cs; main reason both groups: high mobility.	50% Cs, 25% Cs; not random: Ts tended to lose women returning to work.
Principal findings	On nonsocial stress situation: T mothers comforted children more at 24 mo, refrained more from verbal control at 24 and 36 mo. In teaching situation: T mothers better at 24 and 36 mo on quality of instruction, praise. Exit interview: T mothers reported greater life-satisfaction, more use of community resources; T children scored 8 points higher on Bayley at 24 mo, 8 points higher on S-B at 36 mo.	On teaching situation: T mothers talked and elaborated more to children, used less criticism at 36 mo. On HOME: Ts higher at 36 mo especially on provision of play materials, emotional responsiveness; T children scored 8 points higher on Bayley at 24 mo, 4 points higher on S-B at 36 mo.	On waiting room situation: T mothers more sensitive, accepting, cooperative at 24 and 36 mo. On teaching situation: T mothers used more positive language with children and more play stimulation at 36 mo; T children scored 6 points higher on S-B at 36 mo.

Source: Andrews, Blumenthal, Johnson, Kahn, Ferguson, Lasater, Malone, & Wallace, 1982.

chapter. The positive findings of the initial experiment led to the initiation of replication activities. But the replication was initiated in a context of growing budgetary pressures on OCD's successor, the Administration for Children, Youth, and Families. Thus, the experiment was soon abandoned.

Nevertheless, all the wind was not yet out of the sails of large-scale federally funded parenting demonstrations. New breezes were stimulated by renewed political and scientific interest in "the family," as well as the need to demonstrate that Head Start was on the cutting edge of new ideas and deserved funding to explore them. One such set of new ideas argued that in order for parenting programs to promote child development, they had to concentrate equally on specific parenting competencies and on the full range of family and neighborhood conditions that impinged on parenting (Hewett, 1982). This could best be accomplished through a mix of focused child development-oriented intervention and broad multifaceted social support. This argument, integrated with the community action tradition of outreach by indigenous paraprofessionals, became the foundation for the Child and Family Resource Programs (CFRP), initiated in 1973 – one of the last major federal early childhood demonstrations.

The Child and Family Resource Programs

The heart of the CFRP model was a 2-year program of monthly home visits for families with children from birth to 3 years. The CFRP home visitors were specially trained community members who were encouraged to address the full range of family needs found in each of their families, in addition to focusing on parenting knowledge and competencies. Each of the 11 local programs was supposed to be linked to an affiliated Head Start center that would provide the resources for provision of health and social services.

In 1977 an evaluation contract was awarded to Abt Associates, with a mandate to focus both on program effects and on patterns of implementation in five of the eleven local CFRPs (those that could generate adequate sample sizes). The Abt team produced a series of reports that provided an unusually rich portrait of lay home visiting programs for low-income families (for a summary, see Travers, Nauta, & Irwin, 1982).

In their on-site observations, the Abt team found that the relative focus on parenting and broader social needs, the frequency of home visits, and the quality of the linkage of Head Start varied significantly across the local programs. For example, the frequency of home visits, although averaging three every 4 months, ranged from once a month to once every 2 months. They found that home visitors at some of the sites had difficulty getting to their program's parent education agenda. In some cases home visitors personally preferred the service brokerage and problem-solving aspects of their role; in others pressing family needs impelled such a focus.

The CFRP summative evaluation design is described in Table 2. It included a variety of child development measures and measures of parents' child-rearing attitudes, teaching skills, use of community resources, general coping and sense of self-efficacy, and personal development.

Within the interpretive constraints of high, nonrandom attrition, (controlled in the analyses), the evaluators found significant program-favoring effects on use of community resources, maternal self-reported control of events and general coping, and maternal participation in job training and employment. There were no documented effects on child development, for the whole sample or various subsamples, and only very modest program-favoring effects in selected areas of parental teaching skills.

Table 2. *Child and Family Resource Program: Evaluation design and findings*

Domain/timing	Measures	Findings
Child development and achievement at baseline, 6, 18, and 36 mo after entry	Bayley, Preschool Inventory, Schaeffer Behavior Inventory	No program effects
Parent teaching skills and parent–child interaction at baseline and 6 mo after entry; observation at 18 mo	Parent-as-Teacher Inventory, Maternal Attitudes Scale, Carew home observation system	Marginally significant program-favoring effects on total PAT score; at 18 mo T mothers observed at home showed more and more stimulating interaction
Child health	Birth records, height and weight at two time points, parental report of preventive health care use	No program effects
Family functioning at baseline and 36 mo after entry	Parental interviews, documentation of how services were used, five-item locus of control scale	No effects on "independence" (recognizes needs and finds resources to meet them); significant program-favoring effects on feelings of efficacy, ability to control events, locus of control
Family circumstances	Parent interviews at four time points	Significant program-favoring effects on percentage of mothers employed, in training, or both – 37% increase in T group and 28% increase in C group from baseline to exit

Notes: Sampling strategy – 82 families from each of five sites randomly assigned to treatment (T) and control (C) conditions, yielding a total evaluation sample of 409 families; initially more C families ($N = 210$) than T families ($N = 199$). *Sample characteristics* – 39% white, 47% black, 4% Hispanic, 10% other; 70% single parents living alone or with extended family, 30% two parents; 505 mothers had completed high school; average maternal age 22 years. *Sample attrition* – 40% for combined sample, 45% for Ts, 35% for Cs.
Source: Travers, Nauta, & Irwin, 1982.

What explains this pattern of effects? One key assumption of CFRP was that home visitors' attention would shift over time from service brokerage and meeting parents' personal needs to child development-focused activities, as the former needs were met or at least stabilized. But this shift only occurred for those mothers who were coping at a high level at the outset of the program. Moreover, the Abt team observed that time devoted to child development activities was overly focused on talking, and not sufficiently focused on modeling, demonstration, and joint activity with the child. One apparent reason for this was inadequate training and supervision of the lay workers (see Musick & Stott, this volume).

The PCDC and CFRP experiences in perspective

The experiences of these and similar programs of the era (see Hewett, 1982; Zigler & Weiss, 1985) suggest that parent support and education for low-income families can improve parenting in domains relevant to child development. Such domains include more reciprocal play and verbalization, more positive and less restrictive control techniques, and greater emotional responsiveness. But effects potent enough to leave a meaningful residue in parents' and children's lives may depend on interventions of such skill, expense, and intensity as to be unreplicable in the average context; unaffordable without a significant redeployment of public resources toward prevention; and unmanageable by the growing proportion of low-income parents facing overwhelming personal, familial, and situational problems. Moreover, it has proven difficult in practice to establish a reasonable balance in emphasis among families' survival needs, parents' personal adjustment and development, and the specific developmental needs of children (Weiss & Halpern, 1988).

Of the two programs reviewed, PCDC clearly had the stronger parenting effects. These appeared to be related to the PCDC programs' more detailed attention to maternal–child interaction, the length and intensity of the intervention, requiring tremendous maternal involvement, and professional participation in service delivery. But these very features, along with the high rates of attrition, raise numerous questions about the generalizability of the PCDC models. The CFRP's responsive lay helping model was in many respects more "typical" of its genre in quality and quantity of services provided. In its efforts to combine attention to a wide range of family needs with a more specific focus on parenting, it also reflected the direction in which the field of parent support and education was heading. As such, its finding that modest gains in parental coping skills and family circumstances do not automatically translate into enhanced parenting and child development raises questions about how best to focus the resources of parenting programs.

At a more basic level, the parenting demonstrations of the 1970s provided another illustration of the persistent American propensity to address inequality in the conditions that shape child development with tools that are incommensurate with the nature of the problem itself. As de Lone (1979) notes of social services in general, they "can counter some of the injuries of inequality, but they cannot destroy inequality itself. Services are insufficient by themselves to alter the powerlessness, the limited life options, and the hardships of everyday experience that are the bottom line of inequality" (p. 68). Intervening to strengthen the early family care received by low-income children without also attending to the social, economic, and institutional context shaping that parenting is at best a problematic proposition (Halpern, 1988). Poverty certainly can and frequently does undermine the capacity and resources of patterns to protect, nurture, and guide their children. But parent-focused early intervention has to be promoted in the context of consensus about children's and families' entitlement to adequate housing, health care, child care, education, and other basic supports (Halpern, 1988).

COMMUNITY-BASED EARLY INTERVENTION IN THE 1980S

Why community-based early intervention?

The early childhood parenting demonstrations of the 1970s straddled a major shift in the locus, concerns, and strategies of social problem solving. During this period, the notion of poverty as a massive social problem requiring massive federal action was gradually replaced by a more disaggregated view of the problems and populations involved. Nonetheless, within the more cautious social problem-solving climate that has emerged in recent years, community-based early intervention has continued to be viewed as a promising strategy for addressing specific support needs of low-income families and young children. Continued interest in this program genre has been stimulated by four principal factors:

1. the deteriorating well-being of young families as a group, which has provided an overall climate for renewed attention and exacerbated specific problems whose causes or consequences seem susceptible to early parenting interventions;

2. growing recognition among professionals in different formal helping systems that their existing services are not equipped to reach out to young families under stress and provide sustained, multifaceted, and nonstigmatizing support;

3. growing recognition of the limitations of informal social supports in providing low-income parents with young children the role models, encouragement, and assistance underlying optimal parenting; and

4. growing appreciation within the early childhood field of the need for models of practice that work with the family in a more integrated manner, attending to the interrelationships among families' basic life conditions, parents' well-being as individuals, specific parenting skills and knowledge, and healthy child development.

The deteriorating well-being of families with young children

The overall climate for continued interest in community-based early intervention programs has been set by the deteriorating well-being of growing numbers of families with young children (see Garbarino, this volume). Three social trends underlie this decline in well-being. The first and most important of these is the growth since the late 1970s of the percentage of children in the United States conceived and born in poverty, currently about 25% of all young children and close to 50% of nonwhite children (Halpern, 1987). The second, an important cause of the growth in poverty among young children, is an increase in the percentage of female-headed families with young children. The rate of poverty among such families is 60%, the highest of any group in our society (Kamerman, 1985). The third trend is a long-term decline in the availability and real-dollar value of means-tested services and supports, including Aid to Families with Dependent Children, Food Stamps, subsidies for child care, and housing (Reischauer, 1986). The effect of this real-dollar decline has been exacerbated by a significant increase in the cost of necessities, especially housing.

As noted earlier, community-based early intervention alone cannot hope to alter fundamentally the difficult life conditions of growing numbers of families with young children. Many of the causes of those conditions, such as negligent housing policies and wage levels inadequate for families to meet basic needs, are not susceptible to family-level interventions. But the information, psychological support, and practical assistance typically provided in community-based programs may serve to buffer the effects of poverty and its attendant stresses by strengthening families' capacities to cope with them, and altering their subjective response to them as well.

Inherent limitations in our public helping systems

There has been a growing recognition in a variety of sectors that mainstream public and private services are not equipped by mandate, caseload, location, or dominant modes of practice to address preventively the inattentive parenting and resulting child health and developmental problems associated with the increasingly stressful life situation of many young families (Schorr, 1988). For example, intervention is usually not authorized until problems have reached a crisis stage, and may have become intractable. The narrowly focused mandate of each individual helping service makes it difficult for providers to address simultaneously the interconnected problems of multiply-stressed young families – problems as diverse as lack of planning skills, lack of food, inadequate housing, inadequate health care, lack of job skills or aspirations, and emotional unavailability to the infant. Providers have demonstrated limited capacity to reach out to families who are unwilling or unable to seek help themselves, and nurture their capacity to identify problems and use help. Most professional helping systems have been unwilling or unable to go halfway toward bridging cultural, linguistic, and social gaps, by starting with families' own child-rearing and coping traditions (see Musick & Stott, this volume).

A number of defining features of community-based early intervention programs address the limitations to preventive community work that are built into many formal helping services. Community-based programs provide multifaceted support, orchestrated to address a variety of family needs. By preference as well as timing, they focus on promoting development rather than treating dysfunction. They have the flexibility of mandate and strategy to mold to the unique patterns of stress and support needs of different populations in different community contexts. Most consider it their responsibility to reach out to isolated or distrustful families and nurture their capacity to use support. The lay family workers in most programs share the same culture as the families they serve, and can function as "culture brokers" to the larger society; many have experienced firsthand the poverty facing the families with whom they work. Finally, family preferences and program agendas tend to receive equal weight in community-based early intervention programs.

Increasing recognition of the limitations of informal social supports

It has frequently been argued that poor families, particularly minority families, have access to strong informal networks of kith and kin that compensate for lack of support from formal helping institutions. But there is growing recognition that as income declines, the relative balance between the benefits and the costs of informal support often shifts to the latter. The presence of informal support does not, in and of itself, promote attentive, nurturant parenting and healthy child development (Bronfenbrenner, 1987). Support that helps a young low-income parent master personal developmental tasks and gain a sense of esteem in parenting, and that provides assistance and encouragement in the face of daily difficulties, may not be available to many poor families, both because it may be objectively lacking in the immediate environment and/or because a young parent may lack the personal psychological resources to use it where it is available (Belle, 1982; Garbarino & Sherman, 1980).

Moreover, highly stressed young parents, usually single mothers, tend to make demands on their informal social networks that are especially draining and often nonreciprocal, such as emergency care for a sick child. Meeting such demands "drains resources from other people in the network and thereby limits their availability" (Pilisuk & Parks, 1986, p. 89). Mutual support demands may on balance be more stressful then beneficial in the resource-scarce environments in which poor families live.

Such demands can even undermine the efforts of individuals in the network to devote time, energy, and money to getting ahead themselves (Stack, 1974).

Community-based early intervention programs strive to reproduce the mixture of nurturance, guidance, and practical assistance characteristic of informal support systems. But they generally can draw on a wider range of community resources and are better prepared to manage the drain of chronic pressing needs. At the same time, they provide an alternative but still secure context for a young mother to explore goals, expectations, and roles for herself that are different from those predominating in her intimate support network.

Growing awareness of the need for models of practice that address families' life conditions

Whereas the defining features of the current social situation for young families suggest a complex set of obstacles to nurturant parenting, the central tendency in the early intervention field historically has been to focus on the mother–infant dyad as the source of all or most problems that must be addressed (Schlossman, 1978). In the extreme, this tendency has resulted in making the mother the "guilty party, . . . guilty because she is creating the situation for her own failure" (Sigel, 1983, p. 12). More commonly, focusing on the mother–infant dyed has meant seeing only a few of the many obstacles to attentive parenting and healthy child development facing most low-income families.

This tendency has defined most early intervention work despite the fact that family workers have found repeatedly that as a practical matter they cannot avoid addressing the broader range of stresses that impinge on the mother–infant relationship and healthy child development (see Musick & Stott, this volume). Parents frequently ask for assistance with housing, food, child care, medical care, and related problems. When they are preoccupied with these problems, and perhaps feeling overwhelmed, it is difficult, if not inappropriate, to focus solely on the relationship between the mother and the infant.

The chronic stress associated with poverty also affects maternal psychological well-being. Recent studies have reported an unexpectedly high rate of depression in low-income mothers with young children, especially single mothers (Belle, 1982). This depression appears to be significantly correlated with a sense of lack of control over difficult life conditions, and a further sense that these conditions are not going to improve. These subjective responses to chronic stress infuse all areas of maternal behavior. They limit the physical and emotional energy affected mothers can invest in parenting (Lyons-Ruth, Zol, Connell, & Odom, 1987). They further limit the mother's personal resources and ability to protect her children from the effects of unsupportive extrafamilial environments.

Community-based early intervention programs appear well suited, by virtue of the defining features discussed thus far, to address the range of obstacles to nurturant and stimulating parenting facing low-income families. They work at the family level, but in a fashion that is particularly sensitive to environmental stresses that impinge on that family. At their best, community-based programs pursue a reasonable balance in emphasis among families' basic survival needs, parents' personal adjustment and development, and children's developmental needs. Rather than providing authoritative instruction that single-mindedly seeks to promote current child-rearing norms, the programs strive to support poor families in their self-determined efforts to care for and nurture their children.

EXAMPLES OF COMMUNITY-BASED EARLY INTERVENTION
PROGRAMS

Three program descriptions are presented to illustrate how the premises, principles, and defining features of community-based early intervention are implemented in practice. The three programs chosen are the lay home visiting programs of the Ford Foundation's Child Survival/Fair Start Initiative, AVANCE of San Antonio, and the Family Focus programs in the Chicago area. Although the former two programs have summative evaluations under way, their findings are not yet available.

Child Survival/Fair Start lay home visiting programs

In 1982 the Ford Foundation launched the Child Survival/Fair Start (CS/FS) Initiative, through which it has sponsored community-based strategies to improve pregnancy outcomes and infant health and development among low-income families. At the heart of this initiative is a network of lay home visiting programs, independent in sponsorship and operation, but linked by Ford's overarching goals and a variety of cross-project communication mechanisms. Each program is conducting its own independent evaluation, but has committed itself to measuring a common core of variables that emerged from discussions with the other programs and a third-party technical assistance team (Bond & Halpern, 1988; Halpern & Larner, 1987).

The five programs currently under way work with a heterogeneous group of high-risk populations: migrant Mexican-American farmwork families in two farm labor camps in Florida; Haitian immigrants and refugees in Ft. Lauderdale and Immokalee, Florida; young black (mostly unmarried) mothers in the three poorest counties of west Alabama; isolated rural families in six Appalachian counties; and urban Mexican-Americans in Austin, Texas. Home visitors generally come from the target community; for example, in the migrant program they are either former farmworkers or members of farmworker families. In all cases, they are trained and supervised by a professional – a nurse practitioner, child development specialist, or social worker.

Home visiting typically begins during pregnancy, and continues biweekly to monthly until the target child is 12–24 months of age. During pregnancy the substantive focus is on enrolling women in prenatal care and Medicaid (when necessary), promoting good nutrition and other health habits, keeping prenatal care appointments, and preparing for childbirth and for the baby. After the baby is born, the focus shifts to supporting the development of the mother–infant relationship, physical care of the new baby, infant feeding, management of infant illness, immunization, infant stimulation activities, and, especially with very young mothers, planning for the future. Instructional materials, activities, objectives, and so forth are embodied in written curricula and home visit planning forms.

During a typical visit the home visitor "catches up" with the expectant or new mother on significant events since the last visit; checks on follow-through with past scheduled appointments; discusses particular health and/or child development topics relevant to the stage in pregnancy or age of the infant; demonstrates and asks the mother to try out infant care and stimulation activities; reminds the mother of coming appointments; generally makes herself available to listen to the mother's immediate concerns, questions and concrete problems; helps forge strategies to address those problems; and encourages and helps the mother formulate plans for achieving personal goals.

Beyond the common substantive concerns of the local programs, each program addresses the special obstacles to nurturant parenting and healthy child development faced by the population served, and attempts to complement special strengths in the community. For the migrant farmworkers, for example, this includes helping families integrate Western medical care into traditional therapeutic systems, thus not waiting until problems are critical to seek treatment. It includes case advocacy to ensure that when a mother does bring her infant to the clinic, the infant is seen within a reasonable time. At the same time, guidance in child rearing is undertaken with a sensitivity to the role of traditional beliefs and behaviors in providing stability to migrant family life. Similarly, advocacy is undertaken with sensitivity to the frequently delicate legal status of participants.

To take another example, the Maternal and Infant Health Outreach Worker (MIHOW) project has developed program strategies responsive to the conditions of life in Appalachia, notably extreme social and geographic isolation, and absolute lack of human services in many small rural communities. This lack of local human service systems made it difficult to identify sponsoring agencies in some of the communities served. Thus, core staff at Vanderbilt University evolved a model in which a professional focused on developing local capacity for self-help and mutual support (Clinton & Larner, in press). This professional (usually a community member) would start out as the home visitor. Through her community work she would then identify local women with untapped personal capacity and recruit them to become home visitors. Over time she would focus a growing proportion of her energies on the personal and professional development of these women, who eventually would become the main service providers and a community resource for young families in the future.

The MIHOW staff used the specific substantive concerns of the program, the focus on healthy pregnancies and babies, to address women's lack of hope and diminished sense of control. Home visitors helped women see that their actions can have an effect on their own health and their children's well-being, and by extension on other aspects of their lives. The networks formed between visitors and parents, and eventually among parents, have begun to be mobilized around other community development concerns, ranging from day care to adequate water supplies.

Each of the CS/FS projects has refined its focus over time, as it has learned first-hand the pressing issues in the lives of families served, and as the program staff has decided which of these issues could and should be addressed with program resources. Both common goals and a common philosophy of augmenting rather than replacing families' current modes of child-rearing and coping have given the CS/FS initiative a measure of continued coherence. At the same time, CS/FS is demonstrating already that no single policy prescription or programmatic approach to early intervention will prove useful to all families.

AVANCE educational programs for parents and children

AVANCE is a center-based parent support and education program serving low-income Mexican-American families in San Antonio, Texas. It was established in 1973, and now has two centers, one in a federal housing project and one in a low-income residential neighborhood. AVANCE was initiated and is still directed by Gloria Rodriguez, who grew up in the barrio of San Antonio, left to pursue higher education and teaching, and then returned. It is staffed largely by former program participants who have been trained by core professional staff; funding is mostly local.

Parents enroll in AVANCE when their children are between birth and 3 years of age.

All community families are welcome. About 50% of the participants are recruited through door-to-door canvassing by AVANCE staff, and 50% by word-of-mouth, especially by past participants. Of families served by AVANCE, half are supported by AFDC, and average monthly income is less than $500. Most participants have an eighth-grade education, less than half are married, the mean family size is six, and the majority were born in the United States. A community survey conducted by AVANCE in 1980 found a lack of knowledge of children's developmental needs; a history among many parents of abuse and neglect as children; lack of job skills and aspirations, little sense of control over events, and extreme isolation.

These findings and accumulating experience led the AVANCE staff to develop a guiding philosophy for services that places equal emphasis on parents' personal development – notably improved self-esteem, higher aspirations, and improved decision-making skills – and very specific knowledge and skill-building in parenting, including encouraging play, and "learning to correct in positive ways." The formal program components are highly structured, with clear expectations regarding participation and personal contribution, a variety of rewards for attendance, timeliness, and the like, all designed to counter the personal disorganization and lack of structure in many women's lives, and to foster a sense of achievement. AVANCE staff members communicate the message that it does matter whether mothers come to the program or not. At the same time, AVANCE, like other community-based programs, has an "underlife," that is, an informal side. Current and past participants and other community members reportedly view AVANCE as a natural part of their social support network. Dropping in just to chat, discuss problems, or share accomplishments is common and encouraged. AVANCE also sponsors community events throughout the year.

The central program component of AVANCE is a 9-month parent education program consisting of weekly $2\frac{1}{2}$-hour sessions (1 hour toymaking, 1 hour child development instruction, $\frac{1}{2}$ hour community resource speaker). Some 80 mothers per year in each center participate in these classes. Toymaking includes an emphasis on the importance of play for children, and on parents' roles as facilitators and teachers. It also allows for informal sharing and conversation with peers. Parenting and child development instruction is provided in lecture and group discussion, embedded in the real-life situations and culture of participants. Class leaders focus on creating a secure climate for discussion of questions and concerns.

During the classes, young children of participants receive developmental child care in another room. Participating mothers are responsible for helping out in the child-care setting 12 times a year, an experience that allows them to observe the child-care specialist at work and to be observed interacting with children. Participants also receive monthly home visits, during which the home visitor videotapes a segment of mother–infant interaction using an AVANCE toy (these segments are used in subsequent classes), checks on how the family is doing, and helps with problem solving. Transportation to the centers is provided.

Graduates of the 9-month parent education program can participate in a variety of AVANCE adult education activities, including English classes and Graduate Equivalent Degree classes, jointly sponsored college classes, and job placement assistance. These activities reportedly serve 395 women a year. AVANCE runs periodic parenting classes at a community center, a school, and a local factory. There are also two child abuse and neglect programs for specially referred families. One is a prevention program that uses parent aides as home visitors. The other involves joint case management and family support with other agencies for confirmed abuse and neglect cases.

In personal communications with the author (Halpern, 1987), the AVANCE director reports that having a center-based program does not prevent many families from participating, because employment rates are low in the target population of mothers. Of the 100 families recruited per center in the summer, 80 start the program and about 60 complete it. There is a mid-program recruitment period to fill in places vacated by dropouts.

As noted earlier, a major summative evaluation of AVANCE is currently under way (Johnson & Rodriguez, 1987). A modest evaluation was conducted in the early 1980s, comparing AVANCE participants from each site to families in a comparison neighborhood of San Antonio (Rodriguez, 1983). A pre–post parent questionnaire was administered, examining attitudes toward various dimensions of parenting, knowledge of children's developmental needs, maternal psychological well-being, presence of stressors, use of community resources, and self-reported behavior around discipline and play with children. Treatment and control families were similar on most demographics at baseline, although treatment families from one of the two sites were higher risk than the other treatment group and controls on a range of variables. Unfortunately, baseline questionnaire scores are not reported. Analyses of posttreatment questionnaire scores, controlling for maternal age, education, and number of children found program-favoring effects on knowledge of children's developmental needs, on hopefulness about the future, on punitiveness of child discipline attitudes, and on actual self-reported punishment for various specific child behaviors. No effects were found on self-reported play and interaction with the target child.

Family Focus

The Family Focus program is built on a network of seven drop-in centers for parents of children birth to 3 years of age in communities around Chicago. Two of the centers serve black, pregnant and parenting teens; two serve low-income Hispanic communities; two serve a diverse mix of mostly middle-class families; and one is a parent cooperative model serving a multiethnic community. Center locations include schools, churches, and storefronts. Each center offers a variety of services and activities responsive to the population served and neighborhood needs. The staff is composed of a mixture of professionals and paraprofessionals, and most of the centers have some volunteer participation as well.

The range of activities and services provided include peer support groups, discussion groups on specific child-related topics (e.g., toilet training), child development classes, adult-focused activities, and child care. The centers serving teens have high school tutoring, family life education classes, and a variety of pregnancy-prevention activities, including a special program for junior high school students. The centers serving Hispanic families have English and crafts classes. Centers have a monthly calendar of events to help parents plan for specific activities.

The drop-in feature at the heart of Family Focus is premised on the notions of nonstigmatizing, family-controlled participation, and gradually growing commitment. As the founder notes, "the implicit message of a drop-in center, that all parents deserve support, erases special feelings of inadequacy. At the same time, such an environment permits families who might be reluctant to declare themselves at traditional social service agencies to lean on its non-threatening character and gradually become available for more help" (Weissbourd, 1981, p. 180).

Family Focus staffs view participation in formal and informal activities as equally important. For example, child development knowledge is as likely to be acquired through informal conversation with the staff and other parents, or through incidental observation of successful encounters other adults have with children, as in the formal child development classes. Provision of child care is viewed as an important element of the program, beyond its role in facilitating participation in parent activities. It affords stimulation for the children involved, opportunity for early detection of developmental problems, and a setting in which parents can observe "model" interactions with young children.

Summary

Together, the descriptions of the Child Survival/Fair Start programs, AVANCE, and Family Focus illustrate the variety of ways in which the common purposes and elements of community-based early intervention receive expression. The principles that bind the genre together can still be observed in all three programs: attention both to parents' personal developmental needs and their role as parents, the use of community members as family workers, sensitivity to cultural preferences in child-rearing values, and the active role of parents in shaping their own participation in the program. But these elements receive different emphasis, or are provided in different formats in each program. This variability is due in large measure to the responsiveness to local needs and conditions that characterizes the genre. Community-based early intervention programs recognize and respond to the fact that poverty is not a monolithic phenomenon, in cause, manifestation, or effect. Low-income families and communities differ in a number of ways relevant to the provision of interpersonal support.

EVIDENCE OF PROGRAM EFFECTIVENESS FOR COMMUNITY-BASED EARLY INTERVENTION: RECENT FINDINGS

Directions in program evaluation

When the era of major federal investment in experimentation with community-based early interventions ended, no comparable sources of research, development, and evaluation funding became available to replace it. But whereas the scale and amount of evaluation activity has been more modest in the 1980s, approaches taken have demonstrated a growing sensitivity to the complexity of the programs being studied. Evaluations have placed increasing emphasis on understanding the relationship among program contexts, processes, and outcomes. Evaluations have also begun to focus more on systematic collection of "practice knowledge" from veteran practitioners (Weiss & Halpern, 1988). These new emphases have yielded data that clarify the parameters and conditions of program effectiveness, illuminate elements of effective practice, and identify the tensions inherent in the purposes and approaches of community-based early intervention programs.

These new emphases are particularly consonant with the fluid implementation context of a field of practice that continues to develop and evolve. The approaches and techniques of community-based early intervention programs are not well developed, nor do they have well-defined procedures. The staffs involved are often attempting something new for themselves and their agency. Even for the participants, the philosophy and objectives of these programs are usually different from what they have experienced previously with human services. As such, program development often entails 1 to 3 years of trial-and-error, during which intervention objectives, emphases, techniques, and sometimes target populations are refined and sometimes redefined. Even established programs often evolve in response to shifting community needs.

The growing emphasis of evaluation work in this field is on identifying elements critical to program effectivess, examining which approaches and emphases are suited to which populations, attempting to define and measure the program "treatment" as received by families, and attending to the effects of program contexts on implementation and effectiveness. This work is just beginning to appear in the literature. Programs selected for review in this chapter include those that have made some effort to examine program processes and contexts, as well as outcomes, to illustrate the kinds of lessons yielded by richer evaluation approaches.

Review of recent evidence of program effects

The same rationale for an exploratory, illuminative approach to evaluation of discrete programs holds for a review of the evidence provided by different programs. Straightforward generalization in this field of practice – whether about the most appropriate target population, philosophy, intervention focus and techniques, intervention agents, or any other variable – is hampered by the unusual sensitivity of programs to community conditions and by the multifaceted nature of programs themselves, both of which make prediction of critical variables even more difficult than is usually found for helping interventions.

Such problems notwithstanding, Table 3 summarizes program features, targeting and sampling strategies, measures, and evaluation findings from four recently completed evaluations of programs whose features reflect the principles and approaches of the community-based genre. These four evaluations were selected also because their measures reflect the emerging measurement emphases in the field, notably the growing focus on attributes of maternal functioning.

The evidence presented in Table 3 confirms the uneven, modestly promising findings of the earlier PCDC and CFRP experiments. As noted in the PCDC/CFRP summary, community-based parenting programs can influence maternal parenting skills and general coping; but significant effort is required to produce moderate gains in a few discrete domains. Taken together with the two earlier studies, the more recent findings suggest that programs sensitive to contextual stresses, but able to maintain a strong, relatively unambiguous focus on improving parenting styles, skills, and knowledge, and with significant professional involvement in service delivery (e.g., the PCDCs and the Prenatal/Early Infancy Project), will be more likely to have sizable program-favoring effects on parenting variables. The PCDC investigators (Andrews et al., 1982) found program-favoring effects on maternal emotional responsiveness, affection, praise, appropriate control, and encouragement of child verbalization. Olds and colleagues (1986) not only found lower rates of substantiated child maltreatment among their risk program participants, but generally less restrictive maternal behavior and severe disciplinary practices. On the other hand, models employing a noticeably diffuse intervention, not getting beyond parents' personal adjustment (e.g., the CFRPs and the Parent–Infant Project), tended to demonstrate fewer significant effects in general. Measurable short-term effects on child development tend to be modest or absent altogether from studies reviewed, perhaps because of measurement limitations and the fact that programs' influence on the child is indirect, mediated by their influence on the parent and family environment.

Together with the findings of the two earlier studies, the data in Table 3 suggest that programs in this genre do in fact influence those outcome domains closest to their emphases in work with families, whether parenting (PCDCs, Prenatal/Early Infancy Project) or mothers' personal development (CFRPs, United Charities of Chicago/ Mothers' Discussion Groups). The various findings also raise questions about the implications for program effectiveness of different emphases in work with families. Specifically, the causal relationship between improvements in child-rearing skills, knowledge, and attitudes, and various indicators of maternal personal development remains unclear, and merits a good deal of further examination. For example, can success in the parenting role stimulate and consolidate personal development, or is parenting perhaps inextricably bound up with other developmental struggles and more usefully addressed in light of those?

The relatively high, and sometimes differential, attrition that plagued the PCDC and CFRP experiments is apparent also in the studies described in Table 3. The self-selection inherent in demanding programs with voluntary participation presents problems for program design, research, and public policy. The unique strengths of random assignment designs in addressing threats to internal validity have been found to be undermined in community-based early intervention programs, as initially similar treatment and control groups became increasingly dissimilar over time (Andrews et al., 1982; Bond & Halpern, 1988). High rates of attrition raise questions of how broad and what kind of population these programs are best suited to helping. Further, when women drop out to return to school or to take a job, the question arises as to whether the goals of parenting programs – improved family-based care and child nurturance by poor women – are consonant with women's own priorities, not to mention government strategies to enhance family self-sufficiency and reduce dependency.

PROGRAM DESIGN AND IMPLEMENTATION LESSONS FROM
AVAILABLE DATA

As noted, there has been increasing examination in recent evaluations of how different factors interact to influence the implementation and effectiveness of community-based early intervention programs. The following discussion draws on the studies cited in Table 3 and reports from other studies in progress to discuss such factors as selecting a target population, matching population and program features, and characteristic strengths and limitations of different kinds of family workers.

Selecting a target population

Developing an appropriate targeting approach is one of the most difficult, yet critical, dimensions of program design in community-based early intervention. The target population is that which the program ideally would like to reach and serve. Decision making in this area requires juggling a variety of factors, including prediction of which set of risk factors will be most salient locally, categorical mandates, desired program identity in the community, and of course resource limitations. Evidence from the studies cited in Table 3, as well as others (Epstein & Weikart, 1979; Lally & Honig, 1977), suggests that programs should target selectively rather than broadly within low-income populations, that determining the appropriate targeting criteria is largely a community- and population-specific matter, and that targeting choices should be made interactively with decisions involving intervention objectives and emphases.

The Prenatal/Early Infancy Project researchers had a sufficiently diverse sample with

Table 3. *Summary of four recently completed community-based early intervention studies: program features and evaluation findings*

	Parent Infant Project (1)	Prenatal/Early Infancy Project (2)	United Charities of Chicago (3)	Family Support Project (4)
Program features	Weekly home visits by lay home visitors, mid-pregnancy to 12 mo; emphasis on provision of emotional support and concrete assistance with immediate concerns, hypothesized to lead to enhanced self-esteem, personal relations, use of resources; program based in local health department clinics	Biweekly nurse home visits mid-pregnancy till birth of baby, weekly the first month, gradually decreasing frequency till 24 mo; home visits focused on parent education (80% of effort), but included service brokerage and work to involve mothers' significant others; postnatal visits emphasized interpreting infant behaviors, emotional needs, and need for progressively more complex experience	Group I: toy demonstration (TD) home visiting program, premised on importance of mother's role stimulating toddler play; 32 visits (twice weekly) during school year for 2 yr; one for introducing toy, other for practice; Group 2: weekly discussion groups of 10 mothers (MD); based on mothers' own agendas, sharing of personal experiences, child-rearing and other topics, regular presentation of child development activities; both groups run by professional black social workers	Group I: weekly home visits by lay workers: demonstrating parent–child activities and basic care, listening to mother's concerns, joint problem solving, service brokerage, provision of transportation; Group 2: weekly visits by professionals, focused more on exploration of affective material, "kitchen" therapy, but also child development activities, practical assistance, problem solving; group 2 also had periodic parent groups, apparently difficult to get going
Sampling strategy	Random assignment; pregnant women aged 16 or older recruited by health department maternity clinic	Random assignment; women with no previous live births and one or more following risk factors: under age 19, single parent and/or low SES, assigned to one of four treatment conditions; (a) infant health and development screening $N = 90$, (b) screening and transportation $N = 94$, (c) (a) above and prenatal home visits $N = 100$, (d) above, prenatal and postnatal home visits $N = 116$	Clusters of buildings in each of three public Chicago housing projects randomly assigned to TD, MD, or control conditions; all families with a child 8–24 mo in any one cluster offered one program (controls offered toys)	Nonequivalent control group design; treatment groups ($N = 18$ lay visited, $N = 16$ professionally visited) referred by social service and health agencies at child age birth to 9 mo; high-risk controls ($N = 10$; similar to T families) recruited from same sources post hoc; also a low-risk control group ($N = 36$), same demographics as T families
Sample characteristics	$N = 92$ treatment (T), 53 control (C) families; 50% teenagers; 34% never married; 75% white, 25% Hispanic	Sample 47% under age 19, 62% unmarried, 61% low SES; 23% of sample with all three risk factors;	At baseline, 41 in TD group, 53 in MD group, 38 controls; sample 100% black; maternal age average 24 yr;	Multirisk T population: 60% high psychiatric risk; 80% AFDC; 40% reported in past for possible abuse or

	(1) Van Doornink et al.	(2) Olds et al.	(3) Slaughter	(4) Lyons-Ruth et al.
		analytic sample 100% white, excluding 46 black families registered	child age at entry average 20 mo; 67% of TD and MD fathers and 93% control fathers not in home; most sample income AFDC	neglect; high-risk C group: same psychiatric and SES risk
Attrition	32% for T group, 40% for C group	No report	37% (15 of 41 TDs, 27 of 53 MDs, 7 of 38 control)	Minimal after 3rd visit (before 18%)
Principal measures	Maternal self-report of depression, support, coping; maternal ego maturity and IQ: infant feeding and teaching observation using Barnard protocol; Caldwell HOME; Ainsworth attachment; at entry, postpartum, 1, 4, 12 mo	Maternal interviews at baseline, 32nd week pregnancy, 6, 10, 12, 22, 24 mo; medical record abstraction up to 24 mo; infant height and weight at 6, 12, 24 mo; Bayley at 12 mo, Cattell at 24 mo; Caldwell HOME at 10 and 22 mo; review of Dept. of Social Services records for substantiated abuse or neglect	Videotaped observation of maternal teaching style and child behavior in standard living/play room situation at 26 and 39 mo, maternal ego development, self-esteem, personal control (Loevinger Scale), maternal-expressed values about child rearing, achievement, risk taking; child development: Cattell, Peabody, McCarthy	T groups: maternal depression on Center for Epidemiological Studies-Depression Scale stress, social support, infant temperament, videotaped maternal-infant interaction, Ainsworth attachment, Caldwell HOME, Bayley, in various combinations at 6, 12, 18 mo; high-risk Cs 18-mo battery, low-risk Cs 12- and 18-mo battery
Principal findings	Control infants slightly fuller gestation, higher birth weight; T mothers with inadequate baseline diet less likely to improve diet (21% vs. 45%); no overall program-favoring postnatal effects; modest program-favoring trend at 4 mo. on maternal warmth; also stronger effects on higher risk T families generally	No overall prenatal effects, but nurse-visited teens under 16 had babies 324 grams heavier than controls; few overall program-favoring postnatal effects, except emergency room visits 12–24 mo; but low SES, unmarried teens in control group ($N = 32$) and prenatal visit group ($N = 18$) had much higher incidence of abuse and neglect than those visited to 24 mo ($N = 22$), 19%/18% vs. 4%; finding supported by same trend on two Caldwell subscales	General pattern of findings spotty, but favoring MD group most: MD mothers superior to controls at one or two testing points on ego maturity, future orientation, use of community resources, endorsement of risk taking, expectations of children to become self-directing; MD mothers most likely to elaborate on children's play, MD children most likely to use expressive language in play; IQ decline in all three groups 22–41 mo	Pattern and magnitude of effects same for both T groups; strongest treatment effects found where mothers had depressive symptoms at intake: at 18 mo, T infants with high-symptom mothers more securely attached (60% vs. 35%) and had significantly (12 points) higher developmental scores than like controls; no reports yet on HOME scores or dimensions on videotapes

Sources: (1) Van Doornink, Dawson, Butterfield, and Alexander, 1980; (2) Olds, Henderson, Chamberlin, and Tatelbaum, 1986; (3) Slaughter, 1983; (4) Lyons-Ruth, Botein, and Grunebaum, 1984.

enough statistical power to allow for examination of treatment effects for subgroups at different levels of risk (Olds et al., 1986). They found a consistent relationship between magnitude of positive program effects and degree of family risk, with poor unmarried teens benefiting more than other subsamples with only one or two risk factors. Van Doorninck and colleagues (1980) also found moderately stronger treatment effects for the higher risk families in their sample. But the CFRP evaluators' subgroup explorations, especially with respect to coping skills at baseline, found the opposite – participation was more beneficial for those coping well at baseline.

Olds and colleagues did not report any particular difficulty undertaking parenting interventions with teens as a population. But a number of other studies (Halpern & Larner, 1988; Miller, 1988; O'Leary, Shore, & Weider, 1984; Ware, Osofsky, Eberhart-Wright, & Leichtman, 1987) do report such difficulties, especially with group-based interventions. These include problems with recruitment and retention; ambivalence about support, expressed by consenting to participate, and then appearing alternately rejecting and accepting; limited social skills, making group work more difficult; the press and urgency of adolescents' own developmental needs, undermining attention to parenting and infants' needs; and even limitations in cognitive skills.

Basic intervention format

The most general choice that parent-focused programs have regarding intervention strategy involves selection of a basic program format. Holding aside the broader decision about whether to develop a comprehensive center providing an array of services, the basic choice is between an individual format, usually home visiting, and a group format, such as peer support groups or parent education classes. Each approach works through somewhat different mechanisms, and is suited to somewhat different support purposes and population characteristics.

Parent support groups, and to a lesser extent parent education classes, seek to effect change through the mutual influence, sharing, and support of peers facing common developmental tasks. Slaughter (1983) notes in her study that such "socially engineered self-help networks" can provide alternative sources of social influence to women's informal networks and a secure setting for women to clarify and rethink or reaffirm personal, familial, and child-rearing goals. At the same time, program experience with parent support groups among low-income families suggests two major limitations. The first concerns difficulties in recruitment and retention, especially among such specific populations as teenagers and multiply stressed families. The second relates to the demands of group process. Successful participation in and benefit from group process appear to demand a level of personal resources and social skills not available to some high-risk parents (Musick & Stott, this volume; Powell, 1983; Slaughter, 1983; Wandersman, 1987).

Home visiting programs seek to effect change through the sustained personal relationship developed between family worker and family. The family worker not only provides information and practical assistance, but serves as a role model, and often becomes a significant source of psychological support to a young mother. The Family Support Project (Lyons-Ruth, Botein, & Grunebaum, 1984) illustrates in the extreme the point that home visiting may be, initially, a more appropriate approach for higher risk families. Lyons-Ruth and colleagues argue that home visiting provides a means for outreach and relationship-building with women too disorganized and with too few personal resources to help themselves. The home visit communicates to mothers that the visitors are willing and interested in sharing their world. The format itself is suited to a balanced, albeit shifting, focus on the mothers' own needs for nurturance, and the achievement inherent in attending to infants' developmental needs.

Choice of family workers

The studies described in Table 3 directly or indirectly raise a number of points about the strengths and limitations of different kinds of family workers. Ironically, although the field has continued to evolve by choice and necessity toward the lay helping model, one of the clearest signals of the potential effectiveness of community-based early intervention comes from Olds and colleagues' nurse home visiting experiment (Olds et al., 1986). On the other hand, the Family Support Project, which deliberately sponsored lay and professional home visiting side-by-side, working toward the same ends with the same population, found that both lay and professional workers were equally effective, but that each had characteristic strengths and limitations. Combining descriptive data from the Family Support Project with those from other initiatives not included in Table 3, it is possible to draw a clear portrait of these characteristic strengths and limitations (Karl, 1986; Larner & Halpern, 1987; Lyons-Ruth, Botein, & Grunebaum, 1984; Musick & Stott, this volume).

Three characteristic strengths are noted most frequently for layworkers. The first is acceptability, both in terms of initial entry into families' lives and in terms of continuing presence in the community. The second is flexibility and responsiveness in where, how, and when work to meet family needs occurs. The third is affiliation with and intimate knowledge of target population beliefs, life experience, and living conditions. Characteristic limitations of layworkers include a tendency to be selective in what they "see" in families, and the issues they feel comfortable dealing with; a tendency to take on too much responsibility for the well-being of families; and a related tendency not to set boundaries between themselves and families, sometimes leading to enmeshment in complicated family problems. Lay workers' membership in the same informal networks as the families they are serving may lead to family reluctance to share highly sensitive personal and marital problems.

In a simplistic sense, professional family workers' strengths mirror layworkers' limitations, and vice versa. Professionals rely less on personal experience and shared history, more on selective application of formally organized bodies of knowledge that are developed and tested in a range of prior situations. Professionals tend to help in more carefully circumscribed, disciplined, and goal-oriented ways; and they tend to use the "authority" inherent in their specialized expertise. They are often more comfortable than layworkers in dealing with a wide range of sensitive issues. And of course, professionals have had a luxury few layworkers have – a long period of time for skill-building and practice under supervised conditions, yielding a well-developed repertoire of helping and assessment skills that are difficult to acquire quickly.

Professionals' limitations derive from the areas that characterize layworkers' strengths, that is, flexibility, availability, and affiliation with families served. Professionals are not inherently weak in these areas as individuals. But the long period of socialization into a professional role, the large caseloads, the high cost of their time, and other similar factors all serve to limit professionals in these areas. Moreover, it is generally difficult to find professionals willing and able to work out in the community and to devote sufficient time to the kind of elemental helping and support that characterizes community-based early intervention.

MAJOR CHALLENGES IN COMMUNITY-BASED EARLY
INTERVENTION PRACTICE

The defining characteristics of community-based early intervention programs embody tensions and contradictions that pose special challenges for practice in this field. The most critical of these include:

1. implementing non-deficit-oriented interventions, especially in contexts with a variety of obstacles to attentive parenting and healthy child development;
2. balancing family preferences regarding the program's support role and the program's own predetermined agenda;
3. seeking an appropriate balance between a focus on parenting itself and a focus on the personal, familial, and social factors that impinge on parenting;
4. providing support that is of adequate duration and intensity to permit families to internalize the program's messages, role models, encouragement, and support, but that avoids fostering a sense of permanent dependency on the program to help meet needs;
5. supporting the development of a helping role for family workers that is at once effective, acceptable to families, and consonant with family workers' characteristics and goals; and,
6. attracting and maintaining the participation of highly stressed families, while not undermining program resources and capacity to serve better-coping families.

It is inherently difficult to implement non-deficit-oriented interventions that purport to emphasize family strengths but inevitably bring with them an implicit, if not explicit, view of optimal child-rearing values and behaviors. Both family workers and families can get mixed messages, putting a strain on the former's ability to understand and carry out their roles, and complicating for both parties the task of establishing a set of mutual obligations and expectations (Mindick, 1987). The goal of supporting families in their self-determined efforts to manage family life is essential. But it can be difficult to implement in contexts that undermine personal strengths or in family situations where there are obvious and immediate threats to children's well-being.

Parents' own motivations for accepting the intrusion of "friendly strangers" into their lives often are unclear. In social contexts of chronic poverty, such motivations may initially be based more on desire for help in coping with the day-in, day-out struggle to meet basic needs than on a recognition of personal problems or dissatisfaction with parenting goals and behavior. Program staffs have to decide the extent to which willingness to participate implies acceptance of the program's primary focus on attentive parenting and secondary focus on identifying and addressing personal as well as environmental obstacles to such parenting.

Program staffs also have to decide where and how to focus their own intervention agenda in the face of numerous obstacles to attentive parenting in the lives of the families being served. Family workers come face to face with a wide range of family problems, and they often feel an internal pressure to respond, especially when there are few services to which to refer families (Larner & Halpern, 1987). This can lead to a strong desire to take on class- as well as case-level advocacy in domains only loosely linked to the program's primary agenda. It is difficult, but important, for programs to delimit carefully the extent and boundaries of their involvement with broad institutional change in their communities.

Another type of practical challenge can be found in the difficulty of providing long-term help and support that in part is aimed at promoting self-sufficiency and independence. For particularly troubled and/or distrustful families, the long-term nature of many community-based program models clearly is necessary. For these families it may take months for trust to develop and for the mother to begin to internalize the empathy and care being provided and alter her sense of self-worth. But for most families typically served, it is difficult to know when the modeling and messages provided have been internalized. At some point, a mutually gratifying, although non-reciprocal, dependency relationship can develop that conceivably undermines the very goals of the intervention.

The development of the family worker role presents a significant challenge in many community-based early intervention programs. There are inherent ambiguities in the indigenous paraprofessional role, which typically calls for being both friend and professional clinician. As Musick and Stott (this volume) note, neither of these roles lends itself to precise definition or standardization. But integrating the two roles is made even more difficult by the fact that the goal orientation, availability, reciprocity, and equality that define friendship on the one hand and formal helping on the other are in many ways opposed.

In part because of the uniqueness of the helping role itself, and in part because the role is usually being undertaken for the first time, each family worker in a comunity-based early intervention program tends to invent and deliver a somewhat different "treatment." A month or two of preservice training does not allow for the rehearsal nor for the same socializing effect as years of formal training in a discipline. Training and supervision can serve to inform lay family workers' personal helping approach with the knowledge, techniques, and self-awareness that characterize clinical helping. But these have to be integrated gradually into the family worker's existing belief and knowledge system, with sensitivity to the personal qualities that led to a family worker's selection in the first place and that contribute to effective lay helping. Forging appropriate roles, expectations, and tasks for lay family workers, taking into account their characteristics as helpers, as well as the nature of the problems facing the families they serve, will be one of the major challenges confronting community-based early intervention for many years (Larner & Halpern, 1987).

Finally, attracting and maintaining the participation of families is a significant challenge in community-based early intervention programs serving low-income families. Self-selection is an inherent problem in voluntary programs in which participation is demanding. But for low-income families with young children, the prevasively stressful living conditions, and the chronic, exhausting struggle to meet basic needs that characterize their daily life create additional obstacles to participation. These obstacles are often further compounded by parents' struggles for their own personal development, lack of personal resources, and feelings of futility about the future (Musick & Halpern, 1989).

The challenge in this situation is to avoid the extremes of serving only the best and/or the worst functioning families in the community. The former can quickly fill program spaces because they know how to use any resources made available in the community and also because they are easy to serve. The latter often pose a recruitment and retention challenge to which program staff devote too much energy. Such effort, sometimes entailing repeated visits to a home to make contact with a particular program participant, can be frustrating for the family worker. It can raise questions about whether the program is ever going to get through to that family, and whether other families might benefit more from participation.

THE FUTURE OF COMMUNITY-BASED EARLY INTERVENTION:
CONCEPTUAL, ORGANIZATIONAL, AND POLITICAL CHALLENGES

It is clear that we need to learn a great deal more about how, when, and for whom community-based early intervention works. At the same time, this burgeoning, largely community-initiated program movement appears to be responding to a variety of family needs not being addressed by informal support networks or formal helping systems. It also appears to be reaching a growing proportion of young families isolated from informal social supports and out of reach of existing formal services.

Should greater public financial support for this program movement await clearer evidence of the parameters and conditions of its effectiveness? Should significant research and development and significant expansion of public support for community-based programs be urged simultaneously, on the grounds of its apparent responsiveness to family needs? Or is this inherently a grassroots movement, whose effectiveness will remain difficult to capture, whose critical elements will remain difficult to convert to easily replicable procedures, and whose purposes will remain marginal to the goals of our human service system?

The first priority: sustained research and development

By the time the first generation of evaluations of community-based early intervention programs (i.e., PCDC and CFRP) was completed, the era of major federal investment in social experimentation was over. No other major sources of research and development funding have been made available to stimulate further experiments of that magnitude. Moreover, the field itself has continued to evolve and diversify. As a consequence, we do not have a reliable body of evaluated program experience to identify which program emphases and strategies are appropriate for particular populations and community contexts.

A sustained research and development effort is required to address a number of questions. These include: Which approaches and emphases are likely to be most helpful for which populations of families? What is the minimum set of services to constitute a program that is likely to be effective? What are the advantages and disadvantages of different staffing patterns? What contextual conditions are critical to effective program operation? In what family and community situations are direct services to children a critical element of community-based early intervention programs? What are the advantages and disadvantages of more universal versus more selective targeting approaches?

A number of emergent lines of basic research remain to be examined for clues to better understanding of appropriate emphases, contextual obstacles to program effectiveness, better targeting of services, and related issues. One is the gradually maturing body of research on the nature and effects of social support, particularly studies that focus on the relationship of social support to child-rearing styles, competencies, and beliefs (Dunst & Trivette, this volume). A second, related to the broader social support research, examines the effects of loneliness and social isolation on parenting (Polansky, 1981). A third examines the influence of neighborhood and community attributes on parenting (Garbarino & Sherman, 1980). Still a fourth examines how deeply rooted life-conditions affect parenting capacities (Belle, 1982).

Community-based programs themselves provide fertile ground for basic research in these domains. Exploring the helping mechanisms underlying the "deliberately constructed social support" provided in these programs would contribute to basic knowledge, as well as to lessons about program implementation. For example, is it the proper orchestration and balance among information sharing, guidance, emotional support, and practical assistance that is critical to family worker effectiveness, or is it the spirit in which all these are provided? To what extent is the effectiveness of support provided a matter of finding a helping role that matches individual families' preferences and needs? Is change in parental behavior somehow linked to the ongoing presence of the family worker? If so, why? Which changes in parenting styles and behaviors seem to influence child well-being most significantly?

Given their unusual "social" space, somewhere between informal support and professional intervention, it would seem that some effort should go into examining the sociological dimensions of community-based early intervention programs. For example, we need to continue to explore the meaning of participation and nonparticipation, the implications of community ownership of programs, and the ways in which programs alter the resource balance in their communities. We also must learn how to account for the variety of intangibles that seem to underlie successful community-based programs, for example, leadership variables, staff mix and energy, and agency climate.

Research, development, and evaluation efforts focused on these diverse groups of questions will have to include attention to the development of better measures of program processes, contexts, and outcomes. For example, there is a need for measures that describe and evaluate the interaction of family workers and families. There are still few validated observational measures of important attributes of parenting usable under the field conditions common to most community-based programs. There are few good measures of those generic problem-solving and coping skills some programs attempt to strengthen. Up to now, few evaluations have been attempted to measure such apparently important variables as neighborhood stability and cohesiveness, levels of mutual support, human service provider attitudes, employment patterns, fertility patterns, and the like. Such contextual variables are important to program design and target population selection, and to explaining patterns of effects. These may be areas where community based programs have significant effects.

A major research and development effort in this field is not likely to pay off without the development of sustained collaborations between field-based research teams and local community agencies. Traditional external evaluation models are not suitable to the fluid conditions, press of urgent family needs, and centrality of community trust characteristic of most community-based programs. In light of these factors, the necessity of at least a measure of researcher control over implementation conditions, particularly for summative evaluations, will prove a sensitive issue. But if undertaken sensitively, it will likely benefit programs characterized by multiple, diffuse goals, and unscrutinized family worker behavior.

Challenges to an expanded public commitment

A sustained research and development effort is likely to illuminate a number of crucial targeting, strategy, and quality control issues necessary to an expanded public commitment to community-based early intervention. It should also provide evidence of program effects in a wider range of domains than is currently available. But it is possible, given the inherent complexities in this field, that even at the end of such an effort the quantitatively detectable effects of community-based early intervention would be found to be modest, particularly in terms of direct effects on infants and toddlers.

If the historical pattern of quantitative findings continues to hold, proponents of community-based early intervention will have to construct an argument for expanded public commitment based equally on scientific evidence and apparent social utility. In broad terms, community-based early intervention programs can be seen to fill a missing element in the continuum of preventively oriented helping services in communities. They provide a kind of support to young families that other helping services have not chosen or been able to provide. Perhaps equally important, they provide such support in a manner that makes them particularly acceptable to a wide range of families. Nonetheless, in constructing an argument on behalf of community-based early intervention, proponents will have to address the problem of the small number of families typically reached in individual programs, and the challenge in devising strategies for reaching larger numbers of families. Small numbers may be inherent to the design of these programs. But they pose serious problems in many community contexts, notably inner cities, where there are large numbers of families who could be supported.

One approach to expanding the number of service recipients could be sponsorship by one or another of the major service systems – social services, mental health, public health, or education. But such sponsorship, although offering the advantage of large, continuously funded budgets, agency stability, and large numbers of families passing through, would pose risks to core purposes and elements of community-based early intervention. Whatever the public system, all are partly designed to control and limit access – with rules, categories, eligibility procedures, and frequent waiting periods. Such features are not consonant with those that characterize most community-based early intervention programs. Furthermore, the provision of social support is generally not valued as an important or even appropriate function of human service agencies (Richman, 1986).

The future for community-based early intervention, then, is uncertain. Zigler (1986) has noted that the broader family support genre (of which early parenting interventions are an important element) will soon no longer be the country's best-kept secret. More preventively oriented parenting programs appear every day, as communities struggle to respond to the stress experienced by growing numbers of young families. But the long-term viability of both individual programs and the program movement in general will depend on a stronger financial commitment from the public sector, a commitment that will be difficult to secure without a more complete understanding of the potential inherent in the strategies being employed.

REFERENCES

Andrews, S., Blumenthal, J., Johnson, D., Kahn, A., Ferguson, C., Lasater, T., Malone, P., Wallace, D. (1982). The skills of mothering: A study of parent child development centers. *Monographs of the Society for Research in Child Development, 47*, (6, Serial No. 198).

Baratz, S., & Baratz, J. (1970). Early childhood intervention: The social science base of institutional racism. *Harvard Educational Review, 40*, 29–50.

Belle, D. (1982). *Lives in stress*. Beverly Hills: Sage Publications.

Bond, J., & Halpern, R. (1988). The role of cross-project evaluation in the Child Survival/Fair Start Initiative. In H. Weiss & F. Jacobs (Eds.), *Evaluating family programs* (pp. 347–378). Hawthorne, NY: Aldine Publishers.

Bronfenbrenner, U. (1987). Family support: The quiet revolution. In S. Kagan, D. Powell, B. Weissbourd, & E. Zigler (Eds.), *America's family support programs* (pp. xi–xvii). New Haven: Yale University Press.

Chilman, C. (1973). Programs for disadvantaged parents: Some major trends and related research. In B. Caldwell & H. Ricciutti (Eds.), *Review of child development research* (Vol. 3, pp. 403–465). Chicago: University of Chicago Press.

Cicirelli, V. (1969). *The impact of Head Start*. Athens, OH: Westinghouse Learning Corporation.

Clarke-Stewart, A. (1981). Parent education in the 1970s. *Educational Evaluation and Policy Analysis, 3*, 47–58.

Clinton, B., & Larner, M. (in press). Rural community women as leaders in health outreach. *Journal of Primary Prevention.*

de Lone, R. (1979). *Small futures.* New York: Harcourt, Brace, Jovanovich.

Deutsch, M. (1967). *An evaluation of the effectiveness of an enriched curriculum in overcoming the consequences of environmental deprivation.* New York: Institute for Developmental Studies, New York University.

Epstein, A., & Weikart, D. (1979). *The Ypsilanti-Carnegie Infant Education Project: Longitudinal follow-up.* Ypsilanti, MI: High/Scope.

Garbarino, J., & Sherman, D. (1980). High risk families and high risk neighborhoods. *Child Development, 51*, 188–198.

Grubb, N., & Lazerson, M. (1982). *Broken promises.* New York: Basic Books.

Halpern, R. (1987). Key social and demographic trends affecting young families: Implications for early childhood care and education. *Young Children, 42*, 34–40.

Halpern, R. (1988). Parent support and education for low-income families: Historical and current perspectives. *Children and Youth Services Review, 10*, 283–303.

Halpern, R., & Larner, M. (1987). Lay family support during pregnancy and infancy: The Child Survival/Fair Start Initiative. *Infant Mental Health Journal, 8*, 130–144.

Halpern, R. & Larner, M. (1988). The design of family support programs in high risk communities: Lessons from the Child Survival/Fair Start Initiative. In D. Powell (Ed.), *Parent education as early childhood intervention: Consequences for children and families* (pp. 181–207). Norwood, NJ: Ablex Publishing.

Hewett, K. (1982). Comprehensive family service programs: Special features and associated measurement problems. In J. Travers & R. Light (Eds.), *Learning from experience* (pp. 203–253). Washington, DC: National Academy Press.

Johnson, D., & Rodriguez, G. (1987). Proposal submitted to the Carnegie Corporation of New York by AVANCE, San Antonio, TX.

Johnson, D., & Walker, T. (1987). Primary prevention of behavioral problems in Mexican-American children. *American Journal of Community Psychology, 15*, 375–386.

Kamerman, S. (1985). Young, poor, and a mother alone. In H. McAdoo & J. Parham (Eds.), *Services to young families* (pp. 1–38). Washington, DC: American Public Welfare Association.

Karl, D. (1986). *Overview of Neighborhood Support Systems for Infants.* Cambridge, MA: Neighborhood Support Systems for Infants.

Klaus, R., & Gray, S. (1968). The Early Training Project for Disadvantaged Children: A report after five years. *Monographs of the Society for Research in Child Development, 33* (4, Serial No. 120).

Lally, R., & Honig, A. (1977). *The Family Development Research Program: A program for prenatal, infant, and early childhood enrichment* (Final Report to the Office of Child Development). Syracuse, NY: Syracuse University.

Larner, M., & Halpern, R. (1987). Lay home visiting programs: Strengths, tensions, and challenges. *Zero to Three, 8*(3), 1–7.

Levenstein, P. (1971). *Verbal Interaction Project: Aiding cognitive growth in disadvantaged preschoolers through the Mother–Child Home Program* (Final Report). New York: Family Service Association of Nassau County.

Lyons-Ruth, K., Botein, S., & Grunebaum, H. (1984). Reaching the hard to reach: Serving multi-risk families with infants in the community. In B. Coehler & J. Musick (Eds.), *Intervention with psychiatrically disabled parents and their infants* (pp. 95–122). San Francisco: Jossey-Bass.

Lyons-Ruth, K., Zoll, D., Connell, D., & Odom, R. (1987, April). *Maternal depression as a mediator of the effects of home-based intervention services.* Paper presented at the annual meeting of the Society for Research in Child Development, Baltimore.

Miller, S. (1988). *Child Welfare League of America – MELD Young Moms Project: Final technical report.* Washington, DC: Child Welfare League of America.

Mindick, B. (1987). *Social engineering in family matters.* New York: Praeger.

Musick, J., & Halpern, R. (1989). Giving children a chance: What role community-based early parenting interventions? In G. Miller (Ed.), *Giving children a chance: The case for more effective national policy* (pp. 177–194). Washington, DC: Center for National Policy Press.

Ogbu, J. (1985). A cultural ecology of competence among inner-city blacks. In M. Spencer (Ed.), *Beginnings: The social and affective development of black children* (pp. 45–66). Hillsdale, NJ: L. Erlbaum.

Olds, D., Henderson, C., Chamberlin, R., & Tatelbaum, R. (1986). The prevention of child abuse and neglect: A controlled trial of nurse home visitation. *Pediatrics*, *78*, 65–78.

O'Leary, K., Shore, M., & Weider, S. (1984, May). Contacting pregnant adolescents: Are we missing cues? *Social Casework*, pp. 297–306.

Pilisuk, M., & Parks, S. (1986). *The healing web*. Hanover, NH: University Press of New England.

Polansky, N. (1981). *Damaged parents*. Chicago: University of Chicago Press.

Powell, D. (1983). Individual differences in participation in a parent–child support program. In I. Sigel & L. Laosa (Eds.), *Changing families* (pp. 203–224). New York: Plenum Press.

Reischauer, R. (1986, Fall). The prospects for welfare reform. *Public Welfare*, pp. 4–11.

Richman, H. (1986). *Social services for children: Recent trends and implications*. Paper presented at a conference at Harvard University, "Children in a changing health care system: Assessments and proposals for reform."

Rodriguez, G. (1983). *Final report: Project CAN PREVENT*. San Antonio, TX: AVANCE.

Schlossman, S. (1978). The parent education game: The politics of child psychology in the 1970s. *Teachers College Record*, *79*, 788–808.

Schorr, L. (1988). *Within our reach: Breaking the cycle of disadvantage*. New York: Anchor Press.

Sigel, I. (1983). The ethics of intervention. In I. Sigel & L. Laosa (Eds.), *Changing families* (pp. 1–21). New York: Plenum Press.

Skerry, P. (1983). The charmed life of Head Start. *The Public Interest*, *73*, 18–39.

Slaughter, D. (1983). Early intervention and its effects on maternal and child development. *Monographs of the Society for Research in Child Development*, *48* (4, Serial No. 202).

Stack, C. (1974). *All our kin*. New York: Harper & Row.

Travers, J., Nauta, M., & Irwin, N. (1982). *The effects of a social program; Final report of the Child and Family Resource Program's Infant-Toddler component*. Cambridge, MA.: Abt Associates.

Valentine, C. (1968). *Culture and poverty*. Chicago: University of Chicago Press.

van Dooninck, W., Dawson, P., Butterfield, P., & Alexander, H. (1980). *Parent–infant support through lay health visitors* (Final Report). Denver: Parent–Infant Programs.

Wandersman, L. (1987). Parent–infant support groups: Matching programs to needs and strengths of families. In Z. Boukydis (Ed.), *Research on support for parents and infants in the postnatal period* (pp. 139–160). Norwood NJ: Ablex Publishing.

Ware, L., Osofsky, J., Eberhart-Wright A., & Leichtman, M. (1987). Challenges of home visitor interventions with adolescent mothers and their infants. *Infant Mental Health Journal*, *8*, 418–428.

Weiss, H. (1987). Family support and education in early childhood programs. In S. Kagan, D. Powell, B. Weissbourd, & E. Zigler (Eds.), *America's family support programs* (pp. 133–160). New Haven: Yale University Press.

Weiss, H. (1989). State family support and education programs: Lessons from the pioneers. *American Journal of Orthopsychiatry*, *59*, 32–48.

Weiss, H. (1988). Family support and education programs: Working through ecological theories of human development. In H. Weiss & F. Jacobs (Eds.), *Evaluating Family Programs* (pp. 3–36). New York: Aldine.

Weiss, H., & Halpern, R. (1988). *Community-based family support and education programs: Something old or something new?* New York: National Resource Center for Children in Poverty, Columbia University.

Weiss, H. & Jacobs, F. (1988). Family support and education programs: Challenges and opportunities. In H. Weiss & F. Jacobs (Eds.), *Evaluating family programs* (pp. xix–xxix). Hawthorne, NY: Aldine Publishers.

Weissbourd, B. (1981, March–April). Family Focus: Supporting families in the community. *Children Today*, pp. 6–11.

Weissman, H. (1978). *Integrating services for troubled parents*. San Francisco: Jossey-Bass.

Zigler, E. (1986). The family resource movement: No longer the country's best kept secret. *Family Resource Coalition Report*, *3*, 9–12.

Zigler, E., & Valentine, J. (1979). *Project Head Start: A legacy of the War on Poverty*. New York: Free Press.

Zigler, E., & Weiss, H. (1985). Family support systems: An ecological approach to child development. In R. Rapoport (Eds.), *Children, youth, and families* (pp. 166–205). New York: Cambridge University Press.

PART VI

Research perspectives and findings

21 Effects of intervention with disadvantaged and disabled children: A decade review

DALE C. FARRAN

INTRODUCTION

The last thing the field of early childhood education may need at the moment is another "comprehensive" review of the effects of intervention on children. Surely, among the large number of overviews and metaanalyses, everything that could be said about early intervention has already been said, and firm conclusions are readily obtainable. That reasonable assumption, however, is hard to support. In fact, the strongest conclusion that can be drawn is that there are very few studies of intervention efforts with either disabled or disadvantaged children that are scientifically valid enough to summarize (Bryant & Ramey, 1985; Dunst, 1986; Dunst & Rheingrover, 1982; Shonkoff & Hauser-Cram, 1987; Simeonsson, 1985).

There are various approaches to reviewing efficacy literature, the latest of which involves the metaanalytic technique of calculating "effect sizes" for studies, and then adding the effects for experimental children across all programs and comparing them to the effects for controls (or in the absence of controls, comparing posttest scores to pretest scores). Although this procedure assumes that the relevant data have been included in the published studies, it has been our experience that important data are often missing.

Metaanalytic reviews produced by the Early Intervention Research Institute at Utah State University have compiled a database of 447 studies drawn from a diverse set of sources, including published articles, and non-peer-reviewed final reports, ERIC documents, and presented papers (Casto & Mastropieri, 1986a; Casto & White, 1985; White, 1985–86). Casto and White (1985) describe in detail how conventions were written for the 97 items coded for each study, with subsequent reliability determined to be 87% average agreement (although neither the method for determining reliability nor the frequency with which it was checked was reported). Given the paucity of data ordinarily presented, it is hard to imagine how even the published studies could have yielded codes for 97 items, yet many of their analyses were based on the derived codes,

The author gratefuly acknowledges the contributions of Dierdre Yin and Tom Darvill, both doctoral candidates in the Department of Psychology at the University of Hawaii, who gathered and categorized the data-based publications from intervention projects; Yin worked with the material on disabled children, Darvill with the disadvantaged. In addition, gratitude is expressed to Ashlyn Kim-Seu who developed the system for tracking the numerous references and to Terry Rakestraw for her cheerful and excellent typing of the manuscript.

not the actual data presented. The conclusions drawn about the effects of programs for children with disabilities (Casto & Mastropieri, 1986a) and of programs for disadvantaged children (Casto & White, 1985) were similar. According to both reviews, effects appear to be immediate and amount to about a 6 to 7 point difference in IQ; the effects were not shown to be long lasting, though data still need to be collected longitudinally.

The Utah State group concluded that their data demonstrated no particular benefit for parental involvement in the program nor evidence that starting earlier was necessarily better. As might be expected, the reaction to these summary statements was immediate and intense (Dunst & Snyder, 1986; Provence, 1985; Snyder, 1988; Strain & Smith, 1986), with equally robust and vehement rebuttals (Casto & Mastropieri, 1986b; Casto & Mastropieri, 1986c). Shonkoff and Hauser-Cram (1987) analyzed a subset of the Utah State database focusing solely on programs for children younger than 36 months with biological disabilities and concluded that family involvement had a significant impact on child performance and that earlier program enrollment made a difference for children with less severe disabilities.

Although it is true that the data on which any conclusions can be based are weak and most published studies are flawed methodologically (Dunst, 1986; Simeonsson, 1985), they are all we have to work with at the moment. They may not provide the foundation for a rigorous knowledge base, but they do warrant close scrutiny and an attempt to make sense of what is there. Thus, in this review as much attention is paid to what is written between the lines, to ways studies contradict themselves and each other, and to places where studies of different populations agree as is paid to the actual data presented.

This chapter focuses on studies that were published in journals, books, or monographs between 1977 and 1986. They had to be studies of intervention projects with either disabled or disadvantaged children that concentrated at least partly on cognitive outcome data for the children involved. Further description of the studies included is provided in each section. What follows is a discussion first of the effects of intervention efforts with disadvantaged children; second, the effects for disabled children; and third, areas they have in common.

DISADVANTAGED CHILDREN

Study characteristics

NUMBER OF PROJECTS INCLUDED. Thirty-two projects begun during the preschool years with results published between 1977 and 1986 are included in this review and are briefly summarized in Table 1. Those projects with long-term follow-up data were begun in the late 1960s or early 1970s. All involved children were considered at risk for school problems, mild mental retardation, and reading problems, though often the children's risk status was not specified in any detail. In general, low socioeconomic status (SES) alone appears to have been considered risk enough to warrant intervention. The type of intervention received varied, but the focus of all these projects was cognitive remediation or support. More than 5,000 children participated in these efforts as experimental subjects. An additional 2,000 served as controls and were tested periodically.

RACE AND SOCIOECONOMIC STATUS OF CHILDREN. Most of the intervention programs begun in preschool were made up exclusively of black children. A few

Table 1. *Intervention programs for the disadvantaged*

Project (study citation)	Delivery site	Length of follow-up[a]	Number Treated	Number Control	Who delivers intervention to the child
Intervention at age 12 mo or earlier					
Parent–Child Development Centers (Andrews, Blumen-Chal, Johnson, Kahn, Ferguson, Lasater, Malone, & Wallace, 1982)					
Birmingham	Center	Short	71	65	Parents and staff
Houston	Home and center	Short	44	58	Parents and staff
New Orleans	Center	None	32	46	Parents and staff
Abecedarian/Project CARE (Ramey & Campbell, 1984; Ramey, Bryant, Sparling, & Wasik, 1985)					
Abecedarian	Center	None	54	53	Staff only
CARE (day care)	Center	None	15	23	Parents and staff
CARE (parent education)	Home	None	26		Parents only
Family Development Research Program (Honig & Lally, 1982; Honig, Lally, & Mathieson, 1982)	Center	Short	100	71	Parents and staff
The Ypsilanti–Carnegie Infant Education Project (Epstein & Weikart, 1979)	Home	Moderate	20	19	Parents only
The Milwaukee Project (Garber & Heber, 1977)	Center	Moderate	40	20	Staff only
Mailman Center Projects (Field, Widmayer, Greenberg, & Stoller, 1982)					
Home visit, parent training	Home	Short	40	40	Parents only
Nursery, parent training	Center	Short	40		Parents and staff
Intervention beginning between 12 mo and 36 mo					
Family-Oriented Home Visit Program (Gray & Ruttle, 1980)	Home	Long	27	20	Parents only
Gordon Parent Education Infant and Toddler Program (Jester & Guinagh, 1983; Lazar & Darlington, 1982)	Home	Long	107	24	Parents only
Verbal Interaction Program (Levenstein, O'Hara, & Madden, 1983; Lazar & Darlington, 1982)	Home	Long	133	53	Parents only
Harlem Study (Palmer, 1983; Lazar & Darlington, 1982)	Center	Long	180	48	Staff only

Table 1. (*cont.*)

Project (study citation)	Delivery site	Length of follow-up[a]	Number Treated	Number Control	Who delivers intervention to the child
Chicago Housing Projects Programs (Slaughter, 1983)					
Toy Demonstration Program	Home	None	26	31	Parents only
Mother Discussion Group	Home	None	26		Parents only
High/Scope (Schweinhart, Weikart, & Larner, 1986a)					
High/Scope	Center	Long	23	59	Staff only
Distar	Center	Long	22		Staff only
Nursery	Center	Long	23		Staff only
Self Controlled Interactive Learning Systems (Steg, Vaidya, & Hamdan, 1983)	Center	Long	22		Staff only
British Preschool Study (Wadsworth, 1986)	Center	Long	1,374	302	Staff only
Intervention between 37 mo and 60 mo					
Columbia Study (McKay, Sinisterra, McKay, Gomez, & Lloreda, 1978)	Center	Moderate	301	107	Staff only
Head Start (Hebbeler, 1985)	Center	Long	1,915	619	Staff only
Project Social Handicap and Cognitive Functioning (Curtis & Blatchford, 1981)	Center	None	431	232	Staff only
In Vivo Language Intervention (Hart & Risley, 1980)	Center	None	11	20	Staff only
Fantasy Play Tutoring (Smith, Dalgleish, & Herzmark, 1981)	Center	Short	65		Staff only
Early Training Project (Gray & Ramsey, 1985; Gray, Ramsey, & Klaus, 1983; Lazar & Darlington, 1982)	Center	Long	55	45	Staff only
The Philadelphia Study (Beller, 1983; Lazar & Darlington, 1982)	Center	Long	74	35	Staff only
The Louisville Experiment (Miller & Bizzell, 1983; Lazar & Darlington, 1982)	Center	Long	109	18	Staff only
Perry Preschool (Farnworth, Schweinhart, & Berrueta-Clement, 1985; Schweinhart, Berrueta-Clement, Barnett, Epstein, & Weikart, 1985; Lazar & Darlington, 1982)	Center	Long	58	65	Parents and staff
Sigel Distancing Theory (Slater, 1986)	Home	None	40	20	Parents only

[a] None = no follow-up data after the program's end; short = 1 year past program's end; moderate = followed through seventh grade; long = followed through eighth grade and beyond.

included low-income whites and blacks. Two studies included Hispanics, one in this country (Andrews et al., 1982) and one in Central America (McKay, Sinisterra, McKay, Gomez, & Pascuala, 1978). One intervention population was low-income white (Slater, 1986). Another two were large-scale studies in the United Kingdom (Smith, Dalgleish, & Herzmark, 1981; Wadsworth, 1986); ethnicity was not specified, and it is assumed that a diversity of ethnicities was included. It is curious that early intervention efforts have focused so heavily on blacks. Although blacks are disproportionately represented among the poor, and the poor are much more likely to have problems in school (Farran, Haskins, & Gallagher, 1980), in absolute numbers there are more poor white children.

All except two of the studies reviewed were made up exclusively of low SES children. Two large United Kingdom studies were mixed socioeconomically; for one of them, half of the children were classified as "disadvantaged" and the other half were not (the two groups were analyzed separately).

RECRUITMENT OF SUBJECTS. It is not clear who was represented by the populations included in these studies. Typically, projects established relationships with various community agencies and then asked for referrals. Once someone was referred, the project staff recruited them into the study. Thus, one cannot be certain what criteria the agencies used to decide whom to refer or how much self-selection occurred at the outset in potential clients choosing to follow through on the interview.

There are exceptions to this pattern: Gray (Gray, Ramsey, & Klaus, 1983) recruited all children of an eligible age who were in two small towns in Tennessee. Slaughter (1983) canvased entire housing projects attempting to recruit all women with children of the appropriate age. Initially there appear to have been 193 eligible mothers in the three housing projects, 61 of whom refused to participate.

Therefore, it is not possible to know to whom the results should generalize. Another factor to consider is attrition over the course of the study. The initial sample is almost never the final one, especially for long-term studies, where the loss can be devastating. Slaughter (1983) lost almost 50% of her sample over the 2 years of the study. Of the 90 children whom Gray (Gray & Ramsey, 1986) began with, 14 girls were followed through the completion of high school. Although most researchers compare their final sample to the original one and almost never find a difference between the two groups, important distinctions unmeasured by demographics and early developmental status of the child are quite likely. Differences in motivation, mobility, vulnerability to stress, and external control – all important variables for children's development – are likely to distinguish the groups. This problem haunts longitudinal research and cannot be avoided. It must be considered when deciding what the results of these studies mean for a policy on intervention.

Cognitive outcomes from home-based intervention programs

The issue of home-based versus center-based intervention is important. All of the home intervention projects reviewed except one (Slater, 1986) began before the children were 36 months of age; most involved a home visitor who brought materials to the home for the child to play with and then demonstrated to the mother developmentally appropriate ways to help the child play, with particular emphasis on language (patterned after Levenstein's [1970] toy demonstrators). The target in all these home-based intervention programs was the child, in order to distinguish these home visitors from social workers.

One of Slaughter's (1983) groups functioned as a maternal support group and was not led through prescribed discussions of development or materials, but the objective was to improve the child's developmental level.

In terms of their immediate effects, the studies display mixed results. Gray's Home Visit Program (Gray & Ruttle, 1980) and the Project CARE Parent Education Program (Ramey, Bryant, Sparling, & Wasik, 1985) showed no positive effects for home visiting. In fact, Project CARE children who received home visiting alone scored more poorly on the Stanford-Binet at age 3 than both the group that attended day care and the controls. The Field (Field, Widmayer, Greenberg, & Stoller, 1982) home visit group scored higher developmentally than the control children, but was significantly lower than the group of children who received center-based care while their mothers learned job skills at the center. Slaughter's (1983) experimental children in both groups scored about one-half a standard deviation higher than controls on the McCarthy Scales but showed no differences on the Peabody Picture Vocabulary Test. Only the earlier projects of Gordon (Jester & Guinagh, 1983) and Levenstein (Levenstein, O'Hara, & Madden, 1983) and a recent effort by Slater (1986) produced unequivocally positive immediate intervention results. The Slater (1986) intervention was short-term, focused, and theoretically based, in contrast to the others. Mothers were taught strategies for story reading based on Sigel's distancing hypothesis (Sigel, 1971); maternal behavior changes reflected the strategies taught, and children's test scores increased. One would like to see this approach incorporated into a regular full-day program.

Four of the home-based intervention projects collected longitudinal data several years after the program's end (Epstein & Weikart, 1979; Gray & Ruttle, 1980; Jester & Guinagh, 1983; Levenstein et al., 1983). Of these, only Levenstein's program showed long-term positive effects. In analyzing the 1976 follow-up data on this project Lazar and Darlington (1982) characterized it as having a "less randomized design," meaning that a control group was established but not through random assignment. Levenstein, however, described the mothers who participated in training in her earlier cohorts (those in the 1976 follow-up) as being "volunteers" (Levenstein et al., 1983, p. 261). Cohorts entering the program between 1973 and 1976 were subjected to random assignment and their short-term results were much lower. Levenstein et al. (1983) cautioned that "these IQ effects do not provide the same basis for prediction of later effects on school performance as did the quasi-experimental IQ effects" (p. 260).

Whether stronger effects can ever be demonstrated by randomly assigning families to receive home visitation is open to question. Early home-based intervention programs may be a case where capitalizing on volunteerism produces the best effects for children even if it does not produce the best science. Having someone in your home on a regular basis can quickly become more of a burden than a help; the more motivated a mother was to have the home visitor in the first place, the more likely she will be to tolerate and learn from the program. It is doubtful that families should ever be *required* to receive parent education and home visitation (as if they were being given a uniformly effective antibiotic); individual receptivity is of paramount importance in this type of intervention. Even with receptive parents, available data do not demonstrate the effectiveness of home-based intervention as a strategy for disadvantaged children.

Cognitive outcomes from center-based intervention programs

PROGRAMS BEGUN IN INFANCY. Eight of the preschool programs that were center-based begun when the child was 12 months of age or younger (see the first section of Table 1 for the particular projects). With regular assessments of the children, these studies afforded the possibility of comparing the development of experimental and control children during the preschool years and beyond. Unfortunately, the studies vary greatly in how far they have tracked the development of the two groups.

The Syracuse group (Honig & Lally, 1982; Honig, Lally, & Mathieson, 1982) has presented the most complete data. The greatest difference between the treated and untreated group occurred at age three where the two groups were separated by almost a standard deviation in Binet scores. At age four, that difference had reduced to one-half of a standard deviation (the difference most often reported as an effect of early intervention). The Syracuse project also reported data on the children at ages five and six, at which point the control group had begun to improve and there was no longer any significant difference between them and children with preschool experience. It is important to note, however, that this is not a "wash-out" effect – the IQ scores of the intervention group remained about the same from age four on. What happened was that the control group began to improve, and to make up the difference. Since the experience of the control group was not being carefully monitored, it is impossible to know if their improvement was also due to preschool experiences or just the result of general participation in a wider world that comes with age.

The Abecedarian/Project CARE data (Ramey et al., 1985; Ramey & Campbell, 1984) are presented only until age four, the age when, based on the Syracuse data, one would still expect to see a significant difference. At age three the Abecedarian/Project CARE children were most different from the controls, at age four the differences were still significant but the control children had begun to score higher than previously. The data for these children at ages five and six will be very important to see.

Data from the Parent–Child Development Centers (PCDC) are somewhat similar (Andrews et al., 1982). However the difference at age three for these three projects was only about one-half of a standard deviation and it remained at that level for one of the two projects followed until age four. In the other project (Birmingham), the control group had begun to score higher by age four and differences were no longer statistically significant. (The third project was not assessed at age four.) Unfortunately, these children were not followed further. Field (Field et al., 1982) followed her sample only until age two. At that age, the control group was scoring a full standard deviation below the nursery group (in which mothers both learned job skills and brought their babies in for care). Garber and Heber (1977) presented a line graph showing experimental and control differences up through 108 months. However, there is no way to inspect the means or standard deviations; without access to such data, and given the questions raised about data analysis in this project by Page and Grandon (1981), their results must be viewed with caution.

PROGRAMS BEGUN IN THE SECOND AND THIRD YEAR OF LIFE. Eleven programs are listed in Table 1 that began when the child was between 13 and 36 months of age and on which data were published between 1977 and 1986. Four involving home intervention have already been discussed. It is difficult to draw conclusions about the effectiveness of the other seven because the studies lack comparability. Two studies, however, involving four different programs should be comparable: that of Palmer (1983) and a High/Scope study that compared the High/Scope Curriculum to the Direct Instruction Model (Distar [Bereiter & Englemann, 1966]) and a normal nursery program (Schweinhart, Weikart, & Larner, 1986a). The Palmer study is difficult to assess because the control group tested significantly lower than the treated group on a

Stanford-Binet pretest at the outset of the study. Twelve years later, Palmer's project was one of only three in the Consortium for Longitudinal Studies (Lazar & Darlington, 1982) that reported an independent effect for preschool intervention in the 1976 follow-up. This effect was achieved on a combined variable called, "Meeting School Requirements," which included avoiding special education placement and grade retention.

The initial effects of all three approaches assessed by Schweinhart et al. (1986a) were similarly positive. Children appeared to enter the programs with comparable developmental levels, and there was an immediate effect on tested intelligence, with decline by the intervention group in each type of program at age five to a level about one-half standard deviation from the control children. There were no differences later among the three curriculum groups on IQ and school achievement, except that the DISTAR children sustained less loss in their scores during the early elementary grades. There were no differences in performance as a function of the earlier preschool curriculum for the 7-, 8-, and 15-year cognitive assessments.

Wadsworth (1986) conducted a two-generation study in the United Kingdom. He noted a tremendous jump in the use of preschools by the current generation compared to their own childhood, from 13.1% to 81.9% in one generation. Children who had attended community preschools were found to be significantly better prepared for primary school than children who did not attend. Nevertheless, the best predictor of both school readiness and the utilization of preschools was maternal education. Analyses that controlled for maternal education demonstrated that preschool experience remained a significant factor in predicting higher verbal skills by age eight. In terms of implications for intervention, Wadsworth found that preschool experience did not compensate for the presence of a presumed verbally unstimulating mother.

PROGRAMS BEGUN IN THE FOURTH OR SIXTH YEAR OF LIFE. All of the interventions that began when the children were between the ages of 37 and 60 months were center-based and are listed in Table 1. In general, all of these efforts produced an immediate effect on children's tested ability. In some cases, that effect persisted for a short period (Beller, 1983; Gray et al., 1983; McKay et al., 1978; Schweinhart & Weikart, 1983). In very few cases did it last past the fifth or sixth grade. Hebbeler (1985) traced three cohorts of Head Start graduates in the Montgomery County, Maryland, public schools, examining achievement and school progress 4 to 12 years past Head Start graduation (she was able to retrieve 50–60% of each group). Despite Hebbeler's conclusion that the results demonstrated the effectiveness of early intervention, in fact, the only group that performed significantly differently from the controls was the first cohort, and no group came close to matching the performance of children in the district as a whole.

This finding brings up the interesting issue of a "generation effect" in implementing programs. Almost all programs are effective when they are initially developed, especially if they are established during a heightened period of belief that a new solution to this very intractable problem has been found. But as soon as programs pass beyond the hands of the originators – into a second generation – very few have proven of lasting importance. There are important lessons to be learned from this phenomenon. The first is that *belief* in the efficacy of a program and the potential of children to learn and progress rapidly may be the most critical element in any intervention strategy. Belief, however, is hard to export. In training new implementors, it may be less important to train them in the fine points of the curriculum than to imbue them with a strong sense that they will be effective and that change is possible.

The second lesson may be a renewed and expanded discovery of the Hawthorne Effect. Thus, change may have to occur periodically so that teachers and curriculum developers will have renewed interest. When Head Start was first implemented, it rode on a tide of strong belief that the country had come to grips with the problems of poor children and that it could actively solve these problems. Rather quickly, though, Head Start was battered with findings that questioned its ability to live up to its promise. Funding never reached the levels originally intended, and the program became mired in bureaucracy. Second generation effectiveness has yet to be established.

CONCLUSION. The conclusion suggested by a review of this most current intervention research goes against the now popular wisdom about how early to intervene with disadvantaged children. There is no strong evidence for "the earlier, the better" despite the commonsense appeal of this homily. Many of the projects that began in early infancy have not had long-term follow-up, however, and there may be effects on school performance measures such as grade retention and special education placement that will surface later. Also, despite its intrinsic appeal, there are few data to suggest the long-term beneficial effects on school performance from preschool intervention *that is not continued into the public schools* (the "booster shot" notion). Thus, although experience with a structured schoollike environment appears to raise tested performance immediately, without continued intervention, test scores fall gradually until they reach a level of difference from controls that is neither statistically nor educationally significant.

A great deal has been written about the effects on school measures that were not IQ or achievement test scores. These are proportional comparisons of grade retention and special education placement, especially those identified in the Consortium study (Lazar & Darlington, 1982). There are several problems with those analyses: (1) Only three Consortium studies found the effect, although there was a general trend in seven of the eight; (2) the length of time children were followed varied greatly, and no high school graduation data are reported for any; and (3) large numbers of children were lost in the follow-up of several of the studies, leaving relatively small groups of possibly atypical students. Small numbers can have a pronounced effect when *proportions* are presented as the outcomes.

These cautions should not be taken as a conclusion that early intervention has not been successful nor as a recommendation that such efforts cease. On the contrary, there are very strong and positive published data (not reviewed here) supporting intervention in the early elementary grades (Becker & Gersten, 1982; Gersten & Carnine, 1984; Meyer, 1984; Meyer, Gersten, & Gutkin, 1983). These data indicate that children in schools in impoverished neighborhoods can perform at grade level and graduate at high rates from high school. The "intervention" consisted of monitoring the teachers to assure that children received instruction for 60% of the school day.

Alternative outcomes

In the search for noncognitive effects of early intervention programs, attention has been focused on what Zigler and Balla (1982) have called "society variables." They write, "If it can be demonstrated that long after participants have left the program they are more adequate adults and contributors to society than they would have been without the program, powerful evidence for program continuation has been provided" (p. 19). The society variable that has received the most attention recently is juvenile delinquency. Unfortunately, results concerning this important issue have been obtained only from the work of the High/Scope Perry Preschool projects, and the controversy surrounding their findings has been substantial.

A review of the three different reports from Michigan highlights the difficulties of drawing firm conclusions in this area. In 1985, Farnworth, Schweinhart, and Berrueta-Clement published a methodologically sophisticated article that presented the results of several multiple regression analyses. Various school measures, including attendance at preschool, were used as predictors; the criterion variables were summary scores (derived from factor analysis) of an 18-item self-report on delinquent behaviors. The premise tested in the analyses was whether "school bonding" was a contributor to delinquent behavior. Despite the title of the article, an investigation of the effects of preschool attendance appeared to have been a secondary, although interesting, aspect. The adolescents surveyed included 99 of the original 123 Perry Preschool graduates; they appeared to be all the subjects available for follow-up. Preschool attendance (defined as attending the Perry Preschool, with no data reported on the possible attendance of the control subjects at other preschools) contributed in interaction with two other variables to two of the four outcomes. One of the outcomes was labeled "Dishonesty": "Individuals who spent more years in special education were more likely to report dishonest forms of delinquency, and preschool attendance interacted with assignment to special education to decrease the likelihood of this type of delinquent involvement" (Farnworth et al., 1985, p. 455). Preschool attendance in interaction with attitudes toward school was a minor contributor to lessening another factor – "Escape," which included reports of running away from home, smoking marijuana, and using drugs.

Several features of this report should be noted. First, from the data reported, it appears that preschool attendance by itself had a simple correlation only with the factor of dishonesty, ($r = -.25$). Second, it is difficult to sort out what an interaction term could mean. Preschool attendance was a dichotomous variable, as were several others in the model, including "relative school attitude," a variable that was based on a yes or no response to a single item. When two dichotomous variables are used in an interaction term and the direction of their effects is different (for preschool attendance, a higher score indicated "yes," but for school attitude, a higher score indicated a *poorer* school attitude), it is difficult to know what to make of their contribution. Third, no data on the validity of the self-reported delinquency are presented, and no information is presented on who did the interviewing and whether it was likely that the adolescents would self-disclose and would do so without bias in terms of their previous preschool experiences. Fourth, the reader cannot assume that the control group had no preschool experiences, given that significantly more of their mothers worked during the preschool years. It would have been better to have arrayed the children on a continuum of preschool experiences from the Perry Preschool to others of different types and amounts in order to investigate the effect of preschool. Without data on the preschool experiences of the other children, it is difficult to conclude anything about the effects of preschool per se on self-reports of delinquent behavior.

A second article by Schweinhart, Berrueta-Clement, Barnett, Epstein, and Weikart (1985) raises further questions. This article is a report of Perry Preschool graduates when they were 19 years of age; all but two of the children were available for follow-up, although there is no explanation of how the 20 who were lost before were recovered.

This article provides information on random assignment to groups, a key aspect of the study. It is apparent that true random assignment did not occur. Siblings were taken into the project and assigned to the same groups, and "between three and six single parents employed outside the home had to be transferred from the preschool group to the no-preschool group because of their inability to participate in the classroom and/or home-visit components of the preschool program" (p. 29). Numbers are not given for the first situation and are inexact for the second. One cannot determine how many children were thus not actually randomly assigned. But the principle was certainly violated, and unless these children are excluded from analyses, one cannot call this a randomized design. In a small sample, the exchange of 6 to 10 children can have a profound effect. Data are presented on several dichotomous outcome measures in terms of percentage comparisons between the two groups. The sources of these variables, however, and the interviews of the youths are not described. Thus, one cannot tell whether the data presented on detention and arrest records are from the interviews or from actual court and police records. It should be noted that all of the percentages favor the graduates of the Perry Preschool. The trend in the direction they obtained is certainly impressive, but near probabilities in small samples beg for replication.

Finally, another study of this same issue but with a different population was published by the same investigators (Schweinhart et al., 1986a). Three waves of children from Ypsilanti were assigned to one of three preschools supervised by Weikart in 1967–69. The random assignment seems cleaner than in the previous study, although allowance was still made for siblings, and 9 of the original 68 children were affected. Despite random assignment, the Nursery Curriculum group was of a higher socio-economic status with fewer single parents than the High/Scope and DISTAR (more properly called direct-instruction) group. Analysis of variance of the responses to a self-report of delinquent behaviors by fifty-four 15-year-olds available at follow-up favored the High/Scope children. They reported fewer delinquent acts overall and were significantly different in the areas of property damage and status offenses. However, these are small samples, the standard deviations are uniformly higher than the means, the instrument is a self-report measure of unknown reliability and validity, and the assessors were individuals with a vested interest in one of the programs being compared. As might be expected, proponents of the other marketed curriculum under consideration (DISTAR) have been highly critical of the findings (Bereiter, 1986; Gersten, 1986, but see reply by Schweinhart, Weikart, & Larner, 1986b).

Two other studies, whose populations have not yet reached adolescence, have findings relevant to the issue of aggression and preschool attendance. These studies may increase our understanding of this complex phenomenon.

Both the Abecedarian Project (Haskins, 1985) and the Syracuse Project (Honig et al., 1982) reported increased rates of aggression in children who attended preschool compared to controls once the children entered the public schools. Haskins (1985) observed the Abecedarian experimental and control children (who had varying amounts of preschool experience in community programs) in their classrooms. The children who attended the preschool were found to be more aggressive in all four settings surveyed (classroom, lunchroom, playground, and hallway) and to engage significantly more in 10 of 11 aggressive acts. There was evidence that the differences between the groups diminished somewhat during the third year of school, because the control children began to be more aggressive and the experimental children became less so. The effect appeared to have been related to participation in the Abecedarian program and not preschool in general because the other control children with equal amounts of preschool experience did not show increased aggression. Furthermore, Finklestein (1982) demonstrated experimental control over the development of aggressive behavior during 1 year of the Abecedarian preschool when he introduced a social skills curriculum. The Syracuse project (Honig et al., 1982) found similar results based on teacher ratings when the children entered public schools. Haskins speculates that his findings were a function of the academic nature of an intervention preschool environment, lending credence to the possibility that a more heavily academic program like DISTAR could be associated with negative behavioral outcomes as well.

Caution must be used in interpreting these findings, and firm policy decisions should not be made on the basis of small samples surveyed by a small number of researchers. Nevertheless, the issue of the possible positive effects to some kinds of preschool experiences or the possible negative effects of other kinds on delinquency should be explored seriously and systematically as quickly as possible.

Conclusion

It is currently popular to argue that studies such as those just reviewed provide strong evidence for the value of early intervention for children who are disadvantaged by poverty and/or social disorganization. For example, a recent article in a local newspaper was geared toward eliciting support for state-funded preschools for the disadvantaged: "Students who get early starts in good programs that stress language and social development are less likely to drop out, get pregnant, use drugs and become trouble-makers" (Avery, 1988). In truth, there is little support for statements that are either so absolute, so long-term, or so inclusive regarding the effects of early intervention. Available data suggest a range of potential benefits from carefully planned and well-implemented early intervention efforts. Such services, however, must be continued if short-term gains are to be sustained. In the area of cognitive growth and school achievement, for example, it appears that improvement in the educational program provided for low-income children in the first four years of elementary school will be more effective than simply providing 1 year of preschool. In the social domain, only juvenile delinquency has been studied, and it has only been studied by a small group of researchers. Before we make sweeping claims for the effects of early intervention (Committee for Economic Development, 1987; Schorr, 1988), it is of paramount importance that the database be firm.

CHILDREN WITH DISABILITIES

Study characteristics

Included in this review and summarized in Table 2 are data published on 42 projects that involved the provision of intervention to children with disabilities; 29 of these projects served a mixed population of children, and 13 were exclusively for children with Down syndrome. Although the effects of any intervention are better understood the more homogeneous the subject population, many handicapping conditions are relatively rare and, therefore, projects often serve a wide variety of children. Of the 29 projects reviewed that had a mixed population, many had a large percentage of children with cerebral palsy; the next most frequently cited category was general developmental delay of unknown etiology. The results of the projects with a mixed population have been summarized separately from those with Down syndrome. There are more research studies than there are projects. Projects that have existed for several years have sometimes led to a number of different investigations. Where there was no way to determine the degree of overlap in different research studies stemming from the same project, the numbers of children involved have been listed separately in Table 2. Where it was clear that the children were the same, all the citations have been given, but the children have been listed only once.

In general, for all the studies the age of entry of children in the program varied widely and, consequently, so did the length of treatment, information on both is provided for all projects in Table 2. Even for children with Down syndrome (which is recognizable at birth), the range of entry into the project for one study was from 20 to 162 months (Hayden & Haring, 1977). Clearly, within a single program the intervention provided for such a heterogeneous group of children would have to be highly individualized. In contrast to the studies of disadvantaged children, little information is usually provided on the families of children with disabilities. Parental age, education, and occupational status are rarely reported; consequently it is difficult for many of these studies to determine what other factors might be affecting the child's development, either positively or negatively, in conjunction with the disabling condition.

Pre–post comparisons with mixed population programs

GAIN SCORES. Pre–post comparisons that assess only the children who receive intervention have been computed in various ways. The simplest involves subtracting pretest scores from posttest scores to compute the gains achieved by the children. Of the 29 projects whose sample populations were mixed, 20 used pre–post data as their outcome evaluation. Six of the 20 report only immediate gain scores (Bailey & Bricker, 1985; Bricker & Dow, 1980; Bricker, Bruder, & Bailey, 1982; Maisto & German, 1979; Rosen-Morris & Sitkei, 1981; Shapiro, Gordon, & Neiditch, 1977). As Rosenberg, Robinson, Finkler, and Rose (1987) point out, "In the absence of a control group or reference comparison group, gain scores lack meaning" (p. 214). Reporting on the children in their programs in 1978–80, Bricker et al. (1982) and Bricker and Sheehan (1981) used an index developed by Abt Associates for determining "educationally significant change." Acknowledging that interpretation of change data is hampered by the lack of a control group, they asserted that this index is a means of deciding whether the gains achieved had educational meaning. If the gains from pre- to posttesting exceeded one-quarter of the pooled standard deviations of the pre- and posttest scores, they were considered educationally significant.

Whether "educational significance" can be determined statistically from the changes in a single group is an important question when thinking about the utility of the measure. This system appears to be an indirect attempt to investigate if there is a main effect of the treatment, that is, if the treatment is exerting an effect substantially above the variation in the sample as a whole. At best, a measure like this should be used as preliminary feedback for indicating the need for a more substantial study of the curriculum. It is clearly too dependent on the variation in a sample to be useful as the sole evaluation of a program.

RATES OF DEVELOPMENT. In 10 other projects (11 studies), change was measured by creating indices of rates of development and comparing preintervention rates to those obtained during the intervention, at the posttest, or both (Bagnato & Neisworth, 1980; Barna, Bidder, Gray, Clements, & Gardner, 1980; Brassell, 1977; Cocks, 1982; Hewitt,

Table 2. Intervention programs for disabled children

Project (study citation)	Design	N^a (Control)	Type of Intervention	Age of entry[b] in mo	Length in mo	Who delivers intervention to the child
Projects with mixed populations						
Early Intervention Program (Bailey & Bricker, 1985)	Gain scores	70	Center and home	$1\frac{1}{2}$–12	5–7	Parents and staff
Mailman Center (Bricker & Dow, 1980)	Gain scores	40	Center	7–54	8	Parents and staff
Center on Human Development Preschool Program[c]						
(Bricker, Bruder, & Bailey, 1982)	Gain scores	41	Center and home	18–60	7	Parents and staff
(Bricker & Sheehan, 1981)	Gain scores	63	Center and home	5–69	7	Parents and staff
Parent Infant Training Program (Maisto & German, 1979)	Gain scores	32	Center	X = 10.8	12	Parents only
Project Shape (Rosen-Morris & Sitkei, 1981)	Gain scores	20	Center	18–72	12	Staff only
Infant Program at the Institute of Rehabilitation Medicine (Shapiro, Gordon, & Neiditch, 1977)	Gain scores	20	Residential	18–36	NS[d]	Staff only
IEI Sample Preschool (Bagnato & Neisworth, 1980)	Rate of development	16	Center	16–20	24	Staff only
South Glamorgan Home Advisory Service[c] (Barna, Bidder, Gray, Clements, & Gardner, 1980)	Rate of development Differential areas	35	Home	3–48	7–23	Parents only

515

Program (citation)	Focus	N	Setting	Age range		Delivery
(Hewitt, Newcombe & Bidder, 1983)	Rate of development / Differential areas	38	Home	5–45	3	Parents only
(Revill & Blunden, 1979)	Curriculum comparison	19	Home	8–48	4–6	Parents only
Western Carolina Infant Program[c] (Brassell, 1977)	Rate of development	73	Home	$X = 20.8$	10	Parents only
(Brassell & Dunst, 1978)	Curriculum comparison	24	Home	$X = 21.0$	4–5	Parents only
Perth Division for the Intellectually Handicapped (Cocks, 1982)	Rate of development / Differential areas	49	Home and center	$X = 30.9$	7	Parents and staff
Wyoming Infant Stimulation Program (Jelinek, 1985)	Rate of development	38	Home and center	3–30	NS	Staff only
Infant and Toddler Learning Program (LeLaurin, 1985)	Rate of development	16	Center	3–31	15.6	Staff only
Program for Down Syndrome and other Developmental Delays (Oelwein, Fewell, & Pruess, 1985)	Rate of development	164	Center	11–168	8–9	Staff only
Kindling Individual Systems (Turner & Rogers, 1981)	Rate of development / Differential areas	78	Home and center	Birth–108	12	Parents and staff

Table 2. (*cont.*)

Project (study citation)	Design	N^a (Control)	Type of Intervention	Age of entry^b in mo	Length in mo	Who delivers intervention to the child
Infant/Parent Training and Early Childhood Development Program (Wolery & Dyk, 1985)	Rate of development	34	Center	17–55	12	Parents and staff
Preschool Instruction for the Exceptional (Zeitlin, 1981)	Rate of development Follow-up	19	Center	$X = 52$–56	7–9	Parents and staff
Children's Evaluation and Rehabilitation Center (Kaminer & Chinitz, 1982)	Differential areas	18	Center	26–60	9	Staff only
Joint Early Education Program for the Handicapped (Karnes, Schwedel, Lewis Ratts, & Esry, 1981)	Pre–post Follow-up	86	Center	NS	36	Staff only
Regional Demonstration Program for Preschool Handicapped (Koen, Musumeci, & Toole, 1982)	Pre–post Follow-up	66	Center	NS	13	Staff only
The DEBT Project (Macy, Solomon, Schoen, & Galey, 1983)	Pre–post Follow-up	103	Home	Xs = 14.9– 19.7	13–15	Parents only
Institute for Psychophysiological and Speech Disorders (Fitzgerald, Brajović, Radicević, Djurdjević, Djurdjić, Novak, Bojanović, 1980)	Treatment study: parents	48	Home and center	NS	12	Parents and staff

Program	Study type	N	Setting	Age range	Duration (months)	Participants
Parent Education Home Program (Moxley-Haegert & Serbin, 1983)	Treatment study: parents	39 (13)	Home	4–36	12 (1 yr. follow-up)	Parents only
Teaching Skills Inventory Program (Infants) (Rosenberg & Robinson, 1985)	Treatment study: parents	16	Center	3–34	Max = 14	Parents only
Parent Training Program (Sandler, Coren & Thurman, 1983)	Treatment study: parents	21	Center	24–68	3	Parents only
University of Hull Pre-School Intervention (Sandow & Clarke, 1978; Sandow, Clark, Cox, & Stewart, 1981)	Treatment study: parents	32 (15)	Home	$X = 30$	36	Parents and staff
Children's Hospital of Philadelphia (Goodman, Cecil, & Barker, 1984)	Treatment study: comparison group	35 (36)	Center	$X = 33.7$	16	Parents and staff
Oregon Mental Health Division Preschool Study (Moore, Fredericks, & Baldwin, 1981)	Treatment study: comparison group	83 (68)	Center	36–60	12–24	Staff only
Dubnoff Center Program (Tymchuk, Dahlman, & Asher, 1981)	Treatment study: comparison group	35	Center	$Xs = 47.2$–54.2	8	Parents and staff
Optimal Learning Environments (Warren, Alpert, & Kaiser, 1986)	Curriculum comparison	20	Center	3–36	NS	Staff only

Table 2. (*cont.*)

Project (study citation)	Design	N^a (Control)	Type of Intervention	Age of entry^b in mo	Length in mo	Who delivers intervention to the child
Projects for children with Down syndrome						
Preston Institute of Technology (Clunies-Ross, 1979)	Developmental patterns	36	Home and center	3–37	4–24	Parents and staff
Down's Syndrome Infant–Parent Program (Hanson, 1981; Hanson & Schwarz, 1978)	Developmental patterns	15	Center	NS	24.4	Parents only
Early Intervention Programmes (Piper, Gosselin, Gendron, & Mazer, 1986)	Developmental patterns	32	Home	6–24	Max = 24	Parents only
Jerusalem Child Development Center (Sharav & Shlomo, 1986)	Developmental patterns	51	Home and center	Birth	72	Parents and staff
Clwyd Home Advisory Service for Families (Woods, Corney, & Pryce, 1984)	Developmental patterns	28	Home	0–24	6–30	Parents only
Early Intervention Program (Connolly, Morgan, Russell, & Richardson, 1980; Connolly, Morgan, & Russell, 1984)	Comparison group	15 (36)	Center	NS	12–36	Parents only
Model Preschool Center for Handicapped Children (Hayden & Haring, 1977)	Comparison group	94	Center	20–162	24	Staff only

Study	Group	n[a]	Setting	Age of entry[b]	Duration (mo)	Who intervened
Early Education Project (Kysela, Hillyard, McDonald, & Ahlsten-Taylor, 1981)	Comparison group	22 8	Home Center	3–18 18–36	NS	Parents and staff
Kent County Council (Ludlow & Allen, 1979)	Comparison group	72 (112)	Center	NS	24	Parents and staff
Project Edge (Rynders & Horrobin, 1980)	Comparison group	17 (18)	Center	NS	60	Parents and staff
Swedish Developmental Training Prospective (Aronson & Fallstrom, 1977)	Comparison group	15 (8)	Residential	21–69	18	Staff only
McGill University (Piper & Pless, 1980)	Prospective comparison group	21 (16)	Center	X = 9.33	6	Parents and staff
Greater Manchester Program (Sloper, Glenn, & Cunningham, 1986)	Prospective comparison group	12 (11)	Home	9–12	9	Parents only

[a] Number who received intervention; number in contrast/control group included in parentheses

[b] Age of entry in months; range or mean

[c] Children in the studies probably overlap; no way to distinguish

[d] NS = not specified

Newcombe, & Bidder, 1983; Jelinek, 1985; LeLaurin, 1985; Oelwein, Fewell, & Pruess, 1985; Turner & Rogers, 1981; Wolery & Dyk, 1985; Zeitlin, 1981). Each of the studies constructed and/or tested the indices in slightly different ways. Nevertheless, according to empirical tests conducted by Rosenberg et al. (1987), the particular means of constructing the rate of development is unimportant; they are all highly intercorrelated.

All of the projects report higher rates of development while children were involved in the treatment than the children had displayed before intervention, but there are several problems with the logic of a rate of development measure. First, a "rate" of development cannot be constructed from one data point. Testing children at intake, deriving their mental ages, and dividing by chronological age is the procedure used to arrive at a preintervention rate of progress. The inherent assumption in this procedure is that development has been linear, even though there is good evidence that development is not linear for normally developing children (McCall, Appelbaum, & Hogarty, 1973; McCall, Eichorn, & Hogarty, 1977) and most unlikely to be linear for children who have suffered developmental insults and whose pattern is uneven across domains of development. The number of measurement occasions that would be necessary to construct an existing developmental growth curve with accuracy is not known; there is evidence that even 10 data points do not describe the curve accurately when plotted against already determined patterns of development (M. Appelbaum, personal communication, May, 1988).

Apart from statistical concerns, there are other problems with using rate of development as an index of evaluation. All the rates were based on a combination of "mental age" and chronological age (CA). The concept of mental age has presented problems for normally developing children; even when derived from the same test, mental ages at different ages are unstable and have different standard deviations. The prediction of mental age for handicapped children presents even greater problems. Brassell (1977) found pre–post correlations of .17 for the Bayley Psychomotor Scale and .29 for the Mental Scale after 10 months of intervention. Even if there had been a substantial effect for intervention, an increase in the mean should not have created such low correlations between pre- and posttesting. In the Wolery and Dyk (1985) project, the older children (CA around 40 months) had higher rates of development than the younger children (CA around 20 months) before intervention began. Younger children may lag further behind for a while as they adjust to their particular handicap and then may move ahead more rapidly as certain developmental systems are more under control.

If investigators are serious about using the idea of rate of development, they must collect data from enough children with varying handicaps to construct projected developmental patterns, against which patterns obtained in specific programs could be compared. Without this information and in the absence of multiple assessment occasions, using a rate of development index is no better than using pre–post scores alone.

DIFFERENTIAL AREAS OF DEVELOPMENT. In an attempt to go beyond pre–post comparisons, five of the studies (from four projects) compared children's progress in different areas of development (Barna et al., 1980; Cocks, 1982; Hewitt et al., 1983; Kaminer & Chinitz, 1982; Turner & Rogers, 1982). This is a promising approach; it is conceivable, for example, that intervention programs are more successful in certain domains of development than they are on overall scores. Unfortunately, these studies are more illustrative of the difficulties in such an effort than they are of its value. One problem in summarizing the finding is that the populations and interventions vary. If the interventions provided had been even remotely similar and the measurement devices somewhat related, a comparison across studies of the reactions of children with different conditions would have been helpful. However, the populations, the intervention approaches, *and* the length of the intervention varied considerably in the five studies. For example, after 3 months of intervention, Hewitt et al. (1983) found no progress for any of their groups on motor skills, whereas after 6 months of intervention, Cocks (1982) found the greatest gain in the motor area. One possible conclusion, of course, is that one should intervene longer in order to affect motor skills. Unfortunately, after 6 months of intervention, Kaminer and Chinitz (1982) achieved no gains in the motor area; yet they did record gains in self-help, an area unaffected by the program of Hewitt et al.

An additional problem in knowing how to interpret this work is that skill areas are measured differently in each of the studies. Several made up their own skill assessment inventories, and then divided the skills into variable numbers of groups, from 4 to 12. It is impossible to draw conclusions from this work when the skills being assessed are different or, if they are the same, are grouped differently for the purpose of assessing gain.

LONG-TERM FOLLOW-UP. Another variation of the pre–post design is pre–post assessment with long-term follow-up (Karnes, Schwedel, Lewis, Ratts, & Esry, 1981; Koen, Musumeci, & Toole, 1982; Macy, Solomon, Schoen, & Galey, 1983; Zeitlin, 1981). Longitudinal data can be most helpful to program developers, indicating areas in need of improvement in the programs. Without comparison groups, however, these studies suffer from the same general problems as the other pre–post designs. Two of the most comprehensive follow-up attempts both used placement in a mainstream setting as the outcome measure (Karnes et al., 1981; Koen et al., 1982). From 50% to 80% of the children were placed in regular mainstreamed elementary classrooms. The difference in percentage placement is probably due more to a difference in populations served than to the effectiveness of the intervention. When children left each of these programs the teachers recommended specific types of subsequent placements. The prediction "error" rates (recommendations for regular placements that later had to become special placements) were similar in the two projects, 12% and 8% respectively. Zeitlin's program (1981) achieved a comparable rate of 64% regular education placement for 36 children; she did not report her error rate.

All of these longitudinal studies had a substantial proportion of children whose handicaps were considered mild, at risk, or borderline; one wonders whether the successfully transitioned children came disproportionately from these subgroups than from those that were more moderately or severely impaired. Clearly more longitudinal work is needed, not just to evaluate programs, but to provide information about ways children could be better prepared to handle mainstreamed classrooms or to adjust to special placements.

CONCLUSION. In general, studies that have used pre–post assessments on a single group show gains in the children's skills at the end of the program and achievement long-term. These gains, however, are not always reflected in increased developmental quotients (indices that take mental age, chronological age, and the norm group into consideration), nor are they found in all areas of development. With no other children to which to compare the gains that were achieved, it is difficult to evaluate the success of these projects. There is no evidence that any particular programs were *more* successful than any others. Finding appropriate comparison groups for disabled children is an extremely difficult task, one that meets with great legal and ethical resistance if it means withholding services. Bricker and Sheehan (1981) have made excellent suggestions about how different kinds of comparison groups could be set up for children with disabilities. In the next section, studies are reviewed that made use of various types of internal control groups.

Treatment studies with mixed population programs

PARENT INTERVENTION PROGRAMS. Eleven projects reported comparative data assessing parent involvement, comparison groups, or different types of curricula. Of these 11 projects, 5 were studies comparing different levels and types of parent involvement (Fitzgerald et al., 1980; Moxley-Haegert & Serbin, 1983; Rosenberg & Robinson, 1985; Sandler, Coren, & Thurman, 1983; Sandow & Clarke, 1978; Sandow, Clarke, Cox, & Stewart, 1981). Fitzgerald et al. (1980) concluded that their work in Yugoslavia showed that parents were likely to be the most effective therapists (especially if both mother and father were involved) and that the home was a better rearing environment for mastery of skills by mentally retarded children. Although this study involved large numbers of children, the way it is reported makes it difficult to assess the reliability of these findings. For example, comparisons are provided between children who are reared at home, in home–nursery combinations, and in foundling homes. Comparisons are made as well among children who have only professional therapists, who have one parent as therapist, or who have both parents as therapists. In none of these comparisons was information given on similarities or differences among the groups of infants on such measures as developmental status and diagnosis. Nor was information provided on the relationship of the two major areas of comparison. Were the children who had only professional therapists also the children who were in the foundling home? The data look convincing, but clearer reporting would have led to less equivocal conclusions.

Several studies examined what parents in intervention programs are asked to do with their infants and how much individualized and specific feedback they are given. In general, it appears that developmentally based approaches (i.e., those that train parents to recognize small developmental progressions in their children) are the most effective, especially if they are coupled with specific feedback to the parents on interacting with their own children. Moxley-Haegert and Serbin (1983) randomly assigned parents to one of three conditions: those who received developmental education, those who received general child management training, and those who received home visits but no parent education. After 4 weeks of training, children in the developmental education group were demonstrating more of the targeted skills than the other two groups; moreover, 9–15 months later the occupational therapist reported those parents to be participating more in carrying out home intervention activities.

Rosenberg and Robinson (1985) assessed the effect of targeted intervention through a multiple baseline study. They used videotapes of mothers playing with their babies prior to the introduction of specific training suggestions based on the actual behaviors observed during the videotaped sessions. A repeated measures analysis of variance established a significant change across time. There were no changes in mothers' behaviors during the preintervention phase, but a significant change when the specific intervention was introduced. Prior to the focused training, parents had been receiving a standard home visitation curriculum, one that emphasized developmental content and used the home visitor as a model. The dramatic increase in quality of parenting behavior and child interest following an intervention that was more specific to the dyad makes one question the utility of general, homogenous, home visit programs, even when developmentally based.

Sandler et al. (1983) tried a similar approach but did not obtain the same dramatic results. In the Sandler et al. study, data are presented following only three months of intervention and without videotape feedback, which may account for its lack of success. It does suggest that the Rosenberg and Robinson (1985) study should be replicated carefully to determine if the findings can be achieved by others.

Sandow et al. (1981) compared different levels of parent intervention over a longer time period (3 years) and concluded that intense visiting (2–3 hours per week) produced more change in children than less intense visiting (2–3 hour visits every 2 months) but that these differences disappeared after the second year. They suggest that the intensity of parent intervention "should gradually decrease as parents become capable of taking charge" (p. 140), and that the eventual withdrawal of the therapist should indicate confidence in the parents' ability to carry on independently.

Parent intervention is a key component of most of the 29 projects that involved a mixed population of children, yet only these five attempted to assess variations in how or what actually was delivered to the parents. Three of these (Moxley-Haegert & Serbin, 1983; Rosenberg & Robinson, 1985; and Sandow et al., 1981) are carefully reported studies that should be helpful to practitioners. Together they suggest that intervention should focus on helping parents become better observers of their children, and should be accompanied by directed attention to the particular child and parent. Given the individual variations among most children with disabilities, this seems to be a sensible approach. Moreover, as parents develop skills in working with their children, the home visitor should gradually retreat and allow the parents to become more independent. One would hope that similar issues important in planning parent involvement would also be assessed by researchers and practitioners so that other generalizations could be reported.

COMPARISON GROUP STUDIES. Three studies involved comparing children in intervention programs to groups that did not receive intervention (Goodman, Cecil, & Barker, 1984; Moore, Fredericks, & Baldwin, 1981; Tymchuk, Dahlman, & Asher, 1981). All three of these studies indicate that the provision of treatment was linked to better outcomes for children with disabilities when compared to children who received little or no intervention. What two of them also indicate is the difficulty of finding appropriate contrast groups in order to make this determination. For example, in the Tymchuk et al. (1981) study, children in the contrast group were much less disabled at the time of their first assessment than either of the treatment groups, suggesting that children were taken into the program on the basis of the severity of their handicap and the immediacy of their needs. Moore et al. (1981) also used a retrospective contrast group, choosing children at school age who had not had preschool. The reason that these children had not had preschool, however, is of paramount importance. If it was because their parents were uninterested, unmotivated, or unwilling, that factor could be a more important influence on outcome than any particular preschool or curriculum.

Goodman et al. (1984) had the advantage of access to a large hospital population; although random assignment was not possible, they were able to match their intervention population with a group receiving treatment in community preschools that did not emphasize parent involvement. Children's Hospital in Philadelphia, where Goodman et al. carried out the research, strongly focused on parental involvement. This more intensively treated group made significantly more progress after 16 months than children in the other projects. Because of the care taken in matching, this was the best treated comparison study we found.

Another means of creating contrast groups is to admit all children to the intervention program, but then to assign them to different kinds of curricula. The three studies that attempted to carry out this type of design are reviewed.

CURRICULUM COMPARISONS. Three studies directly assessed the effects of different curricula. Revill and Blunden (1979) conducted a delayed introduction study of the Portage curriculum using the South Glamorgan Home Advisory Service population about whom we have included two other studies. Taking two areas of the community, they collected 2 months of baseline data for one group and 4 months of baseline for the other before focusing the home visits on skills derived from Portage. In both cases, the rate of acquisition of Portage checklist skills increased faster after the service was introduced. The Portage checklist skills, however, did not translate into much higher scores on the Griffiths for the children.

Brassell and Dunst (1978) studied the impact of a Piagetian-focused curriculum on children's object-relations during the Western Carolina home visit intervention program. Concerns about this study include the reason 24 children were chosen from the 91 to receive the special focus and why, since all children eventually were given the curriculum, further data were not collected to demonstrate the general effectiveness of the program. It should be possible in a large intervention program such as the Western Carolina Infant Program to assign children randomly to a new curricular approach at different times and to collect comparative data from all groups as the curriculum is introduced.

Warren, Alpert, and Kaiser (1986) did not obtain measures of child development outcomes but focused instead on differences in the delivery of the intervention and child engagement in classrooms with different curricular foci. They found that teachers using their Optimal Learning Environment model spent a far greater proportion of the day teaching, and the children in those classrooms were more engaged with their teachers or materials than was found in two contrast classrooms without a specialized approach. This is a good implementation study, showing that a curriculum is actually being carried out as planned. Now one would like to see data on the consequences of intervening in that fashion for the children.

The work on comparative curriculum is disappointing. Whereas there are legitimate disagreements among professionals on the best way to work with disabled children, most of the studies seem to be done only by those who believe in a particular approach. Karnes et al. (1981) have argued, on the other hand, that the particular curriculum content is less important than the general approach, which should be focused, specific, and intense for individual children.

Programs for children with Down syndrome

GENERAL OVERVIEW. Children with Down syndrome present a special case of exceptional development. They are identifiable at birth, and the prevalence of the disorder is high enough to yield adequate numbers of children for study. Nevertheless, conclusions about patterns of development to be expected of children with Down syndrome are hard to draw. It appears that females make better progress than males (Piper, Gosselin, Gendron, & Mazer, 1986; Rynders & Horrobin, 1980; Sharav & Shlomo, 1986; Woods, Corney, & Pryce, 1984), but most studies do not report testing for sex differences, and it is not clear from the four that demonstrated differences what could account for them (e.g., physiologic differences, parental reactions, general male vulnerability).

Available studies disagree on the pattern of developmental growth for children with Down syndrome. Three investigators found evidence of a rapid decline for the children in developmental attainments, but cite different patterns: The decline persists either until 15 months, the last age tested by Piper and Pless (1980); until 18 months in the work by Sharav and Sholmo (1986) when it reversed until age 5 years; or until age 36 months (Ludlow & Allen, 1979). Woods et al. (1984) argue for the evidence of a quadratic function with the lowest point in development at 30–40 months when the trend reverses. However, other studies (Hayden & Haring, 1977; Clunies-Ross, 1979) find generally lower functioning but no decline, and in one case actually cite an increase in developmental attainments (Hayden & Haring, 1977). Berry, Gunn, and Andrews (1984) have been tracking the progress of 39 Down syndrome children during their first 5 years of life. All are home-raised; Berry et al. (1984) are not involved in intervention. Their careful assessment efforts suggest generally lower functioning for Down syndrome children, but no decline. Theirs is probably the best recent longitudinal data available.

Generally, the areas of development that seem most affected are motor, language, and personal–social. It is also clear that the variation among children with Down syndrome is more extreme than in normally developing children. Compared to children without disabilities, the standard deviations are larger and the range within which various milestones are achieved is much greater. Thus, some of the difficulty in plotting an accurate developmental function must be due to small samples, the lack of uniformity within the population, and different developmental areas emphasized by different assessment devices.

COMPARING PROGRESS TO DEVELOPMENTAL NORMS. In the absence of any control group, several investigators assessed the effectiveness of their intervention programs by comparing the progress of the children in the program to norms that had been reported earlier in the literature from Down syndrome children who were reared at home but without any specific intervention (e.g., Carr, 1975). All argue that the children in their programs made more progress than would have been expected and that therefore the interventions were successful (Hanson, 1981; Hanson & Schwarz, 1978; Kysela, Hillyard, McDonald, & Ahlsten-Taylor, 1981; Sharav & Shlomo, 1986; Woods et al., 1984).

Given the lack of agreement already noted among studies that have more recently attempted to plot developmental functions for children with Down syndrome, such comparisons are neither sufficient nor even meaningful. It might be possible for a collaborative effort to be mounted, patterned after the efforts of Berry et al. (1984), to collect data from enough Down syndrome children to constitute a large standardization sample; it is probable that the range of "normal" for these children would turn out to be so large that most of the differences found in the studies cited would appear to be normal variations.

COMPARISON GROUP STUDIES. Eight of the projects reported findings from comparison groups, and these can be divided again into those five that constituted a comparison group after the fact or had no control over who was included in the group and those three prospective studies that provided for group assignment before treatment began. Kysela et al. (1981) compared children who began intervention at a younger age to the entry skills of older children; this approach makes an unwarranted assumption – that children whose parents enroll them in early intervention programs are the same as those whose parents do not. The same criticism holds for Hayden and Haring (1977) and Ludlow and Allen (1979). In the Ludlow and Allen project, parents actually had refused to participate in the early intervention project, making it absolutely certain they were different to begin with. The comparison children in Hayden and Haring are never described in enough detail to know why they did not participate in an early intervention program.

Rynders and Horrobin (1980) used a distal comparison group from another city where an intervention program was not offered. That comparison did not yield positive findings, leading them to conclude that the intervention had been a failure.

The work by Connolly and her colleagues represents an ambitious effort to follow both a treated and controlled group from infancy through age nine (Connolly, Morgan, & Russell, 1984; Connolly, Morgan, Russell, & Richardson, 1980). The treatment provided was an extensively developed physical therapy approach with the children, focusing on early locomotor development. Initially there were 40 in the intervention program; 20 were assessed at age four and a half, 14 were tested at age nine. One of the first problems with this work concerns sample attrition, especially the first time when parents were dropped for not being able to continue consistently with the educational program.

The children treated were compared in the first study to 53 who had not participated in the program, but who otherwise were not described. By the second follow-up, there were only 36 control children left with no explanation of what happened to the others. Although significant differences were found at age nine between the treated and the comparison groups on IQ scores, Vineland Scores, and in the percentage of children in various categories of retardation, even Connolly et al. (1984) conclude that "we are dealing, then, with a select sample of the original group of children whose parents are generally highly motivated, as reflected by their pursuit of appropriate educational programs and their participation in this follow-up study" (p. 1518). Given that condition, it is difficult to accept differences in the children's development as being due to the intervention.

Three studies of children with Down syndrome created a matched control group from the same population as the treated group before treatment began (Aronson & Fallstrom, 1977; Piper & Pless, 1980; Sloper, Glenn, & Cunningham, 1986). In two of these there were immediate effects in favor of the treatment; Piper and Pless, on the other hand, found no immediate effects. In none of the three were there long-term effects. The absence of long-term effects led Sloper et al. (1986) to conclude that the intensive training provided was "neither altering the processes that lie behind development nor accelerating development by reducing cumulative handicaps" (p. 158).

CONCLUSION. It is clear that in no prospective study has any particular intervention effect been established for children with Down syndrome. Rather, individual programs have only been "validated" by reference to comparison groups that are demonstrably different from the treated group, or through a comparison to published norms that have not been appropriately standardized on a large enough population of children with Down syndrome. Therefore, in the research conducted so far, the evidence for the superiority of any particular treatment of Down syndrome children is inconclusive. A similar conclusion was reached in earlier reviews by Simeonsson, Cooper, and Scheiner (1982) and Gibson and Fields (1984). Each review, however, interpreted that conclusion differently. Simeonsson et al. argued for a greater use of the clinical study model, in effect concluding that the concentration on achieving effects through parametric designs is futile. Gibson and Fields strongly urged the development of interventions that are focused on the interaction of the physical and psychological aspects of the syndrome and that are tested rigorously through more sophisticated multivariate analyses.

A third position seems more appropriate. Despite efforts in a variety of domains (physical, linguistic, social, cognitive), development comparable to normal children has not been achieved for children with Down syndrome. With deinstitutionalization, the developmental pattern for this syndrome has moved away from a prognosis of severe/profound retardation to a mild/moderate level of disability – a remarkable accomplishment. Perhaps the field of early intervention should concentrate now on those strategies that would prove most effective in supporting family adaptation as well as on the task of gathering information about the functional abilities of older children with Down syndrome.

Measuring developmental progress in children with disabilities

Table 3 lists all the instruments that were used in the 42 intervention projects with handicapped children (29 for mixed populations and 13 for children with Down syndrome). Twenty different published instruments were used in studies with children in these projects; no instrument was used by more than 32% of the studies (the Bayley Scales of Infant Development was the instrument used most frequently, with the Stanford-Binet second). There was a heavy concentration on infant developmental measures; 31 projects used one of the seven measures that assess development in infancy.

In addition to the plethora of published instruments, a number of instruments were developed by various researchers and practitioners and were used by others in the field. Although these have not been formally published, they have been distributed beyond the boundaries of the projects that first used them. Eleven of these instruments are included in Table 3; 16 of the projects used them. In addition, 12 projects (or more than one-fourth of those surveyed) generated their own assessments of the children's development; eight that the staff completed, and four that were filled out by parents or teachers. Finally, three projects developed other ways of measuring the effectiveness of the intervention.

Obviously, using such a vast and varied number of instruments makes comparing projects difficult and summarizing across them for general effectiveness almost impossible. One factor that contributes to the lack of concentration on a single instrument, and probably to the temptation to continue developing new instruments, is the fact that none of the published general developmental instruments has been standardized on a disabled population. The justification for using instruments standardized on a normally developing population is that it is helpful to know how children with disabilities compare to children without disabilities. However, this justification has its problems.

First, good agreement is lacking among the "standard" instruments concerning when

Table 3. *Measurement instruments used in projects with handicapped children, in alphabetical order*

Instrument	Number of projects
Published instruments (norm-referenced)	
Alpern-Boll	2
Boehm Test of Basic Concepts	1
Bayley Scales of Infant Development	15
Bruininks Oseretsky Test of Motor Proficiency	2
Brunet-Lezine	1
Bzoch-League Receptive Expressive Emergent Language Scale	1
Cattell Infant Intelligence Scale	2
Denver Developmental Screening Test	1
Early Intervention Developmental Profile	1
Early Learning Accomplishment Profile	1
Gesell Developmental Scales	3
Griffiths Scales of Mental Development	8
McCarthy Scales of Children's Abilities	3
Merrill-Palmer Scale	1
Peabody Picture Vocabulary Test	4
Preschool Attainment Record	2
Portage Project Checklist	2
Reynell Developmental Language Scales	2
Stanford-Binet	11
Uzgiris-Hunt Ordinal Scales of Psychological Development	1
Vineland Social Maturity Scale	5
Unpublished instruments and their developers (local norms)	
The HI-COMP Curriculum Sequence (Willoughby-Herb, Neisworth, & Laub, 1977)	1
The Coping Inventory (Zeitlin, 1978)	1
Developmental Sequence Performance Inventory (Oelwein, Fewell, & Pruess, 1985)	1
Irrabeen Early Intervention Scales (Cocks, 1982)	1
Koontz Child Development Program (Koontz, 1974)	1
Perceptions of Developmental Skills (Bagnato, Eaves, & Neisworth, 1977)	1
Sewall Early Education Development Profile (Herst, Wolfe, & Jorgensen, 1975)	1
Student Progress Record (Moore, Fredericks, & Baldwin, 1981)	3
Uniform Performance Assessment System (White, Edgar, & Haring, 1978)	3
Vulpe Assessment Battery (Vulpe, 1979)	1

Table 3. *(cont.)*

Instrument	Number of projects
Program-generated developmental checklists (Hanson, 1981 and Hanson & Schwarz, 1978; Hayden & Haring, 1977; Hewitt, Newcombe, & Bidder, 1983; Kysela, Hillyard, McDonald, & Ahlsten-Taylor, 1981: Rynders & Horrobin, 1980; Sandler, Coren, & Thurman, 1983; Turner & Rogers, 1981; Zeitlin, 1981)	8
Program-generated parent-teacher ratings of child skills (Kaminer & Chinitz, 1982; Karnes, Schwedel, Lewis, Ratts, & Esry, 1981; Moore, Fredericks, & Baldwin, 1981)	4
Other measures Teaching Skills Inventory (Rosenberg & Robinson, 1985); Anecdotal Record Coding System (Shapiro, Gordon, & Neiditch, 1977); Classroom Observation Code (Warren, Alpert, & Kaiser, 1986)	3

certain skills are mastered. For example, walking independently is a later skill in the Griffiths (standardized on a fairly homogeneous United Kingdom sample) than it is on the Bayley (standardized on a mixed ethnic American sample). Therefore, a child with orthopedic disabilities looks more delayed when assessed with the Bayley than with the Griffiths.

Second, these tests are measuring what is ordinary, not what is critical. There are many attainments of normal children that can be measured precisely, especially under the psychometric pressure to make the number of items uniform at each age. However, not all of that precision is meaningful. Within the large number of skills measured there are likely to be only a few that are truly critical to future development (see Farran & Harber, 1989; and McCall et al., 1977, for further discussions of critical areas). These will probably be different for different developmental areas. Thus, if one were concerned about the future educability of a child, the critical skills to which to attend would likely be perceptual alertness, receptive language, and, later, expressive language. If one were concerned about a child's ambulatory capability, then the use of any of the several motor proficiency indices would be advised. A specific, single number (IQ or DQ) is of minimal value for children whose development is not proceeding smoothly across all areas; rather, it is more important to examine progress separately by developmental area.

Conclusion

Most parents of children with disabilities need support and guidance from experienced professionals. Most of the studies reviewed in this section have labored under the burden of proving they had some positive effect on specific skills, or of showing that the child would have fared less well had they not intervened. Studies to prove the effectiveness of the programs have been rushed; for most of the projects reviewed the length of intervention was less than 1 year, much shorter intervention time than disadvantaged children were given. Showing success over such a short time span with children whose problems are often severe is expecting a great deal. Moreover, some children will never show substantial improvement; the field should not be judged by how far along it moves all the of the children it serves or how much children with disabilities improve in a few months time. If such a judgment were made, services could be denied to families who are most in need, those coping with severely impaired, retarded, and multiply handicapped children.

COMMON ISSUES

Theoretical rationale

Meisels (1985) observed that one of the difficulties of summarizing data across intervention projects is that they do not derive from comparable theories about the process of development. The studies included in this review reflect an astounding number of different ideas about what needs to be "fixed" or helped through the intervention process. For disadvantaged children, efforts range from general intervention, to a nursery school approach, to targeted language instruction, to parent support groups, to direct, focused instruction at elementary school age. For children with disabilities examples of interventions include focusing on parental interactions, providing sensorimotor experiences, and developing Piagetian-based concepts.

It is clear that precise solutions for the most appropriate form of intervention for children with disabilities have not been found. Most services are based on a "good idea" for the most part, not on empirically established treatment approaches. It could be argued that many of the studies reviewed here were designed to generate data that would demonstrate their effectiveness. However, the studies are generally too poorly done to yield reliable information, and almost none of them has been replicated. Little information is available in these studies that would support focusing intervention on any one of the approaches tried over the others. As Simeonsson (1985) pointed out, the enthusiasm of proponents for one type of intervention or another is not matched by data supporting their efforts. Those who are working with handicapped children should be drawn into an even tighter network (like the one established by the Handicapped Children's Early Education Programs) for the purpose of exchanging information and insights. The data collected should not be restricted to mean-outcome data, but to data related to the questions posed by Sheehan and Gallagher (1983), and Anastasiow (1986), seeking to determine for whom the program worked best and under what conditions. It ought to be possible to centralize assessment of program effectiveness through the use of common procedures and measurement instruments.

No breakthrough has been reported regarding the appropriate focus for intervention with disadvantaged children either. Services have most commonly focused on changes within individual children, and occasionally their parents, in an effort to strengthen the individual to face the continuing exigencies of poverty, poorly run public schools, and bleak life chances (Farran, 1982). Yet, most would agree that it is the surrounding environment that places the child at risk for school failure and retardation (Ogbu, 1986; Wilson, 1987).

An alternative approach for minority children, best exemplified by the work at the Kamehameha Schools in Hawaii, is to "tinker" with the educational environment, assessing carefully along the way, until the right approach for helping children achieve is found (Au, 1980; Kawakami-Arakai, Oshiro, & Farran, 1988; Farran, 1988; Tharpe et al., 1984). This program had the luxury of assured funding during an experimental phase in which a variety of approaches could be tried in the classrooms until one was found that consistently raised children's achievement scores closer to the national norm.

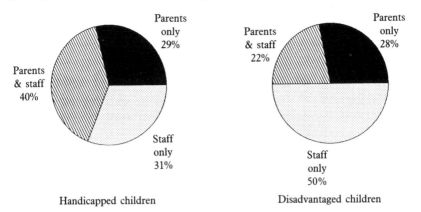

Figure 1. Who delivers intervention to children in preschool intervention projects

If there are going to be more preschool programs for the disadvantaged, then there will need to be more experimentation with the type of teaching and educational environment provided both at the preschool and school-age levels. Much more serious attention has to be paid to the environmental side of the child–environment interaction. For too long, attention has been focused almost exclusively on the child.

Parent involvement

Figure 1 provides a comparison of the 42 intervention programs for disabled children and the 32 programs for disadvantaged children in terms of the amount of parental involvement in intervention activities they include in the program. Programs were characterized by whether the intervention was delivered to the children only by the staff, only by the parents (staff worked with parents and then the parents worked with their children), or by a combination of staff and parents (staff worked with children, and also instructed parents in intervention techniques for the children). The classification of each program is provided in Tables 1 and 2.

Different philosophies appear to have guided the type of interventions planned for the two groups of children. Frequently in programs for disadvantaged children, the parents are seen as part of the problem; children are enrolled in the programs on the basis of low maternal IQ and/or education, previous parent and sibling involvement in special education placement, or other indices that indicate poor achievement on the part of the parents. Trained staff members, therefore, are seen to be the best deliverers of intervention. When parents are involved, it is most often as a recipient of general home visits once per week from the teachers in the program, as in the Perry Preschool (Lazar & Darlington, 1982), or as demonstrators of how to play more appropriately with materials, as in Slaughter (1983) and Levenstein (1970). One exception to this pattern is the very focused and successful intervention of Slater (1986) that concentrated on specific verbal interaction patterns following story reading and story telling.

In general, equal participation of parents and professionals in determining the intervention approaches with the children is not a part of these projects. In fact, the disadvantaged infant has probably not demonstrated any problems to "solve" through intervention; these projects are *preventive*, and everything in the child's normal environment, sometimes especially the parents, is viewed as a probable contributor to poor long-term development without intervention.

A different attitude prevails in programs for disabled children. There the *child* is viewed as the problem; the child has a disability, a physical reason that purportedly explains why interactions with the parent will be different from those of normally developing children. Staff members are seen as models, people who by virtue of training and experience know more about a particular handicapping condition than the parents under any circumstances. Thus, only one-fourth to one-third of the programs for disabled children relied *solely* on professional staffs to provide the intervention. In these programs, parental visitation to the program sites is often mandatory, and the staff observes and feeds back to parents on a regular basis suggestions about their interaction with the child. Parents in such programs are considered to be the most appropriate intervenors for their handicapped children. Moreover, the goal of these programs is to teach parents the skills that will make appropriate, compensatory behavior possible, that is, those skills that relate to the child's particular disability (e.g., diapering a child with cerebral palsy; motor exercises for children with Down syndrome, etc.).

CONCLUSION

Reviews of intervention effectiveness have usually focused either on children who are disabled biologically or those considered vulnerable by virtue of their social and economic environment. It is appropriate to maintain that distinction.

For the physically disabled, there is a biological trajectory (to use Clarke & Clarke's [1988] phrase) that limits the impact of the social environment. Although it is true that more impact from the social environment has been demonstrated since deinstitutionalization than anyone would have suspected, for many children normal development cannot be the goal. Rather, the goal is to improve their adaptation within the limits of their disability. Innovative treatment approaches should continue to receive research funding, but only if there are clear expectations that the design and procedures will dramatically improve. There must not be a subsequent 10-year review that notes the same difficulties when drawing conclusions from this work. Small, precise, well-grounded studies should become the norm. Services, on the other hand, should be offered to all families of children with disabilities, and those service providers should not have to prove their right to exist through individually mounted evaluation efforts. Evaluation should be for the purpose of improving service and thus could be done in a comprehensive fashion on a contract basis.

It is also important to realize that children with disabilities themselves exert a profound influence on their social environments, environments that must adapt to accommodate their special needs. The adaptation of the physical and social environment is the area where interventionists may be the most helpful. Parents and teachers profit from the knowledge of professionals about specific ways to work with children with various disabilities. This work needs to be extended beyond the preschool years, to adolescence and adulthood. Providing information to parents and others at these later developmental periods is critical.

For children who are potentially at risk from a social environment that is less than adequate (the second trajectory that Clarke & Clarke [1988] define), most of the intervention efforts have focused on strengthening the individual child so that his or her growth curve can resist the impact of a negative social environment. When the intervention does not work, interventionists have a tendency to throw up their hands (at least privately) and to say, "What can you do? We can't be with the child 24 hours a day." In truth, the nation's social problems (drugs, delinquency, teenage pregnancy) and work force problems (school failure, drop-outs, adult illiteracy) cannot be solved simply through programs for its disadvantaged 4-year-olds. Currently, too much is expected of preschool intervention programs.

There is no doubt that with time to experiment, better curricular approaches could be found, approaches that would send children forward to kindergarten better prepared to manage the expectations of the public schools. Whether these programs can ever go beyond their "first-generation" effects into general dissemination has not been established by anyone. Even with an effective preschool program, a great deal of work remains to be done to guarantee the children that the schools will be ready to work with them when they enter. The most effective intervention for disadvantaged children may be making the early elementary schools accountable for teaching the children they have (Comer, 1980; Edmonds, 1986). No child should leave the fourth grade unable to read, and being able to read at fourth grade cannot be assured solely by one year of preschool.

Finally, for children whose social and economic environments threaten their development, intervention should focus more directly on those environments themselves: job training for parents, adult literacy sessions, parental support groups, and PTA groups in low-income schools that empower parents rather than disenfranchise them. These kinds of interventions are much more difficult, time-consuming, and possibly expensive than establishing preschool programs, but they may have more chance of lasting success. The cost of school failure for poor and minority children is so high that one would hope the country would find resources both to provide preschool and to strengthen their elementary school programs.

In summary, the provision of support to parents of biologically disabled children should not be open to debate. Further, systematic explorations are needed to determine how best to deliver specific interventions and which disabling conditions are most responsive to which kinds of programs. For the preschool child who is disadvantaged by poverty or family disorganization, the picture is less clear. Too much has been promised about preschool programs and their long-term effects. Much more has been promised than there are data to support. Children from low-income homes should have the same access to high-quality early child care and positive, productive elementary school experiences that children from middle income homes have – not because they will then be held accountable for any future problems they may encounter with jobs, the law, drugs, or the educational system, but because of equity and the established efficacy of these experiences. Problems that develop in adolescence and adulthood must be dealt with by the nation as a whole in a more coherent, systematic fashion.

REFERENCES

Anastasiow, N. (1986). The research base for early intervention. *Journal of the Division for Early Childhood, 10*, 99–105.
Andrews, S., Blumen-Chal, J., Johnson, D., Kahn, A., Ferguson, C., Lasater, T., Malone, P., & Wallace, D. (1982). The skills of mothering: A study of parent–child development centers. *Monographs of the Society for Research in Child Development, 47*(6, Serial No. 198).
Aronson, M., & Fallstrom, K. (1977). Immediate and long-term effects of development training in children with Down's syndrome. *Developmental Medicine and Child Neurology, 19*, 489–494.

Au, K. (1980). Participation structures in a reading lesson with Hawaiian children: Analysis of a culturally appropriate instructional event. *Anthropology and Education Quarterly, 11*, 91–115.

Avery, S. (1988, June 19). Center says state-aided preschools could help disadvantaged youngsters. *Greensboro News & Record*, pp. C1, C7.

Bagnato, S. J., Eaves, R. C., & Neisworth, J. T. (1977). *Perceptions of developmental skills: A multi-source rating profile of functional skills for the preschool child.* University Park: The Pennsylvania State University, HICOMP Preschool Project.

Bagnato, S. J., & Neisworth, J. T. (1980). The intervention efficiency index: An approach to preschool program accountability. *Exceptional Children, 46*, 264–269.

Bailey, E. J., & Bricker, D. (1985). Evaluation of a three-year early intervention demonstration project. *Topics in Early Childhood Special Education, 5*, 52–65.

Barna, S., Bidder, R. T., Gray, O. P., Clements, J., & Gardner, S. (1980). The progress of developmentally delayed pre-school children in a home-training scheme. *Child: Care, Health, and Development, 6*, 157–164.

Becker, W. C., & Gersten, R. (1982). A follow-up of a follow through: The later effects of the direct instruction method on children in 5th & 6th grades. *American Educational Research Journal, 19*, 75–92.

Beller, E. K. (1983). The Philadelphia Study: The impact of preschool on intellectual and socioemotional development. In The Consortium for Longitudinal Studies (Ed.), *As the twig is bent* (pp. 333–376). Hillsdale, NJ: L. Erlbaum.

Bereiter, C. (1986). Does direct instruction cause delinquency? *Early Childhood Research Quarterly, 1*, 289–292.

Bereiter, C., & Englemann, S. (1966). *Teaching the disadvantaged in the preschool.* Englewood Cliffs, NJ: Prentice-Hall.

Berry, P., Gunn, V. P., & Andrews, R. J. (1984). Development of Down's syndrome children from birth to five years. In J. M. Berg (Ed.), *Perspectives and progress in mental retardation: Vol. 1. Social, psychological, and educational aspects* (pp. 167–177). Austin, TX: PRO-ED.

Brassell, W. R. (1977). Intervention with handicapped infants: Correlates of progress. *Mental Retardation, 15*, 18–22.

Brassell, W. R., & Dunst, C. J. (1978). Fostering the object construct: Large scale intervention with handicapped infants. *American Journal of Mental Deficiency, 82*, 507–510.

Bricker, D., Bruder, M. B., & Bailey, E. (1982). Developmental integration of preschool children. *Analysis and Intervention in Developmental Disabilities, 2*, 207–222.

Bricker, D. D., & Dow, M. G. (1980). Early intervention with the young severely handicapped child. *Journal of the Association for the Severely Handicapped, 5*, 130–142.

Bricker, D., & Sheehan, R. (1981). Effectiveness of an early intervention program as indexed by measures of child change. *Journal of the Division for Early Childhood, 4*, 11–27.

Bryant, D., & Ramey, C. T. (1985). Prevention-oriented infant education programs. In M. Frank (Ed.), *Infant intervention programs: Truths and untruths* (pp. 17–35). Binghampton, NY: Haworth Press.

Carr, J. (1975). *Young children with Down's syndrome: Their development, upbringing, and effect on their families.* London: Butterworth.

Casto, G., & Mastropieri, M. (1986a). The efficacy of early intervention programs: A meta-analysis. *Exceptional Children, 52*, 417–424.

Casto, G., & Mastropieri, M. (1986b). Much ado about nothing: A reply to Dunst and Snyder. *Exceptional Children, 53*, 277–279.

Casto, G., & Mastropieri, M. (1986c). Strain and Smith do protest too much: A response. *Exceptional Children, 53*, 266–268.

Casto, G., & White, K. (1985). The efficacy of early intervention programs with environmentally at-risk infants. In M. Frank (Ed.), *Infant intervention programs: Truths and untruths* (pp. 37–50). Binghampton, NY: Haworth Press.

Clarke, A. M., & Clarke, A. D. B. (1988). The adult outcome of early behavioral abnormalities. *International Journal of Behavioral Development, 11*, 3–19.

Clunies-Ross, G. G. (1979). Accelerating the development of Down's syndrome infants and young children. *The Journal of Special Education, 13*, 169–177.

Cocks, E. (1982). Measures of outcome in an early intervention program. *Australia and New Zealand Journal of Developmental Disabilities, 8*, 15–20.

Comer, J. P. (1980). Relationship between school and family – Policy implications of an inner-city school program. In R. Haskins & J. J. Gallagher (Eds.), *Care and education of young children in America.* Norwood, NJ: Ablex Publishing.

Committee for Economic Development. (1987). *Children in need: Investment strategies for the educationally disadvantaged.* New York: Author.

Connolly, B. H., Morgan, S., & Russell, F. F. (1984). Evaluation of children with Down syndrome who participated in an early intervention program. Second follow-up study. *Physical Therapy, 64,* 1515–1519.

Connolly, B., Morgan, S., Russell, F. F., & Richardson, B. (1980). Early intervention with Down syndrome children. Follow-up report. *Physical Therapy, 60,* 1405–1408.

Curtis, A., & Blatchford, P. (1981). Meeting the needs of socially handicapped children. *Educational Research, 24,* 31–42.

Dunst, C. J. (1986). Overview of the efficacy of early intervention programs. In L. Bickman & D. Weatherford (Eds.), *Evaluating early intervention programs for severely handicapped children and their families.* Austin, TX: PRO-ED.

Dunst, C., & Rheingrover, R. (1982). An analysis of the efficacy of infant intervention programs with organically handicapped children. *Evaluation and Program Planning, 4,* 287–383.

Dunst, C. J., & Snyder, S. W. (1986). A critique of the Utah State University early intervention meta-analysis research. *Exceptional Children, 53,* 269–276.

Edmonds, R. (1986). Characteristics of effective schools. In U. Neisser (Ed.), *The school achievement of minority children* (pp. 93–104). Hillsdale, NJ: L. Erlbaum.

Epstein, A., & Weikart, D. (1979). *The Ypsilanti-Carnegie infant education project.* (Monographs of the High/Scope Educational/Research Foundation, No. 6). Ypsilanti, MI: High/Scope.

Farnworth, M., Schweinhart, L., & Berrueta-Clement, J. (1985). Preschool intervention, school success and delinquency in a high-risk sample of youth. *American Educational Research Journal, 22,* 445–464.

Farran, D. C. (1982). Alternative approaches to intervention with poor children. In L. Feagans & D. C. Farran (Eds.), *The language of children reared in poverty.* New York: Academic Press.

Farran, D. C. (1988). *Reform in kindergarten: A multidisciplinary approach.* (Technical report available from the Center for Development of Early Education, Kamehameha Schools/Bishop Estate, Honolulu, HI 96817)

Farran, D., & Harber, L. (1989). Responses to a learning task at six months and IQ test performance during the preschool years. *International Journal of Behavioral Development, 12,* 101–114.

Farran, D., Haskins, R., & Gallagher, J. (1980). Poverty and mental retardation: A search for explanations. In J. J. Gallagher (Ed.), *New directions for exceptional children* (Vol. 1, pp. 47–65). San Francisco: Jossey-Bass.

Field, T., Widmayer, S., Greenberg, R., & Stoller, S. (1982). Effects of parent training on teenage mothers and their infants. *Pediatrics, 69,* 703–707.

Finklestein, N. (1982). Aggression: Is it stimulated by day care? *Young Children, 37,* 3–9.

Fitzgerald, H. E., Brajović, C., Radicević, Z., Djurdjević, M., Djurdjić, S., Novak, J., & Bojanović, M. (1980). Home-based intervention for infants with developmental disorders. *Infant Mental Health Journal, 1,* 96–107.

Garber, H., & Heber, F. (1977). The Milwaukee Project: Indications of the effectiveness of early intervention in preventing mental retardation. In P. Mittler (Ed.), *Research to practice in mental retardation: Vol. I. Care and intervention* (pp. 119–127). Baltimore: University Park Press.

Gersten, R. (1986). Response to "Consequences of three preschool curriculum models through age 15." *Early Childhood Research Quarterly, 1,* 293–302.

Gersten, R., & Carnine, D. (1984). Direct instruction mathematics: A longitudinal evaluation of low-income elementary school students. *The Elementary School Journal, 84,* 395–407.

Gibson, D., & Fields, D. (1984). Early infant stimulation programs for children with Down syndrome: A review of effectiveness. *Advances in Developmental and Behavioral Pediatrics, 5,* 331–371.

Goodman, J. F., Cecil, H. S., & Barker, W. F. (1984). Early intervention with retarded children: Some encouraging results. *Developmental Medicine and Child Neurology, 26,* 47–55.

Gray, S. W., & Ramsey, B. K. (1985). Adolescent childbearing and high school completion. *Journal of Applied Developmental Psychology, 1,* 167–179.

Gray, S., Ramsey, B., & Klaus, R. (1983). The early training project 1962–1980. In The Consortium for Longitudinal Studies (Ed.), *As the twig is bent* (pp. 33–70). Hillsdale, NJ: L. Erlbaum.

Gray, S., & Ruttle, K. (1980). The Family-Oriented Home Visiting Program: A longitudinal study. *Genetic Psychology Monographs, 102,* 299–316.

Hanson, M. (1981). Down's syndrome children: Characteristics and intervention research. In M. Lewis & L. A. Rosenblum (Eds.), *The uncommon child* (pp. 83–114). New York: Plenum Press.

Hanson, M. J., & Schwarz, R. H. (1978). Results of a longitudinal intervention program for Down's syndrome infants and their families. *Education and Training of the Mentally Retarded, 13*, 403–407.

Hart, B., & Risley, T. (1980). In vivo language intervention: Unanticipated general effects. *Journal of Applied Behavior Analysis, 13*, 407–432.

Haskins, R. (1985). Public school aggression among children with varying day-care experience. *Child Development, 56*, 689–703.

Hayden, A. H., & Haring, N. G. (1977). The acceleration and maintenance of development gains in Down's syndrome school-age children. In P. Mittler (Ed.), *Research to practice in mental retardation: Vol. 1. Care and intervention* (pp. 129–141). Baltimore: University Park Press.

Hebbeler, K. (1985). An old and a new question on the effects of early education for children from low income families. *Educational Evaluation and Policy Analysis, 7*, 207–216.

Herst, J., Wolfe, S., & Jorgensen, C. (1975). Sewall Early Education Development Profile. Denver: Sewall Rehabilitation Center.

Hewitt, K. E., Newcombe, R. G., & Bidder, R. T. (1983). Profiles of skill gain in delayed infants and young children. *Child: Care, Health, and Development, 9*, 127–135.

Honig, A., & Lally, R. (1982). The family development research project: A retrospective review. *Early Child Behavior and Care, 10*, 41–62.

Honig, A., Lally, R., & Mathieson, D. (1982). Personal-social adjustment of school children after 5 years in a family enrichment program. *Child Care Quarterly, 11*, 138–146.

Jelinek, J. A. (1985). A model of services for young handicapped children. *Language, Speech, and Hearing Services in Schools, 16*, 158–170.

Jester, R. E., & Guinagh, B. J. (1983). The Gordon Parent Education Infant and Toddler Program. In The Consortium for Longitudinal Studies (Ed.), *As the twig is bent* (pp. 103–132). Hillsdale, NJ: L. Erlbaum.

Kaminer, R. K., & Chinitz, S. P. (1982). Educational intervention with multiply handicapped preschool children. *Archives of Physical Medicine and Rehabilitation, 63*, 82–86.

Karnes, M. B., Schwedel, A. M., Lewis, G. F., Ratts, D. A., & Esry, D. R. (1981). Impact of early programming for the handicapped: A follow-up study into the elementary school. *Journal of the Division for Early Childhood, 4*, 62–79.

Kawakami-Arakaki, A., Oshiro, M., & Farran, D. C. (1988). *Research to practice: Integrating reading and writing in a kindergarten curriculum* (Tech. Rep. No.145). Champaign, IL: University of Illinois, Center for the Study of Reading.

Koen, S., Masumeci, M., & Toole, A. (1982). The long-range effects of the Regional Demonstration Program for Preschool Handicapped Children. *Journal of the Division for Early Childhood, 6*, 73–83.

Koontz, C. (1974). *Koontz Child Development Program.* Los Angeles: Western Psychological Services.

Kysela, G., Hillyard, A., McDonald, L., & Ahlsten-Taylor, J. (1981). Early intervention: Design and evaluation. In R. L. Schiefelbusch & D. D. Bricker (Eds.), *Early language: Acquisition and intervention* (pp. 341–388). Baltimore: University Park Press.

Lazar, I., & Darlington, R. (1982). Lasting effects of early education: A report from The Consortium for Longitudinal Studies. *Monographs of the Society for Research in Child Development, 47* (2–3, Serial No. 195).

LeLaurin, K. (1985). The experimental analysis of the effects of early intervention with normal, at-risk, and handicapped children under three. *Analysis and Intervention in Developmental Disabilities, 5*, 129–150.

Levenstein, P. (1970). Cognitive growth in preschoolers through verbal interaction with mothers. *American Journal of Orthopsychiatry, 40*, 426–432.

Levenstein, P., O'Hara, J., & Madden, J. (1983). The mother–child home program of the Verbal Interaction Project. In The Consortium for Longitudinal Studies (Ed.), *As the twig is bent* (pp. 237–264). Hillsdale, NJ: L. Erlbaum.

Ludlow, J. R., & Allen, L. M. (1979). The effect of early intervention and pre-school stimulus on the development of the Down syndrome child. *Journal of Mental Deficiency Research, 23*, 29–44.

Macy, D. J., Solomon, G. S., Schoen, M., & Galey, G. S. (1983). The DEBT Project: Early intervention for handicapped children and their parents. *Exceptional Children, 49*, 447–448.

Maisto, A., & German, M. (1979). Variables related to progress in a parent infant training program for high-risk infants. *Journal of Pediatric Psychology, 4,* 409–419.

McCall, R. B., Applebaum, M., & Hogarty, P. (1973). Developmental changes in mental performance. *Monographs of the Society for Research in Child Development, 38* (3, Serial No. 150).

McCall, R., Eichorn, D., & Hogarty, P. (1977). Transitions in early mental development. *Monographs of the Society for Research in Child Development, 42* (3, Serial No. 171).

McKay, H., Sinisterra, L., McKay, A., Gomez, H., & Lloreda, P. (1978). Improving cognitive ability in chronically deprived children. *Science, 200,* 270–278.

Meisels, S. J. (1985). The efficacy of early intervention: Why are we still asking this question? *Topics in Early Childhood Special Education, 5,* 1–11.

Meyer, L. (1984). Long-term academic effects of the direct instruction follow-through. *The Elementary School Journal, 84,* 380–394.

Meyer, L., Gersten, R., & Gutkin, J. (1983). Direct instruction: A project follow-through success story in an inner-city school. *The Elementary School Journal, 81,* 241–252.

Miller, L. B., & Bizzell, R. P. (1983). The Louisvile Experiment: A comparison of four programs. In The Consortium for Longitudinal Studies (Ed.), *As the twig is bent* (pp. 171–200). Hillsdale, NJ: L. Erlbaum.

Moore, M. G., Fredericks, H. D. B., & Baldwin, V. L. (1981). The long-range effects of early childhood education on a trainable mentally retarded population. *Journal of the Division for Early Childhood, 4,* 94–110.

Moxley-Haegert, L., & Serbin, L. (1983). Developmental education for parents of delayed infants: Effects on parental motivation and children's development. *Child Development, 54,* 1324–1331.

Oelwein, P. L., Fewell, R. R., & Pruess, J. B. (1985). The efficacy of intervention at outreach sites of the program for children with Down syndrome and other developmental delays. *Topics in Early Childhood Special Education, 5,* 78–87.

Ogbu, J. U. (1986). Castelike stratification as a risk factor for mental retardation in the United States. In D. C. Farran & J. D. McKinney (Eds.), *Risk in intellectual and psychosocial development* (pp. 83–120). New York: Academic Press.

Page, E., & Grandon, G. M. (1981). Massive intervention and child intelligence: The Milwaukee Project in critical perspective. *Journal of Special Education, 15,* 239–256.

Palmer, F. (1983). The Harlem Study: Effects by type of training, age of training and social class. In The Consortium for Longitudinal Studies (Ed.), *As the twig is bent* (pp. 201–236). Hillsdale, NJ: L. Erlbaum.

Piper, M. C., Gosselin, C., Gendron, M., & Mazer, B. (1986). Developmental profile of Down's syndrome infants receiving early intervention. *Child: Care, Health, and Development, 12,* 183–194.

Piper, M. C., & Pless, I. B. (1980). Early intervention for infants with Down syndrome: A controlled trial. *Pediatrics, 65,* 463–468.

Provence, S. (1985). On the efficacy of early intervention programs. *Journal of Developmental and Behavioral Pediatrics, 6,* 363–366.

Ramey, C., Bryant, D., Sparling, J., & Wasik, B. (1985). Project CARE: A comparison of two early intervention strategies to prevent retarded development. *Topics in Early Childhood Special Education, 5,* 12–25.

Ramey, C., & Campbell, F. (1984). Preventive education for high-risk children: Cognitive consequences of the Carolina Abecedarian Project. *American Journal of Mental Deficiency, 88,* 515–523.

Revill, S., & Blunden, R. (1979). A home training service for preschool developmentally handicapped children. *Behavior Research and Therapy, 17,* 207–214.

Rosen-Morris, D., & Sitkei, E. G. (1981). Strategies for teaching severely/profoundly handicapped infants and young children. *Journal of the Division for Early Childhood, 4,* 81–93.

Rosenberg, S. A., & Robinson, C. C. (1985). Enhancement of mothers' interactional skills in an infant education program. *Educating and Training of the Mentally Retarded, 20,* 163–169.

Rosenberg, S. A., Robinson, C. C., Finkler, D., & Rose, J. S. (1987). An empirical comparison of formulas evaluating early intervention program impact on development. *Exceptional Development, 54,* 213–219.

Rynders, J. E., & Horrobin, J. M. (1980). Educational provisions for young children with Down's syndrome. In J. Gottlieb (Ed.), *Educating mentally retarded persons in the mainstream* (pp. 109–147). Baltimore: University Park Press.

Sandler, A., Coren, A., & Thurman, S. K. (1983). A training program for parents of handi-capped preschool children: Effects upon mother, father, and child. *Exceptional Children, 49*, 355–358.

Sandow, S., & Clarke, A. (1978). Home intervention with parents of severely subnormal, preschool children: An interim report. *Child: Care, Health, and Development, 4*, 29–39.

Sandow, S. A., Clarke, A., Cox, M., & Stewart, F. (1981). Home intervention with parents of severely subnormal children: A final report. *Child: Care, Health, and Development, 7*, 135–144.

Schorr, L. (1988). *Within our reach: Breaking the cycle of disadvantage.* New York: Anchor Press.

Schweinhart, L., Berrueta-Clement, J., Barnett, S., Epstein, A., & Weikart, D. (1985). Effects of the Perry Preschool Program on youths through age 19: A summary. *Topics in Early Childhood Special Education, 5*, 26–35.

Schweinhart, L., & Weikart, D. (1983). The effects of the Perry Preschool Program on youths through age 15 – A summary. In The Consortium for Longitudinal Studies (Ed.), *As the twig is bent* (pp. 71–102). Hillsdale, NJ: L. Erlbaum.

Schweinhart, L., Weikart, D., & Larner, M. (1986a). Consequences of three preschool curricu-lum models through age 15. *Early Childhood Research Quarterly, 1*, 15–45.

Schweinhart, L. J., Weikart, D. P., & Larner, M. B. (1986b). Child-initiated activities in early childhood programs may help prevent delinquency. *Early Childhood Research Quarterly, 1*, 303–312.

Sharav, T., & Shlomo, L. (1986). Stimulation of infants with Down syndrome: Long-term effects. *Mental Retardation, 24*, 81–86.

Shapiro, L. P., Gordon, R., & Neiditch, C. (1977). Documenting change in young multiply handicapped children in a rehabilitation center. *The Journal of Special Education, 11*, 243–257.

Sheehan, R., & Gallagher, R. J. (1983). Methodological concerns in evaluating early intervention. *Diagnostique, 8*, 75–87.

Shonkoff, J. P., & Hauser-Cram, P. (1987). Early intervention for disabled infants and their families: A quantitative analysis. *Pediatrics, 80*, 650–658.

Sigel, I. E. (1971). Language of the disadvantaged: The distancing hypothesis. In C. S. Lavatelli (Ed.), *Language training in early childhood education* (pp. 60–76). Urbana: University of Illinois Press.

Simeonsson, R. (1982). Intervention accountability efficiency indices: A rejoinder. *Exceptional Children, 4*, 358–359.

Simeonsson, R. (1985). Efficacy of eary intervention: Issues and evidence. *Analysis and Interven-tion in Developmental Disabilities, 5*, 203–209.

Simeonsson, R., Cooper, D., & Scheiner, A. (1982). A review and analysis of the effectiveness of early intervention programs. *Pediatrics, 69*, 635–641.

Slater, M. (1986). Modification of mother–child interaction processes in families with children at-risk for mental retardation. *American Journal of Mental Deficiency, 91*, 257–267.

Slaughter, D. (1983). Early intervention and its effects on maternal and child development. *Monographs of the Society for Research in Child Development, 48* (4, Serial No. 202).

Sloper, P., Glenn, S. M., & Cunningham, C. C. (1986). The effect of intensity training on sensori-motor development in infants with Down's syndrome. *Mental Deficiency Research, 30*, 149–162.

Smith, P., Dalgleish, M., & Herzmark, G. (1981). A comparison of the effects of fantasy play tutoring and skills tutoring in nursery classes. *International Journal of Behavioral Development, 4*, 421–441.

Snyder, S. (1988, April). *Structural features of meta-analysis data sets: Issues, evidence and recom-mendations.* Paper presented at the biennial meeting of the Conference of Human Develop-ment, Charleston, SC.

Steg, D., Vaidya, S., & Hamdan, P. F., (1983). Long term gains from early intervention through technology: An eleven year report. *Journal of Educational Technology Systems, 11*, 203–214.

Strain, P. S., & Smith, B. A. (1986). A counter-interpretation of early intervention effects: A response to Casto and Mastropieri. *Exceptional Children, 53*, 260–265.

Tharp, R., Jordan, C., Speidel, J., Au, K. H., Klein, T., Calkins, R., Sloat, K., & Gallimore, R. (1984). Product and process in applied developmental research: Education and the children of a minority. In M. E. Lamb, A. L. Brown, & B. Rogoff (Eds.), *Advances in Developmental Psychology* (Vol. 3, pp. 91–144). Hillsdale, NJ: L. Erlbaum.

Turner, R., & Rogers, A. M. (1981). Project KIDS: Infant education for the handicapped in an urban public school system. *Journal of the Division for Early Childhood, 2*, 40–51.

Tymchuk, A. J., Dahlman, A. Y., & Asher, K. N. (1981). Extending the benefits of a demonstration program for handicapped preschool children to community based programs. *Exceptional Children, 48*, 70–72.

Vulpe, S. (1979). Vulpe Assessment Battery. Ontario, Canada: National Institute of Mental Retardation.

Wadsworth, M. (1986). Effects of parenting style and preschool experience on children's verbal attainment: Results of a British longitudinal study. *Early Childhood Research Quarterly, 1*, 237–238.

Warren, S. F., Alpert, C. L., & Kaiser, A. P. (1986). An optional learning environment for infants and toddlers with severe handicaps. *Focus on Exceptional Children, 18*, 1–11.

White, K. (1985–86). Efficacy of early intervention. *The Journal of Special Education, 19*, 401–416.

White, O., Edgar, E., & Haring, N. G. (1978). Uniform Performance Assessment System. Seattle: University of Washington, College of Education, Experimental Education Unit, Child Development and Mental Retardation Center.

Willoughby-Herb, S. J., Neisworth, J. T., & Laub, K. W. (1977). *COMP-Curriculum.* University Park: Pennsylvania State University, HICOMP Preschool Project.

Wilson, W. J. (1987). *The truly disadvantaged.* Chicago: University of Chicago Press.

Wolery, M., & Dyk, L. (1985). The evaluation of two levels of a center based early intervention project. *Topics in Early Childhood Special Education, 5*, 66–77.

Woods, P. A., Corney, M. J., & Pryce, G. J. (1984). Developmental progress of preschool Down's syndrome children receiving a home-advisory service: An interim report. *Child: Care, Health, and Development, 10*, 287–299.

Zeitlin, S. (1981). Learning through coping: An effective preschool program. *Journal of the Division for Early Childhood, 4*, 53–61.

Zigler, E., & Balla, D. (1982). Selecting outcome variables in evaluations of early childhood special education programs. *Topics in Early Childhood Special Education, 1*, 11–22.

22   *The family as a focus for intervention*

JAMES J. GALLAGHER

The last decade has seen a dramatic increase in research, programs, and policies designed specifically to examine and improve the capabilities of families to cope with the presence of a disabled child (see, e.g., Blacher, 1984; Bricker, 1987; Gallagher & Vietze, 1986; Parke, 1986; Turnbull & Turnbull, 1986). There are many reasons for this accelerated interest. First, practitioners have shown an increased appreciation for the importance of the context or the environment surrounding children with handicaps in determining how well such children develop. Second, a growing body of research has documented the influence of the family on the child's developmental progress. Third, family members may represent the most likely focus for professional attention when the child is very young and/or disabled. Finally, there is a growing recognition that family members may need assistance in their own right and should be recipients of intervention services.

The needs of families for a variety of assistance have appeared in personal documents written by parents themselves (Turnbull & Turnbull, 1985) and in reviews of the literature (see, e.g., Baker, 1984; Bristol & Gallagher, 1986; Gallagher, Beckman, & Cross, 1983; Wikler, 1986). These reviews have found an elevated level of stress in many, but by no means all, families with young children with disabilities. The incidence of divorce or separation in families with a disabled child also seems to be elevated, another index of increased tension and distress (Bristol, Schopler, & McConnaughey, 1984).

An increased interest in the family has also been reflected in laws passed to aid children in various types of unfavorable circumstances (Smith, 1986). Head Start legislation has mandated a strong role for parents in designing programs and policies. The Handicapped Children's Early Education Act, first passed in 1968, created demonstration centers for preschool-age children with handicaps and required that such centers have a parent participation component. P.L. 94-142, The Education for All Handicapped Children Act, mandated greater parental participation in educational planning for the disabled child, and the recent Education of the Handicapped Act Amendments of 1986 (P.L. 99-457) have prescribed an Individualized Family Service Plan than reflects a thorough understanding of family strengths and needs, and generates a plan for specific actions designed to improve each family's situation.

This chapter reviews the evidence that supports the claims of success for these interventions in the family setting. But perhaps more relevant for the professions involved in early intervention are the answers to the following questions: Which

540

family-focused services are effective? In what ways and under what conditions are they effective? Thus, whereas the purpose of this chapter is to provide an overview of research on family intervention, it will focus on specific interventions designed to increase the capacity of family units to meet the needs of their disabled children as well as the needs of all family members.

METHODOLOGICAL CONCERNS IN FAMILY INTERVENTION RESEARCH

As we begin to examine the literature on the effectiveness of family interventions, a number of research design problems become evident that weaken the conclusions that can be drawn from intervention programs. Most of these problems stem from the inability of investigators to control key variables. Many investigators try to evaluate already existing service programs and thus cannot exert influence on the practices of the service providers in order to ensure a more carefully designed research effort. Most of these design problems involve the selection of the sample, the specification of the treatment, and the nature of the measurements.

Selection of samples for study

Many of the families included in past intervention studies are "samples of convenience," that is, they were already present or decided upon before the researcher became involved. In many instances the family treatment programs were ongoing before the research started, so the opportunity to gather baseline data and select randomly chosen experimental and control groups did not exist.

These samples generally consist of families who have sought out treatment and who may differ in many important respects from families with handicapped children who have not sought help from professionals or service agencies. Thus, generalizations of the results of such studies are limited.

Nature of the treatment

In many studies the nature of the treatment received, its intensity, and its level of delivery are not clearly presented. The treatment may be referred to as "parent counseling" or "parent training," with few additional details presented. Also, parents may receive different treatments for different purposes, and, therefore, should not be evaluated by a single outcome measure.

Finally, many service providers are interested in dealing with a wide variety of problems that families face. Treatments might include group parent counseling, training parents to interact with their disabled child, structured interviews with all members of the family, and direct treatment for the disabled child in terms of physical therapy or psychological interventions. Thus, even if a study shows parental gain on some established measures following participation in a program, we are left with many questions about which of the factors, or which combination of factors, might be responsible for the improvement.

Measuring the outcome

What instruments can be used to measure success or improvement? Although some measures of parental stress and knowledge growth are straightforward and well established, others involve gathering the subjective impressions of the parents or of the clinician without providing confirming evidence to support the findings. Few standard measures have been developed to help in such studies and many instruments or procedures do not have well-documented validity or reliability (see Krauss & Jacobs, this volume).

Finally, there may not be agreement among investigators and clinicians on the nature of the outcome that is desired. Is it reduction of stress for the mother or father? Is it change in the developmental progress in the child? Is it demonstrable change in parent–child interactions? Different studies focus on different outcome variables, which makes it difficult to compare results of specific programs.

Common goals and objectives

One of the complicating factors in assessing family intervention projects is the wide variety of goals and objectives that such projects may have. Marfo and Kysela (1985) list five possible goals of early intervention:

1. To help parents overcome feelings of confusion, uncertainty, guilt, or fear associated with the birth and parenting of a handicapped child;
2. To help parents understand the child's handicapping condition and its implications, and prepare them to accept the responsibilities for assisting in planning and implementing ameliorative program activities;
3. To facilitate developmental progress in the child by providing training for parents in specific skill areas;
4. To prevent possible disruption of normal, mutually reinforcing parent–child interaction by training parents to be responsive, and by enhancing reciprocal interactions;
5. To assist families with disabled infants gain access to relevant community services.

Obviously, the "success" of an intervention program for families depends heavily upon which combination of these or other goals has been chosen as the target for intervention. Some of these goals might appear to be easier to attain than others, so that different conclusions regarding the effectiveness of intervention efforts could be reached depending upon the content, direction, and intensity of the program itself (see Shonkoff & Hauser-Cram, 1987).

None of these reservations are meant to denigrate the efforts or the importance of the work included here. These investigations represent a necessary step in obtaining the information needed to improve our approach to family-focused intervention. What these reservations about evaluation design should do is to encourage the reader to delay drawing final conclusions on the basis of the results reported herein, and to expend greater effort on developing more refined studies in the future.

THEORIES, IMPLICIT OR EXPLICIT

Whenever we deliberately intervene in a child's life or in the life of a family, we assume a theoretical position regarding human behavior. Although these assumptions are often implicit (see Argyris & Schon, 1974), they should be made explicit so that their validity can be judged.

Meisels (1985) points out that current ambiguity and confusion regarding the effects of early intervention can be traced, in part, to the differing developmental models or theoretical frameworks being used. Each general treatment strategy has its own rationale, however poorly stated, and the review in this chapter is organized around five of these assumptions:

1. *Changing children will change other family members.* The child who is developmentally delayed is likely to have a negative impact on other family members. Therefore, if the child's problems are ameliorated, improved family interactions will result (see Gray, Ramsey & Klaus, 1982). Also, the family that is in trouble will respond better when the child's needs are being met more effectively.

2. *Providing information and teaching parenting skills can change families.* Family difficulties may be due to inaccurate or incomplete information about child rearing, child development, or associated issues. Therefore, a program that provides parents with accurate information will ease many of the internal relationship problems within the family (see Schlossman, 1983). Parents are also often frustrated by their inability to enhance their child's learning or to control their child's undesirable behaviors. Teaching skills that will make parents more competent in these efforts will also improve family interactions (see Blacher, 1984).

3. *Personal counseling can change families.* The feelings and perceptions that people have about themselves and others can often cloud and distort family interactions. Personal counseling can help individuals become more comfortable with their own feelings and remove barriers to the accurate perception of themselves and others (see Berger & Foster, 1986).

4. *Increasing parent empowerment can change families.* Individuals and families are influenced negatively by feelings of powerlessness, or by the inability to change their circumstances through their own actions. Teaching family members how to exercise power and to use available community institutions can improve family attitudes and interactions (see Zigler & Freedman, 1987).

5. *Providing more support services can change families.* An unhealthy environment can have a negative impact on families. The creation of more positive and extensive resources for the family can result in better family interactions by reducing stress and creating shared responsibilities (see Parke, 1986).

Most intervention studies are based upon a mix of these assumptions or quasi-theories. This review will try to sort out the evidence for each of these proposed strategies as it relates to service impacts on families. Studies that focus primarily upon child outcomes are not included.

Meisels (1985) has summarized the current professional consensus about the family and the importance of the interactions of the family members with the child:

The family and its sociocultural and economic context is the crucible in which forces for good and ill are transformed into developmental patterns for high risk and handicapped children in the first years of life. The evidence from a whole generation of research demonstrates that the quality of parents' behavior as caregivers and as teachers makes a difference in the development of infants and young children (p. 9).

The proper question to pose then is not whether parental intervention makes a difference. Rather, we should ask, Under what sets of conditions does parental intervention make a difference for the child, or for the parents themselves?

Minuchin (1985) presents a powerful case for the use of family systems theory. This approach stresses the critical importance of interactions among the various components of the family system: The child influences the parent, the parent influences the child, and one parent can easily influence another parent, causing a modification in the linkage to the child in the family system (see Bristol, Gallagher, & Schopler, 1988). Minuchin claims that many developmentalists ignore these complex system interactions in their research because they are not sure how to handle them methodologically. She concludes that "complex systems are integral to the understanding of child development, and what is not tackled will not yield" (p. 294).

There is certainly reason to believe that family triads, and even larger systems, change over time as a result of sequential interactions among the members of the system. Yet, the management and analysis of such data, though clinically invaluable, is difficult for the researcher. Nevertheless, if we are to progress further than we are now, the creative development of better methods for working with such data is required (Stainback & Stainback, 1988).

Can child improvement modify family members?

The potential results of any intervention can include side effects or unintended consequences. One of those possible consequences is the impact on the parents of a program that is directed primarily at the needs of disabled children. Thus, even though the major effort of the service may be focused on the child, it is possible that the intervention might have impact upon the other family members in some fashion (see Powell & Ogle, 1985). If we assume that we are intervening in a family system and not just treating the child, then the impact can be measured for all members of that system. In some cases the attention given to a child raises the parents' image of the child or motivates them to do more themselves to help the child. In other circumstances parents might devote less attention to the child, leaving child rearing to the professionals who become incorporated into the family system.

Gray et al. (1982) reported on a follow-up study of an early training program begun in the mid-1960s for poor rural families in the South. Eight-six children were randomly divided into experimental and control groups. The experimental group received intensive summer programs when they were 3 and 4 years of age. These were supplemented by a family-oriented home visit once a week for 9 months.

Although the experimental children showed initial gains on measured achievement and cognitive abilities, and still maintained modest gains in comparison to the control group several years later, these results did not appear to modify parental attitudes or expectations. As Gray et al. (1982) concluded, "Our examination of the interview data shows little in the way of any treatment effects upon the parents, either in attitudes toward their children or in their aspirations and expectations for them" (p. 183).

Changes in these families during the 1960s and 1970s seemed to be the result primarily of significant societal changes. Thus, the civil rights movement apparently resulted in more powerful change for families than did preschool programs for their children. On the other hand, a summary of the literature on efficacy research led Guralnick (1988) to conclude that "improved family functioning may well be a reasonable and appropriate outcome for early intervention programs irrespective of their effects on child development" (p. 81). In other words, we can have confidence that intervention can bring positive results to the entire family and should be a family-focused strategy.

LONG-TERM EFFECTS. Only a few clues are available concerning whether intervention programs targeted toward young children have some continuing effect on the family. A follow-up analysis of data on child-centered programs from a consortium of 11 studies on over 2,100 subjects (70% of the original samples) looked at the long-term effects of preschool enrichment programs (Lazar & Darlington, 1982). Differences after 10 years or more were maintained by experimental groups over comparison groups in academic achievement, grade retention, and referrals to special education, but not in IQ. Lazar (1987) contends that the persistent differences that were observed in these groups of children were due primarily to social or family change. He claims that "it seems likely that the permanence of the change can very well be accounted for as representing a change in the value placed on education by both the child and the parent and that it is this change in values that made the difference" (p. 99). This is an attractive and plausible hypothesis, but it is only a hypothesis. More definitive measurement of actual parental change would have to be documented to prove this point.

Portes, Dunham, and Williams (1986) reported on a 10-year follow-up of 30 mother–child dyads, consisting of an experimental group of 10 low socioeconomic status (SES) families, a control group of 10 low SES families, and a second contrast group of 10 middle SES families. During the experimental period the mothers assisted in a day-care setting that their child attended while the fathers received counseling. Semistructured interviews 10 years later revealed the parents in the experimental group to be interacting more actively with their children and demonstrating less punitive behavior than the lower SES control families, with no differences found between the experimental and middle-class contrast families. Although such findings are striking, the small sample size and the possibility of selective attrition cause us to be cautious about our interpretation of these results and underlines the need for additional follow-up studies from the programs of the 1960s.

Can increased information and enhanced parenting skills change family members?

Whereas some intervention programs have been content to look at the possible incidental effects on parents of services focused primarily on their preschool children, others have made parental change a major intervention objective. The Parent Child Development Centers (PCDC) were among those programs that focused upon parental change as a primary goal (Dokecki, Hargrove, & Sandler, 1983). Conceived as part of the Great Society programs of the Johnson administration, but actually implemented during the Nixon presidency, these programs embodied a family service strategy to complement the prevailing economic approach of the nation's comprehensive antipoverty program.

The PCDC programs placed primary emphasis on the education of poor mothers as well as their children. They also provided a wide array of services for the family, including classes in nutrition, arts and crafts, assistance in budgeting, peer support groups, and medical care. Beginning with three original sites (Houston, Birmingham, and New Orleans) the original plan was to replicate these efforts in a number of other states. Each of these anticipated sites was to serve 60 to 70 families with children from birth to 3 years of age. Since the philosophy of the program was based on an assumption that the child is more likely to change if his or her mother's parenting skills improved, the program emphasis was placed upon improving the parent–child relationship. A randomized design was used in the three original sites in order to estimate the effects of the program.

Dokecki et al. (1983) summarized the evaluation data on these programs and found that PCDC mothers exhibited enhanced positive interactions with their children and the children demonstrated enhanced cognitive, language, conceptual, and abstraction skills compared to control group mothers and children, up to 1 year after the program ended. They concluded that this kind of mother–child stimulation should be a component in a comprehensive program for poor families that would include jobs, modified income, and taxation policies that would have to be adjusted to fit local conditions. Despite the generally favorable results of the PCDC pilot effort, however, a change in political climate resulted in no further expansion (see Halpern, this volume).

Beyond the PCDC program, other investigators have explored the results of parent intervention programs with an eye to the impact of the intensity of the intervention and the type of parental involvement (Schickedanz, 1977). For example, Belsky (1985) reported the "failure" of an intervention program to show an effect on mother–infant, father–infant, and husband–wife interaction when comparing passive versus active exposure to the administration of the Brazelton Neonatal Behavioral Assessment Scale. Belsky stressed caution regarding the interpretation of possible effects of such relatively minor interventions.

An example of more intense parental involvement was provided in a program designed directly to influence fathers (Vadasy, Fewell, Meyer, Schell, & Greenberg, 1984). In this program, fathers and their children with moderate to severe disabilities met with two male program leaders for 2 hours every Saturday morning. The fathers were taught activities and games they could take part in with their children, were able to share their concerns with other fathers, and learned how to help their families cope more effectively with the responsibilities of caring for and educating a child with special needs. Evaluation of this intervention demonstrated that fathers who remained in the program longer had less need to talk with someone about their children and had less need to access more organized assistance than did newly enrolled fathers. Furthermore, not only did this program reduce the fathers' feelings of isolation, it also provided mothers with some much needed respite care (Vadasy, Fewell, Greenberg, Dermond, & Meyer, 1986). This study, as is typical of many investigations in this area, focused on a very small sample (a total of 23 families in both groups) and an atypical population (highly educated fathers and mothers with other strong support in the community). How such a program might succeed with less advantaged fathers remains an open question.

Hanson (1985) reported on a program for 30 infants and toddlers aged 4 weeks to 3 years with multiple moderate and severe handicaps. The families received a combination of public school, center-based, and home-based programs. At school the children received services from speech therapists, occupational and physical therapists, and special education teachers, while the parents were assisted in working with their children in school and in the home. The mothers reported substantial improvements in their parenting behavior and satisfaction with the services that they received. No relationships were found, however, between parent improvement and child change in behavior.

Rosenberg and Robinson (1985) reported on a training program for 16 mothers designed to teach them strategies to improve their interaction with their mildly to severely handicapped infants ranging in age from 4 to 27 months. Ratings of videotapes of mother–child interaction showed significant improvement in mothers' parenting skills and an increase in the children's interest in interaction with their parents. These and other studies indicate that such skills can be taught.

Although the process of family-focused intervention has become increasingly important in serving families with young handicapped children, few interventionists are prepared to design treatment objectives for families without some training. The Family Focused Intervention program is an individualized approach that generates a specific treatment plan based on family assessment and interviews (Bailey et al., 1986). The overall goals of the program are: (1) to help family members cope with the unique needs related to caring for and raising a child with a handicap; (2) to help family members grow in their understanding of the development of their child both as an individual and as a member of the family; (3) to promote parent–child interactions that are sufficient in quantity, sensitivity, and warmth, and are mutually enjoyable and appropriately stimulating at the child's developmental level; and (4) to preserve and reinforce the dignity of families by respecting and responding to their desire for services and incorporating the families into the assessment, planning, and evaluation process.

Bailey and his colleagues (1986) suggest the use of Goal Attainment Scaling that allows for the comparison of progress matched against expected outcomes. When used in conjunction with other objective measures, this approach can be added to the portrait of intervention effectiveness.

The Goal Attainment Scale (see Bailey et al., 1986) is a device for measuring gain when treatments differ. As Table 1 indicates, the scale consists of identifying treatment goals and then estimating what the level of attainment in each goal would be if the treatment were successful. This instrument allows for the aggregation of program results when different goals are being addressed in different families. Although the Goal Attainment Scale has limitations (i.e., estimates of expected outcomes are not always appropriate), approaches to evaluation that allow the investigator to aggregate differing levels or kinds of treatments obviously are needed (see Hauser-Cram, this volume).

Do different methods of intervention change family members?

Some investigators have tried to judge the relative merits of different types of intervention on parents and upon their children. Barrera, Rosenbaum, and Cunningham (1986) tested the effects of a 1-year intervention program with preterm infants randomly assigned to three groups. One group received a developmental intervention program that helped the parents to enhance their child's development in five domains: cognition, communication, gross and fine motor development, socioemotional skills, and self-help skills. A second group of parents was given a program to enhance their general observational skills and mutual responsivity during parent–infant interactions. A third group served as controls for the first two and received no formal program. Data obtained at 16 months showed that both intervention programs positively modified the home environment and the infants' cognitive development, but the investigators believed that the parent–infant interaction model appeared to have a slightly more positive impact.

Baker and Brightman (1984) tried to accomplish two sets of goals in a single parent intervention program. Fifteen families were provided with either a Parents as Teachers program, which was designed to enhance parents' ability to teach their young children developmental skills and to manage behavior problems, or a Parents as Advocates program, which was designed to increase parents' knowledge of their rights and increase their advocacy skills. Participants were assigned at random to one of the training programs. Analysis of outcome data revealed that parents who were taught techniques as teachers learned those skills better than they did the advocacy skills. On the other hand, those taught advocacy skills learned them better than they learned techniques as teachers. In other words, there was little generalization from one training program to the other. Thus, the conclusion derived from this study was that if parents are to learn something, they must be taught directly; one cannot assume that specific skills will be picked up in a more general instructional program. However, high rates of attrition and small sample sizes make such studies only suggestive of directions to be pursued in future research.

PARENTS TEACHING PARENTS. One practical question that has been raised in the family intervention literature is Who will do the intervention? particularly given the limited number of highly trained professionals in this area. As one alternative, Bruder

Table 1. *Sample goal attainment scale for family-related goals*

| Program Families Project | Goal attainment scale for Jason | | | | Date of program plan 9/23/84 |
Scale attainment levels	Goal 1: Quality of handling ($W_1 = 3$)	Goal 2: Awareness of state ($W_2 = 2$)	Goal 3: Community resources ($W_3 = 3$)	Goal 4: Implementing training ($W_4 = 3$)	Goal 5: Sibling relationship ($W_5 = 1$)
2 Best expected outcome	Father almost always handles child in sensitive fashion, never rough or abrupt	Mother almost always differentiates states when child is receptive for social and educational interactions	Family always accesses needed community resources independently	Mother follows training program steps with accuracy of at least 90% (A)	Sibling often participates in a positive fashion in interactions between handicapped sibling and parents
1 More than expected outcome	Usually sensitive handling of child	Usually differentiates states (A)	Usually accesses community resources independently; occasionally needs help	Mother follows training program steps with accuracy of at least 80%	Sibling sometimes participates in a positive fashion in interactions between handicapped sibling and parent
0 Expected outcome	Sometimes sensitive handling; about half the time (A)	Sometimes differentiates states; about half the time	Sometimes accesses needed community resources; about half the time (A)	Mother follows training program steps with accuracy of at least 70%	Sibling rarely interferes with parent-child interactions (A)
-1 Less than expected outcome	Occasionally sensitive handling	Occasionally differentiates state and responds appropriately	Family rarely accesses community resources independently	Mother follows training program steps with accuracy of at least 60%	Sibling sometimes interferes with parent-child interactions
-2 Worst expected outcome	Father never handles child in sensitive fashion; almost always rough or insensitive (I)	Mother never differentiates states when child is receptive for social and educational interactions (I)	Family always depends on others to access community resources (I)	Mother follows training program steps with less than 60% accuracy	Sibling almost always interferes with parent-child interactions (I)

W = Weights, I = initial performance, A = attained performance

Source: Bailey, D., Simeonsson, R., Winton, P., Huntington G., Comfort, M., Isbell, P., O'Donnell, K., & Helm, J. (1986). Family-focused intervention: A functional model for planning, implementing and evaluating individualized family services in early intervention. *Journal of the Division for Early Childhood 10,* 156–171.

and Bricker (1985) proposed training parents who, in turn, could train other parents in methods for enhancing the disabled child's learning skills. The arguments given for this approach are reduced cost, the maintenance of skills among parents doing the training, and the enhancement of a support network.

In one study Bruder and Bricker (1985) identified nine mothers of at-risk toddlers who were selected from a larger longitudinal investigation. Three of the nine mothers were taught techniques of behavior modification and shaping in four 1-hour sessions. Each parent followed a detailed manual and was trained in intervention techniques in a one-to-one session with a trained interventionist. These three parents then trained the other six parents, using the same training techniques they had received. The resul's of this experiment demonstrated that the six parent-trained parents were able to use these skills with their children as effectively as the three parents who were trained by the interventionist. These results were limited to a clinic setting and the investigators pointed out that generalization to the home setting still needed to be demonstrated. Nevertheless, this example suggests a number of potentially encouraging lines of investigation based on the model of an "expert parent" who is able to train other parents. The cost effectiveness of such an approach is extremely favorable if generalization and long-term effects can be documented.

Bailey and Simeonsson (1988) summarized the research on parent training as follows:

1. Parents can be taught to implement correct and consistent behavior change programs, educational interventions, and specific therapeutic techniques.
2. Parent training programs often result in subsequent changes in children in accordance with desired child outcomes.
3. Generalization and maintenance of training efforts have not been adequately documented.
4. Effective training techniques most frequently incorporate modeling, practice, and specific feedback, as well as a system for monitoring performance.
5. Parent and child variables often serve to mediate or to limit the effectiveness of parent training programs (p. 208).

Rosenberg and Robinson (1988), in their review of parent–child interaction, indicated that there are two desirable goals for parent training that may conflict with one another. One of these goals is to prepare the parents to provide directive teaching experiences for their children. The second is to focus on effective emotional interchange between parent and child. The authors suggested that directive teaching instruction often can add an element of strain to the emotional interactions that unfold between parents and their children. The validity of this concern remains an empirical question.

LONG-LASTING EFFECTS? One of the most troublesome questions posed about the efficacy of family intervention programs concerns the persistence of the effects of such programs. After all, if the benefits disappear 6 months after the program terminates, how can a compelling argument be made for the investment of substantial resources in such programs?

Seitz, Rosenbaum, and Apfel (1985) conducted a 10-year follow-up study of the effects of a family support intervention for low SES families with healthy infants with no biological handicaps. A control sample was drawn from the same neighborhood, after the program ended, using the same criteria employed to select the treatment group. Analysis of follow-up data indicates that the children in the treated group had better later school adjustment and fewer negative teacher ratings or referrals for special assistance than did children from the comparison families. No differences were found on IQ or achievement measures. Mothers in the treatment group were found to have changed dramatically, particularly regarding their pursuit of additional education for themselves. However, the majority of the fathers refused to participate in the program. The investigators concluded that the costs of addressing the extensive problems displayed by the study families proved to be a profitable investment over time. Thus, measurable change in the mothers, particularly in the form of greater educational attainment, suggests long-term family benefits. Once again, however, the small sample size and nonrandom selection of the control group calls for caution in interpreting these results.

Baker (1984) reviewed the literature on family intervention programs and found a mixture of significant and nonsignificant results in home training, child gains, skill generalization, and parental attitudes. He proposed the following conclusions and recommendations: First, choosing specific child behaviors to modify, and monitoring the child's progress over time, must be a primary concern. Not unexpectedly, the magnitude of child gains has been shown to be inversely related to the level of disability. Second, it is likely that the most helpful program for parents would be integrated with their child's ongoing school activities and would draw on a variety of related professionals for consultation regarding the selection of objectives and intervention techniques. Third, although intervention with children should be focused on specific skills, productive intervention with parents might be broadened. Parents of severely disabled children are likely to need more support and information than those whose disability is less extensive. Fourth, families should have a choice about their level of involvement in an intervention program. There must not only be greater services but also a wider variety of options. Simply because individuals suddenly find themselves in the role of a parent of a disabled child does not mean that they should be required to participate a half-day every week in a school program or in any other obligatory involvement.

Do increased opportunities for parental decision making change family members?

One of the ideas that has received growing credence in this decade is the assertion that the most important role that professionals can play is in fostering supportive and reciprocal relationships between parents and their disabled children and empowering parents to make informed decisions and take control over their own lives (Dunst, 1985). This represents a significant departure from the dominant professional role that characterized intervention efforts only a few years ago and requires a major shift in the attitudes of service providers in order to establish a more equal parent–professional partnership.

Head Start was one of the first major social programs to place an emphasis on the family and to legitimize parental empowerment – the involvement of parents in decision making for their child's overall treatment program – as a way of reducing family dependence upon social institutions. After the initial phase of Head Start implementation, a series of demonstration programs was developed to illustrate specific aspects of the overall Head Start agenda. One of these programs was the Child and Family Resource Program that was designed to offer a variety of social and educational services according to the needs of the individual family (see Halpern, this volume; Zigler & Freedman, 1987).

These programs stressed four major program components: an emphasis on support and education for parents; a focus on developmental continuity by beginning parental services before birth and continuing service provision to the family into elementary school; an effort to coordinate comprehensive social services by way of direct service provision and referrals; and an attempt to individualize services through needs assessment and goal setting with each family (Zigler & Freedman, 1987). Ironically, one early negative evaluation of the Head Start program (Westinghouse Learning Corporation, 1969), which reported very limited child improvement, placed even more emphasis on those other program dimensions, such as overall family well-being, where favorable findings could be identified. Subsequently, a series of reviews (Abt, 1976; Datta, 1983; Grotberg, 1980) identified a variety of favorable family results, including parents reporting increased satisfaction with their life situation, greater feelings of psychological well-being, and improved job training and employment opportunities.

Even when parental participation in service programs is mandated, however, there is no guarantee that what the legislators intended will be implemented in the field. Hocutt and Wiegerink (1983) studied 28 demonstration projects in the Handicapped Children's Early Education Program whose guidelines mandated that they show clear evidence of parent participation in the program. Although all of the centers complied with the mandate through such activities as parent involvement in the development of the required Individual Education Program (IEP) for their child, and although 90% of the centers involved parents in an orientation to the program, relatively few of the programs granted the parents any kind of real decision-making or policy-making responsibilities. Rather, there was a clear tendency to relegate parents to the role of instructional helper. In those centers administered by public school programs there was even less effort to encourage parent participation in decision making than was true in centers run by private agencies.

Hocutt and Wiegerink (1983) also obtained measures of parental satisfaction with the program and compared the top and bottom quartile from a sample of 68 parents to discover which variables were linked to the highest level of satisfaction. They found that such satisfaction was associated with children who were less likely to be multiply handicapped and more likely to be boys. Even more interesting, given the information noted about professionals' reluctance to share authority with parents, parental satisfaction was related to their level of activity in the program and their feeling that they had influence in its administration. These investigators concluded that increased parental participation in decision-making activities can result in greater parental satisfaction with the program.

Does providing support systems change family members?

With increased attention being paid to the ecology of the child with disabilities (Kirk & Gallagher, 1986; Turnbull & Turnbull, 1986), it is inevitable that interest would extend beyond the family boundaries and include its informal and formal support networks. Parke (1986) reviewed the literature on informal support systems (e.g., extended families, neighbors, and co-workers) and concluded that there is a powerful relationship between family adaptation and the presence of effective informal supports. This, of course, does not necessarily mean that providing such supports will improve the adaptation of those families who do not have them. It is always possible that both good adjustment and the presence of informal support systems are interrelated and integral parts of stable families. A natural question to address in an intervention study would be, Can better family adaptation be achieved by increasing informal family supports?

There is considerable evidence that a common reaction of parents to the presence of a disabled child is to reduce their social and extended family contacts (see Farber, 1960; McDowell & Gabel, 1981). Even grandparents may not be helpful without additional training or counseling (Gabel & Kotsch, 1981), and siblings can be an aid in families of handicapped children only under conditions where they have been prepared for such a constructive role (Powell & Ogle, 1985).

Formal support systems (health care, social services, education, etc.) have also been extended to help the adaptation of families with handicapped children. Parke (1986) reports on a number of studies that indicate improvements in mothers' and fathers' caregiving capabilities as a result of programs specifically designed for that purpose, through such vehicles as counseling, viewing of videotapes, and so on. Fewer studies illustrate such results with families of children with disabilities and, in general, more documented results in this domain are clearly needed. Parke (1986) contends that it is possible to combine informal and formal social support systems to aid families. He notes that one can strengthen the informal network through formal intervention by mobilizing existing social networks in time of stress and by using informal network members to help individuals utilize formal support systems.

Tracy and Whittaker (1987) reviewed the evidence for social support systems intervention and found favorable results reported from family support programs, network facilitation (mobilizing informal family networks), introduction of peer support groups, and parental skills training. They also found a variety of methodological issues that plague the field and compromise many of the studies they reviewed.

Ironically, the increasing number of formal support services available to aid the family in crisis may make it less likely that specific new intervention programs will appear favorable. On the other hand, in a situation where there is literally no help available from family or extrafamilial sources, any program that provides assistance is almost certain to be highly valued by the parent and result in favorable outcomes. The increasing availability of routine prenatal, neonatal, and postnatal services for the family, although still not as prevalent as clinicians might prefer, has changed the baseline from which to evaluate services (Shonkoff, 1987). Now a new intervention program may be only one more support service in an already existing array of services and consequently may not stand out as much, nor have the emotional support value it would have if it were the only available service. The task of service coordination and refinement represents an important challenge for the field in the future (see Harbin & McNulty, this volume).

SUMMARY AND IMPLICATIONS

The evidence seems convincing that parents can be taught both new skills and additional knowledge related to child rearing and can be helped with their child's specific developmental problems. In many instances, this instruction can also be applied to other children in the family and can produce measurable benefits for the entire family unit. Furthermore, evidence suggests that the more specific the skills taught, the more likely that a defined objective can be attained. We also know, however, that parent training or counseling programs do not automatically convey benefits. In general, the more negative factors present in the family environment, the less likely that the usual, single-focus interventions (i.e., periodic visits to the home) will be shown to have an impact. In such circumstances, a more comprehensive strategy appears to be called for.

Whereas many of the parental programs described here have been directed at mothers, some work has been done with fathers that seems to show positive results as well. Too few studies are now available to comment with any confidence on intervention programs focused on extended families or siblings, but the provision of additional social support seems to be helpful in families with extra burdens to bear.

There is little evidence that working with children directly has any direct impact on other family members, except for some possible benefits of respite care and the facilitation of maternal employment. There is some indication that unless there is a major effort on the part of professionals to provide an extensive treatment program lasting over weeks and months, there is little chance for substantial change in family relationships. Thus, professionals in the field of family intervention are discovering what ministers and teachers already know – that a weekly sermon or semiannual teacher–parent conference will not have a significant impact on an unfavorable family situation.

One other solution that often turns out to be less than satisfactory is the establishment of public policy at the state and federal level with an expectation that the policy will be translated adequately at the local level. The "street bureaucrat" (Dokecki & Heflinger, 1989), that is, the professional who deals directly with the family in the local community, has a way of translating policies that may or may not resemble the original intent of the lawmakers. This situation seems to be particularly true about policies that might diminish the authority of the professional vis-à-vis the family. All policy has to be monitored constantly to see that its original intentions are observed.

An argument often heard concerning alternative strategies in psychotherapy has relevance in the field of family-focused early intervention as well. Some therapists believe that if a person is feeling incompetent, the major task is to allow that person to play out those feelings in interaction with the therapist so that he or she can cope with them more effectively. An alternative view suggests that the way to deal with perceived incompetence is to train people to become more competent. Though these conflicting views can be oversimplified, as they have been here, they reflect a significant philosophical and theoretical difference. The small body of available knowledge from the field of early intervention suggests that in the process of helping parents gain concrete parenting skills, their attitudes toward their child and themselves generally become more positive.

One other observation recorded about parent intervention programs is the fact that positive feelings are generally expressed by the parents about the program, whatever its nature. This near unanimity of positive parental response, when compared with the abundance of uncertain and highly variable findings recorded by more objective measures, is worthy of greater consideration than it is usually given. Either parents are so grateful for any kind of effort that is generated on their behalf, or on behalf of their child, that they report feeling good about all programs, or significant changes are not documented adequately by the more objective measures that are usually chosen by evaluators. It may well be that the most significant changes that take place are in the perceptions of the parent rather than in the objective reality. Such changes are fundamental to feelings of well-being and long-term family adjustment, even if they are hard to measure (Bristol et al., 1988).

Unintended consequences of policy intervention

The world of public policy is crowded with examples of results that are unexpected by-products of well-meaning legislative or administrative initiatives. An intervention program may stigmatize families or make them more dependent on others, even though its intent is to help them.

Dokecki and Moroney (1983) call attention to one unintended consequence that emerges from a quarter century of societal concern for children and families who are in need of special help. They point out that the primary purpose of legislation for the poor or the disabled has been to help them adapt more effectively in society. Such legislation, however, may give the impression that the state has no responsibilities for helping families who have special needs that fall outside those narrow boundaries defining handicapping conditions.

Generally, it is easier to pass legislation and obtain appropriations earmarking funds for subgroups in special trouble because of their observable needs and the public sympathy they engender. In this context it is especially easy to support programs for families of disabled children because their problems are perceived clearly to be not of their own making. Most often there is less sympathy for those families who find themselves in poverty. Such families are sometimes accused of causing their own unfavorable circumstances and, therefore, are seen as less deserving of public sympathy and support. Hence, the expression, "the undeserving poor."

Dokecki and Moroney (1983) have suggested that a policy that earmarks funds for a special group stigmatizes those who receive the resources and implies that families with adequate income, housing, and health provisions are unlikely to need support in carrying out basic family functions. They go on to propose an alternative strategy characterized by shared responsibility between families and the state and the adaptation of social policies that are not limited to crisis intervention but reflect the proposition that the role of the state is to support all families in the task of child rearing and family development.

There is yet another disturbing, possibly unintended consequence of a public policy of earmarking resources for special groups. In the process of trying to help families cope with adversity, are we weakening the family system by making it too dependent upon professionals and bureaucrats? In the end, are we defeating the very purpose for which the public policy was established? We have long since abandoned the position that good intentions are a sufficient defense for bad policy. A continued careful analysis of the various outcomes of these programs, both positive and negative, is clearly needed.

REMAINING ISSUES

This review has highlighted several persistent issues that will have to be dealt with in the near future. Each of these will be described.

Parents and professionals

The blunt and simple way to describe the issue of parents and professionals is, Who is in charge? Who has primary responsibility for the child? Is it the professional with his or her specialized training and experience who may use a parent as just another (not very well paid) assistant to carry out a professionally driven intervention program? Or are the parents in charge of child rearing and the determination of when to call upon a variety of expert help, as seems appropriate or needed? Questions about the relative responsibilities of parents and professionals toward the needs of the disabled child and toward each other must receive more systematic attention.

Clinical versus public health approaches

Until recently there has been one predominant intervention strategy used for families with disabled children. This strategy was built upon the established medical practice of individual diagnosis followed by a treatment program based upon that diagnosis. The patient was provided treatment in a one-to-one relationship and the treatment was directed at the target child or adult. Increasingly, however, the value of a public health approach is being considered to facilitate a healthy environment in which the family can more easily function. More thought is now being given to providing extended support systems for families and to creating a social environment that increases the likelihood that a family will be able to cope with the special problems of rearing a child with a disability.

McCall (1987) refers to the different environments found within a particular home for the various children who reside there. Obviously, that home environment is not the same for a child with moderate to severe disabilities as it is for a normal sibling. These different psychological environments within the same physical setting, what McCall (1987) calls the "discontinuous, nonshared, within-family environments," should be major topics for future research. Interactions between physical risk factors, such as a child with low birth weight, and environmental contingencies must also be analyzed more carefully (see Sameroff & Chandler, 1975). It is increasingly apparent that we live in a multivariate, interactive world in which few declarative statements about families can be made without substantial qualifiers. One cannot assert, for example, that having a disabled child results in crippling family stress. There are too many other environmental factors that can challenge the validity of that statement for a given family.

Research design

Attempts to conduct research in service programs for families of children with social or biological disabilities have often resulted in poorly designed studies, not because of the incompetence of the investigators but because of their inability to control important aspects of the situation (Bailey & Simeonsson, 1986; Tracy & Whittaker, 1987). In less than desirable circumstances, some investigators may well conclude that some information is better than no information at all, while others believe that given the constraints, a study may not be worth doing.

In a review of early intervention programs for organically impaired children, Dunst and Rheingrover (1981) concluded that "flaws in the experimental designs employed make most of the results from most of the studies uninterpretable from a scientific point of view" (p. 319). Nevertheless, other researchers have proceeded to analyze these data. Ottenbacher and Petersen (1985) examined the same group of studies as Dunst and Rheingrover, conducting a metaanalysis on the effect sizes derived from their outcome variables. After reviewing 118 hypotheses from 38 studies, they concluded that there was strong support for the efficacy of early intervention. One of the areas that showed the strongest evidence of effects was that of successful home training of parents.

There seems to be reason to believe that mothers who have more social support engage in more effective mother–child interactions (see Dunst, Trivette, & Cross, 1986). Thus, it may be tempting to conclude that providing more social support for a family is the answer to better family relationships. But as Tracy and Whittaker (1987) point out, it could well be that more effective parents also seek out and secure more social support. It will not be until some investigator intervenes with strong social support for families that are lacking in such support, and demonstrates subsequent change, that we can infer some causal relationship.

A remaining question concerns the most appropriate design for future investigators of family intervention effectiveness. That basic question is not Is parental intervention effective? but rather What are the dimensions of successful parental intervention for various situations? Under such circumstances, the use of a standard experimental-control group design would seem to yield limited results because the variation within each of the groups (experimental and control) is likely to be so great. With such wide variance, the magnitude of difference required to demonstrate statistically significant treatment effects becomes difficult to achieve and, even if achieved, difficult to interpret. If we have reason to believe, as we do, that there are multiple interactive factors determining outcomes for different families, then combining such data in group analyses may have the effect of obscuring such idiosyncratic interactions – the very discovery we are seeking – that explain success for a particular family.

It is for this reason that the case study approach with replications (see Yin, 1984) may be considered a promising research design because it allows for the careful analysis of interactive factors in a given situation. It is more likely that specific time series, single subject, idiographic designs with replications may provide an even more sensitive means of charting program intervention characteristics in interaction with specific family factors.

Marfo and Kysela (1985) decry the limited use of process measures in outcome evaluation studies. They point out that many of the studies they reviewed used child gains on developmental tests as an outcome measure, even when the intervention program was devoted to parent goals. When a child fails to gain in development, one does not know whether the parent-training procedures were ineffective or inappropriate, or whether the parents never learned the teaching techniques properly in the first place. The danger of labeling an intervention method as ineffective when, in fact, the "intervention" was never really implemented is a significant problem.

A much broader range of outcome measures would seem to be required as well, so that social, temperamental, and emotional factors in the family can be charted along with the cognitive abilities of the child. We have not paid systematic attention to the development of instrumentation despite its obvious importance in scientific research. It is clearly time for a deliberate and long-term commitment to the development of measurement techniques. A more tolerant approach to the use of qualitative measures and to measures of process as well as outcome seems to be needed as we try to find ways to strengthen our parental assistance strategies and seek to measure the effectiveness of our attempts to create positive change in families.

A final word

The next decade will surely see a substantial increase in both the quantity and quality of family intervention studies. The range of variables and outcome measures is also likely to increase. By the end of this century we should be able to produce a literature review of impressive specificity and documentation on this topic. At the moment, however, we must discuss clues, trends, and suggestions for future research. The definitive studies lie ahead of us.

REFERENCES

Abt, C. (1976). *The evolution of social programs.* Beverly Hills: Sage Publications.

Argyris, C., & Schon, D. (1974). *Theory in practice: Increasing professional effectiveness.* San Francisco: Jossey-Bass.

Bailey, D., & Simeonsson, R. (1986). Design issues in family impact evaluation programs. In L. Bickman & D. Weatherford (Eds.), *Evaluating early intervention programs for severely handicapped children and their families* (pp. 209–230). Austin, TX: PRO-ED.

Bailey, D., & Simeonsson, R. (1988). Home-based early interventions. In S. Odom & M. Karnes (Eds.), *Early intervention for infants and children with handicaps* (pp. 199–216). Baltimore: P. H. Brookes.

Bailey, D., Simeonsson, R., Winton, P., Huntington, G., Comfort, M., Isbell, P., O'Donnell, K., & Helm, J. (1986). Family focused intervention: A functional model for planning, implementing, and evaluating individualized family services in early intervention. *Journal of the Division for Early Childhood, 10,* 156–171.

Baker, B. (1984). Intervention with families with young, severely handicapped children. In J. Blacher (Ed.), *Severely handicapped young children and their families* (pp. 319–376). Orlando: Academic Press.

Baker, B., & Brightman, R. (1984). Training parents of retarded children: Program-specific outcomes. *Journal of Behavioral Therapy & Experimental Psychiatry, 15,* 255–260.

Barrera, M., Rosenbaum, P., & Cunningham, C. (1986). Early home intervention with low birth weight infants and their parents. *Child Development, 57,* 20–33.

Belsky, J. (1985). Experimenting with the family in the newborn period. *Child Development, 56,* 407–414.

Berger, M., & Foster, M. (1986). Applications of family therapy theory to research and interventions with families with mentally retarded children. In J. Gallagher & P. Vietze (Eds.), *Families of handicapped persons* (pp. 251–261). Baltimore: P. H. Brookes.

Blacher, J. (Ed.). (1984). *Severely handicapped young children and their families.* Orlando: Academic Press.

Bricker, D. (1987). Impact of research on social policy for handicapped infants and children. *Journal of the Division for Early Childhood, 11,* 98–105.

Bristol, M., & Gallagher, J. J. (1986). Psychological research on fathers and young handicapped children: Evaluation, review, and some future directions. In J. Gallagher & P. Vietze (Eds.), *Families of handicapped persons* (pp. 81–100). Baltimore: P. H. Brookes.

Bristol, M., Gallagher, J., & Schopler, E. (1988). Mothers and fathers of young developmentally disabled and nondisabled boys: Adaptation and spousal support. *Developmental Psychology, 24,* 441–451.

Bristol, M., Schopler, E., & McConnaughey, L. (1984, December). *The prevalence of separation and divorce in families of young developmentally disabled children.* Paper presented at Handicapped Children's Early Education Program Conference, Washington, DC.

Bruder, M., & Bricker, D. (1985). Parents as teachers of their children and other parents. *Journal of the Division for Early Childhood, 8,* 136–150.

Datta, L. (1983). A tale of two studies: The Westinghouse-Ohio evaluation of Project Head Start and the Consortium for Longitudinal Studies Report. *Studies in Educational Evaluation, 8,* 271–280.

Dokecki, P., Hargrove, E., & Sandler, H. (1983). An overview of the Parent Child Development Center social experiment. In R. Haskins & D. Adams (Eds.), *Parent education and public policy* (pp. 80–111). Norwood, NJ: Ablex Publishing.

Dokecki, P., & Heflinger, C. (1989). Strengthening families of young children with handicapping conditions: Mapping backward from the "street level" pursuant to effective implementation of Public Law 99-457. In J. Gallagher, R. Clifford, & P. Trohanis (Eds.), *Policy implementation and P.L. 99-457: Planning for young children with special needs.* (pp. 59–84). Baltimore: P. H. Brookes.

Dokecki, P., & Moroney, R. (1983). To strengthen all families: A human development and community value framework. In R. Haskins & D. Adams (Eds.), *Parent education and public policy* (pp. 40–64) Norwood, NJ: Ablex Publishing.

Dunst, C. (1985). Rethinking early intervention. *Analysis and Intervention in Developmental Disabilities, 5,* 165–201.

Dunst, C., & Rheingrover R. (1981). An analysis of the efficacy of infant intervention programs with organically handicapped children. *Evaluation and Program Planning, 4*, 287–323.

Dunst, C. J., Trivette, C. M., & Cross, A. F. (1986). Roles and support networks of mothers and handicapped children. In R. Fewell & P. Vadasy, *Families of handicapped children* (pp. 167–172). Austin, TX: PRO-ED.

Farber, B. (1960). Family organization in crisis: Maintenance of integration in families with a severely mentally retarded child. *Monographs of the Society for Research in Child Development, 25* (1, Serial No. 75).

Gabel, H., & Kotsch, L. S. (1981). Extended families and young handicapped children. *Topics in Early Childhood Special Education, 1*, 29–36.

Gallagher, J., Beckman, P., & Cross, A. (1983). Families of handicapped children: Sources of stress and its amelioration. *Exceptional Children, 50*, 10–19.

Gallagher, J., & Vietze, P. (Eds.). (1986). *Families of handicapped persons*. Baltimore: P. H. Brookes.

Gray, S., Ramsey B., & Klaus, R. (1982). *From 3 to 20: The Early Training Project*. Baltimore: University Park Press.

Grotberg, E. (1980). *The federal role in parenting*. ERIC Clearinghouse on Elementary and Early Childhood Education.

Guralnick, M. (1988). Efficacy research in early childhood intervention programs. In S. Odom & M. Karnes (Eds.), *Early intervention for infants and children with handicaps* (pp. 75–88). Baltimore: P. H. Brookes.

Hanson, M. J. (1985). An analysis of the effects of early intervention services for infants and toddlers with moderate and severe handicaps. *Topics in Early Childhood Special Education, 5*, 36–51.

Hocutt, A., & Wiegerink, R. (1983). Perspectives on parent involvement in preschool programs for handicapped children. In R. Haskins & D. Adams (Eds.), *Parent education and public policy* (pp. 211–229). Norwood, NJ: Ablex Publishing.

Kirk, S., & Gallagher, J. J. (1986). *Educating exceptional children* (5th ed.). Boston: Houghton Mifflin.

Lazar, I. (1987). Changing views on changing children. In J. Gallagher & C. Ramey (Eds.), *The malleability of children* (pp. 97–102). Baltimore: P. H. Brookes.

Lazar, I., & Darlington, R. (Eds.). (1982). Lasting effects on early education: A report from the Consortium for Longitudinal Studies. *Monographs of the Society for Research in Child Development, 47* (2–3, Serial No. 195).

Marfo, K., & Kysela, G. (1985). Early intervention with mentally handicapped children: A critical appraisal of applied research. *Journal of Pediatric Psychology, 10*, 305–324.

McCall, R. (1987). Developmental function, individual differences, and the plasticity of intelligence. In J. Gallagher & C. Ramey (Eds.), *The malleability of children* (pp. 25–36). Baltimore: P. H. Brookes.

McDowell, J., & Gabel, H. (1981). Social support among mothers of retarded infants. Unpublished manuscript, George Peabody College, Nashville.

Meisels, S. J. (1985). The efficacy of early intervention: Why are we still asking this question? *Topics in Early Childhood Special Education, 5*, 1–11.

Minuchin, P. (1985). Families and individual development: Provocations from the field of family therapy. *Child Development, 56*, 289–302.

Ottenbacher, K., & Petersen, P. (1985). The efficacy of early intervention programs for children with organic impairment: A quantitative review. *Evaluation and Program Planning, 8*, 135–146.

Parke, R. (1986). Fathers, families, and support systems: Their role in the development of at-risk and retarded infants and children. In J. Gallagher & P. Vietze (Eds.), *Families of handicapped persons* (pp. 101–114). Baltimore: P. H. Brookes.

Portes, P., Dunham, R., & Williams, S. (1986). Preschool intervention, social class and parent-child interaction differences. *Journal of Genetic Psychology, 147*, 241–255.

Powell, T., & Ogle, P. (1985). *Brothers & sisters: A special part of exceptional families*. Baltimore: P. H. Brookes.

Rosenberg, S. A., & Robinson, C. C. (1985). Enhancement of mothers' interactional skills in an infant education program. *Education and Training of the Mentally Retarded, 20*, 163–169.

Rosenberg, S. A., & Robinson, C. C. (1988). Interaction of parents with their handicapped children. In S. Odom & M. Karnes (Eds.), *Early intervention for infants and children with handicaps* (pp. 159–178). Baltimore: P. H. Brookes.

Sameroff, A., & Chandler, M. (1975). Reproductive risk and the continuum of caretaking casualty. In F. D. Horowitz, M. Hetherington, S. Scarr-Salapatek, & G. Siegel (Eds.), *Review of child development research* (Vol. 4, pp. 187–244) Chicago: University of Chicago Press.

Schickedanz, J. (1977). Parents, teachers, and early education. In B. Persky & L. Colubcheck (Eds.), *Early childhood*. Wayne, NJ: Avery Publishing Group.

Schlossman, S. (1983). The formative era in American parent education: Overview and interpretation. In R. Haskins & D. Adams (Eds.), *Parent education and public policy* (pp. 7–39). Norwood, NJ: Ablex Publishing.

Seitz, V., Rosenbaum, L., & Apfel, N. (1985). Effects of family support intervention: A ten year followup. *Child Development, 56,* 376–391.

Shonkoff, J. (1987). Family beginnings: Infancy and support. In S. Kagan, D. Powell, B. Weissbourd, & E. Zigler (Eds.), *America's family support programs* (pp. 69–98). New Haven: Yale University Press.

Shonkoff, J. P., Hauser-Cram, P. (1987). Early intervention for disabled infants and their families: A quantitative analysis. *Pediatrics, 80,* 650–658.

Smith, B. (1986). *A comparative analysis of selected federal programs serving young children.* Unpublished report. Chapel Hill: University of North Carolina.

Stainback, S., & Stainback, W. (1988). *Understanding and conducting qualitative research.* Reston, VA: Council for Exceptional Children.

Tracy, E., & Whittaker, J. (1987). The evidence base for social support interventions in child and family practice: Emerging issues for research and practice. *Children and Youth Services Review, 9,* 249–270.

Turnbull, A., & Turnbull, H. (Eds.). (1985). *Parents speak out* (2nd ed.). Columbus, OH: Merrill.

Turnbull, A., & Turnbull, H. (1986). *Families, professionals, and exceptionality.* Columbus, OH: Merrill.

Vadasy, P., Fewell, R., Greenberg, M., Dermond, N., & Meyer, D. (1986). Follow-up evaluation of the effects of involvement in the Fathers Program. *Topics in Early Childhood Special Education, 6,* 16–31.

Vadasy, P. F., Fewell, R. R., Meyer, D. J., Schell, G., & Greenberg, M. T. (1984). Involved parents: Characteristics and resources of fathers and mothers of young handicapped children. *Journal of the Division for Early Childhood, 8,* 13–25.

Westinghouse Learning Corporation. (1969). *The impact of Head Start: An evaluation of the effects of Head Start on children's cognitive and affective development.* Athens, OH: Ohio University.

Wikler, L. (1986). Family stress theory and research on families of children with mental retardation. In J. Gallagher & P. Vietze (Eds.), *Families of handicapped persons* (pp. 167–196). Baltimore: P. H. Brookes.

Yin, R. K. (1984). *Case study research.* (Applied Research Review 5). Beverly Hills: Sage Publications.

Zigler, E., & Freedman, J. (1987). Head Start: A pioneer of family support. In S. Kagan, D. Powell, B. Weissbourd, & E. Zigler (Eds.), *America's family support programs* (pp. 57–78). New Haven: Yale University Press.

23 *Economic costs and benefits of early intervention*

W. STEVEN BARNETT AND
COLETTE M. ESCOBAR

Public policy choices regarding early intervention can be viewed from a variety of perspectives, one of which is economics. It is not the only, or even the preeminent, perspective that one might wish to use. Ethical, legal, and educational perspectives have much to offer that may elude the economic perspective. The unique contribution of the economic perspective is that it insists that policymakers attend to all of the resources consumed as well as the outcomes produced by alternative policy choices. Interest in the economic perspective on early intervention has increased recently for two reasons. One is the heightened intensity of the debate over the level of government spending. The other is new empirical evidence that early intervention produces important economic benefits (Barnett, 1985a).

The purpose of this chapter is to introduce the methods and findings of economic research on early intervention and to explore the implications of those findings for research, policy, and practice. Thus, the chapter begins with an overview of the methodology and terminology of economic analysis. This is followed by an introduction to principles of cost analysis and a comprehensive review of research on the costs of early intervention. To make the cost information as accurate as possible, cost estimates have been corrected whenever it was found that the research cited in the literature had departed from accepted principles. The next section provides an introduction to cost-benefit analysis and a review of research on the economic benefits of early intervention. A detailed example of cost-benefit analysis is explored. The review of research on the benefits of early intervention is selective in that it does not discuss studies with findings that are severely compromised by methodological problems. Comprehensive critiques of the literature that include these studies have been provided elsewhere (Barnett & Escobar, 1987, 1988). Finally, general conclusions are drawn regarding the economics of early intervention, and recommendations are made for research, practice, and policy.

Work reported in this publication was carried out in part with funds from the U.S. Department of Education (Contract No. 300-82-0367) to the Early Intervention Research Institute at Utah State University.

560

WHAT IS ECONOMIC ANALYSIS?

From the economic perspective, early intervention is an investment with both immediate and future benefits. Economic analysis can be used to measure the net economic gain or loss from early intervention and to describe the accompanying distribution of gains and losses; that is, who gains or loses. If an activity produces a net gain in economic value for society as a whole, it is said to be "economically efficient." Economic analysis provides specific criteria for measuring efficiency and identifying the most efficient alternative. However, economic analysis does not provide criteria regarding the equity, or fairness, of distribution. The best that economic analysis can do is describe the distribution produced by each alternative. Policymakers must use their own values to judge the fairness of those distributions.

Practically, economic analysis is an extension of underlying studies of program operation and program effectiveness. A cost analysis is possible only if there is a program description. An economic analysis that goes beyond cost is desirable only if there is evidence of program effectiveness. Ideally, an economic analysis should be built upon the data provided by an ecological or systems study of the type recommended by Sameroff (1983) and Bronfenbrenner (1986), because economic analysis is concerned with all costs and effects of a program, no matter who bears the costs or is affected and regardless of whether or not the results are intended. Thus, economic analysis should include measures of costs borne by a program's clients and their families as well as costs in the program budget. For instance, the cost to parents of providing transportation to a center should be included. Measurement of program effects should be expanded beyond measures of child progress to include effects on others such as the family, children's peers, the school system that children enter after intervention, and the intervention staff. For example, it might be found that two programs have similar costs and child outcomes, but that one is more economically efficient because it produces less staff stress.

A variety of terms have come to be used more or less interchangeably to refer to economic analysis in educational research (Levin, 1983): cost analysis, cost-effectiveness analysis, and cost-benefit analysis. However, the terms have distinctly different meanings in economics. Although in educational research the term "cost analysis" is sometimes used to refer to any economic analysis, the term more properly refers to studies of only the resources used by an activity (Barnett, 1986). Cost-benefit (or benefit-cost) analysis and cost-effectiveness analysis are both used to study the resources used *and* the outcomes produced by an activity. These two techniques differ in their treatment of program outcomes and in the circumstances in which they are most useful.

In cost-benefit analysis, monetary values are estimated for both the resources used (costs) and the effects produced (benefits). For example, it might be determined that the economic value of benefits from Program A is $5,000 per child more than its cost. In cost-effectiveness analysis, programs are evaluated on the basis of program costs and effects alone; there is no attempt to estimate the monetary value of program effects. For example, it might be determined that children in Program A gain 10 points on a standardized test at a cost of $3,000 per child, and children in Program B gain 5 points at a cost of $2,500. This type of analysis is obviously easier to perform because, practically speaking, it is an incomplete benefit-cost analysis.

Whether cost-benefit analysis or cost-effectiveness analysis should be used in a particular situation depends on the resources available to conduct the analysis, the program outcome measures, and the amount of information required by the decision makers. Benefit-cost analysis is more time-consuming and costly to perform. The underlying effectiveness study may or may not yield outcome measures that can be translated into monetary terms. For example, reductions in the need for special education can be assigned a dollar value quite easily; increases in self-esteem cannot. On the other hand, cost-effectiveness results alone may provide less information than decision makers want. If a single program is studied, is it enough to conclude that later special education needs are reduced, or will decision makers want to compare the cost of the program to the cost savings? If two programs are compared, will the decision makers be satisfied with cost estimates and a specified number of program outcome measures for each program, or will they want some summation that says how much those outcomes are worth?

COSTS AND COST ANALYSIS

The most basic question in the economics of early intervention is: How much does early intervention cost? Yet, it is not a simple question to answer. One reason is that early intervention programs are extremely diverse. A wide range of programs exist to serve a wide range of children and families who vary greatly in their needs. Local variations in salaries, rents, and other prices are also a source of differences in costs (Grubb, 1987). For example, teacher salaries differ considerably from New York to Mississippi. Another reason is that relatively few cost studies have been conducted, and many of those that have did not follow standard practices of economics. Thus, the lack of information makes it difficult to generalize about average national costs, and inconsistencies across studies compound the problem and make it difficult to compare accurately the costs of different approaches to early intervention.

Cost analysis methodology

The goal of cost analysis is to determine the economic value of all resources used in the activity or program studied. Levin (1983) has described the standard economic approach to cost analysis as an "ingredients model." The first step in the use of this model is to develop a list of all the ingredients and the amounts of each that are needed by the program. One can think of this as a recipe for producing the program. The second step is to determine the cost of each ingredient. When the cost of each ingredient has been established, these costs can be summed to produce a measure of the total cost of the intervention.

The first step in the ingredients model is straightforward if one is careful not to omit any of the ingredients. A program description can be used to produce a list of the ingredients needed to produce all of the intervention's activities, and the ingredients can be categorized by type. Almost all early intervention program ingredients will fall into one of the following categories: personnel, facilities, equipment, materials and supplies, utilities, communications, and insurance. Programs also tend to have a few small items left for a miscellaneous ingredients category. Transportation is sometimes thought of as an additional category, but the ingredients used to provide transportation can be sorted into the various categories already listed.

The second step in the model is to determine the cost of each ingredient. The key to correctly determining costs is understanding that the true cost of an ingredient is its "opportunity cost," that is, the value of an ingredient in its best alternative use. When a resource is used in an early intervention program, its cost is the value of the foregone opportunity to use that resource in another way. Most people understand and apply the concept of opportunity cost in daily life. For example, people often say that they "can't afford the calories" in something. The cost of an afternoon snack is giving up dessert after dinner, running an extra mile, or gaining weight. The amount paid for the snack is only of secondary importance. Opportunity cost is important in determining the cost of early intervention programs precisely, because what is paid does not always represent the full cost there as well.

Costs of early intervention

We reviewed the early intervention research literature in order to bring together all of the published information on the costs of early intervention. The results are summarized in Tables 1 and 2, with center-based and home visit programs categorized separately. Some center-based programs had home visit components as noted in Table 1. To make the various estimates as comparable as possible, two adjustments were made to the original estimates. First, all estimates were converted to 1986 dollars, using a price index for state and local government purchases, to correct for inflation (Bureau of Economic Analysis, 1982, 1987). Second, estimates that omitted major ingredients or miscalculated costs were corrected based on information from other studies that used standard procedures to estimate the complete costs of all ingredients.

As can be seen, there was wide variation in the estimated costs of early intervention programs. Center-based programs ranged from $4,000 to $9,000 per child annually, with programs for infants and handicapped children toward the high end of the range. Home-based programs tended to be less expensive, $1,500 to $4,500 per child, and cost did not vary with age or handicapping condition. Some of the variation in program costs is due to local differences in program circumstances. However, a substantial amount of variation in costs is due to differences in program characteristics that are matters of choice. Four program characteristics were identified that can significantly influence program cost: duration, intensity, number of services, and reliance on parents to bear part of the cost.

COST AND DURATION OF SERVICES. One source of variation in cost of early intervention is the difference in the duration of intervention services. Programs that serve children in classroom settings vary in the length of day and number of days per year. The day may be $2\frac{1}{2}$ hours (half-day), 6 hours (full school day), or 9 or more hours (day care). The number of days per year may reflect a school year or year-round program. Programs that serve children through home visitors vary in the length of visits and the number of visits per year. For studies reporting duration, the number of hours per year varied from 380 to 2,438 for center-based programs and from 50 to 94 for home-based programs.

The cost-per-hour figures in Tables 1 and 2 indicate the relative costs of programs holding duration constant. One seemingly obvious conclusion is that home visit programs provide many fewer hours of service at a much higher cost per hour of service. However, it must be cautioned that only the home visitor's time is included. If the intent of the program is to enable parents to deliver intervention services (in a formal program or through natural interaction), the actual hours of intervention may be greatly underestimated. Of course, the costs to parents are not included either.

Table 1. *Cost per child of center-based programs*

Program	Age in years	Condition	Annual cost (1986 dollars)	Cost/hour (1986 dollars)
1. Public Preschool Special Education – $3,526 (1977 dollars)	3–5	handicapped	$6,174	$ 8.60
2. Perry Preschool – $4,963 (1981 dollars)	3–5	disadvantaged & handicapped	6,341	15.50
3. Head Start – $3,032 (1981 dollars)	0–3	disadvantaged	4,451	5.00
4. National Daycare Study – $2,112 (1985 dollars)	0–3	disadvantaged	3,964	2.10
5. Sioux City Schools (1985 dollars)	3–5	handicapped		
half-day: $5,340			5,979	11.10
full day: $8,417			9,424	8.30
6. Toledo Public Schools – $6,152 (1982 dollars)	3–5	handicapped	7,227	19.00
7. Early Lifestyle Program – $3,627 (1979 dollars)	3–5	handicapped	5,324	n/a
8. Abecedarian – (1986 dollars)				
Infant program: $8,495	$0–1\frac{1}{2}$	disadvantaged	8,495	3.50
Preschool program: $7,943	$1\frac{1}{2}–5$	disadvantaged	7,943	3.30
9. INREAL – $175 (1976 dollars)[a]	3–6	disadvantaged & handicapped	1,294	2.90
10. Yale Family Support Program – $3,000 (1970 dollars)[b]	0–3	disadvantaged	8,566	n/a
11. Social Integration Program – $4,048 (1985 dollars)	3–5	handicapped	5,166	4.80
12. Triple T Infant Consortium – $2,272 (1979 dollars)[b,c]	0–3	handicapped	7,250	n/a
13. HCEEP – (1976 dollars)[b,c]	0–6	handicapped		n/a
High cost (7 programs): $1,542–4,113			6,726–17,941	
Medium cost (15 programs): $943–1,344			4,113–5,863	
Low cost (6 programs): $353–821			1,539–3,580	

[a] Omitted indirect service costs, omitted nonpersonnel resources costs, and day-care cost.
[b] Omitted fringe benefits and nonpersonnel resource costs.
[c] Includes some home-based programs.
Sources: (1) Kakalik, Furry, Thomas, & Carney (1981). (2) Barnett (1985a, 1985b). (3) Aurora Associates, Inc. (1982). (4) Ruopp, Travers, Glantz, & Coelen (1979). (5) Barnett & Pezzino (1987). (6) Weiss & Jurs (1984, October). (7) Frakes (1981). (8) Escobar & Barnett (1986, October). For simplicity, the cost of the infant program is based on 12 months although infants were typically not enrolled until 6 weeks of age. (9) The cost of the INREAL intervention is from Weiss (1981). The cost of $2\frac{1}{2}$ hours of day care for 180 days was estimated based upon the cost of private day care ($1.55/hour) in the National Day Care Study (Ruopp et al., 1979). (10) Seitz, Rosenbaum, & Apfel (1985). (11) Rule, Stowitschek, Innocenti, Striefel, Killoran, Swezey, & Boswell (1987). (12) Macy & Carter (1980). (13) Stock, Wnek, Newsborg, Schenck, Gabel, Spurgeon, & Ray (1976).

Table 2. *Cost per child of home-based programs*

Program	Age in years	Condition	Annual cost (1986 dollars)	Cost/hour (1986 dollars)
1. Early Lifestyle Program – $1,642 (1979 dollars)	0–3	handicapped	$2,410	$ 48.20
2. DARCEE (1970 dollars)[a]	3–5	disadvantaged		
professional: $440			2,907	n/a
paraprofessional: $288			1,902	n/a
3. SKI*HI – $1,450 (1980 dollars)[b]	0–5	handicapped	2,891	55.60
4. Project Sunrise – $625 (1979 dollars)[b]	0–5	handicapped	1,310	n/a
5. MAPPS – $1,640 (1977 dollars)[b]	0–3	handicapped	2,980	62.10
6. Macomb 0–3 – $2,237 (1979 dollars)[b]	0–3	handicapped	4,691	99.80
7. Home Start – $1,750 (1974 dollars)	3–5	disadvantaged	4,194	116.50
8. Clinch-Powell Educational Co-op (1980 dollars)	3–5	disadvantaged & handicapped	2,315	60.90
weekly: $1,433			1,293	68.10
biweekly: $800				

[a] Omitted fringe benefits and nonpersonnel resource costs.
[b] Omitted nonpersonnel resource costs.
Sources: (1) Frakes (1981). (2) Barbrack & Horton (1970). (3) Antley & DuBose (1981). (4) Walker (1981). (5) Casto & Tolfa (1981). (6) Hutinger (1981). (7) Love, Nauta, Coelen, Hewlett, & Ruopp (1976). (8) Burkett (1982).

One aspect of duration that is not captured in Tables 1 and 2 is the number of years of intervention that may be required. Two years of a program cost twice as much as 1 year. Programs that begin at birth and continue until school entry can be expected to cost much more than programs that begin at 2 or 3 years of age. However, some programs that work through the parents may not need to be repeated every year until school age if they transfer to parents the knowledge or other resources necessary to continue the intervention's success.

COST AND INTENSITY OF SERVICES. Variation in the intensity of services is another important source of variation in the cost of early intervention and the primary reason that cost per hour of service is so highly variable. Program intensity, which we define as the quality and quantity of service delivered in a given period of time, is determined by the number of staff and their qualifications. Because staff accounts for about 70% of program costs (Coelen, Glantz, & Calore, 1979; Kakalik, Furry, Thomas, & Carney, 1981; Ruopp, Travers, Glantz, Coelen, 1979), substantial increases in program intensity imply substantial increases in program cost.

Program intensity tends to vary with the characteristics of the children served. The two most important characteristics in this respect are age and the type of severity of handicapping condition. Younger children and more severely handicapped children require higher staff–child ratios. The effects of handicapping condition are somewhat obscured in Tables 1 and 2 because the estimates are heavily influenced by the greater prevalence of mild and moderate conditions. Thus, it is instructive to examine the cost

Table 3. *Preschool (ages 3–5 yr) special education in public
schools, cost per child by handicapping condition
(in 1986 dollars)*

Handicapping condition	Cost per child
Speech impairment	$ 4,360
Learning disability	5,939
Educable mental retardation	6,067
Trainable mental retardation	8,256
Severe mental retardation	9,371
Emotional impairment	5,708
Deaf	13,441
Partial hearing loss	10,249
Blind	11,562
Partial sight loss	5,698
Orthopedic impairment	8,925
Other health impairment	4,061
Multiple handicaps	16,428
All conditions	6,174

Source: Kakalik, Furry, Thomas, & Carney (1981, p. 34)

estimates provided by Kakalik et al. (1981) for public school preschool (ages 3 to 5 yr) special education programs by handicapping condition. The cost estimates have been adjusted for inflation and are presented in Table 3.

Clearly, there is a very strong difference between most center-based programs and home visitor programs with respect to intensity. Home visitor programs all have a staff–child ratio (or staff–parent ratio) of one to one. When home visitor programs train parents to be intervenors, the object generally is to have parents work with the child one to one. This ratio is constant for home visitor programs, so these tend to make the most economic sense for infants and severely handicapped children who require the most intense services. At the same time, the intensity of home visits makes the cost per hour very high. Thus, home visitor programs tend to provide relatively few hours of care in order to keep cost down.

The cost estimates presented in Tables 1 and 2 cover the range of likely policy options but should not be considered a measure of the average cost of early intervention programs. Many of the programs included in the cost review were specially designed as research projects, and had unusually high staff–child ratios and exceptionally qualified (and well-paid) staff. For example, the Perry Preschool had a 1:6 ratio with two teachers per classroom. Its cost would have been even higher, except that there was no transportation cost because children walked to the school. Recent state initiatives providing preschool programs for disadvantaged preschoolers commonly set much lower ratios, 1:10 with one teacher and an aide per classroom (Grubb, 1987). Whether these less intensive programs can produce the same benefits as the research programs is an open question.

One study that sheds some light on the importance of intensity in center-based programs is the National Day Care Study (NDCS) (Ruopp et al., 1979). The NDCS investigated the links between cost, program characteristics, and program quality that were measured by observing caregiver and child behavior and administering standardized tests at the beginning and end of the year. The NDCS researchers concluded that staff–child ratio was the most important influence on cost per child, but was not strongly related to caregiver behavior, child behavior, or test scores of 3- to 5-year-old disadvantaged children. Class size and staff training were strongly related to caregiver and child behavior and children's test scores, but not to cost. Their conclusions were similar for infant and toddler programs, except that staff–child ratio was more strongly related to caregiver behavior (the only outcome measure because tests were not given to infants).

As with any study, the findings of the NDCS require cautious interpretation. As the NDCS researchers recognized, in practice it is difficult to decrease class size without increasing staff–child ratio (Ruopp et al., 1979, pp. 137–157). Whereas it might be possible to trade two classes with a teacher and an aide in each for three classes with one teacher in each, this arrangement might create problems for safety or for responding to individual needs and could preclude integration of handicapped children into a class. Also, the meaning of the findings depends on the types of comparisons they were based on. Was the comparison that of one teacher and an assistant with 20 children to one teacher with 12 children, or was it of two teachers who work as a team with 14 children to one teacher with 7 children? The latter comparison seems unlikely. Finally, the absence of a strong relationship between staff qualifications and compensation can only be expected to hold over a very limited range. It should be noted that the NDCS results were heavily influenced by a single training program in one city (Ruopp et al., 1979, p. 161). Furthermore, although there are always a small number of highly qualified persons willing to work in early intervention programs no matter how poor the pay, it would be unreasonable to expect to attract and keep large numbers of highly qualified staff unless salaries are competitive.

COST AND NUMBER OF SERVICES. Other things being equal, programs that provide more services are more costly than those that are more limited. Thus, early intervention programs that provide classroom services for children and home visit services for children and/or parents tend to cost more than programs that deliver only one or the other of these options. Costs are also increased by offering health care, nutrition, family counseling, transportation, and other services that address child and family health and development more generally. Head Start is the best known example of a program that offers a wide range of services. To keep costs down, Head Start tends to offer low salaries, a short year, and partial day care. The Yale Family Support Project (Seitz, Rosenbaum, & Apfel, 1985) provides another example of comprehensive services. It offered prenatal care, pediatric care, social work, and infant day care. Not surprisingly, the Yale program was among the most expensive reviewed.

COSTS TO PARENTS. The costs of programs may appear to vary because parents bear some of the costs. The cost estimates in Tables 1 and 2 include only the costs borne by the public. Often, parents are used in the roles of intervenors at home or in classrooms, in other volunteer roles, or as providers of transportation for their children. Frequently overlooked is the opportunity cost to parents of the time consumed by these activities; the omission of this cost causes some programs to appear more economical than they are in reality.

Home-based programs can be thought of as reducing cost per child by separating child development services from child care services and focusing resources on the former. The cost of child care is then "shifted" to the parents, resulting in a program that costs the taxpayer less. Programs that provide early intervention services in ordinary day-care settings such as INREAL (Weiss, 1981) and SIP (Social Integration Program) (Rule et al., 1987) similarly reduce the cost per child. In this case, child development and child care services are, in effect, separated by having a lower paid child-care staff provide the child-care services. Additional cost shifting occurs if parents pay for the day-care services. (The cost of day care is included in the Table 1 cost estimates for INREAL and SIP.) Of course, in practice, child-care and child development services cannot be completely separated, and the provision of child care by parents, poorly paid child-care providers, or more highly qualified (but more expensive) teachers may have implications for program outcomes as well as cost.

Whether parents should bear part of the cost of intervention is an ethical, practical, and legal question. Whereas the ethical issue is not one about which we have particular expertise, we can shed some light on the practical and legal issues. Parent involvement is often desirable, and in some cases, the use of parents as intervenors may be more effective and economically efficient than the alternatives. Yet, the costs to parents of participating in an intervention program can be very substantial. Policymakers and the public should not confuse cost shifting, which decreases the public cost but increases the costs to parents, with cost reduction; the total cost to society could be higher. In addition, costs to parents may discourage participation so that children do not receive the desired type or amount of service.

From a legal perspective, the 1986 amendments to the Education of the Handicapped Act (P.L. 99-457) require that a "free appropriate education" be provided to handicapped 3- to 5-year-old children. In the past, this has been interpreted to mean that parents of handicapped children should not pay out-of-pocket costs or be required to provide their own transportation, but the opportunity costs of parent time have been largely ignored. We suggest that this point of view is inconsistent. Regardless of how parents choose to spend their time (in the labor force, caring for children at home, in active or passive leisure, etc.), their time has value, and if they are required to give it up, they incur cost. As we have argued elsewhere, the economic value of parent time is, at the very least, what they could earn if they chose to be in the labor force (Barnett, Escobar, & Ravsten, 1988).

The cost of transportation is an issue that may be receiving increased attention in the near future. Prior to the passage of P.L. 99-457, center-based programs for young handicapped children often relied on parents to provide transportation. Now programs must provide the transportation, and the cost may turn out to be fairly high. We have no way of estimating national costs, but we are concerned by an initial study of transportation costs in Utah that found a range of $400 to $2,000 per child for one school year, with a significant number of programs reporting costs toward the high end (Escobar, Peterson, Lauritzen, & Barnett, 1987). If such costs prove to be typical, a search for ways to reduce transportation costs may be a high priority.

BENEFITS AND BENEFIT-COST ANALYSIS

From an economic perspective, early intervention for handicapped and disadvantaged children is an activity with two conceptually distinct products: child development services and family support services. The primary product is child development services because the definitive aim of early intervention is to improve child outcomes. At the same time, many early intervention programs also include family support services that aim to improve family functioning and well-being. Child care is the most common form of family support. Child care relieves parents from custodial responsibilities so that they can pursue such other activities as work, rest, and recreation without distraction. In recent years, there has been a movement toward broader family support programs that address a variety of family needs (Kysela & Marfo, 1983; Weissbourd, 1983; Zigler & Berman, 1983).

Family support services are provided for a variety of reasons, one or all of which may apply to a given intervention program. Family support may be viewed as an important indirect avenue of intervention for the child. An intervention program also may have goals for family outcomes in their own right (Bristol, Reichle, & Thomas, 1987). Family support can even be an incidental by-product of child-directed intervention, as when programs provide out-of-home child care because they use a classroom model to deliver intervention. However, from an economic perspective, the rationale for family support services is irrelevant. Family support services produce outcomes that are economically valuable, and estimates of program benefits should include the value of services to all family members whenever it is possible.

Benefit-cost analysis methodology

Benefit-cost analysis is essentially the application of economic theory, primarily microeconomics, to the problem of estimating the economic value of a program's effects. A complete introduction to the methodology of benefit-cost analysis is beyond the limits of this chapter, and the reader is referred to the excellent texts by Levin (1983) and Thompson (1980). As the application of economic methods to the study of early intervention has been discussed in detail elsewhere (Barnett, 1986), only a brief outline of the procedures involved is presented prior to our consideration of research findings regarding the benefits of early intervention. Cost-effectiveness analysis may be viewed as an incomplete benefit-cost analysis and is not discussed separately.

The process of conducting a cost-benefit analysis of an early intervention program can be described in a series of steps. The first is to identify and estimate the resources used and the effects produced by the program. The second is to translate resource and effect estimates into monetary measures of costs and benefits. The third is to aggregate those monetary estimates of costs and benefits in a way that meaningfully depicts the net economic value of the program to society as a whole. The fourth is to describe the distributional consequences, that is, who gains and who loses. The final step is to consider how the underlying assumptions and any other limitations of the analysis might affect the findings. An example using these steps is presented. It serves a dual purpose, illustrating the methodology and describing the benefits of early intervention.

Benefits of early intervention: the Perry Preschool Project

The most extensive evidence to date of the benefits of early intervention is provided by a benefit-cost analysis based on the Perry Preschool Project (Barnett, 1985a, 1985b). The Perry Preschool Project is a longitudinal study of the effects of a preschool program that was begun with 3- and 4-year-olds in the early 1960s. Its findings through age 19 were recently published (Berrueta-Clement, Schweinhart, Barnett, Epstein, &

Weikart, 1984). The 123 subjects of the study were children with low IQs from low-income black families. Many of the children had IQs that would classify them as mentally retarded, and half of the control group eventually received special education. Thus, the subjects can be considered to come from a disadvantaged population that has many handicapped members, and the study is relevant to intervention with handicapped as well as disadvantaged children.

The Perry Preschool program ran from October to June and consisted of a $2\frac{1}{2}$-hour daily classroom program that met 5 days per week and $1\frac{1}{2}$-hour weekly home visits by the teachers. Children attended the program at ages 3 and 4, except for a small group of children the first year who attended only at age 4. Two public school teachers with early childhood and special education training served each classroom of 8 to 13 children. Teachers taught in the morning and conducted home visits in the afternoon. A cognitive-developmental curriculum was used as described by Weikart, Kamii, and Radin (1967). Study subjects entered public kindergarten at age 5.

PROGRAM EFFECTS. The Perry Preschool Project employed an experimental design to study immediate and long-term effects. Subjects were assigned in a manner approximating random assignment either to an experimental group that entered the program or to a control group that did not enter the program (Weikart, Bond, & McNeil, 1978). Analyses indicate that no biases were introduced by incidental initial differences between the groups of subsequent attrition (Berrueta-Clement et al., 1984). Thus, comparison of the two groups can be considered to yield unbiased estimates of the effects of the preschool program. Measures of child development and success in a variety of areas have been obtained periodically since the first year of preschool. Most recently, the findings of the project were reported through age 19 (Berrueta-Clement et al., 1984).

The Perry Preschool Project found a chain of lasting effects that stretches from preschool to early adulthood. Some of the most important effects are displayed in Table 4 as comparisons of means for the experimental and control groups. As can be seen, the intervention's effects were pervasive as well as persistent. The intervention's first measured effects were IQ gains for the experimental group at ages 3 and 4. The IQ differences between experimental and control groups began to decline after school entry and ceased to be statistically significant by second grade. Despite the decline in IQ, the initial IQ gains were associated with later success. The experimental group performed better on achievement tests and on teacher ratings throughout the school years and was less likely to be placed in special education (Schweinhart & Weikart, 1980). By the time they were young adults, it was clear that the experimental group was also experiencing nonacademic as well as academic advantages. They were not only more likely to be pursuing higher education, but they had higher employment rates and higher incomes, less involvement in crime and delinquency, and as teenagers, girls had borne fewer children (Berrueta-Clement et al., 1984).

THE MONETARY VALUE OF COSTS AND BENEFITS. The heart of the economic analysis was an estimation of the program's economic value based on the resources used by the program and estimated program effects. A very complete cost estimate was produced based on program records. As reported in Table 1, annual cost was about $6,300 per child (in 1986 dollars). The economic value of benefits was estimated for child care, elementary and secondary education, postsecondary education, earnings and employment, crime and delinquency, and welfare. The estimated value of benefits was

Table 4. *Major findings of the Perry Preschool Project*

Category	Number of subjects[a]	Preschool group	No-preschool group	p
Mean IQ at age 5	123	95	83	<.001
Age 15 achievement test	95	122.2	94.5	<.001
Percentage of all school years in special education	112	16%	28%	.039
High school graduation (or equivalent)	121	67%	49%	.034
Postsecondary education	121	38%	21%	.029
Arrested or detained	121	31%	51%	.022
Females only: teen pregnancies per 100	49	64	117	.084
Receiving welfare at age 19	120	18%	32%	.044
Employed at age 19	121	50%	32%	.032

[a] Total *n* = 123
Source: Berrueta-Clement, Schweinhart, Barnett, Epstein, & Weikart (1984)

in each case based on observed program effects, although in some cases it was necessary to predict continued benefits beyond age 19.

The value of day care was estimated based on the number of hours of center-based care provided. For the Perry Preschool program, this was relatively small because it was only a morning program. Moreover, because the parents were relatively poor, their ability and willingness to pay for day care was low. With these limitations, the estimated value of day care to parents was only $385 per year (this and all other benefit figures are in 1986 dollars).

The effect of intervention on the costs of elementary and secondary education was estimated by calculating the cost of each year of education for each child based on school placement and comparing average costs for the experimental and control groups. The intervention reduced total educational costs by about $9,000 per child as the result of two opposing effects. First, cost was reduced because children who attended preschool required less expensive placements (e.g., less special education). Second, cost was increased because preschool attendees were less likely to drop out and so had more total years of schooling. Thus, the overall cost savings was achieved despite the cost of increased educational attainment.

The effect of intervention on the costs of postsecondary education demonstrates that it is possible to have "negative benefits." The intervention increased the costs of public higher education by about $1,500 per child because experimental subjects were more likely to graduate from high school and enter postsecondary education. As the study provided data only through age 19, entry to postsecondary education was known, but most postsecondary students had not completed their education. Thus, the number of years of education completed was predicted for each subject with the aid of national data.

The Perry Preschool program increased the employment rate and earnings of the experimental group. The effect on total compensation (wages plus fringe benefits) was based on actual earnings data through age 19 and predicted from educational attainment beyond age 19. Total earnings were roughly $1,300 higher per experimental subject through age 19. Obviously, they were just barely beginning their earning careers, and some had postponed work in order to continue their education. The effect on compensation over the balance of the lifetime was estimated using U.S. Census data that linked educational attainment to earnings by race, age, and sex. The estimated benefit was more than $100,000 per child.

Crime and delinquency were reduced as a result of the preschool program. This finding was based on self-report data and police and court records. Because official records data were gathered later than interview data, information concerning involvement with the criminal justice system was available through age 20. Costs to victims and costs to the police, court, and prison systems were estimated for each arrest. A comparison of average cost of the two groups indicated that the cost of crime and delinquency had been reduced by about $2,400 per child. National data on patterns of arrests by age were used to project arrest rates and crime costs beyond age 20, producing an estimate of over $6,800 per child in additional cost reductions over the subjects' lifetimes.

The Perry Preschool program's effect on welfare costs was estimated from the subjects' reports of welfare payments at age 19. The estimated effect on annual welfare payments was $1,050 per child. The effect of the program on welfare payments beyond age 19 was predicted to be about $40,400. Projecting welfare payments beyond age 19 was a difficult task because much less is known about long-term patterns of welfare assistance than about other patterns over the life cycle – income, for example. Thus, this estimate is the least certain of those made in the benefit-cost analysis. However, the estimated cost savings to society is only a small fraction of the reduction in welfare payments. This is because welfare is primarily a shift of resources from one person to another. Only the administrative cost of welfare is a cost to society as a whole, and that amounts to roughly 10% of the payments.

AGGREGATION AND INTERPRETATION. A summary of the Perry Preschool program's costs and benefits is presented in Table 5. Benefit estimates before and after age 19 are presented separately so that the importance of each can be assessed. The figures presented in Table 5 have been discounted at a real rate of 5% annually. Discounting is necessary because even after dollar values from different years have been adjusted for inflation (as all the figures in this chapter have been), they are not equivalent in value. Discounting converts all dollars to their "present value," which is their value at the beginning of the project, and in this way makes the money value of all costs and benefits comparable over the years. The calculation of present value is central to economic analysis. In general, a program is said to be economically efficient, a good investment, if the net present value is positive (the present value of benefits is greater than the present value of costs). When two programs are compared, the one with the greatest net present value is the most economically efficient and the best investment

To illustrate discounting and the calculation of net present value, a hypothetical example is presented in Table 6. In this example, the discount rate is a real rate of 5%. The top part of Table 6 presents the undiscounted, but inflation corrected, dollar values of cost and benefit figures by year. The bottom part of the table presents discounted figures and the calculations used to derive them. Thus, the undiscounted

Table 5. *Present value of costs and benefits of the Perry Preschool Project discounted at 5% (in 1986 dollars)*

Benefits through age 19	
Child care	$ 714
School cost savings	5,082
Earnings increase	574
Crime reduction	1,164
Welfare reduction	46
Total	$7,580
Benefits beyond age 19	
College costs	$ −621
Earnings increase	14,403
Crime reduction	1,386
Welfare reduction	993
Total	$16,160
Total benefits	$23,740
Total cost	$11,614
Net benefits	$12,126

Source: Barnett (1985b, p. 98)

Table 6. *Calculating net present value of costs and benefits with a 5% discount rate*

Real dollar value	Year	Costs		Benefits	
Undiscounted	1		$ 5,000		$ 500
(inflation already	2		4,000		500
factored out)	3		1,000		1,000
	4		0		3,000
	5[a]		0		3,000
	10		0		3,000
Total			$10,000		$11,000
Discounted	1	$5,000 ÷ 1.05 =	$ 4,762	$ 500 ÷ 1.05 =	$ 476
	2	$4,000 ÷ (1.05)^2 =	3,628	$500 ÷ (1.05)^2 =	454
	3	$1,000 ÷ (1.05)^3 =	864	$1,000 ÷ (1.05)^3 =	864
	4			$3,000 ÷ (1.05)^4 =	2,468
	5[a]			$3,000 ÷ (1.05)^5 =	2,351
	10			$3,000 ÷ (1.05)^{10} =	1,842
Total			$ 9,254		$ 8,455
Net present value = $8,455 − $9,254 = −$799					

[a] In this hypothetical example there are no costs or benefits between years 5 and 10.

dollar value of benefits in Year 2 is $500. The present value of benefits in Year 2 is $454. As can be seen from the calculations, discounting is an exponential process (the present value of a dollar is $1.00/1.05 in Year 1, $1.00/1.05^2 in Year 2, $1.00/1.05^3 in Year 3, and so on). Thus, in Year 4, $3,000 of benefits had a present value of $2,468. By Year 10, $3,000 of benefits had a present value of only $1,842. The example of Table 6 shows how forgetting to discount can alter the results of an analysis. Undiscounted benefits are greater than undiscounted costs. However, discounting reveals that net present value is negative and that the hypothetical project is not a good investment. Readers who want to learn more about discounting and discount rates are referred to Gramlich (1981) and Thompson (1980).

The bottom line in Table 5 indicates that the net present value of the Perry Preschool program to society was positive. Thus, the Perry Preschool program was a sound economic investment. It is the kind of investment that requires a long time horizon, however. The investment in 2 years of this fairly expensive program was not "paid off" until some years after the participants left school and became adults. Benefits through age 19 were sufficient to offset somewhat more than the cost of 1 year of preschool. Nevertheless, it is noteworthy that the conclusion that the program was a sound investment requires only a small part of the estimated benefits beyond age 19 – a quarter of the estimated effect on lifetime earnings alone would suffice.

One of the questions that was not answered by the Perry Preschool Project is: Are 2 years of preschool needed to generate the long-term benefits, or would 1 year be sufficient? There was no statistically significant difference in effects between the 1-year and 2-year subjects, but because the 1-year sample was so small, the power to detect differences was relatively slight. Obviously this is an important question from an economic perspective. One year would cost just about half as much as 2 years (slightly more because such costs as screening tests are incurred just once), which is a very large savings.

DISTRIBUTIONAL CONSEQUENCES. Having determined that society as a whole gained, further analysis was directed to the question of the distribution of costs and benefits from the Perry Preschool program. Barnett's (1985a) analysis investigated the distribution to two conceptually distinct groups: taxpayers (that is, people in the role of taxpayer) who paid for the program, and participants who attended the program (and their families). It was found that most of the present value of the benefits accrued to the taxpayers, and that taxpayers' benefits more than justified the program's cost. The participants and their families received relatively small monetary benefits because the primary source of these was increased earnings, and these were largely offset by decreased welfare payments. Welfare is much more important in the distributional analysis than it is in the analysis of efficiency. As noted earlier, welfare payments themselves are not a cost or benefit from the perspective of society as a whole. Welfare payments are just a transfer of funds from one part of society to another. The net effect of welfare on society as a whole is limited to administrative costs, which are only about 10% of the amount of the payments. However, in the distributional analysis, both the payment and administrative cost are relevant – in their role as program participants, some people no longer qualify for welfare and lose it; in their role as taxpayers, some people have their taxes reduced. Note that from the viewpoint of welfare recipients, the value of welfare payments, per se, are important, not just the administrative costs.

There are two salient public policy implications of the distributional analysis. First, the Perry Preschool program appears to have been a social program in which everybody was a winner. Both participants and taxpayers came out ahead. Such a program should be very popular politically. Second, the distribution of benefits offers a strong rationale for public funding. There is no economic incentive for families like those in the Perry Preschool Project to buy preschool services on their own, because their economic benefits are much less than the cost. The economic incentive for early intervention clearly lies with the taxpayers who receive more than enough economic benefits to make it an attractive investment.

ASSUMPTIONS AND LIMITATIONS. Extensive analysis were conducted to investigate the effects of departures from the various assumptions required to conduct the benefit-cost analysis of the Perry Preschool program. One of the most crucial assumptions in any benefit-cost analysis is the rate used in discounting. Thus, net present value was calculated using a wide range of discount rates. The net present value of 2 years of the program was positive over the entire range of reasonable real (without inflation) discount rates (3% to 7%). The net present value of 1 year (assuming the same benefits except for child care) was positive even at unrealistically high discount rates (over 11%). Extensive analyses were also conducted varying the assumptions used to project benefits beyond age 19. Even radical changes in assumptions did not alter the conclusion that the program was a sound investment. Details of all of the alternative analyses have been provided by Barnett (1985b).

Perhaps the most serious limitation of the benefit-cost analysis was that cost was more completely estimated than benefits. This tends to be true generally in benefit-cost analysis of early intervention because the economic value of many benefits is difficult to assess. In the Perry Preschool study, some benefits could not be valued at all: (a) early IQ gains and school success, per se; (b) increased satisfaction with high school; (c) reduced teenage childbearing; and (d) increased adult social competency. Other benefits were incompletely valued. The estimated benefits from reduced crime did not include the value of increased feelings of safety; reduced pain and suffering by victims; or decreased expenditures on locks, guards, and other security measures. When weighing the program's value, it is useful to bear in mind those indicators of increased well-being that were not monetarily valued but are important to children, their parents, and society generally.

Other longitudinal studies

Although the Perry Preschool study is the most comprehensive of its kind, its findings are supported in some measure by two other studies that estimated long-term economic benefits, and by more than a dozen experimental and quasiexperimental studies of the long-term effects of early intervention. These studies are briefly reviewed here. Note that the subjects in all of these studies were economically disadvantaged, and similar studies have not been conducted with children whose handicapping conditions are associated primarily with observed biological impairments. The extent to which studies with disadvantaged children contribute to the knowledge of the economics of early intervention for biologically impaired children is a matter that will be taken up later.

Weiss (1981) conducted a benefit-cost analysis of the effects of adding INREAL, which is a language intervention program, to ordinary preschool and kindergarten classrooms. The study's subjects were 3- to 5-year-old disadvantaged children in seven matched pairs of classrooms. One classroom from each pair was randomly assigned to receive INREAL. The INREAL program was delivered by language specialists who were assigned to classrooms for one school year. Each specialist worked with one preschool class in the morning and one or two kindergartens in the afternoon. A major goal of the INREAL program is to provide language therapy in the classroom in a way that minimizes the stigmatizing of children needing therapy. A 3-year follow-up of study participants revealed that children in the intervention group experienced fewer grade retentions and fewer and less restrictive special education placements than children in the control group.

To assess the intervention program's economic value, Weiss (1981) compared the program's cost to the benefits from reductions in later educational costs over the 3-year follow-up period. Despite some flaws in the economic analysis and the inclusion of only 3 years of benefits, it is clear that the present value of benefits exceeded that of costs. This finding suggests that early intervention programs for disadvantaged children (17% of the sample was identified as handicapped at study entry) can have a substantial economic impact (Weiss & Heublein, 1981). Of course, the INREAL study did not measure the economic benefits of the preschool and kindergarten programs alone, but its results indicate that there are substantial economic benefits to be obtained from early intervention (beyond those already yielded by the basic programs), and that ordinary early childhood programs serving disadvantaged children might significantly increase their economic value by adopting such language interventions as INREAL.

Seitz et al. (1985) reported the results of a 10-year follow-up study of economically disadvantaged families who participated in the Yale Family Support Project. The intervention program provided medical and social services and an educational day-care program for about $2\frac{1}{2}$ years beginning at birth. Some parents received prenatal services as well. A comparison group was obtained by applying the procedures used to select the treatment group to later births at the hospital from which the treatment group was drawn. Comparison families were matched with treatment families on sex of child, income, number of parents in the home, and mother's ethnicity. Together, the two groups contained 28 families. Program effects were measured by comparing parent and child outcomes of the two groups.

Seitz et al. (1985) found evidence of positive effects on parent and child at the age 10 follow-up. Treatment group mothers had a higher employment rate, a higher level of educational attainment, and a lower birth rate. Children had better school attendance records and fewer special education placements. Although a complete benefit-cost analysis was not conducted, the monetary value of costs and some benefits was estimated. Cost was reported to be approximately $20,000 (1982 dollars) per family over the program's $2\frac{1}{2}$-year life. The estimated value of benefits from increased employment and reduced special services in the follow-up year was $2,125 (1982 dollars) per family. The present value of those benefits discounted at 5% was $1,337. It would be difficult to extrapolate accurately the value of benefits from a single follow-up year, although the effect on lifetime income might be estimated based on educational attainment. It is interesting that the educational cost savings accounted for about half of the 1-year benefit and were similar in magnitude to the average annual educational cost savings estimated for the Perry Preschool program.

Additional evidence of economic benefits comes from early intervention studies that have found long-term effects similar to those that produced economic benefits in the

Perry Preschool Project. The Consortium for Longitudinal Studies (1983) conducted analyses of pooled data from 11 long-term studies of early intervention (including the Perry Preschool Project). Eight studies provided information about school success at grade 7, and four studies provided information about school success through grade 12. The pooled analyses indicated that there was significantly less grade retention and special education placement for children who had received early intervention, and the results were not dependent on the inclusion of the Perry Preschool results in the analyses.

The evidence that early intervention with disadvantaged children increases school success (and thereby reduces the costs of schooling) is quite strong. This finding has been replicated in a variety of locations and times with programs that differed in theoretical approach, service delivery model, and the age at which intervention begins. Direct empirical support for the other economic benefits found in the Perry Preschool study is not as broad-based, but a substantial body of research in economics links educational success to key variables for economic benefits: earnings and employment, criminal activity, childbearing, and health (Haveman & Wolfe, 1984). This research and the finding by the Yale Project of effects on parental economic success suggest that the economic benefits of early intervention might be even greater and more far-reaching than the Perry Preschool Project indicated.

Benefits for biologically impaired children

Longitudinal studies comparable to the studies with disadvantaged children have not yet been conducted on early intervention for biologically impaired children with moderate to profound handicapping conditions (Casto & Mastropieri, 1986; Dunst, 1986; Shonkoff & Hauser-Cram, 1987). Thus, the case for long-term benefits to biologically impaired children rests on other kinds of evidence and on generalization from studies with disadvantaged children. The evidence that is available has been reviewed extensively elsewhere, with generally positive conclusions (e.g., Bricker, Bailey, & Bruder, 1984; Guralnick & Bennett, 1987). There appears to be a substantial basis for concluding that early intervention can produce immediate benefits for biologically impaired children, and that these are of the same order of magnitude as initial benefits for disadvantaged children (Casto & Mastropieri, 1986; Shonkoff & Hauser-Cram, 1987). This at least leaves open the possibility of similar long-term benefits for biologically impaired children.

Given the evidence of immediate benefits, it is worth considering what the long-term benefits of early intervention for biologically impaired children might be, and how these might compare to the benefits estimated for the Perry Preschool program. Benefits for disadvantaged children and their parents were found in the areas of child care, educational costs, employment and earnings, crime and delinquency, and welfare. Benefits to biologically impaired children and their families seem possible in all of those areas except for crime and delinquency. Criminal activity by persons with more severe handicaps is undoubtedly negligible. In addition, it seems likely that the benefits to parents would differ, as parents' needs are principally related to the child's condition rather than to the family's economic circumstances.

Although benefits to biologically impaired children and their families can be expected to vary with type and severity of handicapping condition, some useful generalizations may be made regarding potential economic benefits to this group as a whole. The child care provided by center-based programs probably has a relatively high value. Child care is likely to be more difficult and costly to obtain for these children, and parents frequently report that the time demands of a handicapped child are a major problem (Dunlap & Hollinsworth, 1977). The costs of special education are very high and tend to increase with the severity of the handicap. Even modest decreases in the intensity of required special education might generate significant cost savings. Increases in cognitive and social abilities, and in daily living skills in particular, might generate significant benefits to families of handicapped persons and generally reduce costs to society to the extent that the ability for independent living (even if not completely independent) is increased.

On the whole, it seems quite possible that early intervention with biologically impaired children can be economically efficient. Consideration of the potential benefits suggests that the economic value of benefits from early intervention for biologically impaired children could equal or even exceed the value estimated for disadvantaged children. The cost of early intervention for biologically impaired children is, on average, likely to be higher than for disadvantaged children, but it is still within the range that might yield a positive economic return (positive net present value).

As always, it is important not to slight potential benefits of early intervention that are difficult to value economically. Parents may highly value such benefits as an increased understanding of their child, improved family relationships, reduced stress, and relatively small increases in their child's abilities that might hardly be noticed by others. The value of increased integration of biologically impaired persons in school, work, and community might be as much or more than the associated cost savings to families and taxpayers. Handicapped persons, their families, and society in general would benefit from such effects on the life courses of handicapped people.

CONCLUSION

The available empirical evidence indicates that early intervention for disadvantaged children and their families can be a sound economic investment. Moreover, it is an investment that should be undertaken by taxpayers because they are the primary economic beneficiaries. Less is known about the economic benefits of early intervention for biologically impaired children and their families, but there is clearly the potential for benefits that would more than justify the costs of early intervention on economic grounds. Certainly, the evidence does not preclude this possibility. These conclusions are broad generalizations over highly diverse populations and may not hold true for every subpopulation. However, it seems to us that this is the level of generality at which policy decisions are made, and these conclusions are therefore useful.

Early intervention is an expensive investment, which makes cost an important policy consideration. The challenge is to restrain cost without jeopardizing benefits; indeed, from an economic perspective, the object is to set cost at the level that yields the maximum net gain to society, regardless of how high or low that cost. From this perspective, the key policy variables are (a) duration (age at start, hours per year), (b) intensity (quantity and quality of staff time devoted to each child), (c) number of services (how broadly the child and family are served), and (d) cost shifting (the extent to which cost is borne by the family). These variables can be manipulated by public policy, but there is a need for more information regarding the relationships between these variables and program benefits as a basis for policy decisions. However, existing research does suggest some questions regarding current public policy.

The costs of the center-based programs for disadvantaged preschoolers provided by federal and state agencies are considerably lower than the costs of the programs that provided most of the evidence for long-term benefits. Costs are lower because Head Start and state programs tend to have lower staff–child ratios and lower staff qualifications, and tend to be provided for only 1 year at age 4 (Grubb, 1987; Head Start Bureau, 1987). The effects of the reductions in intensity and duration on child outcomes are unknown, but the potential for reduced benefits cannot be ignored. These programs should be subject to careful evaluation, and research on the effects of number of years (which provides the greatest cost reduction), staff–child ratio, and staff qualifications should be assigned high priority.

Given the high costs of early intervention, low-cost options that have some demonstrated success should be the subject of research and practical experiments. Home-based programs are one low-cost option and are particularly well suited for early intervention with infants. They can be highly efficient if parents can, in a short time, learn effective methods for improving their child's development in natural interactions. However, there are several issues that should be weighed when considering this choice. First, there may be a trade-off with benefits. The number of hours of service is much lower than in center-based programs, and, by definition, home-based programs do not provide day care, which may have important benefits for parents. Second, as infant day care becomes more common, home-based programs may be a poor fit for families where a parent is not the primary caregiver during the day. Third, if parents must spend substantial amounts of time in intervention activities that are not intrinsically valuable, then a substantial cost may be imposed on the family. That cost is not in principle different from the cost incurred when parents provide transportation to a center or pay for a day-care program in which intervention is delivered. Another low-cost option is to provide intervention in a day-care setting, as with the INREAL program. This may be useful when home-based programs are problematic. However, the evidence for success with this type of intervention is primarily for disadvantaged and mildly handicapped children (Weiss, 1981; Rule et al., 1987).

Although low-cost options are of obvious interest, they are not the only options that deserve closer attention. In particular, the Yale Family Support program, which is broader and more expensive than most early intervention programs, has been found to generate substantial long-term economic benefits to parents as well as the kinds of long-term benefits that other intervention programs have produced for children. The promise of persistent benefits for both parents and children suggests that family-focused interventions should receive increased attention in both research and practice.

In our view, a problem arises because early intervention programs for handicapped children tend to limit enrollment to children who already manifest the outcome that is to be prevented or ameliorated (i.e., a handicap), primarily those with biological impairments. For many children whose handicap is an outcome that results in large part from environmental disadvantage, this means that they are excluded from early intervention. In fact, most of the children who will need special education later if they do not receive early intervention are not served in preschool special education programs (Barnett, 1988). These children are not necessarily served elsewhere. Despite the political rhetoric regarding Head Start, programs that serve disadvantaged children are not as well funded as programs for handicapped children and they serve only a small portion of the eligible population (Schweinhart, 1985). With the provision of early intervention services so limited, a great many of the potential benefits of early intervention are foregone.

In reviewing the evidence on the costs and benefits of early intervention, it is evident that a great deal remains to be learned regarding the economic efficiency of early intervention strategies with specific types of children and families. We do not say this to minimize the contributions of previous research, nor do we wish to overemphasize the importance of economics as a source of public support for early intervention. As noted earlier, economics is only one of many perspectives from which to view early intervention, and few enterprises have stronger economic evidence to support their claim on a share of society's resources. Rather, we believe that further economic research should be pursued because it can continue to make important contributions to both policy and practice if it is based on sound longitudinal research and adheres to accepted economic methods.

REFERENCES

Antley, T. R., & DuBose, R. F. (1981). *A case for early intervention: Summary of program findings, longitudinal data, and cost-effectiveness.* Unpublished manuscript, University of Washington, Experimental Education Unit, Seattle.

Aurora Associates. (1982). *Study of Head Start unit costs: Final report.* Rockville, MD: Weststat Research.

Barbrack, C. R., & Horton, D. M. (1970). Educational intervention in the home and paraprofessional career development: A second generation mother study with an emphasis on costs and benefits. *DARCEE Papers and Reports, 4*(4), 1–45. (George Peabody College)

Barnett, W. S. (1985a). Benefit-cost analysis of the Perry Preschool program and its policy implications. *Educational Evaluation and Policy Analysis, 7,* 333–342.

Barnett, W. S. (1985b). The Perry Preschool program and its long-term effects: A benefit-cost analysis. *High/Scope Early Childhood Policy Papers* (No. 2). Ypsilanti, MI: High/Scope.

Barnett, W. S. (1986). Methodological issues in economic evaluation of early intervention programs. *Early Childhood Research Quarterly, 1,* 249–268.

Barnett, W. S. (1988). The economics of early intervention under P.L. 99-457. *Topics in Early Childhood Special Education, 8,* 12–23.

Barnett, W. S., & Escobar, C. M. (1987). The economics of early educational intervention: A review. *Review of Educational Research, 57,* 387–414.

Barnett, W. S., & Escobar, C. M. (1988). The economics of early intervention for handicapped children: What do we really know? *Journal of the Division for Early Childhood, 12,* 169–181.

Barnett, W. S., Escobar, C. M., & Ravsten, M. (1988). Parent and clinic early intervention for children with language handicaps: A cost-effectiveness analysis. *Journal of the Division for Early Childhood, 12,* 290–298.

Barnett, W. S., & Pezzino, J. (1987). Cost-effectiveness analysis for state and local decision making: An application to half-day and full-day preschool special education programs. *Journal of the Division for Early Childhood, 11,* 171–179.

Berrueta-Clement, J. R., Schweinhart, L. J., Barnett, W. S., Epstein, A. S., & Weikart, D. P. (1984). *Changed lives: The effects of the Perry Preschool program on youths through age 19.* Ypsilanti, MI: High/Scope.

Bricker, D., Bailey, E., & Bruder, M. B. (1984). The efficacy of early intervention and the handicapped infant: A wise or wasted resource. *Advances in Developmental and Behavioral Pediatrics, 5,* 373–423.

Bristol, M., Reichle, N., & Thomas, D. (1987). Changing demographics of the American family: Implications for single-parent families of young handicapped children. *Journal of the Division for Early Childhood, 12,* 56–69.

Bronfenbrenner, U. (1986). Ecology of the family as a context for human development: Research perspectives. *Developmental Psychology, 22,* 723–742.

Bureau of Economic Analysis. (1982). *The national income and product accounts of the United States, 1929–1982: Statistical tables.* Washington, DC: U.S. Government Printing Office.

Bureau of Economic Analysis. (1987). *Survey of current business, 67*(7), 74.

Burkett, C. W. (1982). Effects of frequency of home visits on achievement of preschool students in a home-based early childhood education program. *Journal of Educational Research, 76,* 41–44.

Casto, G., & Mastropieri, M. A. (1986). The efficacy of early intervention programs: A meta-analysis. *Exceptional Children, 52*, 417–424.

Casto, G., & Tolfa, D. (1981). Multi-agency project for preschoolers. In T. Black & P. Hutinger (Eds.), *Cost-effective delivery strategies in rural areas: Programs for young handicapped children* (Vol. 1, 28–35). (HCEEP Rural Network Monograph)

Coelen, C., Glantz, F., & Calore, D. (1979). *Day care centers in the U.S.: A national profile 1976–1977.* Cambridge, MA: Abt Associates.

Consortium for Longitudinal Studies. (1983). *As the twig is bent.* Hillsdale, NJ: L. Erlbaum.

Dunlap, W. R., & Hollinsworth, J. S. (1977). How does a handicapped child affect the family? Implications for practitioners. *The Family Coordinator, 26*, 286–293.

Dunst, C. J. (1986). Overview of the efficacy of early intervention programs. In L. Bickman & D. L. Weatherford (Eds.), *Evaluating early intervention programs for severely handicapped children and their families* (pp. 79–147). Austin, TX: PRO-ED.

Escobar, C. M., & Barnett, W. S. (1986, October). *Benefit-cost analysis of the Abecedarian preschool program.* Paper presented at the Council for Exceptional Children, Division of Early Childhood Annual National Conference, Louisville, KY.

Escobar, C. M., Peterson, A., Lauritzen, V., & Barnett, W. S. (1987). *Transportation options and costs for preschool special education in Utah* (Report to the Utah State Office of Education). Logan: Utah State University, Early Intervention Research Institute.

Frakes, P. (1981). Early lifestyle program, King's Daughters' School. In T. Black & P. Hutinger (Eds.), *Cost-effective delivery strategies in rural areas: Programs for young handicapped children* (Vol. 1, 11–17). (HCEEP Rural Network Monograph)

Gramlich, E. M. (1981). *Benefit-cost analysis of government programs.* Englewood Cliffs, NJ: Prentice-Hall.

Grubb, W. N. (1987). *Young children face the states: Issues and options for early childhood programs.* Center for Policy Research in Education (CRPE) Joint Note. New Brunswick, NJ: Rutgers, Eagleton Institute of Politics, CPRE.

Guralnick, M. J., & Bennett, F. C. (1987). *The effectiveness of early intervention for at-risk and handicapped children.* Orlando: Academic Press.

Haveman, R. H., & Wolfe, B. L. (1984). Schooling and economic well-being: The role of nonmarket effects. *Journal of Human Resources, 19*, 377–407.

Head Start Bureau. (1987). *Head Start Program Information Report* (Report to federal government). Washington, DC: Author.

Hutinger, P. (1981). The Macomb 0–3 regional project. In T. Black & P. Hutinger (Eds.), *Cost-effective delivery strategies in rural areas: Programs for young handicapped children* (Vol. 1, 19–27). (HCEEP Rural Network Monograph)

Kakalik, J. S., Furry, W. S., Thomas, M. A., & Carney, M. F. (1981). *The cost of special education* (Report No. N-1792-ED). Santa Monica: The Rand Corporation.

Kysela, G., & Marfo, K. (1983). Mother–child interactions and early intervention programmes for handicapped infants and young children. *Educational Psychology, 3*, 201–212.

Levin, H. (1983). *Cost-effectiveness: A primer.* Beverly Hills: Sage Publications.

Love, J., Nauta, M., Coelen, C., Hewlett, K., & Ruopp, R. (1976). *National Home Start evaluation final report: Findings and implications.* Cambridge, MA: Abt Associates.

Macy, D. J., & Carter, J. L. (1980). *Triple T infant consortium follow-up study.* Dallas: Macy Researach Associates.

Rule, S., Stowitschek, J., Innocenti, M., Striefel, S., Killoran, J., Swezey, K., & Boswell, C. (1987). The Social Integration Program: An analysis of the effects of mainstreaming handicapped children into day care centers. *Education and Treatment of Children, 10*, 175–192.

Ruopp, R., Travers, J., Glantz, F., & Coelen, C. (1979). *Children at the center: Summary findings and policy implications of the National Day Care Study.* Cambridge, MA: Abt Associates.

Sameroff, A. J. (1983). Developmental and theory systems: Contexts and evolution. In P. Mussen (Ed.), *Handbook of child psychology: Vol. 1. History, theory, and methods* (pp. 263–288). New York: Wiley.

Schweinhart, L. J. (1985). Early childhood development programs in the eighties: The national picture. *High/Scope Early Childhood Policy Papers* (No. 1). Ypsilanti, MI: High/Scope.

Schweinhart, L. J., & Weikart, D. P. (1980). *Young children grow up: The effects of the Perry Preschool program on youths through age 15.* Ypsilanti, MI: High/Scope.

Seitz, V., Rosenbaum, L. K., & Apfel, N. H. (1985). Effects of family support intervention: A 10-year follow-up. *Child Development, 56*, 376–391.

Shonkoff, J. P., & Hauser-Cram, P. (1987). Early intervention for disabled infants and their families: A quantitative analysis. *Pediatrics, 80*, 650–658.

Stock, J. R., Wnek, L. L., Newborg, J. A., Schenck, E. A., Gabel, J. R., Spurgeon, M. S., & Ray, H. W. (1976). *Evaluation of the Handicapped Children's Early Education Program.* Columbus, OH: Battelle Memorial Institute.

Thompson, M. A. (1980). *Benefit-cost analysis for program evaluation.* Beverly Hills: Sage Publications.

Walker, K. (1981). Project Sunrise. In T. Black & P. Hutinger (Eds.), *Cost-effective delivery strategies in rural areas: Programs for young handicapped children* (Vol. 1, 28–35). (HCEEP Rural Network Monograph)

Weikart, D. P., Bond, J. T., & McNeil, J. T. (1978). *The Ypsilanti Perry Preschool Project: Preschool years and longitudinal results through fourth grade.* Ypsilanti, MI: High/Scope.

Weikart, D. P., Kamii, C. K., & Radin, N. L. (1967). Perry Preschool Project progress report. In D. P. Weikart (Ed.), *Preschool intervention: A preliminary report of the Perry Preschool Project* (pp. 1–61). Ann Arbor, MI: Campus Publishers.

Weiss, R. S. (1981). INREAL intervention for language handicapped and bilingual children. *Journal of the Division for Early Childhood, 4*, 40–51.

Weiss, R. S., & Heublein, E. A. (1981). Colorado school district INREAL experimental study. In B. A. McNulty, D. B. Smith, & E. W. Soper (Eds.), *Effectiveness of early special education for handicapped children* (Appendix). Denver: Colorado State Department of Education.

Weiss, S., & Jurs, S. (1984, October). *Cost-effectiveness of early childhood education for handicapped children.* Paper presented at the Annual Meeting of the Atlantic Economic Society, Montreal.

Weissbourd, B. (1983). The family support movement: Greater than the sum of its parts. *Zero to Three, 4*, 8–10.

Zigler, E., & Berman, W. (1983). Discerning the future of early intervention. *American Psychologist, 38*, 894–906.

24 *Designing meaningful evaluations of early intervention services*

PENNY HAUSER-CRAM

The enterprise of evaluating human service programs has evolved considerably during the past two decades. Knowledge gained from previous evaluations of such programs as Head Start and from the growing body of research on young children with disabilities and their families enables evaluators to avoid the pitfalls of past evaluations by taking advantage of recent advances in analytical approaches and employing measures of child and family change that are based on a broad view of human development.

Evaluation differs from other forms of research in that it focuses primarily on questions of efficacy – that is, on how change has occurred as a result of a program or specific treatment. Although understanding the mechanisms and impact of change forms the basis of our knowledge of human development, in evaluation research the critical task is to disentangle the impacts of services from other effects. Nevertheless, the logic of inquiry is the same in evaluation research as in other research endeavors. Evaluation demands the conceptualization of research questions and hypotheses, development of an appropriate and feasible design, selection of valid and reliable measures, application of systematic and unbiased procedures for data collection, determination of precise analyses of data, and accurate interpretation of results.

Well-designed evaluations require investigators to progress through a series of steps, beginning with understanding the purpose of the evaluation, proceeding with conceptualization of the questions and study design, followed by selection of appropriate data analysis strategies, and culminating in interpretation of the results. Following these various steps, this chapter reviews the methodological decisions, dilemmas, and limitations that guide evaluation of early intervention programs and suggests new directions that evaluation research may take.

UNDERSTANDING THE PURPOSE OF EVALUATION

The functions of evaluation of service programs like early intervention are many and varied. Evaluation may serve to justify the existence or expansion of a program, improve its functioning, or demonstrate impact of a specific set of services on participants and the wider community. Each of the "stakeholders" (that is, individuals concerned with a program) may have different questions that evaluators could legitimately address. For example, state legislators may ask questions about a program's cost-benefit ratio, program developers may be concerned with cost-effectiveness, service providers may wonder about the relative benefits of various program features, such as

583

parent groups, and parents may ask whether their child's motor needs are met as well by an educator as by a physical therapist. Each of these questions requires a different design, analytical strategy, and level of resources and skills.

In general, it has been considered useful to dichotomize the purpose of program evaluation into serving either formative or summative goals (Scriven, 1967). In formative (or process) evaluation, questions are asked that will aid in the improvement of a program. For example, evaluators might focus on parent satisfaction with parent groups or staff recommendations for improving the assessment process. This is sometimes referred to as "use-based" evaluation (Bryk & Raudenbush, 1983), because it yields information that is immediately useful to service providers and participants.

In contrast, summative (or outcome) evaluation provides evidence of the benefits (or absence of benefits) of a program. Generally, it responds to questions about whether the goals of the program were achieved in terms of positive gains for participants. Information relating to input (i.e., various elements of the program), process (i.e., ways in which program implementation occurs), and outcome (i.e., effects on participants) is collected. Data are reported with a view toward the importance of generalizability of the program should the results be promising. This is termed "need-based" evaluation, because it produces information about programs, like early intervention, that respond to social needs (Bryk & Raudenbush, 1983).

Although useful heuristically, the formative–summative dichotomy has been criticized for being overly simplistic (Beer & Bloomer, 1986). Programs require different types of evaluation at different stages in their growth (Jacobs, 1988). Newly developed services may need to concentrate on collecting data about the characteristics of program participants (such as educational and marital status of parents and age, gender, birth order, and disability of the child) and about the range of services provided (including hours of service and discipline of the service provider). Although such data may seem only rudimentary, they can be used to respond to important questions about families a program is and is not serving, and when used in conjuction with census and prevalence data, about whether large pockets of children exist who are not receiving services.

Programs that have been functioning for awhile may find most useful evaluations that focus on the program's goals and objectives. For example, a program's stated goals may be to provide family-focused services, and an evaluation can establish to what extent the planned services are actually implemented. As Patton (1978) emphasizes, a discrepancy frequently exists between the stated goals of a program and the conflict-laden realities of implementation. While incorporating information about participants and implemented services, more mature programs may use evaluations to focus on the effects of the program on the participants. Program directors and staff may want to know, for example, if services have resulted in a reduction in stress in families or enhanced functional abilites in children.

A program's stage of development, particular needs, and fiscal constraints will suggest the form evaluation should take and the type of data to be collected. Yet, policymakers ask questions about the efficacy of early intervention programs that demand evaluations that yield information across programs and participants. Although some evaluations should be designed to respond to specific questions about the functioning of a particular program, others should be developed with a broader view toward the types of information about early intervention that are of value to those creating programs and establishing policies. Thus, one of the first tasks of the evaluator is to determine the extent to which the investigation can yield broad-based findings that will aid in the accumulation of knowledge about early intervention programs.

CONCEPTUALIZING THE QUESTIONS

Any human service program must respond to the question, Is this program successful? This question, which might appear simple and straightforward, at closer glance reveals its complexity. First, we need to be more precise about the definition of "this program." What is early intervention, and is one early intervention program similar to another? Second, what is meant by "success" and how can it be measured? Third, "success for whom?" Is the program targeted only on children or do parents also benefit? Each of these questions will be considered in turn.

What is the program?

Descriptions of early intervention programs often do little more than differentiate between "home-based" and "center-based" services. Although such descriptions indicate the location of service delivery, they tell little about the theoretical bases underlying service provision or about the actual content of the services. One home-based program may differ substantially from another, as was revealed in a metaanalysis of studies on early intervention programs (Shonkoff & Hauser-Cram, 1987). Programs classified as home-based varied substantially in the number of hours of service, discipline of provider (e.g., educator, physical therapist, social worker), type of curriculum (developmentally based, language-based, behavioral), and model of service provision (transdisciplinary or multidisciplinary). Even more problematic was the finding that few studies reported sufficient information about program components to allow systematic study of these critical variables.

The question of defining services is not unique to early intervention programs and, to some extent, is relevant to all human service programs that are multifaceted in scope and multidimensional in purpose. One solution would be to code written information about a program's goals or model of service provision. Yet, as was found in the evaluation of the Follow Through program, written information shares only some characteristics with the actual program (House, Glass, McLean, & Walker, 1978). Even similarly labeled models may have as much variation in service components as do models with different labels (Bock, Stebbins, & Proper, 1977). An additional problem occurs in defining services provided to participants in early intervention programs. Many programs may offer a similar array of features but individualize these services to families based on the family's needs and desires, the child's age and disability, and the program's philosophy and staffing pattern. Individual variation may indeed be the hallmark of these programs, and suitable and efficient ways of documenting such variation need to be found.

Finally, as in all human service programs, because the services that are planned for a child and family are often quite different from those actually received, it is important that implemented services be considered. Patton (1978) delineates three aspects of implementation that require attention in an evaluation. The first, termed "effort evaluation," concentrates on questions about whether there has been a sufficient quantity of service to allow the possibility of impact. Although the lack of effort seems clear in cases of individuals who terminate medical treatment before they are advised to do so, it is not as clear in cases where families enrolled in a program have an uneven rate of participation. The next phase, "process evaluation," involves an analysis of how the program produces its results. For example, what actually occurs during a home visit that is likely to have an effect on a child or family? In the third phase, "treatment specification," the independent variables (services) are identified and specified in a way that allows them to be measured precisely.

Delineating the various program components may require a multistage process. Through that process, features of a program that have the potential of promoting beneficial changes in children and families should become evident. The need to reconceptualize the simple question of the effectiveness of early intervention into a more complex, but more meaningful, question also becomes apparent as evaluators strive to understand the differential effects on children and families produced by various aspects of an early intervention program.

What is success?

Most evaluations of early intervention have defined program success as cognitive gain for children (Casto & Mastropieri, 1986; Dunst & Rheingrover, 1981; Shonkoff & Hauser-Cram, 1987; Simeonsson, Cooper, & Scheiner, 1982). Yet cognitive gain on a standardized test is a limited and, in some cases, misguided choice as the predominant outcome measure for evaluating early intervention programs. Conventional measures of intelligence quotient (IQ) or developmental quotient (DQ) for infants and toddlers have poor predictive validity (Lewis, 1976). Since such measures are unstable indicators of development, it would be difficult to determine aspects of development attributable to program input.

Traditional developmental assessments for children younger than school age suffer from a range of technical problems. The most important drawback for application to children with disabilities is the inability of the test to distinguish between normal and disabled children within the youngest age groups for whom the test is intended (Bracken, 1987). For example, on the McCarthy Scales of Children's Abilities (McCarthy, 1972), the average $2\frac{1}{2}$-year-old child is expected to fail to answer a single item correctly on 11 of the 18 subtests. Furthermore, certain tests, such as the Battelle Developmental Inventory (Newborg, Stock, Wneck, Guidubaldi, & Svinicki, 1984) have steep item gradients, meaning that small differences in the number of correct items can yield large changes in a child's score. A more general criticism of the use of norm-referenced tests for assessment of the development of children with disabilities is the inability to locate tests with an appropriate reference population (Hamilton & Swan, 1981). Few traditional standardized measures have included children with disabilities in their norming population. In a comparison of 27 such measures, including the McCarthy Scales of Children's Abilities (McCarthy, 1972) and the Stanford-Binet Intelligence Scale (Terman & Merrill, 1973), Fuchs, Fuchs, Benowitz, and Barringer (1987) found only 5 reported the proportion of disabled children who participated in some aspect of test development.

Another problem with the application of IQ measures to infants with atypical development is the heavy dependence on motor and perceptual-motor skills in most infant IQ tests (Garwood, 1982; Shonkoff, 1983). Such measures are misleading indicators of cognitive competence, especially for children with motor impairment (see Cicchetti & Wagner, this volume; McCune, Kalmanson, Fleck, Glazewski, & Sillari, this volume). Finally, IQ tests are so global in nature that they often are insensitive to the types of specific changes in development that might occur as the result of intervention. Changes in a target area of development, such as language skills, for example, may be obscured by the lack of change in other areas, such as motor skills, resulting in a statistically nonsignificant increase in overall IQ.

Reliance on IQ as an outcome measure has overshadowed other critical areas of child development affected by early intervention programs. Such programs often seek to have an effect on a range of domains of development, such as functional skills, social competence, self-regulatory behaviors, motivation, and curiosity (Bricker & Kaminski, 1986). Although measures are not as well developed in these areas of development as in the area of cognition, they should not be neglected by evaluators (Zigler & Balla, 1982). Given the multifaceted goals of early intervention programs, an array of child outcomes is often required to understand program effects sufficiently (Meisels, 1985).

Evaluators may need to seek creative ways of measuring change in domains of development for which there are no standardized measures. A number of new instruments have been reported in the research literature that deserve careful consideration (Hauser-Cram & Shonkoff, 1988). Because such measures often lack sufficient documentation of their psychometric properties and standardization for atypical populations, admittedly there is an element of risk associated with their selection as outcome measures. Such risk is diminished if multiple measures are employed, with each sharing a portion of the theoretically relevant factors but each having different loadings of irrelevant factors or "noise" (Isaac & Michael, 1978). This approach, often referred to as triangulation of measurement (Miles & Huberman, 1984), offers more powerful evidence of effects than would reliance on a single measure alone.

For example, many early intervention programs aim to increase children's motivation and curiosity during self-initiated or self-directed activities. A measure, such as an IQ test, in which an examiner elicits a child's performance would be a poor choice as a means of measuring this outcome. Instead, a valid evaluation of this program goal might require observation of children during spontaneous play. The research literature on spontaneous play in normally developing children (Belsky & Most, 1981) and in children with disabilities (Hill & McCune-Nicolich, 1981) offers some promising examples of measures of the level of play (ranging from mouthing to pretense) in which a child may engage. Assessments of mastery motivation (Morgan & Harmon, 1984) in which task persistence is assessed during play with a problem-presenting toy, would further strengthen knowledge about children's self-directed activity. Finally, a questionnaire about task persistence and behavior during self-initiated activites (Morgan, Maslin, Harmon, Jennings, & Busch-Rossnagel, in press) could be completed by parents and service providers to marshall more evidence of children's behavior in this domain.

In operationalizing "success," evaluators need to consider both short-term, immediate gains and long-term advantages. Most evaluations of early intervention services for disabled infants focus on short-term skill development, and virtually none have considered sufficiently the long-term benefits of such programs (Shonkoff & Hauser-Cram, 1987). The value of short-term effects should not be minimized, and individual programs may well strive for short-term gains that evaluations should acknowledge. Equally important questions exist, however, about the stability of such gains and about latent effects that emerge after a child leaves an early intervention program.

Examples of investigations of persistent effects have emerged in the literature on early education programs for economically disadvantaged children. These benefits usually include a range of policy-relevant variables, such as the avoidance of delinquency, successful employment, and decreased need for remedial services in school (Berreuta-Clement, Schweinhart, Barnett, Epstein, & Weikart, 1984; Lazar & Darlington, 1982). Evaluations of early intervention services would benefit from careful thought about appropriate measures of their long-term effects. For example, it may be valuable to investigate whether participation in early intervention affects later school adjustment, peer interaction, amount and type of additional services, placement in an integrated or segregated setting, parental advocacy, and parent–school relationships.

Success for whom?

Early intervention programs serve a wide range of children and families. Some children may have no documented delays but be "at risk" for problems, others may have delays of unknown etiology, and still others may have nervous system dysfunction related to a specific diagnosis. It would be naive to assume that the effects of early intervention programs would be similar across such a wide range of disabilities.

A central question facing evaluators is how best to define subgroups of children for purposes of elucidating the differential effectiveness of a program (Adelman, 1986). When subgroups have been determined in past evaluations of early intervention services, they have generally been based on diagnostic groups (e.g., Down syndrome, cerebral palsy, and so on). The value of this classification scheme is not yet known, and there may be better approaches. For example, Stein and Jessop (1982) recommended that the traditional categorical approach to the study of the impact of chronic illness on children and families be replaced by an approach that focuses on differences in functional status. It may be that for certain questions about the effectiveness of early intervention, differences may emerge by severity of the child's disability rather than by the type of disability. A hint of this possibility has occurred in the developmental literature, but has not yet been investigated in relation to program effects. In a study of a young children with Down syndrome, cerebral palsy, and developmental delay, Brooks-Gunn and Lewis (1984) found that maternal responsivity was more related to a child's mental age than to diagnostic status. Such data point to the value of thinking carefully about subgroup classifications and about possible interactions among interventions and characteristics of children and families.

In most early intervention programs, the participants are not only children but their parents as well. Despite a fair amount of literature on the impact of raising a handicapped child on families (Blacher & Meyers, 1983; Simeonsson & McHale, 1981), few evaluations of service programs have considered their effects on families aside from measures of satisfaction (Bailey & Simeonsson, 1986). Satisfaction measures may be useful to formative evaluations in helping to improve a program's functioning, but such measures do not lead to objective understanding of a program's effects. Measures of satisfaction can, however, help evaluators understand parents' views of the benefits of a program and how such views vary based on characteristics of the family and child. For example, parents of children with mild disabilities may be satisfied if they believe the program helps to advance their child developmentally, whereas satisfaction for parents of children with severe disabilities may rely on a program's ability to provide support and respite from caretaking tasks (Sandow, Clarke, Cox, & Stewart, 1981).

A program's theoretical model should guide the selection of outcome measures of family impact. Several different models have been posited to explain how early intervention programs affect families. They share a reliance on the ecological view of the child and family (Bronfenbrenner, 1979) and on the transactional nature of development (Sameroff & Chandler, 1975). Marfo and Kysela (1985) isolate three distinct approaches to the characterization of the role of parents in early intervention programs. In the first, the parent therapy model, parents are assisted through counseling or support groups to help resolve stress related to raising a child with disabilities. A more didactic approach is taken in the second, the parent training model, which emphasizes the role of parent behavior in teaching skills to a child. The third, the parent–child interaction model, focuses on assisting the parent in learning to read the child's cues and in being sensitive to the child's needs. The outcomes selected would follow from the model, but each would relate to changes in parents.

Another result of evaluators recognizing the importance of families in early intervention programs is that more precise and accurate findings can be generated if data are analyzed in terms of subgroups of families. Families vary in many ways, and determining the critical characteristics of families that differentiate the impact services will have on them is no easy task. Demographic grouping (by income or educational attainment) is a common strategy. Another approach would be to group families according to differences along a dimension thought to be theoretically important, such as extent and satisfaction with a support network (Shonkoff, 1984). An empirical approach has been suggested by Mink, Nihira, and Meyers (1983). They applied cluster analysis, which is a statistical procedure for defining groups such that they vary on a number of theoretically important variables and each subject is a member of only one group (Anderberg, 1973). Mink et al. (1983) found five distinct patterns of family life, varying from cohesive and harmonious to disadvantaged and low morale. Such differences may help explain how families differ in their response to programs like early intervention.

Evaluators who consider such issues are forced to move from a unitary view of services and a dichotomous notion of success to a better elaborated picture of a program and its participants in which the complexities of each can emerge. Before developing a research design for evaluating a program as multifaceted as early intervention, a series of questions should be addressed. Aspects of a program that are thought to relate to its success must be delineated in a way that will allow replication in future programs. Definitions of success that relate to a program's goals should be sought and appropriate measures selected. Finally, targets of success should be clarified and ways of determining subgroups of children and families need to be considered. The task for evaluation thus becomes one of determining which aspects of a program are valuable, for whom, and in what way. The challenge for the researcher is to design an evaluation that responds to such questions.

DEVELOPING THE RESEARCH DESIGN

Research methodology and statistical analysis emerged as a topic of study in the fields of agriculture and biology (Mark, 1958). It is not difficult to randomly assign seeds to various soil conditions or to control a range of variables, such as amount of daylight or water, to study effects on plant growth. Through random assignment, threats to a study's validity (such as history, maturation, instrumentation, testing, and statistical regression) can be controlled adequately (Campbell & Stanley, 1966). Some researchers (Gilbert, Light, & Mosteller, 1975; White & Mott, 1987) contend that only by conducting controlled randomized field trials can we understand and demonstrate the true effects of innovative programs. But randomized trials are a contentious issue in discussions of research on such programs as early intervention.

Few studies of early intervention have employed a true experimental design. In a review of 49 studies of early intervention programs for children under school age, Dunst and Rheingrover (1981) reported finding only four studies that could be considered true experiments and only one that employed random assignment of subjects to an intervention or control group. Randomized designs have been applied more successfully to studies of early education programs for children likely to have developmental delays as a result of their family's socioeconomic circumstances (e.g., Berrueta-Clement et al., 1984; McKay, Sinisterra, McKay, Gomez, & Lloreda, 1978; Ramey et al., 1976) than to programs for children with disabilities.

Ethical concerns about withholding services from children with disabilities pervade questions regarding the desirability of employing randomized designs in early intervention research. Travers and Light (1982) maintain that legislation such as the Education for All Handicapped Children Act (P.L. 94-142) carries with it a climate of entitlement that tends to extend beyond the boundaries of the legislation. A similar climate is likely to accompany P.L. 99-457, even though it does not mandate services for infants and toddlers but rather offers incentives for the provision of such services. Withholding services for research purposes within such a sociopolitical context may obstruct, rather than facilitate, evaluation efforts. The trust established among evaluators, service providers, and program participants is crucial to a successful evaluation. If participants think they should be receiving more or different services or if service providers believe families should be given a different array or intensity of services, it is unlikely that either will view the evaluation effort as more important than the perceived needs of the child and family. Such beliefs can erode the structure of even the best designed randomized study. Thus, examples exist of service providers' unwillingness to follow the dictates of a randomized study (e.g., Ward, 1973) based on their perception of the need for services by members of the control group. Moreover, participants in a control group themselves may find ways of compensating for the lack of services (known as compensatory rivalry) or may express resentment and demoralization (Cook, Cook, & Mark, 1977). In either case the control group changes as a result of the study, allowing the treatment (or program) to look more or less promising than it should. In sum, randomized evaluation studies conducted within a climate of belief in participants' rights to the services have many risks, not the least of which is the inability to demonstrate the true value of the services.

Evaluation of early intervention programs is at a point where efforts can move beyond questions of general efficacy. Metaanalyses of studies of early intervention programs for infants and toddlers with disabilities (Shonkoff & Hauser-Cram, 1987) and extending into the preschool years (Casto & Mastropieri, 1986) consistently demonstrate moderate effects on general measures of intelligence for children enrolled in these programs. Rather than struggling with practical and ethical concerns about withholding services to children and families in order to design yet another study of the general efficacy of early intervention, evaluators would be wise to concentrate their efforts on answering the current critical questions about the value of specific features of such programs. A host of questions deserve further investigation, for example:

1. What is the range of effects produced by early intervention programs?
2. How do effects vary based on characteristics of the child (e.g., age, disability, severity of disability) and the family (e.g., income, style of coping, satisfaction with support network)?
3. What is the optimal match of service features to the individual needs of children and families?

Evaluations in which such questions are explored can ultimately optimize efficacy by suggesting ways in which services can best be targeted. Ideally, such studies should be preceded by a series of correlational studies that indicate which services are associated with specified beneficial outcomes (Cook & Campbell, 1979). Then, promising program features can be selected for systematic evaluation. Although beyond the scope of this chapter, studies of cost-effectiveness (see Barnett & Escobar, this volume) would complement such investigations.

Design issues are as critical in responding to the questions posed as in developing more general efficacy studies. As an example, suppose an evaluator were investigating the value of parent support groups in reducing stress in families. The true experimental design approach to this question would demand that subjects be randomly assigned to either a treatment group (i.e., to a parent support group) or a control group (i.e., the absence of a parent support group). Unless a large sample of participants were to be involved in the investigation, subjects should be paired (or matched) based on their stress scores on a pretest measure and possibly on demographic characteristics assumed to be related to outcome, such as gender. One member of each matched pair would be selected randomly to attend parent support groups. The evaluation would proceed to document aspects of the support group interaction, attendance levels, and other related process variables. A posttest measure of stress would then be given to members of each group. Finally, analyses would be developed to determine whether participation in support groups was associated with a reduction in level of stress.

When the value of a service is not well documented, as in the case of parent support groups (McGuire & Gottlieb, 1979; Wandersman, 1987), a true experiment, such as the one just described, may be feasible. However, if participants and/or service providers regard the service as valuable, then withholding it from some families touches on ethical issues. Moreover, a randomized study of one feature of an early intervention program is prone to certain weaknesses. First, it often establishes an artifical situation, which makes generalization of its results questionable. Perhaps parents are more or less likely to attend parent support groups when they are "assigned" to do so; thus, their actual behavior is quite different from what it would be if they could simply opt to select attendance at such a group. Second, whenever random assignment occurs within a program in which participants interact with each other, contamination can occur. For example, support group participants may carry on their support group discussion topics with members of the control group, creating, in effect, an underground treatment group.

Several creative options for designing evaluation studies that take into account the constraints of conducting a study within an ongoing program exist (Cook & Campbell, 1979). Although not yet well tested in the early intervention literature, quasiexperiments cater to situations in which treatments (or services) have been provided to participants in some nonrandom fashion (Cook et al., 1977). Four quasiexperimental designs would have particular relevance to investigations of the value of a particular feature of early intervention services, such as parent support groups: (1) the untreated control group with pretest and posttest scores, (2) the cohort design, (3) the nonequivalent dependent variables design, and (4) the planned variation design. An example of the application of each of the four designs to the question of the value of parent support groups in reducing stress is described briefly.

UNTREATED CONTROL GROUP DESIGN. This design would be feasible if more parents in an early intervention program wished to join parent support groups than there were staff members available to lead such groups. Since some parents would need to be placed on a waiting list, they would serve as a natural comparison group. Legitimate comparisons could be made only if members of each group were given a pretest and a posttest and analyses of changes could be made (Cook & Campbell, 1979).

Otherwise, differences between groups at the end of the support group intervention may be attributable to initial differences, rather than to the intervention itself. Other threats to validity exist with this design, such as regression to the mean; if either group has exceptionally high or low scores, their scores are likely to drift toward the mean even in the absence of intervention. A possible selection-maturation effect also exists if members of the two groups are likely to change at different rates irrespective of the intervention. Finally, this strategy is best for interventions that produce effects rather rapidly, for it is unlikely that programs will be willing to keep individuals on a waiting list for a specified service for a long period of time.

COHORT DESIGN. Cohort design takes advantage of knowledge of characteristics of families before a new service, such as parent support groups, is introduced. Changes in stress scores over time could be recorded for one cohort of participants in a program. Parent support groups could then be offered to the next cohort and changes in their stress scores compared to changes in those of the prior cohort. Such a design requires a great deal of patience and prior planning if sufficient data for a cohort are to be gathered before the introduction of a new service. Threats to validity, such as history (i.e., effects on the second cohort that did not exist for the first due to changes in legislation, public information, etc.), need to be considered in the application of this design.

NONEQUIVALENT DEPENDENT VARIABLES DESIGN. This design involves only one group, but comparisons on different outcome measures are made within the group. For example, suppose father support groups are hypothesized to reduce stress for fathers but not to affect other aspects of their social support network. Pretest–posttest changes would be expected to occur for measures of stress but not for a measure of the size of the support network. This approach has the advantage of avoiding the problem of selecting a comparison group, yet still can provide some evidence of change associated with participation in a support group. Dunst describes his use of this strategy in evaluating an intervention program in which changes were targeted on only certain aspects of development (Dunst & Rheingrover, 1981). A difficulty inherent in this design involves the determination of one set of discrete outcomes that are assumed to be affected and another set of outcomes assumed not to be affected by the intervention. Many interventions, such as parent support groups, may produce changes in one area of a child's or family's functioning that, in turn, affect changes in other areas.

PLANNED VARIATION DESIGN. Planned variation is appropriate for analyzing questions about the relationship between the intensity of a service and the outcome. Individuals are assigned to groups that receive different levels of service. For example, one parent support group might meet weekly and another only monthly. Changes in stress scores from pretest to posttest associated with these different levels of service would be analyzed. Ideally, the assignment to groups would be random (or would be a matched pair with random assignment), although some of the same concerns about random assignment discussed previously could occur, such as compensatory rivalry and resentment. If not random, selection-maturation effects and regression effects would need to be considered, as in the untreated control group design. Ideally, the evaluator would need to strive to ensure that the difference in level of treatment was large enough to be maintained. For example, a difference between weekly and biweekly group meetings may be inadequate because it is likely that parents in the weekly group may miss some meetings and, therefore, attend at about the same frequency as the biweekly group, obscuring the difference in level of intervention.

Each of the designs described has the potential of responding to questions about the value of a particular feature of early intervention services. Each also possesses potential weaknesses, as does even the randomized study. The evaluator's task is to anticipate such weaknesses and garner evidence that counters alternative explanations for findings.

Statistical power

Regardless of the design selected, evaluators need to consider issues of statistical power. Power is the ability to detect differences statistically when such differences exist in the population (Cohen, 1977). In statistical terms, it is the ability to reject the null hypothesis when, in fact, it should be rejected. In the two-group comparison case, the null hypothesis can fail to be rejected due to one of three reasons: (1) The difference in sample means is small enough to suggest with a high degree of probability that there is no true difference in the population; (2) the within-group variation is large and the difference between group means is moderate or small; or (3) the sample size is small and the mean differences between groups in moderate. In the latter case, it is said that there was insufficient power to allow the analysis to detect the moderate differences that actually exist in the population.

Problems of insufficient power plague evaluation research on early intervention. Unless studies are done using particularly large programs, sample sizes are small, making it unlikely that moderate effects will be demonstrated. Samples of at least 70 subjects per group are needed to detect differences of one-half standard deviation 90% of the time (Cohen, 1977). Yet, very few studies on early intervention have samples of that size. In a metaanalysis of early intervention studies, 82% of samples had 40 or fewer subjects (Shonkoff & Hauser-Cram, 1987).

Sample size questions to some extent intersect with questions about design. For example, designs that call for matching of subjects may mean that many potential sample participants are ineligible simply because no "match" can be found for them. This may necessitate summative evaluations to occur across programs in order to develop samples of sufficient size. An added benefit of this appoach may be that the results of such studies can be generalized to a wider array of programs and not restricted to a particular site that may have an unusually dedicated staff or other idiosyncratic features that may account for differences.

ANALYTICAL APPROACHES

Measuring change

One of the greatest dilemmas for those evaluating early intervention programs is how to measure the effects of services in the absence of research designs with randomized or rigorously selected control groups. Documenting and analyzing change is indeed the central task of evaluation research, yet it is an exceedingly difficult undertaking when causal inferences are not readily apparent. Children and families naturally change over time, and there are many influences on such change, including environmental forces, genetic or biological influences, and support services. The question facing evaluators is how to disentangle the influences on change so that changes due to early intervention services above and beyond (or in interaction with) those due to other causes can be isolated. Several approaches to partitioning change into its various components have been proposed and applied, although infrequently, to early intervention research. Each has its appealing aspects and its drawbacks.

NORM-REFERENCED MODELS. One popular approach in educational evaluation work has been the norm-referenced model. Much of the evaluation of Title I (now, Chapter I) programs has relied on this strategy (Linn, 1979). In the norm-referenced model the performance of children in a program is compared to national norms or standardized test norms. It is reasoned that if children in a program demonstrate greater gains than those of the norming population, the program has been effective. The assumption is that in the absence of the program the expected rate of development would be the same for all children.

The appeal of this approach to the evaluation of early intervention programs is limited. First, it relies heavily on the use of standard psychometric measures of development. As discussed earlier, such reliance is unwise given the properties of such tests and the lack of a comparable norming population. Second, it assumes a linear rate of development for all children. Many have questioned whether this assumption holds for children with disabilities (Fuchs et al., 1987; Meisels, 1987).

INDEXES OF CHANGE. Another approach to measuring change that has particular application to the evaluation of early intervention programs involves the development of an index that measures development as a function of disability. Generally, these indexes quantify how rapidly development changes over a specified period of time, usually the time the child is enrolled in an early intervention program. The indexes have tended to become more sophisticated over time. One of the first was the Intervention Efficiency Index developed by Bagnato and Neisworth (1980). This index involves the calculation of the ratio of months of developmental gain divided by months of intervention. For example, if a child gained 4 months developmentally over a 6-month period of intervention, the child's rate of development could be calculated as .67. The drawback to this approach is the lack of comparison to the child's rate of development prior to entering early intervention.

A second type of index was thus developed to compare current development rates with prior ones. Several versions exist, but most are similar in structure. For example, Dunst (1986) proposed the following formula:

$$\frac{DA_2 - DA_1}{CA_2 - CA_1} \bigg/ \frac{DA_1}{CA_1}$$

where DA is developmental age and CA is chronological age. Wolery's Proportional Change Index (Wolery, 1983), which was employed in the evaluation of a center-based early intervention program (Wolery, 1985), has a similar structure:

$$\frac{\text{Developmental gain}}{\text{Time in intervention}} \bigg/ \frac{\text{Pretest DA}}{\text{Pretest CA}}$$

Other related indexes have been recommended (Irwin & Wong, 1974; Simeonsson & Wiegerlink, 1975). Rosenberg, Robinson, Finkler, and Rose (1987) compared some of these indexes and found high correlations among them. They concluded that "there is little basis for recommending one formula over another" (p. 217).

This approach has certain limitations, however. First, it is useful only for the measurement of change using standardized assessment measures in which developmental ages can be calculated. Second, it is based on the assumption that the ratio of developmental age to chronological age would be stable in the absence of intervention. This assumption is critical in the application of such indexes, yet lacks empirical verification.

The measurement of change in early intervention programs needs to be considered over a wide range of measures and not restricted to assessments of IQ and DQ. What methods are proposed for dealing statistically with such data?

DIFFERENCE SCORES. The most straightforward approach to the analysis of change is to use difference scores (also called gain scores). This involves subtracting the pretest score (before intervention) from the posttest score (after intervention). Although computationally appealing, there is debate among methodologists as to the wisdom of this approach. For some time it has been argued that a simple difference score lacks reliability (Cronbach & Furby, 1970; Linn & Slinde, 1977). Reliability indicates to what degree individuals can be distinguished from one another based on the measure. Moreover, a measure is said to be unreliable if it produces a different value for the same individual when the test is replicated. Some contend that difference scores are more unreliable than the scores themselves (Lord, 1956) and that in most cases, difference scores correlate negatively with pretest scores (Linn & Slinde, 1977). That is to say, those with low pretest scores would tend to have large difference scores even in the absence of effects of intervention.

Most recently, the assumption of the lack of reliability of difference scores has been questioned (Rogosa & Willett, 1983). Such scores may have value if external information about the test-retest reliability of the measure is employed. For example, Webster and Bereiter (1963) proposed a reliability-weighted measure of individual change. Such alternatives have not been used widely in the research literature, which instead has turned to the use of residual change scores as the standard approach to the measurement of change.

Cronbach and Furby (1970) defined the residual change score as "primarily a way of singling out individuals who have changed more (or less) than expected" (p. 70). The key to understanding such analyses is in how the "expected" (or predicted) scores are calculated. An equation (a regression equation) can be developed that describes the relation between the posttest scores and the pretest scores for the entire sample; a linear relation between pretest and posttest is assumed in developing the equation. For each individual a score can then be calculated that represents the difference between the actual posttest score that individual obtained and the score that would be predicted for the individual inserting the individual's pretest score into the regression equation. This difference score is termed the "residual." As with any regression equation, demographic and other critical variables can be put into the equation first to respond to questions of change above and beyond that accounted for by differences in characteristics of sample participants (such as income or education). The critical question for evaluators is whether there is a relationship between certain aspects of early intervention services (say, intensity of service) and the size of the residuals. In other words, did individuals who received home visits more frequently change more than predicted? The prediction in this case is purely empirical, not based on clinical judgment.

Even advocates of this approach to measuring change admit that residual regression has limitations. Two specific drawbacks are relevant to the application of this approach to the evaluation of early intervention programs. First, as Rogosa, Brandt, and Zimowski (1982) point out, residual regression tells us little about how an individual actually changes on a certain dimension. Instead, it tells us how a person would have changed on that dimension *if* all persons in the sample had had the same pretest scores. The lack of utility of this hypothetical situation applied to children (or families) in early intervention programs is obvious, as variation not only exists but, in fact, is the very question of interest: How do various program features affect children and families of varying characteristics? Second, regression relies heavily on group data and large samples and is relatively insensitive to the individualized nature of services provided in most early intervention programs.

GOAL ATTAINMENT SCALING. In response to this criticism, a method termed Goal Attainment Scaling (GAS) (Kiresuk & Lund, 1976) has been developed that takes advantage of the evaluation of progress of participants toward unique goals. GAS is a procedure for the development of a quantitative outcome measure based on levels of success in meeting individualized goals of program participants. The GAS score is in essence a measure of how close the individual's progress on a particular goal comes to that predicted by service providers. It has the advantage of being sensitive to unique goals and of providing a quantitative outcome that lends itself to statistical analysis.

There are several different approaches to GAS (e.g., Bailey et al., 1986; Romney, 1976), but each involves a similar series of steps. The first four steps occur before an intervention commences. First, a set of goals is specified for each child and family. Next, each goal is weighted, based on its priority, although several goals may be given the same weight. Third, a continuum of expected outcomes is developed (from "worse than expected" to "better than expected"), using criteria for the attainment of each level. Fourth, initial performance is assessed for each objective. Finally, after the participant has received intervention services for a specified period of time, performance is again assessed so determination of level of outcome can be made. Outcomes can be standardized (i.e., converted to a common metric that has a specified mean and standard deviation) so comparisons can be made and statistical tests applied.

The apparent attraction of GAS – its ability to incorporate the reality of programs that individualize services – may at first glance mask its shortcomings. Programs that have attempted to use this method of evaluation have not always met with success. One consistent problem has been the question of the validity of goals, especially in areas of development where there is no agreed-upon measure of progress, such as socioemotional development (Meisels, 1987). An equally perplexing problem became apparent in the application of GAS to the evaluation of the Child and Family Resource Program (Nauta & Hewett, 1988), a federally funded demonstration project. Goals were not always a reflection of a family's true needs, and reliability in goal determination was questionable. Some have found correlations between staff on goal attainment decisions to be as low as .12 (Woodward, Santa-Barbara, Levin, & Epstein, 1978).

Another problem with the application of GAS is that the meaning of the outcome measure at the program level is obscure (Maher, 1983). How do we interpret a program's mean goal attainment? Although the mean attainment can be represented by a single number, the wide range of goals that make up that mean make it an "apples and oranges" type of outcome. Moreover, in comparing two programs, can we be sure the one with the higher attainment had better methods or simply lower expectations or more trivial goals? Such questions cast doubt on the utility of this approach to program evaluation. GAS may have its greatest promise, however, as a method of helping service providers monitor their work.

Understanding change

As methodologists struggle with improvements in analyzing change scores, developmental psychologists wrestle with refinements in understanding what causes changes in children and families. Such understanding can lead to predictions about how various aspects of intervention affect patterns of development. Predictions can, in turn, guide us in knowing the characteristics of families and children that benefit from various aspects of intervention. Two approaches to understanding change during development that are rapidly gaining visibility are growth modeling and structural equation modeling. Each is described, although only briefly, here.

GROWTH MODELING. Bryk and Raudenbush (1987) contend that to really understand change, data must be collected over more than two time points. Growth modeling makes maximum use of data collected over several time points and highlights the different rates of growth of different individuals (Willett, 1988). It involves a two-stage process, beginning with the calculation of a mathematical model that summarizes each individual's change across all data points. Next, differences in these changes across individuals are analyzed. This analysis involves examining whether differences in change are a function of selected characteristics of the child (such as gender, type of disability), the family (such as income), or the services (such as intensity).

The advantage of growth modeling applied to the evaluation of early intervention services is that it allows ways of testing whether development occurs in a linear or other (curvilinear) fashion. This is a contrast to other approaches that assume a linear model. Moreover, growth modeling allows researchers to test whether development approaches an asymptote (i.e., levels off) at a certain point, and, if so, whether this occurs for certain subgroups and not others (Goldstein, 1979). Although growth modeling has not been applied to evaluations of early intervention or other similar programs, it warrants serious consideration by evaluators.

STRUCTURAL EQUATION MODELING. Structural equation modeling (SEM) is a method of both model building and model testing that requires specification of the temporal relations among a set of variables (Duncan, 1975). It is also sometimes referred to as path analysis (because of the links, or paths, assumed between variables) or as causal modeling. The latter term is misleading because this analytical procedure does not yield definite confirmation of cause-and-effect relations (Biddle & Martin, 1987).

Although not an inherent requirement of SEM, a visual diagram of the hypothesized relations among variables is generally presented. The diagram is drawn so that by left-to-right inspection the reader can understand the temporal ordering of variables: Independent variables are on the left, followed by one or more sets of intervening variables in the middle, and concluding with dependent variables on the right. Paths are drawn only among variables assumed to be related. A series of hierarchical regression equations are developed to test the predicted relations. For each equation, the question is asked whether the new variable accounts for a significant proportion of the variance above and beyond that contributed by those variables already in the equation. A final step involves a statistical test of the "goodness of fit" of the data to the entire model.

The advantage of SEM is that it offers a way of examining the multiple influences on change in children and families. It provides a way of moving from a simplistic notion of the impact of early intervention to one that more closely represents its multifaceted nature. A schematic representation of the multiple variables and their empirical relations is an appealing feature of this approach.

Currently, only a few examples exist of structural equation modeling applied to analyses of programs for young children, and none has focused exclusively on early intervention services. Tietze (1987) followed a group of 203 children through 4 years of elementary school and analyzed the effects of attending a preschool program on retention and assignment to a special class placement. He specified a model that included various context variables (e.g., socioeconomic characteristics, religion, etc.), several process variables (e.g., class size, hours of instruction per week, etc.), and criteria as outcomes (assignment to a retention class, retention in grade, and special class placement). He found that enrollment in a preschool program had the strongest influence on school success.

Although SEM has many advantages over more simplistic analytical approaches, enthusiasm for it needs to be tempered by a realistic understanding of its limitations. In order to specify a sufficient number of assumed relations among variables in a model, a large number of cases is required. Tanaka (1987) reports that some contend that as many as 200 cases are required to provide adequate estimates using SEM, although, based on simulations, Gebring and Anderson (1985) have questioned whether such a large sample is mandatory. There is general agreement that the more variables specified in the model, the larger the sample size required. Sophisticated questions about the multiple effects of early intervention programs on children and families with differing characteristics will clearly require studies with large samples if SEM is the analytic strategy of choice.

The most important limitation of SEM, however, is conceptual, not statistical. In a variation of the "correlation does not imply causation" theme, Biddle and Martin (1987) contend that confirmation of a model does not imply proof of the model's validity. Even with models that appear to fit the data well, we do not necessarily know if we have failed to specify a critical variable that accounts for the relations among other variables. Therefore, even when researchers claim a model has been confirmed, they need to consider other possible explanations of the results.

Finally, some concern exists about whether SEM will replace the theoretical development of models (Connell, 1987). In the extreme, our knowledge of human development would be data-driven and atheoretical. Like the application of other analytical techniques, SEM can be misused. The critical steps in determining which variables to include, hypothesizing their relations in the model, and interpreting results are important challenges that can best be met by those working from theoretical frameworks. The possibility of using SEM for mere "fishing" or data exploration should not restrict its application to appropriate data sets by researchers armed with a set of specific questions. Further refinements in analytic technique may permit its application to smaller data sets with well-specified hypotheses.

DERIVING MEANING FROM DIVERSITY

When the full impact of P.L. 99-457 is felt, there is bound to be a heightened focus on the need to understand the effects of programs for infants and toddlers with special needs. Past evaluations, for the most part, have been unidimensional in their view of participants, programs, and impacts. More meaningful evaluations of early intervention services will occur only if those undertaking the evaluation enterprise attempt to develop new ways of understanding and explaining diversity.

In evaluating early intervention services, diversity occurs at many levels. First, children with disabilities are not all the same. Rather than relying on a categorical view of disabilities, typologies need to be developed that take into account a range of important characteristics, such as severity of disability and temperament or behavior. Prior research can guide decisions about the selection of those critical variables, but others are likely to emerge as research results accumulate. Second, families rearing a disabled child are not all the same. Our view of families needs to be multidimensional, include "protective" and "regenerative" factors (see Werner, this volume; Whittacker & Garbarino, 1983), and incorporate theories of family development and adaptation (see Krauss & Jacobs, this volume). Third, all early intervention programs are not the same, and services vary for families within programs. Evaluators need to find ways of describing models of service provision and ways of classifying services that are individualized and vary over time. Finally, outcome measures need to be determined that are responsive to program goals and that reflect a broad view of child development and family adaptation.

It is unlikely that any one evaluation of early intervention services can enlist and fully incorporate such diversity. Instead, evaluators should aim for the development of a series of carefully designed studies with well-chosen outcomes on a tightly determined set of subgroups. We can then search for patterns across studies that take advantage of different ways of defining subgroups, services, and outcomes. Rather than more unidimensional evaluations, investigators should provide evidence of the different ways early intervention services affect children and families. Evaluations can play a critical role in such knowledge accumulation.

REFERENCES

Adelman, H. S. (1986). Intervention theory and evaluating efficacy. *Evaluation Review, 10,* 65–83.
Anderberg, M. R. (1973). *Cluster analysis for application.* New York: Academic Press.
Bagnato, S. J., & Neisworth, T. J. (1980). The Intervention Efficiency Index: An approach to preschool accountability. *Exceptional Children, 46,* 264–269.
Bailey, D. B., & Simeonsson, R. J. (1986). Design issues in family impact evaluation. In L. Bickman & D. L. Weatherford (Eds.), *Evaluating early intervention programs for severely handicapped children and their families* (pp. 209–230). Austin, TX: PRO-ED.
Bailey, D. B., Simeonsson, R. J., Winton, P. J., Huntington, G. S., Comfort, M., Isbell, P., O'Donnell, K. J., & Helm, J. M. (1986). Family-focused intervention: A functional model for planning, implementing, and evaluating individualized family services in early intervention. *Journal of the Division for Early Childhood, 10,* 156–171.
Beer, V., & Bloomer, A. C. (1986). Levels of evaluation. *Educational Evaluation and Policy Analysis, 8,* 335–345.
Belsky, J., & Most, R. (1981). From exploration to play: A cross-sectional study of infant free play behavior. *Developmental Psychology, 17,* 630–639.
Berreuta-Clement, J. R., Schweinhart, L. J., Barnett, W. S., Epstein, A. S., & Weikart, D. P. (1984). *Changed lives: The effects of the Perry Preschool Program on youths through age 19.* Ypsilanti, MI: High/Scope.
Biddle, B. J., & Martin, M. M. (1987). Causality, confirmation, credulity, and structural equation modeling. *Child Development, 58,* 4–17.
Blacher, J., & Meyers, C. E. (1983). A review of attachment formation and disorder of handicapped children. *American Journal of Mental Deficiency, 87,* 359–371.
Bock, G., Stebbins, L. B., & Proper, E. C. (1977). *Education as experimentation: A planned variation model.* Cambridge, MA: Abt Associates.
Bracken, B. A. (1987). Limitations of preschool instruments and standards for minimal levels of technical adequacy. *Journal of Psychoeducational Assessment, 4,* 313–326.
Bricker, D., & Kaminski, R. (1986). Intervention programs for severely handicapped infants and children. In L. Bickman & D. L. Weatherford (Eds.), *Evaluating early intervention programs for severely handicapped children and their families* (pp. 51–75). Austin, TX: PRO-ED.

Bronfenbrenner, U. (1979). *The ecology of human development by nature and design.* Cambridge, MA.: Harvard University Press.

Brooks-Gunn, J., & Lewis, M. (1984). Maternal responsivity in interactions with handicapped infants. *Child Development, 55,* 782–793.

Bryk, A. S., & Raudenbush, S. W. (1983). The potential contribution of program evaluation to social problem solving: A view based on the CIS and Push/Excel experience. In A. S. Bryk (Ed.), *Stakeholder-based evaluation* (pp. 97–107). San Francisco: Jossey-Bass.

Bryk, A. S., & Raudenbush, S. W. (1987). Application of hierarchical linear models to assessing change. *Psychological Bulletin, 101,* 147–158.

Campbell, D., & Stanley, J. (1966). *Experimental and quasi-experimental designs for research.* Chicago: Rand McNally.

Casto, G., & Mastropieri, M. (1986). The efficacy of early intervention programs: A meta-analysis. *Exceptional Children, 52,* 417–424.

Cohen, J. (1977). *Statistical power analysis for the behavioral sciences.* New York: Academic Press.

Connell, J. P. (1987). Structural equation modeling and the study of child development: A question of goodness of fit. *Child Development, 58,* 167–175.

Cook, T. D., & Campbell, D. T. (1979). *Quasi-experimentation: Design and analysis issues for field settings.* Chicago: Rand McNally.

Cook, T. D., Cook, F. L., & Mark, M. M. (1977). Randomized and quasi-experimental designs in evaluation research: An introduction. In L. Rutman (Ed.), *Evaluation research methods: A basic guide* (pp. 103–139). Beverly Hills: Sage Publications.

Cronbach, L. J., & Furby, L. (1970). How should we measure "change" – or should we? *Psychological Bulletin, 74,* 68–80.

Duncan, O. D. (1975). *Introduction to structural equation models.* New York: Academic Press.

Dunst, C. J. (1986). Overview of the efficacy of early intervention programs. In L. Bickman & D. L. Weatherford (Eds.), *Evaluating early intervention programs for severely handicapped children and their families* (pp. 79–147). Austin, TX: PRO-ED.

Dunst, C. J., & Rheingrover, R. (1981). An analysis of the efficacy of infant intervention programs with organically handicapped children. *Evaluation and Program Planning, 4,* 287–323.

Fuchs, D., Fuchs, L. S., Benowitz, S., & Barringer, K. (1987). Norm-referenced tests: Are they valid for use with handicapped students? *Exceptional Children, 54,* 263–271.

Garwood, S. G. (1982). (Mis)use of developmental scales in program evaluation. *Topics in Early Childhood Special Education, 1,* 61–69.

Gebring, D. W., & Anderson, J. C. (1985). The effects of sampling error and model characteristics on parameter estimation for maximum likelihood confirmatory factor analysis. *Multivariate Behavioral Research, 20,* 255–271.

Gilbert, J. P., Light, R. J., & Mosteller, F. (1975). Assessing social innovation: An empirical base for policy. In A. K. Lumsdaine & C. A. Bennett (Eds.), *Evaluation and experiment* (pp. 39–193). New York: Academic Press.

Goldstein, H. (1979). *The design and analysis of longitudinal studies: Their role in the measurement of change.* London: Academic Press.

Hauser-Cram, P., & Shonkoff, J. P. (1988). Rethinking the assessment of child-focused outcomes. In H. B. Weiss & F. H. Jacobs (Eds.), *Evaluating family programs.* Hawthorne, NY: Aldine Publishing.

Hamilton, J. L., & Swan, W. W. (1981). Measurement references in the assessment of preschool handicapped children. *Topics in Early Childhood Special Education, 1,* 41–48.

Hill, P., & McCune-Nicolich, L. (1981). Pretend play and patterns of cognition in Down's syndrome children. *Child Development, 52,* 611–617.

House, E. R., Glass, G. V., McLean, L. D., & Walker, D. F. (1978). No simple answer: Critique of the Follow Through evaluation. *Harvard Educational Review, 48,* 128–160.

Irwin, J. V., & Wong, S. P. (1974). Compensation for maturity in long-range intervention studies. *Acta Symbolica, 5,* 34–45.

Isaac, S., & Michael, W. B. (1978). *Handbook in research and evaluation.* San Diego: Edits.

Jacobs, F. H. (1988). The five-tiered approach to evaluation: Context and implementation. In H. B. Weiss & F. H. Jacobs (Eds.), *Evaluating family programs.* Hawthorne, NY: Aldine Publishing.

Kiresuk, T. J., & Lund, S. H. (1976). Process and measurement using Goal Attainment Scaling. In G. V. Glass (Ed.), *Evaluation studies review manual* (Vol. 1, pp. 383–399). Beverly Hills: Sage.

Lazar, I., & Darlington, R. (1982). Lasting effects of early education. *Monographs of the Society for Research in Child Development, 47* (2–3, Serial No. 195).

Lewis, M. (1976). What do we mean when we say "Infant intelligence scores?" A socio-political question. In M. Lewis (Ed.), *Origins of intelligence* (pp. 1–17). New York: Plenum Press.

Linn, R. (1979). Validity of inferences based on the proposed Title I evaluation models. *Educational Evaluation and Policy Analysis, 1,* 23–32.

Linn, R. L., & Slinde, J. A. (1977). The determination of the significance of change between pre- and posttesting periods. *Review of Educational Research, 47,* 121–150.

Lord, F. M. (1956). The measurement of growth. *Educational and Psychological Measurement, 47,* 421–437.

Maher, C. A. (1983). Goal attainment scaling: A method for evaluating special education services. *Exceptional Children, 49,* 529–536.

Marfo, K., & Kysela, G. M. (1985). Early intervention with mentally handicapped children: A critical appraisal of applied research. *Journal of Pediatric Psychology, 10,* 305–324.

Mark, L. M. (1958). *Statistics in the making.* Columbus, OH: Bureau of Business Research.

McCarthy, D. (1972). McCarthy Scales of Children's Abilities. New York: The Psychological Corporation.

McGuire, J., & Gottlieb, B. (1979). Social support groups among new parents: An experimental study in primary prevention. *Journal of Clinical Child Psychology, 8,* 111–116.

McKay, H., Sinisterra, L., McKay, A., Gomez, H., & Lloreda, P. (1978). Improving cognitive ability in chronically deprived children. *Science, 200,* 270–278.

Meisels, S. J. (1985). The efficacy of early intervention: Why are we still asking this question? *Topics in Early Childhood Special Education, 5,* 1–11.

Meisels, S. J. (1987). Using criterion-referenced assessment data to measure the progress of handicapped children in early intervention programs. In G. Casto, F. Ascione, & M. Salehi (Eds.), *Perspectives in infancy and early childhood research* (pp. 59–64). Logan, UT: DCHP Press.

Miles, M. B., & Huberman, A. M. (1984). *Qualitative data analysis.* Beverly Hills: Sage Publications.

Mink, I. T., Nihira, K., & Meyers, C. E. (1983). Taxonomy of family life styles: I. Homes with TMR children. *American Journal of Mental Deficiency, 87,* 484–497.

Morgan, G., & Harmon, R. J. (1984). Developmental transformations in mastery motivation: Measurement and validation. In R. N. Emde & R. J. Harmon (Eds.), *Continuities and discontinuities in development* (pp. 263–291). New York: Plenum Press.

Morgan, G. A., Maslin, C. A., Harmon, R. J., Jennings, K. D., & Busch-Rossnagel, N. A. (in press). Assessing mothers' perceptions of mastery motivation: The development and utility of the dimensions of mastery questionnaire. In P. Vietze & R. MacTurk (Eds.), *Perspectives on mastery motivation in infancy and childhood.* Norwood, NJ: Ablex Publishing.

Nauta, M. J., & Hewett, K. (1988). Studying complexity: The case of the Child and Family Resource Program. In H. B. Weiss & F. H. Jacobs (Eds.), *Evaluating family programs.* Hawthorne, NY: Aldine Publishing.

Newborg, J., Stock, J. R., Wnek, L., Guidubaldi, J., & Svinicki, J. (1984). Battelle Developmental Inventory. Allen, TX: DLM/Teaching Resources.

Patton, M. Q. (1978). *Utilization-focused evaluation.* Beverly Hills: Sage Publications.

Ramey, C. T., Collier, A. M., Sparling, J. J., Loda, F. A., Campbell, F. A., Ingram, D. L., & Finkelstein, N. W. (1976). The Carolina Abecedarian project: A longitudinal and multidisciplinary approach to the prevention of developmental retardation. In T. D. Tjossem (Ed.), *Intervention strategies for high-risk infants and young children* (pp. 629–665). Baltimore: University Park Press.

Rogosa, D. R., Brandt, D., & Zimowski, M. (1982). A growth curve approach to the measurement of change. *Psychological Bulletin, 76,* 726–748.

Rogosa, D. R., & Willett, J. B. (1983). Demonstrating the reliability of the difference score in the measurement of change. *Journal of Educational Measurement, 20,* 335–343.

Romney, D. M. (1976). Treatment progress by objectives: Kiresuk's and Sherman's approach simplified. *Community Mental Health Journal, 12,* 286–290.

Rosenberg, S. A., Robinson, C. C., Finkler, D., & Rose, J. S. (1987). An empirical comparison of formulas evaluating early intervention program impact on development. *Exceptional Children, 54,* 213–219.

Sameroff, A., & Chandler, M. J. (1975). Reproductive risk and the continuum of caretaking casualty. In F. D. Horowitz (Ed.), *Review of child development research* (Vol. 4, pp.

187–243). Chicago: University of Chicago Press.

Sandow, S. A., Clarke, A. D. B., Cox, M. V., & Stewart, F. L. (1981). Home intervention with parents of severely subnormal preschool children: A final report. *Child: Care, Health, and Development, 7*, 135–144.

Scriven, M. (1967). The methodology of evaluation. In R. W. Tyler, R. M. Gage, & M. Scriven (Eds.), *Perspectives of curriculum evaluation* (AERA Monograph Series on Curriculum Evaluation No. 1, pp. 39–83). Chicago: Rand McNally.

Shonkoff, J. (1983). The limitations of normative assessments of high-risk infants. *Topics in Early Childhood Special Education, 3*, 29–43.

Shonkoff, J. (1984). Social support and the development of vulnerable children. *American Journal of Public Health, 74*, 310–312.

Shonkoff, J. P., & Hauser-Cram, P. (1987). Early intervention for disabled infants and their families: A quantitative analysis. *Pediatrics, 80*, 650–658.

Simeonsson, R., Cooper, D., & Scheiner, A. (1982). A review and analysis of the effectiveness of early intervention programs. *Pediatrics, 69*, 635–641.

Simeonsson, R. J., & McHale, S. M. (1981). Review: Research on handicapped children–sibling relationships. *Child: Care, Health, and Development, 7*, 153–171.

Simeonsson, R. J., & Wiegerink, R. 1975. Accountability: A dilemma in infant intervention. *Exceptional Children, 4*, 474–481.

Stein, R., & Jessop, D. (1982). A noncategorical approach to chronic childhood illness. *Public Health Reports, 97*, 354–362.

Tanaka, J. S. (1987). "How big is big enough?": Sample size and goodness of fit in structural equation models with latent variables. *Child development, 58*, 134–146.

Terman, L., & Merrill, M. (1973). Stanford-Binet Intelligence Scale. Boston: Houghton Mifflin.

Tietze, W. (1987). A structural model for the evaluation of preschool effects. *Early Childhood Research Quarterly, 2*, 133–153.

Travers, J. R., & Light, R. J. (1982). *Learning from experience: Evaluating early childhood demonstration programs.* Washington, DC: National Academy Press.

Wandersman, L. (1987). Parent–infant support groups: Matching programs to needs and strengths of families. In C. F. Boukydis (Ed.), *Research on support for parents and infants in the prenatal period* (pp. 139–160). Norwood, NJ: Ablex Publishing.

Ward, D. H. (1973). Evaluation research for corrections. In L. E. Ohlin (Ed.), *Prisoners in America* (pp. 184–206). Englewood Cliffs, NJ: Prentice-Hall.

Webster, H. & Bereiter, C. (1963). The reliability of changes measured by mental test scores. In C. W. Harris (ED.), *Problems in measuring change* (pp. 39–59). Madison: University of Wisconsin Press.

White, K. R., & Mott, S. E. (1987). Conducting longitudinal research on the efficacy of early intervention with handicapped children. *Journal of the Division for Early Childhood, 12*, 13–22.

Whittacker, J., & Garbarino, J. (1983). *Social support networks: Informal helping in the human services.* Hawthorne, NY: Aldine Publishing.

Willett, J. B. (1988). Questions and answers in the measurement of change. In E. E. Rothkopf (Ed.), *Review of research in education* (Vol. 15, pp. 345–422). Washington, DC: American Educational Research Association.

Wolery, M. (1983). Proportional Change Index: An alternative for comparing child change data. *Exceptional Children, 50*, 167–170.

Wolery, M. (1985). The evaluation of two levels of a center-based early intervention project. *Topics in Early Childhood Special Education, 5*, 66–77.

Woodward, C. A., Santa-Barbara, J., Levin, S., & Epstein, B. (1978). The role of goal attainment scaling in evaluating family therapy outcome. *American Journal of Orthopsychiatry, 48*, 464–471.

Zigler, E., & Balla, D. (1982). Selecting outcome variables in evaluations of early childhood special education programs. *Topics in Early Childhood Special Education, 1*, 11–22.

PART VII

Policy issues and programmatic directions

25 *Who should be served? Identifying children in need of early intervention*

SAMUEL J. MEISELS AND BARBARA A. WASIK

Defining and identifying the potential recipients of early childhood intervention services constitutes one of the principal tasks facing those charged with implementing P.L. 99-457. As defined by the law, potential service recipients may include disabled children and their families, as well as those who are "developmentally delayed" and those children "at-risk" for developmental problems. Whereas definitions of traditional disability categories exist, there are no clear definitions of developmental delay or risk. Furthermore, there is relatively limited experience nationally in identifying young disabled children. For example, prior to the passage of P.L. 99-457, during the first decade of services that were regulated by the Education for All Handicapped Children's Act (P.L. 94-142), only six states guaranteed services to all birth to 3-year-olds with disabilities (Meisels, Harbin, Modigliani, & Olson, 1988). An additional nine states mandated services to infants and toddlers with specific handicapping conditions, but nationwide the majority of disabled and developmentally vulnerable young children clearly were not receiving intervention.

Now, all of the states have begun to confront the critical issues of early identification, including such problems as how many handicapped infants and toddlers there are in the state; what the prevalence is of specific disabling conditions in the birth to 3-year-old population; how to define the at-risk category; whether all disabled and developmentally at-risk children should receive services; when and how often at-risk children should be assessed; which valid screening and assessment instruments are available; and how developmentally vulnerable children and their families can be assessed meaningfully. This chapter will attempt to respond to these issues and problems. Many of them can only be addressed partially, because of incomplete knowledge and undeveloped methodology. Nevertheless, because these issues are fundamental to identifying the recipients of early intervention services, they are among the most critical questions that will be faced in the coming decade.

THE BENEFICIARIES OF EARLY INTERVENTION

Epidemiologic considerations

Annually, the U.S. Department of Education (USDOE) submits a report to Congress concerning the implementation of P.L. 94-142. As in previous reports the 1987 document notes that approximately 12% of all children between ages 3 and 21 received

605

Table 1. *Number of handicapped children by age (Michigan, 1986–1987)*

Age	N	Percentage of general education total[a]
Birth–2	1,826	0.7
3	2,276	1.8
4	4,206	3.2
5	7,163	5.3
6	9,431	7.5
7	11,581	10.0
8	13,213	11.9
9	13,543	12.6

Based on data supplied by the Michigan Department of Education, January, 1988.
[a] Birth to 4 years percentages are based on an annual birth cohort of 130,000. Ages 5 to 9 percentages are based on actual 1986–87 school year totals.

special education services (USDOE, 1987). The handicapping conditions of these children and youths follow the traditional epidemiological order of prevalence: speech impairment, mental retardation, learning disabilities, emotional disturbance, crippling conditions and other health impairments, hearing impairment, visual impairment, deafness, and multihandicapped problems.

Unfortunately, no incidence or prevalence data are available nationally for birth to 3-year-olds. Indeed, tentative conclusions drawn from national surveys (cf. Meisels et al., 1988) indicate that very little is known regarding the epidemiology of risk and disability in the first 3 years of life.

Table 1 illustrates the limitations of the identification process for young children. This table supplies data regarding the number of handicapped children, birth to age 9, who received special education services in the state of Michigan during 1986–87.

In reviewing this table one should realize that since 1971 the state of Michigan has had legislation entitling all disabled children from birth through age 26 to comprehensive special education services. Hence, the exceedingly low rates of identification for children younger than school age, shown as a proportion of the general population, cannot be attributed simply to lack of state-funded services. Indeed, Michigan is a leader in the provision of these services. Nevertheless, the table demonstrates that relatively few young children are enrolled in early intervention. Moreover, since it is unlikely that substantially fewer disabled infants and toddlers would reside in Michigan as compared to the rest of the United States, and since there is no reason to believe that the number of such children would nearly double by age 4 and more than double again by age 6, there are apparently several factors in the Michigan early intervention service system, as well as in those of other states, that must be clarified so that the low rates of identification shown in Table 1 can be understood.

Defining risk and disability in the first 3 years

Several reasons can be advanced to explain the disparity between prevalence rates reported in early childhood and those for school-age children. One reason lies with the categories used for reporting handicapping conditions. For example, children who are diagnosed to have "speech handicaps," "learning disabilities," or "attention deficit disorder," or those who are "educationally or trainably mentally retarded" cannot be identified accurately in the first year or two of life. Yet, these categories account for nearly half of the prevalence or "child count" at school age. Since many of the traditional categorical labels are generally inapplicable to the population served by early intervention programs, it follows that identification and prevalence rates would differ.

A second reason for differences between early and later childhood identification rates concerns differences in point prevalence rates. "Point prevalence" refers to the number or proportion of individuals in a community or population with a given condition at any particular point in time (see Eaton, 1980; Scott & Masi, 1979). The point prevalence rate is constantly in flux during the first 3 years of life, depending on the basis for the risk itself, external circumstances, and interventions. Bell (1986) describes this phenomenon as "Age Specific Manifestations" (ASM) of risk, claiming that "we can assume that ASM may change from one developmental period to the next, even though the individuals may remain at risk as far as the fixed or overriding basis for risk is concerned" (p. 177). Thus, children who are at risk for language disorder because of birth trauma may only manifest these problems in the second or third years of life, but with remediation may demonstrate a lowered risk status in the early elementary years (see Lock, Shapiro, Ross, & Capute, 1986). In contrast, a deaf baby may show few adaptive problems in the early sensorimotor period, but as the child grows older, socioemotional and cognitive issues may become more pressing. Finally, children whose problems can be traced to abusive or neglectful home environments may go in and out of risk status, dependent on a variety of childhood, familial, or other external variables (see Garbarino, this volume).

In contrast, school experience, for all of its diversity, functions as a relatively constant developmental context for most disabled children. Children who function in the mildly mentally retarded range, while performing at different levels in different life contexts, are still generally considered to be retarded in school (Bogdan & Taylor, 1976). Similarly, those children with sensorial deficits (e.g., vision or hearing impairment) that pose major learning difficulties will, in most instructional settings, show much less of the fluidity of risk that Bell (1986) suggests characterizes very young children. In short, estimates of the number of disabled infants and toddlers fluctuate and are subject to wide variation when compared with older children.

A third explanation for the differences in early and late prevalence concerns the mechanisms that are available for identification. A wide array of assessment devices can be used for diagnosis and evaluation of school-age children (Sattler, 1988). The situation with young children is decidedly different, with few valid instruments available for use with birth to 3-year-olds (Cicchetti & Wagner, this volume; McCune, Kalmanson, Fleck, Glazewski, & Sillari, this volume; Meisels, 1988). Added to this problem is the notoriously poor predictive power of infant intelligence tests (Brooks-Gunn & Weintraub, 1983; Honzik, 1983; Kopp & McCall, 1982) that casts doubt on the predictive validity of judgments about disability in early childhood.

Still other issues that distinguish early and late prevalence rates can be raised. For example, since relatively few intervention services are available, the incentive to identify young children is not very great. Nor is there much incentive from an economic or sociopolitical perspective. This follows because as increased numbers of infants and toddlers are identified, public agencies will be confronted with the responsibility to establish publicly funded services for these children and their families. This also has an impact on considerations of eligibility. That is, if criteria for eligibility for services are narrowly defined, and if etiological factors are construed correspondingly narrowly, then fewer children will qualify for services.

Indeed, the etiology of risk in the first 3 years of life is of crucial importance. Children of school age who appear in government prevalence charts as receiving special education services can typically be described in terms of one or more of the accepted handicapping conditions. However, the nosology, or classification of problems that is utilized with younger children, differs markedly. In particular, as suggested already, services to birth to 3-year-olds are frequently focused on those who are at risk for developmental problems. For example, given the extensive literature linking parent–child interactive disorders to subsequent disabling conditions in childhood (see Beckwith, this volume; Sameroff & Fiese, this volume), one could describe a high-risk dyad as one involving a sick premature infant and the infant's parents. The parents of this newborn, high-risk, preterm infant, may themselves be potentially beset by grief, anxiety, and premature projection into the role of parenting. They, in turn, may be confronted by a tiny, physiologically poorly regulated, fragile, and possibly unattractive infant

who may be critically ill and who is being cared for in an ambience of emergency medical care. Such an infant may appear to be unreadable, unpredictable, and unresponsive. This situation may further increase the parents' sense of anxiety, frustration, and incompetence after the child is discharged from the NICU [neonatal intensive care unit], and may contribute to less-optimal developmental outcomes for the infant and to further psychosomatic reactions to stress for both baby and caregivers over time (Meisels & Plunkett, 1988, p. 107).

Should a baby such as this be considered disabled, or at risk for disability? How long must the problems described be manifested before the child and family should begin receiving services? What type of measures would be appropriate for predicting this child's disorders and the family's potential maladaptations? In short, etiological considerations heavily influence who is and who is not considered a potential recipient of early intervention services. Available information regarding incidence and prevalence of disabling conditions among older children appears to have only a tenuous relationship to the task of defining the population of at-risk and disabled children in the first 3 years of life. In particular, the "risk" category is the most difficult to operationalize.

Classifying risk

The most widely used approach to classifying risk conditions in infancy and early childhood was introduced by Tjossem in 1976. His tripartite classification included children at established medical risk, biological risk, and environmental risk. These categories have been adapted by many researchers (see Guralnick & Bennett, 1987), and can be defined as follows:

1. *Established diagnosis* refers to children whose early developmental disabilities are presumed to be related to diagnosed medical disorders. Examples of such disorders include Down syndrome, inborn errors of metabolism (e.g., untreated PKU and other disorders of the body's chemical system), multiple congenital anomalies (e.g., spina bifida), and morphological anomalies (e.g., cleft palate).
2. *Biologically vulnerable* refers to children who have a history of biological factors during their prental, neonatal, or postnatal periods that could have developmental sequelae. Such factors include metabolic disease and nutritional deficiencies in the mother, obstetrical complications, low birth weight, anoxia, and prematurity, among many others.

3. *Environmentally at-risk* refers to children whose experiences are significantly limited during early childhood in areas of maternal attachment, family organization, health care, nutrition, and in opportunities for physical, social, and adaptive stimulation. Such factors are highly correlated with a probability of delayed development (Meisels & Anastasiow, 1982, p. 26).

These three classifications of risk are not mutually exclusive. A child may have an established diagnosis, be biologically vulnerable because of birth trauma, and may be at risk environmentally. This clearly limits the potential usefulness of these categories in assigning prevalence figures to each risk factor. But there are other reasons that reduce their epidemiologic value as well.

ESTABLISHED DIAGNOSIS. Children with established diagnoses are, as already noted, those whose early developmental disabilities are presumed to be related to disorders that are medically diagnosed or, in other words, have a recognizable biological substrate or cause. Such disorders are extremely varied and include, for example, children with Down syndrome, cystic fibrosis, spina bifida, cerebral palsy, and inborn errors of metabolism. Each of these conditions is characterized by a different prevalence rate. Furthermore, many of the handicapping conditions that are associated with these causes, for example, mental retardation, orthopedic disorders, or speech and language delays, carry with them extensive variation concerning etiology and outcome. In other words, even the category of "established medical diagnosis" does not yield clear and definitive prevalence data. This issue becomes even more complex as one explores the categories of biological vulnerability and environmental risk.

BIOLOGICAL RISK. Biologically vulnerable infants are those who are at risk for developmental delay or disability as a result of several factors occurring during pregnancy, at birth, or in the postnatal period. Chief among the factors that can contribute to a child's developmental problems are those associated with preterm birth. The list of risk factors that are related to prematurity includes the following major illnesses: respiratory distress syndrome, bronchopulmonary dysplasia, intraventricular hemorrhage, periventricular leukomalacia, and retinopathy of prematurity.

Preterm infants survive today who only a few years ago would have been too young gestationally, and too small in birth weight, to be viable. The risk for their experiencing one or more of the conditions noted generally increases in inverse proportion to their birth weight and gestational age. As a result, the mortality and negative effects on developmental abilities of these increasingly surviving, extremely immature infants is an issue of great concern. Several studies have now reported the presence of major handicaps (e.g., hypotonic quadriplegia, dyskinetic cerebral palsy, spastic diplegia, neuromotor abnormalities, etc.) among infants born weighing less than 1,250 grams (i.e., 2.75 lb) (Britton, Fitzhardinge, & Ashby, 1981; Buckwald, Zorn, & Egan, 1984; Hack & Fanaroff, 1986; Knobloch, Malone, Ellison, Stevens, & Zdeb, 1982; Scott, Ment, Ehrenkranz, & Warshaw, 1984). However, because of the rapid advances in neonatal care and the concomitant problem of generalizing about future risk status from studies completed before improved technology was available, these findings still leave unanswered many critical questions. Specifically, we do not know which infants born under which conditions will thrive, and which will not. Prematurity is not a unitary construct, nor is it a typical syndrome with well-defined characteristics and developmental sequelae (see Meisels, Plunkett, Pasick, Stiefel, & Roloff, 1987). Two premature infants may begin life in similar situations of physiological, neurological, and psychological risk, but one infant may develop well, and one poorly. Moreover, research concerning the developmental consequences of preterm birth is confined principally to the first 2 years of life, and is focused generally on cognitive, motoric, and linguistic outcomes (see Meisels & Plunkett, 1988). Hence, predictions about the long-term risk status of preterms, and statements about the prevalence of developmental disorders in this population – particularly regarding socioemotional adaptation – are highly probabilistic. Furthermore, investigations of the outcomes of biologically at-risk children frequently cite factors in the caregiving environment as decisive for explaining differences in development. Thus, biological and environmental risk cannot easily be separated, and epidemiologic conclusions must be considered ambiguous at best.

ENVIRONMENTAL RISK. The difficulty in determining prevalence rates for children who can be classified as environmentally at risk may be even greater than for the other two etiological categories. This follows in part from the range of risk factors – their type and degree – that are included in typical definitions of this category. For example, one such description includes children who are at risk because of parental mental retardation or psychiatric disorder, parental substance abuse, suspected child abuse or neglect, maternal age less than 15; children who are economically disadvantaged and whose primary caregivers have less than a twelfth grade education; and "children whose parent(s) or regular caregiver have significant concerns regarding their development" (Division for Early Childhood, 1987, p. 6).

These categories are not definitive of developmental problems because so many individuals who could fulfill these criteria do not demonstrate developmental sequelae. Ramey and MacPhee (1986) point out that "although 75% of mild mental retardation occurs among the poor, only 2% to 10% of the poor are likely to become mentally retarded by traditional criteria" (p. 63). Similarly, children of adolescent mothers are at risk for developmental problems for a host of potential reasons (e.g., poor maternal nutrition, small maternal size, limited prenatal care, impoverished caregiving skills, drug abuse, unstable familial setting). However, research evidence does not support the presumption of a one-to-one relationship between adolescent parenting and childhood developmental disorder (Furstenberg, Brooks-Gunn, & Morgan, 1987; Zuckerman et al., 1983).

At most, one can safely assume developmental vulnerability among children who are environmentally at risk, particularly those who are reared in poverty. As Werner (1986) points out in reviewing the data from her 18-year longitudinal study,

Poverty alone was not a sufficient condition for the development of serious coping problems. A low standard of living, especially at birth, increased the likelihood of exposure of the infant and young child to *both* biological and psychosocial risk factors. But it was the *joint* impact of perinatal stress and early family instability that led to serious and persistent learning and behavior problems in both middle-class and lower-class children (p. 23).

SUMMARY. The three risk categories defined by Tjossem (1976) constitute potential etiological factors. They do not describe developmental disorders or developmental pathways. They do not indicate the type or severity of developmental problems for which the child is at risk. Nor do they imply necessarily that a child who can be included in one of these categories will experience developmental problems. In most cases these risk factors – particularly when taken in isolation – serve as probabilistic indicators of the potential for developmental vulnerability.

The factors discussed can be used to identify some of the elements that contribute to and may be related to developmental disorders. But the "predictive risk" is that they will result in high proportions of misclassifications, particularly overinclusion in the risk category. For example, 7% of all live births are premature (National Academy of Sciences, 1985), but only a small proportion of these preterm infants are delayed in development at school age (Cohen, 1986; Klein, Hack, Gallagher, & Fanaroff, 1985). Similarly, more than a quarter of all children living in the United States reside in poverty (Edelman, 1987), but most poor children are free of handicapping conditions (Ramey & MacPhee, 1986; Werner, 1986).

Whereas there may be a higher incidence of disabling conditions among populations of poor children and preterm children when compared with those born into families with greater economic advantages and better neonatal health status, it would be highly inaccurate to generalize from these single markers of risk to developmental problems in general. Thus, the problem that must be addressed is not one of defining or listing the characteristics of risk. Rather, the task is that of identifying those children who, because they are developmentally vulnerable, in fact demonstrate developmental problems. In other words, which risk factors, or which constellation of risk conditions, in what severity and intensity, are most frequently associated with developmental disorders? The balance of this chapter will be devoted to trying to answer these questions, first by reviewing research about single-factor predictors of risk, then by examining psychometric devices designed as predictors, and finally by analyzing risk indexes, or multifactorial predictions of developmental disorder.

IDENTIFYING CHILDREN AT RISK

Two techniques appear to govern most approaches to early identification of risk and disability. In simplistic terms the techniques refer to the number of data sources utilized for making a decision about who is at risk. *Single-source*, single-factor, or univariate approaches rely on demographic or medical variables (e.g., socioeconomic status, age of parent, birth status) as chief indicators of risk, or else they use the results of a screening test to accomplish this purpose. *Multiple-source*, or multifactorial, approaches utilize data from a number of sources, often arranged in a weighted index, to characterize the population of at-risk children.

Single-factor approaches

The etiological categories discussed earlier can generally be characterized as single-factor or single-source approaches to identification. As noted, children are typically considered to be at developmental risk if they have experienced a recognized high-risk condition (e.g., preterm birth, NICU admission, anoxia, poor prenatal care, etc.). Alternatively, the environment in which children are reared, including their family's economic situation, and the age and education of their mothers may have negative developmental consequences. However, although many children who have been exposed to these conditions display problems in development, most do not. Thus, the danger of making predictions based on single risk factors is that large numbers of children will be overreferred. In short, single-factor predictors – particularly when they are of the types recognized in the Tjossem categories of risk – are too inclusive to be used in isolation to make accurate predictions of developmental problems. Some type of composite index appears to be indicated.

PSYCHOMETRIC APPROACHES AND OTHER SCREENING TESTS. Another technique that can be described as a single source of identification is represented by psychometric tests and other screening devices. The purpose of developmental screening tests is to identify at an early stage those children who have a high probability of exhibiting delayed or abnormal development. Psychometric tests refer to the quantitative assessment of individuals' psychological traits or abilities (Sattler, 1988). However, a number of other electrophysiological, perceptual, and behavioral techniques can also be used to identify children at risk (Vietze & Vaughan, 1988).

Developmental screening tests can be classified as single-source or univariate techniques of identification because it is claimed that failing such a test signifies that the child is at risk for developmental problems, and typically no further information or sources of data are needed for referral to further evaluation. In fact, most psychometric scales tap several areas of development (e.g., fine-motor and adaptive, language, gross motor, and cognition), although some tests can be construed as being less representative of development, focusing, for example, solely on language acquisition or on perceptual recognition memory. The same point can be made for such other single-factor variables as socioeconomic status (SES). As a latent or marker variable, SES stands for a host of other factors (see Wilson, 1987), although in some situations very narrow indicators of SES (e.g., number of rooms in a family's household) are utilized. Nevertheless, when not used in a battery of tests or in combination with other types of data, the tests to be reviewed in this section will be considered a single source of data.

SCREENING VERSUS EVALUATION. At the outset of this discussion it is important to recognize what is *not* a developmental screening test. Full-scale developmental evaluation instruments (e.g., the Bayley Scales of Infant Development [Bayley, 1969]; Uzgiris-Hunt Scales of Infant Psychological Development [Uzgiris & Hunt, 1975]; Griffiths Mental Development Scales [Griffiths, 1954]) should not be used for the purpose of identifying children potentially at risk. Such assessments are to be used to confirm that a child's development is disordered or delayed.

The most widely used assessment of infant development is the Bayley Scales of Infant Development (Bayley, 1969). The Bayley consists of three components: a Mental Development Index, a Psychomotor Development Index, and the Infant Behavior Record (see McCune et al., this volume). The Bayley is not a screening test. The purpose of the Bayley scales is to measure a child's developmental status at a given point in time. A child receives a developmental quotient (DQ) for both the mental and the motor components of the test. (The Infant Behavior Record [IBR] consists of 25 categories of behavior and 5 clinical impressions that assess the child's attitudes, interests, emotions, energy, activity, and tendencies to approach or withdraw from stimulation during testing. Unfortunately, easily computed and interpreted summary scores from the IBR are not available [see Meisels, Cross, & Plunkett, 1987].) The DQ is not an IQ score. Unlike an IQ, which is expected to be a stable characteristic of intellectual ability, the DQ measures the concurrent performance of children compared to others their age.

The lack of predictability of performance on the Bayley to later cognitive abilities highlights its lack of usefulness for identifying children at risk. Considerable research has shown that there are only low to modest correlations between Bayley scores and later cognitive measures (Kopp & McCall, 1982; Lewis & Sullivan, 1985). Therefore, using performance on the Bayley scales as an index of long-term developmental risk could be misleading.

The Bayley also is not a sensitive measure for children who fall below the limits of the test. The lowest DQ that an infant can receive on the Bayley is 50 (with 100 being average). Thus, the test does not allow for qualitative differences to be made for children who perform at the low end of the developmental continuum.

DEVELOPMENTAL SCREENING TESTS. As noted earlier, developmental screening tests are brief assessments intended to identify children who are at risk for developmental problems. Developmental screening instruments must meet a number of criteria that have been described elsewhere (Barnes, 1982; Lichtenstein & Ireton, 1984; Meisels, 1985, 1989). The tests should be brief, norm-referenced, inexpensive, standardized in administration, objectively scored, broadly focused across all areas of development, reliable, and valid. In addition, all tests intended to screen for a condition during a presymptomatic period must be sensitive to the sample of children who are developmentally at risk, and specific to the portion of the screening population that is not at risk.

Although these criteria indicate the methodological criteria that must be met in designing a screening test, of even greater concern are decisions about which variables are important for predicting developmental outcomes (Murphy, Nichter, & Linden, 1982). For example, some researchers suggest that language development is a reliable predictor of developmental outcome (Capute & Accardo, 1978). However, there is no evidence to suggest a one-to-one correspondence between delay in language acquisition and subsequent developmental delay in childhood.

In describing the construction of screening tests, Aiken (1988) emphasizes the importance of making a detailed analysis of the activity or end-goal for which screening is being used. He uses the example of designing a screening test for performance on a specific job. Successful construction of a screening test for job performance would entail conducting a task analysis of the job, and then selecting or creating items based on that analysis that are likely to predict success on that job. Using this model, one can see how difficult is the task of identifying items in early childhood that best predict later normal development. Research in this area suggests that little is known about all of the necessary and sufficient components that ensure healthy development (Emde & Harmon, 1984). This problem is all the more exaggerated during the first 3 years of life, when rapid changes in development are taking place. Indeed, developmental theorists argue that although there is some continuity in development, the discontinuity that is present creates problems for designing screening tests that assume a regularity in development (Kopp & McCall, 1982; McCall, 1982).

PSYCHOMETRIC TESTS. Relatively few screening tests can be used reliably and validly with infants and toddlers. Two of the most widely known tests, the Denver Developmental Screening Test (Frankenburg, Dodds, Fandal, Kazuk, & Cohrs, 1975) and the Minnesota Child Development Inventory (Ireton & Thwing, 1974), will be discussed briefly.

The Denver Developmental Screening Test (DDST) is the test most widely used by physicians, clinicians, and other public health professionals. It was originally introduced by Frankenburg and Dodds in 1967 and has since been revised twice. In addition to the DDST, there are two abbreviated versions of the test, the Denver

Developmental Screening Test – Revised (Frankenburg, Fandal, Sciarillo, & Burgess, 1981) and the Prescreening Developmental Questionnaire (Frankenburg, van Doorninck, Liddell, & Dick, 1976).

The DDST consists of 105 items that are arranged in developmental sequence similar to the Gesell scales. It includes items that are intended to sample four behavioral domains: personal-social, fine motor-adaptive, language, and gross motor. The screening test can be used from 2 months to 6 years of age.

The DDST has a number of positive features. Administration of the test requires a minimal amount of training. Therefore, people with varying degrees of experience can learn to give the test. Moreover, the test gives practitioners an excellent overview of developmental milestones in the first 6 years of life. The portion of the DDST appropriate for a particular age range can be administered in approximately 20 minutes.

The DDST has a high specificity, referring few children for further evaluation who are not at risk for developmental problems. However, because the test appears primarily to refer children who are "obvious" candidates for further evaluation, the test has been criticized as being "largely unnecessary" (Carmichael & Williams, 1981). Based on findings from a longitudinal study, these researchers argue that the infants identified as "abnormal" on the DDST were identified with equal accuracy by clinical assessments conducted by pediatricians. They and other researchers (e.g., Applebaum, 1978) conclude that the DDST does not add any information not already provided by a clinical assessment. Indeed, Sciarillo, Brown, Robinson, Bennett, and Sells (1986) found that screeners' qualitative impressions were a better indicator of children at risk than the DDST, and Diamond (1987) demonstrated that parents' concerns were at least as effective as the DDST in predicting subsequent school problems of 4-year olds.

In short, the DDST appears to be constructed in such a way that its high specificity (the proportion of children not at risk who are correctly excluded from further assessment) comes at the cost of only referring children at very high risk, and also at the cost of a very low sensitivity (i.e., the proportion of at-risk children who are correctly identified). Indeed, one of the major criticisms of the DDST is that it is not sensitive and therefore fails to identify a significant proportion of children who are developmentally at risk (Cadman et al., 1984; Meisels, 1988, 1989).

Questions about the sensitivity of the DDST have arisen from Frankenburg's own data as well as from other research on the DDST. Recalculating findings presented by Camp, van Doorninck, Frankenburg, and Lampe (1977), one report showed that although the DDST had an overreferral rate of only 2%, its underreferral rate was 46% (Walker, Bonner, & Milling, 1984).

Other studies have also highlighted the problem of the sensitivity of the DDST as a screening test for potential developmental delay. Table 2 shows the sensitivity and specificity of the DDST for 11 samples. The pooled sensitivity and specificity of the concurrent studies were .41 and .93, respectively; for the longitudinal studies these values were .18 and .98 (see Meisels, 1988, 1989, for elaboration of these findings). In other words, these studies indicate that the DDST underrefers at nearly a two-to-one ratio. Clearly, the test should be used with considerable caution.

The *Minnesota Child Development Inventory (MCDI)* (Ireton & Thwing, 1974) differs from the DDST by relying on parental report of behavior, rather than on clinical assessment. The MCDI is a standardized instrument for 1- to 6-year-olds that consists of 320 statements describing development and behavior. The statements are divided into eight basic categories: general development, gross motor, fine motor, expressive language, comprehensive conceptual, situation-comprehension, self-help, and personal-

Table 2. *Concurrent and longitudinal predictive value of the Denver Developmental Screening Test*

Study	Criterion	Test interval	N	Age range	Sensitivity	Specificity	False negative ratio (%)
Applebaum (1978)[a]	Bayley MDI	concurrent	76	2–30 mo	.38	1.0	62
	Bayley PDI	concurrent			.46	1.0	54
Sciarillo, Brown, Robinson, Bennett, & Sells (1986)[a]	MDI and PDI	concurrent	62	M = 7.7 mo	.13	.87	87
Borowitz & Glascoe (1986)[c]	Preschool Language Scale	concurrent	71	18 mo–5.5 yr	.46	1.0	54
Camp, van Doorninck, Frankenburg, & Lampe (1977)[b]	School perform. and IQ	3 yr	65	4–6 yr	.41	.93	59
van Doorninck, Dick, Frankenburg, Liddell, & Lampe (1976)[b]	School problems	5–6 yr	44	2–24 mo	.33	.87	67
			45	2–4 yrs	.28	1.0	72
			62	4–6 yrs	.39	.95	61
Harper & Wacker (1983)[b]	IQ	14 mo	555	M = 3.9 yr	.39	.95	62
Cadman, Chambers, Walter, Feldman, Smith, & Ferguson (1984)[b]	Teacher report	14–16 mo	2,569	4–5 yr	.06	.99	94
Diamond (1987)[b]	Special class placement	4 yr	150	M = 3.5 yr	.17	.93	83

[a] Screen positive = DDST abnormal
[b] Screen positive = DDST abnormal or questionable
[c] Screen positive = Failure on the DDST language sector

Source: Meisels (1988). Reproduced, with permission, from the *Annual Review of Public Health*, Vol. 9. © 1988 by Annual Reviews Inc.

social. Caretakers are expected to describe the child's present behavior by responding to each statement.

The MCDI is both cost- and time-efficient. Since it is based on caretaker report, professionals are not needed to administer the test. Further, it takes into account a wide range of behaviors, such as daily living skills, that are often disregarded in screening and assessments, yet can often provide important information about a child's functioning.

There are, however, several problems with the MCDI that raise serious questions about its use as a screening test. One major criticism of the MCDI is that it can be used reliably only with middle-class parents. This criticism emerges not only from the limited population on which the test was normed, but also from the more general concerns of using parental reports as assessment measures regardless of the educational backgrounds of the parents.

The MCDI was originally normed on a sample of 769 white suburban children from a Minneapolis suburb (Ireton & Thwing, 1974). SES data on this sample indicate that the parents were relatively well educated (fathers' mean education = 14.1 years; mothers' mean education = 13.1 years). Additional validation of the MCDI (Ireton, Thwing, & Currier, 1977) was completed on 109 Caucasian preschool-age children. Again, SES was in the average to above average range, and 99% of the mothers were at least high school graduates. Because of this limited sample, Ireton (1982) suggested that caution be used in generalizing results of the test, asserting that its "validity remains to be determined" (p. 55).

Despite Ireton's cautionary words, research on the MDCI continues to take place with selective populations. For example, in attempting to determine the predictive validity of the MCDI, Guerin and Gottfried (1987) sampled white middle-class families. The average years of education of the mothers and fathers were 14.2 and 15.2, respectively. Additional research by Gottfried and his colleagues (Gottfried, Guerin, Spencer, & Meyer, 1983, 1984) was based on the same sample of children.

Other researchers attempted to use families from diverse SES groups, yet the samples still represent small select groups. Kenny, Hebel, Sexton, and Fox (1987) report that their families represented a broad range of SES backgrounds. However, they did not use any standardized measures to verify this, and the average education of the mothers in their study was 12.3 years with only 4% having less than 9 years of school. Similar sample problems are found in studies by Dean and Steffen (1984), Saylor and Brandt (1986), and Ullman and Kausch (1979). (For a more detailed review of these studies, see Meisels, 1988.)

A related problem endemic to the MCDI concerns the question of the reliability of parental reports of children's behavior. Recent research has shown that when pediatricians, mothers, and school professionals were asked to report on the same child's behavior, the mother was the least accurate in her descriptions (Gradel, Thompson, & Sheehan, 1981). Although Nezerka and Mangelsdorf (1988) report that mothers are quite accurate in reporting how well their child will do in a stressful situation, their sample focused once more on mothers who were middle-class and highly educated. Additional data are needed to determine the reliability of parental report in both low- and high-SES groups as well as for a range of severity of disabilities. Clearly, a screening test that uses maternal report as an index of behavior should demonstrate how well mothers understand specific questions and if the information they provide is reliable. Further research must be conducted on the reliability and validity of the MCDI.

PERCEPTUAL AND PSYCHOPHYSIOLOGICAL SCREENING INDEXES. With increased interest in screening for at-risk infants, a variety of alternative approaches have been presented in the literature. Before discussing these approaches, it must be stated that the authors of these new techniques have only proposed these approaches as possible means of detecting developmental problems in infants. With one exception (i.e., Fagan) they have not yet proposed standardized tests in the form of the DDST or the MCDI. Therefore, data on norms or test validation are, in most cases, unavailable.

Fagan and his colleagues (Fagan & Singer, 1983; Fagan, Singer, & Montie, 1985; Fagan, Singer, Montie, & Shepherd, 1986) have developed a screening device for early detection of intellectual deficits. The *Fagan Test of Infant Intelligence* (FTI) consists of 12 pairs of perceptual recognition items that can be administered to infants between the ages of 3 and 7 months. The screening test assesses the infant's ability to discriminate familiar stimuli (those to which the infant has habituated) from novel stimuli. The stimulus consists of abstract black-and-white patterns. After the habituation sequence the infants are presented with the familiar item paired with a new item. Infants are expected to attend to the new item longer because it is a new stimulus. This differential attention to the novel stimulus is interpreted in terms of the infant's ability to detect differences and the infant's capacity to habituate to the familiar item.

The rationale for this test lies in Fagan's theory of the development of intelligence. Fagan and other researchers (Caron & Caron, 1981; Fagan, 1982, 1983; Rose & Wallace, 1985) argue that early visual discrimination and recognition memory is the basis of intellectual development. The display of competence in early visual information processing is believed to provide an index to future cognitive functioning. Indeed, Fagan argues that tests, such as the Bayley, that assess sensorimotor abilities in the infant do not assess those abilities that will predict later intelligence (Fagan & Singer, 1983). In contrast, the FTI is described as an accurate measure of discrimination ability in infants and as a window on more complex cognitive processes.

One issue raised by the FTI concerns how it should be categorized. Although Fagan has labeled it an infant intelligence test, an IQ or DQ score cannot be obtained, and it does not measure achievement or qualitative strengths and weaknesses in cognitive functioning. Instead, the Fagan test is perhaps most appropriately described as a secondary screening test. As Fagan et al. (1986) state, this test should be used "as a selective screening device, i.e., one that is applied only after an infant is suspected to be at risk for later cognitive delay" (p. 1026).

There are some positive aspects to such a second-level screening test. If a suspicion of risk is indicated because of prenatal or perinatal factors, such a test – if negative – could alleviate anxiety for parents who were alerted that their child may be at risk for developmental problems. However, as a selective screening device, it is essential that the test be highly sensitive and specific so that children who are identified because of other risk conditions are not mistakenly screened negative, and thus deprived of or delayed in receiving needed follow-up (see Meisels, 1988).

There are several problems with the FTI. One problem concerns the standardization sample. As reported in Fagan et al. (1986), subjects were preselected to be at risk for mental retardation based on the following problems: prematurity (birth weight < 1,500 g), intrauterine growth retardation, treated hypothyroidism, diagnosis of failure to thrive, or history of maternal diabetes. The problem with this sampling is that these factors cannot be given equal weight in predicting whether a child will be mentally retarded later in life. Different problems at birth may result in different outcomes in development. Therefore, it seems potentially misleading to group all subjects together and compare their performance on the novelty problems. Data on how infants with different risk factors (e.g., diabetes vs. failure to thrive) compared on their performance on the novelty problems are not presented. This heterogeneous grouping of infants with varying types of problems could explain why, of the 62 children who were described as at risk according to the factors listed previously, 49 were predicted to be normal. It is unclear if these infants were, in fact, developmentally at risk. Further, SES and maternal education were not analyzed as possible mediating variables that might be involved in predicting risk. Indeed, Fagan presents no demographic data of this type. Finally, the screening device is based on data from only 92 infants, and predictive validity of the instrument was assessed based on the performance of only 62 subjects. This small sample size raises substantial concern about the test's reliability and validity.

Calculation of the index used to determine if a child is at risk is also open to question. Each infant is assigned a mean novelty preference score. A percentage is determined based on the time an infant spends looking at a new item compared to the time spent looking at both the new and old item. Therefore, in a 60-second period, an infant who devotes 10 seconds to looking at the new pattern and 6 seconds to looking at the old pattern would obtain a novelty score of 63% [10/(10 + 6)]. But such an approach does not appear to be sensitive. For example, an infant could spend 2 seconds looking at the familiar item and 3 seconds looking at the new item and still receive a novelty score of 60%. It is unclear what this novelty score measures or how it can discriminate between infants. A novelty score of 60% compared to one of 63% does not appear to be significantly different, yet the performance of the infants could be quite dissimilar. Considerably more methodological development is needed before this test can be used with confidence to identify children at risk (see McCall, 1988).

ALTERNATIVE APPROACHES TO ASSESSING INFANTS. Caron, Caron, and their colleagues (Caron, Caron, & Glass, 1982; Caron, Caron, & Myers, 1982) also examined infant perceptual processing as an indicator of current cognitive functioning. Although the rationale for their procedure is similar to Fagan's, they differ from him on several important issues regarding the basis for intellectual functioning in infancy.

Caron and Caron (1981) propose that infants' abilities to interrelate elements of experience are an essential ingredient of intellect. This differs from Fagan's perceptual processing theory because Fagan regards visual preference for novelty or visual recognition as the basis for intellectual development. For Caron and Caron, it is the infant's ability to detect and abstract relational aspects of environmental information that is fundamental to intelligence. Examples of relational information are the ability to detect sameness and difference, contours and shapes, and so on. (For a complete review see Caron & Caron, 1981.) Although Caron and Caron's findings are not yet conclusive, measurement of this relational ability in infants may provide an early index of future cognitive functioning.

Another area of research that shows potential as an assessment technique is the analysis of infant cries. Early investigations suggested that characteristics of an infant's cry may reflect the capacity of the infant's nervous system to process and to inhibit stimulation. In particular, this research documented the unusually high-pitched and short cry of infants with brain damage (Fisichelli & Karelitz, 1963; Karelitz & Fisichelli, 1962; Parmelee, 1962). Several recent studies have reported the unusual cries of infants who later succumbed to sudden infant death syndrome (Colton & Steinschneider, 1981; Stark & Nathanson, 1975), and other research has attempted to analyze infant cries systematically with the intention of isolating patterns that are indicative of infant neurological problems (Golub & Corwin, 1982, 1985).

Extensive research has been directed toward using infant cry as an index for assessing infants at risk. For example, Lester and Zeskind (1981) examined the cry features of infants with differential fetal growth. Results indicated that underweight- and overweight-for-length infants showed distinctively different cry patterns from infants who were average weight for length. These results, and findings that abnormal variability in the pattern of newborn cries is related to 18-month Bayley scores (Lester, 1988; Zeskind & Lester, 1981), suggest that this distinctly different crying pattern could be used as a screening measure to identify infants who are at risk (see Zeskind & Marshall, 1988).

Still another approach to infant screening that differs from the traditional cognitive and sensorimotor approaches was presented by Porges (1983). His research focused on the use of psychophysiological tests to provide a method for evaluating infants' qualitative changes in behavior prior to their acquisition of complex verbal or motoric behaviors.

Porges used heart rate patterns as his physiological index. This approach differs from the simple measurement of heart rate acceleration or deceleration in infants. By examining patterns in heart rate, Porges (1988) argues that he is using a highly sensitive measure, a "noninvasive window to the brain" (p. 150), of the functioning of the central nervous system (CNS). In one study, Porges, McCabe, and Yongue (1982) examined the heart rate pattern in preterm and full-term infants. Results showed a relationship between heart rate patterns and gestational age. Although additional research is needed in this area, Porges's work suggests that examining heart rate patterns may provide important information for identifying children at risk during the early development of the nervous system.

DISCUSSION. Screening devices representing both a psychometric and a perceptual and psychophysiological perspective have been reviewed. Unfortunately, there are few candidates available for adoption in either category, and none with adequate standardization and predictive properties to recommend wide-scale use. Moreover, all of the psychophysiological approaches are still experimental, and are not yet appropriate for use in mass screening efforts. Despite the paucity of research in this area, one need not be overly pessimistic about the emergence of better screening instruments. As early intervention programs continue to expand, the need for better instrumentation will become more apparent, and it is likely that more comprehensive research efforts will be expended on this issue.

Nevertheless, one still can question the wisdom of these efforts if they are intended to produce a test that can unilaterally predict developmental problems. Our review of research supports the need to develop more sensitive and specific instruments that can accurately identify children whose developmental difficulties are still in a preclinical or asymptomatic stage. But, by virtue of the brevity and highly inferential nature of screening tests, and the dynamic changes in development that occur during the first 3 years of life, it is unlikely that any test will be adequate to the task of identifying the vast range of potential developmental problems that were enumerated earlier in the chapter. Furthermore, problems that have their origin in the caregiving environment, or that are late-appearing manifestations of risk, cannot be expected to be detected by a single data source, particularly a source that focuses exclusively on the intactness of the central nervous system. Rather, what may be called for is a multifactorial approach to screening, combined with a carefully devised periodicity schedule.

Multiple-factor approaches

For some years researchers have attempted to construct a "risk index" in order to solve some of the problems of over- and underidentification that are endemic to single-factor screening approaches (Bee et al., 1982; Field at al., 1978; Kochanek, Kabacoff, & Lipsitt, 1987; Littman & Parmelee, 1978; Minde, Whitelaw, Brown, & Fitzhardinge, 1983; Sameroff, Seifer, Barocas, Zax, & Greenspan, 1987). Such indexes may combine biologic risk data (e.g., prenatal care, Apgar scores, birth weight, and gestational age) with environmental variables (e.g., parental education and occupation, social support, economic status, family size, and life events). Some practitioners suggest using a risk index to select at-risk children and families, and then administering a screening test to the children identified in this manner (Saltzman & Shea, 1983). These efforts at combining multiple data sources into an index, or weighted formula, may prove to be most successful in isolating those factors that have the highest probability of placing certain children at risk. But there seems to be little agreement about the composition of the "best" index of risk.

BIOLOGICAL INDEXES. Littman and Parmelee (1978) attempted to correlate developmental outcome with medical complications affecting the fetus and the infant. They devised three scales, known as the Obstetric, Postnatal, and Pediatric Complications Scales. The most widely used of these is the Obstetric Complications Scale (OCS), which records 41 events reflecting the mother's medical history, the child's gestation, and the labor, delivery, and immediate postnatal course of the child. The items on the scale are unweighted, that is, they do not differentiate the severity of the medical condition, and they are quite heterogeneous, including such factors as birth weight, gestational age, duration of labor, Apgar score, marital status, and so on. Whereas it is reported that the pediatric scales at 4 and 9 months bear some relationship to developmental outcome, Littman and Parmelee (1978) note that "neither the obstetric nor the postnatal scales correlated with developmental quotient or mental performance at 4, 9, 18, or 24 months" (p. 473). Thus, although the scales may be used to characterize a newborn's health status, they cannot be used effectively as a screening device.

Minde, Whitelaw, Brown, and Fitzhardinge (1983) devised a Morbidity Scale that appears to be more sensitive than the Obstetric and the Postnatal Complications Scales. They combined 20 common neonatal diseases and pathophysiological states (e.g., convulsions, hydrocephalus, sepsis, respiratory distress syndrome, etc.) into an index that permits the severity of each condition to be rated daily on a 4-point scale. The infant receives a total score reflecting the day's complications, as well as other global scores representing the severity and duration of his or her neonatal course. Although the Morbidity Scale was not devised to predict future neurological or behavioral functioning, Minde et al. (1983) showed that it was effective in characterizing the contribution of the infant's illness to shaping the caregiving environment. However, the intensive effort required to record daily morbidity ratings may preclude the use of this scale as one factor in a multiple-risk index.

The "cumulative risk scales" devised by Littman and Parmelee and by Minde et al. suffer from the limitations of the data they sample. Whereas both scales assess initial biological insult, neither one can characterize adequately or predict accurately the infant's neurological functioning or rate of recovery of neurological function. As Thoman (1982) notes,

> The problem of predicting the outcome of individuals on the basis of pregnancy and perinatal problems has not been solved. It is simply not possible to know the infant's developmental status from the infant's prior exposure to risk factors or even the infant's prior distress conditions. As each infant has an individual pattern of early trauma, each will show an individual course in central nervous system compensation (p. 167).

Risk indexes that focus principally on the child's biological status at birth and postnatally are apparently too static to account for the self-righting mechanisms within the child and the compensating factors within the child's environment. Even if the biological condition is particularly influential on development, such as is the case with moderate to severe intraventricular hemorrhage, an infant's quality of performance and specific skill patterns are not assessed by biologic risk conditions and may need to be included before accurate predictions can be made (Shonkoff & Marshall, this volume; Sostek, 1988).

ENVIRONMENTAL INDEXES. Another type of risk index, derived from easily available environmental data, is reported by Ramey and his colleagues (Ramey, Stedman, Borders-Patterson, & Mengel, 1978). They focused on data available from birth certificates: race, parity, month prenatal care began, mother's educational level, birth weight, legitimacy of birth, and previous child mortality. However, in a first-grade follow-up study of those children who were predicted to be a high risk, this method was found to overrefer low-risk children by a six-to-one ratio (Finkelstein & Ramey, 1980). Apparently, the factors included in this index were all tapping elements that were highly related to the same social class variable – a variable that proves not to be very specific.

Previous research (Bradley & Caldwell, 1984; Broman, Bien, & Shaughnessy, 1985; Broman, Nichols, & Kennedy, 1975; Werner, Bierman, & French, 1971) has shown that less-optimal developmental status can be predicted by lower SES, less maternal education, higher birth order, and larger family size. But evidence is also available that indicates that SES and its correlates are not sufficient indicators of psychosocial and intellectual risk (see Farran & McKinney, 1986; Gallagher & Ramey, 1987). Rather than focus attention on a single factor, regardless of how complexly defined, the fact that development is multidetermined implies that predictive measurements should be correspondingly multifactorial. Adopting a suggestion of Ramey, MacPhee, & Yeates (1984), we must attempt to combine "measures of individual vulnerability with assessments of environmental forces that influence the range of stability" (p. 358). Such an approach holds out the promise of improving our ability to identify individuals who are at risk for maladaptive or disabled functioning (see Meisels & Provence, 1989).

MIXED MULTIFACTORIAL INDEXES. Several researchers have sought to link performance data regarding children's developmental attainments with measures of their social environment and indicators of their neonatal and postnatal health status. The purpose of devising these mixed risk indexes is to discover efficient and relatively accurate means of identifying children who are at developmental risk. A corollary purpose is that of creating a set of risk indicators sufficiently broad to include the majority of the children we are seeking to identify, regardless of their etiology.

Two such risk indexes were developed as part of longitudinal studies of preterm development. Field et al. (1978) studied 151 infants, 46 with respiratory distress syndrome (RDS), 46 who were described as having "post" term postmaturity syndrome," and 59 full-term infants. Field and her colleagues conducted discriminant function analyses of the data from the first year of these infants' lives in order to identify the most efficient predictors and accurate discriminators of continuing risk.

The discriminant function analyses comparing the full-term with the postterm and the preterm infants showed that "although the same general group of predictors entered the analyses for both groups and for both mental and motor outcome scores, the order of their significance...changed from stage to stage, from group to group, and from outcome variable to outcome variable" (Field et al., 1978, p. 128). Among the variables that best predicted 12-month Bayley mental and motor scales were the OCS, PCS, and Brazelton motoric process scores at term; these perinatal variables plus temperament and infant interaction at 4 months; and temperament, the Brazelton, and Bayley scores at 8 months. However, the proportion of false positives and negatives was fairly high until the 8 month assessment.

Some stability was suggested by the common core of variables used at each stage of development, but problems with this index remain. One such problem is that the study's conclusion that predictions become more accurate as additional assessments are conducted and as the outcome period nears is not very helpful. It can be interpreted as saying that since accuracy is difficult to achieve with brief risk indexes, the closer one is to the point of outcome assessment, that is, the shorter the period of prediction, and the more data one has, the better will be one's estimates of risk. But, the purpose of a risk index is to predict outcomes over time and with limited data. Furthermore, the outcome used in this study – 1-year Bayley scores – is itself of questionable predictive validity.

Siegel, also studying a group of preterms, sought to overcome some of these problems by using more varied outcomes and by following her subjects for 5 years. Like Field, she found that different combinations of variables predicted differently at various ages. In an investigation of the outcome of 53 preterms and 51 full-terms, she constructed a risk index that predicted IQ and language expression and comprehension at 36 and 60 months of age. SES, birth order, maternal smoking, and for preterms, severity of illness in the perinatal period, were consistently the best predictors of development at 3 years (Siegel, 1982a). At 5 years of age the predictors were similar, with maternal and paternal educational levels also included in the analysis (Siegel, 1982b).

The percentage agreement between risk index and Stanford-Binet IQ at 3 years was 76.3 for preterms and 84.0 for fullterms (Siegel, 1982a). However, these figures are somewhat misleading because they do not permit analysis of the proportions of over- and underreferrals. Such analyses are possible through computation of sensitivity and specificity ratios. For preterms these figures are .62 and .70, respectively; for fullterms they are .75 and .85. Although these proportions indicate an underreferral rate of 38% for preterms and 25% for fullterms, these figures are better than those obtained with single predictors or with other indexes. Yet to be conducted, however, is a replication of these findings with another sample. Until this is accomplished the generalizability of the index cannot be determined. Nevertheless, these findings lend strong support to the position that predictions of risk should combine data from multiple sources.

Another study that arrived at similar conclusions is reported by Kochanek et al. (1987). They used data from the National Collaborative Perinatal Project to determine

Table 3. *Variables used for calculating cumulative risk scores for families of 4-year-olds*

Risk variable	Source of data
Maternal mental health	Psychiatric interviews during pregnancy and at 30 months, information from psychiatric registry
Maternal anxiety	Average of the standardized scores of three measures
Parental perspectives	Combined scores of three measures
Maternal interactive behavior	Home observations at 4 and 12 months
Maternal education	Determined during prenatal interviews
Occupation	Determined during prenatal interviews
Minority group status	White vs. nonwhite
Family social support	Father present or absent
Family size	Four or more children constitute risk
Stressful life events	Life Events Inventory

Source: Sameroff, Seifer, Barocas, Zax, & Greenspan (1987)

if a combination of prenatal, perinatal, and early developmental variables can identify children at risk for intellectual difficulties and academic problems. The subjects consisted of 536 children, half of whom were disabled upon evaluation as adolescents, and half of whom were not. The groups were matched for sex, race, and age. Using stepwise logistic regression analysis, four early childhood variables considered as potential predictors of risk during adolescence were identified. These included maternal education (reported at the birth of the child), placing or stepping at 4 months, physical development at 8 months, and the presence or absence of neurological abnormalities at 12 months. Sensitivity and specificity for these four variables were 42.3 and 84.3. In other words, although the risk index overreferred relatively few children, it underreferred nearly 60% of those later found to be handicapped. In further analyses the authors report that none of the prenatal and perinatal data yielded significant results when examined as single predictors. Indeed, they note that maternal education was "a more accurate predictor of adolescent functioning than the child's own developmental status from birth to 12 months" (Kochaneck et al., p. 418). Thus, ecological factors, specifically maternal education, are identified as critical variables in predicting outcomes.

Similar results are presented by Sameroff et al. (1987). Seeking to show that combinations of risk factors provide the best prediction of outcome, they assessed a set of 10 environmental variables that they contend are correlates of socioeconomic status. Kochanek et al. (1987) had also noted the preeminence of environmental factors in their risk index, but they had pointed out that such variables as maternal education are typically static and uninformative about maternal behaviors or patterns of interactions that could be related to specific child competence. In contrast, Sameroff et al. (1987) sought to capture the details of the child's environmental context by identifying a number of variables that describe comprehensively the caregiving environment. These variables are listed in Table 3.

The sample consisted of 215 families, all with a 4-year-old child. Half of the families were selected because of maternal emotional problems; the other half were matched controls. Children were tested when they were 4 years old with the verbal scales of the Wechsler Preschool and Primary Scales of Intelligence (WPPSI). Results showed that as the number of risk factors increased, performance decreased for children at 4 years (see Sameroff & Fiese, this volume). In other words, these findings support the notion of a cumulative burden of risk. As risk factors multiplied, their combination "resulted in a nearly threefold increase in the magnitude of differences found among groups of children relative to the effect of most single variables" (Sameroff et al., 1987, p. 347). As we have seen in other studies, no single variable determined outcome. Rather, more than 50% of the variance in 4-year-old verbal IQ scores could be explained when the environmental context of the child was broadly considered. Although sensitivity and specificity proportions are unavailable, the authors report that "the probability of falling into the low IQ category was 24 times as great in the high-risk group compared to the low-risk group" (Sameroff et al., 1987, p. 348).

These results are further strengthened by data from a 1982 study by Bee et al. They followed 193 healthy working-class and middle-class families through a 4-year longitudinal study. Their findings recapitulate the major conclusions of all the studies of risk indexes reported thus far:

1. Measures of perinatal status are extremely weak predictors of later IQ or language development;
2. Standardized measures of the child's performance are of limited value during the first year of life;
3. Mother–infant interaction and assessments of environmental factors are good predictors of long-term outcomes;
4. "Family ecology" variables (level of stress, social support, maternal education) predict later intellectual functioning better than any combination of measures from the first year of life, and about as well as measures obtained at 2 years of age.

Bee and her colleagues suggest that, if one were only to assess children and families once, the best timing would be either at birth or at 2 years. However, they recommend that different information be obtained at these different time points. At birth the most useful and predictive information would concern family functioning and the parents' perception of the child; at 2 years one would seek to measure the child's performance on standardized tests in combination with observations of the home environment. In short, early identification requires that data be obtained from multiple sources; that it combine caregiving and environmental information with data about the child's biological status; and that in the first 2 years of life, psychometric measures of child development be used in combination with other sources of data.

CONCLUSION

A contextual approach to early identification

Identifying infants and toddlers at risk for developmental problems remains a task in which more is known about what doesn't work than what does. The evidence reviewed in this chapter supports the assumption that most isolated events or factors that occur early in a child's life do not have an inevitable impact on the child's development. (Such a statement excludes events that involve significant damage to the central nervous system, or the presence of chromosomal anomalies.) In other words, events such as preterm birth, neonatal hospitalization, or being born into poverty do not in themselves imply that a child's developmental potential will be compromised.

Nevertheless, few events occur in isolation. The child born into poverty will probably experience material deprivations throughout the first several years of life. The corolaries of poverty, including poor nutrition, poor pre- and postnatal care, potential drug addiction, inadequate housing, disorganized family life, and limited social support may also be present. Similar contexts of continuity can be assumed to exist for children who are born with other types of problems or risk conditions.

It has been suggested (Sameroff, 1975, 1986) that the environmental context of child development carries forward the impact of risk factors. Furthermore, this context is ultimately responsible for both the amelioration and the magnification of early problems. Such a view has several important implications for early identification. First, it helps us understand why predictions from infancy are so tenuous. If development is affected by subsequent environmental interactions, and if infant screening can capture only a momentary "snapshot" of this developmental process, it is not surprising that many errors of prediction are made. Hence, it can be concluded that the process of early identification should occur on a recurrent or periodic basis. As stated earlier, children go in and out of risk on a fairly frequent, though irregular, basis. Also, some developmental problems are only manifested later in childhood. Thus, continuing vigilance is justified if the complexity of the factors that influence development is to be properly evaluated (see Meisels & Provence, 1989).

A second implication of the contextual view of how risk factors arise and evolve focuses on the importance of multiple sources of data. The research reviewed in this chapter demonstrates that "no single factor is always present or always absent when high levels of social-emotional and intellectual incompetency are found" (Sameroff, 1986, p. 197). Rather, developmental disorders are generally attributable to multiple factors or multiple causes. Even very low birth weight preterm children who demonstrate clear developmental sequelae are probably evidencing the effects of a number of biological and environmental insults. For example, children who develop chronic lung disease (bronchopulmonary dysplasia, or BPD) and later have less than optimal cognitive and socioemotional development may have been exposed to a host of pre-, peri-, and postnatal risk factors, as well as caregiving problems during the first several years of life (Meisels, Plunkett, Roloff, Pasick, & Stiefel, 1986; Plunkett, Meisels, Stiefel, Pasick, & Roloff, 1986). Development is multidetermined, and assessments of those at risk for nonoptimal development should reflect this.

A third implication concerns the number and weighting of risk factors that must be present before the probability is heightened of a child demonstrating delayed development. The precise number of such factors is, of course, both unknown and probably unknowable, due to the interaction of individual child and family differences with risk conditions. However, in Werner's 18-year longitudinal study on the island of Kauai, the presence of four or more predictors of risk by age 2 years "appeared to be a realistic dividing line between most children...who developed serious learning and/or behavior problems by age 10 or 18 and most of the boys and girls who were able to cope successfully with the developmental tasks of childhood and adolescence" (Werner, 1986, p. 16). These predictors included biological variables (e.g., moderate to severe perinatal stress, congenital defect at birth); caregiving factors (e.g., low level of maternal education, low standard of living, low rating of family stability between birth and 2 years of age); and other behavioral variables (e.g., maternal ratings of very low or very high infant activity level, delayed development as assessed by psychometric examination). Thus, systems of early identification should be sensitive to the cumulative nature of risk, especially when the risk factors represent a range of potential developmental influences.

Still another implication of the research reviewed in this chapter concerns the status and usefulness of standardized tests. It is abundantly clear that none of the existing psychometric instruments have sufficient stability over time to be used in isolation as accurate predictors. However, most predictive indexes include psychometric devices among the cluster of variables used for prediction. Tests can be used to assess a child's current level of functioning and to make qualitative judgments about areas of strength and areas in need of intervention. Effective infant screening devices, i.e., tests with adequate stability and validity, do not currently exist. One reason for the lack of effective tests is that developmental status is so vulnerable to environmental and familial influences. As a result, what may be needed is not a single test, but a sequence of brief assessment devices, used perhaps at 6-month intervals in order to add an important behavioral dimension to risk indexes.

The final implication of the contextual view of development concerns which children and families should be targeted for casefinding or child find efforts. If it is true that unitary variables do not, in isolation, provide a justification for assigning risk, then simple categorical models of risk must be discarded. No longer should we assume that all preterms, all poor children, or all infants born to adolescent mothers are at risk for less optimal development. That is, we should not make this assumption unless we know something else about the family or the child that constitutes a risk factor. For example, in addition to knowing that a child's family is very poor, other factors central to the child's development include whether the child was exposed to drugs in utero, whether either of the parents or the infant tested HIV positive, and "enduring characteristics of the family (e.g., number of children, marital and minority status), psychologic characteristics of the parents (e.g., mental health, education, child-rearing attitudes, beliefs and coping skills), and stressful life events that interfere with the family's ability to provide a nurturant context for the child" (Sameroff, 1986, pp. 196–197). More refined risk registers will lead to more sensitive and specific identification of children in need of early intervention services.

Four stages of identification

It is possible to recapitulate these points by describing a four-stage conceptual process, or research strategy, leading to future identification of children at highest risk for developmental problems. The first stage involves defining *eligibility* and determining which child and family characteristics are most likely to be related to developmental disorders. This stage of inquiry focuses on basic research already accomplished about normative and atypical development. In this stage we identify the elements of optimal and suboptimal development, concentrating on sensorimotor skills, perceptual and language development, cognitive abilities, socioemotional growth, and patterns of familial adaptation.

The second phase focuses on *methods*: How can the characteristics identified be defined and made operational? For example, how should we assess language acquisition in the first 2 years, or infant–mother attachment, or any of the other constructs that are intended to characterize development? Much of the work in this area has already been described extensively in the research literature.

The third stage concerns *identification*: Which combinations or clusters of characteristics can be used with accuracy to identify children who have a high probability of experiencing developmental problems? This aspect of the process entails the construction of various risk indexes, and the empirical application of these indexes, using the methods described, so that efficient, accurate, and age-appropriate indexes can be developed.

Finally, the task of establishing and managing *risk registers* must be undertaken: How can the identification process be made most efficient? Everyone with one or two risk factors should not go through an identification process. How can the most likely candidates be selected? Which combination of factors should lead to preventive efforts? Which children are the best candidates for psychometric screening? Who should be followed-up soon, and who should be followed later?

These questions – particularly those in the latter two phases – will require intensive research. Only after we have answers to them will we know who should be served in early intervention programs, and it is only then that the potential of these programs can be realized.

Identifying the "right" children – those in greatest need of remediation, those experiencing the most debilitating social environments, those who are very likely to lead lives filled with despair and unfulfilled promise – is a complex matter. No longer can we be satisfied with relatively simple etiological classifications. No longer can we assume that the right test will come along someday. Our knowledge of how children develop and change has been unalterably affected by our awareness of the multiplicity of factors that shape children's lives. The task before us is to devise methods of identification that reflect this multiplicity and that are sensitive to the combinations and clusters of factors that are most likely to compromise or to enhance a child's development.

REFERENCES

Aiken, L. R. (1988). *Psychological testing and assessment* (6th ed.). Boston: Allyn & Bacon.
Applebaum, A. (1978). Validity of the revisied Denver Developmental Screening Test for referred and non-referred samples. *Psychological Reports, 43*, 227–233.
Barnes, K. E. (1982). *Preschool screening: The measurement and prediction of children at-risk.* Springfield, IL: Charles C. Thomas.
Bayley, N. (1969). Bayley Scales of Infant Development. New York: The Psychological Corporation.
Bee, H. L., Barnard, K. E., Eyres, S. J., Gray, C. A., Hamond, M. A., Spietz, A. L., Snyder, C., & Clark, B. (1982). Prediction of IQ and language skill from perinatal status, child performance, family characteristics, and mother–infant interaction. *Child Development, 53*, 1134–1156.
Bell, R. Q. (1986). Age-specific manifestations in changing psychosocial risk. In D. C. Farran & J. C. McKinney (Eds.), *Risk in intellectual and psychosocial development* (pp. 169–186). Orlando: Academic Press.
Bogdan, R., & Taylor, S. (1976). The judged, not the judges: An insider's view of mental retardation. *American Psychologist, 31*, 47–52.
Borowitz, K. C., & Glascoe, F. P. (1986). Sensitivity of the Denver Developmental Screening Test in speech and language screening. *Pediatrics, 78*, 1075–1078.
Bradley, R. H., & Caldwell, B. M. (1984). 174 children: A study of the relationship between home environment and cognitive development during the first 5 years. In A. W. Gottfried (Ed.), *Home environment and early cognitive development* (pp. 5–56). Orlando: Academic Press.
Britton, S. B., Fitzhardinge, P. M., & Ashby, S. (1981). Is intensive care justified for infants weighting less than 801 g at birth? *Journal of Pediatrics, 99*, 937–943.
Broman, S., Bien, E., & Shaughnessy, P. (1985). *Low achieving children: The first seven years.* Hillsdale, NJ: L. Erlbaum.
Broman, S. H., Nichols, P. L., & Kennedy, W. A. (1975). *Pre-school IQ: Prenatal and early developmental correlates.* Hillsdale, NJ: L. Erlbaum.
Brooks-Gunn, J., & Weintraub, M. (1983). Origins of infant intelligence testing. In M. Lewis (Ed.), *Origins of intelligence: Infancy and early childhood* (2nd ed., pp. 25–66). New York: Plenum Press.

Buckwald, S., Zorn, W. A., & Egan, E. A. (1984). Mortality and follow-up for neonates weighing 500 to 800 g at birth. *American Journal of Diseases of Children*, *138*, 779–782.

Cadman, D., Chambers, L. W., Walter, S. D., Feldman, W., Smith, K., & Ferguson, R. (1984). The usefulness of the Denver Developmental Screening Test to predict kindergarten problems in a general community population. *American Journal of Public Health*, *74*, 1093–1097.

Camp, B., van Doorninck, W., Frankenburg, W., & Lampe, J. (1977). Preschool developmental testing in prediction of school problems: Studies of 55 children in Denver. *Clinical Pediatrics*, *16*, 257–263.

Capute, A. J., & Accardo, P. J. (1978). Linguistic and auditory milestones during the first two years of life. *Clinical Pediatrics*, *17*, 847–853.

Caron, A. J., & Caron, R. F. (1981). Processing of relational information as an index of infant risk. In S. L. Friedman & M. Sigman (Eds.), *Preterm birth and psychological development* (pp. 219–240). New York: Academic Press.

Caron, A. J., Caron, R. F., & Glass, P. (1982). Responsiveness to relational information as a measure of cognitive functioning in nonsuspect infants. In T. M. Field & A. M. Sostek (Eds.), *Infants born at risk: Psychological, perceptual, and cognitive processes* (pp. 181–210). New York: Grune & Stratton.

Caron, A. J., Caron, R. F., & Meyers, R. (1982). Abstraction of invariant face expression in infancy. *Child Development*, *53*, 1008–1015.

Carmichael, A., & Williams, H. E. (1981). Developmental screening in infancy – A critical appraisal of its value. *Australian Paediatric Journal*, *17*, 20–23.

Cohen, S. E. (1986). The low-birthweight infant and learning disabilities. In M. Lewis (Ed.), *Learning disabilities and prenatal risk* (pp. 153–193). Urbana: University of Illinois Press.

Colton, R. H., & Steinschneider, A. (1981). The cry characteristics of an infant who died of sudden infant death syndrome. *Journal of Hearing Disorders*, *46*, 359–363.

Dean, R. S., & Steffen, J. E. (1984). Direct and indirect pediatric screening measures. *Journal of Pediatric Psychology*, *9*, 65–75.

Diamond, K. E. (1987). Predicting school problems from preschool developmental screening: A four-year follow-up of the revised Denver Developmental Screening Test and the role of parent report. *Journal of the Division for Early Childhood*, *11*, 247–253.

Division for Early Childhood. (1987). *Position statements and recommendations relating to PL 99-457 and other federal and state early childhood policies*. Arlington, VA: Council for Exceptional Children.

Eaton, W. W. (1980). *The sociology of mental disorders*. New York: Praeger.

Edelman, M. W. (1987). *Families in peril: An agenda for social change*. Cambridge: Harvard University Press.

Emde, R. N., & Harmon, R. J. (Eds.). (1984). *Continuities and discontinuities in development*. New York: Plenum Press.

Fagan, J. F. (1982). New evidence for the prediction of intelligence from infancy. *Infant Mental Health Journal*, *3*, 219–228.

Fagan, J. F., & Singer, L. T. (1983). Infant recognition memory as a measure of intelligence. In L. P. Lipsitt & C. K. Rovee-Collier (Eds.), *Advances in infancy research* (pp. 31–77). Norwood, NJ: Ablex Publishing.

Fagan, J. F., Singer, L. T., & Montie, J. E. (1985). An experimental selective screening device for the early detection of intellectual deficit in at-risk infants. In W. K. Frankenburg, R. N. Emde, & J. W. Sullivan (Eds.), *Early identification of children at risk: An international perspective* (pp. 257–266). New York: Plenum Press.

Fagan, J. F., Singer, L. T., Montie, J. E., & Shepherd, P. A. (1986). Selective screening device for the early detection of normal or delayed cognitive development in infants at risk for later mental retardation. *Pediatrics*, *78*, 1021–1026.

Farran, D. C., & McKinney, J. D. (Eds.). (1986). *Risk in intellectual and psychosocial development*. Orlando: Academic Press.

Field, T., Hallock, N., Ting, G., Dempsey, J., Dabiri, C., & Shuman, H. (1978). A first-year follow-up of high-risk infants: Formulating a cumulative risk index. *Child Development*, *49*, 119–131.

Finkelstein, N. W., & Ramey, C. T. (1980). Information from birth certificates as a risk index for educational handicap. *American Journal of Mental Deficiency*, *84*, 546–552.

Fisichelli, V., & Karelitz, S. (1963). The cry latencies of normal infants and those with brain damage. *Journal of Pediatrics*, *62*, 724–734.

Frankenburg, W. K., Dodds, J., Fandal, A., Kazuk, E., & Cohrs, M. (1975). Denver Developmental Screening Test. Denver: University of Colorado Medical Center.

Frankenburg, W. K., Fandal, A., Sciarillo, W., & Burgess, D. (1981). The newly abbreviated and revised Denver Developmental Screening Test. *The Journal of Pediatrics, 99*, 995–999.

Frankenburg, W. K., van Doorninck, W. J., Liddell, T., & Dick, N. P. (1976). The Denver Prescreening Developmental Questionnaire (PDQ). *Pediatrics, 57*, 744–753.

Furstenberg, F. F., Brooks-Gunn, J., & Morgan, S. P. (1987). *Adolescent mothers in later life.* New York: Cambridge University Press.

Gallagher, J. J., & Ramey, C. T. (Eds.). (1987). *The malleability of children.* Baltimore, MD: P. H. Brookes.

Golub, H. L., & Corwin, M. J. (1982). Infant cry: A clue to diagnosis. *Pediatrics, 69*, 197–201.

Golub, H. L., & Corwin, M. J. (1985). A physio-acoustic model of the infant cry. In B. M. Lester & C. F. Z. Boukydis (Eds.), *Infant crying: Theoretical and research perspectives* (pp. 59–82). New York: Plenum Press.

Gottfried, A. W., Guerin, D., Spencer, J. E., & Meyer, C. (1983). Concurrent validity of Minnesota Child Development Inventory in a nonclinical sample. *Journal of Consulting and Clinical Psychology, 51*, 643–644.

Gottfried, A. W., Guerin, D., Spencer, J. E., & Meyer, C. (1984). Validity of Minnesota Child Development Inventory in screening young children's developmental status. *Journal of Pediatric Psychology, 9*, 219–230.

Gradel, K., Thompson, M., & Sheehan, R. (1981). Parental and professional agreement in early childhood assessment. *Topics in Early Childhood Special Education, 1*, 31–40.

Griffiths, R. (1954). *The abilities of babies.* London: University of London Press.

Guerin, D., & Gottfried, A. W. (1987). Minnesota Child Development Inventories: Predictors of intelligence, achievement, and adaptability. *Journal of Pediatric Psychology, 12*, 595–609.

Guralnick, M. J., & Bennett, F. C. (1987). A framework for early intervention. In M. J. Guralnick & F. C. Bennett (Eds.), *The effectiveness of early intervention for at-risk and handicapped children* (pp. 3–32). Orlando: Academic Press.

Hack, M. H., & Fanaroff, A. A. (1986). Changes in the delivery room care of the extremely small infant (< 750 g). Effects on morbidity and outcome. *The New England Journal of Medicine, 314*, 660–664.

Harper, D. C., & Wacker, D. P. (1983). The efficiency of the Denver Developmental Screening Test for rural disadvantaged preschool children. *Journal of Pediatric Psychology, 8*, 273–283.

Honzik, M. P. (1983). Measuring mental abilities in infancy: The value and limitations. In M. Lewis (Ed.), *Origins of intelligence: Infancy and early childhood* (2nd ed., pp. 67–106). New York: Plenum Press.

Ireton, H. (1982). Early identification of developmentally delayed children by maternal report: The Minnesota Child Development Inventories. In N. J. Anastasiow, W. K. Frankenburg, & A. W. Fandal (Eds.), *Identifying the developmentally delayed child* (pp. 53–61). Baltimore: University Park Press.

Ireton, H., & Thwing, E. (1974). The Minnesota Child Development Inventory. Minneapolis: Behavioral Science Systems.

Ireton, H., Thwing, E., & Currier, S. (1977). Minnesota Child Development Inventory: Identification of children with developmental disorders. *Journal of Pediatric Psychology, 2*, 18–22.

Karelitz, S., & Fisichelli, V. (1962). The cry threshold of normal infants and those with brain damage. *Journal of Pediatrics, 61*, 679–685.

Kenny, T. J., Hebel, J. R., Sexton, J. M., & Fox, N. L. (1987). Developmental screening using parent report. *Journal of Developmental and Behavioral Pediatrics, 8*, 8–11.

Klein, N., Hack, M., Gallagher, J., & Fanaroff, A. A. (1985). Preschool performance of very low birthweight children with normal intelligence. *Pediatrics, 75*, 531–537.

Knobloch, H., Malone, A., Ellison, P., Stevens, F., & Zdeb, M. (1982). Considerations in evaluating changes in outcome for infants weighing less than 1,501 grams. *Pediatrics, 69*, 285–295.

Kochanek, T. T., Kabacoff, R. I., & Lipsitt, L. P. (1987). Early detection of handicapping conditions in infancy and early childhood: Toward a multivariate model. *Journal of Applied Developmental Psychology, 8*, 411–420.

Kopp, C. B., & McCall, R. B. (1982). Predicting later mental performance for normal, at-risk, and handicapped infants. In P. B. Baltes & O. G. Brim (Eds.), *Life-span development and behavior* (Vol. 4, pp. 33–61). New York: Academic Press.

Lester, B. M. (1988). Neurobehavioral assessment of the infant at risk. In P. M. Vietze & H. G. Vaughan (Eds.), *Early identification of infants with developmental disabilities* (pp. 96–120). Philadelphia: Grune & Stratton.

Lester, B. M., & Zeskind, P. S. (1981). A biobehavioral perspective on crying in early infancy. In H. Fizgerald, B. Lester, & M. Yogman (Eds.), *Theory and research in behavioral pediatrics* (Vol. 1, pp. 133–180). New York: Plenum Press.

Lewis, M., & Sullivan, M. W. (1985). Infant intelligence and its assessment. In B. D. Wolman (Ed.), *Handbook of intelligence: Theories, measurement, and applications* (pp. 505–600). New York: Wiley.

Lichtenstein, R., & Ireton, H. (1984). *Preschool screening: Identifying young children with developmental and educational problems.* Orlando: Grune & Stratton.

Littman, B., & Parmelee, A. M. (1978). Medical correlates of infant development. *Pediatrics, 61,* 470–474.

Lock, T. M., Shapiro, B. K., Ross, A., & Capute, A. J. (1986). Age of presentation in developmental delay. *Journal of Developmental and Behavioral Pediatrics, 7,* 340–345.

McCall, R. B. (1988). Identifying developmental disabilities: Resume and future. In P. M. Vietze & H. G. Vaughan (Eds.), *Early identification of infants with developmental disabilities* (pp. 385–401). Philadelphia: Grune & Stratton.

McCall, R. B. (1982). A hard look at stimulating and predicting development: The case of bonding and screening. *Pediatrics in Review, 3,* 205–212.

Meisels, S. J. (1985). *Developmental screening in early childhood: A guide* (rev. ed.). Washington, DC: National Association for the Education of Young Children.

Meisels, S. J. (1989). Can developmental screening tests identify children who are developmentally at-risk? *Pediatrics, 83,* 578–585.

Meisels, S. J. (1988). Developmental screening in early childhood: The interaction of research and social policy. In L. Breslow, J. E. Fielding, & L. B. Lave (Eds.), *Annual review of public health* (Vol. 9, pp. 527–550). Palo Atlo, CA: Annual Reviews.

Meisels, S. J., & Anastasiow, N. J. (1982). The risks of prediction: Relationships between etiology, handicapping conditions and developmental outcomes. In S. Moore & C. Cooper (Eds.), *The young child: Reviews of research* (Vol. 3, pp. 259–280). Washington, DC: National Association for the Education of Young Children.

Meisels, S. J., Cross, D. R., & Plunkett, J. W. (1987). Use of the Bayley Infant Behavior Record with preterm and full-term infants. *Developmental Psychology, 23,* 475–482.

Meisels, S. J., Harbin, G., Modigliani, K., & Olson, K. (1988). Formulating optimal state early childhood intervention policies. *Exceptional Children, 55,* 159–165.

Meisels, S. J., & Plunkett, J. W. (1988). Developmental consequences of preterm birth: Are there long-term effects? In P. B. Baltes, D. L. Featherman, & R. M. Lerner (Eds.), *Lifespan development and behavior* (Vol. 9, pp. 87–128). Hillsdale, NJ: L. Erlbaum.

Meisels, S. J., Plunkett, J. W., Pasick, P. L., Stiefel, G. S., & Roloff, D. W. (1987). Effects of severity and chronicity of respiratory illness on cognitive development of preterm infants. *Journal of Pediatric Psychology, 12,* 117–132.

Meisels, S. J., Plunkett, J. W., Roloff, D. W., Pasick, P. L., & Stiefel, G. S. (1986). Growth and development of preterm infants with respiratory distress syndrome and bronchopulmonary dysplasia. *Pediatrics, 77,* 345–352.

Meisels, S. J. & Provence, S. (1989). *Identifying and assessing disabled and developmentally vulnerable young children and their families: Recommended guidelines.* Washington, DC: National Center for Clinical Infant Programs.

Minde, K., Whitelaw, A., Brown, J., & Fitzhardinge, P. (1983). Effects of neonatal complications in premature infants on early parent–infant interactions. *Developmental Medicine & Child Neurology, 25,* 763–777.

Murphy, T. F., Nichter, C. A., & Linden, C. B. (1982). Developmental outcomes of the high-risk infant: A review of methodological research. *Seminars in Perinatology, 6,* 353–364.

National Academy of Sciences. (1985). *Preventing low birthweight.* Washington, DC: National Academy Press.

Nezerka, M. M., & Mangelsdorf, S. (1988, April 24). Predictive validity of maternal reports of infant behavior. Paper presented at the International Conference on Infant Studies, Washington, DC.

Parmelee, A. (1962). Infant crying and neurological diagnosis. *Journal of Pediatrics, 61,* 801–802.

Plunkett, J. W., Meisels, S. J., Stiefel, G. S., Pasick, P. L., & Roloff, D. W. (1986). Patterns of attachment among preterm infants of varying biological risk. *Journal of the American Academy of Child Psychiatry*, *25*, 794–800.

Porges, S. W. (1983). Heart rate patterns in neonates: A potential diagnostic window to the brain. In T. M. Field & A. M. Sostek (Eds.), *Infants born at risk: Psychological, perceptual, and cognitive processes* (pp. 3–22). New York: Grune & Stratton.

Porges, S. W. (1988). Neonatal vagal tone: Diagnostic and prognostic implications. In P. M. Vietze & H. G. Vaughan (Eds.), *Early identification of infants with developmental disabilities* (pp. 147–159). Philadelphia: Grune & Stratton.

Porges, S. W., McCabe, P. M., & Yongue, B. G. (1982). Respiratory-heart-rate interactions: Psychophysiological implications for pathophysiology and behavior. In J. Carioppo & R. Petty (Eds.), *Perspectives in cardiovascular psychophysiology* (pp. 283–301). New York: Guilford Press.

Ramey, C. T., & MacPhee, D. (1986). Developmental retardation: A systems theory perspective on risk and preventive intervention. In D. C. Farran & J. D. McKinney (Eds.), *Risk in intellectual and psychosocial development* (pp. 61–82). Orlando: Academic Press.

Ramey, C. T., MacPhee, D., & Yeates, K. O. (1984). Preventing developmental retardation: A general systems model. In L. A. Bond & J. M. Joffe (Eds.), *Facilitating infant and early childhood development* (pp. 343–401). Hanover, NH: University Press of New England.

Ramey, C. T., Stedman, D. J., Borders-Patterson, A., & Mengel, W. (1978). Predicting school failure from information available at birth. *American Journal of Mental Deficiency*, *82*, 525–534.

Rose, S. A., & Wallace, I. F. (1985). Visual recognition memory: A predictor of later cognitive development in preterms. *Child Development*, *56*, 843–852.

Saltzman, E. J., & Shea, D. W. (1983). Management of pediatric practice. Elk Grove, IL: American Academy of Pediatrics.

Sameroff, A. J. (1975). Early influences on development. *Merrill-Palmer Quarterly*, *21*, 267–294.

Sameroff, A. J. (1986). Environmental context of child development. *Journal of Pediatrics*, *109*, 192–200.

Sameroff, A. J., Seifer, R., Barocas, R., Zax, M., & Greenspan, S. (1987). Intelligence quotient scores of 4-year-old children: Social-emotional risk factors. *Pediatrics*, *79*, 343–350.

Sattler, J. (1988) *Assessment of children* (3rd. ed.). San Diego: Jerome M. Sattler.

Saylor, C. F., & Brandt, B. J. (1986). The Minnesota Child Development Inventory: A valid maternal report form for assessing development in infancy. *Journal of Developmental and Behavioral Pediatrics*, *7*, 308–313.

Sciarillo, W. G., Brown, M. M., Robinson, N. M., Bennett, F. C., & Sells, C. J. (1986). Effectiveness of the Denver Developmental Screening Test with biologically vulnerable infants. *Journal of Developmental and Behavioral Pediatrics*, *7*, 77–83.

Scott, D. T., Ment, L. R. Ehrenkranz, R. A., & Warshaw, J. B. (1984). Evidence for late developmental deficit in very low birth weight infants surviving intraventricular hemorrhage. *Child's Brain*, *11*, 261–269.

Scott, K. G., & Masi, W. (1979). The outcome from and utility of registers of risk. In T. M. Field, A. M. Sostek, S. Goldberg, & H. H. Shuman (Eds.), *Infants born at risk: Behavior and development* (pp. 485–496). Jamaica, NY: Spectrum Publications.

Siegel, L. S. (1982a). Reproductive, perinatal, and environmental variables as predictors of development of preterms (< 1,501 grams) and fullterm children at 5 years. *Seminars in Perinatology*, *6*, 274–279.

Siegel, L. (1982b). Reproductive, perinatal, and environmental factors as predictors of the cognitive and language development of preterm and full-term infants. *Child Development*, *53*, 963–973.

Sostek, A. M. (1988). The utility of risk indices: Intraventricular hemmorhages as a model. In P. M. Vietze & H. G. Vaughan (Eds.), *Early identification of infants with developmental disabilities* (pp. 53–70). Philadelphia: Grune & Stratton.

Stark, R. E., & Nathanson, S. (1975). Unusual features of cry in an infant dying suddenly and unexpectedly. In J. Bosma & J. Showacre (Eds.), *Development of upper respiratory anatomy and function: Implications for sudden infant death syndrome* (pp. 323–352). Washington, DC: U.S. Department of Health, Education & Welfare.

Thoman, E. B. (1982). A biological perspective and a behavioral model for assessment of premature infants. In L. A. Bond & J. M. Joffe (Eds.), *Facilitating infant and early childhood development* (pp. 159–179). Hanover, NH: University Press of New England.

Tjossem, T. D. (Ed.), (1976). *Intervention strategies for high risk infants and young children.* Baltimore, MD: University Park Press.

Ullman, D., & Kausch, D. (1979). Early identification of developmental strengths and weaknesses in preschool children. *Exceptional Children, 46,* 8–13.

U. S. Department of Education. (1987). *Ninth annual report to Congress on the implementation of the Education of the Handicapped Act.* Washington, DC: U.S. Government Printing Office.

Uzgiris, I., & Hunt, J. (1975). *Assessment in infancy: Ordinal scales of psychological development.* Urbana: University of Illinois Press.

van Doorninck, W. J., Dick, N. P., Frankenburg, W. K., Liddell, T. N., & Lampe, J. M. (1976, April). *Infant and preschool developmental screening and later school performance.* Paper presented at the Society for Pediatric Research, St. Louis.

Vietze, P. M., & Vaughan, H. G. (Eds.). (1988). *Early identification of infants with developmental disabilities.* Philadelphia: Grune & Stratton.

Walker, L. E., Bonner, B., & Milling, L. (1984). Denver Developmental Screening Test. In D. J. Keyser & R. C. Sweetland (Eds.), *Test critiques* (pp. 239–251) Kansas City, MO: Test Corporation of America.

Werner, E. E. (1986). A longitudinal study of perinatal risk. In D. C. Farran & J. D. McKinney (Eds.), *Risk in intellectual and psychosocial development* (pp. 3–28). Orlando: Academic Press.

Werner, E. E., Bierman, J. M., & French, F. E. (1971). *The children of Kauai.* Honolulu: University of Hawaii.

Wilson, W. J. (1987). *The truly disadvantaged: The inner city, the underclass, and public policy.* Chicago: University of Chicago Press.

Zeskind, P. S., & Lester, B. M. (1981). Analysis of cry features in newborns with differential fetal growth. *Child Development, 52,* 207–212.

Zeskind, P. S., & Marshall, T. R. (1988). The relation between variations in pitch and maternal perceptions of infant crying. *Child Development, 59,* 193–196.

Zuckerman, B., Alpert, J. J., Dooling, E., Hingson, R., Kayne, H., Morelock, S., & Oppenheimer, E. (1983). Neonatal outcome: Is adolescent pregnancy a risk factor? *Pediatrics, 71,* 489–493.

26   Early intervention as preventive intervention

CAROLE C. UPSHUR

The notion that the type and nature of early experience to which human infants are subjected will make a measurable and permanent difference in their developmental life course as children and adults has been supported by a convergence of research findings from widely disparate disciplines: animal research, human genetics, and neuroanatomy. Continually debated are such issues as the degree of malleability or plasticity in development, the age at which intervention is necessary or useful, which types of intervention activities are beneficial, and the cultural relativity of outcome parameters. Some contend that development below age 2 years is highly canalized (i.e., there is a predetermined, genetically based pathway for infant development that exhibits strong "self-righting" tendencies and resists outside influences) and therefore intervention during early infancy may not be very useful (McCall, 1987). Others point out that recent evidence supports a probabilistic versus linear view of development (i.e., simple one-to-one relationships cannot adequately explain which factors or combination of factors actually account for developmental change) and that changes throughout the life span as well as individual differences play as much of a role as early experience in determining developmental outcome (Lerner, 1987; Scarr & Arnett, 1987). However, these same authors support early prevention and intervention activities because of a belief that it is easier to change or prevent problems and deficits the earlier one starts, although it is not necessarily impossible to intervene effectively later in life.

There is thus a spectrum of belief as to the relative importance of early experience, the degree of malleability of development, and the rigidity of "critical" or "sensitive" periods during which intervention may or may not produce results. One's position on this spectrum dictates one's belief as to the roles early intervention programs can play in preventing or treating developmental problems. Although there is currently common agreement that early intervention programs should be provided to infants with documented handicapping conditions (Guralnick & Bennett, 1987) and to those at some level of identifiable risk of developmental problems (Bennett, 1987), little attention is paid to the need for primary prevention programs for all young children. This chapter will discuss the prevention roles currently played by early intervention programs and the potential for expanding the range of prevention services in order to reach a larger number of infants and families. The discussion will begin by presenting traditional definitions of prevention and move to a discussion of the problems in defining the concept of risk. The current evidence for the preventive impact of early intervention programs will then be reviewed, followed by a discussion of the need to

633

develop a broader national policy oriented toward prevention of child and family dysfunction.

TRADITIONAL CONCEPTS OF PREVENTION

Traditionally, health services have been conceptualized as encompassing three levels of prevention: primary, secondary, and tertiary (Keogh, Wilcoxen, & Bernheimer, 1986). These three levels can be thought of as three progressively narrowing nets, with the largest number of individuals caught in the first net, fewer in the second, and the fewest in the last. However, when the net at either of the first two levels has gaps, that is, fails as a preventive agent, more individuals end up at the next level, requiring more intensive and costly services than if prevention efforts had occurred. Primary prevention thus involves providing services to the broadest group of individuals in order to prevent health-threatening conditions from occurring. Such services attempt to stem the conditions that give rise to the causes of illnesses and psychosocial problems – in other words, to stop the process before it starts. A program to provide prenatal care and education classes to all first-time mothers would be an example of a primary prevention effort to reduce birth complications that place infants at risk for later developmental problems. Immunizations and health screenings are other good examples of primary prevention services.

Secondary prevention involves services provided once a condition is identified, but before symptoms or problems become evident (i.e., in the asymptomatic or preclinical stage). Service delivery at this level is designed to prevent progression of the disease or problem and the development of more extensive symptoms that will require more intensive and costly intervention. For example, despite the best primary prevention efforts, some pregnancies will develop complications. Specialized management of these pregnancies, however, may still prevent insults to the fetus or neonate (as well as detrimental effects on the mother), thus constituting secondary prevention. Another example of secondary prevention is the provision of a special infant formula and subsequent specialized diet for children who screen positive for phenylketonuria (PKU). In early infancy these children show no symptoms, but without a special diet they will develop mental retardation due to an inability to process one of the nine amino acids, necessary for growth, present in many protein foods. Secondary prevention targets individuals whose characteristics or symptoms place them at risk of developing further problems if some type of intervention is not undertaken at that point.

Tertiary prevention is the smallest net – the one into which an individual falls if things go wrong or fail to be identified at an earlier stage of symptom or disease development. In some cases, despite our best efforts at earlier stages of identification and prevention, or because prevention efforts did not reach everyone or were flawed in methodology, the disease or problem will fully manifest itself. Tertiary prevention is thus not really "prevention" at all; rather, it is the treatment and management of the disease, disability, or problem once it has occurred. The goal is to ameliorate or "cure" the condition, to restore the earlier healthier condition, or to prevent continued deterioration or death.

Along this continuum of service delivery, early intervention services for infants and toddlers can most often be described as tertiary services because they primarily target children with a clearly identified medical or developmental problem. The goal is to manage the problem and provide services to mitigate the effects of the condition. In some instances, however, early intervention programs have also been utilized to provide secondary prevention services to young children, who at the time of referral, do not exhibit specific deficits or developmental problems. For example, premature infants often have poorly developed abilities for self-regulation that are implicated in later attention deficit and behavior problems (Als, Duffy, McAnulty, & Badian, in press). Whereas no identifiable problems may be evident at a few weeks of age, programs can assist parents to understand the subtle cues of their premature infant and can teach them special handling techniques. This intervention constitutes secondary prevention directed at a "risk" group prior to the development of symptoms.

Primary prevention services are rarely delivered by early intervention programs because legislative and funding mandates for these programs, as is the case with most health and social services, require that target populations with a specified need for services be identified before services are delivered. Since the concept of primary prevention implies that services be provided *before the need develops*, it has always been difficult to muster resources and support for any service that is described as a primary prevention (Healy, Keesee, & Smith, 1985). Some would say that primary prevention is not a wise use of resources because lack of specificity as to risk groups means that some children will be served who did not require preventive services, and others will be served who do not benefit from these services because they require different, more intensive services (Gardner, Karmel, & Dowd, 1984; Kaye, 1986). Current political thinking holds that government roles should be limited rather than limitless, thus placing great emphasis on using resources for those most in need or most likely to benefit (Singer & Butler, 1987). Short of offering services only at the tertiary level, the problem then quickly becomes one of being able to accurately identify target groups most likely to need intensive services without earlier preventive activities.

THE EVOLVING CONCEPT OF RISK

The determination of which interventions prevent developmental delay in childhood requires some knowledge of causation of handicapping conditions (Keogh et al., 1986). Attempts to identify families and children at risk for later problems, however, are quite imprecise. For example, Ramey and MacPhee (1986) report that about 75% of mildly mentally retarded children are from low-income families, but only 2–10% of low-income children are mentally retarded. Similarly, infants infected with cytomegalovirus (CMV) are reportedly at much greater risk of developing long-term problems if they are from low-income families (Haskins, 1986). But attempts to use straightforward socioeconomic indicators from birth certificates to identify children with later school problems have resulted in highly inaccurate predictions (Finkelstein & Ramey, 1980; Ramey, Stedman, Borders-Patterson, & Mengel, 1978).

Chamberlin (1984) notes that childhood problems occur in families where little experience or knowledge about childbirth or child care is present, where there is limited emotional support for parents, and under conditions of economic, health, or emotional stress. In a summary of several British studies, Chamberlin concludes that about 80% of children identified with school problems come from only 20% of all families with children. This would seem to indicate that it is relatively easy to identify risk. However, both sensitivity (the degree to which children with problems are correctly identified) and specificity (the degree to which children are correctly excluded from intervention if they do not need services) are at issue in defining risk. What is most desirable is to have a method for identifying children at risk that includes the highest percentage who actually need help (i.e., high sensitivity), but at the same time limits the number who are falsely identified as at risk (i.e., high specificity).

A number of studies have hypothesized the direct relationship of certain perinatal factors, such as prematurity or low birth weight, to the appearance of later developmental problems, but only with limited success. For example, Rogers (1968) determined that 41% of children from a birth register had to be followed in order to accurately identify only 65% of the children who later developed chronic handicaps. Davie, Butler, and Goldstein (1972) found that only 51% of the children who later evidenced mental retardation were identified by selectively following 25% of a geographic cohort of children whose early characteristics indicated they were at risk (representing higher specificity, but lower sensitivity than the Rogers method). Werner, Bierman, and French (1971) reported that only 15% of all school problems in a birth cohort followed through age 18 were contributed by the group of children with high perinatal risk indicators (representing quite low sensitivity). The sensitivity of the birth register or perinatal identification methods for determining children at risk for later developmental problems is thus not high. Many children who are at risk are not identified through these methods while, at the same time, large numbers of children are tracked who do not evidence problems (low specificity).

Although these simple risk register methods that isolate either socioeconomic factors or perinatal health risks do not appear fruitful, there is evidence that by considering the interactive, or "transactional," nature of perinatal risk and the caregiving environment, a better understanding of which infants are likely to develop later problems can be achieved (Sameroff & Chandler, 1975). For example, Alberman (1973) found that birth order and social class were better predictors of reading problems in school than was birth weight alone. Both Honig (1984) and Beckwith (1984) found significant interactions among developmental competence of infants and family sociodemographic status, with infants from higher income families consistently showing more optimal developmental outcome than those from lower socioeconomic status families, regardless of initial risk indicators.

More recent work has also indicated that developmental delay may be best explained by multiple risk factors that extend beyond even the major influence of socioeconomic status (Sameroff, Seifer, Barocas, Zax, & Greenspan, 1987). These factors include maternal mental health status, level of anxiety, belief in control, and educational level; number of children in the family; racial status; father absence; and stressful life events. No single risk factor was found to be related to a child's IQ in this study. Rather, multiple risks were required to predict lower scores. This may be explained in part by the hypothesis that there are strong species-specific developmental patterns at work in early infancy (i.e., highly canalized patterns) that result in adaptability and self-righting tendencies in the face of most environmental and biological insults (Brownell & Strauss, 1984). There is thus a strong and somewhat elastic template for normal development, although there are limits to this adaptability in the face of such major trauma as central nervous system damage or multiple environmental assaults (Brownell & Strauss, 1984; Lerner, 1987; McCall, 1987; Scarr & Arnett, 1987).

Werner (1986) and Ramey and MacPhee (1986) note that even with a sophisticated, interactional model of risk, the risk approach only examines the deficit aspects of development, rather than simultaneously examining both deficits and strengths in individual children and families. Thus, a simultaneous look at "protective" factors and risk factors would yield more insight into why certain children and families do well and others do not (see Werner, this volume). For adequate development to occur, Werner indicates that such protective factors as sources of social support and a sense of competence must be balanced against such risk factors as stress and biological insult.

When risk factors accumulate and cannot be compensated for through a variety of protective factors, child development is impaired. We thus need to consider an even broader array of issues in order to predict developmental outcome.

The evidence for the powerful roles of social support and stress in influencing child development is mounting and provides us with additional clues as to why some families and children thrive, even in the presence of traditional risk factors, and others do not (see Dunst & Trivette, this volume). For example, studies have shown that the quality of infant attachment can be predicted by mothers' level of social support, isolated families are more likely to evidence child abuse, and verbal and emotional responsivity to children occur more often in mothers who have more contact with friends (Crockenberg, 1981; Powell, 1980, 1982). In another study, mothers without social support systems were found to be more restrictive and punitive toward their preschoolers (Colletta, 1979). The possibility of causal links between adequate parental social networks and children's cognitive outcomes has also been raised (Cochran & Brassard, 1979). In a study of mothers with less than high school education, social support, life stress, and measures of expectations for the child significantly predicted IQ at 48 months and language facility at 36 months (Bee et al., 1982). Better pregnancy outcomes have also been found for mothers who experienced high emotional support during pregnancies when prenatal stress was present. Only 33% of mothers with both high stress and high social support evidenced pregnancy complications, whereas 91% of those with high stress but low social support experienced complications (Nuckolls, Cassel, & Kaplan, 1972).

As we have seen, the concept of "risk" for developmental problems in children grows more complex with new research findings. Yet there are even other levels of risk that must be considered. These involve the broader institutional, social, and cultural impacts on families and children that play a role in developmental outcome (Bronfenbrenner, 1979, 1986; Garbarino, 1982, this volume). In particular, recent sociodemographic changes have created different, more stressful conditions for child rearing than existed in the past. These changes include increased employment of mothers due to economic necessity as well as new opportunities for women, increased divorce rates, decreasing family size, and family mobility, all of which create the need for more nonfamilial supports in order to provide adequate child-rearing environments (Bronfenbrenner & Weiss, 1983; Kagan, Klugman, & Zigler, 1983). Communities, schools, and government have been slow to respond to these changes, holding on to a traditional ethic of nonintervention in family life and a traditional, but outmoded, definition of what constitutes a family. The pervasiveness of these changes comes into startling focus when it is projected that by 1990 as many as one-third of the children in this country will have experienced the divorce of their parents (Kagan et al., 1983).

Particularly in the last decade this country has witnessed an erosion of family income that has caused middle-income families to slip into low-income groups; a substantial increase in the number of families below the poverty line; a 75% increase in teenage, out-of-wedlock pregnancies; an increased teen suicide rate; and widespread substance abuse. These phenomena mean that fewer families and children are immune to conditions that may impair healthy functioning (Kagan et al., 1983). At the same time, informal sources of family support are less available and public services have been cut back to target only the most desparately in need (Bawden, 1984). As Margaret Mead (1980) points out, "What we have failed to realize is that even as we have separated the single family from the larger society, we have expected each couple to take on a range of obligations that traditionally have been shared within the larger community" (p.

102). The consideration of these broader social issues as part of the "risk index" for predicting child developmental problems illustrates precisely just how difficult it is to identify which children require and can benefit from prevention activities.

In short, the concept of what constitutes risk to healthy child development has evolved into a complex understanding concerning cumulative and dialectical interactions among the characteristics of the infant, the infant's parents, and other environmental factors. Rather than fixed and linear, infant development is viewed as "plastic" and "probabilistic," with strong tendencies to self-correction in the face of biological and environmental insults. This more multifaceted understanding of the factors that will predict poor child development outcomes must also then dictate our understanding of the types of prevention and intervention activities that will likely have an impact on these outcomes. The simple, linear, main effect model is clearly not very useful. It is within this context that we will now examine the evidence that has accrued concerning the successful prevention activities of early intervention.

TRADITIONAL TARGET GROUPS FOR EARLY PREVENTION SERVICES

As discussed, early intervention programs typically serve specific groups of children, often with a priority placed on infants and toddlers with moderate-to-severe readily identifiable disabilities. For infants with clear medically diagnosed disorders, the role of early intervention programming is to provide tertiary services, that is, to treat or manage the existing condition. For most of these children, the goal is not to cure the disability but to prevent secondary handicaps, that is, to avoid additional disabilities by providing environmental facilitation and support designed around the specific capabilities of the infant. For example, without active intervention in the early months, a child with cerebral palsy may develop contractures and experience less range of movement and motor control than indicated by the initial central nervous system insult.

However, the potential for the true "preventive" roles of early intervention programs is best exemplified by services to groups of children with less well-defined disabilities or risks. By examining the secondary prevention activities of early intervention programs in serving children who are at risk for developmental delay, but who in early infancy are not yet manifesting problems, we can more clearly understand the potential benefits of broader primary prevention activities for young children. The two risk groups most often served by such early intervention efforts are preterm or low birth weight infants and infants from low-income families.

Preterm and low birth weight infants

The risks for developmental problems in preterm, or low birth weight infants (gestational age under 37 weeks; birthweight less than 2,500 grams) have been well documented (Als, 1986; Bennett, Chandler, Robinson, & Sells, 1979; Hagberg, 1978; National Institute of Health, 1979). A high correlation has been demonstrated between low birth weight and such conditions as cerebral palsy, mental retardation, epilepsy, visual problems, motor coordination problems, and learning disabilities (Hayden & Beck, 1982). Differences in temperament and arousal state between preterm and full-term babies are also frequently noted (Field, 1983; Gardner et al., 1984). However, it is difficult to predict from neonatal complications due to premature delivery and/or low birth weight which individual infants will have later developmental problems (Cohen, Sigman, Parmelee, & Beckwith, 1982; National Institute of Health, 1979).

Intervention for premature or low birth weight babies is designed to provide developmental facilitation for the infant and caretaking information for the parents to meet the unique needs of these infants. Because of their difficult temperament and neurological immaturity, it is postulated that special services can prevent or lessen developmental problems (Field, Widmayer, Stringer, & Ignatoff, 1980). For example, Barrera, Rosenbaum, and Cunningham (1986) reported on a home visiting program for a group of preterm infants compared to matched controls and full-term infants. Developmental activities and parent–infant interaction were the focus of the curriculum. Although differences in cognitive development were not identified between the program and control preterm infants, the control group mothers were noted to be significantly less responsive to their infants at age 16 months, and scores on a measure of the caretaking environment (the HOME, Caldwell & Bradley, 1984) were significantly higher for the intervention group.

Bromwich and Parmelee (1979) reported on a 2-year study of a center-based intervention program for preterm infants from families of varied socioeconomic status. Infants receiving programming had more positive social interactions and social skills. Minde, Shosenberg, Marton, Thompson, Ripley, and Burns (1980) provided weekly group meetings with a veteran mother and nurse for parents of premature infants and compared the infants and mothers to a control group during the hospital stay and at 1, 2, and 3 months postdischarge from the hospital. Mothers who participated in the in-hospital groups visited their infants significantly more, had more positive discharge reports, and were more active with their infants than the controls. Once home, the program mothers talked to and looked at their infants more, and more often participated in social activities for themselves. In a study of low birth weight and preterm infants from low-income families who were matched to controls and were provided with a year of home visiting services, Ross (1984) reported significantly higher 12-month developmental and home environment scores for the intervention group, although no overall differences were found on maternal ratings of infant temperament or maternal attitudes. Similar findings concerning better developmental and home environment scores for home-visited mothers were reported by Field et al. (1980) in a study that compared black, lower-class, preterm and full-term babies and their teen mothers (some receiving intervention, others not) to babies with older mothers. In addition, this latter study found the intervention mothers to return to work more frequently and to have fewer repeat pregnancies. The babies of intervention mothers were also reported by mothers to have easier temperaments.

The studies described thus far focus on mother–infant interactions. More recent studies of the developmental outcome of very low birth weight infants (less than 1,250 grams) have found that a critical factor may be overstimulation of these infants in the first few days and weeks of life (Als, 1986; Als, Lawhon, Brown, Gibes, Duffy, McAnulty, & Blickman, 1986; Thoman, 1987). It is postulated that due to neurological immaturity, preterm infants are hypersensitive to the extraordinary level of sensory stimulation of the neonatal intensive care nursery, that is, the bright lights, noise, frequent handling, and painful medical interventions. This overstimulation may have an impact on the organization of neural pathways and can cause hemorrhages in different areas of the brain, thus accounting for some of the common developmental problems associated with prematurity (Als, 1986).

The intervention proposed by Als and her colleagues is less, rather than more, stimulation, particularly directed toward assisting the neonate to develop self-regulatory behaviors. This includes allowing for more quiet sleep, prone positioning, nonnutritive sucking, and self-regulated feeding. Evidence of the outcome of such an approach to caring for preterm infants extends to age 3 years, when verbal ability, memory, and motor skills have been found to be significantly better than in control infants (Als et al., in press). Of further interest, Als et al. (in press) have assessed both premature and full-term infants and found that they could be differentiated into three distinct groups based on their self-regulatory behavior. Although a large number of premature infants were found in the "highly reactive/sensitive" group, as were a few full-term infants, other preterms were categorized as "moderately well modulated," and even a few as "well modulated." This method of evaluating neonates appears to hold promise for explaining some of the variance in the developmental outcomes among infants, whether premature or full-term, as well as providing a new model for early intervention.

This brief review of recent reports of the impact of intervention for preterm and low birth weight infants and their families illustrates that positive changes appear to be engendered in individual infant development and in parenting behaviors when early intervention services are provided. The question to raise next is whether these early changes are correlated with the prevention of future deficits in development, school performance, and adult functioning. There is some evidence from longitudinal studies that environmental factors are better predictors of outcomes for preterm infants than are perinatal problems. For example, Beckwith (1984) monitored 126 preterm infants through age 2 years and then again at age 5. Developmental quotients for infants from English-speaking (primarily middle-income) families were within the normal range. Higher socioeconomic status predicted improving developmental quotients over time, while low socioeconomic status was correlated with declining developmental quotients, this being most evident for Hispanic infants. Very low birth weight (less than 1,500 grams in this study) or other perinatal complications were not significantly related to developmental quotients over time. There were gender and birth order differences as well as interactions among these variables and maternal characteristics. More verbal interaction, physical contact, and attention by mothers correlated with higher child developmental quotients at 4, 9, and 24 months and at 5 years for all ethnic groups.

The Beckwith study points to socioeconomic status and mother–infant interaction as major factors in the development of preterm infants. The substantial influence of the environment, as contrasted with perinatal insults, is further supported by the longitudinal study (birth through age 18) of 698 children from the island of Kauai (Werner, 1986). This study concluded that middle-class infants who sustained severe perinatal complications (although not all were low birth weight) did *not* demonstrate, on the average, significant developmental or intellectual deficits. In addition, children identified as resilient, even though from lower income families, were from smaller families and had more than one adult caretaker at home, more attention in childhood, and an informal support network beyond their parents. There were also interactive effects among difficult infant temperament and poor infant health and presence in a disorganized family, which led to poorer outcomes for certain children. This study thus points to additional factors that may serve as intervention points in the prevention of developmental deficits for biologically vulnerable infants, that is, family functioning and social support.

Infants from low-income families

The previous discussion concerning prevention of developmental problems in preterm and low birth weight infants concluded that environmental factors, particularly socioeconomic status, may have an equal, if not predominant, influence on an infant's developmental outcome. (Of course, due to lack of access to adequate health care among low-income groups, socioeconomic status may also be one of the best predictors of prenatal and perinatal complications that result in higher numbers of low birth weight and preterm infants.) Whereas the relationship between environmental factors and developmental outcome for infants with severe central nervous system impairment is not as strong, the relationship between socioeconomic status and child development status has been investigated extensively (Caldwell & Bradley, 1984; Honig, 1984; Ramey & MacPhee, 1986; Whiteman, Brown, & Deutsch, 1967; Whiteman & Deutsch, 1967). Haskins (1986), for example, summarized the child rearing techniques that discriminate among low- versus middle-income families and that seem to have an effect on child development. These include verbal responsivity, avoidance of punitive control, warmth, and environmental stimulation.

The importance of early childhood experience in terms of lasting impact on lifetime development has also been widely described, and has served as the theoretical basis for the development of preschool compensatory education and early intervention programming since the mid-1960s (Bloom, 1964; Fowler, 1968; Hunt, 1964; Lazar & Darlington, 1982). An early review of the effectiveness of compensatory education (Bronfenbrenner, 1974) reported that IQ gains, although evident in the first few years after intervention, tended to fade after intervention ceased and long-term gains were rarely found. However, a more recent review of the lasting effects of preschool compensatory education that reported follow-up studies of 11 groups of children at ages 9–19 found major long-term impacts on children, including less need for special education, less grade retention, better achievement test scores, and more achievement-oriented attitudes (Lazar & Darlington, 1982). In a 10-year follow-up of a program of home visits, center activities, and day care provided at birth through 30 months of age to a group of low-income, predominately minority families, similar results were also found (Provence & Naylor, 1983; Seitz, Rosenbaum, & Apfel, 1985).

Berrueta-Clement, Schweinhart, Barnett, Epstein and Weikart (1984) described non-school-related impacts of the Perry Preschool Project for their study sample at age 19. They cite evidence that the treatment group experienced a higher percentage of employment, fewer arrests, and fewer teen pregnancies. This group (which received either 1 or 2 years of preschool beginning at ages 3 or 4) also had higher high school graduation rates, higher rates of enrollment in college or vocational training, better high school grades, and better scores on competency tests.

In another study of early intervention with infants from low-income families, group day care provided to randomly assigned, at-risk infants from 3–36 months of age maintained IQs in the normal range, whereas a control group that did not receive day care showed declines in IQ starting at age 12 months (Ramey & Haskins, 1981). Follow-up until age 5 showed continued declines in the cognitive scores of control infants, but intervention children's scores remained in the normal range (Ramey & Campbell, 1984). The risk factors utilized to identify children eligible for the study included family income; parental education, welfare, and employment histories; school-age siblings evidencing school problems; social service histories; and father absence. A study of day-care intervention supplemented by home visiting, compared to home visiting alone, found that children from home-visited families did no better than controls (Ramey, Bryant, Sparling, & Wasik, 1985).

These studies on an extremely intensive intervention of full-day infant care, year-round for several years, can be contrasted to results found by Slaughter (1983) that compared mother discussion groups versus in-home toy demonstration activities provided to two groups of randomly assigned, low-income black mothers. Slaughter found that the discussion group mothers showed significantly better ego development and maternal teaching styles compared to controls at the end of the second year of the program. Differences found in favor of both treatment groups on openness and flexibility toward child rearing at the end of the first year of the program disappeared by the end of the second year. However, scores on the McCarthy Scales of Children's Abilities (McCarthy, 1972) for children from both treatment groups were higher compared to controls at final testing. All children evidenced declining cognitive and verbal assessment scores. However, the scores of children in the treatment group did not decline as much. Slaughter concludes that the discussion group had broader-ranging impacts because of its greater impact on the mothers (i.e., social support, assistance with multiple aspects of child rearing), as compared to the situation-specific "infant stimulation" focus of the home-visiting, toy demonstration intervention.

The Slaughter study presents somewhat counterintuitive results in favor of a less intensive intervention with at-risk infants that nevertheless holds promise of significant impact on maternal behavior. Maddan, Ottara, and Levenstein (1984). the researchers who originated the toy demonstration–home visit model of early intervention with economically disadvantaged families, recently studied a cohort of families who participated in their early treatment groups. Prevention of school disadvantage through developing early positive mother–child interactive patterns and parent responsiveness to the child has been the major focus of their work. They note that although IQ differences of 13–15 points were found among children participating in early cohorts of the project, evidence of lack of impact was also found. First-grade follow-up of children indicated maternal interaction differences for only one of three cohorts and no long-term effects of the intervention on cognitive development, teacher ratings, retention in kindergarten, or attendance in special education. The researchers concluded that selection factors in the original cohorts may have eliminated potential differences and that preschool program participation by the majority of children in both treatment and control groups probably resulted in the similar performance of the groups in kindergarten and first grade. Further, they point out that depending on socioeconomic status alone to identify children and families in need of intervention may not be an adequate selection criterion.

In a review of 12 prevention programs for at-risk infants that employed an experimental design (i.e., random assignment of infants to treatment and nontreatment groups), it was found that more intensive, center-based infant activities produced the largest IQ differences at age 2 years (Bryant & Ramey, 1984). However, six of ten studies reported statistically significant differences in treatment versus control group IQ, primarily due to the lack of decline in developmental scores for the treatment group as compared to the controls. Seven of ten studies reported statistically significant differences in cognitive scores at age 3 years. Some differences in the home environment and in mother–child interactions were found favoring the treatment groups in these studies. However, Bryant and Ramey conclude that these differences are modest and their long-term value is unknown.

In contrast to focusing solely on child IQ outcomes, at least some studies also investigated such functional impacts on families as education and income. Field (1983) reported that intervention mothers more often returned to work and had fewer repeat pregnancies. Gutelius, Kirsch, MacDonald, Brooks, and McErlean (1977) reported that treatment group mothers finished school more often. Garber and Heber (1981) reported more stable employment and higher incomes for treatment groups mothers. Olds (1984) reported similar findings for low-income and teenage mothers involved in a home visiting program that began prenatally for first pregnancies and continued until the infant was 2 years of age. A 10-year follow-up of children and their mothers who participated in an infancy support program (including 30 months of home visits, day care, and center activities) found that mothers of program children had fewer children and better housing, education, and employment status compared to controls (Provence & Naylor, 1983; Seitz et al., 1985).

Nauta and Travers (1982), in reporting the findings of the Child and Family Resource Program (CFRP), indicated that there were no differences in infant developmental scores for program versus control children, but that program mothers showed greater awareness of their role as educators of their own children and interacted more with their toddlers. They also reported higher employment among single black teenage mothers enrolled in the program as compared to controls. The CFRP program consisted of comprehensive family support services such as referrals to jobs, counseling, health, and housing resources as well as a home visiting program and center-based group activities for parents and children aged birth to 8 years.

This review of preventive and compensatory interventions directed at socioeconomically disadvantaged infants illustrates that intervention can have specific impacts on the child's development, the mother's child-rearing style, and the mother's subsequent education and employment. Further, there is evidence of a substantial long-term impact on children's lives in terms of functional outcome (employment and educational achievement, level of need for public services, and delinquent behavior), although there is no evidence for long-term change in IQ scores.

There is thus substantial documentation of the potential for early intervention services to have an effective preventive impact for a range of risk groups. It can be argued that this does not constitute evidence of "primary" prevention because of the strong association of problematic child development outcomes that are identified with these high-risk groups. In contrast, since the concept of risk is quite complex, it is often necessary to serve a large number of children and families who may not have required assistance in order to catch the few who would have progressed to more intense needs without early services. Thus, the question remains as to whether the role of early intervention services can or should be expanded to become a primary prevention system for all infants and families.

A BROAD VIEW OF PREVENTION

When the risks to healthy child development are recognized as multifacted and dependent on the interaction of both detrimental and nurturing factors, it becomes apparent that prevention programs must be prepared to provide a wide variety of services. In addition, it must be recognized that although there may be different targets of prevention, initiation of programs at one level of risk (e.g., individual family) will not be very effective unless programs are initiated simultaneously at other levels that directly or indirectly affect that quality of the child's caretaking environment. Garbarino (1982, this volume), drawing on Bronfenbrenner's (1979) work on the ecology of human development, describes a systems approach to identifying risk that encompasses four levels: microsystem (individual family), mesosystem (child's school, service system), exosystem (parent's work place and government agencies that set policies that affect the child indirectly), and macrosystem (broad cultural or policy assumptions such as racism, sexism, federal support of national health insurance or day care).

At the microsystem level, primary prevention consists of such activities as family planning and education in parenting, childbirth, and child development (Healy et al., 1985). These should be designed to assist parents in understanding the qualities of interaction with their children that promote healthy development, although it should be recognized that the impact of other systems may prevent even the most well-intentioned parents from carrying out their role adequately (Garbarino, 1982; Zigler & Weiss, 1985). The Minnesota Early Learning Design (MELD) program, which consists of parent-facilitated groups meeting twice a month, starting during pregnancy and continuing until the infant is 2 years old, is a good example of a communitywide primary prevention program aimed at educating individual families as well as providing informal support (Ellwood, 1983).

At the mesosystem level, appropriate services need to be provided that are oriented toward health issues and social support. These include comprehensive prenatal, perinatal, and well-child care. Periodic screening of all children for health and developmental problems provides the greatest promise of adequate sensitivity in identifying children who need help, as contrasted to the risk factor approach discussed earlier in this chapter (Chamberlin, 1984; Meisels, 1984). Specific parent support services such as access to home visitors, homemaker or aids services, transportation, day care, drop-in day care, and respite care are additional preventive services that address the risks of family stress (Chamberlin, 1984). The Brookline Early Education Project (BEEP) is a good example of a program that attempted to provide both parent education services and instrumental support in terms of parent groups, home visits, and day care to all children in a particular birth cohort from one community, randomly assigned to differing intensity of services (Pierson et al., 1983). Documented outcomes for children included more optimal social skills and better use of time in kindergarten and second grade, as well as more advanced reading skills.

Schools themselves need to be more attuned to individual differences and be able to provide supportive, nonthreatening environments for learning. Reasons for school failure need to be identified as much in the organization, curriculum, and climate of the schools as in the problems of individual children or their families. Other mesosystem issues include coordination and communication between the formal service systems and the home so that parents, other caregivers, and teachers can engage in complimentary and not contradictory interactions with the child. Attention must be paid to cultural, ethnic, racial, and religious differences in order to accomplish this aim (Ogbu, 1987).

Exosystem issues concern policies at the formal, regulatory level (e.g., official government, corporate, health, social welfare, and educational policies) that can help facilitate individual family functioning as a supportive caregiving environment. For example, school curriculum policies are needed for sex education and parenting education, including the introduction of these topics early enough to prevent adolescent pregnancy (National Research Council, 1987). Similarly, the corporate sector must examine its policies with regard to day care, parental leaves subsequent to a birth or adoption, flex time, and so on (Galinsky, 1986; Garbarino, 1982). To the extent that a parent's work setting does not accommodate the parenting role, children may be deprived of adequate high-quality interaction with a caring adult, which is essential to the prevention of child development problems (Bronfenbrenner & Weiss, 1983).

Perhaps even more important and basic to adequate child development are exosystem-level policies that keep welfare benefits below the poverty level, ignore labor market trends that create conditions of high unemployment, focus on private profit in housing so that displacement and homelessness of families becomes common, and ignore public transportation and recreation needs of lower income families. Even when policies that are favorable to children and families are established, a lack of coordination of services, inconsistent or contradictory eligibility rules, and poor implementation present major roadblocks to delivering preventive services (Healy et al., 1985). Meisels (1984) aptly notes that the Early Periodic Screening, Diagnosis and Treatment program (EPSDT), a federal prevention program that is designed to identify and treat physical and mental problems in poor children, ages birth though 21, has not fulfilled its promise because few physicians and eligible families know about the program, eligibility criteria are unclear, and there are inadequate standards, monitoring, and funding. Moreover, evidence from a Michigan study shows that EPSDT has very limited impact on tertiary health-care utilization (Meisels & Margolis, 1988).

Finally, at the macrosystem level, we are talking about the absence of a national climate or policy that is inclined to take seriously the systems view of examining developmental risk in infancy and childhood. We continue to view family life primarily as if it exists in the context of small-town America where extended families provide support and services to each other. In this view, family life is considered to be a private affair in the context of a social Darwinism approach to family needs, with policies that provide minimum services only for those in most dramatic need (Garbarino, 1982, this volume). This alternative is a climate that provides broad-based support for child development and family life activities, and includes national health insurance, a national day-care policy, and a comprehensive continuum of child and family support services that are available to all families when needed.

CONCLUSION

This chapter has reviewed the definitions of prevention traditionally utilized in the health care field and has examined the role that early intervention programs have played in preventing developmental problems in infants and young children. We have seen that there is a rich research literature describing both the short- and long-term impact on children and their families through participation in such early intervention services as home visiting, parent groups, and day care. Although these effects have been quite dramatic in some cases (e.g., Berrueta-Clement et al., 1984), the substantive impact of such programs as the Perry Preschool Project represent less of a "miracle," than a more socially constructive and less impoverished outcome for a selected group of economically disadvantaged children. Nevertheless, whereas many such programs undoubtedly have provided preventive services, they have been directed toward specific risk groups, which limits their potential as true tests of primary prevention. The programs have not been opened wide enough to capture in their nets a majority of the children and families who need and could benefit from early services.

How do we know that early intervention services delivered to a broad range of children is a good investment of national resources? We have seen that it is quite difficult to predict developmental outcomes for children from the variety of well-established risk indicators, including birth weight, perinatal health status, and socioeconomic status. The work of Als et al. (in press) has shown that there are subtle, but identifiable, individual differences in the self-regulatory behavior of any infant that may predict later developmental outcomes. Although there is a higher percentage of poor indicators in premature infants, a commonly targeted risk group, these indicators are also found in full-term infants who are not likely to be identified as being at risk for developmental problems. Other studies have identified a broader range of factors that can be influential in child development, including social support, family functioning, and mothers' attitudes and education (Colletta, 1979; Crockenberg, 1981; Powell, 1980, 1982; Sameroff et al., 1987; Werner, 1986). Still other research has pointed out such potential influence as divorce, family size, and mobility that impinge on the family system and, indirectly but powerfully, on the environment of the growing child (Bronfenbrenner, 1979, 1986; Bronfenbrenner & Weiss, 1983; Garbarino, 1982; Zigler & Weiss, 1985). Our understanding of the concept of risk has evolved from a focus on single, intuitively obvious factors to a multifaceted, transactional model. Thus, simple screening methods, such as risk registers, are not sensitive or specific enough to detect children and families in need of services when this newer understanding of risk is adopted.

Experience suggests that we cannot assume that programs aimed at specific, commonly targeted risk groups will be sensitive enough to identify most of the children and families who can benefit from early services. By failing to detect developmental problems in their earliest stages, that is, by failing to support the goals of primary prevention, we set the stage for having to serve larger numbers of children with more complex and costly intervention needs at the secondary and tertiary levels. School failure, delinquency, and teen pregnancy are but a few of these most common, costly results.

Current early intervention programs have substantial experience in serving disabled children and other young children identified as being at risk for later developmental problems. Many of the services developed by such programs can play a wider role in primary prevention if they are made available to all families and in the context of recognition of a multilevel system of influences on child developmental outcome. This is not to say that the only solution is for federal or state government to provide comprehensive, free support services to any family requesting help. Rather, national policy should reflect the lessons learned from research on the impact on children of the broadly conceived caregiving environment. Attention must be paid to developing an infrastructure that makes available appropriate medical, educational, therapeutic, recreational, housing, and child-care help to all families, and at the same time thoughtfully attacks the fundamental causes of poverty. This means developing government policy that provides resources for training paraprofessionals and professionals to deliver a variety of care-giving services; capital expenditures for housing, schools, clinics, recreation facilities, and community centers; health and social insurance mechanisms; better unemployment and welfare programs; and further research and demonstration projects. At the same time there is clearly a role for private sector participation, both in terms of resources and policies.

Families will have a range of needs for child support services, from mimimal and infrequent to more intense and ongoing, and a range in ability to seek out and pay for services. Currently, families at the two economic extremes are those most likely to be able to access services, although the lack of fundamental agreement on the broader social need to be supportive of children and families makes services sometimes unavailable, at any cost, and poorly delivered when designed entirely for the disenfranchised. This situation leaves many children, regardless of socioeconoic status, at risk for developmental difficulties. The lessons learned from early intervention research demonstrate that it may be possible to prevent many of these problems.

REFERENCES

Alberman, E. (1973). The prediction of learning disorders. *Developmental Medicine and Child Neurology, 15*, 202.

Als, H. (1986). A synactive model of neonatal behavioral organization: Framework for the assessment of neurobehavioral development in the premature infant and for support of infants and parents in the neonatal intensive care environment. *Physical and Occupational Therapy in Pediatrics, 6*, 3–55.

Als, H., Duffy, F. H., McAnulty, G. B., & Badian, N. (in press). Continuity of neurobehavioral functioning in preterm and fullterm newborns. In M. Bornstein & N. Krasnegor (Eds.), *Continuity in development*. Hillsdale, NJ: L. Erlbaum.

Als, H., Lawhon, G., Brown, E., Gibes, R., Duffy, F. H., McAnulty, G., & Blickman, J. G. (1986). Individualized behavioral and environmental care for the very low birth weight preterm infant at high risk for bronchopulmonary dysplasia: Neonatal intensive care unit and developmental outcome. *Pediatrics, 78*, 1123–1132.

Barrera, M. E., Rosenbaum, P. L., & Cunningham, C. E. (1986). Early home intervention with low birth weight infants and their parents. *Child Development, 57*, 20–33.

Bawden, D. L. (1984). *The social contract revisited*. Washington, DC: Urban Institute Press.

Beckwith, L. (1984). Parent interaction with their preterm infants and later mental development. *Early Child Development and Care, 16*, 27–40.

Bee, H., Barnard, K. E., Eyres, S. J., Gray, C. A., Hammond, M. A., Spietz, A. L., Snyder, C., & Clark, B. (1982). Prediction of IQ and language skill from perinatal status, child performance, family characteristics, and mother–infant interaction. *Child Development, 53*, 1134–1156.

Bennett, F. C. (1987). The effectiveness of early intervention for infants at increased biologic risk. In M. J. Guralnick & F. C. Bennett (Eds.), *The effectiveness of early intervention for at-risk and handicapped children* (pp. 79–112). Orlando: Academic Press.

Bennett, F. C., Chandler, L. S., Robinson, N. M., & Sells, C. J. (1979, December 3). Spastic diplegia: Perplexing "disease of prematurity." *Child Development and Mental Retardation Center Newsletter*, University of Washington, Seattle.

Berrueta-Clement, J. R., Schweinhart, L. J., Barnett, W. S., Epstein, A. S., & Weikart, D. P. (1984). *Changed lives: The effects of the Perry Preschool Program on youths through age 19* (Monographs of the Educational Research Foundation, No. 8). Ypsilanti, MI: High/Scope.

Bloom, B. S. (1964). *Stability and change in human characteristics*. New York: Wiley.

Bromwich, R., & Parmelee, A. (1979). An intervention program for preterm infants. In T. M. Field, A. M. Sostek, S. Goldberg, & H. H. Shuman (Eds.), *Infants born at risk* (pp. 389–412). New York: SP Medical/Scientific Books.

Bronfenbrenner, U. (1974). *A report on longitudinal evaluations of preschool programs. Vol. 2: Is early intervention effective?* (DHEW Pub. No. [OHD] 74–29). Washington, DC: Office of Child Development.

Bronfenbrenner, U. (1979). *The ecology of human development*. Cambridge: Harvard University Press.

Bronfenbrenner, U. (1986). Ecology of the family as a context for human development: Research perspectives. *Developmental Psychology, 22*, 723–742.

Bronfenbrenner, U., & Weiss, H. B. (1983). Beyond policies without people: An ecological perspective on child and family policy. In E. F. Zigler, S. L. Kagan, & E. Klugman (Eds.), *Children, families and government: Perspectives on American social policy* (pp. 393–414). New York: Cambridge University Press.

Brownell, C. A., & Strauss, M. S. (1984). Infant stimulation and development: Conceptual and empirical considerations. *Journal of Children in Contemporary Society, 17*, 109–130.

Bryant, D. M., & Ramey, C. T. (1984). Prevention oriented infant education programs. *Journal of Children in Contemporary Society, 17*, 17–35.

Caldwell, B. M., & Bradley, R. H. (1984). *Home observation for measurement of the environment*. Little Rock: University of Arkansas.

Chamberlin, R. W. (1984). Strategies for disease prevention and health promotion in maternal and child health: The "ecologic" versus the "high risk" approach. *Journal of Public Health Policy, 5*, 185–197.

Cochran, M., & Brassard, J. (1979). Child development and personal social networks. *Child Development, 50*, 601–616.

Cohen, S. E., Sigman, M., Parmelee, A. A., & Beckwith, L. (1982). Perinatal risk and developmental outcome in preterm infants. *Seminars in Perinatology, 6*, 334–339.

Colletta, N. (1979). Support systems after divorce. *Journal of Marriage and the Family, 41*, 837–846.

Crockenberg, S. (1981). Infant irritability, mother responsiveness and social support influences on the security of infant–mother attachment. *Child Development, 52*, 857–865.

Davie, R., Butler, N., & Goldstein, H. (1972). *From birth to seven.* London: Longman.

Ellwood, A. (1983). Preparing for parenthood during pregnancy and early infancy. In *Programs to strengthen families: A resource guide* (pp. 123–147). Chicago: Family Resource Coalition and Bush Center in Child Development and Social Policy.

Field, T. (1983). High risk infants "have less fun" during early interactions. *Topics in Early Childhood Special Education, 3*, 77–87.

Field, T., Widmayer, S., Stringer, S., & Ignatoff, T. (1980). Teenage lower class black mothers: An intervention and developmental follow-up. *Child Development, 50*, 426–436.

Finkelstein, N. W., & Ramey, C. T. (1980). Information from birth certificates as a risk index for educational handicap. *American Journal of Mental Deficiency, 84*, 546–552.

Fowler, W. (1968). The effect of early stimulation in the emergence of cognitive processes. In R. D. Hess and R. M. Bear (Eds.), *Early education: Current theory, research, and action.* Chicago: Aldine.

Galinsky, E. (1986). Family life and corporate policies. In M. W. Yogman and T. B. Brazelton (Eds.), *In support of families* (pp. 109–145). Cambridge: Harvard University Press.

Garbarino, J. (1982). *Children and families in the social environment.* Hawthorne, NY: Aldine Publishing.

Garber, H., & Heber, R. (1981). The efficacy of early intervention with family rehabilitation. In M. Begab, H. C. Haywood, & H. L. Garber (Eds.), *Psychosocial influences in retarded performance* (pp. 71–87). Baltimore: University Park Press.

Gardner, J. M., Karmel, B. Z., & Dowd, J. M. (1984). Relationship of infant psychobiological development to infant intervention programs. *Journal of Children in Contemporary Society, 17*, 93–108.

Guralnick, M. J., & Bennett, F. C. (1987). A framework for early intervention. In M. J. Guralnick & F. C. Bennett (Eds.), *The effectiveness of early intervention for at-risk and handicapped children* (pp. 3–29). Orlando: Academic Press.

Gutelius, M. F., Kirsch, A. D., MacDonald, S., Brooks, M. R., & McErlean, T. (1977). Controlled study of child health supervision: Behavioral results. *Pediatrics, 60*, 294–304.

Hagberg, R. (1978). The epidemiologic panorama of major neuropaediatric handicaps in Sweden. In J. Apley (Ed.), *Clinics in developmental medicine: Care of the handicapped child* (pp. 111–124). Philadelphia: Lippincott.

Haskins, R. (1986). Social and cultural factors in risk assessment and mental retardation. In D. Farran & J. McKinney (Eds.), *Risk in intellectual and psychosocial development* (pp. 29–60). Orlando: Academic Press.

Hayden, A. H., & Beck, G. R. (1982). The epidemiology of high risk and handicapped infants. In C. T. Ramey & P. L. Trohanis (Eds.), *Finding and educating high-risk and handicapped infants* (pp. 19–51). Baltimore: University Park Press.

Healy, A., Keesee, P. D., & Smith, B. (1985). *Early services for children with special needs: Transactions for family support.* Iowa City, IA: University Hospital School.

Honig, A. S. (1984). Risk factors in infancy. *Early Childhood Development and Care, 16*, 1–8.

Hunt, J. McV. (1964). The psychological basis for using preschool enrichment as an antidote for cultural deprivation. *Merrill-Palmer Quarterly, 10*, 209–248.

Kagan, S. L., Klugman, E., & Zigler, E. (1983). Shaping child and family policies: Criteria and strategies for a new decade. In E. F. Zigler, S. L. Kagan, & E. Klugman (Eds.), *Children, families and government: Perspectives on American social policy* (pp. 415–438). New York: Cambridge University Press.

Kaye, K. (1986). A four-dimensional model of risk assessment and intervention. In D. C. Farran & J. D. McKinney (Eds.), *Risk in intellectual and psychosocial development* (pp. 273–286). Orlando: Academic Press.

Keogh, B. K., Wilcoxen, A. G., & Bernheimer, L. (1986). Prevention services for risk children: Evidence for policy and practice. In D. C. Farran & J. D. McKinney (Eds.), *Risk in intellectual and psychosocial development* (pp. 287–316). Orlando: Academic Press.

Lazar, I., & Darlington, R. (1982). Lasting effects of early education: A report from the consortium for longitudinal studies. *Monographs of the Society for Research in Child Development, 47* (2–3, Serial No. 195).

Lerner, R. M. (1987). The concept of plasticity in development. In J. J. Gallagher & C. T. Ramey (Eds.), *The malleability of children* (pp. 3–14). Baltimore: P. H. Brookes.

Maddan, J., Ottara, J., & Levenstein, P. (1984). Home again: Effects of the mother–child home program on mother and child. *Child Development, 55*, 636–647.

McCall, R. B. (1987). Developmental function, individual differences and the plasticity of intelligence. In J. J. Gallagher & C. T. Ramey (Eds.), *The malleability of children* (pp. 25–35). Baltimore: P. H. Brookes.

McCarthy, D. (1972). McCarthy Scales of Children's Abilities. New York: Psychological Corporation.

Mead, M. (1980). Can the American family survive? In R. Metraux (Ed.), *Aspects of the present* (pp. 93–105). New York: Morrow.

Meisels, S. J. (1984). Prediction, prevention and developmental screening in the EPSDT program. In H. W. Stevenson & A. E. Siegel (Eds.), *Child development research and social policy* (pp. 267–317).Chicago: University of Chicago Press.

Meisels, S. J., & Margolis, L. H. (1988). Is the Early Periodic Screening, Diagnosis and Treatment Program effective with developmentally disabled children? *Pediatrics, 81*, 262–271.

Minde, K., Shosenberg, N., Marton, P., Thompson, J., Ripley, J., & Burns, S. (1980). Self-help groups in a premature nursery – A controlled evaluation. *Pediatrics, 96*, 933–940.

National Institute of Health. (1979). *Antenatal Diagnosis*, Report of a Consensus Development Conference sponsored by the National Institute of Child Health and Human Development, Office for Medical Applications of Research and the Fogarty International Center (NIH Pub. No. 79–1973). Bethesda, MD: Author.

National Research Council. (1987). *Risking the future: Adolescent sexuality, pregnancy and childbearing* (Vol. 1). Washington, DC: Author.

Nauta, M. J., & Travers, J. (1982). The effects of a social program: Executive summary of CFRP's infant–toddler component. Washington, DC: Administration for Children, Youth and Families, Office of Human Development, U.S. Department of Health and Human Services.

Nuckolls, C., Cassel, J., & Kaplan, B. (1972). Psychosocial assets, life crises and the prognosis of pregnancy. *Journal of Epidemiology, 95*, 432–441.

Ogbu, J. U. (1987). Cultural influences on plasticity in human development. In J. J. Gallagher & C. T. Ramey (Eds.), *The malleability of children* (pp. 155–169). Baltimore: P. H. Brookes.

Olds, D. L. (1984). Case studies of factors interfering with nurse home visitors' promotion of positive caregiving methods in high-risk families. *Early Child Development and Care, 16*, 149–166.

Pierson, D., Bronson, M., Dromey, E., Swartz, J., Tivnan, T., & Walker, D. (1983). The impact of early education measured by classroom observation and teacher rating of children in kindergarten. *Evaluation Review, 7*, 191–216.

Powell, D. R. (1980). Personal social networks as a focus for primary prevention of child maltreatment. *Infant Mental Health Journal, 4*, 232–239.

Powell, D. R. (1982). From child to parent: Changing conceptions of early childhood intervention. In W. M. Bridgeland and E. A. Duane (Eds.), *The annals of the American Academy of Political Science* (pp. 135–144). Beverly, Hills: Sage.

Provence, S., & Naylor, A. (1983). *Working with disadvantaged parents and their children.* New Haven: Yale University Press.

Ramey, C. T., Bryant, D. M., Sparling, J. J., & Wasik, B. H. (1985). Project CARE: A comparison of two early intervention strategies to prevent retarded development. *Topics in Early Childhood Special Education, 5*, 12.

Ramey, C. T., & Campbell, F. A. (1984). Preventive education for high-risk children: Cognitive consequences of the Carolina Abecedarian Project. *American Journal of Mental Deficiency, 88*, 515–523.

Ramey, C. T., & Haskins, R. (1981). The modification of intelligence through early experience. *Intellgience, 5*, 5–19.

Ramey, C. T., & MacPhee, D. (1986). Developmental retardation: A systems theory perspective on risk and preventive intervention. In D. C. Farran & J. D. McKinney (Eds.), *Risk in intellectual and psychosocial development* (pp. 61–81). Orlando: Academic Press.

Ramey, C. T., Stedman, D. J., Borders-Patterson, A., & Mengel, W. (1978). Predicting school failure from information available at birth. *American Journal on Mental Deficiency, 82*, 525–534.

Rogers, M. (1968). Risk registers and the early detection of handicaps. *Developmental Medicine and*

Child Neurology, 10, 651–661.

Ross, G. (1984). Home intervention for premature infants of low-income families. *American Journal of Orthopsychiatry, 54,* 263–270.

Sameroff, A. J., & Chandler, M. J. (1975). Reproductive risk and the continuum of caretaking casualty. In F. D. Horowitz (Ed.), *Review of child development research* (Vol. 4., pp. 187–244). Chicago: University of Chicago Press.

Sameroff, A. J., Seifer, R., Barocas, R., Zax, M., & Greenspan, S. (1987). Intelligence quotient scores of 4-year-old children: Social-environmental risk factors. *Pediatrics, 79,* 343–350.

Scarr, S., & Arnett, J. (1987). Malleability: Lessons from intervention and family studies. In J. J. Gallagher & C. T. Ramey (Eds.), *The malleability of children* (pp. 71–84). Baltimore: P. H. Brookes.

Seitz, V., Rosenbaum, L. K., & Apfel, N. H. (1985). Effects of family support intervention: A ten-year follow-up. *Child Development, 56,* 376–391.

Singer, J. D., & Butler, J. A. (1987). The Education for All Handicapped Children Act: Schools as agents of social reform. *Harvard Educational Review, 57,* 125–152.

Slaughter, D. T. (1983). Early intervention and its effects on maternal and child development. *Monographs of the Society for Research on Child Development, 48* (4, Serial No. 202).

Thoman, E. B. (1987). Self-regulation of stimulation by prematures with a breathing blue bear. In J. J. Gallagher & C. T. Ramey (Eds.), *The malleability of children* (pp. 51–69). Baltimore: P. H. Brookes.

Werner, E. E. (1986). A longitudinal study of perinatal risk. In D. C. Farran & J. D. McKinney (Eds.), *Risk in intellectual and psychosocial development* (pp. 3–27). Orlando: Academic Press.

Werner, E., Bierman, J. M., & French, F. (1971). *The Children of Kauai: A longitudinal study from the prenatal period to age ten.* Honolulu: University of Hawaii Press.

Whiteman, M., Brown, D., & Deutsch, M. (1967). Some effects of social class and race on children's language and intellectual abilities. In M. Deutsch (Ed.), *The disadvantaged child* (pp. 319–335). New York: Basic Books.

Whiteman, M., & Deutsch, M. (1967). Social disadvantages are related to intellective and language delays. In M. Deutsch (Ed.), *The disadvantaged child* (pp. 337–356). New York: Basic Books.

Zigler, E., & Weiss, H. (1985). Family support systems: An ecological approach to child development. In R. N. Rapoport (Ed.), *Children, youth and families: The action research relationship* (pp. 166–205). New York: Cambridge University Press.

27 Paraprofessionals, parenting, and child development: Understanding the problems and seeking solutions

JUDITH S. MUSICK AND FRANCES M. STOTT

Community-based early intervention programs are primarily concerned with the modification or improvement of the caregiving environment for young children at developmental risk. The challenge inherent in this goal lies in the attempt to bring about change in the complex process of parenting. This chapter addresses the use of paraprofessional or lay helpers, those service providers chosen to be the principal agents of change in the majority of community-based intervention efforts. The chapter seeks to further our understanding of the factors that underlie the more serious problems of lay helping, and to explore new modes of training that are called for in the design and implementation of future programs.

No simple, clear-out solutions are offered; no final conclusions reached. Far too few data currently exist for any such certainty. Rather, the search for answers must be preceded by the raising of thought-provoking and meaningful questions. This chapter is an attempt to raise such questions.

THE PARAPROFESSIONAL IN HUMAN SERVICES

Even a cursory glance indicates that few direct service providers in early intervention and prevention programs are psychiatrists, educators, psychologists, nurses, pediatricians, or masters-level social workers. Whereas some such mix of professionals may function in consulting or supervisory roles, rarely do they serve as a participant's primary link to a community-based program. Rather, it is lay or paraprofessional helpers who develop the personal relationships with program participants. These people

The preparation of this paper was supported in part by a grant to Judith S. Musick from the Rockefeller Foundation.
The authors would like to thank Victor Bernstein of the University of Chicago and Vicki Magee, Candice Percansky, and Katherine Kamiya Rubino of the Ounce of Prevention Fund for the significant contributions they have made to the programs described in this paper. Thanks also to Barbara Bowman of the Erikson Institute for her helpful and supportive comments on an earlier draft of this paper, and for her wise and valued counsel on the issue of cultural embeddedness. A final word of thanks goes to Lynn Olsen of Northwestern University for her generous offer of editorial help, which was greatly appreciated.

651

come from the same community and share many of the same values and experiences as the participants they serve. They form the web of structured social support that is the heart of the community-based approach. How did lay helpers become linchpins of the early intervention movement? What were the social and political antecedents of the current reliance on paraprofessionals?

The paraprofessional, or lay helper, is an individual who has not received training in a traditional baccalaureate or postbaccalaureate, professional training program. Although paraprofessionals have always been involved in the delivery of social services, their widespread use has only emerged since the mid-1960's War on Poverty. The initial impetus for the use of paraprofessionals was the rapid growth of human service programs and the resultant shortage of trained workers (e.g., Albee, 1968; Austin, 1978; Gartner, 1971). Indigenous paraprofessionals began to be employed in such fields as mental health, health care (e.g., drug abuse and chronic hospitalized patients), Head Start and other early intervention programs, education, juvenile corrections, welfare and law, and community action programs.

Further motives for the utilization of paraprofessionals have been to increase the efficiency and effectiveness of services (Austin, 1978). It was reasoned that efficiency would be increased if professionals were freed from work that might be done as well by persons with less training and/or skill. Similarly, paraprofessionals were thought to provide a more cost-effective system of service delivery.

Paraprofessionals were also assumed to have a greater understanding of their clients, whose background more closely resembles their own. Paraprofessionals were thus viewed as providing a "bridge" between programs and clients because they generally shared the same cultural backgrounds and lived in similar neighborhoods. Further, since paraprofessionals did not rely on the use of roles and techniques that produce distance between helper and client, they were able to gain entry and establish rapport with a variety of individuals who might otherwise be unapproachable (Kalafat & Boroto, 1977; Reiff & Riessman, 1965; Sobey, 1970). The enthusiasm behind this grass-roots involvement of people has sometimes led to an antiprofessional bias and an unrealistic belief that paraprofessionals can serve as change agents of the social system (Austin, 1978). It was thought that through client participation and community action, paraprofessionals might influence preexisting beliefs about clients, the design of services, and agency and social policy (Halpern, 1986).

A final pair of related motives for the use of paraprofessionals concerns the benefits that accrue to the paraprofessionals themselves. One such benefit is jobs that are provided for the poor and the chronically unemployed. This goal was implicit in such legislation as the Economic Opportunity Act of 1964 (Austin, 1978). An extension of the employment motive is a new careers philosophy that emphasizes continuous employment and personal advancement opportunities (Riessman, 1965; Reiff & Riessman, 1965). Riessman's "helper therapy principle" holds that through their training and attempts at helping others, nonprofessional helpers often experience significant personal growth. This growth results from increased opportunity for skill building as well as improvement in such aspects of psychological health as self-esteem, aspirations, and the ability to engage in effective interpersonal relationships (Pearl & Riessman, 1965). As the paraprofessional realizes these therapeutic benefits, he or she will become more effective and have a positive effect on the client. More recently it has been noted that paraprofessionals' newly gained interactive skills can help them in their own parenting (Halpern & Convey, 1983).

Difficulties in the paraprofessional role

Effectiveness of paraprofessionals has been assessed by a number of investigators (e.g., Austin, 1978; Gartner, 1971, 1979; Gordon, 1976). In general, such research has found them to be both effective in the delivery of services and satisfied with their work. Reports from experiences with paraprofessionals in a wide variety of fields, however, suggest that there are a number of issues and problems that emerged in the 1960s and continue to exist today.

One of the most basic of these issues is the specification of the particular roles to be assumed by paraprofessionals. Programs often do not provide specific training and job descriptions for lay workers, and there is much ambiguity of role (Gartner, 1979). Further, the demands made by the community often conflict with those of the professional agency, resulting in what Austin (1978) has termed "psychic stretch." Two of the common problems of this role confusion are inappropriate evaluation of paraprofessionals based on professional criteria and the increasing identification of paraprofessionals with the professionals, resulting in the development of an "armor" that acts as a barrier between the helper and the client (Kalafat & Boroto, 1977).

Another major factor that has mitigated the effectiveness of paraprofessionals to some degree involves the attitudes and behaviors that they bring to their roles. These may include overidentifying with the client, imposing their own values on the client, and difficulty sharing power with the client (Austin, 1978). Cowen (1973) has further identified such other problems as excessive dependency, panicking, and projecting one's problems onto others.

A final difficulty in the use of paraprofessionals involves the tension between professionals and paraprofessionals. By definition, professionalism implies special expertise based on abstract principles selectively applied to concrete problems (Goode, 1965). The knowledge and skills required are obtained, for the most part, in a university setting. A paraprofessional, by contrast, generally does not need a high level of skill in handling abstract concepts and receives his or her training on-the-job (Richan, 1978). Hence, a major issue is the extent to which professional training and credentials are necessary for the performance of social service functions. As paraprofessionals have begun to perform traditionally professional functions, this issue has been dramatically brought to the surface (Austin, 1978).

Other difficulties have arisen when professionals try to serve as role models although they may lack the experience of an indigenous layworker, have an entirely different background, or are younger than the paraprofessional. Austin comments further that professional values, career objectives, and reference group identification can also become problems. Contrasting cultural styles and education may also result in differing goals and expectations of program participants. Both the professional and paraprofessional may feel threatened if salary increases and new positions are in short supply. Finally, differences have been noted in the expectations of the two groups concerning their informal relations. If, for example, paraprofessionals are barred from the professionals' reference group, they may in turn exclude the professionals from the paraprofessionals' reference group.

In contrast, several conditions have been identified over the years that appear to promote effective performance by paraprofessionals (Gartner, 1979). Such personal qualities as high levels of empathy and nonpossessive warmth toward clients seem to be critical factors in positive performance, as does a carefully designed selection procedure that emphasizes these qualities (Truax, 1965). A final factor conducive to effective performance is a well-executed, long-term program of training and supervision designed to fit the paraprofessionals' learning styles. Thus, under the proper conditions, many of the difficulties of the paraprofessional role can be overcome. This point will be illustrated in a later section in the description of an innovative training model.

RATIONALE FOR COMMUNITY-BASED EARLY INTERVENTION PROGRAMS

Halpern (1986) notes that an outgrowth of the paraprofessional movement in recent years has been the incorporation of lay helpers in community-based family support programs. These programs are based on the continuing belief that a paraprofessional can provide a bridge to the community. The theoretical rationale for these family support programs is drawn from the relatively new literature on social support that emphasizes informal helping (e.g., Weiss & Jacobs, 1984) and the tenets of clinical infant intervention that address specific obstacles to adequate parenting (e.g., Fraiberg, 1980; Greenspan, 1981). The establishment of clear roles for paraprofessionals is very difficult in such programs. Informal social support and clinical intervention do not easily lend themselves to precise definition. Beyond this, as Halpern and Larner (in press) have noted, the paraprofessionals need to "invent" their new role; to tailor it to each family in a way that is acceptable to that family. Paraprofessionals must accomplish this task while balancing personal responsiveness to the needs and concerns expressed by the participants with the agenda and goals of the program.

These programs require a reconceptualization of the ways in which role delineation, recruitment, training, and supervision of paraprofessionals are conceived of and implemented. Before we consider these factors, we need to examine the notions of child development and parenting that form the theoretical rationale and framework for these programs.

What do infants need?

What do all infants need in order to grow and develop to their optimal potential? They need protection from physical and psychological harm, adequate nourishment, help in regulating their own biological rhythms, and at least one special responsive adult to whom they can become attached, and who will act as a mediator between them and and the world. Infants must also have adult caretakers who treat them as *people*, creating positive expectations and prophesies that the children will slowly come to fulfill. As infants develop there is an increasing need for guidance, structure, and experiences that will help them to develop a sense of who they are and what they can do. They need opportunities to explore the world, test autonomy, and feel personally effective. Capacities for later learning such as language use, focused attention, and interaction with people and objects are then further consolidated and differentiated during the second and third years of life. What might cause these elements to be absent or only minimally present in a child's life? What factors may place a child "at risk"?

Infants at risk

Two major pathways can create or exacerbate vulnerability and dysfunction. One pathway is some form of biological impairment sustained either prenatally or during the perinatal period, or as a result of a genetic disorder. Such impairments can either act *directly* to limit the growth-facilitating aspects of the environment, *indirectly* through diminished parental responsivity, or, as is so frequently the case, from a complex interaction of both direct and indirect factors.

Infants with a less than intact nervous system, those who are physically malformed, biologically impaired, or seriously ill, and those with a difficult temperament all to some degree present a parenting problem. Such children may offer formidable challenges that even the most loving, mature, and knowledgeable parents – those having considerable psychological and material resources – will be unable to meet (Beckwith, this volume). Clearly, such children and their parents will require a variety of specialized intervention services in order to promote optimal child development and healthy parent–child relationships, to ameliorate handicapping conditions, and to prevent increasing developmental failure.

The second route to developmental vulnerability – environmental risk – is an equally serious threat to a child reaching full capacity and becoming a competent member of society. Environmental risk describes a situation where the child-rearing milieu is either deficient in certain key resources and functions, or is actively harmful to the developing child. This chapter addresses issues of intervention for these environmentally at-risk children and specifically their teen parents. Although the populations and approaches for biological and environmental risk overlap, each requires different techniques and calls for special perspectives.

Environmental risk is manifested in three general ways: (1) the social context and material constraints of living in poverty; (2) community differences or values that affect patterns of child rearing and may, in turn, be related to later success in school, work, and life roles; and (3) psychological factors within the family that affect parents' capacities to adequately nurture and guide their children. Early intervention programs must address all three manifestations of risk to some degree. The principal means used by most programs to accomplish this is through the supportive and helping relationships that providers establish with the parents.

There can be little doubt about the importance and impact of the total ecology of risk. This ecology includes the influences of such variables as extended family, community and society (Sameroff & Fiese, this volume), and poverty and social isolation (Garbarino, this volume). Although they acknowledge the power of these more societal-level variables, program designers also recognize that during infancy parents are the most significant and salient forces in a child's environment. Parents are the *mediators* of the effects of poverty, community values, social isolation, psychosocial pathology, and relationships within the family and other social networks. For example, a mother who feels defeated by life and helpless to control her own destiny may pass on that sense of powerlessness to her child through her lowered expectations (Clark, 1983), her inability to assert herself in protecting her child from harm, or through her depression, emotional unavailability, and insensitivity to the child's needs. Similarly, the child of 17-year-old parents in an isolated and impoverished rural area may suffer from his or her parents' lack of knowledge about and access to material or human resources and lack of adequate role models to guide them in appropriate parenting.

As already suggested, the multiple interlocking components that constitute the sociocultural context of risk do not act directly to harm children in any simple, easily comprehensible ways. Parents filter and give meaning to the various experiences of poverty, family and community norms, and available support systems. Many of these experiences will have a profound influence on parental perceptions and thus on the patterns of child rearing through which parents interact with their children. But at the same time, the needs of today's children have an immediacy that cannot be ignored. In the long run, vulnerable children and their parents would benefit most from such broader social and economic changes as better education and training programs; greater employment possibilities; eradication of racial barriers; more two-parent families; and less social isolation. In reality, however, changes such as these occur slowly and are intimately tied to the political agenda-setting process (Kingdon, 1984; Weiss & Bucinvalos, 1980).

Changing the caregiving environment

The overarching goals of most early intervention and prevention programs for environmentally at-risk children have long been to help the child optimize development, promote educability, and ensure later school success (see Zigler & Weiss, 1985). To a large degree, programs rely on environmental manipulations to meet these goals. This approach has generally meant an emphasis on the parents as the "window" into the life of the child, and a tacit acknowledgment that in infancy and early childhood the parents constitute the child's primary environment. Research on the community-based, family-support efforts that make up the major portion of programs for environmental risk yields mixed or equivocal results (Halpern, 1986; Powell, 1987; Weiss & Jacobs, 1984). Perhaps this is because the enormity of the task – *changing the caregiving environment* – has not been fully grasped.

A review of the family support and parent education literature, such as that recently undertaken by Powell (1987), as well as our many years of direct experience in designing, directing, and evaluating service models, has led us to the conclusion that whereas these programs may successfully reach and support parents as people, most have yet to effectively and consistently reach them as *parents* (Musick & Barbera-Stein, 1988). This is the case despite the existence of numerous parenting curricula and parent education models (Clarke-Stewart & Fein, 1983). Indeed, there is currently little evidence of medium or long-term maintenance of changes in either parental behavior or infant development (Halpern, 1986). It seems clear that the time has come to reformulate some of our questions about the tasks of early intervention programs, and to reexamine our approaches to working with parents.

We believe that parenting is a relationship – a way of interacting with, nurturing, and guiding a young and initially dependent human being. As such, parenting cannot be learned in the same way that we learn an academic discipline. Nor can it result from the kinds of training required for vocational competence. This would appear to be self-evident yet most early intervention programs seem to be predicated on the notion of parenting as analogous to a job, that is, something that can be taught or retaught if it has not been "learned" well initially. In truth, the processes by which the capacity for parenting normally develops are poorly understood, and so it is not surprising that failures to bring about significant change are widespread. Scholars and practitioners compare techniques, but seldom look at what underlies the goals they have set for bringing about change.

If changing the early caregiving environment involves changing the parent, this can best be accomplished in the context of a *relationship* with the parent. Where issues revolve around relationships, the change agents are not the methods, or curricula; they are other *people*. It is these other people and the quality of the relationships they are able to establish and sustain that will be the critical elements in any intervention. These relationships provide the scaffolds for building or rebuilding parenting strength.

The paraprofessional in early intervention programs

As suggested previously, largely because paraprofessionals can provide a bridge to the community, they are uniquely qualified to be the most effective change agents. However, the success of such an approach rests on two central assumptions. The first assumption is that paraprofessional staffs have been wisely recruited. Just as professional service providers are not a homogenous group, neither are paraprofessionals. They may range from farmers' wives seeking to bring additional income into the family to meet growing economic stress, to women with some college experience reentering the work force after raising children, to single parents who may be independent of public assistance for the first time in their lives. Some will require far more extensive training than others; some may regard the position as a temporary "way station," and others will view it as a career with long-term growth potential. Although this variation is unavoidable and may even be desirable, reflecting, as it does, sensitivity to the diversity of individual communities, there are certain personal qualities about which there should be no compromise. Lay helpers, like professionals, should be caring, intuitive people who develop positive relationships with others. They also need to have the capacity for reflection about themselves and their work, and to be open to new ways of thinking and doing. Most of all, they need to be emotionally strong people with a good deal of common sense. These are not rare qualities, but they must be carefully looked and listened for during the recruitment and early supervisory process. Such qualities constitute the foundation for successful use of paraprofessional staff.

The second assumption of successful community-based programming that utilizes paraprofessional staff is that good, not just adequate, training and supervision are provided. Although a professional-level supervisor may understand the psychology of parents and children, he or she may fail to grasp the complexities involved in staff development of lay helpers. No training, no matter how excellent, can possibly overcome serious errors in recruitment or lack of well-articulated ongoing supervision. It seems evident that concerted effort must also be devoted to training professional supervisory-level staff in community-based early intervention initiatives, lest programs fail because of a vital but missing link in the chain of enablement.

The following section explores certain key problems that surround the implementation and effectiveness of services that appear to be related to the use of lay helpers. It also posits new modes of training designed specifically to address these problems.

TRAINING AND SUPERVISING PARAPROFESSIONALS: UNDERSTANDING THE PROBLEMS AND SEEKING SOLUTIONS

In this section we draw on the experiences of the Ounce of Prevention Fund to illustrate problems that can arise when programs use paraprofessionals and to offer concrete suggestions for training and supervising layworkers. In examining the patterns of lay helping that undergird community-based early intervention programs, we seek first to isolate those elements or processes that may be implicated in unevenly implemented and ineffective services. Such services may help parents feel somewhat better about themselves, but they often do little more than scratch the surface of dysfunctional parenting and subsequent developmental failure. Whereas little "hard" data exist on factors underlying the enduring problems of lay helping, clinical research and systematic observations conducted by the Ounce of Prevention Fund have raised certain issues that should be addressed before the next generation of interventions for children and parents is designed. Raising such issues is the logical next step in the process of developing more coherent and thoughtfully designed programs.

The Ounce of Prevention Fund

The Ounce of Prevention Fund is a statewide system of service, research, training, and technical assistance in Illinois. It is dedicated to helping families raise strong and healthy children through community-based programs for preteens, teens, young parents, and their children. Created as a joint public–private agency, it works to prevent family problems that can result in child abuse and neglect, infant mortality, delayed development in children, and repeated cycles of teenage pregnancy and parenthood. The organization designs, develops, monitors, and evaluates projects that address these family problems and conducts research to help identify causes and potential solutions.

Domains of silence

Ounce programs use professionals in training and supervisory roles, but the majority of direct service work is carried out by paraprofessional staff members living in (or very near) the community that houses the program. Halpern's (this volume) notion of "domains of silence" aptly describes a phenomenon much noted among these paraprofessional staff members. For example, in teen parent programs home visitors and parent-group facilitators seldom deal strongly or consistently with such loaded topics as sexuality, family planning, adoption, domestic violence, or child abuse. This is especially the case in regard to parenting practices and decisions that affect the well-being of children. In a study of the attitudes of service providers and adolescent mothers toward the option of placing their children for adoption (Musick, Handler, & Waddill, 1984), staff as well as teens remarked that the issue of adoption was almost never broached, even when the teen mother and her family were highly ambivalent about the child. Several teen mothers remarked that they wondered why nobody ever brought up adoption despite their clearly expressed messages about the conflict they felt in regard to being a parent at such an early age.

Another study that looked at providers' attitudes toward teens as parents gives striking evidence of how difficult it is for many paraprofessionals to even talk about the adolescent as a parent (Musick & Mosena, 1988). When specifically asked to describe their participants as parents, the majority of the paraprofessional respondents focused instead on nonparenting aspects of their behavior (e.g., their problems with families, boyfriends, or personal insecurities), almost as if they had failed to hear the clearly and directly spoken questions. Only after prompting and additional questions did they speak of parenting, and then only in terms of such behaviors as "they never take them downtown" or "they usually keep them clean." Both this study and the adoption study were conducted with well-qualified staff members, most of whom had participated in earlier Ounce training sessions on the subject matter under discussion. Such findings resulted in our making significant changes in the Ounce's system of training and technical assistance, some of which will be discussed.

What are the origins of the domains-of-silence phenomenon as it manifests itself in staff reluctance to deal with the parent as a parent, that is, as the caregiver of a child? Certainly, cultural and community norms about what can and cannot be discussed are major factors, particularly with regard to such issues as adoption or physical punishment of children. However, although the effects of cultural embeddedness are often overlooked by program developers, once they are acknowledged they can generally be addressed in a straightforward and mutually satisfactory manner. Such factors are not, we believe, the primary barrier to intervention in the parenting process. In examining this question over a number of years and across a variety of contexts, we conclude that there are two other, more complex and subtle impediments to direct and consistent focus on promoting good parenting and improving child outcomes. The first is best described as a countertransference issue; the second as an issue of expectations.

Countertransference

The term *countertransference* is used here to describe difficulties in maintaining psychological distance or objectivity in regard to the participant. The term countertransference was originally used to designate the emotional reactions of a psychoanalyst to a patient's transference toward him or her. It was considered to be a disturbing factor in that it interfered with the therapist's ability to be objective in regard to the patient (Gitelson, 1952). Today, however, the term is used more broadly to refer to distortions or emotional interference on the part of a therapist that may result in failures of empathy, failure to notice, understand, or adequately interpret what is going on with a patient, including idealizing some patients and "advertently" disliking others. Countertransference phenomena have their roots in a wide variety of external and internal psychological factors. For the purposes of this chapter, countertransference generally refers to the possibility that a paraprofessional may inadvertently harm or fail to help a client because of his or her unrecognized feelings (Richan, 1978). It may, for example, be particularly painful to acknowledge that a young mother's attitude and/or behavior toward her child is truly harmful, if that is the way you were raised or the way you felt and behaved toward your child. Developmental issues around dependency, autonomy, negativism, separation, assertiveness, aggression, and the expression of strong emotions can become spheres of conflict in parent–child relationships, especially in troubled or multiproblem families. Such issues can have strong psychological reverberations for service providers because they are very heavily affect-laden and may threaten to bring into awareness feelings that are so painful that they have been denied or repressed.

In theory, professional clinical training is expected to take into account such psychological phenomena. The social worker, psychiatrist, or other human service professional is supposed to be armed with the tools to recognize when countertransference is interfering with the helping relationship by preventing the therapist from seeing what is really going on and by distorting clinical perception and interpretation of behavior. Such training has not generally been part of the paraprofessional experience, nor do we advocate that it should be provided in precisely the same manner as for professional-level staff. However, some carefully designed and well-implemented training of this nature is both useful and necessary in order to guard against a layworker either ignoring or seriously exacerbating a problem when it reverberates with the worker's own issues. Further, this training can be conducted in such a way that it will not undermine the very real strengths that lay helpers bring to high-risk families. An example of how such training is carried out may be illustrative.

Several years ago, in response to multiple disclosures of sexual abuse among teen mothers in our programs, the Ounce of Prevention Fund developed Heart-to-Heart, a prevention program with the goal of strengthening teen parents' abilities to protect themselves and their children against sexual abuse (Gershenson, Musick, Ruch-Ross, Magee, Rubino, & Rosenberg, in press). Using a specially designed curriculum for mothers, group members discuss childrens' sexual development, sexual abuse and its prevention, and the indicators and treatment of sexual abuse. Trained group leaders are community women who were once teen mothers. Many of them are also adult survivors of childhood sexual abuse.

The lengthy and intensive training for group leaders integrates the presentation of educational material on sexual abuse and related topics with an emphasis on building the capacity to effectively handle psychologically complex and powerful subjects. The training provides opportunities for group leaders to confront their own feelings and conflicts about sexuality, sexual abuse, and parenting, and permits them an opportunity to be reflective about their personal values and experiences. These opportunities have proven to be critical safeguards against the lay helpers' tendencies to confuse their own emotions and needs with those of the group members. Training such as this concerning countertransference issues is clearly not carried out in a way that is either structurally or functionally identical to that which would be undertaken with professional staff. Rather, it is part of a program that combines structured learning experiences, group leader guides, audio-visual and written materials, modeling, interactive exercises (such as role playing), journal writing, and the opportunity for personal reflection and sharing of feelings. Both didactic and interactive components are necessary, and each nourishes the other. Whereas the term countertransference may never acutally have been used by the trainers, the issue premeates the training agenda, in hopes that it will eventually become an integral part of the lay helpers' repertoire. Participants frequently refer to the healing nature of the Heart-to-Heart training experience, and consequently appear to bring more objectivity to their work with the young parents and their families.

A word of caution is called for in regard to techniques such as these that allow for the expression of painful emotions. Any context in which this expression occurs must also contain safeguard elements of limit setting and boundary maintenance, lest the groups deteriorate into "encounter" sessions. For example, one group member should not be allowed to confront another in a deliberately hurtful way, nor to otherwise control or monopolize the discussion. The supervisor or trainer needs always to keep in mind the purpose of the group, providing an invisible but critically important structure. Here the guiding role of the professional will always be key, first as the trainer, and later as the supervisor of the lay helper's work.

Expectations

A second impediment to the paraprofessional's capacity for dealing with participants as parents is lowered expectations. Lowered expectations are manifested on two levels: one, the expectations paraprofessionals had or continue to have of their own children; and, two, the expectations they have of their clients, both parents and children. Lowered expectations are most likely derived from internalizations of the experience of poverty and discrimination. The sense of powerlessness or helplessness that is the outcome of such internalizations is the result of a number of interconnected factors. It can come directly from experiences both in the past and in the present. It can also come indirectly from observing the ways in which one's parents coped with their particular life circumstances.

The psychological experience of being poor or of minority status all too frequently results in lowered expectations for one's children and a dim view of their chances for a different and better life. This is especially the case when a parent's family of origin was characterized by psychologically devastating experiences, repeated trauma, multiple life-event stresses, and limited social support (Clark, 1983). In describing the parents of the low-achieving high school students whose families he studied, Clark noted that these parents "have experienced severe psychologically debilitating events at earlier stages in their lives. Past (and contemporary) experiences in their own family of origin and in the market place have had a trickle down effect which have left mental scars so deep as to have rendered them unable or unwilling to stay deeply commited to quality parental functioning" (p. 192). They have, Clark noted, "sustained immeasurable strain and pain, and they now have an impoverished human spirit" (p. 192). They sense little chance for a better tomorrow and, although they may be interested in their children, they lack hope, a sense of power, and expectations that they can have a positive influence on their children's potential for more than mere survival. Such parents "just can't see how they can do any better" (p. 190). Interestingly, such parents' life circumstances are not always qualitively worse then those of Clark's contrast group – the parents of successful high school students. Rather, their "sense of powerlessness and hopelessness was markedly different" (p. 191).

Since many community-based paraprofessional helpers have psychological backgrounds similar to those oberved by Clark, one must be concerned about whether it is realistic to expect them to be "naturally" adroit at the complex task of improving the child-rearing environments provided by young parents. The efforts involved, for example, in enabling parents to actively promote language development, encourage curiosity, and tolerate striving for autonomy are all predicated on the notion that these behaviors will lead somewhere – that the child can some day be somebody. In addition, they are intimately tied to the lay helper's expectations that the young mother is actually capable of being a good parent, or of changing her negative parenting behaviors.

In the light of such issues, one of the greatest strengths of using lay workers – shared background and understandings between staff and participants – can also be viewed as a potential weakness in the fabric of these programs. Many paraprofessionals find themselves working with young mothers who are not too different from the young mother they were in the not so distant past. Although they have achieved some success in moving forward in school, work, or community roles, they may have been far less successful in their roles as parents. For example, Brooks-Gunn and Furstenberg (1986) found that although a group of former adolescent mothers had achieved a level of success as adults, their children fared more poorly than the offspring of older child-bearers. Whereas the intellectual differences found between the groups of children were relatively small at first, they became increasingly pronounced as the children got older. In the early years such behavior problems as hostility, activity level, and under-control of behavior had more strongly differentiated younger from older childbearers.

The monumental effort to pull oneself up out of generations of poverty, with little or no support from near or extended kin, may take its toll on the capacity for being an enabler of one's children and being able to promote their best interests. The negative self-images established in childhood remain, despite success experiences, and manifest themselves psychologically and behaviorally in lowered expectations for one's children. Children are self-objects of their parents; that is, they represent an extension of the parent's own self (Kohut, 1971). As self-objects, the paraprofessional's children may thus beome the unwitting victims of her unacknowledged or unconscious feelings about herself as an incompetent or ineffective person. She cannot promote her child's optimal development if she does not at some level believe that the child can succeed; and this she cannot believe if that child represents her own worst feelings or gravest fears about herself. In sum, the challenge for program developers is to effectively utilize paraprofessional helpers as change agents, recognizing that some lay helpers will themselves require strengthening of certain socioemotional resources of critical importance for the task ahead.

Just as parents are a heterogeneous group, so too are paraprofessional helpers. Clearly, a service provider who has higher expectations to begin with will be in the best position to act as a facilitator of positive growth for parents. Certainly there are paraprofessionals with healthy expectations for themselves, their own children, and for the families they serve. Such persons may have high expectations, but nevertheless lack some of the means to fulfill them or to help others do the same. The fortunate (and skillfull) program developer will have recruited at least some of these individuals whose training and supervision can focus primarily on gaining new knowledge and access to resources and on expanding their existing repertoire of skills. Unfortunately, such characteristics do not typify the majority of paraprofessional service providers. For them the issue of expectations must be addressed in a meaningful way, because no amount of education about child development or child-rearing principles can be effective if it conflicts with a provider's deeply held views of parents and children. The first step in solving the problem of paraprofessionals' lower expectations (of both parents and children) should come from new training approaches. As was the case in dealing with the countertransference issues described earlier, well-conceptualized and well-implemented training for lay helpers who work with at-risk parents and children offers considerable promise for breaking transgenerational cycles of maladaptive and growth-thwarting parenting patterns. Again, an example may be illustrative.

In 1986 the Ounce of Prevention Fund made the decision to begin providing both traditional developmental screening and ongoing observation of the parent–child (and in many cases, grandparent–child) relationship for all of the children born to adolescent parents in the programs we administer. The creation of the unique Developmental Program (Musick, Bernstein, Percansky, & Stott, 1987), as it has come to be called, grew out of a recognition of the need for direct service staff to have useful techniques for understanding and assessing children's development. Underlying the actual methods devised for the Developmental Program was our commitment to identifying more subtle problems in the realm of socioemotional development. Equally as important was the pressing need for the mostly paraprofessional staff in these programs to be more confident and skillful in enabling teens to function effectively in their parenting roles.

As alluded to previously, on many occasions we had observed how lay helpers failed to intervene or even notice a variety of potentially serious problems, in either the child or in the parent–child relationship. Indeed, the previous 3 years had been marked by repeated, but largely unsuccessful, attempts to improve staff performance in this area. Although, for example, we had expanded the child development and parent–child aspects of our parenting curriculum, we found very little generalization or carry-over into practice. This was true for participants and for staff alike. After exploring a number of possible reasons for this phenomenon, we concluded that participants' apparent lack of interest was due, in part, to staff reluctance (or inability) to fully accept these topics.

We next added a series of parenting and child development workshops that incorporated modeling and hands-on experience with parent–child activities into the expanded training curriculum. However, while program staff members were enthusiastic about these parent–child workshops, they were unable to sustain their new skills once the Ounce of Prevention Fund child development specialists had stepped back into more supervisory roles. In like manner, the teen mothers who had been eager participants in the workshops when they were led by Ounce trainers suddenly lost interest when these activities were taken over by the program staff.

After lengthy discussions with all levels of the field-based program staff, we better understood the barriers to intervention efforts in this content area. We came to believe that lay helpers' expectations about themselves and about the children and families they served were playing a significant role in "blocking" them from truly grasping, let alone using, the material presented. This observation, in combination with our dissatisfaction with our efforts to date, led us to the decision to create a developmental screening program that would include extensive and qualitatively different methods of training for paraprofessional staff.

The Ounce of Prevention Developmental Program combines the use of the Denver Developmental Screening Test (DDST) (Frankenburg & Dodds, 1967) with an instrument designed specifically to assess early socioemotional adjustment, the Parent–Infant Observation Guide (PIOG) (Bernstein, Percansky, & Hans, 1987). The PIOG was developed to capture the more subtle, early precursors of developmental impairment that lie within the realm of socioemotional development. During infancy this development is best observed within the context of parent–child interaction. Problems in this domain have been found to be predictive of developmental lags (e.g., Erickson, Sroufe, & Egeland, 1985; Greenspan, 1982; Greenspan & Poisson, 1983) and can be noted early in the first year of life (Bernstein, Jeremy, & Marcus, 1986).

The DDST and the PIOG are each, in their own way, key elements in the Developmental Program. This is due not only to their usefulness as screening instruments, but perhaps more significantly to their efficacy as training tools for community-based staff. Both techniques have provided the opportunity for staff members to see children and parents in a new light – not just areas of vulnerability and possible deficit, but strengths and competencies as well. "I didn't know little babies could do that," say providers, as they watch the unfolding of the infant's behavioral repertoire during assessments on videotapes of parent–child interaction. The need to communicate with children is underscored by observing the exquisite responsiveness of even very young infants to the sound of their mother's voice, and the sight of her smiling face. Such experiences appear to bring about subtle shifts in providers' perceptions of babies and parents as important and effective beings. One can reasonably expect that such beings are capable of growing and changing in positive ways. At the same time, the gradually increasing ability to notice and better understand developmental or interactional difficulties raises a paraprofessional's personal sense of competence and efficacy. This in turn helps her to view herself as an intervenor, and motivates her to become involved in the parent–child relationship. In this stimulating and empowering process expectations begin to change.

The Developmental Program enables service providers to focus more directly on children and to feel more comfortable entering the parent–child relationship. Additionally, the entire training protocol has been structured to model the kinds of reciprocal, interactive roles we expect the staff to fulfill vis-a-vis the teen parents, who will then it is hoped, behave in similar ways with their children. Training includes observation of parents and children, modeling, and supervised hands-on experiences in both assessment and intervention. Such training experiences have resulted in staff members gaining a better understanding of their roles as change agents. They also have more realistic notions of their abilities, as well as their limitations in facilitating change.

Above all, the trainers stress the centrality of the *relationship* between the staff and parent. The training is designed to help service providers make empathic connections with parents and children. For example, although our ratings of temperament are rudimentary (see Bernstein et al., 1987), they were included to help staff members become more sensitive to individual differences among the children, and to stimulate them to think about what these difficulties may mean to the parents. Pointing out a parent's strengths or skills instead of ignoring or criticizing is a key step in building a strong relationship. Paraprofessional staff, with knowledge gained from the training and parent–infant observations, are in a stronger position to judge when and how to intervene. Because of their experiences with the Developmental Program, staff members are now ready for more information about child development and a broader range of techniques for observing parent–child relationships.

THE CHALLENGE AHEAD

Both the Heart-to-Heart and Developmental programs seek to create a chain of enablement that fosters positive growth in paraprofessional staff, so that they in turn can foster such growth in teen parents, who in turn can facilitate the growth of their children. This method of training paraprofessionals to focus on the teen as a *parent* is structured to ultimately result in more enabling and nurturing parenting as the teen begins to do for her child what was done for her. Both programs are highly interactive, encouraging the paraprofessionals (and parents) to participate actively in their own learning process. Trainers assist, encourage, and model the critical elements to be acquired. For example, they assume competence, capitalize on uncertainty, know the learner, and share interests. They also help the staff come to terms with and effectively use the strong emotions that may surface.

Unlike most educational or training techniques the Heart-to-Heart and Developmental programs do not minimize or bypass relationship issues. Rather, they are incorporated within the training process. Experience with our earlier training efforts had illustrated the shallowness of purely intellectualized approaches and convinced us of the need for new modes of training. Since we observed that emotions had sometimes been implicated as barriers to staff effectiveness, discounting lay helpers' feelings while increasing "knowledge input" would clearly have been a futile exercise. Instead, the process of bringing affective reactions into the training context allows the paraprofessional to make the experience more fully her own. We believe our approach shifts the training context from one that stresses only *learning*, to one that facilitates *acquisition*.

The psycholinguist James Paul Gee distinguishes these two processes. He states, "Acquisition is a process of acquiring something subconsciously by exposure to models and a process of trial and error, without a process of formal teaching" (Gee, 1987, p. 4). Participating in meaningful and natural settings, the acquirer is motivated to acquire what he or she is exposed to in order to function. Gee suggests that this is how most people come to control their first language. We believe that parenting shares many elements of this acquisition process.

In contrast, learning involves conscious knowledge gained through teaching. Although this instruction does not have to come from an officially designated teacher, it does involve explanation and analysis. In creating metaknowledge about the matter at hand, learning creates a distance between the learner and what is learned. Formal learning has traditionally constituted the training for professionals and, by extension, paraprofessionals.

It is our contention that training and supervision of paraprofessionals in early intervention programs should include techniques that foster both the acquisition and learning processes. Acquisitional approaches that include meaningful participation in newly created reference groups are more likely to foster empathy and enhance self-esteem, thereby facilitating change on a deeper level. At the same time, training and supervision should be structured to help community-based lay helpers gain some psychological distance from the parents and children they serve and to help them abstract general principles from immediate experience. In this way, paraprofessional staffs can use both what they have acquired and what they have learned to influence families' lives in more meaningful and lasting ways. Then, for example, the lay helper may be able to set limits when she observes a teen parent cruelly teasing or slapping her toddler for no apparent reason. The lay helper will be able to propose and model alternatives based on empathy, as well as knowledge of both parent and child.

Training and supervising paraprofessionals in this manner is a costly and complicated process that requires substantial commitment. Nevertheless, the community of available workers is a natural resource that should be tapped if we wish to significantly reduce environmental risk for parents and young children in high-risk communities. Where else shall we look for the large numbers of helping individuals needed to support the literally tens of thousands of parents and young children under stress? Does it seem likely that there will be an available pool of social work, medical, or psychology professionals for the job? Do we have adequate funds for such a large-scale professional-level endeavor? Even if we did, are professionals really the best people to meet the challenges ahead? If the role of the service provider is to fulfil certain key familylike functions, who is more appropriate for carrying this out than a lay helper from the extended "near-kin" network that makes up the community?

In the absence of a national commitment to radically change the social and economic conditions that contribute so heavily to dysfunctional parenting and developmental failures, well-trained lay helpers can provide the skill building and inspiration that raise individual, family, and community expectations and motivate positive change. It is our hope that community-based, trained paraprofessionals will function as catalysts, parent by parent, child by child, and family by family.

REFERENCES

Albee, G. W. (1968). Conceptual models and manpower requirements in psychology. *American Psychologist. 23*, 317–320.

Austin, M. J. (1978). *Professionals and paraprofessionals.* New York: Human Sciences Press.

Bernstein, V., Jeremy, R., & Marcus, J. (1986). Mother–infant interaction in multi-problem families: Finding those at risk. *Journal of the Academy of Child Psychiatry, 25*, 631–640.

Bernstein, V., Percansky, C., & Hans, S. (1987, April). *Screening for social-emotional impairment in infants born to teenage mothers.* Paper presented at the biennial Conference of the Society for Research in Child Development, Baltimore.

Brooks-Gunn, J., & Furstenberg, F. (1986). The children of adolescent mothers: Physical, academic, and psychological outcomes. *Developmental Review, 6*, 224.

Clark, R., (1983). *Family life and school achievement: Why poor black children succeed or fail.* Chicago: University of Chicago Press.

Clarke-Stewart, A., & Fein, G. (1983). Early childhood programs. In P. Mussen (Ed.), *Handbook of child psychology* (4th ed.) (Vol 2, pp. 917–999). New York: Wiley.

Cowen, E. L. (1973). Social and community interventions. In P. H. Mussen & M. R. Rosenzweig (Eds.), *Annual review of psychology* (Vol. 24). Palo Alto, CA: Annual Reviews, Inc.

Erickson, M., Sroufe, L., & Egeland, B. (1985). The relationship between quality of attachment and behavior problems in preschool in a high-risk sample. In I. Bretherton & E. Waters (Eds.), Growing points in attachment theory and research. *Monographs of the Society for Research in Child Development, 50* (1–2, Serial No. 209), 147–166.

Fraiberg, S. (Ed.). (1980). *Clinical studies in infant mental health,* New York: Basic Books.

Frankenburg, W., & Dodds, J. (1967). Denver Developmental Screening Test. *Journal of Pediatrics, 71,* 181–191.

Gartner, A. (1971). *Paraprofessionals and their performance.* New York: Praeger.

Gartner, A. (1979). The effectiveness of paraprofessionals in service delivery. In S. Alley, J. Blanton, & R. Feldman (Eds.), *Professionals in mental health: Theory and practice.* New York: Human Sciences Press.

Gee, J. P. *What is literacy* (1987, March). Unpublished manuscript prepared for Mailman Foundation Conference on Families and Literacy. Harvard Graduate School of Education, Cambridge.

Gershenson, H., Musick, J., Ruch-Ross, Magee, V., Rubino, K., & Rosenberg, D. (in press). The prevalence of sexual abuse among teenage mothers. *Journal of Interpersonal Violence.*

Gitelson, M. (1952). The emotional position of the analyst in the psychoanalytic situation. *International Journal of Psycho-Analysis, 33,* 1–10.

Goode, W. (1965). Encroachment, charlatanism, and the emerging professions. *American Sociological Review, 25,* 902–927.

Gordon, M. T. (1976). *Involving paraprofessionals in the helping process: The case of federal probation.* Cambridge, MA: Ballinger.

Greenspan, S. (1981). *Psychopathology and adaptation in infancy and early childhood: Principles of clinical diagnosis and preventive intervention.* New York: International Universities Press.

Greenspan, S. (1982). Developmental morbidity in infants in multi-risk factor families. *Public Health Reports, 97,* 16–23.

Greenspan, S., & Poisson, S. (1983). *Greenspan-Lieberman Observation System for Assessment of Caregiver–Infant Interaction During Semi-structured play (GLOS).* Rockville, MD: DHHS, Division of Maternal and Child Health.

Halpern, R. (1986, Summer). Community-based support for high risk young families. *Social Policy,* pp. 17–18, 47–50.

Halpern, R., & Convey, L. (1983). Community support for adolescent parents and their children: The parent-to-parent program in Vermont. *Journal of Primary Prevention, 3,* 160–173.

Halpern, R., & Larner, M. (in press). The design of family support programs in high risk communities: Lessons from the Child Survival/Fair Start Initiative. In D. Powell (Ed.), *Parent support and education: Consequences for children and families.* Norwood, NJ: Ablex Publishing.

Kalafat, J., & Boroto, D. R. (1977). The paraprofessional movement as a paradigm community psychology endeavor. *Journal of Contemporary Psychology, 5,* 3–12.

Kingdon, J. (1984). *Agendas, alternatives, and public policies.* Boston: Little, Brown.

Kohut, H. (1971). *The analysis of the self.* New York: International Universities Press.

Musick, J., & Barbera-Stein, L. (1988). The role of research in an innovative preventive initiative. In D. Powell (Ed.), *Parent education and support programs: Consequences for children and families* (pp. 209–227). Norwood, NJ: Ablex Publishing.

Musick, J., Bernstein, V., Percansky, C., & Stott, F. (1987). A chain of enablement: Using community-based programs to strengthen relationships between teen parents and their infants. *Zero to Three, 8,* 1–6.

Musick, J., Handler, A., & Waddill, K. (1984). Teens and adoption: A pregnancy resolution alternative? *Children Today, 13,* 24–29.

Musick, J., & Mosena, P. (1988). *Teens as parents: The providers' perspective.* Unpublished research report, The Ounce of Prevention Fund, Chicago.

Pearl, A., & Riessman, F. (1965). *New careers for the poor.* New York: Free Press.

Powell, D. (Ed.). (1987). *Parent education and support programs: Consequences for children and families.* Norwood, NJ: Ablex Publishing.

Reiff, R., & Riessman, F. (1965). The indigenous nonprofessional: A strategy of change in community action and community mental health programs. *Community-Mental Health Journal* (Monograph).

Richan, W. (1978). Training of lay helpers. In F. Kaslow (Ed.), *Supervision, consultation and staff training in the helping professions* (pp. 115–132). San Francisco: Jossey-Bass.

Riessman, F. (1965). The "helper" therapy principle. *Social Work, 10,* 26–32.

Sobey, F. (1970). *The nonprofessional revolution in mental health.* New York: Columbia University Press.

Truax, C. B. (1965). *An approach toward training for the aide therapist: Research and implications.* Fayetteville, AR: Arkansas Rehabilitation Research and Training Center.

Weiss, C. H., with Bucinvalos, M. (1980). *Social science research and decision-making.* New York: Columbia University Press.

Weiss, H., & Jacobs, F. (1984). *The effectiveness and evaluation of family support and education programs.* Final report to the Charles Stewart Mott Foundation.

Zigler, E., & Weiss, H. (1985). Family support systems: An ecological approach to child development. In R. Rapoport (Ed.), *Children, youth and families: The action-research relationship* (pp. 166–205). New York: Cambridge University Press.

28 *Parent advocacy: A resource for early intervention*

PEGGY PIZZO

Organized parent advocacy combines the efforts of parents who share the common activity of making government and child-serving institutions respond better to the individual needs of children and families. Parent advocates have many goals, including the establishment of mutual support among themselves, institutional reform, and new laws that provide a fairer distribution of resources for all children who share a particular experience. This shared experience might center on special health care needs, adoption, single parenthood, or on some special handicapping condition or life event.

In early intervention, parents in mutual support of one another seek to change health care agencies, school systems, and the institutional practices of pediatrics, special education, nursing, physical therapy, occupational therapy, and child development to achieve several objectives. These include making it more possible for very young children with disabilities and developmental and medical vulnerabilities to live at home, receive multidisciplinary services within the family context, and, in the earliest months and years of life, obtain specialized health and educational services to stimulate their linguistic, motoric, intellectual, emotional, and social development (Association for the Care of Children's Health, 1987; National Center for Clinical Infant Programs [NCCIP], 1988).

Parent advocates favor the establishment of early intervention services in every community so that children can receive the services they need without traveling great distances, which can create additional stress for the family. Parent advocates also seek to use the power of government and organized consumer action to reform established institutions so that the services of those institutions will validate and empower parents and families as the center of young children's lives. Fueling this reform movement is the powerful sense of responsibility that many parents of disabled and special-needs children feel toward the development of these children, who may eventually be evaluated and treated by a hundred or more professionals over the course of their lifetimes.

This chapter will address three issues: first, the origins of parent advocacy for early intervention services within the context of the parent advocacy movement in general; second, the sensitive issue of anger between parent advocates and professionals during both advocacy and the delivery of early intervention services; and third, the implications of this movement for the creation of new models of human services.

668

ORIGINS OF PARENT ADVOCACY AND THE SHARED EXPERIENCE

Parent advocacy originates from a shared participation in events that span a spectrum of parental experiences. On one end of the scale there are anxious waits for diagnoses and prognoses; powerful feelings of helplessness as one's child repeatedly undergoes physical or emotional pain; the "roller coaster" uncertainty of sometimes relentlessly unpredictable medical complications to a child's chronic condition; and feelings of entrapment in a web of negative cultural images about parents. The shared experiences on the other end of the spectrum include moments of victory, joy, and relief at challenges mastered, assaults to health overcome, and encounters with hope-sustaining breakthroughs (NCCIP, 1985; Turnbull & Turnbull, 1985).

It is the unique nature of this shared experience as parents of children with discernible impairments that causes parent advocates to believe that only they can truly articulate their special perspective to policymakers, professionals, researchers, and others. Their point of view seems inherently justified by the obvious shared experience that appears in written and verbal accounts by parents (Pizzo, 1983). This shared experience distinguishes parents of children with special needs and even separates them into a world (or as social scientists might say, a subculture) where they are insiders. Those who do not participate in this shared experience are inevitably, no matter how sympathetic, outsiders.

The sociological origins of parent advocacy: Exclusion and denial of opportunity

Exclusion of their children from the mainstream and denial of opportunities for a fair start in life are conditions experienced by many parents who advocate expanded and improved early intervention services. These experiences of exclusion give birth in part to the commitment to create a sense of inclusion among parent advocates. Exclusion from decision making that affects their children also intensifies parent anger.

Inevitably, organized mutual support and advocacy by parents creates an even stronger distinction between insiders (i.e., parents of children with special needs) and outsiders. This is particularly true when parents propose that groups of advocates should include only individuals who have undergone the unique parental experience of coping with the challenges already described. When a shared developmental condition or life event is the basis for organizing a group, the additional experience of participating in planned mutual support and advocacy bonds parent advocates together powerfully and helps them to create a strong sense of family among themselves.

There is, as well, another source for the advocacy experience. Like mutual help, advocacy emerges from an experience of stress – either one's own or someone else's. There have always been concerned human beings who have advocated proper care for homeless or sick children and for the children of the poor (Bremner, 1970–1974). All advocacy is fueled by feelings of caring and commitment, but the first-hand knowledge of the suffering of children, of their exclusion from a fair opportunity for normal development, is a special motivation.

Self-advocacy, the assertion of one's own rights in a sustained effort to systematically improve unfair social and economic conditions, is also a long-standing American tradition. The exploitation of industrial laborers by factory owners; the many prohibitions directed at blacks; the denial to women of equal pay for equal work – all of these conditions illustrate that in the history of organized self-advocacy in America, the shared experience of exclusion and denial of equal opportunity is a basis for effective action.

Although it has roots in activities initiated during the 1930s and 1940s, parent advocacy for children with special needs began to flower in the 1960s and 1970s, at a time when the civil rights and women's movements were also spreading a belief in equality deep within our national culture. Parent advocacy, thus, is imbued with the notion that people experiencing protracted obstacles to their opportunities for healthy, productive lives have a natural right – and as parents, virtually a responsibility – to speak out, to object strongly, and to remove those obstacles to equal opportunity from their own paths and those of their children (Turnbull & Summers, 1985). In the sixties, seventies, and eighties, hundreds of parent support and advocacy groups, inspired to no small degree by the success that parents of children with special needs had in winning new laws and obtaining needed services, sprang up to address issues of single parenting, adoption, child custody, drunk driving, drug use among teens, childbirth, and many other issues (Pizzo, 1983).

The psychological origins of parent advocacy

The psychological origins of this movement among parents lie in the powerful force that parent–child bonding and attachment gives to the normal adult impulse to protect children from harm and to achieve and sustain both physical and psychological proximity to a child when harm seems likely to occur. To parent advocates this psychological proximity – a sense of closeness based on a sense of understanding the child – is so critical that parent advocacy efforts often begin when parents feel that their psychological proximity to their children is thwarted by actions or attitudes adopted by institutions or professionals. Parent advocates want to establish policies, procedures, and practices that guarantee respect for parental psychological proximity in relationships between professionals and children, as well as in relationships between professionals and parents.

Parents of children with special needs often have children whose behavior is difficult to understand. Autistic children, children with aggressive or unpredictable outbursts caused by neurological damage, and children who do not seem to "tune in" to the world profoundly challenge a parent's sense of competence and self-worth. Such children elude psychological proximity. At the same time, these children cause parents to feel the need for even greater proximity than do other children because they are so clearly at risk for emotional harm. Parents then find themselves trapped in the uncomfortable dilemma of knowing that they need to achieve psychological proximity in order to realize the powerful desire to protect their child from harm, and yet finding it enormously difficult to understand their child's behavior and to be psychologically close.

Thus, parents strongly object when relationships between professionals and children in early intervention and other services are established without respect for the parents' responsibility and desire to achieve psychological proximity to the child, even when there is good rapport between the professional and the child. Such a situation is described by Akerley (1985) in her harrowing account of conflicts with psychotherapists who attempted to "rescue" her autistic child from her. Detailing incident after incident of painful disregard of her own understanding of her child's behavior, she recounts one situation in which the physicians involved seem to be disappointed that her autistic son, who had finally learned to kiss, kissed his parents first before the medical staff. She says:

> If those child therapists really wanted to help Eddie, I believe they should have tried to make themselves psychologically invisible. They should have done all in their power to enhance the normal relationships in his life. Instead, motivated by Technicolor rescue fantasies, they charged between a child and the people who loved him most in an egocentric effort to make themselves paramount (Akerley, 1978, p. 28).

To some extent, all individuals involved with a young child become attached to the child. That is a desirable outcome. Competition between parents and professionals may thus be an inevitable consequence of the young child's powerful capacity to quite literally make people fall in love with him or her – a capacity finely honed over thousands of years of human evolution and one that is essential to the sheer survival of young children.

Parent advocates believe that some professionals understand proximity-seeking behavior in children as a normal result of parent–child attachment, but do not understand that parents, too, engage in proximity-seeking behavior as a healthy, inevitable consequence of parent–child attachment. Normal proximity-seeking impulses are one reason that parents of children with special health and developmental vulnerabilities want laws, regulations, and judicial decisions that acknowledge parents' rights to primacy in the lives of their young children. For example, parent advocates often seek hospital policies that guarantee 24-hour physical access by parents to children who are hospitalized. These policies address the right to physical proximity. Parent advocates also seek hospital policies that require professionals to offer clear verbal and written explanations (in the parents' native language) of the child's diagnosis and prognosis. These policies address the right to psychological proximity and to an informed understanding of the child. When professionals misread parental proximity-seeking behavior as "neurotic" or abnormal, they fuel parental anger, disrupt parent–professional collaboration, and intensify parent advocates' determination to secure legal and policy guarantees in all decisions regarding their dependent children's lives.

Cultural origins of parent advocacy: Negative images of parents

Among other influences, parent advocacy is a response to three cultural images of parents that recur continually in the literature describing policies and programs established to help children. Fundamental and sometimes unconscious beliefs about the relationship between parents and "experts" often become clearer as one analyzes these images in the language and writing of policymakers, professionals, and scholars who concern themselves with children and families. In particular, three images – the Incompetent Parent, the Victimized Parent, and the Resourceful Parent – reflect sentiments that guide the assumptions upon which services to children have been and continue to be built. These images reveal attitudes that have influenced the perspectives professionals are taught (subtly or overtly) to have about parents. Finally, these images shape our feelings about ourselves as parents, our interactions with each other, and our fundamental relationships with our children. Thus, they are strong currents in the headstream of parent activism (Pizzo, 1983; Pizzo, 1987).

The image of the Incompetent Parent portrays a person who is incapable of meeting essential requirements of child rearing. In this portrayal, moral defects, ignorance, emotional inadequacies, and deficient skills cause incompetence. Parental incompetence in turn "results" in misfortune and harm to children, or thwarts some basic right of the child, such as the right to equal opportunity. Typically, the Incompetent Parent image appears in discussions about why professionals, programs, public and private service, and government in general should do more to help children.

The Victimized Parent image portrays a person who is well meaning but a helpless victim of powerful forces, warped by events he or she is unable to influence or control in the rearing of his or her children. Parents here fail to raise children well because external pressures prevent them from doing so, not because of personal incapacity or moral torpor. Traditionally, the Victimized Parent is treated as a sympathetic figure, struggling with oppressive economic and social conditions that obstruct good child development. Victimized Parents typically are overwhelmed by these conditions, which can be countered chiefly by professionals, programs, and government. More recently, however, in some scholarly works, legislative testimony, public statements, and advocacy bronchures, parents are described as victims of the very forces that are supposed to aid them: professionals, experts, helping institutions, and government (Lasch, 1977).

There is now a third parental image, the Resourceful Parent (Pizzo, 1983), which many parent advocates have constructed for themselves. The Resourceful Parent is first of all a decision-maker who works hard to discover what resources are available for rearing children and what choices can be made, often in defiance of powerful forces. When few options for children exist, the Resourceful Parent generates new choices by combining forces with other parents to establish halfway houses, peer counseling, support groups, or preschool programs. Parents also generate alternatives through advocacy for institutional change or for a law that provides new authority and appropriations for fairer, more effective services, and for protection of children. Resourceful Parents want help that is more accessible, more responsive, more humane, and more accountable to parents.

The central shared characteristic of the Incompetent Parent image and the Victimized Parent image is passivity. In contrast, Resourceful Parents are contributors to public policy, not just beneficiaries of it. They are valued partners with professionals in the delivery of public services to children; they are mediators, protective buffers between vulnerable children and powerful institutions; they are final arbiters (or at least the parties with the most rights to that position) of all decisions about the child.

Activism, then, is the central shared characteristic of the Resourceful Parent image, in contrast to the passive and negative images that prevailed previously. In creating this active image, parent advocates helped to fuel advocacy for a whole new type of human service – early intervention programs in which parents are members of the multidisciplinary team.

In this process parent advocates have also actively expressed their feelings about early intervention services. Whereas earlier generations of parents might have been more inclined to be passive and to endure interactions with professionals and helping institutions toward which they felt anger, this is no longer the case. Thus, early intervention professionals have had to learn to deal with painful feelings that probably always have existed but may never have been directly expressed before.

THE ISSUE OF ANGER

One obstacle to parent–professional collaboration in advocacy and in the provision of early intervention services is parental anger. Professionals involved in early intervention services often encounter parent advocates who express anger more easily than other parents and who may seem more angry in general. This seems paradoxical, in that parent advocates fight for the early intervention services which they subsequently seem to criticize. Why would parents work so hard for something that they seem to be angry about?

There are a number of reasons for parental anger. First, the nature of the diagnostic process creates anxiety, which provokes anger. Second, the knowledge needed to carry out early intervention services is not immediately accessible to parents. Third, undesirable professional activities sometimes intensify parental anxiety and self-blame. And, finally, the very experience of advocacy can sometimes temporarily increase parental anger. However, in the long range, parent advocacy equalizes the relationships between parents and professionals and carries great potential for reducing anger in parent–professional collaborations.

Parental anger and competence during diagnosis and early intervention services

Parent–professional interaction during diagnosis and the delivery of early intervention services is typically controlled by the professionals' exercise of power. The reasons for this are straightforward. Parents cannot make an objective diagnosis, they cannot provide objective treatment, and they cannot simply "fix" the child's problem. When diagnosis and treatment of a professional's child is required, even the most knowledgeable professional must turn to another professional for help. In most cases, this is not what provokes anger. Rather, having to turn to a professional who does not know what to do, does not care enough, or who insensitively exacerbates the self-blame that many parents feel as they come to terms with a diagnosis is what sparks anger.

Parents cannot just assume control of the situation in cases like these. For most individuals, the knowledge needed to competently assess and remediate health and developmental conditions is not accessible. It is highly technical knowledge that is locked within the language of biological and chemical science and therapeutic and developmental practice. Without advanced formal schooling most individuals cannot master that language nor attain the requisite clinical skills. Consequently, parents must – for something absolutely essential to their well-being – depend on a professional who can (and might) walk away. This dependence can be felt very keenly during the weeks and days following diagnosis, and the child's earliest years and in the period when parent and child participate in early intervention programs.

Thus, parental anxiety during early intervention emerges from at least three sources: (1) threatened loss of the child, loss of proximity to the child, or loss of one's dreams for the child; (2) dependence on other human beings for actions sometimes absolutely essential to the child's safety or development; and (3) damage to feelings of competence and self-worth and to one's identity as a parent. This anxiety, when sufficiently heightened, can trigger intense anger.

Not every parent experiences anger and sadness around the time of diagnosis of the child, but many do. Consider the realization reached by a physician and mother of two whose third child was diagnosed to be mentally retarded (Ziskin, 1985). First, she blamed herself and thoroughly reviewed every aspect of her pregnancy, looking for junctures where she might have eaten something, taken a medication, or been in contact with an illness that could have resulted in her daughter's mental retardation. Subsequently, she turned to her husband and blamed him, but he refused to accept the blame. She recounts:

In an attempt to get me away from my problem, my husband took me along on a convention trip to Toronto. On that long drive through the mountains of New York State and Canada, I remember feeling that I had become a completely different person. I felt that my ego had been wiped out. My superego with all its guilts had become the most prominent part of my personality and I had completely lost my self-esteem. Any credits of self-worth that I could give myself from any of my personal endeavors meant nothing. Graduating from college and a first-rate medical school, surviving an internship, practicing medicine, and having two beautiful sons and a good marriage counted for nil. All I knew at this point was that I was the mother of an abnormal and most likely retarded child (Ziskin, 1985, p. 68).

The self-blame and anger experienced by some parents as they come to terms with a diagnosis that is difficult and painful is less intense, however, than the anger experienced while ricocheting from one uncertain diagnosis to another. In situations like these, anxiety and anger are exacerbated by a sense of helpless dependence on a professional who is seemingly invested with quasi religious powers but whose diagnoses are uncertain and unreliable. Akerley (1985) describes the frustration of searching for a diagnosis, especially after months or years of believing that something is wrong with a child. Parents who spend the early years of a child's life trying to persuade the primary health care provider that development is not occurring as it should harbor particularly strong hopes for a definitive diagnosis during the first in-depth evaluation – hopes that can be shattered in ways particularly difficult for parents to bear.

With luck our pediatrician refers us to an appropriate specialist, and we are (or should be) on our way. We transfer our trust to the new god and wait expectantly for the oracle to speak. Instead of the strong, authoritative voice of wisdom, we more often hear an evasive stammer 'Can't give you a definite diagnosis...uh [mumble, mumble]...virtually untestable...Let us see him...[cough, cough]...again in a year' (Akerley, 1985, p. 24).

The rarer the diagnosis, or the more uncertain the outcome, the more some parents are likely to repress their feelings of anger and anxiety; professional good-will is simply too important to risk. Parents of premature infants have described a similar situation after discharge of their infants from the hospital.

The doctors and therapists who follow these tiny babies look for benchmarks and try to identify obvious conditions, but generally present an attitude of wait and see to the parents, who are anxious for definite answers. These parents don't dare question the medical staff too much for pressure leads to resistance, and parents need the professionals as their allies and sources of comfort (Gould & Moses, 1985, p. 14).

Undesirable professional activities may also spark parental anger, principally because they intensify parental anxiety about some powerful professional's competence and degree of caring for both the parent and the child. Some actions described in the literature of parent advocates (Kupfer, 1985; NCCIP, 1987; Pizzo, 1983; Roos, 1978; Turnbull & Turnbull, 1978, 1985) include:

1. mistakes in dosage or computation of critical test results;
2. failure to read the child's history, records or file before important junctures in the diagnostic process;
3. reluctance to share information on the theory that it would be too unpleasant for parents and would provoke them into behavior harmful to the child;
4. patronizing overemphasis on therapy for parents, to the detriment of straightforward sharing of information;
5. defeatist attitudes and "giving in" by professionals to feelings of hopelessness;
6. use of confusing and sometimes frightening jargon; and
7. resorting to judgmental attitudes, particularly when a situation includes diagnosis or treatment.

Finally, the very experience of advocacy can temporarily exacerbate tension in parent–professional relationships because parent advocates may come to realize their own personal power. In fact, they have the power to influence both the way those services are offered and the budgets that control them.

A parent advocate who has felt, perhaps for the first time in his or her life, a new identity as a powerful rather than powerless individual may expect this feeling almost automatically to carry over into the period of assessment and treatment services. This expectation, however, can be frustrated for two reasons. First, professionals possess an inherent power, particularly during diagnosis. Second, even though parents learning to become advocates may change their sense of identity, professionals who have not been through any similar transformations may not have changed the way they view themselves or parents. If anything, the passage of a new law or an increase in the commitment of funds validates the belief that professionals are providing a much-needed and significant service and solidifies the professional identity as an admired, respected helper, and even as a saver of children.

For decades professional schools have trained people to assist the powerless and to be helpers, givers, and assessors. When professionals break with this tradition and enter into consultant roles, or into co-case manager or cotherapist and group leader partnerships with parents, the new skills needed to be successful at navigating new interactions have to be acquired. If formal retraining is not required, certainly time is (Gartner & Reissman, 1977). However, even if change does not occur on the professional side of the partnership or if it is slow to occur, there is still inherently more equality during parent–professional collaboration during advocacy activities than there is during diagnosis and early intervention services.

The roots of this increased equality are threefold. First, as long as parents apply themselves with persistence and find a veteran advocate to teach them, they can attain the expert knowledge needed to be successful advocates without advanced formal schooling. In fact, many parents can attain this type of expert knowledge about advocacy as well as or better than professionals. Second, the elimination of judgments about a parent's individual child also facilitates equality of relationships. Third, skilled parent advocates who can organize a constituency group and who know how to move a law toward passage can, when they choose to do so, exercise power to obtain increased appropriations for service, training, and research – power that professionals respect, sometimes need, and often admire (Biklen, 1974; Pizzo, 1983). Thus, as a result of advocacy efforts, professionals may become more dependent on parent advocates, equalizing the relationships even more.

It is important to note that anger is often felt and expressed by parents who greatly appreciate the actions of professionals and helping institutions. Some of the same parent advocates who express anger are also profoundly relieved that new opportunities for early intervention services finally exist (NCCIP, 1985; Turnbull & Turnbull, 1985).

In addition, some personal relationships between professionals and parent advocates become so strong and so positive that they are a source of deep satisfaction to both sides of the partnership. And many parents understand the stresses involved in working with children who have special needs. Parent advocates sometimes try to articulate what they see as the viewpoint of professionals who are criticized by parents. One special educator who is also the mother of a mentally retarded son explains:

While I have been offended as a parent, I have also been rebuffed as a teacher. I have found that many parents think that no one else knows their problems, no one else has experienced their heartaches, no one else understands. In conferences the parents of my students would frequently say, "but you don't know what we go through." While I could empathize on one level as a parent, I also was angered as a teacher. . . . To say the teacher does not understand is insulting. Moreover, the teacher sometimes spends hours outlining remedial or developmental procedures which should be continued at home. In many cases, it is obvious that the procedures have not been followed (Schulz, 1985, p. 7).

To work as equals in advocating expanded and improved early intervention services, and in the actual delivery of services, professionals need to gain insight into the sensitive issue of anger between parent advocates and professionals. Professionals need to understand that parent advocates may say out loud what many parents who participate in early intervention services feel but do not articulate. Both the degree of sensitivity that exists around anger and the degree to which its existence is rarely discussed openly indicate that professionals seeking to gain these insights will find it difficult to do so.

IMPLICATIONS: REVOLUTION IN THE HUMAN SERVICES

Acting in concert with sympathetic professionals, parent activists in the 1970s revolutionized hospitalized childbirth practices, special educational opportunities for handicapped children, hospital policies regarding parental presence during a child's hospital stay, opportunities for adoption of older, minority, or handicapped children, and drug abuse prevention and treatment programs. This revolution accomplished several objectives. First, more services were created where too few previously existed. Second, profoundly different services were authorized, funded, and/or promoted, services where parents are to be accorded a respected partnership role in deciding what happens to their children. Third, the laws, judicial decrees, regulations, and nongovernmental policies that were established as part of winning both new services and different services fundamentally changed the perceptions about the rights parents can now exercise on behalf of their children (Pizzo, 1983). Laws such as the Amendents to the Education of the Handicapped Act (P.L. 99-457), the Adoption Assistance and Child Welfare Reform Act of 1980, and the proposed Act for Better Child Care codify the rights that were previously a privilege for only a few.

These rights vary. Scattered amidst the laws and regulations of the past decade are provisions that strengthen the rights of parental access to children and to information collected about them, and that call for direct regular discussions between parents and the professionals involved with their children, parental involvement in decisions that affect children, and parental oversight of the policies and administrative practices that ultimately shape those services. The continued exercising of these rights will create an even more profound revolution in the expectations, attitudes, and behavior that characterize human services for children.

Already, models of new partnerships between parents and professionals have emerged. Parents now function in the following positions: evaluators and members of the multidisciplinary team developing the Individualized Family Service Plan (IFSP) and the Individual Education Plan (IEP); consultants to the treatment team in pediatric cancer services; cosigners (even for parents reported as abusive) to contracts designed to improve the safety and well-being of the child in foster care and child-welfare services; members of parent policy or advisory councils with responsibility for approving budgets, grant applications, and personnel decisions; coleader of parent education courses; and cotherapists in groups of parents struggling with severe stress (Pizzo,

1983, 1987). In early intervention services, these new roles reflect an understanding that an essential goal of early intervention is to foster parent closeness to the child – both the physical proximity and the psychological proximity or closeness that results from a deeper, more confident understanding of the child.

One of the most important revolutions is taking place in the process of diagnosis. Parents who once felt excluded and helpless during the diagnosis of their child's condition have the right now, because of the IFSP mandated under P.L. 99-457, to be participants – Resourceful Parents – in the assessment of their own children. The congressional report accompanying the Education of the Handicapped Act Amendments of 1986 – the document that spells out congressional intent – states that " ach handicapped infant or toddler and the infant's or toddler's family must receive a multidisciplinary assessment of unique needs and the identification of services appropriate to meet such needs and a written individualized family service plan developed by a multidisciplinary team, which includes the parents or guardian" (NCCIP, 1987, p. 12).

In short, early intervention professionals who wish to work collaboratively with parent advocates need to understand the sociological, psychological, and cultural origins of parent advocacy; the reasons for parental anger and its relationship to parent advocacy; and the ramifications of human services that include parents as decision makers in all that happens to their young children. Given that early intervention itself is a growing area of human service, the possibilities for a great diversity of new collaborations and benefits to children and families are vast. Two decades ago these types of human services were just being launched on a wide scale (see Shonkoff & Meisels, this volume). Two decades from now parent advocates and their sympathetic professional allies will undoubtedly have completed a revolution. They will have extended to the nation's youngest children and their parents early intervention services that minimize disability as much as possible and that support parents who deal with significant life challenges. That will be but one revolution. The other will be the one that accords to parents their rightful role at the heart, rather than at the periphery, of services to their children.

REFERENCES

Akerley, M. (1985). False gods and angry prophets. In A. P. Turnbull & H. R. Turnbull (Eds.), *Parents speak out: Then and now* (pp. 23–33). Columbus, OH: Merrill.

Association for the Care of Children's Health. (1987). *Family centered care for children with special health care needs.* Washington, DC: Author.

Biklen, D. (1974). *Let our children go.* Syracuse, NY: Human Policy Press.

Bremner, R. (1970–1974). *Children and youth in america: A documentary history* (Vols. 1–3). Cambridge: Harvard University Press.

Gartner, A., & Reissman, F. (1979). *Self-help in the human services.* San Francisco: Jossey-Bass.

Gould, P., & Moses, L. (1985). Mild developmental delays from a parent's perspective. In National Center for Clinical Infant Programs, *Equals in this partnership* (pp. 14–18). Washington, DC: Author.

Kupfer, F. (1985). Severely and/or multiply disabled children. In National Center for Clinical Infant Programs, *Equals in this partnership* (pp. 18–25). Washington, DC: Author.

Lasch, C. (1977). *Haven in a heartless world: The family besieged.* New York: Basic Books.

National Center for Clinical Infant Programs. (1985). *Equals in this partnership.* Washington, DC: Author.

National Center for Clinical Infant Programs. (1987). *Report accompanying the Education of the Handicapped Act Amendments of 1986 and commenting on P.L. 99-457.* Washington, DC: Author.

National Center for Clinical Infant Programs. (1988). *The open door: Parent participation in state policymaking about children with special health needs.* Washington, DC: Author.

Pizzo, P. (1983). *Parent to parent: Working together for ourselves and our children.* Boston: Beacon Press.

Pizzo, P. (1987). Parent to parent support groups: Advocates for social change. In L. Kagan, D. Powell, B. Weissbourd, & E. Zigler (Eds.), *American family support programs* (pp. 228–245). New Haven: Yale University Press.

Roos, P. (1978). Parents of mentally retarded children: Misunderstood and mistreated. In A. P. Turnbull, & H. R. Turnbull (Eds), *Parents speak out: Growing with a handicapped child.* Columbus, OH: Merrill.

Schulz, J. (1985). The parent–professional conflict. In A. P. Turnbull & H. R. Turnbull (Eds.), *Parents speak out: Then and now* (pp. 3–11). Columbus, OH: Merrill.

Turnbull, A. P., & Summers, J. (1985, April). From parent involvement to family support: Evolution to revolution. Paper presented at the Down's Syndrome State of the Art Conference, Boston.

Turnbull, A. P., & Turnbull, H. R. (Eds.). (1978). *Parents speak out: Growing with a handicapped child.* Columbus, OH: Merrill.

Turnbull, A. P., & Turnbull, H. R. (Eds.). (1985). *Parents speak out: Then and now.* Columbus, OH: Merrill.

U.S. Congress, House. *Education of the Handicapped Amendments of 1986: Report to Accompany H.R. 5520.* 99th Congress, 2nd session, Report 99-860, p. 12.

Ziskin, L. (1985). The story of Jennie. In A. P. Turnbull & H. R. Turnbull (Eds.), *Parents speak out: Then and now* (pp. 67–75). Columbus, OH: Merrill.

29 Preparing personnel to serve at-risk and disabled infants, toddlers, and preschoolers

NANCY K. KLEIN AND PHILIPPA CAMPBELL

The passage of P.L. 99-457, the Education for All Handicapped Children Act Amendments of 1986, with its accompanying requirements for early intervention services for infants, toddlers, and preschoolers with disabilities, provides a unique opportunity. This new law, the most far-reaching federal policy ever mandated for early intervention services, strengthens incentives for states to serve 3- to 5-year-old children with disabilities by school year 1990–91. Furthermore, it establishes discretionary programs for states that wish to serve infants and toddlers from birth to 3 years of age. States choosing to participate in the state grant program must designate a lead agency, develop a statewide plan, establish agreements for interagency cooperation, and require Individualized Family Service Plans for each child and family.

Closely related to the successful implementation of this comprehensive mandate, which provides both an opportunity and a challenge for professionals and advocates who have long sought such services, is the design, implementation, and evaluation of high-quality personnel preparation programs. Indeed, given the diversity and complexity of problems of the target population defined in P.L. 99-457, one might assume that successful implementation of both the spirit and letter of the law will be a direct result of the quality of personnel available to provide such early intervention programs.

States today face a critical shortage of qualified personnel to serve young children at risk and with handicaps, and the requirements of P.L. 99-457 will magnify the problem (Weiner & Koppelman, 1987). In a survey of the 50 states and the District of Columbia, Meisels, Harbin, Modigliani, & Olson (1988) found that 88% of the states had a current documented shortage of early childhood special education personnel to serve children from birth to 3, and 81% anticipated the shortage to continue into the foreseeable future. Similarly, 81% of the states reported current shortages regarding personnel to serve 3- to 5-year-old children, whereas 65% reported anticipated shortages until 1989. Moreover, trained clinicians needed to provide services mandated by the new law, including speech, occupational, and physical therapists, were reported by Meisels et al. (1988) as in even shorter supply. Current estimates by the states indicate that more than 95% have personnel shortages in these specialties and approximately 80% of the states expect these shortages to continue to the end of the decade. Clearly there is a pressing national need for highly qualified early childhood special education personnel to provide early intervention services for young children with disabilities.

The purpose of this chapter is to explore several issues related to personnel preparation in Early Childhood Special Education (ECSE). These issues will include a review

679

of prevailing theories and philosophies from both early childhood and special education that can guide the development of models for personnel preparation, various roles for ECSE personnel, bodies ~f knowledge from which personnel preparation content can be drawn, and selected competencies associated with high-quality ECSE personnel. A model for a dual specialization personnel preparation program will be described and, finally, recommendations for future research will be suggested.

EARLY CHILDHOOD SPECIAL EDUCATION – A NEW ENDEAVOR FOR PERSONNEL PREPARATION ACTIVITIES

Since the late 1960s, there have been many types of early intervention programs available for young children at risk for developmental delay or those with established disabilities (Guralnick & Bennett, 1987c). The effectiveness of these programs has been well documented (Casto, White, & Taylor, 1983; Clark-Stewart & Fein, 1983; Hanson, 1984; Hayden & Haring, 1977; Lazar & Darlington, 1982; Meisels, 1985a; Schweinhart & Weikert, 1981; Shonkoff & Hauser-Cram, 1987). Although service delivery models, target populations, goals, evaluation designs, and outcome measures vary considerably across programs (Guralnick & Bennett, 1987b), there is a clear research base for early intervention (Anastasiow, 1986). The unique needs of at-risk children and those with disabilities from birth to 5 years and their families have implications for training personnel (Beckman & Burke, 1984). And, finally, issues have emerged from research that can guide the development of models for personnel preparation in ECSE (Guralnick & Bennett, 1987a).

Target populations

The first question to be addressed in considering components in ECSE personnel preparation programs is the nature of the target populations. Children who have been and who will be identified for services include the following: (1) infants, toddlers, and preschoolers with identified handicapping conditions (e.g., Down syndrome, spina bifida); (2) infants, toddlers, and preschoolers at increased environmental risk (e.g., extreme poverty, teenage parent); and (3) infants, toddlers, and preschoolers at increased biological risk (e.g., history of very low birth weight, asphyxia). Early intervention programs for these groups of children are intended to "enhance development, minimize potential developmental delays, remediate existing problems, and prevent institutionalization by providing developmental and therapeutic services to children and support and instruction to families" (Meisels, 1985b, p. 115).

Credentials

Although there has been a substantial increase in the numbers of early intervention programs during the past decade, this increase has not been accompanied by state credentialing of personnel to work in these programs. Stile, Abernathy, Pettibone, and Wachtel (1984) reported that a survey of 50 states, the District of Columbia, Samoa, and Puerto Rico regarding the certification of ECSE personnel indicated that only 20 (37%) states reported a separate early childhood special education endorsement or certificate, and three (6%) states reported that such requirements were under development. Although few data exist regarding the relationship of certification requirements to increased quality of ECSE personnel and the services they provide (Smith & Powers,

1987), it is clear that an ECSE credential will be created, similar to other areas of education. Many states are using a "band-aid approach to dealing with shortages" (Weiner & Koppleman, 1987, p. 69) by issuing emergency temporary teaching certificates. However, a much more organized effort at the state level will be required to reduce the current personnel shortage. Universities can help alleviate the problem, but are reluctant to do so unless states mandate services and programs to train early childhood special education personnel.

Efforts to develop certification are hindered by the fact that the lead agency required for the state grants to serve infants and toddlers is often not the education agency (Meisels, 1985b; Meisels et al., 1988) and credentials are likely to be differentiated for those serving infants and personnel serving preschool age children (McCollum, 1987). Furthermore, standards for personnel have been or will be developed separately for early childhood and special education. For example, the Council for Exceptional Children is developing standards for special education training and the National Association for the Education of Young Children has guidelines for training early childhood education personnel (Bredekamp, 1987). The issue of certification is further complicated by the fact that many teachers currently employed in programs for 3- to 5-year-olds have associate degrees from 2-year programs, and/or Child Development Associate (CDA) certification. If state certification is mandated, will these requirements also be applied to personnel in private, proprietary, or Head Start programs that currently serve both at-risk preschool age children and those with disabilities? Similar questions could be posed regarding personnel working with target populations in agencies other than education, that is, departments of heatlh.

Credentials will also have to be developed for allied health professionals who are certified in their own discipline but who need special training to work with infants and young children. These standards must be cast in a manner that ensures both quality and quantity of personnel to provide clinical early intervention services.

Professionalism and research

The field of early childhood special education is a combination of two disciplines, each of which is associated with differing philosophies, and educational and treatment orientations. Theoretical and philosophical perspectives in early childhood education, for example, are derived from a constructivist – developmental view (DeVries, 1987) that is associated with high-quality programs (e.g., Hawkins, 1974; Seefeldt & Barbour, 1986; Yonemura, 1986). A focus on fostering development and using developmental principles to guide classroom activities has been described as "developmentally appropriate practice" and is widely accepted as the cornerstone of early childhood education (Bredekamp, 1987).

Special education, on the other hand, is derived from a behavioral orientation (Sulzer-Azaroff & Mayer, 1977), and classroom activities are associated with direct instruction of skills (Bailey & Wolery 1984; Snell, 1987). Thus, a combination of these fields must evolve into a blend of theories and practice in order for this partnership to be synthesized and integrated as a new professional alliance emerges (Mallory, 1983).

The issue of professionalism has been a topic addressed by many writers in early childhood education (Almy, 1982; Raths & Katz, 1982). The level of professionalism and the nature and variety of services provided influence how practitioners will be prepared (Spodek & Saracho, 1982). Katz (1984b) found that the professionally trained teacher is more than merely a manager, as is often the case with the nonprofessionally trained teacher. Katz described the professionally trained teacher as one who has the ability to capitalize on classroom incidents for purposes of instruction, who engages in creative decision making, and who demonstrates leadership and flexibility. Katz (1984b) further notes that the education of early childhood teachers appears to be following a trend noted in teaching at the upper levels – longer periods of training and greater emphasis on theoretical or foundational subjects.

A review of the literature on the education of early childhood teachers finds it to be largely descriptive in nature, with virtually no research on the relative effectiveness of alternative teacher education models (Katz, 1984a). Katz (1984a) argues for research that would test the relative impact of various kinds of content, child observation skills, and the application of developmental stage concepts on preservice training.

Similarly, in ECSE there is an absence of research on the effectiveness of personnel training models. Whereas the needs of handicapped infants and their parents have been well documented (Bricker & Sheehan, 1981; Fraiberg 1977; Horton, 1974), data related to the effectiveness of training personnel to work with handicapped infants, toddlers, and preschoolers and their parents is almost nonexistent. In an extensive review of literature on personnel preparation for working with handicapped infants, Bricker and Slentz (1988) concluded that although there is common content across programs surveyed nationally, research is needed to identify the impact of specific content on trainees and service recipients.

ISSUES IN THE TRAINING OF ECSE PERSONNEL

With the passage of P.L. 99-457, there is an expansion of both ages and levels of severity of young children to be served. Therefore, ECSE personnel must be trained to use new skills in a variety of settings and for a variety of roles (Bailey, Farel, O'Donnell, Simeonsson, & Miller, 1986). Models for ECSE personnel preparation must be predicated upon the many roles in which personnel are expected to function, and should provide training for the age span and diversity of problems of children and families who are or will be service recipients. These diverse roles evolve from the purposes of early intervention, the ages of children to be served, the needs and problems of families, team-based service and delivery, and advocacy.

Purposes of early intervention

The roles that emerge for ECSE personnel emanate from the purposes of early intervention, that is, the goals and expectations for services to parents and children that undergird the mandates of P.L. 99-457. Bond (1982) proposes an orientation for viewing early intervention programs that focuses on the promotion of development. She suggests that "promoting development might be best approached by promoting the motivational system underlying infants' own active, adaptive interaction with the environment" (p. 6). Fewell and Vadasy (1987) provide strong evidence for placing renewed emphasis on enhancing the quality of life of the child and the family, and Zigler and Trickett (1978) argue for enhancing social competence as additional purposes. Another view of early intervention comes from the field of developmental psychopathology and work with multirisk families (Cicchetti & Toth, 1987). The purpose of these efforts is to modify family interactions in order to foster optimal development in young children. These researchers have used the transactional model that views the child within the context of social transactions rather than focusing on the child as the sole target of intervention (Sameroff, 1975). Kopp and Parmelee (1979) and Sameroff (1975) have shown that the mutual transactions between children and their caregiving environments have a marked effect on children's developmental progress. Closely related is the work of Sroufe (1979), and Sroufe and Rutter (1984), that has described the development of a secure attachment relationship with the primary caregiver as the central stage-salient developmental issue between 6 and 12 months of age. Several investigators have found that maltreated infants are more likely to form insecure attachment relationships (Egeland & Sroufe, 1981; Schneider-Rosen, Braunwald, Carlson, & Cicchetti, 1985), findings that have implications for preventive early intervention programs.

Personnel working in early intervention programs will require training to prepare them to assume specific roles and related responsibilities for working with children and families. One such role will be promoting development and increasing the quality of life for children. Another role will be supporting and enhancing the quality of life for families and promoting mutually satisfying interactions between parent – infant and parent – child dyads and child – family interactions.

Age as a factor in role delineation

Infants and toddlers differ significantly from preschool age children. The types of services required by infants from birth to 3 years of age differ markedly with regard to types of intervention strategies, targets for intervention, and settings for services. Early intervention with infants at biologic and environmental risk, including risk for psychopathology (Bennett, 1987; Bromwich, 1981; Sander, 1983), as well as infants with disabilities (Fraiberg, 1977), has used intervention models and strategies that differ from those used with older children (e.g., Weikart, Rogers, Adcock, & McClelland, 1971). Therefore, as roles are defined in ECSE, the ages of children to be served need to be a consideration in role development (McCollum, 1987).

Family focus: A requirement of P.L. 99-457

As stipulated in P.L. 99-457, parents of the infants, toddlers, and preschoolers in early intervention programs have a significant role in the design and implementation of their child's educational program. The law mandates services at a much earlier age than previous legislation, and is designed to affect the role of parents positively, enabling them to become full partners with professionals in supporting their child's development. Data from the Yale Project (Trickett, Apfel, Rosenbaum, & Zigler, 1982), Head Start (O'Keefe, 1979), and programs for children with handicaps (Cartwright, 1981; Filler & Kasari, 1981; Rosenberg, Robinson, & Beckman, 1984; Sheehan, 1981) have demonstrated the positive effects of early intervention and preschool programs on both children and families. This requirement supports the already prevailing practice in early childhood education and special education, both of which have a long history of commitment to parent involvement (e.g., Bredekamp, 1987; Seefeldt & Barbour, 1986; Smith, 1987; Turnbull & Turnbull, 1986).

The new state grant program for infants and toddlers is based on a family-centered case management model. This approach views services from the perspective of families and requires professionals to work with the family as an integral part of the team. So important is the family in adequately serving infants and toddlers that an Individualized Family Service Plan (IFSP) is mandated for each family that has an infant receiving services. Specific family goals as well as child goals must be included in the IFSP, thereby requiring ECSE personnel to engage in mutual goal setting with parents (Wolery, 1987). A model for family-focused intervention described by Bailey, et al. (1986) presents a systematic approach to assessment, planning, intervention, and evaluation of services to families. The type of organized approach described by those authors is essential to successful implementation of the mandate and has direct implications for personnel preparation including subject matter and roles.

Congress clearly intended that parents should have an important and central role in early intervention and preschool programs at each level of programming. The IFSP must establish plans for transition for the child and family to preschool services and must provide a mechanism for coordinating the IFSP of early intervention with the Individualized Education Plan (IEP) required in programs for children 3 to 5 years of age. Parents are expected to be decision makers, teachers, evaluators, and monitors of their child's services. These new roles and responsibilities for parents have direct implications for tasks required of ECSE professionals. That is, identified family needs must be addressed in service plans. In addition, ECSE personnel are responsible for teaching parents to be advocates for their children, and to evaluate and monitor the quality of services that their children are receiving. These are new types of behaviors expected from professionals and careful, thoughtful planning and development activities will be critical to the success of such endeavors.

Team-based service delivery

Occupational and physical therapists, speech and language pathologists, and other professionals are an important source of clinical services for infants, toddlers, and preschoolers with disabilities (Fewell, 1983). Training that is focused only on discipline-specific skills for each professional is thus insufficient. Clearly, ECSE personnel training will necessitate the inclusion of specific strategies that enable professionals from several disciplines to work together with families, using a variety of models (e.g., consultant, transdisciplinary, and interdisciplinary).

Courtnage and Smith-Davis (1987) surveyed special education training programs to determine whether Interdisciplinary Team Training (ITT) was an integral part of training programs. Of those programs that responded, 48% indicated that such training was not included. ITT is vitally important because many barriers to effective team functioning have been identified in the literature when the team process is left to chance (Bray, Coleman, & Gotts, 1981; Golin & Ducanis, 1981). These barriers include confusing jargon from other disciplines, a lack of understanding of the work of other disciplines, and ineffective interpersonal relations. Therefore, well-functioning teams must be developed (Courtnage & Healy, 1984). Providing team training should be a key feature in ECSE personnel preparation programs in order to ensure that professionals from various disciplines can productively collaborate and effectively implement the interdisciplinary requirements of P.L. 99-457.

Several studies have made recommendations for improving the team process that can guide the development of training procedures (e.g., Bailey, Helsel-DeWert, Thiele, & Ware, 1983; Knoff, 1983; Rhode, Leininger, Egan, & Bluhm, 1981). For those teacher-training institutions that have no allied health preservice programs, Courtnage and Smith-Davis (1987) recommend collaborative efforts between training programs and community agencies and schools.

ESSENTIAL CONTENT FOR ECSE PERSONNEL TRAINING

The successful implementation of roles and responsibilities presupposes that trainees will have mastered bodies of knowledge essential to their competence in such roles. This knowledge base can be drawn from research in early childhood, developmental psychology, and special education that has been synthesized within a conceptual framework that is cognitive and developmental in orientation (e.g., Kohlberg & Mayer, 1972, Meisels, 1979). This orientation is then supplemented with knowledge and skills for accommodating infants and young children with handicapping conditions (e.g., Bricker, 1982; 1986; Guralnick & Bennett, 1987b; Neisworth & Bagnato, 1987). The work of Meisels (1979) has shown the applicability of the developmental approach for children with atypical development. Rather than viewing the child with handicaps as deficient, from the developmental perspective all children "can be seen as occupying a position on a developmental continuum. Although age and experience significantly influence development, the developmental approach admits of finer gradations of ability and hence helps to identify the similarities as well as differences among children" (Meisels, 1979, p. 4). The value of a cognitive-developmental approach reminds us that the exceptional child functions no less as a coordinated, self-regulated person than the nondisabled child (Reid, 1978).

Information concerning normal child developmental theory and related research is important for all trainees. This includes such diverse bodies of knowledge as attachment and social development (e.g., Sroufe, 1979); cognitive development (e.g., Flavell, 1977); emotional development (e.g., Campos, Barrett, Lamb, Goldsmith, & Stenberg, 1983); communication and language development (e.g., Menyuk, 1971; deVilliers & deVilliers, 1979); types, importance, and the role of play in development (e.g., Garvey, 1977; Vandenberg, 1978; Johnson, Christie, & Yawkey, 1987); and behavioral theory (e.g., Sulzer-Azaroff & Mayer, 1977). Further, this knowledge base must be merged with information from other fields, such as sociology and medicine, and include topics such as factors that place the child at risk, and the impact of a child with disabilities on caregiving and family functioning. Information related to assessment of infants (Sheehan & Klein, 1988), young children and families, current trends in early intervention and preschool programs, creation and management of developmentally appropriate learning environments, collaboration among team members and across agencies, and information regarding community services and advocacy should also be included. This interdisciplinary approach to content selection provides the breadth of basic knowledge essential for highly qualified ECSE personnel.

Competencies needed to deliver high-quality services

Competency-based teacher training is an outgrowth of behavioral technology and is more frequently associated with special education than general early childhood education. Such an approach maintains that teachers demonstrate specific competencies that are observable and measurable. In contrast, early childhood programs focus on a teacher's ability to create environments that are responsive to the developmental needs and interests of each child, that foster physical well-being, and that nurture emotional health (Hendrick, 1984). Qualities such as these do not easily lend themselves to measurement. Nevertheless, although these perspectives have traditionally differed, it is possible to specify early childhood competencies that reflect the prevailing values of both fields. For example, the requirements of developmentally appropriate classrooms (Bredekamp, 1987) could be translated into measurable competencies. Competencies expected of well-qualified ECSE personnel must combine and reflect both early childhood and special education values for professional competence as well as theoretical and research knowledge bases.

The following provides a brief, although noncomprehensive, listing from which ECSE competencies may be generated. Additional attention regarding training competencies must be directed toward program directors and paraprofessionals who will have different responsibilities in early intervention and preschool programs (Linder, 1983).

ECSE professionals must demonstrate knowledge of

1. development of typical infants and young children;
2. development of atypical infants and young children including those with sensory, motor, cognitive, and socioemotional disabilities;
3. function and structure of families, family dynamics, and the role of families in promoting development; and
4. roles and responsibilities of ECSE personnel, including team and interagency collaboration, service coordination, and advocacy.

ECSE professionals must be able to

5. assess infant, child, and family needs;
6. demonstrate use of effective intervention strategies, and apply current thinking in early intervention and preschool programs;
7. create developmentally appropriate learning environments using strategies to adapt environments, activities, and materials to the needs of atypical children;
8. collaborate with parents and professionals in the design and delivery of services; and
9. perform service coordination (case management) responsibilities jointly with families.

ROLES FOR EARLY CHILDHOOD SPECIAL EDUCATION PERSONNEL

Geik, Gilkerson, and Sponsellor (1986) presented a personnel preparation model for early intervention that describes the essential roles for personnel who work with children from birth to age 3 years and their families. This section presents modifications of those roles, and includes differentiated responsibilities for personnel in early intervention programs for children from birth to 3, as compared to services for children 3 to 5 years of age. Furthermore, the roles are an outgrowth of the purposes of early intervention cited earlier and the need to work with families and professionals from several disciplines. Given that the purposes of specific programs and age of children served differ across ECSE services, three specific roles have been identified: developmental specialist, parent consultant, and team member, all of which are essential to the delivery of comprehensive early intervention services.

To a great extent, the responsibilities of the early childhood special educator is broader than the traditional role of the teacher, thereby reflecting the more comprehensive view of a "developmental specialist." As described by Stedman (1973):

[A] developmental specialist [is one who is] competent in child development theory and its application in educational settings (home, nursery, school, playground, neighborhood, day-care center, specialized educational intervention program, etc.), methods of educating and training young children, methods of assessing children and converting assessment data into educational treatment prescriptions and daily educational strategies, utilization of educational research information, ability to apply knowledge and some treatment in the area of child health, childhood illness, and human growth and development from both the physical and biobehavioral points of view, counseling parents and children, utilizing consultation and technical assistance, and assuming a place in the community where the educator is viewed as a person with special skills with children and families (pp. 157–158).

Whereas the concept of the developmental specialist relates to educators, the same skills are important for clinical personnel as well.

Developmental specialist: Infants and toddlers; preschoolers

The developmental specialist selects, uses, and interprets data from appropriate developmental assessment instruments in order to plan, implement, and evaluate Individualized Family Service Plans and individualized educational programs. The developmental specialist creates and modifies programs to meet the needs of children and their families, while adhering to developmentally appropriate practices from early childhood education. Whether located in home-based or center-based settings, the developmental specialist works with families to help them understand their child's development and the implications of their child's disability on developmental progress, in order to facilitate productive parent–child interaction (Bromwich, 1981; Richard, 1986).

The developmental specialist is knowledgeable about the developmental needs of infants, toddlers, and preschoolers and assists parents in arranging the home environment to maximize learning opportunities, select appropriate toys and activities, and implement adaptive techniques suggested by the transdisciplinary team. At the forefront of the developmental educator's work with parents should be the developmental and socioemotional needs of young children and families. The developmental specialist will help parents place the special considerations created by handicapping conditions into a framework that presupposes that a child with a disability is a child first, who secondarily has a handicapping condition.

Parent consultant

The development of mutually satisfying relationships between infants and parents is of major importance during the early years. Research has identified the important role that infants play in initiating and maintaining relationships with caregivers and parents (e.g., Lewis & Rosenblum, 1974), and has identified specific infant characteristics that influence dyadic relationships (Richard, 1986). Studies of infants who are at risk or handicapped and their parents indicate that compared to low-risk dyads, such infants may contribute differently to the relationship (DiVitto & Goldberg, 1979; Krakow & Kopp, 1983). Infants with Down syndrome, for example, show significantly fewer social responses and infants with disabilities give less feedback in general (Rothbart & Hanson, 1983; Walker, 1982). Fraiberg (1975) found that blind children are less responsive than infants without disabilities. Not suprisingly, several studies have shown that parents' behavior with their disabled infants differs from that observed of parents whose children do not have handicapping conditions (Jones, 1977; Rondal, 1977). Increased family stress in families with handicapped children has also been well documented (Featherstone, 1980).

Some early intervention programs have focused on facilitating mutually satisfying parent–infant interactions (Bromwich, 1981; McCollum & Stayton, 1985). As a parent consultant, the major responsibilities for personnel include assisting parents to interpret and respond to infant signals, and to understand infant temperament and communication systems. In this role, the focus is on the infant within the family, with the expectation that the better able the family is to respond to the infant's needs, the better the infant will grow and develop and the better the family constellation will function. The parent consultant assists the family in setting goals and in establishing an individualized family service plan. Turnbull and Turnbull (1986) have described strategies for developing productive parent–professional relationships. The degree to which parents are able to choose to be involved in programs, however, will differ widely (Winton & Turnbull, 1981). Parental strengths and interests should be considered in the goal-setting process.

Team contributor

The importance of the participation of a variety of professional disciplines in early intervention services has been clearly stated in P.L. 99-457. Comprehensive early intervention service delivery teams will include occupational, physical, and speech therapists, educators, and in some cases, nurses and physicians. Whether within a transdisciplinary, interdisciplinary, or multidisciplinary model, the team contributor role requires collaboration and consultation among team members (Bailey et al., 1983). All team members, regardless of professional discipline, are likely to require specialized training and experiences to acquire skills necessary to collaborate and consult with families and other professionals.

A MODEL FOR ECSE PERSONNEL PREPARATION

The model described here incorporates training related to the roles and responsibilities of the developmental specialist, parent consultant, and team member, and the competencies associated with each role. It reflects an integration of content from early childhood and special education with the view that direct teaching strategies should be employed in developmentally appropriate classroom settings. And, finally, the model focuses training on the needs of young children, their parents, and their mutual interactions.

The model is based on graduate-level training. The breadth and depth of knowledge essential for trainees to demonstrate competence in each of the roles requires both undergraduate training as prerequisite knowledge and the experience associated with graduate students. It is assumed that trainees will be drawn from many different baccalaureate programs including regular education, special education, early childhood education, nursing, and clinical fields.

This model is a dual-track specialization model – birth to 3 and 3 to 5 – with training focused on the three primary roles for ECSE personnel to work with both infants and toddlers and with preschool children and their families previously described. The ECSE model is predicated on the belief that a common core of knowledge is essential for all students, supplemented by additional knowledge and skills specific to work with each age group. Table 1 presents the core and supplemental content for each specialization.

Core courses and specializations

All trainees will be required to complete core foundation courses prior to their specialization work. Content in this core requirement will include typical and atypical child

Table 1. *Competency-based ECSE Training Model*

Core course content required of all trainees	Specialization tracks	
	Infant and toddler specialization	Preschool specialization
1. Cognitive, affective, language, and psychomotor development from birth to 5 years of age	1. Methods of developmental assessment; team-based program planning	1. Methods of developmental assessment and related program planning; team consultation
2. Atypical child development: cognitive, sensory, socioemotional, environmental, biological, and medical factors	2. Team-based service delivery models	2. Creating a developmentally appropriate classroom environment
3. Interdisciplinary programming for at-risk and handicapped infants, toddlers, and preschool children; participating on the team	3. Support, consultation, education, and advocacy for parents	3. Support, consultation, education, and advocacy for parents
4. Family systems and functioning		4. Consultation and least restrictive environments
5. Research in early childhood special education		

development, interdisciplinary team planning, family systems functioning, and research in early childhood special education.

Infant-toddler specialization

Personnel trained to work with handicapped and at-risk infants and toddlers at the masters level will presumably be drawn from many fields (e.g., special education, early childhood, nursing, psychology, etc.). Given these varied backgrounds, their ECSE preparation will focus on knowledge and skills required to deliver services, either center-based or home-based, as part of an interdisciplinary team. The structures currently available to deliver team services vary, ranging from educationally based approaches to models where related services are an adjunct to transdisciplinary services (Campbell, 1987). Therefore, the infant-toddler specialization should prepare personnel to work in a variety of service delivery models.

Programs serving handicapped infants and toddlers are characterized by the team approach (Campbell, 1987) and a focus on the family (Healy, Keesee, & Smith, 1985). The infant-toddler specialization will incorporate training activities that place special emphasis on knowledge of family dynamics, family functioning, and family systems. This emphasis is necessary both because of the service mandates in P.L. 99-457 and because work with infants and toddlers inherently requires close family collaboration. Furthermore, training will include writing IFSPs in order to assure that family and child needs are met. Campbell and Hanson (1987) and Gilkerson, Hilliard, Schrag, and Shonkoff (1987) urge the inclusion of parents as part of the training team and suggest that courses on families and family systems be cotaught by parents of children with disabilities.

Training for the infant-toddler specialization must also include a focus on knowledge and skills related to multidisciplinary assessment of child and family functioning. Such intervention approaches should be directed toward supporting families in ways that enable them to optimize the growth and development of their children. These approaches include facilitating satisfying mother–child interactions, assisting parents to understand and respond to their children's needs and signals, teaching parents to modify home settings to effectively accommodate children's needs, helping them to select appropriate toys and materials, and supporting parents through difficult periods in their lives.

The focus of this specialization is on behaviors that are associated with the sensorimotor stage and related implications for constructing developmentally appropriate learning environments in center-based programs for infants and toddlers. Trainees must learn to create environments that optimize development and function, based on principles related to developmentally appropriate practice (Bredekamp, 1987). This must include opportunities for exploration and play in environments that are modified to accommodate the special needs of children with disabilities (Olds, 1979).

Training also includes knowledge and skills related to consultation with providers of day-care services for infants and toddlers (Jones & Meisels, 1987). For infants and toddlers enrolled in day care, their teachers will have to work with early childhood special educators in a consultation model in order for day-care personnel to modify activities to accommodate children with disabilities into their programs (Klein & Sheehan, 1987). And, finally, training should include skills for providing support to families and staff for transitions from infant to preschool programs (Hains, Fowler, & Chandler, 1988; Hanline, 1988; Hanline & Knowlton, 1988).

Preschool specialization

Whereas the focus of the infant-toddler specialization is primarily on parent–infant interaction, transactional family patterns, and working on teams, the focus of the preschool specialization will be different. McCollum (1987) reported that a survey of teachers of handicapped children from birth to 5 years indicated that teachers of infants spent most of their time supporting families and working in team contexts, and teachers of 3- to 5-year-olds spent more time arranging and managing the classroom environment. Although the role and influence of the family in the lives of 3- to 5-year-old children continues to be vital, family dynamics change due to the age, developmental needs, and interests of these older children, and their families' responses to these changes. Knowledge and skills for working with families, assessing family needs, and engaging in parent education and collaborative activities must certainly be included in this track. In addition, however, the preschool specialization should focus on regular early childhood educational programming to ensure that trainees have the ability to provide for the needs of nonhandicapped children participating in integrated preschool programs as well as to use effective early childhood practices in programs that serve handicapped children (Meisels, 1979; Odom, DeKlyen, & Jenkins, 1984; Winderstrom, 1986).

This specialization will focus on characteristics and behaviors associated with the preoperational child and learning activities that facilitate cognitive and language development, motivation and inquiry, and basic elements of a developmentally appropriate classroom. Within this context, trainees learn strategies for modifying activities to accommodate the special needs of disabled children, to design interdisciplinary team strategies, and to implement individualized interventions (Safford & Rosen, 1981). The roles and importance of play are also stressed.

An important aspect of working with 3- to 5-year-old children includes planning of transitions for individual children to less restrictive settings (Noonen & Kilgo, 1987; Polloway, 1987) and/or to subsequent services in different settings. Such planning includes involvement of the parent in consultation with staffs from other programs.

Consultation in least restrictive settings

Programs for at-risk and disabled preschoolers are provided in separate special education settings and in mainstreamed settings, that is, Head Start and day-care centers. Some children will be enrolled in both types of programs (Klein & Sheehan, 1987) or only in day care (Bagnato, Kontos, & Neisworth, 1987; Jones & Meisels, 1987). Training therefore must promote development of the knowledge and skills required for successful consultation with regular early childhood preschool programs (Safford, 1988).

Additional experience for all trainees

After coursework has been completed, a supervised internship should be devised. This extended field experience permits the translation of theory into practice, the application of newly acquired skills and knowledge for working with children and families, and team participation supported by ongoing feedback from field site personnel and university faculty. The internship is an opportunity for the trainee to demonstrate skills and knowledge and to synthesize and evaluate the training experiences.

Specialist roles – Special considerations for personnel preparation

The educator role in programs for young children allows for infant-toddler or preschool specialization and prepares educators to perform roles as developmental specialists, parent consultants, and team members. The roles of physical and occupational therapists, speech and language pathologists, and other specialists who are involved in addressing the needs of families and young children vary in relation to the ages of the children involved. Traditionally, these disciplines have been viewed as "related services" personnel in programs for children aged 3 through 5 years, as well as in special education programs for school-aged students. In other words, these services are provided only to the extent that their provision is necessary for children to benefit from special education. In programs for children from birth through age 2 years, all services are classified as early intervention services. An infant may receive early intervention services provided only by a physical or occupational therapist, for example, if that discipline best addresses the needs of the family and infant. The team of professionals required to meet each infant's unique needs may vary from infant to infant and may include any combination that best addresses those needs.

Flexibility in team membership and the "equality" of all services in an early intervention program results in two primary issues related to competencies and preparation of personnel. The first is that each discipline must require additional training sufficient to match current competencies with those skills required for quality service provision for families, infants, and toddlers. Most physical and occupational therapists, for example, receive limited training in working with families. In contrast, social workers are likely to have received a great deal of experience with families as part of basic professional preparation, but little training in developmental assessment of young children.

A second issue involves the degree of professional skill required to intervene with infants and toddlers. The three most common therapeutic disciplines, for example, are trained in basic professional programs oriented toward the problems presented by a wide variety of disabilities within a broad age range (e.g., infant through geriatric). Thus, a physical or occupational therapist is likely to be licensed or credentialed on the basis of general competence across disabilities and age groups. Specialization training must then follow basic professional preparation to provide the skills necessary to work with specific age groups or disabilities. Although many professionals may benefit from graduate education, such as a master's-level program in ECSE, pursuing such a course will not necessarily provide the professional with the specialist skills necessary to work with infants and toddlers. At some point, the competencies specific to the practice of each discipline must be delineated. Appropriate graduate-level coursework or programs, or well-designed in-service training programs, can then be developed to address the training needs of professionals other than educators.

Addressing in-service training needs

The proposed training model for ECSE personnel at the masters level is designed to prepare a cadre of highly qualified staff to provide early childhood special education services. However, it will take time for universities to create such programs. In order to alleviate current personnel shortages and to meet the ECSE training needs of professionals from the several disciplines currently employed in early intervention programs, in-service training models that combine didactic and practical experiences are a mechanism immediately available to prepare qualified personnel. Professional standards will both influence practice and suggest areas for in-service training (Dunn, Campbell, Berger, Hall, & Otter, 1987; Smith, 1987; Wilcox, 1987). In-service training activities and associated models will also be shaped by the Part H regulations of P.L. 99-457 that require the lead agency in each state to establish personnel standards and a comprehensive system of personnel development for a statewide system of early intervention.

In-service training models will require cooperation and collaboration among institutions of higher educations, state agencies, and professional organizations. Crossland, Hasselbring, and O'Brien (1980) reported that summer training institutes taught by university faculty, followed by one semester of on-site supervision of trainees in their places of employment, were more successful than isolated didactic experiences. Other in-service models that have reported effective outcomes include coursework and didactic instruction in combination with supervised field experiences (Crain, 1980).

Several factors have been identified by Lawrence (1974), Brinkerhoff, (1980), and Browder (1983) that influence the effectiveness of in-service training. These include the identification of specific training needs and related goals and objectives for training; qualified training staff; and supervision and on-site monitoring of application of skills. These factors can be used to guide the development of a variety of in-service, community-based models.

The development of innovative in-service training models, including the use of computerized modules and interactive videodiscs and videotape, holds potential for alleviating current personnel shortage. These efforts cannot substitute over time for state-based documentation of ECSE personnel needs and related development of university-based preservice programs (Campbell, 1987). However, they may be necessary in order to remedy the immediate shortage of qualified personnel (Smith & Powers, 1987).

RECOMMENDATIONS FOR FUTURE RESEARCH

In this chapter we have attempted to explicate the contrasting philosophies that prevail in early childhood and special education. In many ways, these differing philosophies are in conflict with regard to the central role of "development" as contrasted to "learning" in young children; the structure and organization of learning environments, roles, expectations, and competencies of teachers; and the freedom of the child in a classroom setting. We urge a synthesis of these multiple orientations to permit broad theoretical reformulations that can be tested with all young children. Such theories would provide a framework for applied research and for testing theories related to child development, family adaptation, and intervention strategies. Theory-based intervention efforts, accompanied by meticulously designed research studies, could provide a valuable research base for both early intervention and personnel preparation.

The dearth of useful research related to teacher effectiveness in schools in general, and teacher effectiveness in early childhood and early childhood special education programs in particular, defines a research area in need of attention. Systematic study efforts are needed to validate personnel preparation models empirically, to explore the relationship of various preservice and in-service training methods of professional performance, and to examine the relationship of professional performance to child and family outcomes. A teacher, for example, may demonstrate all of the competencies considered essential for a highly qualified ECSE teacher, and yet not be "competent."

Empirical descriptions of highly competent teachers will provide guidelines for personnel preparation.

Research efforts should be directed toward the study of theory-based classroom organizations and of curricula that focus on infants and young children at risk and those with disabilities. Generating such activities from theoretical models would provide a framework within which to test hypotheses. Similarly, research related to the "matching" of infant, child, and family characteristics to specific program models holds potential for enhancing program effectiveness and has important implications for personnel preparation. The effects of professional standards and credentialing on the quality of services is also an unexplored issue. Historically, in the area of education for children with mild mental retardation, the presence of a teaching credential did not result in program excellence (Dunn, 1968). It is our hope that we can learn from the past and carefully study the effects of credentialing on service effectiveness, specifically in order to identify those credential requirements that have the greatest impact on outcome.

And, finally, a prospective, longitudinal research agenda that specifies appropriate contrast groups, identifies valid and reliable outcome measures, and incorporates cost factors, program characteristics, and ECSE personnel competencies will permit comparisons across regions of the country and will contribute significantly to our knowledge base in early intervention. Such efforts should differentiate among service recipients regarding types of problems, (e.g., very low birth weight, failure to thrive, cerebral palsy), demographic factors, and family organizations, and should identify specific competencies related to child and family outcomes.

The current service mandate provides a valuable opportunity for professionals, advocates, and parents to use the existing knowledge base to help infants and young children and to generate new knowledge regarding ECSE personnel training and services. It is hoped that this new legislation will serve as a catalyst for the articulation of new theories, innovative interventions, applied research, and data-based personnel preparation models that will benefit service recipients directly. Congress has done its job; the ball is now in our court.

REFERENCES

Ableson, M. A., & Woodman, R. W. (1983). Review of research on team effectiveness: Implications for teams in schools. *School Psychological Review, 12,* 125–138.

Allen-Meares, P., & Pugash, M. (1982). Facilitating interdisciplinary collaboration on behalf of handicapped children and youth. *Teacher Education and Special Education, 5,* 30–36.

Almy, M. (1982). Daycare and early childhood education. In E. Zigler & E. Gordon (Eds.), *Daycare: Scientific and social policy issues* (pp. 476–495). Boston: Auburn House Press.

Anastasiow, N. J. (1986). The research base for early intervention. *Journal of the Division for Early Childhood, 10,* 99–117.

Bagnato, S., Kontos, S., & Neisworth, J. (1987). Integrated day care as special education: Profiles of programs and children. *Topics in Early Childhood Special Education, 7,* 28–47.

Bailey, D. B., Helsel-DeWert, M., Thiele, J. E., & Ware, W. B. (1983). Measuring individual participation on the interdisciplinary team. *American Journal of Mental Deficiency, 88,* 247–254.

Bailey, D. M., Farel, A. M., O'Donnell, K., Simeonsson, R., & Miller, C. A. (1986). Preparing infant interventionists: Interdepartmental training in special education and maternal and child health. *Journal of the Division for Early Childhood, 11,* 67–77.

Bailey, D., Simeonsson, R., Winton, P., Huntington, G., Comfort, M., Isbell, P., O'Donnell, K., & Helm, J. (1986). Family focused intervention: A functional model for planning, implementing, and evaluating individualized family services in early intervention. *Journal of the Division for Early Childhood, 10,* 156–171.

Bailey, D. B., & Wolery, M. (1984). *Teaching infants and preschoolers with handicaps.* Columbus, OH: Merrill.

Beckman, P., & Burke, P. (1984). Early childhood special education: State of the art. *Topics in Early Childhood Special Education, 4,* 19–32.

Bennett, F. C. (1987). The effectiveness of early intervention for infants at increased biological risk. In M. J. Guralnick & F. C. Bennett (Eds.), *The effectiveness of early intervention for at-risk and handicapped children* (pp. 79–112). New York: Academic Press.

Bond, L. (1982). From prevention to promotion: Optimizing infant development. In L. A. Bond & J. M. Joffe (Eds.), *Facilitating infant and early childhood development* (pp. 5–39). Hanover, NH: University Press of New England.

Bray, N., Coleman, J., & Gotts, E. (1981). The interdisciplinary team: Challenges to effective functioning. *Teacher Education and Special Education, 4,* 44–49.

Bredekamp, S. (1987). *Developmentally appropriate practice in early childhood programs serving children from birth through age eight* (expanded edition). Washington, DC: National Association for the Education of Young Children.

Bricker, D. (Ed.). (1982). *Intervention with at-risk and handicapped infants: From research to application.* Baltimore: University Park Press.

Bricker, D. (1986). *Early education of at-risk and handicapped infants, toddlers and preschool children.* Glenview, IL: Scott, Foresman.

Bricker, D., & Sheehan, R. (1981). Effectiveness of an early intervention program as indexed by measures of child change. *Journal of the Division for Early Childhood, 4,* 11–27.

Bricker, D., & Slentz, K. (1988). Personnel preparation: Handicapped infants. In M. C. Wang, M. C. Reynolds, & H. J. Walberg (Eds.), *Handbook of special education: Research and practice* (Vol. 3, pp. 319–345). Elmsford, NY: Pergamon Press.

Brinkerhoff, R. O. (1980). Evaluation of inservice programs. *Teacher Education and Special Education, 3,* 27–37.

Bromwich, R. (1981). *Working with parents and infants: An interactional approach.* Baltimore: University Park Press.

Browder, D. (1983). Guidelines for inservice planning. *Exceptional Children, 49,* 300–307.

Campbell, P. H. (1987). The integrated programming team: An approach for coordinating professionals of various disciplines in programs for students with severe and multiple handicaps. *Journal of the Association for Persons with Severe Handicaps, 12,* 107–116.

Campbell, P. N. (In Press). Meeting needs of infants and toddlers and their families. In A. Kaiser & C. McWhorter (Eds.), *Preparing personnel to work with persons who are severely handicapped.* Baltimore: P. H. Brookes.

Campbell, P., & Hanson, M. (1987). *Early intervention guidelines.* Seattle: The Association for Persons with Severe Handicaps.

Campos, J., Barrett, K., Lamb, M., Goldsmith, H., & Stenberg, C. (1983). Socioemotional development. In M. M. Haith & J. J. Campos (Eds.), *Infancy and developmental psychobiology* (Vol. 2, pp. 783–915). New York: Wiley.

Cartwright, C. (1981). Effective programs for parents of young handicapped children. *Topics in Early Childhood Special Education, 1,* 1–10.

Casto, G., White, K., & Taylor C. (1983). An early intervention research institute: Studies of efficacy and cost effectiveness of early intervention at Utah State. *Journal of the Division for Early Childhood, 7,* 37–48.

Cicchetti, D., & Toth, S. L. (1987). The application of a transactional risk model to intervention with multi-risk maltreating families. *Zero to Three, 7,* 1–8.

Clarke-Stewart, K. A., & Fein, G. G. (1983). Early childhood programs. In M. M. Haith & J. J. Campos (Eds.), *Infancy and developmental psychobiology* (Vol. 2, pp. 917–999). New York: Wiley.

Courtnage, L., & Healy, H. (1984). Interdisciplinary team training: A competency and procedure-based approach. *Teacher Education and Special Education, 7,* 3–11.

Courtnage, L., & Smith-Davis, J. (1987). Interdisciplinary team training: A national survey of special education teacher training programs. *Exceptional Children, 53,* 451–458.

Crain, E. J. (1980). A generic practicum: A seven week program for mildly handicapped learners. *Teacher Education and Special Education, 3,* 33–36.

Crossland, C. L., Hasselbring, T. S., & O'Brien, K. (1980). Project IMPACT: Inservice plan assisting classroom teachers. *Teacher Education and Special Education, 5,* 53–58.

de Villiers, P. A., & de Villiers, J. G. (1979). *Early language.* Cambridge: Harvard University Press.

DeVries, R. (1987). *Programs of early education: The constructivist view*. White Plains, NY: Longman.

DiVitto, B., & Goldberg, S. (1979). The effects of newborn medical status on early parent–infant interaction. In T. M. Field, A. M. Sostek, S. Goldberg, & H. H. Shuman (Eds.), *Infants born at risk: Behavior and development* (pp. 311–322). Jamaica, NY: Spectrum Publications.

Dunn, L. (1968). Special education for the mildly retarded: Is much of it justifiable? *Exceptional Children, 35*, 5–22.

Dunn, W., Campbell, P., Berger, E., Hall, S., & Otter, P. (1987). *Guidelines for the Practice of Occupational Therapy in Early Intervention*. Rockville, MD: American Occupational Therapy Association.

Egeland, B., & Sroufe, L. A. (1981). Developmental sequelae of maltreatment in infancy. *New Directions for Child Development, 11*, 77–92.

Featherstone, H. (1980). *A difference in the family: Living with a disabled child*. New York: Basic Books.

Fewell, R. (1983). The team approach to infant education. In S. G. Garwood & R. R. Fewell (Eds.), *Educating handicapped infants* (pp. 299–320). Rockville, MD: Aspen Systems.

Fewell, R., & Vadasy, P. F. (1987). Measurement issues in studies of efficacy. *Topics in Early Childhood Special Education, 7*, 85–96.

Filler, J., & Kasari, C. (1981). Acquisition, maintenance and generalization of parent-target skills with two severely handicapped infants. *Journal of the Association for Severely Handicapped, 6*, 30–38.

Flavell, J. H. (1977). *Cognitive development*. Englewood Cliffs, NJ: Prentice-Hall.

Fraiberg, S. (1975). The development of human attachment of infants blind from birth. *Merrill-Palmer Quarterly, 21*, 315–334.

Fraiberg, S. (1977). *Insights from the blind*. New York: Basic Books.

Garvey, C. (1977). *Play*. Cambridge: Harvard University Press.

Geik, I., Gilkerson, L., & Sponseller, D. (1986). An early intervention training model. *Journal of the Division for Early Childhood, 10*, 42–52.

Gilkerson, L., Hilliard, A., Schrag, E., & Shonkoff, J. (1987). Commenting on P.L. 99-457. *Zero to Three, 7*, 13–17.

Golin, A. K., & Ducanis, A. J. (1981). *The interdisciplinary team: A handbook for the education of exceptional children*. Rockville, MD: Aspen Systems.

Guralnick, M. J., & Bennett, F. C. (1987a). Early intervention for at-risk and handicapped children: Current and future perspectives. In M. J. Guralnick & F. C. Bennett (Eds), *The effectiveness of early intervention for at-risk and handicapped children* (pp. 364–382). New York: Academic Press.

Guralnick, M. J., & Bennett, F. C. (Eds.). (1987b). *The effectiveness of early intervention for at-risk and handicapped children*. New York: Academic Press.

Guralnick, M. J., & Bennett, F. C. (1987c). A framework for early intervention. In M. J. Guralnick & F. C. Bennett (Eds.), *The effectiveness of early intervention for at-risk and handicapped children* (pp. 3–29). New York: Academic Press.

Hains, A., Fowler, S., & Chandler, L. (1988). Planning school transitions: Family and professional collaboration. *Journal of the Division for Early Childhood, 12*, 118–125.

Hanline, M. F. (1988). Making the transition to preschool: Identification of parent needs. *Journal of the Division for Early Childhood, 12*, 98–107.

Hanline, M., Fowler, S., & Chandler, L. (1988). A collaborative model for providing support to parents during their child's transition from infant intervention to preschool special education public school programs. *Journal of Special Education, 12*, 126–136.

Hanline, M. F., & Knowlton, A. (1988). A collaborative model for providing support to parents during their child's transition from infant intervention to preschool special education public school programs. *Journal of the Division for Early Childhood, 12*, 116–125.

Hanson, M. J. (1984). Parent–infant interaction. In M. J. Hanson (Ed.), *Atypical infant development* (pp. 179–106). Baltimore: University Park Press.

Hawkins, F. P. (1974). *The logic of action: Young children at work*. New York: Pantheon.

Hayden, A., & Haring, N. (1977). The acceleration and maintenance of developmental gain in Down's syndrome school-age children. In P. Mittler (Ed.), *Research to practice in mental retardation: Care and intervention* (pp. 129–142). Baltimore: University Park Press.

Healy, A., Keesee, P., & Smith, B. (1985). *Early services for children with special needs: Transitions for family support*. Iowa City: University of Iowa Hospitals and Clinics.

Hendrick, J. (1984). *The whole child: Early education of the eighties* (3rd ed.). St. Louis: Mosby.

Horton, K. B. (1974). Infant intervention and language learning. In R. L. Schiefelbeusch & L. L. Lloyd (Eds.), *Language perspectives: Acquisition, retardation, and intervention* (pp. 211–232). Baltimore: University Park Press.

Johnson, J. E., Christie, J., & Yawkey, T. (1987). *Play and early childhood development.* Glenview, IL: Scott, Foresman.

Jones, O. (1977). Mother–child communication with prelinguistic Down's syndrome and normal infants. In H. R. Schaffer (Ed.), *Studies in mother–infant interactions: Proceedings of the Loch Lomond Symposium* (pp. 379–401). London: Academic Press.

Jones, S., & Meisels, S. J. (1987). Training family day care providers to work with special needs children. *Topics in Early Childhood Special Education, 7*, 1–12.

Katz, L. G. (1984a). The education of preprimary teachers. In L. G. Katz (Ed.), *Current topics in early childhood* (Vol. 5, pp. 209–225). Norwood, NJ: Ablex Publishing.

Katz, L. G. (1984b). The professional early childhood education teacher. *Young Children, 39*, 3–10.

Katz, L., & Raths, J. D. (1985). A framework for research on teacher education programs. *Journal of Teacher Education, 5*, 9–15.

Klein, N., & Sheehan, R. (1987). Staff development: A key issue in meeting the needs of young handicapped children in day care settings. *Topics in Early Childhood Special Education, 7*, 13–27.

Knoff, H. M. (1983). Investigating disproportionate influences and status in multidisciplinary child study teams. *Exceptional Children, 49*, 367–370.

Kohlberg, L., & Mayer, R. (1972). Development as the aim of education. *Harvard Educational Review, 42*, 449–496.

Kopp, C. B., & Parmelee, A. H. (1979). Prenatal and perinatal influences on infant behavior. In J. D. Osofsky (Ed.), *Handbook of infant development* (pp. 29–75). New York: Wiley.

Krakow, J., & Kopp, C. (1983). The effects of developmental delay on sustained attention in young children. *Child Development, 54*, 1143–1155.

Lawrence, G. (1974). *Patterns of effective in-service education.* Tallahassee: Florida Department of Education.

Lazar, I., & Darlington, R. (Eds.). (1982). Lasting effects of early childhood education: A report from the Consortium for Longitudinal Studies. *Monographs of the Society for Research in Child Development, 47* (2–3, Serial No. 195).

Lewis, M., & Rosenblum, L. A. (1974). *The effect of the infant on its caregiver.* New York: Wiley.

Linder, T. (1983). *Early childhood special education: Program development and administration.* Baltimore: P.H. Brookes.

Mallory, B. (1983). The preparation of early childhood special educators: A model program. *Journal of the Division for Early Childhood, 7*, 32–40.

McCollum, J. (1987). Early interventionists in infant and early childhood programs: A comparison of preservice needs. *Topics in Early Childhood Special Education, 7*, 24–35.

McCollum, J. A., & Stayton, V. D. (1985). Infant/parent interaction: Studies and intervention guidelines based on the SIAI Model. *Journal of the Division for Early Childhood, 9*, 125–135.

Meisels, S. J. (Ed.). (1979). *Special education and development: Perspectives on young children with special needs.* Baltimore: University Park Press.

Meisels, S. J. (1985a). The efficacy of early intervention: Why are we still asking this question? *Topics in Early Childhood Special Education, 5*, 1–11.

Meisels, S. J. (1985b). A functional analysis of the evolution of public policy for handicapped young children. *Educational Evaluation and Policy Analysis, 7*, 115–126.

Meisels, S., Harbin, G., Modigliani, K., & Olson, K. (1988). Formulating optimal state early childhood intervention policies. *Exceptional Children, 55*, 159–165.

Menyuk, P. (1971). *The acquisition and development of language.* Englewood Cliffs, NJ: Prentice-Hall.

Neisworth, J., & Bagnato, S. (Eds.). (1987). *The young exceptional child: Early development and education.* New York: Macmillan.

Noonan, M. J., & Kilgo, J. L. (1987). Transition services for early age individuals with severe mental retardation. In R. N. Ianacone & R. A. Stodden (Eds.), *Transition issues and directions* (pp. 25–37). Reston, VA: Council for Exceptional Children.

Odom, S. L., DeKlyen, M., & Jenkins, J. (1984). Integrating handicapped and non-handicapped preschoolers: Developmental impact on non-handicapped children. *Exceptional Children, 51*, 41–48.

O'Keefe, A. (1979). *What Head Start means to families* (HEW Publication No. OHDS 79-31179). Washington, DC: U.S. Government Printing Office.

Olds, A. (1979). Designing developmentally optimal classrooms for children with special needs. In S. J. Meisels (Ed.), *Special education and development: Perspectives on young children with special needs* (pp. 91–138). Baltimore: University Park Press.

Polloway, E. (1987). Transition services for early age individuals with mild mental retardation. In R. N. Ianacone & R. A. Stodden (Eds.), *Transition issues and directions* (pp. 11–24). Reston, VA: Council for Exceptional Children.

Raths, J. D., & Katz, L. (1982). The best intentions for the education of teachers. *Journal of Teacher Education, 8*, 276–283.

Reid, D. K. (1978). Genevan theory and the education of exceptional children. In J. M. Gallagher & J. A. Easly (Eds.), *Knowledge and development* (Vol. 2, pp. 199–241). New York: Plenum Press.

Rhode, V., Leininger, J., Egan, M., & Bluhm, H. (1981). Perceptions of effectiveness as perceived by members of multidisciplinary elementary school teams. *Teacher Education and Special Education, 4*, 39–43.

Richard, N. B. (1986). Interaction between mothers and infants with Down's syndrome: Infant characteristics. *Topics in Early Childhood Special Education, 6*, 54–71.

Rondal, J. (1977). Maternal speech to normal and Down's syndrome children. In P. Mittler (Ed.), *Research to practice in mental retardation: Education and training* (Vol. 2, pp. 239–243). Baltimore: University Park Press.

Rosenberg, S., Robinson, C., & Beckman, P. (1984). Teaching skills inventory: A measure of parent performance. *Journal of the Division for Early Childhood, 8*, 107–113.

Rothbart, M., & Hanson, M. (1983). A caregiver report comparison of temperamental characteristics of Down syndrome and non-retarded infants. *American Journal of Mental Deficiency, 89*, 124–132.

Safford, P. (1988). *Integrated teaching in early childhood: Starting in the mainstream.* White Plains, NY: Longman.

Safford, P., & Rosen, L. (1981). Applications of a philosophical perspective in an integrated kindergarten program. *Topics in Early Childhood Special Education, 1*, 1–10.

Sameroff, A. J. (1975). Early influences on development. *Merrill-Palmer Quarterly, 21*, 267–294.

Sander, L. (1983). A twenty-five year follow-up of the Pavenstedt Longitudinal Research Project. In J. D. Call, E. Galenstin, & R. L. Tyson (Eds.), *Frontiers of infant psychiatry* (pp. 225–231). New York: Basic Books.

Schneider-Rosen, K., Braunwald, K., Carlson, V., & Cicchetti, D. (1985). Current perspectives in attachment theory: Illustration from the study of maltreated infants. In I. Bretherton & E. Waters (Eds.), Growing points in attachment theory and research. *Monographs of the Society for Research in Child Development, 50*, (1–2 Serial No. 209).

Schweinhart, L., & Weikart, D. P. (1981). Effects of the Perry Preschool Program on youths through age 19: A summary. *Journal of the Division for Early Childhood, 4*, 29–39.

Seefeldt, C., & Barbour, N. (1986). *Early childhood education: An introduction.* Columbus, OH: Merrill.

Sheehan, R. (1981). Issues in documenting early intervention with infants and parents. *Topics in Early Childhood Special Education, 1*, 67–75.

Sheehan, R., & Klein, N. K. (1988). Infant assessment. In M. C. Wang, M. Reynolds, & H. J. Walberg (Eds.), *Handbook of special education: Research and practice* (Vol. 4, pp. 243–258). Elmsford, NY: Pergamon Press.

Shonkoff, J. P., & Hauser-Cram, P. (1987). Early intervention for disabled infants and their families: A quantitative analysis. *Pediatrics, 80*, 650–658.

Smith, B. J. (Ed.). (1987). *Position statements and recommendations relating to P.L. 99-457 and other federal and state early childhood policies.* Alexandria, VA: Division for Early Childhood, Council for Exceptional Children.

Smith, B. J., & Powers, C. (1987). Issues related to developing state identification standards. *Topics in Early Childhood Special Education, 7*, 12–23.

Snell, M. E. (Ed.). (1987). *Systematic instruction of persons with severe handicaps* (3rd ed.). Columbus, OH: Merrill.

Spodek, B., & Saracho, O. N. (1982). The preparation and certification of early childhood personnel. In B. Spodek (Ed.), *Handbook of research in early childhood education* (pp. 399–425). New York: The Free Press.

Sroufe, L. A. (1979). The coherence of individual development: Early care, attachment, and subsequent development issues. *American Psychologist, 14*, 834–841.

Sroufe, L. A., & Rutter, M. (1984). The domain of developmental psychopathology. *Child Development, 48*, 1184–1199.

Stedman, D. J. (1973). Training: The need for getting it all together. In J. B. Jordan & R. F. Dailey (Eds.), *Not all little wagons are red: The exceptional child's early years* (pp. 154–171). Arlington, VA: Council for Exceptional Children.

Stile, S., Abernathy, S., Pettibone, T., & Wachtel, W. (1984). Training and certification for early childhood special education personnel: A six-year follow-up study. *Journal of the Division for Early Childhood, 11*, 69–73.

Sulzer-Azaroff, B., & Mayer, G. (1977). *Applying behavior-analysis procedures with children and youth*. New York: Holt, Rinehart, & Winston.

Trickett, P., Apfel, N., Rosenbaum, L., & Zigler, E. (1982). A five-year follow-up of participants in the Yale Child Welfare Research Program. In E. Zigler & E. W. Gordon (Eds.), *Day care: Scientific and social policy issues* (pp. 200–222). Boston: Auburn House.

Turnbull, A. P., & Turnbull, H. R. (1986). *Families and professionals: Creating an exceptional partnership*. Columbus, OH: Merrill.

Vandenberg, B. (1978). Play and development from ethological perspectives. *American Psychologist, 33*, 724–738.

Walker, J. (1982). Social interactions of handicapped infants. In D. Bricker (Ed.), *Intervention with at-risk and handicapped infants: From research to application* (pp. 217–232). Austin, TX: PRO-ED.

Weikart, D., Rogers, L., Adcock, C., & McClelland, D. (1971). *The cognitively oriented curriculum: A framework for teachers*. Washington, DC: National Association for the Education of Young Children.

Weiner, R., & Koppleman, J. (1987). *From birth to 5: Serving the youngest handicapped children*. Alexandria, VA: Capital Publications.

Wilcox, M. J. (1987). *Report of the American Speech and Hearing Infant Committee*. Rockville, MD: American Speech and Hearing Association.

Winderstrom, A. H. (1986). Educating young handicapped children: What can early childhood education contribute? *Childhood Education, 63*, 78–83.

Winton, P., & Turnbull, A. (1981). Parent involvement as viewed by parents of preschool handicapped children. *Topics in Early Childhood Special Education, 1*, 11–19.

Wolery, M. (1987). Program evaluation at the local level: Recommendations for improving services. *Topics in Early Childhood Special Education, 7*, 111–123.

Yonemura, M. V. (1986). *A teacher at work: Professional development and the early childhood educator*. New York: Teachers College Press.

Zigler, E., & Trickett, P. (1978). IQ, social competence, and evaluation of early childhood intervention programs. *American Psychologist, 33*, 789–798.

30 *Policy implementation: Perspectives on service coordination and interagency cooperation*

GLORIA L. HARBIN AND BRIAN A. MCNULTY

Infants and toddlers with handicaps often require the services of a variety of disciplines and agencies. Since no single discipline or agency can serve every child's needs, both parents and professionals have noted the need for a multidisciplinary, interagency approach to service provision (Featherstone, 1980; Steiner, 1976). Nevertheless, the various disciplines and agencies that work with individual children and their families often have difficulty with mutual coordination and cooperation. This chapter will focus on the sources of this problem, paying particular attention to the implementation of P.L. 99-457. It will discuss the importance of interagency coordination and will make recommendations for its enhancement.

Public Law 99-457 contains several important mechanisms to ensure both the development and the implementation of a coordinated system of services. A State Interagency Coordinating Council appointed by the governor is the primary mechanism for developing an interagency, coordinated, statewide service system. The Individualized Family Service Plan and a case manager are the mechanisms designed to coordinate the multidisciplinary, interagency services to individual families and children. Thus, the concept of coordinated services has been written into federal policy in such a way that it must become state policy as well. P.L. 99-457 contains the mandate and the mechanisms that encourage coordination, but does not explain the "why" nor the "how" of coordination. As with the implementation of any legislation or policy, the realization of this critical concept will depend upon how well each state understands the rationale and the means for enhancing coordination.

SERVICE COORDINATION INITIATIVES

More than a decade ago, Elliot Richardson, then the secretary of the Department of Health, Education, and Welfare (HEW), predicted that the human service sector would face a crisis in both control and performance (Brewer & Kakalik, 1979). Richardson recognized that the human service system was not a system at all, but a collection of independent, political, and highly specialized public agencies whose number and magnitude were expanding beyond anyone's ability to understand or manage them effectively (Brewer & Kakalik, 1979).

The authors would like to thank Catherine Daguio for her contributions in the preparation of this chapter.

700

Richardson (1978) identified comprehensive planning and programming as major policy changes required to increase integration and replace fragmentation. As part of this framework, HEW contracted for a comprehensive 2-year cross-agency evaluation of collaboration within federal and state programs for handicapped children. This study documented the disorganization, complexity, and fragmentation of the existing service delivery system (Brewer & Kakalik, 1979). It specifically identified five major problems: (1) inequity (i.e., unevenness in accessibility of services); (2) gaps in service (found to occur by state, age, type of handicap, and geographic areas within a state); (3) insufficient information (i.e., lack of reliable data for planning); (4) inadequate control (referring to the lack of a national policy resulting in a varied, uncoordinated, fragmented, and unresponsive service system); and (5) insufficient resources (i.e., the need for dollars, personnel, and facilities, as well as improved and coordinated services and changes in the organizational structure of the service delivery system) (Brewer & Kakalik, 1979).

Whereas Brewer and Kakalik's (1979) study documented the extent of the problems in coordinating services, other federal studies confirmed that service integration, or coordination, has a positive effect on the accessibility, continuity, and efficiency of service provision (Gans & Horton, 1975). These studies concluded that, if coordination efforts were to be successful, they must be undertaken at both the federal and state levels. Consequently, in recognition of the need for better coordination of services to young children with handicaps, four different types of initiatives were developed by federal agencies to encourage interagency service coordination. The first type was the development of federal Interagency Agreements and Memoranda of Understanding among agencies. Unfortunately, the general nature of these federal interagency agreements has done little to change the fragmented and disparate policies that hamper coordination at the state and local levels. The second type of initiative provided incentives through funding a variety of local demonstration projects, intended to coordinate services to young children with handicaps and their families. Six of these collaborative projects were funded jointly by the Division of Maternal and Child Health and the former Bureau of Education for the Handicapped. The third type of initiative involved technical assistance in which the Division of Maternal and Child Health funded a program to assist federally funded projects to develop community-based, coordinated services. The fourth type of initiative focused specifically on the use of federal regulations. The regulations for programs from most of the federal agencies include provisions requiring coordination through such activities as joint planning and sharing information, staff, services, and facilities.

Despite all of these federal coordination initiatives, the specific requirements of federal policies concerning eligibility for services, service delivery, and funding remained unchanged. Although the federal agencies mandated and encouraged interagency coordination, the method of determining just how coordination would occur was left to the discretion of states and local communities.

In further recognition of the critical contribution of state agencies to service coordination for disabled children, Congress passed P.L. 98-199. This bill provided grant money to each state to develop a comprehensive service delivery system for all young handicapped children from birth through age five. The legislation required states to coordinate service delivery, but Congress also demonstrated an understanding that a coordinated system of services takes time to evolve. The legislation allowed 2 years for planning, 3 years for developing the system, and an additional 3 years for implementation.

Congress, however, decided that states needed more direction in the development of a coordinated service system for handicapped infants and toddlers. Hence, in 1986 Congress passed P.L. 99-457, which superceded P.L. 98-199 and required participating states to develop a comprehensive, coordinated, multidisciplinary, interagency system of services. The legislation also provided an incentive for participation through increased appropriations to each state taking part in this program.

This legislation recognizes that infants and toddlers with handicaps frequently require services that should be provided by professionals from different disciplines and agencies. There are several aspects of P.L. 99-457 that facilitate the coordination of services to individual children as well as the coordination of the system of services. The law recognizes the need for early intervention services to be integrated into a single plan for each child, called the Individualized Family Service Plan (IFSP). Professionals and parents have come to realize that it is not enough merely to provide multidisciplinary services. It is critical that someone be responsible for analyzing all of the recommendations from all professionals involved and then synthesizing and integrating those recommendations into a single service plan. This plan must then be translated or explained to the family. P.L. 99-457 incorporates an additional mechanism that is designed to further ensure the coordination of early intervention services to both the child and family. That mechanism is the required appointment of a case manager to assist in the coordination of services for the infant or toddler and his or her family.

P.L. 99-457 also addresses the need for a statewide coordinated service system for all infants and toddlers with handicaps. This requires the coordination of programs and agencies, both public and private. The law sets forth a minimum of 14 components for the service system in each state. One of the requirements is for a lead administering agency – not to provide all of the services alone, but to administer the system of services and finances. The legislation also requires that the Interagency Coordinating Council, which is appointed by the governor, ensures the development and implementation of a statewide system of services that is coordinated across agencies.

THE CONCEPT OF COORDINATION

The concept of coordination affects both the disciplines and the agencies that provide services to handicapped children and their families. Multidisciplinary coordination focuses on decisions concerning an individual child, and interagency coordination focuses on decisions concerning programs. Both require the participation of individuals with different points of view and expertise, based on the belief that a single discipline or agency is insufficient to determine and understand the needs of handicapped infants and toddlers and their families. Coordination, then, requires the effective communication of one's own perspective and the ability to hear and understand the perspectives of others. The two approaches (multidisciplinary and interagency) are also similar in terms of decision making. That is, once individuals from different disciplines and agencies have presented their points of view, the multidisciplinary team or the interagency council must then make a group decision before taking action.

There have been many attempts over the years to coordinate services among various human service agencies. The complex (Magrab, Flynn, & Pelosi, 1985), multidimensional (Agranoff, 1977; Martin, Chackerian, Imershein, & Frumkin, 1983; Rogers & Farrow, 1983) nature of the concept of coordination has made it extremely difficult to implement effectively (Flynn & Harbin, 1987). In their review of the literature on interagency coordination, Flynn and Harbin (1987) discovered that research efforts generally had not addressed the complexity of the concept. The focus of such studies was often upon a single aspect, such as the individuals involved in the coordination effort, the process used to coordinate services, or the number of contacts made. Thus, Flynn and Harbin (1987) articulated the need for a conceptual model to better describe the complexities and breadth of the concept of interagency coordination. They presented a multidimensional, interactional, developmental paradigm that contains five broad dimensions: climate, resources, policies, people, and process. A sixth dimension, identified by McNulty (1986), is agency structure. Each of these dimensions will be discussed briefly.

Climate

The general atmosphere in which cooperative efforts are attempted can greatly influence the success or failure of these efforts. A variety of factors contribute to the nature of the climate. The attitudes, priorities, and support of key decision makers, as well as those of direct service providers and the general populace, can enhance collaborative efforts or render them nearly impossible. The extent to which children are valued and seen as a priority is a part of the climate and will influence whether dwindling resources will be allocated to programs. Attitudes concerning the need and value of collaboration and concerning the roles of the public and private sectors are also key factors in determining the supportiveness of the climate.

Resources

The availability and the nature of assets has a profound influence upon interagency collaborative efforts. At least three factors contribute to the level of resources available to support such endeavors: money, people, and facilities. The amount of fiscal resources available and then committed is obviously crucial. The number and quality of available professionals also contribute greatly to the level of resources. The quality and number of intervention and specialized settings (i.e., diagnostic clinics, surgical hospitals, neonatal intensive care units, etc.), are a final and important part of the resource pool.

Policies

Policies consist of those sets of governing principles that have been established within and among agencies. These include laws, regulations, standards, guidelines, licensing, certification, and formal interagency agreements. Numerous sets of policies have been developed in each state, and their effects upon interagency cooperation are substantial. These governing principles can have a major impact on the ability of programs to work cooperatively. All too often existing policies at the state and federal levels are in conflict with one another, encouraging competition among agencies.

People

The ability of the interagency group to accomplish its goals and achieve its mission is dependent to a large extent on the people involved in the effort. Three main categories of participants are involved: the facilitator-leader, group members, and key decision makers. They vary in skills, attitudes, and amount of involvement. A skilled facilitator-leader is a critical part of this dimension. This person guides the group and can be very influential in determining its effectiveness. The group members play a crucial role in the interagency coordination effort. They are involved in planning, developing, and influencing others to accept the plan. Key decision makers also contribute to the eventual acceptance or rejection of interagency efforts.

Process

The series of actions and operations used by an interagency group has a critical impact on the success of interagency collaborative efforts. Actions taken by the group can either promote cooperation or engender competition and dissension. Communication, proper planning, and mechanisms for conflict resolution are critical to the proper functioning of an interagency group and can have profound effects, both positive and negative, on the entire interagency effort.

Agency

The structure and flexibility of the administering agency, as well as the agency's history concerning change, will have an influence upon successful coordination. Most governmental agencies operate within the classic pyramidal, bureaucratic model. Many of these agencies have grown larger, more rigid, and less adaptable in meeting the needs of consumers (Glazer, 1983; Kotler, 1982). For example, the Special Education Agency in many state departments of education began as a small agency with a few programs serving a few children. The staff was small and its organization was often flexible. As state Special Education Agencies added more programs, they added more personnel. The increased size and number of programs required more rules and regulations, and often necessitated more time to both make and change decisions. These larger agencies often are less likely to be able to meet the immediate needs of children and families. The ability of agencies to adapt to needed changes in agency structure, as well as policies, will have considerable effects on the successful coordination of services among agencies.

Within the paradigm presented by Flynn and Harbin (1987), these six dimensions (climate, resources, policies, people, process, and agency) are interactive. These interactions can range from simple to complex. In some circumstances, two of the dimensions interact (climate and policies); at other times, all of the dimensions may interact with one another. The relationship among these dimensions is often multi-directional, because an event or factor in one dimension may influence change in another dimension, which in turn influences the first dimension. The six dimensions are dynamic, with the possibility for change occurring at any time.

The concept of interagency coordination is hard to define and understand. Its broad, complex, multidimensional, interactional, developmental nature makes implementation difficult. Many previous approaches to defining the concept of interagency service coordination have been too simplistic. Future implementation efforts must systematically address the complexity of the concept if they are to be successful.

DIFFICULTIES IN COORDINATION

Although federal initiatives have increased efforts of service coordination at the state and local levels, much remains to be accomplished before each state has a coordinated system of services for handicapped infants and toddlers. When P.L. 99-457 was passed, most states did not have a mandated lead agency to coordinate a system of services. A study of all 50 states and the District of Columbia found that the administration and provision of services was divided among several agencies in most states (Meisels, Harbin, Modigliani, & Olson, 1988). The study indicated that, on the average, every state had three to four agencies with primary responsibilities for managing early intervention services. In some states there were as many as seven agencies operating semiautonomously in the delivery of early intervention services. Adding to the difficulties in coordination, the funding patterns for such services were found to be as diverse as the administrative arrangements designed to manage them.

States were presented with a list of services (public awareness, screening, diagnostic assessment, intervention programs, parent training, and case management) and asked to identify the services in greatest need of coordination. Responses indicated that all of these services were in need of extensive coordination. However, those services in greatest need for improved coordination were case management, staff training, diagnostic assessment, and intervention programs. Respondents to the Meisels et al. (1988) survey were also asked to address the obstacles to coordination. States reported numerous problems that prevented coordination of services to infants and toddlers with handicaps. Those problems most frequently cited as substantial barriers were the lack of available funds, limitations in the use of funds, inconsistent eligibility criteria, lack of interagency coordination, and inconsistent regulations across agencies.

One of the most compelling survey findings was that even those states that had an entitlement to services and a designated lead agency still listed numerous serious problems that hindered service coordination. For example, one state with legislation that entitles infants and toddlers with handicaps to services under the P.L. 94-142 categorical definition, reported numerous and substantial problems in the ability to coordinate with other agencies. This lack of coordination might result, for instance, in parents being presented with conflicting instructions from the pediatrician, physical therapist, nurse, and early intervention specialist. In such cases, a family can become overwhelmed because it is being asked to do more than it feels is possible while not really understanding precisely what it is that is being requested. Both parents and professionals become frustrated, and the child fails to receive all of the indicated services. Thus, those states participating in P.L. 99-457 had much to overcome in the area of service coordination.

In addition to the study by Meisels et al. (1988), other reports document the difficulties in coordinating service provision at the local and state levels (Foltz, 1982; Hayes, 1982; Knitzer, 1982; Meisels, 1985; Steiner 1976). The interagency coordination paradigm developed by Flynn and Harbin (1987) will be used to delineate those problems most often mentioned in the literature.

Climate

One of the most frequently mentioned problems is the lack of support from the various agencies, especially high-level decision makers (Hayes, 1982; Meisels, 1985). In many instances, agency administrators, the legislature, the governor, and even the electorate view the problems of infants and toddlers with handicaps and their families as insignificant in comparison to other problems facing the state. Interagency coordination would be nice, they seem to say, but we must put our energy elsewhere in order to resolve really important issues. In other instances, a competitive and mistrustful climate may exist, in which the key decision makers argue and compete openly for control and resources. This competitive and mistrustful attitude filters through to everyone involved with the agencies. In this situation, even if an interagency group has been appointed to fulfill the requirements of a federal program, the agency's suggestions for program changes may be ignored. Interagency service coordination requires support from key decision makers to plan cooperatively and change existing programs and policies as needed. Lack of support from administrators, as well as the public, makes the task of coordinating services very difficult. The best that can be done under these circumstances is an occasional success in which local service providers agree to solve the service coordination problems for an individual child and his or her family.

Resources

Lack of staff time and scarce fiscal resources are frequently mentioned as barriers to interagency coordination (Meisels, 1985) and are associated with the resources dimension of the Flynn and Harbin (1987) paradigm. All too often agency staff members are assigned to work on an interagency group, but are still required to perform all of the other responsibilities they had prior to their appointment to this group. An interagency group that is trying to resolve such difficult problems as eligibility criteria, a coordinated screening and tracking system, or the development of policies to support these coordinated services requires a great deal of time and effort. If the agency staff is not allotted the time necessary to work on interagency service coordination, its efforts are likely to fail. Similarly, interagency activities require financial support. In some cases, this lack of financial support and staff time results from a lack of understanding by agency administrators concerning the need for this type of support. In other instances, attitudes (i.e., the climate dimension) influence the amount of resources assigned. In either case, the result all too frequently is an eventual termination of interagency activities with no improvement in the coordination of services to children and families.

Policies

Associated with the policy dimension are the many complaints associated with disparate and often conflicting policies at the state and federal levels (Steiner, 1976). These policies lead to inconsistent eligibility criteria, so often a stumbling block to the coordination and availability of services to all infants and toddlers with disabilities. When agencies differ in their definition of who should receive services, it means that some children who need services from both agencies may only be eligible for services from one. Existing policies in many states perpetuate this "patchwork quilt" approach to service provision. Unless the policies are examined, and more complementary policies developed, the service system will remain fragmented.

One of the most needed policies concerns interagency agreements. Yet, these agreements have often been criticized for being so general that they communicate nothing of real substance. Many such agreements only state that interagency coordination is necessary, and agree to "foster" cooperation and share information. These generalities, although setting a positive tone, do little to delineate services and financial responsibilities. Service coordination, once again, is left to informal arrangements by service providers, which affects only a portion of the children and families truly in need of service coordination.

People and process

The lack of leadership and vision is frequently mentioned as a barrier to interagency service coordination (Hayes, 1982). Even in the presence of a supportive climate, if no one directly involved has leadership skills, this complex interagency effort is likely to become directionless and its membership disenchanted. A vision is needed to provide direction to the efforts to plan a system of coordinated services. Unfortunately, too many interagency groups have floundered and eventually dissolved because no one shared a vision of how the current service system elements could be put together. Furthermore, once the interagency planning group has developed a vision and direction, another type of leadership becomes critical. This is the leadership that is necessary to get the plan and policies adopted by the administration and the legislature, but all too often this important leadership is lacking.

The individuals who are directly involved in planning a coordinated service system often possess what Boshier (personal communication, July 24, 1982) refers to as professional narcissism. That is, these people believe that their perspective or the way their agency provides programs is the only "right way." To compound this problem, interagency members often lack (1) experience in interagency work (Pollard, Hall, Keeran, 1979); (2) the competencies needed to deal constructively with interpersonal problems (Baumheir, 1979); (3) negotiation skills (Northwest Regional Educational Laboratory [NWREL], 1980); and (4) conflict resolution skills (Elder & Magrab, 1980). The lack of vision and leadership of individuals directly managing the interagency process, as well as failures in the process itself, are the most frequently mentioned problems within the people and process dimensions.

Agency

Agency rigidity has been described as another barrier to the successful coordination of services (Pollard et al., 1979). Agency administrators are often either unable or unwilling to undertake the difficult task of changing the structure of their agencies, programs, or responsibilities in order to be more responsive to the needs of young children with disabilities and their families. Rigid bureaucracies are slow to change and, when more than one of them is involved, service coordination becomes even more difficult. The current service system structure is designed around separate, single agencies that are accustomed to "doing their own thing." Interagency coordinated service delivery requires a change in the structure of the current system to incorporate multiple agencies, coordinated roles, and shared responsibilities. The inability of state agencies to adjust or change their structures often results in a continuation of a fragmented service system.

Numerous factors pose difficulties for the coordination of services. The task is made even more complex because quite frequently several of these factors operate simultaneously. As described in Flynn and Harbin's (1987) paradigm, these factors interact and influence one another. The need to identify all of the contributing factors, understand their interaction, and develop strategies (including the identification of key individuals) to alleviate the barriers is a critically important set of tasks.

REASONS FOR THE CURRENT FOCUS ON SERVICE COORDINATION

Despite the various federal and state initiatives, the logic of the concept, and the common acceptance of the need for service coordination, interagency services that are coordinated and multidisciplinary remain elusive. Nevertheless, as seen in such recent federal initiatives as P.L. 99-457 and the Maternal Child Health Block Grant, there is a major impetus to develop programs that reflect substantial interagency coordination. The desire for change in this direction can be linked to four primary factors: (1) a conservative political climate combined with reduced fiscal resources, (2) an increase in the public's awareness of problems posed by ineffective bureaucracies, (3) changes in consumer demands, and (4) expectations concerning service delivery based on the conceptual understanding of the transactional nature of the development of children and families.

Political climate and fiscal resources

One of the most significant reasons or motivations for an increased interest in inter-agency coordination is the overall conservative political mood of the 1980s (McNulty, 1988). Because of increasingly scarce resources, the rejection of local bond issues, tax reduction initiatives, and federal cutbacks and block grants, state and federal legislatures are reflecting their constituencies by demanding more efficient operation and clearer proof of nonduplication of services before establishing new or continuing appropriations. Legislators often believe that the coordination of fiscal resources is the best strategy to reduce or hold the line on costs, while continuing to provide human services.

Public awareness of ineffective bureaucracies

High expectations have been set through legislation and litigation promising education, social services, health care, public assistance, and other services to consumers. Concurrently, consumers have become more knowledgeable and demanding of the service delivery system and more aware of the problems inherent in the present human services system. As a result, there is a sense that public agencies and institutions are not living up to expectations (Glazer, 1983). This has been especially true of the human services sector because rapid and massive increases in services and expenditures have resulted in the creation of a maze of highly specialized public programs, some of which are so complex and disorganized that they seem to defy effective operation (Brewer & Kakalik, 1979). Many parents and professionals believe that the only logical and practical method for creating a more effective and efficient system is through the coordination of existing programs. It is felt that interagency coordination can result in a more well-managed and coherent delivery system (Baumheir, 1979; Flynn & Harbin, 1987).

Changes in consumer demands

Given the rapid rise in expenditures for human services during the past decade, one would expect a high degree of consumer satisfaction, yet just the opposite appears to be true. The results of a Rand Corporation study on services to the handicapped (Brewer & Kakalik, 1979) clearly documented that both providers and consumers of these services found the system to be so complex and disorganized that it often seemed inaccessible. Although there appeared to be a wide range of services available, fully two-thirds of all consumers had difficulty finding them, let alone actually receiving them. Professionals clearly documented their frustrations in trying to match appropriate and available services with eligible clients. Unfortunately, many believe that the service system has become even more inaccessible during the 1980s (Meisels, 1985). All too often professionals are faced with the frustrating dilemma of a child who obviously needs services not being eligible for a particular program because of the parents' income level, or the child's type or severity of disability, age, residence, or lack of insurance.

At the other end of the spectrum the opposite problem may occur – a client or family may be "over identified" by an array of agencies and consequently receive too many or conflicting services. Agencies that are unaware of each other's services and shared clients may, and often do, "overload" a particular family with too many intervention services; or they may provide conflicting requests to the family. An example of this overload is the family with a young handicapped child who receives health, education, and social services. Under the direction of one agency, the parent spends the day transporting his or her child from one therapy to another. Simultaneously, mothers are counseled by another agency that in order to meet the emotional needs of their child, they must feel more fulfilled personally and should therefore seek employment and stimulation outside the home. They are informed by a third agency, however, that if they increase the family income they will no longer be eligible for certain benefits such as Medicaid or food stamps. Traditionally, although such families have been labeled multiproblem families, in actuality they may be dealing with a multiagency problem (Selig, 1976).

In addition to these difficulties, there is also the issue of clients not receiving the full range of diversity of services that they may require and for which they are eligible. Since many agency personnel do not always understand the eligibility criteria or the services provided by other agencies, referrals across agencies are limited. This lack of direction or information about the array of available services is the problem most frequently cited by parents (Brewer & Kakalik, 1979; Meisels, 1985). Although families may be grateful for the services they receive, they have expressed the need for significant improvement in the way these services are provided.

With the societal trends toward increased personal affluence and higher education, many parents are also demanding opportunities for greater involvement and more personal choices from the service delivery system. Naisbitt (1982), Toffler (1980), and Glazer (1983) all find this to be especially true for the activist "baby-boom" generation. These individuals are demanding more adaptability, responsiveness, diversity, and accountability from governmental organizations. Glazer (1983) suggests that this desire for more personal choice and diversity is resulting in more private citizens requesting a greater role in managing governmental services that affect them.

Transactional nature of child and family development

Increased knowledge of family systems theory has demonstrated the complex, interactional relationships between parents and their children (Gallagher & Vietze, 1986). This knowledge has also more recently created an awareness of the impact of service providers on the family system. Interventions with young children affect not only the child, but the family system as well. Therefore, it is critical to realize that "it is impossible to separate intervention aimed at a child from intervention specifically aimed at families" (Berger & Foster, 1986, p. 255). Given these facts, interventionists must be able to gain access directly to a variety of services, refer families to other service providers, and be able to assist families in dealing with a variety of agencies. Further, services should not be planned separately for families and children, but in a more integrated manner, across agencies and programs (see Sameroff & Fiese, this volume). All of these skills require a knowledge of interagency services and the ability to access services across agencies.

RECOMMENDATIONS FOR IMPROVING SERVICE COORDINATION

If the intent of P.L. 99-457 is to be realized, extensive improvements in coordination of services, whether for an individual child or within a state system, must be made. The coordination of services needs to be undertaken by a group of individuals involved in and responsible for service provision. This group may be located at either the local or state level or at both levels. The group may consist of members representing service agencies, consumers, and providers, as mandated for the 15-member P.L. 99-457 State Interagency Coordinating Council. In contrast, the group may be a small policymaking group of high-level decision makers (e.g., agency commissioners). Interagency service coordination may be undertaken by some combination of these various types and levels of groups. The preceding analysis of this complex (Magrab et al., 1985; Meisels et al. 1988), multidimensional (Martin et al., 1983; Bailey, 1984; Flynn & Harbin, 1987), poorly defined (Hagebak, 1979; Zald, 1969) concept indicates that several areas must be addressed by any interagency service coordination group if its implementation is to be successful. These areas include (1) attention to all six interagency dimensions, (2) use of a systems approach, (3) leadership and participation, (4) coordinated policy development, (5) multidisciplinary and multiagency training, (6) case management, and (7) federal interagency coordination. Each of these items will be discussed briefly, using as an example the provision in P.L. 99-457 for implementing an Interagency Coordinating Council. These recommendations apply to other efforts at coordinating services for young infants and toddlers with handicaps as well.

Systematically addressing all dimensions

Efforts at service coordination have been as haphazard, fragmented, and unsystematic as those services they are attempting to coordinate (Meisels, 1985). If service coordination is to be successful, an increased understanding of the complexities and multidimensional nature of this concept is needed. Successful leaders of interagency service coordination groups will assist the group in systematically addressing all dimensions that affect the successful coordination of services at the state and local levels (climate, resources, policies, people, process, and agency structure). Previous efforts have often focused on a single dimension, much like the famed story of the blind men and the elephant (Churchman, 1968). Those individuals providing leadership in the development of service coordination must be able to see the "whole elephant," or the big picture, so that efforts will not become simplistic.

For example, if interagency efforts are to be more successful, the chair of the State Interagency Coordinating Council, in conjunction with council members and staff, need to examine each dimension carefully. They should discuss the general climate within the state concerning support for services for infants and toddlers with handicaps, as well as identify support for the coordination of services and the barriers to this coordination. Then strategies can be developed and individuals identified who can be helpful in improving the climate.

The chair, staff, and members of the Interagency Coordinating Council need also to examine the resources they have been given to accomplish the task. Furthermore, they should urge agencies to coordinate their requests for appropriations from the legislature. When agencies agree and support one another's requests as a result of joint fiscal planning, it is a powerful statement to legislators who are relieved of the difficult task of choosing among competing interests and programs. It is also extremely important to analyze the existing policies for gaps, overlaps, and contradictions. Then a process of joint policy development, such as the one described later in this section, can be undertaken.

Also needed is an individual or small group of people who can provide leadership, vision, and direction in the development of a service system. A variety of leaders is needed to gain support and obtain official approval (i.e., legislation, interagency agreements, regulations). Many constituencies (i.e., parents, local service providers from different agencies and disciplines, private providers, the medical community, state agency staff, agency administrators, legislators, and the governor) should be involved in the planning, kept informed of the plans, and be expected to provide support for the coordinated services plan. Areas such as case management and the IFSP will be especially controversial. For coordination attempts to be successful, it is important that both parents and service providers understand and support the plans that have been developed for development of the IFSP and case management, including selection of the case manager. If not, the plans and policies may be doomed from the outset.

Finally, there should be at least one individual – and it is helpful if there is more than one – who understands the larger political climate and has a good grasp of group dynamics. It is critical that the individual be skilled in helping a group of this nature develop and work productively. If not, the group may become overwhelmed by the scope of the task. Most people are accustomed to working on smaller, short-term tasks as a part of a group, or working out the problems of a single child and family. The development of a large, complex service system is more difficult and time-consuming than other group planning tasks. Therefore, leadership is an essential ingredient for assisting the group to understand the scope, sustain motivation, and provide a productive working climate over a prolonged period of time.

Systems approach

Most professionals have been trained in a single discipline and have knowledge about service provision from the perspective of a single agency, rather than the entire service system. The development of a coordinated system of services requires knowledge and use of a systems approach (Mittenthal, 1976). Systems theory and technology is relatively new to most human services personnel, including agency administration (Mittenthal, 1976). To complicate matters even further, when compared to a systems model, the 14 components of a service system required for P.L. 99-457, Part H, do not constitute a complete system.

Some of the components listed separately actually would form only one component (i.e., the several components that are related to funding). Others listed as components would not be considered as discrete components within a systems model. For example, a "central directory of services" would be part of a larger component perhaps, such as an information and tracking system, an essential part of Child Find.

Finally, the 14 components listed in P.L. 99-457 do not form an organic whole. There is no way to diagram them to illustrate how they relate or function together to make a complete system. Within the required 14 components, some, but not all, of the pieces or components needed to develop a system exist.

The use of a systems approach in planning and developing coordinated early intervention services is critical to eliminating redundancy, fragmentation, and gaps. When developing a system for comprehensive, coordinated, multidisciplinary, interagency services for children with handicaps, birth through age two, states should ask two important questions: (1) What components, including the elements within those components, are involved in developing a system of statewide services for young children with special needs and their families? (2) How do these components and elements interact and relate to the roles and responsibilities at both the state and local levels?

Harbin (1987), utilizing a systems approach, has delineated a framework for the development of comprehensive, coordinated early intervention services. This framework contains five interrelated components (see Figure 1).

1. *Ensure public awareness, understanding, and support.* Create an environment in which the public and key decision makers understand the value and benefits of comprehensive services, support these services, and are aware of their availability.
2. *Identify and locate eligible children and families.* Locate, screen, and determine through multidisciplinary assessment which children and families are eligible to receive services.
3. *Provide an array of appropriate services to children and families.* Develop and utilize an IFSP for eligible children and families in addition to providing an array of multidisciplinary and multiagency services, which are coordinated by a case manager, that meet the individual needs of children and families.
4. *Specify agencies' roles, functions, policies, and procedures to manage and provide support for comprehensive services.* Develop a system with complementary policies for funding, personnel, administration, and interagency coordination.
5. *Evaluate and improve services provided to children and families.* Determine the effectiveness of programs in order to improve their quality.

Each of the five components of a service system contains one or more elements. For example, the fourth component contains six elements: system planning, interagency coordination, administration and management (which involves the administrative structure for the system), funding, personnel, and policies. In turn, each of these elements can be compared against a list of quality indicators for enhancing comprehensive services at both the state and local levels. For example, within the funding element quality indicators at the local level include identification of all possible funding sources, knowledge of how to access funds, and recording information on costs and expenditures. At the state level quality indicators include policies that facilitate the coordination of funds at the state and local levels, accounting mechanisms that allow for funds and payments to be coordinated, and procedures for regulating disputes concerning funding.

The development of a comprehensive, multidisciplinary, coordinated, early intervention service system is a complex, difficult, and time-consuming task. It is very difficult for interagency groups, such as the State Interagency Coordinating Council, to start from the beginning in developing such a system. The councils may be hindered by infrequent meeting schedules, by not having worked together enough to become a productive cohesive group, and by lack of experience with systems design and early intervention. Efforts at designing a state and local coordinated system of services will be enhanced if some individual or individuals – either affiliated with or outside of the interagency group – can provide examples of a system of services to which the Interagency Coordinating Council can react.

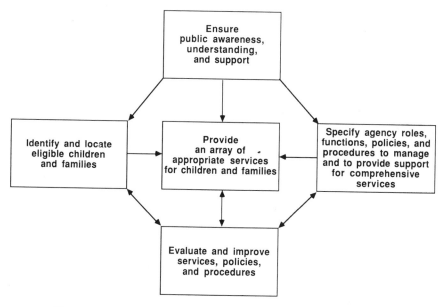

Figure 1. A framework for the development of comprehensive services for young children with special needs and their families.

Leadership and Participation

The creation of coordinated early intervention services is influenced by the nature and amount of both leadership and productive participation. The creation of the State Interagency Coordinating Council and its working groups and task forces offers both new opportunities and challenges for identifying sufficient leadership and stimulating participation. Traditionally, the role of leadership was considered to rest with a single powerful person, which is consistent with hierarchical, bureaucratic agencies that operate primarily in isolation from other agencies. However, for interagency coordination of early intervention services to be successful, individuals must assume leadership positions that transform related activities at all levels. The transformational leader creates purpose and builds on an individual's need for meaning (Burns, 1987). The transformational leader creates a new vision of and for the organization (Bennis, 1984; Tichy & Ulrich, 1984).

If interagency efforts are to be effective, several types of leaders and facilitators are needed in the legislature, among agency administrators, in the State Interagency Coordinating Council, among direct service personnel, and among parents. Leadership is needed to help develop policies and obtain passage of legislation, to provide vision in designing the comprehensive coordinated service system, and to facilitate constructive group dynamics and productive group functioning and decision making. Another major role of the leader or leaders is to encourage and manage broad-based participation. Leaders or facilitators need to provide structures that value diverse perspectives from which to view and understand issues and yet achieve consensus regarding common goals.

In interagency policy development, broad-based participation at both the state and local level is critical. Participation facilitates the development of a broader and more comprehensive picture. Involving individuals in the planning process reduces the resistance to change. In order for change to be effective, it must involve those who will be affected by the proposed change (Sarason, 1971). In addition, successful implementation of any such plans depends upon the development of internal and external support groups (Huff, 1980). Greater representation on planning groups enhances the likelihood of diffusion, and consequently the development of needed support groups. The diversity of the group can build on the existing communication networks, and through increased contacts can build an even larger base of support.

Improvement in interagency service coordination requires an interactive effect between leadership and participation. It appears that effective groups typically have a number of common characteristics (Kast & Rosenzweig, 1974). These include characteristics that pertain to individual group members (e.g., impartiality and critical evaluation of ideas); to use of outside groups and experts to test and validate the ideas developed by the group; and to communication with other relevant groups, decision makers, and recipients of group plans (Kast & Rosenweig, 1974). Efforts at coordinating services, whether at the local or state level, are likely to be more successful if interagency groups have effective leadership and productive participation.

Joint Policy Development

Many issues, such as who is disabled and how to locate and identify children with disabilities, cross agency boundaries. In order to solve these critical problems, there is a need for a more coordinated policy analysis and development across agencies at all levels of government. This joint policy development process will promote cohesion and continuity of policies that have been developed by individual agencies, as well as those policies developed together. The process forces both agency personnel and consumers to think about the purposes and directions of their organizations. Statements that define goals or a mission can provide a more standardized and cohesive framework for dealing with shared problems across agencies.

Unlike many of the interagency efforts described earlier, which focused on "agreeing to agree," joint policy development focuses on identifying and achieving common goals and missions through the adoption of common policy statements. An example of this type of policy initiative comes from a recent report of the National Council on the Handicapped (1986). This report recommends a restructuring of disability aid programs to promote independence and self-sufficiency and to reduce the current overemphasis on income support. The report delineates clear policy priorities and makes recommendations for accomplishing these priorities through the reduction of existing barriers, as well as better utilization of existing resources.

It is not uncommon within a state to find interagency groups functioning at different levels. There may be a formalized group of human services cabinet members (e.g., commissioners) established to address interagency concerns and initiatives. At another level of government, division directors of mental health, special education, health developmental disabilities, and social services may have begun to address shared state policy issues. At the next level is the State Interagency Coordinating Council. Joint policy planning documents can be and should facilitate coordinated planning among all three of the levels described.

In Colorado the document *Interagency Public Policy Principles* (Colorado Department of Education, 1987) was developed to establish goals that affect each department and that could be addressed in a cooperative effort. A multiagency policy document was developed that addressed transition services for disabled young adults. Colorado's *Interagency Transition Policy Document* (Colorado Department of Education, 1986) outlines a series of common policy statements, objectives, and outcomes to be addressed by all state and local providers. The adoption of these interagency policy statements was meant to provide a unified direction for all participating agencies. The policy statements were purposefully kept broad-based, for example, "All Colorado citizens, including youth with disabilities, will have opportunities for full participation in work and community life" (p. 3). However, following these broad statements is a series of more specific policy objectives to which all collaborating agencies agreed. The purpose of the objectives is to define the outcome of the process. These objectives can and should address both philosophical and programmatic issues:

All young people with disabilities will be prepared for and offered "real work" settings for "real wages" with access to necessary support services.... All youth with disabilities shall have access to "functional" likeskills curriculum designed to prepare them to live and function in domestic, recreational, social, community, and vocational environments.... All youth with disabilities will have a written individual transition plan developed by the transition team. All young people with disabilities will have access to appropriate residential options in integrated, community-based settings (pp. 3–4).

Clearly, these statements can set specific systems objectives toward which all agencies and individuals can make a commitment. It becomes the responsibility of the participating agencies to work together to remove barriers and create incentives for reaching these goals. Readers of the document can gain an understanding of what the outcomes are meant to be because it places performance expectations on all of the participating agencies.

An example of a policy document that could be developed to design a system of early intervention services that is coordinated across agencies and that addresses both the public and private sector would include the following topics.

1. *Definitions*. Who are the target populations and what are early intervention services? The council may choose to be either specific or general, depending on the needs and direction of the state.

2. *Policy goals*. These statements should reflect the philosophy, purposes, and outcomes of intervention services, for example, "It is the policy of all human services agencies to provide for an integrated service delivery system that will support families and assist young children with disabilities and their families to achieve maximum independence, integration, and self-sufficiency." Such statements should set the goals toward which all agencies will work. The policy should also assist in defining the purpose of intervention. Is it to provide support to families, to improve school placements, to provide for social integration, or all of these? The question to be addressed here is, What are the purposes of early intervention services? By defining our purposes, we help to define the composition of such programs and how to intervene more effectively (Bricker, 1987). Finally, program evaluation strategies become more evident when purposes are well defined.

3. *Policy objectives*. In order to achieve policy goals, the collaborating agencies must identify and work to achieve certain performance objectives cooperatively. These objectives might state that services are to be family-focused and, as such, should provide for information, support, and involvement of families. They might address the

need for placements that allow for, facilitate, and maximize interaction with nonhandicapped siblings and peers, or they might address the need for flexibility in the delivery
of services to meet the needs of individual children and families. They could focus on
issues, such as the roles and responsibilities of service providers and parents, and
describe how the single line of authority is to be implemented. They may define a
timely evaluation, the role of private providers, personnel standards, and the availability of ongoing training. Ultimately, however, these policy objectives will provide
conceptual guidance concerning how the system should be structured and how it should
operate. As stated earlier, the objectives can and should address philosophical and
programmatic issues. It is also important to realize that the policy document is a "living
document" and, as such, can be amended and clarified as new issues or concerns
emerge.

   4. *Services.* This section of the document should describe how to implement
the policy objectives and components of the statewide system. The framework for a
comprehensive delivery system developed by Harbin (1987) and mentioned earlier
could provide a basis for selecting and delineating services. The key is to provide
conceptual guidance without being overly prescriptive. In many cases, the actual development should be left to local communities, providers, and consumers. Although not an
exhaustive list, at least five areas of services and issues that require coordination should
receive attention by the Council.

> a. *Case finding and management.* A system must be established and implemented for an
> active and effective public awareness campaign and child-find services that include
> screening, assessment, and multidisciplinary planning. Case management should
> help families gain access to early intervention services, ensure the timely delivery of
> these services, and coordinate their provision, including services from medical and
> health care providers.
> b. *Provision of direct and support services.* The intent of the new legislation clearly
> identifies the family as the primary learning environment for all young children
> (U.S. House Committee on Education and Labor, 1986). Therefore, all providers
> must collaborate with parents and the family. Among the primary purposes of inter-
> vention services are to provide families with information, support, and meaning-
> ful opportunities for involvement. In addition to family services and direct interven-
> tion services to the child, policies also should be developed and implemented for
> therapy services, advocacy services, and procedural safeguards. Finally, policies and
> procedures should address the utilization of existing public and private community
> providers.
> c. *Transitional services.* Transitional services must be provided to all eligible children. A
> transitional service can be defined as a carefully planned, outcome-oriented process,
> initiated by the primary service provider, that establishes and implements a written
> multiagency service plan for each child moving to a new program.
> d. *Interagency issues.* The responsibilities for a coordinated service delivery system rest
> with the state and with local communities. At a minimum, the state must develop a
> directory of services and available resources, define contractual and reimbursement
> responsibilities among agencies, and establish a process for dispute resolution
> through formal, written interagency agreements. In addition to implementing these
> agreements, local providers also should ensure the coordinated delivery of services to
> all handicapped children and their families.
> e. *Training.* The lead agency and the Interagency Coordinating Council, in conjunc-
> tion with institutions of higher education, should develop a comprehensive plan for
> personnel development in both pre- and in-service training as well as establish and
> adopt standards for the certification and licensing of personnel.

   5. *Methodology.* This particular component should address implementation
and evaluation of the interagency plan. It is highly recommended that such a plan be

implemented initially on a pilot basis. By holding a trial run, implementors can reduce resistance to change, operationalize the policy concepts more effectively, allow for the integration of practical information prior to full implementation, test the utility of the concepts, and measure observable outcomes. In addition, both the model and the system can be modified in a way that imposes minimal burden on the individuals, organizations, and systems involved. Research completed at the Diffusion Research Center at Stanford University supports the need for piloting new approaches if they are to be successfully implemented (Randall, 1981).

Case management

The role of the case manager, as well as the system developed for case management, is critical to early intervention services coordination for children and their families. It is essential that the case manager be aware of services and resources across agencies in order to facilitate greater family access to them. If the intent of the new legislation is to be realized, the case manager must coordinate services actively across agencies and disciplines. Unfortunately, most of the case management models currently in use are directed primarily at a single agency (Bailey, in press). Furthermore, the caseload of many managers is so large that it prevents them from accomplishing their purpose.

As states develop a case management system, regardless of which model they select, the individuals who are assigned the case management responsibility must be knowledgeable about all available resources. The Central Directory of Services required as part of P.L. 99-457, Part H, should be developed in such a way that it is a useful tool for case managers. To encourage a more effective interagency approach, states might wish to examine the possibility of sharing the costs for case management across agencies.

The revision of current policies and the development of coordinated policies is an essential ingredient in increasing service coordination. However, these policies require qualified individuals to implement them. Unless there is adequate case management, the ultimate goal of comprehensive, coordinated, multidisciplinary, interagency early intervention services for disabled and at-risk infants, toddlers, and their families will go unmet.

Training

In a recent national survey, more than 68% of the states reported that they lacked sufficient training programs, more than 80% are now reporting shortages of trained early childhood special education teachers, and nearly 100% are experiencing shortages of therapists (Meisels et al., 1988). Significant new initiatives are required in both preservice and in-service training. Most current training approaches do not prepare professionals to work effectively as members of a multidisciplinary team or on an interagency planning group (Bailey, 1984; Magrab et al., 1985). New approaches to training should be developed to find ways to help professionals understand and appreciate the perspectives and expertise of professionals from other disciplines. University training programs should examine models and strategies for joint training of professionals across disciplines, such as the multidisciplinary training program implemented at the University Affiliated Program of the University of Southern Mississippi (Siders, Riall, Bennett, & Judd, 1987) and the joint training program between the Department of Maternal and Child Health and the Department of Special Education at the University of North

Carolina at Chapel Hill (Bailey, Farel, O'Donnell, Simeonsson, & Miller, 1986; Farel, Bailey, & O'Donnell, 1987).

The ability to play the role of case manager or service coordinator will also require skills not usually taught in the training programs of the traditional disciplines. In order to coordinate services for an individual infant and his or her family to form an integrated whole, a case manager or service coordinator must be able to understand the programming suggestions of professionals from different disciplines, analyze them carefully, synthesize them into an integrated, cohesive program, and then translate the goals of that program for the parents and for the other professionals involved. It is probably too early to determine whether these essential case management skills should be addressed in preservice or in-service training programs. However, the case manager training program developed by Dunst and Trivette (1989) could serve as an exemplary model for future training programs. This model is based on the belief that parents of infants and toddlers with handicaps vary along a continuum from dependent to independent in their ability to utilize the resources available to them and their handicapped child. The case manager should be trained to take the parents from where they begin and facilitate their movement toward increased independence.

Parents have done much to enlighten professionals concerning the limitations of many approaches to parent training and parent involvement (National Center for Clinical Infant Programs [NCCIP], 1986; Turnbull & Turnbull, 1985). Training programs for individual disciplines would be wise to examine their approach to parent–professional interaction and involvement. All too frequently these programs are based upon the philosophy of finding the pathology or deficiency in both the child and the family, and then instructing the family in how better to "teach" their child. Based upon the last 15 years of experience and dialogues with families, a philosophical shift is certainly needed. Instead of the philosophy of "experts know best" or "doing something to or for parents," our training programs must do a better job of preparing professionals who know how to involve parents as important members of the team (Healy, Keesee, & Smith, 1985; Shelton, Jeppson, & Johnson, 1987; Simeonsson & Bailey, this volume). Service coordination for individual children, as well as the coordination of a statewide system of early intervention services, will surely fail unless there is widespread understanding and acceptance of this shift in philosophy.

Increased coordination at the federal level

All of the major efforts at evaluating the effectiveness of interagency service coordination have recommended the need for coordination of policies at the federal level (Brewer & Kakalik, 1979; Gans & Horton, 1975). Furthermore, it is well documented that conflicting and disparate federal policies are a major barrier to early intervention service coordination (Meisels et al., 1988). Despite this important information, federal agencies have done little to examine and change their own policies in order to enhance the possibilities of better service coordination. They have focused most of their efforts on strategies to encourage states to take on this task and to assume the responsibility for solving the dilemma of coordinating these disparate federal programs. To date, the federal agencies have been unwilling to undertake the rigorous process that is currently demanded of states under P.L. 99-457. For the most part, the federal interagency agreements have been much too general to be of assistance to states that are earnestly attempting better policy coordination for early intervention services. Furthermore, these interagency agreements are often established between only two agencies, rather than among all concerned parties. This approach fails to recognize that an agreement between two agencies often addresses only a part of the problem of service delivery. In many cases this creates additional problems in coordinating with the agencies that were not a part of the agreement.

If service coordination is to be more than an empty mandate developed as a politically expedient way to quiet a powerful constituency, then the relevant federal agencies (Office of Special Education Programs, Bureau of Maternal and Child Health and Resources Development, Administration for Children, Youth and Families, the Administration on Developmental Disabilities, etc.), need to enter into a process of coordinated policy development similar to that required of the states participating in Part H of P.L. 99-457. It is essential that federal agency representatives attain agreement concerning common goals of service delivery. These common goals or missions regarding the philosophy of services should also be followed with objectives and expected outcomes. Unless the federal agencies are willing to tackle the problems of service eligibility, funding, and certification, the promise of service coordination may never come to fruition.

CONCLUSION AND RECOMMENDATIONS

The past 10 years taught us that interagency coordination is a much more complex endeavor than first imagined. The human services system often performs as anything but a system. Rather, it frequently appears to be a labyrinth of disparate individual providers and services.

The expansion of services under P.L. 99-457 has provided new opportunities and expectations for both parents and professionals. To actualize these opportunities it will be essential to utilize all of the available resources in a more effective and efficient way. Traditional interagency problems, such as agency autonomy, divided responsibilities, short-term perspectives, and the lack of focus on external issues can all begin to be rectified through the use of interagency policy planning groups. Such groups can provide a forum for shared experiences to highlight common values, perceptions, and goals, and, therefore, to facilitate communication within and between agencies. They can provide professionals with a more comprehensive view of the service delivery system and the needs of families. These interagency groups can also assist all of the participating agencies in defining their shared goals. As a result, the agencies can better meet the complex and changing needs of families with young disabled children.

Interagency coordination of services is now a federal policy as delineated in Part H of P.L. 99-457. However, this legislation places upon each participating state the responsibility to replace currently conflicting policies with new, more compatible state policies that ensure coordination. This effort requires a dramatic change in early intervention service delivery. Given the magnitude of needed change in most states, it is essential to develop a climate that supports this major interagency effort. It is also essential that those involved in the policy development process identify the various policy options and carefully analyze the consequences of those options. It is critical that policy developers understand the choices they are making, because once they are instituted, policies are difficult to change.

The complex and critical nature of this policy development effort requires that it not be undertaken in haste. The traditional approach of an interest or advocacy group trying to push through its legislation or agenda quickly is an inappropriate strategy for a policy development process that seeks more coordinated policies. If service coordination is to take place and be more than a hollow promise, the needs of disabled or at-risk infants and toddlers and their families must always remain uppermost in the focus of policy development activities.

REFERENCES

Agranoff, R. (1977). Services integration. In W. F. Anderson, B. J. Rieden, & M. J. Murphy (Eds.), *Managing human services* (pp. 527–561). Washington, DC: International City Management Association.

Bailey, D. B. (1984). A triaxial model of the interdisciplinary team and group process. *Exceptional Children, 51*, 17–25.

Bailey, D. B. (in press). Case management in early intervention. *Journal of Early Intervention.*

Bailey, D. B., Farel, A. M., O'Donnell, K. J., Simeonsson, R. J., & Miller, C. A. (1986). Preparing infant interventionists: Interdepartmental training in special education and maternal and child health. *Journal of the Division for Early Childhood, 11*, 67–77.

Baumheir, E. C. (1979). *Interagency linkages in the field of developmental disabilities.* Paper presented at the meeting of the American Association of Mental Deficiency, Miami Beach.

Bennis, W. G. (1984). Transforming power and leadership. In T. T. Sergiovanni & J. E. Corbally (Eds.), *Leadership and organizational culture* (pp. 64–71). Urbana: University of Illinois Press.

Berger, M., & Foster, M. (1986). Applications of family therapy theory to research and interventions with families with mentally retarded children. In J. J. Gallagher & P. M. Vietze (Eds.), *Families of handicapped persons: Research, programs, and policy issues* (pp. 251–260). Baltimore: P. H. Brookes.

Brewer, G. D., & Kakalik, J. S. (1979). *Handicapped children: Strategies for improving services.* New York: McGraw-Hill.

Bricker, D. (1987). Impact of research on social policy for handicapped infants and children. *Journal of the Division for Early Childhood, 11*, 98–105.

Burns, J. M. (1987). *Leadership.* New York: Harper & Row.

Churchman, C. W. (1968). *The systems approach.* New York: Delacorte Press.

Colorado Department of Education. (1987). *Interagency public policy principles.* Denver: Author.

Colorado Department of Education. (1986). *Interagency transition policy document.* Denver: Author.

Dunst, C. J., & Trivette, C. M. (1989). An enablement and empowerment perspective of case management. *Topics in Early Childhood Special Education, 8*, 87–102.

Elder, J. O., & Magrab, P. R. (Eds.). (1980). *Coordinating services to handicapped children: A handbook for interagency collaboration.* Baltimore: P. H. Brookes.

Farel, A. M., Bailey, D. B., & O'Donnell, K. J. (1987). A new approach for training infant specialists. *Infant Mental Health Journal, 8*, 76–85.

Featherstone, H. (1980). *A difference in the family: Life with a disabled child.* New York: Basic Books.

Flynn, C., & Harbin, G. (1987). Evaluating interagency coordination efforts using a multidimensional, interactional, developmental paradigm. *Remedial and Special Education, 8*, 35–44.

Foltz, A. M. (1982). *An ounce of prevention: Child health policies under Medicaid.* Cambridge: MIT Press.

Gallagher, J. J., & Vietze, P. M. (Eds.). (1986). *Families of handicapped persons: Research, programs, and policy issues.* Baltimore: P. H. Brookes.

Gans, S. P., & Horton, G. T. (1975). *Integration of human services: The state and municipal levels.* New York: Praeger.

Glazer, N. (1983). Toward a self-service society? *The Public Interest, 70*, 66–90.

Hagebak, B. R. (1979). Local human service delivery: The integration imperative. *Public Administration Review, 39*, 575–582.

Harbin, G. (1987). *Framework for a comprehensive service system for young children with handicaps and their families.* (Available from NEC*TAS, CB# 8040, 500 NCNB Plaza, Chapel Hill, NC 27599)

Hayes, C. D. (Ed.). (1982). *Making policies for children: A study of the federal process.* Washington, DC: National Academy Press.

Healy, A., Keesee, P. D., & Smith, B. S. (Eds.). (1985). *Early services for children with special needs: Transactions for family support.* Iowa City: University of Iowa.

Huff, A. S. (1980). Planning to plan. In D. L. Clark, S. McKibbin, & M. Malkas (Eds.), *New perspectives on planning in educational organizations* (pp. 33–48). San Francisco: Far West Laboratory for Educational Research and Development.

Kast, F. E., & Rosenzweig, J. E. (1974). *Organization and management: A system approach* (2nd ed.). Englewood Cliffs, NJ: Prentice-Hall.

Kotler, P. (1982). *Marketing for non-profit organizations* (2nd ed.). Englewood Cliffs, NJ: Prentice-Hall.

Knitzer, J. (1982). *Unclaimed children: The failure of public responsibility to children and adolescents in need of mental health services.* Washington, DC: Children's Defense Fund.

Magrab, P., Flynn, C., & Pelosi, J. (1985). *Assessing interagency coordination through process evaluation.* (Available from NEC*TAS, CB# 8040, 500 NCNB Plaza, Chapel Hill, NC 27599)

Martin, P. Y., Chackerian, R., Imershein, A. W., & Frumkin, M. L. (1983). The concept of "integrated" services reconsidered. *Social Science Quarterly, 64,* 747–763.

McNulty, B. A. (1986). *Interagency cooperation: The state of the art.* Unpublished manuscript, Colorado Department of Education, Denver.

McNulty, B. A. (1988). Leadership and policy strategies for interagency planning: Meeting the early childhood mandate. In J. J. Gallagher, P. L. Trohanis, & R. M. Clifford (Eds.), *Policy implementation (P.L. 99-457): Planning for young children with special needs* (pp. 147–167). Baltimore: P. H. Brookes.

Meisels, S. J. (1985). A functional analysis of the evolution of public policy for handicapped young children. *Educational Evaluation and Policy Analysis, 7,* 115–126.

Meisels, S. J., Harbin, G., Modigliani, K., & Olson, K. (1988). Formulating optimal state early childhood intervention policies. *Exceptional Children, 55,* 159–165.

Mittenthal, S. D. (1976). A system approach to human services integration. *Evaluation, 3,* 142–148.

Naisbitt, J. (1982). *Megatrends: Ten new directions transforming our lives.* New York: Warner Books.

National Center for Clinical Infant Programs. (1986). *Equals in this partnership: Parents of disabled and at-risk infants and toddlers speak to professionals.* (Available from: National Maternal and Child Health Clearinghouse, 38th and R Streets, Washington, DC, 20057)

National Council on the Handicapped (1986). *Toward independence.* Washington, DC: U. S. Government Printing Office.

Northwest Regional Educational Laboratory. (1980). *Proceedings: Dissemination, processes seminar, collaboration – A promising strategy for improving educational practice.* Portland, OR: Northwest Regional Educational Laboratory.

Pollard, A., Hall, H., & Keeran, C. (1979). Community service planning. In P. R. Magrab & J. O. Elder (Eds.), *Planning for services to handicapped persons: Community, education, health* (pp. 1–39). Baltimore: P. H. Brookes.

Randall, A. (1981). Human nature: Resistance and survival. *Science Digest, 89,* 32.

Richardson, E. (1973). *Responsibility and responsiveness (II): A report on the H.E.W. potential for the seventies.* Washington, DC: U.S. Department of Health, Education, and Welfare.

Rogers, C., & Farrow, F. (1983). *Effective state strategies to promote interagency collaboration* (Vol. 1, Contract No. 300-82-0829). Washington, DC: The Center for the Study of Policy Analysis.

Sarason, S. B. (1971). *The culture of the school and the problem of change.* Boston: Allyn & Bacon.

Selig, A. (1976). The myth of the multi-problem family. *American Journal of Orthopsychiatry, 46,* 526–532.

Shelton, T. L., Jeppson, E. S., & Johnson, B. H. (1987). *Family-centered care for children with special health care needs.* Washington, DC: Association for the Care of Children's Health.

Siders, J. Z., Riall, A., Bennett, T. C., & Judd, D. (1987). Training of leadership personnel in early intervention: A transdisciplinary approach. *Teacher Education and Special Education, 10,* 161–170.

Steiner, G. Y. (1976). *The children's cause.* Washington, DC: Brookings Institute.

Tichy, N. M., & Ulrich, D. O. (1984). The leadership challenge: A call for the transformational leader. *Sloan Management Review, 26,* 59–68.

Toffler, A. (1980). *The third wave.* New York: Bantam Books.

Turnbull, H. R., & Turnbull, A. P. (1985). *Parents speak out: Then and now* (2nd ed.). Columbus, OH: Merrill.

U.S. Congress. House. Committee on Education and Labor. (1986). *Report on the Education of the Handicapped Act Amendments of 1986.*

Zald, M. (1969). The structure of society and social services integration. *Social Science Quarterly, 50,* 557–567.

Name Index

722

Cline, M. G., x
Clunies-Ross, G. G., 518, 525
Coates, D., 278, 280, 283, 385
Cobb, S., 331, 334
Cobeliner, W. G., 459
Cochran, M., 54, 314, 326, 637
Cochran, N., 183
Cocks, E., 513, 515, 520, 521, 528
Cocozza, J. J., 313
Coe, R., 84
Coelen, C., 564, 565, 566
Cohen, D., 45
Cohen, J., 593
Cohen, L. B., 256, 257, 259, 261
Cohen, L. H., 332
Cohen, M. A., 387
Cohen, S., 57, 208, 220, 242, 278, 280, 281,
    283, 285, 286, 287, 326, 327, 328, 331,
    334, 338, 458, 611, 638
Cohler, B., 54, 65, 98, 99, 100, 101, 103
Cohn, J. F., 57, 64
Cohrs, M., 221, 613
Cole, J. G., 377
Cole, J. T., 185
Cole, R. E., 100
Coleman, J., 353, 684
Coleman, R., 357
Coles, R., 99
Collard, R., 224
Colletta, N., 327, 637, 646
Collins, A., 89
Collis, G. M., 59, 286
Collmer, C. W., 66, 67
Colona, A., 99
Colorado Department of Education, 714, 715
Colton, R. H., 618
Comer, J. P., 533
Comfort, M., 279, 294, 317, 548
Committee for Economic Development, x, 512
Comptroller General, 357
Conboy, T. J., 43
Condon, W. S., 153
Conger, R. D., 68
Conn-Powers, M., 189, 190
Connell, D., 64, 67, 480
Connell, J. P., 598
Conners, C. K., xiii
Connolly, B., 518, 526
Connors, R. E., 376
Consortium for Longitudinal Studies, 577
Convey, L., 652
Cook, F. L., 590
Cook, T. D., 590, 591
Cook-Gumperz, J., 190
Cooper, C., 327
Cooper, D., 392, 419, 428, 527, 586
Cooper, L. Z., 43
Coppel, D., 331
Copple, C. E., x
Coren, A., 433, 517, 522, 529
Corman, H. H., 219, 231
Corney, M. J., 518, 525

Cornwell, J. C., 344
Corrigan, R., 201, 231
Corsaro, W. A., 190
Corter, C., 62
Corwin, M. J., 619
Coster, W., 265
Cotman, C. W., 199
Courtnage, L., 684
Couvreur, J., 44
Covitz, F. E., 280
Cowen, E. L., x, 653
Cox, G. B., 331
Cox, M., 99, 517, 522, 588
Cox, R., 99
Craft, M., 14
Crain, E. J., 693
Crane, R., 353
Cravioto, J., 137, 154
Crawford, A. G., 99, 106
Crichton, L., 60, 67
Crissey, M. S., 10
Crittenden, P. M., 66, 67, 68, 265
Crnic, K. A., 54, 62, 184, 281, 304, 312, 313,
    314, 327, 361
Crnic, L. S., 196
Crockenberg, S., 57, 61, 62, 99, 106, 283,
    637, 646
Crocker, A. C., 388
Crocker, R. W., 304, 316
Cronbach, L. J., 595
Crook, C. K., 61
Cross, A., 184, 327, 540
Cross, A. F., 555
Cross, A. H., 134, 312, 314, 317, 332
Cross, D. R., 612
Crossland, C. L., 693
Crouchman, M., 356
Crouter, A., 82, 85, 87, 91
Crow, R. E., 184
Crowder, J., 318, 332, 340
Crowe, T. K., 241
Crutcher, D. M., 388
Cummings, E. M., 58, 265
Cummings, M., 65, 264
Cummings, S., 352
Cunningham, C., 296, 364, 547
Cunningham, C. C., 286, 287, 312, 431,
    519, 526
Cunningham, C. E., 415, 639
Cunningham, S., 85
Curd, K., 129
Curley, R., 211
Currier, S., 616
Curtis, A., 504
Cutler, C., 67, 139, 376
Cutright, P., 127
Cutrona, C. E., 331
Cytryn, L., 65

Dahlman, A. Y., 517, 523
Dalgleish, M., 504, 505
Dallas, J. R., 421

Subject Index